MILLER'S

antiques

MILLER'S antiques

ELIZABETH NORFOLK *GENERAL EDITOR*

2003
VOLUME XXIV

MILLER'S ANTIQUES PRICE GUIDE 2003

Created and designed by
Miller's
The Cellars, High Street
Tenterden, Kent, TN30 6BN
Tel: 01580 766411
Fax: 01580 766100

General Editor: Elizabeth Norfolk
Production Co-ordinator: Kari Reeves
Editorial Co-ordinator: Deborah Wanstall
Assistant to General Editor: Gillian Charles
Editorial Assistants: Joanna Hill, Maureen Horner
Production Assistants: Clare Gillingham, Ethne Tragett
Advertising Executive: Jill Jackson
Advertising Co-ordinator & Administrator: Melinda Williams
Advertising Assistants: Elizabeth Ellender, Carol Woodcock
Designer: Philip Hannath
Advertisement Designer: Simon Cook
Jacket Design: Victoria Bevan
Indexer: Hilary Bird
Additional Photographers: Ian Booth, Dennis O'Reilly, Chris Rutter, Robin Saker

First published in Great Britain in 2002
by Miller's, a division of Mitchell Beazley,
imprints of Octopus Publishing Group Ltd,
2–4 Heron Quays, London E14 4JP

A CIP catalogue record for this book is
available from the British Library

ISBN 1-84000-6129

Illustrations: CK Litho, Whitstable, Kent
Lab 35, Milton Keynes, Bucks
Printed and bound: Lego SPA, Italy

Front cover illustrations:
An etched glass silver-plated and parcel gilt claret jug, by Elkington & Co, 1887, 11in (28cm) high.
£1,350–1,500 ⊞ PAY
A set of eight mahogany dining chairs, including a pair of armchairs, c1810. **£15,000–20,000 ⚒ S**
An Adams blue and white plate, decorated with lions, c1815, 9½in (24cm) diam. **£350–400 ⊞ SCO**

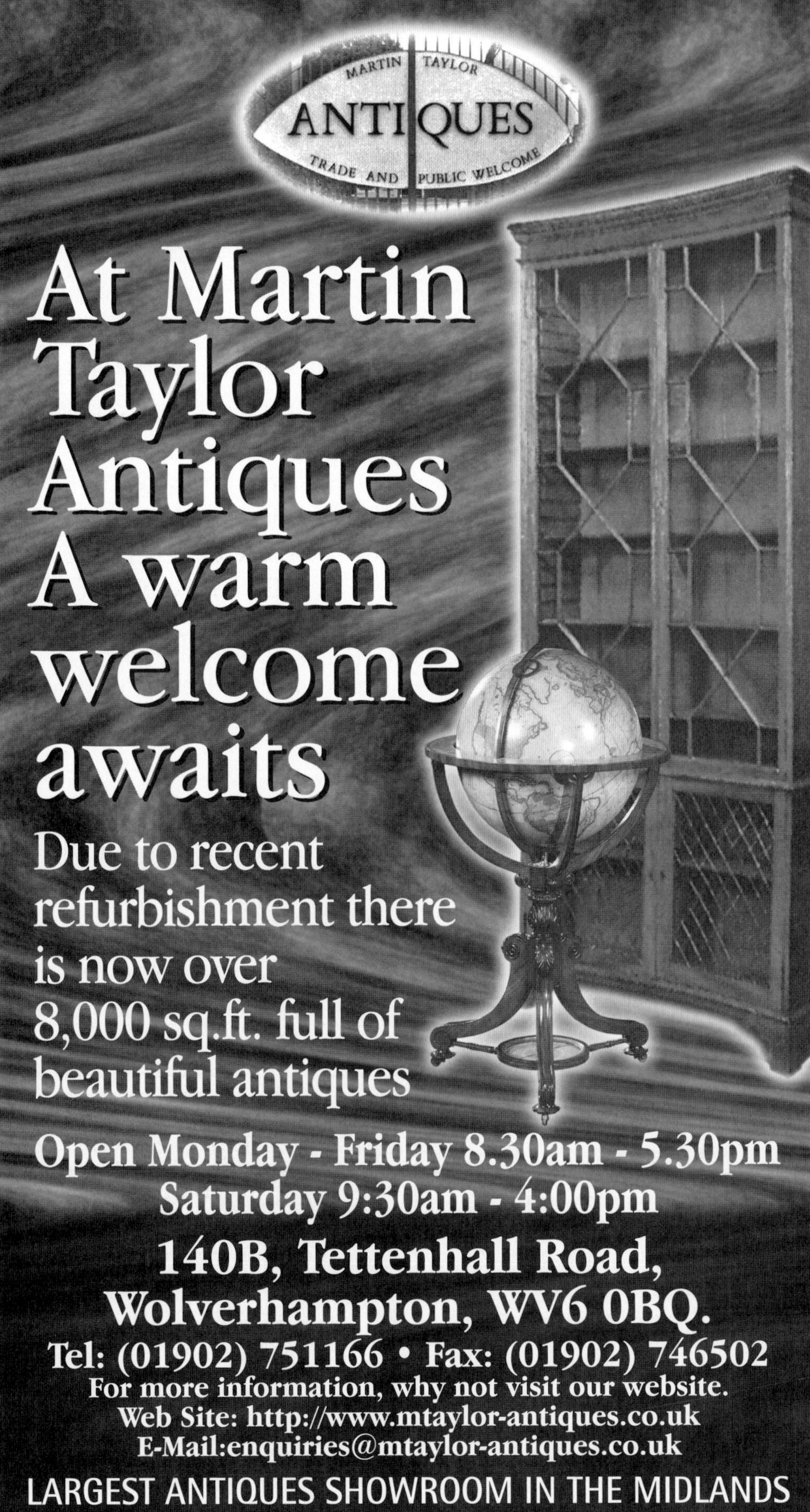
MARTIN TAYLOR
ANTIQUES
TRADE AND PUBLIC WELCOME
At Martin Taylor Antiques A warm welcome awaits
Due to recent refurbishment there is now over 8,000 sq.ft. full of beautiful antiques
Open Monday - Friday 8.30am - 5.30pm
Saturday 9:30am - 4:00pm
140B, Tettenhall Road,
Wolverhampton, WV6 0BQ.
Tel: (01902) 751166 • Fax: (01902) 746502
For more information, why not visit our website.
Web Site: http://www.mtaylor-antiques.co.uk
E-Mail:enquiries@mtaylor-antiques.co.uk
LARGEST ANTIQUES SHOWROOM IN THE MIDLANDS

Dates	British Monarch	British Period	French Period
1558–1603	Elizabeth I	Elizabethan	Renaissance
1603–1625	James I	Jacobean	
1625–1649	Charles I	Carolean	Louis XIII (1610–1643)
1649–1660	Commonwealth	Cromwellian	Louis XIV (1643–1715)
1660–1685	Charles II	Restoration	
1685–1689	James II	Restoration	
1689–1694	William & Mary	William & Mary	
1694–1702	William III	William III	
1702–1714	Anne	Queen Anne	
1714–1727	George I	Early Georgian	Régence (1715–1723)
1727–1760	George II	Early Georgian	Louis XV (1723–1774)
1760–1811	George III	Late Georgian	Louis XVI (1774–1793) Directoire (1793–1799) Empire (1799–1815)
1812–1820	George III	Regency	Restauration Charles X (1815–1830)
1820–1830	George IV	Regency	
1830–1837	William IV	William IV	Louis Philippe (1830–1848) 2nd Empire Napoleon III (1848–1870) 3rd Republic (1871–1940)
1837–1901	Victoria	Victorian	
1901–1910	Edward VII	Edwardian	

<table>
<tr><th>German Period</th><th>U.S. Period</th><th>Style</th><th>Woods</th></tr>
<tr><td rowspan="2">Renaissance</td><td rowspan="3">Early Colonial</td><td>Gothic</td><td rowspan="12">Oak Period (to c1670)
Walnut period (c1670–1735)
Early mahogany period (c1735–1770)
Late mahogany period (c1770–1810)</td></tr>
<tr><td rowspan="3">Baroque (c1620–1700)</td></tr>
<tr><td rowspan="3">Renaissance/ Baroque (c1650–1700)</td></tr>
<tr><td>William & Mary</td></tr>
<tr><td>Dutch Colonial</td><td rowspan="3">Rococo (c1695–1760)</td></tr>
<tr><td>Baroque (c1700–1730)</td><td>Queen Anne</td></tr>
<tr><td>Rococo (c1730–1760)</td><td>Chippendale (from 1750)</td></tr>
<tr><td>Neo–classicism (c1760–1800)
Empire (c1800–1815)</td><td>Early Federal (1790–1810)
American Directoire (1798–1804)
American Empire (1804–1815)</td><td>Neo–classical (c1755–1805)
Empire (c1799–1815)</td></tr>
<tr><td>Biedermeier (c1815–1848)</td><td rowspan="2">Late Federal (1810–1830)</td><td>Regency (c1812–1830)</td></tr>
<tr><td rowspan="3">Revivale (c1830–1880)
Jugendstil (c1880–1920)</td><td rowspan="2">Eclectic (c1830–1880)
Arts & Crafts (c1880–1900)</td></tr>
<tr><td>Victorian</td></tr>
<tr><td>Art Nouveau (c1900–1920)</td><td>Art Nouveau (c1900–1920)</td></tr>
</table>

Contents

MILLER'S 2003

Acknowledgments

The publishers would like to acknowledge the great assistance given by our consultants. We would also like to extend our thanks to all auction houses and their press offices, as well as dealers and collectors, who have assisted us in the production of this book.

FURNITURE:	Jonty Hearnden, Dorchester Antiques, The Barn, 3 High Street, Dorchester-on-Thames, Oxfordshire OX10 7HH
OAK & COUNTRY FURNITURE:	Denzil Grant, Drinkstone House, Drinkstone, Bury St Edmunds, Suffolk IP30 9TG
POTTERY:	Mark Law, Law Fine Art, Fir Tree Cottage, Church Lane, Brimpton, Berkshire RG7 4TJ
TOBY JUGS:	Judi Bland, Quills, Bagshott Road, Cobham, Surrey GU24 8DE
BLUE & WHITE TRANSFERWARE:	Gillian Neale, P O Box 247, Aylesbury, Buckinghamshire HP20 1JZ
PORCELAIN:	John Sandon, Bonhams, 101 New Bond Street, London W1Y 0AS
ASIAN CERAMICS:	Peter Wain, Anglesey
GLASS:	Jeanette Hayhurst, 32a Kensington Church Street, London W8 4HA
PAPERWEIGHTS:	Anne Metcalfe, Sweetbriar Gallery, Sweetbriar House, Robin Hood Lane, Helsby, Cheshire WA6 9NH
SILVER & SILVER PLATE:	Hugh Gregory, Tennants, The Auction Centre, Harmby Road, Leyburn, Yorkshire DL8 5SG
CLOCKS:	John Jillings, Croft House, 17 Church Street, Newent, Gloucestershire GL18 1PU
BAROMETERS:	Derek & Tina Rayment, Orchard House, Barton, Nr Farndon, Cheshire SY14 7HT
DECORATIVE ARTS:	Mark Oliver, Bonhams, 101 New Bond Street, London W1Y 0AS
ART DECO:	Anne Mitofsky-Citron & Laurance B. Citron, Mitofsky Antiques, Rathfarnham Road, Terenure, Dublin 6, Republic of Ireland
	Irish Antique Dealers Association, Adare, Co. Limerick, Republic of Ireland
RUGS & CARPETS:	Desmond North, The Orchard, Hale Street, East Peckham, Nr Tonbridge, Kent TN12 5JB
ASIAN WORKS OF ART:	Peter Wain, Anglesey
ARCHITECTURAL ANTIQUES:	Rupert van der Werff, Sotheby's Sussex, Summer's Place, Billingshurst, West Sussex RH14 9AD
SCULPTURE:	William Bevan, Bevan Fine Art, P O Box 60, Uckfield, East Sussex TN22 1ZD
MUSICAL INSTRUMENTS:	David Winston, Period Piano Company, Park Farm Oast, Hareplain Road, Biddenden, Kent TN27 8LJ
ANTIQUITIES & TRIBAL ART:	Siobhan Quin, Bonhams, Montpelier Street, London SW7 1HH
PHOTOGRAPHS:	Richard Meara, Jubilee Photographica, 10 Pierrepoint Row, London N1 8EE
SCIENTIFIC INSTRUMENTS & MARINE:	Charles Tomlinson, Chester
FOCUS ON SCANDINAVIA:	Håkon Groth, Rupert Cavendish Antiques, 610 King's Road, London SW6 2DX

How to use this book

It is our aim to make this book easy to use. In order to find a particular item, consult the contents list on page 19 to find the main heading – for example, Pottery. Having located your area of interest, you will find that larger sections have been sub-divided. If you are looking for a particular factory, designer or craftsman, consult the index which starts on page 804.

TOBY & CHARACTER JUGS 50

Toby & Character Jugs

How to identify early Yorkshire Toby jugs

Look out for the following typical characteristics:
- The scalloped top on his hat.
- A black fringe (even when hair is brown).
- Dotted eyebrows.
- Curled pipe on his chest.
- Raised octagonal cup.
- Caryatid (figurehead) handle.
- Sponged underglaze colours on the base.

A Yorkshire Toby jug, decorated in Pratt colours with a manganese face, blue coat and yellow breeches and a sponged green, black, with a caryatid handle, c1790, 10in (25.5cm) high.
£950–1,050 ⊞ JBL
This Toby still retains his measure which is used to drink from when passing around the jug of strong ale.

► **A Yorkshire Toby jug,** decorated with a reddish-brown coat and yellow breeches, with a translucent blue scalloped edge to his hat, a brown, yellow and green sponged base and hat, his pipe moulded flat to his chest, with a caryatid handle, c1830, 10in (25.5cm) high.
£450–550 ⊞ JBL

A Yorkshire Toby jug, with blue-glazed coat and yellow breeches, raised octagonal cup and caryatid handle, c1910, 10in (25.5cm) high.
£80–100 ⊞ JBL
By the early 20th century the Yorkshire Toby had lost his fringe, dotted eye-brows and curled pipe. The only features which distinguish it as being a Yorkshire piece are the raised octagonal cup and caryatid handle.

POTTERY

A Prattware Toby jug, wearing a yellow coat, pale blue breeches, striped stockings and brown and ochre hat, holding a jug, on a sponged base, c1800, 10in (25.5cm) high.
£200–240 ⚒ P(Ba)

An enamelled pearlware Martha Gunn Toby jug, her dress painted with red and green sprigs with a pink *fichu* and yellow bodice, hat restored, c1810–20, 10½in (26.5cm) high.
£370–400 ⚒ P(Ba)
Martha Gunn was the 'Queen of Dippers', well known and greatly sought after in late 18th– early 19th-century Brighton. A 'dipper' was someone who provided a service by assisting his patron or her patroness into the sea to bathe with the use of a bathing machine brought from the water's edge.

◄ **A creamware Toby jug,** wearing a green translucent coat, blue waistcoat and yellow breeches, with brown hat and shoes, hat restored, c1800, 10in (25.5cm) high.
£400–500 ⊞ JBL

Miller's Compares

I. A Neale & Co enamelled creamware Toby jug, wearing a brown coat, turquoise waistcoat, pale yellow breeches, and black shoes and hat, some damage and repainting, impressed mark and incised number 35, c1790–95, 10in (25.5cm) high.
£750–900 ⚒ P(Ba)

II. A Staffordshire pearlware Toby jug, wearing a pale dove-grey coat, turquoise waistcoat, lime green breeches, black hat and shoes, hat repaired and repainted, c1800–20, 10in (25.5cm) high.
£250–300 ⚒ P(Ba)

Toby jugs marked with a maker's name such as Item I are rare and this will substantially increase their value. Furthermore, Neale & Co pieces are of particularly good quality – a close study of Item II will reveal that it is not as finely finished off as Item I. Item II has also sustained more damage than Item I, although the price of both pieces has been adversely affected by this. Item I is also earlier in date than Item II – those 20-odd years will make a difference to the price.

Further reading

Miller's Collecting Pottery & Porcelain: The Facts At Your Fingertips, Miller's Publications, 1999

Information Box
covers relevant collecting information on factories, makers, care and restoration, fakes and alterations.

Price Guide
this is based on actual prices realized. Remember that Miller's is a price guide not a price list and prices are affected by many variables such as location, condition, desirability and so on. Don't forget that if you are selling it is quite likely you will be offered less than the price range. Price ranges for items sold at auction tend to include the buyer's premium and VAT if applicable.

Page Tab
this appears on every page and contains the main heading under which larger sections have been sub-divided, therefore, allowing easy access to the various sections.

Miller's Compares
explains why two items which look similar have realized very different prices.

Source Code
refers to the Key to Illustrations on page 794 that lists the details of where the item was photographed.
The ⚒ icon indicates the item was sold at auction.
The ⊞ icon indicates the item originated from a dealer.

Caption
provides a brief description of the item including the maker's name, medium, year it was made and in some cases condition.

Further Reading
directs the reader towards additional sources of information.

BaCa

BRITISH ANTIQUES AND COLLECTABLES AWARDS

presented by

MILLER'S

Celebrating the Winners of BACA 2002

The third annual Awards Ceremony took place on 26 June 2002 at The Dorchester, Park Lane, London. After a champagne reception, the 300+ guests enjoyed a 3 course meal and, after eagerly awaiting the presentation ceremony, learned of the winners for the first time during the evening. Eric Knowles, Chairman of BACA, presented each winner with a certificate on stage.

The evening was a tremendous occasion continuing on into the early hours with guests and winners alike sharing in the celebrations.

Congratulations to all the short-listed nominees and winners!

Eric Knowles with guest, Michael Aspel

PROUDLY SPONSORED BY

The BACA *Winners...*

CATEGORY 1
General Antiques Dealer

LONDON (INSIDE M25)
sponsored by ebay.co.uk
Alistair Sampson Antiques Ltd
120 Mount Street

UK (OUTSIDE M25) ***sponsored by***
Richard Gardner Antiques
Swan House, Market Square, Petworth, West Sussex

CATEGORY 2
Specialist Antiques Dealers

FURNITURE
sponsored by AON Artscope Incorporating Needham Jobson
Huntington Antiques Ltd
Church Street, Stow-on-the-Wold, Glos

MUSICAL INSTRUMENTS
Vintage and Rare Guitars
6 Denmark Street, London

ART NOUVEAU/ART DECO
The Fine Art Society plc
148 New Bond Street, London

COLLECTABLES
Manfred Schotten Antiques
The Crypt, 109 High Street, Burford, Oxon

SILVER & PLATE
Lowe & Sons
11 Bridge Street Row, Chester

SCULPTURE
Robert Bowman
8 Duke Street, St Jame's, London

PRINT
The O'Shea Gallery
120a Mount Street, London

WATERCOLOUR
Abbott & Holder
30 Museum Street, London

COSTUME & TEXTILES
Antique Textiles & Lighting
34 Belvedere, Lansdown Road, Bath, Somerset

POST WAR DESIGN
Target Gallery
7 Windmill St, London

CERAMICS
Andrew Dando
4 Wood Street, Bath, Somerset

CATEGORY 3
Auction Houses

LONDON (INSIDE M25)
sponsored by AON Artscope Incorporating Needham Jobson
Christie's South Kensington
85 Old Brompton Road, London

UK (OUTSIDE M25)
sponsored by AON Artscope Incorporating Needham Jobson
Gorringes incorporating Julian Dawson
15 North Street, Lewes, East Sussex

SPECIALIST DEPARTMENT WITHIN AN AUCTION HOUSE
Woolley & Wallis Ltd (Ceramics)
51–61 Castle Street, Wiltshire

CATEGORY 4
Associated Awards

FAIR OF THE YEAR
The Grosvenor House Art & Antiques Fair (June 2001)

AWARD FOR: IN-HOUSE EXHIBITION
John Walker, The English Joined Backstool 1660–1720

JOURNALIST OF THE YEAR
Brian Sewell, Evening Standard

AUCTIONEER OF THE YEAR
Rodney Tennant
Tennant Auctioneers, The Auction Centre, Leyburn, N Yorkshire

SERVICES AWARD: THIS YEAR FEATURING ANTIQUES ON THE INTERNET
www.christies.com

AWARD FOR: FRIENDLY ANTIQUES SHOP
Megarry's
Jericho Cottage, The Duckpond Green, Blackmore, Essex

AWARD FOR: BEST ANTIQUES TOWN/VILLAGE
Saffron Walden

Introduction

Whether we accept it or not the lives of private collectors, antique dealers and auctioneers are all undeniably linked by one key factor: the international art market. We all experience the roller-coaster effects of the ever-changing market and, now of all times, it would be a mistake to apply a rigid set of tried and tested rules that in the past have determined the value of art, antiques and collectables. As many in the trade have experienced over the last year, the market can sometimes appear unfathomable, with months of exceptional trade figures being followed by a trading month worse than any in the last ten years. The factors affecting the market continue to change, and whatever the reason some of the following certainly affect the value of what we buy and sell.

Over the last year, events indirectly linked to our market have had a major impact on prices. Nationally dealers and auctioneers felt the effects of foot-and-mouth disease, and broadly speaking trade had dipped and was only starting to stabilize by 11 September.

Even the most pessimistic predictors could not have imagined that fairs, auctions and exhibitions would be cancelled and postponed and that the American postal service would be totally disrupted. With virtually all areas within this guide relying on trans-Atlantic trade few escaped the impact.

The global economy plays the fiddle and the art market dances to the tune. Last year the fall in share prices reached beyond the confines of the dot coms, and while this has led to a general dip in confidence across the fine art and antiques trade, the top end of the market has been buoyed by investors adding top-quality objects to their portfolios in an effort to diversify their risk.

Our market has always been subject to the fickle trends of fashion and style. As the move towards contemporary design and minimalism continues to surge, objects designed with a timeless look are at a premium. Many of the pieces designed by Dr Christopher Dresser exemplify the quality of simplicity, whether it be a plated claret jug or a pottery vase, and such items seem to go from strength to strength. Likewise unfussy furniture of a clean line from almost any period appeals to designers and young buyers – no doubt spurred on by the plethora of interior design magazines and television programmes aimed at consumers who have continued to spend despite events.

The age of an object perhaps, then, plays a less significant part in the process of valuation. Consider, for example, differences between the average values of a late 17th-century oak coffer and a late 19th-century painted satinwood work table; a mid-18th-century Chelsea figure and a late 19th-century Moorcroft vase; or an 18th-century drinking vase and a late 19th-century Gallé vase. In many such cases the later objects may command the higher values.

The effects were undoubtedly minimized by the technology that we now increasingly take for granted. After the initial hype and expectations of the internet it is now a dependable aid and an established channel for buyers and sellers alike. Speedy global communication with detailed images and sourcing services allow an interaction across the market that even the best marketing campaigns could not hope to achieve. Long-distance buying and selling, while applicable to almost any object, can be particularly successful for small pieces that are easy to ship – these range from postcards and books to jewellery and medals. There is of course no substitute for examining objects first hand, but when events have curtailed traditional habits and when other services have been interrupted, the internet has provided a cost effective and increasingly trusted transaction mechanism.

One unforeseen quirk resulting from the proliferation of computers has been the fate of the George III mahogany bureau. While early walnut examples continue to be in demand, others have fallen from favour because of their functional incompatibility with desktop technology and its associated peripherals. Unsurprisingly in a world where computers are owned by anyone from teenagers to octogenarians, the rise of flat-surfaced writing tables and desks seems to have counterbalanced the fall of bureaux.

The last year has been a selectively strong year for exceptional quality and workmanship. High prices have been achieved across the board but the secret must be to be selective. Never imagine that anyone can assess the value of any object without knowledge and a keen pair of eyes. If you are considering an item take your time and have a critical and questioning point of view.

On the open market demand for top of the range goods has never been stronger: auctioneers fight for the best collections and dealers and private collectors cluster around select lots, prepared to pay substantially higher sums for items that display the right qualities, while being able to leave anything that appears mediocre.

This Guide seeks to impart the knowledge of specialists in areas as diverse as Toby jugs, Asian furniture, sculpture, paperweights and architectural antiques; giving practical examples with values and introductions to each section with constructive facts and backgrounds.

The strongest thread of advice from the contributors is unanimous: in any area buy the best pieces you can afford, as time and time again they give the most pleasure and prove overall to be the best performers. A good test is whether or not something has to apologize for itself.

Miller's Antiques Price Guide 2003 contains images and data from the past year of objects sold at auction and dealers' stock and is representative of the market. The range and content of each Miller's publication is down to you – enjoy your researching and buying, and if you discover a new area of art and antiques it may even be in the next price guide.

Elaine Binning

Furniture

International terrorists have done their best to disrupt confidence in world trade, stock markets have fallen, and for a while whole areas of the English countryside were under flood-water, to then be followed by severe restrictions due to foot-and-mouth disease. So what effect has all this had on the buying and selling of antique furniture in the last 12 months?

For once one can say that the meteoric rise in prices for furniture has indeed slowed and a welcome check has entered the market, but with strong signals that world economies are regaining confidence it may only be a matter of time before furniture prices strengthen again.

Throughout these uncertainties, what has remained is the insatiable thirst for furniture that is rare, of exceptional quality and/or with pedigree or provenance. This includes all good-quality late 17th- and early 18th-century walnut, and good English mahogany of the 18th-century.

In recent years Irish 18th-century furniture, an often neglected collecting area, has seen increases in prices thanks largely to the growth in the Irish economy and Irish-American interest.

In the mid-1980s Georgian furniture became too expensive for many collectors, so Regency furniture saw price increases, thanks largely to the fact that it fulfilled the buyer's desire for sobriety and classicism without the heavy price tag. These days Regency furniture made by Gillows of Lancaster (often easily identified as they were one of the few makers of the time to stamp their furniture) can command significantly higher prices than similarly designed furniture of the same period.

Style and utility are still important factors that determine values – for instance dining room furniture, sideboards, extending tables and long sets of chairs all command intense interest when they enter the market. Occasional furniture is still desirable, along with sofa tables, chiffoniers and bookcases.

With the increase in home computing and working from home, pedestal desks and writing tables gained in value recently, while bureaux and davenports have remained static. With the demand for a more minimalist look furniture with a clean line has proved popular: this includes furniture made in the Arts and Crafts period, Art Deco, and now furniture made in the 1950s and 1960s.

However, all is not doom, gloom and inflated prices – there are still bargains out there. Just look to the Victorian period and you can find furniture offering excellent design and high-quality craftsmanship as well as providing real value for money. **Jonty Hearnden**

Beds

A mahogany French bed, attributed to Mack, Williams & Gibtoun of Dublin, the panelled head- and footboards with turned rails, Irish, 42in (106.5cm) wide.
£625–700 MEA

A William IV mahogany four-poster bed, the spiral-reeded and foliate-carved turned posts with leafy baluster sections headed by gadrooned knops, 64in (162.5cm) wide.
£4,500–5,000 S

◀ **A Victorian mahogany four-poster bed,** the turned and reeded front posts with rectangular panel between, with a shell- and scroll-carved pediment, draped with gold and red fabric, 72in (183cm) wide.
£2,500–3,000 Mit

A Victorian brass bedstead, the top-rail with turned finials, above a pierced stylized wheel motif, 60in (152.5cm) wide.
£900–1,100 DD

A Victorian brass half-tester bed, 60in (152.5cm) wide.
£3,200–3,500 ⊞ DUK

A cast-iron bedstead, finished in black, c1875, 48in (122cm) wide.
£520–575 ⊞ SeH

Miller's Compares

I. A cast-iron and brass bedstead, in black, with convex brass rail and plaque decoration in foot panel, c1890, 54in (137cm) wide.
£1,100–1,200 ⊞ SeH

II. A cast-iron and brass bedstead, finished in black, with straight brass top rails, c1895, 54in (137cm) wide.
£625–700 ⊞ SeH

Item I is more desirable because it is a rarer design, whereas beds such as Item II were made in large quantities for both the domestic and overseas markets. The foot panel of Item I is particularly attractive with its bowed brass top-rail and rosettes, compared with the plainer design of Item II. The uprights of Item I are also sturdier than those of Item II, which renders it not only more pleasing to the eye, but also a more substantial piece of furniture than Item II.

A Victorian mahogany bedstead, the moulded headboard with a deeply buttoned panel, 56in (142cm) wide.
£1,000–1,200 ⚒ MEA

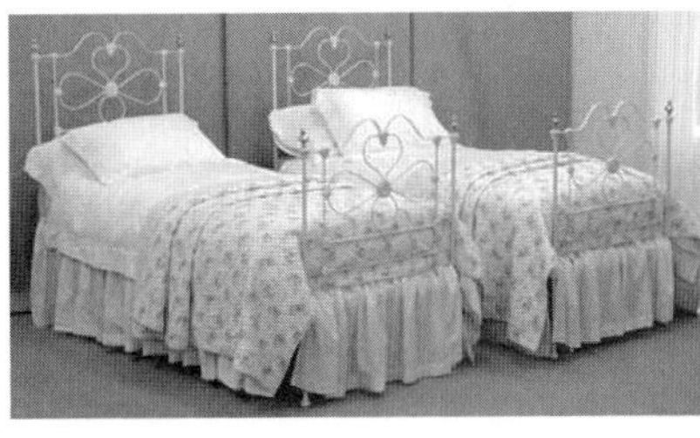

► **A pair of cast-iron bedsteads,** finished in cream, c1875, 36in (91.5cm) wide.
£1,350–1,500 ⊞ SeH

A cast-iron four-poster bed, finished in black, the head and foot panels with decorative brass plaque, c1875, 54in (137cm) wide.
£1,700–1,900 ⊞ SeH

A Victorian mahogany bed, the headboard with deeply buttoned panel, 54in (137cm) wide.
£900–1,100 ⚒ MEA

Items in the Furniture section have been arranged in date order within each sub-section.

◄ **A Victorian brass and iron double bed,** with brass ball finials and top-rails, the foot with brass flowerheads within pierced iron scrollwork and central brass ornament, slight damage, 54½in (138.5cm) wide.
£300–350 ⚒ PFK

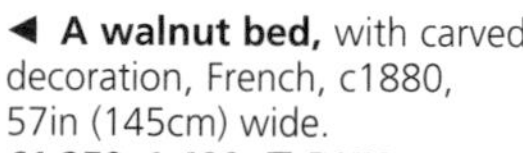

◄ **A walnut bed,** with carved decoration, French, c1880, 57in (145cm) wide.
£1,250–1,400 ⊞ DUK

A Renaissance-style walnut bed, with carved crown and Corinthian capitals on turned and reeded posts with quartered veneers and gilded embellishments, French, c1890, 39in (99cm) wide.
£620–680 ⊞ SWA

A child's iron folding cot, painted white, with brass headboard rails and finials, late 19thC, 24in (61cm) wide.
£250–300 ⚒ WW

A mahogany *lit en bateau*, with applied moulded borders and the ends with trefoil and flower edge, French, c1900, 50in (127cm) wide.
£600–720 ⚒ HOLL

A Louis XV-style solid walnut bed, with original carved side-rails and scroll to head, the inside of the footboard also carved, c1890, 60in (152.5cm) wide.
£1,700–1,900 ⚒ SWO

An 18thC-style iron bed, the headboard surmounted by a scrolling crest, with conforming footboard, Spanish, c1900, 36in (91.5cm) wide.
£700–800 ⚒ NOA

A cast-iron and brass bedstead, c1910, 48in (122cm) wide.
£500–550 ⊞ SeH

A burr-walnut bedstead, with *bombé* front and boxwood marquetry, Italian, c1920, 60in (152.5cm) wide.
£2,000–2,200 ⊞ SWA

A pair of Louis XV-style upholstered beds, with tapestry-effect covers, mid-20thC, 36in (91.5cm) wide.
£1,000–1,150 ⊞ SWA

Benches

A Gillow-style mahogany seat, with ribbed side lifts and leaf-carved knuckles, on turned ribbed tapering legs, early 19thC, 36in (91.5cm) wide.
£3,500–4,200 ⚒ WW

► A mahogany hall bench, the seat with turned ornament, on turned tapering baluster legs, c1835, 35½in (90cm) wide.
£1,100–1,200 ⚒ S(O)

◄ A mahogany long bench, with upholstered seat above a shaped apron, on bobbin-turned legs, American, c1840, 48in (122cm) wide.
£900–1,100 ⚒ SK

Bonheurs du Jour

► A rosewood bonheur du jour, with ivory inlay, the raised back with domed lid enclosing a stationery compartment over a hinged writing surface and two frieze drawers, late 19thC, 32¾in (83cm) wide.
£3,500–4,200 ⚒ AH

An Edwardian figured mahogany bonheur du jour, crossbanded in satinwood, inlaid with boxwood stringing, the back with two cupboards over a writing surface above a single drawer, 24½in (62cm) wide.
£2,500–3,000 ⚒ DD

A late Georgian mahogany bonheur du jour, the hinged fall-front revealing a writing surface, the interior of semicircular design with pigeonholes and drawers, supported on a table base with one long frieze drawer, 28in (71cm) wide.
£2,000–2,400 ⚒ TMA

◄ A Victorian walnut and marquetry bonheur du jour, the back with mirrored door and seven drawers, over a central drawer, on cabriole legs, 36in (91.5cm) wide.
£1,200–1,450 ⚒ G(L)

Bookcases

A pair of George III mahogany bookcases, with astragal-glazed doors, the bases with pairs of panelled cupboard doors, some repolishing to sides and possible adaptations, 46½in (118cm) wide.
£4,250–5,250 P(L)

A George III mahogany bookcase, with astragal-glazed doors, the lower section with a pair of crossbanded panelled cupboard doors enclosing three short drawers above a pair of removable modern compartments, 55½in (141cm) wide.
£3,250–4,000 S

A mahogany bookcase, with two astragal-glazed doors over two short drawers above two panel doors, early 19thC, 55in (139.5cm) wide.
£4,000–5,000 P(Ba)

A Louis XVI-style mahogany bookcase, with a drawer with blond-wood banding over two trellis-set doors, Dutch, c1800, 39¼in (99.5cm) wide.
£1,400–1,600 S(Am)

A mahogany breakfront bookcase, with four astragal-glazed panel doors above four panelled doors, 19thC, 90½in (230cm) wide.
£6,000–7,000 P(Ba)

Checkpoints: Bookcases

- Glazing bars should be of the same style, age and timber as the carcass. Mid–late 19th century breakfront wardrobes have been converted into bookcases by replacing the solid panels in the doors with glass.
- A bookcase on a bureau or cupboard base should be slightly smaller than the base and the retaining moulding preferably fixed to the base, not the top. The bureau fall should be steeper than on a normal bureau to create greater depth to accommodate the upper section.
- A bureau which has been made to carry a bookcase will usually not have a veneered top.
- In the late 19th century the glazed sections of bookcases were often removed and feet added to turn them into 'Georgian' bookcases. The correct version was much taller and often had frieze drawers to the base.

A William IV mahogany bookcase, the astragal-glazed doors flanked by turned column uprights, with acanthus-carved terminals, the drawer below inlaid with brass arabesques, 61½in (156cm) wide.
£2,400–2,700 P(E)

► **A mahogany bookcase,** with two astragal-glazed doors, on a base with two moulded panelled doors, 19thC, 55¼in (140.5cm) wide.
£4,500–5,500 LFA

A Biedermeier mahogany bookcase, with glazed doors flanked by columns, over a plinth drawer, German, 1800–50, 45¼in (115cm) wide.
£2,700–3,200 S(Am)

A carved mahogany bookcase, the two glazed doors over conforming panelled doors, c1860, 58in (147.5cm) wide.
£6,000–6,750 MTay

► **A Victorian mahogany breakfront bookcase,** the four-door glazed upper section over a four-panelled door base, labelled 'James Phillips, Union Street, Bristol', 101¼in (257cm) wide.
£9,000–11,000 JNic

A mid-Victorian mahogany bookcase, with glazed panel doors, the lower section fitted with two short and one long drawer, above a pair of arch panel doors, 52in (132cm) wide.
£1,100–1,300 P(Ba)

A figured walnut book-case, the two glazed doors over two inlaid doors, c1870, 83in (211cm) high.
£5,200–5,800 ⊞ MTay

An Edwardian inlaid mahogany bookcase, with floral marquetry frieze and two astragal-glazed doors, 27in (68.5cm) wide.
£1,200–1,500 G(L)

A mid-Victorian mahogany breakfront bookcase, 76in (193cm) wide.
£4,000–5,000 Bon(C)

A Sheraton revival mahogany bookcase, satinwood and chequer crossbanded with boxwood and ebony stringing, the astragal-glazed doors above a projecting base with a frieze drawer above a pair of doors, bellflower and leafy scrollwork panels, late 19thC, 35½in (90cm) wide.
£1,250–1,500 P(S)

An Edwardian Sheraton revival mahogany bookcase, satinwood crossbanded, the arched centre astragal-glazed doors over a projecting base fitted with two frieze drawers and cupboards under, 42in (106.5cm) wide.
£2,200–2,600 DMC

A Victorian oak library bookcase, the four astragal-glazed doors flanked with fish-scale moulded pilasters headed with leaf capitals, probably Irish, 106in (269cm) wide.
£3,700–4,200 MEA

A Victorian carved oak bookcase, with a pair of arched leaded and coloured-glass panelled doors, the projecting base with one long drawer, above a pair of panelled doors carved with fruit-filled urns, the whole profusely carved with scrolls, mask heads and floral drapery, 56¼in (143cm) wide.
£1,300–1,600 DD

Cross Reference
See Colour Review
(page 101)

◄ **An oak bookcase,** carved in high relief with figures, mythical beasts, masks and foliage, late 19thC, 45in (114.5cm) wide.
£700–850 SWO

Bureau Bookcases

A walnut and herringbone-banded bureau bookcase, the top with single mirror door enclosing shelves and four drawers, two candle slides below, the fall flap revealing a fitted interior, two short and two long drawers under, Dutch, early 18thC, 41in (104cm) wide.
£5,500–6,500 ⚒ E

A George III inlaid mahogany bureau bookcase, the astragal-glazed doors enclosing removable shelves and two short drawers, the lower part with a fall-front, with central floral marquetry inlaid oval panel enclosing a fitted interior, two short and two long graduated drawers below, the whole inlaid with chequered stringing lines and raised on carved lion's paw feet, Irish, 46in (117cm) wide.
£3,200–4,000 ⚒ PF

A George III inlaid mahogany bureau bookcase, the astragal-glazed doors above a sloping fall enclosing a fitted interior, the base with two short over three long drawers with original handles, later top, 50in (127cm) wide.
£2,000–2,400 ⚒ Bri

A Victorian burr-walnut cylinder bureau bookcase, with arched panelled doors, the cylinder fall below with slide-out writing surface, two panelled doors under, flanked by applied scrolling motifs, 47½in (120.5cm) wide.
£2,600–3,200 ⚒ AG

◄ An Eastlake walnut and flame birch bureau bookcase, with glazed doors and two small drawers above a slant lid and three long drawers, American, c1875–80, 43in (109cm) wide.
£1,000–1,200 ⚒ SK

Charles Locke Eastlake (1836–1906)

Although Eastlake trained as an architect, he never practised. His theories of design, outlined in his book *Hints on Household Taste*, published in England in 1868, found an immediate following in Britain and subsequently in the United States, where his influence on furniture design was profound and where his name is still synonymous with the Gothic revival. His second book, *A History of the Gothic Revival in England*, appeared in 1872, and it is mainly on the strength of these two volumes that his reputation rests. He deplored the shoddiness of mass-produced furniture and favoured hardy and solid designs of a somewhat rustic nature.

Eastlake's designs are not marked, and many pieces of furniture are attributed to him, some of them erroneously. Some documented proof can be gleaned from the records of contemporary cabinet makers, but as his pieces are not stamped, even by makers, this could be laborious.

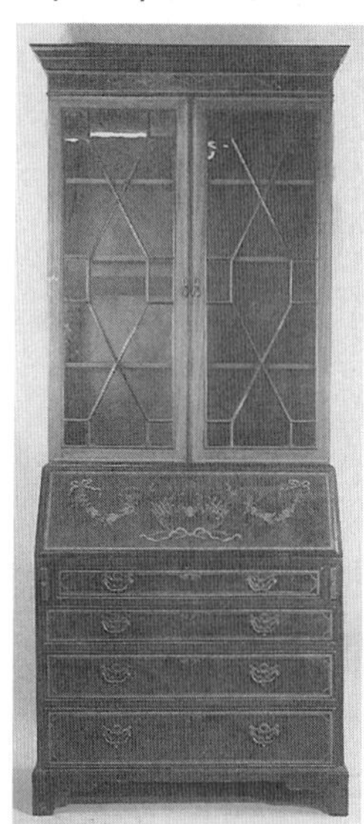

A Sheraton revival mahogany bureau bookcase, the astragal-glazed doors enclosing three adjustable shelves, the fall-front inlaid with ribbon-tied swags of foliage, enclosing a fitted interior, with four long graduated drawers below, c1900, 39½in (100cm) wide.
£2,300–2,750 ⚒ CGC

An Edwardian mahogany bureau bookcase, satinwood crossbanded, with twin 13-pane astragal doors, the fan-inlaid fall above four long drawers, 36in (91.5cm) wide.
£1,500–1,800 ⚒ DMC

► A William and Mary-style walnut bureau bookcase, the astragal-glazed double doors over a featherbanded fall enclosing a fitted interior, over two short and two long drawers, 29in (73.5cm) wide.
£1,200–1,500 ⚒ P(Ba)

Low Bookcases

A Regency rosewood open bookcase, with later green marble top, and long frieze drawer above two adjustable shelves, 47½in (120.5cm) wide.
£1,800–2,200 ⚒ AH

A Victorian burr-walnut bookcase, the top with three-quarter gilt-brass gallery above two glazed doors enclosing three gilt-tooled green leather-fringed shelves, 48in (122cm) wide.
£900–1,100 ⚒ BR

A Victorian mahogany dwarf bookcase, with inverted breakfront, the centre with two adjustable shelves flanked by arch panel doors applied with twist split pilasters, 66¼in (168.5cm) wide.
£750–900 ⚒ Bri

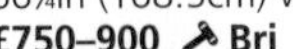

A breakfront dwarf open bookcase, of figured walnut and amboyna, inlaid with stringing, the top with a pierced brass gallery, above adjustable shelves flanked and divided by turned and fluted pilasters, c1880, 80in (203cm) wide.
£2,700–3,000 ⚒ S(S)

A mahogany bookcase, by Maple & Co, with astragal-glazed doors raised on ogee feet, c1900, 48in (122cm) wide.
£1,350–1,500 ⊞ RAN

◄ **An Edwardian two-tier bookcase,** the turned spindles terminating in pad feet, 19in (48.5cm) wide.
£300–350 ⚒ P(Ba)

Open Bookcases

A mahogany dwarf waterfall bookcase, c1810, 31in (78.5cm) wide.
£1,500–1,700 ⊞ F&F

◄ **An Empire-style mahogany bookcase,** with grey and white marble top above a frieze drawer and shelves, Dutch, c1820, 39in (99cm) wide.
£900–1,100 ⚒ S(Am)

► **A Victorian mahogany stepped open bookcase,** 30in (76cm) wide.
£320–380 ⚒ SWO

► **A Victorian mahogany bookcase,** the three bays of adjustable open shelves above three fret panel doors, two hinged, the centre sliding, 77½in (197cm) wide.
£2,200–2,600 ⚒ LAY

A walnut open bookcase, the serpentine front with gilt highlights to foliate scroll-carved friezes, and gilt flutes to the adjustable shelves, French, late 19thC, 72in (183cm) wide.
£900–1,100 ⚒ WW

Revolving Bookcases

A mahogany revolving bookcase, the two tiers each fitted with four compartments, late 19thC, 24in (61cm) wide.
£400–500 GAK

An inlaid mahogany revolving bookcase, the top of serpentine ebonized outline, above two shelves united by ebonized slats, late 19thC, 20½in (52cm) wide.
£400–500 PF

◀ **An inlaid mahogany revolving bookcase,** early 20thC, 12in (30.5cm) wide.
£250–300 SK

An Edwardian oak revolving bookcase, the four square tiers with slatted sides, on casters, 23½in (59.5cm) wide.
£500–600 P(Ba)

▶ **An Edwardian mahogany revolving bookcase,** the top banded in satinwood, the two shelves each fitted with four compartments sectioned by slatted dividers, 19½in (49.5cm) wide.
£620–700 WW

An Edwardian mahogany and marquetry revolving bookcase, 15in (38cm) wide.
£675–750 S(S)

Secretaire Bookcases

A George III mahogany secretaire bookcase, with astragal-glazed panelled doors, the lower part with a fall-front enclosing a fitted interior, 44½in (113cm) wide.
£3,700–4,500 P(EA)

A George IV mahogany secretaire bookcase, the glazed doors enclosing adjustable shelves, the fitted secretaire above two solid panelled doors, 44in (112cm) wide.
£1,850–2,200 RBB

A mahogany-veneered secretaire bookcase, the glazed doors with reeded brass trim enclosing four shelves, the lower section with a secretaire drawer with tooled-leather writing surface, on original bracket feet and with original brasses, c1840, 49in (124.5cm) wide.
£8,000–8,800 HA

A Victorian walnut secretaire bookcase, with ebonized mouldings, the glazed doors above a secretaire fitment with a fall-front, with two panelled doors below, 49¾in (126.5cm) wide.
£1,600–2,000 P(S)

◀ **A secretaire bookcase,** the glazed tracery doors enclosing adjustable shelves, the base with a fall-front enclosing fitted drawers, above panelled doors to sliding trays, mid-19thC, 35½in (90cm) wide.
£3,200–3,800 WW

▶ **A mahogany secretaire bookcase,** the satinwood interior with original tooled-leather writing surface, c1850, 54in (137cm) wide.
£5,000–5,750 MTay

Buckets

► **A George III mahogany and brass-bound peat bucket,** with brass swing handle and liner, 11¾in (30cm) high.
£600–720 ⚒ P

A pair of George III mahogany and brass-bound peat buckets, with brass loop handles, 15½in (39.5cm) high.
£1,500–1,800 ⚒ AH

► **A George III mahogany and brass-bound peat bucket,** with brass swing handle, 12½in (32cm) wide.
£700–800 ⚒ S(S)

► **A mahogany and brass-bound bucket,** with two broad and two narrow brass bands and later brass liner, 1780–1820, 13¾in (35cm) high.
£800–950 ⚒ S

A mahogany and brass-bound plate bucket, the body with two brass bands and brass loop handle, late 18thC, 14¼in (36cm) diam.
£2,700–3,000 ⚒ S

A Georgian mahogany and brass-bound plate bucket, with brass swing handle, Irish, 25in (63.5cm) high.
£700–850 ⚒ MEA

Buffets

A Regency rosewood-veneered buffet, on turned and banded baluster columns, 34in (86.5cm) wide.
£1,500–1,800 ⚒ L&E

A William IV mahogany buffet, the three graduated tiers with scroll-carved brackets, 40½in (103cm) wide.
£1,000–1,200 ⚒ P(O)

A William IV mahogany three-tier buffet, the centre with two cutlery drawers, on semi-fluted supports, 45in (114.5cm) wide.
£900–1,100 ⚒ HOLL

A Victorian mahogany three-tier buffet, with shaped tray top and scroll ends, on cabriole front supports with scroll toes, 45in (114.5cm) wide.
£1,300–1,600 ⚒ CAG

Miller's is a price GUIDE not a price LIST

A Victorian walnut two-tier buffet, the three-quarter galleried top over four baluster uprights and two-door enclosed cupboard, 44¾in (113.5cm) wide.
£400–500 ⚒ Bri

A Victorian mahogany two-tier buffet, with a foliate-pierced galleried back on turned and fluted columns, above twin panelled cupboards, 48in (122cm) wide.
£220–250 ⚒ DMC

A mahogany three-tier buffet, the three tiers flanked by pierced supports and scroll terminals, a long drawer to centre, 19thC, 24in (61cm) wide.
£425–500 ⚒ Bon(W)

An Edwardian mahogany and inlaid two-tier buffet, with a frieze drawer and two panel doors to base, 41¾in 106cm) wide.
£850–950 ⚒ S(S)

Bureaux

A Queen Anne figured walnut and featherbanded bureau-on-stand, the fitted sloping fall-front above a shaped frieze drawer enclosing five compartments above a quarter-veneered hinged slide, with brass carrying handles to sides, restored, 18¼in (46.5cm) wide.
£5,000–5,500 ⚒ Bon

► **A walnut bureau,** with a crossbanded and herringbone-banded fall-front enclosing a fitted interior above four graduated drawers, 18thC and later, 36¼in (92cm) wide.
£2,000–2,400 ⚒ HYD

A mahogany writing bureau, the fall-front enclosing a fitted interior, c1780, 36in (91.5cm) wide.
£2,000–2,250 ⊞ DOA

A Queen Anne walnut bureau, the lower section with three short drawers above a single drawer inlaid to simulate three drawers, partially inlaid with ebonized and boxwood stringing within crossbanding, later alterations, 23½in (59.5cm) wide.
£2,300–2,600 ⚒ S

◄ **A inlaid walnut bureau,** the fall-front enclosing canopied pigeonholes, mostly original brass, c1760, 36in (91.5cm) wide.
£3,000–3,350 ⊞ TWh

Cross Reference
See Colour Review (page 97)

A George III mahogany bureau, the fall-front enclosing a fitted interior, above two short and three long graduated drawers, 41¾in (106cm) wide.
£600–720 ⚒ CGC

A walnut and boxwood-strung bureau-on-stand. the hinged fall-front enclosing a fitted interior, the lower part containing three small drawers, early 18thC, 27½in (70cm) wide.
£3,200–3,800 ⚒ P(EA)

A George III mahogany bureau, the fall-front with boxwood and ebony-strung decoration enclosing a fitted interior above four long boxwood and ebony-strung chevron-banded drawers, 36in (91.5cm) wide.
£1,100–1,300 ⚒ Mit

Origins of English bureaux and buying tips

Bureaux first appeared in France in the latter part of the 17th century and soon became popular in England. In early examples the fall-fronts were supported by gatelegs, but these were replaced by sliding slopers by c1700. The slope concealed an interior fitted with drawers, pigeonholes and sometimes a well with a sliding top in which to hide documents. Timbers most commonly used were walnut veneer on a carcass of oak or pine. When buying a bureau the main features to look for are:

- Quality of construction
- Good proportions and compact size
- Original brassware and feet
- Attractive colour and patination
- Stepped interior and central cupboard
- Fitted well and slide
- Secret compartments
- Oak drawer linings

Many of these points will apply to most items of good furniture.

A George III mahogany bureau, the fall-front enclosing a fitted interior, the four long drawers fitted with later brass handles, some damage, 43in (109cm) wide.
£650–800 WW

A George III faded mahogany bureau, the fall-front enclosing a fitted interior, above four long drawers with original brass handles, interior door missing, 44¾in (113.5cm) wide.
£800–950 WW

A mahogany bureau, the fall-front enclosing a fitted boxwood-strung and inlaid interior, above two short and three long cockbeaded drawers, c1790, 48in (122cm) wide.
£3,750–4,250 JC

A floral marquetry *bombé bureau à cylindre,* the fitted cylinder compartment above a pull-out writing slide and one long and two short drawers, the sides with ormolu carrying handles, Continental, probably French, 18thC, 34½in (87.5cm) wide.
£2,700–3,200 MEA

A Chippendale-style cherrywood bureau, the fall-front enclosing a fitted interior, above four cockbeaded graduated long drawers, American, 1780–1820, 39in (99cm) wide.
£2,000–2,200 BB(S)

A mahogany bureau, the satinwood banding with neo-classical-style marquetry, the fall-front enclosing an inlaid fitted interior, above two frieze drawers with brass handles, 19thC, 42in (106.5cm) wide.
£600–720 WW

► **A painted satinwood cylinder bureau,** the cylinder front depicting a young girl and lambs within a floral surround, enclosing a fitted interior and pull-out writing surface, above three graduated long drawers, late 19thC, 24in (61cm) wide.
£500–600 MCA

An Edwardian mahogany cylinder bureau, decorated with inlaid satinwood crossbanding and boxwood stringing, the cylinder enclosing a fitted interior above a pull-out slide and two short drawers, 29½in (75cm) wide.
£425–525 AG

An Edwardian mahogany and satinwood-banded cylinder bureau, the fitted interior with pull-out writing surface, 29¼in (74.5cm) wide.
£525–625 P(S)

Cabinets

A mahogany estate cabinet, the fielded panel doors enclosing 17 drawers, the lower section with fielded panel doors enclosing one long and six short drawers, c1755, 50in (127cm) wide.
£18,000–22,000 ⚒ S
This cabinet was almost certainly supplied to William Wrightson (d.1760), Cusworth Hall, Yorkshire and remained in the family until after 1952. It is because of this provenance that it fetched a top price at auction.

A George III mahogany collector's cabinet, the upper panelled doors enclosing 22 short drawers, the lower panelled doors enclosing five long graduated drawers, with brass carrying handles to sides, 29in (73.5cm) wide.
£2,700–3,000 ⚒ Bon

A pair of mahogany pedestal cabinets, with panelled doors, c1830, 21¼in (54cm) wide.
£1,250–1,500 ⚒ HOK

A mahogany estate cabinet, the fielded panel doors enclosing an interior with door, file slots and small drawers, the hinged flap above four long drawers, later brass handles, carrying handles, early 19thC, 38½in (98cm) wide.
£1,150–1,400 ⚒ WW

A rosewood-veneered pedestal cabinet, with polished slate top, the frieze drawer above shelves enclosed by a panelled door flanked by turned pilasters, brass handles, 19thC, 15in (38cm) wide.
£230–275 ⚒ WW

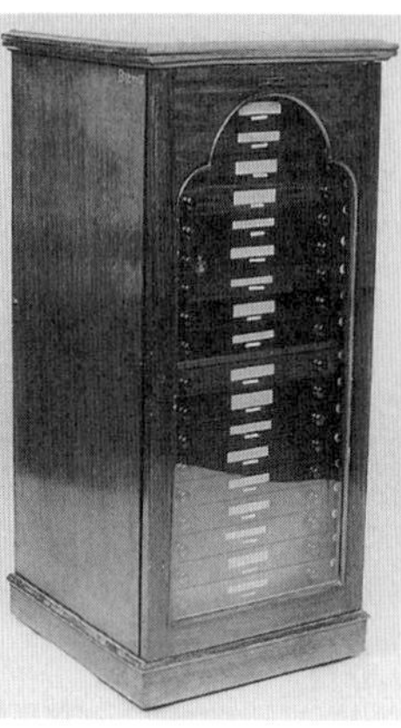

A Victorian mahogany specimen cabinet, the glazed door with Gothic trefoil arch enclosing 20 drawers with glazed lids, 23½in (59.5cm) wide.
£1,500–1,800 ⚒ P(Ed)

A Biedermeier mahogany cabinet, the top with a serpentine-shaped drawer above a door simulating a fall-front and various drawers, flanked by columns headed by Ionic capitals, German, 19thC, 43¼in (110cm) wide.
£1,350–1,600 ⚒ S(Am)

An ebonized and ivory inlaid cabinet, with two panelled doors flanked by reeded pillars, the lower part with panelled doors, all inlaid with figures, grotesques, acanthus foliage and engraved ivory, some damage, Italian, 19thC, 41½in (105.5cm) wide.
£2,300–2,750 ⚒ L

Biedermeier

Biedermeier furniture was made principally in the 1820s and 1830s in Austria, Germany and parts of Scandinavia. It was named after a fictional character who symbolized the German bourgeoisie of the early 19th century. Designed for a relatively mass market, it was constructed mainly of blondwoods such as ash, maple, cherry and other fruitwoods. In Austria and Germany mahogany was also used, and these designs tended to be more sophisticated and elaborate, whereas Scandinavian forms were simple and relatively austere. Ornamentation was generally restricted to columns and palmettes, and these were often applied in ebony to contrast with the pale colour of the carcass.

A Victorian stained mahogany collector's cabinet, the glazed door enclosing nine drawers with turned wooden handles and brass indices, 22in (56cm) wide.
£340–400 ⚒ DD

A mahogany cabinet, the shelved interior enclosed by bowed panelled doors flanked by stop-fluted pilasters, c1905, 60in (152.5cm) wide.
£9,500–10,500 ⚒ S

Bedside Cabinets

A Chippendale period mahogany night table, c1780–90, 21in (53.5cm) wide.
£3,200–3,500 ⊞ CAT

A mahogany tray-top night commode, with a door above a pull-out drawer, brass handles, early 19thC, 22in (56cm) wide.
£260–320 ⚒ LFA

A mahogany tray-top night table, with a tambour sliding door above a cockbeaded drawer, now with a removable shelf with a compartment below, c1780, 22in (56cm) wide.
£2,200–2,450 ⊞ JC

A George III mahogany bedside commode, the cupboard door above a pull-out commode seat enclosing a white ceramic pot, with brass fittings, 20½in (52cm) wide.
£1,350–1,600 ⚒ TMA

◄ A Louis XVI mahogany night table, with white marble top, above tambour door and drawer, with all-over inlay and gilt-brass banding, signed 'E. Avril, ME', French, 14¼in (36cm) wide.
£1,500–1,800 ⚒ S(Am)
Etienne Avril (1748–91) was received master on 23 November 1774. He is known as Avril the Eldest and his workshop was at rue de Charenton, Paris. It is known that he was commissioned by Marie-Antoinette for her apartment in the Château de Saint-Cloud.

A mahogany Lancashire bedside cabinet, with inlaid bow front, c1790, 31in (78.5cm) wide.
£950–1,050 ⊞ BMi

A mahogany bedside cabinet, with arched door panel, c1860, 30in (76cm) wide.
£575–635 ⊞ RAN

Bureau Cabinets

► A mahogany bureau cabinet, associated, with architectural pediment, c1800, 38½in (98cm) wide.
£3,750–4,350 ⊞ MTay

A Gothic revival walnut bureau cabinet, c1890, 82in (208.5cm) high.
£2,000–2,250 ⊞ APO

◄ A tiger maple bureau cabinet, the doors enclosing eight valanced compartments, two adjustable shelves and three drawers, above a fall-front enclosing a fitted interior, three further drawers, 19thC grain paint, American, 1750–1800, 35½in (90cm) wide.
£8,500–10,000 ⚒ SK(B)

A mahogany bureau cabinet, the panelled doors opening to reveal three adjustable shelves, the lower section with a fall enclosing pigeonholes and small drawers, c1760, 39¾in (101cm) wide.
£2,200–2,500 ⚒ S(O)

Cabinets-on-Chests

A walnut cabinet-on-chest, with a cushion-moulded frieze drawer above two doors enclosing a fitted interior, the chest with two drawers, early 18thC, 38in (96.5cm) wide.
£10,000–12,000 ⚒ S

A burr-walnut-veneered cabinet-on-chest, outlined with featherbanding, with two crossbanded doors enclosing 11 drawers and a cupboard, the base with four drawers, on later bracket feet, early 18thC, 37½in (95cm) wide.
£7,500–9,000 ⚒ Bea(E)

A walnut and feather-banded cabinet-on-chest, early 18thC, 39¾in (101cm) wide.
£6,500–8,000 ⚒ Bon(C)

A walnut and burr-walnut serpentine cabinet-on-chest, with two panelled rocaille-carved doors above two short and two long drawers, on claw feet, Dutch, 18thC, 76¾in (195cm) wide.
£2,500–3,000 ⚒ S(Am)

◄ **A walnut cabinet-on-chest,** with foliate-carved cresting, the *bombé*-shaped base with three drawers, on claw feet, altered, Dutch, mid-18thC, 71¾in (182.5cm) wide.
£3,800–4,500 ⚒ S(Am)

► **A walnut serpentine-fronted cabinet,** with a pierced and carved scroll and foliate crest centred by an armoured mask, the doors carved with foliate spandrels, above a frieze drawer and two panel doors, on knurl feet, German, 19thC, 36¼in (92cm) wide.
£900–1,100 ⚒ P(Ba)

Corner Cabinets

A mahogany standing corner cabinet, the astragal-glazed door enclosing a shaped shelved interior, with panelled door below, c1760, 39½in (100.5cm) wide.
£2,250–2,750 ⚒ S(S)

A George III black lacquered bowfronted corner cupboard, the doors gilt-decorated with a chinoiserie scene, enclosing three shelves, 54¼in (138cm) high.
£1,150–1,400 ⚒ CGC

► **A George III mahogany corner cupboard,** with a boxwood- and ebony-inlaid frieze, with two shaped shelves and three small drawers enclosed by arched three-panel fielded doors, 37½in (95.5cm) wide.
£825–1,000 ⚒ DMC

Cross Reference
See Colour Review (page 101)

◄ **A George III mahogany bowfronted corner cupboard,** with stringing, the frieze with three marquetry cameos depicting a bird and two lions, the doors enclosing shelving and three small drawers, 30in (76cm) wide.
£850–1,000 ⚒ AH

A mahogany hanging corner cupboard, with glazed door, c1790, 26in (66cm) wide.
£2,200–2,400 ⊞ HA

A William IV mahogany bowfronted hanging corner cupboard, the cornice applied with acorn drops, the doors with rosewood-framed reserves above a small apron drawer, 49¼in (125cm) high.
£350–420 ⚒ P(S)

An Edwardian mahogany and satinwood cross-banded corner cabinet, the top with a frieze inlaid with scrolling acanthus and an astragal-glazed door enclosing shelves, the base with similarly-inlaid frieze and panelled door, 27¼in (69cm) wide.
£900–1,100 ⚒ P(Ed)

A satinwood, tulipwood and maple corner cupboard, with later white marble top, restored, Dutch, c1800, 26¾in (68cm) wide.
£1,600–2,000 ⚒ Bon(C)

A Georgian-style mahogany corner cupboard, the astragal-glazed door above a panelled door, on carved ogee bracket feet, c1890, 35in (89cm) wide.
£1,750–2,000 ⚒ MCA

An Edwardian inlaid mahogany corner cabinet, the astragal-glazed door enclosing two shelves, 22in (56cm) wide.
£500–600 ⚒ Bri

A George III bowfronted hanging corner cupboard, with moulded broken pediment, 47in (119.5cm) high.
£1,000–1,200 ⚒ HOLL

▶ A Victorian George II-style mahogany standing corner cabinet, with a green velvet-lined display cupboard, above an arched open compartment, shallow drawer, two panelled doors and open base, the pilasters and frieze with blind Chinese fretwork, 32in (81.5cm) wide.
£400–500 ⚒ N

A mahogany corner cupboard, with tambour door, original casters, Dutch, c1820, 28in (71cm) wide.
£3,300–3,650 ⊞ RGa

Display Cabinets

A George III mahogany china cabinet, the glazed doors crossbanded and enclosing shelves, above two short and one long drawer, top and base possibly associated, 54in (137cm) wide.
£6,750–8,000 S

A mahogany floral marquetry vitrine, with two glazed doors, a *bombé* drawer to base, inlaid throughout with engraved floral decoration, outlined with stringing, Dutch, 19thC, 41in (104cm) wide.
£1,000–1,200 N

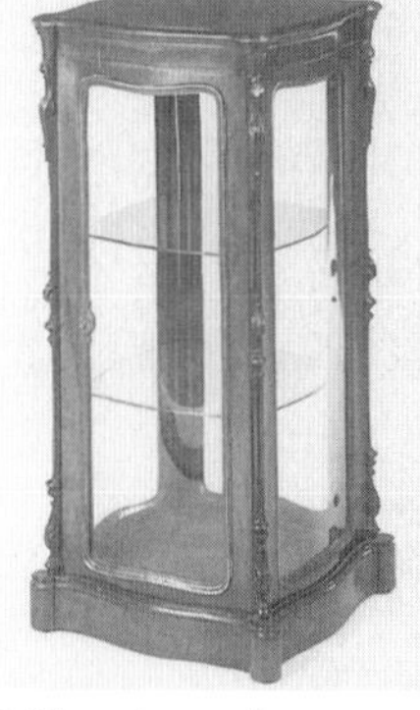

A Victorian walnut freestanding vitrine, with bowed glazed panel sides, one forming a door, the corners with scroll-carved fluted mouldings, the interior with two glass shelves, 19¼in (49cm) wide.
£1,200–1,350 S(S)

► **A walnut floral marquetry display cabinet,** Dutch, late 18thC, 67in (170cm) wide.
£6,750–8,000 Bon(C)

A George III mahogany alcove cupboard, the domed reeded cornice above two arched panelled doors with wooden astragals and centre brass edging strip, 44in (112cm) wide.
£700–850 Mit

A floral marquetry hanging cabinet, the arched top above a glazed barred door, Dutch, 19thC, 24in (61cm) wide.
£550–650 HOLL

A single door mahogany display cabinet, c1870, 56in (142cm) high,
£3,000–3,400 MTay

A pair of amboyna, ebony and parcel-gilt display cabinets, by Gillow & Co, with pierced brass galleries, two shaped glass shelves and mirrored back, inlaid throughout with ebony banding, boxwood and ebony stringing and brass beading, c1870, 33½in (85cm) wide.
£11,000–13,000 S

The firm of Gillows, based in Lancaster, was founded in the 1730s by Robert Gillow. His sons Richard and Robert II became partners in 1757 and 1767 respectively, Robert II managing the London branch which opened in 1770. Robert II's son and Richard's three sons became partners in the business between 1785 and 1795, and Richard's grandson, Richard Thomas (b.1806), was the last member of the family to be directly associated with the company, retiring in 1830. The firm was taken over by the partners Redmayne, Whiteside and Ferguson in 1813, but traded with 'late Gillows' after their names until 1829 when they adopted the firm's old name of Gillow & Co. After once more reverting to their own names between 1834–54, they finally changed back to Gillow & Co in 1855.

A mahogany and applied brass vitrine, with a brass astragal-glazed door flanked by two fluted columns enclosing two shelves above a concave frieze drawer, the base with a cupboard door enclosing a shelf, flanked by columns, Russian, early 19thC, 29½in (75cm) wide.
£4,000–5,000 Bon

A pair of Chippendale revival mahogany display cabinets, each with an astragal-glazed door and projecting bowfronted base with shallow drawers above an undertier, applied throughout with blind Chinese fretwork, pierced key pattern brackets and gallery of interlaced ovals, late 19thC, 24in (61cm) wide.
£3,800–4,500 N

Miller's is a price GUIDE not a price LIST

A kingwood serpentine front vitrine, with a single glazed door, the projecting base with panel door painted with a study of lovers in a garden landscape, the sides painted with rural scenes, the whole ormolu moulded, late 19thC, 29in (73.5cm) wide.
£1,750–2,000 DD

A display cabinet, with two glazed doors and swag and bellflower inlay, c1910, 42in (106.5cm) wide.
£1,400–1,550 MTay

An Edwardian mahogany bowfronted display cabinet, with satinwood and chequer line-inlaid decoration, with leaded glazed door and sides, 39¼in (100cm) wide.
£500–600 JNic

A Biedermeier fruitwood cabinet, the two glazed doors enclosing a fitted interior, 19thC, 43in (109cm) wide.
£400–500 P(Ba)

A mahogany *vernis Martin*-style vitrine, inlaid with panels of floral marquetry and stringing and applied with gilt-metal mounts, the glazed front and sides enclosing fitted plush-lined shelves, early 20thC, 27½in (68.5cm) wide.
£800–950 GAK

A Transitional-style kingwood vitrine, applied with gilt-metal mounts, the glazed door enclosing glass shelves and a mirrored glass backing, with glazed sides, French, early 20thC, 27½in (70cm) wide.
£700–800 P

An Edwardian mahogany and crossbanded display cabinet, the back with cartouche bevelled mirror, astragal-glazed door, 22½in (57cm) wide.
£340–400 WL

A gilt-metal-mounted mahogany bowfronted vitrine, with glazed door and *vernis Martin* panels, French, early 20thC, 27in (68.5cm) wide.
£900–1,100 G(L)

◄ **An Edwardian mahogany display cabinet,** with crossbanded and string-inlaid frieze and two glazed and gothic-beaded doors enclosing two shelves, over two base drawers, 42in (106.5cm) wide.
£700–850 DA

Music Cabinets

A Regency rosewood music cabinet, with two panelled doors enclosing an adjustable shelved interior with three long base drawers, 26½in (67.5cm) wide.
£1,750–2,000 TMA

► **A rosewood serpentine music cabinet,** with boxwood line inlay and panels of musical trophies, late 19thC, 19in (48.5cm) wide.
£450–550 E

► **A Victorian rosewood music cabinet,** with stringing and marquetry, the raised mirrored back above a fall-front inlaid with a musical trophy enclosing a fitted secretaire interior, the glazed door below enclosing shelves, 22½in (57cm) wide.
£775–900 AH

A Victorian walnut music cabinet, inlaid with boxwood lines, with a pierced brass three-quarter gallery above an arched glazed panel door enclosing four shelves, 22½in (57cm) wide.
£400–500 P(Ba)

◄ **An Edwardian satinwood serpentine music cabinet,** painted with classical urns among foliage and ribbon-tied floral swags within chequer-banded borders, enclosed by a frieze drawer above a panelled door, 21¼in (54cm) wide.
£1,100–1,300 P(S)

Secretaire Cabinets

► **A Queen Anne walnut secretaire *escritoire*,** the cushion-moulded long drawer over a herringbone-banded fall-front enclosing a central door, drawers and pigeonholes, above two short and two long drawers, on later bun feet, 39¾in (101cm) wide.
£2,500–3,000 P(E)

A Federal mahogany-veneered secretaire cabinet, the panelled doors enclosing two adjustable shelves, above a bowfronted lower case of cockbeaded graduated drawers, the top one fitted with a felt-lined sliding writing surface, American, 1800–10, 34½in (87.5cm) wide.
£22,000–26,000 SK(B)

A rosewood writing cabinet, with leather top and six drawers, c1840, 23in (58.5cm) wide.
£5,500–6,000 GBr

A mahogany and inlaid secretaire cabinet, the upper part with fitted shelves and three drawers enclosed by a pair of tambour doors, above a concave long drawer and fall-front enclosing a fitted interior, Dutch, early 19thC, 44in (112cm) wide.
£3,500–4,200 MCA

► **Two mahogany and gilt-metal-mounted Louis XVI-style *secrétaires à abattant*,** each with a marble top above a drawer, the fall-front with a floral porcelain roundel, French, c1880, 19in (48.5cm) wide.
£3,700–4,200 S(S)

A mahogany marquetry *secrétaire à abbatant*, with a single drawer above a trellis-patterned inlaid fall-flap enclosing a fitted interior, the base with two conforming doors, Dutch, 19thC, 33½in (85cm) wide.
£1,800–2,200 E

Side Cabinets

A George III mahogany side cabinet, with two re-entrant panel doors, 39¾in (101cm) wide.
£650–800 P(Ba)

A Regency rosewood side cabinet, the superstructure fitted with a mirrored back and drawers, the lower section with an arrangement of five frieze drawers, above two cupboard doors with pleated fabric-lined brass grilles, enclosing a shelf, 35¾in (91cm) wide.
£4,250–5,250 S

Cross Reference
See Colour Review (page 104)

A mahogany chiffonier, the two panelled and crossbanded doors enclosing three mahogany-faced adjustable shelves, c1880, 40in (101.5cm) wide.
£2,000–2,250 JC

A Louis XVI mahogany and gilt-steel commode, by M. G. Cramer, the white marble top above two short drawers and two panelled doors centred by bosses, applied overall with bands of cut and gilded steel beadwork, maker's stamp, 51in (130cm) wide.
£14,000–17,000 Bon
M. G. Cramer was born on 4th September 1771 in Germany, but moved to Paris where he opened a workshop in the rue du Faubourg Saint Antoine, before later moving to the rue du Bac.

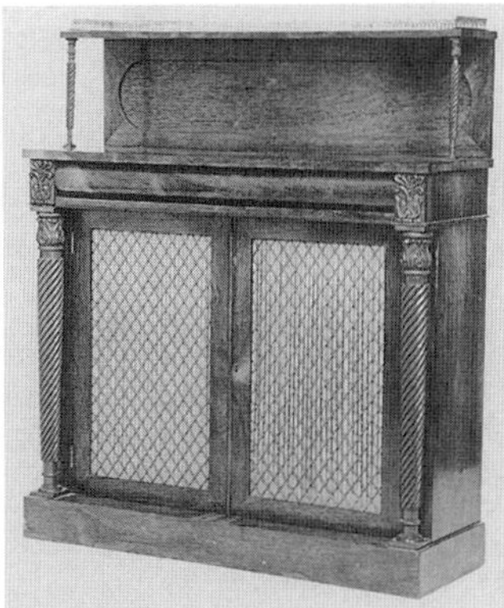

A late Regency rosewood chiffonier, with a pierced brass gallery, and a frieze drawer above two brass trellis-patterned doors flanked by carved and applied honeysuckle motifs and acanthus-leaf-carved spiral twist pilasters, 43in (109.5cm) wide.
£2,300–2,750 AG

A William IV rosewood chiffonier, with single shelf back and foliate scroll brackets, the two doors with brass lattice enclosing fabric, 36in (91.5cm) wide.
£550–650 G(L)

A Regency gilt-metal-mounted rosewood breakfront chiffonier, with a gilt-metal three-quarter galleried back above three green silk-lined cupboard doors with gilt-metal grills, divided by acanthus-leaf-carved scroll columns, 64in (162.5cm) wide.
£5,250–6,250 HYD

A brass-inlaid chiffonier, the doors with brass grilles, on turned rosewood feet, c1820, 40in (101.5cm) wide.
£5,000–5,650 HA

A William IV mahogany chiffonier, the base fitted with a frieze drawer above two arched panelled doors enclosing a shelf, 46½in (118cm) wide.
£650–800 CAG

A mahogany chiffonier, with two drawers above two doors, c1840, 49in (124.5cm) wide.
£1,500–1,650 RPh

A carved mahogany chiffonier, in original condition, c1850, 49½in (125.5cm) wide.
£2,000–2,250 ⊞ MTay

An ebonized credenza, with bone inlay, c1860, 69in (175.5cm) wide.
£2,800–3,200 ⊞ DUK

An Eastlake carved mahogany side cabinet, the upper section fitted with a mirror and shelves, the lower section with glazed door enclosing shelves, with frieze drawer, all-over carved with geometric designs, American, 1880, 44in (112cm) wide.
£1,700–2,000 ⚒ SK

A mahogany dining room cupboard, the top with a shaped gallery, the frieze drawers with later brass handles, above two panelled doors enclosing a sliding linen tray, Scottish, 19thC, 42in (106.5cm) wide.
£500–600 ⚒ WW

A Victorian walnut pier cabinet, with gilt-metal mounts and mirrored door, 30in (76cm) wide.
£2,000–2,350 ⊞ RAN

◄ **A Victorian figured mahogany chiffonier,** with two frieze drawers above chamfered arched panelled doors, 47in (119.5cm) wide.
£450–550 ⚒ DMC

A Louis XVI-style commode, inlaid with maplewood, with white marble top, c1890, 23¾in (60.5cm) wide.
£900–1,100 ⊞ HA

► **An Edwardian mahogany and satinwood-banded side cabinet,** of bowed outline, with a central door and a shaped undertier, 36¼in (92cm) wide.
£800–1,100 ⚒ P(Ba)

A mahogany chiffonier, with one long drawer above two cupboard doors, c1860, 45in (114.5cm) wide.
£1,800–2,000 ⊞ RPh

A Victorian mahogany chiffonier, with three short frieze drawers above three arched panel doors, 46in (117cm) wide.
£1,450–1,750 ⚒ AG

A Victorian mahogany breakfront side cabinet, the shaped red marble top fitted with a central frieze drawer, above a pair of panelled doors, flanked by conforming curved doors, 72in (183cm) wide.
£2,000–2,400 ⚒ P(Ba)

Cabinets-on-Stands

An ebonized, tortoiseshell and ivory-inlaid cabinet-on-stand, the top with a hinged lid enclosing three mirrored panels, one missing, above ten ripple-moulded drawers around a central panelled door enclosing a parquetry-veneered interior, faults, Flemish, early 18thC, later stand, 31½in (80cm) wide.
£2,700–3,200 ⚒ S(S)

A George III coromandel lacquered cabinet-on-stand, with incised decoration of polychrome flowers, birds and insects and with brass mounts, the doors enclosing an arrangement of ebonized drawers, decoration refreshed, 32in (81.5cm) wide.
£3,400–3,750 ⚒ S

A floral marquetry cabinet-on-stand, the top centred by a stylized chequerboard within a frame surrounded by floral sprays, above two small drawers and one long drawer decorated with similar marquetry, stand altered, late 18thC, later stand, 16½in (42cm) wide.
£4,500–5,500 ⚒ Bon

A Louis XIII-style ebony-veneered and ebonized writing desk, by Collier & Plucknett, ivory-inlaid with lines and marquetry of urns, birds, a mask, and a cornucopia of fruit and leaf scrolls, fitted with a superstructure enclosed by two panel doors above a sliding top and frieze drawer, 30in (76cm) wide.
£1,100–1,300 ⚒ P(WM)

A cream-painted mahogany cabinet-on-stand, painted in coloured enamels with baskets of flowers, doves and gardening trophies, the base with an inset writing surface and two frieze drawers, French, late 19thC, 40½in (103cm) wide.
£900–1,100 ⚒ LFA

Coromandel lacquer, with its characteristic incised decoration, was made in central and northern China from the latter part of the Ming Dynasty, and exported to Europe before the end of the 17th century through the English East India Company's trading posts on the Coromandel coast of India. The technique involved overlaying a base of wood with a series of increasingly fine white clays and fibrous grasses. Over this surface lacquer was applied and polished before the design was incised and the hollowed-out portions filled with colour and gilding. An English version of the technique was known as 'Bantam work', probably named after the Dutch settlement in Java, thought to have been the initial market for this type of Chinese incised lacquer.

A chinoiserie lacquer cabinet-on-stand, with gilt-painted scenes of figures, willow trees and buildings, the two doors enclosing shelves, alterations, 1885–1915, 74in (188cm) high.
£1,300–1,600 ⚒ RTo

A green lacquerware cabinet-on-stand, with gilt cabriole legs, c1900, 16in (40.5cm) wide.
£600–680 ⊞ RAN

◀ **A William and Mary-style walnut escritoire,** by Maple & Co, c1910, 44in (112cm) wide.
£2,250–2,500 ⊞ NAW

▶ **A Queen Anne-style walnut drinks cabinet-on-stand,** with cabriole legs, c1910, 33in (84cm) wide.
£1,100–1,250 ⊞ MTay

A Georgian-style scarlet lacquer cabinet-on-stand, with hinged lid over twin doors, decorated with gesso relief in gilt and polychrome, on a giltwood blind fretwork stand, 1920s, 25½in (65cm) wide.
£850–1,000 ⚒ Bri

Table Cabinets

A stained fruitwood miniature cabinet, the two doors enclosing a fitted interior with seven drawers applied with reverse glass paintings depicting landscapes, minor damage, Germany, c1700, 7½in (19cm) wide.
£1,600–1,800 ⚒ S(Am)

A late Regency rosewood, penwork and transfer-printed table cabinet, decorated with classical figural ovals, the top opening to a compartment workbox section, the twin doors enclosing two short and two long drawers, 12¼in (31cm) wide.
£700–850 ⚒ P(Ba)

A Regency rosewood table-top cabinet, with mother-of-pearl inlay, pewter line and egg-and-tongue moulded edges, the hinged lift-up top over silk-lined ring and jewellery compartments and fitted with four drawers with lift-out jewellery tray, a needlework tray, a writing box and one open drawer, 13½in (34.5cm) wide.
£500–600 ⚒ TMA

A mahogany table cabinet, with cupboards, drawers and fitted writing tray, c1830, 28in (71cm) wide.
£2,000–2,250 ⊞ RGa

A Victorian rosewood-veneered accessories cabinet, the lidded sewing compartment with mirror and two drawers, one for jewellery, and a writing slope enclosed by two doors inlaid with mother-of-pearl, one handle damaged, 12in (30.5cm) wide.
£650–800 ⚒ WW

◄ **An Edwardian carved oak smoker's cabinet,** fitted with four interior drawers, enclosed by panelled doors with bevelled glass tops, 16in (40.5cm) wide.
£140–170 ⚒ HOLL

Canterburies

A Regency mahogany canterbury, the four-division top with crossed supports, above a single drawer, 19½in (49.5cm) wide.
£1,200–1,500 ⚒ B(Ed)

Sheraton, in his *Cabinet Dictionary,* 1803, explained that the name Canterbury has been applied because the Bishop of that See first gave orders for the pieces: 'the legs are ... turned or plain, tapered, with castors, and are adapted to run in under a piano forte'.

A mahogany canterbury, with a single drawer, c1800, 18in (45.5cm) wide.
£2,750–3,250 ⚒ S

► **A rosewood canterbury,** with Prince of Wales feather, scroll- and shell-carved divisions, on a base with one long drawer, early 19thC, 29½in (75cm) wide.
£650–900 ⚒ TMA

A Regency rosewood canterbury, with curved dividers and cross-filled sides over a drawer, some damage, 20½in (52cm) wide.
£1,150–1,400 ⚒ Bea(E)

A Regency mahogany scoop-top canterbury, with a central carrying handle and a frieze drawer, 20in (51cm) wide.
£1,600–1,800 DMC

A rosewood canterbury, after a design by Loudon, with three folio sections and frieze drawer, mid-19thC, 19¼in (49cm) wide.
£1,200–1,400 Bon

A Victorian walnut canterbury, with three divisions over a single drawer, 20¼in (51.5cm) wide.
£700–850 HYD

A Victorian walnut music canterbury, with pierced fret divisions, the base with a frieze drawer, 25in (63.5cm) wide.
£750–900 WW

A late Regency mahogany canterbury, the four-division top with ring-turned supports above a single drawer and opposing false drawer, 21¾in (53.3cm) wide.
£1,500–1,800 P(Ed)

A Victorian walnut canterbury, with a gilded gallery rail, turned columns, decorative inlay and fretwork, the base incorporating a drawer, 23½in (59.5cm) wide.
£650–800 HOLL

► **A Victorian walnut whatnot canterbury,** the upper section with pierced three-quarter gallery supported on barley-twist turned uprights and spindle-divided based above a frieze drawer, on turned legs, 21in (53.5cm) wide.
£600–720 RFA

A rosewood canterbury, with pierced dividers and turned supports, one drawer under, 19thC, 24in (61cm) wide.
£600–720 E

► **A Victorian rosewood music canterbury,** with barley-twist uprights and pierced lyre-shaped panels above two divisions with pierced sides, above a frieze drawer, 25½in (65cm) wide.
£1,500–1,800 P

A mahogany canterbury, with four divisions above a drawer, c1830, 19in (48.5cm) wide.
£1,200–1,400 S(O)

A Victorian inlaid burr-walnut-veneered canterbury/music cabinet, with pierced gilt-brass gallery, two fret-carved divisions and a compartment below, 25¼in (64cm) wide.
£1,100–1,300 Bea(E)

Open Armchairs

A pair of William and Mary walnut open armchairs, the pierced S-scroll crests with central shell motifs above caned backs, later arms and embossed leather seats.
£600–700 ⚒ CGC

A George III mahogany Gainsborough armchair, the seat back and arms in worn tapestry.
£2,000–2,400 ⚒ TRM

A pair of George III mahogany elbow chairs, with pierced vase-shaped splats and padded seats, later arms.
£450–550 ⚒ LFA

► **A marquetry armchair,** with vase-shaped splat and scrolled arms, damaged, Dutch, 18th–19thC.
£1,000–1,100 ⚒ S(Am)

A pair of carved and parcel-gilt walnut armchairs, Italian, 17thC.
£2,700–3,200 ⚒ S(Mi)

A mahogany Raeburn chair, Scottish, c1790.
£2,200–2,400 ⊞ BMi

A walnut armchair, the cresting rail with acanthus carving above a harebell-carved splat, the cabriole legs with acanthus carving to the knee, c1715.
£14,500–16,000 ⊞ REI
The chair can be accurately dated to the beginning of the reign of George I due to the paper scrolling of the cresting rail which was in vogue at this date.

A Hepplewhite-style hoop-back mahogany elbow chair, with rope carving to the back and front legs, c1790.
£1,300–1,475 ⊞ RGa

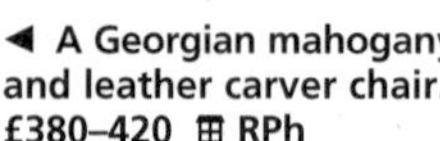

◄ **A Georgian mahogany and leather carver chair.**
£380–420 ⊞ RPh

► **A Sheraton period mahogany commode armchair,** with plumed back splats, late 18thC.
£200–240 ⚒ WW

A mahogany Yorkshire chair, with original inset boxwood casters, c1770.
£1,250–1,400 ⊞ RGa
This chair is known as a 'drunkard's chair'. As the story goes, the casters inset in the base stretchers enabled the master of the house to be wheeled to his bedroom when he was too incapacitated to walk.

A pair of George III giltwood open armchairs, with oval padded backs and beaded frames, re-gilded.
£2,000–2,400 ⚒ Bon

◄ **A set of six Directoire-style mahogany open armchairs,** upholstered in green velvet, Belgian, c1800.
£3,400–4,000 ⚒ S(Am)

A Regency open armchair, button-upholstered in black leather.
£400–480 ⚒ MAR

A mahogany-framed 'Daw's Patent Recumbent Easy Chair', the arms with leaf-scroll ornament, upholstered in brown moquette with reclining back, adjustable seat and pull-out footrest, with original label to underside, dated January 1821.
£850–1,000 ⚒ CAG

An elbow chair, upholstered in brown leather, c1830.
£1,100–1,250 ⊞ RPh

A giltwood open armchair, the carved back and scroll arms decorated with acanthus in pale green, c1840.
£1,300–1,450 ⊞ RAN

A Victorian foliate scroll-carved mahogany-framed open armchair, with button upholstered back, arm pads and serpentine front seat.
£600–720 ⚒ MCA

A walnut open armchair, upholstered in black leather, c1860.
£900–1,000 ⊞ SIE

An early Victorian mahogany-framed easy armchair, upholstered in a sand-coloured fabric.
£400–500 ⚒ CGC

A Renaissance revival rosewood armchair, the crest with a cartouche-centred cabochon, American, 1875–1900.
£380–450 ⚒ NOA

A Victorian mahogany armchair, with buttoned roll-over back, padded arms and stuff-over seat, upholstered in gold-coloured velvet-type material.
£450–550 ⚒ Mit

► **A Victorian ornately carved open armchair,** with scrolling acanthus frame and pink patterned fabric upholstery.
£330–400 ⚒ HOLL

A Victorian walnut-framed open armchair, with a foliate-carved top-rail, carved back and seat with padded arms.
£400–500 ⚒ Mit

A pair of Victorian lady's low elbow chairs, the rosewood frames inlaid with stringing, the padded back with a marquetry-inlaid splat over an upholstered sprung seat.
£300–350 ⚒ WW

A pair of Chippendale-style mahogany elbow chairs, c1900.
£900–1,000 ⊞ NoC

A Queen Anne-style carver chair, stamped 'Shoolbred', c1900.
£550–625 ⊞ RPh

A pair of early George III-style mahogany elbow chairs, with carved shaped crests, pierced gothic tracery splats, leaf-carved arms and padded serpentine seats, 19thC.
£2,200–2,700 ⚒ LFA

A pair of Edwardian Sheraton revival-style satinwood open armchairs, with floral and foliate polychrome decoration, caned panels and seats with squab cushions.
£2,800–3,200 ⚒ P

◀ **An Edwardian inlaid mahogany open armchair,** with a sycamore and harewood-inlaid shaped and pierced splat, over an upholstered seat.
£280–350 ⚒ BLH

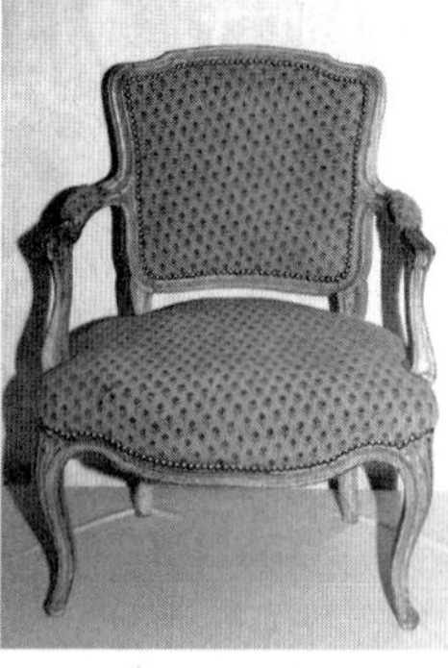

A pair of Louis XV-style open painted armchairs, French, c1880.
£1,200–1,350 ⊞ TDS

A turned-mahogany rocking chair, American, c1890.
£550–625 ⊞ RPh

An Edwardian mahogany open armchair, the shaped pierced back with floral-carved decoration above shaped crook elbow supports, restored.
£150–180 ⚒ BLH

A late Victorian mahogany and satinwood open armchair, by Christopher Pratt & Sons, the top-rail with a satinwood tablet inlaid with scrolling acanthus above a similarly-inlaid lozenge splat flanked by rams' heads, over an upholstered seat.
£1,000–1,200 ⚒ P(Ed)

A pair of walnut *fauteuils*, with foliate-carved top-rails, open scroll arms and serpentine seats, French, 19thC.
£1,500–1,800 ⚒ CGC

An Edwardian stained beech chair, the T-shaped splat upholstered in ochre plush fabric, on a foliate-pierced support, the arms on similar supports, over a shaped upholstered seat.
£100–120 ⚒ PFK

◀ **A pair of Edwardian *faux* bamboo side chairs.**
£1,200–1,350 ⊞ RAN

Upholstered Armchairs

A George II walnut and beechwood wing armchair, upholstered in apricot damask, on cabriole legs and pad feet, restored.
£3,800–4,500 S

A mahogany elbow chair, the arms terminating in scrolls, on short front supports with scrolled feet, upholstered in puce Regency stripe, 19thC.
£300–350 GAK

A pair of Victorian easy armchairs, the buttoned backs, scrolled arms and serpentine seats covered in a figured buttermilk fabric, on ebonized and gilt-metal-mounted cabriole legs.
£950–1,150 CGC

A Hepplewhite-style mahogany armchair, in the French manner, on moulded cabriole front legs headed with a carved shell, with rounded, shaped legs to the back, re-upholstered, left seat rail and back right leg replaced, the front legs restored, c1780.
£2,000–2,250 JC

A George IV oak and grained rosewood armchair, with scroll arm fronts raised on front turned legs.
£820–1,000 MEA

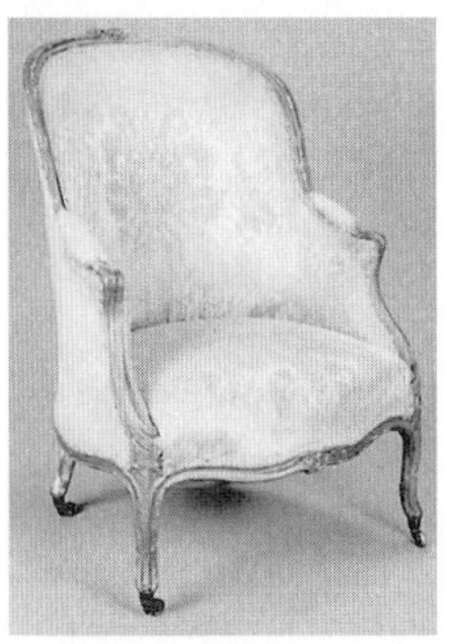

A giltwood armchair, the crest and seat rail carved with flowers and leaves, upholstered in blue damask, on leaf-carved cabriole legs, 19thC.
£820–1,000 LFA

◄ **A pair of stained beech armchairs,** upholstered in cream *faux* suede, French, c1920.
£2,800–3,100 BMi

An Empire mahogany *fauteuil,* the top-rail with an ormolu mount cast as a foliate patera flanked by palmettes over dolphin-carved arm supports, French, early 19thC.
£750–900 HYD

A rosewood chair, reupholstered in leather, c1835.
£2,500–2,750 RGa

A Victorian mahogany elbow chair, upholstered in pale green, the scrolled uprights joined by a serpentine apron, on lobed baluster front supports with peg feet.
£240–300 GAK

► **An Edwardian mahogany-framed armchair,** with floral and swag inlay to the top-rail and string inlay to the front legs.
£180–220 FHF

A wing armchair, with ribbed back, a cushion to the later sprung seat, on mahogany legs, the back legs repaired, early 19thC.
£350–420 WW

A mid-Victorian rosewood-framed chair, the upholstered buttoned back above a seat raised on cabriole legs with shell decoration.
£160–200 Bon(W)

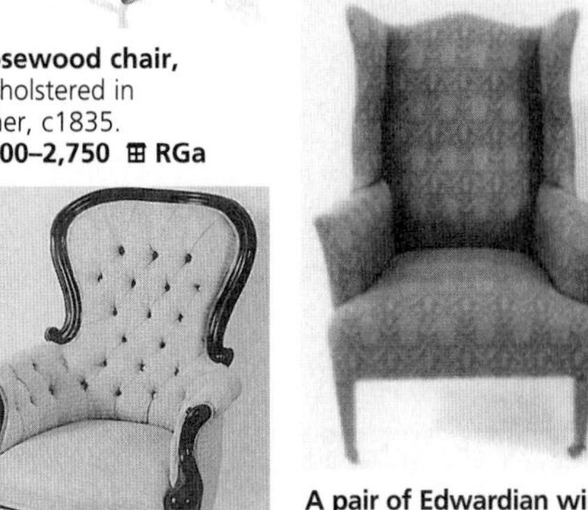

A pair of Edwardian wing armchairs, upholstered in a red floral-patterned fabric, on square tapered mahogany legs.
£270–330 DA

Bergères

A mahogany bergère, the caned back with leather head and arm pads, raised on front sabre legs, c1810.
£4,500–5,500 ⊞ RGa

An Empire mahogany bergère, with red fabric upholstery and circular leaf-carved legs, French, c1815.
£1,600–2,000 ⚒ S(Am)

A mahogany bergère, with caned sides and seat, on front square tapering legs, early 19thC.
£950–1,150 ⚒ WW

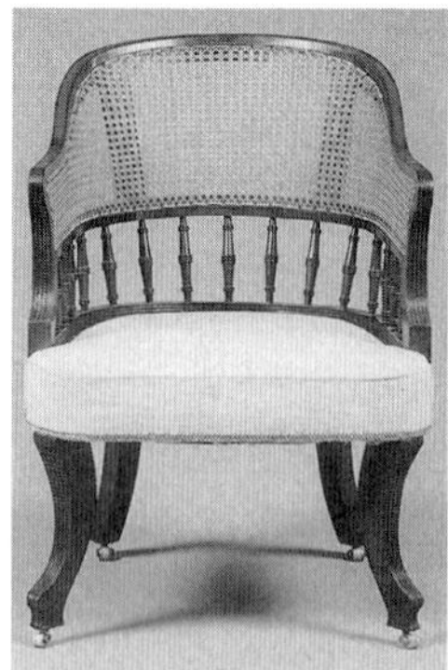

A mahogany bergère, the caned back above a spindle-turned gallery, the moulded and reeded top-rail with incurved reeded supports, the button cream-upholstered seat on reeded sabre legs, c1820.
£3,800–4,250 ⚒ S

Bergères

First introduced in France c1725, and soon produced in many other European countries, a bergère was originally any armchair with upholstered sides. Nowadays the term is more often used to describe a particular type of armchair or settee, with a square or round back leading down to the armrests and with caned sides, back and seat, usually fitted with a squab cushion. This style was popular during the Regency period, but upholstered examples generally date from a little later.

A George IV mahogany-framed bergère, on carved, turned and tapering forelegs and outswept back legs.
£1,650–2,000 ⚒ AAR

A rosewood bergère, the panelled arms carved with rosettes, lotus and anthemia beneath axehead crestings, the tapering lobed legs headed by rosettes, c1825.
£1,400–1,700 ⚒ N

A mahogany and caned bergère, with scroll arms and a gold striped stuff-over seat, on faceted turned tapered legs, faults, c1830.
£1,450–1,600 ⚒ S(S)

A pair of William IV mahogany bergères, on fluted supports.
£4,000–5,000 ⚒ HOLL

A William IV mahogany bergère, with woven cane infill and squab cushion, on stylized lotus-carved turned tapered front supports.
£1,250–1,500 ⚒ Bri

A mahogany bergère, the downswept arms with rosette-carved terminals and wrap-around down-curved sides, above a leather-covered drop-in seat, 19thC.
£1,100–1,250 ⚒ Bri

A pair of inlaid bergères, with green leather upholstery, c1890.
£1,650–1,850 ⊞ MTay

A pair of mahogany-framed bergères, on cabriole legs, early 20thC.
£350–420 ⚒ FHF

◄ **A pair of Empire-style inlaid mahogany and parcel-gilt bergères,** the top-rails inlaid with foliage, with gilded chimera supports, Italian, early 20thC.
£1,600–1,800 ⚒ SK

Children's Chairs

A child's George I-style mahogany open armchair, the carved shell seat rail on shell-carved hip cabriole legs, terminating in claw-and-ball feet, 19thC.
£2,600–3,000 BLH

◄ **A child's George III mahogany chair,** with a pierced vertical splat, out-swept arms and solid seat.
£320–380 CGC

A child's Victorian mahogany high chair, on a stand, the foliate-carved outscroll arms over a serpentine seat, and scroll legs terminating in knurled toes.
£500–600 HYD

◄ **A child's Victorian beech rocking chair,** with spindle frame.
£350–400 PSA

A child's mahogany bergère high chair, the stand forming a low table, c1830.
£450–500 F&F

A child's Edwardian mahogany corner chair, the satinwood-strung top-rail inlaid with musical trophies above outswept arms, pierced vertical splats, ring-turned arm supports and an upholstered seat.
£220–280 CGC

◄ **A child's Regency-style ebonized chair,** with sabre legs and spindle gallery top-rail, c1880.
£160–175 MTay

A child's beechwood correction chair, with spindle back, oval caned seat and turned tapering legs joined by multiple stretchers, mid-19thC.
£200–240 AH

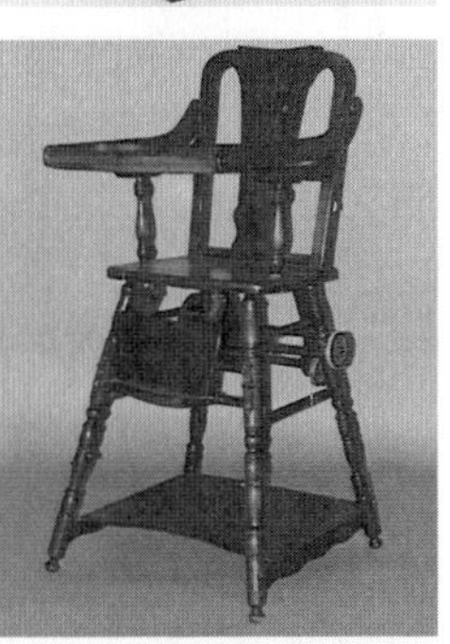

A child's Victorian mahogany high chair.
£160–200 Hal

Corner Chairs

A George II walnut corner chair, with a solid seat on turned legs terminating in braganza feet.
£900–1,100 HYD

A maple and cherry commode corner chair, with a frontal cabriole leg and two rear turned legs, minor imperfections, American, early 19thC.
£1,700–2,000 SK(B)

An Edwardian inlaid corner chair, with stuff-over seat and turned tapering legs joined by cross-stretchers.
£160–200 WilP

Dining Chairs

A pair of walnut dining chairs, with solid vase-shaped splat backs above drop-in seats, on cabriole legs with hoof feet, American, early 18thC.
£300–360 G(L)

A pair of Sheraton-style mahogany dining chairs, with carved Prince of Wales feathers, c1780.
£1,000–1,100 DJH

A set of six George III mahogany dining chairs, each with a yoke cresting rail, pierced vase-shaped splat back and drop-in seat.
£1,500–1,800 TRM

A pair of carved mahogany dining chairs, the acanthus- and paterae-carved serpentine top-rails above conforming pierced vase-shaped splat backs, the drop-in seats now upholstered in red damask, above cabriole legs with acanthus-carved knees, Irish, c1750.
£2,700–3,000 S

A set of six George III Hepplewhite-style mahogany dining chairs, with foliate-carved triple-splat backs centred by paterae.
£2,300–2,750 G(L)

A pair of George III mahogany dining chairs.
£130–145 NAW

A set of four mahogany dining chairs, with central pierced vase-shaped splat backs, above solid dished and shaped seats, on square moulded and chamfered legs, c1770.
£2,500–2,850 JC

A set of six George III mahogany dining chairs, with pierced vertical leaf-capped splat backs above drop-in seats.
£1,100–1,300 CGC

◄ **A set of six George III Sheraton-style mahogany dining chairs,** including one elbow chair, with stringing, reeded-bar back and uprights, and drop-in upholstered seats.
£900–1,100 AH

A set of six George III Hepplewhite-style mahogany dining chairs, including one open armchair, with pierced wheatsheaf splat backs, the stuff-over seats on square fluted and tapering legs, some restoration.
£650–800 P(Ba)

Facts in brief

In general, the larger the set of chairs (number of original matching chairs) the greater the value. However, harlequin sets (closely matched sets of period chairs) can be a fraction of the cost of a fully matching set, and often represent good value for money.

- Always look out for old repairs, especially to the legs, as this often weakens the chair and can often make it unusable.
- Check the condition of the upholstery as replacing this can increase the overall cost of the set considerably.
- Check that all the chairs are original to the set as later copies can often be introduced.

A set of six Regency mahogany dining chairs, with lyre-shaped horizontal splats and stuff-over seats on turned front and sabre rear legs.
£2,000–2,400 ⚒ HYD

A set of six Regency mahogany dining chairs, including one armchair, the crest rails with inlaid ebony lines above a spiral-turned horizontal bar, on sabre front legs.
£1,600–2,000 ⚒ LAY

A set of six simulated rosewood and brass-inlaid dining chairs, by John Gee, the gadroon-carved top-rails inlaid with cut-brass scrolling foliage above pierced scroll-carved mid-rails centred by a cut brass-inlaid tablet, the caned seats with later squab cushions, c1815.
£4,500–5,500 ⚒ S

These chairs are stamped with the letters 'GEE', indicating that they were produced by the leading London chair-maker and turner John Gee. John Gee is first recorded in 1779, when he entered into partnership with Benjamin Crompton, Turner-in-Ordinary to George III. In 1787 Gee was appointed Turner to the King and, although he retired from active business around 1824, he retained his royal warrant for a further seven years.

A set of six Regency mahogany dining chairs, with rope-twist scroll backs, carved splats and drop-in seats, on reeded turned legs.
£2,600–3,200 ⚒ F&C

► **A set of six Regency rosewood dining chairs,** with carved top-rails, foliate-pierced backs and drop-in seats on turned tapering legs, one leg restored.
£1,600–2,000 ⚒ BLH

► **A set of four burr-birchwood dining chairs,** the back rests with small parcel-gilt fan-shaped motifs, above drop-in seats, on sabre legs, South German or Austrian, c1820.
£2,000–2,400 ⚒ S(Am)

A set of six late Regency Gillows-style rosewood dining chairs, the shaped top-rails carved with scrolls and gadrooning, above caned seats, on turned and reeded legs.
£1,100–1,250 ⚒ P(L)

A pair of mahogany chairs, c1820.
£700–785 ⊞ RPh

A set of six George IV rosewood dining chairs, with scroll-carved rail backs and pink upholstered and cane seats, on turned and fluted tapering front legs.
£1,300–1,500 RBB

A set of six Chippendale-style mahogany dining chairs, with pierced vase-shaped splat backs above red leather drop-in seats and serpentine seat rails, 19thC.
£1,000–1,200 P(Ba)

A pair of Victorian mahogany balloon-back chairs.
£400–450 MLL

A pair of walnut chairs, on cabriole legs, c1870.
£650–725 RPh

A set of eight Biedermeier mahogany dining chairs, including two armchairs, on sabre legs, Dutch, 1800–25.
£3,250–4,000 S(Am)

A set of eight William IV mahogany dining chairs, including two armchairs, with lotus-moulded horizontal splat backs and drop-in seats, on ring-turned tapering legs.
£2,750–3,300 DD

A set of six Victorian mahogany balloon-back chairs, with cartouche-form horizontal bar splats, the serpentine-front stuff-over seats on melon fluted legs with peg feet.
£800–950 P(Ba)

A set of four walnut dining chairs, with stuff-over seats on cabriole legs, c1865.
£1,500–1,650 JC

A set of four Biedermeier cherry-wood dining chairs, the pierced back rests with ebonized splats, German, 1800–50.
£1,700–2,000 S(Am)

A set of five Victorian balloon-back dining chairs, with pierced and scrolled bar back, stuff-over seat and cabriole front legs with peg feet.
£500–600 AH

A set of eight Victorian Gothic-style oak dining chairs, with central shield motif depicting a bust of a lady, in need of reupholstering.
£300–350 FHF

A set of eight Victorian oak dining chairs, the S-scroll and foliate-carved top-rails above interlaced and quatrefoil vertical splats, the leather stuff-over seats on block-turned baluster legs.
£1,100–1,250 CGC

◄ **A set of six Victorian rosewood dining chairs,** with stuff-over seats and turned and fluted front legs.
£550–650 L&E

A set of six rosewood dining chairs, c1870.
£2,000–2,350 ⊞ MTay

A set of eight Sheraton-style mahogany dining chairs, including two armchairs, with central husk-carved slender baluster splats flanked by conforming slats, above drop-in seats, 19thC.
£2,000–2,400 Bri

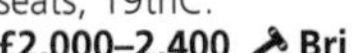

A set of six Victorian mahogany balloon-back dining chairs, with drop-in green leather seats and turned front legs.
£650–800 FHF

A set of four Chippendale-style mahogany dining chairs, c1900.
£675–750 ⊞ NoC

A set of eight Edwardian mahogany dining chairs, including two armchairs, with shaped oval backs with pierced splats, above serpentine-front padded seats, on cabriole legs.
£950–1,100 MEA

A set of six Edwardian satinwood and rosewood-banded dining chairs, with triple spindle and ovoid form splat backs, the padded seats on tapered square legs.
£420–500 P(Ba)

A set of six Georgian-style dining chairs, with original leather seats, early 20thC.
£1,100–1,250 ⊞ CGA

Hall Chairs

A pair of Regency Grecian-style mahogany hall chairs, the moulded panelled tapering square backs on scroll supports, the solid seats on moulded sabre legs.
£1,100–1,300 ⚒ P(S)

A pair of mahogany hall chairs, the pelta-shaped pierced backs with carved eagle-head corners flanking a double scroll finial, c1815.
£2,300–2,600 ⚒ S
This form of back, headed by eagles, is derived from a design published by Thomas Sheraton in his *Cabinet Dictionary* of 1803, although this chair is distinguished by the strictly classical pelta form rather than Sheraton's more simple semi-circular back.

A pair of mahogany hall chairs, on turned reeded front legs, c1830.
£1,300–1,450 ⊞ DUK

A pair of oak hall chairs, with carved heraldic coat-of-arms, c1830.
£1,750–2,000 ⊞ F

A pair of mahogany hall chairs, by L. Dowler, with cartouche backs and solid seats on faceted legs, stamped maker's mark, c1840.
£820–900 ⚒ S(O)

► **A pair of Victorian mahogany shield-back hall chairs,** with panelled seats on turned front legs.
£360–430 ⚒ WilP

A pair of oak hall chairs, c1840.
£700–780 ⊞ SSW

► **A mid-Victorian oak double hall chair,** the backs decorated with foliate scrolls above a serpentine moulded seat on ring-turned tapering front legs.
£500–600 ⚒ P(Ba)
This is a very unusual design for a hall chair.

A set of four Victorian oak hall chairs, the backs carved and pierced in the shape of grotesque masks, above solid seats, on foliate-carved and turned front legs.
£420–500 ⚒ CGC

◄ **A pair of Victorian mahogany hall chairs,** with cartouche backs and turned front legs.
£200–240 ⚒ P(S)

Cross Reference
See Colour Review
(page 108)

► **A pair of mahogany wheel-back hall chairs,** with round seats, on turned front legs, c1810.
£2,200–2,500 ⚒ E

A Gothic-style oak hall chair, 19thC.
£200–225 ⊞ NoC

Library Chairs

A Regency mahogany metamorphic library chair, the caned back and seat flanked by down-sweeping arms on bobbin supports, the hinged seat opening to reveal four treads.
£2,500–3,000 B(Ed)

◄ **A William IV mahogany library open armchair,** the adjustable seat mechanism working on arched supports, with leather button-upholstered back, seat and padded arms.
£1,100–1,200 P(S)

A mahogany library armchair, by G. Minter, with reclining back upholstered in red leather, the apron with a sliding foot-rest, on lappet-carved turned tapered legs, c1835.
£2,750–3,250 S
This chair bears the stamp of George Minter of Soho, a cabinet-maker and upholsterer specializing in patent reclining chairs. He was first recorded in 1829 and traded from various addresses in the Soho area until 1854, when he apparently ceased trading.

► **A pair of early Victorian mahogany show-frame library armchairs,** the top-rails cornered with acanthus-leaf scrolls above leather button-upholstered backs and seats.
£800–950 RTo

Nursing Chairs

A Victorian walnut-framed nursing chair, with floral carved detail and buttoned fabric upholstery, on shell-carved cabriole legs.
£360–430 DMC

A Victorian nursing chair, with a sprung bell-shaped seat, upholstered in old red plush, with a loose cover, on carved walnut cabriole legs.
£130–160 WW

A rosewood-framed nursing chair, with cabriole legs, c1870.
£500–550 ⊞ MTay

A Victorian walnut-framed nursing chair, with needlework upholstery, the back with pierced and carved scrolling foliate surmount.
£360–430 AH

Salon Chairs

◄ **A Victorian mahogany show-frame salon chair,** with button back and turned supports.
£140–170 Bon(W)

► **A pair of giltwood salon chairs,** with carved backs and fluted tapering legs, French, late 19thC.
£575–625 ⊞ RPh

A pair of rococo-style giltwood salon chairs, with floral and foliate cartouche, 19thC.
£4,400–4,850 ⊞ RAN

Side Chairs

A pair of George III mahogany side chairs, with three wheatsheaf-carved vertical splats and central paterae motifs flanked by reeded uprights.
£260–320 ⚒ CGC

A pair of floral marquetry side chairs, with shaped splat backs and serpentine seats, Dutch, late 18thC.
£500–600 ⚒ P(O)

A stained beech George Jacob-style side chair, with a pierced anthemion top-rail and trellis-filled back, over a stuffed seat and sabre legs, French, 1770–1820.
£470–565 ⚒ S(O)

George Jacob, received master in 1765, was one of the most important French cabinet-makers of the 18th century and had many royal and aristocratic clients. His descendants carried on the business until well into the 19th century.

A set of four Empire mahogany side chairs, with floral motif and acanthus-carved top-rails, the padded backs and stuff-over seats upholstered in cream and red stripes, with gilt-highlighted foliate-carved seat rails, French, c1800.
£320–380 ⚒ P(Ba)

A set of four neo-classical fruitwood side chairs, with shaped pierced backs and serpentine-front stuff-over seats, Italian, early 19thC.
£900–1,100 ⚒ SK

A pair of mahogany side chairs, reupholstered, c1835.
£750–850 ⊞ RPh

► **A pair of Victorian ebonized side chairs,** with simulated bamboo frames, the buttoned padded backs and seats covered in red fabric, the backs with later strengthening.
£50–60 ⚒ WW

Miscellaneous Chairs

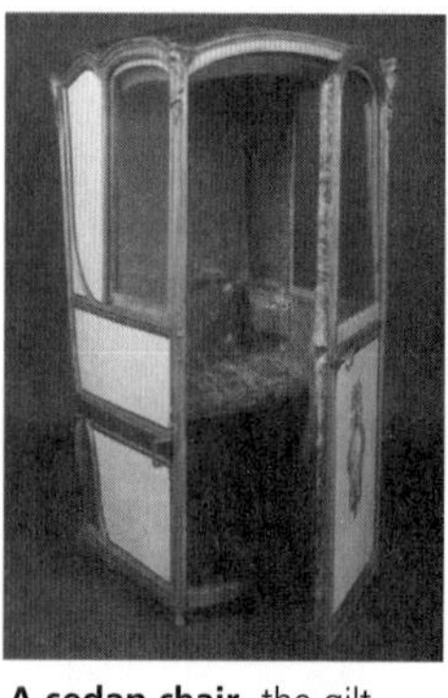

A sedan chair, the gilt-painted frame with leaf-scroll mounts and later painted panels, the roof in old black leather, the interior with original cut gold velvet lining and seat, missing carrying arms, French, 1770–1820, 60¼in (153cm) high.
£900–1,100 ⚒ B(WM)

► **A mahogany desk chair,** upholstered in green hide, c1850.
£800–875 ⊞ RPh

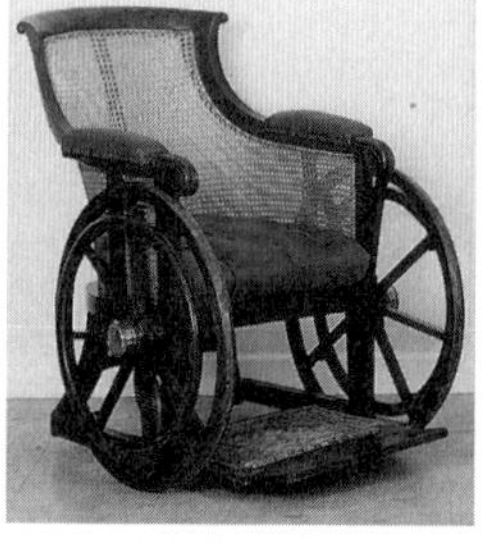

◄ **A Regency mahogany-framed bergère invalid chair,** with padded and scrolled arms and button-upholstered seat.
£430–520 ⚒ RBB

◄ **A Victorian walnut prie-dieu chair,** the padded back with ring-turned supports, above a padded seat, on turned front legs.
£400–500 ⚒ LFA

► **A Victorian carved oak parlour chair,** with tan hide upholstery.
£700–850 ⚒ SWO

Chaises Longues & Daybeds

◀ **A Biedermeier walnut daybed,** upholstered in brown and beige floral fabric, early 19thC, 80¾in (205cm) long.
£1,000–1,100 ⚒ S(Am)

A mahogany chaise longue, with leaf-carved scroll back and side, on reeded tapering turned legs, c1840, 60¼in (153cm) long.
£1,150–1,400 ⚒ HOK

▶ **A William IV chaise longue,** the Brazilian rosewood show-frame with floret and rococo spray carving, with modern fawn damask upholstery including bolster and squab cushions, 84in (213.5cm) long.
£500–600 ⚒ WW

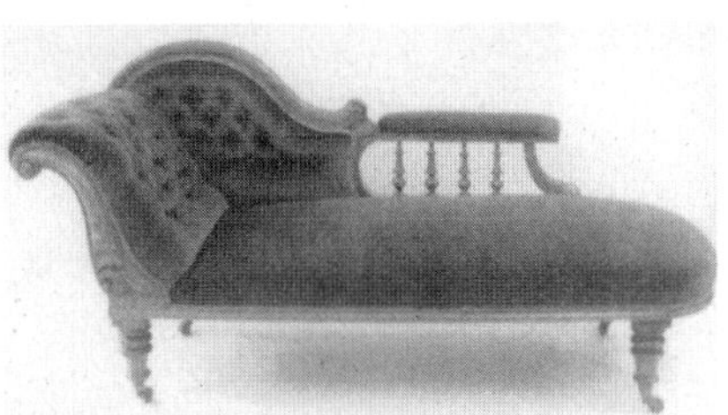

◀ **A Victorian mahogany chaise longue,** with scrolled buttoned back to part-upholstered arm rest over four turned spindles, upholstered in bottle green velvet.
£520–625 ⚒ DA

A daybed, upholstered in beige and cream fabric, late 19thC, 70¾in (179.5cm) long.
£825–1,000 ⚒ S(Am)

Chests & Coffers

A walnut *cassone*, the hinged lid with bead-and-dart edge, the front carved with an armorial cartouche flanked by unicorns, radiating volutes and caryatids, with iron carrying handles, Italian, 17thC, 62½in (159cm) wide.
£2,600–3,200 ⚒ WW

▶ **A walnut coffer,** the plinth with geometric carving, some restoration, Spanish, 17thC, 72in (183cm) wide.
£700–850 ⚒ L

◀ **A walnut, pewter and marquetry-inlaid casket,** on a gilt-metal-mounted stand, restored, casket 18thC, stand 19thC, 23¾in (60.5cm) wide.
£2,500–3,000 ⚒ Bon(C)

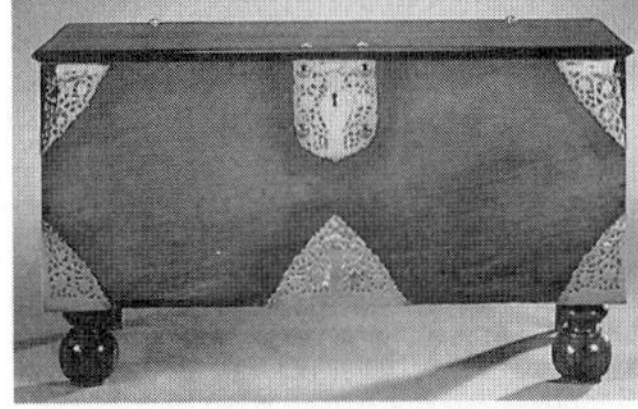

A colonial teak chest, the hinged lid with ebonized border, the chest with foliate-cast mounts and handles, Dutch, 18thC, 58in (147.5cm) wide.
£3,000–3,600 ⚒ S(Am)

A painted walnut chest, decorated on both the interior and exterior with scenes from the life of Horatio Nelson, 19thC, 49¼in (125cm) wide.
£1,600–2,000 ⚒ Bon

◀ **A camphorwood travelling chest,** covered with dark green close-nailed and brass-bound leather, the hinged top bearing the initials 'A.P.', with brass carrying handles, early 19thC, 43½in (110.5cm) wide, on a later ebonized stand.
£900–1,100 ⚒ Bea(E)

Chests of Drawers & Commodes

A Tuscan walnut chest, the frieze with a concealed compartment above three long drawers with brass loop handles and escutcheons, now with bracket feet, late 17thC, 58in (147.5cm) wide.
£3,200–3,850 N

A serpentine commode, with later veneered top, parquetry sides and four graduated long drawers, on bun feet, German, c1700, 28in (71cm) wide.
£700–850 G(L)

A walnut bedside chest, with ivory inlay, Sicilian, c1675–1725.
£2,400–3,000 S(Mi)

A walnut chest, the crossbanded top with reeded edge, above three short and three long graduated drawers, early 18thC, 40½in (103cm) wide.
£1,000–1,200 TMA

Styles of furniture feet

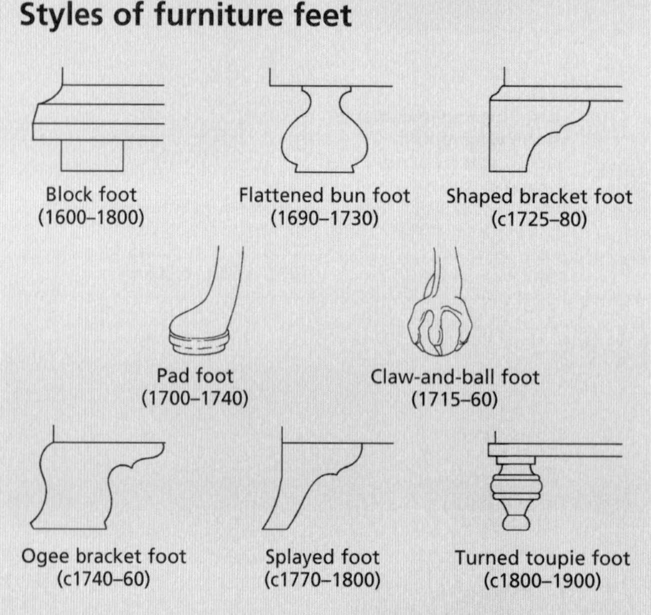

A walnut chest of drawers, with two short drawers above four long drawers, c1760, 44in (112cm) wide.
£2,000–2,200 REF

► **A George II mahogany bachelor's chest,** the twin-flap fold-over top with additional ratchet mechanism, pull-out candle slides, three small drawers, one fitted for writing, above three long drawers, original brass handles, 28in (71cm) wide.
£2,400–3,000 DMC

A mahogany dressing chest, the top fitted with lidded toilet boxes, central mirror on ratchet, inset writing slide with pen drawer beneath, mid-18thC, 38in (96.5cm) wide.
£4,300–5,200 WBH

► **A figured mahogany-veneered commode chest,** with serpentine front and original French-style brasses, c1760, 53in (134.5cm) wide.
£6,750–7,500 HA

A three-drawer chest, with three long graduated drawers and later chinoiserie decoration, 18thC, 37½in (95.5cm) wide.
£750–900 AG

A George III mahogany bachelor's chest, of serpentine outline, with a crossbanded brushing slide above three graduated drawers, with gilded handles, 37½in (95.5cm) wide.
£1,800–2,200 M

Miller's Compares

I. A mahogany chest, the four long graduated drawers with original brass swan-neck handles, bracket feet restored, c1770, 31in (78.5cm) wide.
£2,000–2,400 WW

II. A mahogany-veneered chest, the top with strips of veneer, a slide above four long graduated drawers, with later brass swan-neck handles, late 18thC, 33in (84cm) wide.
£950–1,150 WW

Both these chests of drawers are compact, making them more desirable as they will fit into any size room, but Item I realized more at auction because of its particularly good proportions. Its almost square shape is very pleasing to the eye, while the addition of the brushing slide to Item II, although a desirable feature, has increased the height. Item I is also of a slightly earlier date, probably c1770, and virtually original. Further factors enhancing the price of Item I are its attractive colour and its feet, which are more pleasing in shape than those of Item II. The strips of veneer on the top of Item II are also less desirable than the more usual solid veneer, indicating that this is probably a provincial piece.

A walnut serpentine commode, with banded top and three long drawers, Italian, 18thC, 29in (73.5cm) wide.
£2,000–2,400 G(L)

◄ **A George III mahogany chest of drawers,** with two short above three graduated long cockbeaded drawers, on swept bracket feet, 47in (119.5cm) wide.
£1,500–1,800 WL

► **A mahogany chest of drawers,** the two short and three long drawers with original handles, restored, c1780, 45in (114.5cm) wide.
£1,600–1,750 MTay

A mahogany chest of drawers, with slide above two short and three long drawers, c1770, 38in (96.5cm) wide.
£1,500–1,650 NoC

A mahogany chest of drawers, 18thC, 29in (73.5cm) wide.
£2,500–2,850 NAW

Commodes

A commode is a Continental chest of drawers or side cabinet. English versions of these, in the French taste, were fashionable from the mid-18th century, but they were not made in great quantities due to the expense of producing the elaborate shapes and decoration. In Victorian times this name was given to any piece of furniture that concealed a chamber pot.

A mahogany chest of drawers, on splay bracket feet, c1800, 29in (73.5cm) wide.
£3,300–3,650 BERA

A mahogany bowfronted chest of drawers, the one-piece rectangular top with a crossbanded edge, above two short and three long graduated drawers, cockbeaded and lined with pine, faced with vertical book-matched veneers, c1800, 45¾in (116cm) wide.
£2,400–2,650 ⊞ JC

A mahogany chest, with baize-lined brushing slide above two short and three long graduated cockbeaded drawers, the brass handles stamped with nautical symbols, early 19thC, 36in (91.5cm) wide.
£600–700 ⚒ DD

An Empire fruitwood commode, with marble top and lion's paw feet, French, c1815, 51in (129.5cm) wide.
£2,700–3,000 ⊞ SIE

A late Federal tiger-maple chest of drawers, with projecting top drawer above three further drawers, flanked by inlaid stiles, American, c1820, 40in (101.5cm) wide.
£1,200–1,400 ⚒ SLN

A mahogany bowfronted chest of three drawers, c1800, 45in (114.5cm) wide.
£1,300–1,450 ⊞ DUK

A Regency mahogany bowfronted chest, the two short and three long graduated drawers flanked by reeded columns, 48¾in (124cm) wide.
£1,100–1,300 ⚒ CGC

A mahogany bowfronted chest of drawers, the two short and three long drawers above a shaped frieze, 19thC, 37in (94cm) wide.
£750–900 ⚒ TRM

A George IV mahogany chest of drawers, with four short and three graduated long drawers, on turned legs, 30in (76cm) wide.
£600–720 ⚒ G(B)

A cherrywood bowfronted chest of drawers, with four cockbeaded graduated drawers, replaced brass, minor repairs, American, c1800, 39in (99cm) wide.
£2,200–2,500 ⚒ SK(B)

A mahogany chest of four drawers, by Smith of Kirkgate, Leeds, with original handles and reeded sabre legs, 1829, 32in (81.5cm) wide.
£1,800–2,000 ⊞ CGA
An inscription on the carcass of this chest reads '1829, Smith, Kirkgate, Leeds'.

A mahogany bowfronted chest of drawers, with a slide and three long graduated drawers with matched veneers, the front corners with reeded and turned columns, with label of George Simson, c1820, 38in (96.5cm) wide.
£8,750–9,500 ⚒ S
The cabinet-maker George Simson was apprenticed to Noah Chivers in 1772, and by 1787 had established a flourishing business in the City of London, trading as an upholder, cabinet-maker and undertaker from premises at 19 St Paul's Churchyard. The business later expanded, taking over seven adjoining properties, and continued to trade until 1840. Although it is not certain that the label on this item is original to the piece, stylistically the chest falls within the period when George Simson was active as a cabinet-maker.

A fruitwood chest of drawers, with five long drawers, the canted corners with tassel pendants, with square tapering front feet and bracket back feet, Continental, 19thC, 40in (101.5cm) wide.
£480–575 WW

A Biedermeier-style satinwood chest of drawers, with geometric marquetry inlay, the three long graduated drawers flanked by chamfered corners with block and turned pilasters, 19thC, 48¾in (124cm) wide.
£700–805 BLH

Drawer knobs & escutcheons

Wooden drawer knobs and mother-of-pearl escutcheons (key-hole surrounds) are desirable features on Victorian furniture. They are also a useful dating guide, as both were first introduced c1850.

A mahogany chest of drawers, with two short above three long drawers, with brass handles, c1870, 42in (106.5cm) wide.
£1,100–1,200 RPh

A William IV mahogany chest, the two short and three long drawers flanked by rounded reeded corners, 48in (122cm) wide.
£800–950 P(Ba)

A Louis XV-style kingwood and burr-walnut serpentine-fronted commode, the white and grey marble top above two long drawers with shaped burrwood panels, boxwood scrollwork and kingwood borders, with conforming side panels, French, 19thC, 36in (91.5cm) wide.
£720–825 CAG

A late Victorian gentleman's mahogany linen chest/valet, the top hinged at the rear and opening to an interior fitted with trouser and tie press, above two runs of three short graduated drawers over two long graduated drawers, 45in (114.5cm) wide.
£475–575 Mit

A mahogany commode, in the style of Henri II, the case fitted with a frieze drawer over three long drawers, all inset with marble panels, the sides with conforming panels, with label for 'J-B Klein', French, 1855–60, 47¼in (120cm) wide.
£9,000–11,000 NOA
Jean-Baptiste Klein (1796–1878) established his third shop at 115 Faubourg Saint Antoine under the name 'l'Acajou sans Pareil' in 1855. In 1860 the business changed its name to Klein Père et Fils. Klein exhibited and received prizes at the 1839, 1844 and 1849 Paris World Fairs, and in 1853 he received the grand prize at the Paris Exposition Universelle.

A Victorian mahogany tall chest of drawers, with a frieze-shaped drawer above five graduated drawers, 48in (122cm) wide.
£300–350 FHF

A serpentine mahogany chest of four drawers, with canted corners and bracket feet, c1920, 34in (86.5cm) wide.
£2,000–2,250 MTay

◀ **A black lacquered chest of drawers,** decorated with chinoiserie scenes, c1920, 36in (91.5cm) wide.
£415–460 RAN

Chests-on-Chests

A walnut-veneered and oak chest-on-chest, fitted with three short and six long drawers, early 18thC, 43¾in (111cm) wide.
£2,700–3,200 ⚒ P(O)

A George III mahogany chest-on-chest, the upper section fitted with three short and three long drawers, the lower section with three long drawers, 45¼in (115cm) wide.
£1,100–1,200 ⚒ P(Ba)

A George III mahogany chest-on-chest, the three short and three long graduated drawers flanked by reeded canted sides, the base with brushing slide and three long drawers, 43¾in (111cm) wide.
£1,100–1,300 ⚒ CGC

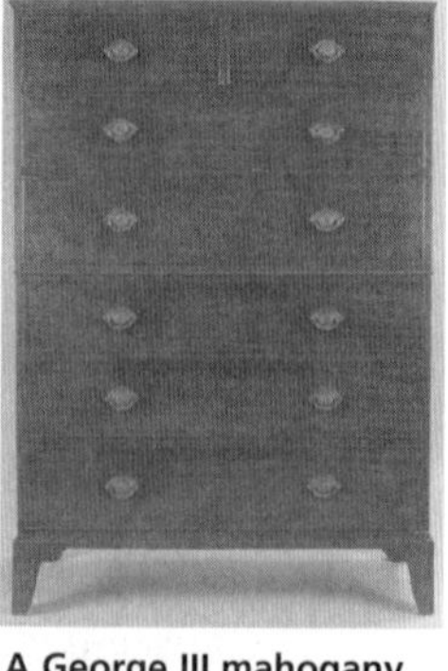

A George III mahogany chest-on-chest, fitted with two short and five long drawers, 45¾in (116cm) wide.
£1,700–2,000 ⚒ P(S)

A George III mahogany bowfronted chest-on-chest, with diamond and round satinwood inlaid panels, above two short and six long drawers, 42in (106.5cm) wide.
£1,500–1,800 ⚒ E

A George III mahogany chest-on-chest, with original handles, 70in (178cm) wide.
£2,800–3,250 ⊞ NoC

A mahogany chest-on-chest, the two short and three long cockbeaded drawers flanked by fluted and canted corners over a base with three long drawers, the front with book-matched vertical veneers, c1777, 43½in (110.5cm) wide.
£6,000–6,750 ⊞ JC

A George III mahogany chest-on-chest, the upper section with two short cockbeaded drawers flanking a wider central drawer, each with replacement brass escutcheons and handles, the bottom section with three graduated long drawers, on shortened bracket feet, 44½in (113cm) wide.
£2,000–2,400 ⚒ PFK

Facts in brief

A development of the chest-on-stand, chests-on-chests were very fashionable from c1710–1830. The upper section has two or three short drawers above three long, often graduated, drawers with a protruding moulded cornice.

The lower section has three drawers, and additional features can include a secrétaire to the top drawer, a brushing slide and early examples sometimes have a decorated concave niche to the bottom drawer.

In the early 18th century, canted corners were introduced, often carved as pilasters. Decoration included Gothic revival mouldings and due to the influence of Thomas Chippendale, Chinese fretwork became popular.

Early pieces, often highly prized, are made of walnut and from c1740 onwards were almost exclusively constructed from mahogany. Until recently these chests were relatively unfashionable and were often split up.

The reverse is common today, so check for identical construction, matching backboards, correct numbers of drawers and matching timbers to both upper and lower sections.

A cherrywood chest-on-chest, some repairs and losses, American, New England, probably Connecticut, c1790, 42¼in (107.5cm) wide.
£3,500–4,500 ⚒ WcH

A Regency mahogany bowfronted chest-on-chest, the upper section with two short and three long graduated drawers flanked by quarter round twist columns and with gadrooned borders to the dividing edge, the bottom part with three long graduated drawers, 50in (127cm) wide.
£3,200–3,800 ⚒ M

Military Chests

A mahogany double military chest, with secretaire drawer, c1820, 42in (106.5cm) wide.
£2,500–2,800 ⊞ DUK

A mahogany brass-bound campaign chest, on later bun feet, 19thC, 39½in (100.5cm) wide.
£1,000–1,200 ⚒ HOK

A mahogany campaign chest, with two short and three long drawers, 19thC, 39in (99cm) wide.
£1,100–1,300 ⚒ Bea(E)

◄ A teak and brass-bound military chest, the upper section with two short and one deep drawer, the bottom section with two long drawers, c1900, 36in (91.5cm) wide.
£600–700 ⚒ S(S)

► A walnut military chest, by Ross & Co, the hinged top revealing two folding serpentine shelves, the secretaire drawer with fall-front enclosing a fitted interior, flanked by two small drawers above three long drawers, Irish, 19thC, 44in (119cm) wide.
£4,500–5,500 ⚒ AH

Secretaire Chests

A George III figured mahogany secretaire chest, with two blind drawers enclosing a fitted satinwood and inlaid interior, over three graduated drawers, damaged, 46½in (118cm) wide.
£800–950 ⚒ Bri

A Federal mahogany inlaid secretaire chest, with fitted secretaire drawer over three graduated long drawers, with serpentine sides and original brass handles, American, c1805, 45¼in (115cm) wide.
£2,000–2,400 ⚒ SK(B)

A mahogany secretaire chest, with boxwood stringing and a satinwood interior, c1810, 46in (117cm) wide.
£2,350–2,600 ⊞ NoC

◄ A George IV mahogany secretaire chest, the top with rope-fronted edge, over a drop-front drawer, enclosing a fitted interior over three long graduated drawers, flanked by half spiral reeded pilasters, probably Irish, 45in (114.5cm) wide.
£1,800–2,200 ⚒ MEA

A mahogany secretaire chest, with a fall-front fitted drawer, above three long graduated drawers, the fronts satinwood-banded with stringing, Scottish, mid-19thC, 44in (112cm) wide.
£700–850 ⚒ WW

Chests-on-Stands

◀ **A walnut chest-on-stand,** with three herringbone-veneered frieze drawers above three long drawers, the base with three drawers on twist columns joined by concave stretchers, basically late 17thC, 44in (112cm) wide.
£1,800–2,200 HYD

A George I walnut chest-on-stand, the top with two short and three long graduated drawers, the base with three drawers on barley-twist legs joined by a waived stretcher, 38¼in (97cm) wide.
£1,650–2,000 P(Ed)

A maple and birch chest-on-stand, the upper section with two short drawers and four long drawers, the bottom section with one long drawer and three short drawers, replaced brasses, minor restoration, American, c1750–70, 38in (96.5cm) wide.
£6,000–7,000 SK(B)

An 18thC-style lacquered chest-on-stand, c1910, 33in (84cm) wide.
£2,000–2,250 MTay

A walnut and cross-banded chest, with three long featherbanded drawers, on a later stand with three short drawers, early 18thC with later alterations, 41¾in (106cm) wide.
£1,600–2,000 P(S)

American styles

American furniture termed, for example, 'Queen Anne' does not necessarily date from the actual period of Queen Anne. This is because the latest fashions took about 20 years to cross the Atlantic, but the style is nevertheless of that period.

Wellington Chests

◀ **A William IV rosewood secretaire Wellington chest,** with two drawers, double fake secretaire drawer and arch panelled cupboard, 25in (63.5cm) wide.
£1,800–2,200 G(B)

A Victorian mahogany Wellington chest, with seven graduated drawers, 18¾in (47.5cm) wide.
£700–850 Mit

A Victorian mahogany and satinwood-banded Wellington chest, with seven drawers, 23¾in (60.5cm) wide.
£2,400–3,000 P(EA)

A late Victorian/ Edwardian mahogany Wellington chest, with six graduated drawers, 22½in (57cm) wide.
£800–950 HOLL

◀ **A late Victorian mahogany Wellington chest,** the seven drawers with ring handles, flanked by brass-capped Corinthian pilasters, 19in (48.5cm) wide.
£800–960 G(L)

▶ **A late Victorian walnut Wellington chest,** with eight drawers, one stamped 'J W Hammond, Worcester St, Birm', flanked by side-locking pilasters, 20in (51cm) wide.
£750–900 WW

Clothes & Linen Presses

A mahogany linen press, the outset base with two short and one long drawer, Irish, mid-18thC, 48in (122cm) wide. **£6,500–8,000 HOK**

A George III mahogany linen press, the two panelled doors enclosing a series of slides, the lower section fitted with two short over two graduated long cockbeaded drawers, 50in (127cm) wide. **£1,650–2,000 WL**

A George III mahogany linen press, the two fielded panel doors with crossbanding, above two long and two short drawers, 49½in (125.5cm) wide. **£1,000–1,200 L&E**

A George III mahogany linen press, the two flame-mahogany panelled doors surrounded by ebonized reeded moulding, enclosing four sliding trays, above two long and two short drawers, 44in (112cm) wide. **£1,400–1,700 HAM**

A Chippendale-style mahogany linen press, the two panelled doors above nine cockbeaded drawers, American, late 18thC, 48in (122cm) wide. **£22,000–25,000 SK(B)**
Early American furniture in good condition invariably sells for high prices in the United States.

A mahogany and ebony-strung linen press, Scottish, c1800, 55¼in (140.5cm) wide. **£1,400–1,700 Bon(C)**

A mahogany linen press, the two panelled doors with applied beading, above two short and two long drawers, 19thC, 49½in (125.5cm) wide. **£1,000–1,200 AH**

A mahogany linen press, the two doors enclosing sliding trays, above a fitted secretaire drawer and four further drawers, 19thC, 53in (134.5cm) wide. **£1,800–2,200 E**

► **A mahogany linen press,** Dutch, c1860, 99in (251.5cm) high. **£5,750–6,500 APO**

Linen presses

The linen press first appeared c1750 as a cupboard in which to store clothes and lay linen flat on sliding trays. These were enclosed by panelled doors over a chest of two short and three long drawers, on bracket or ogee feet. It was not until c1870 that spaces were made for vertical hanging and later still before coat hangers became universally used.

Mahogany was the principal timber used for construction. The most refined examples are lined with cedarwood both for fragrance and to keep the moths at bay. In the second half of the 19th century, walnut and birch became fashionable alternatives, and pine for 'below stairs'.

Many fine Regency presses were gutted in the mid-19th century to make them into wardrobes, consequently a piece which retains all its original fittings will usually command a premium.

◄ **A mahogany linen press cupboard,** attributed to Gillows, with two banks of four drawers flanking two panelled and bead-moulded cupboard doors enclosing four sliding tray shelves, three shelves missing, c1820, 72in (183cm) wide. **£5,500–6,000 S**

► **A serpentine-shaped mahogany linen press,** c1910, 44in (112cm) wide. **£1,800–2,000 NAW**

Davenports

A Regency mahogany davenport, inlaid throughout with geometric ebony stringing, the upper section folding open to form a desk, each side with a slide, one side with four drawers, 18¼in (46.5cm) wide.
£2,200–2,700 HYD

A George IV bird's-eye maple davenport, the sliding top with inset tooled green leather hinged slope enclosing two drawers and a secret locking hinged inkwell and pen holder, the panelled door enclosing four drawers, with two side slides, 20in (51cm) wide.
£1,000–1,200 Gam

A Victorian rosewood davenport, with scroll-carved mirror superstructure above a serpentine inset writing slope enclosing a fitted interior, the side with a slide-out hinged stationery drawer above a fretwork-decorated cupboard door enclosing drawers, 24¾in (63cm) wide.
£1,250–1,400 S(S)

A rosewood davenport, with sliding top, c1820, 38in (96.5cm) wide.
£3,400–3,800 NoC

A rosewood davenport, the top with a hinged slanting crossbanded lid, over a fitted interior, the base with four graduated drawers to the right side, and false ones to the left below a full width leather slide, c1835, 21½in (54.5cm) wide.
£3,800–4,200 JC

A late Victorian walnut davenport, the stationery compartment with hinged cover decorated with inlaid stringing and brass balustrade, the leather-lined writing surface opening to reveal storage compartments and a small drawer, with four drawers and four dummy drawers to the side, 21in (53.5cm) wide.
£620–750 AG

A George IV rosewood davenport, the sliding top above a fall enclosing a bird's-eye maple-veneered interior, with writing fitment and four graduated long drawers to the side, 20in (51cm) wide.
£1,800–2,200 P(S)

A Victorian walnut davenport, with fitted drawers and writing surface, the piano lid over a drawer with ratcheted back, press-action operating stationery compartment enclosing three drawers and compartments, piano front closing lid, four side drawers, 20in (51cm) wide.
£3,200–3,800 L&E

A Victorian inlaid walnut davenport, the slope with leather inset interior, fitted drawers and pigeonholes to the right, a small drawer with fitted inkwell above four drawers, 21in (53.5cm) wide.
£700–850 HOLL

A George IV rosewood-veneered davenport, with brass gallery, fitted interior and leather inset easel writing top above drawers, the sides with slides above a door enclosing four drawers, 20in (51cm) wide.
£1,700–2,000 WW

A Victorian burr-walnut davenport, with sloping leather writing surface and side drawer, with four graduated drawers to one side and dummy drawers to the other, 21in (53.5cm) wide.
£1,000–1,200 HYD

LOCATE THE SOURCE

The source of each illustration in Miller's can be found by checking the code letters below each caption with the Key to Illustrations, pages 794–800.

A lady's davenport, with tooled-leather writing surface above a lidded stationery compartment, with foliate-carved moulding to the front and three drawers to the right with dummy drawers to the left, late 19thC, 22in (56cm) wide.
£300–360 Mit

Desks

A walnut kneehole desk, the top inlaid with geometric herringbone banding over a brushing slide, with an arrangement of eight drawers surrounding a recessed cupboard, early 18thC and later, 31½in (80cm) wide.
£1,300–1,500 ⚒ HYD

A mahogany kneehole desk, the long drawer and two pedestals of three drawers with cockbeaded mouldings, the kneehole recess with a cupboard below an apron drawer, faded, c1740, 31½in (80cm) wide.
£1,000–1,200 ⚒ N

A yew and burr-yew kneehole desk, with frieze drawer above a vacant compartment with shelf, flanked by six drawers, on later bracket feet, Irish, c1750, 37in (94cm) wide.
£6,200–7,500 ⚒ MEA

▶ **A mahogany estate desk,** c1760, 83in (211cm) wide.
£7,250–8,000 ⚒ S(O)

A George III mahogany kneehole desk, with a fitted frieze drawer and six short graduated drawers flanked by a recessed cupboard, 41¾in (106cm) wide.
£2,700–3,200 ⚒ CGC

◀ **A mahogany kneehole desk,** with long frieze drawer, eight small drawers and recess cupboard, the underside of the brushing slide inscribed 'Thos. Gannaford, 1782', restored, 31¾in (80.5cm) wide.
£1,350–1,500 ⚒ Bea(E)

▶ **A parquetry desk,** with tambour and fall-front enclosed top, with partially fitted interior, over one long and two short drawers, Italian, 18thC, 49in (124.5cm) wide.
£1,200–1,500 ⚒ G(L)

◀ **A burr-walnut inlaid and veneered desk,** minor damage, Italian, c1800, 48¾in (124cm) wide.
£6,000–7,200 ⚒ S(Mi)

A mahogany writing desk, with six frieze drawers on column-shaped supports on a shaped base fitted with two further drawers, the frieze decorated with painted arabesques, upper part missing, damaged, German, early 19thC, 43¼in (110cm) wide.
£3,300–3,700 ⚒ S(Am)

A walnut pedestal desk, by Holland & Sons, the top with replaced gilt-tooled leather inset, above three frieze drawers, kneehole recess flanked by six graduated drawers, with opposing panelled cupboard doors, maker's mark, c1840, 56in (142cm) wide.
£6,000–7,200 ⚒ S

A mid-Victorian mahogany twin pedestal desk, by Edwards & Roberts, the top with inset leather writing surface above three frieze drawers, with three drawers to each pedestal, 48in (122cm) wide.
£2,200–2,800 ⚒ P(L)
The London firm of Edwards & Roberts was established in 1845 as cabinet makers and sellers of antique and modern furniture.

A Victorian mahogany pedestal desk, with three frieze drawers on pedestals, each with three drawers, 46in (117cm) wide.
£350–420 ⚒ P(Ba)

► **A Regency mahogany pedestal desk,** the top inset with a green leather writing surface above an arrangement of drawers and opposing panelled cupboard doors, 52in (132cm) wide.
£5,000–6,000 ⚒ CGC

An early Victorian mahogany clerk's desk, the hinged top opening to reveal a leather insert, fitted with two opposing small end drawers, one fitted with pen and ink wells with four simultaneously opening lever-action compartments, Holland & Sons maker's stamp, 29¼in (74.5cm) wide.
£1,000–1,200 ⚒ P(Ba)

Patination

This is the term used to refer to the build-up of polish, dirt, dust and grease on the surface of an antique through years of handling. It is difficult to fake, and pieces that have an attractive patina will usually sell at a premium.

- Patination varies in different timbers, but one piece of wood will form a uniform colour, apart from areas which have been subject to different conditions, such as bleaching by sunlight.
- Areas around drawer handles, chair arms etc should have a darker colour due to frequent contact, and accumulated dirt will create dark patches around carving and crevices – if this is not the case, beware! Inexplicable dark patches may well conceal old repairs, replacement parts or even conversions.
- Replacement of components or a conversion can be concealed by repolishing and destroying the original patina.
- Walnut furniture often had an oil varnish applied to provide a good base for wax polish. This produced a mellow patina which is almost impossible to fake.

A Victorian oak twin pedestal desk, the top with faded gilt-tooled brown leather-inset writing surface, the frieze fitted with three drawers, supported by two pedestals fitted with six further drawers, 48in (122cm) wide.
£300–360 ⚒ GAK

A mid-Victorian figured-walnut twin pedestal desk, with later green tooled-leather insert, with two frieze drawers, the pedestals with three short drawers, one side with expansion crack, 48in (122cm) wide.
£1,850–2,200 ⚒ TMA

A Victorian burr-walnut pedestal desk, the red leather-inset writing surface above three short drawers to the frieze, each pedestal with two arched panelled doors, 50in (127cm) wide.
£500–600 ⚒ AG

A Victorian mahogany desk, with three frieze drawers, the open front on two baluster-turned legs, the rear comprising a series of cupboards and opening and dummy drawers, 32in (81.5cm) wide.
£900–1,100 ⚒ WL

A Victorian mahogany Georgian-style pedestal desk, with leather-inset top, the central frieze drawer flanked by three drawers to each pedestal, 60in (152.5cm) wide.
£2,500–2,800 ⊞ RPh

A late Victorian mahogany partner's pedestal desk, the inset leather top above three frieze drawers, three drawers to each pedestal, floret-wood knob handles, the reverse with a frieze above cupboard doors, 60in (152.5cm) wide.
£3,400–4,000 ⚒ WW

A lady's rosewood writing desk, the superstructure inlaid with urns forming a stationery compartment, with leather-inset top and one drawer, late 19thC, 36in (91.5cm) wide.
£650–800 ⚒ E

An oak pedestal desk, with embossed hide writing surface, 19thC, 59in (150cm) wide.
£4,750–5,300 ⊞ HA

Prices

Desks and writing tables have steadily increased in price in recent years because a personal computer can be placed on them and still leave working space. For this reason the price of bureaux has remained static.

A mahogany pedestal desk, the hinged superstructure enclosing three pigeonholes and a hinged compartment, with elevating tooled brown leather-inset top, flanked by hinged outward folding leather-inset leaves enclosing various compartments, the frieze with two dummy drawer sliding lopers opposing two further panelled pedestals fitted with eight drawers opposing four long drawers and two cupboards, 19thC, 72½in (184cm) wide.
£3,200–3,800 ⚒ P(Ba)

A late Victorian Carlton House desk, with satinwood line inlay and tulipwood crossbanding, stamped 'Gillows', 54½in (138cm) wide.
£7,000–8,500 ⚒ Bon(C)

A late Victorian walnut pedestal desk, the tambour fall enclosing an inset writing surface and fitted interior, above a central frieze drawer and two banks of four graduated drawers with brushing slides flanked by fluted pillars, 60¼in (153cm) wide.
£950–1,150 ⚒ CGC

A walnut desk, the superstructure with a sloped panel door and shelf on outswept acanthus-carved feet, French, c1900, 45¼in (115cm) wide.
£230–275 ⚒ P(Ba)

A late Victorian oak pedestal partner's desk, 59in (150cm) wide.
£3,750–4,200 ⊞ RAN

A late Victorian mahogany knee-hole desk, with blind fret decoration, the raised back with small cupboards, drawers and an open shelf, the base with three frieze and four pedestal drawers, on cluster column legs, 47¾in (121.5cm) wide.
£900–1,100 ⚒ P(S)

A late Victorian lady's mahogany writing desk, with ebony stringing, the superstructure with brass gallery over a tooled-leather writing surface, above a bowfronted drawer flanked by two further drawers, stamped 'Maple & Co Ltd', 39½in (100.5cm) wide.
£700–850 ⚒ P(L)

A late Victorian mahogany partner's pedestal desk, the top with a tooled red leather insert, with three drawers opposing three further drawers, the pedestals fitted with six short drawers opposing two cupboards, 54¼in (138cm) wide.
£1,000–1,200 ⚒ P(Ba)

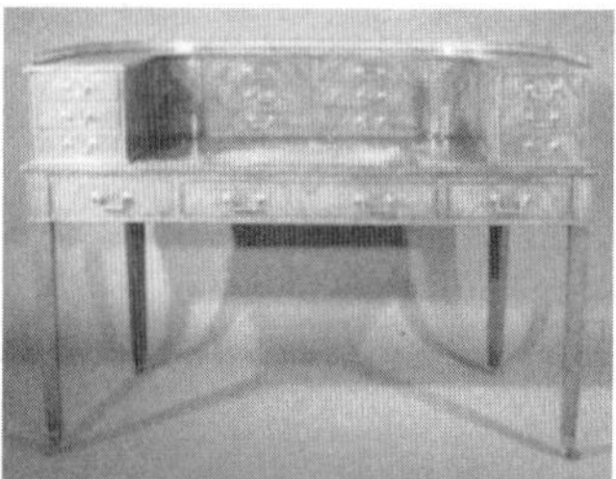

A mahogany Carlton House desk, with inlaid stringing, the brass galleried superstructure and leather-inset writing surface over three frieze drawers, early 20thC, 56in (142cm) wide.
£4,000–5,000 WW

An Edwardian rosewood writing desk, with two panelled doors enclosing stationery compartments centred by a bevelled mirror-back fitted with ebonized pilasters, the leather-lined writing surface above five drawers, 42in (106.5cm) wide.
£1,100–1,300 AG

An Edwardian oak roll-top desk, the tambour lid enclosing pigeonholes, the kneehole with a shallow drawer, the pedestals with three short drawers above a deep drawer, 42in (106.5cm) wide.
£450–550 DA

An 18thC-style mahogany kidney-shaped desk, with original leather inset, c1920, 42in (106.5cm) wide.
£1,650–1,850 MTay

An Edwardian satinwood and marquetry Carlton House desk, decorated with urns and scrolling foliage, the superstructure with a gilt-metal gallery, the inset leather writing surface above a frieze drawer and four short drawers, leather distressed, 53½in (136cm) wide.
£7,000–8,000 P

The distinctive design of this desk, with its superstructure of two or three tiers of small drawers rising from the back and curving around the sides, dates from the late 18th century. It was first seen in a plate published by George Hepplewhite in 1792, and Thomas Sheraton illustrated a similar desk in his *Cabinet Maker's and Upholsterer's Drawing Book* in 1793. It was not until 1796 that the term 'Carlton House' desk was first used by the firm Gillow. A similar desk at Buckingham House was thought to have originated from the Prince Regent's Carlton House mansion. Possibly this location was given to Robert Gillow by one of his clients and the term perpetuated.

An Edwardian mahogany officer's desk, by Parkins & Gotto, with a rising top and a pull-down front enclosing a fitted interior, the stand with a drawer fitted with recessed brass handles over an undertier, 28½in (72.5cm) wide.
£1,500–1,800 HYD

An Edwardian mahogany writing desk, the serpentine-shape break-front with three drawers, 40in (101.5cm) wide.
£1,700–1,875 CGA

An Edwardian mahogany desk, the raised satinwood crossbanded superstructure with a central mirror, pen tray, inkwells and two drawers flanking bowfronted glazed doors, enclosing paper racks above an inset writing surface and three drawers, 39in (99cm) wide.
£600–700 CGC

An Edwardian rosewood and inlaid desk, the mirror-back superstructure and central shelf flanked by two hinged inlaid compartments above a dummy drawer, the serpentine-front leather-inset top above a frieze drawer flanked by two deep drawers, 40¼in (102cm) wide.
£1,200–1,400 P(Ba)

◄ **A figured walnut pedestal desk,** the inverted breakfront top with triple leather inset and gadrooned edge above three frieze drawers, each pedestal with three graduated drawers, on claw-and-ball feet, 1900–50, 60¼in (153cm) wide.
£1,000–1,100 S(S)

Dumb Waiters

A three-tier mahogany dumb waiter, c1770, 45in (114.5cm) high.
£4,250–4,750 ⊞ F

A George III mahogany dumb waiter, with three graduated dished tiers on a wrythen-turned column, 42¼in (107.5cm) high.
£2,800–3,300 ⚒ CGC

A fruitwood dumb waiter, with two graduated tiers on a turned spiral-cut column, tiers cracked and warped, late 18thC, 19in (48.5cm) diam.
£400–500 ⚒ WW

A late Georgian mahogany dumb waiter, with three graduated tiers on a turned column, 40in (101.5cm) high.
£1,000–1,200 ⚒ RBB

A mahogany three-tier dumb waiter, c1835, 53in (134.5cm) wide.
£2,200–2,600 ⊞ GBr

A mahogany three-tier dumb waiter, c1835, 42in (106.5cm) wide.
£1,750–2,000 ⚒ S(O)

► **A George III-style mahogany dumb waiter,** the three graduated tiers on a balustrade-turned column, late 19thC, 27¼in (69cm) diam.
£350–420 ⚒ P(Ba)

A Victorian walnut dumb waiter, the fixed top above two graduated revolving tiers, veneered in burr-figured walnut, slight damage, 23in (58.5cm) diam.
£600–700 ⚒ WW

Etagères

A William IV coromandel and ebonized *étagère*, with brass three-quarter gallery, the four tiers with brass-beaded edges on gilt-highlighted, fluted and lotus leaf-carved columns, 27½in (70cm) wide.
£3,800–4,200 ⚒ P(Ba)

A mahogany and parquetry three-tier *étagère*, applied with gilt-metal mounts, the tiers with pierced gilt-metal galleries, the legs with gilt-metal banding, mid-19thC, 26in (66cm) wide.
£1,400–1,600 ⚒ P

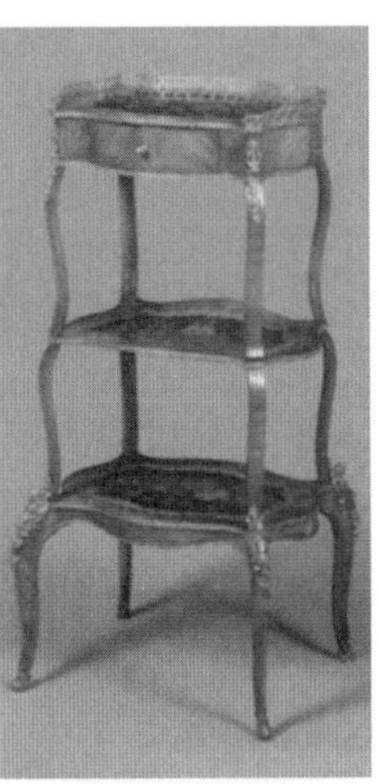

A marquetry *étagère*, c1860, 16in (40.5cm) wide.
£1,800–2,000 ⚒ S(O)

A three-tier *étagère*, with parquetry inlay, the top with an ormolu gallery and a frieze drawer, c1880, 32in (81.5cm) high.
£2,200–2,475 ⊞ BERA

Items in the Furniture section have been arranged in date order within each sub-section.

FURNITURE

Frames

A carved and gilded frame, with cavetto sight, finger panels to the reverse cushion-moulded hollow with leaf and flower centres and corners, scotia, ribbon-twist and demi-flowerhead back edge, late 17thC, 49 x 39½in (124.5 x 100.5cm).
£600–720 Bon

Cross Reference
See Colour Review
(page 113)

► **A carved giltwood frame,** with later mirror plate, the surround carved with putti, putti masks and scrolls entwined with floral and foliate festoons issuing from cornucopiae, re-gilded, originally a picture frame, probably Dutch, late 17thC, 37½ x 46½in (95.5 x 118cm).
£12,000–14,000 S

A mahogany frame, the later bevelled plate within a frame carved with egg-and-dart, Greek key and foliate mouldings, the corners with flowerheads and leaves, c1740, 25¼ x 19in (64 x 48.5cm).
£2,700–3,000 S

A pierced, swept and gilded frame, with foliate sight, sanded frieze and rocaille hollow with rocaille cartouche centres and flowerhead cartouche corners, mid-18thC, 20 x 14in (51 x 35.5cm).
£350–420 Bon

A carved and gilded frame, with egg-and-dart sight, leaf scotia and flower palmette, with strapwork to the crosshatched ogee and cabochon corners, Italian, 18thC, 21¼ x 16¼in (54 x 42cm).
£700–850 Bon

A gilded frame, with plain wedge sight, scotia, cluster-reeded cushion-moulded frieze with corner cassettes and plain top taneia, 19thC, 49 x 33½in (124.5 x 85cm).
£900–1,100 Bon

A carved wood and gilded frame, with rococo acanthus and pierced decoration, early 19thC, 34 x 30¼in (86.5 x 77cm).
£400–500 B&L

A gilded composition Carlo Maratta frame, with cavetto sight, leaf-and-shield ogee, plain hollow, and centred pin and leaf-twist below plain top knull, 19thC, 16 x 12¾in (40.5 x 32.5cm).
£260–320 Bon

A carved and gilded frame, with cavetto sight, double bead-and-reel, sanded hollow and repeat demi-flower to top knull, 19thC, 18 x 12½in (45.5 x 32cm).
£160–200 Bon

Hall Stands

◄ **A Victorian oak hall stand,** the S-scroll carved back with four branches above a lion-mask carved apron, the base fitted with a drip pan, 94½in (240cm) high.
£260–320 CGC

► **A pine and oak hall stand,** in the shape of a garden gate, surmounted with a painted spelter figure of a cat, the base with a red-painted brick wall surmounted by a dog, restored, late 19thC, 26in (66cm) wide.
£5,000–6,000 S(S)

An Edwardian mahogany hall stand, with mirrored centre and two umbrella stands, 47in (119.5cm) wide.
£1,000–1,150 RPh

Jardinières

A mahogany jardinière, the slatted container on a turned column support above a trefoil base, liner missing, restored, early 19thC, 15in (38cm) diam.
£320–380 ⚒ BLH

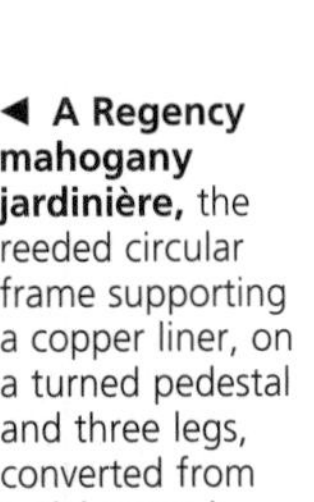

◄ **A Regency mahogany jardinière,** the reeded circular frame supporting a copper liner, on a turned pedestal and three legs, converted from a globe stand, 24½in (62cm) diam.
£600–700 ⚒ CGC

A burr-yew veneered serpentine jardinière, with a pierced bronze gallery and pierced cast bronze mounts, the ebonized border with brass studs, liner missing, French, 19thC, 17½in (44.5cm) wide.
£170–200 ⚒ WW

LOCATE THE SOURCE
The source of each illustration in Miller's can be found by checking the code letters below each caption with the Key to Illustrations, pages 794–800.

◄ **A kingwood and ebonized jardinière,** with marquetry inlay, detachable cover, and undertier, on cabriole legs, French, 19thC, 22¾in (58cm) wide.
£575–700 ⚒ S(S)

A satinwood and polychrome-decorated jardinière, the repainted metal liner within a panelled surround, each panel decorated with a floral spray, the ends decorated with ribbon-tied swags, c1900, 20½in (52cm) wide.
£900–1,100 ⚒ P(Ba)

An Edwardian brass and mahogany jardinière, with crossbanding and stringing, the body with pierced brass panels and slat supports, 18½in (47cm) high.
£825–1,000 ⚒ AH

Lowboys

A George II mahogany lowboy, with four drawers and ogee-arched apron, on cabriole legs with ball-and-claw feet, 29½in (75cm) wide.
£2,200–2,500 ⚒ Bea(E)

► **A mahogany lowboy,** with one long drawer above three short drawers, on cabriole legs, c1740, 29in (73.5cm) wide.
£3,300–3,650 ⊞ F&F

A George III mahogany lowboy, the crossbanded top above two short and one long drawers, on chamfered square legs, 29½in (75cm) wide.
£800–950 ⚒ GAK

◄ **A George III mahogany lowboy,** with three drawers, two with circular veneers, around a recess with carved brackets, 35¾in (91cm) wide.
£1,000–1,200 ⚒ P(L)

A mahogany lowboy, with a long frieze drawer over a kneehole flanked by two short drawers, on square tapering legs, early 19thC, 32¼in (82cm) wide.
£400–480 ⚒ BLH

Miniature Furniture

A walnut miniature chest of drawers, with original brasses, c1730, 6½in (16.5cm) wide.
£750–825 F&F

A mahogany miniature bureau, with marquetry inlay, Dutch, 18thC, 17in (43cm) wide.
£2,150–2,400 SuA

A mahogany and parquetry bowfronted miniature commode, in the style of Louis XVI, the sides with rounded columns, Dutch, c1800, 12¾in (32.5cm) wide.
£2,500–3,000 CAG

A mahogany miniature chest of drawers, in the Sheraton style, with bone handles and escutcheons, c1800, 11in (28cm) high.
£580–650 F&F

A Victorian flame-mahogany miniature chest of drawers, the three drawers with ivory knobs, 9in (23cm) wide.
£160–200 OTT

A mahogany miniature chest of drawers, edged in ebony stringing, the four drawers with replaced brass handles, on later softwood bracket feet, 19thC, 11½in (29cm) wide.
£160–200 WW

► **A walnut and amboyna miniature breakfast table,** with turned column base and carved sabre legs, c1860, 13in (33cm) diam.
£2,000–2,300 BBo

A Victorian mahogany miniature press cupboard, the panelled cupboard door with applied gadroon-moulded spandrels and turned boss, flanked by beaded pilasters, above a projecting base with four graduated cockbeaded and crossbanded drawers flanked by spiral carved quarter-cut pilasters, 15in (38cm) wide.
£900–1,100 P(NW)

A Victorian oak miniature Wellington chest, with nine graduated long drawers, the locking stile and opposing column with carved leaf scroll bracket, 15in (38cm) wide.
£800–950 CAG

A walnut miniature Sutherland table, c1880, 30in (76cm) wide.
£1,000–1,150 MTay

◄ **A Victorian miniature specimen chest,** veneered in fiddle-back mahogany, the four drawers with wooden knob handles, 11¾in (30cm) wide.
£320–380 WW

A Louis XV-style tortoiseshell miniature vitrine, with gilt-metal mounts, the bowfronted glazed door and sides enclosing glass shelves, 1850–1900, 14in (35.5cm) high.
£800–950 S(S)

Cheval Mirrors

A Regency mahogany cheval mirror, in the style of Trotter of Edinburgh, the plate within a broad frame with a reeded border, 62¼in (158cm) high.
£1,500–1,800 CGC

A William IV mahogany cheval mirror, the adjustable plate supported by turned columns with conical finials, 30¼in (77cm) wide.
£800–900 P(Ba)

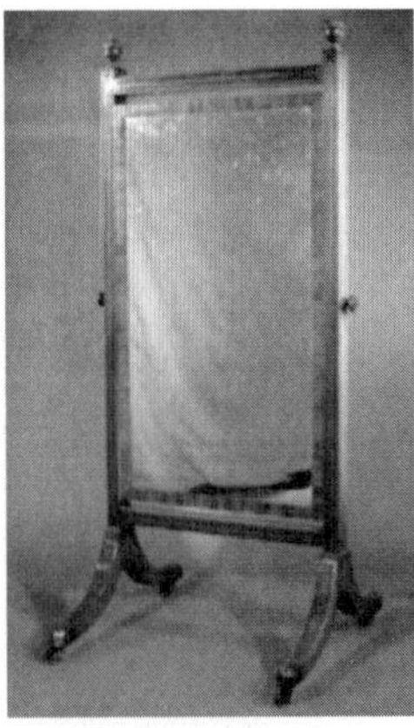

A William IV mahogany cheval mirror, the outline-moulded frame with ribbed cup finials, the ribbed splay legs with brass sabots on casters, 29in (73.5cm) wide.
£850–1,000 WW

A mahogany cheval mirror, the columnar uprights surmounted by a shaped pediment, on scrolling supports, 1800–50, 42in (107cm) wide.
£620–700 S(Am)

Dressing Table Mirrors

A Federal dressing mirror, the original plate in a frame supported by two turned and carved uprights, on reeded legs with carved paw feet, American, 1800–25, 35in (89cm) wide.
£1,000–1,200 NOA

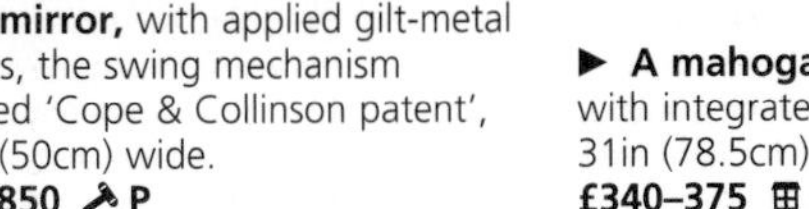

A mid-Victorian Louis XV-style walnut and tulipwood crossbanded toilet mirror, with applied gilt-metal mounts, the swing mechanism stamped 'Cope & Collinson patent', 19¾in (50cm) wide.
£700–850 P

A mahogany swing dressing table mirror, in the style of Gillows, the frame with turned ribbed supports and stretchers, early 19thC, 19½in (49.5cm) wide.
£200–240 WW

A mahogany dressing mirror, c1850, 26in (66cm) wide.
£330–365 NoC

► **A mahogany toilet mirror,** with integrated lidded box, c1870, 31in (78.5cm) wide.
£340–375 MTay

An early Victorian mahogany dressing table mirror, by James Mein of Kelso, with lotus-carved semi-circular support headed by rosettes, on a breakfront chamfered base, 21½in (54.5cm) wide.
£500–600 B(Ed)

The family business of James Mein is known to have supplied furniture for the 5th and 6th Dukes of Roxburgh at Floors Castle, as well as to the Earl of Haddington at Mellerstain. Mein's furniture is often remarkably sober and stylized in appearance, avoiding fussy decoration.

Wall Mirrors

A William and Mary walnut mirror, the later plate within a cushion-moulded frame, 23¼in (59cm) wide.
£650–800 ⚒ CGC

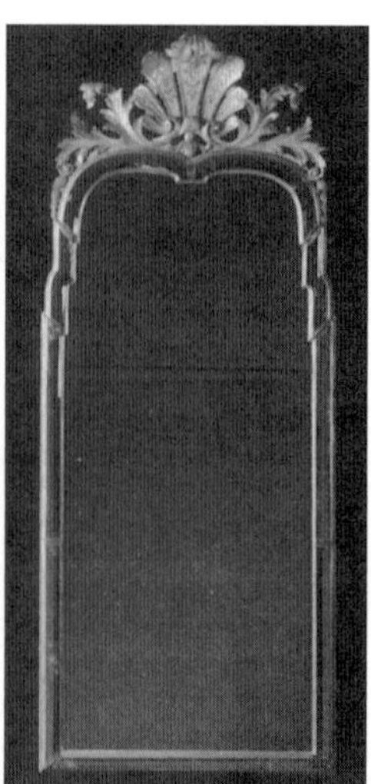

► A walnut oyster-veneered wall mirror, cushion-framed, with bevelled rectangular plate, early 18thC, 28in (71cm) wide.
£2,000–2,400 ⚒ RBB

◄ A Queen Anne giltwood pier mirror, the cresting carved with leaves and scrolls, regilded, some later glass, 24¼in (61.5cm) wide.
£6,500–8,000 ⚒ S

A painted wood mirror, the frame fitted with floral painted and *verre églomisé* panels, Continental, 18thC, 8½in (21.5cm) wide.
£730–800 ⚒ BB(S)

A George II carved giltwood mirror, the later plate within a bead-and-reel and egg-and-dart carved frame, surmounted by a broken arched pediment centred by a cabochon cresting, 30in (76cm) wide.
£7,500–9,000 ⚒ P

Miller's is a price GUIDE not a price LIST

A carved and giltwood mirror, damaged, Italian, late 18thC, 28¾ in (73cm) wide.
£2,000–2,400 ⚒ S(Mi)

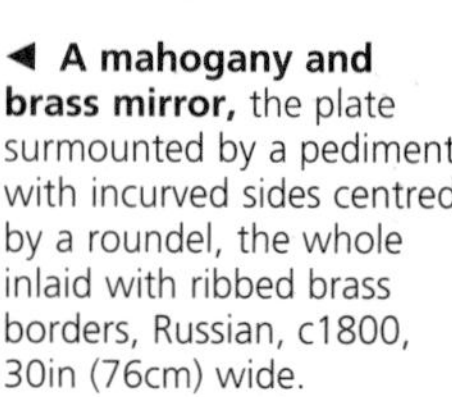

◄ A mahogany and brass mirror, the plate surmounted by a pediment with incurved sides centred by a roundel, the whole inlaid with ribbed brass borders, Russian, c1800, 30in (76cm) wide.
£3,800–4,500 ⚒ S(Am)

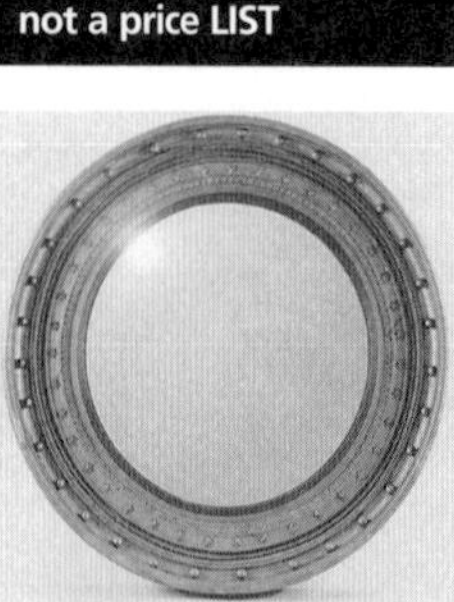

A Regency giltwood wall mirror, the border with gilt balls, beaded decoration and stars, with an ebony reeded slip and convex plate, 52¾in (134cm) diam.
£13,500–16,000 ⚒ HAM

An Empire mahogany mirror, with parcel-gilt, black-polished and blue-plastered decorative panels, the arched panel with medallion depicting a bust of the Marquis of Wellington, flanked by vines, damaged, French, early 19thC, 22in (56cm) wide.
£750–825 ⚒ S(Am)

A carved giltwood convex wall mirror, the crest with an eagle on a rocky outcrop above a central shell, flanked by flowers and foliage, with foliage base, early 19thC, 17in (43cm) high.
£1,150–1,400 ⚒ E
This mirror would probably have realised at least double this price if the plate had been in good condition.

A Federal gilt and *verre églomisé* wall mirror, the top panel reverse-painted on glass with a neo-classical female figure seated on a chair with surrounding red drapery, above a lightly bevelled plate flanked by turned split-baluster columns, original paint and gilt, American, 20in (51cm) wide.
£1,400–1,600 ⚒ SK(B)

◀ **A Regency Grecian-style gilt overmantel mirror,** by W. Froom, the frame with reeded split-column pilasters, lotus capitals and bases, the angles set with rosettes beneath a shallow cornice, 59in (150cm) wide.
£2,000–2,400 ⚒ N
Pasted to the back of this mirror is a label for 'W. Froom, late Fentham & Co, Looking Glass Manufacturer, Carver and Gilder and Picture Frame Maker, 136 Strand, near Somerset House, glasses conveyed to any part of the Country on spring machines constructed for the sole purpose'.

A Regency gilt and gesso breakfront mirror, the plate within a reeded ebonized slip flanked by leaf-capped columns, 24¾in (63cm) wide.
£300–360 ⚒ CGC

A gilt and parcel-ebony overmantel mirror, by Del Vecchio of Dublin, the original plate in a bead and leaf-moulded frame, signed and dated, with trade label on reverse, Irish, 1818, 59in (150cm) wide.
£3,750–4,500 ⚒ MEA
In recent years Irish furniture has greatly increased in value. This is a good example and has proof of origin.

A gilded overmantel mirror, c1820, 22in (56cm) wide.
£3,000–3,300 ⊞ HA

▶ **A mahogany mirror,** the frieze with applied scrolling botanical forms and a central brass boss above the two glass plates enclosed in reeded frames flanked by ring-turned rope-carved columns, American, 1825–35, 37½in (95.5cm) high.
£675–800 ⚒ SK(B)

A wall mirror, the frame decorated with Dieppe ivory, c1830, 23in (58.5cm) wide.
£1,250–1,400 ⊞ DJH

An overmantel mirror, with original plate and giltwood frame, back panels restored, c1870, 56in (142cm) wide.
£1,150–1,250 ⊞ ASH

A carved giltwood and gesso overmantel mirror, in the style of Louis XVI, with original bevelled plate, French, 1850–75, 41in (104cm) wide.
£1,600–1,800 ⚒ NOA

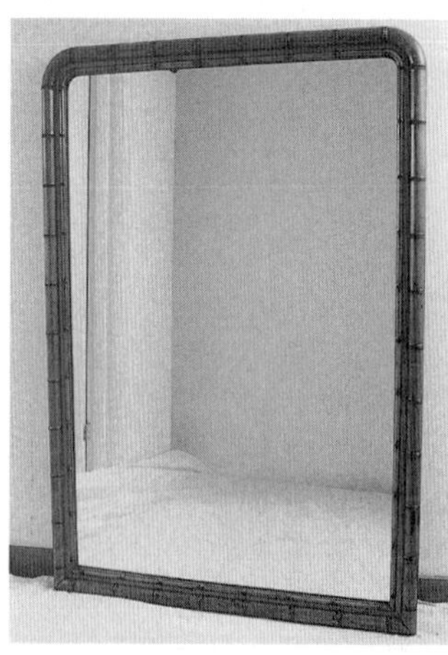

A mahogany wall mirror, the everted moulded frame with applied ebonized paterae motifs, c1835, 35¾in (91cm) wide.
£1,800–2,200 ⚒ S(O)

A carved giltwood mirror, Italian, 1850–75, 25¾in (65.5cm) wide.
£550–650 ⚒ NOA

A pair of George III-style giltwood mirrors, with feather plumes and acanthus cresting rails, the stippled frames further carved with foliage, c1900, 31in (78.5cm) wide.
£800–950 ⚒ P(Ba)

◄ **A cherrywood on pitch-pine *faux* bamboo mirror,** with original plate and back, French, c1910, 40in (101.5cm) wide.
£850–950 ⊞ OFM

► **An overmantel mirror,** with beaded frame painted gold on red, regilded, French, c1920, 41½in (105.5cm) wide.
£550–600 ⊞ OFM

An early Victorian mahogany breakfront overmantel mirror, flanked by turned columns with stylized tulip capitals, 46in (117cm) wide.
£330–400 ⚒ Mit

A wall mirror, the carved giltwood frame with ribbon-tied fruiting bellflowers and an open scrolling foliate border with fleur-de-lys corners, French, 19thC, 43in (109cm) wide.
£1,300–1,600 ⚒ WW

A carved and gesso wall mirror, applied with putti among swagged drapes adorned with pink flowers and painted to simulate bronze and ivory, Continental, 19thC, 39in (99cm) wide.
£1,100–1,250 ⚒ G(L)

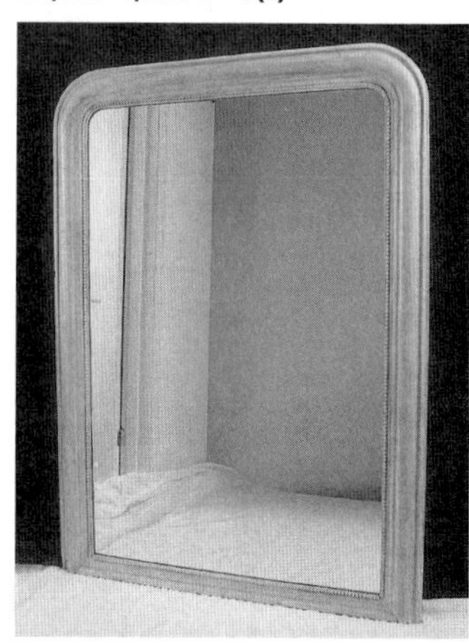

Pedestals

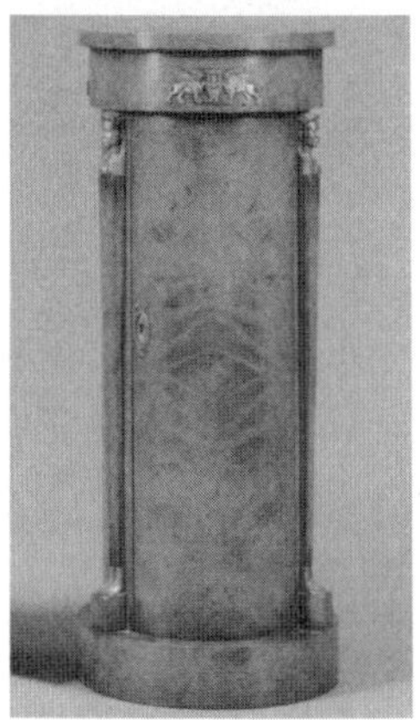

A pair of Empire burr-oak and gilt-metal mounted pedestals, with quarter-veneered tops, each pale green painted interior with a shelf, pilaster mounts later, French, c1830, 41¾in (106cm) wide.
£3,750–4,500 S(O)

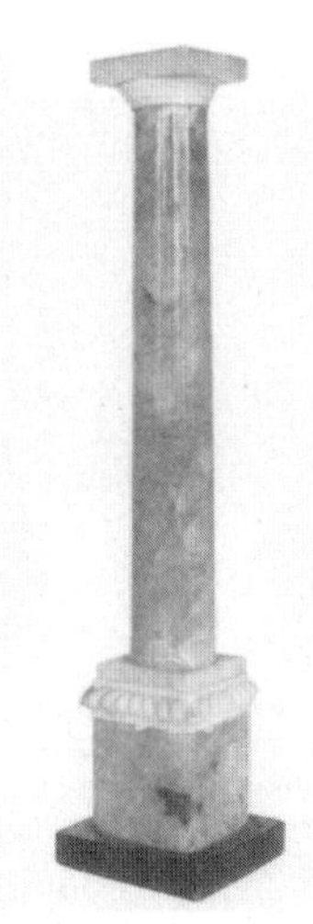

A pair of blue john pedestals, with alabaster capitals and slate bases, some damage, 19thC, 17½in (44.5cm) high.
£2,000–2,400 F&C

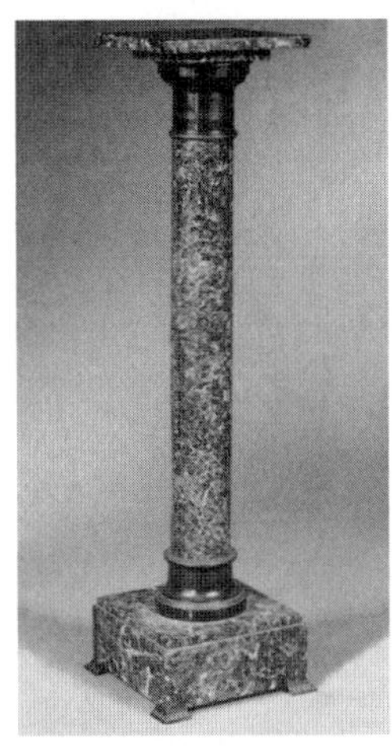

A green marble and patinated bronze pedestal, with engine-turned capital and base, Italian, late 19thC, 45½in (115.5cm) high.
£850–1,000 NOA

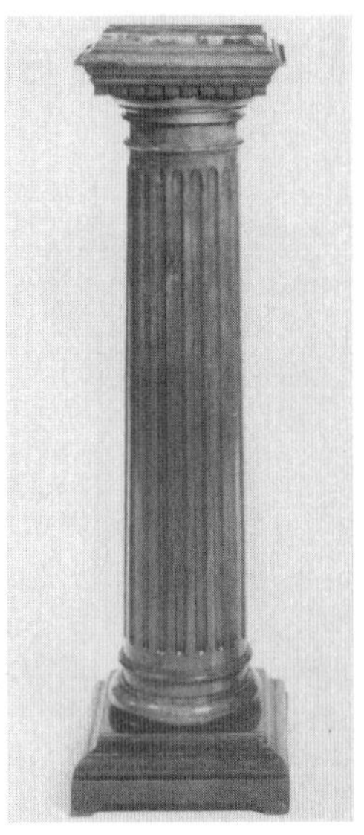

An oak pedestal, the grey and red marble top above a fluted cylindrical column on a square plinth, late 19thC, 45in (114.5cm) high.
£500–600 P(Ba)

Screens

A painted-leather four-fold screen, each leaf with brass studding and painted with birds, probably Dutch, 18thC, 84¼in (215cm) high.
£4,000–4,800 HOK

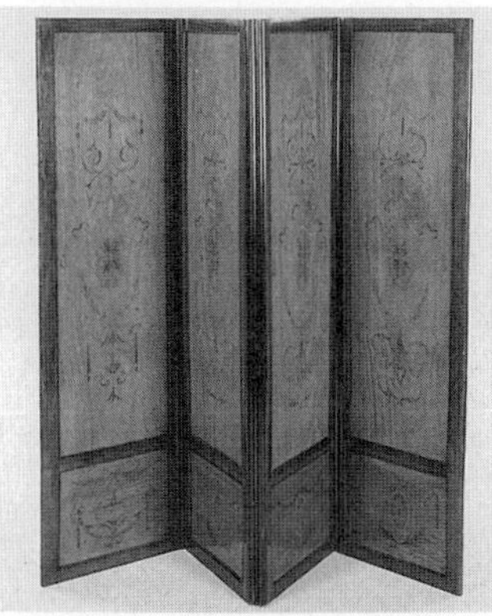

A George III-style satinwood, mahogany and marquetry four-fold screen, each panel decorated with neo-classical motifs of ribbon-tied swags and scrolling foliage, centring on paterae and urns, missing cresting, late 19thC, 61in (155cm) high.
£3,600–4,300 S

A painted-leather four-fold screen, painted with a scene believed to be Fleet Street, London, with a C-scroll and floral garland border, mid-19thC, 84in (213cm) wide.
£1,500–1,800 P(E)

An embossed hide six-fold screen, each panel decorated in Regency style, with polychrome and gilt cartouches surmounted by parrots and fruit entwined with flowers, on a turquoise and dark green ground, the reverse panels painted black with turquoise and pink borders, tears to leather, late 19thC, 70½in (179cm) high.
£4,000–5,000 S

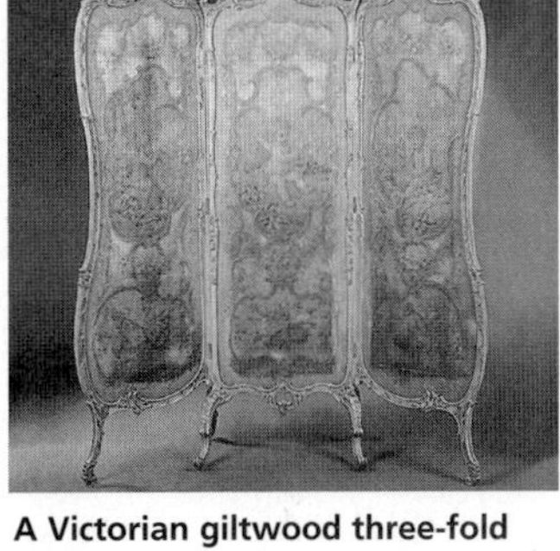

A Victorian giltwood three-fold screen, the leaves with tapestry panels depicting cherubs in cartouches, 84in (213cm) wide.
£900–1,100 B(Ed)

A four-fold screen, the panels covered with Spanish tooled-leather, 19thC, 74in (188cm) high.
£900–1,100 WW

Prices

The value of screens is very much dependent on condition. Often the leather has perished, and as leather is almost impossible to restore, the value decreases dramatically.

Fire Screens

A pair of mahogany pole screens, with needlework panels, c1795, 54in (137cm) high.
£1,750–2,000 ⊞ DJH

A Louis XV-style mahogany fire screen, the frame surmounted by flower-carved cresting, Dutch, 18thC, 29½in (75cm) wide.
£750–900 ⚒ S(Am)

A rosewood fire screen, with needlework panel depicting two girls, c1830, 28in (71cm) wide.
£450–500 ⊞ NoC

A rosewood fire screen, the tapestry panel depicting a hawk among flowers, flanked by barley-twist supports, c1840, 31in (78.5cm) wide,
£550–625 ⊞ NoC

A Victorian Berlin-tapestry fire screen, depicting a hunter with game and two dogs, the frame with foliate and scroll-carved top and base, with barley-twist column supports, 26in (66cm) wide.
£500–600 ⚒ Mit

A mid-Victorian walnut fire screen, the pierced scrolling pediment with carved phoenix crest above a tapestry depicting a Spanish scene of a cardinal being greeted by an abbot, flanked by barley-twist columns, 39½in (100.5cm) wide.
£550–650 ⚒ P(L)

A Victorian ebonized fire screen, the pierced cresting rail above a glazed panel inset with a stumpwork-style scene of a cat on a chair, with two dogs below, flanked by barley-twist uprights, 30in (76cm) wide.
£500–600 ⚒ GAK

A Victorian rosewood screen, the figural needlework panel in a scroll-carved frame, on a turned baluster shaft, 45¼in (115cm) high.
£380–450 ⚒ P(NW)

Settees & Sofas

A George II two-seater sofa, the reeded show-frame with berry, leaf and foliate terminals, on leaf- and scroll-carved cabriole legs, with ball-and-claw feet and rear swept legs on pad feet, 60in (152.5cm) wide.
£6,000–7,200 ⚒ TMA

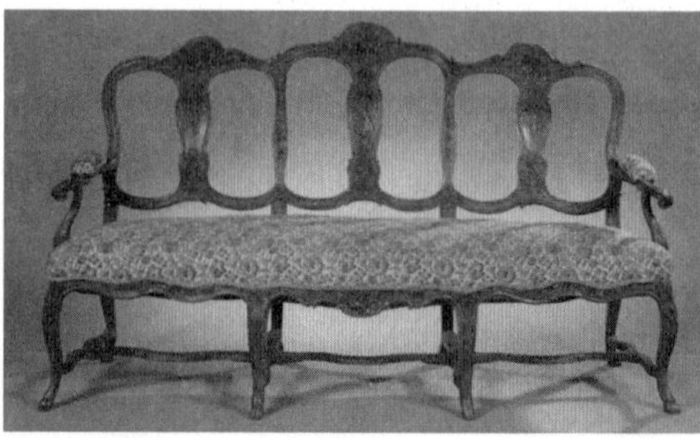

A rococo walnut settee, carved with foliage and floral sprays with scrolled padded arms above a padded serpentine seat, German, mid-18thC, 72in (183cm) wide.
£1,800–2,200 ⚒ S(Am)

► **A Regency mahogany-framed settee,** the arms ending in turned and reeded terminals, on turned and reeded legs, with a loose cushion, 76in (193cm) wide.
£1,400–1,700 ⚒ P(L)

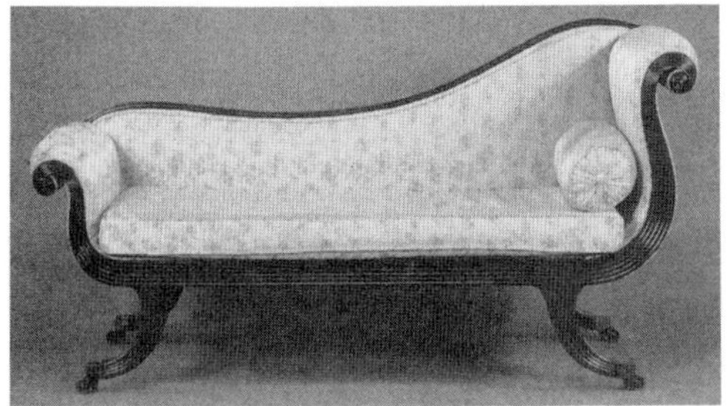

A Grecian-style mahogany sofa, the reeded frame with scroll ends and sabre legs, upholstered in yellow floral silk, c1810, 74in (188cm) wide.
£1,100–1,300 N

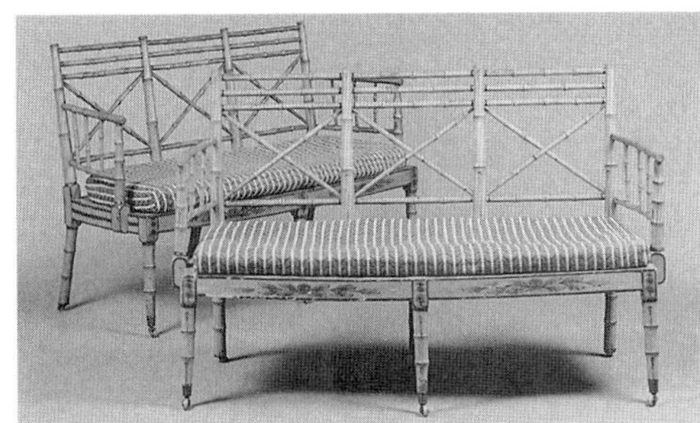

A pair of simulated bamboo and painted chairback settees, the triple panel backs with X-shaped splats and spindle-filled open arms, the bowed seat-rails decorated with panels of oak leaves, c1810, 54in (137cm) wide.
£3,250–4,000 S

A giltwood settee, after a design by Thomas Hope, the pediment carved with double roundels, arabesques and acanthus leaves above a frieze of anthemia, flanked by square uprights with pineapple-shaped terminals, each of the turned reeded armrests terminating in rams' heads over an acanthus-wrapped scroll and arabesque-carved panel topped by seven spheres, the removable cushions covered in old green velvet, the seat-rails carved with paterae, the underside pierced for original tassels, c1810, 44½in (113cm) wide.
£56,000–67,000 G(L)
It is thought that this settee may be one of a pair sold by Christie's in 1917 at Deepdene House in Dorking, that was purchased by Thomas Hope in 1807 and furnished with pieces made to his designs. Included in the 1917 auction was 'a pair of Empire gilt settees with rams' head and honeysuckle ornament, the seats covered with green velvet, 3ft 9ins wide' and referenced as Plate 22 in Hope's *Household Furniture and Interior Decoration*, published in 1807.

Regency furniture

- Designs were influenced by the neo-classical taste fashionable in Europe since the late 18th century, and styles from the French Consulate (1799–1804) and Empire (1804–15) periods.
- Decoration was based on classical forms such as Egyptian, Greek, Etruscan and Roman, which were often all used on one piece.
- Excellent brass inlay was often a key feature.
- Mahogany and rosewood were the main timbers used, the latter often simulated by painting on beech. It was also often French polished.
- Thomas Hope was one of the greatest English exponents.

◀ **A Regency mahogany double-ended settee,** the scroll back with a centre shell flanked by two C-scroll ends, Irish, 87in (221cm) wide.
£1,400–1,700 MEA

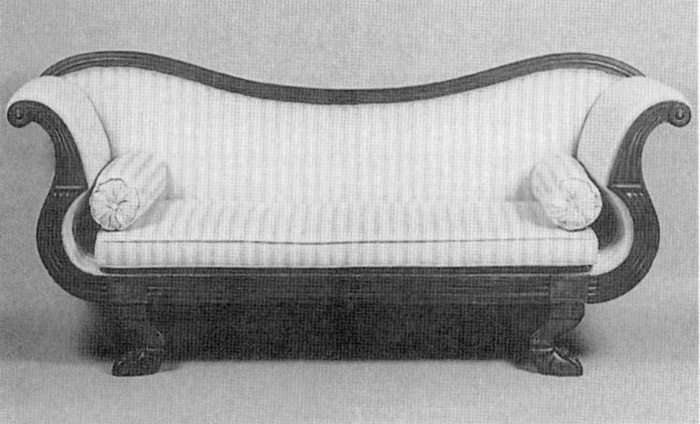

▶ **A Regency mahogany-framed sofa,** the reeded serpentine back above two scrolling arms and a cushion seat, on lappet-headed lion's paw feet, Irish, 82in (208.5cm) wide.
£1,450–1,750 RFA

An early Victorian ebonized and gilt-painted chair-back settee, the scrolling top-rails above pierced scrolling horizontal rails, the canework seat with a squab cushion, 45¼in (115cm) wide.
£370–450 B(Ed)

◀ **A Biedermeier walnut sofa,** c1820, Austrian, 87in (221cm) wide.
£2,200–2,500 S(O)

▶ **A William IV rosewood sofa,** the dipped upholstered back above a button cushion seat with bolsters, flanked by padded arms with floral carved rests, on turned lotus-carved tapering legs, Scottish, 76¾in (195cm) wide.
£2,000–2,400 P(Ed)

A Louis XV-style giltwood canapé, with a cresting of ribbon-tied foliage to the moulded and husk-decorated frame, French, mid-19thC, 70in (178cm) wide.
£3,500–3,850 ⊞ RAN

A Victorian walnut sofa, the top-rail carved with a floral crest, flanked by pierced and carved foliage, the serpentine stuff-over seat on foliate-carved cabriole legs terminating in knurl feet, 74in (188cm) wide.
£900–1,000 ⚒ P(Ba)

A Victorian walnut four-seater conversation seat, with button back and padded seat, four pierced and moulded dividers, on moulded cabriole legs, 51in (129.5cm) wide.
£1,100–1,300 ⚒ MEA

A Victorian mahogany sofa, the back crested with acanthus-leaf and scrolled mount, upholstered in a puce buttoned fabric, on short lobed and fluted tapering legs, 62in (157.5cm) wide.
£650–800 ⚒ GAK

A Victorian walnut chair-back settee, with foliate-carved moulded show-frame, buttoned back and corded upholstery, 68in (172.5cm) wide.
£600–720 ⚒ WW

A walnut sofa, with carved back, cabriole legs and serpentine seat rail, c1860, 78in (198cm) wide.
£2,600–3,000 ⊞ NoC

An oak and mahogany caned folding campaign sofa bed, with brass mounts, 19thC, 76½in (194.5cm) wide.
£1,200–1,500 ⚒ L&E

A mid-Victorian carved walnut show-framed conversation seat, comprising four conjoined seats, 38in (96.5cm) wide.
£670–800 ⚒ AAR

An Edwardian 18thC-style satinwood two-seater settee, painted all over with lines and floral sprays, the twin trellis splat back over a cane and squab seat, 39½in (100.5cm) wide.
£1,100–1,300 ⚒ P

◀ **An Edwardian mahogany-framed settee,** with satinwood marquetry and boxwood string inlaid decoration, 65in (165cm) wide.
£420–500 ⚒ AAR

An Edwardian boxwood-strung mahogany two-seater settee, the crossbanded top-rail centred by an inlaid flowerhead medallion flanked by bellflowers, the pierced interlaced back between satinwood-crossbanded uprights and similar downswept arms, the seat upholstered in a printed fabric, 42in (106.5cm) wide.
£350–420 ⚒ PFK

Shelves

A four-tier mahogany waterfall hanging shelf, c1800, 25in (63.5cm) wide.
£340–375 ⊞ F&F

► **A George III mahogany wall shelf,** the shaped sides pierced with Chinese-style fretwork, the base with two drawers, one divided, 28¼in (72cm) wide.
£2,700–3,300 WW
This shelf shows the influence of Thomas Chippendale who popularized the pierced fretwork seen here on the supports. This shelf is 18th century and has never gone out of fashion, therefore such pieces are always sought after.

► **A painted and parcel-gilt free-standing corner shelf,** the white marble top over two mirror-backed shelves flanked by lion monopodia supports, early 19thC, 18in (45.5cm) wide.
£1,700–2,000 Bon

► **A pair of carved and composition gilt-gesso hanging corner shelves,** on acanthus scroll frames and winged putto supports, both damaged, one missing an arm, Italian, c1900, 39½in (100.5cm) high.
£600–720 P(Ba)

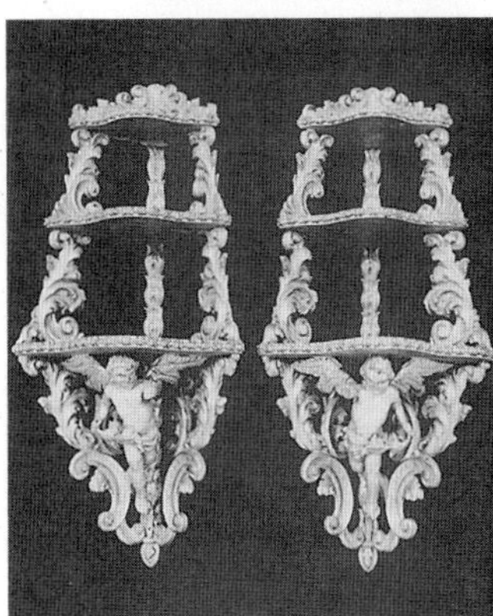

Sideboards

► **A George III Sheraton-style serpentine sideboard,** the central drawer flanked by two further drawers, with inlaid spandrels, crossbanding and boxwood stringing, the tapering legs on spade feet, 72½in (184cm) wide.
£3,200–3,800 Gam

A mahogany crossbanded and boxwood-line-inlaid serpentine sideboard, with a breakfront and bowed frieze drawer above a shaped apron with central shell inlay flanked by concave drawers and deep drawers, with inlaid paterae, late 18thC, 54in (137cm) wide.
£2,300–2,600 HOK

◄ **A Regency satinwood-strung bowfronted sideboard,** the central drawer flanked by a pivoted cellaret and a cupboard, altered, 45in (114.5cm) wide.
£1,350–1,500 CGC

► **A late Regency mahogany sideboard,** with a later undulating gallery over three frieze drawers, 84¾in (215.5cm) wide.
£650–750 P(Ba)

A Regency mahogany and satinwood crossbanded bowfronted sideboard, inlaid with ebonized, boxwood and harewood lines, the frieze drawer and recessed apron drawer flanked by two short and one deep cellaret drawer, 79¼in (201.5cm) wide.
£7,000–8,500 Bon
The legs on this sideboard are of an unusual design.

A late Georgian figured mahogany breakfront sideboard, the central slightly bowed drawer over a further central drawer and base cupboard with fitted shelves, flanked by side cupboards below deep bottle drawers with twist-carved and lobed pilasters with gilt-metal winged paw feet, 85in (216cm) wide.
£2,500–3,000 TMA

◄ **A George IV mahogany pedestal sideboard,** with brass rail back, the rectangular top decorated with inlaid ebonized stringing, above three freeze drawers with lion mask ring handles, each pedestal with a panelled door, 66in (167.5cm) wide.
£1,800–2,200 AG

A crossbanded mahogany sideboard, the breakfront top above a frieze, with inset centre drawer and applied lion mask ring mounts, early to mid-19thC, 85in (216cm) wide.
£20,000–24,000 HOLL
This sideboard is in a good state of preservation and of elegant proportions and sold for ten times its lower estimate. There is currently a ready market for individualistic pieces in good condition, while middle range items are tending to be more difficult to sell.

► **A Federal mahogany sideboard,** the scrolled back flanked by gallery sides above a case of three cockbeaded drawers over four recessed panel cupboard doors flanked by reeded pilasters, replaced brasses, restored, American, c1820, 72in (183cm) wide.
£2,200–2,700 SK(B)

A William IV mahogany sideboard, the top with applied crossbanded edge above a central bowfronted frieze drawer flanked by spiral fluted pillars, with two short drawers to the right and a cellaret drawer modelled as two short drawers to the left, Scottish, 66in (167.5cm) wide.
£2,000–2,400 Mit

A William IV mahogany double pedestal breakfront sideboard, with two panelled doors, four drawers and blind fret carving, 86in (218.5cm) wide.
£1,500–1,800 Gam

► **A mahogany carved serpentine sideboard,** the mirrored back surrounded by grape and vine carving, c1860, 77in (195.5cm) wide.
£4,000–4,350 MTay

A Victorian figured mahogany sideboard, the panel back with foliate-carved crest over inverted breakfront frieze drawers with two panel doors to the recessed centre, flanked by further doors with applied scroll-carved corbels, 72¾in (185cm) wide.
£1,300–1,600 Bri

► **An Edwardian oak sideboard,** the superstructure with a shaped mirror and shelf flanked by tapering lobed columns, two shelves and two arched mirrors, the base fitted with a central carved panel door above two drawers, flanked by two frieze drawers and two carved panel doors, 59½in (151cm) wide.
£700–800 P(Ba)

A Victorian mahogany pedestal sideboard, the raised back centred by a shield-shaped motif, above three fitted frieze drawers, each pedestal with a panelled door, the right-hand door enclosing a revolving decanter stand, 84in (213.5cm) wide.
£800–950 AG

A camphorwood and brass-bound campaign sideboard, the raised sides with hinged lids, one fitted as a cellaret, enclosing a single drawer, the lower sections with arched panel cupboard doors, 19thC, 62¼in (158cm) wide.
£3,400–4,000 B(Ed)

Stands

A Georgian mahogany cutlery box, on a later stand, 20in (51cm) high.
£350–385 ⊞ RAN

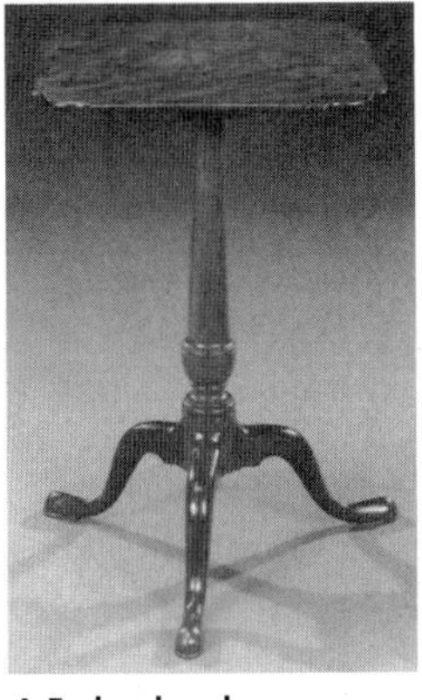

A Federal mahogany candlestand, the square top with shaped corners, American, c1800, 17in (43cm) wide.
£1,700–2,000 ⚒ SLN

► A Federal walnut stand, with a single drawer, pull possibly replaced, American, 19thC, 18½in (47cm) wide.
£400–500 ⚒ SK(B)

A rosewood folio stand, the adjustable folio section on turned columns and reeded outswept legs, early 19thC, 24½in (62cm) wide.
£2,100–2,500 ⚒ Bon

A mahogany boot and shoe rack, with arched top and wooden pegs, 19thC, 24in (61cm) wide.
£220–270 ⚒ MEA

An Empire mahogany and poplar stand, with two drawers, French, 1850–1900, 21¾in (55.5cm) wide.
£200–240 ⚒ SLN

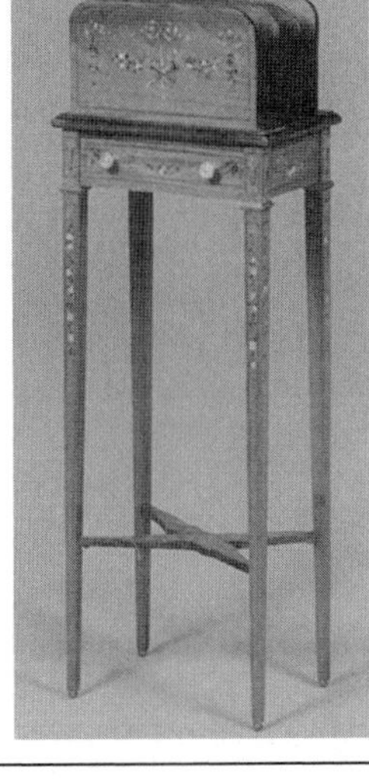

► A painted satinwood magazine stand, c1910, 13in (33cm) wide.
£1,200–1,500 ⚒ S(O)

► A Victorian figured walnut folio stand, the hinged top above a glazed front and back, 37in (94cm) wide.
£900–1,100 ⚒ P(S)

Hat & Stick Stands

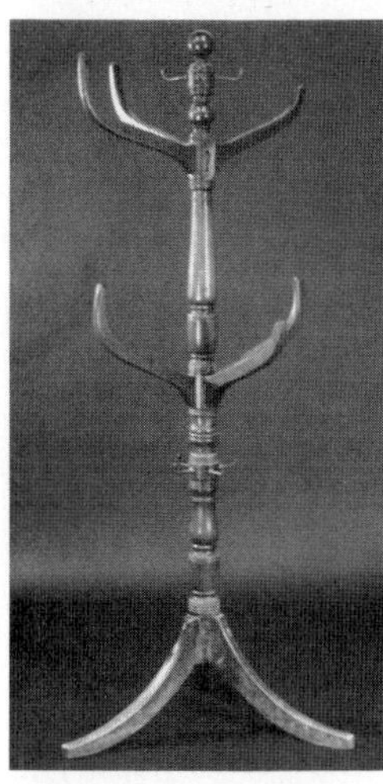

A Regency mahogany hat stand, missing two arms, 70½in (179cm) high.
£280–320 ⚒ CGC

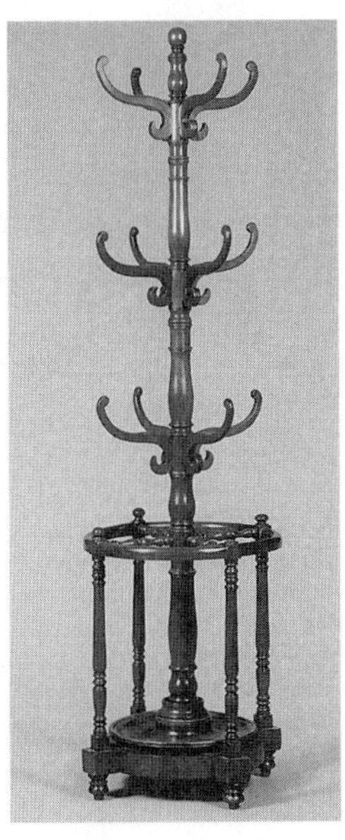

► A maple wall-hanging bonnet rack, c1860, 19in (48.5cm) wide.
£100–125 ⊞ GBr

◄ A William IV mahogany hat, coat and stick stand, 84¼in (214cm) high.
£6,000–7,200 ⚒ S

► A Victorian painted cast-iron stick stand, with flower, fox and shell-cast top and base, 27½in (70cm) high.
£380–450 ⚒ LFA

A mahogany and brass-bound stick stand, with lion mask handles and tin liner, 19thC, 11¾in (30cm) diam.
£1,000–1,200 P(E)

A carved oak stick stand, modelled as a standing bear holding a branch to retain the canes, on a rocky plinth base, German, 19thC, 45¾in (116cm) high.
£4,000–5,000 P(EA)

◄ **A mahogany and brass-mounted stick stand,** 19thC, 24in (61cm) high.
£2,000–2,200 S

► **A Victorian mahogany hat and coat stand,** restored, 67in (170cm) high.
£675–800 S

► **A Victorian cast-iron umbrella stand,** later painted, 40½in (103cm) wide.
£270–300 P(Ed)

A Victorian painted cast-iron Coalbrookdale hat, coat and stick stand, the central section cast with floral bouquet caryatids, face masks, lion head and vacant cartouches, tray missing, 79¼in (201.5cm) high.
£500–600 P(E)

Condition

The condition is absolutely vital when assessing the value of an antique. Damaged pieces on the whole appreciate much less than perfect examples. However a rare desirable piece may command a high price even when damaged.

Kettle & Urn Stands

► **A mahogany kettle stand,** restored, c1740, 10¾in (27.5cm) diam.
£2,500–2,750 S(O)

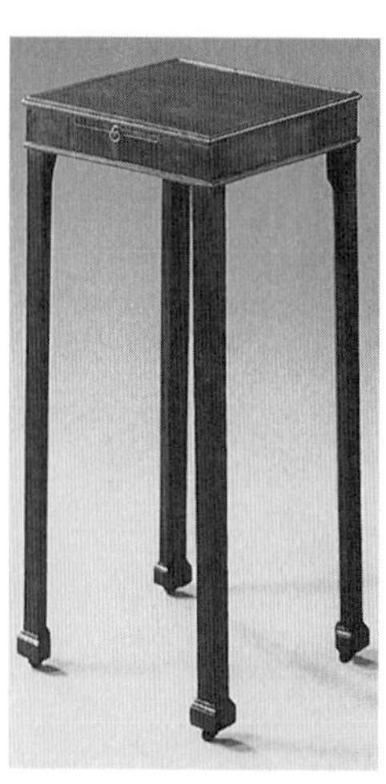

◄ **A mahogany Chippendale period urn stand,** with a moulded gallery above a crossbanded frieze with a pull-out slide centred by an axe-head handle, c1760, 11½in (29cm) wide.
£3,750–4,250 REI

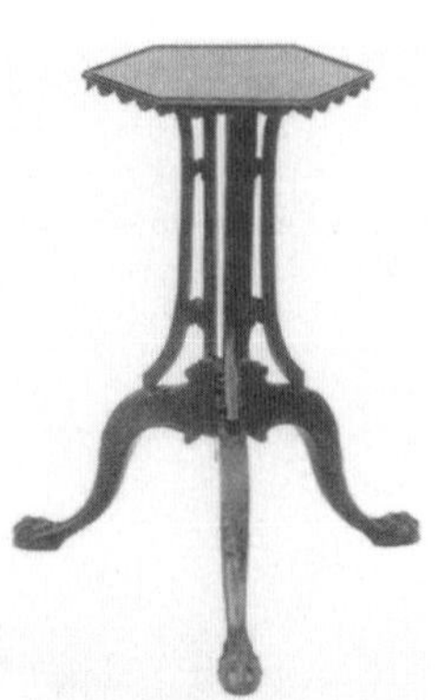

A pair of Chippendale-style mahogany kettle stands, with octagonal tops, late 19thC, 12½in (32cm) diam.
£650–800 F&C

Miller's is a price GUIDE not a price LIST

An Edwardian mahogany and marquetry urn stand, the octagonal top inlaid with floral paterae, the ribbon swag-inlaid frieze with slide, 16½in (43cm) wide.
£550–650 P(S)

Music Stands

A tripod music stand, with adjustable turned column, c1835, 52in (132cm) high.
£1,650–2,000 ⚒ P(O)

◀ **A mahogany music stand,** for four musicians, French, mid-19thC, 59in (150cm) high.
£2,350–2,750 ⚒ S(Am)

Items in the Furniture section have been arranged in date order within each sub-section.

▶ **A Victorian ebonized duet music stand,** the fluted stem on three splayed legs and scrolled rosette feet, 48in (122cm) high.
£170–200 ⚒ DA

Plant Stands

A pair of carved and painted figural plant stands, in the form of two boy satyrs holding baskets of flowers, losses, restored, Italian, late 19thC, 56in (142cm) high.
£2,000–2,400 ⚒ Bon(C)

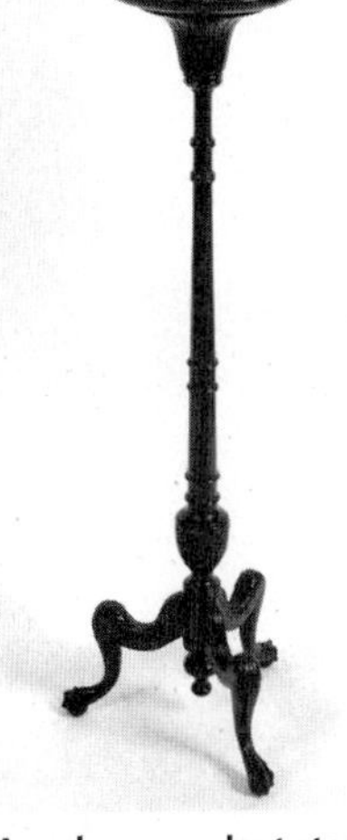

A mahogany plant stand, with carved tripod legs and claw-and-ball feet, c1900, 47in (119.5cm) high.
£425–475 ⊞ MTay

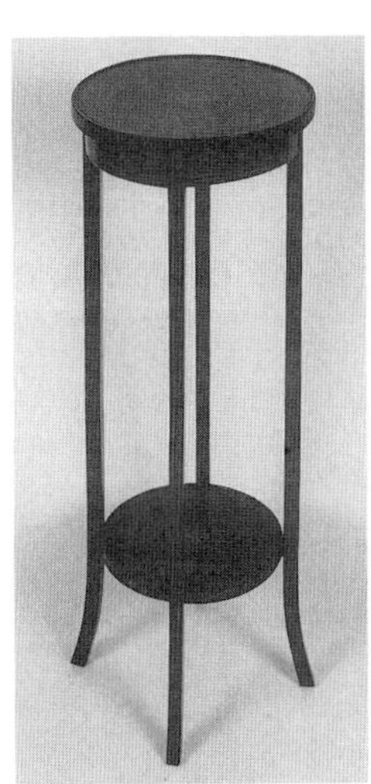

An inlaid mahogany plant stand, c1910, 38in (96.5cm) high.
£225–250 ⊞ RPh

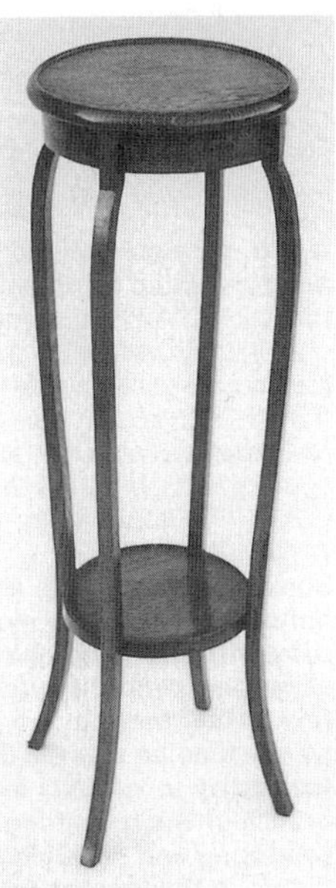

An oak two-tier plant stand, c1920, 37in (94cm) high.
£70–75 ⊞ NAW

Shaving Stands

◀ **A Biedermeier blond-wood and ebony shaving stand,** the mirror plate on a turned adjustable column support, on an octagonal table with hinged flaps, 19thC, 62in (157.5cm) high.
£400–500 ⚒ AH

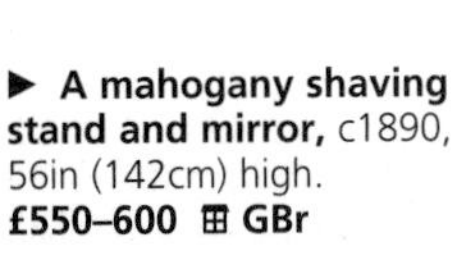

▶ **A mahogany shaving stand and mirror,** c1890, 56in (142cm) high.
£550–600 ⊞ GBr

A mahogany shaving stand, c1890, 45in (114.5cm) wide.
£650–750 ⊞ SWA

Stools

A George II walnut stool, with upholstered drop-in seat, later repairs and additions, 21in (53.5cm) wide.
£1,350–1,500 ⚒ TMA

A pair of rosewood and gilt-brass-mounted footstools, in the style of Matthew Gregson, the sides with flowerhead and scroll-cast mounts joined by leaf-cast turned stretchers, on rope-twist cast bases and brass ball feet, upholstered in brown suede, c1820, 17in (43cm) wide.
£7,000–8,500 ⚒ S

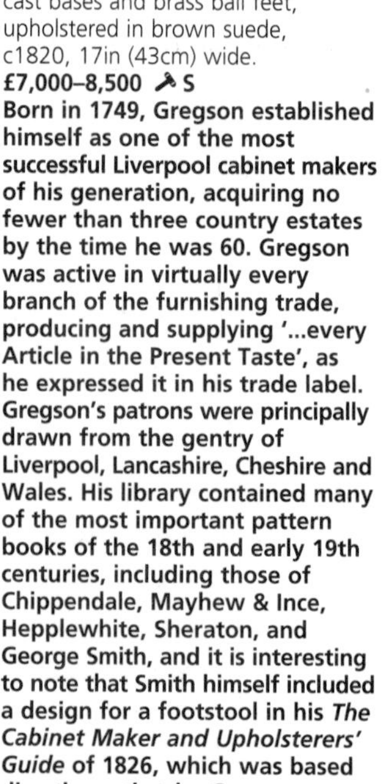

Born in 1749, Gregson established himself as one of the most successful Liverpool cabinet makers of his generation, acquiring no fewer than three country estates by the time he was 60. Gregson was active in virtually every branch of the furnishing trade, producing and supplying '...every Article in the Present Taste', as he expressed it in his trade label. Gregson's patrons were principally drawn from the gentry of Liverpool, Lancashire, Cheshire and Wales. His library contained many of the most important pattern books of the 18th and early 19th centuries, including those of Chippendale, Mayhew & Ince, Hepplewhite, Sheraton, and George Smith, and it is interesting to note that Smith himself included a design for a footstool in his *The Cabinet Maker and Upholsterers' Guide* of 1826, which was based directly on that by Gregson.

A mahogany stool, the upholstered seat on four turned round tapering legs, early 19thC, 24in (61cm) wide.
£550–650 ⚒ DMC

A footstool, the brass hoof feet with original gilding, upholstered with a beadwork panel, c1825, 15in (38cm) wide.
£1,150–1,300 ⊞ HA

A pair of upholstered box stools, c1840, 21½in (54.5cm) wide.
£1,500–1,650 ⊞ JC

A Victorian carved walnut stool, with cabriole legs, 19in (48.5cm) wide.
£530–585 ⊞ RAN

◄ **A Victorian carved walnut stool,** the stuff-over seat upholstered in a floral embroidered fabric, with a scroll frieze on leaf-carved cabriole legs with scrolled feet, 34½in (87.5cm) wide.
£500–600 ⚒ AH

A Regency rosewood stool, 21¾in (55.5cm) square.
£320–400 ⊞ SWA

A William IV rosewood stool, the upholstered seat above carved X-frame scroll legs joined by a turned stretcher, faults, 29¼in (74.5cm) wide.
£750–900 ⚒ RTo

A carved oak ottoman, with upholstered hinged lid, the corners with carved lion's head supports, the sides carved with acanthus and strapwork and central cartouches of a rose, a thistle, a shamrock and a woman playing a harp, Anglo-Irish, 19thC, 45½in (115.5cm) wide.
£1,300–1,500 ⚒ LAY

LOCATE THE SOURCE

The source of each illustration in Miller's can be found by checking the code letters below each caption with the Key to Illustrations, pages 794–800.

A mahogany X-framed stool, with original rush drop-in seat, c1890, 26in (66cm) wide.
£600–675 ⊞ MTay

Music Stools

◀ **A rosewood adjustable cellist's chair,** inlaid with brass foliage, the bar back with a lyre-carved splat above a padded seat, c1815.
£1,000–1,200 ⚒ S(S)

A mahogany adjustable music stool, c1820, 21in (53.5cm) high.
£440–485 ⊞ DJH

◀ **A walnut piano stool,** c1860, 21in (53.5cm) high.
£340–375 ⊞ MTay

A gilt piano stool, with fluted handles and a lift-up seat, the interior with three compartments, 19thC, 25in (63.5cm) wide.
£230–275 ⚒ MEA

An inlaid mahogany piano stool, c1890, 18in (45.5cm) wide.
£300–340 ⊞ RPh

◀ **A walnut revolving piano stool,** c1875, 19in (48cm) high.
£135–150 ⊞ NAW

◀ **A rosewood adjustable duet stool,** c1900, 24in (61cm) high.
£2,250–2,500 ⊞ PPC

Bedroom Suites

A rosewood two-piece bedroom suite, comprising an armoire and a bedstead, French, late 19thC, armoire 45in (114.5cm) wide.
£2,200–2,500 ⚒ NOA

A late Victorian mahogany three-piece bedroom suite, comprising a kidney-shaped dressing table, a secretaire wardrobe and a night cabinet, wardrobe 58¼in (148cm) wide.
£2,000–2,400 ⚒ P(NW)

A lacquer bedroom suite, comprising wardrobe, dressing chest, washstand, bedside cabinet, cheval mirror, towel horse, pair of chairs, dressing stool and a pair of bedsteads, decorated in a chinoiserie pattern, 1920s, wardrobe 76½in (194.5cm) wide.
£3,500–4,200 ⚒ DD

Salon Suites

A Victorian walnut-framed three-piece salon suite, comprising a gentleman's spoon-back chair, button-upholstered in cream draylon, a matching lady's chair and a chaise longue, 68in (173cm) wide.
£2,500–3,000 ⚒ AH

A carved walnut-framed salon suite, comprising a chaise longue, button-upholstered in a lilac fabric, with matching gentleman's open armchair and a lady's chair, 19thC.
£1,350–1,500 ⚒ L&E

► **An ebonized chinoiserie lounge suite,** retailed by Maple & Co, probably produced by Hille, comprising a china cabinet, two open armchairs, a standard lamp and an occasional table, early 20thC, china cabinet 34¾in (88.5cm) wide.
£3,200–3,500 ⚒ P

The firm of Hille was founded in 1906 by Salamon Hille. Their Old Street workshop, London, aimed at high quality production with an emphasis on materials and craftsmanship. They produced furniture in a number of revivalist tastes, supplying retailers such as Hamptons, Waring & Gillows and Maples. Salamon spent a great deal of time in the Victoria & Albert Museum looking at 18th-century furniture, especially Chippendale period pieces that were greatly admired at the time. The Chinese Chippendale lacquer suites were introduced in 1914, mostly in red but also in blue, black and ivory. The most exclusive pieces in the range were produced in the finest satinwood with lacquer panels and gold leaf decoration. Salamon's daughter, Ray, a notable designer who produced the firm's acclaimed 'Art Deco', 'Moderne' and 'Hollywood' styles, was painting the lacquer designs for this range by her early teens. By 1932, in a male-dominated world, she had assumed the role of director of the firm, designing, running the large workshop and dealing with the firm's many clients both in Britain and overseas, supplying furniture to match the sophisticated tastes of the time.

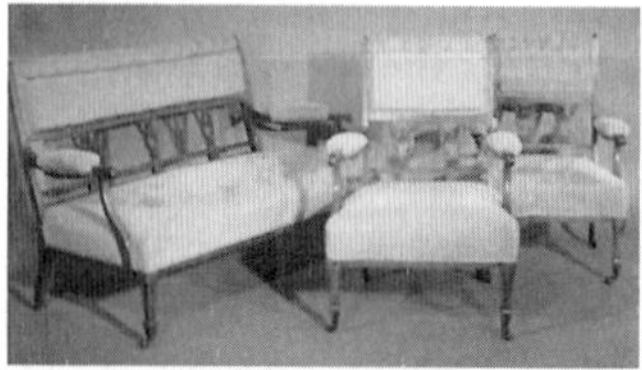

An Edwardian rosewood three-piece suite, with inlaid stringing, comprising a settee and two armchairs, with padded and marquetry-decorated slat backs, padded arms and sprung seats, settee 54in (137cm) wide.
£400–500 ⚒ WW

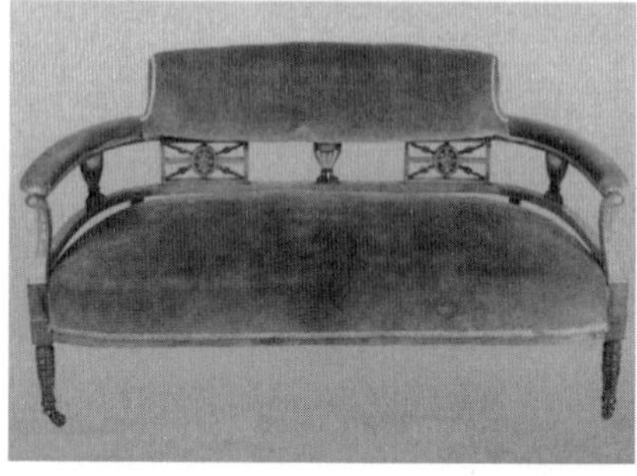

► **A late Victorian Sheraton revival inlaid rosewood drawing room suite,** comprising a settee, a lady's chair, a gentleman's chair, four occasional chairs and two nursing chairs, each with classical urn decoration, the settee, lady's and gentleman's chairs with boxwood and ebony stringing.

£1,300–1,600 ⚒ Mit

T

INDEX

Colour Review

A satinwood, painted and inlaid bonheur du jour, possibly with some later decoration, early 19thC, 45in (114.5cm) wide.
£35,000–42,000 S

An Edwardian mahogany bonheur du jour, in the Sheraton revival style, on tapered spade feet, with satinwood inlay, 30in (76cm) wide.
£900–1,000 ⊞ CGA

A rosewood bonheur du jour, late 19thC, 40in (101.5cm) wide.
£2,000–2,200 ⊞ RAN

A walnut bureau, with herringbone banding, brasses replaced, early 18thC, 38½in (98cm) wide.
£5,500–6,000 ⊞ BMi

A lacquered bureau, in original condition, early 18thC, 29½in (75cm) wide.
£60,000–65,000 ⊞ REI

A Chippendale period mahogany bureau, with original handles, c1750–60, 44in (112cm) wide.
£7,500–8,500 ⊞ JC

A walnut marquetry *bombé* bureau, Dutch, 18thC, 39½in (100.5cm) wide.
£5,500–6,500 JNic

A George III mahogany and inlaid roll-top bureau, with satinwood-banded top, 41¼in (105cm) wide.
£3,700–4,500 P(E)

A provincial kingwood parquetry bureau, restored, French, c1770, 39½in (100.5cm) wide.
£4,000–5,000 Bon

◄ **A walnut and parquetry bureau,** with central fall-front enclosing six drawers, Italian, 18thC, 50in (127cm) wide.
£4,000–5,000 G(L)

► **A Louis XV-style rosewood lady's bureau,** the inlaid fall-front enclosing small drawers and a well, on cabriole supports with ormolu mounts, 19thC, 32in (81.5cm) wide.
£1,800–2,000 RBB

A neo-classical walnut and mahogany painted and parcel-gilt bed, Italian, early 19thC, 84in (213.5cm) wide.
£7,000–8,000 S(NY)

A mahogany tall-post bedstead, American, 19thC, 61in (155cm) wide.
£8,500–10,000 NOA

An Empire-style mahogany, parcel-gilt and green-painted cradle, Dutch, early 19thC, 43¼in (110cm) long.
£5,000–5,500 S(Am)

A carved walnut bed, French, c1860, 54in (137cm) wide.
£2,200–2,500 DUK

A tiger-maple bed, with metal tester, American, c1830, 45in (114.5cm) wide.
£1,200–1,400 SLN

A William IV four-poster bed, frame extended, 78in (198cm) wide.
£12,000–13,000 SeH

A cast-iron bedstead, finished in green verdigris, the head and foot panels with brass plaque decoration, c1875, 60in (152.5cm) wide.
£1,350–1,500 ⊞ SeH

A half-tester bedstead, with original canopy and foot panel, back posts and head panel replaced, c1890, 60in (152.5cm) wide.
£3,500–4,000 ⊞ SeH

A four-piece walnut bedroom suite, comprising half-tester bed, double-door armoire, dresser and mirrored washstand, bed length extended, American, late 19thC, bed 66in (167.5cm) wide.
£10,000–11,000 ⚒ NOA

A Biedermeier mahogany, stained wood, giltwood and brass-inlaid bed, 19thC, 76½in (194.5cm) wide.
£850–1,000 ⚒ S(Am)

An Edwardian mahogany bedstead, 60in (152.5cm) wide.
£1,350–1,500 ⊞ SeH

A mahogany bookcase, with broken-arch pediment and original cartouche, c1760, 96in (244cm) high.
£27,000–30,000 ⊞ DJH

A mahogany inverted breakfront library bookcase, c1835, 86½in (219.5cm) wide at the base.
£22,000–25,000 ⊞ JC

A George III mahogany bureau bookcase, 41¾in (106cm) wide.
£7,500–9,000 ⚒ LFA

A Victorian mahogany breakfront bookcase, 84in (213.5cm) wide.
£5,000–6,000 ⚒ AH

◄ **A mahogany bookcase,** with two glazed doors, late 19thC, 40in (101.5cm) wide.
£1,350–1,500 ⊞ DOA

A walnut and crossbanded cylinder bureau bookcase, with later glazed doors, Italian, early 19thC, 45¾in (116cm) wide.
£2,000–2,500 ⚒ P

A pair of rosewood open bookcases, with mirrored backs and brass galleries to tops, c1810, 36in (91.5cm) wide.
£18,000–19,500 ⊞ APO

A kingwood and parquetry-inlaid *cartonnier*, by Jean François Leleu, maker's stamp, French, mid-18thC, 38in (96.5cm) wide.
£23,000–27,000 ⚒ G(L)

A satinwood cupboard/ bookcase, kingwood-banded in the Sheraton style, c1790, 32in (81.5cm) wide.
£11,000–12,250 ⊞ F&F

A Regency mahogany secretaire bookcase, 45in (114.5cm) wide.
£3,000–4,000 ⚒ Bon(C)

A mahogany, mahogany-veneered and bird's-eye maple secretaire bookcase, c1840, 36in (91.5cm) wide.
£1,500–1,800 ⚒ SLN

A mahogany secretaire bookcase, with satin birch interior and cast-metal mounts, French, c1850, 57in (145cm) wide.
£3,400–3,750 ⊞ MTay

A Victorian rosewood book press, with six separation plates, 28in (71cm) wide.
£875–1,000 ⚒ LJ

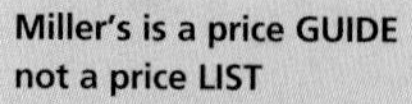

Miller's is a price GUIDE not a price LIST

A walnut cabinet-on-chest, with figured burr veneers, c1710, 44in (112cm) wide.
£27,000–30,000 ⊞ RGa

A veneered walnut cabinet-on-chest, late 17thC, 42in (106.5cm) wide.
£30,000–33,000 ⊞ HA

Cross Reference
See Furniture
(page 26–155)

◄ A George III black-japanned hanging bow-fronted corner cupboard, heightened in gilt chinoiseries and simulated brown tortoiseshell, 23¾in (60.5cm) wide.
£1,000–1,200 ⚒ P(Ba)

A late George III mahogany standing corner cupboard, 42¼in (107.5cm) wide.
£2,800–3,500 ⚒ Bri

A mahogany standing corner cupboard, missing finial, 19thC, 38in (96.5cm) wide.
£2,500–3,000 ⚒ TRM

COLOUR REVIEW

A walnut and marquetry display cabinet, Dutch, c1800, 36in (91.5cm) wide.
£2,200–2,700 G(L)

A late Victorian ebonized and amboyna-veneered corner cabinet, 34in (86.5cm) wide.
£800–1,000 TMA

► **A late Victorian Sheraton revival satinwood breakfront display cabinet,** 92½in (235cm) wide.
£6,200–7,500 Bri

A mahogany Wooton desk, American, late 19thC, 48in (122cm) wide.
£4,750–5,750 BWe

An Edwardian carved mahogany and floral marquetry corner display cabinet, 28¾in (73cm) wide.
£1,000–1,200 P(S)

A mahogany breakfront display cabinet, with carved and pierced decoration, c1900, 104in (264cm) wide.
£18,000–20,000 MTay

A Louis XVI-style gilt vitrine, c1900, 58in (147.5cm) wide.
£8,000–10,000 B&L

A William and Mary walnut and marquetry cabinet-on-stand, marquetry restored, later elements to stand, 43¾in (111cm) wide.
£21,000–25,000 S

A mahogany open pot stand, c1760, 20in (51cm) wide.
£4,500–5,000 REI

A walnut music cabinet, with boxwood inlay, c1860, 22in (56cm) wide.
£1,450–1,600 DUK

◄ **A pair of mahogany bedside cabinets,** c1885, 14in (35.5cm) wide.
£3,200–3,500 DOA

► **A pair of Louis XVI-style *encoignures*,** with ormolu mounts and marble tops, 19thC, 24½in (62cm) wide.
£14,000–16,000 JNic

A Victorian burr-walnut veneered music cabinet, 27¼in (69cm) wide.
£1,250–1,500 Bea(E)

◄ **A rosewood collector's cabinet,** with later intaglios, marbles and hardstones within the interior drawers, early 19thC, 17in (43cm) wide.
£10,000–12,000
S

► **A papier mâché table cabinet,** inlaid with mother-of-pearl, c1870, 8in (20.5cm) wide.
£1,350–1,500
CAT

◄ **A Regency carved rosewood canterbury,** 19¼in (49cm) wide.
£2,200–2,700
P

► **A mahogany canterbury,** c1820, 20in (51cm) wide.
£3,200–3,500 RGa

A Regency rosewood canterbury, 21in (53.5cm) wide.
£3,200–3,800 P
This piece is particularly desirable because of its stylized, elegant appearance. A good-quality item with provenance (this canterbury was the property of the Countess of Coventry) will invariably achieve a high price.

A figured walnut music canterbury, by Charles Hindley & Sons, c1850, 26in (66cm) high.
£3,750–4,250 F

A mahogany breakfront side cabinet, with later top, early 19thC, 61in (155cm) wide.
£22,000–27,000 Bon

A Regency Grecian-style rosewood side cabinet, with patinated bronze mounts, 80¼in (204cm) wide.
£20,000–22,000 P

A rosewood chiffonier, with twin glazed doors enclosing a shelved interior, c1840, 47in (119.5cm) wide.
£950–1,100 Bri

A Victorian figured walnut and kingwood serpentine credenza, with marquetry inlay and gilt-metal mounts, 73¼in (186cm) wide.
£4,250–5,250 P(S)

A pair of boulle work side cabinets, mid-19thC, 44in (112cm) wide.
£7,000–7,800 RAN

A pair of Victorian walnut side cabinets, with gilt-metal mounts, 30¾in (78cm) wide.
£4,500–5,500 P(NW)

A Victorian burr-walnut credenza, with gilt-metal mounts, inset porcelain plaques, beaded edging and marquetry-inlaid frieze, 92in (233.5cm) wide.
£2,500–3,000 AH

A Victorian burr-walnut pier cabinet, with floral marquetry inlay and applied ormolu mounts, 40½in (103cm) high.
£2,600–3,200 G(L)

A Victorian credenza, with burr-walnut veneered panels, central solid panelled door and cast floral gilt-metal mounts, 60in (152.5cm) wide.
£1,100–1,300 RBB

A mahogany side cabinet, inlaid with boxwood urns and swags, c1900, 60in (152.5cm) wide.
£1,000–1,200 L

◄ **A George III-style satinwood and painted commode,** inlaid with kingwood crossbandings and stringing, c1890, 59¾in (152cm) wide.
£21,000–25,000 S

A mahogany chiffonier, c1870, 42in (106.5cm) wide.
£1,500–1,650 MTay

A pair of Hepplewhite period mahogany open armchairs, c1790.
£9,000–10,000 ⊞ DJH

A pair of mahogany and inlaid armchairs, in the style of Thomas Hope, c1810.
£40,000–50,000 ⚒ S

A set of four Regency painted open armchairs, decoration refreshed.
£1,500–1,800 ⚒ Bon

A neo-classical mahogany, painted and parcel-gilt armchair, attributed to Andrei Voronikhin, Russian, early 19thC.
£11,000–12,000 ⚒ S(NY)

A pair of walnut armchairs, French, c1860.
£2,000–2,200 ⊞ SIE

A suite of eight Sheraton-style painted chairs, decorated with gilt and polychrome stencilling, American, mid-19thC.
£3,500–4,200 ⚒ NOA

A Sheraton revival lady's satinwood occasional armchair, c1890.
£2,000–2,250 ⊞ RGa

A lady's Edwardian inlaid mahogany armchair.
£475–525 ⊞ MTay

A George I wing armchair, on carved walnut front legs and elm rear legs, later upholstery.
£15,000–18,000 ⚒ TMA

An upholstered wing armchair, on mahogany legs, c1780.
£2,300–2,650 ⊞ JC

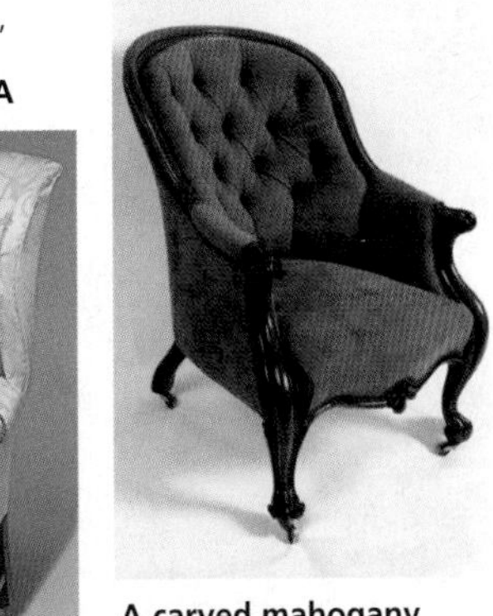

A carved mahogany upholstered armchair, c1860.
£1,300–1,500 ⊞ MTay

A beech-framed upholstered armchair, by Louis Delanois, stamped, French, mid-18thC.
£14,000–16,000 ⚒ S(P)

◀ **A carved rosewood library bergère,** c1825.
£8,000–9,000 ⊞ F

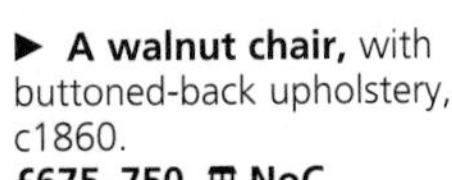

▶ **A walnut chair,** with buttoned-back upholstery, c1860.
£675–750 ⊞ NoC

A set of six mahogany dining chairs, c1750.
£13,000–14,500 ⊞ F

A set of six Chippendale period mahogany chairs, with spindle backs, c1790.
£11,000–12,500 ⊞ DJH

A set of four neo-classical mahogany chairs, with ebony line inlay, c1810.
£750–875 ⊞ CGA

A set of four Victorian walnut chairs.
£900–1,000 ⊞ RPh

A set of eight Hepplewhite-style inlaid mahogany dining chairs, c1900.
£2,200–2,700 ⚒ Bri

A pair of Renaissance revival walnut and burr-walnut hall chairs, American, late 19thC.
£400–500 ⚒ NOA

A set of six Regency mahogany hall chairs, attributed to Gillows.
£8,250–10,000 ⚒ CGC

A pair of giltwood salon chairs, with moulded and husk-decorated frame, c1840.
£2,500–2,850 ⊞ RAN

A white cedar side chair, American, c1750.
£3,000–3,500 ⚒ SLN

A carved walnut side chair, American, 1740–85.
£7,000–8,500 ⚒ SK(B)

A pair of Chippendale mahogany side chairs, of Gothic design, c1760.
£13,000–14,500 ⊞ JC

◄ **A pair of mahogany side chairs,** the interlaced backs decorated with carvings, c1760.
£7,500–8,500 ⊞ REI

A pair of giltwood seats, probably Italian, c1890.
£12,500–15,000 ⚒ S

◄ **A pair of rococo-style giltwood side chairs,** with needlework-panel backs and stuff-over seats, c1840.
£1,300–1,450 ⊞ RAN

An early George III mahogany low linen press, 49¾in (126.5cm) wide.
£2,500–3,000 Bri

A bird's-eye maple and rosewood-banded serpentine-front wardrobe, late 19thC, 87in (221cm) wide.
£3,500–4,000 EH

A chinoiserie-style japanned clothes press, 18thC with 19thC additions, 52in (132cm) wide.
£6,500–8,000 P(E)

► **A Sheraton revival mahogany and painted wardrobe,** by Walker & Edwards, London, late 19thC, 74¼in (188.5cm) wide.
£3,200–4,000 AH

A carved cherrywood linen press, American, late 18thC, 47in (119.5cm) wide.
£7,000–8,500 BB(S)

A Victorian mahogany breakfront wardrobe, 104in (264cm) wide.
£1,400–1,700 DD

A chest of drawers, with olivewood and holly geometric inlay, c1690, 36in (91.5cm) wide.
£30,000–33,000 ⊞ HA

A fiddle-back mahogany chest of drawers, with mahogany crossbanding and boxwood and ebony stringing, original handles, c1790, 39in (99cm) wide.
£2,500–3,000 ⊞ CGA

A George III mahogany serpentine chest, crossbanded with stringing, 42½in (108cm) wide.
£2,200–2,500 ⚒ AH

A Federal mahogany and birchwood bowfronted chest of drawers, American, 1800–10, 41in (104cm) wide.
£1,600–2,000 ⚒ BB(S)

A Genoese walnut chest of drawers, Italian, 17thC, 60¼in (153cm) wide.
£5,750–7,000 ⚒ S(NY)

A walnut and marquetry commode, Continental, 18thC, 70in (178cm) wide.
£12,000–15,000 ⚒ RBB

A Louis XV-style burr-walnut commode, damaged, restored, Dutch, 18thC, 37½in (95.5cm) wide.
£1,500–1,800 ⚒ S(Am)

A walnut commode, with figured walnut veneer, French, c1820, 45in (114.5cm) wide.
£2,300–2,600 ⊞ SIE

A Hepplewhite period amboyna and kingwood serpentine commode, with original gilt-brass handles, c1785, 38¼in (97cm) wide.
£30,000–36,000 ⚒ Bri

A marquetry and ormolu-mounted commode, stamped 'J.H. Riesener J M E', French, late 18thC, 52½in (133.5cm) wide.
£75,000–90,000 ⚒ JNic

A carved mahogany chest of drawers, American, c1800, 41in (104cm) wide.
£2,400–3,000 ⚒ SLN

A burr-walnut commode chest, with marble top, French, c1840, 51in (129.5cm) wide.
£3,800–4,350 ⊞ RAN

◄ **A cherrywood with fruitwood inlay commode,** with three drawers, Austrian, early 19thC, 53in (134.5cm) wide.
£8,750–9,750 ⊞ DOA

A walnut-veneered chest-on-chest, with original locks and handles, c1725, 36in (91.5cm) wide.
£17,000–20,000 ⊞ RGa

A George I walnut chest-on-stand, with boxwood-strung drawers, 45½in (115cm) wide.
£750–900 ⚒ CGC

A George II walnut and featherbanded chest-on-chest, restored and altered, 42½in (108cm) wide.
£6,000–7,200 ⚒ Bon

A mahogany chest-on-chest, with rococo handles, c1770, 43in (109cm) wide.
£1,500–1,650 ⊞ NoC

A tiger-walnut veneered chest-on-stand, with original handles, c1720, 61in (155cm) wide.
£8,000–8,850 ⊞ BMi

◀ **A George III mahogany secretaire chest-on-chest,** with original brasses, 43¼in (110cm) wide.
£3,000–3,500 ⚒ DMC

A burr-walnut chest-on-chest, with original brass handles, c1730, 74in (188cm) high.
£18,000–20,000 ⊞ DJH

A walnut chest-on-stand, the drawers inlaid with featherbanding, c1730, 41in (104cm) wide.
£25,000–30,000 ⚒ S

A figured walnut davenport, with matched sunburst veneer, c1840, 18in (45.5cm) wide.
£5,750–6,500 ⊞ F

A walnut pedestal davenport, with original brass handles, original condition, c1850, 25in (63.5cm) wide.
£8,500–9,500 ⊞ JC

A walnut and pollarded oak davenport, c1850, 21in (53.5cm) wide.
£2,000–2,200 ⊞ CGA

A Victorian burr-walnut harlequin davenport, 22in (56cm) wide.
£2,500–3,000 ⚒ AH

A Victorian walnut piano-top davenport, 21¾in (55.5cm) wide.
£1,500–1,800 ⚒ P(E)

A George III mahogany serpentine kneehole desk, with a later hinged rear flap, 67¾in (172cm) wide.
£15,000–18,000 ⚒ S

A yew wood kneehole desk, 18thC, 30in (76cm) wide.
£4,750–5,750 ⚒ RBB

Miller's is a price GUIDE not a price LIST

A red-painted slant-lid desk, with original brasses, American, late 18thC, 36in (91.5cm) wide.
£8,500–10,000 ⚒ SK(B)

A carved oak congressional desk, by Doe, Hazleton & Co, American, c1850, 29½in (75cm) wide.
£6,500–8,000 ⚒ BB(S)

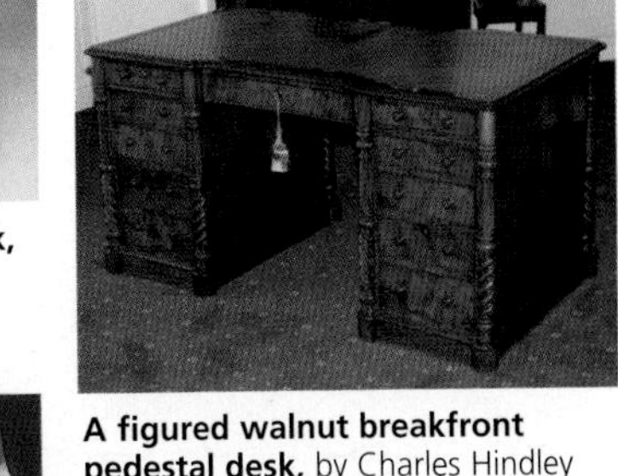

A figured walnut breakfront pedestal desk, by Charles Hindley & Sons, London, c1860, 58in (147.5cm) wide.
£22,000–26,000 ⊞ F

► **A late Victorian mahogany Carlton House desk,** by Maple & Co, with satinwood banding and marquetry, later writing surface, 52¾in (134cm) wide.
£9,500–11,500 ⚒ P

◄ **A mahogany pedestal desk,** with original locks and handles, leather top replaced, 19thC, 53in (132cm) wide.
£5,500–6,000 ⊞ RGa

A mahogany cylinder top desk, with rosewood banding and stringing, late 19thC, 45½in (115.5cm) wide.
£1,000–1,200 ⚒ AH

A mahogany cheval mirror, American, 19thC, 38½in (98cm) wide.
£3,500–4,200 NOA

A mahogany ebonized cheval mirror, with gilt-bronze mounts, 19thC with possibly 20thC restorations to stretcher, 43¾in (111cm) wide.
£2,200–2,700 P

A gilt-bronze swing frame mirror, 19thC, 14¼in (36cm) wide.
£550–650 P

A mahogany toilet mirror, c1825, 30in (76cm) high.
£1,000–1,150 F

LOCATE THE SOURCE
The source of each illustration in Miller's can be found by checking the code letters below each caption with the Key to Illustrations, pages 794–800.

◄ **A Charles II carved giltwood wall mirror,** with later plate, re-gilt, 46in (117cm) wide.
£25,000–30,000 S

A George II giltwood mirror, in the style of William Kent, later plate, 33in (84cm) wide.
£7,000–8,500 P

A carved mahogany mirror, with satyr's mask, c1740, 21in (53.5cm) wide.
£4,000–4,500 HA

A Federal giltwood and wire wall mirror, American, 1780–1800, 14½in (37cm) wide.
£18,000–20,000 SK(B)

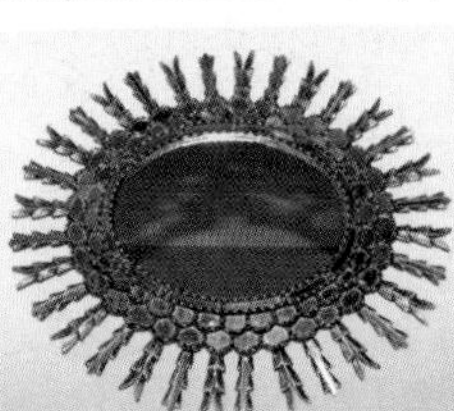

A gesso and glass sunburst mirror, c1920, 30in (76cm) diam.
£675–750 DOA

A Regency carved giltwood convex wall mirror, 34¾in (88.5cm) wide.
£3,800–4,500 Bri

A gilded *trumeau,* French, early 20thC, 30¼in (77cm) wide.
£650–720 OFM

► **A pair of giltwood convex mirrors,** surmounted by eagle-shaped finials, 19thC, 35¾in (91cm) high.
£3,500–4,000 P(B)

A mahogany chimney mirror, glass replaced, c1825, 19½in (49.5cm) wide.
£600–650 JC

► **A Renaissance revival walnut pier mirror,** with gilt decoration, American, late 19thC, 34¼in (87cm) wide.
£1,600–2,000 NOA

An ebonized and parcel-gilt chaise longue, c1815, 77in (195.5cm) wide.
£7,250–8,500 S

A beechwood canapé, by Martin Delaporte, French, mid-18thC, 76¼in (193.5cm) wide.
£6,500–8,000 S(P)

A pair of Regency rosewood settees, 68in (172.5cm) wide.
£23,000–26,000 RGa

A Regency settee, with brass inlay and simulated rosewood scroll ends, 89½in (227.5cm) wide.
£3,200–3,800 DMC

► **A Regency mahogany-framed settee,** 82in (208.5cm) wide.
£1,100–1,300 RBB

◄ **An Empire mahogany love seat,** with brass mouldings and ormolu mounts, French, c1810, 58in (147.5cm) wide.
£10,000–11,000 ⊞ F

A pair of rococo-style giltwood canapés, the frames centred by a floral and foliate cartouche, probably French, 19thC, 62in (157.5cm) wide.
£7,000–7,800 ⊞ RAN

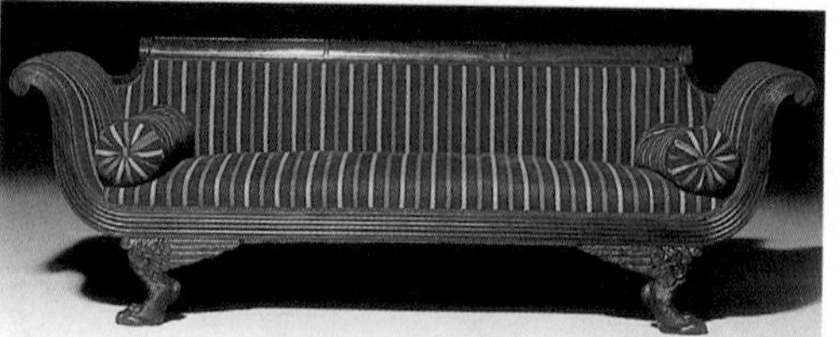

A Federal carved mahogany sofa, in the Empire style, American, mid-19thC, 93¾in (238cm) wide.
£1,800–2,200 ⚒ Bon

A mid-Victorian conversation seat, 92½in (235cm) wide.
£2,000–2,400 ⚒ P

◄ **A late Victorian sofa,** with mahogany frame, 50in (127cm) wide.
£220–260 ⚒ TRM

A Sheraton period mahogany side-board, c1780, 61½in (156cm) wide.
£15,000–16,500 ⊞ JC

A Sheraton period inlaid mahogany sideboard, with kingwood crossbanded top, c1790, 50in (127cm) wide.
£4,750–5,500 ⚒ Bri

A late George III mahogany and ebony-inlaid bowfronted sideboard, 72¾in (185cm) wide.
£4,000–5,000 ⚒ Bon(C)

A Regency mahogany breakfront sideboard, with satinwood, brass, boxwood and ebony inlay, later alterations, 82½in (209cm) wide.
£8,000–9,000 ⚒ S

A William IV mahogany pedestal sideboard, repolished, 56¾in (144cm) wide.
£2,500–2,850 ⊞ JC

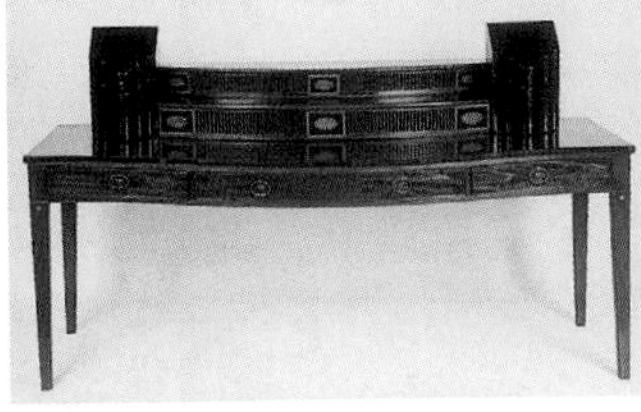

A George III inlaid mahogany serving table, with two knife boxes between the later Edwardian superstructure, original cast-brass handles, 76¾in (195cm) wide.
£3,500–4,200 ⚒ Bri

A mahogany sideboard, with boxwood stringing, handles replaced, late 18thC, 37in (94cm) wide.
£3,500–4,000 ⊞ BMi

A Regency mahogany pedestal sideboard, in the manner of Thomas Hope, 70in (178cm) wide.
£4,000–4,600 ⊞ RAN

A mahogany pedestal sideboard, c1820, 66in (167.5cm) wide.
£2,200–2,500 ⊞ RPh

A mid-Victorian carved oak sideboard, with brass and copper mounts, 78in (198cm) wide.
£4,750–5,250 ⊞ MTay

A George III mahogany serpentine breakfront sideboard, 66in (167.5cm) wide.
£2,500–3,000 ⚒ G(L)

A Federal mahogany-inlaid serpentine sideboard, attributed to John Shaw, Annapolis, one leg repaired, American, c1797, 71in (180.5cm) wide.
£55,000–65,000 ⚒ SK(B)

A Regency mahogany breakfront sideboard, with ebony stringing, 84in (213.5cm) wide.
£2,200–2,700 ⚒ Bri

A mahogany bowfronted pedestal sideboard, with satinwood inlay, Irish, c1830, 57in (145cm) wide.
£8,000–9,000 ⊞ HA

A Victorian carved mahogany sideboard, 56in (142cm) wide.
£500–600 ⚒ WW

A mahogany breakfast table, on reeded swept legs, c1800, 63¼in (160.5cm) wide.
£10,000–11,500 ⊞ RAN

A mahogany and parcel-gilt card table, American, c1815, 36in (91.5cm) wide.
£5,500–6,250 ⚒ BB(S)

A rosewood and parquetry centre table, the top inlaid with a geometric design in specimen woods, c1845, 54in (137cm) diam.
£8,500–10,000 ⚒ S

A Regency rosewood breakfast table, with foliate cut-brass inlay, 49¾in (126.5cm) diam.
£6,000–7,200 ⚒ P(EA)

A lacquered card table, attributed to Jennens & Bettridge, c1840, 38in (96.5cm) wide.
£7,000–8,000 ⊞ RGa

A kingwood, burr-walnut and marquetry-inlaid centre table, in the manner of Howard & Son, applied with gilt-metal mounts, mid-19thC, 51¼in (130cm) wide.
£3,000–3,500 ⚒ P(S)

◀ **A Sheraton period satinwood pier table,** c1790, 48in (122cm) wide.
£7,500–8,500 ⊞ BMi

◀ **A Regency mahogany telescopic action extending dining table,** 53½in (136cm) extended.
£3,500–4,200 ⚒ Bri

A mahogany breakfast table, with rosewood crossbanding, 19thC, 42in (106.5cm) wide.
£2,800–3,400 ⚒ RBB

A rosewood card table, c1840, 37in (94cm) wide.
£3,500–4,000 ⊞ BERA

A mid-Victorian rosewood and boxwood-inlaid centre table, centre of top reveneered, 55½in (141cm) diam.
£4,750–5,750 ⚒ P(L)

A William IV mahogany dining table, 60in (152.5cm) diam.
£15,000–16,500 ⊞ JC

A tiger-maple dressing table, American, 1710–20, 29¾in (75.5cm) wide.
£15,000–18,000 ⚒ SK(B)

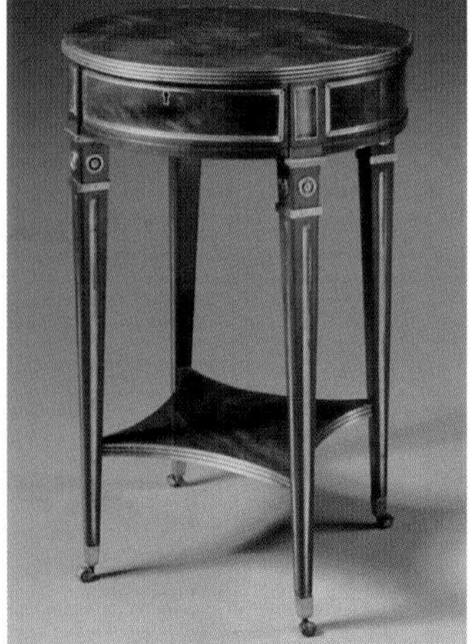

A neo-classical mahogany *guéridon*, with ormolu mounts, Russian, early 19thC, 20¼in (51.5cm) diam.
£10,000–11,000 ⚒ S(NY)

A kingwood, walnut and ormolu-moulded side table, in the style of Jean-François Oeben, the top with crossbanded and marquetry inlay of satinwood, ebony, partridge wood and tulipwood, mid-19thC, 31½in (80cm) wide.
£4,000–5,000 ⚒ P(S)

A pair of mahogany tea tables, in the French Hepplewhite-style, 1780, 36in (91.5cm) wide.
£19,000–21,000 ⊞ APO

A mahogany dressing table, American, mid-19thC, 38½in (98cm) wide.
£630–700 ⚒ NOA

A kidney-shaped occasional table, in thuyawood and various exotic woods, c1880, 38in (96.5cm) wide.
£12,500–14,000 ⊞ REI

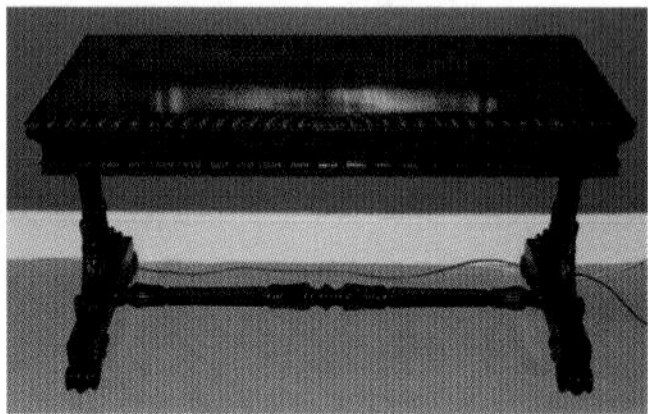

A rosewood library table, original condition, 1829–30, 30in (76cm) wide.
£6,800–7,600 ⊞ BMi

A lacquered tripod table, French, c1840, 32in (81.5cm) diam.
£3,500–3,850 ⊞ DJH

► **A Renaissance-style carved oak writing table,** mid-19thC, 66½in (169cm) wide.
£7,500–8,250 ⚒ Bon

A mahogany library table, with inset leather-lined top, c1790–1800, 60in (152.5cm) wide.
£16,000–18,000 ⊞ CAT

A Sheraton period laburnum Pembroke table, with satinwood crossbanding, Scottish, c1800, 25in (63.5cm) wide.
£3,000–3,500 ⊞ RGa

A burr-walnut Sutherland table, c1860, 36in (91.5cm) wide.
£2,000–2,350 ⊞ BERA

A rosewood sewing table, c1830, 20in (51cm) wide.
£850–950 ⊞ NoC

A carved and gilt mirror-back wall unit, 19thC, 22½in (57cm) wide.
£1,000–1,150 ⊞ MTay

A George III mahogany washstand, with hinged splashback, 25in (63.5cm) high.
£1,500–1,650 ⊞ RGa

Miller's is a price GUIDE not a price LIST

A mahogany washstand, attributed to Ince & Mayhew, with pine dished top, c1765, 38in (96.5cm) high.
£2,300–2,750 ⚒ WW

A mahogany bidet, the back panel applied with a gilt-brass female mask mount, French, c1820, 18½in (47cm) wide.
£650–750 ⚒ S(O)

A walnut commode, 19thC, 16in (40cm) wide.
£150–160 ⊞ NoC

A mahogany teapoy, inlaid with ebony, c1820, 29in (73.5cm) wide.
£1,500–1,700 ⊞ BMi

A Regency mahogany whatnot, with three tiers incorporating drawers, 46in (117cm) high.
£9,000–11,000 ⚒ G(L)

A Victorian rosewood corner whatnot, 54in (137cm) high.
£1,000–1,200 ⚒ AH

An ebonized *étagère*, with neo-classical inlays of sycamore and satinwood, c1890, 17in (43cm) wide.
£1,000–1,150 ⊞ CGA

A late Regency mahogany and ebony-inlaid cellaret, attributed to Gillows, 28in (71cm) wide.
£4,500–5,000 ⚒ Bon

► **A mahogany wine cooler,** Irish, c1830, 32¼in (82cm) wide.
£3,000–3,600 ⚒ S

Architects' Tables

An early George III mahogany architect's table, with adjustable top and a pivoting circular candle tray to each side, the pull-out drawers with an adjustable surface enclosing compartments and small drawers, distressed, 42in (106.5cm) wide.
£2,000–2,400 LAY

An early George III mahogany architect's table, the hinged top on an adjustable easel above a pull-out frieze drawer enclosing a baize-lined writing surface and fitted interior, 39in (99cm) wide.
£4,000–5,000 RFA

A George III mahogany architect's table, with adjustable hinged top and three fall leaves, above a single cockbeaded drawer, 54in (137cm) wide.
£1,800–2,200 DD

◀ **A mahogany architect's table,** German, c1800, 35in (89cm) wide.
£1,800–2,200 S(O)

▶ **A mahogany architect's table,** with hinged and ratcheted top above two candle slides and a sliding drawer with leg supports, the interior fitted with a leather surface sliding to reveal a fitted interior, late 18thC, 36in (91.5cm) wide.
£3,200–3,500 SK

Breakfast Tables

A mahogany drop-leaf breakfast table, each end with a cockbeaded drawer, on a turned column with four downswept reeded legs, c1810, 50in (127cm) wide.
£2,800–3,250 JC

A mahogany breakfast table, with crossbanded top, one leg spliced, early 19thC, 54in (137cm) wide.
£700–850 P(Ba)

A William IV rosewood breakfast table, the top with matched figured veneer panels, the swept-in square base with carved scroll and shell-pattern feet, 54in (137cm) diam.
£2,400–3,000 CAG

A mahogany drop-leaf breakfast table, with two opposing frieze drawers, the platform base with scrolled paw feet, c1835, 42in (106.5cm) wide.
£1,800–2,200 S(O)

A William IV mahogany breakfast table, the faceted baluster support over a shaped platform base, 48in (122cm) diam.
£1,100–1,300 DA

► **A rosewood breakfast table,** the concave triform base with carved lion's paw feet, 19thC, 48in (122cm) diam.
£1,850–2,200 AH

A mid-Victorian figured-walnut breakfast table, quarter-veneered and supported on a carved baluster column, on four foliate- and leaf-carved cabriole legs, 57in (145cm) wide.
£700–850 TMA

Miller's Compares

◄ **I. A Victorian rosewood breakfast table,** the tilt-top inlaid with a central octagonal figured walnut and floral marquetry panel within a conforming marquetry-banded edge, on an octagonal baluster column and tripod base, with acanthus-carved scroll legs, 46½in (118cm) diam.
£1,600–1,800 P(S)
With a label verso for Allen & Smith, Lough & Grimsby, with name and address of the purchaser.

► **II. A Victorian burr-walnut breakfast table,** the tilt-top centred by a floral marquetry medallion within a foliate-inlaid border, on a turned column and outswept legs and scroll feet, 50½in (128.5cm) diam.
£950–1,150 P(Ba)

Both of these tables were made c1860 and are of similar size and proportions, but Item I has a far more sophisticated inlaid top using both rosewood and walnut in its construction. Although each has a pleasing central marquetry-inlaid floral panel, Item I has a larger and more intricately worked floral band to the edge than Item II. A further advantage is that Item I bears the maker's label and the details of the purchaser.

A Victorian figured-walnut breakfast table, the tilt-top on a turned revolving pedestal and four moulded cabriole legs, 41in (104cm) diam.
£550–650 CGC

A Victorian walnut extending breakfast table, the top with ebonized edge, on turned tapering supports with ebonized flutes, with three additional leaves, 66¼in (168.5cm) diam.
£620–750 DD

Card Tables

An early George III mahogany card table, the hinged top above a frieze on cabriole legs with pad feet, 29¼in (74.5cm) wide.
£1,200–1,500 P(Ed)

A George III mahogany card table, with baize-lined fold-over top, one leg with a remaining pierced fret bracket, 36in (91.5cm) wide.
£300–360 WW

A Regency rosewood card table, the top with inlaid brass stringing and enclosing a green baize lining, the frieze with inlaid brass honeysuckle motifs, on a tapering column with quatreform base and splay feet, 36in (91.5cm) wide.
£1,500–1,800 AG

A Regency rosewood card table, 36in (91.5cm) wide.
£2,000–2,200 ⊞ RPh

A Hepplewhite period inlaid mahogany demi-lune card table, with carved legs, c1780, 37in (94cm) diam.
£6,000–6,500 ⊞ REI

A mahogany fiddle-back card table, inlaid with rosewood cross-banding and boxwood stringing, the tapering legs with geometric inlay, c1795, 35in (89cm) wide.
£4,400–4,800 ⊞ F

A demi-lune rosewood crossbanded mahogany card table, c1785, 35in (89cm) wide.
£3,200–3,550 ⊞ RGa

A Sheraton period mahogany card table, strung with boxwood and holly, with a band of figured satinwood and edged with tulipwood crossbanding, the fold-over top with a re-baized interior, c1790, 35½in (90cm) wide.
£3,800–4,200 ⊞ JC

Miller's Compares

I. A Regency oak and pollarded oak card table, in the style of William Trotter, the hinged top with brass lines and crossbanding above a frieze with foliate cast-brass beads, on scrolling supports ending in rosettes, the concave platform base on splayed legs headed by anthemia, Scottish, 36in (91.5cm) wide.
£5,500–6,500 P(Ed)

II. A Regency oak and pollarded oak card table, in the style of William Trotter, the rosewood crossbanded top with trailing anthemion brass inlay enclosing a baize-lined interior, above a frieze with egg-and-dart border, with a foliate clasped pedestal on a quadripartite concave base, the hipped splay legs with foliate capitals and brass oak leaf-cast caps, Scottish, 38¼in (97cm) wide.
£3,600–4,200 P(Ed)

These two tables are similar in style, but Item I realized a higher price because it is in original condition, whereas Item II had been cleaned and regilded resulting in a less pleasing colour and a rather too bright appearance to the gilding. Moreover, the quadripartite supports on Item I give it an altogether more elegant appearance in contrast to the central, rather bulky, pedestal and over exaggerated outswept legs on Item II.

A late Regency rosewood swivel-top folding card table, the interior with a baize-lined panel on a turned tapering foliate-carved column, the shaped platform base with four claw-and-ball feet, 36in (91.5cm) wide.
£750–900 E

A Sheraton-style mahogany card table, with boxwood inlay, c1820, 36in (91.5cm) wide.
£1,250–1,400 DUK

A mahogany and crossbanded card table, the D-shaped swivel top above a frieze with applied ovoid decoration, the turned and reeded acanthus-carved column on an oval base with four paw feet, 36¾in (93.5cm) wide.
£1,400–1,700 B&L

A mahogany-veneered card table, the carved lyre base above a veneered pedestal with four leaf-carved scrolled and panelled legs on brass hairy paw feet, American, 1825–35, 34¾in (88.5cm) wide.
£2,000–2,400 SK(B)

A pair of pollarded oak card tables, the fold-over swivel tops with crossbanded edges, enclosing green baize-lined interiors, c1830, 36in (91.5cm) wide.
£7,500–8,500 JC

A William IV rosewood card table, with fold-over top, the shaped apron with leaf and scroll mouldings, on a melon lobed baluster pedestal, the lotus-carved platform above four outswept paw feet, 35¾in (91cm) wide.
£850–1,000 WL

A William IV rosewood card table, retailed by W. Williamson & Sons of Guildford, the folding top with a baize-lined interior, above a frieze drawer, 36in (91.5cm) wide.
£1,100–1,300 CAG

A campaign card table, in a padouk/rosewood box, c1840, 23in (58.5cm) wide.
£2,800–3,200 RGa

An early Victorian rosewood card table, with fold-over top and acanthus-carved frieze, 35¾in (91cm) wide.
£650–800 Bea(E)

Facts in brief

To quench the thirst of the 18th and 19th century upper and middle classes for gambling, card tables were made in relatively large numbers. Horace Walpole wrote in 1770 of 'young men losing five, ten and fifteen thousand pounds in an evening'.

The tables were made with hinged tops so that they could stand against a wall when not in use. Early examples (c1700–50) have protruding rounded corners to stand candles, and sunken dishes for counters.

From c1750–1800 tops were more usually D-shaped or semi-circular with square tapering legs, the more elaborate examples having inlay to the top and frieze. From c1800 the folded top was often supported by a single pedestal, and this in turn was mounted on a plinth, outswept legs and brass casters.

From c1850, with the revival of the rococo style, tables with serpentine tops and matching curvaceous supports and feet became popular.

A Victorian burr-walnut serpentine card table, the folding top enclosing a baize-lined interior, on a turned carved column with four downswept legs and carved shell feet, 36¾in (93.5cm) wide.
£1,700–2,000 HYD

A Victorian burr-walnut folding card table, the quarter-veneered top enclosing a baize-lined playing surface, on two foliate-carved baluster end uprights above two cabriole supports with scroll-carved feet, 36¼in (92cm) wide.
£750–900 ⚒ Bri

A Victorian burr-walnut fold-over card table, the quarter-veneered fold-over top inlaid with a geometric and foliate border in various woods, and enclosing a baize-lined interior, on ring-turned uprights joined by a foliate-carved finial and turned stretcher, on downswept legs, 37½in (95.5cm) wide.
£1,250–1,500 ⚒ M

A rosewood loo table, c1860, 56in (142cm) wide.
£3,400–3,750 ⊞ MTay

A walnut card table, c1865, 33in (84cm) wide.
£1,600–1,750 ⊞ NAW

A Victorian walnut folding card table, the swivel top quarter-veneered with crossbanding and stringing, on four turned columns, the quadripartite base with turned finial and leaf-carved scroll feet, 36in (91.5cm) wide.
£600–700 ⚒ AH

A Victorian burr-walnut and marquetry loo table, the quarter-veneered tilt-top on a turned and carved column, the four downswept legs carved with foliage, 56½in (143.5cm) wide.
£2,000–2,400 ⚒ HYD

A Victorian mahogany loo table, the veneered octafoil tilt-top on a turned tapering column above ribbed scroll legs, the toes carved with bunches of grapes, 53in (134.5cm) diam.
£1,100–1,300 ⚒ WW

A boulle ebonized card table, the serpentine folded top enclosing a baize inset and brass inlay, French, c1860, 35in (89cm) wide.
£1,000–1,200 ⚒ S(S)

A late Victorian inlaid rosewood envelope folding card table, 21¾in (55.5cm) wide.
£550–650 ⚒ P(S)

An inlaid mahogany folding bridge/card table, the baize-lined top with bezique and cribbage board, late 19thC, 30in (76cm) wide.
£900–1,100 ⚒ MEA

An ebonized and brass card table, on fluted turned tapering legs, late 19thC, 33in (84cm) wide.
£400–500 ⚒ P(Ba)

An Edwardian inlaid mahogany envelope card table, with a single drawer, 22in (56cm) wide.
£1,250–1,400 ⊞ RPh

Centre Tables

A George II mahogany centre table, the later top above a shell-carved frieze, on cabriole legs and pointed pad feet, Irish, 29¼in (74.5cm) wide.
£2,000–2,400 B

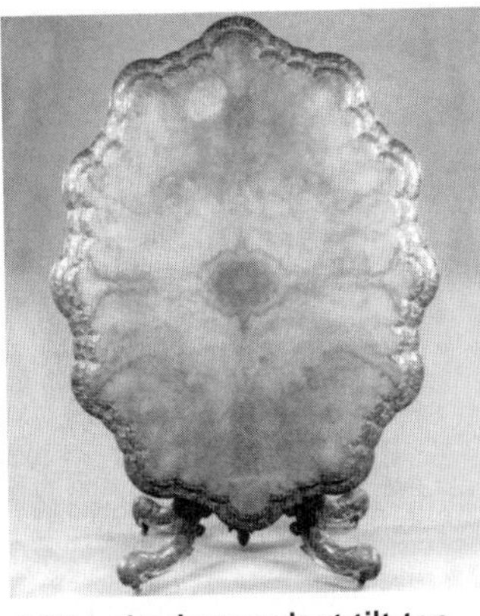

A Victorian burr-walnut tilt-top centre table, the figured multi-lobed top quarter-veneered, 62¼in (158cm) wide.
£1,650–2,000 PFK

A Biedermeier walnut-veneered centre table, c1860, 51in (129.5cm) diam.
£3,500–3,850 SIE

A George IV rosewood centre table, with two short frieze drawers, on turned and lobed trestle legs with scrolled toes, veneer damaged, 47½in (120.5cm) wide.
£700–850 L

A Victorian ebonized and burr-yew centre table, with satinwood banding and stringing, and gilt decoration, the top with radial veneers, on four turned and fluted legs joined by X-stretchers, 39in (99cm) wide.
£600–720 AH

A Renaissance revival walnut centre table, the marble top over a moulded and carved frieze, on a turned and carved pedestal supported by foliate- and scroll-carved legs, American, c1850–75, 40½in (103cm) wide.
£2,500–3,000 NOA

By tradition, tables of this form have been attributed to the workshop of Thomas Brooks, of Brooklyn, New York. However, similar tables appear to have been manufactured by Brooks' contemporaries, including Kingman and Murphy and the Grand Rapids companies.

◄ **A satinwood pedestal centre table,** the tilt-top with a brass-banded border, on a baluster-turned pillar, the triform base with carved giltwood feet, north European, 19thC, 41in (104cm) diam.
£1,000–1,200 S

A William IV mahogany centre table, the tilt-top with radiating veneers, on an octagonal tapered column with lotus mouldings terminating in a three-sided platform, on scroll moulded feet, 48in (122cm) diam.
£1,600–2,000 PF

A Victorian walnut centre table, on turned tapered fluted legs, joined by a turned stretcher with central urn, 43¼in (110cm) wide.
£200–240 TRM

A Renaissance revival fruitwood marquetry centre table, with gilt-metal mounts, the floral- and insect-inlaid top above a frieze drawer inlaid with trelliswork, on foliate-carved and fluted legs, American, c1875, 54in (137cm) wide.
£1,850–2,000 SK

A specimen marble table top, on a later *faux* bamboo gilt-metal base, Italian, 19thC, 32¾in (83cm) diam.
£2,000–2,400 Bon(C)

A carved and ebonized centre table, supported on bacchanalian caryatids and atlantes, ending in hairy hoof feet, 19thC, 57in (145cm) wide.
£8,000–8,850 ⊞ RAN

A walnut tilt-top centre table, with ebonized edging, on four turned tapering column supports, with central finial on a carved quadruped base, 19thC, 44in (112cm) wide.
£700–850 ⚒ E

A mahogany centre table, with boxwood and satinwood inlay and penwork detail, c1890, 36in (91.5cm) wide.
£1,300–1,450 ⊞ NAW

A classical revival mahogany centre table, the oval top with a gadrooned edge and fitted at the centre with a felt writing surface, the frieze with a single drawer, above a lotus-carved pedestal on a platform with carved paw feet, American, late 19thC, 42in (106.5cm) wide.
£675–800 ⚒ NOA

◄ **An Edwardian inlaid mahogany and satinwood-banded centre table,** the octagonal top decorated with scrolling foliage and guilloches, bellflowers and beaded swags, with ivorine label to underside inscribed 'Edwards & Roberts', 38½in (98cm) wide.
£1,700–2,000 ⚒ P(O)

Console & Pier Tables

A carved giltwood console table frame, top missing, 19thC, 31in (78.5cm) wide.
£2,500–3,000 ⚒ TMA

A mahogany console table, crossbanded and satinwood banded, on tapered square legs, 19thC, 30¾in (78cm) wide.
£600–700 ⚒ P(S)

► **A pier table,** the plum-pudding mahogany top above a lappet-moulded frieze carved at each corner with foliage, the two scrolling supports carved at the knees with palm leaves and surmounted by roundel motifs, c1820, 26in (66cm) wide.
£3,200–3,500 ⚒ S

A Directoire console table, the black and white marble top with brass gallery, on turned legs, French, c1800, 36in (91.5cm) wide.
£5,000–5,600 ⊞ HA

An oak console table, with black marble top and central armorial plaque, c1860, 56in (142cm) wide.
£3,500–3,850 ⊞ RAN

An Edwardian inlaid fiddle-back mahogany demi-lune pier table, the crossbanded top decorated with an Adam-style vase within festoon swags and foliate scrolls, above a conforming frieze with central drawer, on four husk-inlaid tapered legs with inlaid undertier, 22½in (57cm) wide.
£1,650–2,000 ⚒ Bri

Dining Tables

A George III mahogany drop-leaf dining table, on four square tapering legs, 47½in (120.5cm) wide.
£1,700–2,000 AH

A George III mahogany drop-leaf dining table, on six Marlborough-style legs, 67¾in (172cm) extended.
£3,200–3,800 HAM

Facts in brief

After c1750 it became fashionable to dine guests around one large extending table made up of three or more separate parts. Before this date, guests were accommodated around a number of different tables within the dining room.

The first 18th-century examples of extending tables were D-ended and could serve as pier tables when not in use. From the turn of the 19th century the most common of these were telescopic with interlocking bearers, or tables with a worm screw mechanism.

Until relatively recently large tables were reduced in size and their timbers used for construction of other furniture. However, the reverse is true today due to the vast increase in their value. Many may have been reconstructed from other tables (a marriage) or even parts of other furniture.Check for identical construction throughout the table, the underneath being a good place to start. Tell-tale warning signs are unexplained markings, holes and inconsistent colour.

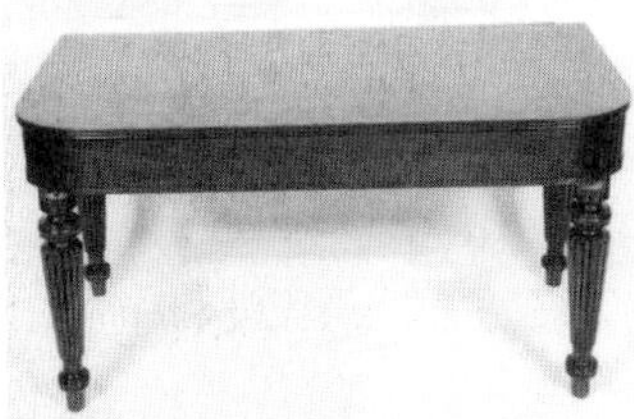

A Regency mahogany patent-action campaign dining table, with a single D-shaped leaf on a pull-out extending frame on turned tapering and fluted legs with toupie feet, with a brass label inscribed 'Stewart, Inventor and Patentee, 115 St Martin's Lane, Charing Cross, London', 48in (122cm) wide.
£2,700–3,000 HYD

A Regency mahogany D-end dining table, the two halves each supported on four turned and tapering legs, with a centre leaf, 72in (183cm) extended.
£900–1,100 FHF

A Regency mahogany extending dining table, by Gillingtons, with two pivoting reeded-end sections each on four turned, tapered and reeded legs, with two additional leaves, altered, Irish, 114in (289.5cm) extended.
£4,500–5,500 S

Gillingtons was among Dublin's most eminent furniture makers during the first half of the 19th century. John Gillington is recorded in the Dublin trade directories at various addresses between 1794 and 1810. From 1810, John worked in partnership with his two sons, George and Samuel, trading under the name of John Gillington & Sons. With their father's departure in 1814, George and Samuel moved to 180 Abbey Street, where they traded as upholders and auctioneers until 1820. From 1820 until 1838, George Gillington apparently continued in business alone, recorded in trade directories at addresses in both Abbey Street and College Green.

A George III mahogany D-end dining table, on 14 square tapering legs, 139¾in (355cm) extended.
£3,000–3,500 CGC

A mahogany dining table, the top above arcaded friezes with drawers, on scroll-top cabriole legs with spade feet, slight damage, 18thC, 58in (147.5cm) wide.
£1,400–1,700 WW

A walnut drop-leaf dining table, with brass casters, French, early 19thC, 51½in (131cm) wide.
£1,800–2,150 SIE

A Regency mahogany extending dining table, with concertina action and single leaf, 72in (183cm) extended.
£3,000–3,600 Mit

A George IV mahogany dining table, by Gillingtons of Dublin, with two leaves, on ten turned and tapered reeded legs, with two extra leaves, 96in (244cm) extended.
£4,000–5,000 MEA

A carved walnut two-part dining table, each section with a hinged leaf over a frieze with acanthus-carved tablets at the centre and corners, on tapering ring- and spirally-turned legs, American, c1825, 47in (119.5cm) wide.
£1,500–1,800 SLN

A William IV mahogany extending dining table, the top with an original extra leaf and a recent further leaf, the frieze on turned petal and faceted tapering legs, 94in (239cm) extended.
£1,400–1,700 WW

Miller's is a price GUIDE not a price LIST

An early Victorian mahogany extending dining table, with telescopic extending action on four lobed inverted baluster uprights, and four extra leaves, 116½in (296cm) extended.
£2,800–3,200 Bri

An extending dining table, the top on a swollen and lappet-carved column, terminating in a quatreform base with double C-scroll legs, 1835–45, 54¼in (138cm) diam.
£1,600–2,000 P(Ba)

A Victorian mahogany extending dining table, the frieze with a hinged flap to one short side, opening to store the two extra leaves, on octagonally faceted tapering legs, 93½in (237.5cm) extended.
£1,750–2,000 PFK

An early Victorian mahogany extending dining table, the top opening to accommodate an extra leaf, on turned legs, 81¾in (207.5cm) wide.
£950–1,150 HYD

► **A mahogany extending dining table,** with three extra leaves, c1860, 93¾in (238cm) extended.
£2,200–2,250 S(O)

◄ **A mahogany extending dining table,** with four extra leaves, c1860, 123½in (313.5cm) extended.
£4,750–5,250 ⊞ MTay

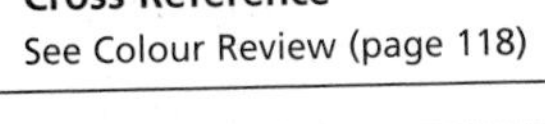

Cross Reference
See Colour Review (page 118)

A Victorian mahogany extending dining table, on fluted baluster legs, with four extra leaves, 120in (305cm) extended.
£5,000–6,000 G(L)

An extending D-end dining table, with a reeded edge, on twin columns with reeded outswept legs, and two extra leaves, early 20thC, 113¾in (289cm) extended.
£800–900 P(Ba)

A mahogany carved extending dining table, the top inlaid with foliate scroll and floral marquetry, opening to take three later mahogany leaves, with later drop down legs, on an octagonal shaft and four inswept putto terms with scroll terminals on a quatreform base with lion's paw feet, with an early 20thC Hungarian fine art transporter's label, possibly Hungarian, 1880–1920, 67¾in (172cm) diam.
£2,750–3,000 P

Display Tables

An ebonized and gilt-metal display cabinet, in Louis XV style, with a glazed hinged top and glazed sides, on turned tapered legs, French, c1870, 35in (89cm) wide.
£350–420 S(O)

An Edwardian mahogany *bijouterie* table, with inlaid stringing and satinwood banding, the glazed lidded top compartment on square tapering legs with undertier, 22½in (57cm) wide.
£400–500 WW

An Edwardian mahogany inlaid and crossbanded vitrine table, with platform stretcher below, 24in (61cm) wide.
£370–450 Bon(W)

An Edwardian mahogany *bijouterie* table, with satinwood-banded and ebonized and boxwood-strung border, with glazed top and sides, 23in (58.5cm) wide.
£400–500 GAK

A mahogany display table, c1910, 24in (61cm) wide.
£875–975 ⊞ MTay

An Edwardian mahogany oval *bijouterie* table, with hinged glazed top, on square tapered supports joined by an undertier, the whole outlined with boxwood stringing and harlequin and lozenge banding, 26¾in (68cm) wide.
£800–950 DD

Dressing Tables

A George III mahogany bowfronted dressing table, the frieze drawer flanked by one deep and two short cockbeaded drawers, on square tapering legs, stamped 'Gillows, Lancaster', 51in (129.5cm) wide.
£2,200–2,700 ⚒ B(Ed)

This table is a good example of Gillows' stylish but understated furniture that was developed to suit Scottish taste in the late 18th century. By producing furniture like this, the company was able to penetrate the south west of Scotland and establish itself as a serious rival to companies such as Trotter of Edinburgh.

A grain-painted and stencil-decorated dressing table, the scrolled splashback above two convex drawers, on a top with convex long drawer below, American, c1820, 33in (84cm) wide.
£1,350–1,600 ⚒ SK(B)

A mahogany dressing table, with three drawers around the arched apron, on ring-turned legs, c1830, 35½in (90cm) wide.
£350–420 ⚒ P(S)

► **A Victorian willow duchess-style dressing table,** the arched mirror above a pair of trinket drawers, fitted with a frieze drawer, on turned tapered columns on an undertier, 45¼in (115cm) wide.
£280–320 ⚒ TRM

A George III bowfronted mahogany dressing table, with arched centre gallery above three frieze drawers each with fan decoration to corners, 48in (122cm) wide.
£1,150–1,400 ⚒ MEA

A mahogany dressing table, with inlaid stringing, the bowfronted top with a gallery, on square tapering legs, early 19thC, 37½in (95.5cm) wide.
£500–600 ⚒ WW

A Regency mahogany dressing table, attributed to Gillows, the central concave drawer and arcaded apron flanked by four short drawers, on reeded turned and tapered legs, top split, early 19thC, 41½in (105.5cm) wide.
£2,400–2,800 ⚒ Bon

A mahogany dressing table, the adjustable mirror plate above a bank of four drawers, the frieze with a central drawer fitted with a leather writing surface, pen tray and compartments for inkwells, Dutch, early 19thC, 46in (117cm) wide.
£500–600 ⚒ CGC

◄ **An Empire dressing table,** the superstructure with an adjustable mirror flanked by brass and ebonized caryatid pilasters with conforming outset columns, the base with a centre frieze drawer and shaped kneehole drawer, flanked by two smaller drawers, French, c1830, 45½in (115.5cm) wide.
£1,100–1,300 ⚒ MEA

A burrwood and tulipwood dressing table, by Paul Sormani, with ormolu mounts, the serpentine top enclosing a mirror and rosewood-lined interior, above a frieze drawer, French, 19thC, 24in (61cm) wide.
£1,300–1,500 ⚒ G(L)

Drop-leaf Tables

A mahogany drop-leaf table, with gateleg support on tapering scallop-capped legs with pointed pad feet, Irish, mid-18thC, 43in (109cm) extended.
£1,250–1,500 HOK

An early George III mahogany corner table, the top with a single flap, on turned legs with pad feet, 41in (104cm) wide.
£400–500 L

A mahogany wake table, the hinged top on eight square-section legs, Irish, 1780–1820, 83½in (212cm) extended.
£4,500–5,500 Bon

A mahogany hunt table, of bowed outline, with removable centre section and hinged flaps to the sides, 19thC, 62¼in (158cm) wide.
£2,500–3,000 P(EA)

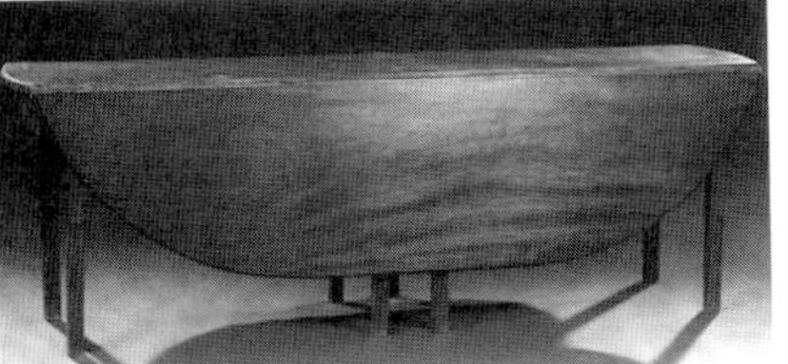

A Federal walnut wake table, with eight square-section legs, American, early 19thC, 88½in (225cm) extended.
£2,200–2,700 SLN

◀ **A George II-style mahogany gateleg table,** the tapered fluted legs joined by bobbin-turned stretchers, with braganza-type feet, 19thC, 22in (56cm) extended.
£500–600 S(S)

Drum Tables

A George III mahogany drum table, the revolving top with a leather-lined surface and crossbanded edge, the frieze with alternate real and false drawers, 42in (106.5cm) diam.
£4,500–5,500 L

A Regency mahogany drum-top library table, with blue skiver and four drawers alternating with dummy drawers, on an octagonal pillar with carved base, triangular platform and scroll feet, 54in (137cm) diam.
£3,000–3,600 G(L)

A mahogany drum library table, the crossbanded top with gilt-embossed green leather inset, eight frieze drawers with brass-mounted turned wood handles, c1810, 50½in (128.5cm) diam.
£3,000–3,600 AH

A mahogany drum table, inlaid with ebony stringing, the top with a tooled green leather inset writing surface above four real and four dummy frieze drawers, c1815, 33½in (85cm) wide.
£2,800–3,200 S(S)

A Regency mahogany rent table, the revolving top with later gilt-tooled leather inset above eight drawers on a panelled and reeded square base with cupboard doors, on hairy paw feet, Irish, 46¾in (119cm) diam.
£6,500–8,000 P

A Sheraton revival rosewood-veneered drum table, boxwood strung, with classical inlay to the centre, above four hinged shield-shaped drawers on tapered legs, joined by an undertier with centre fan medallion, c1900, 27in (68.5cm) diam.
£1,800–2,200 Mit

Games Tables

A figured-rosewood games or needlework table, c1820, 27in (68.5cm) wide.
£5,000–5,500 ⊞ HA

A rosewood games table, the top inlaid as a chequer board, on a turned column support with tripod base, mid-19thC, 20in (51cm) wide.
£1,150–1,300 ⊞ RGa

► A mid-Victorian walnut games table, the swivelling *verre églomisé* top with inset chequer board, one half inlaid with the three lions of England and the cross of St George, the other half with the lion rampant of Scotland and the cross of St Andrew, on a barley-twist column and foliate-carved tripod legs, 27½in (70cm) wide.
£800–950 ⚒ B(Ed)

A Victorian walnut games table, on turned stretchered legs, 36¼in (92cm) wide.
£800–950 ⚒ BLH

A Regency rosewood games table, with brass stringing and specimen marble inset top, 28¾in (73cm) wide.
£1,000–1,200 ⚒ Bon(C)

A Rococo revival rosewood games table, the serpentine fold-over top revealing a felt playing surface, the frieze mounted with foliate carving and raised on reeded scroll supports to a platform base with foliate-carved stylized dolphin feet, American, 36in (91.5cm) wide.
£4,000–5,000 ⚒ NOA

A George IV rosewood games and work table, the top fitted with a sliding reversible panel inlaid on one side with a chequer board and revealing a backgammon well, above a drawer and a pleated fabric work-bag drawer, flanked by two small drawers, 30¾in (78cm) wide.
£1,600–2,000 ⚒ S

An early Victorian rosewood-veneered games table, the swivel fold-over flap top inlaid as a chequer board, above a frieze drawer, 20in (51cm) wide.
£850–1,000 ⚒ WW

A Victorian figured-walnut games table, the hinged top enclosing inlaid backgammon, cribbage and chequer boards above a fitted frieze drawer, with a pull-out work-bag below, 25¼in (64cm) wide.
£1,600–2,000 ⚒ CGC

◄ A mid-Victorian inlaid rosewood games/work table, the hinged bone and boxwood foliate-inlaid top opening to reveal chequer and backgammon inlaid playing surfaces, above a fitted frieze drawer with tapered sliding well below, 24in (61cm) wide.
£1,300–1,500 ⚒ Bri

Library Tables

A Biedermeier mahogany library table, each side with two drawers, restored, north European, c1830, 58in (147.5cm) wide.
£2,200–2,500 ⚒ S(O)

A rosewood library table, the top with two drawers, on two end supports with gadrooned and scrolled bases, c1830, 53¾in (136.5cm) wide.
£1,500–1,800 ⚒ WilP

A Victorian oak Gothic-style library table, by Bulstrode of Cambridge, the top with a tooled leather inset, the frieze fitted with three real opposing three dummy drawers, the shaped panelled end supports joined by a platform stretcher, 66in (167.5cm) wide.
£5,000–6,000 ⚒ S

Christopher Stone Bulstrode (1818–c1895) is recorded in the 1851 census as an upholsterer and employer of 22 men with premises in Bridge Street, Cambridge. His place of birth is given as Marylebone, Middlesex, making it likely that he was a relation of Charles Bulstrode, cabinet-maker and undertaker of 50 Paddington Street, Marylebone (active 1820–39). The 1858 street directory lists Christopher Bulstrode as a cabinet-maker as well as upholsterer, house decorator, appraiser, agent, carpet layer and undertaker. By 1888 he had moved to 38 Sydney Street, Cambridge and by 1892 he disappears from the directories.

A Victorian walnut library table, with two short drawers, on turned end supports with carved lotus-leaf decoration, on splay cabriole legs, 42in (106.5cm) wide.
£525–625 ⚒ MCA

A Victorian walnut library table, with inset leather top, above two short and two false frieze drawers, on octagonal tapering legs, 48in (122cm) wide.
£2,000–2,400 ⚒ AG

Nests of Tables

◄ An inlaid mahogany nest of four tables, the tops with satinwood crossbanding and ebony stringing, on splayed boxwood-strung legs, early 20thC, largest 25in (63.5cm) wide.
£650–800 ⚒ PFK

An Edwardian mahogany nest of three tables, the tops with fan mahogany inlay and satinwood banding with moulded serpentine borders, largest 22in (56cm) wide.
£320–380 ⚒ WW

An Edwardian walnut nest of four spider-leg tables, with crossbanding and raised ebony stringing, c1910, largest 19½in (49.5cm) wide.
£1,650–1,850 ⊞ MTay

An Edwardian mahogany nest of four tables, the tops with a central oak-veneered panel with ebonized cockbeading and crossgrain decoration, largest 19¼in (49cm) wide.
£1,800–2,200 ⚒ BLH

► A mahogany nest of three tables, the largest oval, c1920, largest 25in (63.5cm) wide.
£400–450 ⊞ RPh

Occasional Tables

A mahogany occasional or lamp table, with serpentine-outline frieze, late 18thC, 21in (53.5cm) wide.
£320–380 WW

A mahogany occasional table, with gilt mounts, c1820, 28in (71cm) high.
£1,100–1,200 REI

A satinwood and cross-banded occasional table, c1890, 30in (76cm) diam.
£2,000–2,250 CHE

A walnut and ebonized occasional table, with floral marquetry decoration, c1880, 21in (53.5cm) wide.
£780–875 MTay

◄ **A mahogany coaching table,** early 19thC, 34in (86.5cm) wide.
£1,250–1,400 DOA

A figured burr-walnut occasional table, the top with a central parquetry star motif above a turned carved stem terminating in a triform platform base with bun feet, c1840, 23¾in (60.5cm) diam.
£2,000–2,400 TF

A Victorian burr-walnut veneered occasional table, with tulipwood-banded quarter-veneered top, stamped 'W. Williamson & Sons, Guildford', 25½in (65cm) wide.
£700–850 Bea(E)

A giltwood occasional table, with marble top, late 19thC, 29in (73.5cm) high.
£1,200–1,350 RAN

Miller's is a price GUIDE not a price LIST

A mahogany, ebonized, parcel-gilt and gilt-metal mounted table, with frieze drawer, on concave legs with inward scrolls supporting a pedestal, on a platform base, mounts either restored or replaced, Russian, early 19thC, 26¾in (68cm) diam.
£1,700–2,000 P

A mahogany metamorphic quartet or glee table, the top with a hinged envelope-flap to each side fitted with a removeable rest and two folding brass arms to hold a song-sheet, each flap adjustable by means of brass arms and sliding ratchets, with a mechanism to alter the height of the entire top, the frame with two cockbeaded drawers on opposing sides and removeable and adjustable brass candlestick and drip pan to each corner, c1800, 24in (61cm) square.
£60,000–65,000 JC
The Prince Regent was a great supporter of glee singing and glee clubs, which were most popular and could be found in many major cities in the 18th and early 19th centuries. Fine quality tables were to be found only in gentlemen's private residences, where three or more male singers would perform, unaccompanied by music.

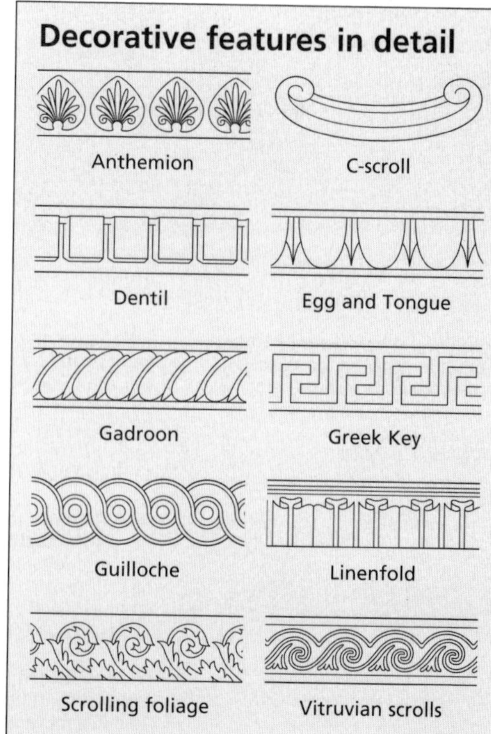

Pembroke Tables

A George III mahogany Pembroke table, 32in (81.5cm) wide.
£550–600 ⊞ NAW

A George III mahogany Pembroke table, with a cockbeaded end drawer and a central undertier with three-quarter spindle gallery, 28in (71cm) wide.
£2,300–2,600 ⚒ DMC

A mahogany-veneered Pembroke table, the repaired top banded in macassar ebony with stringing, over a frieze drawer, early 19thC, 28¼in (72cm) wide.
£500–600 ⚒ WW

A George III mahogany Pembroke table, the frieze with satinwood and ebony banding and one drawer, 36in (91.5cm) wide.
£800–950 ⚒ AH

A Sheraton-style mahogany Pembroke table, the serpentine drop-leaf top crossbanded and inlaid with stringing, with dummy drawers, c1800, 25in (63.5cm) wide.
£2,300–2,600 ⚒ WW

A Regency mahogany Pembroke games table, the satinwood-banded and ebony-strung top with sliding centre section and chequer board to reverse, over satinwood banded ends, 27½in (70cm) wide.
£1,500–1,800 ⚒ P(E)

◄ **A Regency mahogany Pembroke table,** with a frieze drawer, the turned column support on four reeded downswept legs, 41¾in (106cm) wide.
£500–600 ⚒ S(S)

► **A mahogany Pembroke table,** with turned legs, c1820, 20in (51cm) wide.
£4,000–4,500 ⊞ REI

A George III mahogany Pembroke table, with frieze drawer, foliate-carved brackets to the legs, and undertier with fret-carved gallery, gallery damaged, 32in (81.5cm) wide.
£1,100–1,300 ⚒ Bea(E)

A mahogany Pembroke table, c1800, 19¾in (50cm) wide.
£500–550 ⊞ SWA

A Pembroke table, with ebony inlay, with single drawer, c1815, 33in (84cm) wide.
£3,200–3,600 ⊞ HA

Reading Tables

A mahogany reading and writing table, the hinged top with ratchet supports above a candle slide to one side and a pen and ink drawer to the other, restored, altered, late 18thC, 24½in (62cm) wide.
£1,300–1,600 P(S)

A satinbirch reading table, the hinged adjustable top with a serpentine edge above a frieze drawer, early 19thC, 27¾in (70.5cm) wide.
£1,800–2,200 Bon

► **A Regency mahogany reading table,** with twin-flap lectern top, above a divided circular understage and parcel-ebonized ring-turned stem, 15in (38cm) wide.
£800–950 G(L)

◄ **A rosewood reading table,** the top with double ratchet book-rests, on a ring-turned baluster column and a platform base, c1835, 29in (73.5cm) wide.
£900–1,000 S(O)

Serving Tables

A Federal walnut serving table, the top with edge inlaid with stringing and banding above two drawers, cut down, American, c1790–1810, 58in (147.5cm) wide.
£3,500–4,000 SK(B)

A mahogany and line-inlaid bowfronted serving table, with a central drawer flanked by dummy drawers, 19thC, 50in (127cm) wide.
£600–720 P(S)

A carved oak serving table, French, c1880, 70in (178cm) wide.
£1,670–1,850 DUK

► **A Chippendale-style mahogany serving table,** the frieze with blind fret and flowerhead decoration, on leaf-carved cabriole legs with pad feet, 19thC, 57½in (146cm) wide.
£2,200–2,700 F&C

An Edwardian mahogany boxwood-inlaid breakfront serving table, 48in (122cm) wide.
£550–625 NAW

A late Victorian mahogany serving table, the raised back with arched centre and carved shell, the frieze with gadrooned edge and two drawers, on shell-capped cabriole legs with claw-and-ball feet, 72in (183cm) wide.
£3,200–4,000 AH

Side Tables

A walnut side table, with a single drawer, on barley-twist legs, c1690, 28in (71cm) wide.
£3,000–3,400 ⊞ CGA

A George III mahogany spider-leg table, with a fitted frieze drawer, 26in (66cm) wide.
£850–1,000 ⚒ RBB

A Regency rosewood side table, with a pierced brass gallery, on slightly tapering turned legs with brass capitals joined by cross stretchers, 22in (56cm) wide.
£900–1,100 ⚒ P(L)

A walnut side table, on splayed tapering legs united by a shelf, French, c1740, 25½in (65cm) wide.
£11,000–12,500 ⊞ REI

A mahogany side table, with a single drawer, on square tapered legs, c1785, 24in (61cm) wide.
£1,400–1,600 ⊞ RL

◄ **A carved and giltwood side table,** with associated marble top, late 18thC, 41½in (105.5cm) wide.
£3,200–3,800 ⚒ S(Mi)

A painted side table, with speckled rouge marble top above a pierced frieze with oval paterae and a centre panel carved with trophies on fluted and reeded legs, French, 18thC, 45in (114.5cm) wide.
£3,700–4,500 ⚒ MEA

A George III mahogany bowfronted side table, the deep fluted frieze with central moulded tablet, on tapering fluted legs headed by re-entrant panels, 50½in (128.5cm) wide.
£1,500–1,800 ⚒ N

A Georgian mahogany side table, with a single drawer, on square tapered legs, 18¼in (46.5cm) wide.
£380–450 ⚒ WilP

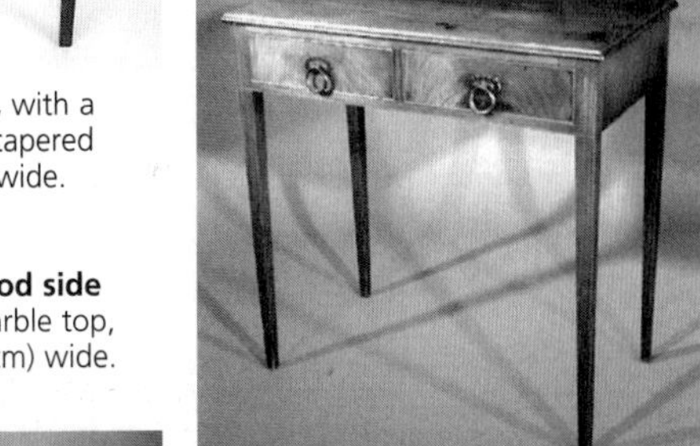

A mahogany side table, the two drawers with later iron handles, on square tapering legs, early 19thC, 33in (84cm) wide.
£450–550 ⚒ WW

A mahogany-veneered brass-mounted side table, on fluted tapering legs, restored, Russian, 19thC, 34in (86.5cm) wide.
£1,400–1,700 ⚒ BUK

◄ **An early Victorian pollarded oak side table,** with moulded decoration, 49½in (125.5cm) wide.
£700–850 ⚒ GAK

A walnut side table, the quarter-veneered top with two frieze drawers on spiral-twist columns and moulded outswept plinth bases, on globular feet, maker's stamp 'Chindley & Sons late; Miles & Edwards, 134 Oxford Street, London', mid-19thC, 48in (122cm) wide.
£1,600–1,750 ⚒ P(Ba)

A walnut and marquetry side table, the top decorated with a flower-filled urn flanked by exotic birds, with a chequerbanded edge, with a similarly decorated frieze drawer, Dutch, late 19thC, 44½in (113cm) wide.
£900–1,100 ⚒ P(Ba)

A Louis XVI-style walnut side table, by Gillow & Co, with two frieze drawers, on fluted tapering legs joined by an H-stretcher, c1884–85, 48in (122cm) wide.
£6,250–7,500 ⚒ Bon

A Victorian carved oak side table, the foliate-carved frieze with a drawer to one long side, the corners with lion masks with brass rings, above turned pendants and a carved apron, on two bulbous carved end standards and four legs shaped as fish, linked by a broad carved stretcher, 37in (94cm) wide.
£320–380 ⚒ PFK

A mahogany side table, by James Hicks of Dublin, the leaf-carved frieze with an incised trellis ground centred by a carved pierced trelliswork basket of flowers flanked by swags of floral garlands issuing from flowerheads, the leaf-carved cabriole legs with lotus leaf and acanthus collars, on claw-and-ball feet, Irish, late 19thC, 59¾in (152cm) wide.
£13,000–15,000 ⚒ S

Born into a family of Dublin chair makers, James Hicks served his apprenticeship in London. By the mid-1890s he had established one of the most successful cabinet making firms in Dublin, producing furniture of superb quality in the styles of Sheraton, Hepplewhite, Chippendale, and the Dublin maker, William Moore. Hicks' patrons included Princess Victoria, the Crown Princess of Sweden, and King Edward VII.

Further reading

Miller's Collecting Furniture The Facts at your Fingertips,
Miller's Publications, 1995

FURNITURE

Silver Tables

A mahogany silver table, with raised edge and cabriole legs, c1750, 28in (71cm) wide.
£5,500–6,250 ⊞ RGa

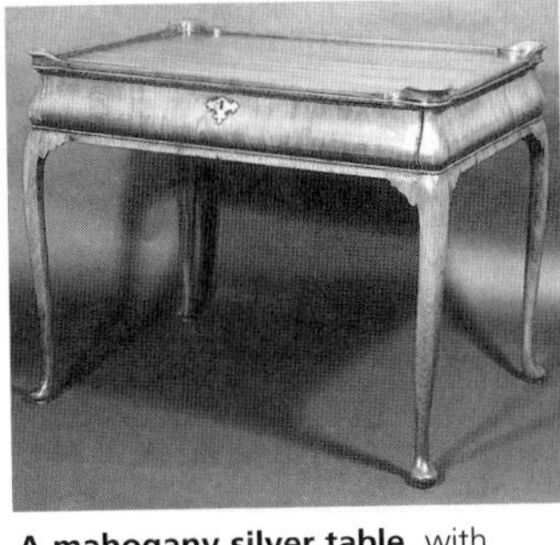

A mahogany silver table, with outswept gallery, the cushion frieze with a single oak-lined drawer, on cabriole legs, c1780, 38in (96.5cm) wide.
£12,000–13,500 ⊞ CAT

A mahogany spider-leg silver table, with a waved solid gallery, c1770, 24½in (62cm) wide.
£5,500–6,500 ⚒ S

A mahogany silver table, the shaped frieze with shell centre on shell-capped cabriole legs, with webbed pad feet, Irish, late 19thC, 29½in (75cm) wide.
£2,000–2,400 ⚒ MEA

A mahogany silver table, on four cabriole legs with claw-and-ball feet, and headed with grotesque masks, Irish, 19thC, 31in (78.5cm) wide.
£625–750 ⚒ MEA

◀ **A Chippendale-style mahogany silver table,** on a turned and carved column and a tripod base, 19thC, 18in (45.5cm) wide.
£1,850–2,200 ⚒ RBB

Sofa Tables

◀ **A mahogany sofa table,** with two frieze drawers and two opposing dummy drawers inlaid with geometric ebonized stringing, c1800, 59¼in (150.5cm) wide.
£3,500–4,200 ⚒ S

A George III satinwood and tulipwood crossbanded sofa table, the hinged top above two frieze drawers, 58¾in (149cm) extended.
£11,000–13,000 ⚒ Bon
This table, made of satinwood with tulipwood crossbanding, is a highly sophisticated piece of furniture.

A Regency brass-inset mahogany sofa table, with frieze drawers, on a twin-pillar stem and downswept legs, 34in (86.5cm) wide.
£1,600–2,000 ⚒ G(L)

A mahogany sofa table, with two frieze drawers and two opposing dummy drawers, the ends joined by a high arched stretcher, early 19thC, 61in (155cm) extended.
£3,500–4,200 ⚒ TF

A mahogany, boxwood and brass-line inlaid sofa table, with two brass inlaid drawers to one side and opposing dummy drawers, Irish, early 19thC, 23¼in (59cm) wide.
£2,500–3,000 ⚒ HOK

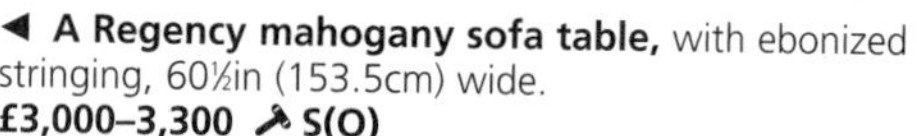

◄ **A Regency mahogany sofa table,** with ebonized stringing, 60½in (153.5cm) wide.
£3,000–3,300 S(O)

An olivewood sofa table, with opposing dummy drawers, c1820, 45in (114.5cm) extended.
£3,500–4,000 S(O)

Facts in brief

- An elegant table first introduced in c1790 for use while sitting on a sofa.
- Identified by its rectangular top and two D-shaped hinged sides, with a pair of full-length drawers backed by dummy drawer fronts.
- Constructed mainly in mahogany, rosewood or satinwood. In Victorian times walnut was more commonly used, or birch as a cheap substitute.
- Bases were originally two trestle ends, and from 1810 onwards a plinth base became popular.
- Look out for reproductions made in the late 19th century, and post-war reproductions made within the last 50 years.

► **A George IV rosewood and satinwood banded sofa table,** with two frieze drawers, inlaid with a brass flowerhead and leaves, on four splayed legs with brass flowerhead roundels, 57¾in (146.5cm) wide.
£2,200–2,700 LFA

A George IV mahogany sofa table, decorated with rosewood crossbanding and ebonized stringing, the frieze with two drawers, 41in (104cm) wide.
£1,500–1,800 AG

A rosewood sofa table, the crossbanded hinged top above a pair of frieze drawers, on a rosewood-grained column, on four scrolled supports, Scottish, early 19thC, 59¾in (152cm) extended.
£5,000–6,000 Bon

A George IV mahogany rosewood crossbanded and line-inlaid sofa, with two frieze drawers, on sabre legs, 36¾ (93½cm) wide.
£2,500–3,000 P

Items in the Furniture section have been arranged in factory order, with non-specific pieces appearing at the end of each sub-section.

A rosewood Regency-style sofa table, the mahogany banded top over two frieze drawers, late 19thC, 59½in (151cm) wide.
£1,600–2,000 P(Ba)

► **A painted mahogany sofa table,** with two frieze drawers, on a trestle support with arched stretcher and sabre legs, painted with foliate sprays throughout, c1895, 31in (78.5cm) wide.
£1,000–1,200 SK

A mahogany sofa table, the frieze fitted with two real and two opposing dummy drawers, c1830, 60¼in (153cm) extended.
£6,250–7,500 S

A mahogany sofa table, inlaid with boxwood stringing, the frieze with two drawers, 19thC, 34½in (87.5cm) wide.
£1,300–1,600 GAK

Supper Tables

A mahogany supper table, the top with two hinged flaps above a frieze drawer and a shaped shelf with pierced trellis sides, c1760, 37¼in (94.5cm) extended.
£3,500–4,200 S

A Regency mahogany supper table, the figured drop-leaf top with burr-birch banding and ebony stringing, with a drawer to each end, 39½in (100.5cm) wide.
£1,100–1,300 WW

A mahogany supper table, with a single hinged flap, c1805, 45in (114.5cm) wide.
£600–720 WW

Miller's is a price GUIDE not a price LIST

Sutherland Tables

A Victorian walnut and burr-walnut Sutherland table, the quarter-veneered oval top on turned end supports joined by a stretcher, on cabriole legs, 27½in (70cm) extended.
£800–900 S(S)

► A Victorian mahogany Sutherland table, the drop-leaf top on a turned folding gateleg frame, 39in (96.5cm) extended.
£230–275 WW

A walnut Sutherland table, c1870, 35in (89cm) extended.
£1,200–1,350 MTay

► A walnut Sutherland table, c1905, 29in (73.5cm) extended.
£200–225 NAW

Tea Tables

A mahogany tea table, with cleated fold-over flap top, the frieze with a concertina action, mid-18thC, 30in (76cm) wide.
£450–550 WW

A George III mahogany tea table, the fold-over top opening onto knuckle-joined double gatelegs, above a frieze drawer, now functioning as a drop-leaf table, with incorrectly fitted hinges, 36¾in (93.5cm) extended.
£280–340 PFK

A George III mahogany tea table, the veneered turn-over top with boxwood and ebony chequer decoration and crossbanded edge, the frieze modelled as two short dummy drawers, on four tapered legs with boxwood-strung decoration and daffodil medallions to the tops, 36in (91.5cm) wide.
£900–1,100 Mit

A mahogany D-shaped folding tea table, with crossbanded borders and boxwood stringing, with a baize-lined interior, c1790, 36in (91.5cm) wide.
£620–750 N

A mahogany tilt-top tea table, refinished, American, c1770–80, 32in (81.5cm) wide.
£1,600–1,750 SK(B)

A mahogany tea table, inlaid with ebonized stringing and stylized anthemia, on quadruple scroll supports, on sabre legs, c1815, 36in (91.5cm) wide.
£1,500–1,800 S(S)

A Georgian mahogany tea table, with fold-over top, 26in (66cm) wide.
£450–550 TMA

A Regency rosewood tea table, the hinged swivel top with inlaid brass stringing, on a spiral-twist column with laurel wreath collar, on four scrolling splay legs, 36in (91.5cm) wide.
£2,000–2,400 AG

A mahogany crossbanded tea table, with boxwood and ebonized stringing, bead-moulded borders and single drop-flap, the frieze with a central drawer, early 19thC, 40½in (103cm) wide.
£650–800 GAK

A mahogany tea table, with fold-over top, c1830, 36in (91.5cm) wide.
£1,100–1,300 ⊞ NoC

◄ **A mahogany single gate-action tea table,** the folding D-shaped top above a cockbeaded frieze drawer, 19thC, 39½in (100.5cm) extended.
£350–420 DD

A mahogany serpentine tea table, the fold-over flap top slightly warped, late 18thC, 36in (91.5cm) wide.
£450–550 WW

A mahogany serpentine-fronted tea table, the fold-over top above a small central drawer, early 19thC, 36¼in (92cm) wide.
£800–900 P(Ba)

A mahogany tea table, the D-shaped fold-over top crossbanded in Brazilian rosewood, with a reeded edge and ebony stringing, over a frieze drawer, Scottish, early 19thC, 39½in (100.5cm) wide.
£600–720 WW

A mahogany tea table, the top crossbanded and strung with boxwood, on double-strung square section legs, 19thC, 35¾in (91cm) wide.
£800–950 P(Ba)

Tripod Tables

A walnut tilt-top table, with a bird-cage support, on a tripod base, c1740, 38in (96.5cm) diam.
£1,600–1,750 ⊞ WELL

A mahogany tripod table, on a reeded stem, c1780, 32in (81.5cm) diam.
£3,200–3,500 ⊞ ChC

A George III mahogany tripod table, with tray form tilt-top, on a bird-cage support, 28in (71cm) diam.
£675–800 ⚒ TMA

Miller's Compares

I. A George III mahogany tripod table, the tilt-top with a moulded pie-crust edge, on a turned and spirally-fluted baluster shaft and a tripod base with elongated pad feet, 24½in (62cm) wide.
£35,000–40,000 ⚒ HYD

II. A George III mahogany pillar table, the tilt-top with a pie-crust edge, on a turned and spirally-fluted baluster shaft and a tripod base with pad feet, 27½in (70cm) wide.
£1,500–2,500 ⚒ HYD

It cannot be stipulated often enough that when considering the purchase of antique furniture for investment, condition is of the utmost importance. This is clearly illustrated by the amounts these two tables realized at auction. Item I achieved an exceptional price because of its wonderful 'skin', as it is termed. It had never been repolished and the mahogany had acquired, over the centuries, a lustrous bronze-like patination, the details of the pie-crust border being accentuated by the build-up of polish. Pie-crust tops are always a desirable feature, and square tops rather than oval are rare, but Item II could have been in the same league as Item I, if not for the fact that the surface had been stripped and repolished. A further plus factor with Item I was that the top quite clearly belonged to the base. Always check this when looking at tripod tables – any tell tale marks on the reverse of the top should ring alarm bells.

A mahogany tripod table, the pie-crust top on a turned reeded baluster column support, on floral-carved tripod legs, 19thC, 34¼in (87cm) diam.
£1,000–1,200 ⚒ BLH

A Victorian mahogany tripod table, with a turned support, on cabriole legs, 35½in (90cm) diam.
£500–600 ⚒ DA

◀ **A Chippendale-style mahogany tripod table,** the octagonal top with a pierced gallery and shaped apron, on a gadrooned baluster stem with leaf-carved cabriole legs, 19thC, 26in (66cm) diam.
£1,100–1,300 ⚒ F&C

Cross Reference
See Colour Review (page 119)

▶ **A rosewood table,** with a marbled top, with drop finials, on a spiral-turned column, 19thC, 20in (51cm) diam.
£500–600 ⚒ E

Two-Tier Tables

A walnut two-tier travelling table, with Sorrento-work panels of musicans and dancers, and a fruit seller, on turned simulated bamboo supports, Italian, early 20thC, 16½in (42cm) wide.
£600–720 ⚒ WilP
Cabinet makers in Sorrento, Italy, specialized in the production of elegantly inlaid occasional tables decorated with rustic scenes.

◄ **A Louis XV-style kingwood and inlaid two-tier table,** inlaid with sprays of flowers and fitted with a drawer, 19thC, 17¾in (45cm) wide.
£550–650 ⚒ P(B)

A Sheraton revival rosewood two-tier table, with boxwood strung decoration, the top with twin drop-flaps, 1880–1920, 21in (53.5cm) wide.
£620–750 ⚒ Mit

A late Victorian ebonized wood and mahogany two-tier table, the top with a trade label 'William Gerrard, Fancy Cabinet Maker, Upholsterer, Lyndhurst, Hants', on three gilt-ringed *faux* bamboo legs with an undertier, 14¾in (37.5cm) diam.
£70–85 ⚒ WW

◄ **A rosewood and marquetry two-tier table,** with gilt-brass mounts, the centre inlaid with floral sprays within a leaf scroll border, with galleried undertier, French, late 19thC, 23in (58.5cm) diam.
£400–500 ⚒ CAG

► **A kingwood and giltwood bronze two-tier table,** attributed to J-E. Zweiner, with quarter-veneered tops within shaped cross-banded borders, the lower section with two frieze drawers applied with mounts cast with scrolling foliage, strapwork and tendrils, French, c1890, 38in (96.5cm) wide.
£14,000–17,000 ⚒ S
Joseph-Emmanuel Zweiner was German by birth but spent most of his working life in Paris, where he is known to have been between 1880–95 at Rue de la Roquette. His work shows an individuality and freedom of design which was taken up by Linke. He exhibited at the 1889 *Exposition Universalle* in Paris, where his work obtained a gold medal.

Work Tables

► **A Regency work table,** with flap top over a drawer, on a turned stem with saltine platform and scroll feet, 21in (53.5cm) wide.
£1,350–1,500 ⊞ RPh

A Regency burr-walnut work table, with ebonized stringing and two drawers, 16in (40.5cm) wide.
£900–1,100 ⚒ G(L)

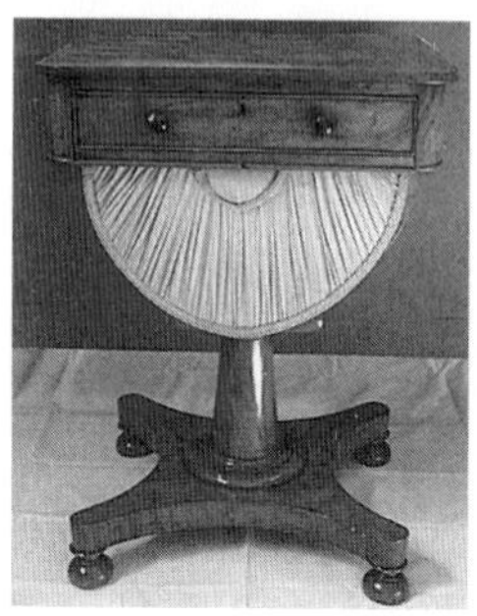

A Regency palisander wood work/games table, with rotating fold-over velvet-lined top over two frieze drawers, one fitted for backgammon, above pleated silk covered well, 21¾in (55.5cm) wide.
£1,800–2,200 ⚒ Bri

A Regency lacquered work table, with well-fitted interior, 25in (63.5cm) wide.
£2,400–2,650 ⊞ RAN

◄ **A satinwood work table,** with a single drawer and pleated silk bag on a turned stem and quatrefoil base with bun feet, early 19thC, 21in (53.5cm) wide.
£1,200–1,500 ⚒ BR

A Federal mahogany inlaid work table, the banded inlaid top above two short drawers flanked by inlaid panels, American, c1810, 19in (48.5cm) wide.
£2,400–2,800 BB(S)

An Empire mahogany and gilt-mounted work table, the hinged top enclosing a fitted compartment with a drawer below, decorated with applied wreaths and fern, French, early 19thC, 21in (53.5cm) wide.
£1,000–1,200 BLH

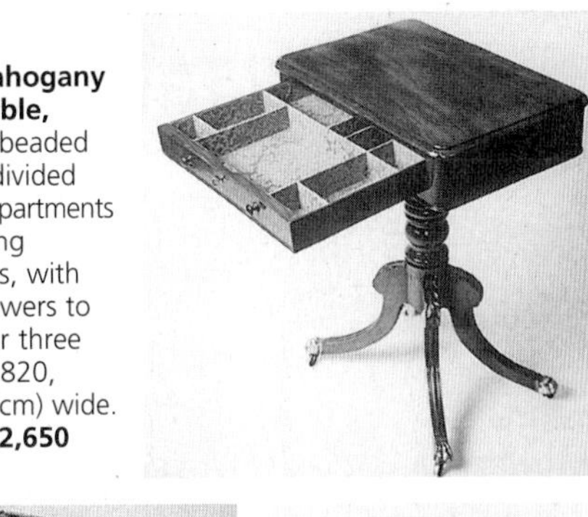

► A mahogany work table, the cockbeaded drawer divided into compartments for sewing requisites, with false drawers to the other three sides, c1820, 22in (56cm) wide.
£2,400–2,650 JC

A George IV mahogany work table, the top with figured veneer and banded in coromandel, with a fitted drawer to the side, 21in (53.5cm) wide.
£1,500–1,800 WW

A mahogany work table, with two drawers, on a rope-twist base, c1830, 14in (35.5cm) wide.
£1,100–1,300 NoC

A mahogany work table, the drop-leaf top above two drawers, on ring-turned legs, c1830, 29in (73.5cm) wide.
£2,000–2,300 RGa

A rosewood work box, on shaped supports with turned stretcher, on bun feet with casters, c1830, 20in (51cm) wide.
£1,800–2,000 BERA

◄ A mahogany work table, c1855, 23in (58.5cm) wide.
£1,700–1,875 NAW

A William IV mahogany work box, with drop-down four-section storage compartment, 18in (45.5cm) diam.
£320–380 FHF

A William IV flame-mahogany work table, the deep central sliding well with a frieze drawer to one side and opposing dummy drawer, 27in (68.5cm) wide.
£1,600–2,000 DA

A walnut work table, the crossbanded hinged top enclosing slide-out compartments with inlaid decoration, over a drawer, German, 19thC, 19¼in (49cm) wide.
£600–720 P(E)

A mahogany work table, the inverse-bowfronted quarter-veneered top opening to reveal 14 lidded compartments, on an acanthus-carved and turned baluster column, with trefoil base and three outsplayed scroll supports, 19thC, 19¾in (50cm) wide.
£800–950 DD

A Victorian mahogany work table, the hinged top in three sections, opening to reveal an interior fitted with covered compartments and pigeon-holes, 29½in (75cm) wide.
£1,500–1,750 LJ

A walnut work table, with applied mouldings, the hinged cover with a concealed locking compartment, opening to reveal a fitted interior, above a frieze drawer with well and one long drawer, 1850–1900, 21in (53.5cm) wide.
£600–720 TMA

Writing Tables

A George III mahogany serpentine writing table, the top now with a leather-lined writing surface, above a fitted frieze drawer, formerly with a slide, 41½in (105.5cm) wide.
£3,500–4,200 ⚒ S

A rosewood writing table, some damage to veneer, Sicilian, 1775–1800, 39¾in (101cm) wide.
£4,750–5,500 ⚒ S(Mi)

A parquetry-inlaid satinwood writing table, the leather inset top with trellis inlay, above a pair of conforming frieze drawers, some damage and restoration, c1780–1820, 36¼in (92cm) wide.
£3,000–3,600 ⚒ Bon

A Regency mahogany lady's writing table, in the Gillows style, the banded top with ebony stringing, above a frieze drawer with baize writing surface on a sliding easel back, and a writing compartment, 22in (56cm) wide.
£2,300–2,750 ⚒ WW

A late Regency lady's mahogany writing table, in the Gillows style, the leather inset top with hinged lid backing interior compartment with a frieze drawer, 25¼in (64cm) wide.
£1,100–1,300 ⚒ P(Ba)

A writing table, attributed to Gillows of Lancaster, c1825, 41in (104cm) wide.
£6,250–7,000 ⊞ F

► **A satinwood and parcel-gilt writing table,** with later leather inset writing surface, c1870, 54in (137cm) wide.
£4,750–5,500 ⚒ S(O)

A mid-Victorian mahogany writing desk, by C. Mellier & Co, with applied gilt-metal mounts, the top with a galleried back above a central frieze drawer and kneehole, flanked by two drawers, maker's stamp to underside, 57in (145cm) wide.
£3,500–4,000 ⚒ P
The London-based company of Mellier & Co took over the Parisian firm of Monboro around 1808. Monboro had established the London arm of their business in 1803 at 2 Frith Street, Soho.

Cross Reference
See Colour Review (page 118)

A lady's writing table, by John Howard & Sons, crossbanded with ebony, with ivory stringing and moulded ebony edging, with velvet writing surface and fire screen, stamped maker's mark, c1865, 27in (68.5cm) wide.
£7,000–7,800 ⊞ HA

◄ **A rosewood drop-leaf writing table,** the top with inset stamped leather panel and hinged lidded stationery compartment, bone stringing and inlaid with engraved bone shellwork, leaf scrolls and phoenix, the frieze with a bow-fronted drawer above pierced brackets, leather distressed, c1890, 24in (61cm) wide.
£800–950 ⚒ N

A late Victorian mahogany travelling writing table, with bottle-green fitted interior, 24in (61cm) wide.
£1,000–1,200 WW

Miller's is a price GUIDE not a price LIST

A Victorian walnut kidney-shaped writing table, the top with shaped leather skivers above two frieze drawers and pierced fret to kneehole, 47¼in (120cm) wide.
£1,100–1,300 B&L

► **A mahogany Rococo-style writing table,** the shaped marquetry-inlaid top within a gilt-brass border, with concave central drawer and side drawers, on cabriole legs headed with carved bearded masks, inlaid with scrolling foliage and games, German, 19thC, 50½in (128.5cm) wide.
£1,200–1,500 S(Am)

An inlaid kingwood writing table, with leather top and gilt-metal mounts, French, 19thC, 63in (160cm) wide.
£3,750–4,500 SWO

Teapoys

A mahogany teapoy, the lid enclosing three lidded compartments and two void wells, c1800, 15¼in (38.5cm) wide.
£1,000–1,200 S(O)

A Regency rosewood teapoy, on a baluster knopped stem over a circular base, 14½in (37cm) wide.
£450–550 P(Ba)

A Regency mahogany teapoy, the hinged gadrooned caddy top enclosing a later fabric-lined interior, adapted, 16in (40.5cm) wide.
£850–1,000 P(NW)

A William IV mahogany teapoy, the *bombé*-shaped hinged box enclosing four compartments for canisters, 15½in (39.5cm) wide.
£500–600 CGC

A William IV mahogany teapoy, the *bombé* top with a gadrooned lid, enclosing two removable lidded canisters flanking a pair of glass mixing bowls, one broken, 16¾in (42.5cm) wide.
£700–850 L

A William IV rosewood teapoy, the sarcophagus-shaped top revealing two lidded caddies and space for mixing bowls, 19in (48.5cm) wide.
£550–650 WW

A walnut and mahogany teapoy, the casket-shaped cover opening to reveal two caddies and two recesses for bowls, 19thC, 14in (35.5cm) wide.
£400–500 HOLL

A Victorian rosewood teapoy, the figured top with applied moulded edge, opening to an interior fitted with a green velvet lining and four compartments, 17in (43cm) diam.
£1,150–1,350 Mit

Torchères

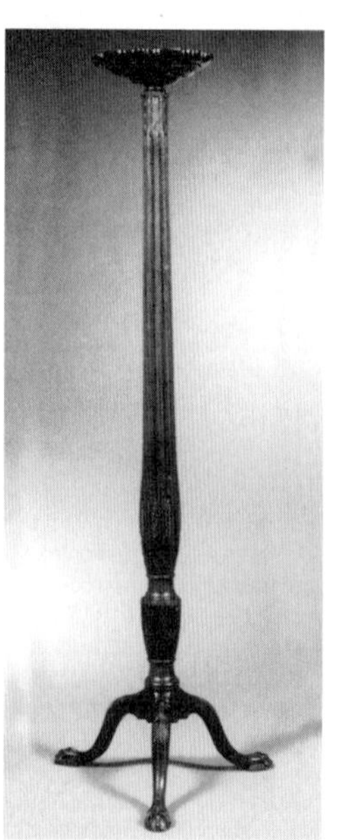

◄ **A George III mahogany torchère,** the piecrust top supported by a bulbous reeded shaft with wheatsheaf carving, 64½in (164cm) high.
£600–700 NOA

LOCATE THE SOURCE
The source of each illustration in Miller's can be found by checking the code letters below each caption with the Key to Illustrations, pages 794–800.

► **A Victorian torchère,** with twist-turned centre column on three short feet, 48in (122cm) high.
£200–240 Mit

A carved mahogany 18thC-style torchère, c1900–10, 42in (106.5cm) high.
£680–760 MTay

Towel Rails

A George III mahogany towel rail/clothes horse, 29in (73.5cm) wide.
£250–285 NoC

A mahogany towel rail, c1870, 36in (91.5cm) wide.
£250–300 GBr

A Victorian mahogany towel rail, the rails on twist-turned end supports with a turned stretcher and scrolling legs, 24in (61cm) wide.
£120–140 WW

Trays

A papier mâché tray, with gilt decoration, on later *faux* bamboo stand, c1820, 31in (78.5cm) wide.
£1,350–1,500 CAT

► **A mahogany butler's tray,** with gallery, 19thC, 28½in (72.5cm) wide.
£250–300 WW

A mahogany butler's tray, with three-quarter gallery on a mahogany turned X-frame stand, late 19thC, 26½in (67.5cm) wide.
£500–600 DMC

Wall Brackets

◀ **A pair of carved giltwood and painted wall brackets,** each supported by a seraphim and carved with scrolling acanthus, Franco-Flemish, gilding worn, late 17thC, 11¼in (28.5cm) wide.
£4,500–5,500 ⚒ S

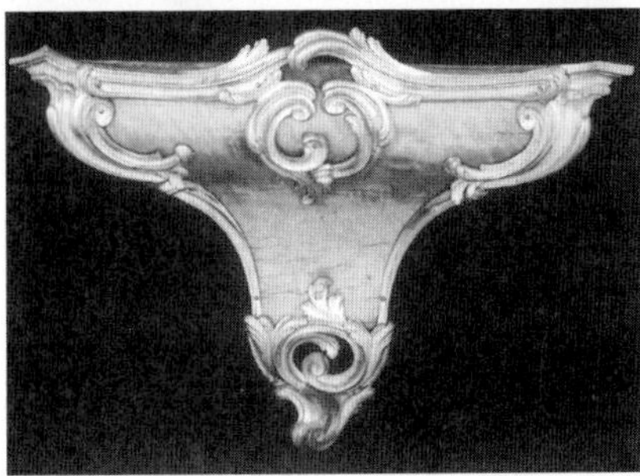

A gilt-bronze-mounted clock bracket, the tapering ogee-scrolled outline applied with acanthus C-scroll mounts, late 19thC, 13¾in (35cm) high.
£1,100–1,200 ⚒ P(Ba)

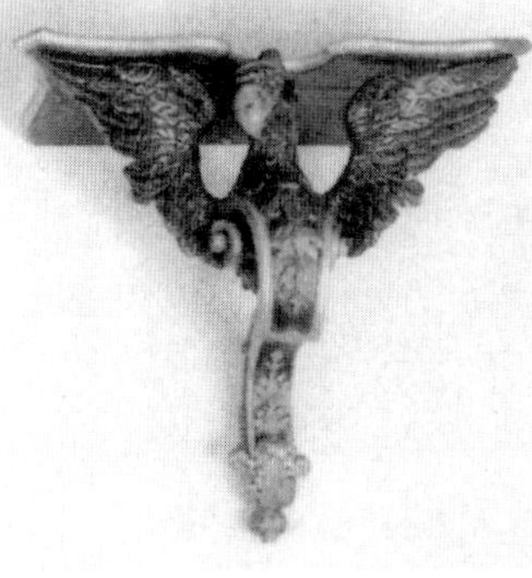

A pair of carved and gilded wall brackets, each supported by a winged eagle and embellished with garlands and acanthus-leaf motifs, 18thC, 31¼in (79.5cm) wide.
£2,500–3,000 ⚒ L&E

A pair of gilt gesso and carved wood mirrored wall brackets, the plates set with C- and acanthus-scroll and turned column surrounds, each mounted to one side with a plateau shelf above a larger undulating shaped plateau shelf, on acanthus-scroll support, early 20thC, 27½in (70cm) high.
£350–420 ⚒ P(Ba)

Wardrobes

A George III mahogany wardrobe, the two doors each with three fielded panels, on ogee bracket feet, 52in (132cm) wide.
£1,700–2,000 ⚒ Bea(E)

A George III walnut wardrobe, the single door enclosing hanging space, 38½in (98cm) wide.
£1,000–1,100 ⚒ S(O)

A mahogany wardrobe, the two reeded doors enclosing a hanging rail and with two false drawers, above a base with one long drawer, c1810, 54in (137cm) wide.
£4,250–4,750 ⊞ JC

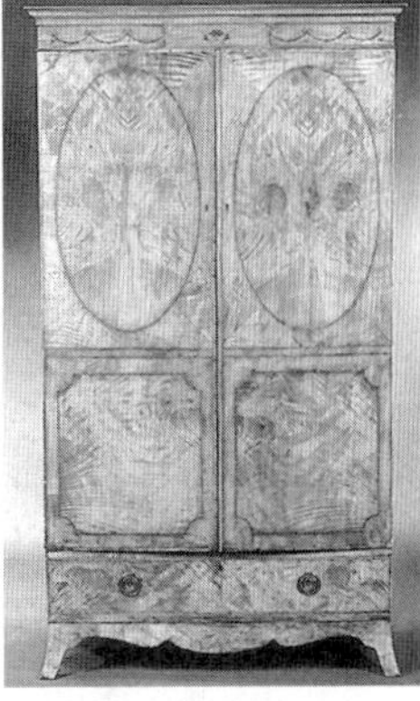

A satinwood and ebony-lined wardrobe, the frieze inlaid with ribbon swags above a pair of oval crossbanded doors enclosing an open interior with a single drawer below, bearing a paper label for Maples Depository, 19thC, 46¾in (119cm) wide.
£1,350–1,600 ⚒ B(Ed)

◀ **A Victorian mahogany-veneered wardrobe,** the left-hand door enclosing hanging space and a series of five short drawers, the right-hand door enclosing hanging space with one drawer below, 56in (142cm) wide.
£550–650 ⚒ Mit

▶ **A mahogany and satinwood-banded breakfront wardrobe,** with boxwood stringing, the central hanging space enclosed above two short and two long drawers, flanked by a door with three false drawers enclosing hanging space, 19thC, 85in (216cm) wide.
£2,500–3,000 ⚒ LFA

A mahogany compactum, with fitted interior, 19thC, 104in (264cm) wide.
£5,750–6,450 ⊞ RAN

◄ **A mahogany wardrobe,** the panelled cupboard doors with cut-corner flowerhead carving embraced by husk-interlaced circle-carved sides, above a pair of *faux* drawers, French, 19thC, 73¾in (187.5cm) wide.
£1,350–1,600 ⚒ P(NW)

An Edwardian satinwood and line-inlaid serpentine wardrobe, 84¾in (215.5cm) wide.
£1,400–1,700 ⚒ Bon(C)

An Edwardian satinwood wardrobe, crossbanded with stringing, the bow-fronted central section with two inlaid oval-panelled doors enclosing slides, over two short and two long drawers, flanked by two long doors enclosing hanging space, 77in (195.5cm) wide.
£2,200–2,500 ⚒ AH

A late Victorian gentleman's walnut wardrobe, the panelled doors enclosing four sliding trays, the base with two short and two long drawers, 48in (122cm) wide.
£750–900 ⚒ CAG
This piece bears the trade label for Pluncknett & Stevens, Cabinet Makers & Upholsterers, Warwick & Leamington.

Washstands

A George II mahogany washstand, on tapering leg supports, 13½in (34.5cm) wide.
£300–360 BLH

A George III mahogany washstand, the hinged flaps opening to reveal cut-out basin and beaker stands and lift-up mirror, above a pair of doors with a short drawer under, 21in (53.5cm) high.
£500–600 AG

A George III mahogany washstand, the faded twin-flap top opening to reveal a lift-up mirror, over a dummy drawer, cupboard door and frieze drawer, 19in (48.5cm) wide.
£350–420 WW

A George III mahogany washstand, the top supported by three scrolling brackets above a concave triangular drawer, on turned columns joined by a dished jug stand, 32in (81.5cm) high.
£400–500 P(Ed)

► **A George III mahogany washstand,** with a gallery back, 37¾in (96cm) wide.
£240–400 WilP

◄ **A mahogany washstand,** with black line decoration, c1800, 18in (45.5cm) wide.
£875–975 MTay

A mahogany corner washstand, with curved splash-back and a quarter shelf with cut-out for toothbrush jar, above a top shelf with a cut-out for jug and basin, the central tier with a drawer flanked by dummy drawers, all edged in ebony stringing, now fitted with removable loose top, c1800, 23in (58.5cm) wide.
£1,100–1,250 JC

A mahogany bowfronted corner washstand, with raised back and one drawer, early 19thC, 22in (56cm) wide.
£280–330 LFA

A bowfronted line-inlaid satinwood-veneered washstand, banded in purple heart, c1790, 15in (38cm) wide.
£3,500–4,000 RGa
An unusual feature of this washstand is that the legs are also veneered.

A Gothic walnut washstand, mid-19thC, 16in (40.5cm) wide.
£450–500 SWA

◄ **A mahogany washstand,** with shaped scrolled marble gallery, the indented front with carved frieze drawer, 19thC, 48in (122cm) wide.
£280–340 HOK

► **An Edwardian walnut washstand,** by Maple & Co, fitted with a bevelled mirror, above a lift-up top enclosing a reservoir over trinket drawers, the fielded panel fall-front section enclosing a tap and lined washstand, above a similar door enclosing recess for slop bucket, with maker's label, 22½in (57cm) wide.
£380–450 BLH

Whatnots

A late Georgian mahogany four-tier whatnot, with a single drawer to the base, 58in (147.5cm) high.
£1,100–1,300 AG

A Regency mahogany whatnot, the base with a single drawer, 60¼in (153cm) high.
£1,600–2,000 HYD

A George IV plum pudding mahogany four-tier whatnot, the top with a three-quarter gallery, the bottom shelf with a full-width drawer, 20½in (52cm) wide.
£2,800–3,250 JC

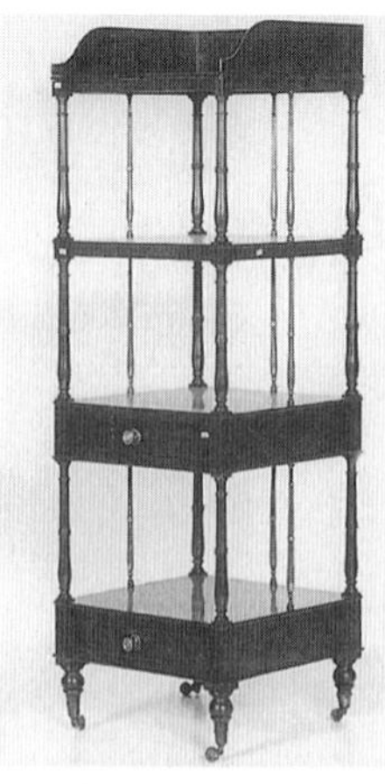

A William IV mahogany whatnot, the three-quarter gallery top above four shelves, two with drawers, 56in (142cm) high.
£2,000–2,400 MEA

A William IV mahogany whatnot, with adjustable reading slope above three tiers, the middle tier fitted with a drawer, 19¼in (49cm) wide.
£900–1,100 P(B)

A mahogany whatnot, each tier with a shaped frieze, the bottom tier fitted with a drawer, c1850, 20in (51cm) wide.
£900–1,100 S(O)

A Victorian rosewood whatnot, with three tiers on turned supports, fitted with two drawers, 23¾in (60.5cm) wide.
£800–950 TRM

A walnut four-tier corner whatnot, of serpentine outline, with turned supports, c1860, 50in (127cm) high.
£750–830 NoC

A Victorian rosewood whatnot, the three tiers with barley-twist supports, the bottom tier with a single drawer beneath, 21in (53.5cm) wide.
£300–360 DA

A walnut three-tier whatnot, with single drawer, c1880, 39in (99cm) high.
£750–820 RPh

A mahogany three-tier whatnot, on ring-turned supports, reduced in height, 19thC, 19¼in (49cm) wide.
£350–420 P(Ba)

A mahogany whatnot, Continental, c1890, 55½in (141cm) high.
£1,400–1,550 APO

Window Seats

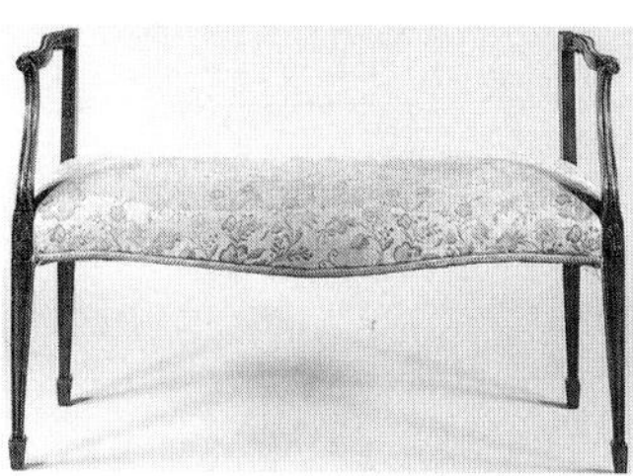

A pair of George III mahogany window seats, the serpentine-fronted upholstered seats flanked by shaped and moulded open arms headed by scrolled paterae-carved terminals, one with a replaced side rail, 44in (112cm) wide.
£10,000–12,000 ⚒ S

► **A mahogany window seat,** with reeded frieze, on tapering legs and axehead feet, brackets later, c1810, 56½in (143.5cm) wide.
£1,500–1,800 ⚒ N

◄ **A Victorian mahogany window seat,** with turned baluster handles and turned tapering legs, 59¾in (152cm) wide.
£1,250–1,500 ⚒ RTo

◄ **A Regency mahogany window seat,** on turned fluted legs and toupie feet, 43¼in (110cm) wide.
£1,500–1,800 ⚒ B

► **A Sheraton-style mahogany-framed window seat,** c1890, 33in (84cm) wide.
£675–750 ⊞ RPh

Wine Coolers

An early George III mahogany cellaret, with fitted interior, 26in (66cm) wide.
£4,200–5,000 ⚒ B(B)

A George II mahogany Irish-style wine cooler, with gadrooned base on lion's mask and acanthus-leaf carved cabriole legs, and hairy paw feet, with a brass liner, 30in (76cm) wide.
£3,500–4,200 ⚒ HYD

A George III mahogany and brass-bound cellaret, with hinged lid and side carrying handles, the tapering legs headed by brackets, partly relined, base partially renewed, Scottish, 16¼in (41.5cm) high.
£1,850–2,200 ⚒ P(Ed)

This type of cellaret is peculiar to Edinburgh. Its identifying features are the hollow brackets at the tops of the legs and the astragal moulding on the lid and the bottom of the frame. Such cellarets were designed for use in the dining room, unlike the rectangular lockable liquor case that was used for drawing room drinking or secure storage of bottled alcohol anywhere in the house.

A George III mahogany wine cooler, with hinged top and brass ring handles, on a stand with thumbnail-carved frieze, one handle lacking, 19¼in (49cm) wide.
£1,500–1,800 ⚒ P(E)

A George III mahogany cellaret, the hinged top enclosing a six-bottle interior, with brass carrying handles, 16½in (42cm) wide.
£1,150–1,350 ⚒ CGC

A late George III mahogany and brass-bound cellaret on stand, with a crossbanded top and brass side-carrying handles, 17¾in (45cm) wide.
£1,000–1,200 P(Ba)

A George IV mahogany wine cooler, sarcophagus-shaped, the hinged top with beaded mouldings, enclosing a zinc-lined interior, 24¾in (63cm) wide.
£1,000–1,200 Bea(E)

A George IV mahogany cellaret, sarcophagus-shaped, 19in (48.5cm) wide.
£650–800 L

An early Victorian mahogany wine cooler, sarcophagus-shaped, the hinged lid enclosing a fitted interior, 22½in (57cm) wide.
£1,500–1,750 P(Ed)

A Regency mahogany wine cooler, sarcophagus-shaped, the hinged lid enclosing an eight-bottle lead-lined interior, 30¾in (78cm) wide.
£1,250–1,500 CGC

A Regency mahogany cellaret, sarcophagus-shaped, the upper section with a hinged lid revealing an altered interior, the base with two cupboard doors, 24½in (62cm) wide.
£1,000–1,200 AH

A mahogany wine cooler, sarcophagus-shaped, the hinged lid enclosing a lead-lined and compartmented interior, on carved paw feet and casters, some faults, c1825, 30in (76cm) wide.
£2,750–3,300 S(S)

A silver plate-mounted oak wine cooler, with lion mask-mounted loop handles, the interior fitted for six bottles, early 20thC, 16½in (42cm) diam.
£1,100–1,300 P

A Regency mahogany cellaret, sarcophagus-shaped, with ebony stringing, lion's head capped fluted pilasters and lion's paw feet, 31in (78.5cm) wide.
£4,000–5,000 G(L)

A Regency mahogany and ebonized wine cooler, sarcophagus-shaped, the hinged top revealing a lead-lined interior with bottle divisions, the lappet-moulded cornice above a slightly tapered body applied with carved anthemia motifs, ebonized decoration restored, 31½in (80cm) wide.
£3,000–3,500 S

A William IV ebony-strung and crossbanded mahogany cellaret, the hinged top with bobbin-turned edge moulding, opening to six compartments, the base fitted with a single drawer, 19½in (49.5cm) wide.
£900–1,100 Mit

A mahogany wine cooler, sarcophagus-shaped, enclosing a fitted lead-lined interior, 19thC, 25in (63.5cm) wide.
£1,650–2,000 GAK

Oak & Country Furniture

Twenty years ago, 18th-century oak and country-made furniture was regarded as slightly lightweight and rather less desirable than oak furniture dating from the 17th century and earlier, but nevertheless a category in its own right. This has now mostly reversed, with 18th-century pieces often making the most money. For example, 18th-century dressers generally fetch more than 17th-century court cupboards, which are still relatively inexpensive.

Continental country furniture, French or otherwise, was not considered important enough to be in a category of its own and was largely unappreciated until recently, when a few pioneering dealers began importing and educating the market. From Scandinavian painted furniture to French provincial, and from the richly painted and carved pieces of central Europe with its Baroque heritage to the simplicity of Swiss country furniture, vernacular European styles are diverse. Each has its own regional stamp and most pieces were produced prior to WWI.

Of all the European styles, French provincial furniture was probably the first type to become popular overseas. Farm tables, armoires, buffets and commodes (chests of drawers) made from marvellous country timbers such as cherry, ash, elm, chestnut, walnut and oak – invariably of peg and tenon construction – are both unpretentious and practical, unlike their formal counterparts, which can be fussy to the extreme. After the French Revolution, in the late 18th century the old system of primogeniture was replaced by a new law stipulating that each child must inherit equally. This led to the division of country estates and farms and the proliferation of working farmers. As children inherited their portion of the farm, they erected their own houses and proceeded to furnish them. Therefore France had a higher proportion of owner-occupiers and consequently more country furniture. Styles were often regional; furniture from the north tends to be more massive in construction, such as heavy, Normandy farm tables and sturdy geometric Breton pieces, compared with much lighter items from the south, for example, the elegant Charentais chairs.

The American market loves the provincial look, having a rich folk tradition of its own. This, coupled with the fact that British country furniture has rocketed in price, has led to the influx of French provincial and other European furniture into Britain. As the demand has grown so have the prices. My only advice is to buy the best you can, as with all things this proves the most pleasurable in the long run. **Denzil Grant**

OAK & COUNTRY FURNITURE

Beds

An oak cradle, in late 17thC/early 18thC-style, 19thC, 37in (94cm) long.
£150–180 ⚒ DN

A rustic oak bedstead, c1910, 60in (152.5cm) wide.
£900–1,100 ⊞ SeH

An oak tester bed, the headboard with lunette-carved bands and an arched flower-filled centre panel embraced by a carved term and leaf-carved panel to either side, 17thC and later, 60¾in (154.5cm) wide.
£8,000–9,500 ⚒ P(NW)

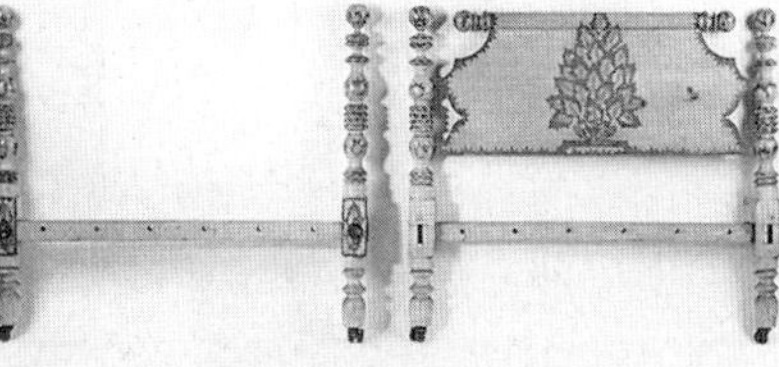

A painted and decorated low post bed, the white paint with gold-leaf stencil decoration, side rails missing, some height loss, American, 1830s, 53¾in (136.5cm) wide.
£850–1,000 ⚒ SK(B)

A chestnut bedstead, with carved and signed panels, Breton, c1890, 78in (198cm) wide.
£3,000–3,300 ⊞ SWA

◀ **A Victorian oak tester bed,** the arcaded footboard incised with rosettes and carved with dentil ornament, the turquoise-lined padded linen draperies, upholstered headboard and cover printed with a colourful design of tree peonies, 60in (152.5cm) wide.
£2,500–3,000 ⚒ N

Bookcases

◄ **An oak bureau bookcase,** the two glazed doors enclosing shelves and pigeonholes, above a cleated fall enclosing a fitted stepped interior, over two short and two long graduated drawers, 18thC, 39½in (100.5cm) wide.
£2,000–2,400 ⚒ TF

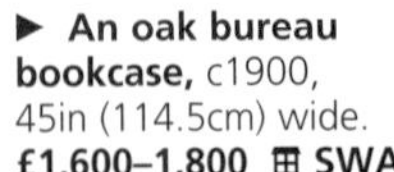

► **An oak bureau bookcase,** c1900, 45in (114.5cm) wide.
£1,600–1,800 ⊞ SWA

A Louis XVI provincial oak bookcase, the two grille doors with green fabric, set with gilt-brass paterae to the angles, Dutch, c1800, 69in (175.5cm) wide.
£1,500–1,800 ⚒ S(Am)

Boxes

A carved oak Bible box, mid-17thC, 16in (40.5cm) wide.
£700–800 ⊞ REF

A chestnut coaching box, with steel brackets, 19thC, 32in (81.5cm) wide.
£450–500 ⊞ MLL

◄ **An oak box,** the lid with carving, c1690, 12in (30.5cm) wide.
£200–230 ⊞ TRI

Buffets

A Louis XV provincial fruitwood buffet, the panelled doors enclosing shelves, French, mid-18thC, 57in (145cm) wide.
£2,750–3,000 SK

A walnut buffet, with marble top, French, mid-19thC, 47½in (120.5cm) wide.
£1,750–2,000 SIE

A cherrywood *buffet à deux corps*, French, c1830, 76in (193cm) high.
£2,700–3,000 TDS

► **A carved cherrywood *buffet à deux corps*,** with stained glass doors decorated with fleur-de-lys, French, c1890, 54in (137cm) wide.
£1,350–1,500 MLL

A cherrywood buffet, with steel locks and hinges, French, c1800, 51in (129.5cm) wide.
£1,900–2,200 GD

OAK & COUNTRY FURNITURE

Bureaux

An oak bureau, with a stepped fitted interior and a concealed well with secret compartment, early 18thC, 35in (89cm) wide.
£1,000–1,200 L&E

An oak bureau, the fall enclosing a stepped interior and a well, with later brass handles, mid-18thC, 36½in (92.5cm) wide.
£700–850 DN

Insurance values

Always insure your valuable antiques for the cost of replacing them with similar items, regardless of the original price paid. Both dealers and auctioneers can provide a valuation service for a fee.

◄ **A George III oak bureau,** the fall enclosing a later mahogany fitted interior, on later bun feet, 37in (94cm) wide.
£450–550 P(Ba)

A George III oak bureau, the fall enclosing a fitted interior, with later brass handles, 37in (94cm) wide.
£500–600 DN

An oak bureau, the fall enclosing an inlaid cupboard door with pilaster compartments, drawers and pigeonholes, late 18thC, 37in (94cm) wide.
£600–700 WW

Chairs

A carved oak panel-back *caqueteuse* armchair, the walnut scroll cresting with a winged cherub mask, the back panel carved with a stylized flowering vase flanked by a heraldic lion, c1600.
£9,000–11,000 ⚒ S

The form of this chair follows the general outline of the 16th-century French *caqueteuse* or *chaise de femme*, a lighter open-frame armchair typified by a trapezoidal seat that is wider in front with arms that follow the seat outwards and a tall, narrow panel back. This style of chair was introduced in Scotland (and later migrated to England) in the 16th century as a result of the close political links between the two countries. Where French *caqueteuses* are generally made of walnut and of a lighter construction, British examples are heavier and constructed in oak. The motif of a winged cherub mask is typically found on French Renaissance furniture and often encountered in the west of England.

A carved oak side chair, with scrolling top-rail and turned finials, over spiral-turned splats, 17thC.
£850–1,000 ⚒ P(EA)

A carved oak Yorkshire/Derbyshire side chair, c1680.
£650–750 ⊞ F&F

A pair of George I oak side chairs, with panelled backs, c1720.
£2,500–3,000 ⊞ PHA

◄ A yew and elm stick-back Windsor elbow chair, with a crinoline stretcher, possibly Nottinghamshire, early 18thC.
£350–420 ⚒ DN

A set of four Charles II carved oak side chairs, late 17thC.
£900–1,100 ⚒ S(O)

An oak open armchair, with a carved top panel and scroll flowerhead-carved cresting, late 17thC.
£1,000–1,200 ⚒ P(NW)

An oak elbow chair, c1720.
£550–660 ⊞ WELL

A carved oak side chair, late 17thC.
£300–340 ⊞ SuA

A set of four oak Yorkshire-style back stools, with two crescent-shaped cross splats, carved with scroll work, with turned pendant, 17thC and later.
£1,200–1,500 ⚒ AH

A black-painted armchair, the top-rail pierced with a heart, American, Milford/Fairfield, Connecticut area, mid-18thC.
£3,300–4,000 ⚒ SK(B)

◄ An oak Lincolnshire ladderback chair, with a split cane seat, 18thC.
£250–280 ⊞ TRI

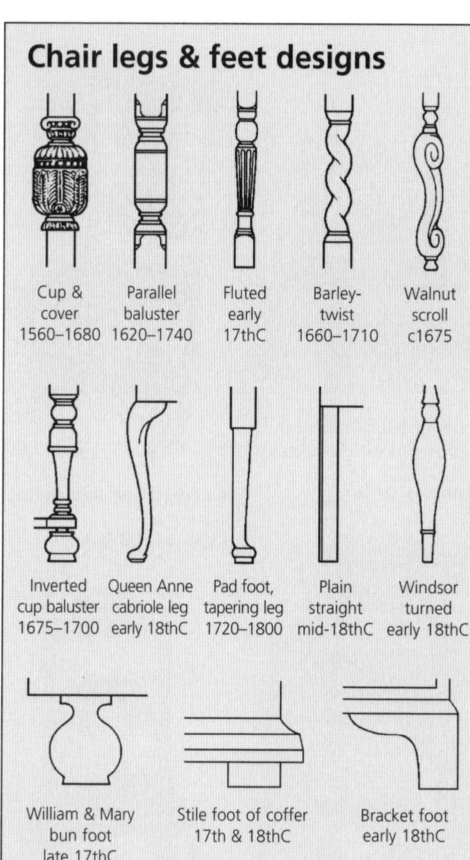

An elm chair, with a rush seat, late 18thC.
£270–300 ⊞ NoC

A painted beech ladderback chair, French, Provence, c1780.
£1,600–1,800 ⊞ RYA

An elm elbow chair, with a pierced splat back, over a blue Dralon drop-in seat, late 18thC.
£220–270 ⚒ WW

An oak elbow chair, with a high back, c1780.
£850–950 ⊞ WELL

A fruitwood elbow chair, possibly East Anglian, c1790.
£550–600 ⊞ WELL

A maple side chair, with a trapezoid rush seat, American, New England, c1790.
£350–420 ⚒ SK(B)

A set of four fruitwood chairs, French, 19thC.
£600–650 ⊞ SIE

A yew wood and elm Windsor elbow chair, with a crinoline stretcher, c1800.
£1,200–1,350 ⊞ REF

◄ **A fan-back Windsor side chair,** American, Pennsylvania, c1800.
£330–400 ⚒ SLN

► **A late George III fruitwood Lowland armchair,** with a padded seat, Scottish.
£620–750 ⚒ P(Ed)

A set of five George III elm provincial dining chairs.
£500–600 ⚒ Bon(W)

A set of six late George III elm dining chairs, with turned crest-rails, rail and sphere backs, and dished seats.
£1,400–1,700 ⚒ LFA

A set of eight yew wood and elm Thames Valley Windsor armchairs, including two open armchairs, with three pierced shaped splats centred by roundels, and crinoline stretchers.
£5,500–6,500 ⚒ P(NW)

Although the chairs are not stamped, they display the quality, distinctive design and constructional characteristics associated with the workshop of the Prior family, Uxbridge, Middlesex. This distinguished dynastic chair-making family made English Windsors for at least three generations from the second half of the 18th century until the third quarter of the 19th. Typically, name-stamped chairs by members of the Prior family are those by Robert Prior (1780–1835), and more rarely by his older brother John Jnr (1761–1846). Recent research has suggested that chairs which display Prior family characteristics without these brothers' identification stamps may have been produced by other family members who apparently did not stamp. Typical features comparable to recorded examples displayed here include the relatively costly use of the triple splats with roundel design made in two lengths to follow the back hoop.

An oak ladderback chair, French, c1820.
£150–165 ⊞ TDS

An ash and elm chair, 1820.
£700–800 ⊞ DJH

A set of six oak dining chairs, the backs with twin horizontal bars joined by three short turned spindles, over solid seats, Welsh, early 19thC.
£550–650 ⚒ PF

An ash and elm spindle-back chair, 19thC.
£165–185 ⊞ DJH

A decorated and yellow-painted chair, the top-rail with gilt stencil and painted fruit and foliate design, American, New England, c1825–30.
£250–300 ⚒ SK(B)

A beech and fruitwood cottage armchair, with an old iron brace repair, 19thC.
£160–200 ⚒ WW

Sets/pairs

Unless otherwise stated, any description which refers to 'a set' or 'a pair' includes a guide price for the entire set or the pair, even though the illustration may show only a single item.

A mahogany Yorkshire knitting chair, the solid seat with a side drawer, 19thC.
£1,200–1,400 ⚒ AH

An oak Windsor chair, 19thC.
£130–145 ⊞ NoC

◄ An ash Windsor chair, 19thC.
£850–950 ⊞ TRI

An ash and elm Windsor rocking chair, with a shaped and pierced splat, 19thC.
£875–1,000 ⚒ AH

OAK & COUNTRY FURNITURE

A fruitwood lambing chair, the solid seat with a side drawer, 19thC.
£625–750 ⚒ DD

A painted ash and pine shepherd's North Country wing armchair, with a drawer, c1840.
£6,750–7,500 ⊞ RYA

A yew wood Christmas tree high-back Lincolnshire Windsor armchair, c1850.
£2,000–2,250 ⊞ DJH

An elm slat-back rocking chair, c1860.
£250–275 ⊞ P&T

► **A harlequin set of six fruitwood chairs,** with rush seats, French, c1860.
£1,900–2,200 ⊞ DeG

A set of six ash ladderback chairs, including two elbow chairs, with rush seats, 19thC.
£1,500–1,800 ⚒ AH

A Victorian oak chair.
£110–125 ⊞ PSA

A set of four beech Oxfordshire Windsor side chairs, with fruitwood turned panel rails and elm seats, 19thC.
£420–500 ⚒ WW

► **A mixed timber country chair,** Irish, 1875.
£130–145 ⊞ Byl

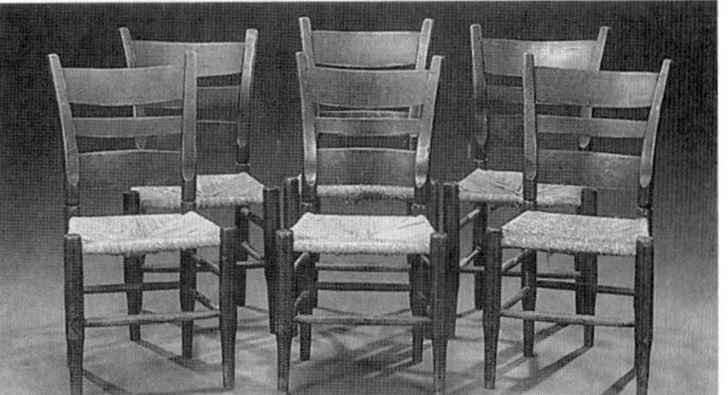

A set of six slat-back side chairs, with tapering cylinder-turned legs, American, 1850–1900.
£475–575 ⚒ SLN

A set of six oak chairs, with leather seats, the backs stamped in gold with a coat-of-arms and fleurs-de-lys, French, 19thC.
£1,100–1,200 ⊞ NGO

► **An oak Orkney chair,** Scottish, c1920.
£1,200–1,350 ⊞ SSW

A carved oak armchair, c1880.
£600–675 ⊞ MTay

A Shaker rocking chair, with a bar incised '6', tape seat replaced with rush, American, Mt Lebanon, New York, 1880–1900.
£350–420 ⚒ SK(B)

OAK & COUNTRY FURNITURE

Children's Chairs

A child's oak joined high chair, with a foliate-carved crest between stiles with pyramid finials, the centre panel carved with a stylized flower and the initials IB, the turned front legs with later foot supports, Lancashire, c1630.
£4,500–5,500 Mit
The pyramid finials are typical of Lancashire chairs.

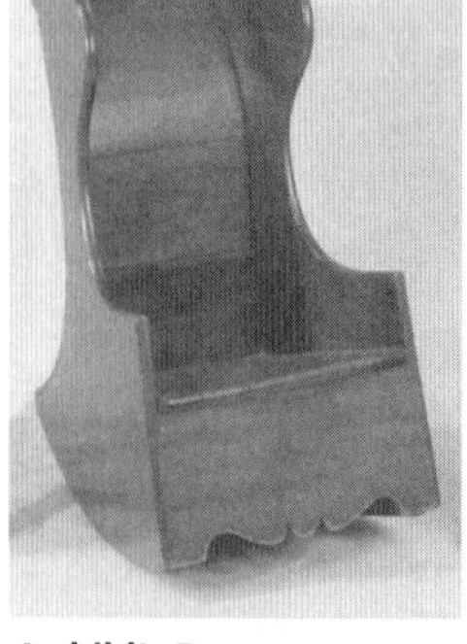

A child's Regency mahogany wing commode chair, with rocking supports.
£160–200 CGC

A child's chair, with a rush seat, French, Provence, c1900.
£350–400 MLL

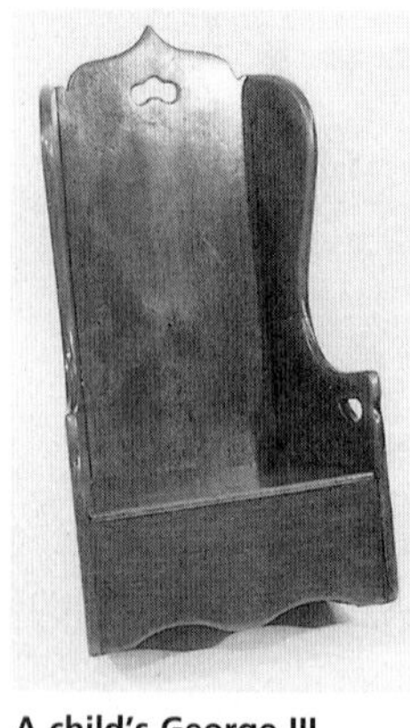

A child's George III mahogany rocking chair, the arched back with ogee crest and pierced handle.
£350–420 AH

A child's stick-back chair, with a solid burr-elm seat, c1800.
£220–245 MTay

A child's painted chair, with a rush seat, French, c1900.
£145–160 MLL

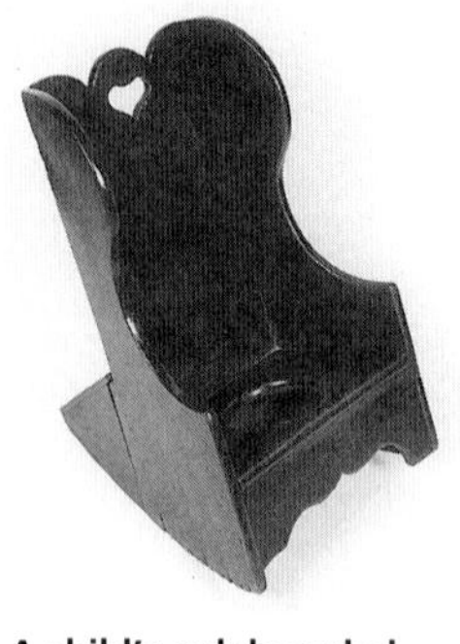

A child's oak boarded rocking chair, Welsh, c1760.
£800–880 CoA

A child's Regency correction chair, in green-painted beechwood and *faux* bamboo, c1810.
£450–500 F&F

◄ **A child's ash and elm comb-back chair,** with a solid wood seat, 19thC.
£200–240 LFA

A child's beech correction chair, early 19thC.
£630–700 DOA

► **A child's beech chair,** c1920.
£70–80 SMI

A child's black-painted armchair, with rush seat, American, New England, 18thC.
£320–380 SK(B)

A child's fruitwood correction chair, c1820.
£530–585 SSW

A child's ash and elm armchair, 19thC.
£440–485 DJH

Chests & Coffers

An oak clamp-front board and stile chest, the front carved with triple geometric chip-carved roundels, restored, 14thC, 44½in (113cm) wide.
£18,000–22,000 ⚒ S

Clamp-front chests are typical English chests of the 14th century. The joint was used for uniting wide boards and took the form of a long mortice-groove down the edge of one board into which a tenon fitted from the end of the other board. The majority of chests of this period have chamfered rails forming a grille tenoned to the stiles. Little medieval furniture of this date survives, and almost none is in private collections. The decoration of chip-carved geometric patterns corresponds to early Gothic architectural decoration, particularly contemporary window tracery such as can be seen in the windows of Magdeburg Cathedral, Germany (c1320) and Albi Cathedral, France (after 1276).

► **An oak coffer,** north of England, c1660, 50in (127cm) wide.
£1,600–1,800 ⊞ REF

◄ **An oak coffer,** the interior with an elm candle box, the diamond-panelled front with carved friezes, 17thC, 47in (119.5cm) wide.
£320–385 ⚒ WW

► **An oak chest,** the front relief-carved with trailing foliate scrolls and two urns flanking a central armorial cartouche depicting a crowned double-headed eagle, with iron side handles, Continental, 17thC, 65in (165cm) wide, on a later oak stand.
£750–900 ⚒ MCA

An oak coffer, the interior with an oak candle box, the front later carved with scrolls, 17thC, 43¼in (110cm) wide.
£400–500 ⚒ DN

An oak mule chest, 17thC, 54in (137cm) wide, on a later stand.
£1,300–1,450 ⊞ SuA

A Charles II oak coffer, with a *guilloche*-carved frieze and three cruciform panels divided by muntins carved with stylized foliage, the ends composed of two rectangular sunken panels below a band of *guilloche*, 60in (152.5cm) wide.
£650–800 ⚒ HYD

A carved oak coffer, c1670, 49in (124.5cm) wide.
£1,150–1,275 ⊞ WELL

An oak two-panelled blanket chest, with a channelled three-panel hinged lid, above a lunette-carved frieze with iron lockplate, base boards replaced, late 17thC, 47in (119.5cm) wide.
£400–500 ⚒ N

A child's oak coffer, late 17thC, 25in (63.5cm) wide.
£1,250–1,375 ⊞ CGA

◄ **An oak six-plank sword chest,** the front panel centred with the carved date '1675', the sides descending to shaped supports, 65in (165cm) wide.
£2,000–2,400 ⚒ P(NW)

A leather-covered domed coffer, decorated throughout with brass-studded stylized flowering plants, *guilloches*, scrolls and star motifs, with wrought-iron carrying handles, late 17thC, 38¼in (97cm) wide.
£400–500 ⚒ Bea(E)

► **A boarded oak coffer,** c1690, 34in (86.5cm) wide.
£675–750 ⊞ WELL

◄ **A joined oak coffer,** the interior with a lidded candle box, the front and sides with a nulled frieze, c1680, 37½in (95.5cm) wide.
£2,250–2,500 ⊞ JC

An oak three-panel blanket chest, with channelled front beneath an ovolo-moulded three-panel hinged lid, c1690, 50in (127cm) wide.
£350–420 ⚒ N

An oak blanket box, the front with three arched panels with leaf, flowerhead and scroll-carved detail, on later turned legs, 17thC, 65in (165cm) wide.
£450–550 ⚒ WL

An oak six-plank chest, with a hinged lid, 17thC, 52in (132cm) wide.
£600–700 ⚒ AH

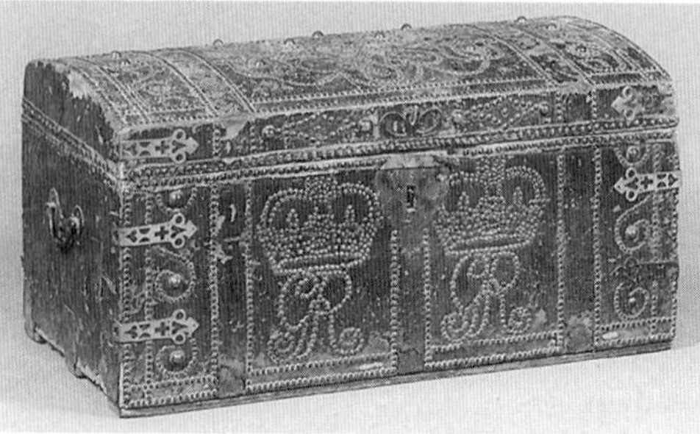

A brass-nailed and leather-bound chest, the hinged domed top above a front with the nailed monogram 'GR', 1700–25, 43in (109cm) wide.
£7,000–8,000 ⚒ S
This chest was used by Vizards, the leading firm of solicitors to store the papers for the famous divorce case between Queen Caroline and George IV. Vizard was appointed solicitor to Caroline sometime between 1811 and 1813. He appears to have first assisted her with her mother's will and then in the search for a central London house. Immediately upon the death of his father, George III, George IV moved to divorce his estranged wife thus depriving her of the title of Queen: it fell to Vizard to organize her defence. The proceedings occupied the House of Lords for most of October 1820 until, on 10 November, the Bill was withdrawn by the Government.

► **An oak mule chest,** with shaped fielded panels, c1730, 57in (145cm) wide.
£2,250–2,500 ⊞ DeG

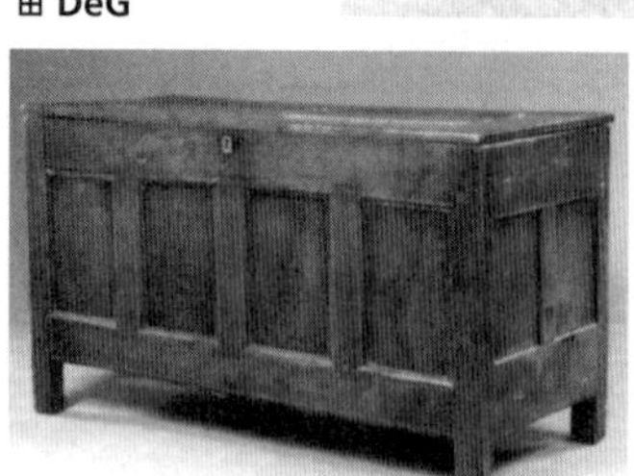

◄ **A George II oak bedding chest,** the four-panelled front with incised ownership initials and date 'S.F.1736', 49½in (125.5cm) wide.
£350–420 ⚒ PFK

► **An oak grain storage bin,** with domed lid, French, Normandy, early 19thC, 37½in (95.5cm) wide.
£600–700 ⊞ AMS
The lid of this coffer lifts off, and therefore the lockplate was for show only.

A George III oak and mahogany-crossbanded mule chest, modelled as a dresser base, the hinged lid over six dummy drawer fronts and three real base drawers flanked by quarter-reeded columns, faults, 62in (157.5cm) wide.
£400–500 ⚒ BR

Chests of Drawers

A Jacobean-style oak chest of drawers, with four graduated block-front drawers, 17thC, 36¼in (92cm) wide.
£800–950 TRL

An oak chest of drawers, with two short and three long drawers with later brass drop handles, re-lined in pine, re-backed, late 17thC, 36in (91.5cm) wide.
£650–800 WW

An oak chest of drawers, with four long drawers, each panelled as two short drawers, on later bracket feet, late 17thC, 35¾in (91cm) wide.
£2,300–2,750 DN

An oak chest of drawers, with three panelled drawers flanked by split turnings, on later bun feet, damaged, adapted, late 17thC, 38in (96.5cm) wide.
£800–950 DN

◄ **A Queen Anne oak chest of drawers,** with two short over three long drawers with double-D moulding, 37in (94cm) wide.
£3,500–4,000 ChC

An oak chest of drawers, in two parts, with four long geometric fielded panelled drawers, restored, early 18thC, 44in (112cm) wide.
£1,100–1,300 Bon(C)

◄ **An oak chest of drawers,** with three short moulded drawers, above two further short and two long graduated drawers, each line-inlaid, early 18thC, 34¾in (88.5cm) wide.
£1,300–1,600 P(NW)

An oak chest of drawers, in two parts, the top with a long twin-panelled drawer and panelled deep drawers, the lower section with two further conforming long drawers, late 17thC, 39¾in (101cm) wide.
£1,650–2,000 P(NW)

A panelled oak chest of drawers, in two parts, with two short and three long geometrically panelled drawers, on later bracket feet, c1700, 41in (104cm) wide.
£700–850 Bea(E)

An oak chest of drawers, with two short and two long drawers with brass handles, early 18thC, 35½in (90cm) wide.
£700–850 DN

Condition

The condition is absolutely vital when assessing the value of an antique. Damaged pieces on the whole appreciate much less than perfect examples. However a rare desirable piece may command a high price even when damaged.

An oak chest of drawers, with six short double-fronted drawers, with later brass handles, feet and crossbanding, early 18thC, 67½in (171.5cm) wide.
£6,000–7,200 ⚒ DN

An oak chest of drawers, the two central small drawers flanked by short deep drawers, above two long drawers, with a reeded frame, early 18thC, 34in (86.5cm) wide.
£1,300–1,600 ⚒ P(NW)

A George III oak chest of drawers, with two short and three long drawers, with later brass handles, 34¾in (88.5cm) wide.
£600–720 ⚒ DN

A George III oak chest of drawers, the two short and three long graduated cockbeaded drawers with brass swan-neck handles, 34½in (87.5cm) wide.
£500–600 ⚒ DA

A cherrywood Directoire commode, with a grey marble top, French, c1790, 50in (127cm) wide.
£3,200–3,500 ⊞ TDS

A George III oak chest of drawers, the two short and three long graduated mahogany crossbanded and moulded drawers with brass swan-neck handles, 38½in (98cm) wide.
£500–600 ⚒ DD

◄ **An oak secretaire chest-on-chest,** with inlaid cornice and frieze above three short and three long graduated drawers, the lower part fitted as a secretaire, with a brushing slide above three long graduated drawers, Welsh, early 19thC, 41in (104cm) wide.
£1,500–1,800 ⚒ PF

Cross Reference
See Colour Review (page 222)

► **An oak chest of drawers,** early 19thC, 43in (109cm) wide.
£675–750 ⊞ WV

◄ **A red-washed birch chest of drawers,** the four drawers with cockbeaded surrounds, American, New Hampshire area, c1810, 37¼in (94.5cm) wide.
£3,800–4,200 ⚒ SK(B)

Chests-on-Stands

A William and Mary oak chest-on-stand, c1700, 37in (94cm) wide.
£21,000–24,000 ⊞ DJH

An oak chest-on-stand, the two short and four long drawers with later brass handles and escutcheons, the base with a deep drawer, on replaced turned feet, 18thC, 38in (96.5cm) wide.
£1,750–2,000 ⚒ WW

◄ An oak chest-on-stand, the top with two short and three long graduated drawers, the reduced base with three pollarded oak-banded drawers, with later brass handles and escutcheons, on later bracket feet, 18thC, 36in (91.5cm) wide.
£1,100–1,300 ⚒ WW

An oak and brass-bound *bombé* chest-on-stand, the top with drawers to each side, above a kingwood-veneered velvet-lined slide above three long shaped drawers, with brass carrying handles to the sides, the stand on cabriole legs with carved knees and traces of inset brass line and dot inlay, probably German, early 18thC, 37¾in (96cm) wide.
£2,000–2,400 ⚒ Bon

► An oak chest-on-stand, with graduated drawers and a shaped apron, on cabriole legs, c1760, 38in (96.5cm) wide.
£5,200–5,750 ⊞ NMA

An oak chest-on-stand, the upper section with two short and three long graduated herringbone-crossbanded drawers, the base with a long single drawer, early 18thC, 42in (106.5cm) wide.
£3,000–3,600 ⚒ HYD

Clothes & Linen Presses

A George III oak linen press, the two panelled doors with reeded borders, the lower section with two short and two long drawers, 44½in (113cm) wide.
£1,300–1,500 ⚒ P(Ba)

► An oak clothes press, the ogee-arched panelled doors enclosing fixed shelves, the lower part with six cockbeaded graduated drawers, Welsh, mid-19thC, 55in (139.5cm) wide.
£1,000–1,200 ⚒ PF

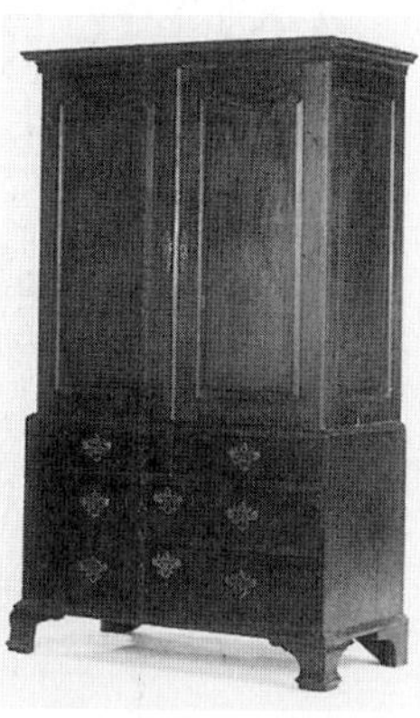

◄ An oak linen press, the fielded panel doors enclosing sliding trays, the lower section with two short and two long graduated drawers, 1750–75, 50½in (128.5cm) wide.
£1,100–1,300 ⚒ S(S)

An oak clothes press, the two ogee-arched panelled doors above three dummy drawers, two short and one long drawer, on reduced stile feet, 19thC, 53½in (136cm) wide.
£1,300–1,600 ⚒ Bea(E)

An oak linen press, with a fitted secretaire drawer, the frieze inlaid with holly and bog oak with a running comma pattern, Welsh, Cardiganshire, c1790, 44in (119cm) wide.
£7,000–8,000 ⊞ CoA

LOCATE THE SOURCE

The source of each illustration in Miller's can be found by checking the code letters below each caption with the Key to Illustrations, pages 794–800.

Cupboards

An oak Yorkshire press cupboard, the frieze centred by the date '1661', above two panelled marquetry-inlaid cupboard doors flanking a conforming central panel, the lower section with a pair of *guilloche*- and lozenge-carved cupboard doors, restored, mid-17thC and later, 59in (150cm) wide.
£1,650–2,000 P(NW)

A carved oak Westmorland press cupboard, c1660–80, 63in (160cm) wide.
£5,000–5,600 TRI

A chestnut provincial armoire, the later cornice above two foliate-carved panelled doors, the apron frieze with a scallop shell and foliage, French, 18thC, 33½in (85cm) wide.
£800–950 WW

► **An oak corner cupboard,** mid-18thC, 26in (66cm) wide.
£700–800 F&F

Miller's Compares

I. An oak press cupboard, the frieze carved with trailing grape and vine, inscribed 'TAT' and dated 1686, the upper section with panelled door cupboards, the lower section with two frieze drawers above panel cupboards, 66in (167.5cm) wide.
£3,800–4,500 HYD

II. An oak press cupboard, the upper section with a panelled door with a groove-moulded border, the lower section with two drawers and a central panelled cupboard, late 17thC, 48in (122cm) wide.
£1,800–2,200 HYD

Colour and patination are prime factors when considering the value of oak furniture. Originality of form and the lack of restoration are also of the utmost importance. Item I boasted a good colour and 'skin', while the surface of Item II had been marred by refinishing. The presence of an original carved date and initials gave an added boost to the value of Item I.

An oak *tridarn*, the recess with baluster-turned supports above two panelled doors flanking a panel with the initials 'H' over 'WG', the base with two panelled doors, alterations, later top tier and feet, 17thC, 54in (137cm) wide.
£2,300–2,750 DN

A Baroque ebony-inlaid oak and rosewood cupboard, with bolection moulded drawer above two doors with raised panels, Dutch, early 18thC, 61in (155cm) wide.
£2,000–2,400 SK

A painted oak and dry-scraped armoire, French, c1760, 71in (180.5cm) high.
£2,700–3,000 TDS
Dry-scraped means that the various paint layers are scraped back with a coin or similar to the first and original colour.

OAK & COUNTRY FURNITURE

Painted furniture

Originality of surface on a painted piece of furniture is extremely important – it can make an enormous difference to the value. For instance, a painted 18th-century commode with original blue paint will be worth three or four times as much as it would with replaced paint. When a piece has been repainted, the previous wear and tear marks are painted over, as are the areas where bits of paint have been chipped off. So for an indication of later paint, look for paint in the wear and tear marks because on an original paint surface there will be no paint in the indentation.

A chestnut armoire, French, Provençal, c1780, 63in (160cm) wide.
£3,250–3,600 ⊞ SSW

A George III burr-elm and walnut cabinet, with two doors enclosing shelves, above two sliding panels simulating drawers, 27½in (70cm) wide.
£1,350–1,500 ⚒ DN

An oak cupboard, the later shelves enclosed by two panelled doors, 18thC, 48in (122cm) wide.
£1,300–1,600 ⚒ LFA

◄ **An oak corner cupboard,** 18thC, 37in (94cm) wide.
£550–600 ⊞ WV

An oak hanging corner cupboard, inlaid with fruitwood, Shropshire, c1770, 20in (51cm) wide.
£1,400–1,600 ⊞ PHA

◄ **An oak glazed corner cabinet,** mahogany banded, c1790, 36in (91.5cm) wide.
£950–1,075 ⊞ F&F

A George III oak bowfronted corner cupboard, crossbanded with parquetry banding and stringing, the two doors with shell marquetry centres and batwing corners, 28½in (72.5cm) wide.
£700–850 ⚒ AH

► **A George III fruitwood hanging corner cupboard,** with shaped shelves, enclosed by one arched fielded panelled door inlaid with a star mask medallion within a chequer band, above one drawer inlaid with stars, flanked by reeded canted corners, 48in (122cm) high.
£700–850 ⚒ LFA

A George III oak food cupboard, Welsh Borders, 42in (106.5cm) wide.
£5,200–5,750 ⊞ NMA

A painted armoire, French, c1780, 49½in (125.5cm) wide.
£1,300–1,450 ⊞ SIE

An oak hanging corner cupboard, with an incised frieze, the interior with shaped shelves enclosed by a shell-inlaid panelled door, early 19thC, 32½in (82.5cm) wide.
£150–180 ⚒ WW

A cherrywood Rennes armoire, French, c1820, 49in (124.5cm) wide.
£1,750–2,000 ⊞ GD

A figured oak wall cabinet, c1870, 27in (68.5cm) wide.
£350–400 ⊞ GBr

A housekeeper's oak cupboard, c1800, 42in (106.5cm) wide.
£3,200–3,600 ⊞ REF

An oak hanging corner cabinet, early 19thC, 31½in (80cm) wide.
£550–650 ⚒ HOK

A cupboard, possibly cherrywood, French, c1840, 22in (56cm) wide.
£525–585 ⊞ SSW
This geometric style of carving is often found in the Auvergne region of France.

An oak glazed standing corner cupboard, Welsh, c1800, 33in (84cm) wide.
£5,000–6,000 ⊞ PHA

A red-stained poplar cupboard, the two glazed doors enclosing two shelves, the lower section with three short drawers over two cupboard doors, American, probably Pennsylvania, early 19thC, 48½in (123cm) wide.
£6,750–8,000 ⚒ SK(B)

A fruitwood armoire, with arched pediment and carved panelled doors, French, c1850, 52in (132cm) wide.
£5,500–6,200 ⊞ HA

◄ **A cherrywood *bonnetière*,** French, Normandy, 19thC, 35in (89cm) wide.
£1,150–1,300 ⊞ NGO

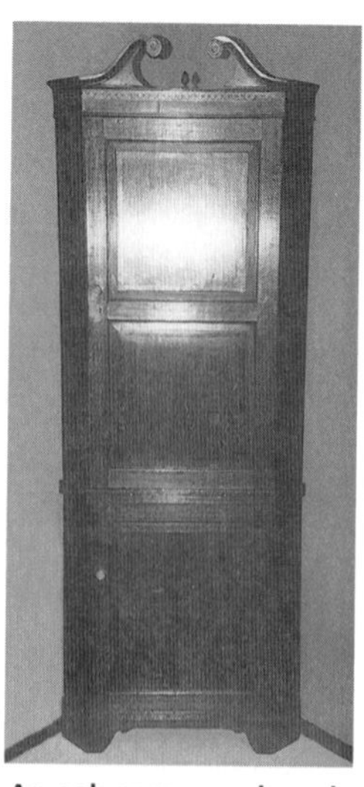
An oak corner cupboard, with inlaid frieze and mahogany banding to frieze and panels, restored feet, c1810, 83in (211cm) high.
£3,500–4,000 ⊞ TWh

A walnut Breton food cupboard, the three-tiered cornice with multiple baluster turnings and central wheel decoration, above a pair of similarly decorated panelled doors enclosing adjustable shelves over a lower section of two short drawers, French, early 19thC, 40in (101.5cm) wide.
£1,100–1,300 ⚒ HAM

An oak and walnut armoire, French, Normandy, c1860, 48in (122cm) wide.
£2,000–2,500 ⊞ ESA

OAK & COUNTRY FURNITURE

Dressers

An oak dresser, the base with four short drawers over two cupboards, c1730, 74in (188cm) wide.
£15,000–16,500 ⊞ REI
This piece retains its original rack and therefore is highly desirable.

An oak pot board dresser, c1780, 75in (190.5cm) wide.
£7,500–8,500 ⊞ F&F

A George III oak dresser, the two cupboard doors enclosing a shelf, 64in (162.5cm) wide.
£2,500–3,000 ⚒ S(O)

A George II oak dresser, 65in (165cm) wide.
£5,000–6,000 ⚒ SWO

A George III oak dresser, the superstructure with open and enclosed shelves with drawers below, the banded base with three frieze drawers, on square tapering legs with side stretchers, 79½in (202cm) wide.
£2,200–2,700 ⚒ HYD

A George III oak dresser, the base with three frieze drawers above three central drawers flanked by panelled doors, the corners with quarter columns, with associated plate rack back, 67in (170cm) wide.
£4,500–5,500 ⚒ HOLL

◄ **A George III oak dresser,** the two-shelf back with iron hooks, the base with three cockbeaded drawers, late 18thC, 59in (150cm) wide.
£2,500–3,000 ⚒ N

An oak dresser, with a three-tier delft rack and three short drawers to the frieze with brass handles and inlaid ivory lock escutcheons, 18thC, 62in (157.5cm) wide.
£3,500–4,200 ⚒ AG

A George III oak dresser, the base with three frieze drawers and arched pot board flanked by panelled cupboard doors, with associated delft rack, 68½in (174cm) wide.
£3,750–4,500 ⚒ AH

An oak dresser, with one long shelf and two smaller shelves flanked by two doors, the base with three mahogany-crossbanded drawers, reduced in height, late 18thC, 73¾in (187.5cm) wide.
£850–1,000 ⚒ DN

Miller's Compares

I. An oak dresser, the base with three drawers above three further drawers flanked by a cupboard on each side, 18thC, 60in (152.5cm) wide.
£3,400–4,000 ⚒ E

II. An oak dresser, the base with three drawers above two cupboard doors and a central dummy drawer panel, 1775–1825, 67in (170cm) wide.
£1,650–2,000 ⚒ E

The wide backboards of Item I point to it being somewhat earlier in date than Item II, and it is also of a more pleasing honey colour. The inlaid decoration to the edge of the base and the frieze of Item I are also appealing, but otherwise its attraction lies in its simplicity, whereas the rather fussy detail to the front of Item II and the mahogany moulded corners are not as universally popular.

An oak dresser, the rack with iron cup hooks, the lower section with three frieze drawers, late 18thC, 75in (190.5cm) wide.
£2,500–£3,000 ⚒ P(NW)

An oak dresser, the removable open rack with brass cup hooks, the base with three drawers over a galleried pot board, c1800, 55½in (141cm) wide.
£5,000–5,750 ⊞ JC

A George III oak dresser, the base with four central drawers flanked by a further drawer and cupboard, c1800, 67in (170cm) wide.
£3,000–3,500 ⚒ WL

An oak dresser, the four shelves flanked by bead-moulded cabinet doors enclosing shelves, the base with six cockbeaded drawers and two bead-moulded cupboard doors with bone-inlaid lozenge keyplates throughout, Welsh, early 19thC, 85in (216cm) wide.
£4,000–5,000 ⚒ PF

An oak dresser, the frieze inlaid with bandings and triangular panels, the three shelves with split-turned columns to sides, the breakfront base similarly inlaid, the centre with four short drawers with turned and spiral-reeded quarter columns to sides, flanked on each side by a drawer and cupboard, 1775–1825, 65in (165cm) wide.
£4,500–5,500 ⚒ CAG
This dresser is thought to originate from North Wales.

A Victorian oak dresser, the plate rack with two arched panelled doors, the base with three drawers, 75¾in (192.5cm) wide.
£900–1,100 ⚒ DN

◄ **A carved chestnut Breton dresser,** the two drawers over two doors with brass hinges and locks, French, c1830, 49in (124.5cm) wide.
£1,750–2,000 ⊞ GD

Low Dressers

An oak low dresser, with two drawers over two fielded panel doors flanking a central raised shielded panel, early 18thC, 56in (142cm) wide.
£5,250–6,000 ⊞ NMA

► **An oak mule chest,** converted to a dresser base, c1760, 54in (137cm) wide.
£2,800–3,200 ⊞ REF

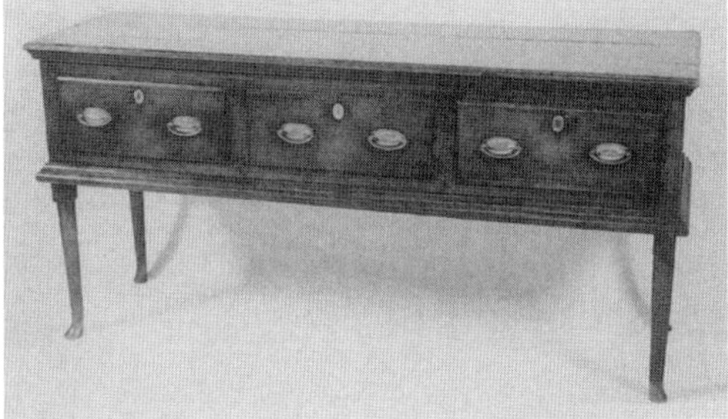

An oak dresser base, the frieze fitted with three drawers, 18thC, 70½in (179cm) wide.
£2,700–3,300 ⚒ GAK

► **An oak dresser base,** with two fielded panel doors flanking four central graduated drawers, later alterations to side panels, 18thC, 56in (142cm) wide.
£850–1,000 ⚒ HOLL

An oak low dresser, with fielded drawers over two doors, Welsh, c1750, 52in (132cm) wide.
£7,000–7,800 ⊞ CoA

An oak dresser base, with three cockbeaded drawers raised on square section legs with C-scroll brackets, originally with rack, 18thC, 63in (160cm) wide.
£1,750–2,000 ⚒ P(E)

A George III oak and mahogany-crossbanded dresser base, inlaid with stringing, with five drawers around the arched apron, faults, restored, 18thC, 65in (165cm) wide.
£2,500–3,000 ⚒ S(S)

A mid-Georgian Westmorland-style oak dresser base, the top with later stained deal back, the five central drawers flanked by two cupboards enclosing a sycamore shelf, 79in (200.5cm) wide.
£2,000–2,400 ⚒ PFK

An oak dresser base, the central bank of three drawers flanked by a fielded panelled cupboard door to either side, the whole with rounded corners, late 18thC, 71in (180.5cm) wide.
£2,300–2,750 ⚒ P(NW)

An oak dresser base, with five moulded drawers around a central arched apron, 1775–1825, 60in (152.5cm) wide.
£1,700–2,000 ⚒ P(NW)

Lowboys

A George II oak lowboy, with one shallow and two deep drawers, on cabriole legs with carved knees and claw-and-ball feet, with later legs, mid-18thC, 31in (78.5cm) wide
£500–600 ⚒ N

A George III oak lowboy, with a shaped apron, crossbanded in walnut, c1760, 35in (89cm) wide.
£5,500–6,500 ⊞ PHA

A fruitwood lowboy, with three frieze drawers, restored, mid-18thC, 29½ins (75cm) wide.
£2,000–2,400 ⚒ Bon(C)

An oak lowboy, with a shallow drawer flanked on either side by a deep drawer, 18thC, 32in (81.5cm) wide.
£900–1,100 ⚒ AH

Marks of authenticity

When buying a piece of furniture always check the hidden surfaces. Wood oxidizes over time, which means that with exposure to the air the surface becomes darker. This oxidization occurs at different rates depending on how close a piece of wood is to another. In other words, the discolouration to the underside of a table will be more pronounced where the surface is open to the air, but the underside – above a drawer, say – will discolour much more slowly, leaving a paler imprint of the drawer on the underside of the table. This is often a good way of determining whether a top belongs to its base.

OAK & COUNTRY FURNITURE

Racks & Shelves

An oak wall hanging delft rack, the cornice with a fret-cut wave patterned frieze above three grooved shelves with shaped sides, fret-cut aprons and refraining bars, c1760, 54¼in (138cm) wide.
£3,200–3,500 ⊞ JC

A set of oak waterfall hanging shelves, c1820, 19in (48.5cm) wide.
£270–300 ⊞ F&F

A set of hanging shelves, pierced and with original cream paint, c1810, 24in (61cm) wide.
£1,600–1,800 ⊞ DeG

Settles & Settees

An elm settle, with fielded panels, c1750, 54½in (138.5cm) wide.
£4,000–4,500 ⊞ DeG

An oak settle, the back with four ogee fielded panels, the seat now panelled, mid-18thC, 73in (185.5cm) wide.
£800–950 AH

An oak and burr-elm bacon settle, with two apron drawers, reduced in height, 1775–1800, 50½in (128.5cm) wide.
£2,000–2,400 S(S)

◄ **A George III elm wing-back box-seat settle,** with two central drawers flanked by two panel doors to the base, 63in (160cm) wide.
£1,400–1,700 S(S)

An oak settle, with one scroll and one downswept solid arm and deep-buttoned squab seat, early 19thC, 74¾in (190cm) wide.
£600–720 DD

► **A Gothic revival oak box-seat settle,** carved with knights, kings and queens, late 19thC, 44in (112cm) wide.
£3,200–3,500 ⊞ REF

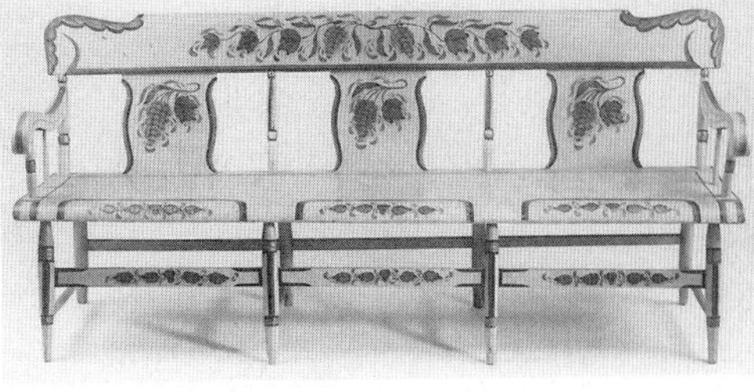

A painted and decorated settee, with original yellow paint, olive green fruit and foliate decoration and black and green striping, American, c1825–35, 78½in (199.5cm) wide.
£2,750–3,000 SK(B)

Stands

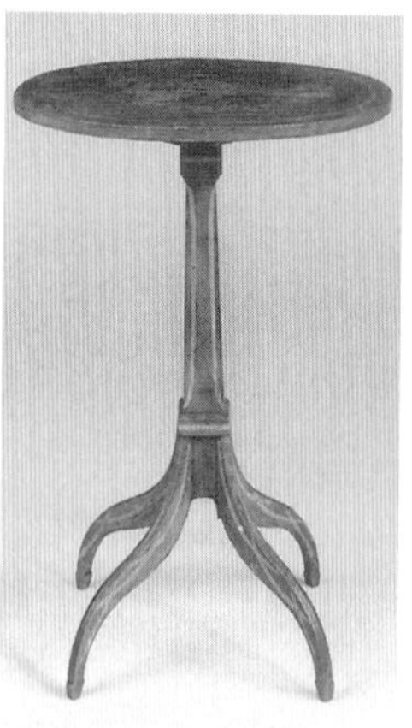

A painted maple candle stand, with light red paint and white striping, American, 19thC, 29½in (75cm) high.
£2,500–2,750 ⚒ SK(B)

A candle stand, in various woods, with a burr-walnut top, French, early 19thC, 26¾in (68cm) high.
£340–375 ⊞ AMS

► **A sycamore book stand,** French, c1880, 21in (53.5cm) wide.
£160–175 ⊞ AL

► **A birch stand,** with a single drawer and four turned legs, American, New England, c1815–25, 19½in (49.5cm) wide.
£600–700 ⚒ SK(B)

A thorn and elm candle stand, c1850, 9in (23cm) wide.
£250–275 ⊞ SEA

Stools

An oak joint stool, with a carved frieze, 17thC, 18in (45.5cm) wide.
£2,200–2,500 ⊞ SuA

A lacemaker's oak stool, the top with one central candle holder surrounded by four holes, 18thC, 10½in (26.5cm) wide.
£180–220 ⚒ TMA

► **An elm stool,** early 19thC, 18in (45.5cm) high.
£160–175 ⊞ F&F

An oak joint stool, the seat upholstered in contemporary *gros point* needlework, late 17thC, 30in (76cm) wide.
£1,700–2,000 ⚒ S

LOCATE THE SOURCE
The source of each illustration in Miller's can be found by checking the code letters below each caption with the Key to Illustrations, pages 794–800.

An oak joint stool, the chip-carved apron with a geometric band, 17thC, 17½in (44.5cm) wide.
£1,350–1,600 ⚒ LFA

A set of six elm stools, c1840, 23in (58.5cm) high.
£600–700 ⊞ SSW

► **A cherrywood stool,** French, c1860, 17in (43cm) high.
£130–145 ⊞ TDS

An oak stool, 18thC, 19in (48.5cm) wide.
£280–320 ⊞ CGA

A West Country ash stool, early 19thC, 16in (40.5cm) wide.
£600–675 ⊞ SEA

Tables

An oak counter table, the associated sliding top above a triple *parchemin*-carved front opposed by three plain panels with linenfold-carved sides, the base with a central rear rising panel enclosing a secret compartment, 16thC, 38½in (98cm) wide.
£13,000–16,000 S

The counter table or counter board is the term used to describe a table which originally had a top marked out with a series of lines and squares representing values and units, which could be used for calculating accounts. It is likely to have stood in the medieval counting house, an office which was attached to the shop or house of most merchants and rich men. It is believed that the earliest counter tables were fitted with a loose top, which slid backwards on two bearers, so that after being counted the coins could be swept into the recess below. As with this piece, few examples retain their original sliding lids and most existing examples now have later hinged tops. From the mid-15th century, cloths (usually green) which bore horizontal lines were sometimes placed over tables to perform the same function.

A cherrywood table, with shaped frieze, American, Long Island or Connecticut, late 18thC, 43¾in (111cm) wide.
£2,500–2,750 SK(B)

An oak side table, with a single drawer, c1680, 28in (71cm) wide.
£2,400–2,650 DJH

An oak gateleg table, supported on bobbin-turned and block-carved legs, with plain and baluster-turned stretcher rails, early 18thC, 60in (152.5cm) wide.
£800–950 TMA

An oak farmhouse serving table, the frieze drawer with brass knob handles, early 19thC, 44½in (113cm) wide.
£500–600 WW

◄ **An oak pedestal table,** the tilt-top on a birdcage and ring-turned, tapered cannon barrel column, on a tripod base and pad feet, late 18thC, 33½in (85cm) wide.
£600–720 AAR

An oak table, the square chamfer legs joined by square stretchers, peg construction, c1700, 19¾in (50cm) wide.
£2,500–2,800 DeG

An oak side table, with a single frieze, early 18thC, 34in (86.5cm) wide.
£600–700 DMC

◄ **An oak centre table,** 18thC, 27in (68.5cm) wide.
£2,500–2,850 NMA

An oak side table, with one long drawer over a central short and two deep drawers, 18thC, 71in (180.5cm) wide.
£900–1,100 P(NW)

A Federal cherrywood drop-leaf table, American, New England, 1800–10, 36in (91.5cm) wide.
£1,200–1,400 SK(B)

A fruitwood table, the top with cleated ends above a drawer to one side, French, early 19thC, 80in (203cm) wide.
£800–950 ⚒ DN

A cherrywood Normandy draw-leaf dining table, French, c1820, 120in (305cm) extended.
£7,500–8,500 ⊞ RYA

A beech farmhouse table, the top made of three wide planks, French, c1830, 105in (266.5cm) wide.
£6,750–7,500 ⊞ DeG

Cross Reference
See Colour Review (page 227)

◄ **A cherrywood side table,** with full length single drawer, French, c1830, 39in (99cm) wide.
£1,650–1,850 ⊞ DeG

A chestnut and oak kitchen table, French, mid-19thC, 52in (132cm) wide.
£400–440 ⊞ AMS

Farm tables

Farm tables are usually constructed out of good or interesting country timbers – cherry, apple, walnut, oak, chestnut, ash and elm are among the favourites. Invariably they are of mortice-and-tenon peg construction. Usually the earlier the table the wider and therefore the fewer the planks, which are sometimes cleated on the ends. The planks are often pegged together with blind tenons with the cleats morticed and tenoned and then pegged into the ends of the planks. Colour is crucial to the value, the better the colour, the higher the price.

► **A fruitwood library drum table,** French, c1840, 37in (94cm) diam.
£2,800–3,200 ⊞ RYA

◄ **An oak table,** with slides, French, c1870, 91in (231cm) wide.
£1,800–2,000 ⊞ MLL

Pine Furniture

Bookcases

A pine graduated and stepped bookcase, with a panelled back, c1800, 48in (122cm) wide.
£450–550 ⊞ TPC

◄ **A pine bookcase cupboard,** c1890, 36½in (92.5cm) wide.
£430–480 ⊞ HRQ

A pine bookcase cupboard, c1880, 45in (114.5cm) wide.
£425–475 ⊞ POT

A Victorian pine open bookcase, with a balustraded gallery, 41in (104cm) wide.
£400–500 ⊞ TPC

◄ **A pine corner bookcase,** with adjustable shelves and fluted uprights, c1880, 40in (101.5cm) high.
£425–475 ⊞ POT

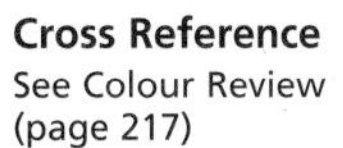

Cross Reference
See Colour Review (page 217)

Boxes

A polychrome-painted and ink-decorated pine box, the lid interior inscribed with name and date, the exterior decorated with country landscape scenes, a basket of flowers and a bowl of fruit, American, 1827, 8in (20.5cm) wide.
£4,200–5,000 ⚒ SK(B)

A pine box, c1860, 42in (106.5cm) wide.
£270–300 ⊞ AL

A pine box, with drawers, c1880, 29in (73.5cm) wide.
£225–250 ⊞ AL

A Victorian pine box, 40in (101.5cm) wide.
£165–185 ⊞ WV

A pine box, c1880, 38in (96.5cm) wide.
£150–165 ⊞ AL

A pine box, 29in (73.5cm) wide.
£145–160 ⊞ WV

► **A pine box,** with iron handles, c1880, 45in (114.5cm) wide.
£220–250 ⊞ AL

Items in the Pine Furniture section have been arranged in date order within each sub-section.

Chairs

A pine and wicker Orkney armchair, with a wickered back and solid seat and drawer below, 19thC.
£320–380 ⚒ Bon(C)

Miller's is a price GUIDE not a price LIST

A pine Caithness chair, the solid seat with a separate rail, 19thC.
£600–700 ⚒ P(Ed)

Caithness chairs are a distinctive Scottish variant with specific features. The back usually contains a panel of turned or whittled banisters and seat rails with rounded-off ends which are tenoned into continuous back stiles and legs. The seat is made up of a narrow board and circular section rails.

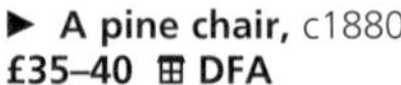

▶ **A pine chair,** c1880.
£35–40 ⊞ DFA

A pine and ash primitive bow-back crofter's chair, with original painted surface, c1830.
£1,800–2,000 ⊞ RYA

▶ **A pine chair,** with original paint, c1890.
£25–30 ⊞ DFA

◀ **A stained pine Orkney chair,** by David Munro Kirkness, late 19thC.
£1,300–1,600 ⚒ P(Ed)

The Orkney chair of today owes its form to the chairs made by the Scottish craftsman David Kirkness (1854–1936). He established himself as a wright and undertaker and set about making improvements on the oat-straw stool that was a common local seating type, particularly on the far northern isles of Westray and Papa Westray. Kirkness opened his workshop in Kirkwall in 1876, but continued to have the oat-straw chair backs made by outworkers on the more remote islands. His workmen made frames which were eventually perfected as a range of four types: child's, lady's, standard and canopied. By replacing the hard board seats with woven sea grass ones and refining the shape of the frame he made the Orkney chair into an aesthetically pleasing and comfortable piece of furniture that could be introduced with ease into the Scottish middle-class drawing room. It appealed particularly to those with an Arts and Crafts sensibility. The workshop continued after the death of Kirkness until it was taken over by the Orcadian Reynold Eunson in 1956.

Chests & Coffers

A painted pine chest, with original blue-grey paint, American, Massachusetts, 1675–1710, 40in (101.5cm) wide.
£3,500–4,000 ⚒ SK(B)

A Georgian pine blanket chest, the interior with a candle box, 32in (81.5cm) wide.
£145–160 ⊞ P&T

A child's red-painted pine and poplar mule chest, American, New England, early 19thC, 17½in (44.5cm) wide.
£1,000–1,200 ⚒ SK(B)

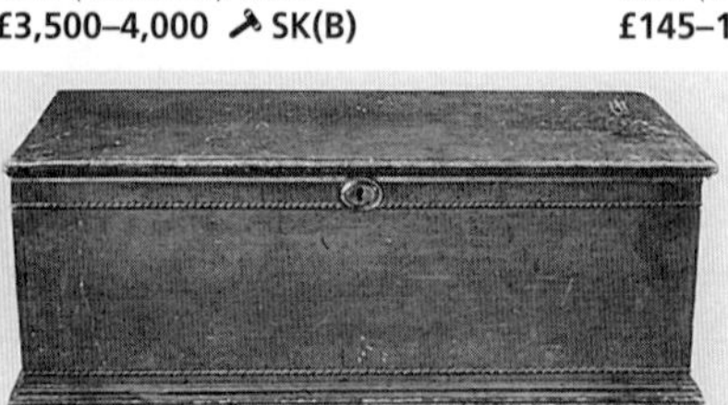

▶ **A Georgian pine mule chest,** 29in (73.5cm) wide.
£350–400 ⊞ TPC

◀ **A blue-painted pine chest,** American, New England, 1775–1800, 44¼in (112.5cm) wide.
£2,500–3,000 ⚒ SK(B)

► **A pine chest,** mid-19thC, 48½in (123cm) wide.
£180–200 ⊞ HRQ

A grain-painted pine chest, the interior with a lidded candle box, the red and gold paint simulating mahogany, one foot repaired, American, probably Maine, 1820–30, 43¼in (112.5cm) wide.
£2,000–2,400 ⚒ SK(B)

A pine blanket box, with original handles and hinges, c1870, 38in (96.5cm) wide.
£115–130 ⊞ POT

A pine blanket box, with a side drawer, c1880, 34½in (87.5cm) wide.
£200–220 ⊞ HRQ

A pine tool chest, c1900, 39in (99cm) wide.
£160–175 ⊞ P&T

A pine sea chest, with a tray and rope handles, c1880, 34in (86.5cm) wide.
£130–145 ⊞ AL

◄ **A late Victorian pine chest,** 39in (99cm) wide.
£225–275 ⊞ TPC

Chests & Banks of Drawers

PINE FURNITURE

A painted pine commode, French, c1780, 55in (139.5cm) wide.
£2,350–2,600 ⊞ SSW

A Regency pine chest of drawers, the six graduated drawers with inset knobs, 51in (129.5cm) wide.
£500–600 ⊞ TPC

A red-painted pine mule chest, with two dummy drawers and two real drawers, American, New England, 18thC, 38in (96.5cm) wide.
£730–900 ⚒ SLN

A pine chest of four drawers, c1840, 35½in (90cm) wide.
£280–320 ⊞ HRQ

◄ **A pine chest of drawers,** with two short over two long drawers and Birmingham-stamped brass locks, c1840, 36in (91.5cm) wide.
£280–320 ⊞ HRQ

A Regency pine chest of drawers, with two short over three long drawers, with original scumble paint and line decoration in blue, 42in (106.5cm) wide.
£600–700 ⊞ TPC

A pine bank of 12 drawers, c1820, 36in (91.5cm) wide.
£450–550 ⊞ TPC

An early Victorian pine chest of drawers, 43in (109cm) wide.
£500–600 ⊞ TPC

top. A Victorian stained pine bank of seed drawers, 41in (104cm) wide.
£800–950
bottom. A Victorian stained pine bank of seed drawers, 71½in (181.5cm) wide.
£300–360 ⚒ CGC

A pine chest of drawers, with two short over two long panelled drawers, c1860, 34in (86.5cm) wide.
£250–280 ⊞ P&T

A pine chest of drawers, with two short over three long drawers, 1860–80, 49in (124.5cm) wide.
£280–320 ⊞ HOA

A Victorian pine chest of drawers, with original mother-of-pearl inlaid knobs, 41in (104cm) wide.
£400–500 ⊞ TPC

A Victorian pine chest of drawers, with two short over three long drawers, c1860, 36in (91.5cm) wide.
£450–550 ⊞ TPC

A pine chest of drawers, with two short over three long drawers, on bracket feet, 19thC, 41in (104cm) wide.
£320–350 ⊞ HOA

◄ **A Victorian pine chest of drawers,** 21in (53.5cm) wide.
£400–500 ⊞ TPC

► **A pine chest of drawers,** with two short over two long drawers, c1880, 33in (84cm) wide.
£400–435 ⊞ AL

◄ **A pitch pine chest of drawers,** with two short over two long drawers, c1875, 38in (96.5cm) wide.
£200–240 ⊞ Byl

A pine chest of drawers, Scottish, 19thC, 47in (119.5cm) wide.
£400–450 ⊞ HOA

A set of pine drawers, with six drawers below a shelf, c1880, 24in (61cm) wide.
£130–145 ⊞ AL

A Victorian pine chest of drawers, 41in (104cm) wide.
£265–300 ⊞ WV

A pine chest of drawers, with two short over two long drawers, on bun feet, c1880, 30in (76cm) wide.
£400–450 ⊞ TPC

A printer's-type chest of drawers, with 11 drawers and original green paint, c1880, 53in (134.5cm) wide.
£450–550 ⊞ TPC

A Victorian pine chest of drawers, 37in (94cm) wide.
£300–330 ⊞ WV

A pine chest of drawers, with two short over two long drawers, with porcelain knobs, c1880, 36in 89cm) wide.
£320–350 ⊞ AL

A Victorian pine chest of drawers, 36in (91.5cm) wide.
£300–330 ⊞ WV

◀ **A pine set of drawers,** c1890, 36in (91.5cm) wide.
£180–200 ⊞ AL

▶ **A pine counter,** with a panelled back and 12 drawers, later paint, 19thC, 52in (132cm) wide.
£1,500–1,650 ⊞ MLL

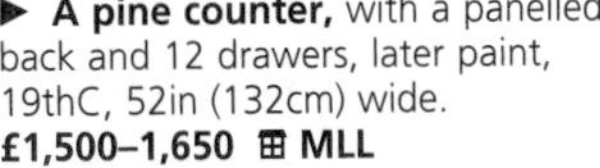

A pine set of drawers, c1880, 28in (71cm) wide.
£180–200 ⊞ AL

A Victorian painted pine chest of drawers, with two short and three long graduated drawers with glass handles, 43in (109cm) wide.
£250–300 ⚒ DA

A pine chest of drawers, with two short over three long drawers, 19thC, 49in (124.5cm) wide.
£375–425 ⊞ HOA

A pine chest of drawers, with two short over three long drawers, with beech knobs, c1880, 39in (99cm) wide.
£350–400 ⊞ AL

Cupboards

A George III stained pine standing corner cupboard, the scroll pediment above a blind fret frieze and astragal-glazed door, faults, restored, 36¼in (92cm) wide.
£1,000–1,100 S(S)

A pine cupboard, the two upper doors enclosing three shelves, with an additional cupboard door to the right and two cupboard doors below, with traces of blue paint, American, probably New England, late 18thC, 54½in (138.5cm) wide.
£3,200–3,800 SK(B)

► **A Regency pine cupboard,** with adjustable shelved interior, 49in (124.5cm) wide.
£600–700 TPC

A Georgian pine panelled cupboard, with two doors, 32in (81.5cm) wide.
£800–900 TPC

A polychrome and *faux-marbre* cabinet, the two doors inset with a raised and shaped panel, flanked to either side by a panelled pilaster, north Italian, 1775–1800, 63½in (161.5cm) wide.
£5,250–6,250 NOA

A pine cupboard, with 10 doors, c1800, 93in (236cm) wide.
£1,500–1,800 TPC

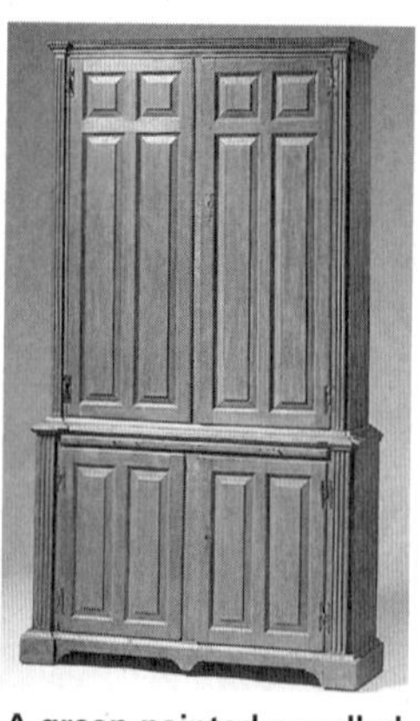

A green-painted panelled pine cupboard, the upper section with two hinged doors enclosing six tiers of red-painted valanced pigeonholes, the lower section with a slide over hinged doors enclosing an unpainted shelf, altered, American, New England, 18thC, 72in (183cm) wide.
£7,000–8,500 S(NY)

A pine corner cupboard, the two doors with fielded panels enclosing three shaped shelves above a single cupboard, replaced iron hinges, American, New England, late 18thC, 47in (119.5cm) wide.
£950–1,150 SK(B)

► **A pine corner cupboard,** with shaped shelves, c1800, 49in (124.5cm) wide.
£1,350–1,500 HRQ

A Regency cupboard, the four doors enclosing a shelved interior, 53in (134.5cm) wide.
£1,200–1,500 ⊞ TPC

A pine corner cupboard, early 19thC, 40in (101.5cm) wide.
£675–750 ⊞ HOA

A pine panelled corner cupboard, American, c1810, 46½in (118cm) wide.
£7,000–8,500 ⚒ S(NY)

A pitch pine cupboard, Irish, Woodford, Co Galway, c1820, 64in (162.5cm) wide.
£1,800–2,000 ⊞ HON

A painted pine cupboard, Irish, c1820, 59in (150cm) wide.
£1,100–1,300 ⊞ HON

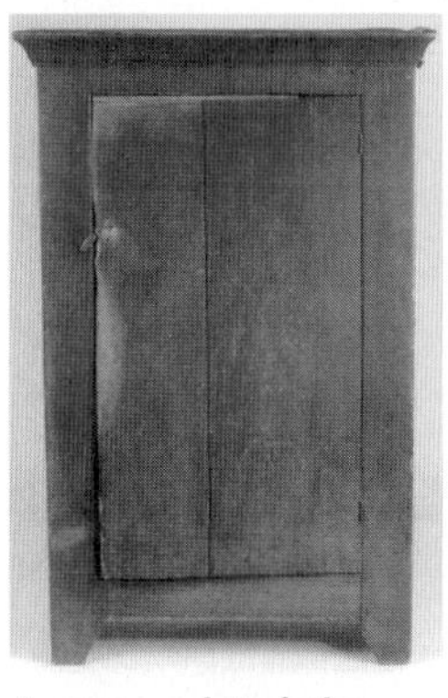

A green-painted pine cupboard, the door enclosing an interior with five shelves, American, New England or New York State, early 19thC, 39in (99cm) wide.
£1,800–2,200 ⚒ SK(B)

A pine housekeeper's cupboard, with original rosewood knobs, c1840, 90in (228.5cm) wide.
£2,250–2,500 ⊞ HRQ

A set of painted pine lockers, c1820, 43in (109cm) wide.
£1,800–2,000 ⊞ SSW

An early Victorian pine cupboard, with two doors, 43in (109cm) wide.
£450–500 ⊞ P&T

A pine meat safe, Irish, c1840, 25in (63.5cm) wide.
£300–360 ⊞ TPC

An upper section of a pine cheese press, Irish, c1840, 54in (137cm) wide.
£200–235 ⊞ DFA

◄ **A Victorian pine miniature display cabinet,** the glazed doors enclosing two shelves, on turned supports with stellar-carved backplate, the lower section with two cupboard doors with applied cut-corner mouldings, 23¾in (60cm) wide.
£500–600 ⚒ P(NW)

A pine cupboard, with four doors, Irish, c1875, 52in (132cm) wide.
£650–800 ⊞ Byl

A pine cupboard, c1880, 48½in (123cm) wide.
£720–800 ⊞ AL

A pine cupboard, with mesh doors, c1880, 73in (185.5cm) wide.
£350–400 ⊞ DFA

A pine cupboard, with two doors above a drawer, Irish, c1880, 46in (117cm) wide.
£330–400 ⊞ Byl

A pine pot cupboard, with a porcelain knob, c1880, 15in (38cm) wide.
£160–175 ⊞ AL

A pine pot cupboard, c1880, 15in (38cm) wide.
£180–200 ⊞ AL

A pine pot cupboard, c1880, 15¾in (40cm) wide.
£150–170 ⊞ AL

Items in the Pine Furniture section have been arranged in date order within each sub-section.

A pine food cupboard, c1890, 42½in (108cm) wide.
£550–600 ⊞ HRQ

A Victorian pine pot cupboard, 14in (35.5cm) wide.
£150–165 ⊞ WV

◄ **A pine cupboard,** with five doors, c1890, 64in (162.5cm) wide.
£600–665 ⊞ AL

A pine cupboard, c1890, 20in (51cm) wide.
£100–110 ⊞ HRQ

A pine cupboard, with two doors, c1890, 29in (73.5cm) wide.
£350–400 ⊞ AL

A pine cupboard, c1890, 41¼in (105cm) wide.
£385–430 ⊞ HRQ

A pine cupboard, with sliding shelves, c1900, 39½in (100.5cm) wide.
£270–300 ⊞ HRQ

A pine double cupboard, with two shelves below, c1890, 33in (84cm) wide.
£240–265 ⊞ AL

► **A pine pot cupboard,** c1890, 15in (38cm) wide.
£120–135 ⊞ AL

A pine pot cupboard, Dutch, c1900, 19in (48.5cm) wide.
£115–130 ⊞ P&T

An Edwardian pine cupboard, with two doors and internal drawers, 42in (106.5cm) wide.
£500–550 ⊞ P&T

Desks

A pine panelled desk, the hinged lid enclosing eight compartments above four small drawers and an open well over a single drawer, with two raised panel doors enclosing a single shelved interior, late 19thC graining to one side, American, New England, 1775–1825, 38½in (98cm) wide.
£1,500–1,800 ⚒ SK(B)

An early Victorian pine writing desk, 47in (119.5cm) wide.
£625–700 ⊞ P&T

A pine kneehole desk, with herring-bone panelling and brushing slide, French, c1890, 48in (122cm) wide.
£800–1,000 ⊞ TPC

◄ **A pine kneehole desk,** Irish, c1860, 42in (106.5cm) wide.
£430–480 ⊞ P&T

A schoolmaster's blue-painted pine desk, the hinged top enclosing a single shaped shelf over open compartments, original paint, American, Long Island, c1840–60, 27¾in (70.5cm) wide.
£1,100–1,200 ⚒ SK(B)

A pine desk, c1880, 51in (129.5cm) wide.
£525–585 ⊞ AL

Dressers

A Georgian pine Cornish dresser, with wood-grain effect paint, 42in (106.5cm) wide.
£1,200–1,500 ⊞ BrH

A Georgian astragal-glazed dresser, with four doors, 99in wide (251.5cm) wide.
£3,500–4,000 ⊞ TPC

A George III pine dresser, with two plate shelves above three frieze drawers, with twin doors flanking a central bank of three further drawers, 67¼in (171cm) wide.
£750–960 ⚒ Bri

► **A pine dresser,** early 19thC, 74in (188cm) wide.
£2,250–2,500 ⊞ WV

◄ **A pine dog-kennel dresser,** with wide boarded rack, c1860, 102in (259cm) wide.
£3,500–3,850 ⊞ POT

A pine dresser, 19thC, 91in (231cm) wide.
£1,600–1,800 ⊞ TPC

► **A pine dresser,** Irish, c1865, 50in (127cm) wide.
£550–650 ⊞ Byl

A painted pine dresser, Irish, 19thC, 86in (218.5cm) wide.
£750–850 ⊞ HOA

► **A Victorian pine dresser,** with replacement plate rack, 58¼in (148cm) wide.
£765–850 ⊞ HRQ

A pine open-rack dog kennel dresser, unrestored, c1870, 60in (152.5cm) wide.
£1,500–1,675 ⊞ POT

A pine dresser, with carved fan and rose decoration, Irish, 19thC, 87in (221cm) wide.
£2,250–2,750 ⊞ TPC

A pine chicken coop dresser, Irish, 19thC, 86in (218.5cm) wide.
£850–950 ⊞ HOA

A pine dresser, the upper section with two glazed doors, Irish, c1875, 44in (112cm) wide.
£400–500 ⊞ Byl

A pine dresser, Irish, c1875, 49in (124.5cm) wide.
£350–420 ⊞ Byl

A pine dresser, Romanian, c1875, 49in (124.5cm) wide.
£400–500 ⊞ Byl

A pine dog kennel dresser, married, c1880, 86in (218.5cm) wide.
£1,575–1,750 ⊞ POT

► **A pine dresser,** with two glazed doors, Irish, 19thC, 62½in (159cm) wide.
£1,150–1,300 ⊞ HRQ

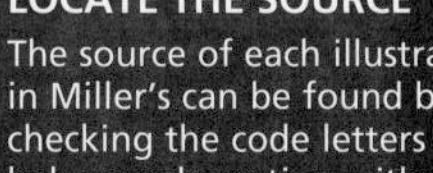

LOCATE THE SOURCE

The source of each illustration in Miller's can be found by checking the code letters below each caption with the Key to Illustrations, pages 794–800.

A pine dresser, with glass top, c1890, 66in (167.5cm) wide.
£1,000–1,150 ⊞ POT

A pine dresser, with turned columns and glazed top, Hungarian, c1890, 48in (122cm) wide.
£580–650 ⊞ MIN

► **A pine kitchen dresser,** c1900, 58in (147.5cm) wide.
£700–800 ⊞ HRQ

Dresser Bases & Side Cabinets

A pine breakfront chiffonier, with gallery back, c1820, 44in (112cm) wide.
£600–700 ⊞ TPC

A Regency pine dresser base, with moulded decoration, 50in (127cm) wide.
£1,200–1,500 ⊞ TPC

A pine dresser base, c1870, 69in (175.5cm) wide.
£800–875 ⊞ POT

Cross Reference
See Colour Review (page 236)

A pine sideboard, c1880, 41in (104cm) wide.
£350–400 ⊞ AL

A pine server, Irish, c1880, 44in (112cm) wide.
£180–220 ⊞ Byl

A pine cabinet, with arched panelled doors flanking central shelving, c1880, 40in (101.5cm) wide.
£250–275 ⊞ TPC

A pine display cabinet, with three doors and glazed tilting top, Irish, c1880, 73in (185.5cm) wide.
£350–420 ⊞ Byl

► **A pine dresser base,** Continental, c1890, 36in (91.5cm) wide.
£250–285 ⊞ HRQ

◄ **A pitch pine low sideboard,** Welsh, c1900, 53in (134.5cm) wide.
£535–600 ⊞ P&T

Dressing Chests & Tables

◄ **A Victorian pine dressing table,** on tapered legs, gesso decorated, 45in (114.5cm) wide.
£500–600 ⊞ TPC

► **A Victorian pine dressing table,** with balustraded decoration, 36in (91.5cm) wide.
£320–400 ⊞ TPC

A pine dressing table, with mirror, c1890, 35in (89cm) wide.
£270–300 ⊞ P&T

Ladders & Steps

A pine step ladder, 1825–50, 109in (277cm) high.
£600–700 ⚒ NOA

A set of pine library steps, c1900, 57in (145cm) high.
£70–80 ⊞ DFA

A pine step ladder, c1930, 40in (101.5cm) high.
£45–50 ⊞ AL

◄ **A pine step ladder,** c1920, 66in (167.5cm) high.
£45–50 ⊞ DFA

Linen Presses

A late Georgian pine linen press, with shaped slides, 42in (106.5cm) wide.
£1,400–1,600 ⊞ TPC

A pine linen press, with new cornice and plinth, c1870, 42in (106.5cm) wide.
£950–1,000 ⊞ AL

A pine linen press, c1870, 72in (183cm) high.
£780–850 ⊞ HOA

A pine linen press, with slides, 19thC, 46in (117cm) wide.
£1,300–1,450 ⊞ WV

Miller's is a price GUIDE not a price LIST

Settees & Settles

A painted pine Windsor settee, on simulated bamboo-turned legs, old black paint with yellow striping, imperfections, American, New England, early 19thC, 73½in (186.5cm) wide.
£2,500–3,000 SK(B)

► **A painted pine settle,** with double hinged lift-top seat, American, New York, early 19thC.
£1,750–2,000 SK(B)

A pine box seat settle, with original painted finish, Continental, c1890, 75in (190.5cm) wide.
£500–600 TPC

◄ **A pine settle,** Irish, Co Kilkenny, c1860, 78in (198cm) wide.
£630–700 Byl

Shelves

◄ **A George III pine corner wall shelf,** with three green-painted open shelves, 36½in (92.5cm) high.
£300–360 LFA

A set of painted pine shelves, with three drawers, c1860, 48in (122cm) wide.
£180–200 DFA

A pine buffet, c1870, 40in (101.5cm) wide.
£780–865 AL

Stools

A pine milking stool, c1870, 15in (38cm) wide.
£45–50 DFA

A painted pine stool, late 19thC, 10in (25.5cm) wide.
£80–100 SMI

A pine stool, c1920, 17in (43cm) wide.
£35–40 DFA

Tables

A pine farmhouse table, with paint remaining on legs, c1780, 35in (89cm) wide.
£2,800–3,200 ⊞ SSW

A Georgian pine table, with two drawers, 72in (183cm) wide.
£500–600 ⊞ TPC

A pine-topped table, on a maple base, drawer missing, American, New England, 18thC, 39½in (100.5cm) wide.
£550–650 ⚒ SK(B)

► **A painted pine chair-table,** with tilting top above a plank seat, American, New England, late 18thC, 49½in (125.5cm) diam.
£2,750–3,000 ⚒ SK(B)

A pine drop-leaf table, Irish, early 19thC, 69in (175.5cm) wide.
£450–550 ⊞ TPC

A pine drop-leaf table, early 19thC, 42in (106.5cm) wide.
£400–500 ⊞ TPC

◄ **A birch and pine card table,** with original red-painted surface, American, New Hampshire or north-eastern Massachusetts, imperfections, c1800–10, 35½in (90cm) wide.
£1,100–1,200 ⚒ SK(B)

◄ **A pine trestle table,** American, 19thC, 102in (259cm) wide.
£1,500–1,800 ⚒ WcH

► **A pine cricket table,** 19thC, 25in (63.5cm) diam.
£350–420 ⊞ TRM

► **A drop-leaf table,** with double stretcher, Irish, c1840, 69in (175.5cm) wide.
£400–500 ⊞ TPC

A pine Pembroke table, c1850, 41in (104cm) wide.
£320–380 ⊞ TPC

A Victorian pine table, 48in (122cm) wide.
£360–400 ⊞ WV

◄ **A pine side table,** with a shaped pot board, c1860, 36in (91.5cm) wide.
£180–200 ⊞ HRQ

A Victorian wind-out pine table, with original handle, 60in (152.5cm) wide.
£600–700 ⊞ TPC

A Victorian pine drop-leaf table, with original paint, 42in (106.5cm) wide.
£320–400 ⊞ TPC

A pine side table, c1880, 36in (91.5cm) wide.
£180–200 ⊞ HRQ

A pine side table, with a drawer, c1880, 25½in (65cm) high.
£75–85 ⊞ AL

A pine and fruitwood kitchen table, with a single drawer, c1880, 48in (122cm) wide.
£200–225 ⊞ POT

A pine kitchen table, with a single drawer, c1880, 48in (122cm) wide.
£215–240 ⊞ POT

► **A Victorian pine draw-leaf table,** with two stowable centrally-hinged leaves, 65in (165cm) extended.
£500–600 ⊞ TPC

A pine wine table, French, c1880, 49in (124.5cm) wide.
£630–700 ⊞ AL

◄ **A pine table,** with a single drawer and original painted legs, c1890, 42in (106.5cm) wide.
£200–220 ⊞ POT

► **A pine gateleg table,** c1900, 54in (137cm) wide.
£380–420 ⊞ TPC

Wardrobes

A gentleman's Regency pine wardrobe, 54in (137cm) wide.
£800–900 ⊞ TPC

A painted pine armoire, Continental, 19thC, 72in (183cm) high.
£1,000–1,100 ⊞ HOA

A pine wardrobe, c1900, 66in (167.5cm) wide.
£750–820 ⊞ HRQ

A pine armoire, repainted, French, Normandy, c1820, 55in (139.5cm) wide.
£2,250–2,500 ⊞ GD

A Victorian pine single wardrobe, 29in (73.5cm) wide.
£400–500 ⊞ TPC

A Victorian pine wardrobe, with a single door over a single drawer, 28in (71cm) wide.
£375–415 ⊞ P&T

◄ A pine wardrobe, with three doors, Continental, c1910, 45½in (115.5cm) wide.
£585–650 ⊞ HRQ

A painted pine and parcel-gilt armoire, the panels painted with figural scenes emblematic of the seasons, the base with a drawer, decoration refreshed, north European, 1800–50, 55in (139.5cm) wide.
£3,000–3,500 ⚒ SLN

► A Victorian pine wardrobe, with a drawer below, 43in (109cm) wide.
£700–770 ⊞ P&T

A Victorian pine wardrobe, 26in (66cm) wide.
£400–500 ⊞ TPC

A late Victorian pine wardrobe, 40in (101.5cm) wide.
£280–320 ⊞ WV

A pine wardrobe, European, 19thC, 47in (119.5cm) wide.
£350–400 ⊞ POT

A pine wardrobe, c1900, 55½in (141cm) wide.
£675–750 ⊞ HRQ

A pair of pine wardrobes, Hungarian, c1900, 40in (101.5cm) wide.
£470–520 ⊞ MIN

Washstands

A pine washstand, c1880, 24in (61cm) wide.
£65–80 ⊞ Byl

► **A Victorian pine washstand,** with gallery back and lyre ends, 38in (96.5cm) wide.
£450–550 ⊞ TPC

A painted pine tray-top washstand, with two small drawers, on simulated bamboo turned legs, 19thC, 42in (106.5cm) wide.
£500–600 LFA

◄ **A pine washstand,** c1880, 36in (91.5cm) wide.
£225–250 ⊞ HRQ

A pine washstand, with gallery back and two drawers, c1880, 36in (91.5cm) wide.
£180–200 ⊞ POT

A Victorian washstand, with a marble top and tiled splashback, 36in (91.5cm) wide.
£220–250 ⊞ P&T

Prices

The price ranges quoted in this book reflect the average price a purchaser might expect to pay for a similar item. The price will vary according to the condition, rarity, size, popularity, provenance, colour and restoration of the item, and this must be taken into account when assessing values. Don't forget that if you are selling it is quite likely that you will be offered less than the price range.

A pine washstand, Irish, c1880, 25in (63.5cm) wide.
£65–80 ⊞ Byl

A pine washstand, c1890, 30in (76cm) wide.
£125–140 ⊞ POT

Bamboo & Wicker Furniture

A Victorian wickerwork basket, with lined interior, 15in (38cm) wide.
£150–200 ⊞ DOA

A Lloyd Loom chair, 1930s, 27in (68.5cm) wide.
£200–220 ⊞ NET

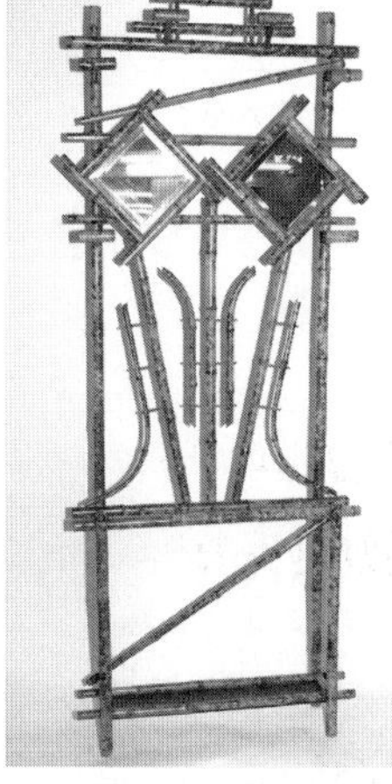

A bamboo and wickerwork sewing basket, the lid enclosing a plush-lined interior, with a fall-front door below enclosing a further plush-lined interior, early 20thC, 16½in (42cm) wide.
£80–100 ⚒ GAK

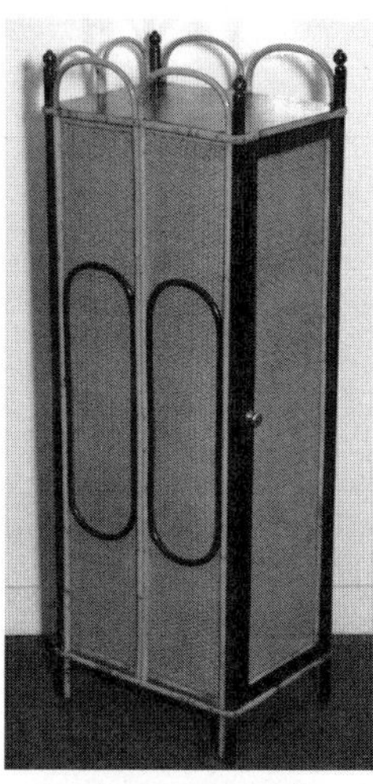

A bamboo cupboard, c1890, 9½in (24cm) wide.
£115–125 ⊞ AL

◀ A bamboo hall stand, c1895, 29½in (75cm) wide.
£200–225 ⊞ NAW

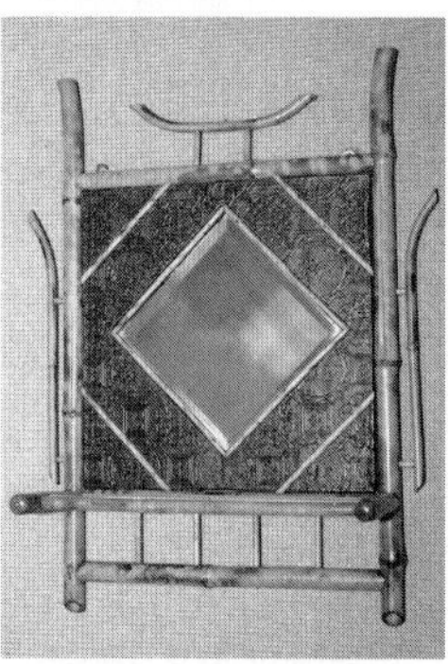

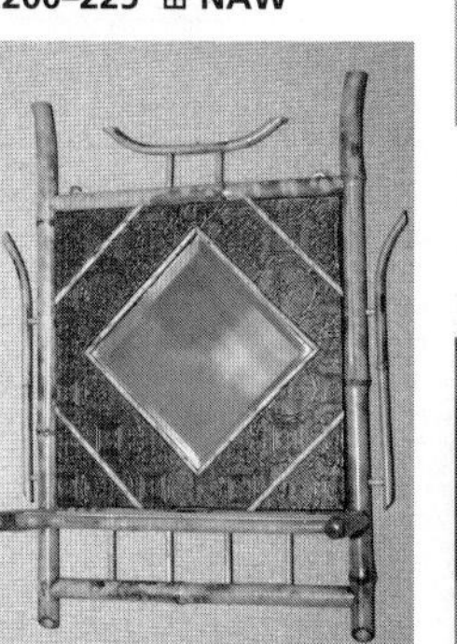

A bamboo and embossed paper hanging mirror, late 19thC, 16in (40.5cm) wide.
£125–140 ⊞ CoHA

◀ A bamboo stick stand, c1880, 37½in (95.5cm) high.
£80–90 ⊞ AL

A Victorian bamboo cabinet, with two glazed doors, 35½in (90cm) wide.
£250–320 ⚒ SWO

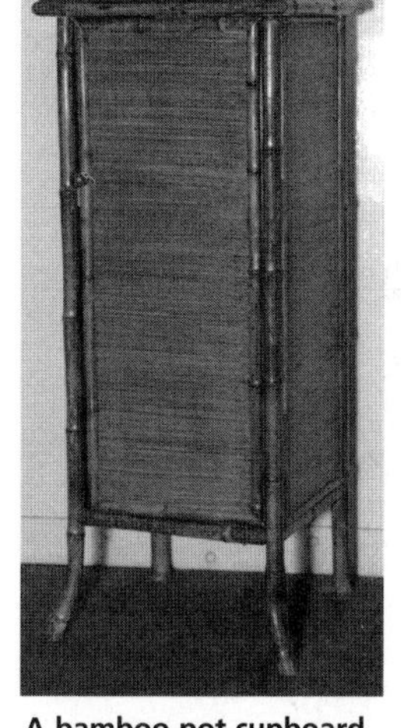

A bamboo pot cupboard, c1885, 36in (91.5cm) high.
£220–235 ⊞ AL

A bamboo magazine stand, c1900, 17in (43cm) wide.
£150–165 ⊞ CoHA

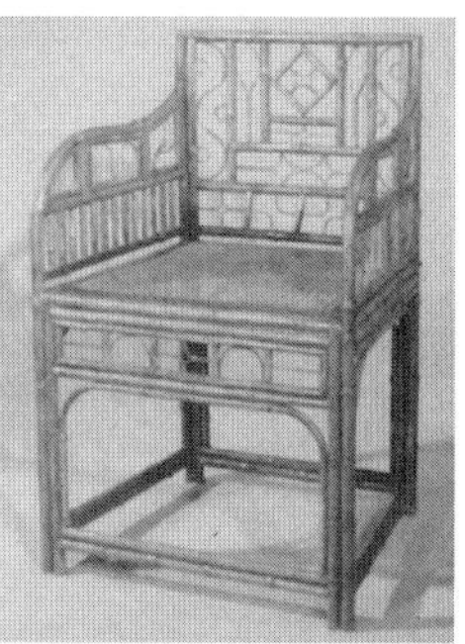

A Regency bamboo elbow chair, with a later rattan seat.
£1,800–2,250 ⚒ WW
The design of this chair was taken from a pattern for a chair made for the Royal Pavilion, Brighton.

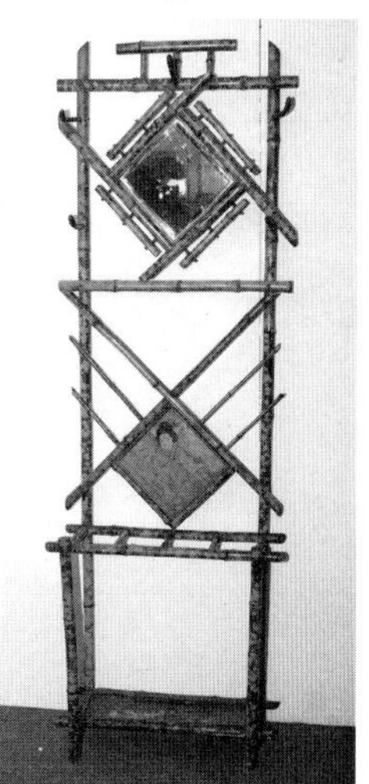

A bamboo hall stand, c1895, 26in (66cm) wide.
£215–240 ⊞ NAW

A set of bamboo shelves, with a canterbury base, c1880, 47in (119.5cm) high.
£300–345 ⊞ AL

◀ A bamboo table, restored, c1900, 17in (43.5cm) wide.
£60–70 ⊞ CoHA

Kitchenware

A carved sycamore bread board, c1870, 12in (30.5cm) diam.
£100–120 ⊞ SMI

A transfer-printed earthenware tile and wood bread box, by Villeroy & Boch, with a hinged lid, the tiles printed with Dutch scenes, German, early 20thC, 18in (46.5cm) wide.
£1,800–2,000 ⚒ SK

A brass-bound oak bucket, with a swing handle, 19thC, 14in (35.5cm) diam.
£150–180 ⚒ GAK

A set of four fruitwood kitchen storage boxes, c1930, largest 8in (20.5cm) high.
£90–100 ⊞ MLL

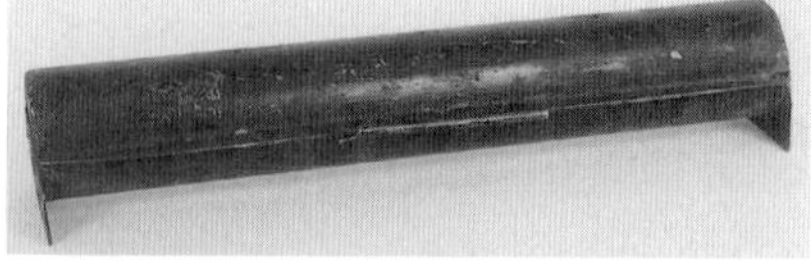

A tin bread pan, American, c1890, 15¾in (40cm) wide.
£150–180 ⊞ MSB

A Victorian black-japanned Golden Syrup dispenser, the centre decorated with a classical ruin, the lettering on a silvered ground, 14¼in (36cm) high.
£300–375 ⚒ P(Ed)

A cast-iron box iron, with a brass sole and wooden handle, late 19thC, 6in (15cm) long.
£100–120 ⊞ SMI

A knife keener and buffer, by H. W. Garrard, 19thC, 16in (40.5cm) diam.
£340–375 ⊞ SEA

A ceramic Mochaware jug, decorated with blue and white bands on a pale yellow ground, c1880, 10in (25.5cm) high.
£225–250 ⊞ SMI

A cast-iron mortar, with raised moulded decoration and initials, late 17thC, 7in (18cm) high.
£250–300 ⚒ WW

A ceramic milk churn, with black transfer printing, early 20thC, 22in (56cm) high.
£1,350–1,500 ⊞ B&R

► **A salt-glazed mould,** late 19thC, 9¾in (25cm) wide.
£40–45 ⊞ B&R

An egg-shaped nutmeg grater, probably by Samuel Meriton II, chased with flowers and swirl fluting, with lift-out grater, c1780, 2in (5cm) diam.
£370–450 ⚒ WW

► **A copper crown mould,** 19thC, 5in (12.5cm) high.
£100–125 ⚒ CGC

An oak wall salt box, with an inlay of a salt cellar to the front, c1790, 14in (35.5cm) high.
£270–300 ⊞ F&F

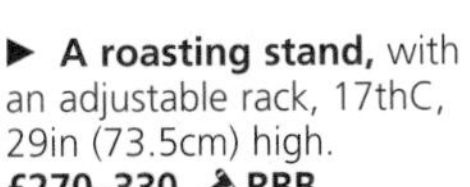

► **A roasting stand,** with an adjustable rack, 17thC, 29in (73.5cm) high.
£270–330 ⚒ RBB

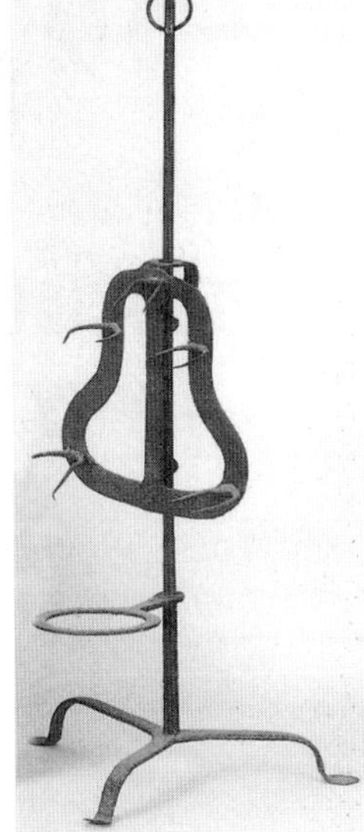

A butter or cheese scale, c1900, 18in (45.5cm) wide.
£88–98 ⊞ B&R

Pottery

In the latter part of 2001, it seemed to many observers that the antiques market in general, and the pottery market in particular, was entering a period of tremendous uncertainty. The events of September 11 had dramatically undermined American confidence in all areas, and as the English pottery market has always had a strong reliance on American collectors, it seemed likely to be hard hit. This was certainly the case immediately after the Twin Towers disaster with sales that contained items very popular in America such as majolica and Staffordshire figures, but this seems in general to have been very short-lived.

Items of quality, particularly those fresh to the market, are experiencing unprecedented demand and a corresponding rise in prices. This trend shows every likelihood of continuing, and already means that the gulf in value between a rare piece and a lesser example can be enormous. Collectors will certainly tolerate damage and restoration if a piece is sufficiently uncommon, but run-of-the-mill pieces with similar faults now need to be priced conservatively if they are to sell. Prices for delftware, creamware and late 18th- and early 19th-century English pottery figures seem very strong, although English delft plates and chargers have not now risen in value for two to three years.

Nineteenth-century Staffordshire pottery figures are proving difficult in general to sell, as prices have increased quite sharply in the last two years following the publication of *Victorian Staffordshire Figures 1835–1875* by A. and N. Harding. Pieces that are still performing well are those incorporating animals, including well-painted pairs of equestrian figures, and, understandably, any figure of real rarity or quality. Sparsely decorated examples made between 1880 and 1900 are currently difficult to market.

Demand for French faïence, particularly Quimper, has increased dramatically in recent years, not least due to active collectors' groups and a number of specialist dealers in this field. It is still, however, an area where discoveries can be made.

It is becoming increasingly rare to find complete dinner or dessert services, and those that are highly decorative and in good condition are keenly sought after. There is now tremendous financial advantage in keeping these services together rather than dividing them into their component parts, as has so often happened in the past.

It has been said that the technological revolution in recent years has made it almost impossible to unearth rarities that others may not have spotted. However, since most sale rooms and dealers have websites, it is now possible to view images of items for sale around the world at the click of a button, allowing buyers regularly to unearth pieces of some importance.

Mark Law

Animals & Birds

A creamware spill vase, modelled as a deer and a squirrel by a tree stump, decorated in green and brown, c1790, 5in (12.5cm) high.
£1,500–1,700 ⊞ JHo

A Prattware bear teapot and cover, wearing a green-brown collar and muzzle, chips and associated crack, tip of spout and nose chipped, late 18thC, 6½in (16.5cm) high.
£1,450–1,600 ⚒ P

◀ **A pair of Wood and Caldwell pearlware models of recumbent lions,** decorated in fawn and brown, on a brown-glazed base, impressed marks, c1810, 5in (12.5cm) wide.
£1,500–1,800 ⚒ LFA

A pair of Prattware birds, decorated with blue and orange feathers, c1795, 3¼in (8.5cm) high.
£2,000–2,200 ⊞ JRe

A pair of Yorkshire pearlware cow groups, one modelled with a milkmaid, the other with a boy, the cows sponged with black-edged manganese patches, the green-glazed base sponged around the sides in ochre, black and blue, female group with restuck section to base and chip to one horn, c1800–20, base 5¾in (14.5cm) wide.
£4,000–5,000 ⚒ S

◀ **A Staffordshire pearlware Napoleonic bear jug and cover,** modelled as a brown bear with a yellow muzzle, holding a monkey wearing French uniform caricaturing Napoleon, chips, hairline cracks, c1810, 10in (25.5cm) high.
£2,000–2,200 P(Ba)
Bear jugs were more usually modelled holding a dog or cub. However, early in the Peninsular War (1808–14), Napoleon Bonaparte became a familiar figure of ridicule in British pottery. As a result, bear jugs were produced for a short time with a monkey in French uniform in lieu of the usual dog. The bear's head was detachable for use as a cup.

A Staffordshire pearlware model of a dog, coloured with brown brushed patches, seated on a green and brown rocky base with applied moss, early 19thC, 6¾in (17cm) wide.
£450–550 WW

A Staffordshire polychrome model of a lion, c1820, 5in (12.5cm) high.
£1,500–1,650 ⊞ JHo

A Staffordshire model of a deer, with bocage, c1825, 5½in (14cm) high.
£560–625 ⊞ DAN

A Staffordshire spill vase, modelled as two sheep standing before a tree stump, tree stump repaired, c1840, 4in (10cm) high.
£250–280 ⊞ SER

A Staffordshire porcellaneous model of an eagle, picked out in gilt, and perched on a base with granitic decoration, 1840–50, 7in (18cm) high.
£180–220 LFA
In granitic decoration, pieces of clay are put through a sieve and then applied to the pot to look like grass.

A Victorian Staffordshire spill vase group, modelled as a brown horse and a black and white dog, on a green base, 7in (18cm) high.
£130–155 G(L)

Staffordshire

By the early 18th century London was being rivalled and then swiftly overtaken by Staffordshire as the hub of the British pottery industry, centred around five main towns that form the area known as the Potteries – Stoke-on-Trent, Burslem, Hanley, Longton and Tunstall. Production of figures and models was particularly prolific due to the popularity of porcelain examples during the 19th century which led to a demand for less expensive versions in pottery. The favourite subject for collectors of animals was the dog, especially the King Charles spaniel, although the opening of the first zoos in the 19th century and the popularity of travelling circuses also fuelled the demand for models of exotic beasts.

Items in the Pottery section have been arranged in date order within each sub-section.

▶ **A Staffordshire polychrome-decorated model of the Princess Royal riding a goat,** c1860, 6in (15cm) high.
£215–240 ⊞ DHA

A pair of Victorian Staffordshire models of zebras, 8¾in (22cm) high.
£900–1,100 G(L)

A Staffordshire tureen and cover, modelled as a hen and chicks, decorated in brown and white, restored, mid-19thC, 7in (18cm) wide.
£320–350 ⚒ S(O)

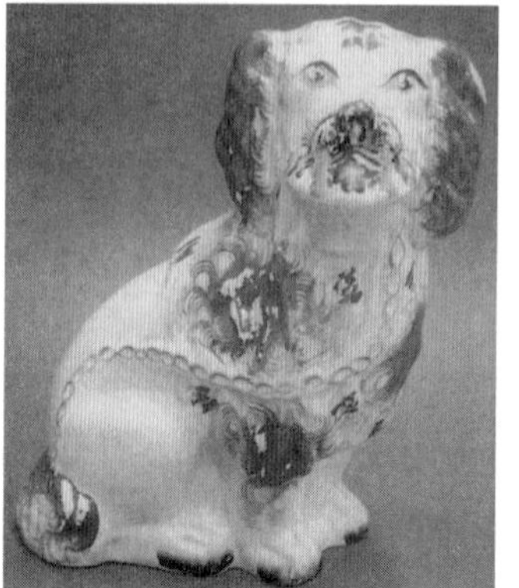

A Staffordshire model of a spaniel, painted with rust-orange patches and holding a basket of flowers in his mouth, 19thC, 9in (23cm) high.
£220–260 ⚒ FHF

A Staffordshire treacle-glazed model of a spaniel, seated on a plinth decorated in brown treacle and green glazes, 19thC, 17in (43cm) high.
£500–550 ⚒ MAT

A black-glazed dog, sitting on a pearlware base, chipped, repainted, 19thC, 5¼in (13.5cm) high.
£200–250 ⚒ SWO

A Staffordshire porcellaneous model of a seated spaniel, decorated with iron-red patches, 19thC, 3½in (9cm) high.
£130–155 ⚒ WW

A Staffordshire model of a jockey, wearing a turquoise coat and seated on a light brown horse, c1860, 9in (23cm) high.
£220–245 ⊞ DHA

► A Staffordshire polychrome model of a giraffe and his keeper, the keeper decorated in red, blue and green, the tree stump with green and red glazes, 1850s, 9in (23cm) high.
£1,100–1,200 ⊞ RGa

◄ A Staffordshire model of a bird on rockwork, c1860, 13in (33cm) high.
£585–650 ⊞ DAN

► A Staffordshire tureen, modelled as a swan on a nest, decorated in white and gilt with a green band, c1860, 9in (23cm) high.
£1,800–2,200 ⊞ ACO

A Staffordhsire model of a greyhound with a hare, naturalistically coloured, on a blue base, c1860, 11in (28cm) high.
£225–250 ⊞ DAN

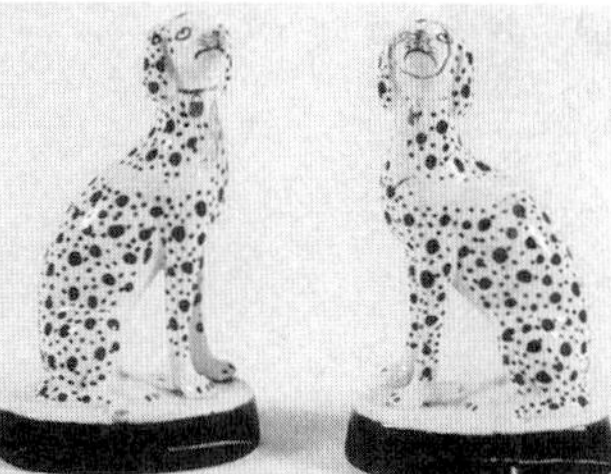

A pair of Staffordshire models of seated dalmatians, with black speckled body markings and gilded collars and leads, on gilt-lined blue bases, one repaired, c1860, 5½in (14cm) high.
£230–275 ⚒ GAK

A pair of Staffordshire models of St Bernards, with orange-brown markings, and gilded collars, one hairline crack, 1885–1900, 10¾in (27.5cm) high.
£450–500 ⚒ P(Ba)

A Wemyss sleeping piglet, painted with green and red thistles, restored, impressed and green script marks, early 20thC, 6½in (16.5cm) wide.
£12,500–14,000 ⚒ S

A Staffordshire model of a spaniel and puppy, on a blue gilt-lined base, c1870, 6in (15cm) high.
£250–275 ⊞ DAN

A Vallauris majolica duck, by Delphin Massier, naturalistically coloured, c1880, 9in (23cm) wide.
£400–445 ⊞ MLL

◄ **A Staffordshire agate ware money box,** modelled as a pig, decorated in green, brown and white, c1880, 5in (12.5cm) wide.
£70–80 ⊞ HUM

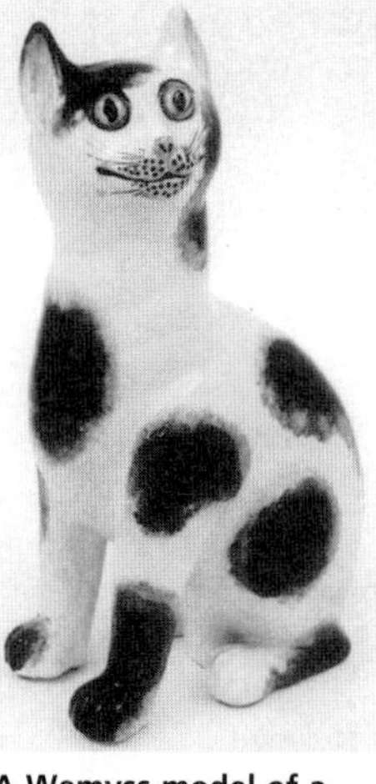

A Wemyss model of a cat, with black sponged markings and pink details to face, ears and one paw, restored, impressed R. H. & S. mark, c1900, 12¾in (32.5cm) high.
£3,000–3,500 ⚒ SH

► **A Wemyss model of a brown pig,** ears restored, impressed marks, c1900, 17¾in (45cm) wide.
£900–1,100 ⚒ SH

A Staffordshire spill vase, modelled as a greyhound standing before a tree stump, with a recumbent hound at its feet, one decorated in brown, the other grey, the tree stump decorated in green and brown glazes, 1865–70, 12in (30.5cm) high.
£400–500 ⚒ LFA

A Staffordshire spill vase, modelled as a group of sheep by a trough, decorated in shades of green, orange, white and brown, 1850–1900, 12in (30.5cm) high.
£230–275 ⚒ G(L)

An Ewenny pig, decorated with a spotted green glaze, chipped, incised mark, dated 1901, 7in (18cm) wide.
£800–900 ⚒ S(S)

Bowls

A Hispano-Moresque bowl, painted in copper lustre with a stylized bird among scrolling foliate decoration on a cream ground, restored crack, glaze chips, Spanish, c1600, 15½in (39.5cm) diam.
£1,300–1,600 S

► **A creamware bowl,** printed in black, French, early 19thC, 9½in (24cm) diam.
£270–300 DHA

A Sunderland pottery bowl, decorated in pink lustre, printed in black and enamelled in colours, the interior with a panel of a ship, two panels of verse and a view of the cast-iron bridge over the River Wear, the exterior with a cartouche for the Crimea, The Sailor's Return and a panel of verse, indistinct impressed mark, c1856, 9¾in (25cm) diam.
£100–120 SAS

An English delft bowl, decorated in underglaze blue with geometric border, the centre inscribed 'Success to Trade', hairline crack, 18thC, 9in (23cm) diam.
£500–600 GAK

A Wedgwood majolica bowl, relief-decorated in Bird and Fan pattern, with blue-green glazed interior, impressed mark, painted No. 2816 and relief-moulded design registration lozenge, 1850–1900, 9½in (24cm) diam.
£80–100 PFK

► **A pottery spongeware bowl,** decorated in blue, green, pink and black, Scottish, c1890, 8in (20.5cm) diam.
£70–80 HUM

A pottery bowl, commemorating the Golden Jubilee of George III, printed in black with a medallion inscribed 'A King Revered, a Queen Beloved, G III C', the inside rim printed in blue with a chinoiserie-style border, the outsides printed in black with cupid scenes, cracks, 1809, 7½in (19cm) diam.
£280–320 DN

A Spode earthenware sucrier and cover, brown-tinted, applied with figures in a wooded landscape, impressed mark, 1815–20, 3½in (9cm) high.
£120–150 LFA

POTTERY

Buildings

A Pratt-style polychrome-decorated money box, the reverse moulded with a band of leafy fronds, chipped, c1800, 5¼in (13.5cm) high.
£700–800 S(O)

A Walton spill holder, modelled as a turret on a mound base applied with flowers and flanked by grassy outcrops, minor damage, losses, c1820, 5¼in (13.5cm) high.
£400–500 P

A slipware model of a mansion, the sides with simulated brickwork, damaged, probably West Country, 1875–1925, 11¼in (28.5cm) high.
£1,700–2,000 WW

A Staffordshire model of a farmhouse scene, decorated in ochre, brown and green, c1830, 5in (12.5cm) high.
£1,100–1,250 ⊞ JHo

A Staffordshire spill vase, modelled as a castle, decorated in salmon pink, with grapevines and a clock above the front door, mid-19thC, 7in (18cm) high.
£70–85 ⚒ CGC

A Staffordshire model of a cottage, decorated in brown, blue and white, c1860, 7½in (19cm) high.
£75–85 ⊞ NAW

A majolica pottery cheese dish, modelled as a castle adorned with vines and ferns, flagpole finial, decorated in coloured glazes, cracked and riveted, chips, minor glaze loss, registration mark, c1872, 9½in (24cm) diam.
£550–650 ⚒ F&C

A Staffordshire model of a cottage, c1870, 6½in (16.5cm) high.
£100–115 ⊞ DAN

A Staffordshire pastille burner, modelled as a gabled cottage, white with coloured decoration, 19thC, 5in (12.5cm) high.
£75–90 ⚒ WBH

Centrepieces

An Avon tazza, moulded in relief with Perseus rescuing Andromeda from the sea monster, decorated in green, blue, brown and yellow, French, c1600, 9in (23cm) diam.
£1,400–1,600 ⚒ S(O)

► **A Minton majolica oyster stand,** the oyster shells with white interiors and brown undersides, surmounted by two purple fish and a turquoise eel handle, green seaweed between each shell, on a separate foot moulded with weed picked out in green against the brown ground, with metal fitting enabling the stand to rotate, some chips and restoration, c1860, 11in (28cm) high.
£4,500–5,000 ⚒ P

A Wedgwood creamware dessert stand, painted in brown with vine bands within brown line borders, impressed mark, 1800–10, 10in (25.5cm) high.
£180–220 ⚒ LFA

A majolica polychrome-decorated centrepiece, 19thC, 16in (40.5cm) high.
£500–550 ⚒ WBH

Cross Reference
See Colour Review (page 290)

A Wedgwood leaf-moulded dessert stand, decorated with a green glaze, c1880,12in (30.5cm) wide.
£220–245 ⊞ DAN

Cow Creamers

A Staffordshire Whieldon-style cow creamer, decorated with brown markings, c1770, 6in (15cm) long.
£3,500–4,000 ⊞ JRe

A pink lustre cow creamer, damaged, Swansea, c1835, 7in (18cm) long.
£175–200 ⊞ NAW

A pottery cow creamer, the cow black-and-white, with a polychrome-decorated milkmaid seated beneath, cover replaced, probably North Country, 1830–40, 5in (12.5cm) high.
£500–600 ⚒ S(O)

POTTERY

Cups

A Neal creamware cup and cover, enamelled in brown, black and iron-red with border designs and armorial for Ferrier-Williams to one side, 1750–1800, 4in (10cm) wide.
£280–335 ⚒ WW

A Wedgwood blue jasper coffee can, the engine-turned ground applied in white with flowerheads beneath a ribbon-and-leaf scroll band, cracked, impressed mark, c1800, 2½in (6.5cm) high.
£250–300 ⚒ LFA

A jasper ware coffee can and saucer, decorated in white on a blue ground with swags suspended from lions' heads, incised and impressed marks, c1881, saucer 4in (10cm) diam.
£40–50 ⚒ WW

Miller's is a price GUIDE not a price LIST

Dishes

A Savona maiolica dish, painted in blue with a man striding in a landscape, flaking to rim, Italian, 1650–1700, 10½in (26.5cm) diam.
£280–320 ⚒ Bon(C)

A Moustier pottery dish, decorated with polychrome sprays of flowers on a cream ground, French, c1740, 14in (35.5cm) wide.
£800–900 ⊞ US

A Hispano-Moresque dish, painted in ruby lustre with carnations, rim chips, 1700–50, 11in (28cm) diam.
£1,000–1,200 ⚒ S(O)

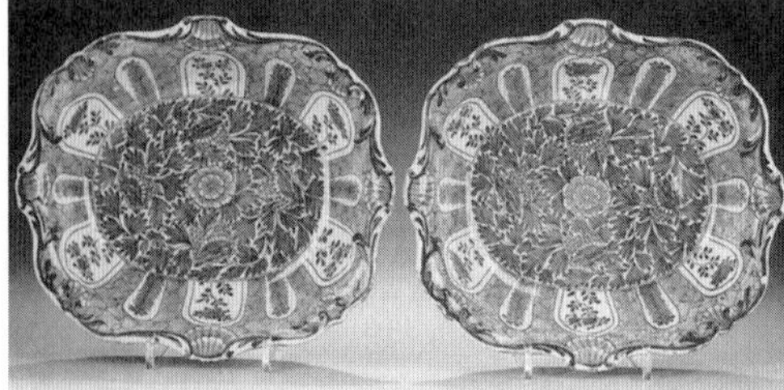

► **A pair of Dutch Delft dishes,** decorated in blue with Parsley pattern, bordered by a series of panels enclosing flowering sprays, marked in underglaze blue for the Factory de Porcelijne Bijl, 1750–1800, larger 13in (33cm) wide.
£800–950 ⚒ S(Am)

A delft blue and white leaf-shaped pickle dish, with serrated rim, painted with a pagoda within a diaper border, minor rim chips, 1750–1800, 3¾in (9.5cm) wide.
£380–450 WW

A faïence dish, polychrome-painted with floral swags and cartouches of doves and flowers, French, late 19thC, 9in (23cm) wide.
£200–240 G(L)

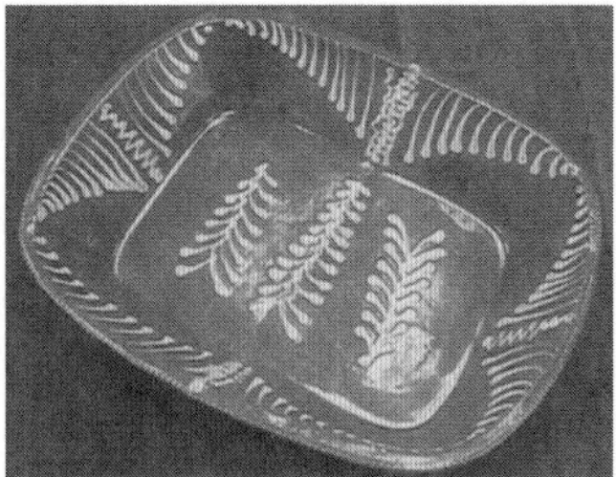

A slipware dish, with cream trailed-decoration on a brown glaze, 19thC, 16½in (42cm) wide.
£150–180 PFK

A pair of George Jones majolica dishes, modelled with a bird perched on entwined branches, the centre moulded in relief with leaves and flowerheads on a turquoise ground within a yellow line, impressed registration diamond and painted pattern No. 2515, late 19thC, 10¼in (26cm) wide.
£630–750 CGC

A pair of Wedgwood creamware pickle dishes, decorated in red and gold with stylized leaf design, c1820, 6in (15cm) long.
£200–220 HUM

A Vallauris dish, with moulded fruits, decorated with a green glaze, c1930, 12in (30.5cm) wide.
£90–100 DAN

POTTERY

Covered Dishes

A Spode New Fayence vegetable dish and cover, No. B218, printed in green and painted with flowers, printed and impressed marks, c1825, 11¾in (30cm) wide.
£80–100 WW

An English majolica game pie dish and cover, relief-moulded with leaves, the cover surmounted by a dead game bird, covered in turquoise, green, ochre and brown glazes with purple interior, chip to base, 19thC, 12in (30.5cm) wide.
£750–900 FHF

A Minton majolica cheese dish and cover, in the shape of a beehive, decorated in brown, green and blue, with flower and leaf decoration and relief-moulded basketweave sides, c1870, 13½in (34.5cm) high.
£1,350–1,500 SHSY

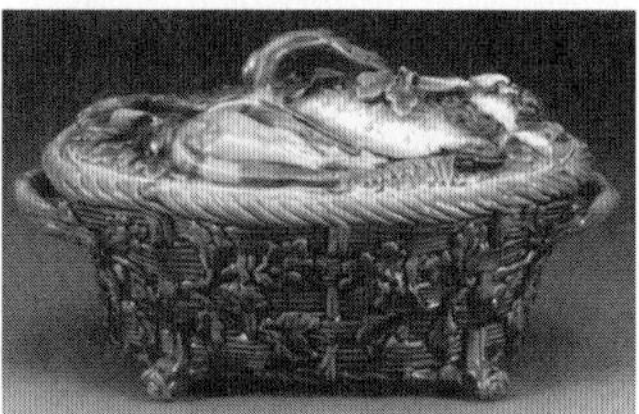

A Minton majolica game pie tureen, cover and liner, the cover moulded with dead game on a bed of leaves, decorated in green and brown, c1875, 12½in (32cm) wide.
£1,300–1,500 S(O)

A Minton majolica game pie dish, the cover modelled with a hare, a mallard and a moorhen, the brown basketwork sides with oak leaves, 1850–1900, 14½in (37cm) wide.
£1,000–1,200 WW

A Wedgwood majolica sardine dish, modelled as a crate bound up with rope and strewn with seaweed, the border moulded as waves lapping around the edge with further seaweed fronds and shells, decorated in blue, yellow, green and brown, hairline cracks, impressed factory marks and date code, applied registration marks, inscribed numerals, dated 1879, 7¼in (18.5cm) wide.
£2,500–2,750 P

Figures

A Ralph Wood group of two figures with a bird cage, decorated in blue, green and magenta, restorations, marked with Wood No. 89, c1790, 11in (28cm) high.
£900–950 ⊞ JRe

Cross Reference
See Colour Review (page 291)

A powder or sand sifter, in the form of a portly gentleman, mainly white with yellow, orange and turquoise detail, c1800, 7in (18cm) high.
£110–120 ⊞ DHA
This would have been used to dry letters written in ink.

A Staffordshire figure of a bagpiper, wearing a yellow coat and black breeches and hat, c1800, 9in (23.cm) high
£560–620 ⊞ DAN

A Staffordshire pearlware model of Andromache, standing beside an urn and weeping over the ashes of Hector, painted with coloured enamels, slight damage, c1800, 9½in (24cm) high.
£160–200 ⚒ WW

POTTERY

► **A set of four pearlware figures,** St Matthew, St Mark, St Luke and St John, each standing before flowering bocage, some restoration, early 19thC, 8¼in (21cm) high.
£1,350–1,500 ⚒ S(O)

Pearlware

Pearlware was developed by Josiah Wedgwood in 1779 as a whiter and more porcelain-like version of his creamware. It was achieved by adding small amounts of cobalt and copper to the transparent lead glaze, which then developed a blue tinge that can be seen most clearly in areas where the glaze gathers more thickly, such as around the footrim. Pearlware was used extensively until the late 19th century and pieces were often painted or printed with underglaze blue chinoiserie or floral subjects.

A Wood-style pearlware spill vase group, decorated in Pratt-style colours, some damage, early 19thC, 8in (20.5cm) high.
£700–850 ⚒ S(O)

A pearlware figure group, modelled as two sleeping girls wearing pink and yellow dresses, beneath a canopy of oak leaves, early 19thC, 4¼in (11cm) wide.
£150–180 ⚒ HAM

A Staffordshire figure of Neptune, in the style of Walton, polychrome-decorated, depicted standing on a shell with a mythical fish spouting water, the base with applied leaves and seashells, losses, early 19thC, 7in (18cm) high.
£80–100 ⚒ PFK

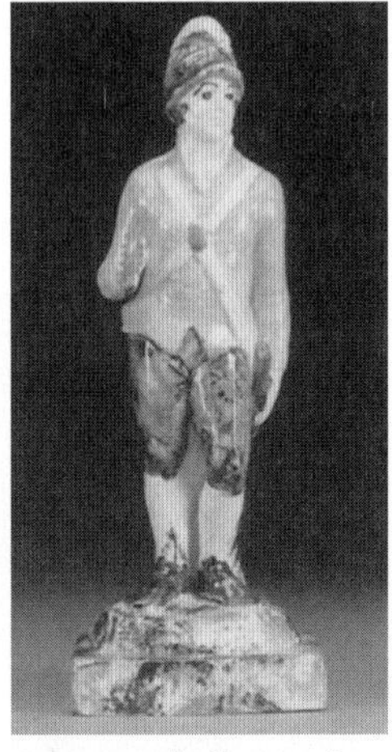

A Pratt-style figure of a soldier, wearing a yellow coat and blue hat and breeches, early 19thC, 8in (20.5cm) high.
£500–600 ⚒ S(O)

A Staffordshire pearlware figure of a Mansion House Dwarf, polychrome-decorated, c1820, 7in (18cm) high.
£400–450 ⊞ JRe

This type of figure was first made at Derby in 1784 and is named after the dwarf figures that stood outside the Mansion House, London, bearing announcements of plays and sales.

A Staffordshire spill vase, modelled as a fruit picker standing by a tree stump, white-decorated with polychrome detail, 19thC, 6in (15cm) high.
£110–125 ⊞ SEA

A Staffordshire pearlware group of rurals, seated before bocage, polychrome-decorated, c1825, 7½in (19cm) high.
£500–550 ⊞ JRe

► **A Staffordshire Sherratt-style figure of a shepherd with lambs,** wearing a brown tunic, before bocage, c1830, 8in (20.5cm) high.
£1,050–1,150 ⊞ DAN

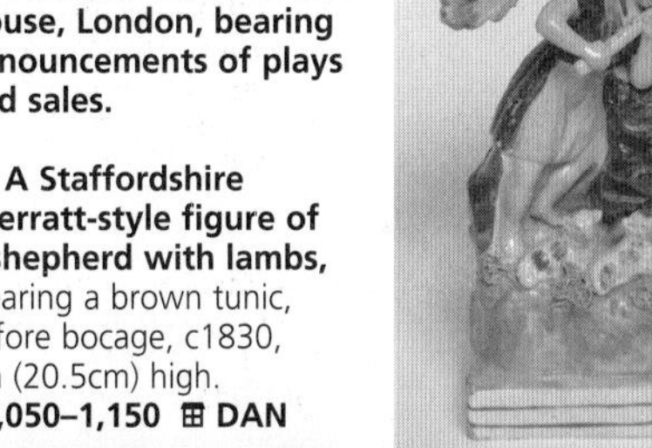

A Staffordshire bocage gardener, polychrome-decorated, damaged, c1820, 6in (15cm) high.
£180–200 ⊞ NAW

► **A pearlware figure of a young woman,** wearing a blue and yellow dress, seated on a tree stump reading a book, on a base applied with enamelled flowers, restored, 19thC, 9½in (24cm) high.
£110–130 ⚒ BLH

A pair of stoneware figures of Punch and Judy, decorated in brown and buff glazes, c1840, 7½in (19cm) high.
£1,600–1,750 ⊞ JHo

A Staffordshire model of John Wesley in a pulpit, 1840, 11½in (29cm) high.
£120–150 WilP

A Staffordshire tobacco jar and cover, modelled as a seated man, wearing a blue coat, red breeches and wearing a yellow hat, some restoration, mid-19thC, 8in (20.5cm) high.
£180–220 WW

► A Staffordshire figural group of Victoria and Albert, she wearing a turquoise skirt with pink trim and white jacket, he wearing a blue coat and white trousers, c1860, 7½in (19cm) high.
£160–175 SEA

A Staffordshire tobacco jar, in the form of a portly gentleman wearing a blue coat, orange breeches, orange and turquoise waistcoat and black hat, c1850, 4½in (11.5cm) high.
£140–155 DHA

A Staffordshire spill vase group, modelled as Paul and Virginia, 1850–1900, 11in (28cm) high.
£110–130 P(S)
Paul and Virginia were characters from a popular romantic novel published in 1787. Virginia drowned in a shipwreck because she would not take off her clothes to swim ashore. Paul died of a broken heart shortly afterwards.

◄ A Staffordshire figural group, with a rabbit, c1860, 7½in (19cm) high.
£180–200 DAN

A Staffordshire figural group, entitled 'Winters Tale', with Jenny Marston as Perdita and Frederick Robinson as Florizel, polychrome-decorated, c1852, 12in (30.5cm) high.
£700–800 RGa

► A Staffordshire spill vase, possibly by Sampson Smith, entitled 'Peace', modelled as a harvester wearing a yellow hat and orange breeches, with a sheep at his feet, restored, c1856, 15in (38cm) high.
£150–180 P(Ba)
This figure and its companion 'War' were probably issued to celebrate the end of the Crimean War.

A Staffordshire equestrian model of the Prince of Wales, wearing a purple jacket, the green and brown base applied with moss, hair cracks, mid 19thC, 10¾in (27.5cm) high.
£120–150 WW

POTTERY

POTTERY

A pepper pot, in the form of a portly gentleman wearing a blue coat, orange breeches and yellow hat, c1860, 6in (15cm) high.
£110–125 ⊞ DHA

A Staffordshire model of the Prince of Wales, standing beside an orange pillar, titled in gilt, the gilt rubbed, 19thC, 17¾in (45cm) high.
£200–240 ⚒ WW

A Staffordshire spill vase, depicting figures from *A Winter's Tale*, c1860, 11in (28cm) high.
£225–250 ⊞ HUM

A Minton majolica model of a gardener pushing a wheelbarrow, the man dressed in 17thC costume, polychrome-decorated, minor repair and chips, impressed marks, c1864, 13in (33cm) high.
£1,800–2,200 ⚒ S(O)

A Staffordshire equestrian group, entitled 'First Ride', white with gilt, black, brown, blue and turquoise detail, wear to enamel, c1870, 12in (30.5cm) high.
£700–850 ⚒ G(L)

A pair of Staffordshire figures, entitled 'Going to Market' and 'Returning Home', modelled as couples on horseback, 1860,
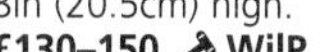
8in (20.5cm) high.
£130–150 ⚒ WilP

► **A Staffordshire spill vase of a huntsman,** his hand resting on his dog's head, standing before a tree trunk and fence, restorations, crazing, some repainting, c1870, 13in (33cm) high.
£150–180 ⚒ P(Ba)

A pair of Staffordshire flatback figures of Dick Turpin and Tom King, painted with coloured enamels, the gilt rubbed, 1870, 9¼in (23.5cm) high.
£250–300 ⚒ WW

◄ **A pair of pottery figures of Gladstone and Disraeli,** by Whitman and Roth, restoration to Gladstone and chip to hat brim of Disraeli, moulded lozenge mark, moulded registration mark for 1876, largest 16¾in (42.5cm) high.
£3,500–4,250 ⚒ SAS

◄ **A Staffordshire spill vase group of a fortune teller,** the red-cloaked lady reading the palm of a young girl beside the tree trunk vase, late 19thC, 12in (30.5cm) high.
£100–120 ⚒ CGC

► **A Staffordshire pottery figure of William Ewart Gladstone,** decorated in coloured enamels on a marbled base, restored, c1890, 11½in (29cm) high.
£200–240 ⚒ LFA

Flatware

A maiolica dish, probably from the workshop of Maestro Domenico, painted with Diana accompanied by a nymph in a rocky landscape, the rim edged with a yellow line, Italian, 1565–70, 9¾in (25cm) diam.
£1,700–2,000 S

An English delft blue and white plate, painted with figures in boats beneath a tree, with buildings in the distance, minor restoration, mid-18thC, 9in (23cm) diam.
£320–385 WW

A Dutch Delft plate, with polychrome decoration, c1760, 9in (23cm) diam.
£160–175 ⊞ BRU

A Dutch Delft Merryman plate, inscribed 'with wyne and mery yests', above a cherub's head, the whole surmounted by a crown and flanked by griffons, in blue, cracks, chips, late 17thC, 8¼in (21cm) diam.
£380–420 Bon(C)

Sets of plates with the Merryman verse were popular both in England and Holland from the last quarter of the 17th century to the first half of the 18th century.

A faïence dish, painted in pink, blue and green with sprays of flowers and scattered leaves, PH monogram, French, c1740, 13¼in (33.5cm) diam.
£500–600 S(O)

◄ **A London delft plate,** with polychrome decoration, probably Lambeth, c1760, 9in (23cm) diam.
£170–190 ⊞ BRU

A Bristol delft plate, probably by Redcliff Back, polychrome-decorated with a bird, rock and flowers, rim chips, c1760, 10½in (26.5cm) diam.
£235–275 S(O)

► **A pair of delft blue and white plates,** possibly London, c1760, 9in (23cm) diam.
£240–265 ⊞ MER

A Dutch Delft blue and white dish, the centre decorated with an exotic bird standing on fruit, the raised crimped rim with a blue floral drop frieze, late 17thC, 8¾in (22cm) diam.
£250–300 P(B)

A Staffordshire salt-glazed plate, printed in black with a pair of seated lovers by a fountain being spied on by a man peeping out from behind a tree, the rim moulded with a trellis border reserved with plumed cartouches, c1755, 9in (23cm) diam.
£350–400 P

A Bristol delft plate, polychrome-decorated with a basket of flowers to the centre, c1760, 8in (20.5cm) diam.
£430–475 ⊞ SEA

POTTERY

A Whieldon plate, glazed with green and ochre patches on a mottled brown ground, the rim moulded with alternating basketweave and latticework scroll cartouches, rim chipped, surface scratches, c1760, 10½in (26.5cm) diam.
£230–275 P(Ba)

A Whieldon plate, decorated in grey with random brown, yellow and green splashes, within a moulded scale border and scalloped rim, c1765, 9½in (24cm) diam.
£250–300 Bon(C)

A creamware plate, painted in black with a twin-masted ship, on a green enamel sea, the flags and sailors picked out in iron-red, the masts in pale yellow, the border painted with a flower spray and with a Dutch inscription, within a feather-moulded rim, dated 1779, 9¾in (25cm) diam.
£700–800 P

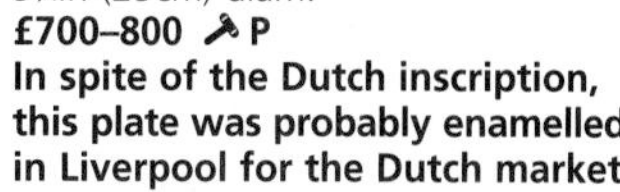
In spite of the Dutch inscription, this plate was probably enamelled in Liverpool for the Dutch market.

A creamware soup plate, painted with an armorial device to the centre and inscribed 'Qua Pote Lucet', late 18thC, 9¾in (25cm) diam.
£200–240 P(Ea)

A Richard Meir Astbury pearlware plate, painted in blue with a figure in a Chinese river landscape, the feather-moulded border picked out in blue, impressed mark, c1790, 9½in (24cm) diam.
£80–100 LFA

A Swansea pottery plate, in the style of Thomas Pardoe, script botanical title in red 'Berry bearing Chinonia', rim chip, c1800, 9in (23cm) diam.
£180–220 GAK

► **A pair of Swansea pottery white ware dessert plates,** painted with brown monochrome landscapes, both cracked and repaired, impressed marks, c1805, 8in (20.5cm) diam.
£80–100 S(O)

Miller's is a price GUIDE not a price LIST

A pair of Dutch Delft plates, polychrome-painted with a floral sprig within a diaper band, the border with three flower sprigs, late 18thC, 9¾in (25cm) diam.
£180–220 DN

A pair of Dutch Delft dishes, the centres decorated in script, the borders with linked circles, dated 1817, 9in (23cm) diam.
£260–320 WW

A pearlware plate, printed in brown with Britannia and two attendants, within garlands of flowers and leaves picked out in blue, green, yellow and ochre, 1810–15, 9½in (24cm) diam.
£90–110 LFA

◄ **A pair of Spode New Stone plates,** in the 18thC Chinese Export style, decorated with a coat-of-arms to the centre, c1820, 8in (20.5cm) diam.
£520–580 HA

◄ **A Southwick pottery plate,** printed in brown and enamelled in red, yellow and green with a sailing ship named *Star of Tasmania*, within a red line and pink lustre border, c1870, 9¼in (23.5cm) diam.
£150–180 SAS

Built by Alexander Hall at Aberdeen and launched in 1856, *Star of Tasmania* traded between London and New Zealand, but foundered off the east coast of the Southern island on 3 February 1868 with little loss of life.

Cross Reference
See Colour Review (page 292)

A set of 12 artichoke and asparagus plates, Continental, c1880, 9½in (24cm) diam.
£750–825 ⊞ MLL

A majolica dish, moulded with a frog and a snake, a butterfly and various other insects, on a seaweed-moulded ground, rim chip, incised mark, late 19thC, Portuguese, 9in (23cm) diam.
£250–300 GAK

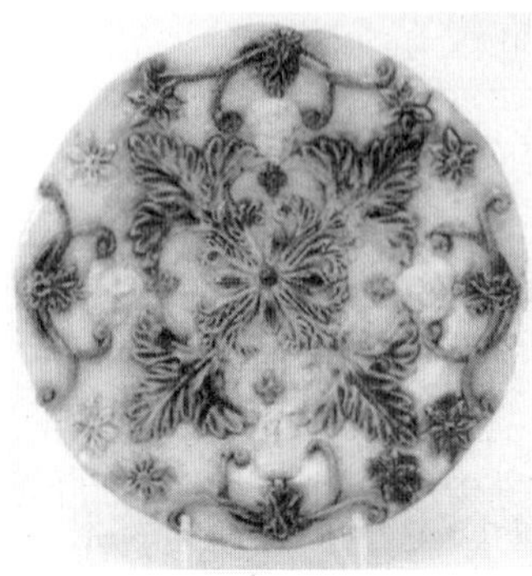

A Castle Hedingham Palissy-style majolica fluted dish, by Edward Bingham, modelled in relief with a flowerhead and radiating leaves, the border with scrolls, masks and flowerheads, impressed and applied marks, c1880, 8in (20.5cm) diam.
£150–180 LFA

A set of seven Wedgwood green-glazed plates, moulded as flowerheads, one cracked, impressed mark, 19thC, 8¾in (22cm) diam.
£140–170 WW

◄ **A Queen Victoria Golden Jubilee plate,** 1887, 9½in (24cm) square.
£75–85 ⊞ NAW

► **A pair of majolica dishes,** painted in coloured enamels with a putto, the blue ground border with a broad band of putti, flowers and masks, Italian, c1900, 9¼in (23.5cm) diam.
£180–220 LFA

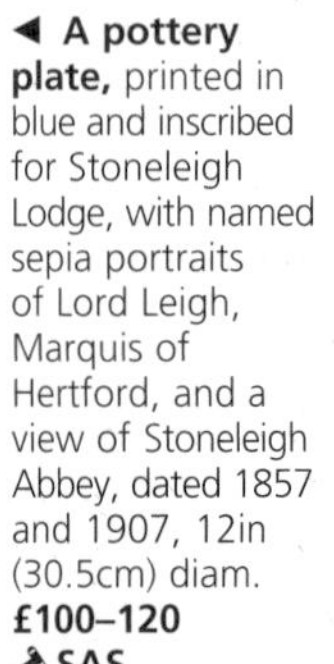

◄ **A pottery plate,** printed in blue and inscribed for Stoneleigh Lodge, with named sepia portraits of Lord Leigh, Marquis of Hertford, and a view of Stoneleigh Abbey, dated 1857 and 1907, 12in (30.5cm) diam.
£100–120 SAS

Footbaths

A Wedgwood creamware footbath, the sides painted with blue and red flowers on a lilac band, impressed mark, early 19thC, 19in (48.5cm) wide.
£400–500 ⚒ CGC

A Wedgwood earthenware footbath, impressed mark, 19thC, 18in (45.5cm) wide.
£350–400 ⚒ S(O)

A Wedgwood pearlware foot-bath, with gilt acanthus leaf handles, painted to each side with brightly coloured floral sprays, mid-19thC, 21in (53.5cm) wide.
£320–380 ⚒ B(EA)

Garden Seats

A Minton majolica garden seat or stand, with fretwork-style panels in pink, pale blue, white and green, the rims picked out in ochre, on an alternating deep and mid-blue ground, cracks and restored damage, impressed factory marks, dated 1867, 19in (48.5cm) high.
£1,000–1,200 ⚒ P

A Minton majolica garden seat, moulded in high relief with flowers and leaves, unmarked, c1870, 15in (38cm) high.
£1,500–1,800 ⚒ S(O)

A Minton majolica turquoise-glazed garden seat, with moulded decoration, impressed mark for 1877, 19in (48.5cm) high.
£320–380 ⚒ SWO

A majolica garden seat, moulded as a bundle of bamboo canes tied with two ribbons, decorated in brown, blue and green, with a pink-glazed interior, chips and cracks, Continental, 19thC, 14in (35.5cm) diam.
£500–600 ⚒ CAG

Inkstands & Inkwells

A Staffordshire porcellaneous inkwell, in the shape of a shoe, with detachable square sander, marbled in purple, pink and blue, damaged, 1820–25, 6in (15cm) wide.
£80–120 ⚒ LFA

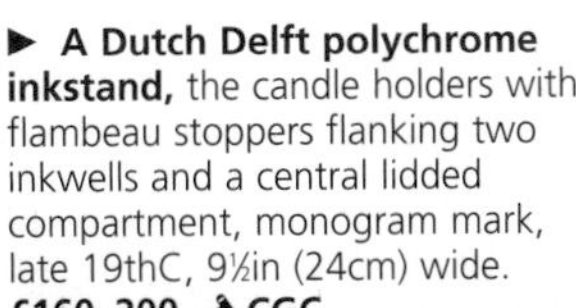

► **A Dutch Delft polychrome inkstand,** the candle holders with flambeau stoppers flanking two inkwells and a central lidded compartment, monogram mark, late 19thC, 9½in (24cm) wide.
£160–200 ⚒ CGC

LOCATE THE SOURCE
The source of each illustration in Miller's can be found by checking the code letters below each caption with the Key to Illustrations, pages 794–800.

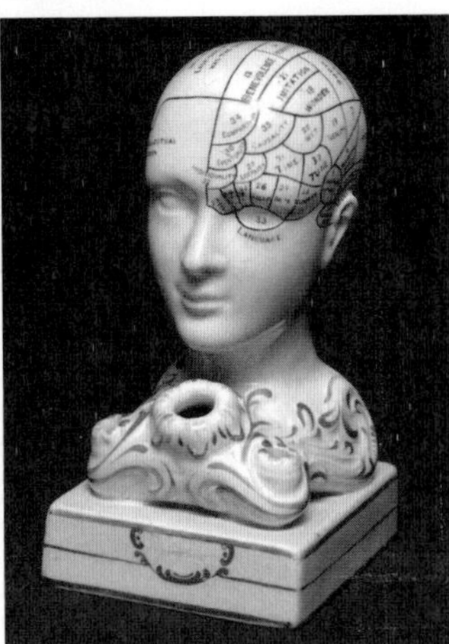

► **A pottery inkwell,** by F. Bridges, modelled as a phrenology head, c1865, 6in (15cm) high.
£630–700 ⊞ HUM

A Wemyss heart-shaped ink stand, painted with strawberries, c1900, 7in (18cm) wide.
£450–500 ⊞ RdeR

Colour Review

An applewood buffet, French, c1780, 54in (137cm) wide.
£2,700–3,000 ⊞ TDS

A cherrywood buffet, French, c1780, 57in (145cm) wide.
£3,200–3,600 ⊞ SSW

A walnut *buffet à deux corps,* French, c1800, 58in (147.5cm) wide.
£2,250–2,500 ⊞ GD

A walnut buffet, with two drawers, French, c1800, 52½in (133.5cm) wide.
£1,300–1,450 ⊞ NGO

A burr-ash *buffet à deux corps,* French, c1840, 77in (195.5cm) wide.
£3,500–4,000 ⊞ TDS

◄ A cherrywood buffet, with steel maritime motifs, French, c1820, 38in (96.5cm) high.
£2,800–3,200 ⊞ RYA

An applewood bureau, the fall-front enclosing a fitted interior, 18thC, 40¼in (102cm) wide.
£1,650–2,000 ⚒ P(NW)

► An oak Bible box, fitted with three small drawers, 17thC, 23in (58.5cm) wide.
£500–600 ⚒ RBB

◄ An oak Bible box, the front carving initialled 'EM' and dated 1742, 24in (61cm) wide.
£350–380 ⊞ TRI

A walnut *buffet à deux corps,* with central drawer, French, 19thC, 39½in (100.5cm) wide.
£1,600–1,800 ⊞ NGO

An oak bureau bookcase, the doors enclosing three adjustable shelves, 1750–75, 40¼in (102cm) wide.
£4,500–5,500 ⚒ S(O)

► An oak close stool, the hinged lid and fall-front enclosing a cavity for a chamber pot, c1820, 27in (68.5cm) wide.
£800–900 ⊞ SEA

Paul Hopwell Antiques

Early English Oak

Dressers, tables and chairs always in stock

A George III oak cabriole leg dresser base. Inlaid with fruitwood and with cupid bow shaped apron. 70" wide x 19" deep x 32" tall. English c1785

A small Charles II oak chest of three drawers. English c1685

An unusual Queen Anne oak side table with three drawers. With moulded stretchers and on ballister turned legs, with original brasses. 35" wide x 21" deep x 30" tall. English c1714

An oak box-seat armchair, with extensive restorations, early 16thC.
£9,000–11,000 ⚒ S
This rare chair is thought to be one of the earliest surviving English armchairs.

An oak panel-back armchair, faults, 1650–75.
£2,500–3,000 ⚒ S(S)

A walnut elbow chair, c1670.
£1,600–1,750 ⊞ WELL

An oak wainscot chair, c1685.
£2,000–2,300 ⊞ REF

A pair of oak side chairs, with vase-shaped splats, c1700.
£1,100–1,250 ⊞ SuA

An oak panel-back armchair, Welsh, c1700.
£1,800–2,000 ⊞ F&F

An oak Lorraine chair, French, c1700.
£250–275 ⊞ AMS

An oak lambing chair, c1725.
£5,500–6,500 ⊞ PHA

An elm corner chair, with upholstered seat, c1740.
£1,600–1,800 ⊞ SWG

A matched set of eight elm side chairs, with cabriole legs, 18thC.
£11,000–12,500 ⊞ REI

A Louis XVI painted cherrywood open armchair, French, c1780.
£450–500 ⊞ TDS

A comb- and splat-back primitive Windsor armchair, East Anglian, c1780.
£4,000–4,500 ⊞ RYA

An ash and oak primitive stick-back armchair, Welsh, late 18thC.
£800–950 ⚒ Bon(C)

A carved and painted banister-back armchair, American, late 18thC.
£7,500–9,000 ⚒ SK(B)

Four painted maple side chairs, one refinished, American, late 18thC.
£1,700–2,000 ⚒ BB(S)

A carved armchair, with hearts and roundels, Welsh, 1828.
£780–875 ⊞ DJH

A carved oak two-panelled coffer, c1670, 32in (81.5cm) wide.
£1,350–1,500 ⊞ F&F

► **An oak coffer,** the scroll-carved frieze with a name and dated 1683, 86in (218.5cm) wide.
£4,250–5,000 ⚒ G(L)

A carved oak coffer, c1680, 53¼in (135.5cm) wide.
£1,100–1,300 ⊞ WELL

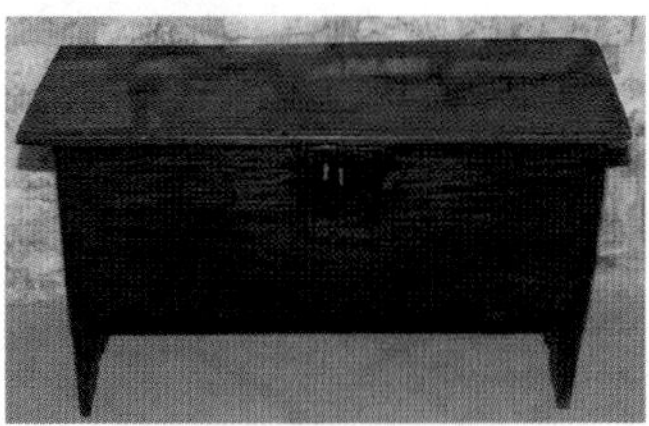

An oak six-plank coffer, early 18thC, 36in (91.5cm) wide.
£700–765 ⊞ F&F

A fruitwood and oak two-part chest, with snakewood moulding to the drawer fronts, c1680, 43in (109cm) wide.
£3,300–3,650 ⊞ SuA

An oak crossbanded chest of drawers, 18thC, 47in (119.5cm) wide.
£1,000–1,100 ⊞ NoC

A carved oak coffer, with iron strap hinges, c1680, 46in (117cm) wide.
£3,200–3,500 ⊞ JC

An oak mule chest, mid-18thC, 53in (134.5cm) wide.
£1,100–1,250 ⊞ DOA

An oak chest of drawers, late 17thC, 36in (91.5cm) wide.
£1,850–2,200 ⚒ RBB

A burr-oak and mahogany crossbanded chest of drawers, 43¾in (111cm) wide.
£1,400–1,700 ⚒ Bon(C)

An oak panelled coffer, late 17thC, 46in (117cm) wide.
£625–750 ⚒ AH

An oak mule chest, with a mahogany crossbanded panel front, 18thC, 56in (142cm) wide.
£900–1,100 ⚒ B(Ed)

An oak chest of drawers, late 17thC, 36in (91.5cm) wide.
£4,000–4,400 ⊞ DJH

An oak and yew wood chest of drawers, early 18thC, 40½in (103cm) wide.
£2,000–2,400 ⚒ P(NW)

◄ **A fruitwood commode,** French, c1800, 46in (117cm) wide.
£2,700–3,000 ⊞ SIE

An oak cabinet, restored, Flemish, early 17thC, 37in (94cm) wide.
£8,500–10,000 ⚒ P(NW)

► **An oak *cwpwrdd deuddarn*,** carved with initials 'WE', dated 1749, 60in (152.5cm) wide.
£8,000–10,000 ⊞ PHA

An oak clothes press, the drawers with later elements, early 18thC, 59in (150cm) wide.
£6,250–7,500 ⚒ S

An oak corner cupboard, cross-banded in mahogany, c1800, 30in (76cm) wide.
£700–785 ⊞ F&F

An oak court cupboard, with later carving, c1700, 64in (162.5cm) wide.
£3,800–4,200 ⊞ REF

A cherrywood armoire, French, early 19thC, 50in (127cm) wide.
£1,700–1,900 ⊞ MLL

An oak *tridarn*, Welsh, c1700, 53in (134.5cm) wide.
£6,750–7,500 ⊞ TRI

An oak panelled cupboard, with dentil cornice, c1780, 40in (101.5cm) wide.
£2,800–3,200 ⊞ CGA

A cherrywood armoire, with steel hinges and brass locks, French, c1800, 51in (129.5cm) wide.
£2,400–2,700 ⊞ GD

◄ **A cherrywood *bonnetière*,** French, c1860, 41in (104cm) wide.
£1,250–1,400 ⊞ NGO

An oak dresser, 18thC, 54½in (138.5cm) wide.
£3,500–4,200 HOLL

An oak dresser, c1800, 68½in (174cm) wide.
£3,200–4,000 TMA

An oak dresser, 18thC, 71in (180.5cm) wide.
£10,500–12,500 TRM

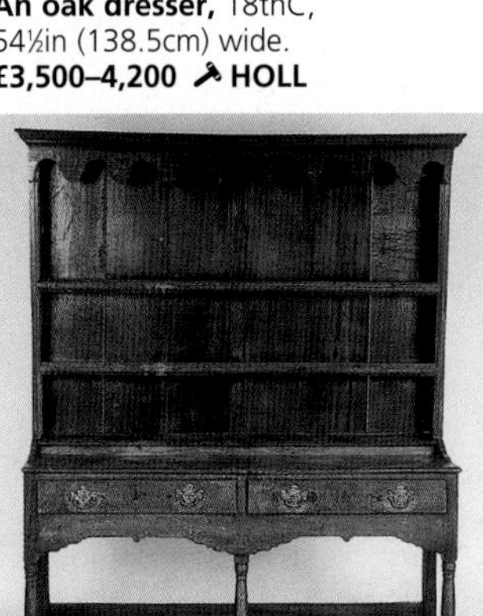

A joined oak dresser, Welsh, probably Glamorganshire, damaged, c1780, 55½in (141cm) wide.
£2,500–3,000 Bri

A yew wood dresser base, early 18thC, 90¼in (229cm) wide.
£28,000–32,000 P(NW)

An oak dresser base, with two cupboards and five drawers, early 18thC, 67in (170cm) wide.
£3,500–3,750 CGA

An oak low dresser, with three drawers, on cabriole legs, c1730, 73in (185.5cm) wide.
£5,500–6,250 F&F

An oak low dresser, c1735, 74in (188cm) wide.
£22,500–25,000 NMA

An oak dresser base, banded in mahogany, c1750–70, 80in (203cm) wide.
£12,500–14,000 AdA

An oak low dresser, with a pierced apron, c1750, 55½in (141cm) wide.
£11,000–12,500 JC

A chestnut server, French, c1840, 69in (175.5cm) wide.
£1,500–1,650 GD

An oak low dresser, with mahogany crossbanding, mainly 18thC, 72in (183cm) wide.
£3,400–4,000 AH

An oak dresser base, possibly originally with a rack, c1810, 61in (155cm) wide.
£3,500–4,000 DUK

An oak gateleg table, the ends of each leaf replaced, c1680, 60¾in (154.5cm) extended.
£5,000–5,750 ⊞ JC

► **An oak refectory table,** faults, restored, mid-17thC, 80in (203cm) wide.
£9,000–11,000 ⚒ S(S)

An oak side table, with wavy stretchers, c1685, 34in (86.5cm) wide.
£2,500–2,850 ⊞ DJH

An oak side table, with X-stretchers and crossbanded drawer front, c1690, 32in (81.5cm) wide.
£2,000–2,350 ⊞ SuA

An oak side table, with baluster ring-turned legs, late 17thC, 33in (84cm) wide.
£1,300–1,600 ⚒ TMA

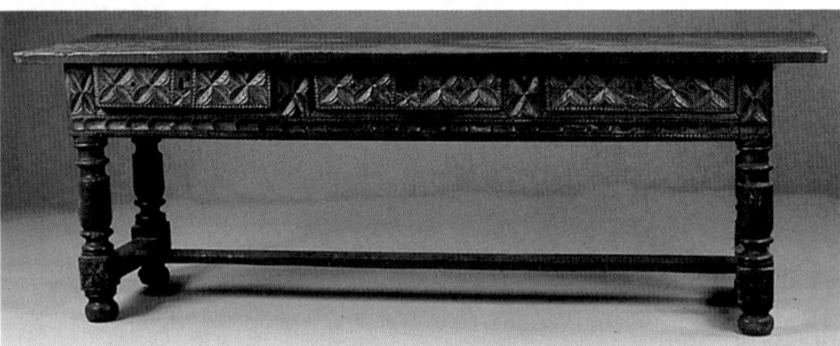

A carved oak refectory table, French, probably Breton, late 17thC, 94½in (240cm) wide.
£4,500–5,500 ⚒ Bon(C)

An oak gateleg table, with a frieze drawer, c1700, 67in (170cm) wide.
£4,200–5,000 ⚒ G(L)

► **A serving table,** painted to resemble wood, French, mid-19thC, 81in (205.5cm) long.
£1,300–1,450 ⊞ SIE

An oak side table, with a single frieze drawer, mahogany banding and corner brackets, c1780, 31in (78.5cm) wide.
£1,000–1,100 ⊞ NoC

A chestnut table, with a shaped rail, French, c1820, 65in (165cm) wide.
£1,750–2,000 ⊞ SIE

An elm table, with a single drawer and square tapered legs, French, c1850, 78in (198cm) wide.
£3,200–3,500 ⊞ DeG

A chestnut and pine farmhouse table, with two benches, French, c1840, table 93in (236cm) wide.
£2,500–3,000 ⊞ TDS

◄ **A drop-leaf dining table,** with figured burr-ash top, c1820, 42in (106.5cm) extended.
£3,500–4,000 ⊞ RYA

A pine bookcase, painted to simulate walnut, c1850, 44in (112cm) wide.
£1,900–2,100 ⊞ DUK

A painted pine folk art box, Hungarian, c1870, 58in (147.5cm) wide.
£200–240 ⊞ Byl

A painted pine folk art box, Hungarian, c1860, 38in (96.5cm) wide.
£250–300 ⊞ Byl

A pine blanket chest, American, c1900, 37in (94cm) wide.
£600–700 ⚒ NOA

A painted pine folk art chest, Hungarian, c1870, 48in (122cm) wide.
£200–240 ⊞ Byl

A painted pine cupboard, Dutch, c1750, 40in (101.5cm) wide.
£720–800 ⊞ KA

A polychrome-painted serpentine cabinet, Netherlands, possibly Haarlem, c1800, with later painting, 59¾in (152cm) wide.
£2,350–2,800 ⚒ S(Am)

A pine marriage cupboard, with original painted decoration, European, c1800, 62in (157.5cm) wide.
£7,750–8,500 ⊞ RYA

A painted pine house-keeper's cupboard, original condition, Irish, Galway, c1800, 60in (152.5cm) wide.
£4,720–5,250 ⊞ NMA

A polychrome-painted pine cupboard, eastern Swiss, 1800–25, 40½in (103cm) wide.
£3,000–3,600 ⚒ S(Am)

A polychrome-painted pine cupboard, eastern Swiss, dated 1825, 53in (134.5cm) wide.
£2,000–2,400 ⚒ S(Am)

A polychrome-painted pine cupboard, French, Alsace, 1850–75, 50½in (128.5cm) wide.
£1,800–2,200 ⚒ NOA

A painted pine demi-lune side cabinet, French, c1780, 43in (109cm) wide.
£2,000–2,200 ⊞ SSW

A painted pine dresser base, 67in (170cm) wide.
£3,500–4,200 ⚒ CGC

► **A Victorian *faux* bamboo and painted pitch pine bedroom suite,** by Howard & Sons, partially stripped.
£1,000–1,200 ⚒ CGC

A roll-top bureau bookcase, c1860, 55in (139.5cm) wide.
£1,500–1,800 ⊞ TPC

A *faux* bamboo bedstead, c1900, 39in (99cm) wide.
£1,200–1,300 ⊞ SeH

A Victorian pine breakfront bookcase, the upper section with two astragal-glazed doors enclosing fixed shelves, the lower section with two panelled doors, on a plinth base, 52in (132cm) wide.
£500–600 ⚒ PFK

A pine box, Irish, c1880, 47in (119.5cm) wide.
£140–170 ⊞ Byl

◄ **A pine seat,** c1870.
£80–100 ⊞ DFA

► **A pine chopping block,** c1900, 16in (40.5cm) wide.
£600–720 ⚒ S

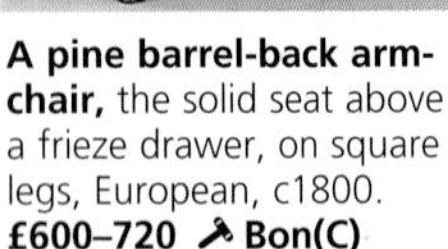

A pine barrel-back armchair, the solid seat above a frieze drawer, on square legs, European, c1800.
£600–720 ⚒ Bon(C)

A child's stained pine Orkney chair, with a woven back, the solid seat above a drawer, on square legs, late 19thC.
£1,350–1,500 DMC

A carved pine clamp-fronted chest, north European, early 17thC, 45¾in (116cm) wide.
£900–1,100 S(O)

A pine chest, with a single drawer, Irish, c1870, 55in (139.5cm) wide.
£160–200 Byl

A pine chest of drawers, Scottish, c1840, 62in (132cm) wide.
£850–950 P&T

◄ **A pine chest of drawers,** with two short and three long graduated drawers, c1820, 30in (76cm) wide.
£500–600 TPC

A pine trunk, with original steel handles, Hungarian, c1890, 23in (58.5cm) wide.
£220–250 MIN

A pine chest of drawers, c1870, 44in (112cm) wide.
£580–650 AL

◄ **A pine multi-drawer chest,** c1860, 38in (96.5cm) wide.
£450–550 TPC

An early Victorian gentleman's pine chest of drawers, 38in (96.5cm) wide.
£500–600 TPC

A pine chest of drawers, with two short over three long drawers, c1870, 41in (104cm) wide.
£350–400 P&T

A Victorian pine chest of drawers, with two short over three long graduated drawers, 39in (99cm) wide.
£425–475 P&T

A Victorian pine chest of drawers, with a gallery back, 36in (91.5cm) wide.
£400–500 TPC

► **A pine chest of drawers,** with two short over two long drawers, c1875, 34in (86.5cm) wide.
£250–300 Byl

A Victorian pine chest of drawers, with four drawers and a small cupboard, 36in (91.5cm) wide.
£320–350 P&T

A Victorian pine chest of drawers, with two short over three long drawers, 39in (99cm) wide.
£450–550 ⊞ P&T

A gesso-decorated pine dressing chest, c1890, 30in (76cm) wide.
£400–500 ⊞ TPC

A pine chest of drawers, with two short over three long drawers, c1880, 36in (91.5cm) wide.
£380–425 ⊞ AL

A Victorian pitch pine chest of drawers, 43in (109cm) wide.
£700–765 ⊞ P&T

▶ A pine chest of drawers, with a shaped top, c1890, 42in (106.5cm) wide.
£250–275 ⊞ P&T

A Victorian pine chest of drawers, 42in (106.5cm) wide.
£280–320 ⊞ WV

A pine chest of drawers, c1890, 35in (89cm) wide.
£330–365 ⊞ AL

A Georgian pine cupboard, with a shelved interior, 33in (84cm) wide.
£400–500 ⊞ TPC

A pine Normandy *buffet à deux corps*, French, c1800, 55in (139.5cm) wide.
£2,800–3,200 ⊞ GD

A pine Normandy *buffet à deux corps*, French, c1820, 55in (139.5cm) wide.
£2,500–2,800 ⊞ GD

A pine astragal-glazed cupboard, Irish, c1840, 52in (132cm) wide.
£1,600–2,000 ⊞ TPC

An early Victorian pine linen press, 45in (114.5cm) wide.
£850–950 ⊞ P&T

A pine shelved cupboard, c1860, 35in (89cm) wide.
£700–800 ⊞ TPC

A Victorian pine linen press, 47in (119.5cm) wide.
£700–800 ⊞ P&T

A pine corner cupboard, with four doors, c1870, 42in (106.5cm) wide.
£950–1,050 ⊞ AL

Cross Reference

See Pine Furniture (page 180–197)

A pine cupboard, with two doors, c1870, 52in (132cm) wide.
£450–500 ⊞ P&T

A pine cupboard, with two central drawers, Irish, c1875, 50in (127cm) wide.
£650–800 ⊞ Byl

◄ **A pine hanging cupboard,** the glazed doors with two drawers below, Hungarian, c1880, 42in (106.5cm) wide.
£425–475 ⊞ MIN

A pine cupboard, with two doors, Irish, c1880, 52in (132cm) wide.
£330–370 ⊞ Byl

◄ **A pine cupboard,** with two drawers, c1880, 26in (66cm) wide.
£350–400 ⊞ AL

A Victorian pine housekeeper's cupboard, 84in (213.5cm) wide.
£1,500–1,800 ⊞ TPC

A pine cupboard, with two doors, Irish, 1880, 47in (119.5cm) wide.
£250–300 ⊞ Byl

A pair of pitch pine pot cupboards, French, c1880, 15in (38cm) wide.
£800–900 ⊞ HA

► **A late Victorian pitch pine vestry cupboard,** 65in (165cm) wide.
£1,000–1,150 ⊞ P&T

A Victorian pine bedside cupboard, 16in (40.5cm) wide.
£180–220 ⊞ TPC

A pine pot cupboard, c1890, 17½in (44.5cm) wide.
£130–145 ⊞ AL

A pine pot cupboard, c1900, 34in (86.5cm) high.
£75–85 ⊞ AL

A pair of pine pot cupboards, Dutch, c1900, 13in (33cm) wide.
£245–275 ⊞ P&T

A pine dog kennel dresser, Welsh, early 19thC, 58in (147.5cm) wide.
£1,800–2,000 ⊞ TPC

A pine dresser, Irish, Co Mayo, c1865, 47in (119.5cm) wide.
£475–575 ⊞ Byl

A pine dresser, 18thC, 70in (178cm) wide.
£1,800–2,000 ⊞ TPC

A pine Pembrokeshire dog kennel dresser, c1870, 54in (137cm) wide.
£1,500–1,675 ⊞ POT

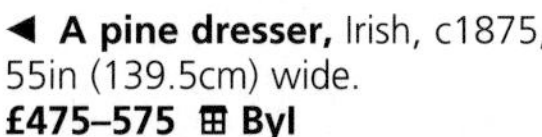

◄ A pine dresser, Irish, c1875, 55in (139.5cm) wide.
£475–575 ⊞ Byl

A pine dresser, Irish, c1880, 48in (122cm) wide.
£475–575 ⊞ Byl

◄ A late Victorian pine dresser, 54in (137cm) wide.
£700–800 ⊞ P&T

► An Edwardian glazed pine dresser, 44in (112cm) wide.
£800–875 ⊞ P&T

A pine dresser, c1840, 72in (183cm) wide.
£1,800–2,000 ⊞ TPC

A pine shop dresser, European, c1870, 98in (249cm) wide.
£1,500–2,000 ⊞ TPC

A pine dresser, Irish, c1885, 49in (124.5cm) wide.
£550–650 ⊞ Byl

A pine sideboard, c1820, 66in (167.5cm) wide.
£1,500–1,800 ⊞ TPC

► **A Victorian panelled shop counter,** 84in (213.5cm) wide.
£800–900 ⊞ TPC

A pine server, Irish, c1875, 50in (127cm) wide.
£250–300 ⊞ Byl

A pine Lincolnshire dresser base, c1880, 41in (104cm) wide.
£380–420 ⊞ P&T

A pine sideboard, with two drawers, c1880, 42in (106.5cm) wide.
£350–400 ⊞ AL

A pine potboard dresser base, c1890, 48in (122cm) wide.
£480–530 ⊞ AL

A pine side cabinet, the seven drawers and single door flanked by four turned columns, c1900, 59in (150cm) wide.
£525–575 ⊞ MIN

A pine stand, French, c1790, 31in (78.5cm) high.
£600–685 ⊞ TDS

◄ **A Victorian pine serving table,** 53in (134.5cm) wide.
£300–345 ⊞ P&T

A stained pine side table, French, late 19thC, 38in (96.5cm) wide.
£430–480 ⊞ AMS

A pine farmhouse table, on tapered legs, early 19thC, 108in (274.5cm) wide.
£800–900 ⊞ TPC

A Georgian pine side table, 33in (84cm) wide.
£300–350 ⊞ TPC

► **A pine drop-leaf table,** c1880, 42in (106.5cm) wide.
£250–280 ⊞ AL

A Victorian pine farmhouse table, with turned legs, 72in (183cm) wide.
£400–500 ⊞ TPC

A pine drop-leaf table, with a mahogany base, c1880, 55in (139.5cm) extended.
£350–400 ⊞ AL

A Victorian pine gateleg table, 35in (89cm) wide.
£350–400 ⊞ P&T

Miller's is a price GUIDE not a price LIST

A pine side table, c1880, 42in (106.5cm) wide.
£380–435 ⊞ AL

A pine wine table, French, c1880, 43½in (110.5cm) wide.
£680–765 ⊞ AL

◄ **A pitch pine refectory table,** c1890, 60in (152.5cm) wide.
£600–665 ⊞ AL

A Victorian pine drop-leaf table, 58in (147.5cm) extended.
£320–400 ⊞ TPC

A Georgian pine breakfront compactum, 84in (213.5cm) wide.
£2,800–3,200 ⊞ P&T

A pine armoire, Continental, c1850, 48in (122cm) wide.
£800–1,000 ⊞ TPC

A late Victorian carved pine two-piece wardrobe, 40in (101.5cm) wide.
£380–425 ⊞ P&T

A pine armoire, French, c1800, 53in (134.5cm) wide.
£1,500–1,650 ⊞ GD

A Victorian pine wardrobe, 65in (165cm) wide.
£1,200–1,400 ⊞ TPC

A pine compactum, c1890, 48in (122cm) wide.
£1,000–1,200 ⊞ TPC

A pine panelled wardrobe, with two doors, Irish, c1800, 52in (132cm) wide.
£1,200–1,400 ⊞ TPC

A pine armoire, with two doors, c1870, 56in (142cm) wide.
£800–900 ⊞ TPC

A pine wardrobe, with two doors, c1900, 48in (122cm) wide.
£350–400 ⊞ P&T

A pine armoire, French, Jura, 19thC, 52in (132cm) wide.
£1,150–1,300 ⊞ MLL

A pine single shoehole wardrobe, c1880, 34in (86.5cm) wide.
£400–500 ⊞ TPC

A pine armoire, the two doors with deep arched panels, c1900, 40in (101.5cm) wide.
£500–600 ⊞ TPC

A pine washstand, c1820, 25½in (65cm) wide.
£300–335 ⊞ AL

A pine washstand, with original marble top, c1875, 36in (91.5cm) wide.
£225–250 ⊞ P&T

A pine washstand, with three drawers, c1880, 42in (106.5cm) wide.
£350–400 ⊞ AL

A bamboo glazed cabinet, with original lacquered top and embossed paper sides, c1880, 20in (51cm) wide.
£375–425 ⊞ MTay

A bamboo cupboard, with lacquered chinoiserie decoration, late 19thC, 27in (68.5cm) wide.
£1,100–1,200 ⊞ CoHA

A pair of rattan garden chairs, c1920.
£120–135 ⊞ MLL

A bamboo dressing table, c1890, 30½in (77.5cm) wide.
£600–665 ⊞ AL

A bamboo table, with restored painted top, c1900, 28in (71cm) wide.
£115–130 ⊞ CoHA

◄ **A bamboo plant stand,** inset with Victorian transfer-printed tiles, c1890, 32in (81.5cm) high.
£420–465 ⊞ NAW

A wicker table, c1920, 36in (91.5cm) wide.
£60–70 ⊞ AL

A Victorian copper two-handled bain-marie, with rounded corners, the removable liner with four pierced holes, 15¾in (40cm) wide.
£100–130 ⚒ PFK

► **A sycamore butter-marking wheel,** the tread carved with leaves and flowerheads, 19thC, 5in (12.5cm) diam.
£90–110 ⚒ PFK

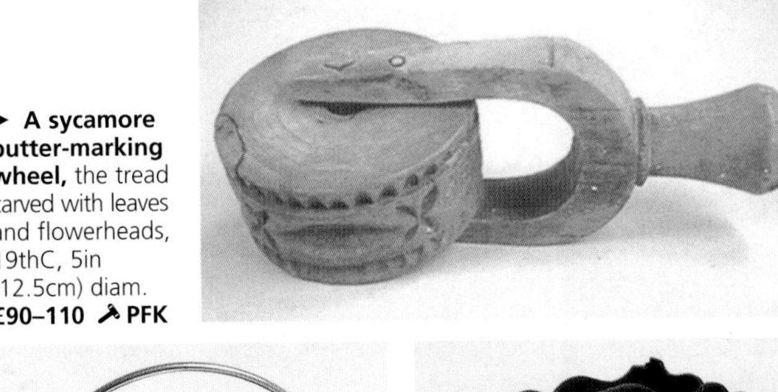

A marble-patterned biscuit tin, by Huntley & Palmers, c1890, 7½in (19cm) high.
£100–120 ⊞ HUM

A steel and brass cream can, 8in (20.5cm) high.
£180–200 ⊞ SMI

A walnut cutlery tray, with two sections, c1800, 14in (35.5cm) wide.
£85–95 ⊞ F&F

A brass and iron preserving pan, c1820, 6in (15cm) diam.
£125–135 ⊞ SEA

An enamel drip tray with ladles, French, c1930, 18½in (47cm) high.
£68–75 ⊞ AL

A marmalade jar, by T. G. Green, 1950s, 4in (10cm) high.
£70–80 ⊞ HSt

A pair of scales, with brass pans and original paint, marked 'W. & T. Loach', c1800, 11in (28cm) wide.
£70–75 ⊞ B&R

A Savoie pottery jug, with a lid, c1920, 7in (18cm) high.
£60–70 ⊞ MLL

An enamel jug, c1920, 14½in (37cm) high.
£90–100 ⊞ AL

A brass pepper or spice pot, 1760–80, 3½in (9cm) high.
£225–275 ⊞ SEA

A fruitwood five-tier spice tower, c1810, 9in (23cm) high.
£350–400 ⊞ F&F

Jars

A maiolica albarello, inscribed 'loch sanu' between bands of oak leaves and acorns in blue on a pale blue ground above an ochre lion's mask, the base inscribed 'TB', Italian, Venice, late 16thC, 9¾in (25cm) high.
£620–750 ⚒ **S(S)**

Cross Reference
See Colour Review (page 290)

A London delft blue and white syrup jar, inscribed 'S:D:Moris' on a winged angel and cockle-shell label, c1700, 7½in (19cm) high.
£1,350–1,500 ⚒ **S(O)**

A Prattware tobacco jar and cover, decorated with the pot lid design Passing the Pipe, Ball 104, on a brick-red ground, with gold-line decoration, c1860, 4¾in (12cm) high.
£200–240 ⚒ **SAS**

Maiolica

Maiolica is the term for tin-glazed earthenwares produced in Italy from the 15th–18th centuries, probably derived from the Tuscan name for the island of Majorca through which Hispano-Moresque wares from Spain were shipped to Italy from the 14th century. Important areas of production include Florence, Faenza, Deruta, Orvieto, Naples, Castelli, Montelupo and Urbino. Sixteenth century pieces were typically decorated in bold, high-fired colours. Maiolica should not be confused with majolica, a heavily-potted moulded ware developed by Minton in the mid-19th century.

◄ **A maiolica syrup jar,** possibly Mantelupo, painted in blue, ochre and green, with a central label 'SIP:DSVG:DACETOSA' damaged, Italian, 1575–1625, 10½in (26.5cm) high.
£400–500 ⚒ **S(S)**

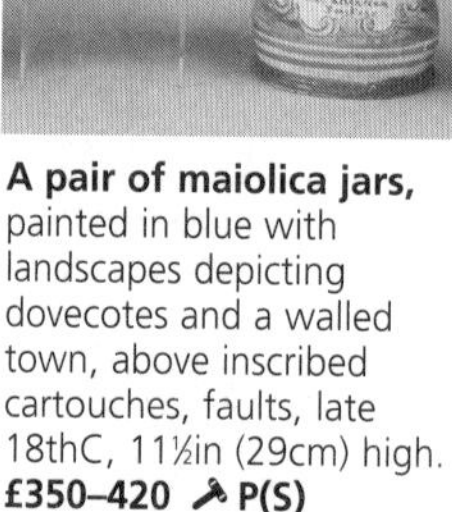

A pair of maiolica jars, painted in blue with landscapes depicting dovecotes and a walled town, above inscribed cartouches, faults, late 18thC, 11½in (29cm) high.
£350–420 ⚒ **P(S)**

A Wemyss preserve jar, painted with oranges, c1900, 6in (15cm) high.
£350–400 ⊞ **RdeR**

A pair of Bassano drug jars and covers, painted with flowers and foliage around oval panels inscribed 'conser di Miole' and 'conser di Genepro', both damaged, late 18thC, 8¾in (22cm) high.
£350–420 ⚒ **P(S)**

A faïence tobacco jar, inscribed 'Tabac' and painted with tobacco leaf sprigs in yellow, green and black, with a pewter mount, screw-on cover and handle, 19thC, 13½in (34.5cm) high.
£300–360 ⚒ **B**

A maiolica jar, possibly Savona, painted in shades of blue with scrolling branches and oak leaves, centred by a banner inscribed 'Nespoli Co Nd' surmounted by a mask, above a winged putto, the handles with mask and scrollwork terminals in relief, foot and handles restored, minor chips, 17thC, 13½in (34.5cm) high.
£900–1,000 ⚒ **S(Am)**

A drug jar, inscribed in blue 'Resumptivum' within a label hung with ropes and flower garlands flanking a winged mask, rim chips, Belgian, probably Brussels, 1750–1800, 10¾in (27.5cm) high.
£1,150–1,300 ⚒ **B**

A Della Robbia faïence drug jar, inscribed 'Safarano di Liverpool', with scrolling foliate panels decorated in green and blue enamels, painted marks to base, c1900, 15in (38cm) high.
£900–1,100 ⚒ **Pott**

Jardinières

A tin-glazed flower or plant holder, with three tiers of apertures, painted in blue with fleurs-de-lys motifs between each aperture, with a chevron pattern around the middle, minor losses, cracked and riveted, 1675–1725, 11¾in (30cm) diam.
£800–950 ⚒ B

Lead-glaze pottery items of this shape have been excavated in Holland, although the glaze on this example would suggest a French or north Italian origin. It was possibly used for growing plants, as the leaves and roots hanging through the holes might be cut for medicinal purposes.

A majolica jardinière, with apple blossom on a basket-moulded blue ground, decorated in green, yellow, brown and white, the interior with a pale turquoise glaze, hair cracks and a foot chip, painted 'L' mark, c1870, 10¼in (26cm) high.
£260–320 ⚒ WW

An orchid jardinière, probably Varage, French, c1880, 10in (25.5cm) high.
£780–865 ⊞ MLL

A pair of Wedgwood jasper ware cachepots and stands, applied with green florets on a brown and white chequerboard ground with scrolling foliage and shells, one foot chipped, one repaired, impressed marks, 19thC, 5½in (14cm) high.
£5,750–7,000 ⚒ S

A pair of Minton majolica jardinières, the handles in the shape of juvenile satyrs, carrying oak leaf foliate swags looped through lion masks, the neck moulded with oak branches, all on a turquoise ground, the interior glazed lilac, No. 1018, impressed mark and date mark for 1867, 10½in (26.5cm) high.
£1,600–2,000 ⚒ P(E)

A Wemyss fern pot, painted with sweet peas, c1900, 3in (7.5cm) high.
£180–200 ⊞ RdeR

► **A Wemyss jardinière,** painted with apples, impressed marks, c1900, 7in (18cm) high.
£580–650 ⊞ RUSK

A Minton majolica cachepot, the basket-moulded body between a pair of cornucopia handles, decorated in shades of blue, yellow, green and cream, with a turquoise interior, impressed marks and date cyphers, c1867, 11in (28cm) high.
£1,100–1,200 ⚒ S(O)

A Victorian majolica jardinière, relief-moulded with a meandering raspberry plant on a brown ground, the interior with a turquoise glaze, painted No. 269, 9in (23cm) high.
£500–600 ⚒ G(L)

A George Jones & Sons majolica jardinière, relief-moulded and decorated with marsh tits and insects among bulrushes, with a band of lily pad leaves and white water lily flowers around the base, on a turquoise ground below a yellow rim, the interior with a pink glaze, extensive riveted repairs, post-1873, 11¾in (30cm) high.
£1,400–1,600 ⚒ S(S)

Jugs & Ewers

A Raeren stoneware jug, decorated with a light brown glaze, possibly German, late 16thC, 6in (15cm) high.
£600–720 BERN

A Raeren stoneware bellarmine, the neck applied with a bearded mask, the body applied with three armorial medallions bearing the double-headed eagle supporting an orb, decorated with a light brown glaze, German, late 16thC, 7in (18cm) high.
£1,000–1,200 B

◄ A stoneware wine jug, decorated with a brown glaze with splashes of tiger glazes, cracked, 17thC, 11½in (29cm) high.
£850–1,000 S

A Cologne stoneware bellarmine, the neck applied with a smiling bearded face, the body applied with three medallions of a crowned shield bearing the arms of Juliet-Kleve-Burg supported by lions, the panels and mask heightened with blue splashes, German, 1590–1610, 10¾in (27.5cm) high.
£1,100–1,200 B

A Montelupo maiolica ewer, pinched at the neck to form a spout, painted with a panel depicting a female saint surrounded by a wreath of foliage with lemons, flanked by calligraphic blue scrolls, extensively cracked and riveted, handle missing, Italian, 17thC, 15½in (39.5cm) high.
£700–800 B

A salt-glazed stoneware bellarmine, modelled with a mask and a floral panel, German, early 18thC, 9in (23cm) high.
£330–400 G(L)

A Hanau faïence jug, with pewter mount, painted in blue, yellow and green with scattered flowers, seeds and an insect, chips, incised 'C' and 'z', German, c1730, 12in (30.5cm) high.
£750–900 S(O)

A Westerwald jug, the grooved neck in manganese, the ground with a chequer pattern in dark blue and grey, the medallion embossed with the crowned cipher 'GR' within a laurel wreath border on a band incised with stylized floral motifs, hairline crack and chip, 18thC, 8in (20.5cm) high.
£320–350 B

A Jackfield-style jug, the body decorated with a black glaze and cold gilding with a figure of a man, possibly William Augustus, Duke of Cumberland, wearing a tricorn hat and holding a sword, the initials D and W to either side, the reverse with a bird among foliage, rim chips, handle cracked, c1760, 7in (18cm) high.
£2,500–3,000 Bon(C)

The Duke of Cumberland was the third son of George II. He commanded the King's army against the Young Pretender, whom he defeated at Culloden in 1746 and was granted an annuity of £25,000 by a grateful Parliament.

A Talavera jug, painted in blue with the Madonna and Child, the reverse inscribed 'VIN', fritting and chipping, hole to base, Italian, 18thC, 12¼in (31cm) high.
£700–800 S(O)

A Leeds creamware jug, the interlaced handle terminating in moulded flowerheads and foliage, the body painted in iron-red and black with a portrait of George III, the reverse with a spray of flowers, spout restored, c1780, 6½in (16.5cm) high.
£2,600–3,200 SAS

A pearlware puzzle jug, with pierced neck and loop handles, painted in blue with leafy stems, handle repaired, c1800, 7½in (19cm) high.
£260–320 WW

A creamware marriage jug, with gilt and transfer-printed decoration depicting a coat-of-arms flanked by a farmer and his wife, with inscription, the handle with full-blown tulip below, the reverse decorated with a group of people dancing next to a farmhouse and field, late 18thC, 12½in (32cm) high.
£900–1,100 ⚒ BLH

A pearlware jug, decorated with a silver lustre resist border, the sides with farming inscription, the red panel below the spout inscribed 'Humphrey Sellman 1812' obscuring an earlier inscription, 6½in (16.5cm) high.
£270–325 ⚒ WW

The decorative technique of silver resist is normally found on pearlwares, particularly jugs and mugs, c1800–20. To achieve the effect, a design is painted onto the object in wax, then the silver lustre is applied to the surface. With the burning off of the wax in the kiln, the painted design appears on a silver lustre ground. Examples in good condition today are scarce, as the silver lustre is prone to rubbing through regular use.

A pearlware jug, commemorating the Peace of Amiens 1801, printed in brownish-black with an allegorical scene depicting Britannia holding named portraits of George III and Bonaparte riding in a carriage, a view of Amiens in the background, c1801, 8in (20.5cm) high.
£650–800 ⚒ SAS

A creamware jug, printed in black with a three-masted ship, the reverse with a compass, entitled 'Come Box the Compass', 1790–1800, 5½in (14cm) high.
£600–700 ⚒ CGC

A pearlware jug, painted in colours with a floral design, within treacle borders, hairline crack, early 19thC, 9in (23cm) high.
£350–420 ⚒ GAK

◄ **A Staffordshire pearlware Parson and Clerk jug,** relief-moulded with figures in a wooded landscape, picked out in coloured enamels within turquoise-glazed stiff-leaf bands, rim chip and hairline crack, 1815–20, 5¾in (14.5cm) high.
£250–300 ⚒ LFA

Commemorative wares

Commemorative wares were produced as early as the 17th century by delft potters, but did not achieve mass popularity until the late 18th and early 19th centuries with the advent of improved transport and industrial techniques. The Victorian era saw a proliferation of pieces issued to celebrate significant occurrences and important individuals. Popular themes were major exhibitions, the first being the Great Exhibition of 1851, and royal, political and military events. Value is dependent on the scarcity and condition of the item.

A cream jug, commemorating Queen Caroline, with a portrait medallion and the motto 'Protect My Mother', beneath a copper lustre band, early 19thC, 3in (7.5cm) high.
£200–240 ⚒ G(L)

A stone china jug, the handle moulded as a serpent, the body decorated with a bird perched among rockwork and flowers, printed mark, c1820, 7in (18cm) high.
£130–150 ⚒ WW

A yellow ground silver resist jug, c1820, 5½in (12.5cm) high.
£450–500 ⊞ RdV

A Sunderland pink lustre jug, probably from the Garrison Pottery, decorated with splashed and scratched pink lustre bands, printed in black with a Masonic design and verse, the reverse with a further verse, cracks, unmarked, 1820–50, 9¼in (23.5cm) high.
£350–420 DN

A Sunderland pink lustre jug, decorated to one side with the 'West View of the Cast Iron Bridge Over The River Wear', the reverse with an oval scenic panel and a motto, 19thC, 5¾in (14.5cm) high.
£180–220 DMC

A Sunderland pink lustre jug, by Dixon & Co, decorated with ships in full sail, damaged, c1830, 7in (18cm) high.
£325–360 NAW

A Mochaware jug, decorated with a broad band of cream slip with blue borders containing pink and blue fern-like fronds above smaller bands, on a coffee ground, hairline crack, 19thC, 7½in (19cm) high.
£425–525 Bea(E)

A set of three graduated copper lustre jugs, with moulded flowers and birds on wide green bands, c1840, largest 7¼in (18.5cm) high.
£130–150 WW

A pottery jug, commemorating the repeal of the Corn Laws, printed in black and enamelled in colour with an agricultural design, the reverse with a scene of a port, c1846, 5½in (14cm) high.
£125–150 SAS

The Corn Laws, a tax on foreign corn, were introduced in 1804 to protect British farmers from competition from abroad.

POTTERY

A stoneware jug, with flow blue decoration, 1850–60, 6in (15cm) high.
£60–70 JOA

An Alcock & Co majolica jug, decorated with a green, brown and mottled lilac glaze, hairline crack, impressed mark, 19thC, 9½in (24cm) high.
£300–360 WL

A stoneware jug, commemorating the Crimean War, relief-moulded with soldiers at home and abroad, c1856, 8in (20.5cm) high.
£400–440 RdV

A scroll-moulded pottery jug, transfer-printed in black with portraits of the Duke of Wellington and his birth and death dates, c1852, 9¾in (25cm) high.
£110–130 SAS

A Sunderland lustre jug, brown transfer-printed with a view of 'The Great Australia Clipper-Ship' and 'Mariner's Arms Verse', and one other view of a ship, within orange lustre zig-zag lines and with a lustre neck, 19thC, 9¼in (23.5cm) high.
£380–420 CAG

A George Jones majolica jug, the body moulded with white orchids and green leaves on a brown and green mottled bark-effect ground, the yellow rim above a turquoise interior, registration lozenge and painted pattern No. 3431, c1870, 5½in (14cm) high.
£1,200–1,400 RTo

A pair of Wedgwood black basalt wine and water ewers, the handles modelled as Neptune and Bacchus, the bodies relief-moulded with foliage and goat and dolphin masks, impressed marks, late 19thC, 14in (35.5cm) high.
£2,400–2,700 M

▶ **A Wemyss ewer and basin,** painted with scattered green shamrock within green line borders, handle of ewer restored, impressed mark, c1900, basin 11¼in (28.5cm) diam.
£550–650 S

A pearlware jug, transfer-printed in black and pink with Bewick's animal prints, c1860, 5½in (14cm) high.
£630–700 JRe

A stoneware jug, probably by Bates, Elliott & Co, relief-moulded with birds nesting, impressed date code for March 1872, 9½in (24cm) high.
£60–70 DN

A Copeland majolica jug, moulded with water lilies, decorated in shades of brown, grey, green, pink and blue, impressed mark and registration mark for 1877, 7½in (19cm) high.
£1,600–2,000 WW

An Elsmore & Forster Staffordshire jug, transfer-printed in colours with clowns, cock fighters and other humorous prints, c1870, 9in (23cm) high.
£650–750 RdV

A Minton majolica jug, with a pewter cover and jester finial, decorated with folk dancers and trailing ivy in green, purple, yellow and brown enamels, hinge damaged, impressed 1231 to base, date code for 1877, 13in (33cm) high.
£900–1,100 Pott

Items in the Pottery section have been arranged in date order within each sub-section.

A pottery jug, transfer-printed in black and decorated in colours with a stylized view of Glasgow International Exhibition, dated 1888, 8in (20.5cm) high.
£50–60 SAS

Loving Cups

A loving cup, with a rhyme, painted with floral sprays, damaged, dated 1829, 8in (20.5cm) high.
£350–420 DA

A Prattware loving cup, with gilt handles, decorated with 'The Best Card', the reverse with an inscription in gilt, gold-line decoration, dated 1864, 6½in (16.5cm) high.
£130–155 SAS

A Staffordshire frog and newt loving cup, printed in puce with figures, chariots and minarets, the interior with a brown and black-spotted frog on the base, the sides with two similarly decorated newts, slightly damaged, 19thC, 6in (15cm) high.
£200–240 TMA

Mugs & Tankards

A Nuremberg faïence tankard, with a pewter mount, painted in colours with a milkmaid milking a cow, with ruins in the background, haircrack and chips, marked with initials in manganese, German, c1760, 8½in (21.5cm) high.
£2,200–2,500 S

A Sunderland mug, depicting 'Jack The Sailor's Return', with a verse and pink lustre detail, c1850, 5in (12.5cm) high.
£415–460 ⊞ RdV

A creamware mug, commemorating Admiral Rodney, sprigged with a profile portrait plaque within a ribboned frame between floral swags, partly picked out in green, reserved on a tortoiseshell-glazed ground, rim chips, 1782–85, 4½in (11.5cm) high.
£1,250–1,400 P
This mug probably commemorates Rodney's promotion to Rear Admiral after his success at the Battle of Saintes in 1782.

A set of three Mason's Ironstone graduated mugs, printed and enamelled in iron-red and underglaze blue with chrysanthemums and foliate scrolls, with serpent loop handles, printed marks in blue, c1820, largest 4¾in (12cm) high.
£475–575 N

► **A child's Wemyss mug,** painted with two geese feeding, within a green line border, restored, impressed marks, early 20thC, 3½in (9cm) high.
£600–720 S

A pottery mug, probably Ferrybridge, transfer-printed in brown with a flower-framed medallion depicting Britannia with two maidens, beneath a floral border, the prints coloured underglaze in orange, blue, green and yellow, rim crack and chip, 1790–1800, 6in (15cm) high.
£160–200 DN

A Staffordshire spongeware mug, decorated in pink and blue, c1850, 6in (15cm) high.
£270–300 ⊞ HUM

Plaques

A Deruta votive plaque, polychrome-painted with the Madonna and Child seated on a throne, flanked by two female saints, within a raised integral frame painted with a stiff-leaf border, Italian, 1575–1625, 7in (18cm) wide.
£1,550–1,850 ⚒ S(O)

A pair of pottery lustre wall plaques, each transfer-printed with an angel musician and a floral wreath, one printed to the centre 'Prepare to Meet Thy God', and the other 'Praise Ye the Lord', both with pale apricot lustre borders, crack to one, 1825–50, 9½in (24cm) wide.
£80–100 ⚒ PFK

A majolica wall plaque, applied in bold relief with lilies, naturalistically decorated in coloured enamels, on a blue and gilt marbled ground, 1880–90, 18½in (47cm) diam.
£260–300 ⚒ LFA

A Prattware plaque, moulded with classical figures playing a harp and lyre above a group of putti and a dog, the border moulded with leaf scrolls, decorated in green, blue, ochre and brown, cracked in half, c1790, 11in (28cm) wide.
£160–200 ⚒ WW

A puce lustre commemorative wall plaque, the centre printed *en grisaille* and decorated with a scene 'A West View of the Cast Iron Bridge over the River Wear', early 19thC, 9in (23cm) wide.
£220–260 ⚒ GAK

An earthenware plaque, printed and painted with children feeding ducks, within a brown marbled band, c1870, 7¾in (19.5cm) diam.
£170–200 ⚒ LFA

◄ **A pair of Cantagalli wall plaques,** moulded in high relief with portraits of a Renaissance man and his lady, cockerel marks in purple, Italian, late 19thC, 12¼in (31cm) diam.
£260–300 ⚒ CGC

A pottery lustre wall plaque, printed 'Thou God See'st Me', within a floral wreath, early 19thC, 9in (23cm) wide.
£100–120 ⚒ PFK

A pair of Victorian Sunderland lustre plaques, with portraits of the preachers Adam Clark and the Rev John Wesley, with inscriptions, 9in (23cm) wide.
£360–430 ⚒ G(L)

A majolica plaque, the centre moulded with a classical scene of female warriors and hunting dogs within a decorated border, decorated in treacle and green with cream and pale blue detail, late 19thC, 17½in (44.5cm) diam.
£280–320 ⚒ GAK

A Wedgwood jasper plaque, decorated by Bert Bentley, with classical figures and a dog in white on a green ground, impressed marks and BB 588, c1920, 5in (12.5cm) wide.
£300–360 ⚒ S(O)

Pot Lids

'Pegwell Bay Established 1760', mounted on a gilt gesso frame, mid-19thC, 4in (10cm) wide.
£50–60 WW

'Holy Trinity Church, Stratford-on-Avon', No. 229, by F. & R. Pratt, multi-coloured lid, chips, c1850, 4½in (11.5cm) diam.
£70–85 BBR

A Prattware pot lid, No. 329A, first edition, depicting a couple, the lady looking coyly down at her needlework, c1865, 5in (12.5cm) diam.
£250–300 JBL

A view of Sandringham House, No.181, with mottled border, c1880, 5in (12.5cm) diam.
£160–190 SAS

'River Scene with Boat', No. 61, c1880, 4in (10cm) diam.
£600–720 SAS

'The Finishing Line', a transfer-printed horse racing scene mounted in a mahogany frame, 19thC, 4in (10cm) diam.
£45–55 HOLL

A view of The Golden Horn, Constantinople, No. 204, with gold-banded border and flange with similarly decorated base, chipped, c1880, 4in (10cm) diam.
£280–340 SAS

POTTERY

Pots & Tubs

◀ **A salt-glazed piggin and spoon,** moulded to resemble a dairy pail, the spoon imitating a ladle, some damage, crack to handle, c1750, 2¾in (7cm) high.
£1,000–1,200 P

▶ **A sgraffito slipware pot,** with incised bands of scrolls and interwoven wavy lines on a cream ground, inscribed 'A.F. 1881', 13¼in (33.5cm) high.
£200–240 PF

◀ **A Wemyss comb pot,** painted with roses, c1900, 7in (18cm) high.
£320–350 RdeR

Services

◄ **A Drabware teapot and cover,** decorated with gilt bands, milk jug and sucrier with cover, small chips to spout, c1815, teapot 3½in (9cm) high.
£200–240 LFA

► **A Mason's Ironstone part dessert service,** comprising 12 pieces, floral decorated in the Oriental style in iron-red, blue and gilt, some pieces repaired, impressed marks, early 19thC.
£1,200–1,500 MCA

A Staffordshire porcellaneous part dessert service, comprising 17 pieces, each applied in white with classical figures, on a lavender-tinted ground, within applied flower and stiff-leaf bands, with gilt line rim, some damage, 1815–20.
£400–500 LFA

◄ **A Mason's Ironstone dinner service,** comprising 85 pieces, printed and overpainted in the Imari palette, damages and repairs, c1835, largest meat platter 20½in (52cm) wide.
£750–900 P(Ba)

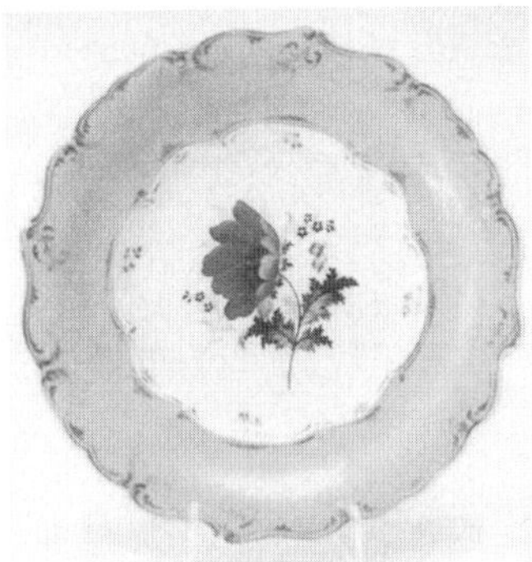

A James Edwards earthenware part dessert service, comprising 12 pieces, painted in coloured enamels, the green ground border picked out in gilt, some damage, c1855.
£350–420 LFA

A Ridgway's Ironstone dinner service, comprising 36 pieces, decorated in iron-red and deep blue with gilded detail, printed marks, damages, 19thC.
£600–720 GAK

A Mason's Ironstone part dinner service, comprising 17 pieces, with oriental floral polychrome decoration in iron-red, blue and green, damaged, 19thC.
£400–480 G(L)

◄ **A Wedgwood dinner service,** pattern No. X7447, after Bartolozzi, signed A. Holland or J. Hodgkiss, comprising 71 pieces, painted in green and purple enamel, the gilded borders acid-etched with a Greek key design, one plate cracked, marks in sepia, c1910, largest plate 9in (23cm) diam.
£3,200–3,800 P

Tea Canisters

A delft tea canister, each side painted with a Chinese figure crossing a bridge, some damage, missing cover, c1730, 4½in (11.5cm) high.
£1,700–2,000 Bon(C)

A Staffordshire creamware tea canister, decorated in shades of green, brown and cream, c1755, 4½in (11.5cm) high.
£1,300–1,450 JHo

A pearlware tea canister, relief-moulded with two dancers and picked out in blue, brown, yellow and ochre, within brown and green borders, rim chips, c1800, 4in (10cm) high.
£250–300 LFA

Tea & Coffee Pots

A Staffordshire red-glazed stoneware coffee pot and cover, engine-turned with chevron bands and horizontal wavy lines, minor chips, c1770, 9in (23cm) high.
£1,200–1,400 S

A Mayer black basalt teapot and cover, the body moulded with flutes beneath a *guilloche* band, impressed mark, c1800, 7¾in (19.5cm) high.
£250–300 WW

► **A Minton majolica turquoise-glazed teapot and cover,** modelled as a Japanese dwarf holding a Noh mask, cover stapled and reglued, chips, No. 1838, impressed mark, c1875, 6in (15cm) high.
£250–300 N

A Wedgwood caneware teapot and cover, the knop modelled as a seated figure, the body formed as a barrel, impressed mark, late 18thC, 6in (15cm) long.
£500–600 WW

A Castleford teapot, polychrome-decorated with swags and urns, with a swan knop, early 19thC, 10in (25.5cm) wide.
£270–300 HUM

A Leeds creamware coffee pot, with cross-band handle and flower knop, c1800, 10in (25.5cm) high.
£520–575 RdV

A Tyneside pink lustre teapot, damaged, c1840, 5½in (14cm) high.
£200–220 NAW

A Staffordshire majolica teapot, modelled as a corn on the cob, c1890, 7in (18cm) high.
£225–250 HUM

Tiles

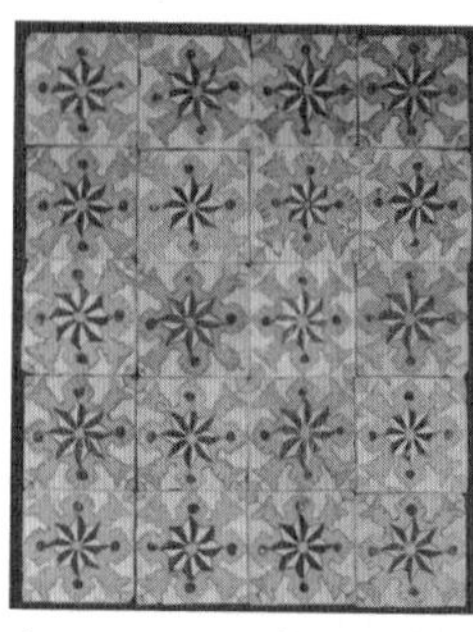

A pavement of Spanish maiolica tiles, comprising 111 pieces, each painted in yellow with a snowflake design, outlined in manganese, most with a manganese and white eight-pointed star in the centre, three similar but with a blue and white star, c1700, tile 5in (12.5cm) square.
£1,250–1,400 B

A Liverpool delft theatrical tile, printed in black, probably by Green, with 'Mr. Lee Lewes in the character of Harlequin', within a diaper border flanked by theatrical trophies, 1770–80, 5in (12.5cm) square.
£450–500 P

Miller's is a price GUIDE not a price LIST

Two delft tiles, transfer-printed in black, one with five figures drinking and smoking pipes, the other with a man riding on another man's back, c1750, 5in (12.5cm) square.
£260–300 WW

► **A set of six Minton pottery tiles,** printed in brown with a farm scene, moulded marks, 19thC, 6in (15cm) square.
£280–335 WW

A delft pottery tile picture, of a bird in a cage, with an oak frame, late 18thC, 15in (38cm) high.
£450–550 S(O)

Toby & Character Jugs

The best Toby jugs were made between 1780 and 1825 and are characterized by sharp, well-defined modelling and subtle colours in the glazes. These glazes were sometimes left to run down the pot into each other (running glaze) or were painted on (translucent glaze). Colours were limited to brown, yellow, green, blue, grey and purple: although the hat will often appear to be black, on closer examination it can be seen to be very dark brown. The best of these translucent jugs were from the Woods factory in Burslem, Staffordshire. A different process used concurrently by William Pratt (1780–1840) obtained very bright yellow, blue, orange, ochre and browns. This palette became generically known as Prattware. Jugs with a cream-coloured pottery body visible through the glaze were called creamware and those with a bluish glaze were called pearlware. Look also for moulded teeth and lips, sometimes painted. The flat painted-on teeth appeared in later pieces, usually Victorian.

The presence of separately applied hollow legs and feet indicate a good early jug. Check inside the body that the clay from face to base is in one piece with no pressed-out shapes of legs. The pressed leg was quicker and therefore cheaper to produce as more moulds were required for applied hollow legs or feet. Pieces of inferior quality were produced because of the great popularity of the Toby jug with poorer people, who bought them to decorate their cottage mantelpieces.

Some early jugs such as the Thin Man, Rodney's Sailor, The Squire and Hearty Good Fellow were decorative rather than functional, as they would have been difficult to clean, as would the examples made in the image of real people such as Martha Gunn and Earl Howe. The Great Plague of 1665 had taught people a lasting lesson in hygiene. In the 18th century, the tavern was often a commercial enterprise, acting as a brewery and a commercial centre where any money-making activity could be carried out. At these bawdy gatherings the Toby jug would have been used to transport the strong ale to the table, its stopper or measure placed on top to protect the contents from candle smuts and dirt. This measure, when filled with strong ale from the Toby, also served as a drinking cup. A small measure you may think, but the ale contained a good portion of ether so it was probably enough to raise the spirits.

As Mr Gabriel Varden says to his daughter Dolly in Dickens' *Barnaby Rudge:* 'Ah well, it's a poor heart that never rejoices. Put the Toby this way my dear.' **Judi Bland**

POTTERY

A Ralph Wood Earl Howe Toby jug, wearing a buff coat and sitting on a translucent-glazed barrel, c1790, 9in (23cm) high.
£2,500–3,000 ⊞ JBL

In the late 18th century the Toby's hat and shoes were always glazed in brown because black was too difficult to achieve and tended to flake off.

A Ralph Wood Thin Man Toby jug, wearing a brown hat, coat and shoes and green waistcoat and breeches, late 18thC, 10in (25.5cm) high.
£2,700–3,000 ⊞ JBL

A Wood-style pearlware Toby jug, dressed in a green hat, coat and breeches and blue waistcoat, stockings and shoes, late 18thC, 10in (25.5cm) high.
£425–475 ⚒ S(O)

A pearlware Toby jug, wearing a brown hat and shoes and pink coat, c1790, 10in (25.5cm) high.
£850–950 ⊞ JBL

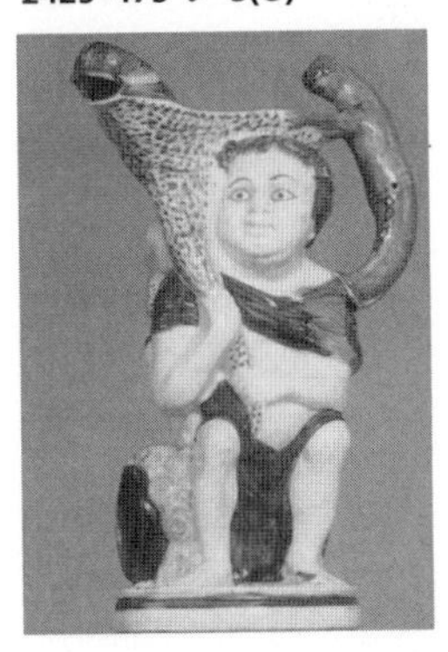

► A Prattware Bacchus and Satyr Toby jug, modelled as Bacchus seated on a blue and yellow wine barrel draped with fruit, wearing a blue robe, the satyr leaning against his back, with a chained monkey handle, restored, c1800, 11¾in (30cm) high.
£250–300 ⚒ P(Ba)

A Pratt-style sailor Toby jug, wearing a blue jacket, yellow waistcoat and striped trousers, restored, c1800, 12in (30.5cm) high.
£800–950 ⚒ S

A Yorkshire Toby jug, decorated in Pratt colours with a manganese face, blue coat and yellow breeches and a sponged green, black, yellow and blue base, hat interior and measure, with a caryatid handle, c1790, 10in (25.5cm) high.
£950–1,050 ⊞ JBL
This Toby still retains his measure which is used to drink from when passing around the jug of strong ale.

A Prattware Toby jug, wearing a yellow coat, pale blue breeches, striped stockings and brown and ochre hat, holding a jug, on a sponged base, c1800, 10in (25.5cm) high.
£200–240 ⚒ P(Ba)

A creamware Toby jug, wearing a green translucent coat, blue waistcoat and yellow breeches, with brown hat and shoes, hat restored, c1800, 10in (25.5cm) high.
£400–500 ⊞ JBL

How to identify early Yorkshire Toby jugs

Look out for the following typical characteristics:

- The scalloped top on his hat.
- A black fringe (even when hair is brown).
- Dotted eyebrows.
- Curled pipe on his chest.
- Raised octagonal cup.
- Caryatid (figurehead) handle.
- Sponged underglaze colours on the base.

► **A Yorkshire Toby jug,** decorated with a reddish-brown coat and yellow breeches, with a translucent blue scalloped edge to his hat, a brown, yellow and green sponged base and hat, his pipe moulded flat to his chest, with a caryatid handle, c1830, 10in (25.5cm) high.
£450–550 ⊞ JBL

An enamelled pearlware Martha Gunn Toby jug, her dress painted with red and green sprigs with a pink *fichu* and yellow bodice, hat restored, c1810–20, 10½in (26.5cm) high.
£370–400 ⚒ P(Ba)
Martha Gunn was the 'Queen of Dippers', well known and greatly sought after in late 18th– early 19th-century Brighton. A 'dipper' was someone who provided a service by assisting his patron or her patroness into the sea to bathe with the use of a bathing machine brought from the water's edge.

◄ **A creamware Toby jug,** some restoration, c1800–10, 9¼in (23.5cm) high.
£700–850 ⚒ LFA

A Yorkshire Toby jug, with blue-glazed coat and yellow breeches, raised octagonal cup and caryatid handle, c1910, 10in (25.5cm) high.
£80–100 ⊞ JBL
By the early 20th century the Yorkshire Toby had lost his fringe, dotted eyebrows and curled pipe. The only features which distinguish it as being a Yorkshire piece are the raised octagonal cup and caryatid handle.

Miller's Compares

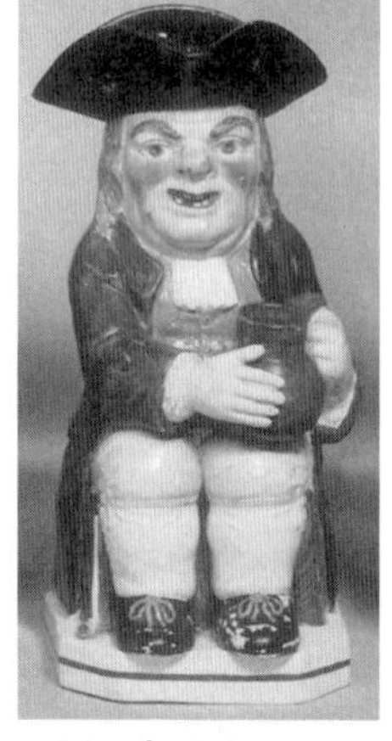

I. A Neale & Co enamelled creamware Toby jug, wearing a brown coat, turquoise waistcoat, pale yellow breeches, and black shoes and hat, some damage and repainting, impressed mark and incised number 35, c1790–95, 10in (25.5cm) high.
£750–900 ⚒ P(Ba)

II. A Staffordshire pearlware Toby jug, wearing a pale dove-grey coat, turquoise waistcoat, lime green breeches, black hat and shoes, hat repaired and repainted, c1800–20, 10in (25.5cm) high.
£250–300 ⚒ P(Ba)

Toby jugs marked with a maker's name such as Item I are rare and this will substantially increase their value. Furthermore, Neale & Co pieces are of particularly good quality – a close study of Item II will reveal that it is not as finely finished off as Item I. Item II has also sustained more damage than Item I, although the price of both pieces has been adversely affected by this. Item I is also earlier in date than Item II – those 20-odd years will make a difference to the price.

POTTERY

A Staffordshire enamelled Drunken Person Toby jug and cover, wearing a black coat and breeches, striped black and white waistcoat and stockings, with black hat and shoes, cover married, hat restored, some repainting, c1820, 9¾in (25cm) high.
£450–550 P(Ba)

It is suggested that the source of this model may be taken from one of the prints in Hogarth's 'A Harlot's Progress' series in which a drunken cleric spills his drink.

A cross-legged Toby jug, wearing a black hat and coat and red breeches, c1880, 10in (25.5cm) high.
£80–100 JBL

A Royal Doulton stoneware Toby-on-a-Barrel jug, wearing a blue coat and grey-green breeches and waistcoat, c1910, 8in (20.5cm) high.
£240–300 G(L)

An Oldfield & Co salt-glazed stoneware Toby jug, the hat picked out in a dark brown glaze, c1838–88, 9¾in (25cm) high.
£370–400 P(Ba)

An unglazed Minton character jug, The Lady with a Fan, c1880, 12in (30.5cm) high.
£320–400 JBL

A Squire Toby jug, dressed in a green coat, blue waistcoat, yellow breeches and manganese hat and shoes, handle replaced, pipe missing, some chips, c1920, 12in (30.5cm) high.
£400–450 P(Ba)

A Copeland Toby jug, wearing a blue-black coat, blue-spotted waistcoat, ochre breeches, black shoes and hat, on a lime green base, hat repaired, impressed mark, c1880, 9¾in (25cm) high.
£140–160 P(Ba)

An Allerton snuff-taker Toby jug, early 20thC, 7in (18cm) high.
£75–85 DHA

A Burleigh Ware character jug, modelled as Winston Churchill seated on a bulldog, the underside impressed 'John Bull Churchill we shall defend every village, every town and every city', green printed mark, c1940, 11in (28cm) high.
£340–400 SAS

A Staffordshire Mr Punch character jug and cover, decorated in coloured enamels, cover with rim chip glued, c1880, 12½in (32cm) high.
£1,000–1,200 LFA

A Toby jug, wearing a blue coat and black-spotted waistcoat, c1900, 6in (15cm) high.
£80–90 DHA

A Winston Churchill Toby jug, by Leonard Jarvis, wearing 18thC dress in shades of brown, green and yellow, holding an artist's palette and three paintbrushes in one hand and making the 'Victory V' sign with the other, a book, quill and builder's trowel at his feet, incised No.151, signed by the artist and titled on base, c1947, 7in (18cm) high.
£500–600 P(Ba)

The various symbols surrounding Churchill represent his skills as war leader, painter, brick layer and writer.

Tureens

A faïence tureen and cover, moulded with mask handles, painted with flower sprays and scattered flowers, the cover surmounted by a horse head finial, French, possibly Bordeaux, c1760, 8in (20.5cm) wide.
£150–180 S(O)

A tureen and cover, decorated with flowers in pale puce on a cream ground with yellow lemon knop, French, Luneville, c1760, 14in (35.5cm) wide.
£2,500–3,000 ⊞ US

A Wedgwood creamware sauce tureen and cover, with leaf moulded knop, painted with brown bands, impressed mark, 1815–20, 8in (20.5cm) wide.
£150–180 LFA

A Mason's Ironstone tureen, stand and cover, decorated with Grasshopper pattern, c1820, 7½in (19cm) wide.
£520–575 ⊞ RdV

A soup tureen, decorated in the Imari palette, c1850, 14in (35.5cm) wide.
£415–460 ⊞ RAN

An Ironstone sauce tureen and cover, decorated mainly in iron-red and blue with gilded detail on a white ground, with matching stand, impressed mark, 19thC, 7in (18cm) wide.
£110–130 GAK

POTTERY

Vases & Urns

A pair of blue and white Dutch Delft vases, damaged, 1675–1725, 13in (33cm) high.
£600–720 BERN

A pearlware vase, painted in underglaze blue, cracked, restored, 1780–1800, 10½in (26.5cm) high.
£220–260 LFA

A pair of Dillwyn's Etruscan ware vases, damaged and repaired, black printed mark, c1847–50, 47½in (120.5cm) high.
£525–625 S(O)

A pottery reproduction Portland vase, by Samuel Alcock, the figures in grey and white transfer on a black ground with brown line edging, 19thC, 10½in (26.5cm) high.
£200–240 AH

► **A maiolica blue and white vase,** painted with a scene of men fishing and with guns, the reverse with a date, the wood stand with presentation inscription, Italian, 19thC, 21in (53.5cm) high.
£450–550 CGC

► **A faïence pot-pourri vase,** the cover modelled as a crown, the sides painted with panels of figures and flowers, on a reticulated foot, damaged, VP mark, 19thC, 11¾in (30cm) high.
£60–75 WW

An earthenware pot-pourri vase and cover, printed in flow blue, 1850–60, 17½in (44.5cm) high.
£180–220 LFA

A Minton majolica double cylinder vase, with blue glaze, moulded with mythological birds, dragons and foliage, c1874, 10in (25.5cm) high.
£450–530 G(L)

◀ A Wemyss flower vase, painted with pink roses, c1900, 5½in (14cm) high.
£320–350 RdeR

A Wedgwood jasper dip vase and cover, with applied white classical relief to a central light blue dip with light green dip socle, footrim and cover, slight relief loss to rim, cover repaired, impressed mark, 19thC, 12¼in (31cm) high.
£1,200–1,300 SK

A pottery vase, decorated with insects and garden flowers, with a gilt band to the shoulder and two gilt ring handles, fitted for electricity, cracked, probably French, late 19thC, 33½in (85cm) high.
£350–420 DN

POTTERY

Wall Pockets

A delft wall pocket, white glazed and moulded in the centre with a female mask flanked by scrolling leaves, a further male mask at the base, chips and losses, 1750–60, 9in (23cm) high.
£800–900 P

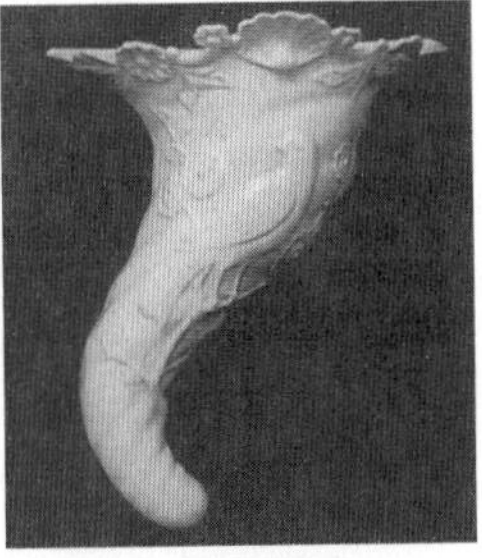

A Staffordshire salt-glazed wall pocket, moulded in relief with a bird perched on a flowering prunus branch, below a scroll, shell- and flower-moulded rim, chips to rim, c1760, 7¾in (19.5cm) high.
£575–700 P

A Minton majolica wall pocket, modelled as a wicker basket resting upon a wooden X-frame with ivy decoration, impressed No.1690, 19thC, 10½in (26.5cm) high.
£950–1,150 G(B)

A pair of Liverpool delftware wall pockets, modelled as fish, decorated in blue and white, glaze chips, c1770, 8in (20.5cm) high.
£7,500–8,500 S(O)

Watch Stands

A Prattware pearlware watch stand, c1800, 10in (25.5cm) high.
£1,350–1,500 JRe

A pearlware watch stand, in the shape of a longcase clock flanked by two figures, minor restoration, probably North Country, early 19thC, 11in (28cm) high.
£400–450 S(O)

A Staffordshire watch stand, polychrome-decorated and modelled as three maidens, c1850, 12in (30.5cm) high.
£120–145 G(L)

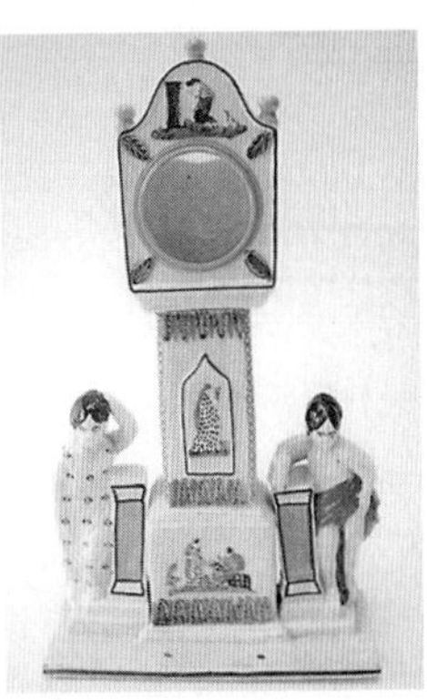

A pearlware watch stand, moulded in relief with figures and stiff leaves, and picked out in blue, green, brown, yellow and ochre, restored, 1815–20, 10½in (26.5cm) high.
£600–720 LFA

Blue & White Transfer Ware

As you can see from the illustrations on the following pages, a great variety of blue and white transfer-printed objects was produced. The more common tableware was made in vast quantities and sizes, and some families commissioned special services that incorporated the family crest or coat-of-arms.

The earliest designs date from the late 18th century and had a very strong Chinese influence (they are known as chinoiserie patterns). These were made in imitation of expensive items of Chinese porcelain, which were out of reach of the less wealthy families. The familiar Willow pattern was introduced by Spode about 1790.

As people travelled further they came back with knowledge of exotic animals which was disseminated through publications. Elephants and zebras were both used by the Rogers pottery in the early 19th century. Country houses, castles, abbeys and ruins were all also used as subjects. Around 1830, patterns became more stylized or floral, because the Acts of Copyright prevented the reproduction of known engravings.

The process of transfer printing involves a design being engraved onto a copper plate by a skilled craftsman using a small mallet and spike. A piece of tissue paper is placed on the ink and the plate plus the paper is passed through a large pair of wooden rollers to distribute the colour evenly. The paper – the 'pull' – is taken from the copper plate and pressed down on the article to be decorated. The paper is then soaked off in cold water and the object is fired at a very high temperature which sets the decoration. The item is then dipped into a glaze and fired again, giving a very shiny glass-like finish. Hence the name 'underglaze transfer-printed pottery'.

Collecting blue and white can become an obsession as I know myself, since this is how I started in the antiques business. My advice is to buy for pleasure rather than investment, although prices have risen quite sharply in the last ten years. It is advisable to buy a book to learn about the different patterns and factories, for instance, *The Dictionary of Blue and White Pottery Vols I* and *II* by Coysh and Henrywood, *Blue and White Pottery, A Collector's Guide* by Gillian Neale and *An Illustrated Guide to Minton Printed Pottery 1796–1836* by G. H. Priestman. You may find a dealer that you like and trust who will search for items for you. Most collections change directions as the collector becomes more interested in a particular theme or factory. On the question of whether you should buy a restored item, if the price reflects the condition, and if you like it and it is for display only, there is no reason not to. However, it is advisable to buy the best you can afford, and get a detailed receipt. **Gillian Neale**

POTTERY

A Herculaneum pearlware blue and white basket and stand, transfer-printed with Charlees Satoon Temple of 40 Pillars pattern from the India series, c1820, 9¾in (25cm) diam.
£630–700 ⊞ GN

A child's J. Meir blue and white bed pan, transfer-printed with Simplon pattern from Byron's Views series, c1830, 9in (23cm) diam.
£750–850 ⊞ GN

A pearlware blue and white bowl, transfer-printed in underglaze blue with Net pattern, the centre with inscription 'Ann Sayers, Southgate, Middlesex, 1807', 13¼in (33.5cm) diam.
£800–950 ⚒ P(EA)

◀ A Minton blue and white bottle coaster, transfer-printed with Bewick Stag pattern, c1815, 5in (12.5cm) high.
£1,000–1,100 ⊞ SCO

A Samuel Alcock blue and white bird feeder, transfer-printed with Ferns pattern, c1830, 4½in (11.5cm) high.
£700–800 ⊞ GN

A blue and white chamber pot, transfer-printed with Highland figures in a rural landscape, with C-scroll borders, c1860, 3¾in (9.5cm) high.
£170–200 ⚒ LFA

A blue and white dessert comport, possibly Herculaneum, transfer-printed in reverse with a view of the Charlees Satoon in the fort of Allahabad on the River Jumna, from the India series, with clips from the central scene on the four outer sides, 1815–25, 12in (30.5cm) wide.
£300–360 DN

A blue and white dish, transfer-printed with a sailing boat before a mill, from the English Scenery series, crowned printed Semi China mark, c1830, 15in (38cm) wide.
£140–170 WW

A Ridgway blue and white egg stand with lid, transfer-printed with Cowman pattern, c1820, 8in (20.5cm) high.
£750–850 ⊞ SCO

A pearlware blue and white jug, transfer-printed with a couple seated at a garden table, the reverse with a swan and waterfowl by the water's edge, minor losses, chipped, 1785–90, 7¼in (18.5cm) high.
£850–950 P(Ba)
Related prints of swans have previously been attributed to Swansea Pottery but the present combination of prints appears to be unrecorded.

A Staffordshire blue and white cow creamer and cover, transfer-printed with Willow pattern, on a green base, chip to one horn, c1900, 6¼in (16cm) wide.
£100–120 WW

A Spode blue and white drainer plate, transfer-printed with Grasshopper pattern, printed mark, 19thC, 14½in (37cm) wide.
£200–240 GAK

A blue and white footbath, transfer-printed with bamboo and flowers, printed Semi China mark, early 19thC, 20in (51cm) wide.
£800–900 S(O)
Semi China has recently been identified by G. H. Priestman in his *Illustrated Guide to Minton Printed Pottery 1796–1836* as being produced by Minton.

A pearlware blue and white jug, transfer-printed with a goldfinch among flowers, fruit and foliage, rim chip, early 19thC, 7in (18cm) high.
£180–220 WW

A Hackwood blue and white cup and saucer, transfer-printed with a rural scene depicting a boy shearing a sheep, c1820, saucer 6in (15cm) diam.
£250–300 ⊞ GN

A Spode blue and white egg cup, transfer-printed with the bird section from the border of the Indian Sporting series, printed mark, 1815–25, 2½in (6.5cm) high.
£500–600 DN

A Spode blue and white beehive-shaped honeypot, transfer-printed with Broseley pattern, c1820, 5in (12.5cm) high.
£500–600 ⊞ GN

A blue and white ewer, transfer-printed with Milkmaid pattern, c1820, 8in (20.5cm) high.
£450–500 ⊞ SCO

◄ **A pearlware blue and white jug,** transfer-printed, commemorating the coronation of Queen Victoria, c1837, 5½in (14cm) high.
£700–780 ⊞ RdV

A blue and white milk jug, transfer-printed with stylized flowers and leaves, c1920, 10in (25.5cm) high.
£225–250 SMI

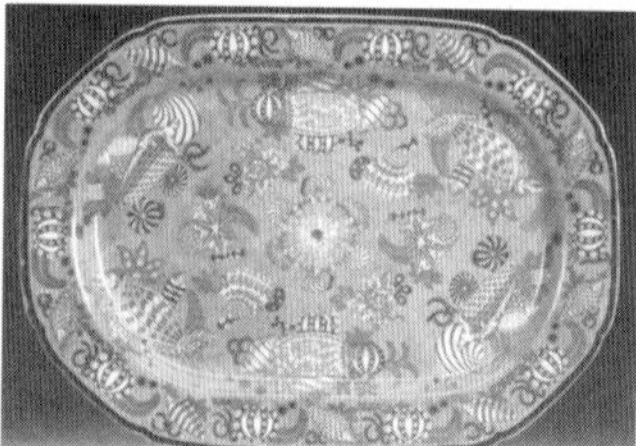

A pearlware blue and white meat dish, transfer-printed with striped and spotted shells, early 19thC, 20½in (52cm) wide.
£525–575 S(S)

A blue and white dish, transfer-printed with Chinese Gardener pattern, c1820, 19in (48.5cm) wide.
£320–350 NAW

A Davenport blue and white meat platter, transfer-printed with Chinoiserie Ruins pattern, within a palm border, impressed mark, early 19thC, 20½in (52cm) wide.
£270–320 GAK

A Spode blue and white earthenware meat platter, transfer-printed with Rome (Tiber) pattern, impressed marks and numeral 10, c1815, 18¾in (47.5cm) wide.
£230–270 S(S)

A blue and white meat plate, by Joseph Stubbs, transfer-printed with Fair Mount near Philadelphia pattern from the Eagle, Scroll and Flowers border series, badly damaged, c1820, 20¾in (52.5cm) wide.
£130–150 WW

A Herculaneum blue and white meat plate, transfer-printed with Etruscan pattern, with gravy gunnel, on bracket feet, early 19thC, 18in (45.5cm) wide.
£450–550 AH

A Staffordshire blue and white meat plate, by H. R. Riley, transfer-printed with Dromedary pattern, within a floral border, crack to rim, 19thC, 18½in (47cm) wide.
£230–275 DMC

◀ **A blue and white mug,** transfer-printed with Cock Inn pattern, c1820, 6in (15cm) high.
£320–350 SCO

▶ **A Spode blue and white pierced tea plate,** transfer-printed with Buddleia pattern, impressed maker's mark, 1790–1805, 7in (18cm) diam.
£320–380 DN

A Staffordshire blue and white meat platter, transfer-printed with a chinoiserie motif and zebra riding, early 19thC, 17in (43cm) wide.
£100–120 L&E

A blue and white meat plate, transfer-printed with the Quarry pattern from the Durham Ox series, c1820, 18½in (47cm) wide.
£3,000–3,250 GN

A Leeds Pottery pearlware blue and white meat dish, transfer-printed with Italian Scenery pattern within a broad stiff-leaf and passion flower border, with gravy gunnel, c1825, 18¾in (47.5cm) wide.
£400–500 LFA

A Staffordshire blue and white meat platter, transfer-printed with Nuneham Courtney near Oxford from the Wild Rose Border series, 19thC, 15in (38cm) wide.
£80–100 MCC

An Adams blue and white plate, transfer-printed with Lions pattern, c1815, 9½in (24cm) diam.
£350–400 ⊞ SCO

A blue and white nursery plate, transfer-printed to the centre with two children, beehives and motto, c1820, 5½in (14cm) diam.
£450–500 ⊞ GN

A Don Pottery blue and white plate, transfer-printed with figures in a landscape within a floral border, from the Italian Views series, 1820–34, 8in (20.5cm) diam.
£140–160 ⊞ CAL

A Spode blue and white part dinner service, comprising 20 pieces, transfer-printed with Jasmine pattern, moulded with ropetwist borders, some damage, impressed and printed mark, c1830, soup tureen 11¾in (30cm) wide.
£500–600 ⚒ P(Ba)

A set of three graduated Davenport blue and white spill vases or match pots, transfer-printed with Rhine View pattern, c1830, largest 5in (12.5cm) high.
£500–550 ⊞ GN

A Staffordshire blue and white Stilton stand, transfer-printed with Willow pattern, 1860–80, 11in (28cm) diam.
£60–70 ⊞ MCC

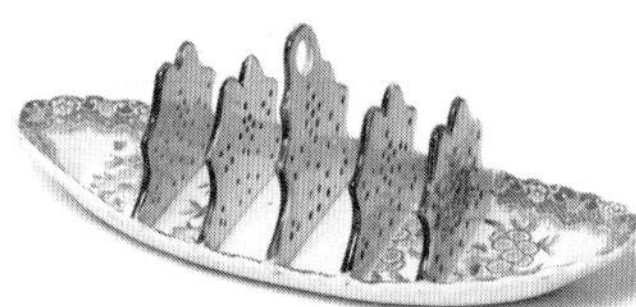

A Spode blue and white toast rack, transfer-printed with Filigree pattern, c1820, 8in (20.5cm) wide.
£450–500 ⊞ SCO

A pair of Ridgway stone china blue and white soup tureens, transfer-printed with Bandanna pattern, one cracked, 1814–30, 13in (33cm) wide.
£400–500 ⚒ N

A blue and white supper set, transfer-printed with an Italianate scene and a narrow border of flowers, the dishes with blue-moulded rose knops, with an ebonized mahogany tray, centrepiece missing, some damage, c1820–30, 19¼in (49cm) wide.
£400–500 ⚒ DN

This supper set is of unusual shape, and while the rose knops are often associated with Rogers, the Italianate scene is particularly reminiscent of the Don Pottery Landscape series, although with a different border.

A Ridgway blue and white soup tureen and cover, transfer-printed with a view of Caius College, Cambridge, from the Oxford and Cambridge College series, c1815, 16in (40.5cm) wide.
£1,600–2,000 ⊞ SCO

A Spode blue and white sauce tureen, cover, stand and ladle, transfer-printed with Jasmine pattern, c1825, bowl 7in (18cm) high.
£500–550 ⊞ GN

◀ **A Mason's Ironstone blue and white tureen and cover,** transfer-printed with Two Man Chinoiserie pattern within a floral and coral diaper border, marks in blue, early 19thC, 14½in (37cm) wide.
£65–80 ⚒ CGC

▶ **A pair of Lakin blue and white garniture vases,** transfer-printed with a stylized chinoiserie design, 1805–10, 9½in (24cm) high.
£675–750 ⊞ GN

POTTERY

Porcelain

Dramatic changes in the auction world have affected porcelain in particular, as sales in London have been shuffled around. Christie's have moved their ceramics department from King Street to South Kensington, while Sotheby's now sell porcelain at Olympia rather than New Bond Street. Phillips and Bonhams have merged their operations, continuing with fine sales in New Bond Street while combining their secondary Bayswater and Lots Road sales at the single location in Chelsea. There is a clear message from all of this: porcelain is not regarded as fine art, to show alongside paintings, or as a luxury investment commodity to mingle with the international jewellery set. Instead, as an applied art, ceramics is viewed as a collectors' market. This change in attitude is a very positive thing. Sale categories have been reassessed, with a return to more specialized auctions. It is appropriate to separate Continental and British porcelain sales, for these appeal to totally different buyers. The buyer's profile has changed too. In a recent fine porcelain sale at Bonhams, private bidders outnumbered dealers by three to one – a complete reversal of the situation just five years ago. These private collectors also attend a growing number of specialist ceramic fairs, where they can peruse the stock of dozens of porcelain dealers in one location. Such fairs are growing in popularity in New York too, as European dealers sell their best porcelain directly to American collectors.

Many porcelain collectors now use the internet to visit dealers' websites or to view auctions on-line, and although most of those who are prepared to spend substantial sums on fine porcelain prefer to hold and feel pieces for themselves, the volume of business carried out over the internet is certainly increasing. With computer technology enabling us to view vast amounts of porcelain on sale around the world at any one time, and the proliferation of specialist auctions and ceramic fairs, collectors are simply spoilt for choice. However, they haven't got bottomless pockets and have to be selective, buying fewer but better pieces. This trend has led to fierce competition for the best porcelain, fresh to the market. The sale of Rudolf Just's collection showed the importance of a well-known provenance, as did the Peter Stephens collection sold at Bonhams. Specialist dealers were pessimistic, predicting that it would be hard to find buyers for so much Plymouth and Bristol porcelain. Instead private collectors were desperate to take home pieces with the Stephens provenance and the sale was a terrific success. There is one noticeable downside, however. As collectors push up the price of the best porcelain, the market for ordinary pieces is static, and in some cases values are falling. It is increasingly difficult to find buyers for damaged porcelain, while over-restored items are almost impossible to sell. **John Sandon**

Animals & Birds

◀ **A Chelsea fable candlestick group,** polychrome-decorated, modelled as two foxes beneath a fruiting grapevine, set before flowers and foliage, some restoration, c1760–65, 12½in (32cm) high.
£900–1,100 WW

▶ **A Derby model of a bird,** polychrome-decorated, perched on a stump applied with flowers, end of tail missing, c1760, 6in (15cm) high.
£850–1,000 WW

A pair of Derby candleholders, modelled as birds in branches, painted with coloured enamels, damaged, 18thC, 9¾in (25cm) high.
£450–540 WW

Cross Reference
See Colour Review (page 296)

A Sampson Hancock Derby group, modelled as three pug dogs, in the white, some faults, marked, late 19thC, 7½in (19cm) wide.
£200–240 N

◀ **A Fürstenberg model of a billy-goat,** modelled by Johann Christoph Rombrich, painted in naturalistic colours, marked, German, 1770–95, 6¼in (16cm) high.
£750–900 S(O)

A Goss model of a Shetland pony, with the arms of the Shetland Isles, 1924–29, 4½in (11.5cm) wide.
£215–235 ⊞ G&CC

A Vienna group of a bear and dog, their coats shaded in brown and black respectively, the base in shades of green, shield mark, c1775, 4½in (11.5cm) high.
£1,300–1,500 ⚒ S(O)
Ex-Rudolf Just Collection. Rudolf Just (1895–1972) was a celebrated collector of ceramics, coins, glass and works of art, who was the inspiration for Bruce Chatwin's novel *Utz*. Living in Prague, he was sent to a concentration camp towards the end of WWII but managed to escape and return home shortly before the Russians liberated the city. All this time his collection had remained in his flat, guarded by the friend who was later to become his second wife. It was again saved from destruction during the four-day uprising in the city, when Just, a native German speaker, persuaded the Germans not to detonate mines laid to blow up an arms depot in a nearby church, which would have destroyed not only the collection, but also the entire square in which the church was situated. The collection was never safe from the authorities, who accused Just in 1962 of speculating in the buying and selling of antiques, although he was later cleared of that charge. Just henceforth ceased publishing articles in the West, and so the existence of the collection became almost a myth, until it was tracked down recently to a tiny flat in Bratislava, inhabited by Just's descendants.

► **A snuff box,** modelled as a stag's head, naturalistically coloured, with a hinged silver-coloured metal lid, Continental, 19thC, 2½in (6.5cm) high.
£170–200 ⚒ WW

A Meissen model of a peacock, naturalistically coloured in green, blue, brown and black, with a gilt-metal ring inserted below one wing, minor chips, crossed swords mark, German, c1770, 5½in (14cm) wide.
£1,100–1,300 ⚒ S

A majolica-glazed porcelain vase, modelled as three birds with yellow baskets on their backs, 19thC, 4¼in (11cm) high.
£140–170 ⚒ WW

A Parian vase, modelled as a pair of owls, entitled 'Match Making', late 19thC, 8in (20.5cm) high.
£100–120 ⚒ G(L)

A pair of Rockingham cats, with tortoiseshell splashed coats in tones of brown, gilt collars, c1830, 1½in (4cm) high.
£900–1,100 ⚒ N

A porcelain fox-mask stirrup cup, picked out in gilt, the rim inscribed 'Tally Ho', 1815–20, 4in (10cm) wide.
£350–420 ⚒ LFA

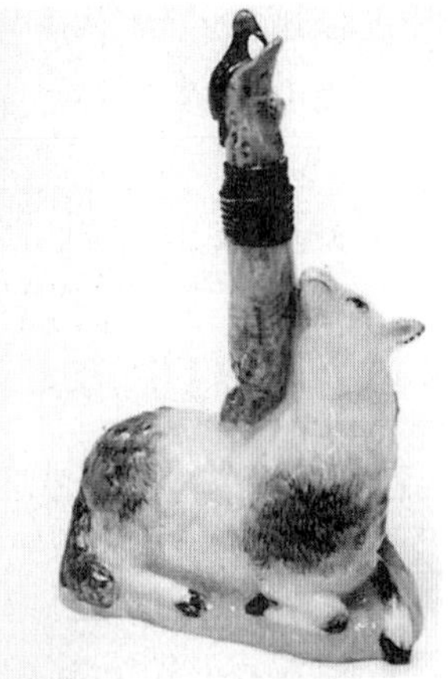

A scent bottle and stopper, modelled as a recumbent lamb looking up at a woodpecker, decorated in coloured enamels with gilt-metal mounts, Continental, c1880, 3¾in (9.5cm) high.
£250–300 ⚒ LFA

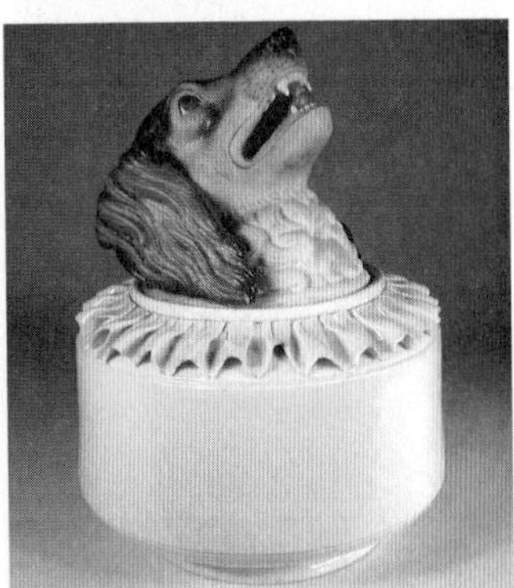

A box, the cover modelled as a spaniel's head, naturalistically decorated, some chips, Continental, early 20thC, 8½in (21.5cm) high.
£80–100 ⚒ WW

Baskets

A Bow basket, painted in blue with bamboo and peony, the reticulated border painted with foliage, damaged and repaired, 1750–55, 6in (15.5cm) diam.
£350–420 WW

A Rockingham basket, moulded with acanthus leaves and flutes, decorated with gilt seaweed, griffin mark in puce, 1830–41, 8in (20.5cm) wide.
£1,150–1,400 N

A Worcester dessert basket, the exterior applied with moulded florets, the centre painted with Anemone and Bellflower Spray pattern, fine crack in one rim section, crescent mark, 1760–62, 6½in (16.5cm) diam.
£700–800 P

On this example one can clearly see how the pierced sides of baskets were produced at Worcester. Concentric lines and a compass have been used to draw the interlaced circles individually prior to cutting out by hand while the clay was still wet. The florets were then separately applied.

▶ **A Royal Worcester basket,** the blush ivory ground with gilt heightening, printed mark, 1908–09, 1½in (4cm) wide.
£30–35 FHF

A Chelsea basket, with reticulated sides, the exterior moulded with yellow flowerheads, the centre painted with pink and yellow flowers, red anchor mark, restored, c1755, 9in (23cm) diam.
£400–500 WW

A pair of Vienna baskets, the exterior applied with florets, the interior with a bouquet of flowers, handles missing, damaged, shield mark, c1800, 8½in (21.5cm) diam.
£750–850 S(Am)

A Worcester yellow-ground basket, painted with flowers within a blue scale border, c1768, 7in (18cm) wide.
£1,800–2,000 ⊞ JUP

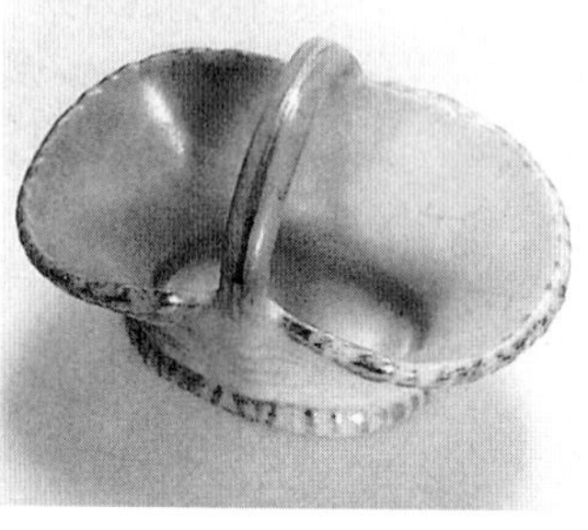

A Lowestoft basket, the sides applied with florets at the intersections, printed in blue with Pinecone pattern, 1775–80, 11in (28cm) wide.
£900–1,100 P

A Worcester blue and white chestnut basket, cover and stand, printed with gooseberries, flowerheads and fruit, the handles with applied floral terminals, the sides of the basket moulded with florettes, scrolling W mark, 1770–72, stand 11in (28cm) wide.
£1,800–2,200 CGC

A Worcester blue and white pierced dessert basket, decorated with Pinecone pattern with a centre spray of autumn fruits and leaves and with daisy heads to each reverse join of the pierced border, crescent mark to base, c1770, 8½in (21.5cm) diam.
£600–720 Mit

A pair of Worcester yellow-ground pierced baskets, the interiors painted with flower sprays, the exterior with a pale yellow ground and moulded at the intersections with florets picked out in puce and green, some restoration, c1770, 5½in (14cm) diam.
£1,600–2,000 S(S)

Bowls

A Bow bowl, painted in blue with a four-clawed dragon reaching out to capture the flaming pearl, the body of the dragon extending to the exterior of the bowl among a series of clouds, painted numeral, 1758–62, 4in (10cm) diam.
£400–500 P

A Lowestoft bowl, painted in red and blue with Redgrave Dolls House pattern, c1780, 6in (15cm) diam.
£250–300 GAK
Redgrave is the name given to this colouring of Lowestoft wares, copying Japanese Imari and named after a family of decorators at the Lowestoft factory.

A Worcester blue and white potted meat pot, decorated with Mansfield pattern, workman's mark, c1758, 5in (12.5cm) diam.
£600–675 WWW

A porcelain bowl, decorated with stylized flowers and leaves, the border with panels of insects and scrolls, 19thC, 12in (30.5cm) diam.
£100–120 WW

▶ **A Philip Christian & Co, Liverpool, blue and white bowl,** painted with stylized flowers and rockwork, chips and cracks, c1765, 7¾in (19.5cm) diam.
£100–120 WW

A Philip Christian & Co, Liverpool, punch bowl, decorated with European landscape prints, rim chips and hairline crack, c1775, 8¼in (21cm) diam.
£350–400 BES
The prints on this bowl were originally used for delft tiles.

A Vauxhall punch bowl, painted in blue with a bridge linking rocks and mountainous islands, including a group of buildings, the interior with further huts on an island with mountains behind, small rim chip, 1755–58, 9¼in (23.5cm) diam.
£1,250–1,500 P
While Worcester and Liverpool punch bowls are reasonably plentiful, Vauxhall examples are extremely rare. Presumably the manufacture of large bowls in Vauxhall porcelain proved too difficult.

A Worcester slop bowl, decorated with Japan pattern, a version of Queen's pattern, gilt rubbed, marked, c1770, 6in (15cm) diam.
£140–170 S(O)

A Lowestoft patty pan, painted in underglaze blue with a moth, surrounded by trailing flowers and leaves, within a berry band, crack, c1780, 3¾in (9.5cm) diam.
£160–200 LFA

A Worcester bowl, painted in turquoise, blue, iron-red and gilt with flowering trees and flowerhead roundels, alternating with blue and gilt diaper bands, with iron-red and gilt flowerhead roundels, the interior with a flowerspray and blue and gilt roundels, foot rim chip, c1768, 9in (23cm) diam.
£700–850 LFA

A Worcester blue and white bowl, decorated with Cannon Ball pattern, crescent mark, c1770, 6in (15cm) diam.
£250–300 G(L)

Care & restoration

Despite its fragile appearance, hard-paste porcelain can safely be washed by hand in luke warm water (never hot) with a little mild detergent added. Soft-paste porcelain may be discoloured and damaged by submerging in detergents, but the surface can usually be wiped gently with a damp cloth. If in doubt consult a professional restorer or specialist dealer.

Pieces of little or no monetary value can be mended at home using glue, but otherwise it is advisable to have repairs carried out by a specialist. It is also wise to obtain an estimate first to determine whether the cost of repair is proportionate to the value of the item.

PORCELAIN

Covered Bowls & Dishes

◄ **A Caughley sucrier and flat cover,** painted in coloured enamels with scattered cornflowers, within gilt-line borders, 1785–90, 4¾in (12cm) high.
£250–300 ⚒ LFA

A two-handled sucrier and cover, by H. & R. Daniel, with flower knop, painted in coloured enamels with birds in branches, the blue ground decorated in gilt with leaves, c1838–40, 5¾in (14.5cm) high.
£150–180 ⚒ LFA

A Derby butter tub and cover, modelled in the shape of a dairy pail, the cover and the base painted in blue with a convolvulus spray on one side and a daisy-like spray on the reverse, separated by insects, 1768–70, 4¾in (12cm) wide.
£1,000–1,100 ⚒ P

► **A Nymphenburg sugar box and cover,** painted to simulate wood, painted *en grisaille* with scenes of a harbour and bridge on two 'tacked' trompe l'oeil panels, some chips, impressed shield mark, German, 1770, 4½in (11.5cm) high.
£650–800 ⚒ S(O)

A Factory Z sucrier and cover, decorated with scrolling foliage in gilt on a pale apricot band, c1800, 6in (15cm) wide.
£300–325 ⊞ MER

When the collector David Holgate researched the New Hall factory he identified three contemporary factories whose names were not known. They were designated Factory X, Factory Y and Factory Z but positive identification is still lacking.

Boxes

A Coalport box and cover, with 'jewelled' decoration, c1900, 4in (10cm) wide.
£1,100–1,250 ⊞ MAA

◄ **A Meissen box and cover,** painted with colourful flower sprays and scattered insects, crossed swords mark, impressed numerals, German, late 19thC, 6in (15cm) diam.
£180–220 ⚒ S(O)
Ex-Rudolf Just Collection.

► **A gilt-metal-mounted snuff box,** possibly Mennecy, moulded with basketwork, the exterior painted with scattered green floral sprigs, the interior of the cover painted with two Cupids in disguise and a couple to one side, French, c1760, 2¾in (7cm) high.
£950–1,150 ⚒ S(O)

Buildings

A Carlton bandstand, entitled 'Lucky White Heather from Margate', with pearl lustre finish, 1902–30, 3½in (9cm) high.
£35–40 ⊞ G&CC

A letter stand, modelled as a castle with a spill vase at each end, the centre panel painted with colourful birds, gilded details, restoration to one tower, c1840, 6¾in (17cm) high.
£250–300 ⚒ WW

A Goss John Knox's House, decorated in colours, unglazed, 1935–39, 3¾in (9.5cm) high.
£315–350 ⊞ G&CC

Busts

► **A Copeland Parian bust of Love,** after R. Monti, impressed mark, c1870, 13¼in (33.5cm) high.
£450–550 ⚒ CAG

A Nymphenburg biscuit bust of Louis XVI, in military dress, impressed shield mark, German, late 19thC, 19in (48cm) high.
£1,000–1,200 ⚒ S(Am)

A biscuit bust of Henry IV, after a model by Bachelier, the metal base with pierced foliate design, incised *faux* Sèvres marks to rear, French, late 19thC, 14½in (37cm) high.
£250–300 ⚒ Bon(C)

A Wedgwood Parian bust of Lord Byron, by E. W. Wyon, c1860, 15½in (40cm) high.
£200–240 ⚒ DMC

A Parian bust of Lord Byron, 19thC, 10in (25.5cm) high.
£150–180 ⚒ WW

► **A pair of biscuit busts of Antinous and a young girl,** after the Antique, impressed marks, Continental, late 19thC, 11½in (29cm) high.
£900–1,000 ⚒ S(O)

Candle Snuffers

◄ **A Copeland snuffer and stand,** with rope-twist decoration in orange and white and gilt line detail, 1850–70, 3½in (9cm) high.
£130–145 ⊞ TH

A Minton snuffer and stand, decorated predominantly in lilac and green with flowers and leaves, c1900, 3½in (9cm) high.
£200–220 ⊞ TH

A Grainger's Worcester candle snuffer and stand, 1875–80, 4in (10cm) high.
£400–450 ⊞ TH

A Kerr & Binns Worcester candle snuffer, modelled as a monk wearing a grey habit and holding an open Bible, 1855–62, 4½in (11.5cm) high.
£1,300–1,500 ⚒ S(S)
This is a rare version of the Kerr & Binns monk.

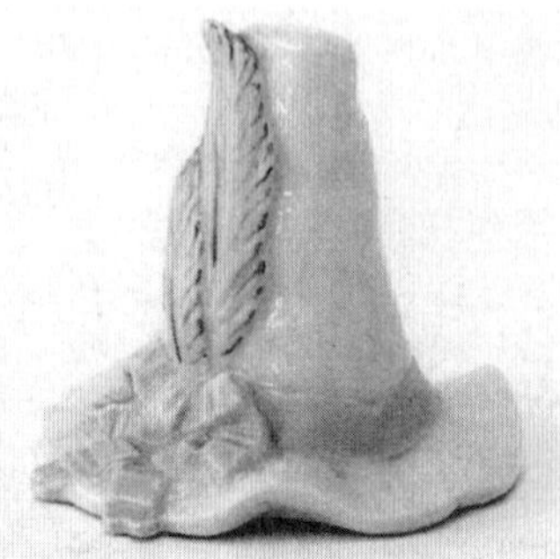

A Royal Worcester candle snuffer, in the shape of a plumed hat, picked out in pink, printed mark in green for 1904 and shape No. G178, 2½in (6.5cm) high.
£100–120 ⚒ LFA

Candlesticks & Chambersticks

A Bow chamberstick, painted in blue with flower sprays and sprigs, cracks, European style, 1765–70, 5¼in (13cm) high.
£1,100–1,300 ⚒ P
Candlesticks were regarded as luxury items and it is not suprising that the few English blue and white examples were decorated in European rather than Chinese taste. The pattern on this Bow candlestick derives from Worcester of similar date.

A pair of Meissen candlesticks, decorated with Onion pattern, German, c1890, 7½in (19cm) high.
£525–575 ⊞ MAA

► **A porcelain chamberstick,** painted with flower sprays in shades of pink and green, 1835–40, 3¾in (9.5cm) high.
£70–85 ⚒ WW

PORCELAIN

Chocolate, Coffee & Teapots

A Frankenthal teapot, reserved on each side in sepia with a putto against a marble ground, with replacement cover, marked, German, c1784, 5½in (14cm) high.
£475–575 S(O)

A Hicks & Meigh teapot, cover and stand, painted with flower sprays within gilded quatrefoil cartouches on blue bands painted with further rose blooms and gilded leaf tendrils, minor cracks, c1820, 6¼in (16cm) high.
£220–280 P(Ba)

A Lowestoft coffee jug and cover, printed in underglaze blue with figures in a Chinese landscape, within flower and cell diaper bands, minor damage, c1785, 8¾in (22cm) high.
£500–600 LFA

Miller's is a price GUIDE not a price LIST

A Ludwigsburg teapot and cover, painted in colours with fruits and flowers, with three paw feet, minor chips, crowned CC monogram, German, c1770, 5½in (14cm) high.
£850–1,000 S(Am)

A pair of Meissen teapots and covers, encrusted with brightly coloured flowers between zoomorphic spouts and scroll-moulded handles, crossed swords marks, German, 1850–1900, 4½in (11.5cm) high.
£2,750–3,000 S(S)

A Tournai chocolate pot, painted in puce *camaieu* with a scene of fishermen in estuary landscapes and ruins, with gilt scrollwork to the spout, turned wooden handle, cover missing, repaired chips to rim, crossed swords and four crosses mark, Belgian, c1760, 5¼in (13cm) high.
£450–550 S(O)

Cross Reference
See Colour Review (page 298)

A New Hall teapot and cover, pattern No. 312, the body painted in colours with flowers and leaves, c1800, 10in (25.5cm) high.
£250–300 WW

A Worcester teapot, painted in underglaze blue with Waiting Chinaman pattern, cover missing, crescent mark, c1765, 3¼in (8.5cm) high.
£140–170 LFA

► **A Worcester teapot and cover,** polychrome-decorated with Chinese Family pattern against a fluted ground, damage to spout, underglaze blue fret mark, 1765–70, 6½in (16.5cm) high.
£250–300 Bon(C)

◄ **A Worcester teapot, cover and stand,** embossed in low relief with Chrysanthemum pattern of intricate flowers and foliage in the Chinese style, with a blue-painted lambrequin border around the rims, the base with a band of blue chrysanthemum petals, the centre of the stand painted in blue with a flowerhead, crescent mark, 1762–65, 5½in (14cm) high.
£1,500–1,700 P

The Chrysanthemum pattern represents Worcester's modelling at its best, for the detail is beautifully crisp even beneath the layer of glaze. A Chrysanthemum tea set would have been far more expensive than other blue and white and would have been aimed at a sophisticated market.

PORCELAIN

Chocolate, Coffee & Tea Services

◀ **A Belleek porcelain part tea set,** comprising 11 pieces, decorated with Shamrock pattern on a cream woven ground, Second Period black mark, Irish, 1891–1926, tray 17½in (44.5cm) wide.
£730–875 ⚒ AH

A Belleek cabaret set, comprising 10 pieces, including an associated pair of plates, Second Period, Irish, 1891–1926.
£600–720 ⚒ HOK

A Copeland bone china cabaret set, comprising 10 pieces, in the Meissen style, decorated with flowers and gilded turquoise borders, c1870.
£200–240 ⚒ WW

A Davenport bone china part tea set, comprising five pieces, with silver-plated mounts, decorated in the Imari style in iron-red and cobalt blue, printed factory marks, c1880.
£280–335 ⚒ WW

A Derby Crown porcelain cabaret set, comprising 26 pieces, decorated in the Imari palette with flowers, c1887.
£800–950 ⚒ CGC

Cross Reference
See Colour Review (page 298)

A Factory Z part tea and coffee service, comprising 10 pieces, each piece bat-printed *en grisaille* with fruits in a gilt urn, within gilt line borders, c1800.
£200–240 ⚒ LFA

◀ **A Royal Crown Derby tea set,** pattern No. 4591, comprising 34 pieces, each decorated in the Imari palette, date code for 1911.
£380–420 ⚒ Bri

A Frankenthal part tea set, comprising five pieces, painted with birds, flowers and fruit embellished with rococco scrolls, German, 18thC, spoon tray 7½in (19cm) wide.
£1,800–2,200 ⚒ HOK

A Limoges cabaret set, comprising 12 pieces, decorated with flowers on a shaded blue ground with gilt highlights, French, early 20thC, tray 20in (51cm) wide.
£130–160 ⚒ DMC

A Meissen Marcolini coffee and chocolate service, comprising 16 pieces, each ribbed and painted in purple with *indianische Blumen* picked out in gilding, crossed swords and star marks, German, c1775, coffee pot 7½in (19cm) high.
£1,600–1,800 ⚒ S(Am)

◀ **A New Hall part tea service,** pattern No. 408, comprising nine pieces, in spiral moulded form, decorated in gilt and blue underglaze with borders and leaf sprigs, c1800.
£450–550 ⚒ WW

A Paris part coffee service, comprising 27 pieces, painted with roses on a solid gilt band, cover of sugar bowl missing, minor damage, marked, French, c1800.
£1,650–1,800 S(O)

A tea and coffee service, possibly Ridgway, No. 8455, comprising 45 pieces, each piece painted with landscape vignettes on a salmon ground with gilt vines, mid-19thC.
£700–850 CGC

A pair of tea bowls and saucers, sugar bowl and cover, possibly Tomaszov, decorated in gilding with bands of scrolling foliage, gilt star marks, Polish, Lubin, early 19thC, sugar bowl cover 3¾in (9.5cm) diam.
£475–575 S(O)
Ex-Rudolf Just Collection.

A Vienna-style cabaret service, comprising eight pieces, painted with panels of classical subjects by Wagner, reserved on a raspberry ground within brightly coloured geometric borders with raised gilt decoration, knops reglued, shield marks, signed, late 19thC.
£900–1,000 B

A Worcester Flight & Barr part composite tea and coffee service, comprising 18 pieces, decorated with puce and gilt flower sprays, incised B mark to some pieces, 1790–1800, teapot stand 7in (18cm) high.
£400–500 P(NW)

A Worcester part tea and coffee service, comprising 41 pieces, each piece painted in underglaze blue with Royal Lily pattern between cobalt and gilt bands, some damage, painted and impressed marks, 1785–1815, milk jug 4½in (11.5cm) high.
£750–900 RFA

A Royal Worcester coffee set, comprising 12 pieces, painted by Harry Stinton with Highland cattle, printed puce marks with date code for 1930, with six silver-gilt coffee spoons in a fitted case.
£3,800–4,200 DN
It is rare to find a full set of this quality by a top artist.

◄ **A tea service,** London shape, comprising 27 pieces, brightly painted with flowers on a gilt ground, some damage, early 19thC.
£1,100–1,300 S(O)

A tea service, comprising 35 pieces, decorated in pink and yellow with butterflies, ribbons and gilt swags, some faults, pattern No. 414 in gilt to base, 1800–10.
£500–600 DMC

A London-shaped part tea service, comprising 17 pieces, each piece polychrome-decorated in the Imari style with a figure on a bridge, in a Chinese river landscape, within gilt line borders, pattern No. 145 in gilt, 1815–20.
£1,650–2,000 LFA

PORCELAIN

Clocks

◄ **A Coalport porcelain-cased mantel timepiece,** by Vulliamy of London, of rococo outline, encrusted in flowers and decorated in mauve and gilt, restored, 1830–35, 11½in (29cm) high.
£1,150–1,350 CAG

A **Dresden Four Seasons clockcase,** modelled in the rococo style with four children emblematic of the seasons applied to the scroll-moulded and pierced case, the scrollwork picked out in gold, pink and turquoise and applied with flowers, a few minor losses, German, late 19thC, 19¾in (50cm) high.
£900–1,000 B

A Meissen mantel clock, moulded with rockwork and *rocailles* picked out in gilding, encrusted with flowers and applied with six various birds, crossed swords mark, German, 20¾in (52.5cm) high.
£3,000–3,500 S(Am)

Clock prices

While not exactly cheap, with porcelain clock cases you do get a lot for your money. Most are based on the rococo designs used at Meissen and by other 18th-century German makers. It is common to find fake Meissen marks on 19th-century clocks, but examples made by Meissen are always of superior quality. The clock movement is usually of secondary importance, but a good maker, such as Vulliamy, will increase the value.

A porcelain clock, in rococo style, French, c1845, 14in (35.5cm) high.
£1,100–1,200 MER

► **A Sitzendorf mantel clock,** decorated in the Dresden style with floral encrusted case, marked, late 19thC, 20in (51cm) high.
£300–360 G(L)

Condiment Pots

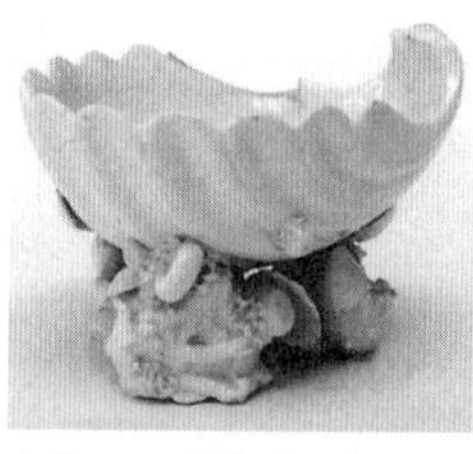

A Bow salt, in the shape of a shell, in the white, on three shell supports applied with shells and seaweed, rim chip, c1755, 4¼in (11cm) wide.
£600–700 LFA

A Meissen salt, decorated with birds and insects, c1750, 4in (10cm) high.
£500–600 US

◄ **A Caughley mustard pot and cover,** printed in underglaze blue with Three Flowers pattern, hatched mark, 1780–85, 3¾in (9.5cm) high.
£500–600 LFA

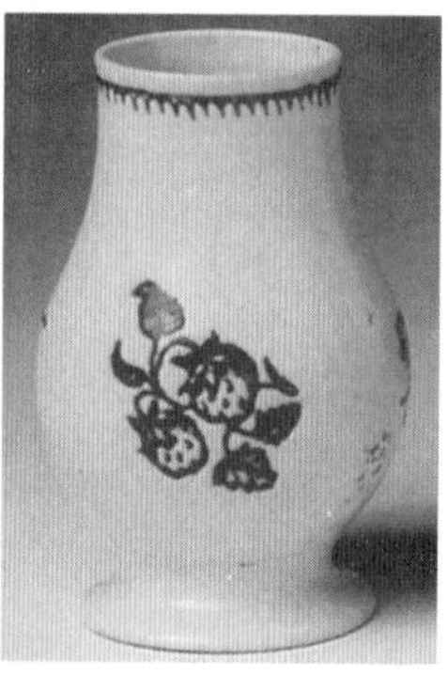

◄ **A John and Jane Pennington, Liverpool, dry mustard pot,** printed in blue with a spray of strawberries and two floral sprigs, cover missing, c1780, 4in (10cm) high.
£250–300 P

► **A Worcester wet mustard pot and cover,** painted in blue with Mansfield pattern of a trailing peony spray, 1756–57, 3¼in (8.5cm) high.
£5,000–6,000 P

The flat cover, glazed underneath, and distinctive handle indicates an early date for this rare mustard pot. The earliest Worcester wet mustard pots did not have openings in the covers for spoons.

Cups

A Bow coffee cup, painted in the *famille rose* style with a lotus below a flower diaper border, cracked, 1755–60, 2½in (6.5cm) high.
£110–130 WW

A Bristol teabowl and saucer, painted in green with swags of flowers and leaves, painted letter and numerals, c1770–75.
£350–420 LFA

A Caughley teabowl and saucer, decorated with Bandstand pattern in an underglaze blue print, 'S' mark to base, c1780, saucer 5in (12.5cm) diam.
£250–300 BES

A Chelsea teabowl, decorated with Lady in a Pavilion pattern in the Kakiemon palette, minor nick to rim, raised anchor mark, 1750–52, 1¾in (4.5cm) high.
£1,500–1,650 S(O)

Three teabowls and two saucers, spirally fluted and painted with floral sprigs and with a cell and garland border within an iron-red outer line border, probably Coalport, two teabowls damaged, one saucer a later replacement, early 19thC.
£40–50 TMA

A Derby teabowl and saucer, decorated with The Boy on a Buffalo pattern in underglaze blue, c1770, saucer 5in (12.5cm) diam.
£700–800 JUP

Chelsea

Production at the Chelsea factory falls into five periods, four of which are named after marks used at the time:

Triangle Period (1744–49)
Mark usually incised or painted in underglaze blue. White, glassy, transluscent body, often left uncoloured, the shape based on British silverware shapes.

Raised anchor period (1749–52)
Mark embossed on a raised pad. Milky white, silky body, containing impurity specks. Decoration based on Japanese porcelain, Vincennes and Meissen.

Red anchor period (1752–56)
Very small mark in red enamel on the backs of figures and bases of plates and cups. Creamy white body with dribbling glaze, often decorated with Meissen-style flowers. When held up to a strong light, so-called Chelsea 'moons' can be seen – bubbles trapped in the paste, which appear as lighter spots in the body.

Gold anchor period (1756–69)
Mark painted in gold. Creamy body, prone to staining. Clear, thickly applied glaze which tends to craze. Rococo decoration, influenced by Sèvres. Use of gilding significantly increased.

Chelsea-Derby period (1770–84)
Mark of a D with an anchor conjoined, usually in gold. Gold anchor mark also continued to be used. Chelsea factory bought and run by William Duesbury & Co, owners of the Derby porcelain factory, until it was closed in 1784. Predominantly neo-classical decoration with a new French look.

► **A Royal Crown Derby urn-shaped cup set,** commemorating a visit to America by George VI and Queen Elizabeth, numbered 162 of 3,000, exclusively for Wm Plummer & Co of New York, c1939, 4¾in (12cm) high.
£800–950 SAS

LOCATE THE SOURCE
The source of each illustration in Miller's can be found by checking the code letters below each caption with the Key to Illustrations, pages 794–800.

A Factory X teabowl and saucer, painted in *famille rose* palette with two figures in a garden, c1790.
£130–160 LFA

PORCELAIN

◄ **A Meissen teacup and saucer,** polychrome-painted with birds and flowers, German, c1750, cup 2in (5cm) high.
£900–1,000 ⊞ US

► **A New Hall-style fluted teabowl and saucer,** painted with a monogram encircled by blue and green flower trails, late 18thC, saucer 4in (10cm) diam.
£150–180 ⚒ WW

A Meissen cup and saucer, decorated with Onion pattern in blue, c1890, saucer 5in (12.5cm) diam.
£75–85 ⊞ MAA

◄ **A Rockingham basketweave teacup, coffee cup and saucer,** decorated with gilt seaweed, red roses and foliage, marked, 1830–41.
£220–260 ⚒ N

A Spode cup and saucer, c1830, cup 3in (7.5cm) diam.
£60–65 ⊞ BES

A lidded chocolate cup and saucer, decorated with flowers and a monogram, Belgian, Tournai, c1765, 4½in (11.5cm) high.
£1,400–1,600 ⊞ US

A pair of Samson chocolate cups and covers, painted with armorials in the *famille rose* style, French, late 19thC, 3¼in (8.5cm) high.
£160–200 ⚒ WW

A Swansea London shape teacup, coffee cup and saucer, painted in purple with scattered flowers and leaves, script marks, c1820.
£350–420 ⚒ LFA

A Vauxhall teabowl and saucer, hairline cracks to teabowl, c1760, saucer 5in (12.5cm) diam.
£750–850 ⊞ BES

A Vienna cup and saucer, decorated with pink roses on a gilt ground, marked, Austrian, 1820, 2½in (6.5cm) high.
£350–420 ⚒ DORO

A cup and saucer, the cup painted with a river and a town landscape, with gilt interior, the saucer painted with a date within a laurel wreath, German, 1860, 3in (7.5cm) high.
£200–240 ⚒ DORO

Custard Cups

A Caughley custard cup, painted in the Chinese style with Willow Nankin pattern in underglaze blue, 1780–85, 2½in (6.5cm) high.
£900–1,100 LFA
This is a very rare shape and therefore realized a high price despite probably missing a lid.

A *pot à jus*, decorated in blue on a white ground, Belgian, Tournai, c1790, 3½in (9cm) high.
£300–350 US

A Caughley Artichoke cup and cover, printed in underglaze blue with Fisherman or Pleasure Boat pattern, knop glued, cover rim chip restored, c1785, 3¼in (8.5cm) high.
£350–420 LFA
Artichoke cups may have been used as custard cups but are distinctive shapes without handles.

► **A Mennecy *pot à jus*,** the cover with a cherry knop, the ribbed white body decorated with flowers, French, c1760, 3½in (9cm) high.
£600–700 US
An extensive exhibition of custard cups was mounted at the Olympia Fair, London, in 2000 which created a great deal of new interest in them.

A Chantilly custard cup and cover, painted with stylized blue flower sprays, painted and incised marks, 1750–1800, 3½in (9cm) high.
£200–240 WW

Dessert & Dinner Services

A Samuel Alcock part dessert service, comprising 15 pieces, painted with flower studies, one dish repaired, painted numeral, c1855.
£1,200–1,500 S(O)

► **A Berlin dessert service,** comprising 13 pieces, each painted with different fruits and leaves, two plates damaged, painted and printed marks, German, 1914–18, serving plate 11in (28cm) diam.
£2,000–2,200 S(S)

A Coalport part dessert service, comprising 18 pieces, painted by Arthur Perry with landscapes on a green ground, with gilding, c1905.
£1,700–2,000 SHSY

A Daniel part dessert service, comprising 15 pieces, painted with flower sprays within blue and gilded borders, some damage, c1830.
£550–650 WW

PORCELAIN

A Davenport dessert service, comprising 20 pieces, with gilt yellow and turquoise blue decoration, c1850.
£600–700 ⚒ G(L)

A Derby dessert service, comprising 30 pieces, painted with sprays of roses, chrysanthemums, tulips and other flowers among foliage, heightened with gilding, some damage, marked, 1816–20.
£950–1,150 ⚒ P(E)

◄ A Minton dessert service, comprising 26 pieces, each painted with a flower specimen within an interlaced band with turquoise 'jewels', c1850.
£1,400–1,700 ⚒ Bea(E)

A Paris dessert service, comprising 71 pieces, with gilt dotted borders, some damage and losses, French, early 19thC.
£3,000–3,600 ⚒ S

A Ridgway dessert service, comprising 28 pieces, with rose pink and gilded grounds, the centres painted in colours with picturesque and rustic landscapes, some damage, c1830.
£1,300–1,500 ⚒ P

A Spode dessert service, comprising 27 pieces, the borders with gold *oeil-de-perdrix* on a soft primrose ground, the centres painted with bouquets, c1830.
£3,200–3,500 ⚒ P

A Royal Worcester vitreous part game service, comprising 16 pieces, each printed and coloured with game birds in landscapes within a brown printed border of scrolls and flowers, some damage, printed marks and date code for 1895.
£800–950 ⚒ Bea(E)

A Staffordshire part dessert service, comprising ten pieces, each painted in purple and green with flowers and leaves, 1835–40.
£250–300 ⚒ LFA

A Grainger's Worcester dessert service, comprising 14 pieces, each decorated with flower sprays within gilt scroll-decorated turquoise borders, 1845–50.
£650–800 ⚒ WW

A dessert service, comprising 18 pieces, decorated with flowers within blue and orange scrolling borders, mid-19thC.
£650–800 ⚒ WW

A part dinner service, comprising 53 pieces, each with a royal blue border containing hand-painted floral sprays within scrolling gilt cartouches, minor damage to some pieces, some with painted letters, 19thC.
£1,300–1,600 ⚒ FHF

Dishes

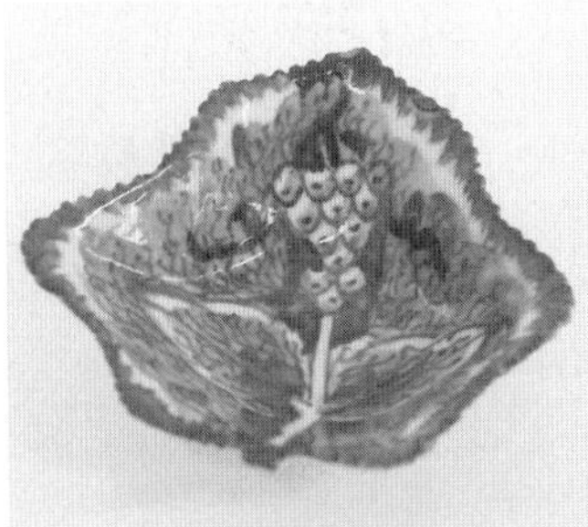

A Bow pickle dish, painted in underglaze blue with grapes and foliage, c1760, 4in (10cm) wide.
£100–120 G(L)

A Lowestoft pickle dish, decorated in underglaze blue with fruiting vines, c1765, 3½in (9cm) wide.
£400–500 G(L)

A pair of Spode Feldspar dishes, c1830, 9in (23cm) wide.
£430–480 HA

A Royal Worcester ashtray, painted in coloured enamels by William Powell with a chaffinch on a branch, within a gilt-line rim, signed, titled, printed mark for 1930, 3½in (9cm) diam.
£90–110 LFA

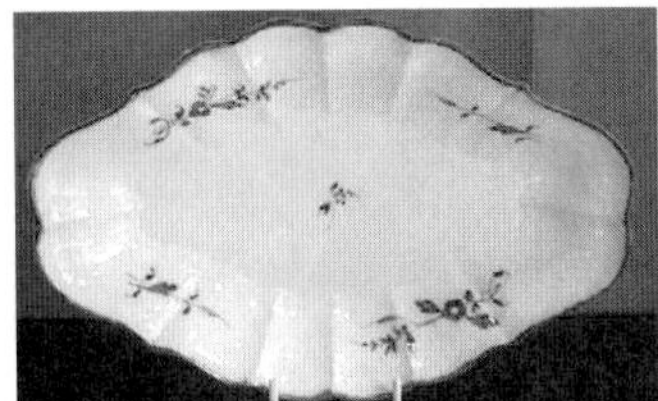

A Caughley dessert dish, painted in the French style with Chantilly sprig design, c1780, 13½in (34.5cm) wide.
£250–275 BES

A Meissen dish, decorated in blue with Onion pattern, German, c1870, 10in (25.5cm) wide.
£120–135 MAA

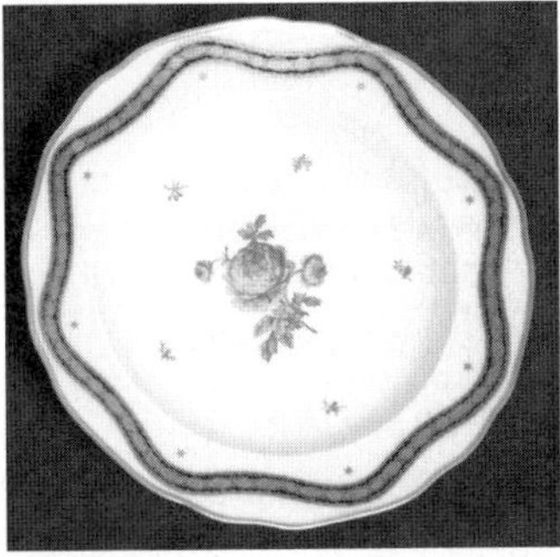

A pair of Vienna soup plates, decorated with floral designs within gilt borders, c1780, 10in (25.5cm) diam.
£330–365 HA

► **A Royal Worcester shell dish,** decorated with flowers on a blush ivory ground, on three feet, date code for 1903, 6¾in (17cm) wide.
£150–180 SWO

An oyster dish, the scalloped rim decorated with flowers, fish and birds in blue and gilt enamel, Austrian, late 19thC, 10in (25.5cm) wide.
£125–150 SK

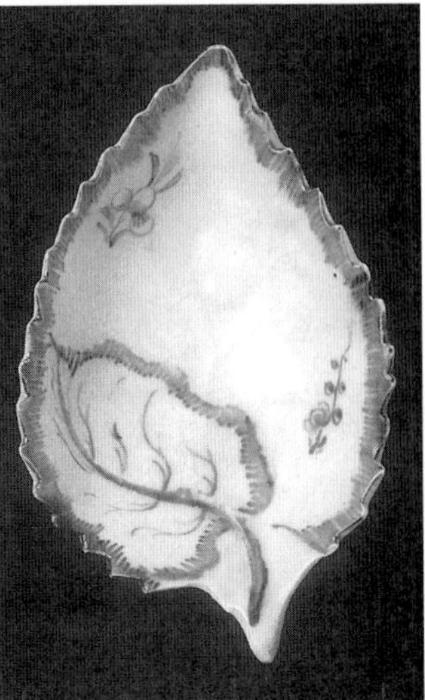

A William Reid, Liverpool, pickle dish, decorated in blue and white, 1756–61, 4½in (11.5cm) wide.
£900–1,100 P

A pair of Ridgway dishes, from a toy or miniature dinner service, painted in coloured enamels with flowers and leaves on a pale blue ground, painted numerals, c1830, 4in (10cm) wide.
£140–170 LFA

A pair of dessert dishes, one with painted fruit, the other with flowers within flower-moulded borders, c1820, 9½in (24cm) wide.
£220–265 WW

Eggs

An Imperial egg, decorated with an angel, Russian, c1880, 2in (5cm) wide.
£2,000–2,250 ⊞ SHa

An Imperial egg, decorated with a bouquet of flowers and an inscription on a pink ground, Russian, c1880, 3½in (9cm) wide.
£675–750 ⊞ SHa

An egg, depicting Maria Magdalena, the reverse with a gilt and blue cross with details in enamel on an orange ground, minor repair, Russian, late 19thC, 4½in (11.5cm) wide.
£525–625 ⚒ BUK

Figures

A pair of Belleek figures of The Belgian Hawkers, the man wearing clogs with a basket on his back, the old woman with a damaged basket, both missing sticks, First Period, 1863–90, Irish, 7in (18cm) high.
£1,500–1,800 ⚒ MEA

◄ **A Bow figure of a young man,** wearing a blue coat and white breeches decorated with cerise flowers, standing on a pink- and blue-veined marble-effect pedestal, c1765, 6in (15cm) high.
£600–700 ⊞ DMa

A Carlton figure of a Yorkshireman, holding a mug of ale, decorated with the City of London arms, 1902–30, 5in (12.5cm) high.
£25–30 ⊞ G&CC

Items in the Porcelain section have been arranged in factory order, with non-specific pieces appearing at the end of each sub-section.

A Chelsea figure of Flora, holding a cornucopia of fruit, with a lion at her feet, painted in brightly coloured enamels with gilt details, minor damage, gold anchor mark, c1765, 8¼in (21cm) high.
£900–1,100 ⚒ WW

A Copeland Parian figure, The Dancing Girl Reposing, modelled by Calder Marshall, impressed 'Art Union of London 1846, Marshall fec, Cheverton sculp', 18¼in (46.5cm) high.
£400–500 ⚒ F&C

A Copeland Parian figure, Sunshine, by W. Brodie, c1860, 18in (45.5cm) high.
£675–750 ⊞ JAK

A Cozzi figure of Neptune with four sea horses, Italian, Venice, c1760, 10in (25.5cm) high.
£1,600–2,000 ⊞ US

A Derby figure of a putto, emblematic of America, from the series of the Continents, decorated in coloured enamels, with an alligator at his feet, before floral bocage, restored, c1775, 8½in (21.5cm) high.
£600–720 LFA

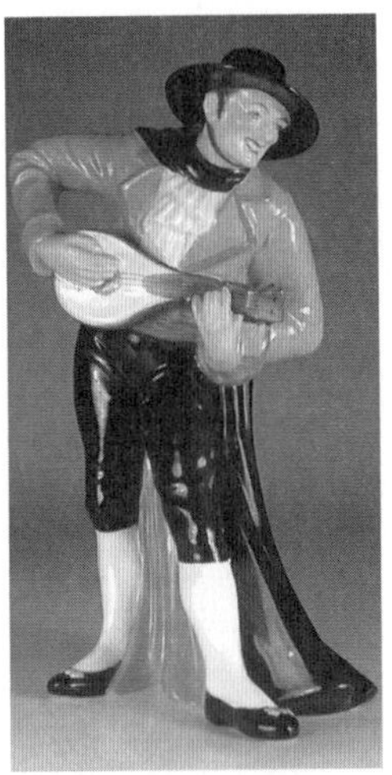
A Royal Crown Derby figure of a Spanish guitar player, decorated in black, orange and cream, red factory mark, c1932, 7¾in (19.5cm) high.
£250–300 WW

A pair of Meissen figures, harvesting grapes, polychrome-decorated, German, c1870, 7in (18cm) high.
£2,250–2,500 MAA

A Derby figure of a lady playing a mandolin, with a sheep by her side, badly damaged, c1770, 5½in (14cm) high.
£100–120 TMA

A Gardner figure of a female water carrier, wearing a blue dress and carrying a yoke and supporting two simulated wooden pails, slight damage, marked, Russian, c1820, 9¾in (25cm) high.
£4,500–5,000 SK

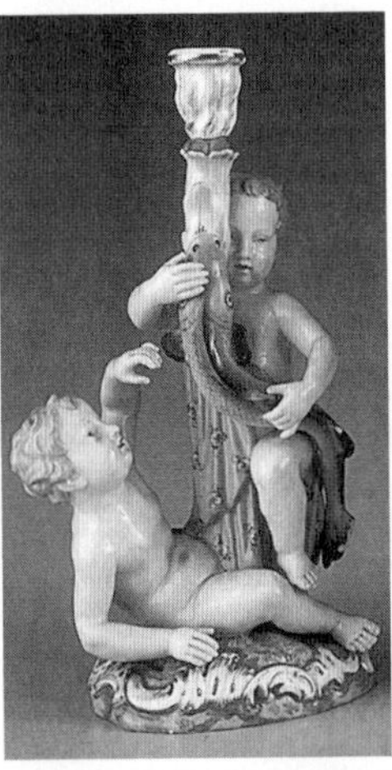
A pair of Meissen figural candlesticks, modelled as two putti supporting a fish, terminating in a rococo foliate stem, severe damage and repairs, incised and painted crossed sword marks, German, 1860–80, 10¼in (26cm) high.
£300–360 HAM

A Derby biscuit group of three maidens, emblematic of Art, Literature and Astrology, standing around a column supporting a flower-garlanded urn, some damage, incised marks, c1785, 14in (35.5cm) high.
£700–850 LFA

A pair of Meissen figures, the gentleman playing a flute, his companion holding a book, decorated in coloured enamels and gilding, severe damage and repairs, German, c1760, 5½in (14cm) high.
£600–700 F&C

A Meissen figure of a lady, playing cards or fortune telling, German, c1880, 6½in (16.5cm) high.
£2,000–2,200 MER

A pair of Derby figural candlesticks of fruit sellers, damaged, c1765, 10in (25.5cm) high.
£450–550 SWO

LOCATE THE SOURCE
The source of each illustration in Miller's can be found by checking the code letters below each caption with the Key to Illustrations, pages 794–800.

A Meissen figural group of three children, playing around a classical herm pillar, the figures painted in colours and gilt, the base with floral encrustation, repaired, marked, c1840, 11in (28cm) high.
£900–1,100 RBB

A Mennecy allegorical figure of Touch, standing beside a swan pecking at her shin, some restoration, incised mark, French, c1755, 6½in (16.5cm) high.
£650–800 S(O)

A Minton Parian figure of Lady Constance Grosvenor, by Albert Carrier de Belleuse, c1854, 20in (51cm) high.
£950–1,150 ⊞ JAK

A Volkstedt figure of a Spanish dancer, wearing a pale yellow petticoat decorated in gilt with a Greek key pattern, under a white dress decorated with sprigs of flowers, German, early 20thC, 11½in (29cm) high.
£375–450 ⚒ DORO

A Royal Dux figure of a female water carrier, wearing a green skirt and pink shawl, and carrying aloft a water jar, with another at her feet, signed 'Hampd', pink triangle mark, stamped '1434', Bohemian, 1890–1900, 31½in (80cm) high.
£1,000–1,200 ⚒ AH

► A Royal Worcester figure of an Italian Musician, by James Hadley, playing a wood-wind instrument, wearing a gilt-edged blue hat, cloak, tunic, trousers and shoes, on a shaped gilt base with obelisk support, marked and date coded for 1920, 12½in (32cm) high.
£450–550 ⚒ PFK

A Samson allegorical figural group of two classical women, on a rocky mound above a sacrificial deer, the base with a pedestal flanked by a bearded man holding a dagger and a kneeling young man holding a bowl, some chips, crossed swords mark, French, late 19thC, 21in (53.5cm) high.
£675–750 ⚒ S(S)

A Vienna figure of a bagpiper, wearing a blue coat, purple breeches and an orange waistcoat, chips to pipes, shield mark in underglaze blue, script numeral, impressed 'O', Austrian, c1760, 7in (18cm) high.
£800–900 ⚒ S(O)
Ex-Rudolf Just Collection.

A pair of Royal Worcester figures of Bringaree Indians, by James Hadley, decorated with some gold and enamelling on an ivory ground, impressed and printed marks, date codes for 1888, 19¼in (49cm) high.
£2,200–2,500 ⚒ Bea(E)

◄ A Parian figure of Innocence, the front impressed 'Art Union of London', impressed 'J H Foley sculp. London 1846', 17in (43cm) high.
£300–375 ⚒ TMA

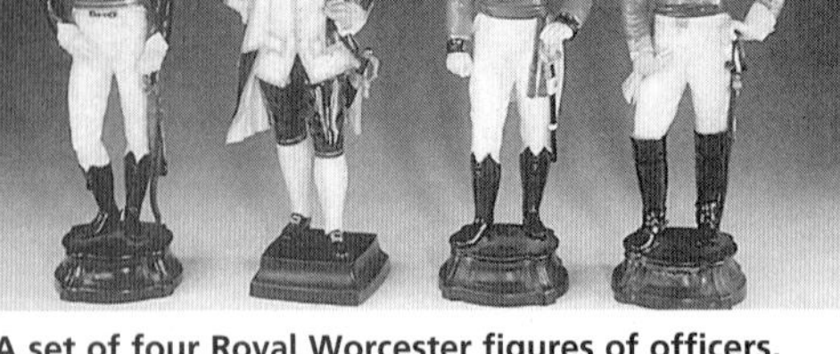

A set of four Royal Worcester figures of officers, decorated in black, white, red and gilt, printed marks, date codes for 1917 and 1918, tallest 11½in (29cm) high.
£900–1,100 ⚒ CGC

◄ A pair of figural perfume bottles, modelled as a European-style lady and gentleman dressed as Orientals, he playing pan pipes and she with a mandolin, each sitting upon a turquoise cushion with gilt bead decoration, 1840–50, 7in (18cm) high.
£700–850 ⚒ Mit

A 'nodder', modelled as a cross-legged figure with moveable head, tongue and hands, decorated with a cream glaze to simulate ivory, Continental, late 19thC, 4¾in (12cm) high.
£300–375 ⚒ RIT

Flatware

A Bow plate, painted in the *famille rose* style with peony flowers and leaves issuing from rockwork, long hairline crack, 1753–55, 8¾in (22cm) diam.
£130–155 ⚒ WW

A Chelsea plate, painted with a flower spray and scattered sprigs, red anchor mark, c1755, 8½in (21.5cm) diam.
£350–420 ⚒ WW

A Copeland 'jewelled' plate, the border embossed with rococo scrollwork heightened with gilding and applied 'jewels' in pink and turquoise, the centre painted with the portrait of a young lady by S. Alcock, signed, marked, impressed date code for 1896, 9in (23cm) diam.
£600–660 ⚒ P

A set of six Derby Imari plates, painted in underglaze blue, iron-red, green and gilding with a tree and flowers, one plate repaired, marked, c1810, 8in (20.5cm) diam.
£330–370 ⚒ S(O)
Ex-Rudolf Just Collection.

LOCATE THE SOURCE
The source of each illustration in Miller's can be found by checking the code letters below each caption with the Key to Illustrations, pages 794–800.

A Du Paquier Vienna plate, painted in enamels and gilding with birds perched on flowering branches issuing from stylized rockwork, the reverse with two trailing flowering branches, rubbing to enamels, Austrian, c1730, 8½in (21.5cm) diam.
£1,880–2,200 ⚒ S(O)
Ex-Rudolf Just Collection.

A Royal Crown Derby berry plate, painted with floral panels signed by Albert Gregory and gilded by George Darlington, from a service made for Judge Elbert Gary of USA, c1910, 6in (15cm) diam.
£675–750 ⊞ JUP

A pair of Gotha plates, each painted with a titled scene, the rim moulded and gilded with foliate scrolls and flowerheads, printed marks and script titles, German, 1834–60, 11¾in (30cm) diam.
£400–500 ⚒ S(S)

► **An Isleworth plate,** painted in bright blue with a Chinese riverscape, the rim painted with four lotus plants, hairline crack, 1765–75, 8½in (21.5cm) diam.
£1,150–1,300 ⚒ P
This unrecorded Isleworth plate has been attributed on the basis of related paintings that have been identified as Isleworth.

A pair of Doccia plates, decorated with flowers, fruits and peas, Italian, c1770, 9in (23cm) diam.
£600–700 ⊞ US

A Höchst plate, with a pierced trelliswork rim, the centre painted with flowers and sprigs, marked, German, 1760–70, 9¾in (25cm) diam.
£160–200 ⚒ WW

PORCELAIN

A set of six dessert plates, by George Jones & Sons, painted by William Birbeck, each with a teal-blue ground with gilt-printed husk swag-and-ribbon pattern, the central reserve hand-painted with roses, 1925–27, 10½in (26.5cm) diam.
£700–850 RIT

A Longton Hall plate, the basketweave-moulded centre decorated in the Trembly Rose style with colourful flowers and moths, two firing faults to rim, one hairline crack, c1755, 7½in (19cm) diam.
£475–525 BES

A Lowestoft saucer, printed in underglaze blue with a Chinese riverscape, two rim chips, c1785, 4¾in (12cm) diam.
£130–160 LFA

A Minton plate, painted with Cupid beside a lily pond, printed and impressed marks, c1895, 8¾in (22cm) diam.
£120–150 WW

A Nantgarw plate, with leaf- and scroll-moulded borders and gilt rim, painted in overglaze blue enamel with flower sprays, a section of rim reglued, impressed mark, 1813–20, 10in (25.5cm) diam.
£130–160 WW

A Paris painted plate, from the John Quincy Adams Presidential Service, decorated with a gilt flower and foliate sprigs within a gilt-banded border with reserves of stylized sea horses, roundels and scrolls, French, 1820–25, 9in (23cm) diam.
£2,200–2,500 BB(S)
A plate from this service is part of the White House collection. This pattern of dinnerware was used in State dinner services during Adams' administration.

A Swansea floral dessert plate, impressed marks, 1814–26, 8in (20.5cm) diam.
£300–360 S(O)

A Vienna Imari plate, painted in underglaze blue, iron-red, yellow and puce with a central flower within a chevron border, the rim with four floral sprays, Austrian, c1745, 9in (23cm) diam.
£235–275 S(O)

A pair of Vienna-style plates, decorated with classical scenes surrounded by a gilt-enriched cobalt-blue border, c1890, 13in (33cm) diam.
£750–820 DeA

Cross Reference
See Colour Review (page 299)

A pair of Worcester fluted dessert plates, decorated with exotic birds on a white ground, 1775–80, 8in (20.5cm) diam.
£850–950 WWW

◄ **A Worcester blue and white plate,** with a scalloped rim, painted with Kangxi Lotus pattern, pseudo Chinese emblem, small rim chip, c1770, 7¾in (19.5cm) diam.
£180–220 WW

Inkstands & Inkwells

A double inkstand, with lift-out wells and inner and outer cover, decorated in green, yellow and gilt, mid-19thC, 8½in (21.5cm) wide.
£320–380 WW

An inkstand, with lift-out well and sander, painted in blue and gilt with birds and pagodas, rubbed, small chip, lids missing, French, 19thC, 6¼in (16cm) wide.
£100–120 WW

A Chamberlain's Worcester drum inkwell, painted in coloured enamels with feathers on a grey ground, with three gilt paw feet, restored, script mark in red, c1820, 3in (7.5cm) high.
£500–600 LFA

Jardinières

◀ **A Belleek jardinière,** cream-glazed and applied with roses, black printed mark, Irish, 1875–1900, 11in (28cm) high.
£250–300 G(L)

A Belleek jardinière, cream-glazed, the sides worked in low relief with branches of cherry blossom, the rim applied with a continuous band of flower blooms, black printed mark, Irish, 1850–1900, 6¾in (17cm) high.
£180–220 P(E)

◀ **A Chamberlain's Worcester jardinière and stand,** decorated with gilt and enamel floral panels on a rich blue ground, c1820, 7in (18cm) high.
£350–400 G(L)

A Herculaneum plant pot and base, decorated with a cottage scene above bands of gilt decoration, c1805, 6½in (16.5cm) high.
£3,200–3,500 ⊞ MER

The Herculaneum Pottery in Liverpool was started in 1796 by Samuel Worthington, who imported 40 potters and their families from Staffordshire to work in his new factory. The pottery quickly developed into a thriving export business and also acted as agents for other Staffordshire potters, including Josiah Spode. A large variety of earthenwares was produced, as well as bone china and a New Hall-type hard porcelain, from 1800 to 1833. The factory closed in 1840.

Chamberlain's Worcester

Robert and Humphrey Chamberlain were in charge of the decorating department at the 18th-century Worcester factory, but in 1788 they broke away and set up on their own in direct competition. Initially they decorated white blanks supplied by Caughley, but by 1791 they were almost certainly making porcelain themselves and by 1793 they ended the relationship with Caughley.

Fine gilding was always a speciality of Chamberlain. The factory was also renowned for its armorial decoration, and in 1802 was commissioned by Lord Nelson to produce an extensive service, which led to other important orders. In the early 19th-century they produced a fine, hard white porcelain body that they named Regent China in honour of the Prince Regent.

Chamberlain employed many fine craftsmen, including Humphrey Chamberlain Jr and Thomas Baxter. Landscape painting became a speciality, in particular views of the city of Worcester and popular spa towns such as Malvern and Cheltenham where customers bought Chamberlain's delightful porcelain souvenirs. Cabinet wares painted with shells and feathers are the most valuable. A range of small animal models, especially cats, dogs and mice are also popular with collectors today.

Humphrey Chamberlain Sr retired in 1827, and the firm suffered declining fortunes. In 1840, Chamberlains amalgamated with old rivals Flight, Barr and Barr to form a new company that traded as Chamberlain & Co. This lasted until 1851 when Kerr and Binns took over, later forming the Worcester Royal Porcelain Co.

Jugs & Ewers

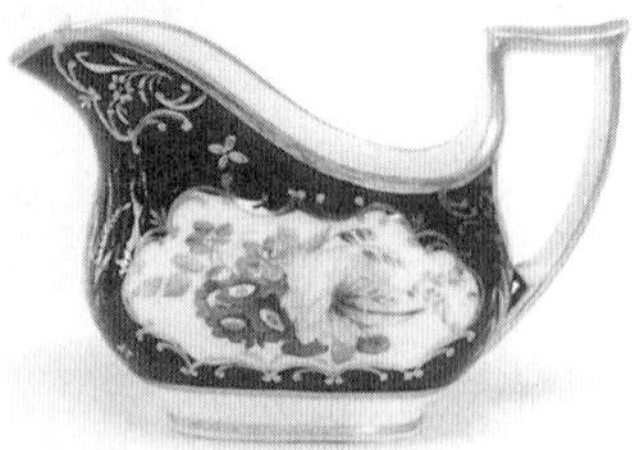

A Coalport London-shape milk jug, painted in coloured enamels with a bird and flowers, within gilt cartouches, on a blue ground, c1820, 3¾in (9.5cm) high.
£140–170 LFA

A Factory Z creamer, the white body decorated with a border of gilt scrolling foliage, c1800, 4¼in (11cm) high.
£165–185 MER

A Gaudy Welsh porcellaneous wash jug and basin, decorated in coloured enamels with flowers and leaves and picked out in purple lustre, c1850, jug 4in (10cm) high.
£130–160 LFA

A Meissen jug, decorated in blue with Onion pattern, c1870, 3½in (9cm) high.
£100–125 MAA

A New Hall milk jug, the fluted body decorated with flowers and leaves, c1800, 5in (12.5cm) high.
£230–275 WW

A Worcester jug, transfer-printed in black with Ruins by a Lake and Ruins with Obelisk patterns, c1765, 3½in (9cm) high.
£475–525 JUP

Loving Cups & Tygs

A Coalport loving cup, commemorating the 1892 general election, printed in gilt with 'Members for Shropshire and their Majorities', hairline crack, printed mark to underside, c1892, 5¼in (13cm) high.
£120–150 SAS

A Staffordshire loving cup, painted with playing cards on a green ground, cracks to base, mid-19thC, 5½in (14cm) high.
£500–550 Bon(C)

► **A Royal Worcester tyg,** decorated with flowers on a shaded ground, puce mark, 1904, 5¼in (13.5cm) high.
£320–380 WW

A loving cup, painted with two landscape panels on a gilded cerise ground, 19thC, 8¾in (22cm) wide.
£275–325 WW

Mugs & Tankards

◄ **A Bow mug,** printed in blue with swans and figures in a pagoda landscape, handle damaged, c1770, 5½in (14cm) high.
£200–230 WW

A John & Jane Pennington, Liverpool, mug, painted in dark blue with two strutting birds walking among rocks and scattered plants, flanked by two stylized flying insects, repaired crack to handle, 1770–75, 13in (33cm) high.
£1,500–1,650 P
This is the only known example of this mug.

A Bloor Derby mug, decorated in the Imari style with flowers and leaves, printed mark, c1830, 5¼in (13.5cm) high.
£250–300 WW

A Longton Hall mug, painted in blue with a two-storey Chinese hut beneath a willow tree growing from a rock, the reverse with a version of Hump Bridge pattern, painted numeral, 1756–60, 3¾in (9.5cm) high.
£2,800–3,200 P

A Liverpool tankard, probably from the Seth Pennington factory, decorated in underglaze blue with a print of roses and butterflies, small chip to rim, c1780, 4¾in (12cm) high.
£350–385 BES

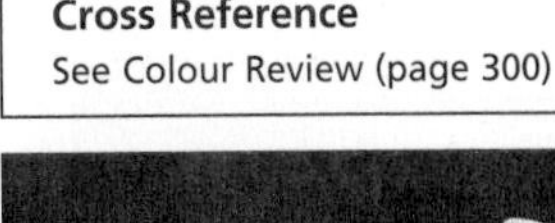

Cross Reference
See Colour Review (page 300)

A Lowestoft mug, polychrome-painted in the style of the Tulip painter, c1775, 5in (12.5cm) high.
£2,200–2,500 S(O)

PORCELAIN

A Vauxhall mug, painted in the Imari style with two islands connected by a bridge, c1757, 3½in (9cm) high.
£1,350–1,500 ⊞ JUP

A Worcester mug, painted in dark blue with Walk in the Garden pattern of a Chinese boy with a bird standing beside a Long Eliza figure holding a *ruyi* sceptre, the reverse with two birds in a pine tree, 1762–65, 3¼in (8.5cm) high.
£750–825 ⚒ P

A Worcester mug, printed in blue with Parrot Pecking Fruit pattern, crescent mark, c1775, 3¼in (8.5cm) high.
£550–600 ⚒ P

◀ **A Worcester mug,** painted in underglaze blue and gilt with sprays of flowers and leaves, below a flower and C-scroll band, crescent mark, c1780, 4¾in (12cm) high.
£350–420 ⚒ LFA

▶ **A Grainger's Worcester mug,** polychrome-decorated with a view of Worcester, printed mark, c1870, 4¼in (11cm) high.
£150–180 ⚒ WW

Plaques

A Berlin plaque, depicting card players, KPM mark, German, 19thC, 12¼ x 16¼in (31 x 41.5cm).
£2,500–3,000 ⚒ DuM

A painted plaque, entitled 'Phyllida', depicting a young lady with blonde hair wearing a cream shawl and a floral dress, the reverse signed 'J. Lesage', 19thC, 11¾in (30cm) diam, framed and mounted.
£600–700 ⚒ WL

A Rockingham plaque, by T. Steel, painted with a still-life of fruits and leaves on a shaded brown ground, signed, dated 1831, 10 x 8¼in (25.5 x 21cm), framed.
£4,500–5,000 ⚒ S

Well known for his paintings of fruit, Thomas Steel (1772–1850) worked at the Derby factory before moving to Rockingham in about 1827. He later moved to Minton and is recorded in a wages book there for 17 March 1832.

Insurance values

Always insure your valuable antiques for the cost of replacing them with similar items, regardless of the original price paid. Both dealers and auctioneers can provide a valuation service for a fee.

A painted plaque, depicting a girl wearing a sailor's outfit, impressed numeral, Continental, 1850–99, 3¼in (8.5cm) high.
£100–120 ⚒ WW

A painted plaque, depicting a young man wearing a yellow-edged white robe, impressed '318', Continental, late 19thC, 5 x 3½in (12.5 x 9cm).
£130–160 ⚒ WW

Pot-Pourri Vases

A pair of three-handled Coalport pot-pourri vases, with covers and liners, painted by Edward Ball, with gilt scroll reserves of titled views of Loch Earn and Loch Tay, the reverse painted with floral reserves, one liner missing, one cover repaired, signed, printed and gilt marks, script titles, c1900, 6½in (16.5cm) high.
£750–900 ⚒ S(O)

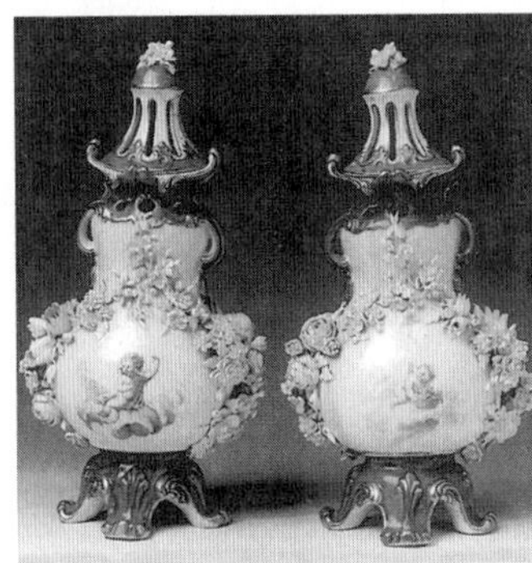

A pair of Derby pot-pourri vases and covers, the feet, necks, handles and covers decorated in turquoise highlighted with gilding, the shoulders applied with white flowers and foliage, with surrounding cherubs frolicking in clouds painted in puce monochrome, covers repaired, minor losses to flowers, c1770, 11½in (29cm) high.
£700–850 ⚒ P

A Derby Crown Porcelain Co pot-pourri vase and cover, painted, gilded and enamelled with bulrushes, lilies and palm leaves below a geometric patterned band, printed iron-red marks, c1887, 14¼in (36cm) high.
£450–550 ⚒ LJ

◀ **A Worcester Locke & Co pot-pourri vase and cover,** the cover pierced with a foliate design, decorated with gilt on a blush ivory ground, the base relief-moulded with acanthus leaves, printed green mark, 1900–04, 5½in (14cm) diam.
£110–130 ⚒ FHF

▶ **A Royal Worcester pot-pourri vase,** decorated with flowers, date code c1911, 7½in (19cm) high.
£500–600 ⚒ SWO

Sauce, Cream & Butter Boats

A Bow sauce boat, painted in blue and white with pagodas, trees and rockwork, damaged, c1760, 4½in (11.5cm) wide.
£100–120 ⚒ WW

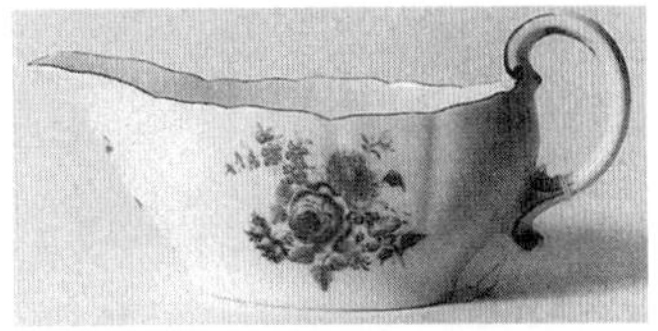

A Bow butter boat, moulded as a geranium leaf, the interior painted in underglaze blue with scattered flowers and leaves, crack, c1765, 3½in (9cm) wide.
£350–420 ⚒ LFA

A Chelsea sauce boat, polychrome-decorated with panels of flowers, hairline crack, red anchor mark, 1755–58, 3½in (9cm) high.
£350–420 ⚒ GAK

Condition

The condition is absolutely vital when assessing the value of an antique. Damaged pieces on the whole appreciate much less than perfect examples. However a rare desirable piece may command a high price even when damaged.

A Derby sauce boat, painted with panels containing birds and insects on a feint feather-moulded ground, rim chips, 1755–65, 7in (18cm) wide.
£270–325 ⚒ WW

A Derby butter boat, moulded as a cabbage leaf, painted in coloured enamels with flowers and leaves, the borders picked out in green and yellow, 1758–60, 4¼in (11cm) wide.
£700–850 ⚒ LFA

PORCELAIN

◀ **A Philip Christian & Co, Liverpool, sauce boat,** finely moulded and painted in underglaze blue with oriental scenes, cracks to base, c1768, 6½in (16.5cm) wide.
£225–250 ⊞ BES

▶ **A Lowestoft butter boat,** painted in blue with a hut and trees on an island, on pad feet, 1775–80, 2¾in (7cm) wide.
£675–750 ⚒ P

Facts in brief

There is much discussion among collectors as to the intended use of these shapes, generally because cream boats are usually more expensive than sauce boats. It is really all a question of size. Sauce, or gravy, was poured from larger boats and these take up more space in a display cabinet. Cream boats (or cream ewers) are small and dainty and most porcelain collectors regard these little pieces as a joy.

Some small sauce boats or large cream boats are hard to classify. Butter boats were used to pour melted butter on asparagus for example. To keep the butter liquid these were placed in dishes of hot water. The shape is therefore shallow rather than rounded.

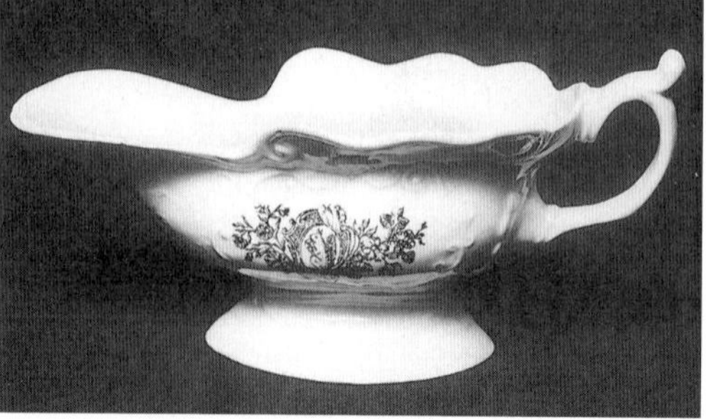

A Worcester sauce boat, printed with a squirrel, a pheasant and a herdsman, with moulded foliate decoration, c1755, 8in (20.5cm) wide.
£1,000–1,150 ⊞ JUP

A Worcester sauce boat, with moulded strap fluting, the side panels painted in blue with Little Fisherman pattern, the reverse with a figure in a sampan passing a rock, the interior with a peony spray, crescent mark, 1762–65, 5¼in (13.5cm) wide.
£600–700 ⚒ P

A Worcester cream boat, painted in underglaze blue with Narcissus pattern, within gadrooned borders, lip restored, crescent mark, 1770–75, 2½in (6.5cm) high.
£400–500 ⚒ LFA

A Worcester sauce boat, decorated in blue and white with floral sprays within foliate-moulded cartouches, the interior with a single foliate spray, open crescent mark, 1776–80, 7in (18cm) wide.
£400–500 ⚒ Mit

PORCELAIN

Scent Bottles

A porcelain scent bottle, depicting a romantic scene, with brass mounts, scallop-formed flip-top and gilt decoration, 19thC, 4in (10cm) high.
£280–320 ⊞ LBr

A Coalport scent bottle, decorated in gilt on a pale pink ground with a central roundel, c1910, 2in (5cm) high.
£550–600 ⊞ TH

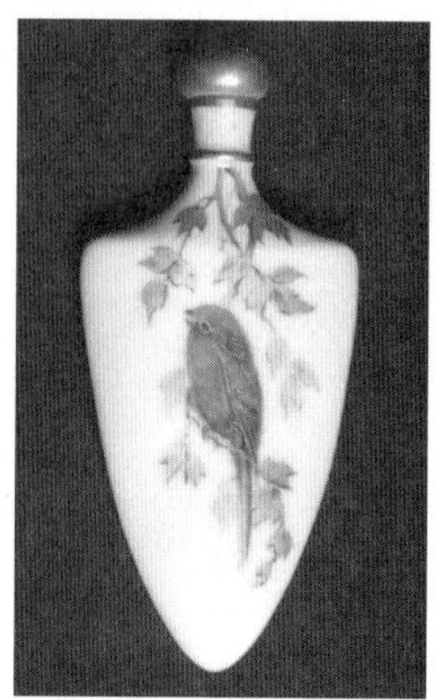

A Worcester scent bottle, decorated with a bird perched on a branch, c1880, 3in (7.5cm) high.
£350–400 ⊞ TH

◀ **A pair of Kerr & Binns Worcester reticulated scent bottles,** in Islamic revival style, the piercing picked out in gold, red and turquoise enamels, with a diamond motif between, one bottle in red, the other in raised and tooled gold, c1860, 6½in (16.5cm) high.
£850–950 ⚒ P

Tea Canisters

A Caughley fluted tea canister and cover, decorated in gilt with leaf scroll and dot-and-pendant leaf bands, inner rim nick, c1785, 4½in (11.5cm) high.
£160–200 LFA

A Nymphenburg tea canister and cover, painted in purple *camaieu* with views of buildings and ruins, minor chips to footrim, impressed shield mark, German, c1765, 5in (12.5cm) high.
£800–950 S(O)

A Worcester tea canister and cover, painted in pink and gilt with flower sprays and sprigs, cover chips, knop missing, c1770, 6in (15cm) high.
£200–250 WW

A Worcester tea canister and cover, decorated in the workshop of James Giles, with a floral spray and smaller sprigs in gold, the rims with a gilt zigzag design, small chips, 1765–70, 6¾in (17cm) high.
£500–550 P

Trays

◄ **A Meissen double-handled tray,** painted in the Kakiemon style with butterflies above sprigs of *indianische Blumen* and stylized rockwork, with an iron-red foliate border interspersed with flowerheads and sprigs, repairs, crossed swords, impressed marks, German, 1730–35, 11¼in (28.5cm) wide.
£7,500–8,500 S(O)
Ex-Rudolf Just Collection.

A New Hall spoon tray, painted with flower sprays and ribbon borders, c1800, 5¾in (14.5cm) wide.
£700–800 WW

◄ **A Worcester spoon tray,** the border painted in black with a pearl and flowerhead band picked out in gilt, on a turquoise ground, 1770–75, 6in (15cm) wide.
£280–320 LFA

Miller's is a price GUIDE not a price LIST

Tureens

► **A pair of Caughley tureens, covers and dishes,** decorated in blue and white with flowers and landscapes in the Chinese style, some faults, 1785–90, dish 8¼in (21cm) wide.
£950–1,150 G(B)

A Royal Crown Derby miniature tureen and cover, decorated with Imari pattern, 1922, 1¾in (4.5cm) high.
£450–550 DA

A Dagoty tureen and stand, with gilt banding on a white ground, c1810, 15in (38cm) wide.
£1,100–1,300 US

Items in the Porcelain section have been arranged in factory order, with non-specific pieces appearing at the end of each sub-section.

◄ **A Vienna tureen,** decorated with single blue flowers and gilt detail, Austrian, c1792, 10in (25.5cm) wide.
£800–900 US

PORCELAIN

Colour Review

A Staffordshire earthenware model of a Suffolk Punch, lead glazed, ears restored, late 18thC, 7½in (19cm) high.
£4,000–4,500 P

A pair of Lunéville faïence recumbent lions, minor glaze chips, 1775–1825, 18in (45.5cm) wide.
£7,500–9,000 S(NY)

A pair of tin-glazed cows, Continental, early 19thC, 6¾in (17cm) wide.
£500–600 AH

A pair of Walton pearlware Royal Supporter groups, minor restoration, impressed marks, early 19thC, 6½in (16.5cm) high.
£3,500–4,000 S(O)

A model of a sheep and lamb beside a tree, by John Walton, slightly chipped, impressed mark, c1825, 7in (18cm) high.
£500–600 G(L)

A Yorkshire drabware cow and milkmaid, 1820, 7in (18cm) high.
£1,350–1,500 JRe

A model of a bulldog, painted with cabbage roses, thorns and foliage, front right paw repaired, c1880, 17¾in (45cm) wide.
£9,500–11,500 SH
This dog is one of only two known, the other example is in the Newport Museum, Wales. Both dogs are unmarked, although painted in the classic Wemyss style.

A Staffordshire pearlware model of a lion, some restoration, minor chip, 1820–30, 11in (28cm) wide.
£3,700–4,000 S(S)

◀ **A majolica model of a grey heron,** modelled by Paul Comolera, minor damage, Minton impressed mark, date cipher for 1876, 39¼in (99.5cm) high.
£7,800–9,350 WW

A majolica model of a spotted frog, 1850–1900, 4½in (11.5cm) high.
£380–450 WW

A pair of Staffordshire cow groups, damaged, c1880, 9in (23cm) wide.
£400–480 SWO

◀ **A pottery vase,** modelled as a cockerel, painted 'Delphin Massier, Vallauris' to base, rim chips, French, 19thC, 26in (66cm) high.
£2,000–2,200 P(EA)

A Wemyss basket, painted with raspberries, 1890–1900, 8in (20.5cm) wide.
£700–800 ⊞ RdeR

A Deruta majolica *crespina*, Italian, c1600, 10in (25.5cm) diam.
£350–420 ⚒ Gam

A Minton majolica jardinière, flaking to ground and wear to interior, impressed mark, date code for 1862, 15in (38cm) high.
£2,000–2,400 ⚒ Bea(E)

A Minton majolica jardinière, c1870, 15½in (39.5cm) diam.
£2,000–2,400 ⚒ LT

A Venice maiolica shallow bowl, cracked and repaired, restorations to rim, Italian, c1550, 11½in (29cm) diam.
£750–825 ⚒ S(Am)

◄ A delft two-handled bowl and cover, fitted with an internal drainer, restored, c1700, 12in (30.5cm) wide.
£300–360 ⚒ DN

A Wedgwood majolica game pie dish and cover, cover repaired, impressed factory marks and registration mark, c1869, 9in (23cm) wide.
£280–320 ⚒ RTo

A Wedgwood majolica cheese dome, 1850–1900, 10in (25.5cm) high.
£900–1,100 ⚒ G(L)

A Wemyss Drummond flower pot, painted with roses, c1900, 6in (15cm) high.
£350–400 ⊞ RdeR

A London delft blue and white punch bowl, repaired, 18thC, 13¼in (33.5cm) diam.
£680–820 ⚒ WW

A Minton majolica centrepiece, bowl restored, impressed mark to base, late 19thC, 21¼in (54cm) high.
£1,750–2,000 ⚒ P(EA)

A Dutch Delft tobacco jar, with associated copper lid, 18thC, 12in (30.5cm) high.
£950–1,150 ⚒ BERN

A maiolica Soupiereau and Fouri jardinière, Italian, 19thC, 14¾in (37.5cm) high.
£135–160 ⚒ L&E

A Ralph Wood glazed figure, stamped '67', c1785, 9in (23cm) high.
£1,450–1,600 ⊞ JRe

A Prattware set of the Four Seasons, c1800, 9½in (24cm) high.
£2,250–2,500 ⊞ JRe

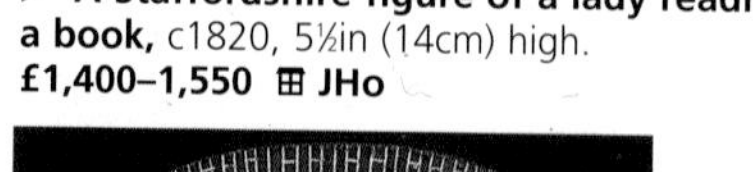

► A Staffordshire figure of a lady reading a book, c1820, 5½in (14cm) high.
£1,400–1,550 ⊞ JHo

◄ A Staffordshire pottery arbour group of the Dame School, teacher's arm missing from elbow, c1825, 6¾in (17cm) wide.
£2,500–3,000 ⚒ Bon(C)

A pair of Staffordshire figures of actors, c1850, 13in (33cm) high.
£950–1,200 ⊞ RGa

A Staffordshire pearlware group of a man and a woman playing flute and mandolin, c1820, 10in (25.5cm) high.
£1,300–1,450 ⊞ JHo

A pair of early Victorian Staffordshire figures of Queen Victoria and Prince Albert, restored, 8¾in (22cm) high.
£140–170 ⚒ BLH

A Staffordshire figure of Napoleon, mid-19thC, 9in (23cm) high.
£325–360 ⊞ DHA

A Staffordshire group of Queen Victoria, Napoleon and King Victor Emmanuel of Italy, entitled 'The Allied Powers', c1854, 12in (30.5cm) high.
£1,750–2,000 ⊞ RGa

A Staffordshire group of a sailor and his girl, c1850, 8in (20.5cm) high.
£260–320 ⚒ G(L)

► A Staffordshire figure of a fish-seller, c1870, 14in (35.5cm) high.
£240–300 ⚒ G(L)

A Staffordshire spill vase group of a fisherman and his wife, c1860, 7½in (19cm) high.
£160–175 ⊞ SEA

A pottery group of a black minstrel band, French, c1880, 8in (20.5cm) high.
£450–500 ⊞ HUM

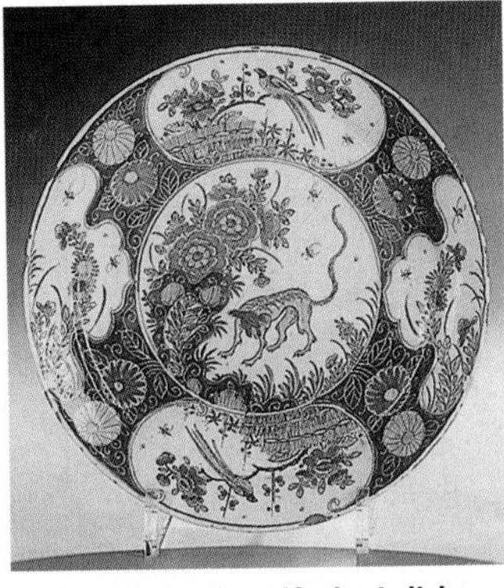

A pair of Dutch Delft doré dishes, after Chinese Kangxi examples, one dish with a hairline crack, the second with a minor glaze crack and minor chips to the rim, marked 'APK' for Pieter Adriaenzoon Kocks, 1701–22, 9in (23.5cm) diam.
£1,500–1,650 ⚒ S(Am)

A Bristol delft plate, c1740, 8½in (21.5cm) diam.
£2,400–2,650 ⊞ JHo

A Staffordshire salt-glazed Jacobite commemorative plate, restored, the pottery c1760, the decoration later, 9¼in (23.5cm) diam.
£400–500 ⚒ P(Ed)

A Bristol delft charger, mid-18thC, 13in (33cm) diam.
£1,350–1,500 ⊞ RdV

A Bristol delft plate, the rim decorated in *bianco-sopra-bianco,* c1770, 13½in (34.5cm) diam.
£1,670–1,850 ⚒ P(B)

A Lambeth delft charger, minor rim chips, c1780, 13½in (34.5cm) diam.
£450–550 ⚒ LFA

A Lambeth delft dish, c1785, 9in (23cm) diam.
£900–1,000 ⊞ JHo

A Swansea pottery plate, by Dillwyn & Co, impressed mark, c1815, 9¾in (25cm) diam.
£700–850 ⚒ WW

A 'malachite' plate, by F. & R. Pratt, entitled 'Hop Queen', c1855, 9½in (24cm) diam.
£260–285 ⊞ DHA

A Minton majolica dish, damaged, impressed mark for 1857, 14in (35.5cm) diam.
£200–240 ⚒ TMA

A Minton majolica Palissy plate or stand, impressed marks, date code for 1863, 9¾in (25cm) diam.
£400–500 ⚒ DN

A majolica Palissy-style dish, impressed mark for Caldas, Portuguese, late 19thC, 7¼in (18.5cm) diam.
£260–320 ⚒ WW

A pearlware puzzle jug, the body decorated with a fox-hunting scene, early 19thC, 8¼in (21cm) high.
£400–500 ⚒ AH

A Sunderland lustre pottery jug, by Dixon Austin & Co, the centre painted with a pseudo-armorial of The Woolstaplers of London, chipped spout, early 19thC, 10¼in (26cm) high.
£600–720 ⚒ CAG

A Bristol pearlware puzzle jug, with hound-head spout, c1820, 6in (15cm) high.
£750–820 ⊞ RdV

A Mason's Ironstone jug, c1820, 12in (30.5cm) high.
£2,500–2,850 ⊞ HA

A Mason's Ironstone Hydra jug, c1840, 8½in (21.5cm) high.
£160–200 ⚒ G(L)

A pottery jug, with a transfer print decoration of Mr Punch and Toby, c1870, 8in (20.5cm) high.
£200–220 ⊞ HUM

A Wemyss mug, painted with daffodils, c1900, 6in (15cm) high.
£630–700 ⊞ RdeR

A Wood family creamware plaque, decorated with a portrait of the Duke of Cumberland, c1770, 4¾in (12cm) wide.
£1,100–1,200 ⚒ S(O)

A Wedgwood blue-dip jasper ware plaque, depicting the Marriage of Cupid and Psyche, hairline cracks to relief-work, impressed mark, dated 1919, 26¼in (66.5cm) wide, in a wooden frame.
£1,200–1,300 ⚒ DN

◄ **A Wedgwood pearlware part dessert service,** comprising 11 pieces, pattern No. A930, some restoration, impressed marks, c1820.
£1,400–1,700 ⚒ LFA

A creamware teapot, probably Cockpit Hill, Derby, c1780, 5in (12.5cm) high.
£850–950 ⊞ HUM

A Portobello plaque, c1825, 10½in (26.5cm) wide.
£900–1,000 ⊞ JRe

An Ironstone part dinner service, comprising 52 pieces, c1875, serving plate 11in (28cm) diam.
£1,700–2,000 ⚒ DA

A Wood-style Toby jug, section of back panel replaced, pipe missing, hat chipped and extensively restored, 1780–90, 10in (25.5cm) high.
£300–360 ⚒ P(Ba)

A Prattware Toby jug, in the form of Martha Gunn, c1795, 10½in (26.5cm) high.
£1,500–1,700 ⊞ JHo

A creamware Toby jug, section of base broken, some chips and crazing, c1790, 9¾in (25cm) high.
£300–360 ⚒ P(Ba)

A Toby jug, c1820, 10in (25.5cm) high.
£400–450 ⊞ JBL

A pearlware character jug, handle restored, c1820, 7¾in (19.5cm) high.
£320–380 ⚒ LFA

A Portobello Toby jug, modelled as a black man, c1830, 10in (25.5cm) high.
£750–850 ⊞ JBL

A Copeland Toby jug, with paint loss and slight damage to handle, c1830, 10in (25.5cm) high.
£220–270 ⊞ JBL

A Staffordshire Toby jug, slight damage to hat brim, 1850–1900, 9in (24cm) high.
£175–200 ⊞ DHA

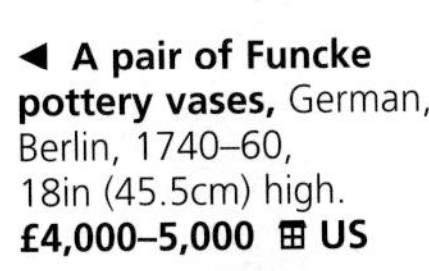

◄ **A pair of Funcke pottery vases,** German, Berlin, 1740–60, 18in (45.5cm) high.
£4,000–5,000 ⊞ US

A pair of Wedgwood majolica Trentham vases, modelled by Roland Morris, one with a fine crack and repair to base, the other with two corners of the base restuck, fine cracks, minor losses, impressed mark, c1870, 11in (28cm) high
£3,000–3,300 ⚒ P
The vase was commissioned by Wedgwood in 1869 to commemorate the Trentham Gardens in Stoke-on-Trent.

A pair of majolica Bodenbach urns, 19thC, 12in (30.5cm) high.
£620–685 ⊞ RAN

◄ **A Staffordshire Morley mazarine two-handled vase,** c1845, 20in (51cm) high.
£1,100–1,200 ⊞ RdV

◄ **A Wemyss vase,** painted with hollyhocks and bees, impressed and painted marks, initials 'KN' for Karel Nekola, dated 1915, 20¾in (52.5cm) high.
£13,000–16,000 ⚒ SH
This was painted the same year that Karel Nekola died. Apparently he was crippled by this time but his painting skills had not diminished.

A Keeling blue and white dog bowl, transfer-printed with Lakeside Meeting pattern, c1820, 9½in (24cm) wide.
£1,300–1,450 ⊞ GN

A blue and white meat plate, transfer-printed with beehive to the centre, early 19thC, 17in (43cm) wide.
£280–300 ⊞ MCC

A Davenport blue and white meat plate, from the Rustic Scenes series, transfer-printed, c1820, 21in (53.5cm) wide.
£1,100–1,250 ⊞ GN
This is the largest dish in the series.

► A pair of blue and white jugs, transfer-printed, 19thC, 7in (18cm) high.
£135–150 ⊞ DHA

A pearlware blue and white plate, transfer-printed with Wandering Monk pattern, c1820, 19in (48.5cm) wide.
£400–450 ⊞ NAW

A Clews blue and white fruit cooler, entitled Dogs on Scent, with brass mount, transfer-printed, c1820, 11in (28cm) high.
£2,000–2,300 ⊞ SCO

◄ A Shorthouse pearlware blue and white teapot, transfer-printed, c1810, 5½in (14cm) high.
£1,100–1,250 ⊞ RdV

A Bow bunch of flowers, with old restoration, c1765, 7in (18cm) high.
£300–360 WW

A pair of Derby models of red squirrels, c1760, 2½in (6.5cm) high.
£1,300–1,600 WW

A Meissen model of an elephant and rider, minor damage, crossed swords mark, German, 1860–80, 16¾in (42.5cm) high.
£3,500–4,200 S

A Derby figural group of the Tithe Pig, c1775, 7in (18cm) high.
£1,350–1,500 JUP

A Bow figure of Earth, some restoration, anchor and dagger mark to reverse, c1765, 9½in (24cm) high.
£500–600 WW

A pair of Samson models of macaws, painted marks, French, late 19thC, 16½in (42cm) high.
£1,600–2,000 P(S)

A Meissen group, modelled as maidens around a sculpture of a girl, crossed swords mark, German, 1860–80, 14in (35.5cm) high.
£2,000–2,400 RBB

A St James's scent bottle, by Charles Gouyn, surmounted by a chained gilt-metal-mounted stopper, 1749–52, 3¼in (8.5cm) high.
£4,000–4,500 P

◀ **A pair of Meissen figures of Malabar musicians,** modelled by F. E. Meyer, restorations, crossed swords marks, German, c1750, largest 12½in (32cm) high.
£4,000–4,500 B

A porcelain allegorical figure of America, attributed to Gille Jeune, French, 1850–75, 19¾in (50cm) high.
£1,250–1,500 NOA

A Rockingham basket, depicting 'North Lodge, St Leonards', 1830–41, 12in (30.5cm) wide.
£2,700–3,300 N

A Worcester reticulated basket, c1770, 5in (12.5cm) diam.
£1,100–1,250 WWW

A Worcester Flight, Barr & Barr sucrier, decorated with vignettes of peasants in rural landscapes, c1820, 5½in (14cm) high.
£600–665 MER

A Royal Worcester bowl, painted by Harold Austin, signed, 1912, 10in (25.5cm) diam.
£700–850 G(L)

A Minton candle snuffer and stand, impressed mark, c1875, 3½in (9cm) high.
£200–220 TH

A Derby card holder, c1810, 6in (15cm) wide.
£600–650 DHu

◄ **A Ludwigsburg sucrier,** German, c1765, 6in (15cm) wide.
£1,150–1,250 US

► **A Longton Hall dish,** c1755, 13¼in (33.5cm) wide.
£2,200–2,500 S

A Worcester teapot and cover, minor damage, incised mark, c1755, 5in (12.5cm) high.
£2,800–3,200 LFA

► **A KPM Berlin cabaret service,** comprising 16 pieces, slightly restored, German, mid-19thC.
£3,700–4,500 Bon(C)

A Belleek tea set on a tray, Irish, late 19thC, tray 16½in (42cm) diam.
£800–950 TMA

A Meissen coffee service, comprising 15 pieces, slight damage, crossed swords mark, impressed numerals, German, late 19thC.
£300–360 P(E)

A pair of Berlin cabinet cups, one with a small chip, saucers or stands missing, sceptre marks, 1820–40, 5¼in (13.5cm) high.
£1,100–1,300 WW

A Chelsea two-handled cup, one handle riveted, c1755, 5¾in (14.5cm) wide.
£800–1,000 WW

A Chelsea tea bowl, small rim chip, red anchor mark, 1752–56, 2¾in (7cm) high.
£300–360 Bon(C)

A pair of Imperial cups and saucers from the Raphael Service, by the Imperial Porcelain Manufactory, gilt crowned marks, Russian, 1895–1902, saucer 6½in (16.5cm) diam.
£8,000–9,000 B

A coffee can, by the Herculaneum Factory, Liverpool, decorated with a rural scene, 1805, 3½in (9cm) high.
£500–550 ⊞ MER

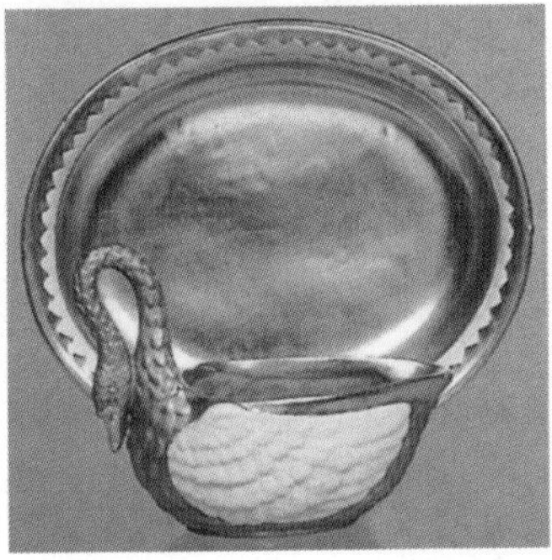

A Minton coffee can, pattern No. 786, pseudo Sèvres mark, c1810, 2½in (6.5cm) high.
£175–195 ⊞ MER

◄ **A swan cup and saucer,** by Carl Thieme, Potschappel, German, 1910–20, cup 3¼in (8.5cm) high.
£235–285 DORO

A pair of Naples cups and saucers, by the Poulard Prad Manufactory, depicting couples wearing regional costume, gilt inscriptions, incised letters, Italian, c1815, 5¾in (14.5cm) high.
£8,500–9,500 B

Three painters were commissioned by Ferdinand IV of Italy between 1782 and 1796 to travel through the kingdom recording regional costumes. Their drawings were then copied by the factory's artists.

A Bow fluted saucer dish, painted with Quail pattern, c1760, 8in (20.5cm) diam.
£450–550 WW

A pair of Chelsea plates, red anchor marks, c1755, 10½in (26.5cm) diam.
£4,000–5,000 US

A Coalport jewelled plate, c1900, 8½in (21.5cm) diam.
£220–250 MAA

An Imperial plate from the Raphael Service, by the Imperial Porcelain Manufactory, gilt crowned mark, Russian, dated 1903, 9½in (24cm) diam.
£6,000–7,000 B
The Raphael Service was first commissioned by Alexander III, the design being inspired by Raphael's frescoes in the Vatican Loggia.

A pair of George Jones plates, signed 'Birkbeck', factory marks, early 20thC, 8½in (21.5cm) diam.
£200–240 WW

A pair of Meissen plates, crossed swords and dot mark, German, c1765, 9½in (24cm) diam.
£1,650–1,800 S(Am)

A London-decorated Nantgarw plate, impressed mark, 1814–23, 9¾in (25cm) diam.
£7,500–9,000 WW

A Naples plate, signed 'Giovine', damaged, painted marks, c1824, 9¼in (23.5cm) diam.
£400–500 JNic

A Worcester saucer dish, 1755–60, 7¼in (18.5cm) diam.
£800–950 LFA

Miller's is a price GUIDE not a price LIST

A Worcester plate, c1770, 9in (23cm) diam.
£120–150 WW

A Worcester dessert plate, with a coloured-in print, 1765–70, 7in (18cm) diam.
£850–1,000 P

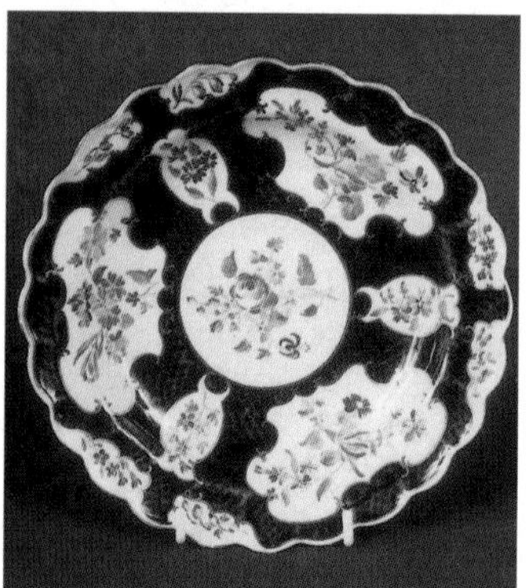
A Worcester blue scale plate, attributed to James Giles, c1770, 7½in (19cm) diam.
£600–700 JUP

A pair of Brussels *seaux à liqueurs*, rim chip, stencilled and incised marks, Belgian, 1791–1803, 12½in (32cm) wide.
£8,000–9,500 S

A pair of Chamberlain's Worcester ice pails, with liners and covers, one cover damaged, script mark, 1795–1805, 11¾in (30cm) high.
£10,000–12,000 Bon(C)

A Royal Crown Derby ewer, red factory mark, c1895, 8¼in (21cm) high.
£170–200 WW

◄ **A Worcester sparrow-beak jug,** c1770, 3¾in (9.5cm) high.
£350–420 WW

A Worcester Flight, Barr & Barr milk jug, 1820, 4½in (11.5cm) high.
£400–450 MER

A Royal Worcester reticulated milk jug, c1871, 5in (12.5cm) high.
£1,250–1,400 JUP

A Bow mug, body crack, c1760, 3½in (9cm) high.
£360–430 WW

◄ **A Vauxhall sauce boat,** 1756–62, 7in (18cm) long.
£3,700–4,000 P

A Caughley mug, with initials inscribed in gilt within a cartouche, flanked by flowers and leaves, 1785–90, 3¼in (8.5cm) high.
£600–700 LFA

A Coalport scent bottle, decorated in gilt, c1910, 2in (5cm) high.
£550–600 TH

A Meissen tankard, painted in the style of J. G. Horoldt, with a hinged silver-gilt cover and footband, area around handle broken and riveted, German, c1725, 7¼in (18.5cm) high.
£25,000–30,000 LFA
Although a damaged piece, the importance of the decoration resulted in the high price.

► **A Meissen armorial tureen and cover,** minor losses, crossed swords mark, incised, impressed and enamelled numerals, German, late 19thC, 10in (25.5cm) wide.
£13,000–16,000 Bon(C)

A Berlin vase and cover, German, 1880, 14in (35.5cm) high.
£1,000–1,200 ⊞ DHu

A pair of Coalport vases, painted with birds in the manner of John Randall, c1835, 11½in (29cm) high.
£1,500–1,800 ⚒ WW

A vase and cover, probably by H. & R. Daniel, cover restored, stress line to body, c1830, 13in (33cm) high.
£280–325 ⊞ MER

A Minton *pâte-sur-pâte* bottle vase, decorated by Lawrence Birks, small firing flaw, impressed factory marks, late 19thC, 7¾in (19.5cm) high.
£2,300–2,750 ⚒ Bon(C)

A pair of Derby vases, with ram's head handles, horns damaged, red painted mark, 1810–15, 9½in (24cm) high.
£1,250–1,500 ⚒ Bea(E)

A Royal Crown Derby vase and cover, painted by Désiré Leroy, signed, red printed marks, c1900, 6½in (16.5cm) wide.
£20,000–24,000 ⚒ HYD

An Imperial Porcelain Manufactory vase, repaired, cracks, Russian, 1825–55, 11¾in (30cm) high.
£1,400–1,700 ⚒ BUK

A Nantgarw or Swansea campana vase, painted by William Billingsley, red painted Nantgarw mark, 1813–23, 10¾in (27.5cm) high.
£30,000–36,000 ⚒ WW
This vase is among the very best pieces of Welsh porcelain. Only one other example of this shape is known (now in the National Museum of Wales) which failed in the firing and so remained undecorated.

A Royal Worcester vase and cover, with griffin handles, painted by Frank Roberts, 1901, 20in (51cm) high.
£2,500–3,000 ⚒ SWO

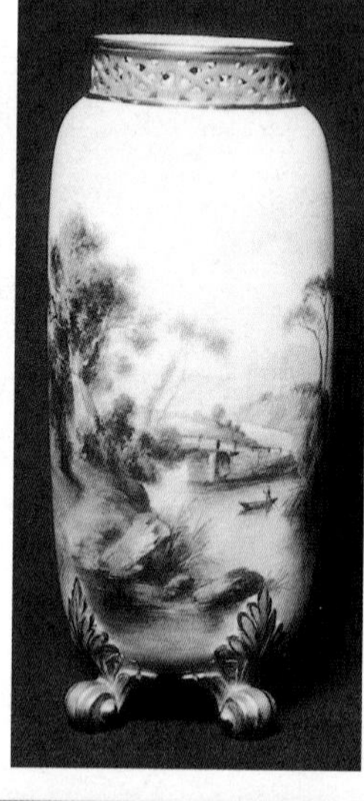

◄ **A pair of Royal Worcester vases,** painted by Frank Roberts, c1912, 9in (23cm) high.
£4,500–5,000 ⊞ JUP

► **A pair of cornucopia vases,** French, 1850–70, 9½in (25cm) high.
£320–380 ⚒ WW

A vase, with gilded goat's head handles, minor flaking, small chip, 1815–20, 19¼in (49cm) high.
£4,000–4,500 ⚒ P
This vase realized a high price because of its exceptional size.

A Sèvres *bleu-céleste* cachepot, with gilt-bronze mounts, interlaced L-mark, French, porcelain 1760–70, mounts contemporary, 4in (10cm) wide.
£5,500–6,500 ⚒ S

A pair of Sèvres pink-ground cups and saucers, painted by Vincent Taillandier, painted and incised marks, 1757–58.
£8,500–9,500 ⚒ S

A Sèvres cup and saucer, painted with Peacock pattern, French, c1760, 2½in (6.5cm).
£1,350–1,500 ⊞ US

A Sèvres cup and saucer, painted by P. Croix, c1768, cup 2½in (6.5cm) high.
£2,500–2,800 ⊞ US

A Sèvres cup and saucer, painted by Guillaume Noel, restored hairline crack, French, c1780, cup 2¾in (7cm) high.
£550–600 ⊞ OKK

A Sèvres cup and saucer, painted by Guillaume Noel, minute chip to footrim, marked, French, dated 1791, saucer 6in (15cm) diam.
£1,750–2,000 ⚒ B

A Sèvres trembleuse cup and saucer, saucer rim chipped, French, dated 1782, cup 3½in (9cm) high.
£250–300 ⚒ G(L)

◄ A Sèvres inkstand, taper holder repaired, one inkwell with chip, red printed factory mark, French, c1810, 8¼in (21cm) wide.
£3,500–4,200 ⚒ S(NY)

A Sèvres part coffee set, comprising five pieces, incised and printed marks, French, 1870–80.
£350–420 ⚒ WW

► A pair of Sèvres *pâte caméléon* vases, French, 1869, 14¼in (36cm) high.
£3,200–3,500 ⊞ JPe
***Pâte caméléon* was first shown at the London Exhibition in 1862, and was remarkable in that it changed from a grey colour in daylight to pink in artificial light.**

A pair of Sèvres ormolu-mounted blue-ground vases and covers, French, c1773, 15in (38cm) high.
£87,000–100,000 ⚒ S
Only one other pair of vases of this exact shape is recorded: a *bleu-céleste* ground pair in the Wallace Collection, London.

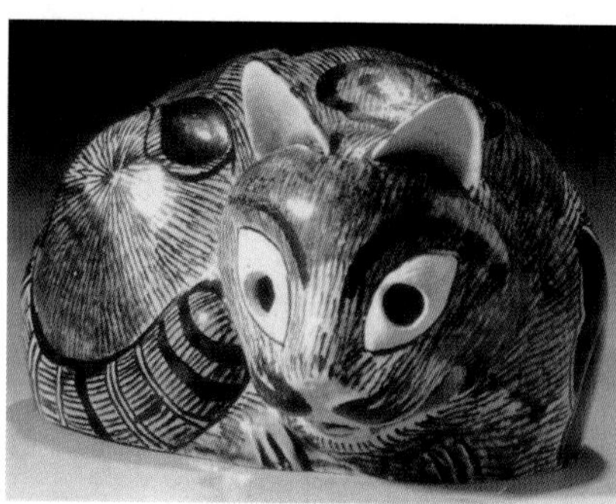

A *famille verte* biscuit cat nightlight, the back pierced with an aperture, ears restored, Kangxi period, 1662–1722, 3½in (9cm) high.
£3,000–3,500 S(Am)

A model of a hawk, early 19thC, 8in (20.5cm) high.
£550–600 FRY

A pair of dogs of *Fo* incense holders, 19thC, 11in (28cm) high.
£700–800 GLD

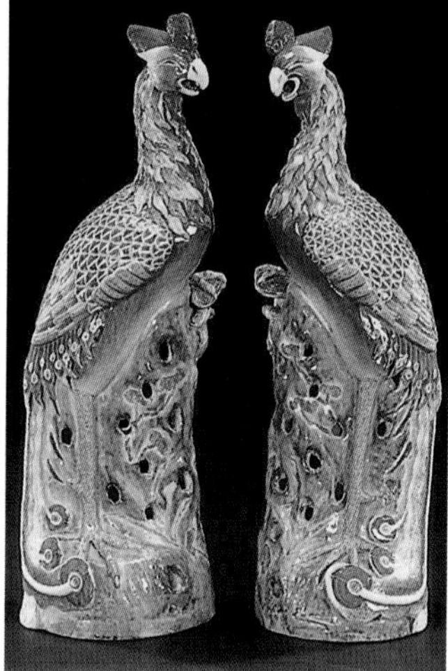

A pair of *famille rose* phoenix, Qing Dynasty, 19thC, 23½in (59.5cm) high.
£4,000–5,000 SLN

A bowl, painted with figures at leisure, minor rim frits, Kangxi period, 1662–1722, 8in (20.5cm) diam.
£1,600–1,750 PCA

A *famille rose* box, with a silver-gilt-mounted lid, Qianlong period, 1736–95, 3in (7.5cm) wide.
£1,600–2,000 WW

► **A pair of gilt-metal-mounted reticulated goblets,** Kangxi period, 1662–1722, 5in (12.5cm) high.
£5,750–6,500 S

A *famille rose* basket and stand, decorated with Rockefeller pattern, some damage, c1795, 10¾in (27.5cm) high.
£750–900 WW

A *famille rose* millefleurs cup, marked, Qianlong period, 1736–95, 3½in (9cm) high.
£13,500–15,000 S(HK)

A carved Qingbai bowl, 12thC, 8in (20.5cm) diam.
£855–950 GLD

◄ **A blue and white bowl,** decorated with a bird in a tree in a rocky landscape, Qianlong period, 1736–95, 15in (38cm) diam.
£500–600 BERN

A Cantonese *famille rose* punch bowl, late 19thC, 14½in (37cm) diam.
£1,150–1,380 BR

A pair of *famille verte* figures of the Ho-Ho twins, c1900, 13in (33cm) high.
£250–300 NOA

A celadon twin fish dish, Song Dynasty, 12th–13thC, 10in (25.5cm) diam.
£1,200–1,400 ⊞ GLD

A turquoise-glazed dish, inscribed, glaze damaged, Ming Dynasty, early 16thC, 9½in (24cm) diam.
£550–600 ⚒ S(P)

A ribbed dish, Kangxi period, 1700–20, 14in (35.5cm) diam.
£1,500–1,650 ⊞ PCA

A *doucai* dish, Kangxi mark and period, 1662–1722, 6in (15cm) diam.
£7,500–8,500 ⚒ S(HK)

A *famille verte* plate, crack, Kangxi period, 1662–1722, 13¾in (35cm) diam.
£700–850 ⚒ DN

A set of five soup dishes, decorated in the *doucai* style, one cracked, 18thC, 8¾in (22cm) diam.
£300–360 ⚒ WW

A set of six *famille rose* plates, mid-18thC, 9in (23cm) diam.
£650–800 ⚒ CGC

A celadon glazed charger, with carved decoration, foot chip, Qianlong mark and period, 1736–95, 16in (40.5cm) diam.
£1,600–2,000 ⚒ BB(S)

◄ **A jar and lid,** decorated with animals, Liao Dynasty, 907–1125, 15in (38cm) high.
£1,550–1,700 ⊞ GLD

A Junyao glazed jar, restored, Song/Jin Dynasty, 960–1234, 5¼in (13.5cm) high.
£800–900 ⚒ S(P)

◄ **A *famille verte* supper set,** Kangxi period, 1662–1722, 17¼in (44cm) diam.
£650–800 ⚒ BUK

A *famille rose* jar and cover, early 20thC, 8in (20.5cm) high.
£160–175 ⊞ FRY

A *Fahua* glazed vase, minor chips, Ming Dynasty, 1368–1644, 9in (23cm) high.
£1,100–1,300 BB(S)

A relief-decorated beaker vase, Kangxi period, 1662–1722, 17in (43cm) high.
£4,000–5,000 S

Miller's is a price GUIDE not a price LIST

A pair of gilded mirror-black vases, Kangxi period, 1662–1722, 8½in (21.5cm) high.
£1,000–1,150 GLD

An Imperial turquoise-ground vase, Qianlong seal mark and period, 1736–95, 22in (56cm) high.
£65,000–70,000 S

A turquoise-glazed vase, Qing Dynasty, 18thC, 13in (33cm) high.
£6,000–7,000 S(NY)

A *famille rose* garniture of five vases, Qianlong period, 1736–95, largest 11in (28cm) high.
£2,800–3,200 Bri

A Canton *famille rose* vase and cover, damaged, mid-19thC, 25¼in (64cm) high.
£600–720 WW

A pair of vases, early 19thC, 14¾in (37.5cm) high.
£4,500–5,500 DMC

A *famille rose* vase or stick stand, moulded with the Hundred Antiques on a yellow ground, late 19thC, 60½in (153.5cm) high.
£320–380 WW

A pair of Canton vases and stands, each with one handle restuck, late 19thC, 30in (76cm) high on wooden base.
£600–720 Bea(E)

A gilt-decorated blue-ground vase, Guangxu mark and period, 1875–1908, 11½in (29.5cm) high.
£7,500–9,000 S(Am)

A pair of Hirado entertainers, Edo Period, c1830, 9in (23cm) high.
£3,000–3,250 ⊞ GLD

A Satsuma bowl, by Yabu Meizan, Meiji period, c1890, 3½in (9cm) diam.
£7,000–8,000 ⊞ MER

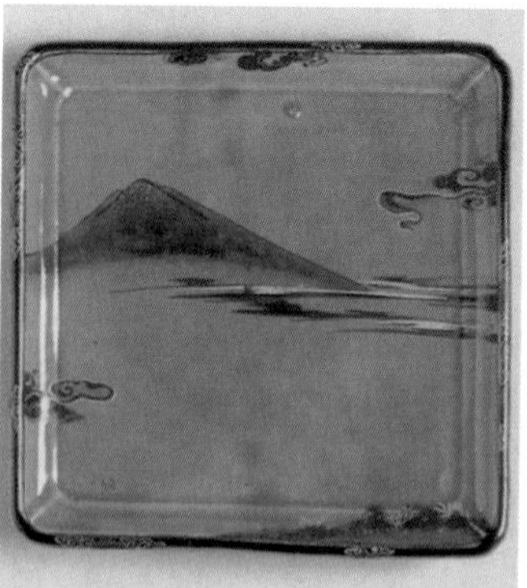

A Kutani plate, mid-17thC, 7½in (19cm) square.
£5,250–6,250 ⚒ S(NY)

An Imari charger, Edo period, 1675–1725, 21¼in (54cm) diam.
£2,000–2,400 ⚒ P(S)

A Kutani three-part food canister, c1890, 8in (20.5cm) high.
£90–100 ⊞ BRU

A jardinière, minor damage, c1900, 16¼in (41.5cm) high.
£550–650 ⚒ WW

◄ A Kakiemon-style teapot and cover, with gilt-metal mounts, hairline cracks and restored chips, late 17thC, 3½in (9cm) high.
£2,750–3,000 ⚒ S

◄ An Imari jar and cover, 19thC, 24in (61cm) high.
£600–700 ⚒ RBB

A Satsuma boxed tea service, c1920, 16in (40.5cm) wide.
£600–700 ⊞ TWr

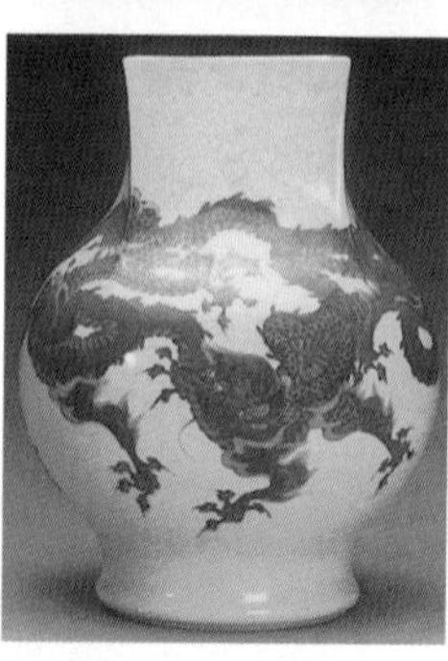

A yellow-enamelled vase, with underglaze blue decoration, signed Makuzu Kozan, minute rim chips, Meiji period, 1868–1911, 12¾in (32.5cm) high.
£6,000–7,000 ⚒ BB(S)

A pair of Kutani vases, marked, Meiji period, 1868–1911, 14½in (37cm) high.
£700–800 ⚒ P(S)

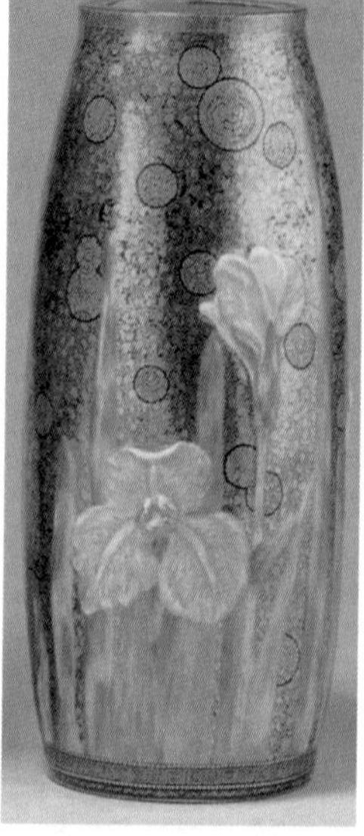

A Satsuma vase, by Kinkozan kore zo, signed, seal, 1875–1925, 16in (40.5cm) high.
£6,500–8,000 ⚒ S(NY)

A reticulated Satsuma vase, by Ryozan & Yasuda Trading Co, signed, Meiji period, 1868–1911, 6½in (16.5cm) high.
£4,000–4,500 ⊞ MER

A green-tinted lead glass roemer, 1700–50, 6¼in (16cm) high.
£1,000–1,100 ⚒ S(O)

A colour-twist wine glass, c1770, 5½in (14cm) high.
£2,700–3,000 ⊞ Del

A ruby-flashed goblet, Bohemian, 19thC, 8¼in (21cm) high.
£320–400 ⚒ WW

An engraved goblet, with blue overlay, attributed to Karl Pfohl, Steinschonau, Bohemian, c1855, 5¼in (13.5cm) high.
£2,200–2,500 ⚒ S(O)

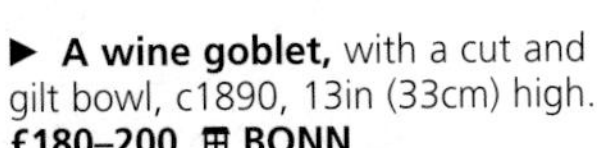

► **A wine goblet,** with a cut and gilt bowl, c1890, 13in (33cm) high.
£180–200 ⊞ BONN

A set of 12 Stourbridge wine glasses, cranberry cut to clear, c1870, 5in (12.5cm) high.
£1,800–2,200 ⊞ ALiN

A goblet and cover, the dished panels engraved with titled vistas, small chips, Bohemian, 1850–75, 9¼in (23.5cm) high.
£350–450 ⚒ DN

Cross Reference
See Glass (page 333–348)

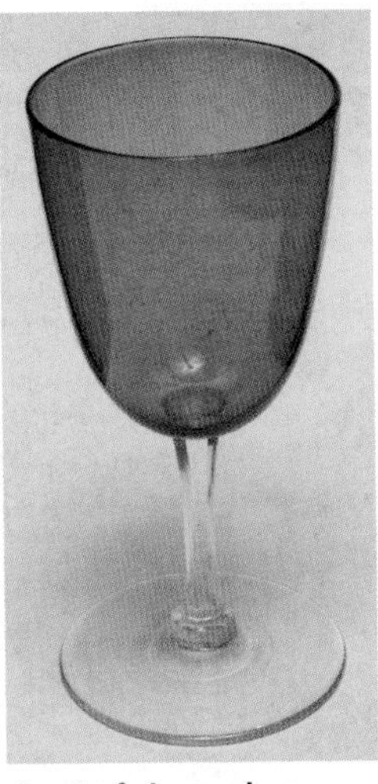

A set of six cranberry glasses, c1880, 5in (12.5cm) high.
£150–180 ⊞ JHa

A glass beaker, decorated with St Caspar with the Virgin and Child, by Anton Kothgasser, Austrian, Vienna, 1825–30, 4½in (11cm) high, in original leather case.
£3,800–4,800 ⚒ DORO

A glass beaker, decorated with enamels and gilt, Bohemian, c1880, 4½in (11.5cm) high.
£375–475 ⚒ DORO

► **A set of four milk glass beakers and stands,** by Imperial Glass Manufactory, St Petersburg, Russian, c1840, 4in (10cm) high.
£1,000–1,200 ⚒ S(Am)

A glass sugar basin, c1800, 5in (12.5cm) diam.
£315–350 ⊞ Del

► **A wrythen-moulded glass cream jug and matching sugar basin,** North Country, c1800, jug 4¼in (11cm) high.
£600–660 ⊞ Som

A gilded glass finger bowl and trembleuse stand, late 18thC, stand 6in (15cm) diam.
£600–775 ⚒ P

A pair of Stuart & Sons glass bowls, c1900, 7in (18cm) diam.
£120–135 ⊞ RUSK

A spirit decanter, c1800, 8in (20.5cm) high.
£180–200 ⊞ Del

A set of three decanters, 19thC, 11in (28cm) high.
£1,600–1,800 ⊞ DJH

An onion-shaped decanter, with mother-of-pearl and cork stopper, c1840, 8in (20.5cm) high.
£200–220 ⊞ GS

A Lithyalin glass cup and saucer, by the Count Buquoy Glassworks, Georgenthal or Silberberg, with gilt decoration, saucer with two rim chips, south Bohemian, 1820–40, saucer 5¼in (13.5cm) diam.
£850–1,000 ⚒ S(O)
Ex-Rudolf Just Collection.

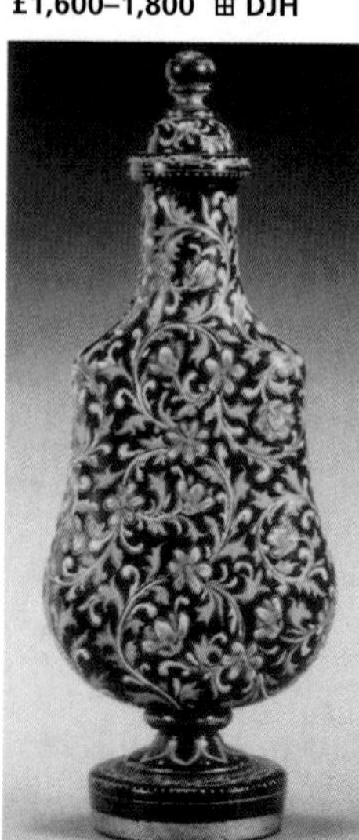

A Persian-style enamelled glass bottle and stopper, rim chips, Bohemian, c1880, 12in (30.5cm) high.
£600–650 ⚒ S(O)

Three Stevens & Williams intaglio-cut glass decanters, 1898–1904, largest 11in (28cm) high.
l. £950–1,250
c. £1,600–2,000
r. £600–800 ⊞ ALiN

A frilled glass preserve dish, in an EPNS stand, c1895, 5½in (14cm) diam.
£120–135 ⊞ GRI

◄ **A Moser enamelled glass cabinet cup and saucer,** Bohemian, c1885, saucer 5in (12.5cm) diam.
£280–350 ⊞ ALiN

A glass flask, rim chips, Alpenland, 17th–18thC, 4¾in (12cm) high.
£1,500–1,650 S(O)
Ex-Rudolf Just Collection.

A white glass flask, with looped decoration, c1850, 9in (23cm) high.
£100–120 Del

► **A glass jug,** with ribbed body and reeded handle, c1880, 8in (20.5cm) high.
£170–185 LHo

A Thomas Webb cameo glass plaque, by George Woodall, signed, c1911, 5in (12.5cm) diam.
£16,000–21,000 S

A double-overlay glass scent bottle and stopper, stopper chipped, finial repaired, c1860, 4¾in (12cm) diam.
£400–500 B

A glass flask and stopper, probably by the Count Buquoy Glassworks, Silberberg or Georgenthal, with gilt chinoiserie decoration, south Bohemian, dated 1834, 4¾in (12cm) high.
£1,300–1,500 S(O)
Ex-Rudolf Just Collection.

A pair of leaded glass windows, German, late 19thC, 19¼ x 16¼in (49 x 41.5cm).
£375–475 DORO

A Nailsea jug, c1810, 7in (18cm) high.
£500–550 Som

A pair of leaded stained glass pictures, Austrian, 1850–1900, largest 18½ x 13½in (47 x 34.5cm).
£700–900 DORO

An overlay glass scent bottle, Bohemian, c1860, 8in (20.5cm) high.
£200–220 LHo

◄ **A Lithyalin glass scent flask and stopper,** possibly by the Egermann Workshop or Harrach Glassworks, highlighted with gilding, chips to the shoulder and neck, north Bohemian, c1830, 2½in (6.5cm) high.
£750–900 S(O)
Ex-Rudolf Just Collection.

► **A Baccarat millefiori paperweight,** with fancy-cut base, French, dated 1848, 3½in (9cm) diam.
£7,000–8,000 ⊞ SWB

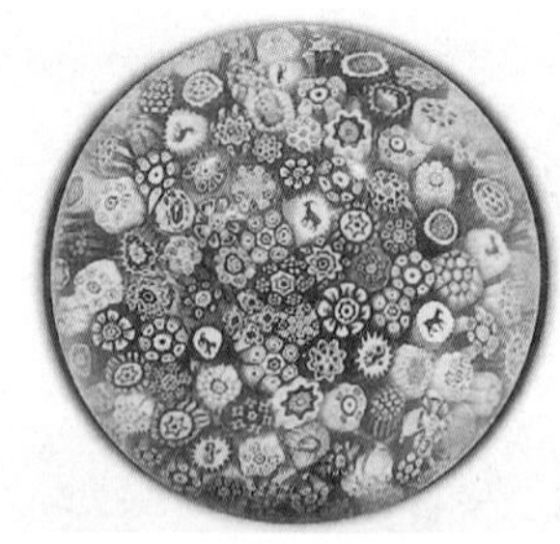

A Pietro Bigaglia scrambled millefiori paperweight, Italian, dated 1845 and 1846, 2¾in (7cm) diam.
£6,000–6,500 ⚒ S(O)

A Baccarat primrose paperweight, minor bruising, French, mid-19thC, 3¼in (8.5cm) diam.
£700–800 ⚒ B

◄ **A Clichy paperweight,** French, 1855, 3in (7.5cm) diam.
£1,600–1,800 ⊞ MLa

A Paul Ysart paperweight, with a butterfly, c1930, 2¾in (7cm) diam.
£600–725 ⚒ RTo

A Clichy concentric millefiori paperweight, French, c1848, 3in (7.5cm) diam.
£5,250–6,250 ⊞ DLP

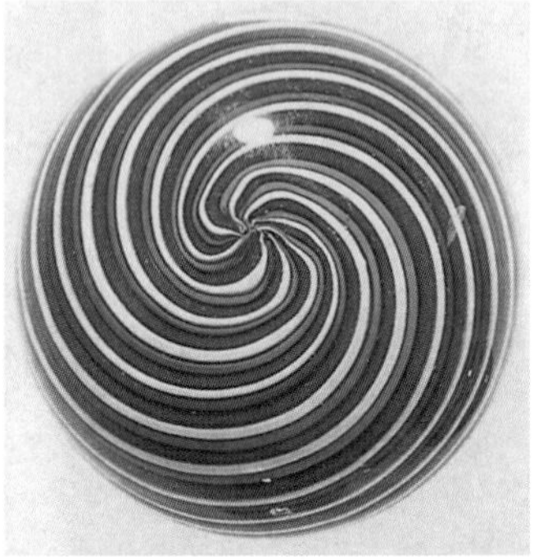

A swirl paperweight, probably St Louis, French, c1850, 3¼in (8.5cm) diam.
£2,750–3,500 ⚒ S

A pair of opaline glass vases, probably by Monot et Cie, decorated with bouquets of flowers, French, c1845, 12in (30.5cm) high.
£2,300–2,750 ⊞ ALiN

A Moser glass vase, decorated with polychrome enamels, Bohemian, Karlsbad, c1875, 8in (20.5cm) wide.
£2,000–2,500 ⊞ ALiN

A Stourbridge cameo glass vase, late 19thC, 6½in (16.5cm) high.
£800–1,000 ⚒ P

A Clichy vase, French, 1845–50, 9½in (24cm) high.
£400–450 ⊞ Del

A Hodgetts, Richardson & Co Paris Exposition glass cameo vase, by Joseph Locke, c1878, 7½in (19cm) high.
£8,000–9,000 ⚒ S(O)

A Lobmeyr Persian-style glass vase, with gilt and enamel decoration, c1880, 7in (18cm) high.
£9,500–12,000 ⚒ S

◄ A shaded cranberry glass vase, possibly by Moser, with enamel decoration, c1910, 8in (20.5cm) high.
£280–320 ⊞ GRI

► A pair of Baccarat crystal vases, with bronze mounts, French, c1930, 13in (33cm) high.
£9,000–10,000 ⊞ MI

An amber-flashed glass vase, monogrammed 'C.A.N.', Bohemian, 19thC, 5¾in (14.5cm) high.
£260–320 ⚒ G(L)

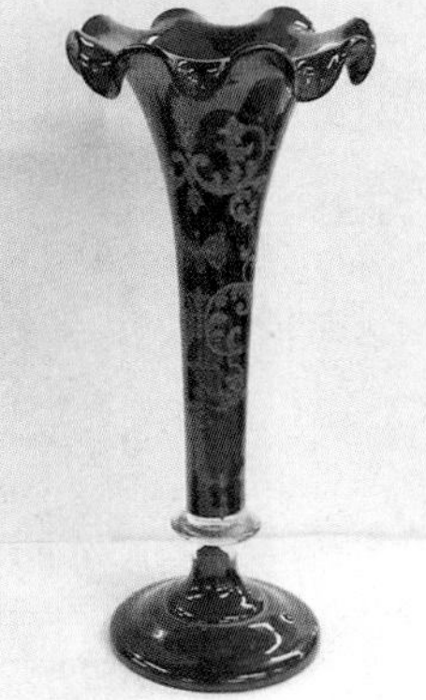

A pair of glass vases, with gilt decoration, late 19thC, 13in (33cm) high.
£230–300 ⚒ G(L)

A three-colour cameo glass vase, probably by Thomas Webb, c1890, 8½in (21.5cm) high.
£4,000–4,500 ⚒ S(O)

A pair of overlay glass vases, with gilt decoration, one damaged, Bohemian, 1850–1900, 8¾in (22cm) high.
£160–200 ⚒ WW

A ruby glass vase, with pinched diagonal trailing, c1880, 8in (20.5cm) high.
£160–175 ⊞ LHo

A pair of glass vases, with gilt decoration, Bohemian, late 19thC, 15½in (39.5cm) high.
£2,000–2,500 ⚒ PFK

Vases & Urns

A Belleek shell vase, First Period, c1860, 9in (23cm) high.
£450–500 ⊞ DeA

A Coalport campana-shaped vase, painted in coloured enamels with a bird within a gilt cartouche, on a blue scale ground, c1820, 3¾in (9.5cm) high.
£200–240 ⚒ LFA

l. A Royal Crown Derby vase, decorated in gilt with foliate sprigs on a maroon ground, printed mark, date code for 1900, 4in (10cm) high.
£75–100 ⚒ N

r. A Royal Crown Derby vase, decorated in gilt with foliate swags and scrolls on a cobalt-blue ground, printed mark, date code for 1896, 5½in (14cm) high.
£150–180 ⚒ N

A Derby campana-shaped vase, painted with summer flowers, damaged, c1825, 12½in (32cm) high.
£1,200–1,350 ⊞ NAW

A pair of miniature Doccia vases, the sides painted with pink flowers, the handles with mask head terminals, some restoration, Italian, c1760, 3in (7.5cm) high.
£300–360 ⚒ WW

A pair of Dresden vases and covers, painted with cavaliers at armed combat and rural backgrounds, with stencilled gilt borders, damaged and repaired, crossed swords mark, German, c1900, 19¾in (50cm) high.
£700–800 ⚒ S(S)

A vase, by Imperial Porcelain Manufactory, the body reserved with a panel of children at play, the reverse with polychrome cellular ground above a moulded matt gold of upright feathers and leaves, the shoulders with two seated Cupids, Russian, c1840, 14½in (37cm) high.
£13,000–15,000 ⚒ S
Pieces by the Imperial Porcelain Manufactory are highly desirable.

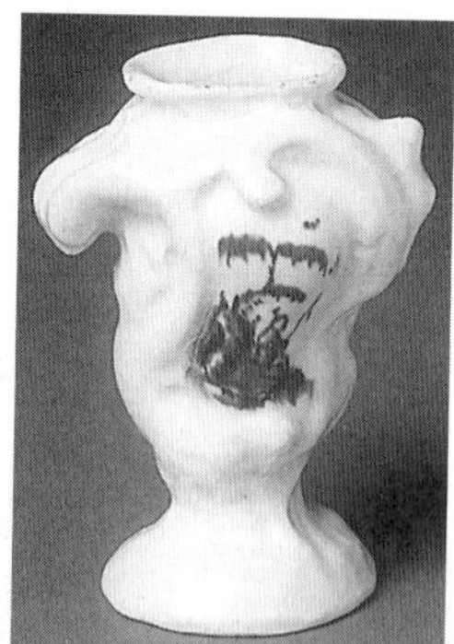

▶ An Isleworth rococo vase, modelled with asymmetric shell scrollwork, the two reserved panels painted in blue with a Chinese fisherman seated beneath a willow tree and a hut, cover possibly missing, c1775, 4in (10cm) high.
£900–1,100 ⚒ P

LOCATE THE SOURCE
The source of each illustration in Miller's can be found by checking the code letters below each caption with the Key to Illustrations, pages 794–800.

A pair of Longton Hall vases and covers, applied with groups of flowerheads, the pierced covers encrusted with flowers, minor damage and restoration, c1760, 7in (18cm) high.
£675–750 ⚒ P

A pair of Minton vases and covers, painted by J. E. Dean with windmills and sailing ships within raised gilt cartouches, on a cobalt-blue ground, finials broken and reglued, signed, printed marks, early 20thC, 11in (28cm) high.
£650–800 ⚒ N

A Paris gilt-metal-mounted campana vase, painted *en grisaille* with classical figures, later mounted with twin serpent handles, French, 19thC, 13in (33cm) high.
£800–950 S(O)

A Royal Worcester posy vase, attributed to James Sherrif, the body painted with colourful feathers, with a row of white enamel pearls and gilding around the rim, with gilt handles, marked, c1875, 3½in (9cm) high.
£630–700 P

Cross Reference
See Colour Review (page 301)

A pair of vases, each painted to one side with a panel depicting rustic courting couples seated in a woodland setting, all reserved on a deep claret ground, Continental, late 19thC, 22¾in (58cm) high.
£500–550 P(Ba)

A Rockingham vase, painted in coloured enamels with a named view of Howick Hall, Northumberland within a gilt cartouche, on a green ground, with gilt stork handles, area of rim restored, printed mark, c1835, 14½in (37cm) high.
£1,400–1,700 LFA

A Royal Worcester vase, with a floral and gilt decoration on a blush-ivory ground, cover missing, date code for 1893, 10½in (26.5cm) high.
£220–250 MAR

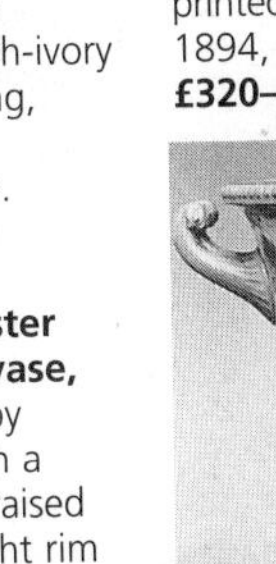

► A Royal Worcester campana-shaped vase, painted with roses by Walter Sedgley, with a bead border and a raised gilt foliate base, slight rim chip, date code for 1919, 8¾in (22cm) high.
£600–720 AG

A pair of Samson vases, decorated in the Imari palette, late 19thC, 21in (53.5cm) high.
£3,500–3,800 US

A Royal Worcester vase, the body painted with daisies on a blush-pink ground, mounted with two lioness handles, cover missing, printed marks, date code for 1894, 14½in (37cm) high.
£320–380 CGC

A Worcester Barr, Flight & Barr vase and cover, painted with a snipe suspended as a game trophy within a panel, within gilded borders of acanthus leaves around the base and neck, chips to base, knop restored, marked, c1805, 13½in (34.5cm) high.
£2,700–3,000 P

A Royal Worcester vase, painted with pheasants by James Stinton, 1904, 5½in (14cm) high.
£1,000–1,135 JUP

A pair of cornucopia vases, encrusted with colourful flowers enriched with green and enamel gilding, some damage, c1840, 6in (15cm) high.
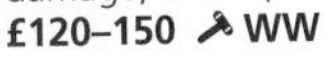
£120–150 WW

A pair of vases, decorated after Worcester's Duke of Clarence pattern, crossed swords mark, Continental, c1900, 8in (20.5cm) high.
£200–240 WW

Sèvres

The soft paste porcelain of Sèvres has a unique beauty. Established at Vincennes, the great French factory moved to Sèvres 250 years ago in 1753. It is best known for its coloured grounds, including a stunning turquoise, glowing rose pink, bright green and several tones of blue. These form rich backgrounds for painted fruit and flowers, landscapes, birds or figures, always framed by exceptional tooled gilding. Under Louis XV and Louis XVI (1715–92), Vincennes and Sèvres enjoyed a state monopoly. Fine vases and magnificent dinner sets were presented as royal gifts, for favour in the French court meant you dined in style. The prestigious Sèvres factory survived the French Revolution, and in turn Napoleon commissioned stunning presentation porcelain. Nineteenth-century production was sporadic, although magnificent sets were made for government and royal commissions. Splendid vases were shown in Victorian exhibitions, and some of the finest Sèvres dates from the Art Nouveau period.

Early Sèvres porcelain was widely collected in the 19th century. Incredible sums were paid for early coloured ground vases, but these high values encouraged a vast number of fakes. It is impossible to collect Sèvres without an extensive knowledge of markings, colours and painting styles. For each genuine Sèvres vase surviving today, there are probably a thousand copies, all bearing fake crossed LL marks. Reproductions can be very decorative and often expensive, but they must not be confused with the real thing. Fortunately, Sèvres marks include a code system that uniquely identifies the painters and gilders, as well as the year of production. Careful checking of these marks is essential, for if the subject matter and date do not match other recorded pieces by that artist, the chances are the piece is a fake.

Values have fluctuated in recent years but there is a very strong demand for 18th- and 19th-century items. Ordinary pieces with simple flowers on a white ground are only moderately priced and very affordable, but any piece with a rich coloured ground is going to be expensive. This is graphically shown by the results of a recent auction, when Christie's Paris sold the Charles Otto Zieseniss collection of single plates from many of the finest services, with most pieces going for considerably more than estimated. Take, for example, a plate from the turquoise ground set made in 1771 for the Prince de Rohan. When the celebrated Firestone collection was sold in New York in 1991 a pair of these plates sold for $16,000 (£11,000). In November 1999 Christie's London sold a similar pair for just £7,000. In the Zieseniss collection one single plate from the same set made an astonishing 32,243 Euros (£19,668). High prices are likely to continue, for the exceptional quality of the best Sèvres is widely appreciated.

John Sandon

A Sèvres-style box, the hinged lid painted with lovers, signed 'A. Gilbert', the sides with raised gilt decoration on a cerise ground, the interior painted with flowers, late 19thC, 9½in (24cm) high.
£350–420 WW

A Sèvres coffee can and saucer, in hard paste, decorated by Ambroise Michel, the cup with a colourful still life of flowers tumbling from a basket, the saucer with fruit and a basket of flowers on a ledge, on a lilac-pink ground overpainted with floral swags and ribbons, footrim chip, marks, French, dated 1778, saucer 5½in (14cm) diam.
£800–950 B

A Sèvres-style cabaret set, comprising 10 pieces, each painted with portrait and floral panels on a gilt-enriched deep blue ground, pseudo Sèvres marks, 1875–1925.
£800–900 S(S)

A Sèvres-style coffee or teapot, with gilt detail on a cobalt-blue ground, French, c1880, 5in (12.5cm) high.
£500–550 MAA

A pair of Sèvres-style cachepots, with gilt detail and jewelled decoration on a *bleu-céleste* ground, French, c1880, 6in (15cm) high.
£2,000–2,300 DHu

Further reading

Miller's Porcelain Antiques Checklist, Miller's Publications, 2001

A Sèvres coffee cup and saucer, painted by Capelle, incised mark, 1756–57, cup 2½in (6.5cm) high.
£1,000–1,300 US

A Sèvres cup and saucer, by Jean Baptiste Tandart, decorated with bouquets of flowers on a gilt-enriched cobalt-blue ground, French, 1789, cup 2¼in (5.5cm) high.
£1,450–1,600 ⊞ DHu

A Sèvres cup and saucer, decorated with flowers on a gilt-enriched ground, French, c1862, cup 2½in (6.5cm) high.
£280–320 ⊞ DHu

A Sèvres-style cup and saucer, the cup with a portrait of Madame La Parabère, on a gilt-enriched cobalt-blue ground, French, c1880, saucer 5in (12.5cm) diam.
£450–500 ⊞ MAA

◀ **A Sèvres cup and saucer,** by Emile-Jacques Ruhlmann, the cream-glazed porcelain with gilt detail, printed mark, c1925, cup 5½in (14cm) diam.
£9,000–11,000 ⚒ S

A Sèvres reticulated white tea cup and saucer, highlighted in gilding, printed factory marks, French, dated 1909.
£650–800 ⚒ S(O)

A Sèvres group of hunting dogs, signed 'AL', probably Armand Lacour, impressed marks, French, c1900, 18¼in (46.5cm) wide.
£600–700 ⚒ BUK

A pair of gilt-metal-mounted Sèvres-style ewers, enamelled with romantic scenes within gilt borders reserved on a *bleu-céleste* ground, on turned wood bases, French, c1870, 12in (30.5cm) high.
£400–500 ⚒ N

A pair of Vincennes plates, by François Binet, decorated with flower sprays, marked, French, 1754, 10in (25.5cm) diam.
£1,600–1,800 ⊞ US

A Sèvres plate, painted with two dogs chasing a stag along a riverbank, the border with gilded cartouches containing birds and insects on a turquoise ground, marked, French, date code for 1771, with mid-19thC decoration, 9½in (24cm) diam.
£150–180 ⚒ P(Ba)

A pair of Sèvres plates, decorated with swags of flowers and bows, French, 1780, 10in (25.5cm) diam.
£800–900 ⊞ US

A Sèvres blue and gilt porcelain dish, French, 1844–45, 16in (40.5cm) diam.
£1,000–1,200 ⚒ S(Mi)

▶ **A Sèvres-style plate,** depicting lovers in a garden setting surrounded by a gilt-enriched *bleu-céleste* border, signed by Lucot, French, c1880, 9¾in (25cm) diam.
£350–400 ⊞ OKK

A pair of Sèvres-style ormolu-mounted cups, painted with bands of flowers above gilt *oeil-de-perdrix*, 1850–1900, 3¾in (9.5cm) high.
£200–240 WW

A Sèvres blue and white biscuit plaque, decorated in high relief with the Triumph of Amphitrite, minor firing cracks, French, c1792, 6½ x 12¼in (16.5 x 31cm), in a giltwood frame.
£3,500–4,200 S
Plaques of this type were recorded for sale at the factory shop from 1791. They were generally used for embellishing furniture, fire surrounds or door cases.

A set of three Sèvres-style tea canisters and covers, with turquoise, red and white jewelled decoration on a blue ground, with gilt and foliate scrollwork motifs, missing some jewels, gilt marks, French, late 19thC, 3½in (9cm) high.
£1,450–1,600 S

A pair of Sèvres porcelain campana vases, gilded with continuous bands of anthemion devices on a mottled blue ground, printed and incised marks, 1928–40, 12in (30.5cm) high.
£2,200–2,500 S(O)

A Sèvres inkstand, decorated in burnished three-colour gold and platinum with chinoiserie scenes on a black ground, probably by Louis-François Lécot, damaged, with later metal ring mount, inscribed mark, French, c1800, 6½in (16.5cm) wide.
£1,200–1,300 B
This type of gilt decoration is usually associated with Louis-François Lécot. He retired from the factory in April 1800, after nearly 40 years service.

A garniture of three Sèvres biscuit vases and pedestals, probably modelled by J. J. Bachelier, on fluted drum-shaped pedestals applied with drapery swags, one vase with minor rim chip, French, c1770, 9½in (24cm) high.
£1,650–1,800 LFA

A Sèvres-style wine cooler, decorated with cartouches of Palais de Versailles and Trianon, on a *bleu-céleste* ground, 1860–70, 12in (30.5cm) wide.
£800–900 OKK

► **A pair of Sèvres-style ormolu-mounted vases,** the bodies painted to one side with an 18thC courting couple, each signed 'Lebell', the reverse with a landscape, on a cobalt-blue ground, set with flat-leaf handles ending in swags, French, 1875–1925, 26in (66cm) high.
£6,750–7,500 SK

A Sèvres-style parfumière, decorated with a cartouche of a classical maiden by a column on a gilt-enriched *bleu-céleste* ground, with jewelled decoration, signed 'Leber', c1860, 12in (30.5cm) high.
£2,250–2,500 DHu

◄ **A Sèvres tea service,** comprising 11 pieces, decorated in gilt with anthemion devices on a blue ground, printed and painted marks, 1813–15.
£1,800–2,000 S(O)

A Sèvres-style vase, decorated with a cartouche of children on a *bleu-céleste* ground, French, c1880, 11½in (29cm) high.
£1,000–1,100 DHu

A Selection of Chinese Dynasties & Marks

Early Dynasties

Neolithic	10th – early 1st millennium BC
Shang Dynasty	16th century–c1050 BC
Zhou Dynasty	c1050–221 BC
Warring States	480–221 BC
Qin Dynasty	221–206 BC
Han Dynasty	206 BC–AD 220
Six Dynasties	222–589
Wei Dynasty	386–557
Sui Dynasty	581–618
Tang Dynasty	618–907
Five Dynasties	907–960
Liao Dynasty	907–1125
Song Dynasty	960–1279
Northern Song	960–1127
Southern Song	1127–1279
Xixia Dynasty	1038–1227
Jin Dynasty	1115–1234
Yuan Dynasty	1279–1368

Ming Dynasty Marks

Hongwu
1368–1398

永樂年製

Yongle
1403–1424

大明宣德年製

Xuande
1426–1435

大明成化年製

Chenghua
1465–1487

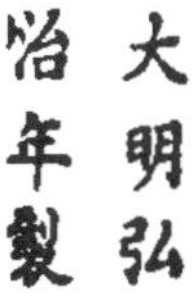

大明弘治年製

Hongzhi
1488–1505

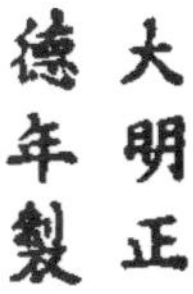

大明正德年製

Zhengde
1506–1521

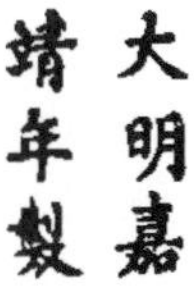

大明嘉靖年製

Jiajing
1522–1566

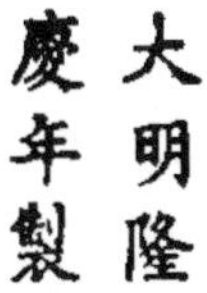

大明隆慶年製

Longqing
1567–1572

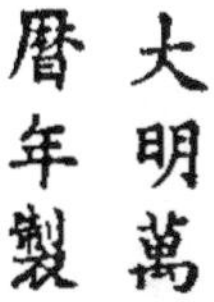

大明萬曆年製

Wanli
1573–1619

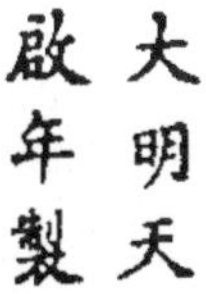

大明天啟年製

Tianqi
1621–1627

崇禎年製

Chongzhen
1628–1644

Qing Dynasty Marks

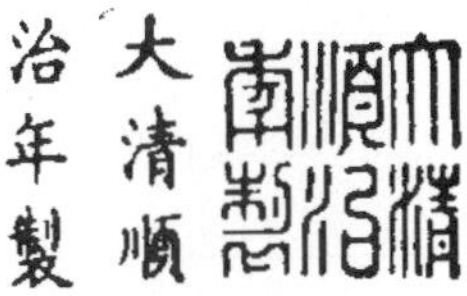

大清順治年製

Shunzhi
1644–1661

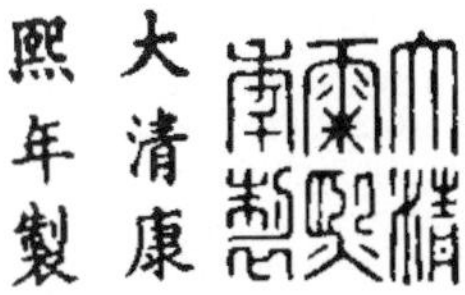

大清康熙年製

Kangxi
1662–1722

大清雍正年製

Yongzheng
1723–1735

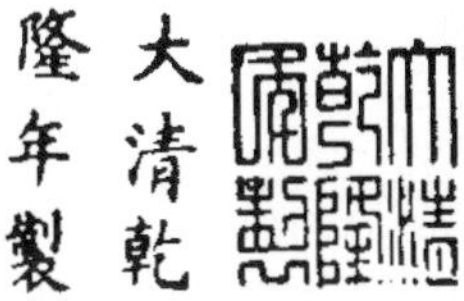

大清乾隆年製

Qianlong
1736–1795

嘉慶年製

Jiaqing
1796–1820

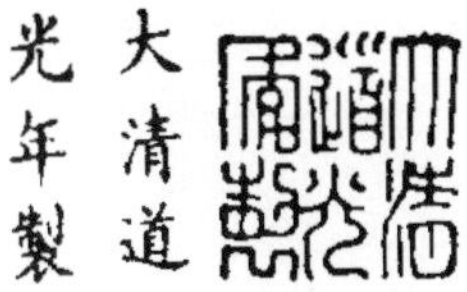

大清道光年製

Daoguang
1821–1850

大清咸豐年製

Xianfeng
1851–1861

大清同治年製

Tongzhi
1862–1874

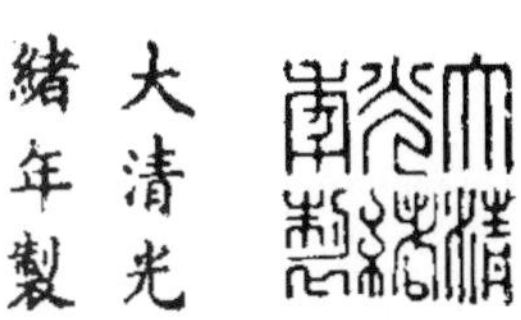

大清光緒年製

Guangxu
1875–1908

大清宣統年製

Xuantong
1909–1911

洪憲年製

Hongxian
1916

CHINESE CERAMICS

Chinese Ceramics
Animals & Birds

A pottery pig, Han Dynasty, 206 BC–AD 220, 8in (20.5cm) high.
£1,400–1,700 ⊞ GLD

A grey pottery figure of a hen, part of a Zodiac series, Yuan Dynasty, 13thC, 5in (12.5cm) high.
£80–100 ⊞ HEL

A *blanc-de-chine* lion dog taperstick holder, taperstick missing, minor chips, early 18thC, 10½in (26.5cm) high.
£300–360 ⚒ S(O)
Ex-Rudolf Just collection.

A red pottery figure of a female polo player, with traces of white, black and red pigment, Tang Dynasty, 618–907, 12½in (32cm) high.
£1,100–1,300 ⚒ SLN

A brush washer, in the shape of a double duck with a central aperture on the back, decorated in blue and white, early 16thC, 4¾in (12cm) wide.
£800–900 ⚒ S(O)

A pair of *famille verte* incense burners, in the shape of Buddhistic lions, decorated in bright enamels with black-line details, one base chipped, Qing Dynasty, 19thC, 9¾in (25cm) high.
£650–800 ⚒ B(Ba)

◄ **A pair of green-glazed ducks,** the wingtips and tailfeathers picked out in red, yellow and blue glaze, small chip to one wing, Qing Dynasty, 19thC 10in (25.5cm) high.
£200–240 ⚒ P(Ba)

► **A Chinese export porcelain figure of a hawk,** perched on a rocky outcrop, decorated in coloured enamels, 1800–50, 8¼in (21cm) high.
£450–550 ⚒ F&C

A glazed duck, decorated in brown and cream, Tang Dynasty, 618–907, 3½in (9cm) high.
£280–320 ⊞ GLD

A pottery ridge tile, in the form of a courtly figure on horseback, covered in thick green glaze, probably late Ming Dynasty, 17thC, 14½in (37cm) high.
£450–550 ⚒ DN

A pair of *sancai*-glazed pottery ridge tiles, modelled as fish, 19thC, 11½in (29cm) high.
£500–600 ⚒ S(O)

Bowls

A creamy white-glazed bowl and cover, Five Dynasties, 907–960, 5in (12.5cm) diam.
£600–650 ⊞ GLD

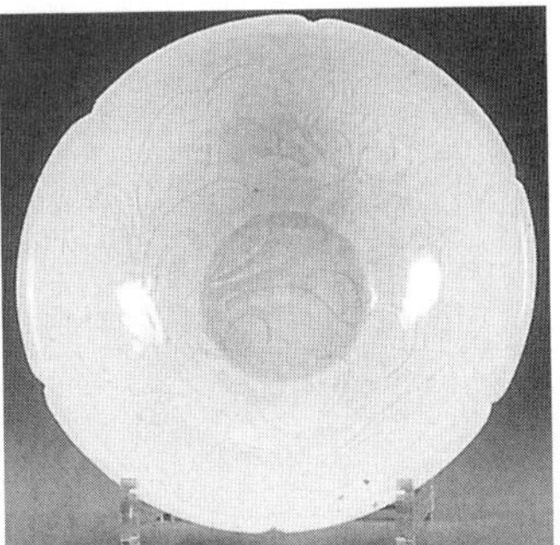

A carved *yingqing* bowl, Song Dynasty, 960–1279, 7½in (19cm) diam.
£375–450 ⚒ S(O)

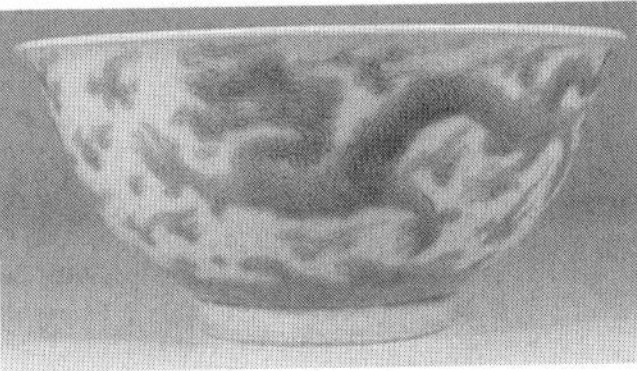

A bowl, decorated with a green dragon on a yellow ground, rim frits, hairline crack, Kangxi mark and period, 1662–1722, 6in (15cm) diam.
£550–650 ⚒ WW

A finely incised white-glazed stem bowl, Yongzheng mark and period, 1723–35, 7in (18cm) high.
£7,000–8,500 ⚒ S(HK)

Some of the finest porcelains of the Qing dynasty were made during the relatively short reign of the Emperor Yongzheng (1723–35). These were made under the direction of Tang Ying, the most famous of the imperial porcelain kiln supervisors.

A Yaozhou celadon bowl, Northern Song Dynasty, 960–1127, 5in (12.5cm) diam.
£850–950 ⊞ GLD

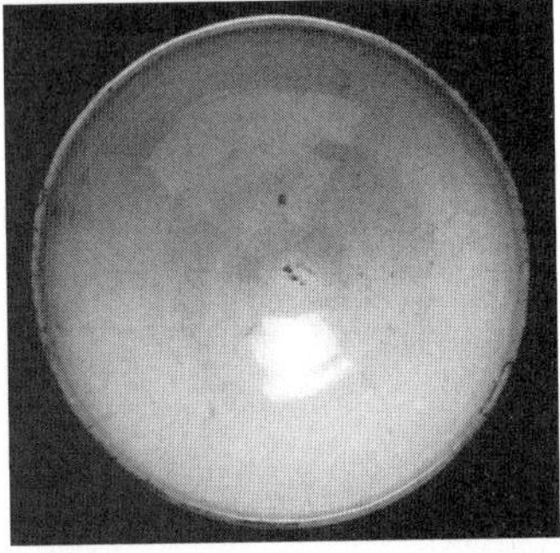

A Junyao bowl, all-over decorated with a lavender blue glaze, 14th–15thC, 7in (18cm) diam.
£600–700 ⚒ S(O)

A *famille verte* bowl, decorated with a procession of children playing in a fenced landscape, cracked, Kangxi period, 1662–1722, 9in (23cm) diam.
£500–600 ⚒ WW

A bowl, painted with two reserves of figures on terraces against a coral-red Y-diaper ground, late 18thC, 10½in (26.5cm) diam.
£400–450 ⚒ CGC

◄ **A *famille rose* punch bowl,** the exterior decorated with a continuous scene of figures at conversation and holding various attributes, accompanied by a Buddhistic lion and cat, repaired, 18thC, 15½in (39.5cm) diam.
£400–500 ⚒ RTo

A brown-glazed bowl, decorated with a phoenix, Song Dynasty, 12th–13thC, 4½in (11.5cm) diam.
£750–850 ⊞ GLD

A blue and white bowl, Ming Dynasty, 1460–1520, 8in (20.5cm) diam.
£675–750 ⊞ GLD

A pair of blue and white bowls, each interior decorated with a bonsai within a stylized flower reserve, the exterior painted with conversational groups and trees, Kangxi mark and period, late 17thC, 8¼in (21cm) diam.
£1,500–1,700 ⚒ P(S)

A pair of armorial soup bowls, the rims hung with festoons of *famille rose* flowers about the armorial, late 18thC, 8¾in (22cm) diam.
£400–500 ⚒ CGC

Cross Reference
See Colour Review (page 303)

CHINESE CERAMICS

A *famille rose* **bowl,** decorated with flowers, c1860, 10in (25.5cm) diam.
£80–90 ⊞ FRY

A *famille rose* **bowl,** cracked, 19thC, 19¼in (49cm) diam.
£250–300 ⚒ WW

A blue and white bowl, decorated in the centre with a hare, from the *Tek Sing* cargo, c1820, 6½in (16.5cm) diam.
£200–220 ⊞ RBA

► **A *famille rose* bowl,** modelled as a lotus flower, with four rows of petals in shades of pink and yellow, with a duck-egg blue interior, hairline crack, Daoguang mark and period, 1821–50, 4in (10cm) high, with hardwood stand.
£280–320 ⚒ RTo

A *doucai* enamelled bowl, the exterior outlined in cobalt highlighted in iron-red, green and aubergine enamels, with lemon yellow applied around the rim above an underglaze blue trifid band, Daoguang mark and period, 1821–50, 6in (15cm) diam.
£2,500–2,750 ⚒ BB(S)

Brushpots

A brushpot, painted in blue and white, Kangxi mark and period, 1662–1722, 6in (15.cm) high.
£3,800–4,200 ⚒ S(Am)

A brushpot, painted in blue and white with two mythical beasts in pursuit, probably 17thC, 4¾in (12cm) high.
£300–360 ⚒ P(Ba)

A blue and white porcelain brushpot, painted with deer under a pine tree issuing from rockery, 17thC–18thC, 6¼in (16cm) high.
£1,400–1,700 ⚒ SLN

Cups

► **A *famille rose* double-walled tea bowl and saucer,** with flower-panelled brown and gilt diaper bands, Qianlong period, 1736–95, 4¼in (11cm) diam.
£400–500 ⚒ LFA

A coffee cup and saucer, probably for the American market, decorated in sepia and gilt, terminal of handle re-touched, early 19thC, saucer 4in (10cm) diam.
£150–180 ⚒ WW

A Batavian *famille rose* tea bowl and saucer, Qianlong period, 1736–95, saucer 5in (12.5cm) diam.
£250–280 ⊞ GLD

Batavian ware

In the early 17th century, the Dutch East India Company was founded and based at Batavia (now Djakarta, Indonesia). One of their more successful exports to Europe throughout the latter part of the 17th and 18th centuries was brown-glazed porcelain tea services with blue and white or *famille rose* decorated reserve panels, subsequently known as Batavian ware.

Dishes

A Longquan celadon dish, cracked, early Ming Dynasty, 15thC, 14½in (36.5cm) diam.
£200–240 WW

A pair of Chinese export dishes, painted in blue and white, rim chips, encircled leaf mark, Kangxi period, 1662–1722, 13¾in (35cm) diam.
£500–600 LFA

◄ **A *famille rose* teapot stand,** c1770, 5in (12.5cm) diam.
£150–165 BRU

► **A dish from the *Diana* cargo,** decorated in blue with a chrysanthemum pattern, c1817, 11in (28cm) diam.
£180–200 RBA

A soup dish, decorated in underglaze blue with pagodas, Qianlong period, 1736–95, 10in (25.5cm) diam.
£65–75 FRY

Figures

Four pottery musicians, Han Dynasty, 206 BC–AD 220, 7in (18cm) high.
£1,250–1,350 GLD

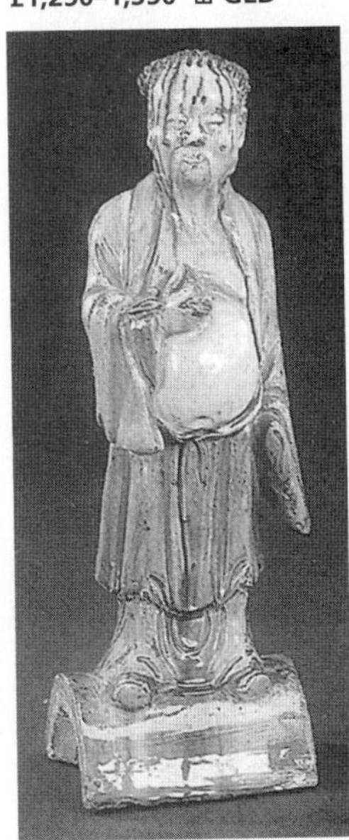

A *blanc-de-chine* figure of a sage, minor losses, 18thC, 6in (15cm) high.
£500–600 S(P)

◄ **A pair of *sancai* pottery roof tiles,** in the form of immortals, each holding fruits in his right hand, 17thC, 16in (40.5cm) high.
£750–900 SLN

A pottery ridge tile figure, modelled with a pig's head and covered with a blue and aubergine glaze and standing on a cloud scroll, restored, part of the base missing, possibly 16thC–17thC, 11½in (29cm) high.
£250–300 DN

► **A figure of Guanyin,** holding a scroll, standing on a base of *ruyi* scrolls with ivory-coloured glaze, some chips, Qing Dynasty, late 19thC, 42in (106.5cm) high.
£500–600 B(Ba)

A pair of pottery court ladies, Sui Dynasty, 581–618, 11in (28cm) high.
£1,200–1,350 GLD

Flatware

A pair of blue and white plates, hallmark to base, Kangxi period, 1662–1722, 8in (20.5cm) diam.
£1,550–1,850 ⊞ GLD

A pair of Chinese Imari plates, Kangxi period, 1662–1722, 9in (23cm) diam.
£600–700 ⊞ GLD

A Swatow blue and white dish, painted with an exotic bird perched among bamboo and other foliage, the border with compartmented panels of flowers and foliage, rim chip, 17thC–18thC, 14½in (37cm) diam.
£200–240 ⚒ P(Ba)

► **A set of six Chinese Imari plates,** early 18thC, 8½in (21.5cm) diam.
£300–360 ⚒ CGC

A Nanking platter, decorated in underglaze blue with a scene of a pagoda, and a figure on a bridge, rim chip, 18thC, 17½in (44.5cm) wide.
£180–220 ⚒ GAK

A blue and white meat plate, 18thC, 12¾in (32.5cm) wide.
£160–200 ⚒ WW

A pair of *famille rose* porcelain plates, the centre decorated with a vase of flowers, cracked, Qianlong period, 1736–95, 8¾in (22.5cm) diam.
£250–300 ⚒ BERN

A Chinese export South Sea Bubble plate, painted in underglaze blue with a figure from the *Commedia dell'Arte,* inscribed 'De Actie-mars op de tang' (The March of the Share Values played on the Tuning Fork), chipped, c1730, 8½in (21.5cm) diam.
£800–950 ⚒ P(Ba)
This subject is taken from a Dutch set of caricatures to commemorate the famous financial scandal. The Scottish financier John Law set up the South Sea Company and proceeded to manipulate the share price to unsustainable heights. At that point the market collapsed, and the financial scam was then repeated in other parts of Europe.

A Chinese export porcelain dish, decorated in underglaze blue, Qianlong period, 1736–95, 14in (35.5cm) diam.
£1,100–1,200 ⚒ BUK

A *famille verte* platter, c1920, 12in (30.5cm) diam.
£70–80 ⊞ BRU

A pair of blue and white plates, decorated with peonies, leaves and flower buds, early 18thC, 8½in (21.5cm) diam.
£425–475 ⊞ NAW

A *Nanking* cargo plate, decorated in underglaze blue with a lakeside pavilion, c1750, 9in (23cm) diam.
£340–370 ⊞ RBA

Garden Seats

A blue and white garden seat, moulded with studs and decorated with birds and foliage, 19thC, 18½in (47cm) high.
£300–360 ⚒ WW

A *famille rose* garden seat, painted with figural scenes of ladies, with pierced cash medallions, Cantonese, late 19thC, 18½in (47cm) high.
£1,000–1,200 ⚒ S(O)

A blue and white porcelain garden seat, painted with floral sprays and precious objects, late 19thC, 18in (45.5cm) high.
£600–720 ⚒ SLN

A Chinese export porcelain *famille rose* garden seat, with pierced cash motifs, surrounded by raised gilt bosses, painted with reserves of courtly figures, alternating with flower and bird panels, late 19thC, 18¾in (47.5cm) high.
£1,500–1,800 ⚒ BB(S)

Jars

A neolithic jar, Qijia culture, c2000–1500 BC, 4in (10cm) high.
£225–250 ⊞ GLD

A covered jar, decorated in underglaze blue with scenes of daily life, Qianlong period 1736–95, 6in (15cm) diam.
£135–150 ⊞ FRY

► **A wine storage jar,** with deep-brown glaze and iron-oxide decoration of bamboo leaves, Song Dynasty, early 13thC, 12in (30.5cm) high.
£1,800–2,200 ⚒ NOA

A straw-glazed stoneware amphora, set with arched double-strap handles applied with studs and dragon's head terminals biting the galleried rim, Tang Dynasty, 618–907, 9¼in (23.5cm) high.
£1,750–2,000 ⚒ S(O)

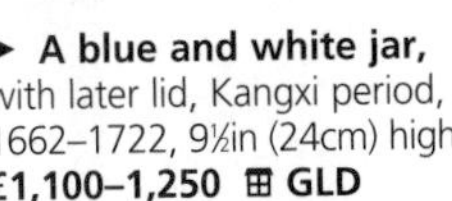

► **A blue and white jar,** with later lid, Kangxi period, 1662–1722, 9½in (24cm) high.
£1,100–1,250 ⊞ GLD

◄ **A blue and white jar,** the sides painted with panels of flowering branches near rockwork, the shoulders with further floral branches, Wanli period, 1573–1619, 15in (38cm) high.
£2,400–2,700 ⚒ S(Am)

A blue and white jar, painted with a warrior standing on a rocky ledge, a further figure standing on a boat, early 17thC, 11½in (29cm) high.
£800–950 ⚒ B(Ba)

A Longquan celadon *guan*/storage jar, carved with a flower scroll above upright stiff leaves, early Ming Dynasty, 15thC, 10¼in (26cm) high.
£450–550 ⚒ WW

A blue and white jar, painted with The Three Friends of Winter, Wanli period, 1573–1619, 5in (12.5cm) high.
£950–1,150 ⚒ S(O)

A *wucai* jar, base crack, Transitional period, 17thC, 12½in (32cm) high.
£750–825 ⚒ S(Am)

A blue and white spice jar, with later white metal mount, Kangxi period, 1662–1722, 5in (12.5cm) high.
£585–650 ⊞ GLD

A blue and white jar, painted in blue with prunus branches on a cracked ice ground, Kangxi period, 1662–1722, 8¼in (21cm) high.
£300–360 ⚒ P(Ba)

► **A blue and white covered jar,** decorated with scholars, c1860, 9in (23cm) high.
£200–230 ⊞ FRY

A blue and white jar, decorated in underglaze blue with panels of symbols, lid missing, chips, Kangxi period, 1662–1722, 13in (33cm) high.
£350–420 ⚒ BUK

A blue and white jar, decorated in underglaze blue with stylized lotus flowers above a stiff-leaf border, 19thC, 12½in (32cm) high.
£700–850 ⚒ BUK

► **A tortoiseshell-glazed storage jar,** 19thC, 30½in (77.5cm) high.
£400–500 ⚒ NOA

Jardinières

A matched pair of *famille rose* jardinières and stands, painted with figural scenes, with flowers and butterflies to the rims and stands, 19thC, 8in (20.5cm) diam.
£1,500–1,650 ⚒ P(S)

A *famille rose* hexagonal jardinière and stand, decorated with alternating panels of figures and flowers, birds and insects, chip to one corner, Cantonese, 19thC, 9¾in (25cm) high.
£380–450 ⚒ WW

A *famille verte* jardinière, the sides decorated with alternating figural panels, c1900, 18in (45.5cm) high.
£450–500 ⚒ S(Am)

Items in the Chinese Ceramics section have been arranged in date order within each sub-section.

Jugs

A wine jar, decorated in underglaze blue with a sage surrounded by servants in a mountainous landscape, Transitional period, 17thC, 8¾in (22cm) high.
£1,600–2,000 ⚒ BERN

A Chinese Imari porcelain jug, the gilt-bronze mounts probably Dutch or German, Kangxi period, 1662–1722, 5¼in (13.5cm) high.
£3,300–4,000 ⚒ S(P)

A European-shaped ewer, with silver mount, decorated in Chinese Imari with ladies in an interior and in a garden, Qianlong period, 1735–40, 8in (20.5cm) high.
£5,000–5,500 ⚒ S(P)

A *famille rose* ewer, painted with stylized exotic birds perched upon rockwork and trees within a fenced garden, with mythical sea beast spout, chip, early 19thC, 14in (35.5cm) high.
£950–1,150 ⚒ P(Ba)

Mugs & Tankards

A tankard, painted throughout in underglaze blue with a lakeside pavilion, 18thC, 5in (12.5cm) high.
£200–240 GAK

A blue and white mug, painted with pavilions, bridges and islands, the handle modelled as a dragon, c1800, 5¼in (13.5cm) high.
£250–300 CGC

A Chinese Imari mug, painted in underglaze red and blue, Qianlong period, 1736–95, 6½in (16.5cm) high.
£550–650 B(Ba)

Services

◀ **A *famille rose* porcelain part dinner service,** comprising 14 pieces, two pieces rivetted, Qianlong period, 1736–95, meat dish 15¾in (40cm) wide.
£3,700–4,200 P(EA)

A *famille rose* part dinner service, comprising 14 pieces, decorated with a roundel of flowers encircling a flowerhead, gilt rim, cracks, Qianlong period, 1736–95, tureen 6½in (16.5cm) wide.
£1,700–2,000 S(Am)

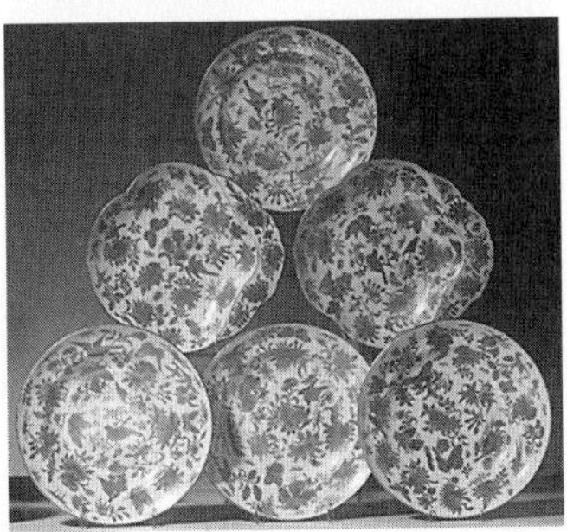

A Chinese export part dessert service, comprising six pieces, crack, 19thC, shell dish 10½in (26.5cm) wide.
£1,000–1,300 S(NY)

A celadon part service, comprising 28 pieces, decorated in *famille rose* enamels with scattered birds, insects and flowers, minor rim chips, Cantonese, late 19thC.
£900–1,000 S(O)

Tea Canisters

A Chinese Imari tea canister, with later white metal lid, Kangxi period, 1662–1722, 4½in (11.5cm) high.
£600–700 ⊞ GLD

A *famille rose* tea canister, decorated with panels of figures in landscapes, Qianlong period, 1736–95, 4¼in (11cm) high.
£50–60 WW

A *blanc-de-chine* tea canister, with wooden cover, 18thC, 4¾in (12cm) high.
£2,200–2,500 S(P)
This is a rare shape of tea canister.

A pair of Chinese Imari tea canisters, decorated with panels of riverside pagodas and distant mountains, surrounded by flowers, the side panels with trailing flowers, covers missing, rim chips, Qianlong period, 1736–95, 4¼in (11cm) high.
£220–270 P(Ba)

Tea & Chocolate Pots

A Qingbai bowl teapot and lid, Song Dynasty, 12th–13thC, 4in (10cm) high.
£1,800–2,000 ⊞ GLD

A blue and white chocolate pot and cover, painted with flowers and foliage, the cover with gilt ball knop, 18thC, 6¼in (16cm) high.
£350–450 ⚒ CGC

A teapot and lid, decorated with panels of figures and flowers, Cantonese, 1880–1900, 7in (18cm) high, with wicker case.
£145–160 ⊞ FRY

Tureens

A blue and white tureen and cover, decorated with a pagoda design, with a pomegranate knop and lotus seed-pod handles, chip, Qianlong period, 1736–95, 13½in (34.5cm) wide.
£500–600 ⚒ WW

A Chinese export tureen and cover, painted with pagodas in landscapes, the cover with foliate lambrequin design within diaper borders, with foliate S-scroll handles, the cover with lotus blossom strap handle, Qianlong period, 1736–95, 14½in (37cm) wide.
£700–850 ⚒ B(S)

◀ **A blue and white soup tureen and cover,** painted with bridges and island reserves within scroll frames, with mythical beast handles and pomegranate finial, 18thC, 13¾in (35cm) wide.
£600–700 ⚒ CGC

A blue and white tureen and cover, with a scroll knop and animal handles, cover possibly associated, Qianlong period, 1736–95, 14¼in (36cm) wide.
£500–600 ⚒ WW

A *Nanking* blue and white tureen and cover, with shell scroll finial and rabbit mask handles, late 18thC, 11in (28cm) wide.
£320–380 ⚒ TRM

Vases

A white-glazed vase, Tang Dynasty, 618–907, 9in (23cm) high.
£1,400–1,600 ⊞ GLD

► **A celadon porcelain incised vase,** with cross-hatch decoration, the neck with lappet leaves, ribs at the base, Ming Dynasty, 15thC, 18in (45.5cm) high.
£1,700–2,000 ⚒ NOA

◀ **A blue and white double-gourd vase,** decorated with shaped panels of flowers and birds, reserved on a wave-pattern ground, neck reduced, Wanli period, 1573–1619, 17¾in (45cm) high.
£2,400–2,700 ⚒ S(Am)

A porcelain blue and white vase, painted with a continuous frieze of figures in a landscape, above a band of pendants, mid-17thC, 16¼in (41.5cm) high.
£825–900 LJ

A blue and white vase, decorated with butterflies and foliage, 1650–1700, 6¾in (17cm) high.
£400–500 WW

A *famille rose* bottle vase, each side painted with a flowering branch, the neck with two flower sprigs, chips to upper rim, Yongzheng/early Qianlong period, early 18thC, 7in (18cm) high.
£500–600 S(O)
Ex-Rudolf Just Collection.

A pair of blue and white vases, the bodies painted with garden panels, and landscapes on the necks, early 18thC, 13¼in (33.5cm) high.
£400–500 CGC

A *famille rose* hexagonal reticulated vase and cover, knop restored, Qianlong period 1736–95, 13¼in (33.5cm) high.
£320–380 WW

A Chinese Imari miniature vase, with silver neck and cover, 18thC, 4in (10cm) high.
£130–155 WW

A porcelain vase, with a straw-coloured glaze, on a wooden base, c1820, 18in (45.5cm) high.
£600–720 NOA

A Yingqing-style vase, with a transparent pale blue glaze, the rim with key-fret border, the body carved with stylized dragon heads and flanked by dragon-shaped ring handles, 18thC–19thC, 18in (45.5cm) high.
£1,000–1,200 S(Am)

◀ **A blue and white vase,** decorated with flowers and scaly dragons, with iron-brown moulded bands, late 19thC, 23½in (59.5cm) high.
£200–230 WW

A porcelain vase, the celadon body with relief blue-scrolled design, the neck modelled as a piece of blue and white decorated material tied with blue-glazed rope, 19thC, 10¾in (27.5cm) high.
£100–120 WilP

A pair of vases, each decorated in typical *famille rose* palette with courtly figures and mounted warriors, with double Dog of *Fo* handles, Cantonese, 19thC, 17in (43cm) high.
£280–320 TRM

A pair of *famille jaune* porcelain vases, decorated with panels of flowers, the shoulders with mask head gilt ring handles, late 19thC–early 20thC, 13½in (34.5cm) high.
£350–420 DMC

◀ **A vase,** polyhrome-decorated with a dragon and a phoenix, late 19th/early 20thC, 15in (38cm) high.
£180–220 WW

Japanese Ceramics

Japanese Chronology Chart

Jomon (Neolithic) period	c10,000–100 BC
Yayoi period	c200 BC–AD 200
Tumulus (Kofun) period	200–552
Asuka period	552–710
Nara period	710–794
Heian period	794–1185
Kamakura period	1185–1333
Muromachi (Ashikaga) period	1333–1568
Momoyama period	1568–1600
Edo (Tokugawa) period	1600–1868
Genroku period	*1688–1703*
Meiji period	1868–1911
Taisho period	1912–1926
Showa period	1926–1989

Animals

A Hirado white-glazed water-dropper, modelled as a mythical sea beast, with feathered upturned tail and scaly body, mid-19thC, 3¾in (9.5cm) high.
£350–420 ⚒ P(Ba)

A Hirado model of a cockerel, 19thC, 5in (12.5cm) high.
£200–240 ⚒ WW

An earthenware model of the sacred toad, the nodulous body decorated with a green glaze, standing on three legs, late 19thC, 11¾in (30cm) high.
£600–660 ⚒ S(O)

A pair of Kutani miniature kittens, Meiji period, 1868–1911, 2½in (6.5cm) high.
£650–700 ⊞ GLD

A Satsuma group of playful *shishis*, Meiji period, 1868–1911, 7in (18cm) high.
£1,100–1,200 ⊞ MER

A Kutani hare, Taisho period, 1912–26, 11in (28cm) high.
£900–1,000 ⊞ GLD

Bottles

◄ **A Kakiemon-style Arita bottle,** painted in underglaze blue, with green enamel and iron-red with black outlines, minor chip, late 17thC, 15in (38cm) high.
£4,000–4,500 ⚒ S

► **An Arita bottle,** decorated in underglaze blue with a band of birds among flowering branches, with flowering branches to the neck, neck chips, 18thC, 9¾in (25cm) high.
£600–720 ⚒ DN

A Hirado tokkuri/sake bottle, painted in blue and white with the Chinese Eight Immortals, the top with *Shoulao* descending on a crane, c1820, 6¼in (16cm) high.
£1,100–1,200 ⚒ S(Am)
***Shoulao* is the star God of Longevity.**

Bowls

An Arita bowl, decorated in blue and white with insects and birds, lid missing, 18thC, 5in (12.5cm) diam.
£380–430 ⊞ FRY

An Imari bowl, brightly decorated with a flowering tree, foot rim chip, Artemesia mark, 18thC, 6in (15cm) diam.
£80–100 ⚒ WW

An Imari bowl, the interior with a central panel of a Dutch ship, bordered by Dutch and Japanese merchants, the exterior similarly decorated with panels among flowers, Meiji period, 1868–1911, 9½in (24cm) diam.
£700–850 ⚒ G(L)

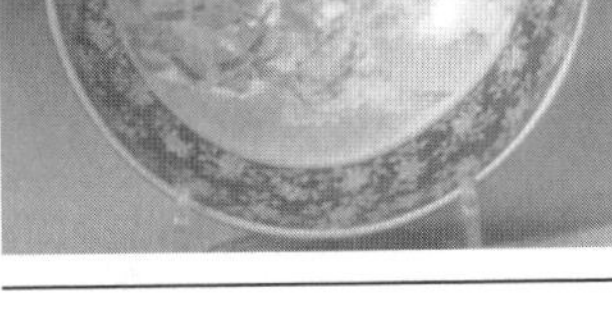

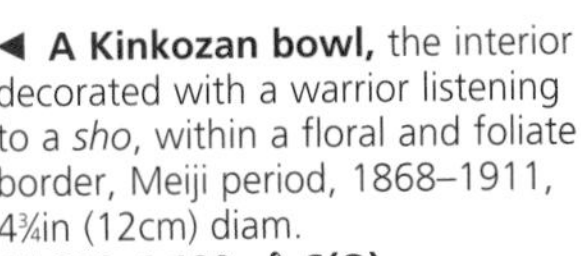

◄ **A Kinkozan bowl,** the interior decorated with a warrior listening to a *sho*, within a floral and foliate border, Meiji period, 1868–1911, 4¾in (12cm) diam.
£1,000–1,100 ⚒ S(O)

► **A Satsuma earthenware bowl,** decorated in enamels and gilt, signed 'Genzan', Meiji period, 1868–1911, 5in (12.5cm) diam.
£4,500–5,000 ⚒ S

Cups

An Imari tea bowl and saucer, decorated in iron-red with flowers and birds, early 18thC, saucer 5in (12.5cm) diam.
£250–275 ⊞ GLD

A Kutani tea cup and saucer, decorated with a floral design, early 20thC, cup 2½in (6.5cm) high.
£20–25 ⊞ FRY

A Satsuma-style Art Pottery tea bowl, decorated in raised gilt and enamels with peony sprays alternating with *kiku mon*, signed 'Harada', early 20thC, 5in (12.5cm) diam, in a black lacquer presentation box.
£1,600–1,750 ⚒ BB(S)

Dishes

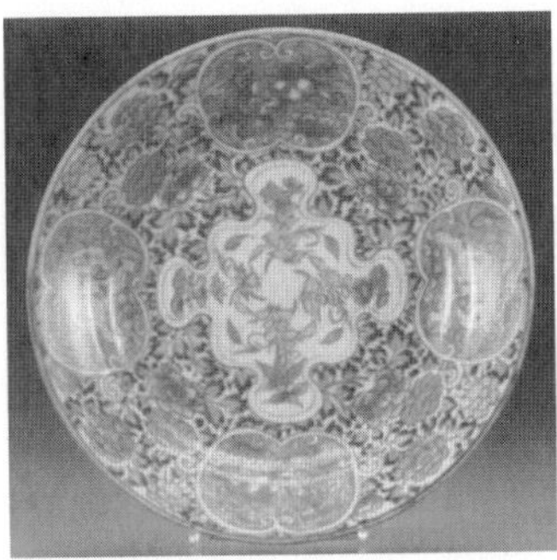

An Imari dish, decorated with *shishi*, peonies and other flowers, c1700, 12in (30.5cm) diam.
£470–570 ⚒ S(O)

Miller's is a price GUIDE not a price LIST

An Arita dish, polychrome-decorated in iron-red and aubergine, chipped, 18thC, 6in (15cm) wide.
£200–250 ⚒ WW

► **A Kakiemon saucer,** decorated in iron-red, turquoise, blue, grey and ochre with a bird among prunus over rockwork, 18thC, 4½in (11.5cm) diam.
£380–450 ⚒ WW

A pair of Imari dishes, from a picnic set, small chip, 18thC, 7¼in (18.5cm) wide.
£170–200 ⚒ WW

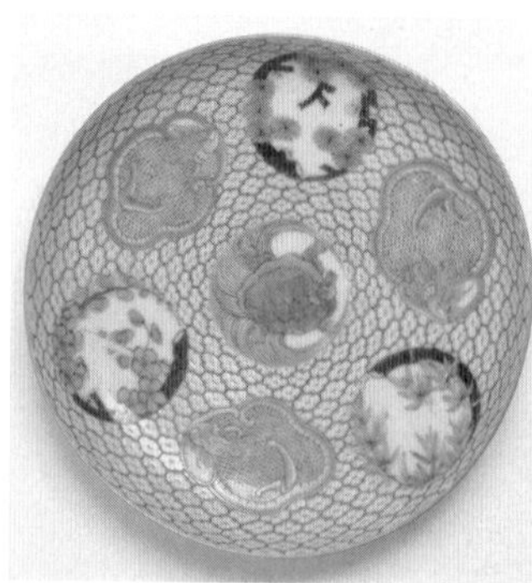

A pair of Arita dishes, decorated with panels of dragons and the Three Friends of Winter in roundels on a millefiori ground, c1820, 8in (20.5cm) diam.
£200–230 ⊞ FRY
The Three Friends of Winter are the pine, prunus and bamboo.

◀ **A Nabeshima dish,** decorated in blue and white with flowers and foliage, 19thC, 6¼in (16cm) diam.
£200–250 WW

A set of three Imari dishes, each decorated with a vase of flowers on a terrace, 19thC, largest 13½in (34.5cm) wide.
£900–1,100 DN

Nabeshima

Nabeshima porcelain was made at Okawachi, north of Arita, and was named after the prince who founded the kilns at the end of the 17th century. The porcelain was of higher quality than that made for export, and was originally made as presentation ware for the local nobility. The decoration on these wares was usually outlined in underglaze blue and infilled with overglaze enamels in iron-red, turquoise, pale manganese, yellow and, rarely, black detailing. Nabeshima wares are never marked.

A pair of Imari chargers, decorated in red, blue and turquoise with panels of wildlife and flowers, late 19thC, 12in (30.5cm) diam.
£160–180 ⊞ FRY

A Satsuma earthenware dish, the centre painted with children at various pursuits, surrounded by maple in autumn colours, the exterior with four garlands of chrysanthemums and tendrils, signed by Yabu Meizan of Osaka, late Meiji period, early 20thC, 8½in (21.5cm) wide.
£3,500–4,200 S

Flatware

An Imari dish, painted in underglaze blue, enamels, iron-red and gilt with a courtesan beneath a parasol held by her attendant confronting three aquatic birds against a background of bulrushes, the underside with mosquitoes in iron-red, c1740, 10¾in (27.5cm) diam.
£3,500–4,000 S
The design is after a drawing by the Dutch artist Cornelius Pronk, commissioned by the Dutch East India Company. Copies of the design were sent from Batavia to both China and Deshima in 1736, but it is thought that the Japanese porcelain dishes with the design were the result of private commissions placed by employees of the East India Company.

An Imari charger, decorated in typical colours with a compartmentalized design, late 19thC, 11½in (29cm) diam.
£100–120 GAK

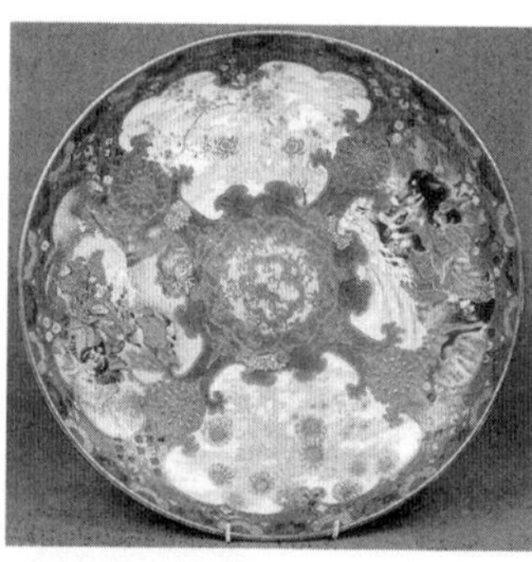

A Satsuma charger, polychrome-enamelled and gilt, Meiji period, 1868–1911, 15¼in (38.5cm) diam.
£350–420 HYD

An Imari charger, richly gilded, Meiji/Taisho period, early 20thC, 18¼in (46.5cm) diam.
£450–500 P(Ba)

A pair of Satsuma chargers, decorated in polychrome enamel heightened with gilding, late 19thC, 16in (40.5cm) diam.
£650–800 Mit

Jars

A pair of Imari jars and covers, painted in underglaze blue, iron-red and gilding, the covers with lion-shaped finials, repairs and restorations, 1675–1725, 23¾in (60.5cm) high.
£2,750–3,000 S(Am)

A Hirado *mizusashi*, painted in underglaze blue with a group of sages, the cover with a *kirin*-shaped knop, Meiji period, 1868–1911, 9½in (24cm) high.
£3,000–3,500 S
A *mizusashi* is a hot-water jar used in tea ceremonies.

A Seto *chatsubo*, painted in blue with swallows and flowers, fitted with an inner cover with chrysanthemum knop, c1900, 12in (30.5cm) high.
£1,100–1,200 S(O)

Cross Reference
See Colour Review (page 307)

A pair of Satsuma jars and covers, with four animal mask handles suspending gilt red tassels, damaged, repaired, Meiji period, 1868–1911, 13¼in (33.5cm) high.
£800–950 B(Ba)

Vases

A pair of Imari vases, painted with a reserve of figures on a pavilion terrace watching frolicking horses opposite a reserve of flowers in a vase, 1675–1725, 13in (33cm) high.
£400–500 CGC

A pair of Satsuma vases, decorated with flowers and hanging branches, c1900, 11in (28cm) high.
£120–135 BRU

An Imari vase, decorated in typical palette with flowers on a blue and white ground, 19thC, 25in (63.5cm) high.
£900–1,100 MEA

A Satsuma vase, by Kinkozan, decorated with processional figures in painted and gilded costumes, within dragon and geometric borders, late Meiji period, early 20thC, 11½in (29cm) high.
£950–1,150 G(B)

A Satsuma garniture, decorated with painted panels of male and female figures, minor restoration, 19thC, largest 9¾in (25cm) high.
£500–600 AG

► **A Hirado porcelain vase,** c1900, 6¼in (16cm) high.
£450–500 MCN

A Satsuma vase, decorated with panels of *bijin* playing cards and egrets beside a floral bordered lake, on a blue and gilt ground, Meiji period, 1868–1911, 4¾in (12cm) high.
£1,100–1,300 DMC

A porcelain vase, polychrome-decorated with herons on the branches of a tree in a landscape, interspersed with polychrome- and gilt-highlighted floral motifs, with lion mask handles, early 20thC, 24½in (62cm) high.
£250–300 BLH

Glass

For the last 18 months there has been an increased interest in antique glass, and prices have risen for all styles, especially 18th-century drinking glasses, attracting numerous and all-important new collectors. These days the price I pay for glasses seems almost what I asked a year ago. So far this has been my best year ever, and the same can be said for many of my colleagues in the field of glass dealing.

It is difficult this year to assess the increases in prices from auction results, as the sales were smaller and there were few collections of note, with the exception of the sale at Phillips of the John Carson collection of British ceremonial goblets. The items were two or three times the size of normal drinking glasses but they did not realize two or three times the price. For example, a mammoth incised twist goblet fetched £965 as opposed to a similar wine glass which would retail at £700–750. The reason was that most of these glasses were too big for collectors' cabinets and this was reflected throughout the sale. A 15½in (29.5cm) high heavy baluster goblet with an acorn knop realized £8000, the same price amount as for an 8in (20.5cm) example.

A recent sale at Sotheby's included the Rinceau Collection of mainly 19th century beautiful engraved glass. This type of glass is rarely found in this quantity, and in such good condition. The collection had been recently purchased, but that did not stop a collector buying a rock crystal engraved vase by William Fritsche for almost £20,000 which Sotheby's only a year previously had sold for £16,600.

Nineteenth-century decanters, water and claret jugs, vases and usable drinking glasses still remain popular and have increased gradually above the rate of inflation, representing very good value for money compared to their more modern equivalents.

There has been a remarkable increase in interest for the use of shallow champagne saucers rather than flutes, following an announcement that it takes longer to get inebriated when drinking from a saucer rather than a flute, because there is less fizz, therefore there has been a price increase of approximately 50 per cent for these pieces.

But the final advice must always be, buy what you like, not as an investment and remember, the pleasure of the purchase always outweighs the pain of the price. **Jeanette Hayhurst**

Ale & Wine Glasses

A heavy baluster goblet, with a rounded funnel bowl over an inverted baluster stem, on a folded foot, c1710, 6½in (16.5cm) high.
£1,350–1,500 ⊞ JHa

◄ **A baluster wine glass,** the thick-walled conical bowl on a teared true baluster stem, on a folded domed foot, c1720, 4½in (11.5cm) high.
£1,200–1,350 ⊞ RAP
This type of glass with its unusually thick outer wall was commonly used by toastmasters so that they could propose a large number of toasts without becoming inebriated.

A baluster wine glass, with a rounded funnel bowl, over drop and ball knops, on a domed foot, c1715, 5½in (14cm) high.
£1,800–2,000 ⊞ WMa

► **A wine glass,** with a trumpet bowl and a tiered light baluster stem, on a folded foot, 1720–30, 6in (15cm) high.
£400–475 ⚒ LFA

◄ **A flammiform dwarf ale glass,** c1740, 4½in (11.5cm) high.
£250–280 ⊞ JHa

A pair of wine glasses, the bell bowls with air beaded bases, on shoulder-knopped multiple-spiral air-twist stems, on folded conical feet, c1745, 6¾in (17cm) high.
£1,000–1,100 ⊞ Som

A wine glass, with a tapered bucket bowl, the shoulder-knopped air-twist stem filled with spiral threads, on a conical foot, c1750, 6¼in (16cm) high.
£425–525 ⚒ DN

A balustroid ale glass, with an engraved rounded funnel bowl, over moulded fluting with a basal knop, on a folded conical foot, c1750, 6¾in (17cm) high.
£350–400 ⊞ WMa

A Newcastle light baluster goblet, with a bell bowl, the composite stem of four knops, two with air beads and two with tears, on a conical foot, c1745, 8in (20.5cm) high.
£1,200–1,350 ⊞ BONN

Newcastle light baluster glasses were made in the north-east of England between c1730 and 1755. They are distinguished by the lightness of the glass of which they were made. These glasses often had knops with tears in them to create the impression of light within the stem.

Miller's is a price GUIDE not a price LIST

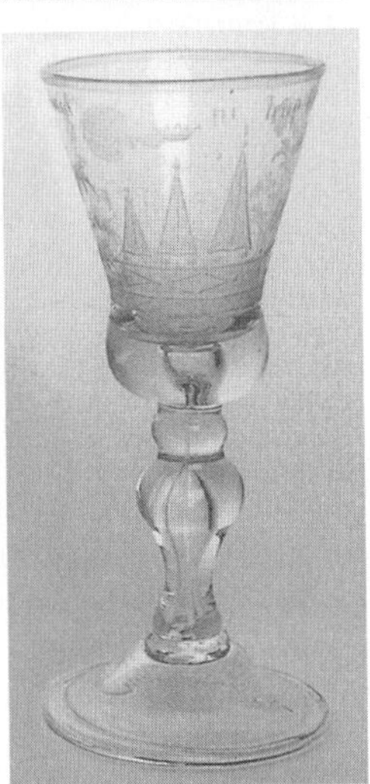

A goblet, the thistle-shaped bowl with solid lower section and engraved with three obelisk devices supported by a sarcophagus base, beneath a device of an arm and a crown, inscribed '*ni trop haut ni trop bas*', on a hollow baluster stem and a domed and folded foot, Dutch, mid-18thC, 7½in (19cm) high.
£250–325 ⚒ DN

A pair of wine glasses, with elongated bell bowls, the multi-spiral air-twist stems extending into the bowl, on conical feet, c1750, 8in (20.5cm) high.
£950–1,050 ⊞ RAP

A wine glass, with a rounded funnel bowl, on a multi-spiral air-twist stem with three knops, c1750, 7in (18cm) high.
£1,300–1,450 ⊞ WMa

A goblet, from St Petersburg Glasshouse, engraved with the Russian Imperial double-headed eagle and the cypher of Elizabeth Petrovna, daughter of Peter the Great, c1750, 8¾in (22cm) high.
£1,150–1,300 ⊞ BrW

A wine glass, with an ogee bowl engraved with a basket of tulips and other flowers, the reverse with a bird in flight, the stem with a central swelling knop, on a folded conical foot, c1750, 5¼in (13.5cm) high.
£340–380 ⊞ Som

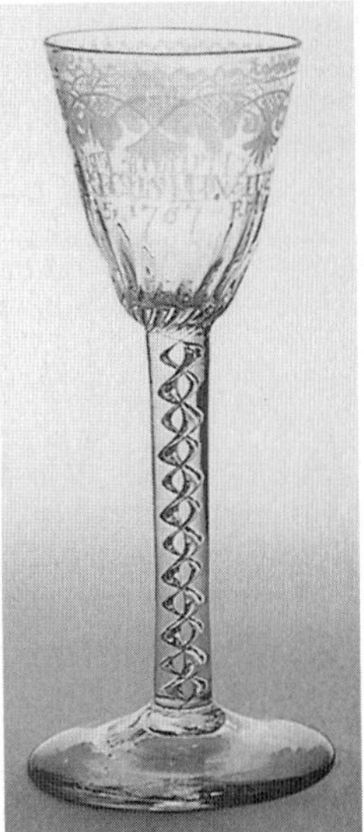

A commemorative wine glass, the double-ogee bowl engraved around the centre 'Fredricus III. (sic) Rex Prussiae Rosbach near Lutzen Nov 5 1757' below a frieze of hatched and foliate ornament, with light spiral rib moulding to the lower part, on a stem containing two corkscrew air twists, c1757, 6in (15cm) high.
£1,400–1,750 ⚒ P

This glass commemorates the victory of Britain's ally, Frederick the Great of Prussia, over the French at Rossbach during the Seven Years War. Frederick was hailed as 'The Prussian Hero' throughout the country, and whereas many porcelain and pottery items survive, it is unusual to find a glass commemorating him.

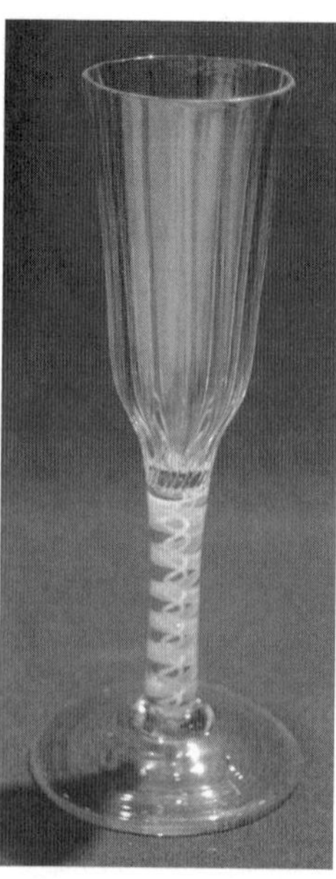

An ale glass, the ogee bowl with vertical fluting, on an opaque-twist stem, c1765, 8in (20.5cm) high.
£1,150–1,285 ⊞ WMa

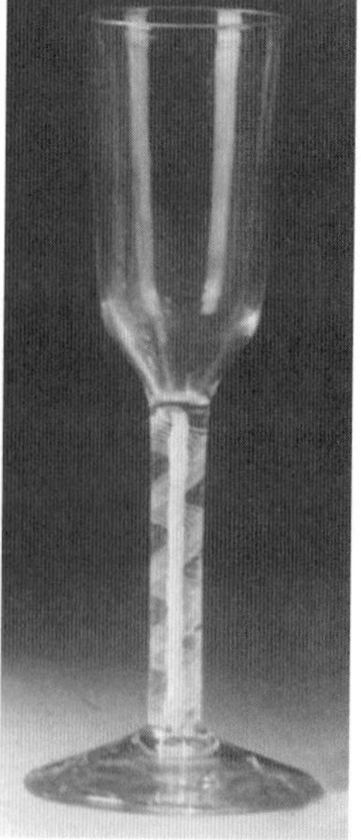

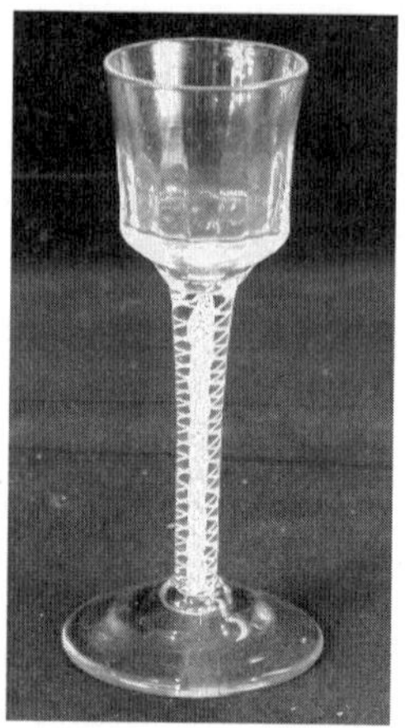

A wine glass, with a fluted bowl, and an opaque-twist stem, 18thC, 6in (15cm) high.
£230–300 ⚒ SWO

◄ **An ale glass,** with a deep ogee bowl, on a double-series opaque-twist stem and a conical foot, c1770, 7½in (19cm) high.
£250–320 ⚒ Bon(C)

A wine glass, the bowl engraved with a tulip border, on a facet-cut stem, c1780, 5in (12.5cm) high.
£70–80 ⊞ JHa

◄ **A glass,** the bucket bowl with an engraved border, on a double-series opaque-twist stem, c1770, 6¼in (16cm) high.
£320–400 ⚒ WW

◄ **A goblet,** with a single-series opaque-twist stem, c1760, 7½in (19cm) high.
£550–600 ⊞ JHa

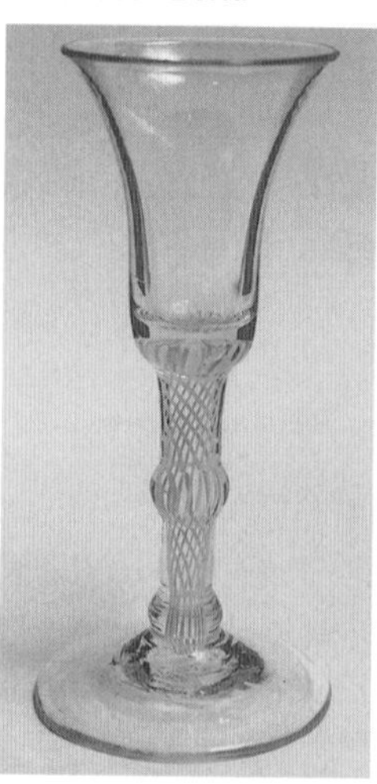

A wine glass, the bell bowl with a solid base, on an opaque-twist stem extending into the bowl, on a conical foot, c1765, 6½in (16.5cm) high.
£650–750 ⊞ GS

► **A punch glass,** the round bowl with an everted rim and applied with a handle, on an opaque-twist stem with two spiral threads, c1770, 4½in (11.5cm) high.
£525–625 ⚒ DN

A wine glass, with a pan-top trumpet bowl, on a double-series opaque-twist stem and a conical foot, c1765, 6in (15cm) high.
£530–600 ⊞ RAP

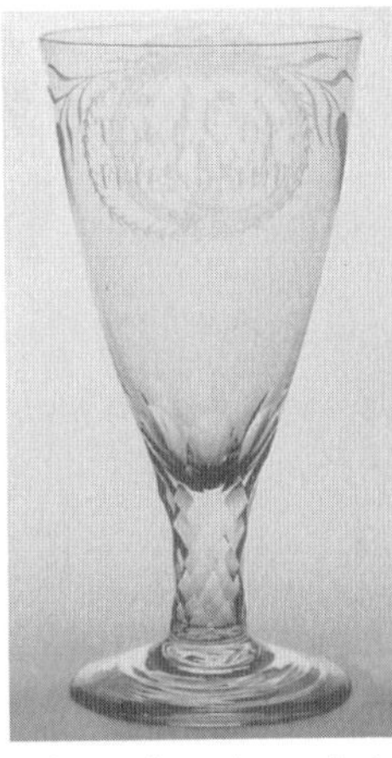

A beer glass, the conical bowl engraved with a medallion flanked by sprigs of barley and inscribed 'A Token of Friendship', the reverse with a panel bearing initials, on a diamond-faceted stem and a heavy circular foot, c1790, 12in (30.5cm) high.
£450–500 P

This glass would have held two full pints of strong beer or 'barley wine' and thus would have offered a very generous toast to a close friendship.

A wine goblet, engraved with Admiral Howe's flagship and 'Queen Charlotte', with a crest above a monogram and 'June 1 1794', on a lemon squeezer base, late 18thC, 6½in (16.5cm) high.
£1,600–2,000 WW

► **A barrel rummer,** with a blade stem, c1810, 5in (12.5cm) high.
£55–60 ⊞ JHa

A dram glass, with a rib-moulded round funnel bowl, on a plain stem and foot, c1800, 8½in (21.5cm) high.
£100–120 ⊞ Som

A rummer, the ovoid bowl engraved with initials within a cartouche, c1800, 5¾in (14.5cm) high.
£135–150 ⊞ BrW

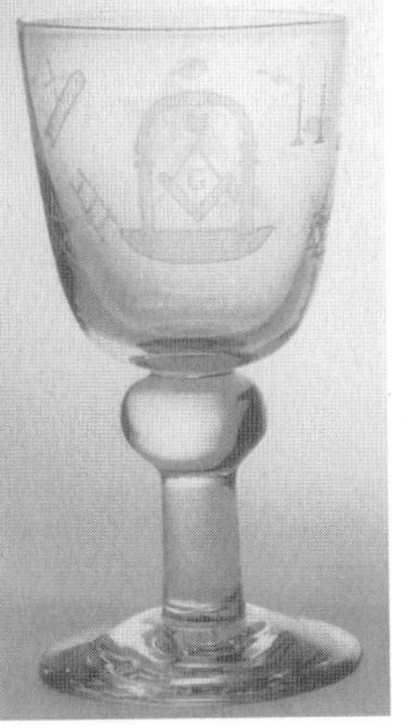

A goblet, the rounded funnel bowl engraved with Masonic emblems, on a ball knop above a plain stem section and a heavy conical foot, probably early 19thC, 11in (28cm) high.
£550–600 P

A diamond- and slice-cut rummer, Irish, c1810, 5in (12.5cm) high.
£80–90 ⊞ JHa

A set of six sherry or port glasses, c1815, 4½in (11.5cm) high.
£225–250 ⊞ Del

A rummer, the bucket bowl engraved with initials within a roundel flanked by floral sprays and a bird in flight below barley sheaves, the reverse engraved with a fruiting vine, on a ball-knopped stem and a reinforced conical foot, c1825, 7¾in (19.5cm) high.
£550–600 ⊞ Som

A slice-cut champagne flute, c1830, 6in (15cm) high.
£50–55 ⊞ JHa

A rummer, with a flute-cut bucket bowl, c1840, 5½in (14cm) high.
£50–55 ⊞ LHo

A pair of goblets, probably by St Louis, one with a sulphide bust of Queen Victoria and one with Prince Albert, French, c1840, 6in (15cm) high.
£700–800 ⊞ BrW

► **A pair of wine goblets,** the funnel bowls cut with bands of diamonds, with knopped stems, on circular feet, 19thC, 6¼in (16cm) high.
£100–140 WW

A part-opalescent goblet, the bell bowl cut with arched flutes, silvered, gilt and enamelled with perching birds, flowers and scrolls, on a hexagonal knopped stem and a scalloped foot with radial-cut base, Bohemian, c1850, 5¼in (13.5cm) high.
£950–1,200 S(O)
Ex-Rudolf Just Collection.

A pair of wine glasses, engraved with passion flowers, possibly by W.H., B. & J. Richardson, c1860, 6in (15cm) high.
£120–135 LHo

A water goblet, the engraved rounded funnel bowl on a hollow-knopped drawn trumpet stem and a foot with a folded edge, c1875, 7½in (19cm) high.
£120–150 JHa

An amber flash overlay glass goblet, the waisted ogee bowl cut with panels, nine engraved with titled scenes, on an octagonal knop stem and a star-cut foot, Bohemian, mid-19thC, 8¼in (21cm) high.
£270–350 JNic

A set of nine Stourbridge wine glasses, engraved with a grape and vine decoration, c1865, 5in (12.5cm) high.
£900–1,200 ALiN

A goblet, acid-etched with a bittern among reeds, c1880, 6in (15cm) high.
£160–180 JHa

A Victorian goblet, commemorating the Crimean War, the bowl engraved with Mars in a horse-drawn chariot watched over by an angel, the reverse with a verse, on a hollow double-knop stem and a plain circular foot, 11½in (29cm) high.
£450–575 P

A Victorian glass goblet, the bowl engraved with a bird, a branch, hops and barley and a monogram, 7in (18cm) high.
£125–160 RBB

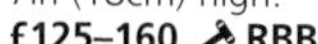

► A Rhineland-style ewer and four wine glasses, olive-coloured and enamelled, with a silver-plated cover dated 1891, Bohemian, ewer 11in (28cm) high.
£1,400–1,700
ALiN

An amber heavy goblet, the bowl with a panel depicting Leonardo da Vinci's Last Supper and an inscription, on a knopped and lobed foot, Bohemian, 19thC, 9in (23cm) high.
£400–500 HOK

A cranberry bowl goblet, on a clear hollow stem and clear foot, c1885, 7in (18cm) high.
£125–140 GRI

A Lobmeyr liqueur set, comprising seven pieces, polychrome-enamelled with baroque ladies and gentlemen, Austrian, Vienna, late 19thC, ewer 9¾in (25cm) high.
£1,000–1,200 DORO

Beakers & Tumblers

A footed tumbler, hexagonal-cut and engraved, Bohemian, mid-18thC, 4in (10cm) high.
£450–500 ⊞ JHa

A tumbler, engraved with a monogram within a floral wreath, the reverse with a bird in flight, reserved on a star ground, c1800, 5in (12.5cm) high.
£160–200 ⚒ DN

A *milchglas* beaker, gilt-tooled with a hunter seated beneath a tree, a deer standing to one side, the reverse with a floral sprig, Bohemian, c1770, 2½in (6.5cm) high.
£200–240 ⚒ S(O)
Ex-Rudolf Just collection.

Miller's is a price GUIDE not a price LIST

A beaker, engraved with the Sunderland Bridge above a ship, the reverse with a cockerel crest, c1825, 5in (12.5cm) high.
£500–550 ⊞ Som

A pair of Jacobite tumblers, engraved with a rose spray with two buds and a bird in flight, c1770, 5in (12.5cm) high.
£350–420 ⚒ B

A ruby glass beaker, with white overlay, decorated with a vine branch, flowers and rocailles in panels, rim slightly ground down, Bohemian, c1850, 4½in (11.5cm) high.
£235–300 ⚒ DORO

A beaker, the conical body engraved with a ship, the reverse with diamond-point 'GL', 'Junior' and 'Leeds' within a wheel-engraved surround, c1800, 4¼in (11cm) high.
£450–500 ⊞ Som

A gilt ruby-overlay cut-glass beaker, possibly Neuwelt, the two rows of bosses cut with strawberry diamonds and heightened with gilt foliate scrolls, Bohemian, c1840, 5in (12.5cm) high.
£600–700 ⚒ S(O)
Ex-Rudolf Just Collection.

GLASS

Bottles & Decanters

A gilded decanter and stopper, by James Giles, 1760–70, 9½in (24cm) high.
£3,000–4,000 ⊞ CB

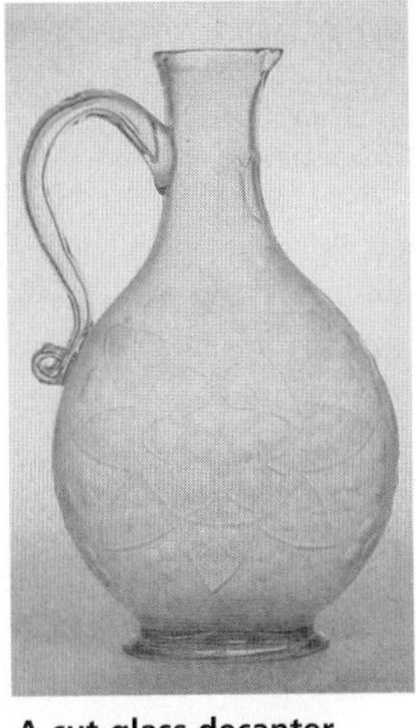

A cut-glass decanter, probably by La Granja de San Ildefonso, Spain, shallow-cut with a geometric flower design to both sides, foot chipped, c1775, 12in (30.5cm) high.
£160–200 ⚒ B

A pair of decanters, with reed-, facet- and diamond-cut bands, three facet-cut neck rings and unmatched bull's-eye stoppers, Anglo-Irish, c1795, 11in (28cm) high.
£900–1,150 ⚒ S

A spirit decanter, with two triple-banded neck rings and banded body, c1800, 10in (25.5cm) high.
£90–100 ⊞ JHa

A set of three dark amber glass spirit flasks, each with an engraved silver mount to the neck, hallmarked Sheffield 1862 with hallmarked contemporary labels, 8in (20.5cm) high.
£900–1,000 ⊞ RAP

An engraved decanter and stopper, with Hebrew inscriptions, matched stopper, Bohemian, early 19thC, 9¼in (23.5cm) high.
£2,500–3,000 ⚒ S(O)
Glass of Jewish interest is very rare.

A wrythen glass decanter, by James Powell, Whitefriars, c1890, 13in (33cm) high.
£200–220 ⊞ JHa

A Moser liqueur decanter and six liqueur glasses, with raised gilding, German, Karlsbad, c1865, decanter 13in (33cm) high.
£800–1,000 ⊞ ALiN

A cranberry glass decanter, with crimped frill handle, c1890, 12in (30.5cm) high.
£215–240 ⊞ GRI

► A lime green intaglio-cut glass liqueur set, by Stevens & Williams, Stourbridge, comprising nine pieces, c1900, decanter 8½in (21.5cm) high.
£2,000–2,500 ⊞ ALiN

A mallet-shaped decanter, with three applied neck rings, the body engraved with a crest, with bull's-eye stopper, 19thC, 11½in (29cm) high.
£170–200 ⚒ WW

A pair of cut decanters, c1870, 13in (33cm) high.
£200–225 ⊞ LHo

A decanter and stopper, engraved with bees beneath a flower and leaf scroll band, on four lion mask and scroll feet, late 19thC, 9¾in (25cm) high.
£550–700 ⚒ LFA

A Prussian-style decanter, with broad-cut flutes and three annular neck rings, with a target stopper, c1830, 8¼in (21cm) high.
£220–240 ⊞ Som

GLASS

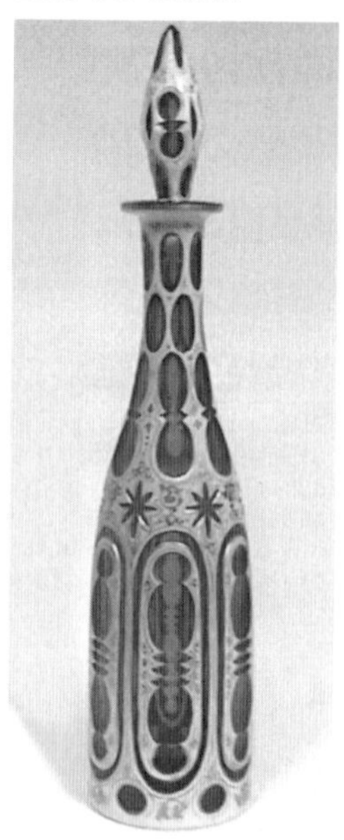

A red cut-glass decanter, with white overlay and gilding, English/Bohemian, c1870, 16in (40.5cm) high.
£320–400 ⊞ CB

A whisky flagon, engraved with thistles, marked 'Libby', American, c1900, 9in (23cm) high.
£450–500 ⊞ JHa

Bowls

An enamelled and gilt shallow bowl, with gadroon-moulded underside, the rim with a gilt band painted with blue, red and white dots, with folded rim and applied footring, Venetian, early 16thC, 7in (18cm) diam.
£4,500–5,000 S(O)

A turn-over bowl, on a lemon squeezer pedestal foot, Irish, c1800, 10¼in (26cm) diam.
£900–1,150 HOK
It is rare to find an uncut example of this typically Irish form.

A blue-tinted glass sugar bowl, with honeycomb moulding, c1800, 4in (10cm) diam.
£150–200 LFA

A turn-over fruit bowl, Irish, c1820, 10in (25.5cm) diam.
£1,100–1,200 Del

An amethyst glass sugar basin, with everted rim, c1800, 3in (7.5cm) high.
£270–300 Som

A glass bowl, with diamond-cut panels, c1840, 6½in (16.5cm) high.
£225–250 JHa

► **A red cut-glass bowl,** with white overlay, painted with panels of flowers and decorated with floral gilding, Bohemian, 19thC, 7½in (19cm) high.
£430–550 F&C

► **A glass pedestal dish,** gilded with scrolling foliate motifs, the pedestal applied with a plaque painted with a portrait of a young lady, chips to base, 19thC, 12in (30.5cm) high.
£160–200 FHF

Boxes

A ruby-flashed casket and cover, with gilt-metal mounts, cut with deer and a fox in a wooded landscape, with stylized scrolling and chequerboard decoration to underside, Bohemian, 19thC, 5½in (14cm) wide.
£450–575 Bea(E)

A Victorian biscuit barrel, the removable cut-glass body with a Parian figure of a sleeping child within a silvered border, the gilt-brass frame with beaded collar and animal mask feet, 9½in (24cm) wide.
£550–700 P(S)

A cranberry glass dressing table box, gilded and enamelled, Bohemian, c1910, 3in (7.5cm) diam.
£100–110 GRI

Miller's is a price GUIDE not a price LIST

GLASS

Celery Vases

A celery vase, with diamond, step and slice cutting, Irish, c1820, 8in (20.5cm) high.
£270–300 ⊞ JHa

A celery vase, cut with a band of diamond lozenges between bands of stylized lozenge foliage, on a turned foot, Irish, early 19thC, 9¼in (23.5cm) high.
£400–525 ⚒ HOK

A bell-shaped celery vase, c1840, 8in (20.5cm) high.
£70–80 ⊞ JHa

A celery vase, engraved with a hunting scene, on a baluster stem and star-cut base, c1860, 9½in (24cm) high.
£350–385 ⊞ BONN

Centrepieces

A four-vase clear glass *épergne*, with turquoise-blue edging, c1890, 22in (56cm) high.
£530–585 ⊞ CB

► **A gravity-fed table fountain and *épergne*,** attributed to F. & C. Osler, the gilt-metal frame with gallery base inset with a mirror centred by a cut-glass reservoir, within three arms, each fitted with a cut specimen vase, rising to a further reservoir with inset cut-glass dish, minor chips, early 20thC, 19¼in (49cm) high.
£3,000–3,500 ⚒ P(WM)
F. & C. Osler (1807–1922) was a Birmingham-based manufacturer with showrooms in London and Calcutta. They produced glass of exceptional quality which was usually heavily cut.

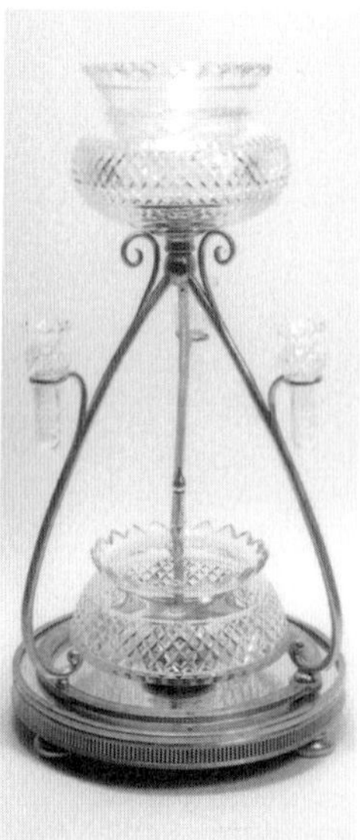

A glass *épergne*, decorated with pink, white and opaque glass spirals, c1900, 17in (43cm) high.
£350–420 ⚒ P(EA)

Miller's is a price GUIDE not a price LIST

Flasks

◄ **A *milchglas* flask,** the opalescent white glass with blue marbling, applied with two trailing spiral bands, with pewter screw-top cover, small chip, German, 18thC, 7in (18cm) high.
£1,300–1,500 ⚒ S(O)
Ex-Rudolf Just Collection.

► **A Stourbridge glass moonflask,** engraved to each side with a mirror monogram below a coronet, c1870, 10½in (26.5cm) high.
£1,000–1,100 ⚒ S(O)

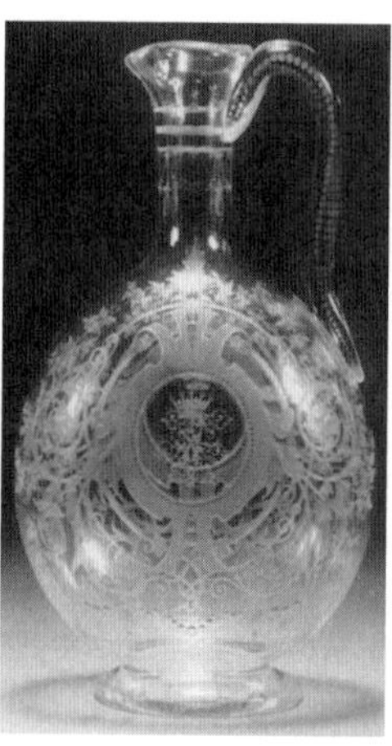

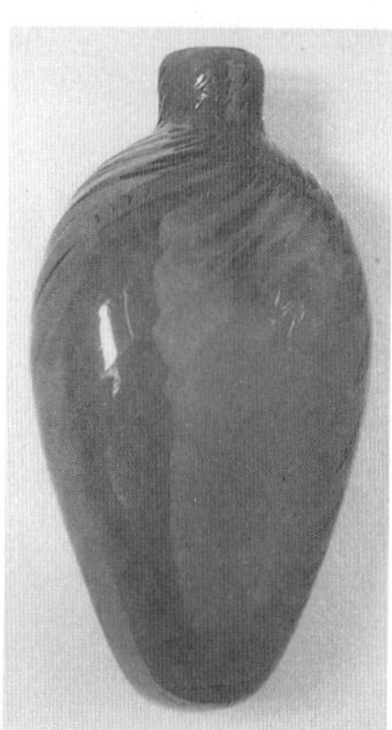

A red glass hip flask, with wrythen moulding, c1880, 5¼in (13.5cm) high.
£160–180 ⊞ Som

GLASS

Jars

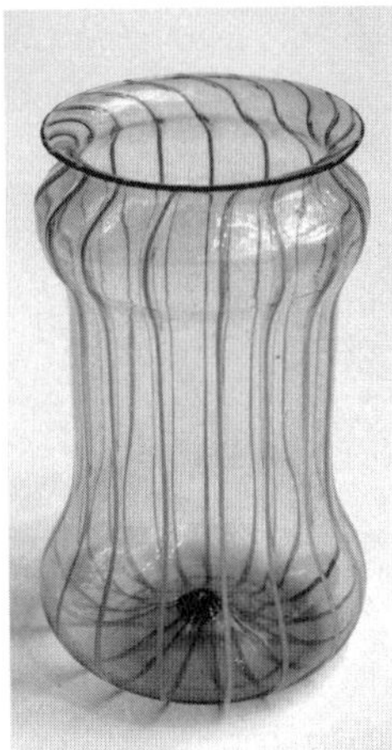

An *arbarello*, Venice, c1600, 6in (15cm) high.
£800–900 ⊞ JHa

A jar and cover, with gilt and hand-enamelled decoration, Bohemian, c1870, 12in (30.5cm) high.
£800–900 ⊞ BONN

A ruby hammered glass jar and cover, c1885, 7in (18cm) high.
£90–100 ⊞ LHo

A faceted and cut-glass storage jar, c1930, 21in (53.5cm) high.
£430–480 ⊞ RAN

Jelly & Sweetmeat Glasses & Jars

A jelly glass, with a folded rim, on a gadrooned base, c1710, 4in (10cm) high.
£90–100 ⊞ JHa

A jelly glass, with a fluted bell bowl, and rudimentary stem, on a gadroon-moulded foot, mid-18thC, 4in (10cm) high.
£100–140 ⚒ DN

► A bonnet glass, with honeycomb moulding, c1800, 3¼in (8.5cm) high.
£45–50 ⊞ LHo

◄ A champagne or sweetmeat glass, with honeycomb-moulded pan-top bowl, on an octagonal stem and similarly-moulded domed folded foot, c1745, 6in (15cm) high.
£1,500–1,650 ⚒ S(O)

A set of six green glass custard cups, c1800, 3in (7.5cm) diam.
£950–1,100 ⊞ Del

► A pair of facet-cut sweetmeat jars and covers, on star-cut bases, c1900, 12in (30.5cm) high.
£300–370 ⚒ TMA

A pair of amber-cased glass sweetmeat jars and covers, engraved with hunting scenes, Bohemian, late 19thC, 11¾in (30cm) high.
£320–400 ⚒ SWO

Jugs

A pair of wine ewers, engraved with stylized egg-and-tulip decoration, with loop handles, on pedestal feet, c1800, 6¼in (16cm) high.
£160–180 ⊞ Som

A glass cream jug, cut with a band of diamonds, Irish, c1800, 8in (20.5cm) wide.
£225–250 ⊞ Del

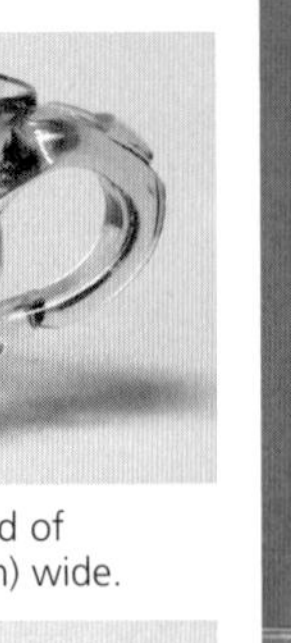

► **A glass cream jug,** with slice-cut foot, c1825, 7½in (19cm) high.
£250–280 ⊞ JHa

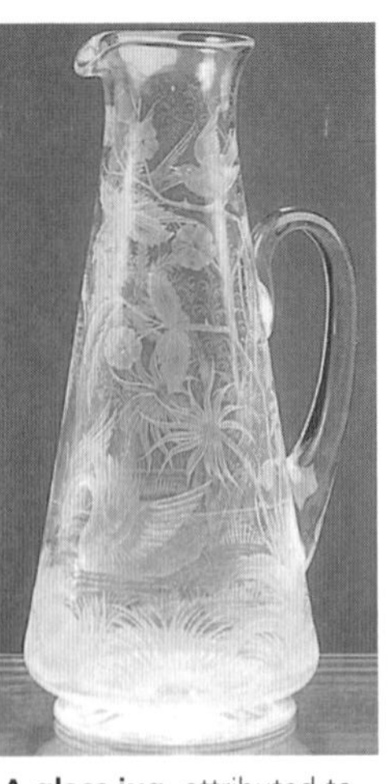

A glass jug, attributed to the Pugh Brothers at The Potters Alley Glass Works, Dublin, engraved by Franz Tieze with a pair of swans by a water lily surrounded by exotic foliage and song birds, on a tucked foot with a star-cut base, signed, 19thC, 10¼in (26cm) high.
£1,800–2,250 ⚒ HOK

Thomas and Richard Pugh took over the Potters Alley Flint Glass Works, also known as The Dublin Flint Glass Works, c1863. They took on the young Bohemian engraver Franz Tieze to produce engravings that could compete with imported wares and also to cater for clients' individual needs, such as crests and inscriptions. After the closure of the Glass Works in 1893, Tieze worked closely with the antiquarian Robert Day to reproduce 'Volunteer' glass.

A ruby glass jug, with a rope-twist handle, c1865, 6½in (16.5cm) high.
£160–175 ⊞ LHo

► **A claret ewer,** by John Baird Glassworks, Glasgow, possibly engraved by Henry Keller with a winged figure holding a child and a branch of laurel below floral festoons, with a shell-moulded handle, c1870, 13½in (34.5cm) high.
£1,750–2,000 ⚒ S(O)

A silver-mounted glass claret jug, both silver and glass engraved with swallows and rushes, maker's mark 'T.S.', London 1874, 7½in (19cm) high.
£700–875 ⚒ BR

GLASS

Lustres

A pair of cut-glass lustre candlesticks, early 19thC, 8¼in (21cm) high.
£450–575 ⚒ Bon(C)

A pair of white overlay glass lustres, on a variegated knopped stem, 19thC, 11½in (29cm) high.
£500–625 ⚒ Mit

A pair of Victorian cut-glass table lustres, 9in (23cm) high.
£650–825 ⚒ G(L)

A Victorian green glass lustre, applied with bands of opaque white panels decorated with portraits and floral sprays, with gilded borders, some damage, 12½in (32cm) high.
£200–250 ⚒ FHF

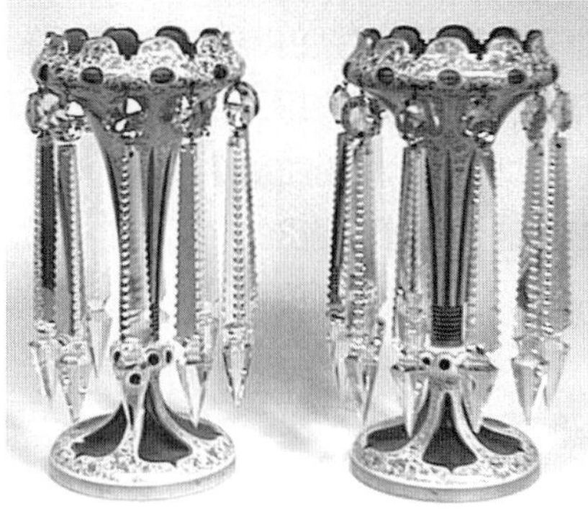

A pair of red overlay on white glass lustre vases, with clear lustre drops and gilding, c1880, 11in (28cm) high.
£1,700–1,850 ⊞ CB

Restoration

Lustres often have replacement drops which is acceptable as long as it is clearly indicated.

► **A glass table lustre,** with a faceted stem, late 19thC, 9½in (24cm) high.
£100–140 ⚒ WW

Further reading

Miller's Glass Buyer's Guide, Miller's Publications, 2002

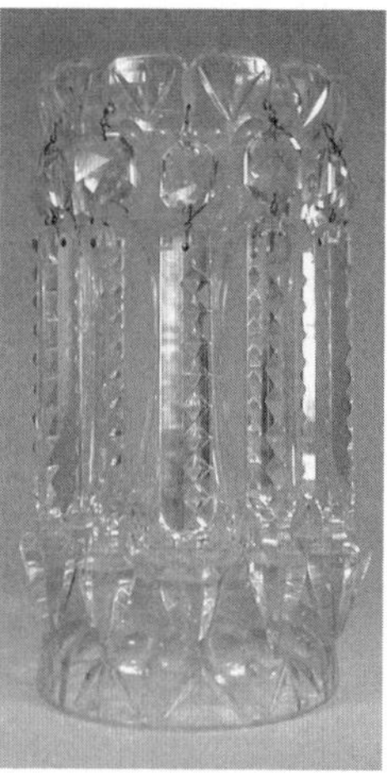

GLASS

Mugs & Tankards

A tankard, engraved and gilded with a coat-of-arms and woodland scenes, with an air-twist handle, Silesian, 1730–40, 4¾in (12cm) high.
£580–650 ⊞ JHa

A *milchglas* mug, with polychrome rococo enamelling, Bohemian, c1790, 4in (10cm) high.
£300–325 ⊞ LHo

A tankard, engraved with a view of the Sunderland Bridge, c1830, 4in (10cm) high.
£225–250 ⊞ Del

Panels & Pictures

A hand-coloured glass panel, depicting two monks flanking a kneeling boy in prayer with his arm in a sling, against a landscaped background, Continental, 17th–18thC, 9½ x 7¾in (24 x 19.5cm).
£100–125 ⚒ Mit

Items in the Glass section have been arranged in date order within each sub-section.

A stained glass panel, depicting Mercury standing next to a brazier, c1900, 18¼ x 12½in (46.5 x 32cm).
£600–700 ⚒ P

► **A leaded stained glass picture,** of a Wild Man, some cracks, German, late 19thC, 15¾ x 26in (40 x 66cm).
£140–175 ⚒ DORO

A reverse glass painting of the Sacrifice of Isaac, depicting Isaac and his son walking in a hilly landscape, a camel in the background, in an acanthus-decorated gilt frame, 18thC, 7½ x 10¼in (19 x 26cm).
£1,100–1,200 ⚒ S(Am)

Paperweights

Every year for the last decade prices for antique glass paperweights have risen, sometimes astronomically such as a few years ago, when Bacchus pieces suddenly shot up from £500 to £2,000. Similarly last year the value of the relatively humble Clichy scrambled weights increased to twice or three times the value of St Louis or Baccarat examples.

One of the rarest antique weights is the Venetian scrambled, which grabs the imagination with its strange little faces peering out at the eager collector. These were among the first millefiori paperweights to be made, so one holds a piece of history when one buys such a weight. A good Venetian scrambled sold for £6,000 recently (see p311). With so few of them around they must be a very good investment.

On the other hand, the pure aesthetic value of the French Clichy weights, which is easy to appreciate, has led to their continued stratospheric price rises. A minimum requirement for these is a pink rose and after that the inclusion of any other colour pushes up the price. The particularly uncommon yellow rose has continued to excite interest. Clichy colour grounds are also very expensive now. Turquoise is the most common, and even so people have been paying over £1,500 for such a weight, while rarer colours have been selling for over £3,000. The price depends, of course, on what other attractions are included in the colour ground, for instance, rare roses, attractive patterns, or quality canes with a good colour balance. Other Clichy weights that are very sought after are the close-packs and close concentrics, which are changing hands for around £7,000.

Baccarat and St Louis weights have for the most part remained steady, although Baccarat close-packs are always appreciated and have consequently seen good price increases.

Weights by Paul Ysart, the Scots master-paperweight maker, continue to be a very popular buy. Any weight with a PY cane has been selling for about £600, and those that include animals or are rare can rise as high as £2,000.

The advent of the internet has had a big impact on the life of serious collectors, particularly in America. The keenest among them tune in daily to dealer's pages, on-line auctions and the internet sales held by the big auction houses, making the market for paperweights completely international. However, many European aficionados are dismayed that the major sales of paperweights have moved to New York. This gives American dealers an advantage over their British and Continental counterparts, who have the added expense of travel to take into consideration. **Anne Metcalfe**

GLASS

An Arculus Chequer paperweight, c1930, 3¼in (8.5cm) diam.
£700–800 ⊞ SWB

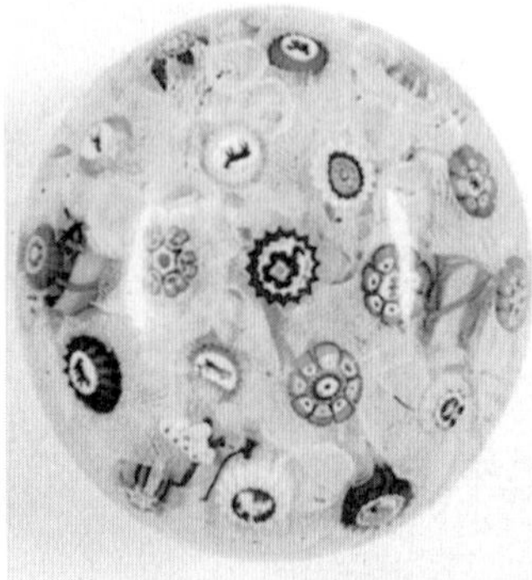

A Baccarat scattered millefiori paperweight, with ten silhouettes and colour-twist ribbons, on a muslin ground, French, dated 1848, 3in (7.5cm) diam.
£1,800–2,250 ⚒ B&L

A Baccarat wheatflower paperweight, French, c1848, 3in (7.5cm) diam.
£2,000–2,500 ⊞ DLP

A Clichy spaced millefiori paperweight, the clear glass set with two concentric circles of canes surrounding a central rose, French, 19thC, 2½in (6.5cm) diam.
£600–750 ⚒ B&L

Technical terms

Close concentric: weight consisting of rings of canes arranged tightly together.
Close-pack: weight characterized by canes closely packed together without a pattern.
Rose cane: resembling an old fashioned cabbage rose, usually with contrasting sepal colour.
Scrambled: weight made up of canes assembled without a pattern.

A Clichy faceted concentric millefiori paperweight, the central green cane within a border of pink and white canes, a further border of purple canes and an outer garland of pink and white canes alternating with a trio of green canes, later faceted and some chips, French, 19thC, 2½in (6.5cm) diam.
£400–475 ⚒ Bon(C)

A St Louis paperweight, with a fuchsia in clear glass above a white latticinio ground, 1845–60, 3in (7.5cm) diam.
£2,100–2,350 ⊞ SWB

A St Louis crown paperweight, with red, green, white and blue canes, French, c1848, 3in (7.5cm) diam.
£1,500–1,800 ⊞ DLP

A flower paperweight, probably by Pantin, the pink flower with cane stamen, French, 1850–1900, 2½in (7cm) diam.
£850–1,100 ⚒ S

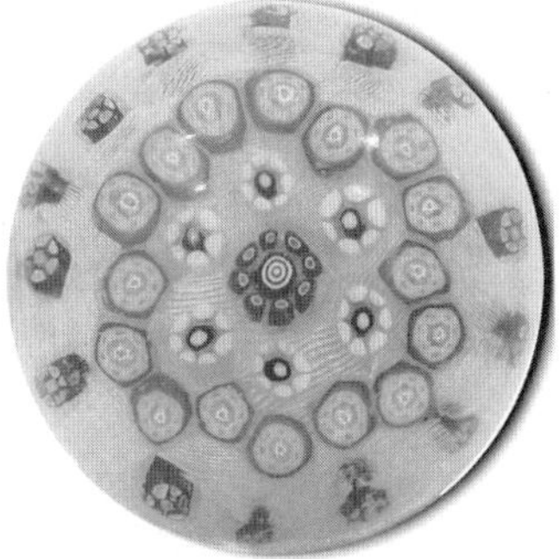

A St Mandé concentric paperweight, the red, white and blue canes on a muslin ground, c1850, 2¾in (7cm) diam.
£450–500 ⊞ SWB

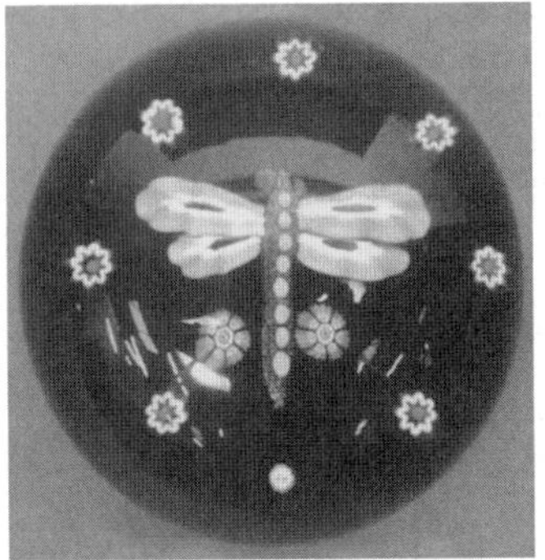

A Paul Ysart paperweight, decorated with a dragonfly on a black ground within a border of seven green, white and red canes, c1930, 3in (7.5cm) diam.
£600–750 ⚒ RTo

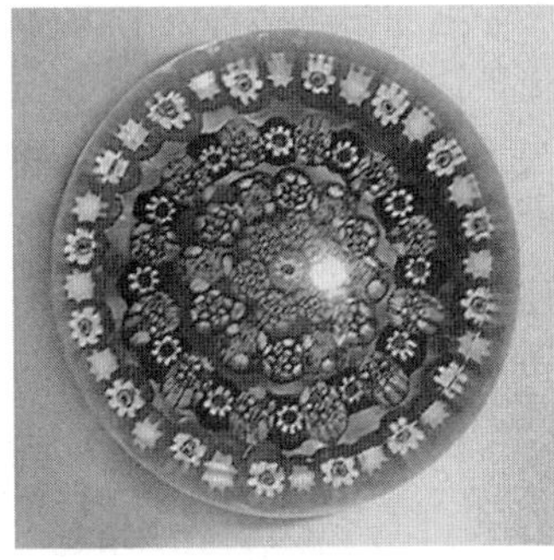

A Paul Ysart paperweight, with four concentric bands of millefiori and single flowerhead canes surrounding a central cane, 1930s, 3in (7.5cm) diam.
£600–750 ⚒ PFK

► **A millefiori inkwell paperweight,** with multi-cane stopper and concentric rings of white, turquoise, pink, red and blue canes, 19thC, 7in (18cm) high.
£350–450 ⚒ G(L)

◄ **A glass paperweight,** 19thC, 6in (15cm) high.
£160–175 ⊞ SEA

A Clichy-style swirl paperweight, with turquoise and white staves radiating from a central white and pink flower, French, 19thC, 3in (7.5cm) diam.
£280–320 ⚒ G(L)

A paperweight, possibly by Riesengebirge, painted or printed with hunters and their dog in woodland beside a dead stag, Bohemian, 1850–1900, 3½in (9cm) diam.
£150–165 ⚒ S(O)
Ex-Rudolf Just Collection.

Salts

An amethyst glass salt, the double-walled bowl on a hollow-knopped stem and a plain domed foot, c1760, 3¼in (8.5cm) high.
£350–400 ⊞ Som

A citrine and cranberry candy-stripe glass salt, with a double clear frill, in an EPNS stand, c1900, 3½in (9cm) diam.
£100–120 ⊞ GRI

A Stourbridge ribbed cranberry glass salt, with a clear glass frill, c1910, 3in (7.5cm) diam.
£80–90 ⊞ GRI

LOCATE THE SOURCE
The source of each illustration in Miller's can be found by checking the code letters below each caption with the Key to Illustrations, pages 794–800.

Scent Bottles & Flasks

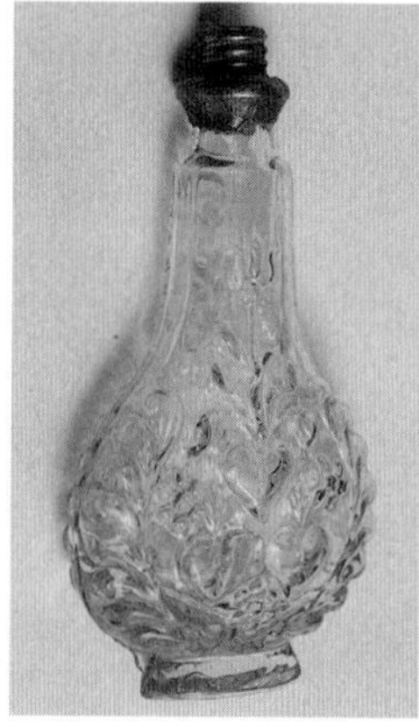

An Orléans clear glass scent bottle, by Bernard Perrot, moulded with a fleur-de-lys design, French, c1680, 3½in (9cm) high.
£600–700 ⊞ LBr

◄ **A cut-glass scent bottle and stopper,** by Apsley Pellatt, with a sulphide bust of Napoleon I, the base cut with hobnail diamonds, c1820, 4½in (11.5cm) high.
£750–850 ⚒ S(O)

► **A late Victorian ruby glass scent bottle,** with a silver top, c1890, 2½in (6.5cm) high.
£135–150 ⊞ GRI

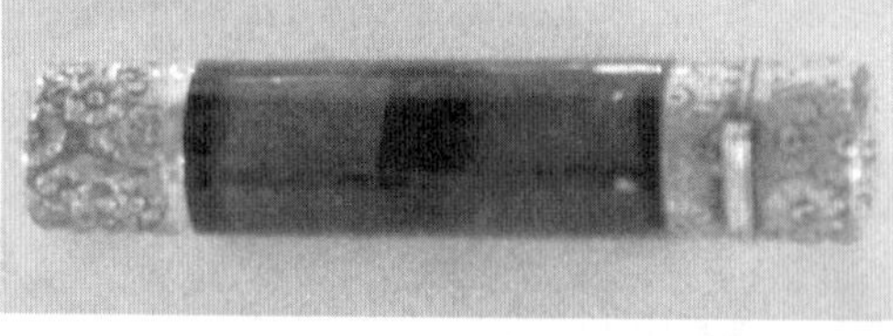

◄ **A Victorian green glass double-ended scent bottle,** with embossed floral decoration and white metal mounts, 4¼in (11cm) long.
£75–90 ⚒ WilP

Vases

A ribbed and cut-glass bulb vase, mid-19thC, 5in (12.5cm) high.
£100–120 ⊞ JHa

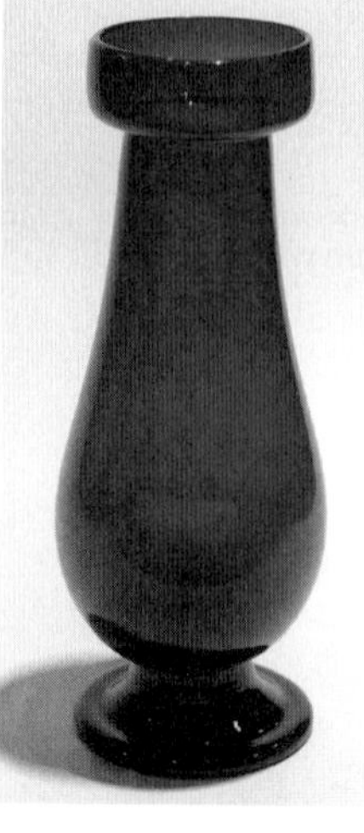

◄ **A blue glass bulb vase,** on a folded foot, c1810, 8½in (21.5cm) high.
£130–145 ⊞ LHo

► **An amber flash overlay vase,** the fold-over petal rim engraved with ivy, the body engraved with a leaping stag within a woodland landscape above a concave stem and cylindrical base, engraved with two further deer grazing beneath trees, minor damage, Bohemian, mid-19thC, 16¼in (41.5cm) high.
£900–1,100 ⚒ RTo

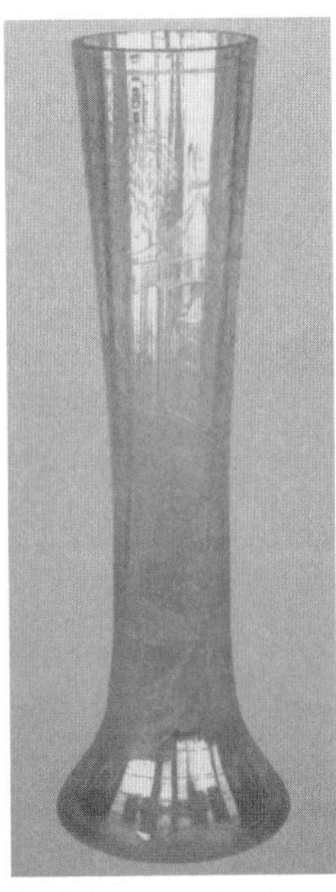

A glass vase, cut and etched with a Chinaman in a pagoda among weeping willows, 19thC, 20in (51cm) high.
£600–750 Mit

A pair of Victorian green and white overlay glass vases, painted with panels of flowers, 12¾in (32.5cm) high.
£425–525 AG

A red and white overlay cut-glass vase, the raised panels painted with a portrait of a lady and flowers, decorated with foliate gilding, Bohemian, 19thC, 12½in (32cm) high.
£575–720 F&C

An opaline glass vase, decorated *en grisaille* with a view of a building, the reverse inscribed in gilt 'Capitol of the U.S., Washington', rim chip, 19thC, 9½in (24cm) high.
£800–1,000 SLN

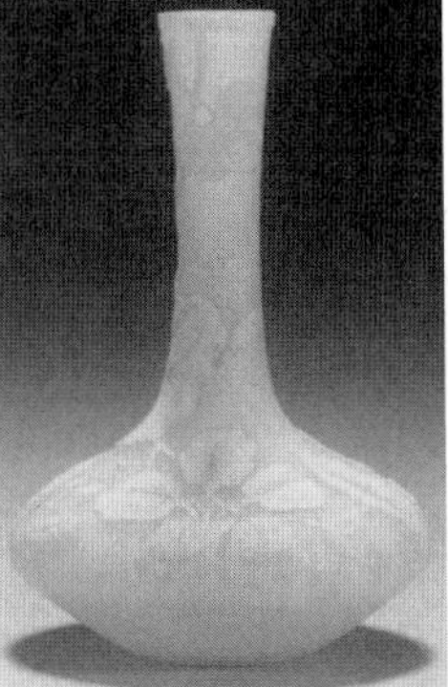

◄ A three-colour cameo bud vase, possibly by Thomas Webb & Co, overlaid in pink and white and carved with convolvulus, c1885, 3¾in (9.5cm) high.
£800–950 S(O)

A cranberry glass vase, with a clear edge, in original brass stand, c1890, 6½in (16.5cm) high.
£180–200 GRI

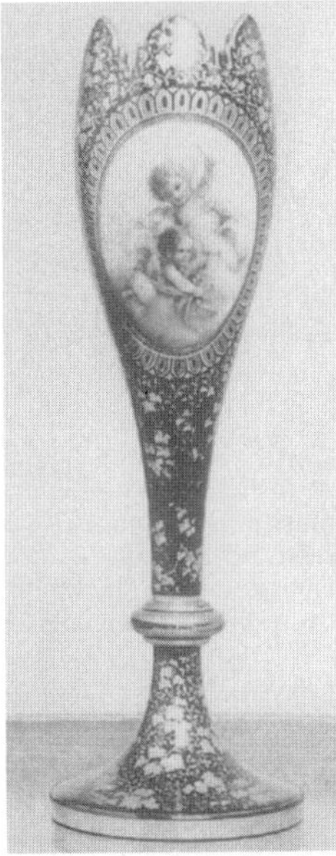

A Victorian green-tinted glass vase, with painted gilt foliage decoration, the raised panel painted with cupids, on a knopped stem, 16¾in (42.5cm) high.
£350–450 AG

A pair of opaque glass vases, decorated with a mixed bouquet of flowers cold-painted in autumnal colours, the reverse with further small sprays of flowers, the rims with gilt pendant borders, Bohemian, late 19thC, 16¼in (41.5cm) high.
£1,500–1,800 P(Ba)

Pairs of vases, like decanters, demand three times the price of a single piece.

A pair of opaque glass vases, with painted decoration of children, Continental, 19thC, 9½in (24cm) high.
£100–125 L&E

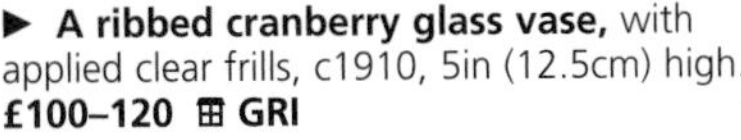

► A ribbed cranberry glass vase, with applied clear frills, c1910, 5in (12.5cm) high.
£100–120 GRI

◄ A pair of clear glass vases, facet-, flute- and diamond-cut, with yellow-metal mounts, French, c1900, 11½in (29cm) high.
£700–850 DORO

Silver

Animals, Birds & Fish

A silver vinaigrette, modelled as an articulated fish, the mouth and head hinged, with red glass eyes, Continental, possibly German, 18thC, 3½in (9cm) wide, in a tooled leather case.
£600–700 ⚒ Bon

Cross Reference
See Colour Review (page 409)

A silver mustard pot, by George Richards, modelled as an owl, with a spoon with deceased mouse terminal, with glass liner, London 1850, 3¾in (9.5cm) high, 5oz.
£2,200–2,500 ⚒ S(S)

A silver model of a cow, 1850–1900, 2in (5cm) high.
£70–85 ⚒ G(L)

► **A silver vesta case,** by Child & Child, modelled as a pig, Birmingham 1908–09, 2¾in (7cm) wide, 0.75oz.
£1,000–1,150 ⊞ NS

A silver pepperette, modelled as a teddy bear, two small dents, maker's mark 'S. & Co', Birmingham 1909, 1½in (4cm) high.
£200–240 ⚒ MCA

A set of four silver place settings, by Sampson Mordan & Co, modelled as owls, with orange glass eyes, one eye missing, Chester 1907, 1½in (4cm) high, in a fitted leather case.
£500–600 ⚒ HAM

A silver pin cushion, by S. Blanckensee & Son, modelled as a pheasant, Birmingham 1913, 4¾in (12cm) wide.
£500–600 ⚒ Bon

Baskets

► **A silver sugar basket,** by Hester Bateman, with pierced and bright-cut decoration and a blue glass liner, London 1784, 6in (15cm) wide.
£1,800–2,000 ⊞ TSC

A silver swing-handled basket, by Samuel Herbert & Co, with pierced and alternate shaped panels of scrolls and crosslets, heavily repaired, London 1763, 12½in (32cm) wide, 22oz.
£400–500 ⚒ Bon

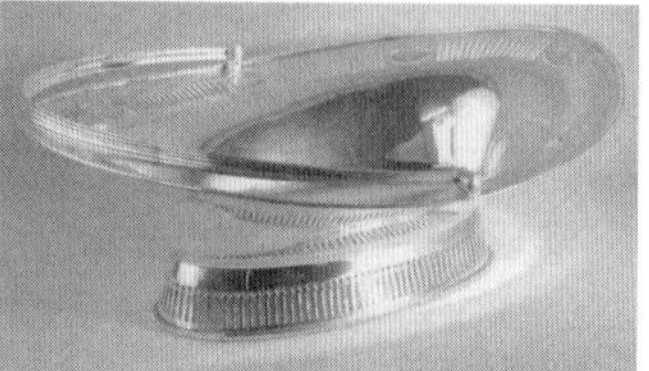

A silver sugar basket, by Richard Sawyer, decorated with an upper band of acorns and oak leaves, oval cartouches now vacant, Dublin 1806, 6¾in (17cm) wide, 8.5oz.
£450–550 ⚒ P(B)

◄ **A silver cake basket,** by Robert Hennell, with engraved and pierced border, London 1806, 14½in (37cm) wide, 31.5oz.
£1,500–1,800 ⚒ CGC

A silver basket, by Robert Gray & Son, embossed and chased with a border of flowerheads and scrolls on a matted ground, Glasgow 1819, 11¾in (30cm) diam, 36.5oz.
£650–800 P(Ed)

Robert Gray, the premier goldsmith in Glasgow in the first half of the 19th century, was also instrumental in establishing the city's assay office in 1819. Gray was appointed one of the four wardens of the newly constituted Glasgow Goldsmiths Company and he chaired its first meeting on 28 May 1819.

A silver cake basket, by Robinson, Edkins & Aston, the body with repoussé scroll decoration and applied floral motifs, Birmingham 1844, 10¼in (26cm) diam, 15oz.
£350–420 B&L

► **A silver-mounted mother-of-pearl basket,** with chased swing handle, Sheffield 1903, 5in (12.5cm) wide.
£140–170 TRM

A silver cake basket, by Martin Hall & Co, the body beaded, pierced and embossed with flowers and festoons, Sheffield 1864, 13in (33cm) diam, 21.5oz.
£500–600 CGC

A George III-style silver basket, with pierced bowl and swing handle, Birmingham 1904, 12¼in (31cm) wide, 17oz.
£160–200 G(L)

Beakers

A silver-gilt beaker, embossed with flowers and leaves, Continental, late 17thC, 5¼in (13.5cm) high.
£650–800 DN

A silver beaker, by Lawrence Twentyman, the body with two wrigglework bands below a frieze with a cartouche containing initials and dated July 1812, 3¾in (9.5cm) high, 5oz.
£800–950 CGC

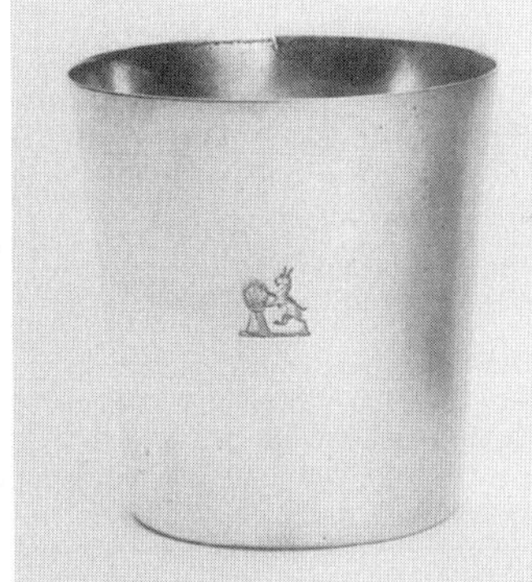

A silver beaker, engraved with a crest and a later inscription, maker's mark E.G., possibly for Emidio Gusimano or Emmanuele Galea, Maltese, c1805, 3¼in (8.5cm) high, 4.5oz.
£500–600 P

A silver and niello beaker, by Vasiliy Semenov, Russian, Moscow 1863, 5½in (14cm) high.
£1,150–1,275 MIR

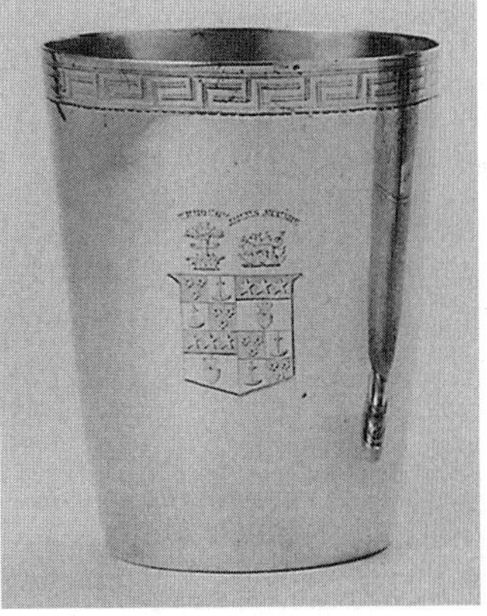

A silver beaker, engraved with a band of Greek key decoration and an armorial shield below two Scottish crests and mottos, maker's mark I.F.T, Portuguese, Lisbon c1810, 4¾in (12cm) high, 8.5oz.
£675–750 B

Many Portuguese beakers of this date are encountered with British arms or crests and it seems likely that some of these were purchased by officers while serving in the Peninsula against Napoleon.

A pair of whisky beakers, by W. M., in the shape of thistles, Edinburgh 1895–96, 2½in (6.5cm) high, 3.5oz.
£600–650 NS

SILVER

Biscuit Boxes

A pair of silver biscuit boxes, retailed by J. Verschuur, one circular, one oval, with tray, Dutch, Amsterdam 1879, oval box 6in (15cm) wide, 45.75oz.
£1,300–1,600 S(Am)

A silver-mounted biscuit box, by James Garrard, the oval cut-glass body with hinged cover, 1894, 6¼in (16cm) high.
£400–500 L

A silver three-compartment biscuit box, by Fenton Bros, with embossed floral and scroll decoration and gilt interior, Sheffield 1898, 9¾in (25cm) high, 57oz.
£1,700–1,850 P(NW)

Bowls

A silver sugar bowl, by John Wakelin and William Taylor, engraved with a band of bright-cut decoration, London 1783–84, 6¾in (17cm) diam, 8oz.
£850–950 NS

A silver bowl, by Richard Sawyer, Dublin 1828, 7in (18cm) diam.
£2,000–2,400 SIL

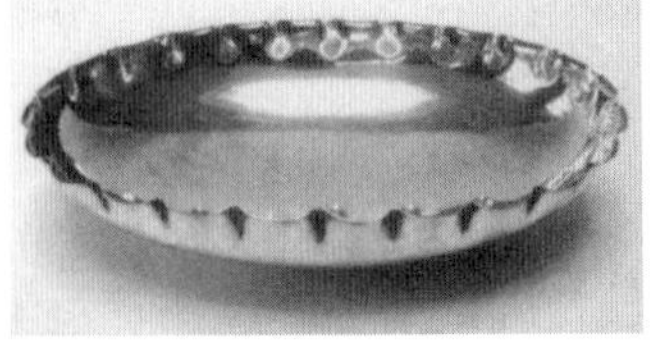

A silver bowl, with fluted rim, London 1900, 9in (23cm) wide.
£140–170 LFA

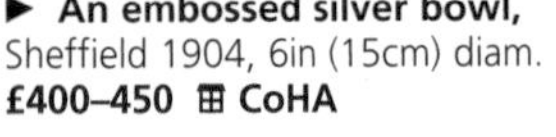

► **An embossed silver bowl,** Sheffield 1904, 6in (15cm) diam.
£400–450 CoHA

Alterations

Bowls have long been modified to meet the demand for good quality silver, a practice which peaked in Victorian times when plain vessels were often chased with lavish ornament of flowers and foliage to help conceal a previous identity. They can be contrived from the bases of coffee pots, loving cups and tankards; larger examples may have started life as entrée dishes or soup tureen liners. Signs to look out for are crude joins with rough soldering, thin patches of metal where an original inscription may have been polished off to make way for new engraving, and excessively thin sides and edges where the metal has been stretched to increase the diameter. Any alteration will significantly reduce the value of a bowl, and become illegal if the original purpose of the item has been changed.

A silver bleeding bowl, by Benjamin Burt, the handle engraved with initials, repaired, American, Boston c1790, 4¼in (11cm) diam, 4oz.
£1,000–1,200 B

Miller's is a price GUIDE not a price LIST

A silver fruit bowl, with impressed and pierced decoration, Birmingham 1898, 11in (28cm) diam, 14oz.
£140–170 L&E

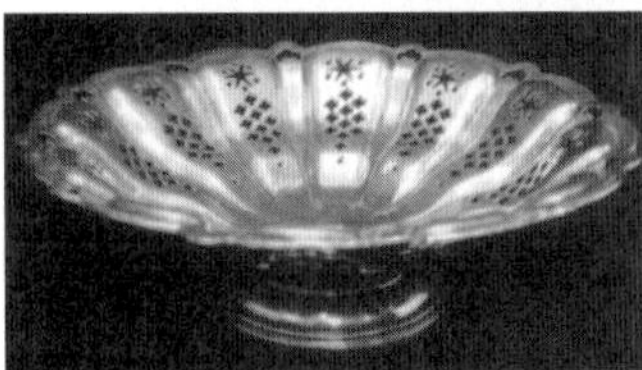

A silver bowl, with star- and lozenge-pierced sides, Birmingham 1899, 9in (23cm) diam, 8.25oz.
£85–100 DA

A sterling silver bowl, by Graff, Washbourne & Dunn, New York 1900–50, 12in (30.5cm) diam.
£320–350 WcH

Boxes

A silver filigree box with counters, the lid enamelled with a playing card, c1800, 1¼in (3cm) high.
£1,250–1,375 ⊞ NOR

A silver-gilt and niello snuff box, by V. G., the lid decorated with a picture of the Kremlin and the base with St Petersburg Stock Exchange, Moscow c1830, 2½in (6.5cm) wide.
£1,000–1,100 ⊞ MIR

A silver box, by Taylor & Perry, engraved with foliate and acanthus leaf decoration, the central cartouche with a presentation inscription, with a gilt interior, Birmingham 1844, 3¾in (9.5cm) wide.
£370–430 ⚒ LJ

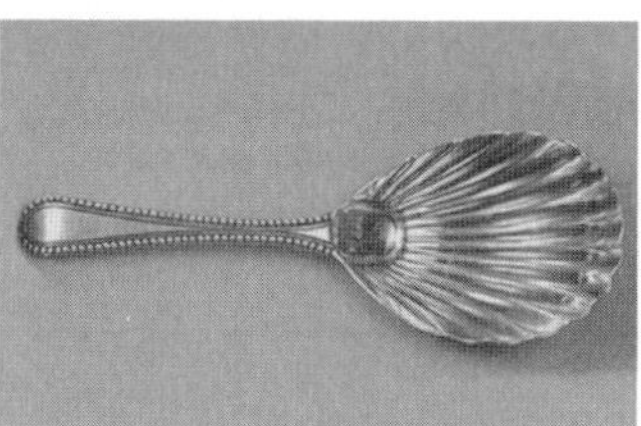

A silver jewellery box, the lid chased with floral and C-scroll decoration framing ownership initials, the interior lined in pleated cream silk, Birmingham 1910, 6in (15cm) wide.
£350–400 ⚒ PFK

A silver trinket box, the cover set with a cameo, the sides embossed with foliate scroll decoration, maker's mark F. H., London 1899, 3¼in (8.5cm) diam.
£220–270 ⚒ Bon

A .950 silver soap box, by C. Becker, German c1890, 3½in (9cm) wide.
£200–225 ⊞ BEX

SILVER

Caddy Spoons

A silver Bead pattern caddy spoon, by George Smith (III), with maker's mark and lion passant on back of stem, London c1780, 4in (10cm) long, 0.5oz.
£180–225 ⚒ WW

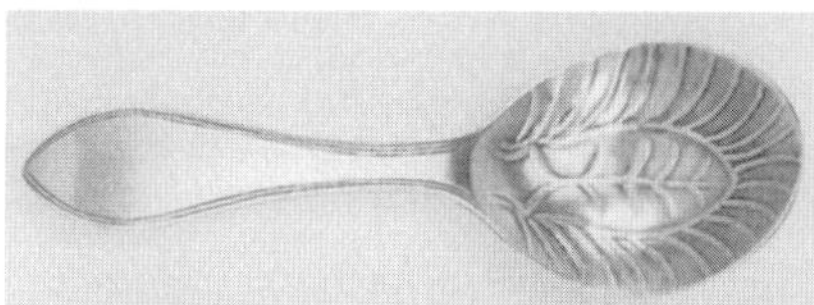

A silver caddy spoon, by Carden Terry and Jane Williams, with leaf-chased bowl, Irish, Cork c1820, 5½in (14cm) long.
£1,500–1,800 ⚒ P

► **A silver Fiddle pattern caddy spoon,** by James Barber & Co, York 1824, 5½in (14cm) long.
£300–350 ⚒ B

Candlesticks & Chambersticks

A pair of cast silver candlesticks, Dublin 1730–40, 8¼in (21cm) high, 24oz.
£2,000–2,400 ⚒ MEA

► **A silver taperstick,** by William Gould, with later nozzle and snuffer attachment, London 1750, nozzle London 1843, 5in (12.5cm) high, 5.5oz.
£550–650 ⚒ S(O)

A silver chamberstick, by John Priest, crested, with shell and scroll edging, London 1752, 13.25oz.
£300–360 ⚒ Bea(E)

A pair of silver candlesticks, one by Richard Syng, the other by John Cafe, with gadrooned knops and bases, partly loaded, 1708 and 1758, 7½in (19cm) high.
£2,000–2,500 TEN

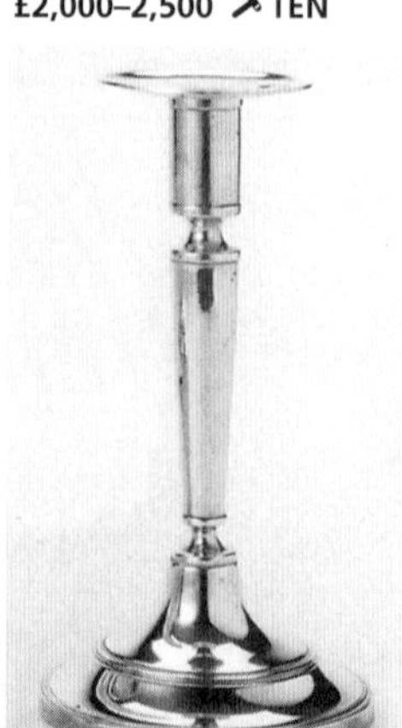

A pair of silver candlesticks, by Pedro Hernandez, adapted for electricity, Spanish, Madrid 1806, 8½in (21.5cm) high, 26oz.
£700–800 B

► **A pair of silver tapersticks,** moulded with palmettes, Chester 1900, 4in (10cm) high, 6oz.
£140–170 AH

A pair of silver Corinthian column candlesticks, with detachable sconces, maker's mark B., Birmingham 1904, 11½in (29cm) high.
£600–700 WL

A pair of silver Corinthian column candlesticks, by Emick Romer, the bases with repoussé decoration of leaves and floral swags, loaded, 1765, 11in (28cm) high.
£1,400–1,700 L

A silver chamberstick, by Smith, Tate & Co, with gadrooned border, Sheffield 1818, with a plated extinguisher and steel candle snuffs.
£320–380 LFA

A silver candelabrum, by Elkington & Co, Birmingham 1907, 16in (40.5cm) high.
£600–700 GAK

Candlesticks

Candlesticks are among the most commonly collected items of silver. Few examples made prior to the mid-17th century are still in existence since most were melted down for coin or as a result of damage. Early candlesticks were raised from thin sheet metal and are usually very light. They were used primarily by the upper classes and the Church. From the late 18th century large quantities of 'loaded' candlesticks were produced in Sheffield and Birmingham, their bases weighted with pitch, wood or plaster of Paris. This mass production made them accessible to the growing middle classes. The plain baluster style on a circular foot and the Corinthian column on a square plinth were particularly popular towards the end of the 18th century.

A silver chamberstick, with a scroll- and leaf-cast border, Sheffield 1841, 6in (15cm) diam.
£300–360 TMA

SILVER

Card Cases

A silver card case, by Taylor and Perry, Birmingham 1836, 2½in (6.5cm) high.
£1,800–2,000 ⊞ BEX

A silver card case, by Wheeler and Cronin, embossed with a scene of Windsor castle, Birmingham 1845, 4in (10cm) high, 2.75oz.
£800–900 ⚒ S(O)

A silver card case, by Edward Smith, engraved with a flower-filled diaper design within scroll borders, Birmingham 1859, 4in (10cm) high, 3oz, cased.
£140–170 ⚒ N

A silver card case, with vacant cartouche and foliate engraving, Birmingham 1902, 4in (10cm) high, 2.5oz.
£100–120 ⚒ DMC

Miller's is a price GUIDE not a price LIST

Casters

◄ **A silver caster,** by William Forbes for Ball, Tompkins & Black, New York 1840–50, 7½in (19cm) high, 7oz.
£700–800 ⚒ WcH

► **A pair of silver casters,** by Gorham Manufacturing Co, chased with marine life, fish and shells, American, Newport, Rhode Island 1882, 4in (10cm) high.
£1,000–1,100 ⚒ S

A silver sugar caster, by Nathan and Hayes, Chester 1911, 8in (20.5cm) high, 8.5oz.
£180–220 ⚒ CGC

Centrepieces

A silver comport, by Emes and Barnard, London 1824, 5in (12.5cm) wide.
£3,800–4,250 ⊞ MCO

A silver repoussé tazza, by The Goldsmiths & Silversmiths Co, with wavy scroll- and shell-cast rim, the border with floral sprays on a chased ground, London 1908, 11in (28cm) diam, 31oz.
£400–500 ⚒ PF

◄ **A silver *épergne*,** by Walker and Hall, the detachable central circular basket and the two hanging baskets with pierced balustrade borders, Sheffield 1917, 11½in (29cm) high, 43oz.
£750–900 ⚒ Bon

A silver nef, with dolphin- and-cherub embossed hull, German, import marks for London 1925, 10in (25.5cm) wide, 20.5oz.
£1,300–1,600 ⚒ AH

LOCATE THE SOURCE

The source of each illustration in Miller's can be found by checking the code letters below each caption with the Key to Illustrations, pages 794–800.

Coffee Pots & Teapots

A Britannia standard silver coffee pot, by Joseph Bell, with a duck's head spout and scrolled wood handle, terminal of handle missing, London 1716, 10in (25.5cm) high, 28oz.
£3,000–3,500 HAM

A silver teapot, by John Hamilton, with engraved decoration, Dublin 1718, 4in (10cm) high.
£25,000–28,000 WELD
There is great demand for Irish silver at the moment and this is a particularly good piece.

A silver crested coffee pot, probably by Richard Beale, with a fruitwood handle, London 1730, 9in (23cm) high, 23oz.
£1,200–1,500 F&C

Teapots

The high price of early 18th-century bullet teapots has resulted in frequent fakes. Such a pot can be made from a coffee pot or mug. A sign that this may have been done is traces of embossing or engraving or thin and patched areas. The lids of early teapots are infrequently marked; however a part mark matching that on the base is an aid to genuineness. Early pots are usually substantial, such weight is difficult to achieve when reshaping another piece and unusually light teapots of this period should be seen with suspicion. Later 18th-century teapots are usually of very light gauge, not in itself a fault. However, such pots are easily damaged and can frequently be seen to have unsightly solder repairs. The elaborately embossed pots of the early 19th century also suffer from similar repairs and, unless in good unrepaired order, should be rejected.

A silver teapot, with an ebonized handle and finial, maker's mark 'I.O.' for James Oliphant, Scottish, Edinburgh 1765, 5½in (14cm) high, 25oz.
£2,300–2,750 MCA

A silver teapot, by Daniel van Voorbis, with engraved monogram and wooden handle, American, Philadelphia c1780–82, 6¾in (17cm) high, 21.25oz.
£6,000–6,500 WcH

A silver teapot and stand, by Peter and Ann Bateman, with pineapple finial, chased crest and coat-of-arms within chased and bright-cut scrolling foliate banding, London 1796, 11¼in (28.5cm) wide, 21.75oz.
£700–850 AH

A silver teapot, with ebonized handle, maker's mark of J. Tolkeri, Russian, St Petersburg 1801, 5½in (14cm) high.
£500–600 Bon

SILVER

► **A silver teapot,** by Samuel Hennell, the body with a reeded band, on four ball feet, with ivory insulators, London 1808, 6in (15cm) high, 20.5oz.
£270–330 DD

A silver coffee pot, by Cattle & Barber, York 1807, 10½in (26.5cm) high.
£2,000–2,300 MHB

A silver teapot, with concealed hinge to lid, London 1820, 4½in (11.5cm) high.
£550–625 GLa

A George I-style silver teapot, by the Barnards, with carved blackwood handle, London 1834, 5¼in (13.5cm) high, 14oz.
£250–300 P(S)

A silver coffee percolator pot, by E. and J. Barnard, London 1859, 13in (33cm) high.
£1,800–2,000 ⊞ PAY

An 18thC-style silver coffee pot, with a wooden handle, London, Britannia standard marks for 1902, 9in (23cm) high.
£300–360 ⚒ LFA

A silver coffee jug, by Wakely and Wheeler, chased with flowers and leaves around a cartouche, Dublin 1916, 7in (18cm) high.
£650–730 ⊞ SIL

Coffee & Tea Services

A three-piece silver tea service, by John Edward Terrey, embossed and chased with a deep band of roses, thistles and scrolling foliage on a matted ground, London 1818, teapot 6in (15cm) high, 55oz.
£800–950 ⚒ N

A silver teapot and sugar basin, by John Tapley, crested, with leaf-capped handles and spout, London 1840, 39.25oz.
£350–420 ⚒ Bea(E)

A five-piece silver tea and coffee service, the coffee pot and slop pot by William Gale & Son, the remaining pieces by Gale and Willis, banded with eight oval cartouches, some engraved 'Maud', New York 1856–59, coffee pot 12in (30.5cm) high, 103.5oz.
£2,500–3,000 ⚒ NOA

This handsome set, an elaborate variation of the highly popular rococo revival style, is exemplary of mid-19th century American silversmithing. William Gale, who began working in 1822 and continued until his death in 1867, was among the first United States firms to work in sterling as opposed to coin silver. His company, always associated with the most prominent in silver production, is currently owned by the Gorham Corporation. Gale was a leading supplier to southern retailers and at the time of his death was one of the wealthiest men in New York.

◄ **A three-piece silver tea service,** with bright-cut decoration, maker's mark 'G.R.' for George Reily, London 1849–50, 45.5oz.
£650–720 ⚒ DD

► **A four-piece silver tea and coffee service,** by William Smily, heavily chased with vacant reserves, birds, C-scrolls and flowering foliage, with conforming C-scroll handles, London 1856, coffee pot 8½in (21.5cm) high, 76.5oz.
£1,800–2,200 ⚒ Bri

Miller's is a price GUIDE not a price LIST

A five-piece coin silver tea and coffee service, by Bigelow Brothers and Kennard, Boston 1850–75, coffee pot 9½in (24cm) high, 92oz.
£1,400–1,700 ⚒ SK

A four-piece silver tea service, by Hunt and Roskell, London 1867, coffee pot 8¾in (22cm) high.
£650–750 ⚒ RTo

SILVER

Condiment Pots

A pair of octagonal silver trencher salts, by James Stone, engraved with a contemporary monogram and initials, London 1730–31, 3in (7.5cm) diam, 5.25oz.
£2,250–2,500 ⊞ NS
These are referred to as trencher salts because they were placed adjacent to each diner's trencher or plate. They were popular from the 1690s to the 1730s.

A pair of silver salt cellars, by Hester Bateman, engraved with initials, gilt interiors, with rope-edge borders, on three hoof feet, London 1773–74, 2½in (6.5cm) diam, 3.5oz.
£850–950 ⊞ NS

A pair of silver salts, the sides pierced with star and scroll panels, with blue glass liners, one stamped with Assay office marks, Irish, 1790–1800, 2½in (6.5cm) diam.
£170–200 ⚒ P(S)

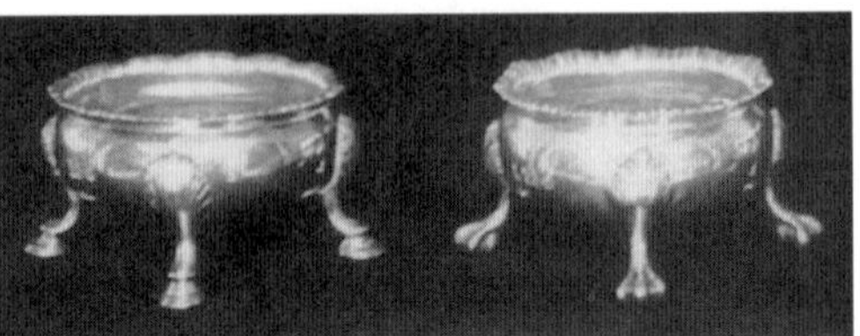

► **A set of four silver salts,** by J.E., with gilt interiors and chased wavy flared edges, London 1805, 4in (10cm) diam, 10oz.
£425–525 ⚒ TRM

A silver mustard pot, by Rebecca Emes and Edward Barnard, with gadrooned rim and blue glass liner, London 1808, 2½in (6.5cm) high.
£250–300 ⚒ GAK

A pair of silver salt cellars, by Richard Sibley I, embossed to simulate a patchwork of punched leatherwork, gilt interiors, crested bases, London 1814, 3¼in (8.5cm) diam, 15oz.
£600–750 ⚒ Bon

A pair of silver salts, by J. Le Bass, Dublin 1825, 2½in (6.5cm) diam.
£900–1,000 ⊞ WELD

◄ **A hexagonal silver mustard pot,** by Hilliard and Thomason, each panel pierced with geometric designs, with a blue glass liner, Birmingham 1866–67, 3in (7.5cm) high.
£700–775 ⊞ NS

► **A pair of silver standing salts,** by Messrs Garrards, commemorating the Diamond Jubilee of Queen Victoria, with the Royal cypher, the dates 1837 and 1897 and the coat-of-arms of the Salters Company, finials missing, London 1897, 5in (12.5cm) high, 12oz.
£1,000–1,200 ⚒ GAK

Cruets

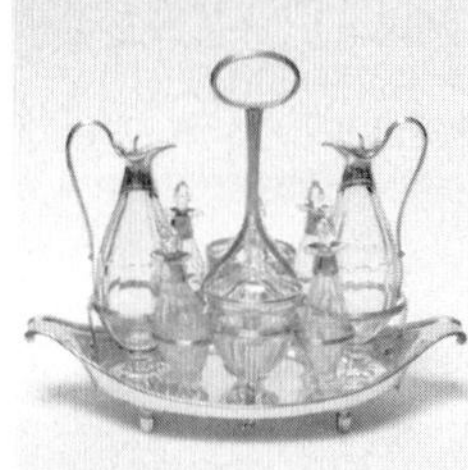

A silver eight-bottle cruet, by John Schofield, London 1789, 14in (35.5cm) wide.
£6,750–7,500 ⊞ TSC
This cruet is by a particularly good maker.

A George III-style silver cruet, comprising 10 pieces, London 1928.
£500–600 ⚒ LFA

A silver cruet stand, by Robert Davies, with a wood base and five glass bottles, three silver-mounted, London 1848, 5¾in (14.5cm) wide.
£270–340 ⚒ DN

SILVER

Cups & Goblets

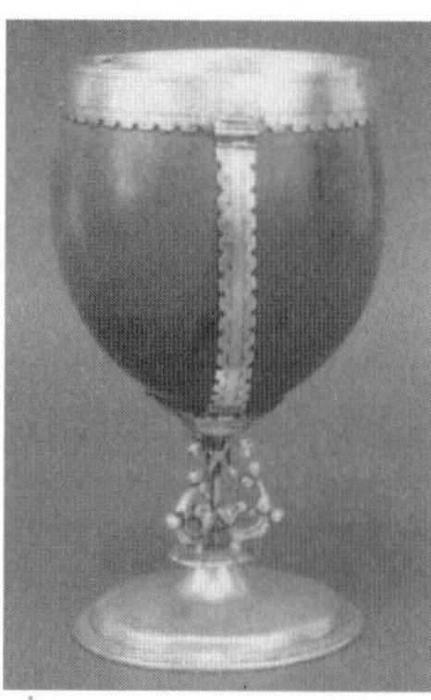

A silver-mounted coconut cup, maker's mark 'B.B', alterations, c1685 and later, 7¾in (19.5cm) high.
£600–750 RTo

A pair of silver loving cups, by Thomas Jones, Dublin 1778, 6½in (16.5cm) high.
£4,800–5,300 WELD

A silver christening cup, by James Sharp, with two S-shaped handles, engraved with initials, London 1779–80, 2½in (6.5cm) high, 3.5oz.
£700–775 NS

Cross Reference
See Colour Review (page 409)

A silver wine goblet, by Richard Cooke, applied with a frieze of fruiting vines, the lower body decorated with gadrooning, crested, gilt interior, London 1812–13, 8in (20.5cm) high, 22.5oz.
£1,600–1,750 NS

Miller's Compares

I. A Channel Islands silver christening cup, engraved with initials, maker's mark 'IH', dated '1779', 1725–85, 3¼in (8.5cm) high.
£2,200–2,750 B&L

II. A Channel Islands silver christening cup, engraved with initials, maker's mark 'IH', 1725–85, 2½in (6.5cm) high.
£800–1,000 B&L

These christening cups are both from the Channel Islands and, even more interestingly, both by the same maker, and yet Item I sold for almost three times as much as Item II. Although Item I is dated and slightly larger than Item II, the main reason for the difference in their realized prices is that Item I is made of a better gauge of silver than Item II, which was a little thin. Moreover, Item I is a better example of the silversmith's work than Item II, the quality of workmanship being superior.

A silver two-handled cup, with an embossed scene of a horse race, maker's mark 'G.W.', Dublin 1795, 6in (15cm) high, 14oz.
£300–375 Bea(E)

A silver two-handled cup, by Joseph Barber and William Whitwell, the body embossed with honeysuckle festoons and floral panels, York 1821, 5¼in (13.5cm) wide, 3oz.
£825–1,000 P(L)
This piece is a typical provincial product; note the festoons and panels fashionable in London almost 40 years previously.

A silver cup, the bowl with a crest and motto, London 1890, 5¼in (13.5cm) high.
£150–180 LFA

► **A sterling silver presentation cup,** the body decorated with repoussé grape clusters surrounding two opposing void cartouches, the lip with cast and applied grapevines, the handles *en suite*, American, c1900, 13in (33cm) high.
£700–850 NOA
Although the underside of this piece is engraved 'Made by Coleman E. Adler, N.O.', it bears the manufacturer's mark of Peter L. Krider Company, Philadelphia, Pennsylvania, active c1870–1903. This suggests that the design by Adler (working in New Orleans from 1898) was supplied to the Philadelphia firm for manufacture. That the style of this piece – rococo revival – was still highly popular in New Orleans but *passé* elsewhere, supports the hypothesis that this piece was commissioned and designed in New Orleans and was one of Adler's earliest.

SILVER

Cutlery

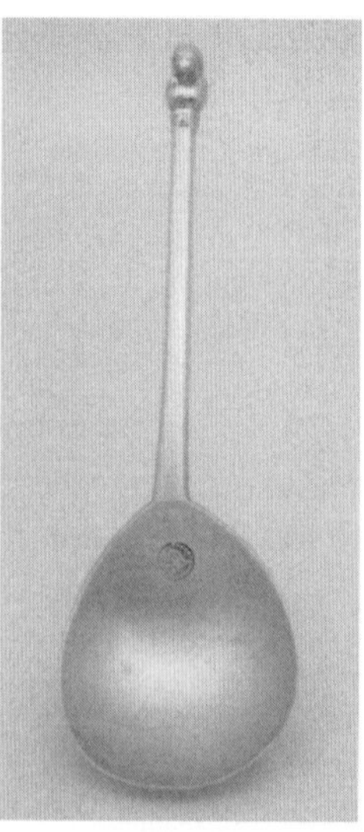

A silver maidenhead spoon, marked 'W.G.', Midlands, 1570–90.
£1,100–1,300 P(WM)

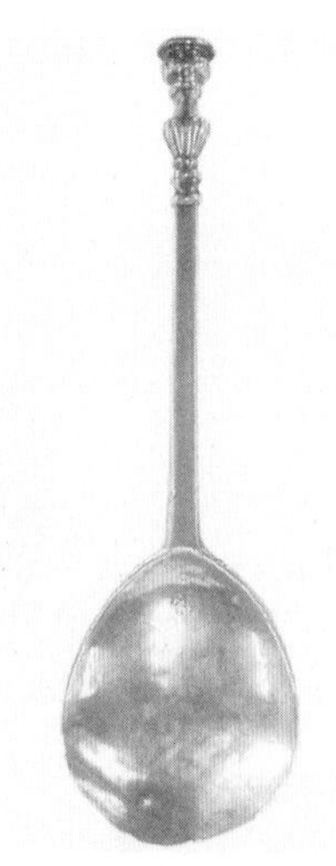

A silver seal-top spoon, marked with a cinquefoil on the bowl, traces of original gilding, Bury St Edmunds district, c1580.
£500–600 F&C

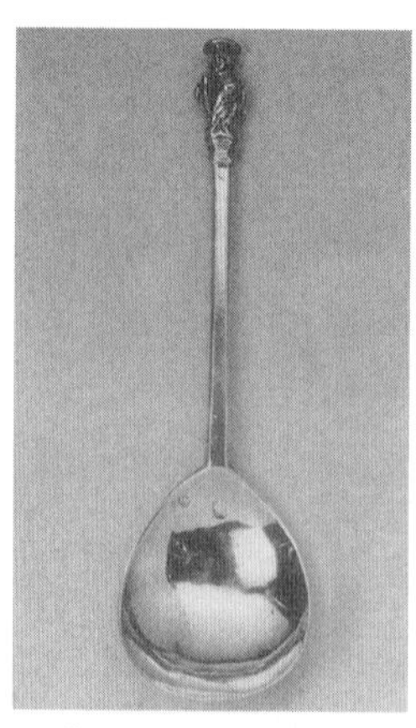

A silver apostle spoon, possibly by John Saunders, with an Esprit nimbus and holding a fuller's bat to represent St James the Less, traces of gilding, London 1616, 7in (18cm) long.
£500–600 AG

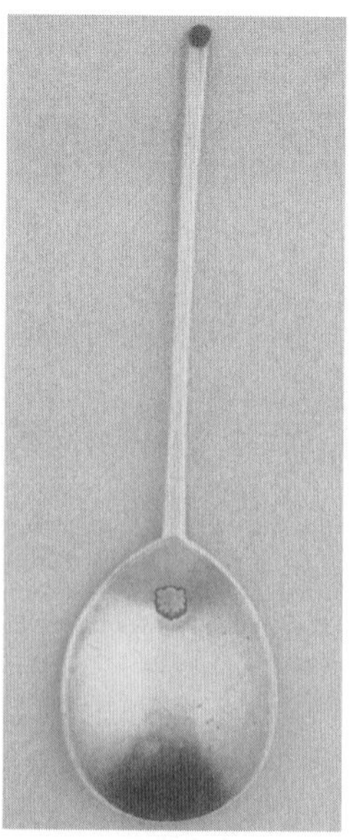

A child's silver slip top spoon, by John Feake, London 1617–18, 4¾in (12cm) long, 0.5oz.
£2,700–3,000 ⊞ NS

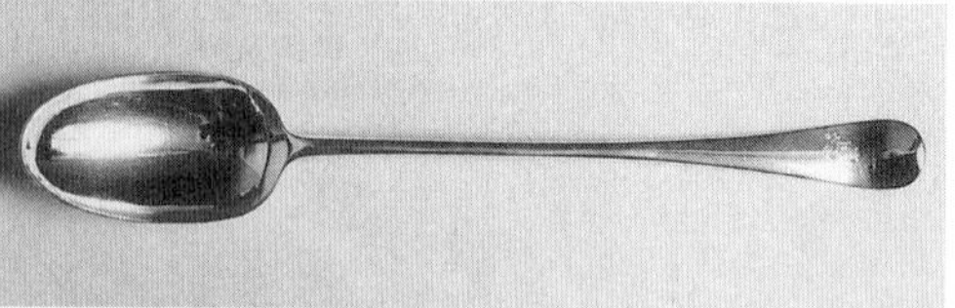

A silver serving spoon, by William Scarlett, London 1731, 14in (35.5cm) long.
£900–1,000 ⊞ BEX

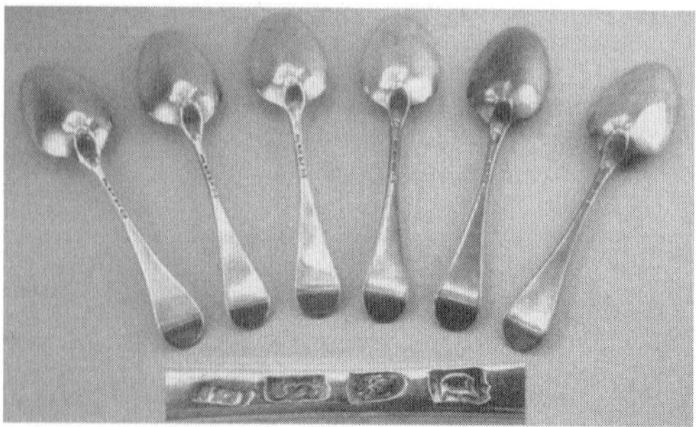

A set of six silver Hanoverian pattern table-spoons, by James Tookey, London 1759, 8in (20.5cm) long, 14.75oz.
£270–330 CGC

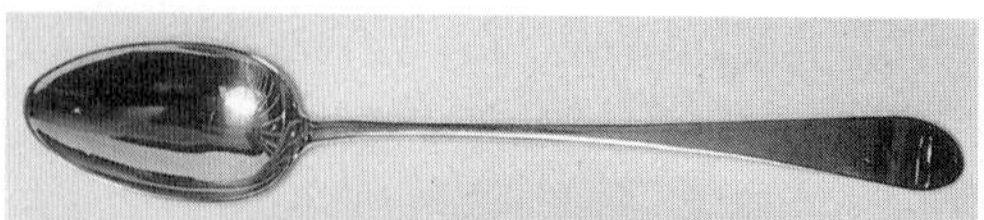

A silver Old English pattern serving spoon, by M. Homer, Dublin 1778, 12in (30.5cm) long.
£300–340 ⊞ SIL

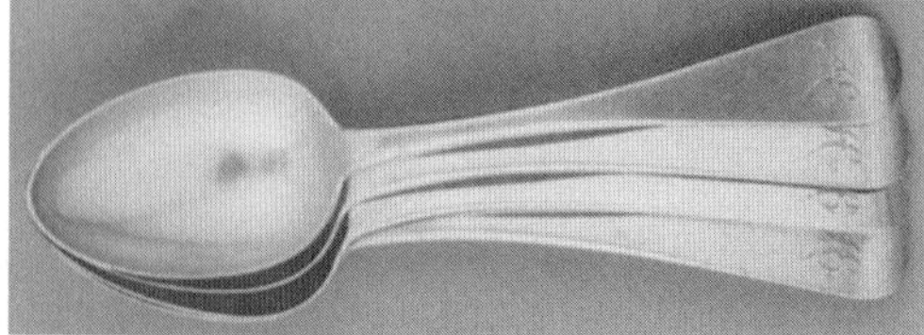

A set of 12 silver Old English pattern dessert spoons, by James Barber, George Cattle and William North, engraved with initials, York 1833–34, 7in (18cm) long, 18.25oz.
£1,200–1,350 ⊞ NS

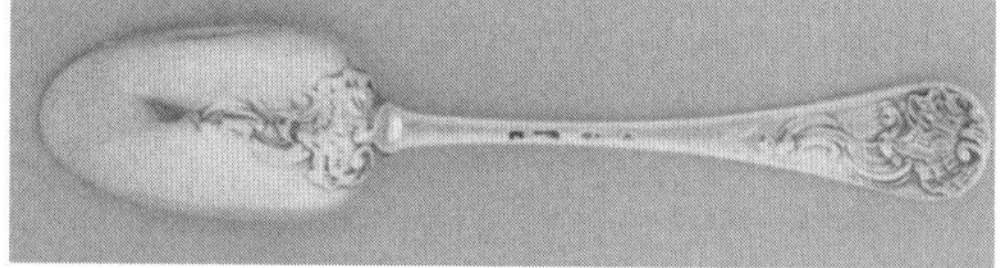

A set of six silver Hanoverian pattern picture-back teaspoons, with foliate and scroll decoration, traces of gilding, missing date letter, maker's mark worn, Dublin, 4¼in (11cm) long, 2oz.
£300–360 Bon

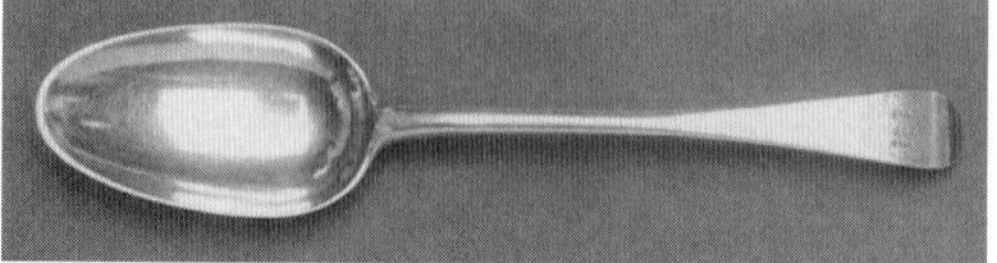

Four silver Old English pattern tablespoons, by Nathaniel Hurd, with galleon crest, American, Boston c1770, 10oz.
£2,000–2,250 S

Nathaniel was the son of Jacob Hurd, the first in a distinguished line of 18th century Boston silver-smiths and engravers. Nathaniel was most active prior to the Revolution and he specialized as an engraver of crests, arms and monograms.

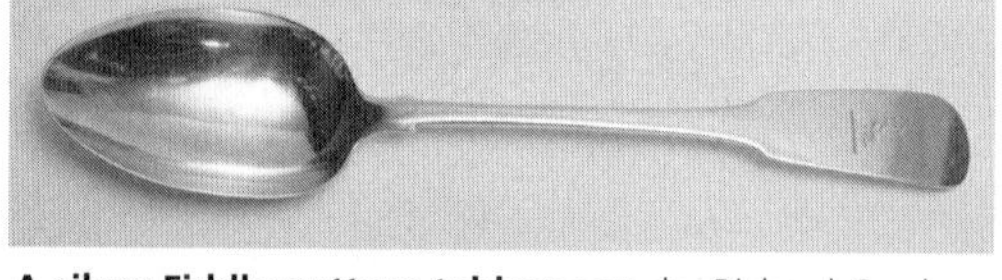

A silver Fiddle pattern tablespoon, by Richard Garde, Dublin 1822, 9in (23cm) long.
£120–150 ⊞ CoHA

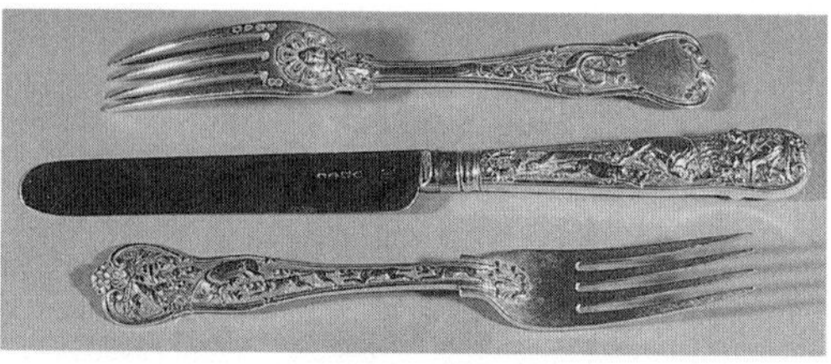

Ten pairs of silver dessert eaters, by George W. Adams for Chawner & Co, the hafts embossed with Stag Hunt pattern, London 1878, forks 23oz.
£350–450 AH

Dishes

A parcel-gilt dish, the border with repoussé flower sprays, with inscription dated 1696, Hungarian, 8½in (21.5cm) diam.
£4,250–5,250 ⚒ L

A parcel-gilt pap boat, by Richard Pearce, decorated with leaves, flowers and shells around the border, London 1826–27, 5in (12.5cm) long, 2.5oz.
£425–475 ⊞ NS

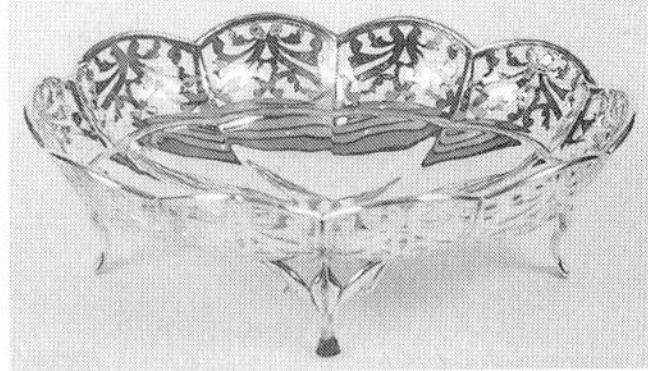

A silver shell-shaped butter dish, by Samuel Herbert, on two stepped paw supports with an engraved armorial, 1756, 5¼in (13.5cm) wide, 4oz.
£450–550 ⚒ P(Ba)

A silver dessert dish, by John Winter, chased with scrolling leaves and flowerheads, Sheffield 1839, 14in (35.5cm) wide, 36oz.
£1,100–1,200 ⚒ S(O)

► **A silver dish,** embossed with flowers and scrollwork, Sheffield 1903, 10½in (26.5cm) diam, 12oz.
£320–380 ⚒ WBH

◄ **A pierced silver bonbon dish,** by H. Vale & Co, Chester 1911, 8in (20.5cm) diam.
£300–350 ⊞ CoHA

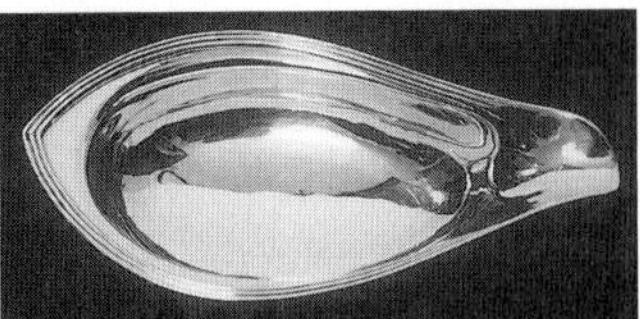

A silver pap boat, by Henry Nutting, London 1804, 5in (12.5cm) long.
£240–265 ⊞ GLa

A silver-gilt fruit dish, by Hunt & Roskill, chased and embossed with flowers and satyr masks, London 1873, 13in (33cm) wide, 19.5oz.
£500–600 ⚒ GAK

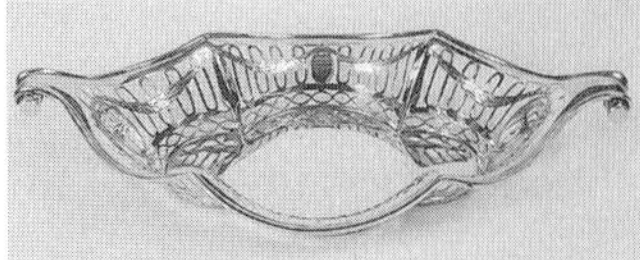

A hand-pierced silver bonbon dish, London 1903, 11in (28cm) wide.
£450–500 ⊞ CoHA

Covered Dishes

◄ **A pair of silver sauce tureens,** by Joseph Cradock and William Reid, engraved with a crest, with scroll loop handles, London 1817, 7in (18cm) long, 34oz.
£1,400–1,750 ⚒ Bri

A silver muffin dish and cover, by John Edward Terrey, cast with a border of C-scrolls, flowers and foliage, 1829, 8in (20.5cm) diam, 21oz.
£450–550 ⚒ P(WM)

◄ **Two silver serving dishes and covers,** by Gorham Manufacturing Co, one circular and one oval, with ram's head handles and engraved monogram, American, Providence, Rhode Island 1875, 12½in (32cm) wide, 109oz.
£2,700–3,500 ⚒ S(NY)

A silver entrée dish and cover, by S. Kirk & Son, American, Baltimore c1846–61, 12¼in (31cm) wide, 96.5oz.
£2,400–2,700 ⚒ WcH

A silver butter dish, cover and stand, by Edward Barnard & Sons, the finial in the form of a milkmaid, London 1856, 7in (18cm) wide, 22oz.
£1,100–1,300 ⚒ S(O)

SILVER

Dish Rings & Stands

A silver dish stand, with turned wood handle above a central burner, London 1785, 4¾in (12cm) diam, 10.5oz.
£300–350 S(O)

A silver dish stand and burner, by John Robins, with reeded decoration, crested, London 1805, 8½in (21.5cm) diam, 18oz.
£450–550 Bon

A silver dish ring, by James Wakely and Frank Clarke Wheeler of London, the body pierced, embossed and engraved with foxes, birds and hounds against a background of scrolls, flowers and berries, with a vacant scroll cartouche, with a blue glass liner, Dublin 1902, 7¾in (19.5cm) diam, 13oz.
£1,600–2,000 Bon
Wakely and Wheeler sent goods to different places for marking although they were based in London. As regards this piece, the company probably had an order from Ireland for Irish-style items and felt that a Dublin mark would be more suitable.

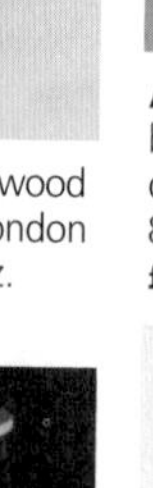

A silver dish ring, maker's mark 'DM', Dublin 1906, 7¼in (18.5cm) diam, 10oz.
£1,300–1,500 S(O)

◀ **A silver dish ring,** by West & Son, Dublin 1908, 7in (18cm) diam.
£2,400–2,700 WELD

Egg Cruets

A silver egg cruet, by Peter and Ann Bateman, the six pedestal cups with pierced borders, in a reeded frame, 1792, 9in (23cm) high, 12oz.
£600–750 P(EA)

A silver egg cruet, by Rebecca Emes and Edward Barnard, with gadrooned rims, the corners raised on Corinthian and foliate columns, with six matching egg cups with gilded liners and six matching spoons, London 1811, 7½in (19cm) wide.
£800–1,000 GAK

A silver egg cruet, by Richard Sibley, with gadrooned borders, on lion's claw, scroll and rosette feet, the four cups with gilt interiors and bright-engraved decoration, 1827, 8in (20.5cm) high, 19oz.
£450–550 B

Ewers & Jugs

◀ **A silver argyle,** by Andrew Fogelberg, engraved with an armorial, pourer repaired, London c1770, 5¼in (13.5cm) high, 12.25oz.
£550–650 CGC
An argyle is used for serving gravy.

▶ **A silver cream jug,** by Hester Bateman, London 1780, 5in (12.5cm) high.
£1,250–1,400 TSC

A silver milk jug, by John Emes, bright-cut and engraved with initials within a shield cartouche, London 1800–01, 3.75oz.
£425–475 NS

SILVER

A silver cream jug, by William Doyle, Dublin 1803, 4in (10cm) high.
£320–400 ⊞ CoHA

A parcel-gilt silver claret jug, by Edward Barnard & Sons, London c1873, 13½in (34.5cm) high.
£1,100–1,300 ⚒ G(L)

A silver hot water pot, by John Clarke II, with fruitwood scroll handle and finial and detachable lid, the body applied with three reeded girdles, London 1811, 7¾in (19.5cm) high, 18.5oz.
£400–500 ⚒ Bon

A silver jug, by W. and J. Barnard, the body semi-reeded and inscribed, the handle with an 18thC-style heart-shaped terminal, London 1889, 5½in (14cm) high, 17.75oz.
£400–500 ⚒ Bea(E)

◀ **A George I-style silver cream jug,** with a raised body band, embossed with animals and birds, Birmingham 1904, 3½in (9cm) high.
£80–100 ⚒ GAK

A silver milk jug, by John Wakefield, chased and engraved with foliage and flowers and a family crest, gilt interior, London 1835–36, 5in (12.5cm) high, 8oz.
£850–950 ⊞ NS

A silver hot water jug, decorated with gadrooned edging and finial, with a cane-clad handle, maker's mark 'W.W.', London 1929, 8¾in (22cm) high, 18.25oz.
£150–180 ⚒ Bea(E)

▶ **A silver jug,** by Dominick & Haff, Newark and New York, American, c1920, 10in (25.5cm) high, 35oz.
£350–420 ⚒ S(O)

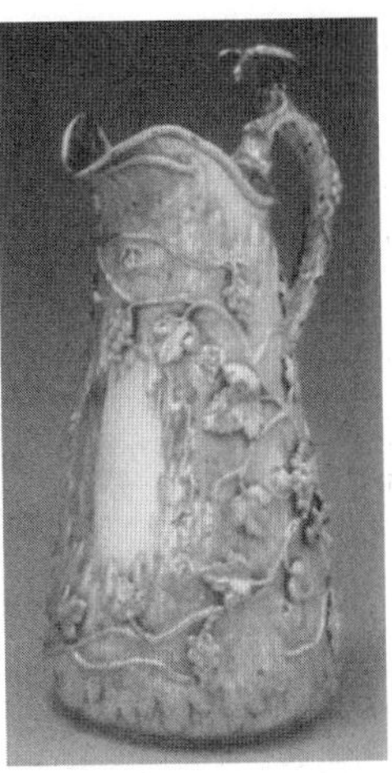
A silver water pitcher, by R. & W. Wilson, in the shape of a tree trunk overlaid with trailing grapevine spreading from the branch handle, applied with salamander and humming birds, the handle topped by a spread-winged eagle, engraved with a monogram, American, Philadelphia c1850, 12¼in (31cm) high, 38oz.
£6,500–8,000 ⚒ S(NY)

SILVER

Figures

A cast silver toothpick holder, modelled as a French north African cavalryman, maker's mark 'IR', Portuguese, Oporto 1853–61, 8½in (21.5cm) high, 11.5oz.
£1,000–1,200 ⚒ P

◀ **A pair of silver novelty match holders,** by Deakin and Francis, in the form of Mr and Mrs Caudle, characters from *Punch* magazine, Birmingham 1892, largest 4½in (11.5cm) high, 5.5oz.
£950–1,200 ⚒ Bea(E)

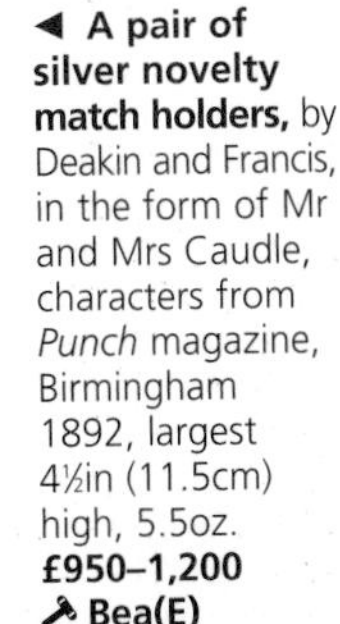

▶ **A pair of silver and ivory figures,** dressed in medieval costume, standing on bases with pierced scrolling floral decoration, with pseudo marks and import marks for Chester 1909 and London 1908, German, largest 8½in (21.5cm) high, 27.5oz.
£2,500–3,000 ⚒ P(E)

A pair of silver and ivory figures, by B. H. M., modelled as Beefeaters, London import marks for 1922 and 1923, 13½in (34.5cm) high including spear.
£1,500–1,800 ⚒ WL

Cross Reference
See Colour Review
(page 409)

Frames

A silver photograph frame, by William Comyns, pierced and embossed with putti and leaf scrolls, London 1900, 7¾in (19.5cm) high.
£220–275 LFA

A silver photograph frame, by William Hutton & Sons, decorated with flowers, shells and leaves, Birmingham 1905–06, 11¾in (30cm) high.
£675–750 ⊞ NS

An embossed silver picture frame, with a pierced border, Birmingham 1901, 9in (23cm) square.
£160–200 F&C

A silver easel photograph frame, with a gadroon scroll and bead embossed frame, Birmingham 1904, 10¾in (27.5cm) high.
£115–145 TMA

A silver photograph frame, by Mappin & Webb, applied on all sides with simulated bamboo scroll edges, 1906, 7½in (19cm) high.
£425–525 P(Ba)

A tortoiseshell picture frame, by Walker & Hall, inlaid in silver with shell and ribbon-tied floral bouquets and centred shells within a palmette-stamped border, Birmingham 1911, 19in (48.5cm) high.
£2,000–2,500 P(L)
This is a good example of how such tortoiseshell pieces are currently realizing high prices.

Inkstands & Wells

A silver reeded inkstand, by Henry Chawner and John Emes, with three silver-mounted glass receivers, one with a taperstick lid, c1796, 10½in (26.5cm) wide.
£1,300–1,600 G(L)

A silver inkstand, by Henry Wilkinson & Co, the tray engraved with strapwork and inscription, the cut-glass hexagonal inkwells with hinged silver covers, a taperstick to the centre, Sheffield 1854, 10¼in (26cm) wide, 13oz.
£450–550 N

A silver-mounted glass inkwell, by John Grinsell & Sons, inscribed, London 1898, 4in (10cm) wide.
£300–375 Bon

◀ **A silver inkstand,** with applied scrolled rim, the faceted glass bottle with a hinged silver lid, Sheffield 1899, 10in (25.5cm) wide.
£160–200 GAK

A silver inkstand, by J. S. and S., with two clear glass and silver-mounted inkwells, Birmingham 1906, 9¼in (23.5cm) wide.
£300–375 Bea(E)

Kettles

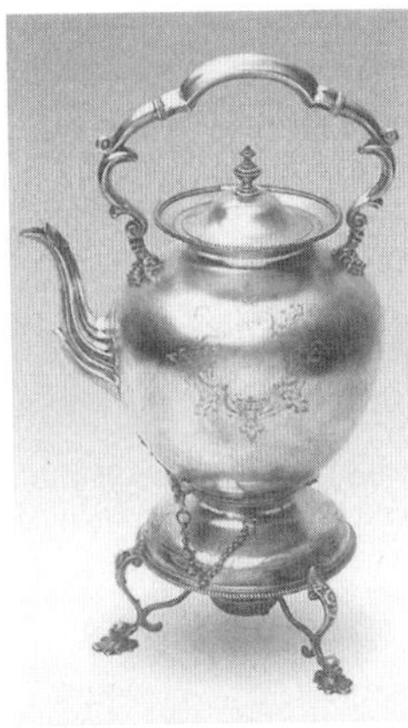

◄ **A silver tea kettle with burner,** by Richard Martin and Ebenezer Hall, with foliate-engraved strapwork, London 1863, 15¾in (40cm) high, 56oz.
£600–750 Bea(E)

► **A silver tea kettle and stand,** with presentation inscription, decorated with chinoiserie embossing incorporating deities and dragons, maker's mark 'W.M.', Edinburgh 1881, kettle 13¼in (33.5cm) high, 53oz.
£330–400 S(O)

A silver tea kettle with stand and burner, by A. and F. Parsons, in the George I style, engraved with an armorial, with a wood finial and turned wood handle, London 1914, 13½in (34.5cm) high, 81.5oz.
£1,200–1,500 DN

Lamps

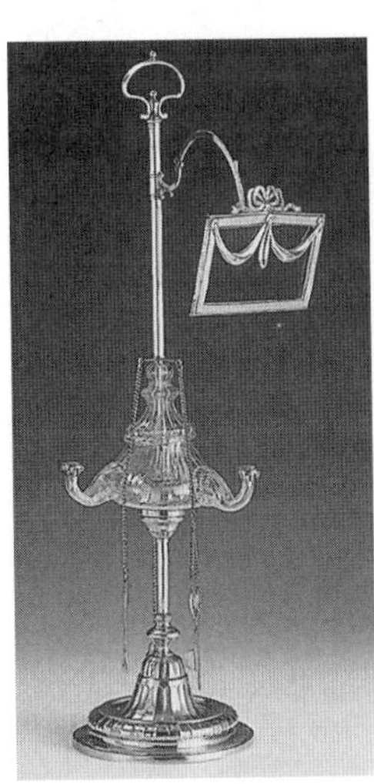

Three silver chamber oil lamps, by Matthew Boulton, with fluted rims and leaf-capped handles, fitted with conical snuffers, crested and initialled, Birmingham 1829, 5½in (14cm) high, with later glass shades.
£6,000–7,500 S

◄ **A silver oil lamp,** Italian, Genoa 1790, 29¼in (74.5cm) high.
£7,000–8,500 S(Mi)

► **A silver oil lamp,** by the Barnards, with cut-glass reservoir and chrysanthemum-etched shade, the column modelled as Triton supporting an urn, the base applied with dolphins and scallop shells, 1871, 27¼in (69cm) high.
£1,500–1,800 B

Menu Holders

A silver menu holder, modelled as an easel, embossed with putti, Birmingham 1900, 3½in (9cm) high.
£85–100 LFA

Miller's is a price GUIDE not a price LIST

A pair of silver menu holders, by George Brace & Co, applied with models of a pheasant cock and hen, London 1910, 1¼in (3cm) high, cased.
£200–250 Bon

A silver menu holder, by Cooper Brothers & Sons, modelled as the mainland of Gibraltar, Sheffield 1925, 7in (18cm) wide.
£200–220 Bea(E)

◄ **A set of four silver menu holders,** by William Base & Sons, pierced and engraved with a running fox and hounds, Birmingham 1929, 1¼in (3cm) diam, 2.5oz, cased.
£400–450 CGC

SILVER

Mirrors

An embossed silver-gilt dressing table mirror, by Lambert, with cartouche cresting, bordered by scrolling foliage set with song birds, London 1874, 22¼in (56.5cm) wide, on a mahogany trestle support.
£650–800 HOK

A silver-mounted green plush easel mirror, openwork-decorated with putti, mythical beasts, flowers, foliate scrolls and beaded cartouches, maker's mark 'J.N.M.', London 1887, 12½in (32cm) diam.
£525–625 MCA

► **A silver easel mirror,** the frame embossed and pierced with a ribbon-tied shield cartouche, birds and foliate scrolls, Birmingham 1908, 15in (38cm) high.
£220–270 N

◄ **A silver-framed mirror,** by Walker & Hall, embossed with scrolls and foliate design, Sheffield 1902, 10in (25.5cm) diam.
£150–180 GAK

Mugs & Tankards

A silver tankard, by George Smith II and Thomas Hayter, with hinged domed cover and gilt interior, later chased with flower scrolls and adapted as a jug, alteration assayed, London 1794, 7½in (19cm) high, 24oz.
£500–600 N

A silver mug, by John L. Westervelt, the central shield cartouche with an engraved inscription flanked by two chased lake scenes with towns, Amercian, New York c1826–50, 3¾in (9.5cm) high, 3.25oz.
£275–320 WcH

A silver christening mug, by Joseph and George Angell, engraved with two flower-bordered cartouches depicting a rustic scene and a castle, London 1847–48, 4¼in (11.5cm) high, 6.25oz.
£500–575 NS

SILVER

Rattles

A child's silver rattle, by Turton & Walblanke, with bells, whistle and coral teether, bright-cut engraved with birds, swags and acanthus, London c1790, 6in (15cm) long.
£500–600 S

A baby's silver rattle, by George Unite, with a tier of bells, foliate and lobed decoration and an ivory teething ring, Birmingham 1906, 5in (12.5cm) long.
£200–250 Bon

► **A child's silver-gilt rattle and whistle,** by Ledsam, Vale & Wheeler, chased with flowers and foliate scrolls, with eight bells and coral teething stick, Birmingham 1826, 6in (15cm) long.
£600–750 P

Salvers & Trays

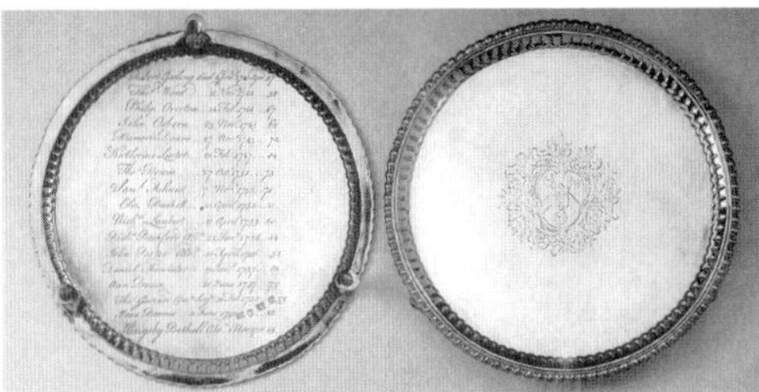

A pair of tontine silver salvers, by Ebenezer Coker, with gadrooned rims, the centres engraved with rococo armorial cartouches, the bases inscribed with a list of names, titles where appropriate, dates of death and their age at time of death, on three hoof feet, 9½in (24cm) diam, 33.25oz.
£2,700–3,000 ⚒ B

A tontine was a form of investment whereby a group of people each contributed a capital sum to a collective pool and derived an annuity for the rest of their lives in the form of interest payments. As the original investors gradually died off, the interest payments were reallocated among the survivors until only one was left, who at that point came into possession of the entire capital sum. Named after Lorenzo Tonti, an Italian financier who devised the scheme during the 17th century, they became increasingly popular, both as private and state-run ventures, in the 18th century. The eventual winding-up of private tontines was frequently marked by the commissioning of a piece of plate, in gold or silver, inscribed with all the names and dates of death of the members of the scheme.

A silver waiter, by Martin & Hall, on three claw-and-ball feet, London 1863, 8¼in (21cm) diam, 9.5oz.
£130–160 ⚒ CGC

A silver salver, by William Adams, with engraved monogram, New York 1829–59, 13in (33cm) wide, 23.5oz.
£550–600 ⚒ WcH

Sauce & Cream Boats

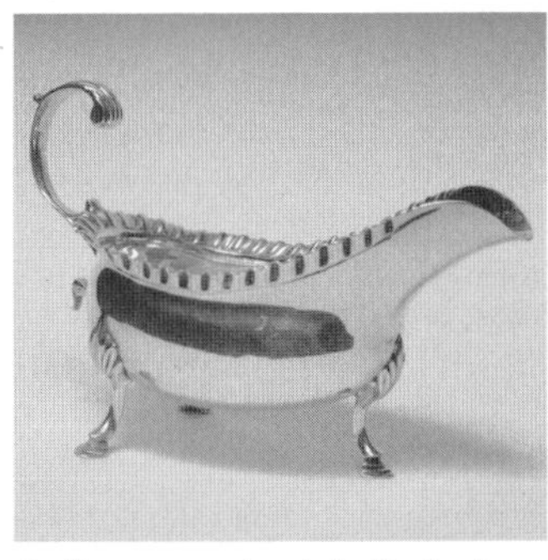

A silver cream boat, by Benjamin Mordecai, 1779, 6in (15cm) wide.
£500–565 ⊞ PAY

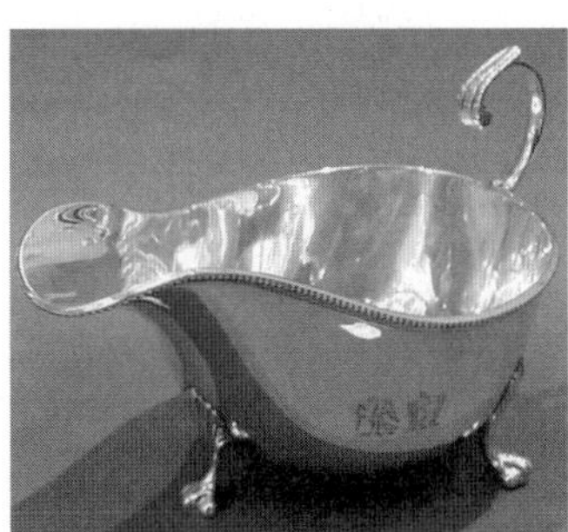

A pair of silver sauce boats, by Horace Woodward & Co, London 1907, 6¼in (16cm) high.
£600–650 ⊞ BEX

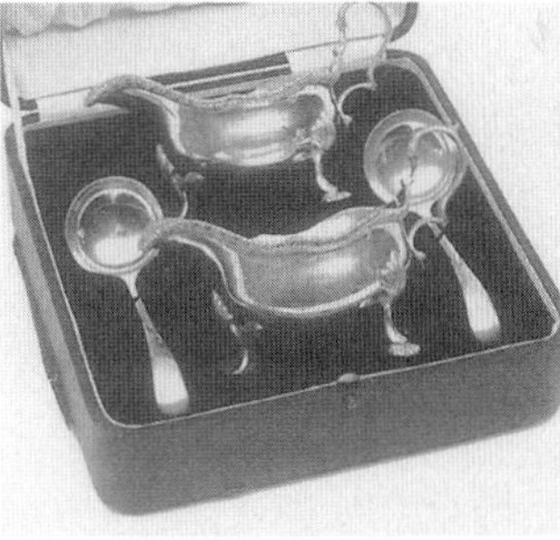

A pair of silver sauce boats, by J. Ramsay, with gadrooned edging and double scroll handles, Sheffield 1929, 6½in (16.5cm) long, with a pair of Old English pattern sauce ladles by Thomas Bradbury, Sheffield 1929, 16oz, in a fitted case.
£500–600 ⚒ Bea(E)

Scent Bottles

A silver scent bottle, with scrolling foliage decoration, maker's mark 'S.B. & S.', c1890, 4½in (11.5cm) high.
£300–350 ⊞ LBr

◄ **A silver-mounted cut-glass scent bottle,** with screw-on cover, Birmingham 1899, 4¾in (12cm) high.
£80–100 ⚒ DMC

A silver-mounted cut-glass scent bottle, with embossed top, London 1901, 3½in (9cm) high.
£65–80 ⚒ WBH

Serving Implements

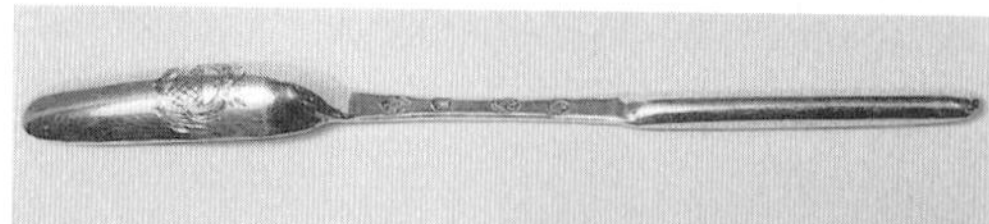

◄ **A silver marrow scoop,** by C. Skinner, Dublin 1759, 9in (23cm) long.
£350–400 WELD

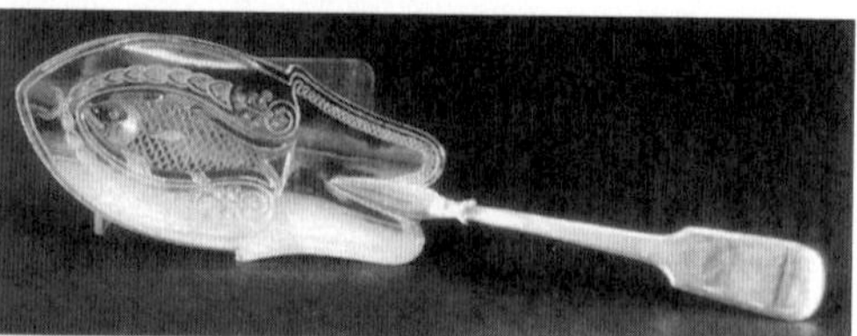

► **A silver Fiddle pattern fish slice,** by William Brown, decorated with a chased and pierced fish, London 1822, 12in (30.5cm) long, 4.5oz.
£200–240 WL

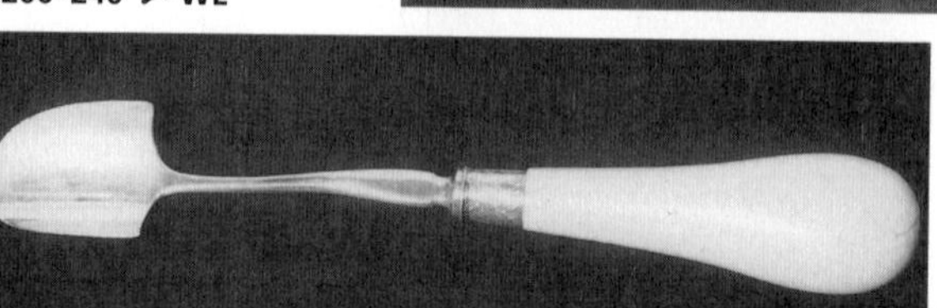

◄ **A silver stilton scoop,** by A. Taylor, with ivory handle, Birmingham 1865, 9in (23cm) long.
£350–400 SHa

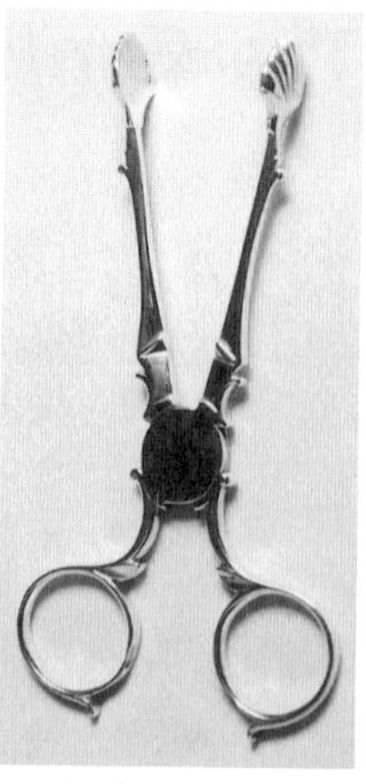

A pair of silver sugar nips, by Richard Morrison, London c1768, 5in (12.5cm) long.
£350–400 BEX

Snuff Boxes

A silver snuff box, niello-decorated with two classical scenes, inscribed Raguses, Neapol, Italian, c1744, 3in (7.5cm) wide.
£380–475 G(L)

A silver-mounted shell snuff box, with scroll, shell and foliate decoration, initialled to one side, unmarked, 18thC, 2¾in (7cm) wide.
£170–200 Bea(E)

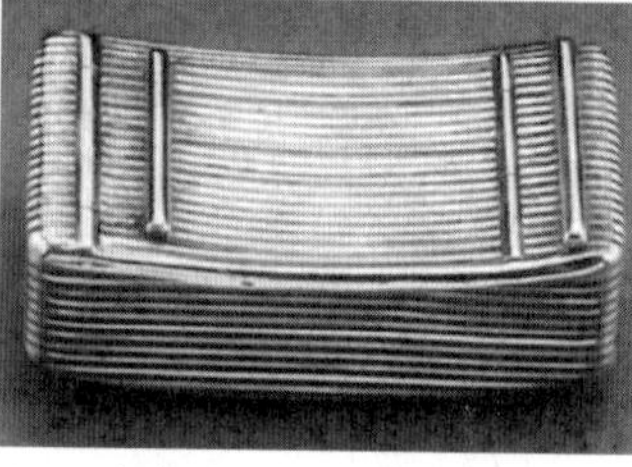

A reeded silver double snuff box, by T. & Co, Birmingham 1807, 2½in (6.5cm) wide.
£400–450 S(O)

◄ **A niello-decorated silver snuff box,** with cheroot cutter, French, c1870, 2½in (6.5cm) wide.
£600–650 BEX

A niello-decorated silver snuff box, Russian, St Petersburg c1882, 3in (7.5cm) wide.
£750–850 SHa

Table Bells

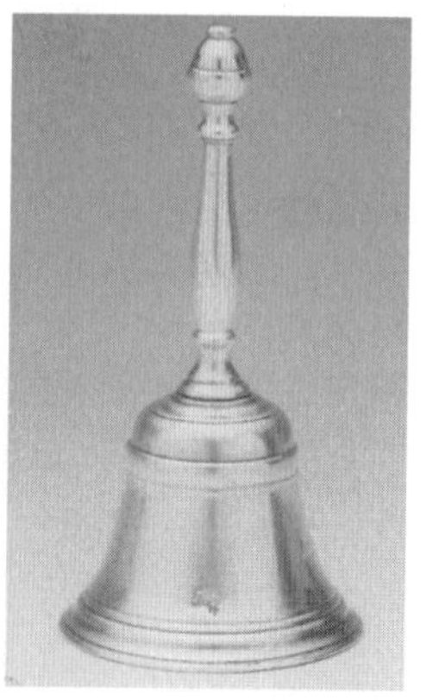

◄ **A silver table bell,** by Robert Calderwood, with acorn-style knop, Dublin c1745, 4½in (11.5cm) high, 4.75oz.
£2,500–2,850 NS

► **A silver table bell,** by Hayne & Cater, engraved with foliate scrolls, crested, 1863, 6in (15cm) high.
£350–450 B(WM)

A silver table bell, pierced with figures among scrolling foliage, with brass liner, London 1890, 4in (10cm) high.
£450–550 AH

SILVER

Tea Canisters

An embossed silver tea canister, by Henry Brind, engraved with a crest and initials, London 1769–70, 5¾in (14.5cm) high, 10.25oz.
£2,500–2,750 ⊞ NS

A silver tea canister, by Hendrik Buysen, with beaded borders and hinged cover, with keys, Dutch, Amsterdam 1789, 3½in (9cm) high, 10.5oz.
£475–575 ⚒ S(Am)

A silver tea caddy, by Henry Charles Freeman, with George II-style sliding top, London 1893, 5¼in (13.5cm) high, 5oz.
£200–250 ⚒ DN

Tea Glass Holders

A silver tea-glass holder, by Gustav Klingert, Russian, Moscow 1896, 3in (7.5cm) high.
£340–375 ⊞ SHa

A silver tea-glass holder, by Grachev Bros, with silver-gilt interior, Russian, St Petersburg 1896–1908, 3in (7.5cm) high.
£1,200–1,350 ⊞ MIR

A silver tea-glass holder, by Pavel Ovchinnikov, with a reeded leaf-chased handle, the bowl chased in high relief with floral swags and cartouches on a diaper ground, Russian, St Petersburg 1850–75, 2¼in (5.5cm) high, with an acid-etched glass beaker, in a fitted case.
£200–250 ⚒ DN

Toast Racks

A silver toast rack, by Aldrige and Green, London 1774, 7½in (19cm) wide.
£525–575 ⚒ S(O)

A silver toast rack, by Naphtali Hart, London 1814, 6in (15cm) wide.
£140–175 ⚒ GAK

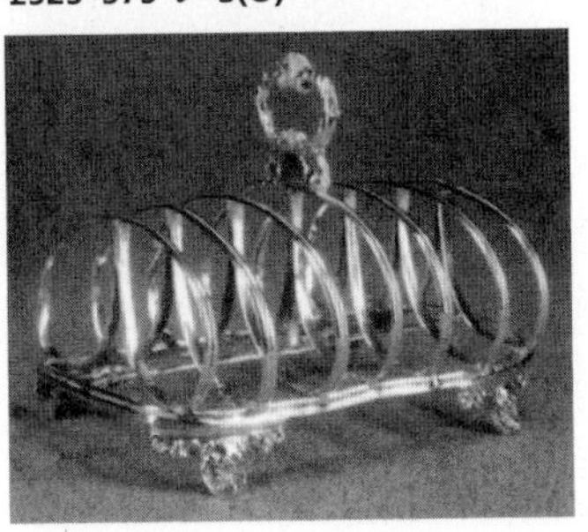

◄ **A silver toast rack,** with a shell and scroll handle and shell and scroll bracket feet, maker's mark 'J.E.', London 1844, 6¾in (17cm) wide, 9oz.
£200–250 ⚒ Bon

A set of six silver-gilt toast racks, by Risler and Carré, with wreath handle, French, Paris c1880, 2½in (6.5cm) wide, 27oz.
£900–1,000 ⚒ S(O)

LOCATE THE SOURCE
The source of each illustration in Miller's can be found by checking the code letters below each caption with the Key to Illustrations, pages 794–800.

Vases

◄ **A silver Warwick Vase,** by Rundell, Bridge & Rundell, the handles in the shape of entwined branches with acanthus decoration, the sides with chased masks of the Green Gods, the base with presentation inscription, London 1768, 15in (38cm) wide.
£11,000–14,000 TRM
The original marble Warwick Vase dates from the 2ndC AD and was excavated in Italy in 1770. It was eventually sold to the then Earl of Warwick, hence the name. It is now in the Burrell Collection in Glasgow.

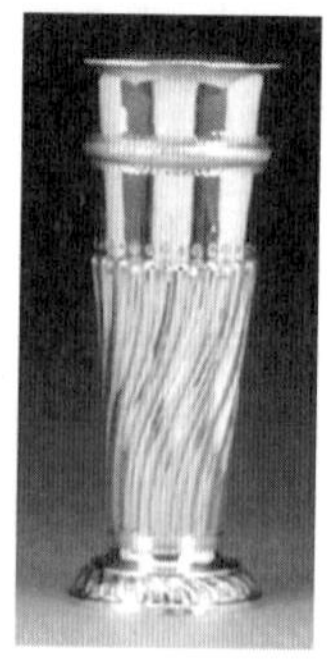

A silver vase, by Hawksworth, Eyre & Co, the gadrooned girdle with stylized punched foliate decoration, the body with swirl-fluted decoration, London 1896, 10in (25.5cm) high, 22oz.
£425–525
Bon

Insurance values

Always insure your valuable antiques for the cost of replacing them with similar items, regardless of the original price paid. Both dealers and auctioneers can provide a valuation service for a fee.

► **A pair of silver vases,** with frilled rims and feet, with applied cast floral decoration, London 1901, 8¼in (21cm) high.
£300–375
WiLP

Vesta Cases

◄ **A silver-gilt combination vesta case, snuff box and wick holder,** by Thomas William Dee, engine-turned, with central crested and monogrammed medallion and slide opening to the base, 1862, 2½in (6.5cm) wide.
£350–450
B(WM)

A silver vesta case, with engine-turned decoration, Birmingham 1907, 2in (5cm) wide.
£75–90 G(L)

A silver vesta case, the front enamelled with primroses, in shades of yellow, orange and green, maker's mark 'W.N.', Birmingham 1885, 2¼in (5.5cm) high.
£200–250 B(WM)

Vinaigrettes

A silver vinaigrette, by Samuel Pemberton, Birmingham 1811, 1½in (4cm) wide.
£375–425 BEX

A silver-gilt vinaigrette, by W.G., in the shape of a book, engraved with foliate designs, the interior fitted with a pierced gilt grille, Birmingham 1842, 1¾in (4.5cm) wide.
£320–400 GAK

A silver vinaigrette, modelled as a book, c1832, 1½in (4cm) wide.
£120–140 G(L)

Miller's is a price GUIDE not a price LIST

A silver and agate vinaigrette, by George Jamieson, Scottish, Aberdeen 1880, 2¼in (5.5cm) high.
£4,275–4,750 NS
The vendor has never seen another agate vinaigrette from a provincial Scottish silversmith.

SILVER

Silver Plate

For an item to be plated rather than silver has always been to brand it as something of a Cinderella. Compared with its hallmarked counterpart, a piece of plate is seen to be something inferior. This is definitely not so.

Plating falls into two main categories. Sheffield plate utilizes copper and silver fused together in the right proportions, approximately one part silver to 12 of copper, which is rolled into sheets and fashioned. Electroplate involves manufacture in a base metal, usually nickel, which is then silver-plated by electrolysis, polished and finished.

In the past, when labour was a smaller proportion of manufacturing costs, the same attention could be given to making pieces of equivalent quality but using less expensive materials. This is obvious in the case of Sheffield plate, where much effort was taken to conceal the base copper. An indication of this is the need to conceal the exposed edge beneath a thin silver cap. In order to hide the copper visible on the underneath the copper was sometimes double-plated. However, many items such as trays and warming dishes had the copper concealed by the means of tinning with solder.

Victorian electroplate was, at its best, quite as good and made in the same way as its equivalent in silver. It does, however, have a poor relation in the form of EPBM (electroplated Britannia metal). This is a pewter-like soft alloy, composed mainly of zinc and antimony and therefore easier to work. However it does not take plating well, is inclined to corrode and is best avoided unless particularly attractive.

In general when selecting plate look for high quality and any unusual items. Avoid pieces that are damaged or worn, particularly in the case of Sheffield plate, which cannot be replated without loss of its integrity. Electroplated pieces, however, can of course be re-electroplated and polished, providing that this is done with care.

Elkington were among the pioneers of the electroplating process and the quality of their wares is superb, with particularly fine engraving. They always marked their pieces including a series of letters or numbers giving the date of manufacture. Other comparable makers are Martin Hall, Walker and Hall and Mappin Brothers, later Mappin & Webb. Among the best of their productions were tea and coffee sets, unfashionable and inexpensive today but worth collecting as the variety is almost infinite.

Items of plate do not have the same appeal as silver but there are many small articles including sets of servers and other cutlery, waiters and cruets that show great originality of design. It is high time that these articles were appreciated for what they are and the craftmanship that they represent.

Hugh Gregory

A late Victorian silver-plated biscuit box, by Daniel and Arter, with electro-chased bands of foliage, the cartouche with initial, the hinged cover with a finial in the form of a seated figure of a Turk, 6¾in (17cm) high.
£120–150 WW

A silver plate and wood brandy barrel, c1910, 9in (23cm) high.
£450–500 CoHA

A Victorian silver-plated butter box, modelled as a straw boater with the lift-off lid as the crown of the hat, kite registration mark, 8¼in (21cm) diam.
£400–450 CGC

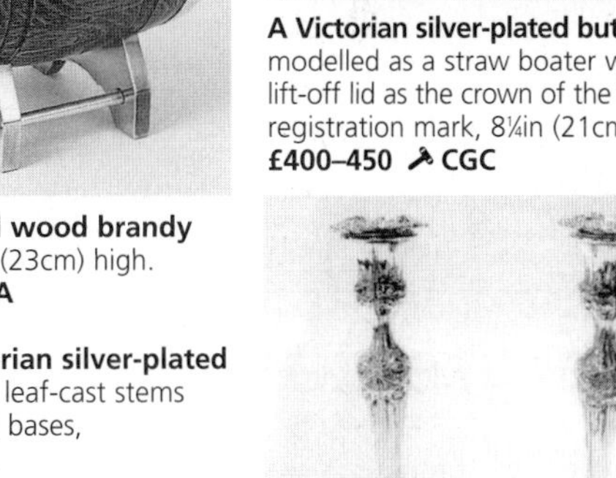

► **A pair of Victorian silver-plated candlesticks,** with leaf-cast stems and scroll-moulded bases, 10¼in (26cm) high.
£100–125 LFA

A pair of Sheffield plate candlesticks, with foliate-patterned stems, c1790, 12in (30.5cm) high.
£150–180 F&C

A set of four Sheffield plate candlesticks, each with a telescopic stem, c1830, 10½in (26.5cm) high, extended.
£700–800 NOA

Marks

Makers of old Sheffield plate occasionally marked their ware, particularly those such as Matthew Boulton and Mappin Brothers, each of whom used a mark depicting a sun; these can be confused. The absence of a mark on Old Sheffield however is of no disadvantage as some of the finest pieces are unmarked.

A pair of silver-plated centrepieces, with frosted glass vases and dishes supported on a base of three laden camels on a platform, on three anthemion and scroll bracket feet, monogrammed and stamped with registration mark for 2 March 1872, 19in (48.5cm) high.
£1,100–1,300 ⚒ P(Ba)

A silver-plated charger, the centre embossed with allegorical scenes featuring a figure of Mars, bordered by panels depicting Abondantia, Inertia, Pax and Bellum, the outer frame featuring the continents, 1875–1900, 18½in (47cm) diam.
£350–450 ⚒ P(NW)

A Sheffield plate coffee pot, embossed with foliate decoration, with applied foliate rim and wooden handle, 1812–30, 11in (28cm) high.
£100–120 ⚒ GAK

A silver-plated moustache cup and saucer, c1930, 2¼in (5.5cm) high.
£100–115 ⊞ MLa

A Sheffield plate cruet stand, the bottle holders with reeded and pierced decoration, with eight matched silver-mounted cut-glass bottles, c1800, 15in (38cm) wide.
£350–425 ⚒ Bon

◀ **A silver-plated cruet,** by Reed and Barton, the stem terminating in a loop handle with two human busts, with two cut-glass bottles with silver-plated caps, American, late 19thC, 13½in (34.5cm) high.
£60–75 ⚒ S(Am)

A suite of silver-plated cutlery, for 12 settings, two salt spoons and a mustard spoon missing, early 20thC, in an oak canteen.
£600–750 ⚒ TRM

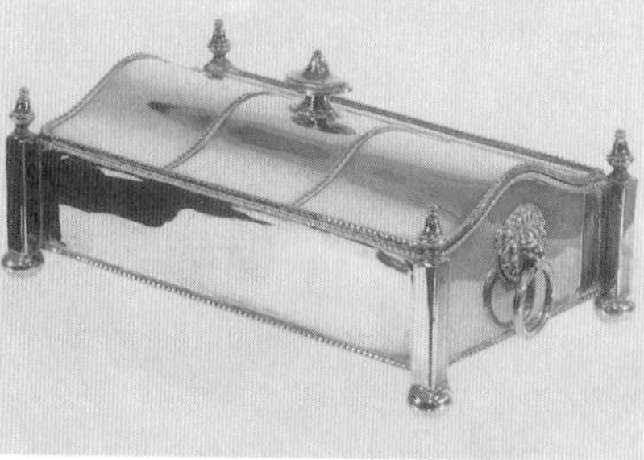

A Sheffield plate desk stand, with beaded edging and lion mask ring handles, the interior with two cut-glass ink bottles flanking a recessed compartment with hinged lid, early 19thC, 8in (20.5cm) wide.
£250–300 ⚒ AH

A silver-plated revolving breakfast dish, the cover engraved with floral strapwork, pierced swag and ram's mask supports and feet, with liner and pierced drainer, c1870, 13½in (34.5cm) wide.
£200–225 ⚒ N

A Victorian silver-plated egg boiler, with burner, 9in (23cm) high.
£45–60 ⚒ WBH

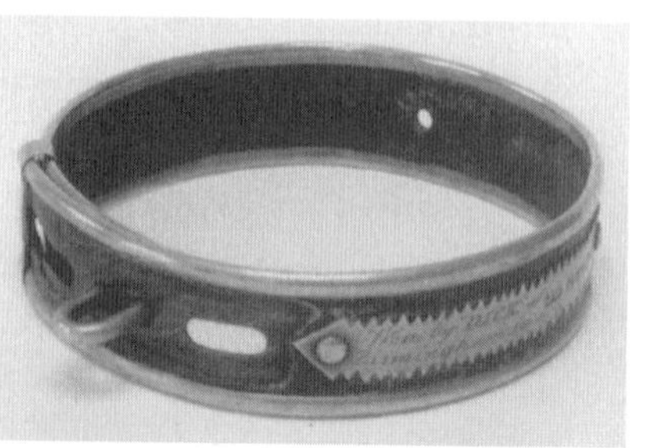

A silver plate and leather dog collar, with plaque inscribed 'Won by "Dick" at Birmingham, in a sweepstake, 12 rats each, dogs of all weight, Nov. 10.1852', mid-19thC, 3¾in (9.5cm) diam.
£850–1,000 ⚒ LFA

A Victorian silver-plated hot water jug, with ribbed foot, girdle and cover, fitted with an insulated scroll handle, 8in (20.5cm) high.
£100–120 ⚒ CGC

A silver-plated cake stand, with chased and embossed edge and mirrored centre, late 19thC, 15in (38cm) diam.
£350–425 GAK

◀ **A silver plate and glass pounce pot,** by Finnigans, modelled as a French bulldog, c1900, 5in (12.5cm) high.
£400–450 ChC

Miller's Compares

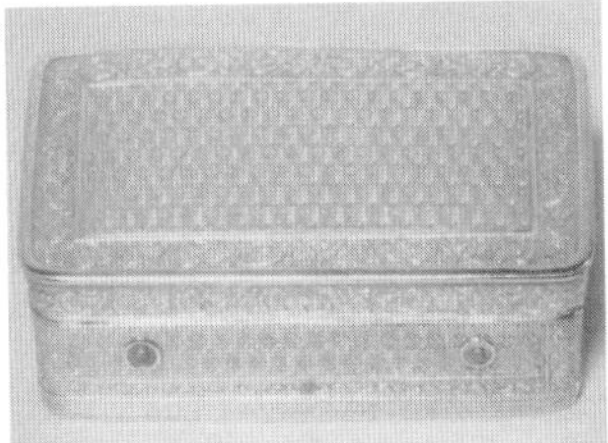

I. A gilt-plated musical snuff box, probably by Nicolas Lecoufle, playing two tunes, French, Paris 1809–19, 3½in (9cm) wide.
£800–900 S(O)

II. A gilt-plated snuff box, by L. Baudin, engine-turned within foliate borders, French, Paris 1809–19, 3¼in (8.5cm) wide.
£400–500 S(O)

Item I is a more substantial piece than Item II, which is quite light, although the exterior of Item II is in better condition. However, the most desirable feature of Item I is the fact that it is a musical snuff box, which is always of more interest to collectors than a plain example such as Item II. Moreover, the value of such pieces will increase with the number of tunes they play.

A silver-plated tea urn, sugar basin and cream jug, embossed with fruit and a repeating floral band, with foliage and reeding to the base, 19thC, 20in (51cm) high.
£300–350 Mit

A Sheffield plate tantalus, the reeded wirework frame containing three contemporary cut-glass decanters and stoppers, 1837–50, 11½in (29cm) high.
£250–300 CGC

A silver-plated toast rack, c1910, 5in (12.5cm) wide.
£40–45 ASAA

A silver-plated tureen, decorated in relief with thistles and flowers, stamped 'W & Hall', early 20thC, 11½in (29cm) diam.
£100–125 PFK

A four-piece silver-plated tea and coffee service, with beaded edging and engraved foliate decoration, late 19thC.
£250–300 Bea(E)

A pair of Sheffield-plated wine coolers, c1825, 9in (23cm) diam.
£2,200–2,550 CAT

▶ **A silver-plated soup tureen and cover,** with flower and scroll cast border, 19thC, 16½in (42cm) wide.
£425–525 LFA

A silver-plated tray, with engraved foliate scrolls, hatched panels and a raised gadrooned border interspersed with shell foliage sprays, with gadroon shell-decorated handles, c1900, 28½in (72.5cm) wide.
£140–180 WW

Wine Antiques

A shaft and globe wine bottle, in deep olive green glass, 18thC, 7in (18cm) high.
£200–225 ⚒ CGC

An octagonal-bodied wine bottle, in deep olive green glass, 1780–1800, 9¼in (23.5cm) high.
£320–400 ⚒ BBR

A cylinder wine bottle, with the seal of the Earl of Mount Edgecombe of Cornwall, c1880, 11in (28cm) high.
£135–150 ⊞ JHa

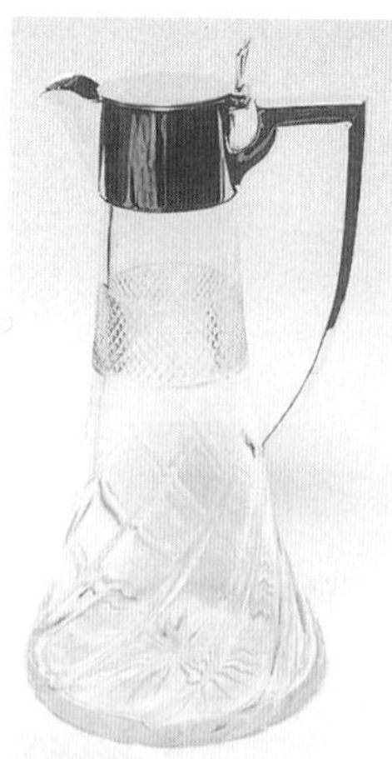

A silver-mounted claret jug, with a cut- and pressed-glass body, Birmingham 1908, 10in (25.5cm) high.
£650–750 ⊞ GLa

A silver travelling cocktail shaker, by Meriden Britannia Co, with three beakers, measurer, condiment box and leather case, American, Connecticut, c1900, case 5¼in (13.5cm) high.
£300–375 ⚒ S

A pair of silver wine coasters, by Hester Bateman, with pierced and bright-cut decoration, London 1786, 5in (12.5cm) diam.
£6,750–7,500 ⊞ TSC

A copper and brass wine cooler, c1900, 14in (35.5cm) diam.
£200–220 ⊞ PICA

Miller's is a price GUIDE not a price LIST

l. A double-action corkscrew, with bone handle and brass barrel, the applied plaque with a royal coat-of-arms with maker's name 'Thomason & Son*Ne Plus Ultra', c1810, 7in (18cm) long.
£150–200

r. A corkscrew, named 'The King Patent 6064', 1904 patent, 6¾in (17cm) long.
£70–90 ⊞ CS

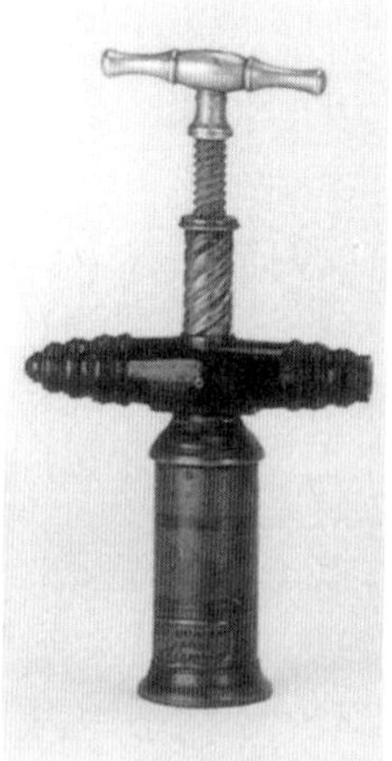

A Thomason Variant-style corkscrew, the turned brass barrel with applied label marked 'Josh. Rodgers & Sons Sheffield,' the main handle of turned *lignum vitae*, the upper handle of plated metal, brush missing, early 19thC, 7in (18cm) long.
£580–725 ⚒ DN

◀ **A narrow rack corkscrew,** with a bone handle and metal side handle, the barrel stamped 'Farrow & Jackson', bone handle cracked, 19thC, 6in (15cm) long.
£260–325 ⚒ P(B)

A steel folding bow corkscrew, with five tools, mid-19thC, 3in (7.5cm) long.
£200–220 ⊞ CAL

A Wulfruma steel corkscrew, German, 19thC, 7in (18cm) long.
£90–100 ⊞ JOL

A silver wine funnel with strainer, the funnel cast and engraved with a band of roses, slight tear to strainer, London 1822, 5½in (14cm) long.
£550–700 TMA

A *tastevin*, by R.B., the side engraved 'M. Gueren', French, Nantes c1760, 3¼in (8.5cm) wide.
£1,200–1,350 NS

A late Victorian silver-plated tantalus, with a biscuit box, fitted with two later decanters, 19in (48.5cm) wide.
£620–775 G(L)

► **An Edwardian oak tantalus,** with pierced brass mounts, the hinged twin flaps enclosing a divided interior above a divided drawer, fitted with three glass decanters, 14¾in (37.5cm) wide.
£260–325 DMC

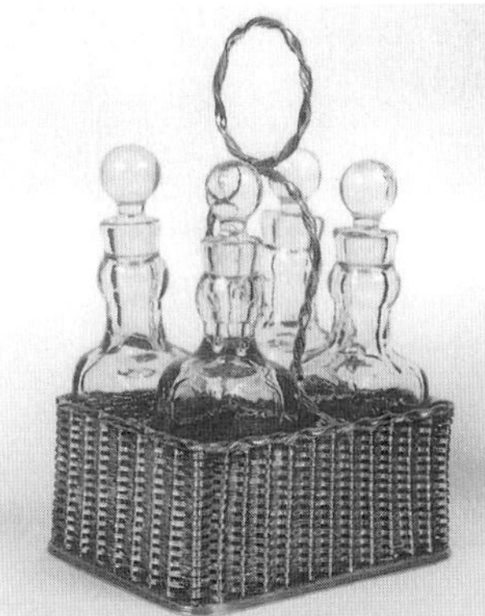

A silver-plated liqueur bottle holder, c1920, 5in (12.5cm) wide.
£200–220 CoHA

► **A George III silver punch strainer,** possibly by Burrage Davenport, London 1780, 6½in (16.5cm) wide.
£275–350 WcH

► **A cast silver wine label,** by Charles Reily and George Storer, in the shape of a vine leaf, 1849, 3¼in (8.5cm) wide.
£120–150 B(WM)

A mahogany cellaret, with a fall-front, 19thC, 18in (45.5cm) wide.
£700–900 LFA

A pair of brown glass spirit bottles, for rum and brandy, in a silver-plated holder, 19thC, 12½in (32cm) high.
£220–275 DA

A late George III mahogany table cellaret, fitted with six square-section spirit bottles, one damaged, 9in (23cm) wide.
£140–175 L

A burr-cedar, tulipwood and sycamore liqueur cabinet, French, c1850, 14in (35.5cm) wide.
£2,200–2,600 MB

A silver spirit flask, by George Unite, with screw-on cap and pull-off base, engraved with geometric decoration and two cartouches, Birmingham 1868, 6in (15cm) high.
£320–360 B

Clocks
British Bracket, Table & Mantel Clocks

An ebonized and gilt basket-top table clock, by Samuel Watson, Coventry, the five-ringed pillar movement with later twin fusee and chain, verge escapement, restored trains, formerly with inside rack, striking altered and striking on a bell, on later bun feet, c1680 and later, 13in (33cm) high.
£3,500–4,500 ⚒ Bon
Samuel Watson was a noted maker, mathematician and designer of many complicated devices, rather than just a clock maker. He worked in Coventry from c1680 and moved to Long Acre, London, c1690.

An ebonized bracket clock, by William Goffe, London, with inlaid brass stringing and brass mounts, two-train fusee movement, with an oak bracket, early 19thC, 17in (43cm) high.
£1,350–1,700 ⚒ Mit

When sold at auction, clocks have sometimes undergone alterations to their movements, or are in unrestored condition, which may be reflected in the prices realized.

◄ An ebonized bracket clock, by John Pepys, London, with brass dial and strike/silent dial, the five-pillar movement with original verge escapement striking on a bell, c1740, 17¾in (45cm) high.
£3,500–4,500 ⚒ Bri

A red japanned chiming table clock, by John Whitehurst, Derby, with brass dial, the two-train fusee and chain movement with verge escapement chiming the quarters on six bells and the hour on a seventh bell, decorated overall with gilt chinoiserie, c1765, 19in (48.5cm) high.
£16,000–20,000 ⚒ S
John Whitehurst, the most famous member of a celebrated clockmaking family, established his business at Derby in 1736. He was an innovative maker who experimented with different forms of clock mechanism, though he showed no interest in protecting any of his inventions and no patent application is filed at the Patent's Office under his name. His interests included astronomy and he published many papers on the subject. He died in 1788 and the business was continued by his nephew, also John, until 1855, when the Whitehurst line became extinct and the firm was purchased by William Roskell of Liverpool.

A George III mahogany bracket clock, by John Crane, Bromsgrove, the twin fusee movement with anchor escapement, on brass ball feet, 20in (51cm) high.
£2,300–3,000 ⚒ G(L)

A brass-mounted mahogany table clock, by Daniel Ray, Battle, the silvered-brass dial with silent/strike dial, the eight-day double fusee movement with verge escapement striking and repeating the hours on a bell, c1800, 15in (38cm) high excluding handle.
£9,000–9,850 ⊞ PAO

CLOCKS

A Regency mahogany, brass-inlaid and brass-mounted bracket clock, by Broderick, Spalding, the later dial with strike/silent and chime/silent subsidiary dials, with an eight-day chiming movement, 23½in (59.5cm) high.
£3,200–4,000 M

► **A Regency brass-mounted mahogany bracket clock,** by Thwaites and Reed, Clerkenwell, London, with double fusee movement, 19in (48.5cm) high.
£400–500 GH

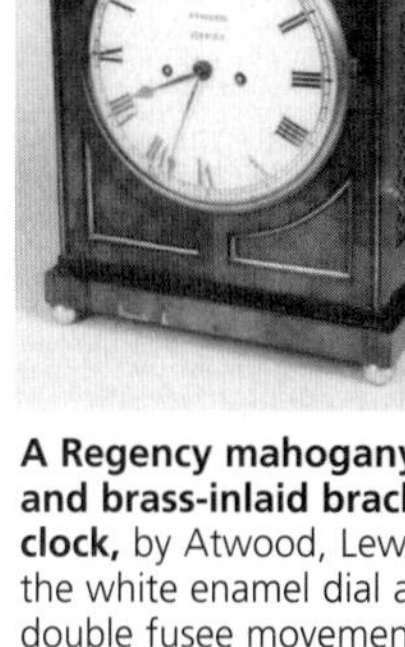

A Regency mahogany and brass-inlaid bracket clock, by Atwood, Lewes, the white enamel dial and double fusee movement striking on a bell, 18½in (47cm) high.
£1,300–1,600 HYD

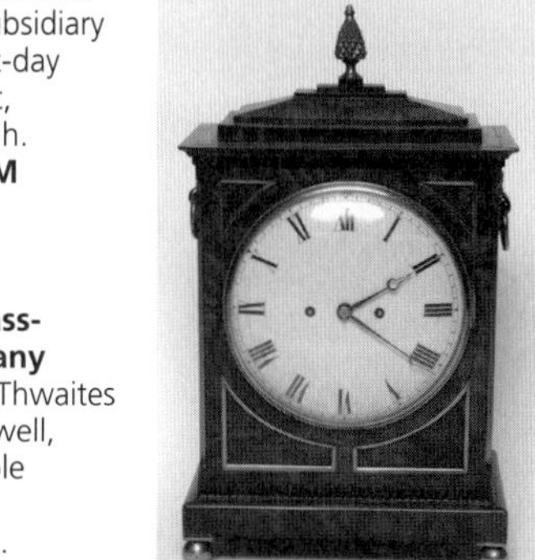

A Regency mahogany and brass-inlaid bracket clock, the painted dial with strike/silent lever, the twin gut fusee movement with anchor escapement striking on a bell, with associated mahogany and brass-inlaid bracket, 33¾in (85.5cm) high.
£2,000–2,400 B

A brass-mounted mahogany table/bracket clock, by Hardeman & Son, Bridge, the white dial with strike/silent feature, the eight-day double fusee movement with anchor escapement striking the hours on a bell with repeat, the pendulum with fine regulator adjustment, c1815, 16½in (42cm) high excluding finial.
£5,750–6,250 PAO

A Regency mahogany and brass-mounted lancet mantel clock, with painted dial, 20in (51cm) high.
£1,000–1,200 G(L)

A brass-inlaid mahogany mantel clock, by Haley, London, with a painted dial, the eight-day movement with anchor escapement, c1820, 16½in (42cm) high.
£2,400–3,000 TEN

A bronze table clock, with silvered dial, the five-pillar two-train and trip repeating fusee movement with anchor escapement striking on a bell, c1835, 15¾in (40cm) high.
£500–600 S(O)

◄ **A Turkish Market bracket clock,** by Maximilian Borrell, with a painted dial, the two-train movement striking on a bell, in a brass-inlaid case, c1835, 17¼in (44cm) high.
£2,000–2,500 SHSY

CLOCKS

A mahogany bracket clock, by James McCabe, Royal Exchange, London, the 8in replacement silvered dial with strike/silent dial to the arch, the triple fusee movement striking on eight bells, sold with original white dial, 19thC, 20½in (52cm) high.
£2,700–3,500 ⚒ GH

A brass-mounted mahogany watchman's timepiece, with silvered dial, the fusee and chain movement with anchor escapement and half-hour passing strike on a bell, c1850, 14¾in (37.5cm) high.
£700–900 ⚒ S(O)

An ebony and silver-mounted desk clock and inkstand, the glass and silver-lidded bottles marked for Robert Garrard, the enamel dial marked 'James Hux 20 Down St Piccadilly', with drum gong-striking movement, dial cracked, dated 1852, 13½in (34.5cm) high.
£700–900 ⚒ CGC

A Victorian mahogany Westminster bracket clock, the brass dial with subsidiary dials for chime/silent, chime selection and regulation, 27in (68.5cm) high.
£2,300–3,000 ⚒ LT

► A Victorian brass and gilt-metal-mounted ebonized mantel clock, by Harry Le Moine, Blackburn, with brass dial and selection dials, with anchor escapement striking and chiming on nine gongs, 28¾in (73cm) high.
£1,400–1,700 ⚒ Bea(E)

◄ A mahogany 18thC-style bracket clock, the dial with 'chime/silent' and 'Westminster/chime on eight bells', subsidiary dials, the triple-train movement with coil gongs and eight bells, the case with chased gilt-brass mounts, c1886, 17in (43cm) high.
£4,000–5,000 ⚒ LAY

CLOCKS

A gilt-metal-mounted walnut bracket clock, with chime/silent and slow/fast dials, with matching bracket, late 19thC, 27½in (70cm) high.
£3,000–3,750 GAK

A bracket clock, the figured walnut case carved with roses and heraldic shields and enclosing a white dial, with double fusee movement, late 19thC, 17½in (44.5cm) high.
£2,000–2,500 GH

► **A silver clock,** by William Comyns, London 1903, 12½in (32cm) high.
£600–750 N

◄ **A gilt-metal-mounted rosewood and inlaid Westminster chiming table clock,** the brass dial with dials for chime/silent, regulation and Westminster chimes/chime on eight bells, the eight-day three-train fusee movement with anchor escapement, c1900, 21½in (54.5cm) high.
£1,800–2,250 DN

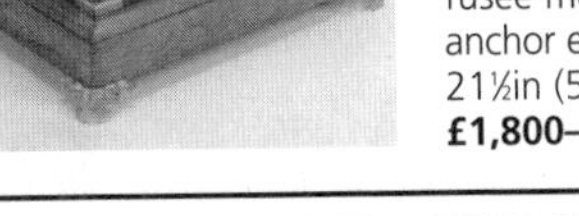

A late Victorian gilt-mounted and ebonized bracket clock, the eight-day triple fusee movement striking on a gong and nine bells, 18¼in (46.5cm) high.
£1,600–2,000 WilP

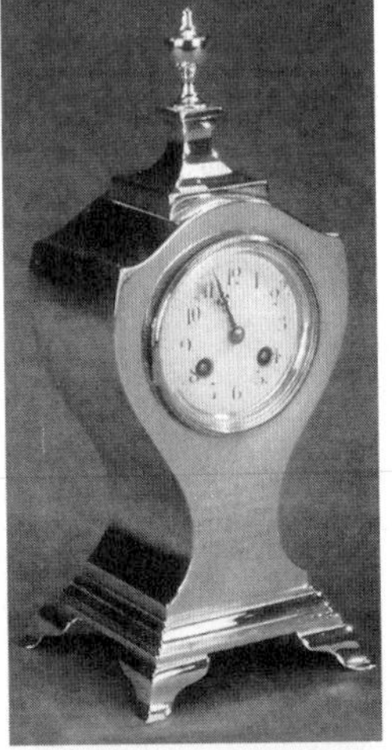

A German-style oak- and walnut-cased Bugler alarm clock, by Thomas Fattorini, Skipton, the brass spring-driven movement striking on a spiral gong, c1900, 19in (48.5cm) high.
£120–150 PFK

An Edwardian George III-style brass-mounted and ebony-strung mahogany bracket clock, by O. Jenkins, Nottingham, with enamelled dial and fusee movement, 16¼in (41.5cm) high.
£320–400 WL

Miller's is a price GUIDE not a price LIST

◄ **A mahogany Willis World clock,** with a painted dial indicating principal worldwide locations, with central 24-hour dial and subsidiary minutes dial, the eight-day movement with lever escapement, c1925, 13½in (34.5cm) high.
£700–900 S(O)

A burr-walnut eight-day mantel clock, retailed by Brights, Scarborough, painted with chinoiserie decoration, 1920s, 10in (25.5cm) wide.
£150–180 DD

CLOCKS

Continental Bracket, Table & Mantel Clocks

Over the past year, both British and Continental clocks have maintained their value and continue to rise, especially in the medium to higher price bracket. Moreover, there has been a significant rise in the prices attained for good quality 18th- and early 19th-century French examples with new collectors entering the field of Empire and earlier period clocks.

The variety of Continental clock designs available is enormous. For the mantelpiece, one could choose between a plain carriage clock and a decorative ormolu mantel clock; on the wall one could hang either an elegant Viennese regulator or an elaborate Louis XV rococo cartel clock.

In Europe, from the mid-17th century, France became the most important and prolific of the Continental clock producers. The casework of French clocks became far more elaborate than English ones. They were treated as works of art, their design involving the sculptor and artist, while their manufacture called upon cabinet maker, bronze caster, gilder, chaser and enameller. The movements were also of high quality, since many of the world's top horologists were French.

During the reign of Louis XIV (1643–1715), table and bracket clocks tended to be quite rectangular in shape with vertical sides. The cases had a wooden carcass veneered with tortoiseshell inlaid with brass and other metals and applied with gilt mounts. This marquetry was developed by the important cabinet maker André-Charles Boulle (1643–1732) and is known as boullework. Towards the end of the reign, the case sides became more curved and the mounts more profuse. At this stage, the dial numerals were on separate enamel cartouches.

In the reign of Louis XV (1715–74) clock cases evolved into a more flamboyant rococo style with asymmetric flowing scrolls and shell shapes. Cases of porcelain or gilded bronze were also introduced, and from c1740 enamel dials started to be made in one piece.

Symmetry and elegance returned to clock design during the reign of Louis XVI (1774–92). Decorative features from Greek and Roman architecture were used and the integration of human and animal sculptures become popular. As well as bronze, unglazed or biscuit porcelain became fashionable, and marble was used extensively in mantel clock cases. This neo-classical style was also evident in the later Directoire and Empire periods.

After the Revolution, mantel clocks portraying scenes from everyday life were in demand. This reflected the new social structure as the tastes of the bourgeosie replaced those of the aristocracy.

Although some high quality and beautiful French clocks can be found that were produced later than c1830, many tend to be copies or 'in the style of' the earlier period clocks. **John Jillings**

CLOCKS

A gilt-bronze-mounted fruitwood table clock, by Kilian Geest, Vienna, the brass and silvered dial flanked by subsidiary dials, the lever movement striking the quarters on two bells, Austrian, 18thC, 25¾in (65.5cm) high.
£1,300–1,600 WW

A boulle mantel clock, by Gilbert, Paris, with an enamel dial, the movement with anchor escapement and outside countwheel striking on a bell, pull quarter repeat missing, French, 1700–50, 27in (68.5cm) high.
£1,800–2,200 B

◄ **An Empire gilt-bronze mantel clock,** by Jn. Jh. Hanser, Brussels, the movement with anchor escapement countwheel striking on a bell, the case surmounted by figures of Amor and Venus, Belgian, c1800, 16¼in (41.5cm) high.
£1,800–2,200 S(Am)

A silvered-bronze and marcasite mantel clock, with white enamel dial and skeleton movement, Russian, c1770, 7¼in (18.5cm) wide.
£14,000–18,000 S
Eighteenth century animal sculptural clocks are highly sought after. This rare and fine Russian example has an unusual silvered bronze case with marcasite decoration and is of a desirable size.

A gilt-bronze-mounted white marble mantel clock, by Gaston Jolly, Paris, the signed white enamel dial with inner concentric calendar ring, the twin barrel movement with verge escapement striking on a bell, c1790, 15¼in (38.5cm) high.
£12,000–14,000 JIL
This is a fine and original 18th-century mantel clock by a good maker with profuse ormolu mounts and original verge escapement.

◄ **A Directoire ormolu-mounted marble clock,** by Lamiral, the eight-day movement striking on a bell, French, c1800, 19¾in (50cm) high.
£6,000–6,750 GDO

An ebonized and gilt-brass-mounted bracket clock, by Jacob Gulda, Pressburg, the brass dial with enamel chapter ring and enamel subsidiaries, the brass four-pillar twin-train movement with verge escapement striking on two bells, on later ball feet, damaged, Hungarian, late 18thC, 17in (43cm) high.
£900–1,100 P(Ba)

A mahogany and alabaster portico mantel clock, the enamel dial with hairline cracks, the movement rack striking on a gong and with anchor escapement, with a mahogany and glass display case, Austrian, c1820, 19¾in (50cm) high.
£525–625 S(Am)

A white marble and gilt-bronze mantel clock, by François Barthet, Marseille, the eight-day twin barrel movement countwheel striking on a bell, French, c1810, 14¼in (36cm) high.
£6,000–8,000 JIL

An ormolu-mounted and patinated bronze Empire clock, by Hemon, Paris, the eight-day movement striking on a bell, French, c1815, 17¾in (45cm) high.
£3,800–4,250 GDO

Cross Reference
See Colour Review (page 412)

► **A gilt-bronze mantel clock,** French, 1815–30, 17in (43cm) wide.
£1,500–1,800 BERN

An Empire ormolu-mounted *tôle peinte* night projection timepiece, by Bofenschen, Paris, with white enamel dial, the backplate with a reverse dial, the back of the case with a magnifying lens, French, c1810, 21in (53.5cm) high.
£11,000–12,500 S(NY)
Bofenschein, recorded working in Paris as an *horloger-mécanicien* in the late 18th and early 19th centuries, was noted for his production of the night projection timepiece. This was operated by placing a small spirit lamp in the centre of the case in front of the reverse dial which was then magnified through the lens and projected onto a wall behind the clock.

An ormolu mantel clock, after a design by Thomire, modelled as Cupid Carrying Time, the eight-day movement striking the hours and half-hours on a bell, French, dated 1811, 15¾in (40cm) high.
£8,750–9,750 GDO

An ormolu mantel clock, by Pre Fen Rouchouze, Bordeaux, with white enamel dial, the eight-day movement with silk-suspended pendulum and countwheel striking on a bell, French, c1815, 12¼in (31cm) high.
£6,500–7,500 JIL

A patinated bronze and ormolu automaton water clock, c1820, 11¾in (30cm) high.
£3,000–3,250 GDO
The water automaton is run by a separate movement in the base and can be set off at will. The water in the fountain is solid silver.

Ormolu (fire-gilded or mercury-gilded bronze)

In France the material used most commonly for clock cases from about 1730 was cast bronze, which was finely finished by the chasers and gilders. After the many constituent parts of a clock case had been cast they were worked on by the chaser (*ciseleur*). Using many different tools, including files and chisels, he was able to create different surface textures in preparation for the gilding process.

Each casting was heated and dipped in various chemical solutions before being coated with an amalgam of mercury and 24 carat ground gold (*or moulu* in French giving us ormolu). The coated pieces were then held over fire to make the mercury evapourate, leaving the deposited gold. This coating and firing procedure was repeated up to four times for the highest quality gilding. Due to the toxic effects of the mercury during the firing process, fire gilding became prohibited and therefore cannot be renewed today.

In the final stage an agate-tipped tool was used to polish (or burnish) selected areas of the gilded bronze thus 'highlighting' the details.

Since ormolu can easily be damaged by incorrect cleaning, this should always be left to a professional.

CLOCKS

A patinated bronze and ormolu clock, by Guyerdet, flanked by Puck from *A Midsummer Night's Dream*, the eight-day movement striking on a bell, French, 1825–30, 15¾in (40cm) high.
£3,375–3,750 ⊞ GDO

A white marble and ormolu clock, the ball timepiece supported by two cherubs standing on a garland-decorated plinth, French, 19thC, 16½in (42cm) high.
£800–1,000 ⚒ FHF

A striking mantel clock, in a gilt-metal- and cloisonné-decorated case, French, 19thC, 13in (33cm) high.
£180–225 ⚒ WilP

► **A gilt-bronze Louis XV rococo-style mantel clock,** French, c1840, 11¼in (28.5cm) high.
£3,000–4,000 ⊞ JIL

An ormolu and bronze mantel clock, by Richond, Paris, surmounted by a cavalier on horseback, 1825–50, 21½in (54.5cm) high.
£950–1,200 ⚒ WL

A brass mantel clock, flanked by a figure of a maiden, with a giltwood socle, French, 19thC, 18in (45.5cm) high.
£160–200 ⚒ GAK

An ormolu and porcelain mantel clock, French, 19thC, 13½in (34.5cm) high.
£500–625 ⚒ TRM

A white marble urn clock, the dial with engine-turned centre and white enamel chapter ring, the eight-day twin barrel movement with countwheel striking on a bell, c1830, 19½in (49.5cm) high.
£2,800–3,200 ⊞ JIL

A silver *grande sonnerie* striking and repeating musical mantel clock with alarm, by A. Oldbrich, Vienna, on an ebonized plinth base containing a single air musical movement, Austrian, mid-19thC, 17¾in (45cm) high.
£1,500–1,700 ⚒ B

CLOCKS

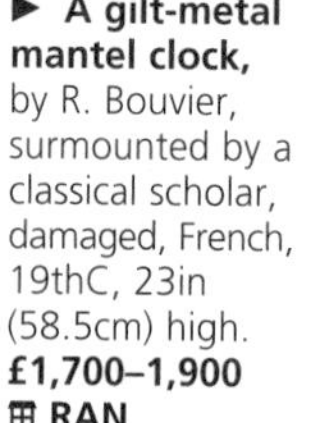

► **A gilt-metal mantel clock,** by R. Bouvier, surmounted by a classical scholar, damaged, French, 19thC, 23in (58.5cm) high.
£1,700–1,900 ⊞ RAN

A carved mahogany cuckoo clock, with bone hour chapters and hands, striking on a gong, German, Black Forest, 19thC, 19in (48.5cm) high.
£800–1,000 FHF

An ebonized portico clock, by Samuel Marti, the enamel dial inscribed 'Leroy à Paris', the eight-day movement striking on a bell, the crest and plinth with brass and polychrome inlay, mid-19thC, 19¾in (50cm) high.
£400–500 CGC

◀ **An ormolu Louis XV-style mantel clock,** with white enamelled dial, the eight-day movement striking on a bell, French, c1860, 14in (35.5cm) high.
£500–625 N

◀ **A carved beech mantel clock,** the case enclosing the French drum movement and surmounted by a pair of pheasants on a modelled ground with chicks below, German, Black Forest, 19thC, 23in (58.5cm) high.
£600–750 Bon

A mantel clock, by Henri Marc, Paris, with white enamel dial, the red boulle case with an eight-day movement striking on a bell, the plinth with chased brass moulding and cast feet, dial cracked and chipped, French, mid-19thC, 13in (33cm) high.
£350–450 WW

A gilt-brass mantel clock, by Popon, Paris, within a dark blue porcelain urn with a white enamel dial, the eight-day movement countwheel striking on a bell, c1850, 25½in (65cm) high.
£4,000–5,000 JIL

A black marble clock, by Potonié, Paris, the eight-day movement with visible escapement, c1865, 12in (30.5cm) high.
£550–625 PTh

A gilt-bronze portico clock, the enamel dial with date calendar above a pierced gilt-brass winged griffin apron, the movement with anchor escapement striking on a bell, French, 1850–1900, 15¾in (40cm) wide.
£500–625 WL

A gilt-bronze mantel clock, by Marti et Compagnie, the eight-day movement with outside countwheel striking on a bell, French, c1870, 22in (56cm) high.
£3,800–4,200 JIL

A gilt-brass and black slate Empire-style mantel clock, the black dial with brass hands, French, c1880, 19in (48.5cm) high.
£875–975 PTh

A patinated metal Louis XVI-style mantel clock, by Japy Fils, with enamel dial and two-train striking movement, on a black marble plinth, French, late 19thC, 17¾in (45cm) wide.
£2,200–2,750 ⚒ SK

A four-glass table clock, the enamel dial with a blue *champlevé* enamel centre and surround, the movement with Brocot escapement striking on a gong, French, c1890, 10in (25.5cm) high.
£750–950 ⚒ Bon

► A gilt-bronze and *champlevé* enamel mantel clock, by Japy Frères, with classical revival enamel decoration, French, c1900, 15¼in (38.5cm) high.
£900–1,150 ⚒ SK

A mantel clock, retailed by Conrad Felsing, Berlin, with two enamel dials, one with hour chapters, the other with day, date, month and phases of the moon behind a chased brass mask, the lever movement with a double-chamber brass mercury pendulum, French, late 19thC, 15in (38cm) high.
£3,700–4,500 ⚒ MEA

A rosewood mantel clock, by Raiter, with French eight-day cylinder platform movement, c1890, 7in (18cm) high.
£800–875 ⊞ PTh

An oak mantel clock, with brass dial and chime/silent and fast/slow dials, the three-train movement chiming and striking on gongs, German, late 19thC, 22in (56cm) high.
£900–1,100 ⚒ N

A gilt-brass four-glass mantel clock, with two-piece enamel dial, the eight-day movement with twin-pot mercury pendulum and Brocot escapement striking on a bell, c1890, 11½in (29cm) high.
£2,000–2,500 ⊞ JIL

◄ A cast gilt-brass eight-day mantel clock, by Japy Frères, with a white enamel face, French, late 19thC, 15in (38cm) high.
£550–650 ⚒ BLH

► A gilt-brass Japanese-style mantel clock, with faïence mounts and enamel dial, the case surmounted by a winged putto, the Japy Frères movement striking on a gong, French, c1895, 20in (51cm) high.
£900–1,100 ⚒ S(O)

A slate mantel clock, with painted landscape panels, French, late 19thC, 13½in (34.5cm) high.
£140–175 ⚒ G(L)

CLOCKS

An oak-cased musical and automaton mantel clock, by Junghans, with enamel dial, the 30-hour two-train open spring movement with anchor escapement, the music train connected to the automaton figure of a violin player causing him to play the instrument and tap his foot, German, c1895, 18¾in (47.5cm) high.
£2,500–3,000 S

A gilt-bronze-mounted walnut mantel clock, the eight-day movement striking the quarters on a gong, the backplate stamped 'Peerless', German, c1900, 17¾in (45cm) high.
£750–950 WW

A lacquered brass four-glass mantel clock, by Japy Frères, with enamel dial, the brass twin drum movement striking on a bell, French, early 20thC, 10in (25.5cm) high.
£400–500 P(Ba)

A mahogany bracket clock, with silvered chapter ring and eight-day striking movement, German, early 20thC, 11½in (29cm) high.
£170–200 GAK

A brass and cloisonné mantel clock, the gilt dial with a jasper ware panel to the centre, the French movement stamped 'RS', Continental, early 20thC, 17½in (44.5cm) high.
£1,100–1,400 Mit

A brass-mounted oak mantel timepiece, with eight-day movement, German, c1910, 11in (28cm) high.
£600–650 ⊞ PTh

Torsion clocks

A torsion clock (or more usually timepiece) is one whose pendulum bob is suspended on a very thin strip of metal (the torsion spring), and slowly rotates or 'twists' in alternate directions. As a general rule of thumb, the earlier pendulum bobs were of 'flat disc' type while later ones consisted of four spheres.

The slow oscillation of the pendulum regulates the clock and due to this 'slow' rate the clocks can be designed to run on one winding for at least a year. This long duration has led to the clocks also being called '400-day' or 'anniversary' clocks.

The first torsion clock produced commercially was patented in 1841 in America. During the late 19th and early 20th centuries production was most prolific in Germany after the first patent was taken out there in 1877.

A silver and blue enamel timepiece, by Rolex, with silvered dials and eight-day circular nickel-lever movement with bi-metallic compensation balance, Swiss, 1920, 4½in (11.5cm) high.
£1,500–1,800 S

► **A silver-gilt and enamel minute repeating boudoir timepiece,** by Cartier, the eight-day movement with lever escapement and repeating on two gongs, in a silver case with engine-turned panels on all sides overlaid with translucent opal enamel, with diamond-set flowerheads, on a polished agate base, French, c1920, 3¼in (8.5cm) high.
£10,000–12,500 S
A highly desirable timepiece by the famous jewellers Cartier, and of extremely high quality. The rare minute repeating function allows the owner to determine the time (to the nearest minute) by pushing the top button and listening to the resulting striking sequence on the two gongs.

A gilt-brass four-glass mantel clock, the enamel dial signed 'Tiffany & Co', the A. D. Mougin movement with Brocot escapement and mercury pendulum striking on a gong, French, c1910, 10¼in (26cm) high.
£950–1,200 S(O)

A Westminster chiming mantel clock, by Winterhalder & Hofmeier, the eight-day movement chiming on gongs, German, c1910, 11in (28cm) high.
£1,100–1,200 ⊞ PTh

A gilt-brass four-glass torsion clock, by Claude Grivolas, Paris, with enamel dial and brass four-pillar movement, French, c1920, 13in (33cm) high.
£1,500–1,800 P(Ba)

A gilt-brass and Sienna marble mantel timepiece, by Longines, the eight-day 17 jewel movement with compensation balance, on a marble plinth, Swiss, c1930, 6in (15cm) high.
£270–350 S(O)

CLOCKS

Carriage Clocks

A rosewood carriage clock, with white enamel dial signed 'Hy Marc, Paris.', the rack and bell striking movement with Jules-type platform escapement with helical spring, French, c1840, 8in (20.5cm) high.
£3,000–4,000 ⊞ JIL

A glazed brass carriage clock, with white enamel dial, the movement with replaced lever platform escapement striking on a gong, French, late 19thC, 7in (18cm) high.
£230–300 ⚒ TMA

► **A carriage clock,** by Richard & Co, Paris, the eight-day movement with lever platform escapement, French, c1900, 6in (15cm) high.
£280–320 ⊞ PTh

◄ **A brass-cased carriage timepiece,** with a porcelain dial and eight-day movement, French, c1910, 6in (15cm) high.
£225–250 ⊞ K&D

A brass caryatid alarm repeat carriage clock, the silvered dial with floral filigree surround, striking on a gong, c1890, 7½in (19cm) high.
£900–1,150 ⚒ GH

An enamel carriage clock, by Andreas Huber, Munich, the platform escapement with bell and alarm, the case set with enamelled panels depicting courting couples, the front panel with putti and doves, German, late 19thC, 5½in (14cm) high.
£2,500–3,000 ⚒ SK

The prestigious clock-making firm of Andreas Huber was founded in 1856. In the 1860s, Ludwig II ordered several costly clocks, which partially accounted for the firm's title of '*Hofuhrmacher*' or 'Court Clockmaker'. The firm is still in existence in Munich.

CLOCKS

Miller's Compares

I. A brass carriage clock, the white enamel dial supporting an eight-day striking movement, French, early 20thC, 6¾in (17cm) high including handle.
£550–650 ⚒ DMC

II. A brass carriage timepiece, with white enamel dial and eight-day movement, French, early 20thC, 7¼in (18.5cm) high including handle.
£270–335 ⚒ DMC

Although both carriage clocks are in similar 'Corniche' cases, Item I has the added feature of a push repeat button (when operated the clock strikes the last hour), and therefore it can be assumed that it strikes on the hour and half hour. Item II does not strike, which renders it less desirable. Item I also has the benefit of the retailer's name and address on the dial.

Cartel Clocks

A gilt-bronze cartel clock, with white enamel dial, the eight-day movement with trip repeat striking on a bell, c1780, 19in (48.5cm) high.
£6,500–7,500 ⊞ JIL

A gilt-bronze cartel clock, by Edmé Causard, surmounted by an antique urn and decorated with a lion's mask and drapery, losses, French, late 18thC, 28¾in (73cm) high.
£4,250–5,250 ⚒ S(P)

A Louis XVI-style gilt-bronze cartel wall clock, with enamel dial, the movement with Brocot anchor escapement, countwheel striking on a bell, c1870, 26½in (67.5cm) high.
£1,350–1,700 ⚒ S(Am)

A gilt-brass cartel clock, with an ivorine dial, the eight-day movement by Japy Frères, Paris, French, c1890, 21in (53.5cm) high.
£340–425 ⚒ N

Electric Clocks

An electric timepiece, by Eureka, London, with enamel dial, brass electric movement with large vertical balance wheel, on a stained wood base under a glass case, c1906, 11in (28cm) high.
£1,100–1,400 ⚒ S(Am)

An electric master clock, by Brillié Frères, in a glazed oak case with a marble backboard, French, early 20thC, 18in (45.5cm) high.
£200–250 ⚒ GH

An electric lantern timepiece, by Eureka, London, the glazed centre revealing the movement with massive balance, bell and spider missing, c1910, 12in (30.5cm) high.
£600–700 ⚒ S(O)

An electric mantel timepiece, by Bulle, the silvered dial with open centre revealing the mechanism, the coil pendulum oscillating over a fixed magnet, on a brass stand and ebonized plinth covered by a cut-glass dome, French, c1925, 15in (38cm) high.
£1,100–1,200 ⚒ S(O)

Garnitures

A gilt-metal and porcelain clock garniture, the twin-train movement with outside countwheel striking on a bell, the *bleu-céleste* panels painted with floral sprays and cherubs, the clock surmounted by a seated female figure holding a mirror, flanked by a pair of cassolettes, French, 19thC, clock 13¾in (35cm) high.
£1,500–1,800 ⚒ P(EA)

► **A gilt-metal clock garniture,** by A.D. Mougin, with eight-day movement, decorated with painted Paris porcelain panels depicting figures and houses, flanked by a pair of urns, French, 19thC, clock 16½in (42cm) high.
£550–650 ⚒ AG

◄ **A gilt-metal clock garniture,** comprising clock and a pair of matching four-branch candelabra, all moulded with scrolls and rococo designs, 19thC, clock 14½in (37cm) high.
£300–375 ⚒ GAK

A marble and ormolu clock garniture, the timepiece surmounted by a bird, flanked by candlesticks, French, 19thC, 7in (18cm) high.
£230–300 ⚒ FHF

An ormolu-mounted dark blue ceramic clock garniture, with enamel dial and bell striking movement, the pair of matching four-light candelabra with paste-set bands, French, 1880s, 19¼in (49cm) high.
£4,250–5,250 ⚒ Bon

A rouge marble and gilt-metal clock garniture, by Sauclierers, Nice, the clock with bell striking movement, with a pair of matching three-light candelabra, French, c1880, 16in (40.5cm) high.
£250–325 ⚒ Bon

A porcelain and gilt-metal-mounted clock garniture, the eight-day movement striking on a bell, the porcelain painted with Watteauesque scenes, the pair of vases and covers on giltwood stands, minor losses, French, late 19thC, clock 17in (43cm) high.
£1,200–1,500 ⚒ DN

A gilt-brass and porcelain-mounted clock garniture, by L. Marti et Cie, the twin-barrel movement striking on a gong, the front with inset plaque painted with two putti, the pair of vases painted with putti and musical trophies, French, late 19thC, 12in (30.5cm) high.
£850–1,100 ⚒ P(Ba)

A cream marble and gilt-mounted clock garniture, with enamel dial, bell striking movement and a pair of matching three-light candelabra, French, early 20thC, 14in (35.5cm) high.
£350–450 ⚒ Bon

Lantern Clocks

A brass lantern clock, by William Bowyer, London, the brass chapter ring formerly silvered, the quarter-striking movement sounding on a bell, case c1650, movement 19thC, 16½in (42cm) high.
£850–1,000 ⚒ Bon

◄ A lantern clock, by Edward Rundell, Norton St Phillips, the engraved dial with an alarm pointer, the eight-day movement with a verge escapement, case restored, with later wall bracket, early 18thC, 10in (25.5cm) high.
£1,500–1,800 ⚒ WW

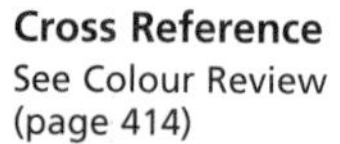

A brass lantern clock, by John Bennett, Plymouth, the brass chapter ring formerly silvered, the 30-hour posted movement with converted anchor escapement, decorated with scrolled foliage, with an oak bracket, 18thC, 15¾in (40cm) high.
£2,400–3,000 ⚒ Bon

► A brass lantern clock, by John Quelch, Oxford, the late 17thC dial engraved with stylized tulips with central alarm dial, the twin fusee spring-driven movement with later replacement plates, 19thC, 15¼in (38.5cm) high.
£900–1,100 ⚒ PFK

◄ A 17thC-style brass lantern clock, probably by Smorthian, Colchester, the eight-day single-train fusée movement with anchor escapement, 1875–1900, 14¼in (36cm) high.
£800–1,000 ⚒ DN

Longcase Clocks

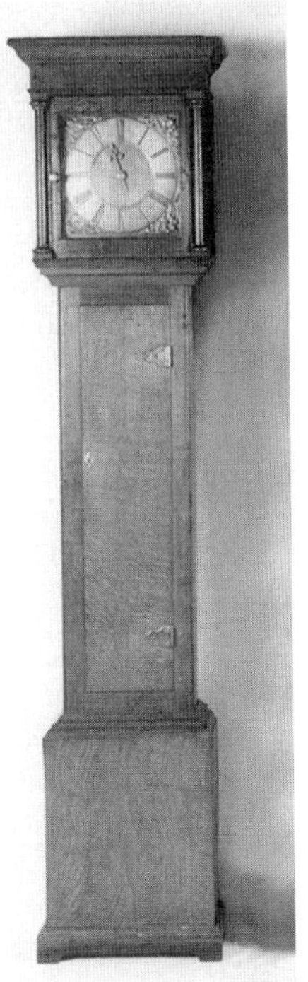

◀ **An oak longcase clock,** by Jonathan Culliford, Bristol, with brass dial and 30-hour bell striking movement, in a later case, c1700, 81½in (207cm) high.
£650–800 ⚒ Bri

An oak longcase clock, by John Williamson, Leeds, the brass dial with seconds dial and date aperture, the eight-day movement striking on a bell, the trunk later carved with flowers, acorns and foliage, 1675–1725, 86in (218.5cm) high.
£4,250–5,250 ⚒ M

A walnut-veneered longcase clock, by John Johnson, London, the brass dial with subsidiary seconds, with five-pillar rack and bell striking movement, case (restored) c1720, movement c1760, 102in (259cm) high.
£6,000–7,000 ⚒ Bon

An oak longcase clock, by Johannes Shepley, Stockport, the brass dial with lunar calendar and penny moon in arch, subsidiary seconds and date aperture, the five-ringed pillar movement with inside countwheel strike and anchor escapement, with inscribed motto below pediment, the trunk door studded with a marriage monogram dated 1719, c1720, 86in (218.5cm) high.
£4,250–5,250 ⚒ P(NW)

A green-and-gilt-japanned longcase clock, by Daniel Barrett, Chatham, the brass dial with seconds dial and calendar aperture, with five-pillar rack and bell striking movement, the case decorated with chinoiserie, replaced finials, reduced plinth, case distressed, c1750, 82½in (209.5cm) high.
£2,400–2,750 ⚒ S(O)

A crossbanded oak longcase clock, by Thomas Hampson, Wrexham, the brass dial with subsidiary seconds and date aperture, with rack and bellstriking movement, the case with turned pillars, c1740, 89½in (227.5cm) high.
£2,300–2,800 ⚒ P(NW)

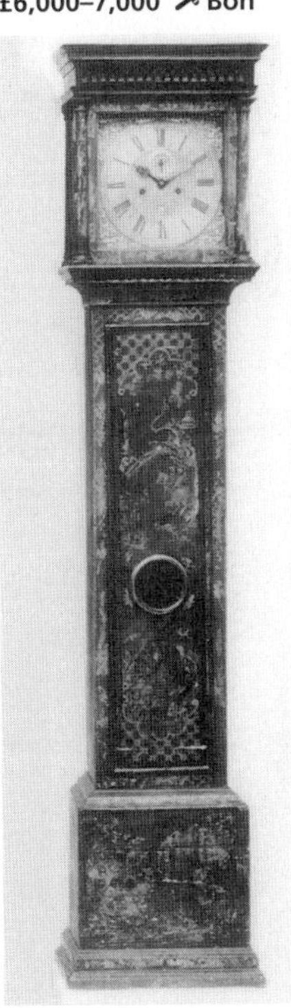

An oak longcase clock, the brass dial with subsidiary seconds and date dials, with an eight-day five-pillar movement striking on a bell, c1750, 82in (208.5cm) high.
£5,500–6,000 ⊞ PAO

◀ **A George II blue-japanned longcase clock,** by David Wyche, London, with brass dial and five-pillar movement, the case front decorated with figures, trees, birds and trailing flowers, 84¼in (214cm) high.
£3,000–3,750 ⚒ P(O)

CLOCKS

A mahogany longcase clock, by Seth Agar, Wisbech, the brass dial with subsidiary seconds dial and date aperture, with eight-day movement, 18thC, 95in (241.5cm) high.
£2,700–3,500 GAK

◄ **A burr-walnut longcase clock,** by Gerrit van der Hey, Amsterdam, the brass dial with date and day apertures, subsidiary seconds and moonphase in the arch, the four-pillar two-train movement with anchor escapement and half hour rack striking on two bells, the possibly associated case surmounted by a giltwood Atlas and two angels, Dutch, c1750, 104¾in (266cm) high.
£7,500–8,250 S(Am)

A stained pine longcase clock, by William Clement, Faversham, the dial with subsidiary seconds and calendar aperture, the brass birdcage-type eight-day movement with outside locking plate striking on a bell, on a reduced base, 18thC, 77in (195.5cm) high.
£550–650 Bon

A black lacquered longcase clock, the brass dial with seconds dial and date aperture with strike/silent to the arch, with eight-day striking movement, in a gilt-decorated case, 18thC, 92in (233.5cm) high.
£1,600–2,000 AG

CLOCKS

An oak longcase clock, by Richard Prew, Tewkesbury, the brass dial with date aperture, the 30-hour movement striking on a single bell, the case with Victorian floral carving, 18thC, 80¾in (207cm) high.
£1,300–1,600 FHF

An oak longcase clock, by E. Sagar, Kirkby Stephen, the brass dial with date sector, the 30-hour four-pillar movement with an outside locking plate striking on a bell, 18thC, 83in (211cm) high.
£1,500–1,800 Bon

A carved oak longcase clock, by James Webster, Shropshire, with brass dial and single-train 30-hour movement, the case with 17thC-style carving, 18thC, 79in (200.5cm) high.
£550–650 HYD

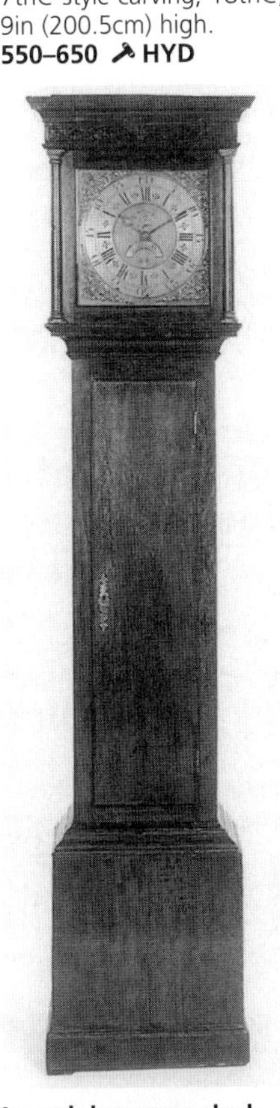

An oak longcase clock, by Phillips, Ashburn, the brass dial with date aperture, the 30-hour, twin-train four-ring turned pillar movement with anchor escapement and countwheel striking on a bell, late 18thC, 75in (190.5cm) high.
£1,600–2,000 P(Ba)

A mahogany longcase clock, by John Ellicott, London, the brass dial with silvered chapter ring, the five-pillar movement with deadbeat escapement and rack striking on a bell, silvered chapter ring, c1765, 103in (261.5cm) high.
£20,000–25,000 ⊞ JIL

John Ellicott was an eminent maker and clockmaker to George III. The case of this clock is predominantly made of solid mahogany and not the more usual veneer. This would have been extremely expensive at the time.

A George III mahogany longcase clock, the gilt-brass dial with moonphase, subsidiary seconds and date aperture and inscribed 'High Waters in Ipswich', the eight-day movement striking on a bell, 84¼in (214cm) high.
£1,800–2,200 P(O)

CLOCKS

A George III oak longcase clock, with brass dial, the case with Victorian foliate carving, the trunk door inlaid with a stellar motif, 79in (200.5cm) high.
£750–950 P(Ed)

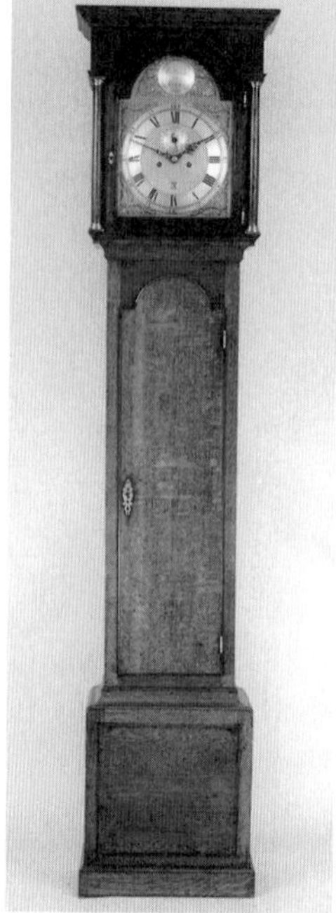

An oak longcase clock, by James Norman, Poole, the brass dial with seconds dial and date aperture, the eight-day movement striking on a bell, the hood with brass-capped pillars, c1770, 91in (231cm) high.
£6,000–6,850 PAO

A George III mahogany longcase clock, by James Gray, Edinburgh, the silvered dial with subsidiary seconds and date aperture, the case with rosewood crossbanding, 85½in (217cm) high.
£4,500–5,500 P(Ed)

A George III walnut longcase clock, by Major Scofield, Rochdale, the brass dial with moonphase and date aperture, with 30-hour movement, the hood with simulated *verre églomisé* panel, 83in (211cm) high.
£2,000–2,500 HYD

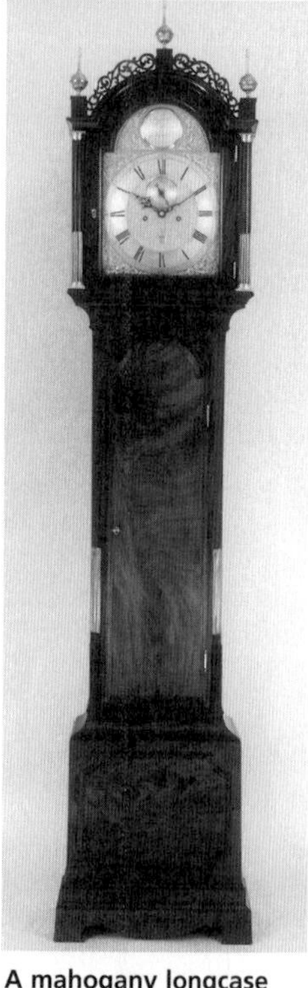

A mahogany longcase clock, by Theophilus Spendelow, Cambridge, the brass dial with date aperture and seconds, the eight-day five-pillar movement striking on a bell, the hood surmounted by brass finials, c1770, 91in (231cm) high.
£12,500–13,750 PAO

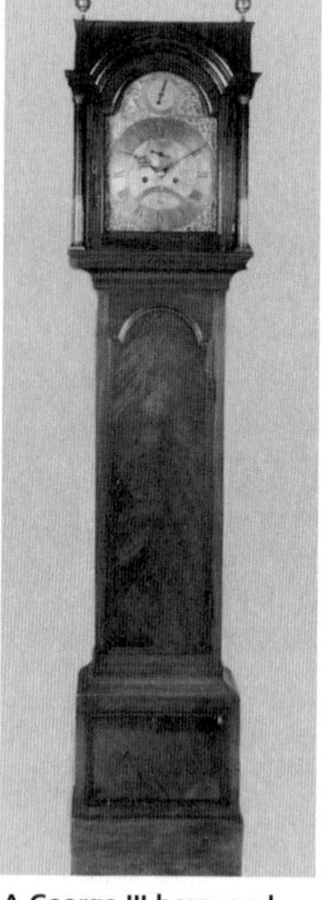

A George III boxwood-banded mahogany longcase clock, by Thomas Hunter, London, the brass dial with date aperture, seconds and strike/silent dials to the arch, with two-train five-pillar movement, the hood with brass stop-fluted columns surmounted by gilt-brass finials, 94in (239cm) high.
£2,600–3,250 HYD

A George III brass-mounted oak longcase clock, by Richard Simpson, Yarmouth, the brass dial with rocking ship to the arch, with eight-day striking movement, the case brass-mounted, 87in (221cm) high.
£2,500–3,200 ⚒ Mit

A George III oak longcase Masonic clock, by T. Femal, Wrexham, the brass dial with date aperture, with eight-day movement, the case mahogany crossbanded, the door inlaid with Masonic emblems, the base inlaid with a vase, 81in (206cm) high.
£1,200–1,500 ⚒ WL

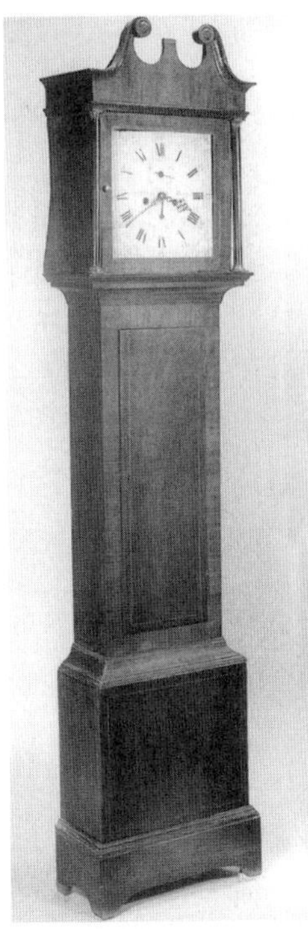

A George III mahogany longcase clock, by W. Bullock, Bath, the painted dial with subsidiary seconds and date dials, the eight-day two-train movement with anchor escapement and rack striking on a bell, 84¼in (214cm) high.
£1,800–2,200 ⚒ DN

A George III mahogany and fruitwood longcase clock, by Thomas Greaves, Quay, Newcastle-on-Tyne, with eight-day bell striking movement, with floral spandrels and hunting scene to the arch, subsidiary seconds and calendar dials, 81¾in (208cm) high.
£1,100–1,400 ⚒ CGC

A mahogany longcase clock, by Andrew Adie, Miln Drummond, the silvered dial with sweep seconds and calendar and painted rolling moonphase in the arch, the four-pillar rack movement with deadbeat escapement striking on a bell, the associated case with brass-inlaid fluted columns, 1750–1800, 95in (241.5cm) high.
£2,800–3,500 ⚒ Bon

A George III oak longcase clock, by Sharman, Melton, the dial with subsidiary seconds and date aperture, with eight-day movement striking on a bell, 79½in (202cm) high.
£1,100–1,300 ⚒ RTo

A George III japanned longcase clock, by John Hodges, London, the brass dial with subsidiary seconds dial and date aperture, strike/silent ring within the arch, the eight-day two-train movement with anchor escapement and rack striking on a bell, the case gilt with chinoiserie panels reserved on a black ground, the hood with two pillars with brass capitals, 97¼in (247cm) high.
£2,000–2,400 DN

A George III crossbanded mahogany longcase clock, by W. Carlton, Kirkham, the dial with date aperture, with painted vase and cover and floral spandrels to the centre in gilt, with eight-day striking movement, flanked by columns with brass capitals, 78in (198cm) high.
£900–1,200 Mit

An oak longcase clock, by William Kettle, Canongate, Edinburgh, the brass dial with seconds dial and date aperture, the eight-day movement striking on a bell, the hood with brass-capped pillars and satinwood blind sound frets, c1780, 89in (226cm) high.
£7,000–7,650 ⊞ PAO

An oak longcase clock, by Lister, Halifax, the brass dial with painted lunar disc, date aperture, with 30-hour movement, c1780, 85in (216cm) high.
£1,700–2,200 TEN

An oak longcase clock, by William Turnbull, Darlington, the brass dial with calendar aperture, the four-pillar pull-chain wind movement with a locking plate striking on a bell, 84in (213.5cm) high.
£1,300–1,600 Bon

A George III oak longcase clock, by Thomas Hammond, the painted dial with calendar aperture, the 30-hour movement striking on a bell, 77¼in (196.5cm) high.
£400–500 RTo

A George III mahogany longcase clock, by Thomas Nevitt, Bristol, the brass dial with subsidiary seconds dial and date aperture with moonphase to the arch, the twin-train movement with anchor escapement striking on a bell, inscribed 'High Water at Bristol Key', 90½in (230cm) high.
£6,000–7,250 P(EA)

CLOCKS

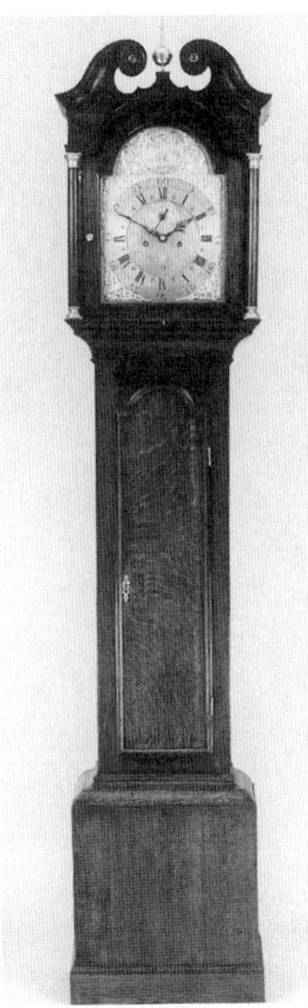

An oak longcase clock, by Valentine Downs, Louth, the brass dial with seconds and date aperture, the eight-day, five-pillar movement striking on a bell, the hood with gilt wood-capped pillars and brass finial, c1785, 90in (228.5cm) high.
£7,000–7,850 ⊞ PAO

An oak longcase clock, by John Draper, Maldon, the brass dial with an automated Old Father Time in the arch, painted decoration, subsidiary seconds dial and date aperture, with eight-day movement, late 18thC, 81½in (207cm) high.
£1,500–1,800 ⚒ HAM

◀ **A mahogany longcase clock,** by Stephen King, Chippenham, the painted dial with seconds dial, calendar aperture and painted moon disc, the movement with rack striking on a bell, case restored, c1785, 87in (221cm) high.
£2,200–2,750 ⚒ S

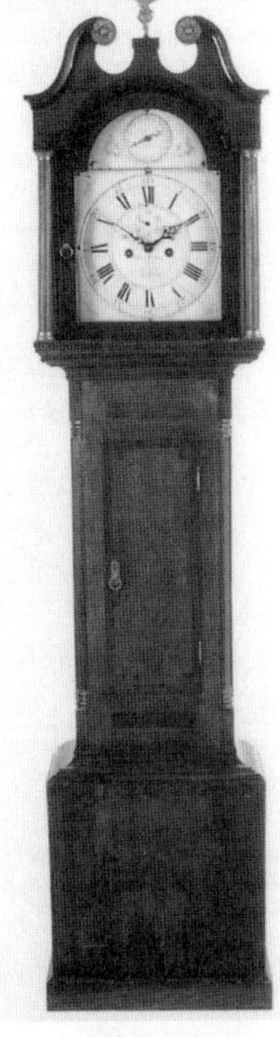

An oak and mahogany-crossbanded longcase clock, by Henry Jenkins, Cheapside, London, the enamelled dial with subsidiary seconds and date dial, the twin-train bell striking movement with anchor escapement, the hood with brass eagle finial and applied brass rosettes, late 18thC, 82in (208.5cm) high.
£1,600–2,000 ⚒ Bea(E)

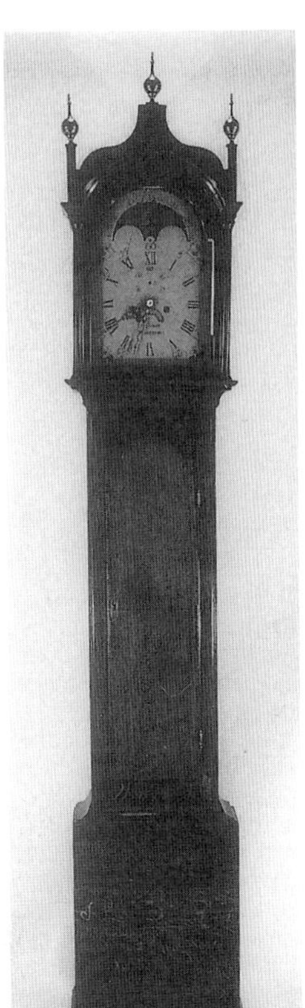

► **An oak longcase clock,** by G. Hewitt, Marlborough, the painted dial with rolling moonphase and painted scene, subsidiary seconds dial and date aperture, with eight-day movement, the hood with three brass finials, late 18thC, 92½in (235cm) high.
£2,200–2,750 ⊞ WL

An oak longcase clock, by Macfarlane, Perth, the white dial with subsidiary seconds and date dials, the eight-day movement striking on a bell, the arch decorated with birds and flowers, the case with boxwood inlay, the hood with brass-capped pillars and brass finial, c1785, 86in (218.5cm) high.
£4,400–4,850 ⊞ PAO

An oak mahogany-crossbanded longcase clock, by Thomas Cottell, Crewkerne, the white-painted dial with seconds and date, with eight-day movement striking on a bell, the case crossbanded in mahogany, c1790, 75in (190.5cm) high.
£4,400–4,850 ⊞ PAO

A George III mahogany longcase clock, by Jonathan Barber, Newark, the painted dial with automata to the arch depicting a butcher and bull, subsidiary seconds dial and calendar aperture, the eight-day movement striking on a bell, the satinwood, harewood and boxwood inlaid case with conch shell inlay to the trunk door, the hood with brass finial and reeded columns with gilt-metal capitals, 90½in (230cm) high.
£3,500–4,500 ⚒ P(L)

A Georgian oak longcase clock, by R. Summerhayes, Ilminster, the enamel dial with gilt shell and leaf spandrel corners, with eight-day movement, 77½in (197cm) high.
£825–1,000 ⚒ DMC

An oak longcase clock, by Samuel Collier, Eccles, the dial painted at the corners with maidens representing the seasons, date and lunar work, with eight-day movement, the case with mahogany crossbanding, the hood with painted *verre églomisé* panel, c1800, 84½in (214cm) high.
£1,400–1,700 ⚒ TEN

► A mahogany longcase clock, by Benjamin Ward, London, the brass dial with strike/silent sector, subsidiary seconds dial and calendar aperture, with eight-day movement, c1800, 87in (221cm) high.
£4,250–5,250 ⚒ G(L)

An oak longcase clock, by Mason, Chesterfield, the painted dial with strawberry and rose spandrels, subsidiary date and calendar, with eight-day movement striking on a bell, defective dials, late 18thC, 87in (221cm) high.
£1,200–1,500 ⚒ DD

A mahogany longcase clock, by Peter Fenwick, Crieff, the silvered-brass dial with subsidiary seconds and calendar, with four-pillar rack and bell striking movement, c1800, 84in (213.5cm) high.
£2,000–2,400 ⚒ Bon

An oak longcase clock, by John Edgecumbe, Bristol, the brass dial with subsidiary seconds dial and calendar aperture, the 30-hour four-pillar movement with outside countwheel striking on a bell, damaged, c1790, 83½in (212cm) high.
£550–650 ⚒ Bri

A George III oak longcase clock, by William Hutchinson, Retford, the painted dial with ship automaton to the arch, subsidiary seconds dial and date aperture, the eight-day movement striking on a bell, the adapted pediment centred by a brass finial, 81in (205.5cm) high.
£800–1,000 ⚒ P(L)

An oak longcase clock, by William Garland, the formerly silvered-brass dial with subsidiary seconds and calendar sectors, with later timepiece movement, 18th/19thC, 74in (188cm) high.
£400–500 ⚒ Bon

An oak and mahogany-banded longcase clock, by J. Nicholas, Daventry, the white-painted dial with a cottage in the arch and painted spandrels, seconds dial and date indicator, with eight-day striking movement, c1830, 84½in (214.5cm) high.
£800–1,000 ⚒ LFA

A Georgian oak longcase clock, by Edward Gartrex, Birmingham, with brass dial and eight-day movement, the hood with brass finials, 86in (218.5cm) high.
£3,800–4,750 ⚒ DMC

A late George III mahogany longcase clock, by Alexander MacWhinnie, the painted dial with subsidiary seconds and date dials and painted with floral spandrels, on a reduced panel base and later ogee bracket feet, 82in (208.5cm) high.
£1,500–1,800 ⚒ P(Ed)

A late George III mahogany longcase clock, by Benjamin Harlow, Lane End, the dial with subsidiary seconds dial and date aperture and painted with moonphase and ship to the arch and bird and floral sprays to the spandrels to the corners, with eight-day striking movement, the case in figured mahogany with kingwood crossbanding and chequer and line inlay, the hood with three brass finials, 92½in (235cm) high.
£3,500–4,500 ⚒ B(WM)

A mahogany and crossbanded longcase clock, by James Craig, Maryport, the painted dial with subsidiary seconds and date dials within shell spandrels surmounted by moonphase, the twin-train movement with anchor escapement striking on a bell, the hood with gilt finial, early 19thC, 92½in (235cm) high.
£2,800–3,500 ⚒ P(EA)

CLOCKS

An oak longcase clock, the dial painted with a girl seated in a cornfield, the spandrels with vignettes of church towers, with 30-hour movement, the case crossbanded and inlaid in mahogany with a centre oval marquetry panel of a bird on a branch, early 19thC, 83½in (212cm) high
£850–1,100 HOLL

Miller's Compares

I. A mahogany long-case clock, by Thomas Lees of Bury, the painted dial with moonphase, four seasons corners and shipping scene to centre, with eight-day movement, the case with inlay of flowers and tracery, c1810, 92in (233.5cm) high.
£5,000–6,000 BL

II. A mahogany longcase clock, by Collingwood, Middlesborough, with black dial and eight-day movement, c1860, 89in (226cm) high.
£2,750–3,250 BL

Both these clocks are in first-class condition, but Item I is earlier in date, slimmer and more elegant than Item II, with a more attractive dial and longer trunk door. The moonphase of Item I is a further desirable feature, as is the very fine inlay, although the value of Item II is enhanced by the rare black-painted dial.

A late Georgian mahogany longcase clock inlaid with boxwood stringing, by D. Robinson, Newcastle, the painted dial with seconds and date dials and with a country scene to the arch and four seasons in the spandrels, 83in (211cm) high.
£1,350–1,700 AG

A Regency mahogany longcase clock with brass stringing, the painted dial with moonphase and painted spandrels depicting either ruins, castles or cottages, with subsidiary date and seconds hands, the eight-day striking movement stamped Wilkes & Son, 90in (228.5cm) high.
£2,600–3,250 Mit

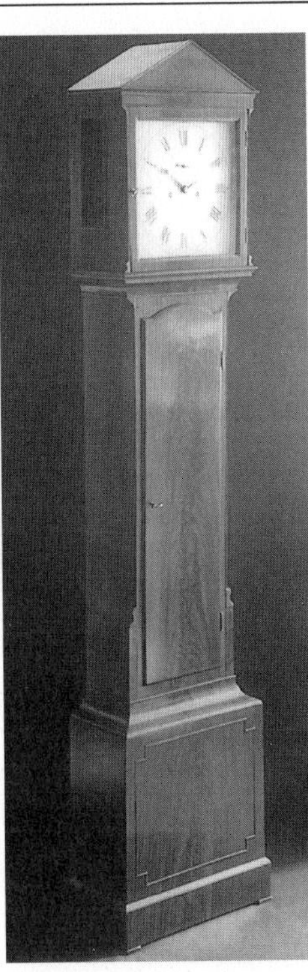

◄ **A mahogany longcase clock,** by Whitehurst & Son, Derby, with silvered-brass 12in square dial, the rack striking movement with a wood rod pendulum and original weights, dated 1818, 82in (208.5cm) high.
£12,000–14,000 JIL
Whitehurst clocks are avidly collected. This Regency example with a well-proportioned and elegant case of flame mahogany has a case of a similar style to that favoured by the famous English clockmaker Vulliamy. The movements of Whitehurst clocks are always of good quality and well finished.

► **A Bristol area mahogany longcase clock,** the white dial with subsidiary seconds dial and calendar aperture, warship cartouche to the arch, the four-pillar eight-day movement striking on a bell, c1820, 83¾in (213cm) high.
£800–1,000 Bri

An oak longcase clock with mahogany crossbanding and boxwood stringing, by R. Fletcher, Chester, with Walker & Hughes falseplate, the painted dial with subsidiary seconds dial and date aperture, the spandrels painted with fruit and foliage and moonphase to the arch, the eight-day movement striking on a bell, c1820, 87¾in (223cm) high.
£1,800–2,200 ⚒ S(S)

A mahogany longcase clock, by Thomas Falle, Jersey, the white dial with seconds and date dials, painted ruin scenes to corners and a lake scene to the arch, the eight-day movement striking on a bell, the hood with brass-capped pillars, brass paterae and central finial, c1830, 87in (221cm) high.
£5,500–6,000 ⊞ PAO

An oak longcase clock, by Alexander Ginlaw, Dunse, the white dial with seconds and date dials, the eight-day movement striking on a bell, the hood with brass bezel, c1830, 80in (203cm) high.
£4,200–4,650 ⊞ PAO

A mahogany longcase clock, by James Howden & Co, Edinburgh, the silvered-brass dial with seconds and date dials, the eight-day movement striking on a bell, c1830, 81in (205.5cm) high.
£6,500–7,250 ⊞ PAO

A William IV mahogany longcase clock, by Blyth & Graham, Birmingham, the painted dial with subsidiary seconds and date dials, the two-train eight-day movement striking on a bell, 84in (213.5cm) high.
£1,100–1,400 ⚒ HYD

◄ **A William IV oak and crossbanded mahogany longcase clock,** by W. H. Davis, Harlech, the painted dial with subsidiary seconds dial and date aperture, the two-train eight-day movement striking on a bell, 84in (213.5cm) high.
£500–625 ⚒ HYD

A figured mahogany longcase clock, by William Bull, Leicester, the white dial with subsidiary seconds dial and calendar aperture, flower and gilt-painted spandrels and conch shell to arch, with eight-day four-pillar movement, c1835, 91¾in (233cm) high.
£1,200–1,500 Bri

► **An oak longcase clock,** by Ross, Epworth, with brass dial, the eight-day movement with anchor escapement and rack striking on a bell, glazed door to hood missing, 19thC, 84¼in (214cm) high.
£800–1,000 DN

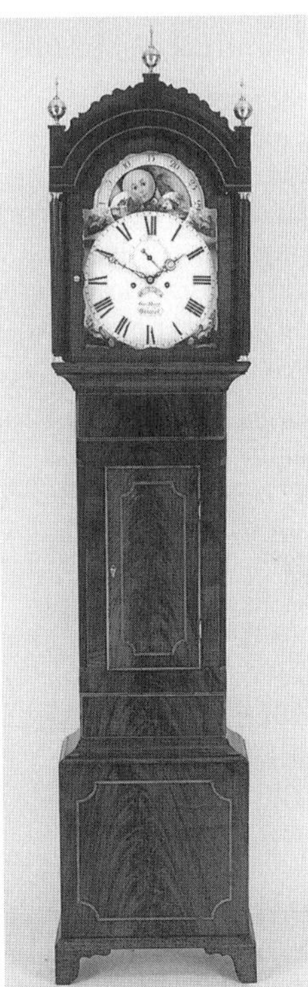

A mahogany longcase clock, by William Dobbie, Falkirk, the white dial with seconds and date dials and decorated with foxhunting scene to the arch and hounds and stags to the corners, with eight-day movement striking on a bell, c1835, 84in (213.5cm) high.
£5,500–6,000 PAO

◄ **A mahogany and boxwood string inlay longcase clock,** by George Hunt, Bristol, the white dial with moonphase, seconds dial and date aperture and the corners painted with squirrels, the eight-day movement striking on a bell, the hood with brass-capped pillars and brass finials, c1840, 89in (226.5cm) high.
£7,500–8,250 PAO

A mahogany longcase clock, the brass dial with subsidiary seconds dial and calendar aperture, with eight-day striking movement, 19thC, 91in (231cm) high.
£2,000–2,500 WW

A mahogany longcase clock, by Ward Dudley, the painted dial with moonphase, subsidiary seconds dial and date aperture and decorated with flower spandrels and a pastoral scene to the centre, with eight-day striking movement, 19thC, 91in (231cm) high.
£1,700–2,000 HOLL

A mahogany drumhead longcase clock, by Bryson, Edinburgh, the silvered dial with subsidiary dials for seconds and date and cast-brass bezel, the eight-day movement with anchor escapement and rack striking on a bell, 19thC, 80in (203cm) high.
£2,750–3,500 B

The Bryson family were a well-respected family of clockmakers working in Edinburgh during the 19th century. Robert Bryson was born in 1778, became a fellow of the Royal Society of Scotland and made a sidereal clock for the Edinburgh Observatory. He died in 1852. His son Alexander was born in 1816 and was also a Fellow of the Royal Society of Scotland and Clockmaker for Scotland to the Queen. He was an eminent maker who invented many devices for electrical and other clocks. After his death in 1866 his brother Robert carried on the business as Robert Bryson & Son until his death in 1886.

◄ **An oak and mahogany longcase clock,** the painted dial decorated with bowls of fruit to the spandrels, the arch painted with a shooting scene, the 30-hour movement with anchor escapement and striking on a bell, some damage and repairs, 19thC, 82in (208.5cm) high.
£600–750 DN

An early Victorian mahogany longcase clock, by Whithers, Halifax, the painted dial with subsidiary seconds and date aperture between painted spandrels depicting landscapes below a scene of a lady rowing beside a bank, with eight-day movement, 92½in (235cm) high.
£750–900 ⚒ WL

A mahogany and boxwood string inlay longcase clock, by J. Jenkins, Tredegar, the white dial with country scenes to the corners and a ruined abbey to the arch, with subsidiary seconds dial and date aperture, the eight-day movement striking on a bell, the hood surmounted by brass eagle finials, Welsh, c1840, 90in (228.5cm) high.
£3,750–4,250 ⊞ PAO

An oak longcase clock, the dial with rolling moon and date aperture, with eight-day movement, the case with mahogany crossbanding and shell and line inlays, c1840, 91½in (232.5cm) high.
£2,500–2,850 ⊞ MTay

A boxwood-inlaid mahogany longcase clock, by Ketterer, Portsea, the white dial with seconds and date dials and painted rural scenes to the corners and arch, the eight-day movement striking on a bell, flanked by reeded brass-capped columns, the hood with brass eagle finials, c1840, 88in (223.5cm) high.
£5,250–5,850 ⊞ PAO

A Victorian mahogany, rosewood and oak longcase clock, by Richard R. Snow, Harewood, the dial painted with rural scenes with subsidiary seconds dial, the eight-day movement striking on a bell, baseboard adapted, 91¼in (232cm) high.
£1,100–1,400 ⚒ P(L)

A crossbanded mahogany longcase clock, by Paul Price, Chester, the painted dial with rolling moon/ paddle steamer, subsidiary seconds, calendar and allegories of continents to spandrels, the fitted rack and bell striking movement with anchor escapement, c1850, 96in (244cm) high.
£2,000–2,500 ⚒ P(NW)

A mahogany longcase clock, by John Jenkins, Swansea, the white dial with seconds dial and date aperture, with painted flowers to the corners and rustic scene to the arch, the eight-day movement striking on a bell, the trunk flanked by brass-capped twisted columns, the top surmounted by brass finials, Welsh, c1845, 89in (226cm) high.
£5,500–6,250 ⊞ PAO

A burr-walnut longcase clock, by Pieter Bramer, Amsterdam, the brass dial with apertures for day, date and month, subsidiary seconds, moonphase to the arch, the quarter-striking four-pillar two-train movement with anchor escapement, Dutch rack striking on two bells, the case surmounted by a giltwood Atlas and two angels, the trunk door with ormolu Father Time lenticle, Dutch, mid–19thC, 115¾in (294cm) high.

£6,500–8,000 ⚒ S(Am)

A boxwood-strung mahogany longcase clock, by Smith, Coleford, the white dial with seconds dial and date aperture, the corners painted with castles and the arch with a fox-hunting scene, the eight-day movement striking on a bell, the hood with brass-capped reeded pillars and brass finials, c1845, 89in (226cm) high.
£4,400–4,850 ⊞ PAO

A Yorkshire mahogany longcase clock, the painted dial depicting Charles I taking leave of his family, with ruined buildings to the spandrels, subsidiary seconds dials, the eight-day movement striking on a gong, mid–19thC, 92in (234cm) high.
£1,350–1,700 ⚒ DD

An oak and mahogany longcase clock, by R. Davies, Ffestiniog, the painted dial with flower corners, calendar sector, seconds dial and *faux* moon dial in the arch, the movement with rack and bell striking, the case with turned mahogany pillars and pilasters and decorated throughout with contrasting woods, the interior signed 'W. Griffith Maker', Bangor, Welsh, c1850, 88¾in (225.5cm) high.
£1,800–2,200 ⚒ S(O)

A rosewood-crossbanded mahogany longcase clock, by Davison, the painted dial with rocking ship feature, subsidiary seconds dial and date aperture, with rack and bell striking movement, c1860, 92in (233.5cm) high.
£1,500–2,000 ⚒ P(NW)

A George III-style mahogany longcase clock, the brass dial with subsidiary seconds dial and chime/silent and Whittington/Westminster dials to the arch, the three-train movement with anchor escapement striking on eight bells and five gongs, the hood surmounted by brass finials and flanked by fluted brass-lined columns, late 19thC, 102¼in (259.5cm) high.
£3,000–3,750 P(EA)

A walnut Vienna longcase clock, the white dial with subsidiary seconds dial, late 19thC, 77¼in (196cm) high.
£800–1,000 P(Ed)

When sold at auction, clocks have sometimes undergone alterations to their movements, or are in unrestored condition, which may be reflected in the prices realized.

A mahogany Sheraton revival longcase clock, the brass dial with subsidiary seconds dial, with eight-day movement striking on a gong, the hood with brass-mounted Corinthian pillars, the case inlaid throughout with ribbon-tied festoons, swags and flowering urns, early 20thC, 98in (249cm) high.
£3,500–4,250 N

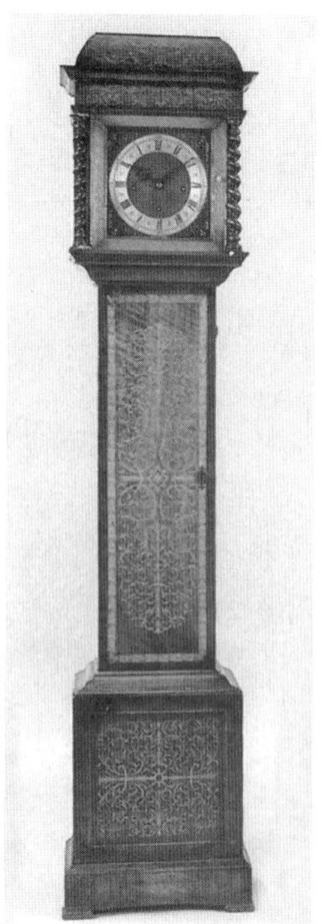

A William and Mary-style walnut granddaughter clock, with brass dial, the triple chain quarter striking movement striking on a gong, the case all-over inlaid with scrolling foliage and seaweed marquetry, early 20thC, 63in (160cm) high.
£2,500–3,000 P(S)

An Edwardian mahogany and walnut Vienna longcase clock, with brass and silvered dial, 88in (223.5cm) high.
£1,250–1,500 MEA

A walnut longcase clock, the metal face with chrome numbers, with chrome pendulum and weights, c1930, 70in (177cm) high.
£580–650 JAZZ

Mystery Clocks

◀ **An ormolu mystery night timepiece,** with replaced glass dial and single hand on a gryphon mount, the eight-day movement with Garnier's two-plane chaff-cutter escapement, the top surmounted with a dolphin candle-holder behind the dial, French, mid-19thC, 13½in (34.5cm) high.
£4,750–5,750 S(O)

▶ **A mystery clock,** by A. R. Guilmet, the black marble dial with incised gilt numerals, with a crank wheel escapement striking on a bell, in a black marble case surmounted by a gilt spelter classical figure of a lady and putto holding the brass and crystal bob pendulum, French, c1875, 21in (53.5cm) high.
£4,250–5,250 Bon

Miller's is a price GUIDE not a price LIST

A mystery clock, by A. R. Guilmet, the cast female figure probably spelter, holding the gilt-brass pendulum with engraved glass bob, the twin-train movement causing the figure to swing the pendulum, with outside countwheel striking on a bell, French, late 19thC, 23½in (59.5cm) high.
£3,500–4,500 B

Novelty Clocks

An automaton picture timepiece, the oil-on-metal village scene with a church tower with a dial, the watch-type verge movement converted to a lever escapement, signed 'Jeffrey Canterbury' fitted to a brass false plate signed 'Wright BIRM', hands missing from dial and sails missing from windmill, 1800–50, 22½ x 17in (57 x 43cm), in a later giltwood frame.
£600–750 Bon
This clock is unusual as the dial must have been a special order for the firm of Wright who were working in the 19th century.

A musical picture clock, the oil-on-metal scene depicting a clock tower with central clock activating musical movement, clock with two-train striking movement, in a giltwood frame, missing automaton movement and alarm train incomplete, musical movement possibly later, German, Black Forest, c1860, 14¾ x 16in (37.5 x 40.5cm).
£500–600 S

A clock, with *tôle peinte* decoration, modelled as a pedlar carrying a timepiece, miniature timepiece to the back missing, pendulum replaced with pocket watch movement, German, 19thC, 16½in (42cm) high, under a glass dome.
£800–1,000 BLH

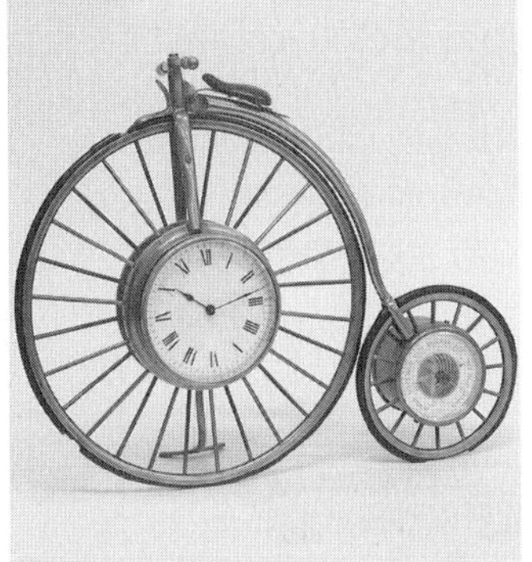

▶ **A turret timepiece,** by J. W. Benson, London, with blue- and gilt-painted convex metal dial, the movement with skeletonized painted iron plates inset with brass bushes, deadbeat escapement maintaining power, hands, pendulum and weight missing, dated 1885, 11¾in (30cm) high.
£575–650 S(O)

◀ **A Victorian brass novelty timepiece and aneroid barometer,** in the shape of a Penny Farthing bicycle, with leather saddle, larger wheel 9¼in (23.5cm) diam.
£720–865 G(L)

Skeleton Clocks

A brass skeleton timepiece, the single fusee movement with anchor escapement, on a rosewood base, 1800–25, 12in (30.5cm) high excluding base.
£450–550 ⚒ Oli

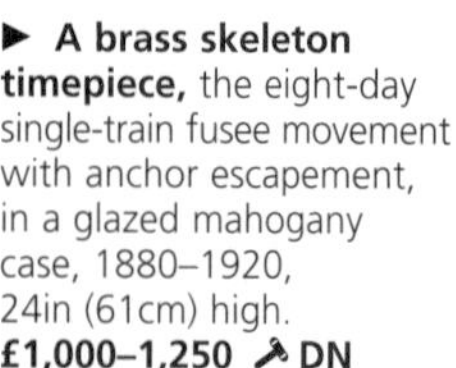

► **A brass skeleton timepiece,** the eight-day single-train fusee movement with anchor escapement, in a glazed mahogany case, 1880–1920, 24in (61cm) high.
£1,000–1,250 ⚒ DN

◄ **A skeleton clock,** with silvered chapter ring, on an ebonized plinth, beneath a glass dome, 19thC, 9in (23cm) high.
£250–325 ⚒ GAK

A brass skeleton clock, by John Williams, Carmarthen, with silvered chapter ring, moon hands and fusee movement, on an ebonized plinth, Welsh, 19thC, 11¼in (28.5cm) high.
£700–900 ⚒ G(L)

A brass skeleton timepiece, with a silvered chapter ring and eight-day fusee movement, on a plush-covered rosewood base, mid-19thC, 14in (35.5cm) high.
£700–850 ⚒ WW

► **A Victorian brass skeleton clock,** fitted with a single fusee movement halberd striking on a bell, on a marble base, beneath a glass dome, 17¾in (45cm) high.
£550–650 ⚒ P(L)

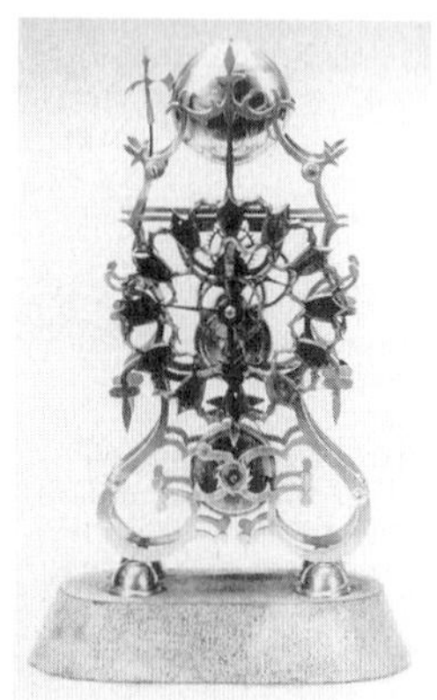

Wall Clocks

A painted iron wall clock, striking the hours on a bell, German, c1700, 13¾in (35cm) high.
£1,300–1,500 ⚒ S(Z)

A George III mahogany drop-dial wall clock, with painted dial and fusee movement, inscribed 'Frankell, King Square', 16¼in (41.5cm) high.
£1,100–1,400 ⚒ RTo

► **A mahogany wall clock,** by Dale & Randall, Newbury, with silvered dial and eight-day movement, case probably re-made, c1800, 19in (48.5cm) high.
£1,000–1,200 ⚒ CAG

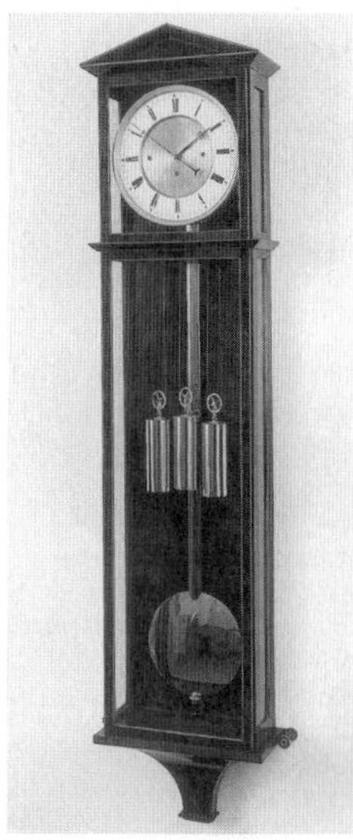

A *grande sonnerie* striking *Dachluhr,* the dial with enamel chapter ring and gilded engine-turned centre and bezel, the eight-day movement striking the quarters on two gongs, with a steel rod pendulum, the mahogany case with boxwood stringing and lift-out trunk door, c1830, 48in (122cm) high.
£12,500–14,000 ⊞ C&A

A brass, mother-of-pearl and red shell inlaid ebonized wall clock by Valéry, Paris, with enamel dial, the bell striking movement with a silk suspension, with applied gilt foliage mounts, c1850, 16in (40.5cm) high.
£700–900 ⚒ Bon

► **A mahogany wall clock,** with a white dial, the eight-day fusee movement with anchor escapement, c1835, dial 10in (25.5cm) diam.
£2,200–2,500 ⊞ PAO
Small dial clocks have become very rare.

A Victorian drop-dial wall timepiece, by Thomas Moore, Derby, with painted dial, in a mother-of-pearl inlaid rosewood case, 22in (60cm) high.
£350–450 ⚒ G(L)

A mahogany and brass-inlaid wall timepiece, signed Beha & Lichard, Norwich, with painted dial, the brass single fusee movement with anchor escapement, case refinished and dial repainted, mid-19thC, 16in (40.5cm) diam.
£350–450 ⚒ P(Ba)

A mahogany wall clock, by Henry Thomas Brown, Islington, London, with a white dial, the eight-day four pillar fusee movement with anchor escapement, c1865, dial 12in (30.5cm) diam.
£1,800–2,200 ⊞ PAO

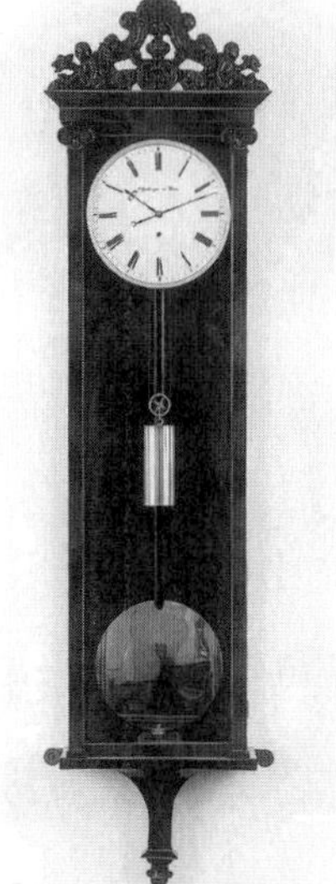

A Biedermeier wall clock, the enamel dial by Effenburger, Vienna, with a gilded engine-turned bezel, with month going movement, Austrian, c1845, 44in (112cm) high.
£5,500–6,300 ⊞ C&A

A Black Forest carved wood cuckoo and musical wall clock, with an enamel dial, the three-train weight-driven brass going striking movement releasing the cuckoo and the music on the hour, the two doors above the dial opening to reveal a colourful carved wooden bird and a composition maiden with fir cone weights, German, c1900, 33in (84cm) high.
£1,300–1,500 ⚒ S(O)

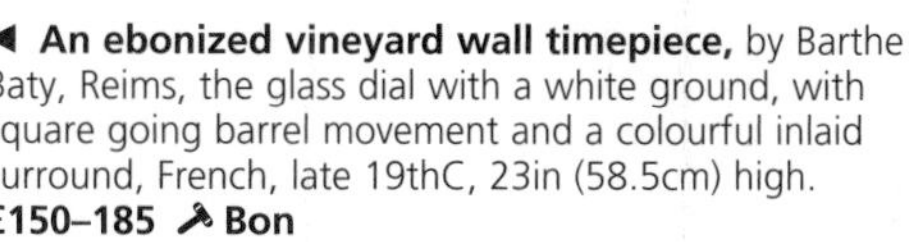

◄ **An ebonized vineyard wall timepiece,** by Barthe Baty, Reims, the glass dial with a white ground, with square going barrel movement and a colourful inlaid surround, French, late 19thC, 23in (58.5cm) high.
£150–185 ⚒ Bon

A musical wall clock, with enamelled dial and three-train quarter striking movement, in a giltwood frame, Austrian, c1840, 16½ x 21in (42 x 53.5cm).
£500–600 ⚒ S

A stained oak alarm *staartschippertje,* the polychrome-painted dial with a landscape in the arch, the brass posted movement with verge escapement, alarm and outer countwheel striking on a bell, surmounted by three turned giltwood finials, Dutch, Frisian, mid-19thC, 21¾in (55.5cm) high.
£4,000–5,000 ⚒ S(Am)
The *staartschippertje* was designed to be used on the vessels using the inland waterways of Holland. The verge escapement and fast-swinging pendulum were less affected by the motion of the boat.

An oak-cased wall clock, by Masters, Rye, the 8in (20.5cm) dial with an eight-day movement, c1900.
£1,150–1,275 ⊞ SO

American Clocks

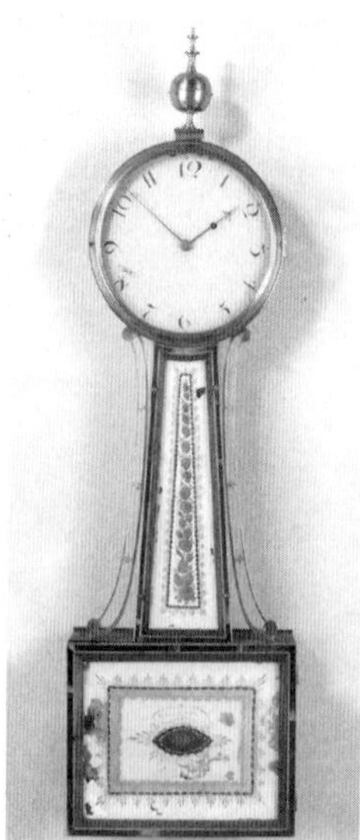

An inlaid mahogany and white and green *verre églomisé* banjo timepiece, by Simon Willard, Roxbury, Massachusetts, with a painted iron dial and eight-day movement, refinished, restored, American, c1805, 33¼in (84.5cm) high.
£3,000–3,750 SK(B)

A rosewood clock, Gale Drop Calendar No. 1, with eight-day time and strike, with D. J. Gale patent astronomical calendar, American, c1880, 30in (76cm) high.
£3,500–4,000 ROSc

This clock was made for sale in another part of the world so the times for sunrise and sunset have been omitted from the inside of the annual calendar at the bottom; it simply shows the day of the month at the end of every seven days starting with 2 January. A chart for the region in which the clock was used could be referred to for the actual sunrise time.

A mahogany-cased Looking Glass clock, by Joseph Ives, the lower tablet requires repainting, mirror old, finials missing, American, c1818, 51in (129.5cm) high.
£2,480–2,750 ROSc

A drop-dial wall clock, with two-train movement, in a walnut case, American, late 19thC, 29in (73.5cm) high.
£200–250 GH

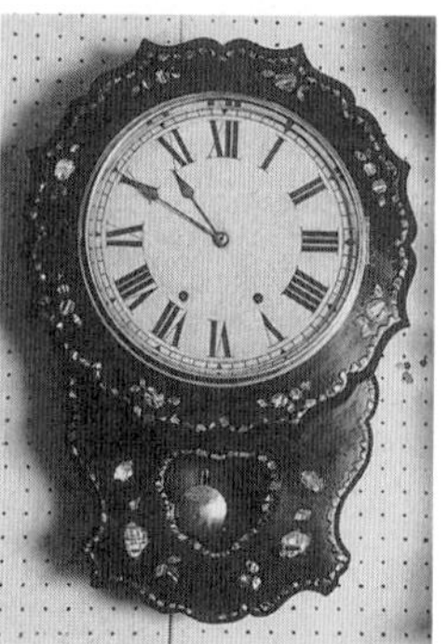

A mother-of-pearl inlaid drop-dial wall clock, with an American eight-day movement striking the hours on a bell, c1890, 24in (61cm) high.
£330–365 K&D

A Federal inlaid cherry-wood longcase clock, the white-painted dial with subsidiary seconds dial and date aperture, maple and ebony stringing throughout, American, possibly Pennsylvannia, 1800–25, 88½in (225cm) high.
£3,500–4,500 SLN

An oak calendar clock, with time and calendar dials, with two-train movement, in an oak case, American, late 19thC, 20½in (52cm) high.
£240–300 GH

A *faux* rosewood, gilt and *verre églomisé* banjo clock, by E. Howard & Co, Boston, with a white-painted metal dial, American, 32in (81.5cm) high.
£2,200–2,700 BB(S)

CLOCKS

A wall clock, inlaid with parquetry bands, American, 19thC, 49¼in (125cm) high.
£300–375 P(S)

A clock, Ansonia, Jumper No. 1, nickel-plated, American, c1894, 15in (38cm) high.
£1,000–1,100 ROSc

◄ **A wall clock,** with a white dial, with two-train movement, the papier mâché case decorated with birds and flowers, American, late 19thC, dial 12in (30.5cm) diam.
£200–250 GH

CLOCKS

British Regulators

A mahogany longcase regulator, signed by James Whitelaw, Edinburgh, with a 12in (30.5cm) silvered-brass dial, the movement with Graham deadbeat escapement and Harrison's maintaining power, c1830, 72¾in (185cm) high.
£11,500–13,500 JIL

► **An ebonized regulator,** by Moore & Sons, Clerkenwell, London, the silvered dial with central minute hand, subsidiary seconds and hour dials, signed for Ham & Huddy, Liskeard, the six pillar high count movement with deadbeat pallets, mid-19thC, 91in (231cm) high.
£3,200–3,750 B
The company of John Moore & Sons succeeded Handley & Moore after the death of G. Handley in 1824. John Moore died in 1842 and the business continued under his son George until his death in 1894. The Ham and Huddy family have been making clocks in Cornwall since the late 18th century.

The mercury pendulum

Invented by George Graham in c1720, this type of pendulum compensates for changes in temperature and is found mainly in precision timepieces called regulators.

The bob consists of a glass or metal container holding a carefully measured quantity of mercury. With a rise in temperature, the mercury expands upwards, the metal pendulum rod expands downwards, and the net result is a pendulum with the same centre of gravity and period of oscillation. With a drop in temperature, the mercury and rod contract in opposite directions, leading to the same result.

► **A centre seconds electric wall regulator,** manufactured by Magneta, invented by Brillié Frères, with an enamel dial, the movement with a pendulum bob fitted with a horse shoe magnet, on a white marble backboard in a glazed oak case, early 20thC, 8¼in (21cm) wide.
£380–475 Bon

Continental Regulators

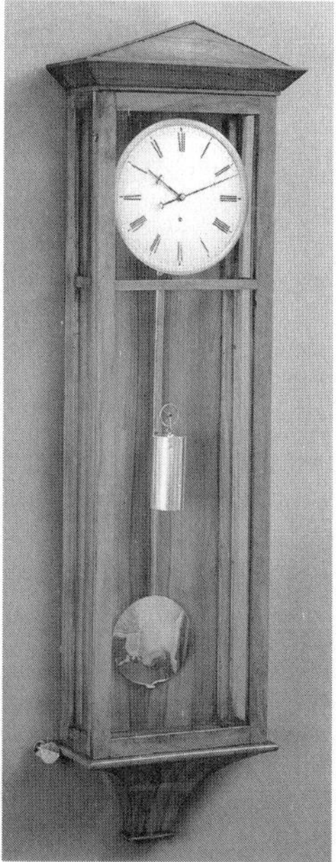

A cherrywood *Dachluhr*, attributed to Elsner & Petrovits, with silvered dial and eight-day movement, Austrian, c1830, 39in (99cm) high.
£5,000–5,500 C&A

A walnut and ebonized Vienna single-weight regulator, the white enamel two-part dial with subsidiary seconds, German, mid-19thC, 45in (114.5cm) high.
£700–900 GH

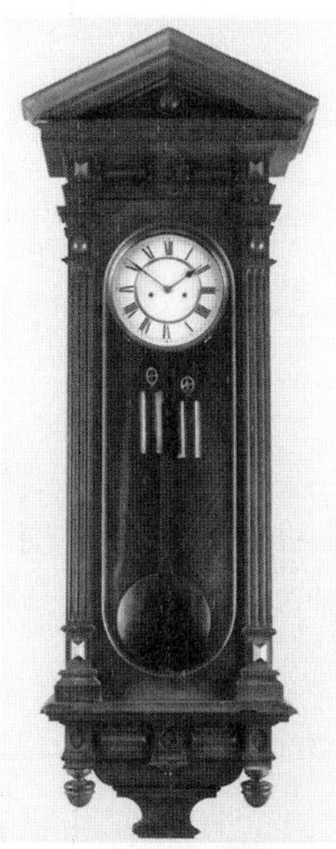

A beech Vienna wall regulator, by Lenzkirch, with enamel dial, the movement with deadbeat escapement, maintaining power and striking on a gong, German, early 20thC, 51in (129.5cm) high.
£600–750 Bon

A mahogany regulator, with ebonized turned finial decoration, German, early 20thC, 48in (122cm) high.
£450–550 FHF

Cross Reference
See Colour Review
(page 429)

Colour Review

A parcel-gilt silver centrepiece, by Gorham Manufacturing Co, American, Providence, Rhode Island, 1872, 13¼in (33.5cm) diam, 71oz.
£10,000–12,000 ⚒ S(NY)

A silver chamberstick, by Sampson Mordan and Gabriel Riddle, London 1828–29, 4in (10cm) high, 6.25oz.
£1,400–1,550 ⊞ NS

A silver cruet, by Paul Storr, London 1816, 10in (25.5cm) high.
£11,000–12,500 ⊞ TSC

A silver desk set, comprising a pair of loaded candlesticks, Sheffield 1892, and an inkstand, possibly by Charles Edwards, 1892, and a red morocco stationery box with repoussé silver cover, by William Comyns, 1892, 12in (30.5cm) wide, contained in a satin-lined red-plush presentation case.
£2,000–2,400 ⚒ L

A set of 12 silver Japanese-style fruit knives and 11 forks, by F. Elkington, the majority damaged, Birmingham 1880, all contained in a lacquered box, the cover decorated in gold leaf.
£1,350–1,500 ⚒ B(Ba)

A silver sauce boat, by William Robertson, London 1753, 4in (10cm) high.
£4,500–5,000 ⊞ MCO

A silver tankard, maker's mark V6, Russian, St Petersburg 1896–1907, 4½in (11.5cm) high.
£1,300–1,450 ⊞ SHa

A William IV silver teapot and cover, by Edward Barnard & Sons, London 1834, slight dents, 6¼in (16cm) high.
£400–500 ⚒ WL

A silver scent bottle, by Gervase Wheeler, c1880, 3in (7.5cm) high.
£300–350 ⊞ LBr

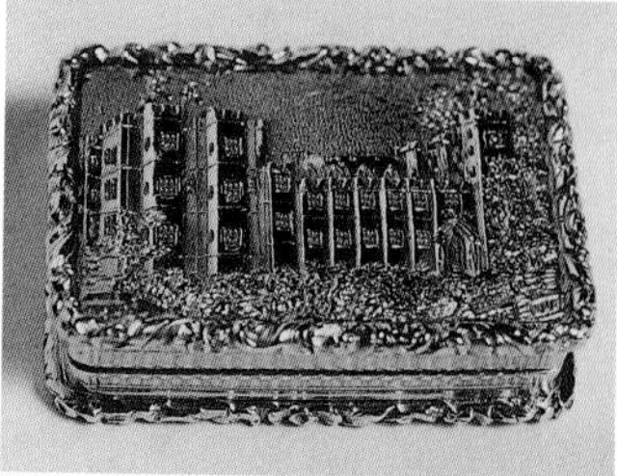

A cast silver-gilt vinaigrette, by Taylor and Perry, depicting Warwick Castle, Birmingham 1832, 1¾in (4.5cm) wide.
£2,000–2,200 ⊞ BEX

A silver tea and coffee set, the teapot by The Goldsmiths & Silversmiths Co, London 1905, 10½in (26.5cm) wide, the kettle stamped Sheffield 1905, 119oz.
£1,100–1,300 ⚒ AH

A Victorian silver-plated folding biscuit box, 9in (23cm) high.
£250–300 ⚒ CGC

► **A Victorian silver-plated candelabrum,** 28in (71cm) high.
£550–650 ⚒ G(L)

► **A Victorian silver-plated *épergne*,** possibly by Elkington & Co, 26¾in (68cm) high.
£1,400–1,700 ⚒ AG

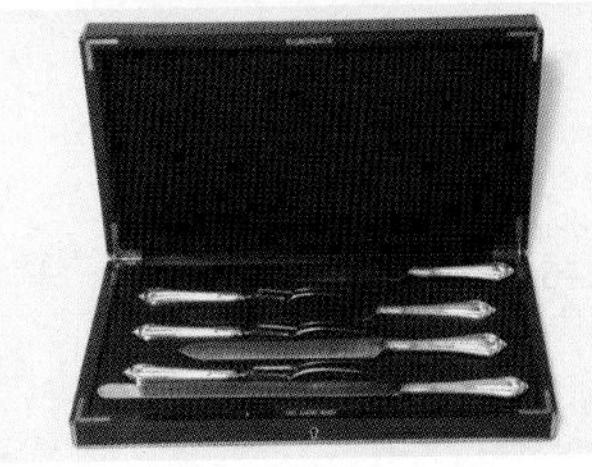

A set of seven silver-plated carving knives and forks, contained in a brass-bound mahogany box, c1905, 20in (51cm) wide.
£700–800 ⊞ HA

A Victorian silver-plated table centrepiece, 21½in (54.5cm) wide.
£1,000–1,200 ⚒ HYD

A Victorian silver-plated double decanter coaster, on ivory rollers controlled by an ivory handle, 16in (40.5cm) wide, with a cut crystal decanter.
£700–850 ⚒ DD

A Victorian silver-plated three-piece tea service, by Walker & Hall, Sheffield, marked EPNS.
£80–100 ⚒ PFK

◄ **A silver-plated tantalus,** by Roswell Gleason & Sons, with three cylindrical segments separated by three smaller ones, the large cylinders each containing a cut-to-clear glass decanter in red, blue and green, the smaller cylinders each containing two cordial glasses, one missing, all decorated with chased flowers and fruit, with a balloon-shaped finial which when turned activates a mechanism that rotates the cylinders, American, Massachusetts, c1865, 21in (53.5cm) high.
£3,000–3,500 ⚒ NOA

A Victorian silver-plated spoon warmer, 8¼in (21cm) long.
£400–500 ⚒ P(B)

A mid-Victorian silver-plated tantalus, with three cut-glass decanters, 11½in (29cm) wide.
£350–420 ⚒ Bon(C)

A Victorian silver-plated sugar sifter, in the shape of a thistle, 6in (15cm) wide.
£400–450 ⊞ SHa

A pair of Sheffield-plated wine coolers, c1820, 9in (23cm) high.
£3,200–3,500 ⊞ TSC

A pair of Sheffield-plated wine coolers, by I. & I. Waterhouse, c1825, 10in (25.5cm) high.
£4,000–5,000 ⚒ P(L)

An ebonized table clock, by George Lindsay, London, the eight-day duration and five-pillar verge movement striking the hours on a bell, c1760, 13¾in (35cm) high.
£13,000–14,750 ⊞ PAO

A musical and quarter-striking table clock, by Jonathan Howlett, London, decorated in ormolu, enamel, paint and paste, with three-train fusee movement and verge escapement, restoration to panel painting, c1790, 12¼in (31cm) high.
£25,000–30,000 ⊞ JIL

◄ A mahogany bracket clock, the five-pillar twin fusee bell striking movement with anchor escapement, c1800, 16¾in (42.5cm) high.
£3,500–4,200 ⚒ Bri

► A Victorian gilt and bronze mantel clock, the movement by Bickerton, Kidderminster, 15½in (39.5cm) high.
£650–800 ⚒ SWO

A mahogany bracket clock, by Thomas Page of Bishop's Stortford, with repeating movement, c1790, 19in (48.5cm) high.
£6,250–7,000 ⊞ DJH

A George III ebonized eight-day bracket clock, the verge movement striking on a bell, 19in (48.5cm) high.
£3,000–3,750 ⚒ WW

An ebonized bracket clock, with triple fusee movement on nine bells, striking the hours on a gong, the brass dial with chime/silent selection subsidiary dials, 19thC, 17½in (44.5cm) high.
£1,300–1,700 ⚒ GH

A mantel clock, signed Etienne Lenoir, in gilt-bronze and porcelain, French, c1760, 18¼in (46.5cm) high.
£7,000–8,000 ⚒ S(Z)

A Louis XV ormolu-mounted boulle bracket clock and bracket, by Jacques Jerome Gudin, decorated with shell, horn and mother-of-pearl, French, 46in (117cm) high.
£45,000–50,000 ⊞ JIL

◄ A porcelain and ormolu mantel clock, the movement with an outside countwheel and striking on a bell, French, c1870, 23½in (59.5cm) high.
£700–900 ⚒ GH

► An ormolu-mounted porcelain mantel clock, the pendulum set with brilliants, French, 19thC, 20in (51cm) high.
£3,400–4,250 ⚒ RBB

A Directoire eight-day *Pendule au Negre,* by Jean-Simon Deverberie, entitled Amerique, with bell striking movement, in original condition, French, c1799, 19¼in (49cm) high.
£32,000–35,000 ⊞ GDO

A ormolu figural mantel clock, by Nicholas Douillon, French, 1820–30, 22¾in (58cm) high.
£1,100–1,400 ⚒ WcH

An ormolu mantel clock, on a marble base, French, late 19thC, 13½in (34.5cm) high.
£320–400 ⚒ G(L)

A brass carriage clock, by Drocourt, Paris, with strike/repeat movement and subsidiary alarm, French, c1890, 6½in (16.5cm) high, in original case.
£2,500–2,800 ⊞ BELL

A silver carriage clock, hallmarked 'W.M.', London 1896, 3in (7.5cm) high.
£700–800 ⊞ JIL

A gilded brass *mignonette* timepiece, by Le Roy & Fils, Paris, with lever escapement, French, c1902, 3in (7.5cm) high.
£2,200–2,500 ⊞ BELL

A gilt-cased hour-repeating carriage clock, with enamel panels, French, early 20thC, 5in (12.5cm) high.
£900–1,100 ⚒ G(L)

A tortoiseshell carriage clock, with silver mounts, c1913, 3in (7.5cm) high.
£3,200–3,500 ⊞ BBo

A porcelain and ormolu clock garniture, the eight-day movement striking on a bell, on original giltwood and velvet bases, French, c1880, 19¾in (50cm) high.
£8,000–8,800 ⊞ GDO

A mantel clock garniture, gilt-bronze and marble, the Mougin movement with cylinder platform escapement, striking on a bell, French, early 20thC, clock 21in (53.5cm) high.
£2,000–2,400 ⚒ S(S)

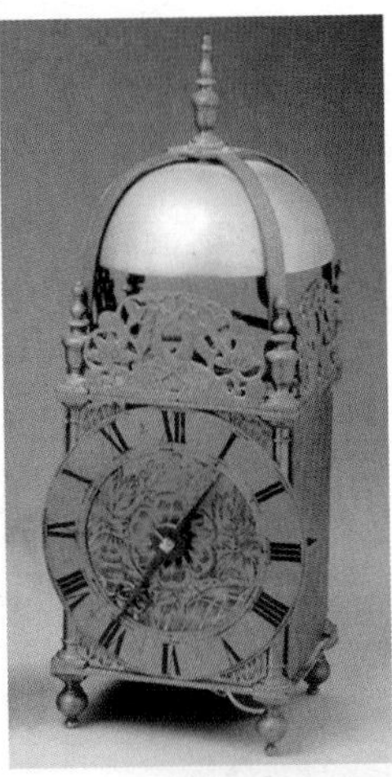

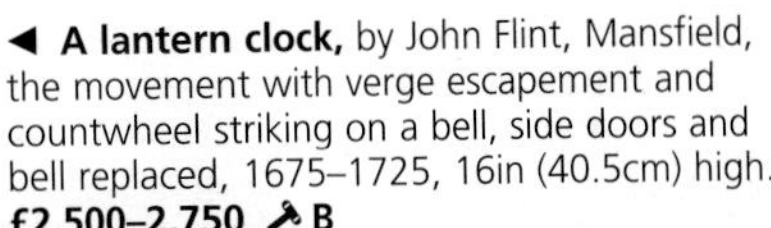

An automaton picture clock, the eight-day square movement striking on a gong, with a curved back-board, missing glass, French, 1800–50, 39 x 28in (99 x 71cm).
£1,800–2,200 ⚒ Bon

◄ **A lantern clock,** by John Flint, Mansfield, the movement with verge escapement and countwheel striking on a bell, side doors and bell replaced, 1675–1725, 16in (40.5cm) high.
£2,500–2,750 ⚒ B

◄ **A brass lantern clock,** by Jonathan Hocker, Reading, the movement with anchor escapement striking on a bell, with later wrought-iron bracket, faults, c1700, 15¼in (38.5cm) high.
£2,250–2,500 ⚒ S(S)

◄ **A brass quarter-chiming skeleton clock,** by J. Smith & Sons, London, the triple-chain fusee movement with dead-beat escapement and gridiron pendulum, on a rosewood plinth with original glass dome and key, mid-19thC, clock frame 16in (40.5cm) high.
£20,000–22,000 ⚒ B

Smith & Sons are perhaps the best-known makers of skeleton clocks in the latter half of the 19th century, but it is extremely rare to find a signed example of their work.

An olivewood marquetry Roman longcase clock, by Joseph Knibb, London, with striking month-going movement, replaced chapter ring and anchor escapement, now striking on two gongs, c1680, 84½in (214.5cm) high, with later cresting and apron. **£75,000–95,000 S(O)**
Roman striking is an ingenious method of accurately indicating the hours by a smaller number of blows than the conventional system.

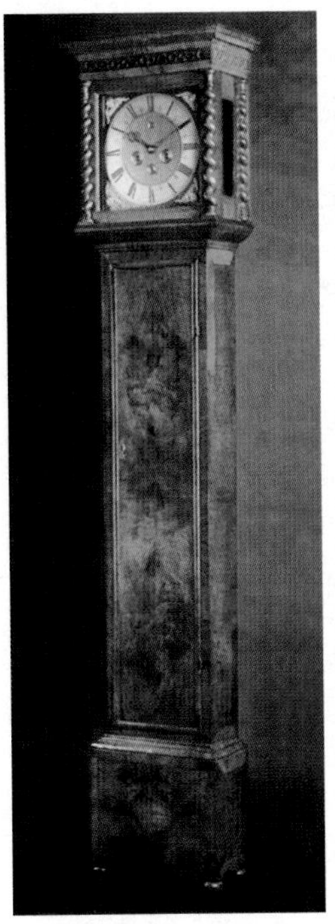

A walnut-veneered cariniana longcase clock, by Joseph Knibb, London, with half-hour passing strike and sunrise/set, case restored, late 17thC, 84in (213.5cm) high. **£45,000–55,000 Bon**

A William and Mary walnut and marquetry eight-day longcase clock, by Manels Bennett, Charing Cross, London, with associated five-pillar bell striking movement, the case with alterations and restorations, 88¼in (224cm) high. **£5,500–6,500 CGC**

A William and Mary walnut and floral marquetry longcase clock, by John Hammers, London, with eight-day striking movement, 88in (223.5cm) high. **£2,500–3,000 SWO**

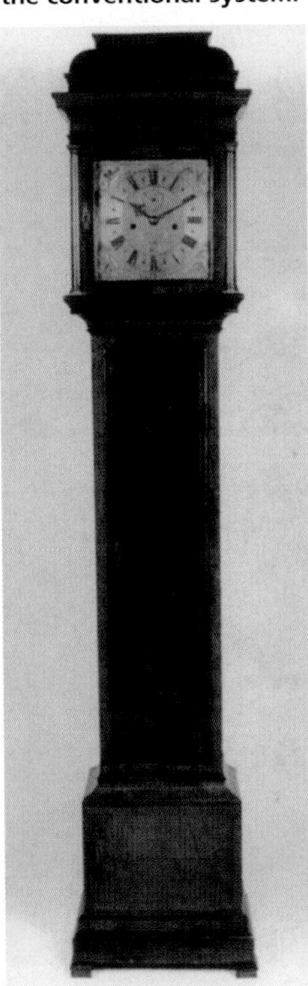

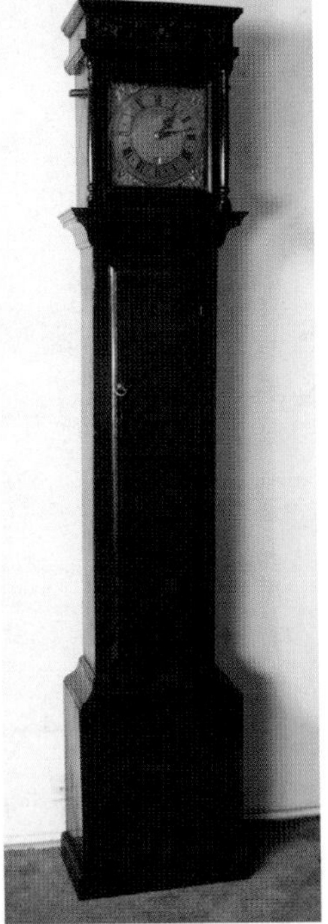

An oak longcase clock, by James Parsons of Presbury, with rack striking movement, 18thC, 87in (221cm) high. **£3,500–4,000 ChC**

◀ **A walnut longcase clock,** by George Graham, with 30-day movement, c1713, 89¾in (228cm) high. **£100,000–110,000 HYD**

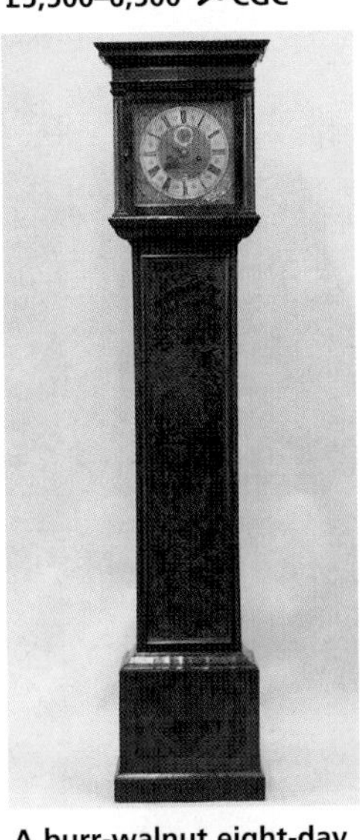

A burr-walnut eight-day longcase clock, by Samuel Watson, London, c1710, 81in (205.5cm) high. **£8,250–10,000 G(L)**

► **A walnut longcase clock,** by Robert Sadler, Redlion Fields, the five-pillar 30-day movement with anchor escapement and rack striking on a bell, moulding and blind fret on hood replaced, cut-down base, early 18thC, 84½in (214.5cm) high. **£10,000–11,000 B**

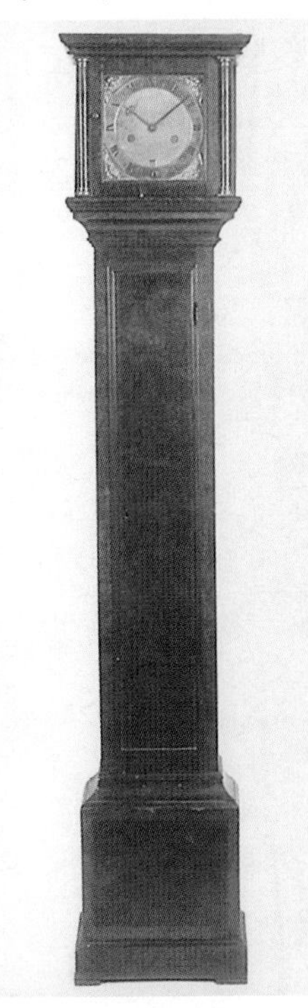

An eight-day longcase clock, by Ahasuerus Fromanteel, London, the movement with bolt and shutter maintaining power and verge escapement, striking on a bell, c1700 with later walnut case, movement c1670, 71¾in (182.5cm) high. **£45,000–55,000 Bea(E)**

Derek Roberts

25 Shipbourne Road, Tonbridge, Kent TN10 3DN
Tel: 01732 358986 Fax: 01732 771842
Email: drclocks@clara.net
Website: http://www.qualityantiqueclocks.com
Member of the British Antique Dealers Associaton

MUSIC BOXES **FINE ANTIQUE CLOCKS** BAROMETERS

A few examples from our very extensive range of fine clocks which may be viewed on our website or details forwarded.

Top left:
Samuel Toulmin, London.
Circa 1770. An extremely rare automaton clock depicting two people playing tennis.

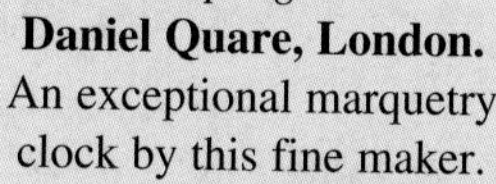

Top right:
Daniel Quare, London.
An exceptional marquetry clock by this fine maker.

Centre left:
Viner, London.
A particularly good quarter chiming rosewood carriage clock.

Centre right:
James McCabe.
A giant striking carriage clock.

Bottom left:
Thomas Bradford, London.
An imposing quarter chiming table clock, with 9" dial, on turntable base; seen here partly rotated. Height 18".

Bottom right:
John Harris, London.
Circa 1690. A very fine ebony veneered table clock with pull-quarter repeat on 5 bells.

Books written by Derek Roberts:
British Longcase Clocks; Carriage & Other Travelling Clocks; Mystery, Novelty & Fantasy Clocks; British Skeleton Clocks; Continental & American Skeleton Clocks.

An oak longcase clock, by William Porterhouse I, Penrith, with 30-hour movement, early 18thC, 82½in (209.5cm) high.
£2,300–2,750 ⚒ PFK

A black-japanned longcase clock, by Thomas Trigg, London, with five-ringed pillar movement striking on a bell, the repainted case decorated with gilt chinoiserie, on a rebuilt base, c1720, 99in (251.5cm) high.
£1,500–1,800 ⚒ Bon

A George I black-japanned eight-day longcase clock, by Henry Baker, Malling, the case decorated with gilt chinoiserie, with two-train movement, 87in (221cm) high.
£2,000–2,400 ⚒ HYD

A red-lacquered eight-day longcase clock, by Peter Dennis, London, the five pillar movement striking the hours on a bell, the case with gilt chinoiserie decoration, c1725, 105in (266.5cm) high.
£13,500–15,000 ⊞ PAO

A walnut longcase clock, by Benjamin Davis, London, with 30-day movement and original mirrored door, c1720, 89½in (227.5cm) high.
£26,000–30,000 ⊞ REI

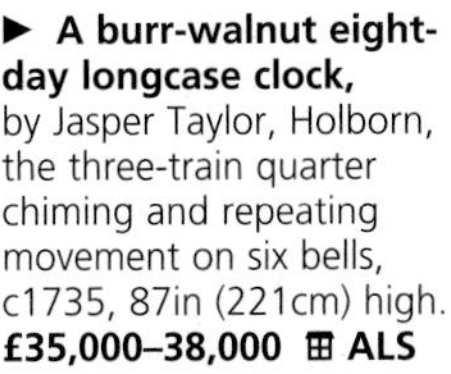

► **A burr-walnut eight-day longcase clock,** by Jasper Taylor, Holborn, the three-train quarter chiming and repeating movement on six bells, c1735, 87in (221cm) high.
£35,000–38,000 ⊞ ALS

A walnut eight-day longcase clock, by Edward Faulkner, London, the five-pillar movement striking the hours on a bell, with mirror trunk door, c1735, 96in (244cm) high.
£18,000–20,000 ⊞ PAO

► **A walnut eight-day longcase clock,** by J. Coelombie, Haarlem, with satinwood floral inlay, Dutch, mid-18thC, 106in (269cm) high.
£8,000–10,000 ⚒ RBB

A black-japanned longcase clock, by William Tomlinson, London, decorated with chinoiserie, c1720, 108¼in (275cm) high.
£15,000–17,000 ⚒ S(P)

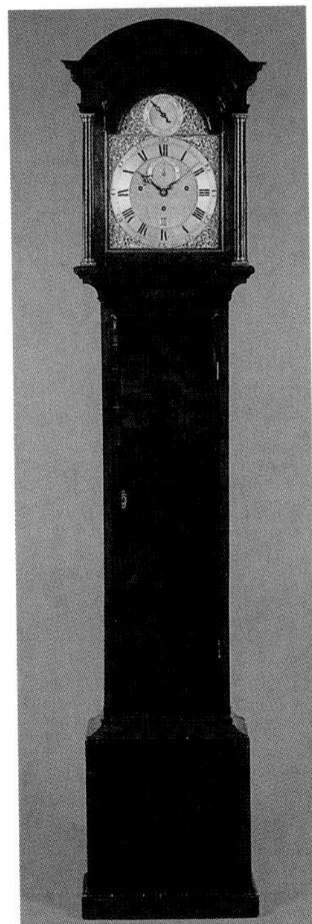

A walnut quarter-chiming longcase clock, by John Ellicott, London, the three-train six-pillar movement with anchor escapement, rack striking the hour on a bell and chiming the quarters on eight bells, 18thC, 94½in (240cm) high.
£16,000–17,500 ⚒ B

A mahogany eight-day longcase clock, by Wm Hawkins, Bury, in need of restoration, 18thC, 99in (251.5cm) high.
£2,300–2,750 ⚒ RBB

A green-lacquered and gilt-decorated longcase clock, by Windmills & Etkins, London, with five-pillar rack and bell striking movement, case distressed, reduced base, 18thC, 94in (239cm) high.
£3,500–4,200 ⚒ Bon

A green-japanned longcase clock, by Robert Allam, London, decorated with gilt chinoiserie, with five-pillar trip repeating rack and bell striking movement, c1760, 96in (244cm) high.
£3,000–3,500 ⚒ S(O)

A red-japanned longcase clock, by William Evill, Bath, the movement with rack and bell striking, decorated with gilt chinoiserie, c1760, 96in (244cm) high.
£12,000–15,000 ⚒ S

A burr-walnut eight-day longcase clock, by John Pyke, London, the five-pillar bell striking movement with original pendulum and brass-cased weights, c1760, 97½in (247.5cm) high.
£12,000–15,000 ⚒ Bri

An oak eight-day longcase clock, by Richard Hornby, Liverpool, the movement striking the hours on a bell, crossbanded in walnut, c1765, 83in (211cm) high.
£7,500–8,500 ⊞ PAO

An oak eight-day longcase clock, by W. Wilson, Kendal, with mahogany banding, c1765, 89in (226cm) high.
£4,000–5,000 ⚒ TEN

A mahogany eight-day longcase clock, by Midwinter, London, with five-pillar movement and pull hour repeat, c1780, 81in (205.5cm) high.
£11,000–12,000 ⊞ ALS

A George III black-lacquered longcase clock, by Joseph Frodsham, Braintree, later plinth, 89in (226cm) high.
£2,000–2,500 ⚒ B(Ed)

► A George III mahogany longcase clock, by William Lundie, Aberdeen, 89½in (227.5cm) high.
£3,200–4,000 ⚒ P(Ed)

An oak and mahogany longcase clock, by Redshaw, Newcastle-under-Lyme, the 30-hour, four-pillar movement with locking plate and bell striking, c1790, 75in (190.5cm) high.
£1,000–1,250 ⚒ Bon

◄ A mahogany white dial eight-day longcase clock, by William & Thomas Chaplin, Bury St Edmunds, the five pillar movement striking the hours on a bell, c1785, 92in (233.5cm) high.
£7,000–7,750 ⊞ PAO

A black-lacquered longcase clock, by Milward, Hammersmith, the five-pillar movement with anchor escapement and rack striking on a bell, later finials, 18thC, 95½in (242.5cm) high.
£2,000–2,500 ⚒ B

A mahogany eight-day longcase clock, by John Distin, Guernsey, the movement striking the hours on a bell, c1785, 79in (200.5cm) high.
£11,000–12,000 ⊞ PAO

◄ A flame mahogany eight-day longcase clock, by Bullock, Marshfield, with satinwood details, c1790, 88in (223.5cm) high.
£7,500–8,250 ⊞ ALS

A George III mahogany eight-day longcase clock, by Thomas Blundell, Dublin, now with gong strike, 92in (233.5cm) high.
£3,200–4,000 ⚒ Oli

A George III mahogany eight-day longcase clock, with lunar and solar dials, 84in (213.5cm) high.
£10,000–12,000 ⚒ G(L)

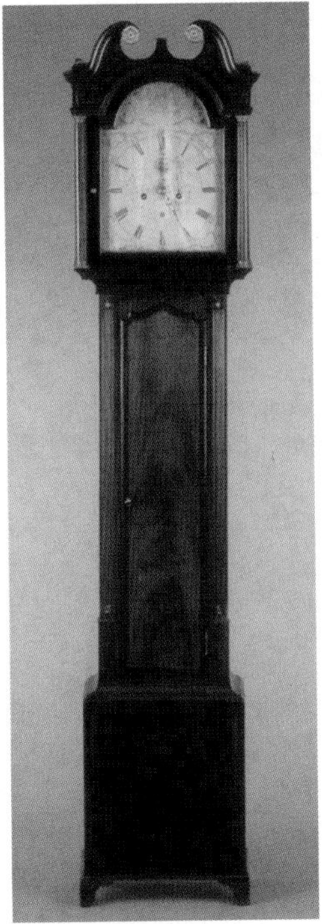

A mahogany eight-day longcase clock, by John Miller, Edinburgh, with boxwood lines and crossbanding, c1780, 83½in (212cm) high.
£3,800–4,750 TEN

A mahogany longcase clock, by Samuel Peacock, Lincoln, with painted panels, late 18thC, 90in (228.5cm) high.
£8,000–8,800 HA

A mahogany automaton longcase clock, by Dirk Wiegels, Amsterdam, the four-pillar movement with anchor escapement and alarm, Dutch rack quarter striking on two bells, Dutch, c1800, 100in (254cm) high.
£10,000–12,500 S(Am)

A late George III mahogany longcase clock, by A. Hunter, Port Glasgow, boxwood lined, 83½in (212cm) high.
£1,350–1,700 B(Ed)

◄ A mahogany eight-day longcase clock, by Stephen Simpson, Preston, with crossbanding, c1810, 90¼in (229cm) high.
£2,000–2,400 TEN

A carved walnut longcase clock, with an associated dial and bell-striking movement, French, early 19thC, 46¾in (119cm) high.
£475–575 S(O)

► An oak and mahogany eight-day longcase clock, by Ralph Cairns, Brampton, with crossbanding, 1825–50, 84¾in (215.5cm) high.
£850–1,000 PFK

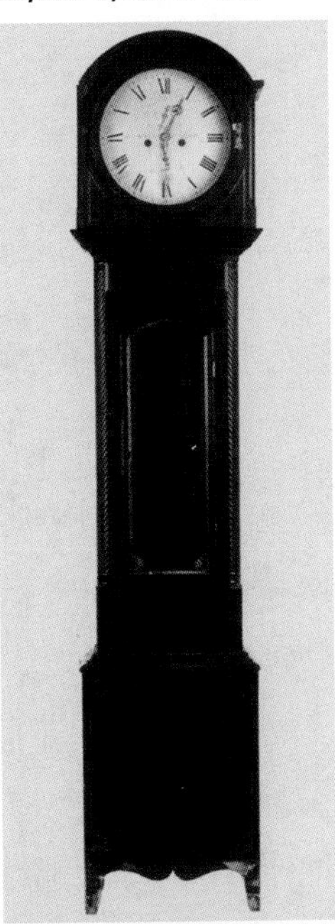

A mahogany longcase clock, by J. McNab, Perth, with four-pillar bell striking movement, Scottish, c1820, 83in (211cm) high.
£1,600–2,000 Bon

A carved oak longcase clock, signed 'Navand', the two-train weight-driven movement with outside countwheel, French, probably Normandy, c1820, 95in (241.5cm) high.
£2,800–3,500 S(O)

◄ **An oak longcase clock,** by J. Mallet, Barnstaple, the 30-hour movement striking the hours on a bell, the case with ebony inlay, c1835, 81in (205.5cm) high.
£1,650–1,850 ⊞ K&D

A cherrywood eight-day longcase clock, with repeating hour and half-hour, French, c1840, 109in (277cm) high.
£3,200–3,500 ⊞ TDS

A mahogany eight-day longcase clock, by Thomas Knight, Bristol, the movement striking the hours on a bell, the case with ebony string inlay, c1845, 90in (228.5cm) high.
£6,750–7,500 ⊞ PAO

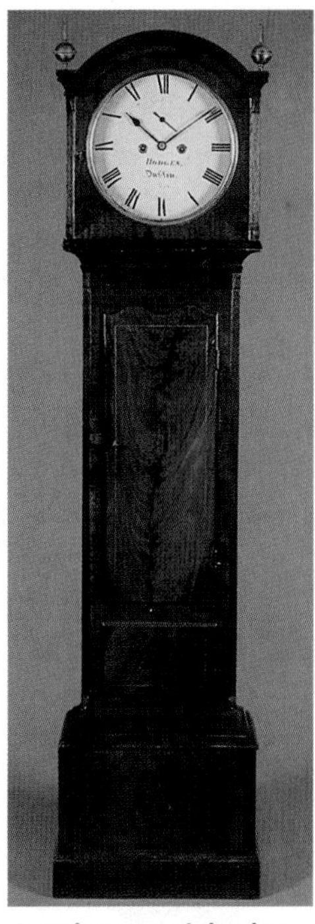

A mahogany eight-day longcase clock, by Hodges, Dublin, with anchor escapement and rack striking on a bell, the associated case with boxwood stringing, base reduced, Irish, 19thC, 75½in (192cm) high.
£1,500–1,800 ⚒ B

► **A mahogany longcase clock,** by Booth, Dublin, the gong striking movement with outside fly, Irish, c1850, 78½in (199.5cm) high.
£1,400–1,700 ⚒ S(O)

A mahogany and kingwood Louis XVI-style longcase clock, by Grieblin, Paris, in the style of Jean-Henri Riesener, the two-barrel spring-driven movement with Graham anchor escapement and countwheel striking on a bell, with ormolu mounts, c1870, 88½in (225cm) high.
£14,000–16,000 ⚒ S(Am)

A crossbanded mahogany longcase clock, by John McConnell, Belfast, 19thC, 93¾in (238cm) high.
£1,250–1,500 ⚒ HOK

► **A mahogany quarter-chiming longcase clock,** the three-train movement with anchor escapement striking the hours and quarters on eight tubular gongs, 19thC, 117in (297cm) high.
£10,000–12,000 ⚒ B

◄ **A carved oak longcase clock,** the four-pillar movement with a deadbeat escapement and maintaining power and striking on a gong, German, c1880, 96in (244cm) high.
£1,500–1,800 ⚒ Bon

► **A stained oak alarm *Zaanse* wall clock,** the brass quarter-striking movement with verge escapement, later weights, Dutch, c1690, 28¼in (72cm) high.
£4,500–5,500 S(Am)

A longcase clock, American, Pennsylvania, late 18thC, 96in (244cm) high.
£5,000–6,250 SLN

A mahogany-cased *Laterndluhr*, by A. Pohl, the engraved silvered dial gilded and engine-turned, with inner and outer bezels and 30-day movement, Austrian, Vienna, c1835, 43in (109cm) high.
£22,500–25,000 ⊞ C&A

◄ **A skeleton clock,** by Terry & Co, Waterbury, with embossed brass decoration, American, c1870, 8in (20.5cm) high.
£800–875 ROSc

An ebonized wall clock, by Diebold, Paris, inlaid with brass, mother-of-pearl and red shell, c1835, 19in (48.5cm) high.
£6,500–7,500 ⊞ JIL

A black and gilt-carved wooden wall clock, French, c1875, 19in (48.5cm) wide.
£700–850 NOA

A mahogany regulator, the silvered dial signed Alois Loeffler, the seven-day movement with Huygens winding, c1840, 73in (185.5cm) high.
£20,000–22,000 ⊞ C&A

A skeleton mantel regulator clock, with calendar, attributed to Verneuil, the weight-driven 30-day movement with visible pin wheel escapement, French, early 19thC, 30¼in (77cm) high.
£35,000–45,000 ⚒ S(O)

A burr-walnut domestic regulator, by Reid & Sons, Newcastle-upon-Tyne, the two-train four-pillar eight-day gong striking movement with shaped plates and deadbeat escapement, c1850, 74¾in (190cm) high.
£3,200–4,000 ⚒ Bri

◄ **A walnut regulator,** by Lewthwaite, the movement with four turned pillars, deadbeat escapement and maintaining power, c1900, 78in (198cm) high.
£3,500–4,200 ⚒ B

A gold pair-cased pocket watch, by John Gordon, London, the case by William Sherwood, c1728, 2in (5cm) diam.
£1,500–1,800 ⚒ B

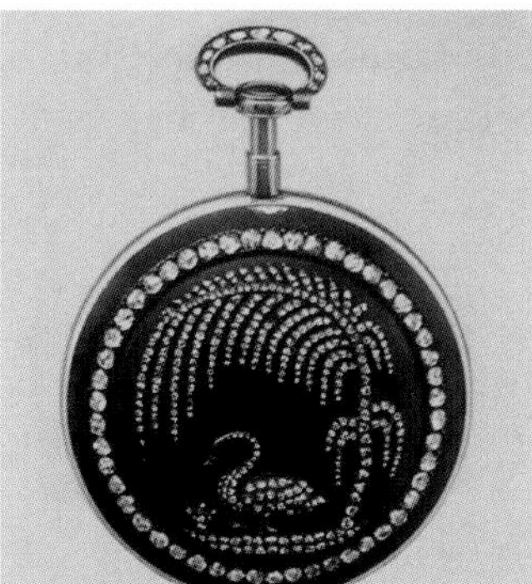

A gold, silver, diamond and enamel watch, by Wm. Keales, London, c1790, 2in (5cm) diam.
£2,200–2,750 ⚒ S(NY)

An 18ct gold and enamel quarter-repeating automaton watch, Swiss, c1820, 2¼in (5.5cm) diam.
£4,000–4,400 ⊞ PT

A lady's 18ct gold and enamel pendant watch, by Patek Philippe & Co, Geneva, Swiss, c1911, 1in (2.5cm) diam.
£2,400–3,000 ⚒ S(G)

A freestanding 22ct repoussé verge watch, London 1764, 2in (5cm) diam.
£5,500–6,000 ⊞ PT

An 18ct gold lever pocket watch, by Taylor & Kennard, London, with an 18ct gold fetter-link chain, c1819, 2in (5cm) diam.
£1,250–1,500 ⚒ B

An 18ct gold, enamel and seed-pearl fob watch, Swiss, c1850, 1½in (4cm) diam.
£1,100–1,400 ⚒ S(HK)

A quarter-repeat lever gold-plated watch, in a gold-plated case with 15 jewels, c1930.
£630–700 ⊞ GLa

A gilt-metal and enamel pair-cased verge watch, by Moricand, Geneva, set with paste stones, Swiss, c1775, 1½in (4cm) diam.
£775–975 ⚒ S(Am)

A silver quarter-repeater watch, by Greguet, French, c1820, 2½in (6cm) diam.
£2,000–2,400 ⊞ PT

An 18ct gold hunting cased watch, by the International Watch Co, with associated chain, American, c1900, 2in (5cm) diam.
£1,600–2,000 ⚒ S(G)

A platinum watch, by Douillard, with painted dial, the movement unsigned, c1927, 1¾in (4.5cm) diam.
£2,250–2,750 ⚒ S(G)

A lady's 18ct white-gold and diamond bracelet watch, by Audemars & Co, Swiss, c1924, 1¾in (4.5cm) long including lugs.
£1,500–1,800 ⚒ S(O)

A platinum and diamond wristwatch, by Cyma, Swiss, c1930, ¾in (2cm) diam.
£550–600 ⊞ GLa

A duo-dial wristwatch, in a gold case, c1930.
£1,600–1,750 ⊞ JoV

A gentleman's 18ct gold wristwatch, by Patek Philippe, retailed by The Goldsmiths & Silversmiths Co, London, Swiss, c1930, 1½in (4cm) diam.
£4,500–5,700 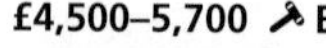 **⚒ B**

A gentleman's 9ct gold Rolex wristwatch, Swiss, c1930.
£780–860 ⊞ TEM

◄ **An 18ct gold wristwatch,** by Vacheron Constantin, Swiss, Geneva, c1935, 1¼in (3cm) diam.
£2,800–3,500 ⚒ S(HK)

► **A gentleman's 18ct gold Patek Philippe wristwatch,** Swiss, c1940, 1¼in (3cm) diam.
£2,200–2,750 ⚒ LJ

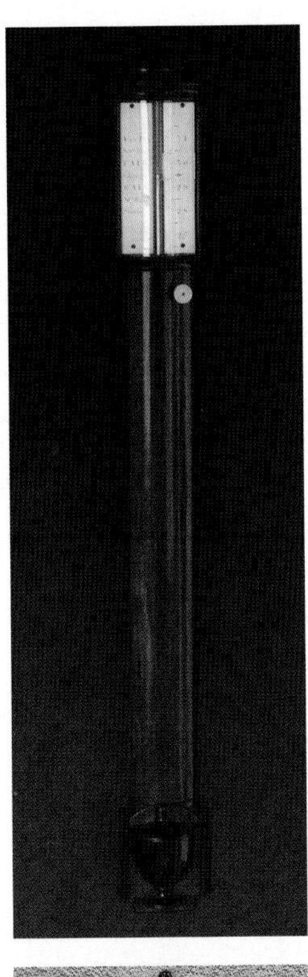

◄ **A mahogany flat-to-the-wall stick barometer,** by Jesse Ramsden, London, c1790, 37in (94cm) high. **£9,500–12,000 ⊞ AW**

A mahogany angle barometer, by Robb, Montrose, with silvered scales, c1800, 38in (96.5cm) high. **£7,500–9,000 ⊞ RAY**

◄ **A mahogany inlaid barometer,** by J. Luvatti, London, c1785, 38in (95.5cm) high. **£3,000–3,500 ⊞ RAY**

► **A mahogany wheel barometer,** by M. Lilly, Edinburgh, with tulipwood crossbanding, Scottish, early 19thC, 43¼in (110cm) high. **£700–875 ⚒ P(Ed)**

An aneroid barometer, by James Hicks of Hatton Garden, London, mounted on a spelter figure, c1875, 16in (40.5cm) high. **£565–625 ⊞ PTh**

A painted rosewood wheel barometer, by Solca, Tunbridge Wells, c1840, 40in (101.5cm) high. **£1,000–1,200 ⊞ DJH**

► **A carved giltwood hunting-theme wheel barometer,** thermometer missing, restoration required, c1850, 47¾in (121.5cm) high. **£700–900 ⚒ S(O)**

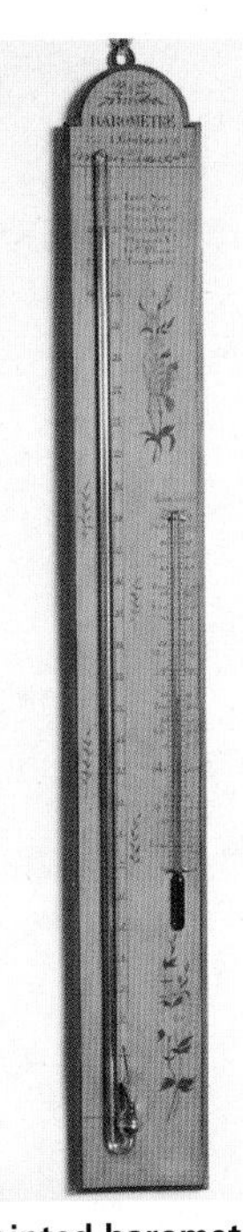

A painted barometer, by A. Coubeaux, Paris, French, c1850, 37in (94cm) high. **£1,600–1,850 ⊞ TRI**

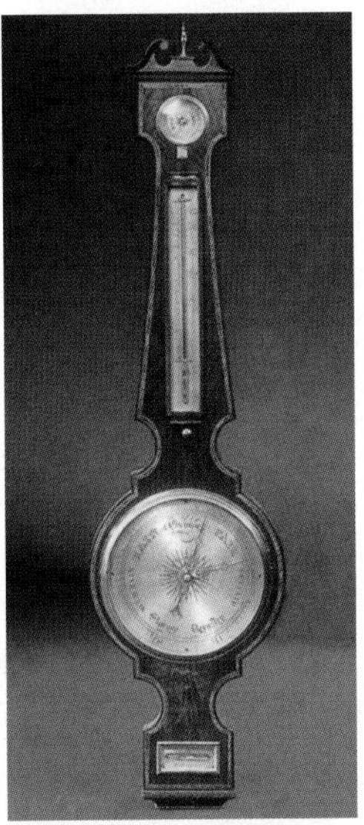

A parcel-gilt wheel barometer, by Brevete, with paper dial, French, c1780, 33in (84cm) high. **£3,400–3,750 ⊞ HA**

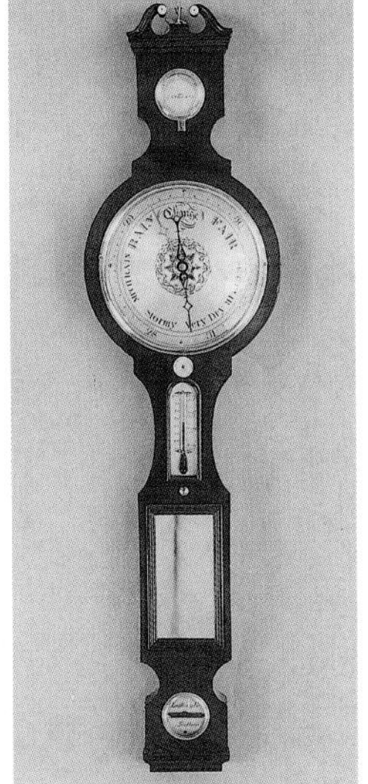

A mahogany inverse wheel barometer, by J. Lanffrancho, Ludlow, c1840, 39in (99cm) high. **£1,600–1,850 ⊞ PAO**

A Victorian figured walnut inverse wheel barometer, by H. Hughes, London, 42in (106.5cm) high. **£1,300–1,600 ⚒ G(L)**

Watches
Pocket Watches

A silver consular-cased verge watch, by Jacob Hueber, Klagenfurth, with tortoiseshell outer, Austrian, c1750, 2½in (6.5cm) diam.
£450–500 ⚒ S(O)
This is a double-bottom watch-case fitted with a high-rounded glass. The term 'consular' was originally applied to single-bottom cases when wound through a hole in the dial. This type of case replaced pair cases and was named in honour of Napoleon, the Consul of France.

A silver pair-cased pocket watch, by Markwick, London, c1800, 1¾in (4.5cm) diam.
£1,750–2,200 ⚒ N

An 18ct gold fusee lever pocket watch, by Ebenezer Thompson, Sloane Street, London, the movement with Harrison's maintaining power, London 1852, 1¾in (4.5cm) diam.
£350–400 ⊞ PT

A gilt-metal and tortoiseshell pair-cased verge watch, by Henry Hindley, York, the outer case containing a printed paper depicting 'an East view of the Iron Bridge at the Wear near Sunderland', mid-18thC, 2in (5cm) diam.
£900–1,100 ⚒ B
Henry Hindley (1701–71) became one of the leading mechanicians and clockmakers of the 18th century. He was probably apprenticed to Arthur Scholefield and was made free of the Clockmakers' Company in 1731. In the same year he presented York City with two eight-day clocks, both of which still survive today. He is credited with having invented the screw-cutting lathe and also an improved wheel-cutting engine. In 1750 he made a clock for York Minster with a 52ft 2in long temperature-compensated pendulum with four-seconds beat.

Miller's is a price GUIDE not a price LIST

A silver and tortoiseshell triple-cased pocket watch, by Edward Prior, London, c1854.
£2,300–2,550 ⊞ AGR

A gold and dark blue translucent enamel verge watch, signed Gregson, depicting a couple in a formal garden, c1780, 2in (5cm) diam.
£2,000–2,350 ⊞ PT

An enamel and gold verge pocket watch, by Romilly, Paris, the reverse cover decorated with a harbour scene, minute hand replaced, French, late 18thC, 1½in (4cm) diam.
£1,500–1,650 ⚒ B

◄ **A silver pair-cased Masonic verge watch,** by William Franklin, London, the dial polychrome-enamelled with Masonic emblems and a large central arch below the All Seeing Eye, c1800, 2¼in (5.5cm) diam.
£1,300–1,450 ⊞ PT

A lady's silver key-wind fob watch, with silver and gold dial, the case hand-chased with flowers and foliage, c1880.
£180–200 ⊞ Bns

A 9ct gold hunter watch, by Waltham Watch Co, Massachusetts, American, hallmarked Chester 1917, 2in (5cm) diam.
£400–450 ⊞ PT

An 18ct gold full hunter, by John Jones, Strand, London, the dust cover secured by two screws taking the place of a cuvette, London 1890, 1¾in (4.5cm) diam.
£375–425 ⊞ PT

An 18ct gold cased demi-hunter fob watch, with 10 jewel cylinder movement, Swiss, c1900, 1¼in (3cm) diam.
£300–325 ⊞ GLa

A 14ct pink-gold hunting cased watch, by Uhrenfabrik-Union, Glashütte, Sachsen, German, c1890, 2¼in (5.5cm) diam.
£1,400–1,600 ⚒ S(G)

A 9ct gold open-faced keyless lever pocket watch, in original case, hallmarked London 1938, 2in (5cm) diam.
£160–200 ⚒ HOLL

Wristwatches

An Audermars Piguet 18ct white gold wrist-watch, Swiss, c1930, 1in (2.5cm) wide.
£750–950 S(HK)

A Cartier 18ct gold Tank wristwatch, French, c1970.
£1,000–1,150 ⊞ JoV

► A Lathin Watch Co regulator-style wrist-watch, the silvered dial with two subsidiary dials in a chrome case, Swiss, 1950s, 1¼in (3cm) diam.
£520–580 ⊞ Bns

Cross Reference
See Colour Review (page 431)

A Longines lady's 18ct gold wristwatch, retailed by Hardy Bros, with white gold lugs and 9ct lined bracelet, Swiss, c1920, ½in (1.5cm) wide.
£180–220 LJ

A Baume & Mercier 18ct pink gold triple-date chronometer wristwatch, with registers and moon-phase, Swiss, c1950, 1½in (3.5cm) diam.
£6,200–7,000 ⊞ AGR
It is very unusual to find this complicated watch in pink gold and even more so in such exceptional condition.

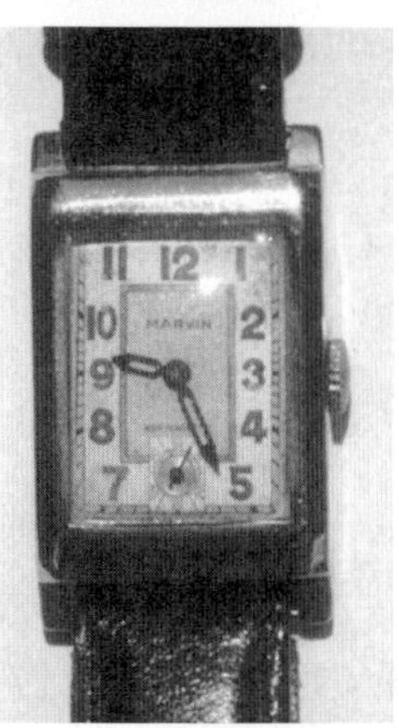

A Marvin gentleman's 9ct gold wristwatch, the gilt dial with subsidiary seconds dial, 1930s.
£500–625 BLH

A Benrus gentleman's 14ct gold wristwatch, c1950, 9in (23cm) long.
£200–240 SK

◄ An Eska 18ct gold wristwatch, folding into an American twenty dollar coin, c1970, 1½in (4cm) diam.
£1,300–1,600 S(NY)

► A Gruen stainless steel duo-dial wrist-watch, retailed by Freccero, Swiss, Geneva, c1935, 1¾in (4.5cm) long.
£2,000–2,500 S(NY)

A Breitling steel Navitimer wristwatch, with 12-hour dial, Swiss, 1960s, 1¾in (4.5cm) diam.
£950–1,050 ⊞ TEM

WATCHES

A Movado 18ct gold wristwatch, retailed by Tiffany & Co, Swiss, 1950s.
£800–900 ⊞ TEM

An Omega stainless steel wristwatch, with original box, Swiss, c1950.
£270–300 ⊞ JoV

An Omega gold automatic bracelet wristwatch, Swiss, c1950, 1¼in (3.5cm) diam.
£470–600 ⚒ S(O)

A Patek Philippe 18ct gold cased wristwatch, with calatrava movement, Swiss, 1950s.
£2,350–2,600 ⊞ JoV

A Piaget lady's 18ct white gold and diamond bracelet watch, with integrated 18ct white gold bracelet, Swiss, c1960, ½in (1.5cm) diam.
£1,600–1,750 ⚒ S(NY)

A Rolex lady's 9ct gold wristwatch, the silvered dial with integral two-colour gold articulated bracelet, signed, Swiss, hallmarked London 1969.
£420–525 ⚒ CGC

A Tissot stainless steel self-winding wristwatch, the dial polychrome-painted with a map of the United States of America with applied star-form numerals, Swiss, c1950, 1¼in (3cm) diam.
£1,800–2,250 ⚒ S(NY)

◄ A lady's Edwardian 18ct gold wristwatch, with diamond-set bezel, on a 15ct gold expanding bracelet, in original fitted case.
£280–350 ⚒ WL

A wristwatch, by Waltham, American, c1930.
£1,100–1,250 ⊞ AGR

An 18ct gold and platinum wristwatch, for The Goldsmiths & Silversmiths Co, the bezel set with rose-cut diamonds and sapphires with Swiss 15 jewel movement, c1922, 1in (2.5cm) diam.
£450–500 ⊞ GLa

Barometers

Stick Barometers

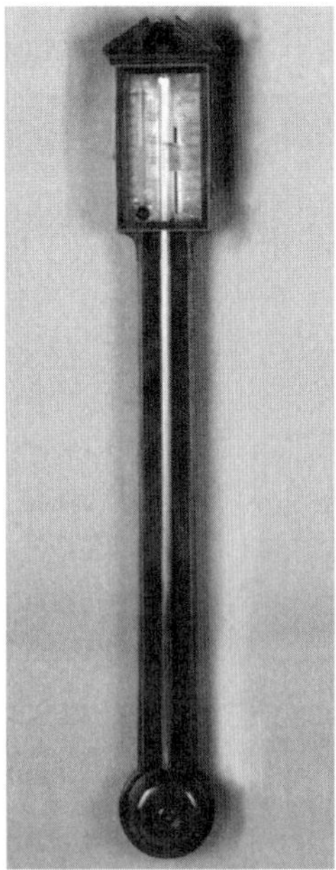

A mahogany stick barometer, by A. Ponti, with silvered scale and boxwood and ebony banding, c1790, 38¼in (97cm) high.
£1,350–1,700 TEN

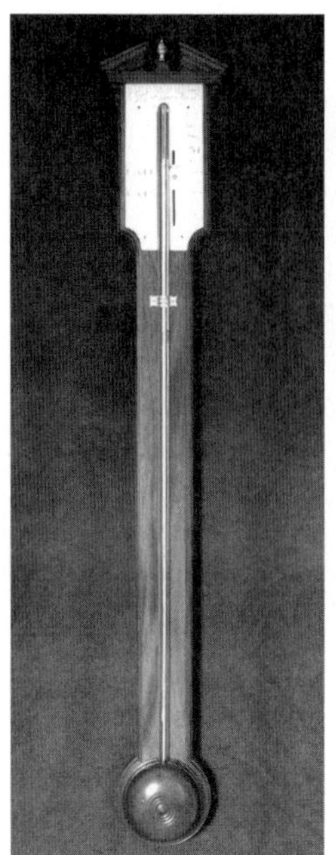

A mahogany stick barometer, by Peter Rabalio, London, with signed register plate and breakarch pediment, c1790, 38in (96.5cm) high.
£2,600–3,000 AW

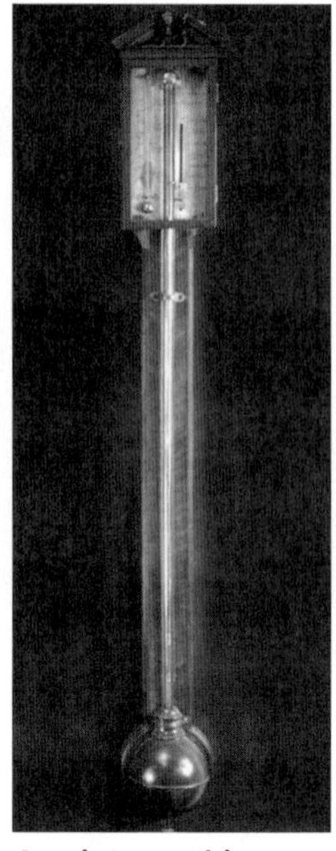

A mahogany stick barometer, by Henry Andrews, Royston, with silvered scale and turned cistern reservoir cover, late 18thC, 39in (99cm) high.
£1,600–2,000 CGC

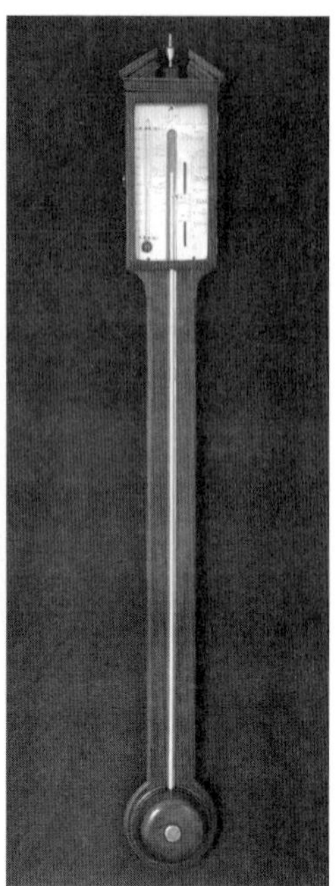

A mahogany stick barometer, by Peter Donegan, London, with signed silvered-brass plate, c1820, 38in (96.5cm) high.
£1,700–2,000 AW

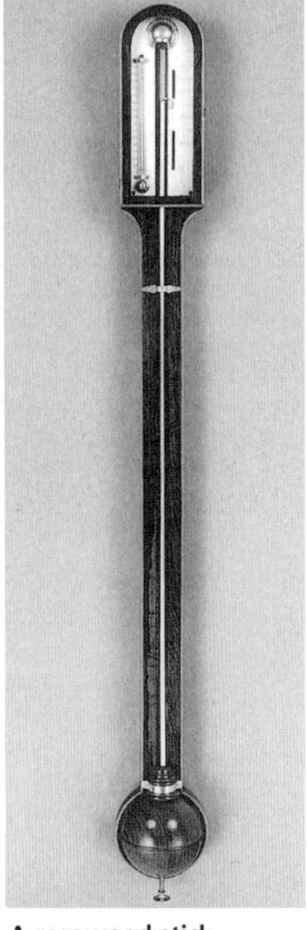

A rosewood stick barometer, with boxwood stringing, by J. Somalvico & Son, London, with silvered-brass scale, glazed access door and domed cistern cover, c1820, 36in (91.5cm) high.
£3,400–3,850 PAO

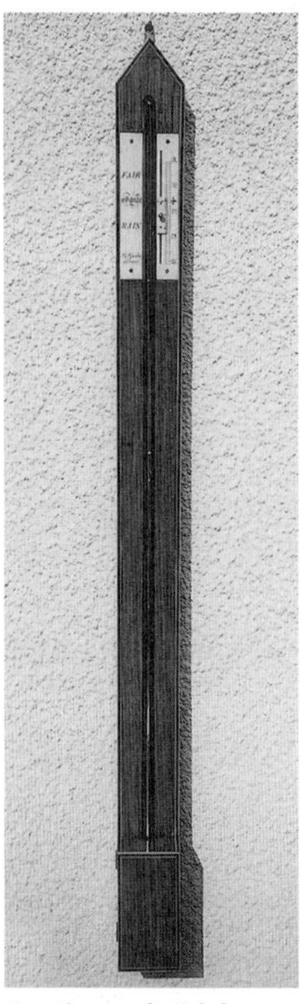

A satinwood stick barometer, by J. J. Gardner, Glasgow, Scottish, c1820, 38in (96.5cm) high.
£2,000–2,500 RAY

BAROMETERS

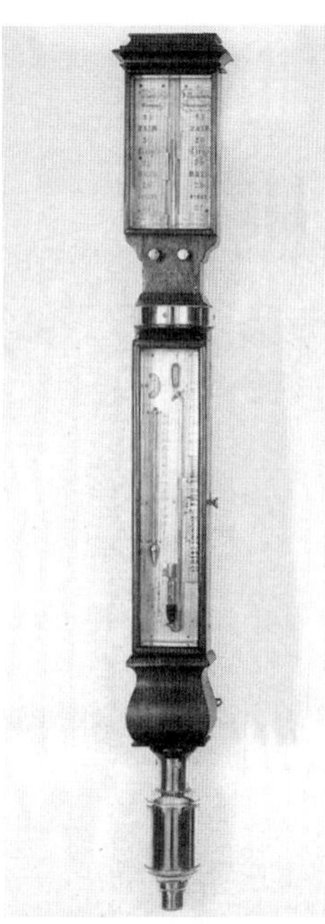

A walnut stick barometer with sympiesometer, by John Thompson, Liverpool, with silvered plate, extended scale, thermometer and recording sector, c1850, 39in (99cm) high.
£4,500–5,500 P(NW)
The combination of barometer and sympiesometer enabled extremely accurate readings to be taken with the latter while permitting checking with the barometer, as the sympiesometer was easily put out of adjustment.

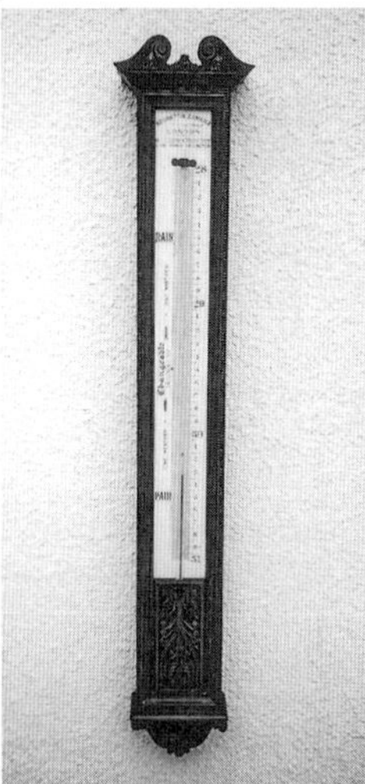

An oak long range mercury/glycerine barometer, by Negretti & Zambra, London, with china scales, signed, c1880, 48in (122cm) high.
£4,500–5,500 RAY
The mercury column behind the scale punches up a spirit/glycerine column which increases the movement and gives a larger rise and fall reading.

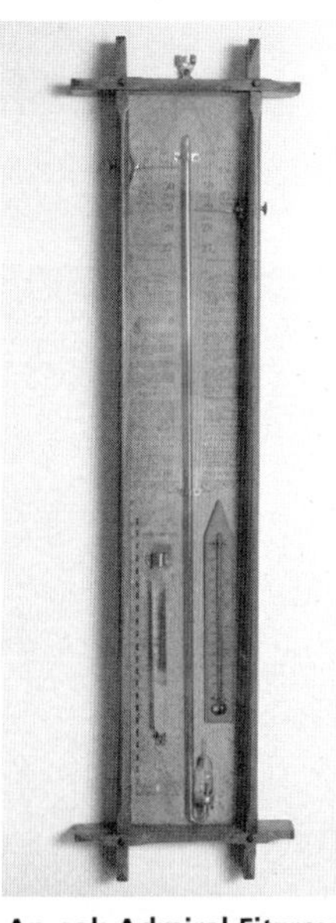

An oak Admiral Fitzroy mercury barometer, c1860, 40in (101.5cm) high.
£850–950 TRI

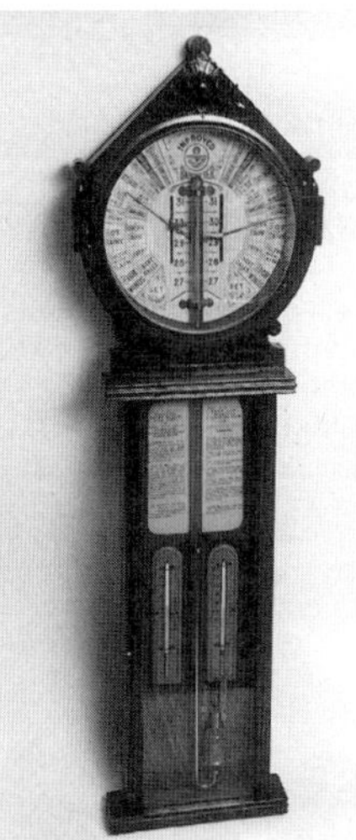

An Admiral Fitzroy Royal Polytechnic barometer, c1880, 42in (106.5cm) high.
£1,200–1,500 TWr

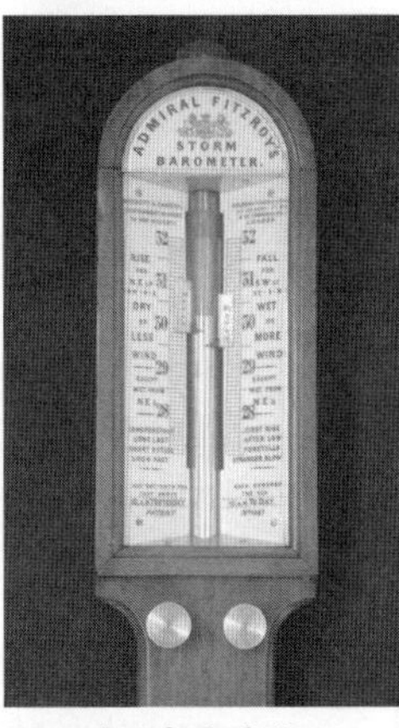

An oak Admiral Fitzroy storm barometer, by Negretti & Zambra, London, with signed porcelain plates, c1880, 40in (101.5cm) high.
£1,500–1,800 AW

An oak Admiral Fitzroy barometer, the paper scales with two-day recorders, explanation of Rising and Falling glass within Gothic tracery, atmosphere glass and associated thermometer, c1875, 42in (106.5cm) high.
£340–425 P(NW)
Admiral Fitzroy (1805–65) was Captain of HMS *Beagle* which took Charles Darwin on his surveying expedition to Patagonia. However, following his retirement from the Governorship of New Zealand, he turned his attention to meteorology and invented his barometer.

An oak stick barometer, by Negretti & Zambra, London, the engraved bone registers with vernier, the case with classical mouldings, the cistern cover carved with a mask, c1900, 42in (106.5cm) high.
£1,600–1,800 N

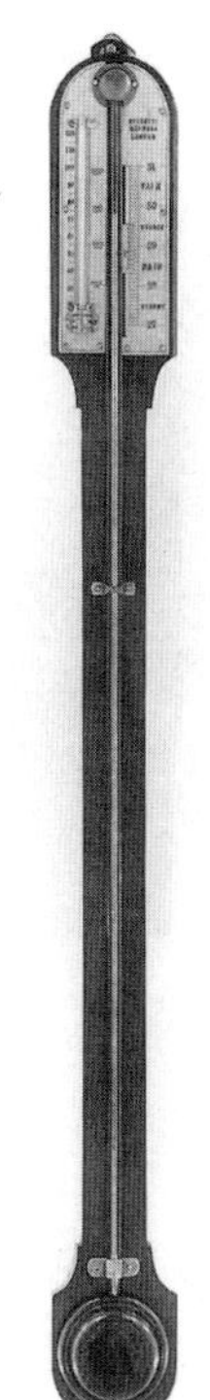

A mahogany Model stick barometer, by Negretti & Zambra, London, with ivory register plate, c1880, 35½in (90cm) high.
£800–950 AW
'Model' was the cheapest stick barometer in a manufacturer's range. Sometimes 'model' was engraved on a bone disc on the cistern cover.

When sold at auction, barometers have sometimes undergone alterations to their mechanisms, or are in unrestored condition, which may affect the prices realized.

A Louis XVI-style painted and giltwood barometer and thermometer, by Secretan, Paris, retored, French, 1850–1900, 53¼in (135.5cm) high.
£2,000–2,400 S(Am)

Wheel Barometers

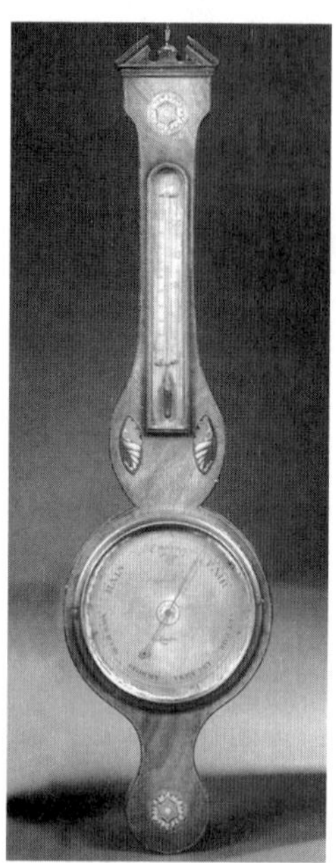

A George III mahogany wheel barometer, by Pastorelli & Co, London, the silvered register dial with thermometer above, with boxwood and ebony lines and inlaid with shells and flowers, 39in (99cm) high.
£550–650 ⚒ B(Ed)

A giltwood wheel barometer, by Bianchy, Paris, with paper dial, some cracking, French, late 18thC, 41½in (105.5cm) high.
£2,000–2,400 ⚒ S(O)

A mahogany-inlaid wheel barometer, by Barbon, London, c1810, 37in (94cm) high.
£1,800–2,000 ⊞ RAY

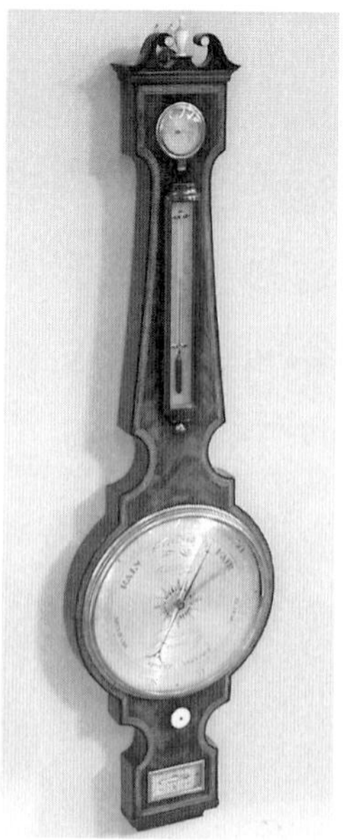

A Regency mahogany wheel barometer, by F. Amadio & Son, London, with boxwood-and-ebony-strung tulipwood banding, silvered hygrometer, thermometer, dial and level, 44in (112cm) high.
£1,800–2,200 ⚒ G(L)

A boxwood-strung mahogany wheel barometer, by Dominick Lione & Co, London, with silvered dial, applied with an alchohol thermometer, c1815, 37¼in (94.5cm) high.
£900–1,100 ⚒ S(O)

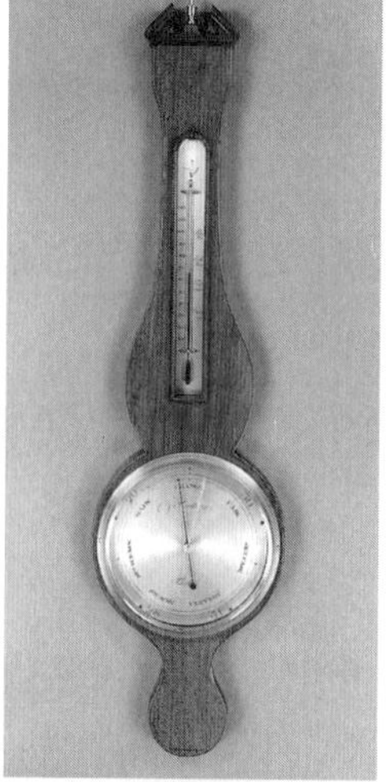

◄ **A mahogany wheel barometer,** by Domco Barelli & Co, Bath, with silvered-brass scale and silvered-brass thermometer scale, c1820, 8in (20.5cm) diam.
£1,600–1,750 ⊞ PAO

► **A mahogany wheel barometer,** by S. Bregazzi, Derby, the silvered dial with integral alchohol thermometer, pediment damaged, c1810, 41in (104cm) high.
£1,000–1,250 ⚒ PFK

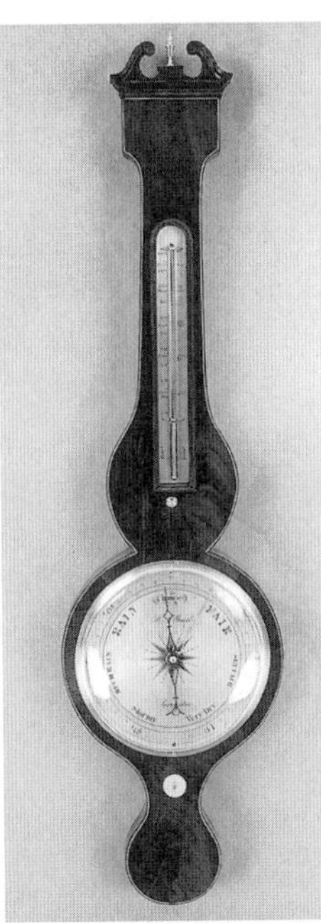

A mahogany boxwood-strung wheel barometer, by R. S. Gough, Servington, with 8in (20.5cm) diameter silvered brass-dial and thermometer, c1820.
£1,100–1,200 ⊞ PAO

► **A mahogany shell-inlaid barometer,** by Molton, Norwich, c1820, 36in (91.5cm) high.
£1,200–1,400 ⊞ RAY

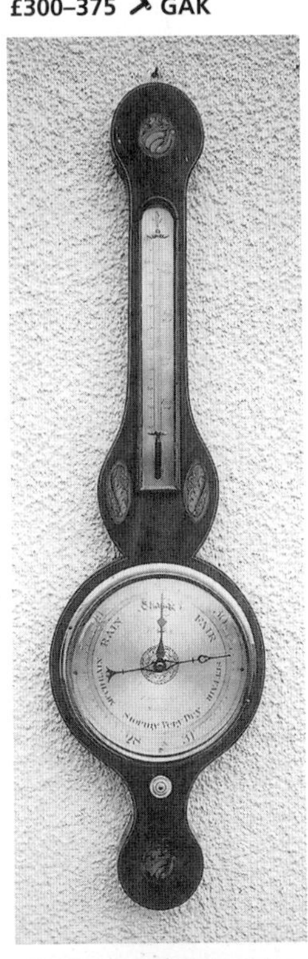

► **A rosewood and mother-of-pearl wheel barometer,** by G. Volanterio, Doncaster, with dry/damp dial and silvered thermometer, 19thC, 40in (101.5cm) high.
£300–375 ⚒ GAK

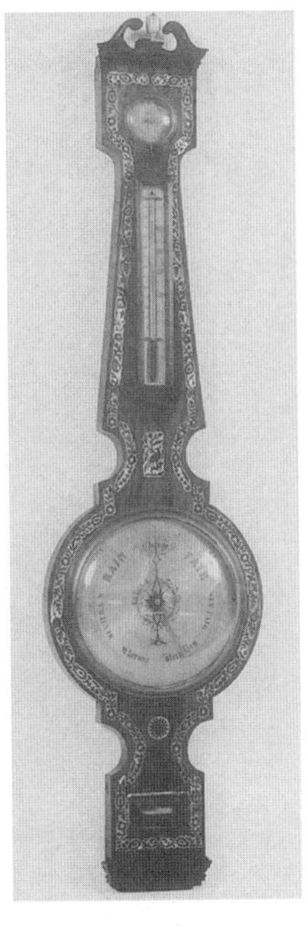

A combination clock barometer, by Lione, London, with 8in (20.5cm) enamel dials, the clock with eight-day movement, c1820, 48in (122cm) high.
£7,200–8,000 ⊞ RAY

► **A string-inlaid mahogany wheel barometer,** by John Leone, Aylesbury, with silvered-brass scale, thermometer, hygrometer and spirit level, c1830, 8in (20.5cm) diam.
£950–1,100 ⊞ PAO

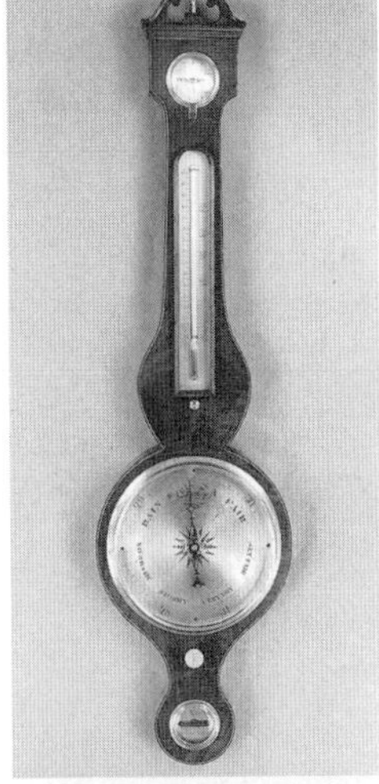

A mahogany and shell-inlaid wheel barometer, with silvered dial, c1830, dial 8in (20.5cm) diam.
£1,100–1,250 ⊞ TRI

► **A rosewood wheel barometer,** by Thomas Saunders, Dorchester, with arched pediment, c1840, 4½in (11.5cm) diam.
£2,800–3,300 ⊞ AW

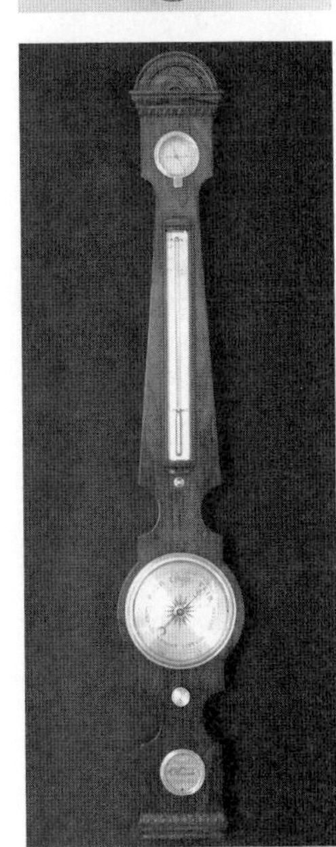

BAROMETERS

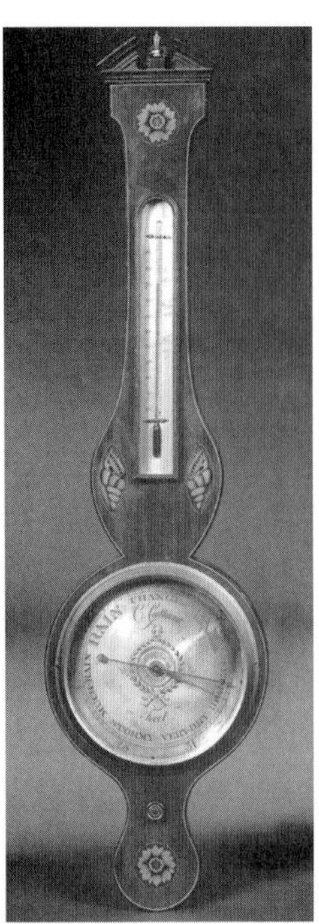

A mahogany and shell-inlaid wheel barometer, by C. Cattani, the silvered registered scale with a thermometer above, 19thC, 39in (99cm) high.
£650–800 B(Ed)

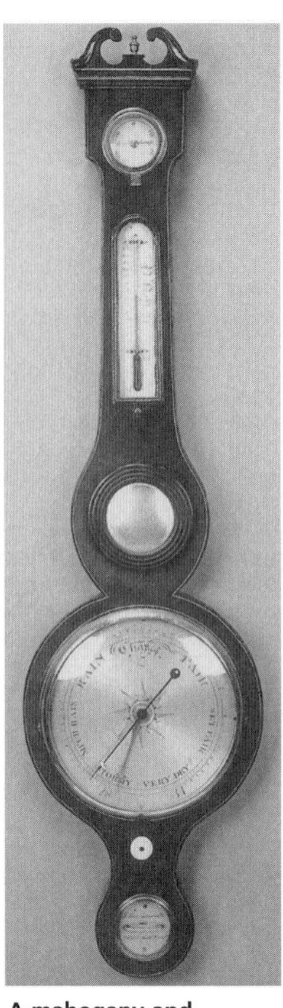

A mahogany and boxwood-banded wheel barometer, by J. Mangiacavalli, London, with silvered dial, thermometer, hygrometer, mirror and spirit level, mid-19thC, 38½in (98cm) high.
£600–750 DN

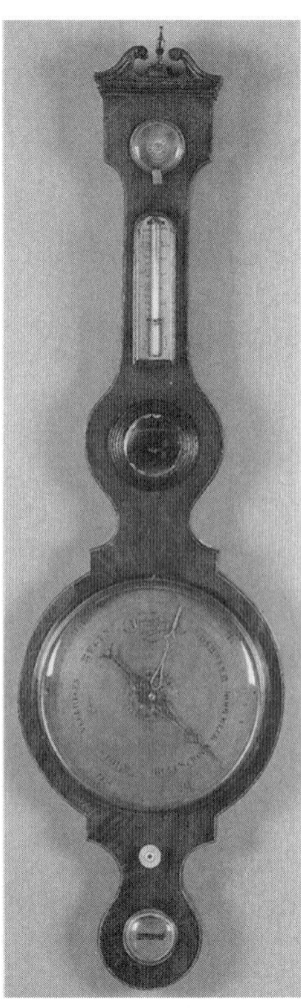

A mahogany inlaid wheel barometer, with silvered dial, hygrometer, thermometer and spirit level, later finial, mid-19thC, 43in (109cm) high.
£600–700 S(Am)

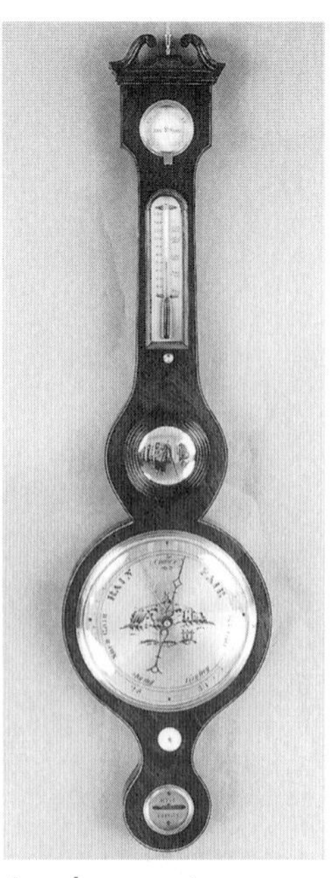

A mahogany-strung wheel barometer, by John Hyde, Bristol, the silvered-brass scale with engraved scene to the centre, with thermometer, mirror and hygrometer, c1850, 39in (99cm) high.
£950–1,100 PAO

Cross Reference
See Colour Review (page 432)

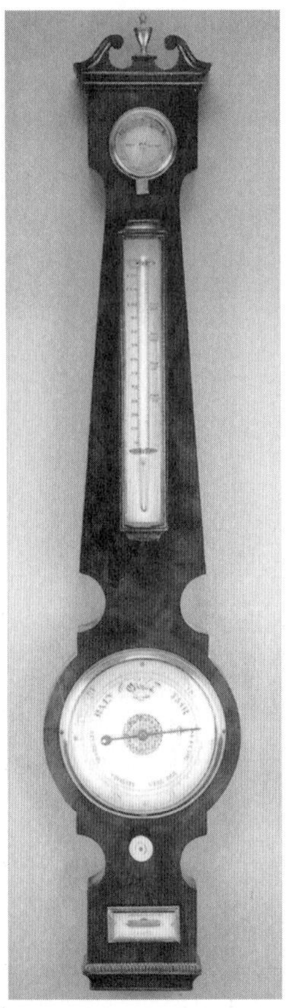

A mahogany wheel barometer, by Sutherland, Derby, with silvered dial, hygrometer, thermometer and spirit level, mid-19thC, 37½in (95.5cm) high.
£850–1,000 DN

A rosewood wheel barometer, by McGregor of Greenock and Glasgow, inlaid with brass, mother-of-pearl and pewter, c1850, 41in (104cm) high.
£3,200–3,500 HA

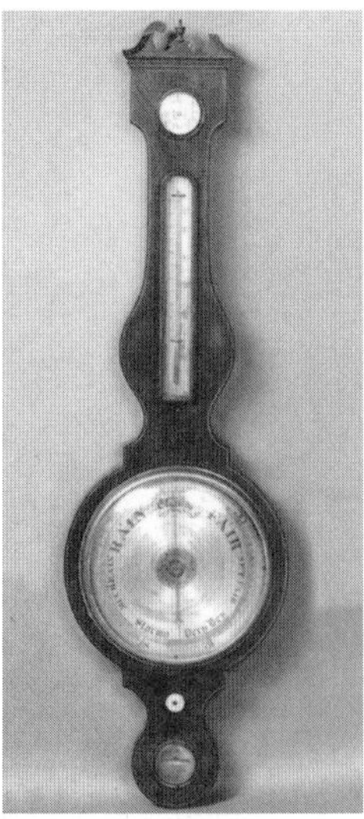

A mahogany wheel barometer, by Tickell, Dublin, with boxwood and ebonized-trim, with silvered-brass dial, thermometer and hygrometer, 19thC, 41¾in (106cms) high.
£350–450 HOK

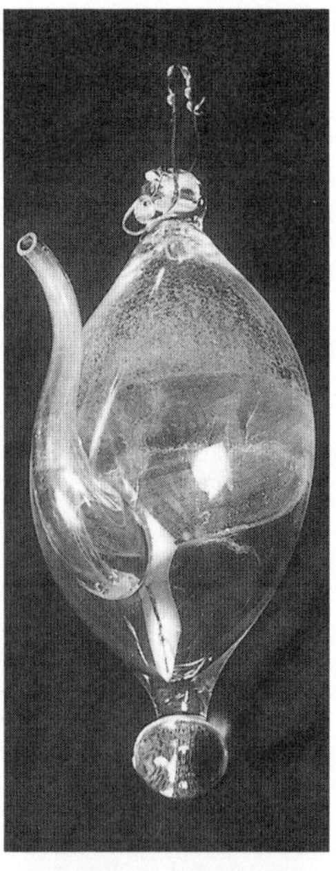

Miller's is a price GUIDE not a price LIST

◀ **A glass water barometer,** c1860, 9in (23cm) high.
£230–300 ⊞ RAY
The Victorians made water barometers that were copies of 18th century Dutch water barometers, called *Donderglass* (Thunderglass). The principle is that with air trapped above the water line, at a constant pressure, the change in pressure outside is reflected by the water level in the spout going up for lower pressure, and down for higher pressure. The entrance from the spout into the chamber must always be covered by the water level in the chamber.

▶ **A rosewood mercurial wheel barometer,** by M. Baumeyer, London, with silvered-brass scale, and thermometer, c1875, 40in (101.5cm) high.
£800–875 ⊞ PAO

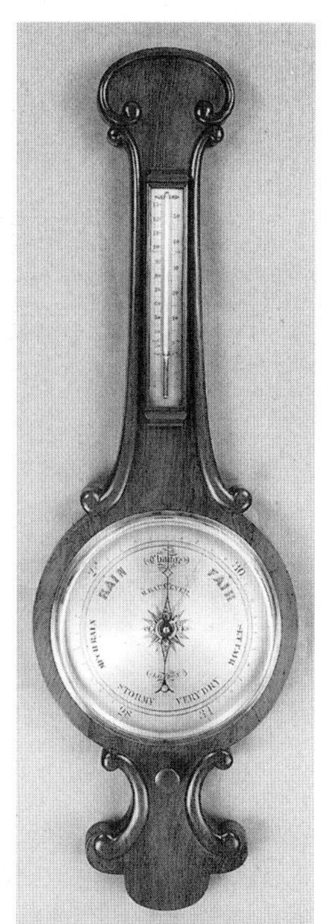

Aneroid Barometers

◀ **A brass-cased aneroid barometer,** by James Hicks, London, with exposed movement, c1880, 8¼in (21cm) diam.
£400–500 ⊞ AW

A holosteric barometer, the dial inscribed 'Apps, London', supported by a gilt-bronze wreath on a foliate black marble plinth, 1875–1900, 4½in (11.5cm) wide.
£700–900 NOA
'Holosteric' is the English translation of 'baromètres holosteriques', meaning wholly solid. These instruments were made in Paris by Naudet, Hulot & Cie, c1860–70.

An architectural oak-cased aneroid barometer and thermometer, by Hinton & Armstead, Oldham, c1880, 36¼in (92cm) high.
£550–650 ⊞ AW

▶ **An aneroid barometer,** in a Black Forest-style walnut case, carved with a mask, cupid and grapes, German, c1900, 29in (73.5cm) high.
£110–135 G(L)

An oak-cased aneroid barometer, by George Wood, London, with engine-turned dial and thermometer, c1880, 17in (43cm) high.
£250–350 ⊞ AW

A Victorian aneroid barometer, with ceramic dial and scale, 35in (89cm) high.
£500–550 ⊞ TRI

An Edwardian oak-cased aneroid barometer, with printed dial, 9½in (24cm) diam.
£80–100 G(L)

BAROMETERS

Barographs

An ebonized self-registering aneroid barograph, by R. & J. Beck, London, sold with original receipt dated July 1870, 23in (58.5cm) high.
£2,350–2,600 ⊞ RTW

An oak-cased self-recording weather station, by Negretti & Zambra, London, the recording drum mounted between the silvered timepiece and barometer dials, faults, c1876, 26in (66cm) wide.
£1,800–2,200 ⚒ S(S)

A mahogany barograph, by Casartelli Bros, Liverpool, with chart drawer to front, c1900, 14½in (37cm) wide.
£500–600 ⚒ Bri

A mahogany-cased barograph, retailed by Lennie & Thomson, Dundee, with additional aneroid dial, early 20thC, 12in (30.5cm) wide.
£1,500–1,800 ⚒ WOM

An Edwardian mahogany-cased barograph, retailed by Dixon & Hempenstall, Dublin, with marquetry and satinwood line inlay, with glazed removable top and fitted with a drawer, 14½in (37cm) wide.
£1,100–1,400 ⚒ RFA

An oak-cased barograph, by Negretti & Zambra, London, retailed by the Army & Navy Co Stores, c1910, 14in (35.5cm) wide.
£1,100–1,300 ⊞ AW

Items in the Barographs section have been arranged in date order.

◄ **An oak-cased Simplex barograph,** by Woodruff & Horsfield, early 20thC, 14¼in (36cm) wide.
£350–450 ⚒ CGC

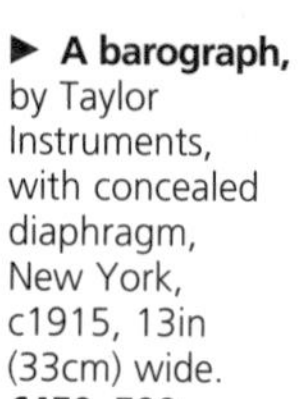

► **A barograph,** by Taylor Instruments, with concealed diaphragm, New York, c1915, 13in (33cm) wide.
£450–500 ⊞ RTW

A walnut-cased barograph, retailed by La Filotechnica, Milan, with bevelled glass to front and back and a single chart drawer, c1920, 14in (35.5cm) wide.
£550–600 ⊞ RTW

Decorative Arts

Aesthetic Movement Furniture

A walnut and ebonized bedroom suite, comprising a triple wardrobe, dressing table, washstand, pot cupboard and a pair of bedroom chairs, with polychrome-decorated panels on a gilt ground, one chair damaged, c1875, wardrobe 74in (188cm) wide.
£1,800–2,250 B

► **An ebonized corner cupboard,** the central mirror-back with frieze drawer below, the base with painted lacquer birds on leafy branches, late 19thC, Anglo-Japanese, 27¼in (69cm) wide.
£1,100–1,400 DN

An ebonized X-frame chair, c1875.
£500–625 B
This chair is clearly an Aesthetic period reworking of Thomas Hope's X-frame chair that was popularized by the publication of his book *Household Furniture and Interior Decoration* (1807) and was produced by Gillows among other manufacturers. The Greek style was to remain one of the most dominant styles for the remainder of the century in both commercial design and the more *avant garde* production of designers such as E. W. Godwin.

An ebonized easy chair, with a padded back panel and stuff-over seat, c1880.
£500–625 P(O)
This was influenced by an Anglo-Japanese chair designed by E. W. Godwin in 1876.

A pair of oak hall chairs, the carved and pierced backs inset with Minton tiles, c1880.
£450–575 P(B)

► **A child's Victorian ebonized chair,** applied with gilt-metal rosettes and mounts, upholstered in burgundy fabric.
£110–140 GAK

Miller's is a price GUIDE not a price LIST

An oak armchair, the back and apron fitted with a Moorish-inspired turned fretwork panel, American, c1885.
£2,800–3,200 NOA

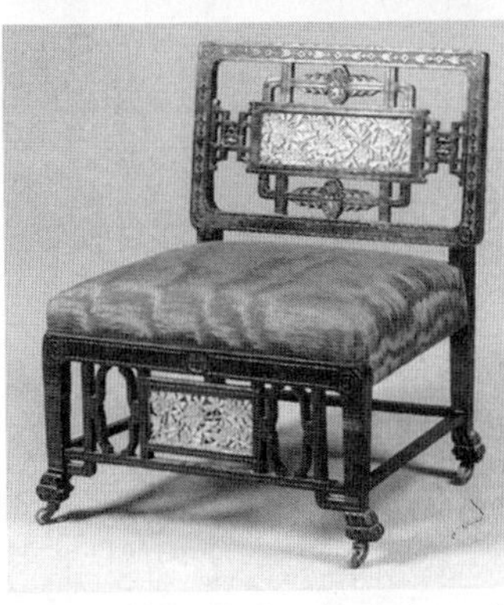

A carved ebonized and upholstered chair, attributed to Herter Bros, with pierced fruitwood panels, American, c1890.
£2,200–2,750 S(O)

A parcel-gilt and porcelain-inset rosewood pier mirror, attributed to Herter Bros, New York, American, c1860, 64¾in (164.5cm) wide.
£5,250–6,500 S(NY)

► **A rosewood and harewood sideboard,** in the style of Collinson & Lock, with a panelled and bevelled mirror-back, the base with two central drawers above a shelf and flanked by two panelled doors, c1880, 78in (198cm) wide.
£3,500–4,000 S(S)

A set of Victorian ebonized wall shelves, with gilt-chamfered borders and pierced fret sides, the cupboard drawers with gilt panels decorated with painted birds, insects and foliage, 26¼in (66.5cm) high.
£280–350 WW

A walnut mirror-back sideboard, by Gillow & Co, in the style of Bruce Talbert, the back with mirror plate above an open shelf and polychrome-decorated tiles, the lower section with a frieze drawer flanked by cupboard doors carved with stylized foliage, maker's stamp, c1880, 72in (183cm) wide.
£825–1,000 S(S)

◄ **A mahogany occasional table,** by E. W. Godwin, c1870, 26½in (67.5cm) high.
£320–400 P(B)

Aesthetic Movement Metalware

A pair of cast-iron andirons, by F. W. Grafton & Co, the stylized supports terminating in flowerheads and rising Gothic pinnacles at the rear with four attached circular shields, one flowerhead missing, c1900, 15½in (39.5cm) high.
£1,100–1,300 S

A brass coal scuttle, with removable tin liner, c1890, 15¾in (40cm) high.
£300–350 S(O)

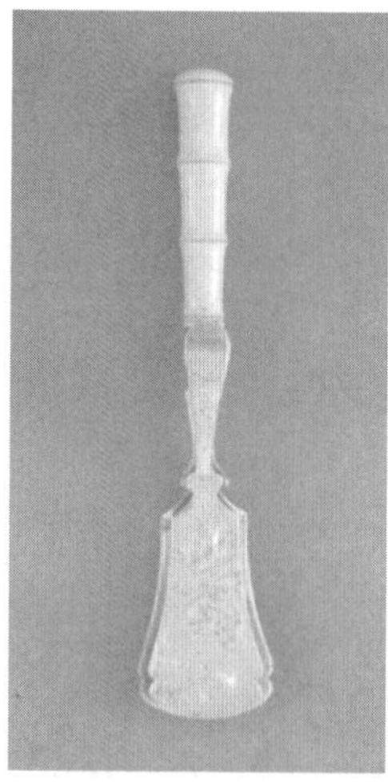

A pair of Aesthetic-style silver serving tongs, by Atkin Bros, with stylized floral decoration, the ivory handle modelled as bamboo, Sheffield 1898, 9½in (24cm) long.
£200–250 Bon

A silver overlay flask, the green glass body covered in an Aesthetic design of birds among bamboo shoots and flowers, probably American, c1890, 19thC, 8in (20.5cm) high.
£600–750 N

A Tiffany & Co silver part flatware service, comprising 17 pieces, American, c1880, 31.25oz.
£1,500–1,700 SLN

A Victorian silver-plated samovar, in the Aesthetic style, with turned ivory handles, 19¼in (49cm) high.
£120–150 P(WM)

► **A *champlevé* enamel vase,** decorated with birds and foliage, on a Japanesque gilt-metal base with stylized mushrooms, maker's mark 'E. & Co', dated 1872, 13in (33cm) high.
£3,700–4,000 RIT

Arts & Crafts Ceramics

A pair of Ault flower shells, modelled as scallops, decorated in yellow and brown, with nine flower holes, c1895, 6½in (16.5cm) high.
£400–435 ⊞ HUN

An Ault vase, attributed to Dr Christopher Dresser, with moulded moths, decorated in olive running to yellow, c1895, 4in (10cm) high.
£170–185 ⊞ HUN

A pair of Brannam pottery vases, decorated with a carved slip design in brown and blue, one with a fox and hounds, the other with goats and birds, c1900, 13in (33cm) high.
£1,200–1,500 ⚒ WW

◄ A Bretby amphora vase with flown blue, green, cream and brown glaze decoration, c1908, 11¾in (30cm) high.
£300–325 ⊞ HUN

► A Bretby spill holder, modelled as a crane and bamboo, naturalistically coloured, c1895, 11in (28cm) high.
£130–145 ⊞ HUN

A William de Morgan pottery tile, painted with blue flowers and green leaves, c1890, 6in (15cm) square, set in a metal mount.
£450–550 ⚒ B

A Linthorpe pottery salad bowl and servers, with plated rim and mounts and mottled green/brown glaze, impressed mark, c1880, 9¾in (25cm) diam.
£110–140 ⚒ LFA

► A Pilkington's vase, decorated in crackled metallic copper lustre glaze, impressed marks, date code for 1908, 6¾in (17cm) high.
£260–325 ⚒ WL

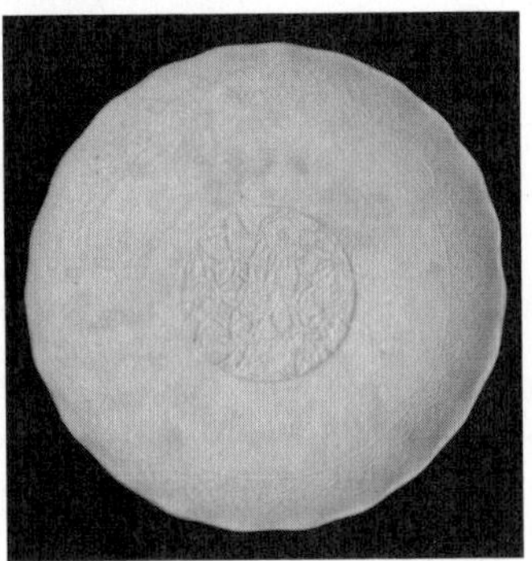

A Linthorpe plaque, the centre moulded with prunus, unglazed, marked 'H. T.' and with Dr Christopher Dresser facsimile signature, c1880, 10in (25.5cm) diam.
£220–250 ⊞ HUN

► A Rockwood vase, by Grace Young, painted with a portrait of 'Weasaw', a Shoshoni chief, with a brown and green glaze, small defects, crazed, American, 10¼in (26cm) high.
£4,500–5,750 ⚒ SWO

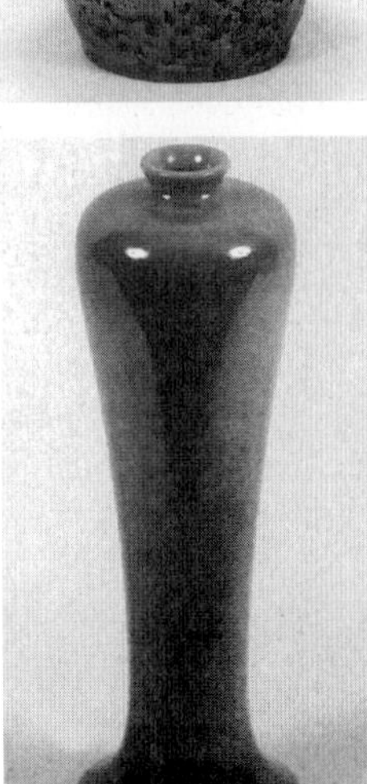

► A Ruskin pottery spill vase, decorated in iridescent pale blue, impressed mark and dated 1918, 10½in (26.5cm) high.
£260–325 ⚒ GAK

Arts & Crafts Furniture

A set of six oak dining chairs, possibly by Liberty & Co, with two open armchairs, the drop-in seats covered in leather.
£1,000–1,250 B

A set of 12 oak dining chairs, designed by William Lethaby, possibly retailed by Morris & Co, including two carvers, c1870.
£6,500–8,000 PVD

A pair of oak chairs, c1880.
£110–125 NAW

A set of 12 oak and rush chairs, by William Birch, c1890.
£7,000–8,000 PVD

Further reading

Miller's 100 Years of The Decorative Arts, Miller's Publications, 1994

► **A Gustav Stickley lady's oak writing desk,** labelled, American, Syracuse, c1912, 38in (96.5cm) wide.
£1,250–1,500 SK

A pair of William Birch oak open armchairs, the design attributed to E. G. Punnett, with rush seats, c1902.
£1,000–1,250 P

The High Wycombe firm of William Birch first appears in trade directories in 1853. William's sons, Walter and Charles, both established furniture businesses in High Wycombe, with Walter taking over his father's firm in 1895. By the end of the 19th century the company had abandoned the standard cheap Windsor and rush or cane seated furniture for a higher quality product and more progressive designs, although they still produced some hybrid revival style pieces. The firm supplied many leading London stores, notably Liberty & Co, with designs produced by designers such as E. G. Punnett and George Walton. Recent research supports the idea that E. G. Punnett was the in-house designer at Birch's as he appears regularly in the wage books for the firm. Punnett's designs show a combination of both Art Nouveau influences and more traditional English vernacular furniture. He often gave his designs Saxon names such as 'Ethelbert' or 'Athelston' and was clearly reacting against some of the more florid examples of English Art Nouveau which were already deemed to have reached unreasonable extremes by the early years of the 20th century.

An ebonized triple chairback settee, by Ford Maddox Brown for Morris & Co, with a rush seat, designed c1865, 48in (122cm) wide.
£1,500–2,000 P

A walnut sideboard, by Shapland and Petter, the raised back with two cupboard doors with three concave glazed panels, decorative brass handles and central plaque embossed with stylized tree motif inlaid with a Ruskin enamel roundel, the base with bowfronted top, early 20thC, 61in (155cm) wide.
£2,300–2,875 P(O)

A Liberty & Co oak stick stand, with chequered inlay and heart-shaped cut-outs, c1900, 31in (78.5cm) wide.
£450–500 ⊞ PVD

A walnut window seat, the splats pierced with stylized seed heads, with rush seat, 47in (119.5cm) wide.
£620–775 N

A two-seater settee, with an upholstered panel seat, late 19thC, 39½in (100.5cm) wide.
£550–700 BLH

An oak side cabinet, with fitted interior enclosed by two panel doors, c1890, 42¼in (107.5cm) wide.
£420–525 L&E

Cross Reference
See Colour Review (page 483)

► **A Stickley Bros single-drawer oak table,** with hammered-copper fittings, American, Fayetteville, New York, c1915, 36in (91.5cm) wide.
£630–700 SK

A Greene & Greene pine settle, with oak detail and hinged seat, American, 1905, 79in (200.5cm) wide.
£5,000–6,250 TREA

An oak smoker's cabinet, c1890, 40in (101.5cm) high.
£430–475 ⊞ NAW

◄ **A mahogany and brass extending dining table,** attributed to Koloman Moser, restored, Austrian, Vienna, 1905, 50¼in (127.5cm) wide.
£3,800–4,750 S(Am)

◄ **A set of oak wall shelves,** by Sir Robert Lorimer, c1928, 48in (122cm) wide.
£900–1,150 P(Ed)
These hanging shelves are designed for plates to lean backwards in the English manner rather than forwards in the Scottish way, so there are no guard rails. This very simple essay in design reflects not only R. S. Lorimer's personal preference for form unencumbered by unnecessary ornament, but also his readiness to experiment with English, as well as Scottish vernacular features.

Arts & Crafts Jewellery

A *plique-à-jour* and green sapphire brooch, designed by Louis Comfort Tiffany, with 18ct gold mount, one bead detached, minor loss to enamel, c1910.
£3,000–3,750 SK

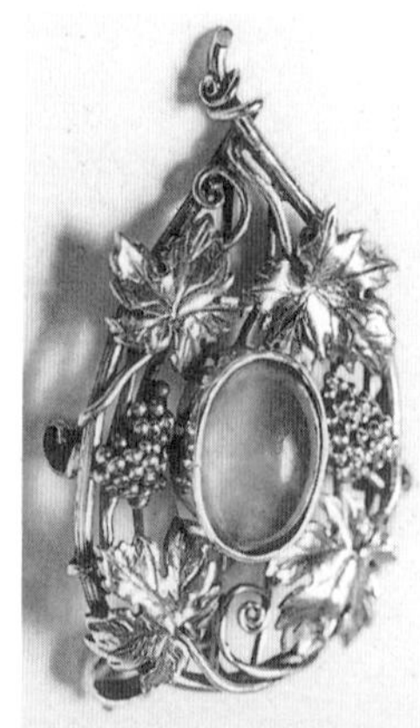

◄ **A Sibyl Dunlop silver brooch pendant,** worked with vine leaves and grape clusters entwined around a chrysoberyl cabochon, c1930, 2in (5cm) long.
£900–1,000 DAD

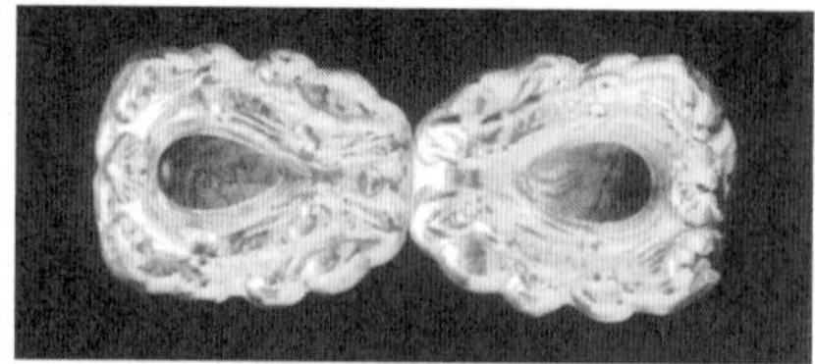

A Newlyn enamel and silver belt buckle, each half embossed with two fish and a scallop shell, set with a teardrop-shaped blue, green and mauve enamel panel, maker's mark of Reginald Thomas Dick, London 1906, 5¼in (13.5cm) wide.
£200–250 Bon

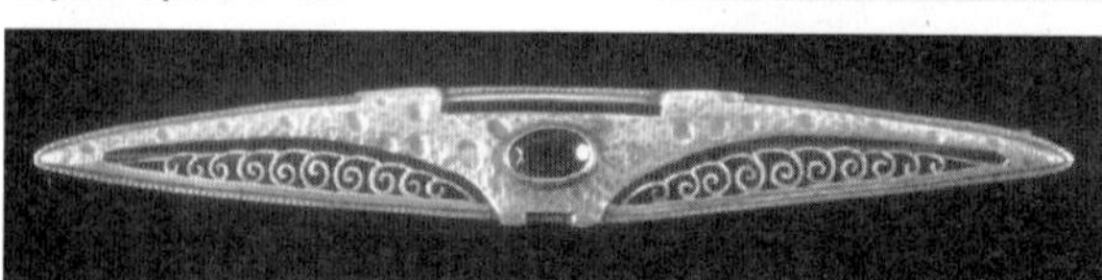

A sterling silver and marcasite bar pin, with hammered finish, hallmarked for Fahrner, German, c1908.
£550–650 SK

► **An Iona silver two-piece cloak clasp,** each piece enclosing scrolling foliage, Chester 1909, 3¼in (8.5cm) wide.
£160–200 DN

Arts & Crafts Metalware

◄ **An Arts & Crafts-style silver bowl,** by Joseph Heming, with hammered finish below a knopped moulded edge, London 1901, 6in (15cm) diam, 11.25oz.
£240–300 CGC

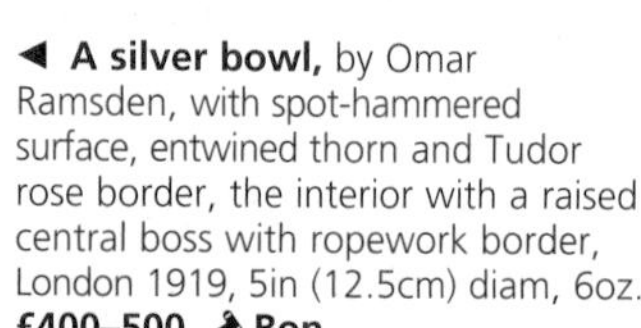

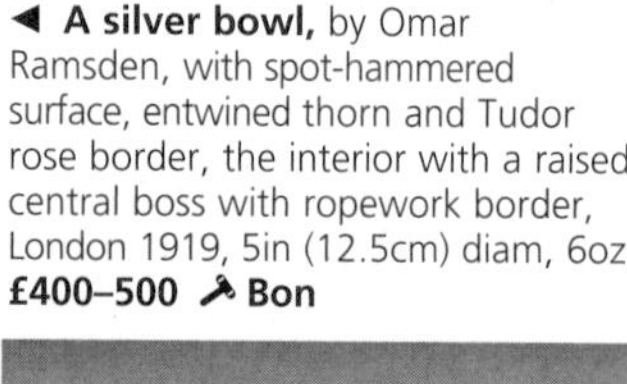

A silver bowl, by Coles and Fryer, the sides chased with stylized leaves, Birmingham 1903, 9¾in (25cm) diam, 23oz.
£250–300 N

A silver sugar bowl, by Nathan and Hayes, with bifurcated loop handle, Chester 1906, 4½in (11.5cm) diam, 5oz.
£500–625 TEN

◄ **A silver bowl,** by Omar Ramsden, with spot-hammered surface, entwined thorn and Tudor rose border, the interior with a raised central boss with ropework border, London 1919, 5in (12.5cm) diam, 6oz.
£400–500 Bon

LOCATE THE SOURCE
The source of each illustration in Miller's can be found by checking the code letters below each caption with the Key to Illustrations, pages 794–800.

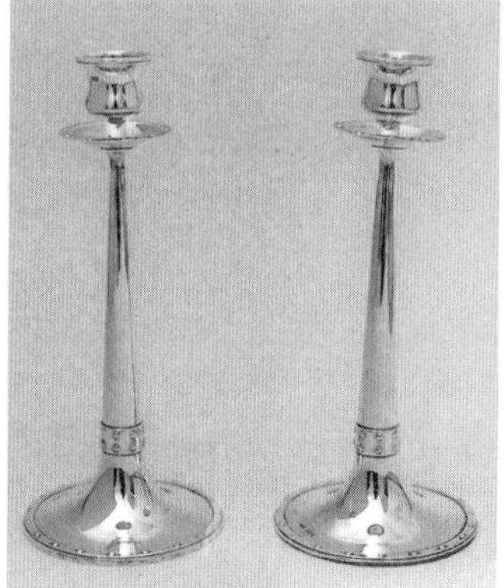

► **A pair of Arts & Crafts silver candlesticks,** by James Dixon & Sons, with beaded motifs to the edges, Sheffield 1905, 9in (23cm) high.
£900–1,100 MCA

A Liberty & Co Tudric pewter and enamel biscuit box, designed by Archibald Knox, early 20thC, 4¾in (12cm) wide.
£950–1,100 S(O)

A wrought-iron three-branch candlestick, attributed to Elizabeth Burton, American, c1910, 24in (61cm) high.
£4,000–5,000 S(NY)

A copper charger, c1895, 15½in (39.5cm) diam.
£500–550 SHa

A silver dish, spot-hammered and applied with a band of pierced foliate decoration, maker's mark of Sybil Dunlop, London 1922, 6¼in (16cm) diam, 8oz.
£500–625 Bon

A silver caddy spoon, Birmingham 1926, 4in (10cm) long.
£500–550 SHa

A silver trinket box, by William Hutton & Sons, with strapwork decoration to the lid and corners, London 1901, 4in (10cm) wide.
£700–900 GAK

A John Pearson copper charger, the centre decorated with five birds in flight among berry-laden vines, the rim with stylized profiles of birds bearing berries, signed and dated 1890, 20¼in (51.5cm) diam.
£3,000–3,800 P(B)

► **A silver cream jug,** by Henry George Murphy, with lightly spot-hammered surface, London 1935, 3in (7.5cm) high, 4oz.
£550–700 Bon

► **A silver seal-top spoon,** by the Guild of Handicraft, with hammered finish, London 1907, 6in (15cm) long.
£100–125 N

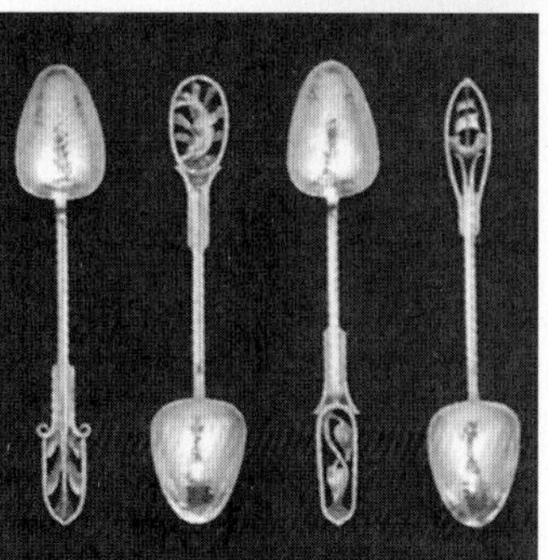

A set of six silver teaspoons, by J. A. B. Linton, with spot-hammered bowls, the various-shaped terminals pierced with flowers, fish, boats and foliate decoration, Australian, Perth c1930, 4¼in (11cm) long.
£220–275 Bon

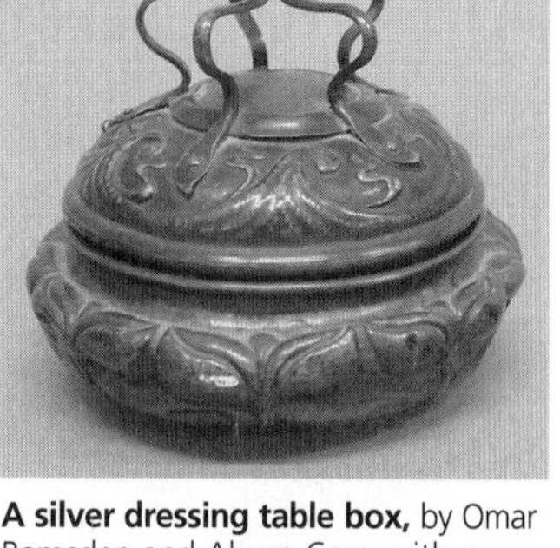

A silver dressing table box, by Omar Ramsden and Alwyn Carr, with a formerly enamelled panel to lid, decorated with waves and stylized motifs, 1901, 4½in (11.5cm) diam, 6.5oz.
£550–700 G(L)

A copper and brass coal scuttle, by Benham & Froud, stamped mark, late 19thC, 20in (51cm) wide.
£350–475 S(O)

A white metal tea caddy, attributed to Friedrich Adler, the cover with a pierced finial set with dark blue lapis lazuli, with gilded interior, German, c1910, 5½in (14cm) high.
£550–700 B

Doulton

A Doulton Lambeth beaker, decorated with green and brown glazes, with presentation inscription, c1902, 5in (12.5cm) high.
£150–165 ⊞ RUSK

A Royal Doulton figure, Tildy, by Leslie Harradine, model No. HN1576, decorated in pink, white and cream, 1933–39, 5in (12.5cm) high.
£350–450 ⚒ BBR

A Doulton salt-glazed brown stoneware figure, The Boer War Soldier, by John Broad, holding a brass rifle, glued repair, firing faults, impressed and incised marks, c1900, 12½in (32cm) high.
£650–725 ⚒ S(O)

A Royal Doulton figure, A Victorian Lady, model No. HN1277, decorated in shades of red, orange, blue and black, withdrawn 1938, 7¾in (19.5cm) high.
£200–250 ⚒ Bea(E)

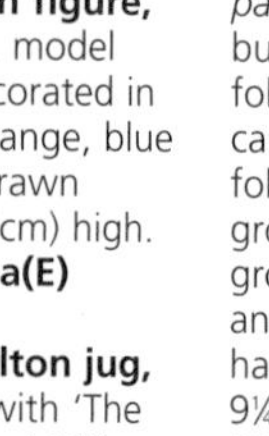

◀ A Royal Doulton jug, transfer-printed with 'The Battle of Hastings 1066 from The Bayeux Tapestry', printed mark, early 20thC, 5¾in (14.5cm) high.
£70–100 ⚒ FHF

A Royal Doulton figure, Chloë, by Leslie Harradine, model No. HN1470, decorated in yellow, purple and green, chip, 1931–49, 5½in (14cm) high.
£160–200 ⚒ BBR

A Doulton Lambeth stoneware jug, by Florence E. Barlow, with a silver rim, decorated in *pâte-sur-pâte* with two budgerigars among brown foliage and a quatreform cartouche with incised foliage on a brown gloss ground, on a stippled ground body, impressed and incised marks, silver hallmarked London 1880, 9¼in (23.5cm) high.
£500–625 ⚒ Mit

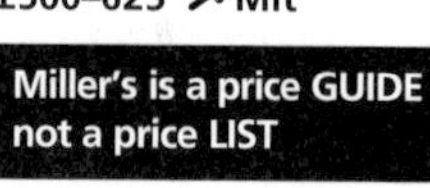

A Royal Doulton figure, Double Jester, decorated in shades of brown, green, blue and black, marked 'Two Heads Are Better Than One' and signed 'C. J. Noke', 1932, 14in (35.5cm) high.
£11,000–14,000 ⚒ MALC
This is a rare colour variation of the Double Jester figure (in its standard colourway it is worth £3–4,000). It has been in private hands for 27 years, the owner having little knowledge of Doulton and no idea of its value. Research by the auctioneers revealed that there were no known photographs of it and only one example recorded. It attracted a great deal of international interest and eventually sold to an overseas buyer.

A Doulton salt-glazed jug, by Hannah Barlow, with a dog chasing two horses wth startled sheep nearby, decorated in blue and brown on a beige ground, artist's mongram, dated 1875, 9in (23xcm) high.
£260–325 ⚒ P

A Royal Doulton stoneware jardinière, c1910, 8in (20.5cm) diam.
£140–175 ⚒ G(L)

A Royal Doulton dinner service, comprising 59 pieces, chinoiserie-decorated with Matsumai pattern in iron-red, dark blue, green and gilt, 19thC.
£1,200–1,500 ⚒ TRM

A Doulton Burslem Holbein Ware porcelain plaque, decorated by William Hodgkinson and Harry Morrey with a man attending a bonfire, watched by three horses, signed, early 20thC, 10½ x 8in (26.5 x 20.5cm), framed.
£900–1,150 S(S)

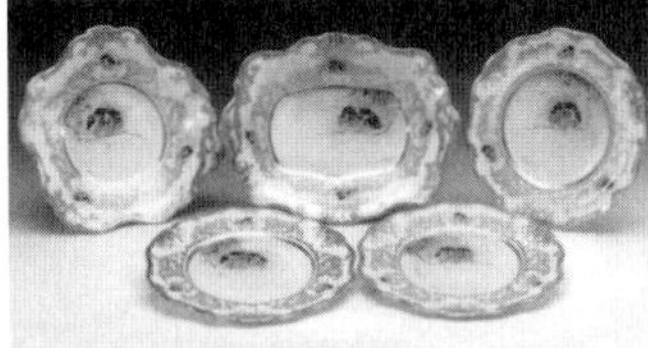

A Royal Doulton dessert service, comprising 16 pieces, each painted with fledgling and blossom, on a buff ground with gilt border, signed H. Allen, c1910.
£1,100–1,200 SHSY

► **A pair of Doulton Lambeth faïence vases,** by Margaret Challis, decorated with autumn leaves in shades of brown and yellow, 1879, 10in (25.5cm) high.
£500–600 GAA

A Doulton Lambeth stoneware mouse group spill vase, by George Tinworth, decorated in blue, pale pink and buff, restored, impressed factory mark, incised monogram, 5½in (14cm) high.
£1,300–1,600 S(NY)
Ex-Harriman Judd collection. Allen Harriman and Edward Judd were American coin dealers who had a passion for British Art Pottery and amassed an extensive collection that was sold in New York in 2001. Due to the size of the collection and fears of flooding the market, the sale was heavily publicized, with the result that the awareness of this type of pottery has greatly increased in the United States.

Cross Reference
See Colour Review (page 486)

A Doulton vase, by Hannah Barlow, decorated with an Old English sheepdog and a flock of sheep, within jewelled floral borders decorated with coloured glazes, marked, post-1891, 12½in (32cm) high.
£675–850 F&C

A Doulton Lambeth stoneware vase, by Florence and Hannah Barlow, decorated with birds and sheep in blue, green and brown, 1895, 13in (33cm) high.
£1,300–1,500 GAA

◄ **A pair of Royal Doulton stoneware vases,** with foliate decoration, c1910, 7¾in (19.5cm) high.
£80–100 G(L)

► **A Royal Doulton Lambeth white stoneware vase,** by Vera Huggins, painted with exotic birds among stylized foliage, restored, impressed and painted marks, 1920s, 22½in (57cm) high.
£800–900 S(NY)
Ex-Harriman Judd collection.

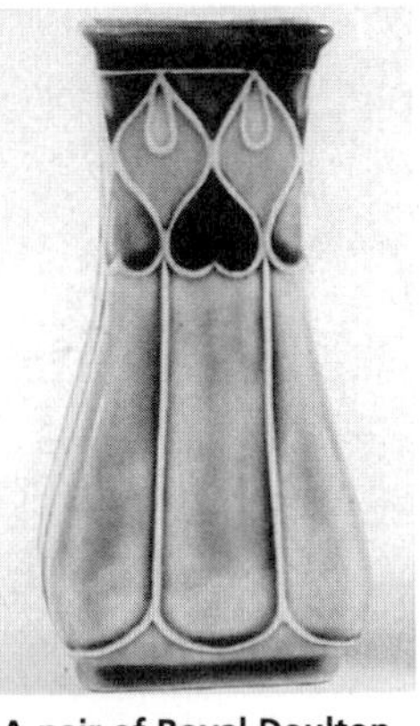

A pair of Royal Doulton vases, decorated in the Art Nouveau style with geometric designs in green, blue and treacle on a washed grey ground, impressed marks, early 20thC, 6in (15cm) high.
£270–340 GAK

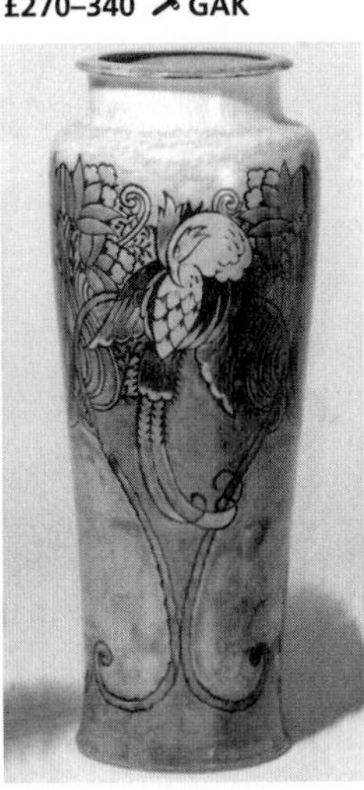

A Royal Doulton vase, hand-painted with sheep grazing in a field at sunset, printed mark, early 20thC, 5¾in (14.5cm) high.
£80–100 FHF

A Royal Doulton Brangwyn Ware vase, with underglaze painted decoration of stylized flower and leaf motifs in blue, green, yellow and purple, printed mark, early 20thC, 9in (23cm) high.
£80–100 FHF

Martin Brothers

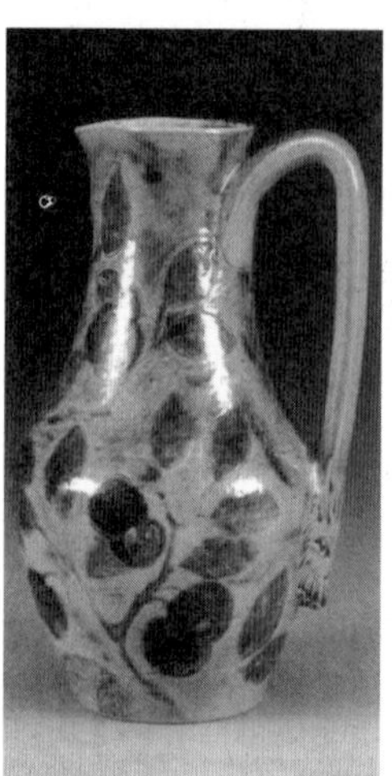

A Martin Brothers stoneware jug, incised with branches bearing plums, incised marks, dated 1880, 10in (25.5cm) high.
£300–360 S(O)

A Martin Brothers stoneware scent bottle, modelled as a bird, chips and repairs, incised mark, c1914, 3½in (9cm) high.
£900–1,150 TEN

► **A Martin Brothers vase,** incised and decorated with crabs in pursuit of a snake on a brown/green ground, now converted to a lamp, incised marks, 1904, 10¾in (27.5cm) high.
£800–1,000 CGC

A Martin Brothers stoneware stand or saucer, incised with foliage beneath a lustrous glaze, incised marks, c1891, 10½in (26.5cm) diam.
£60–75 WW

A Martin Brothers stoneware vase, with stylized seahorse design, incised mark, early 20thC, 6¼in (16cm) high.
£320–400 WilP

Martin ware

The Martin Brothers – Robert, Edwin and Walter – opened their first studio at Pomona House in Fulham in 1873, rapidly expanding the business to open a workshop in 1877 in Southall, Middlesex. Here they concentrated on the production of salt-glaze stoneware. They quickly developed a reputation for producing animal models and decorative wares that embraced the Victorian fascination with the grotesque. Inherent in their work though was a strong element of humour, which has stood the test of time.

Production ceased in 1914, and the public's fascination with Martin Wares was to remain dormant until the early 1970s, when pieces began to trade at auction. Particularly popular were the 'Wally' birds modelled by Robert Martin. These were embraced *en-masse* by two American collectors, Ed Judd and Allen Harriman. When their estate went under the hammer in New York in 2001, the excited audience witnessed some Martin Ware pieces fetching in excess of $40,000.

Moorcroft

► **A Moorcroft bowl,** decorated with Anemone pattern on a dark blue ground, c1900, 9½in (24cm) diam.
£320–400 G(L)

A Moorcroft bowl, decorated with Poppy pattern, signed, 1930, 12in (30.5cm) diam.
£775–850 GAA

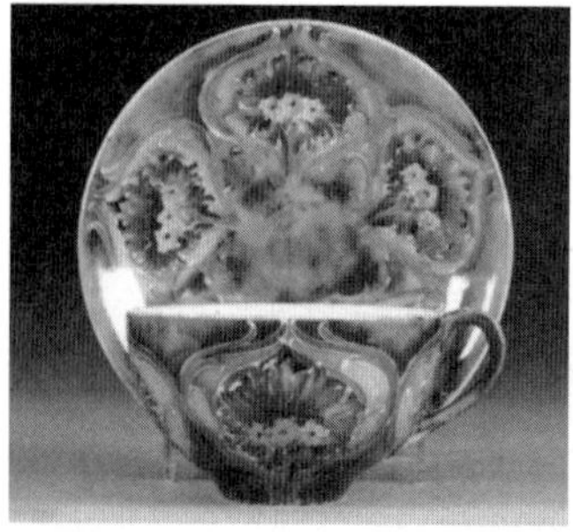

A Moorcroft pottery cup and saucer, decorated with Cornflower or Brown Cornflower pattern, tube-lined with bands of flowers, painted mark, c1913.
£600–700 S(O)

◄ **A Moorcroft pottery box and cover,** decorated with Pomegranate pattern on a dark blue ground, some restoration, impressed and painted marks, 1918–29, 6¼in (16cm) diam.
£470–600 S(O)

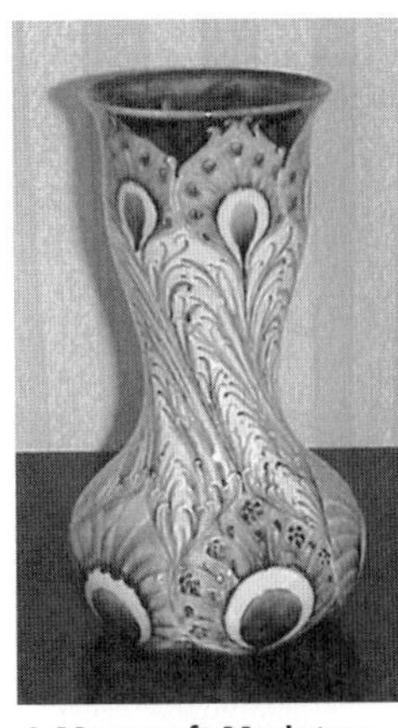
A Moorcroft Macintyre Peacock vase, c1899, 10in (25.5cm) high.
£2,700–3,000 ⊞ MPC

A Moorcroft vase, decorated with Orchids and Cornflowers pattern on a pale green ground, c1900, 12½in (32cm) high.
£600–750 ⚒ G(L)

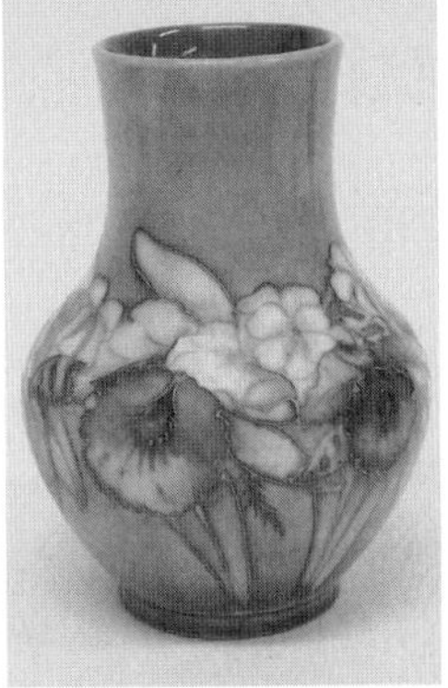
A Moorcroft vase, decorated with Orchids and Cornflowers pattern on a pale green ground, c1900, 7¼in (18.5cm) high.
£320–400 ⚒ G(L)

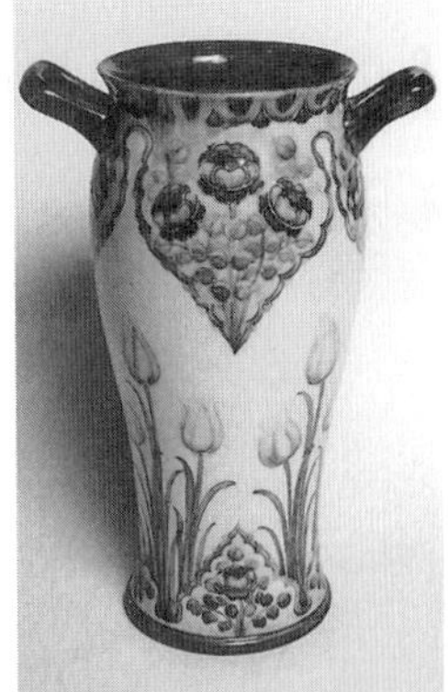
A Moorcroft Macintyre vase, decorated with yellow tulips and blue poppies, c1903, 10in (25.5cm) high.
£3,400–3,750 ⊞ Lan

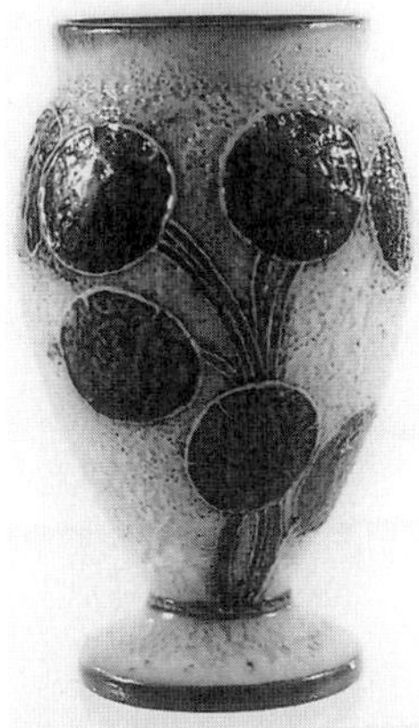
◄ **A Moorcroft Macintyre vase,** decorated with Honesty pattern in shades of blue, two chips, painted and printed marks, c1903, 3in (7.5cm) high.
£750–950 ⚒ WL

► **A Moorcroft Florian ware vase,** decorated with blue and yellow stylized flowers on a light green/blue ground, inscribed and impressed marks, 1915–16, 4in (10cm) high.
£900–1,150 ⚒ Mit

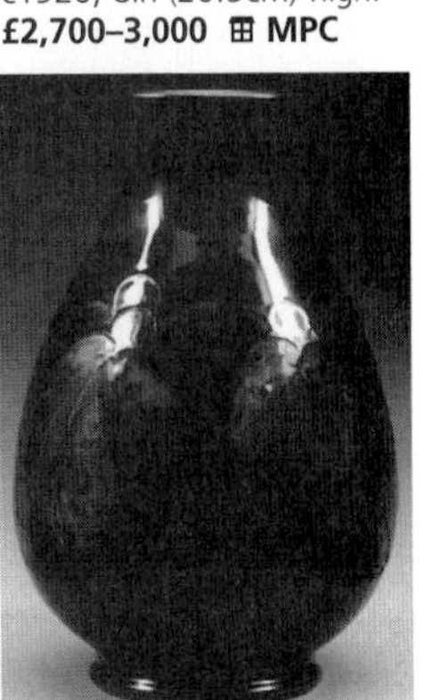
A Moorcroft vase, decorated with Moonlit Blue pattern, signed, c1920, 8in (20.5cm) high.
£2,700–3,000 ⊞ MPC

A Moorcroft vase, decorated with Wisteria pattern on a dark blue ground, signed, c1930, 13in (33cm) high.
£1,100–1,200 ⊞ GAA

A Moorcroft *flambé* vase, decorated with Leaves and Fruit pattern, tube-lined with leaves and berries beneath a mottled deep red glaze, impressed and painted marks, 1928–34, 10in (25.5cm) high.
£900–1,100 ⚒ S(O)

◄ **A Moorcroft vase,** decorated with Anemone pattern in shades of yellow and red, signed, c1940, 5½in (14cm) high.
£720–800 ⊞ GAA

Art Nouveau Ceramics

An Amphora porcelain vase, enamelled and gilded, with a portrait of a young woman on a ground of stylized trees and flowers with jewelled highlights, impressed mark, Bohemian, 20thC, 13in (33cm) high.
£2,500–3,000 S(O)

A pair of Amphora pottery two-handled vases, decorated with stylized armorial devices, impressed marks, Bohemian, early 20thC, 14in (35.5cm) high.
£800–1,000 S(O)

A pair of Boch Frères, Keramis vases, decorated with light green blossoms and foliage with gold accents on a turquoise ground, Belgian, c1910, 11¼in (28.5cm) high.
£675–850 SK

A pair of copper-effect Bretby vases, by David Ash, c1907, 10¼in (26cm) high.
£180–200 HUN

A copper-effect Bretby vase for four flowers, by David Ash, decorated with jewelled cabochons, c1908, 7½in (19cm) high.
£220–250 HUN

A Foley Intarsio biscuit barrel, decorated with scenes from *Hamlet*, stylized Art Nouveau-style flowers and plated mounts and cover, printed mark, early 20thC, 6in (15cm) high.
£180–225 FHF

An Antonin Larroux earthenware figural jardinière, inscribed and impressed marks, French, c1900, 21½in (54.5cm) diam.
£3,300–4,200 S(NY)

A Linthorpe Art Nouveau-style vase, decorated in green and brown glazes with raised panels of classical busts, medallions and flowers and raised collar of brown and turquoise-coloured studs, rim repaired, impressed mark, c1890, 24in (61cm) high.
£850–1,100 AG

A Pilkington's lustre pottery vase, decorated by Richard Joyce, with deer and formalized trees in silver lustre against a deep red ground, impressed and printed marks, c1906, 8in (20.5cm) high.
£1,100–1,300 S(O)

A Minton Secessionist jardinière, tube-lined with flowerheads and stiff leaves picked out in red, green and yellow on a red ground, two chips, impressed and printed marks for 1908, 10in (25.5cm) high.
£380–475 LFA

A Poole Pottery relief-moulded vase, covered in a deep pink lustre glaze, chips, incised signature and date, c1903, 12in (30.5cm) high.
£200–250 FHF

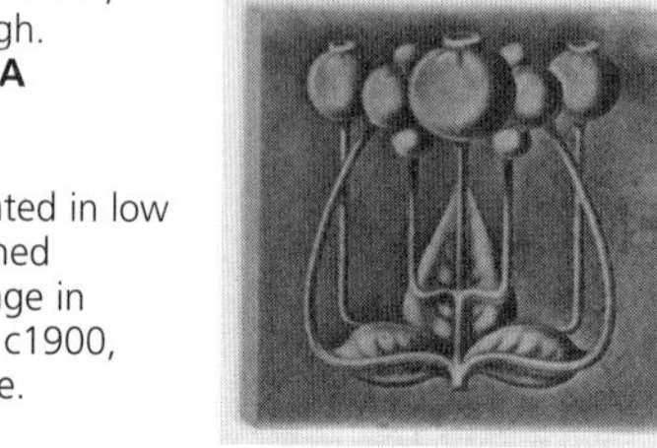

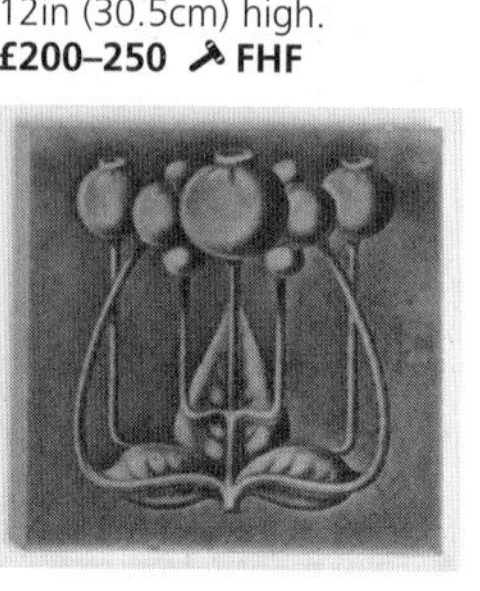

► **A tile,** decorated in low relief with entwined poppies and foliage in shades of green, c1900, 6in (15cm) square.
£40–45 DAD

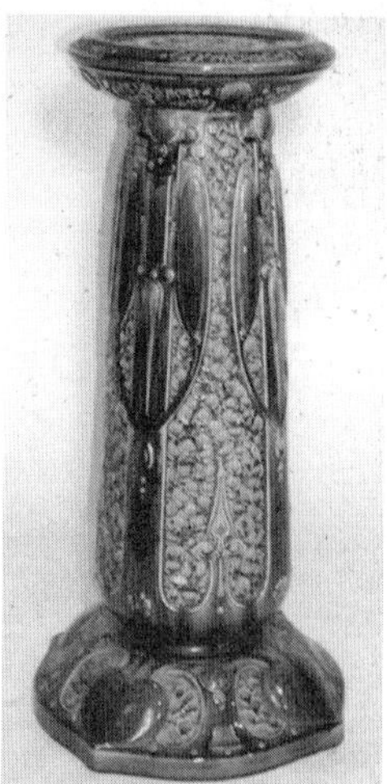

An earthenware jardinière and stand, decorated with stylized floral and heart-shaped motifs in a deep green-coloured glaze, damage to glaze, base marked 'Fiorence', c1900, 29in (73.5cm) high.
£65–85 BLH

Art Nouveau Clocks

A Bagge and Peters silvered-bronze clock, French, c1921, 11¼in (28.5cm) high.
£3,000–3,750 S(NY)

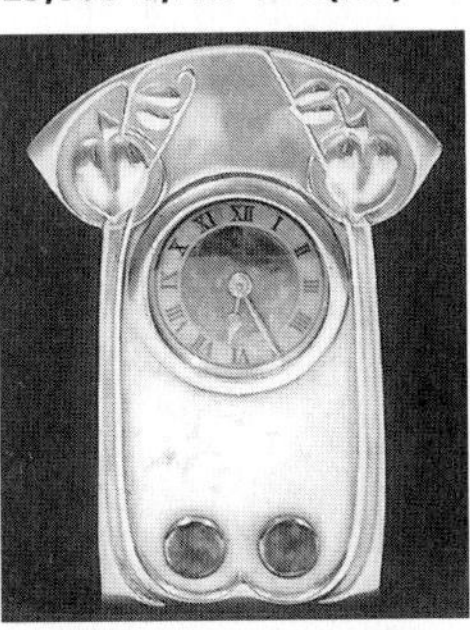

A Liberty & Co Tudric pewter clock, designed by Archibald Knox, 1890–1910, 9in (23cm) high.
£4,000–5,000 ASA

A *grande sonnerie* Vienna wall clock, by Gustav Becker, the enamel dial with brass centre applied with a profile portrait of a girl, the three-train movement with deadbeat escapement, the brass bob and weights applied with Art Nouveau pewter mounts, Czechoslovakian, c1905, 52in (132cm) high.
£1,700–1,850 S(O)

◄ **A Michael Powolny ceramic clock,** manufactured by Wiener Keramik, surmounted by a bird and flowers, impressed marks, Austrian, designed c1907, 7½in (19cm) high.
£1,800–2,200 DORO

A Duchess of Sutherland Cripple Guild silver-plated clock case, with stylized flower motifs enclosing clock aperture, the blue enamel mounts flanked by strapwork supports, c1890, 10¼in (26cm) wide.
£1,000–1,200 S(O)

A Liberty & Co Tudric pewter carriage time-piece, with green and blue enamel plaque within the brass chapter ring, 1905–10, 3½in (9cm) high.
£350–450 G(L)

A Liberty & Co Tudric pewter and enamel clock case, designed by Archibald Knox, enamel dial detached, missing back cover, hands and glass, registered 1905, 5½in (14cm) high.
£3,700–4,000 S(O)

A Wiener Werkstätte walnut wall clock, the spring-driven two-train movement signed 'J. Leroy & Cie, Paris', with Brocot escapement rack half-hour striking on a bell, 1910–20, 24½in (62cm) high.
£1,400–1,700 S(Am)

◄ **A WMF silver-plated clock,** the body decorated with flowers and sinuous strapwork, c1906, 15½in (39.5cm) high.
£2,000–2,200 S(O)

Art Nouveau Figures & Busts

◄ **A French School bronze bust of a young woman,** by De Wever, Ninon, signed, c1900, 23¼in (59cm) high.
£850–1,000 S(O)

► **A bronze group of two dancers,** by Bruno Zach, 1890–1910, 16in (40.5cm) high.
£3,500–4,500 ASA

A Ferdinand Lepcke patinated-bronze figure of a dancer, on a mottled red, green and pink marble base, marked, German, c1900, 21in (53.5cm) high.
£4,500–5,000 S

Art Nouveau Furniture

A mahogany and marquetry display cabinet, the back with a galleried shelf above two mirrors, c1900, 48in (122cm) wide.
£650–800 ⚒ N

A mahogany bowfronted display cabinet, the stained-glass door with pink opalescent stylized flowerheads, floral inlaid with pewter, satinwood and boxwood, c1900, 31½in (80cm) wide.
£1,000–1,250 ⚒ P(B)

An ebonized walnut, copper and leather wall cabinet, by Carlo Bugatti, with tilting mirror inlaid with pewter and bone, Italian, c1900, 14¼in (36cm) wide.
£2,400–3,000 ⚒ DORO

A carved oak side cabinet, attributed to Arthur Simpson, the frieze carved with stylized flowers above two shaped panel doors carved with a stylized motif and inlaid with different monograms, enclosing shelves above two drawers, c1910, 21¾in (55.5cm) wide.
£1,100–1,300 ⚒ B

A beechwood hallstand, probably manufactured by Thonet, Vienna, reveneered and restored, Austrian, designed c1900, 52½in (133.5cm) wide.
£1,650–2,000 ⚒ DORO

A mahogany elbow chair, c1905.
£180–225 ⚒ N

A pair of stained beech open armchairs and a table en suite, by Gustav Siegel for Jacob & Josef Kohn, Vienna, reupholstered, marked, Austrian, c1900, table 21½in (54.5cm) diam.
£1,300–1,600 ⚒ DORO

A walnut, thuyawood and marquetry-inlaid étagère, by Louis Majorelle, indistinctly signed, French, c1900, 19¼in (49cm) wide.
£1,500–1,700 ⚒ S(O)

A Liberty & Co oak sideboard, with central mirror back, flanked by two glazed cupboards, inlaid with ebony and satinwood stringing, c1900, 60in (152.5cm) wide.
£1,200–1,500 ⚒ P(B)

A set of three stained and bent beechwood chairs, attributed to Otto Prutscher, Austrian, c1910.
£6,000–7,500 ⚒ S(NY)
Otto Prutscher was a designer for the Wiener Werkstätte. His pieces were never signed.

◀ **A lady's mahogany writing table,** with inset leather writing surface, c1900, 39in (99cm) wide.
£1,000–1,250 ⚒ AH

▶ **A lady's stained beech-wood writing desk,** minor restorations, designed c1900, manufactured by Thonet, Vienna, after 1922, 37½in (95.5cm) wide.
£3,000–3,750 ⚒ DORO

Art Nouveau Glass

A Benedikt von Poschinger iridescent glass vase, Austrian, c1905, 5½in (14cm) high.
£600–750 DORO

A Daum cameo glass landscape bowl, in grey glass with internal amber mottling overlaid with deep magenta glass, acid-etched with a tree-lined lake shore, signed, French, c1910, 8½in (21.5cm) high.
£2,750–3,000 JAA

A Daum enamelled and etched Winter Landscape glass vase, French, early 20thC, 3½in (9cm) high.
£1,300–1,500 S

A Burgun & Schverer cameo glass vase, the interior decorated with flowers, signed, French, c1895, 7¾in (19.5cm) high.
£5,000–6,000 S(NY)

A Daum enamelled glass dish, the exterior decorated with a winter landscape, French, late 19thC, 3¼in (8.5cm) diam.
£280–350 PFK

A Daum glass vase, etched and enamelled with autumnal trees, painted mark, French, early 20thC, 3¼in (8.5cm) wide.
£475–525 S(O)

◄ **A Daum glass vase,** decorated with an acid-etched and painted lakeside landscape, on a frosted ground, signed, French, c1900, 4¾in (12cm) high.
£2,200–2,750 DORO

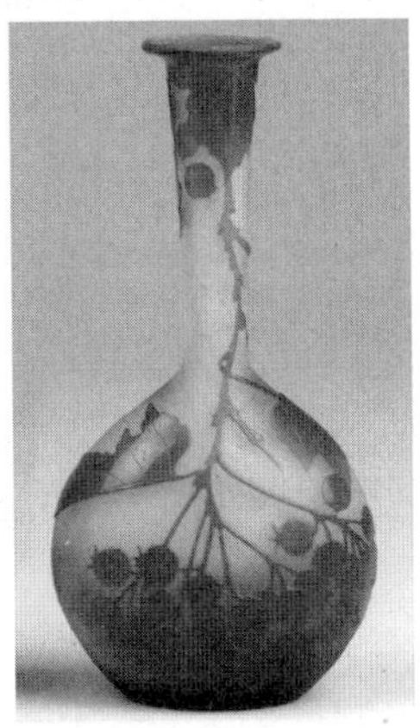

An Emile Gallé glass vase, the clear glass partly cased in ochre, overlaid in strawberry-red with an acid-etched berried branch and a single leaf, signed, French, 1904–06, 6½in (16.5cm) high.
£700–875 DORO

An Emile Gallé cameo glass vase, the milky-white glass with pale blue tint overlaid with deep amber, acid-etched with pine cones and needles, signed, French, c1900, 11½in (29cm) high.
£2,500–3,000 B

An Emile Gallé glass vase, the pink glass overlaid with green and etched with seed pods and leaves, French, c1900, 8in (20.5cm) high.
£950–1,200 M

Miller's is a price GUIDE not a price LIST

An Emile Gallé cameo two-handled glass vase, decorated with plumbago, signed, French, c1900, 8in (20.5cm) high.
£1,000–1,100 S(O)

► **A pair of Jacques Gruber leaded glass doors,** with oak frames, inset with opalescent and polychrome-leaded glass panels, one marked, French, c1910, 28¾in (73cm) high.
£12,000–15,000 S

A glass vase, by Legras & Cie, St Denis, the violet glass decorated with acid-etched and gold-painted poppies on a frosted ground, with gilt rim, French, c1900, 14½in (37cm) high.
£750–950 ⚒ DORO

A glass vase, by Legras & Cie, acid-etched with maple in mauve on a frosted clear surface, French, c1900, 16¾in (42.5cm) high.
£675–850 ⚒ BERN

► **A Loetz iridescent glass box,** with hinged lid, the top decorated with enamel flowers in pink, yellow and black, outlined in gold, Austrian, c1900, 6½in (16.5cm) diam.
£450–550 ⚒ P(B)

◄ **A Loetz iridescent glass centrepiece,** in the shape of a conch shell, covered with mottled blue iridescence over a green ground, Austrian, c1900, 8½in (21.5cm) high.
£700–875 ⚒ RTo

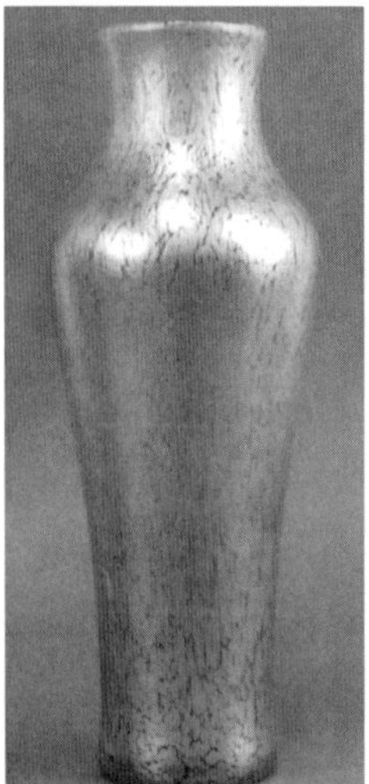

A glass vase, probably by Loetz, covered in dense golden oil spot iredescence over a leaf-green body, c1900, 13in (33cm) high.
£250–320 ⚒ RTo

◄ **A Loetz glass vase,** with streaked iridescent green and ice-blue decoration on an orange ground, printed retailer's mark of Hemming, Montreal, Austrian, 1905–15, 7¾in (19.5cm) high.
£3,000–3,500 ⚒ RIT

A Loetz-style glass vase, with all-over green iridescent dappling, early 20thC, 5in (12.5cm) high.
£250–320 ⚒ PFK

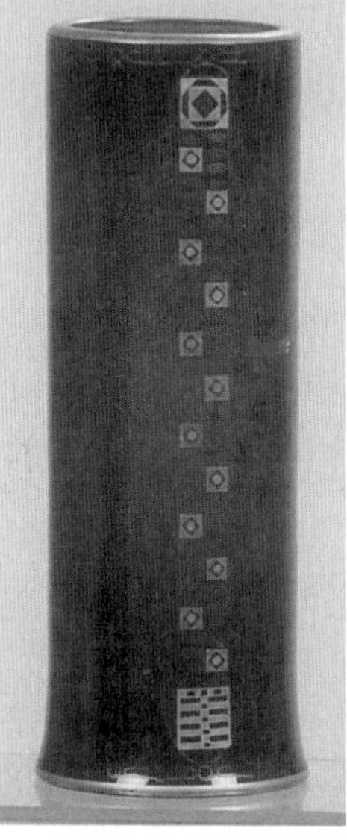

A Steinschönau School of Glassmaking vase, signed 'R.W.', German, c1908, 10½in (26.5cm) high.
£400–500 ⚒ DORO

An iridescent glass vase, probably by Loetz, the leaf-green ground covered in an irregular criss-cross patchwork of mottled peacock blue, Austrian, c1900, 9½in (24cm) high.
£300–375 ⚒ RTo

◄ **A glass vase,** by Camille Tutre de Varreux, Pantin, the clear glass cased in yellow/green, overlaid in dark brown, signed, French, c1910, 17¼in (44cm) high.
£1,200–1,500 ⚒ DORO

A Tiffany Favrile glass vase, inscribed mark, American, 1899–1920, 6½in (16.5cm) high.
£8,500–10,000 ⚒ S(NY)

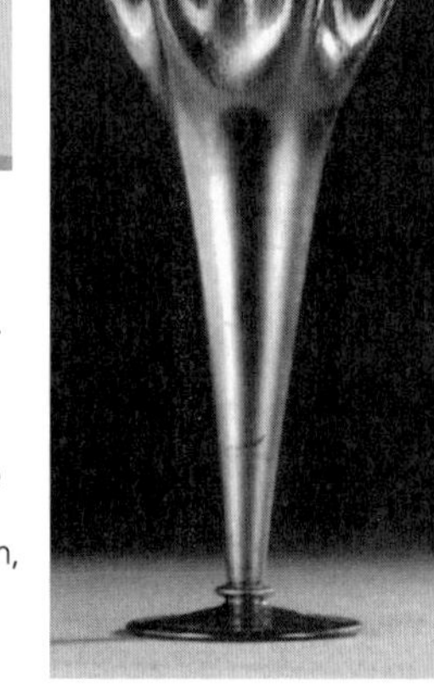

◄ **A Steuben Aurene glass vase,** the wavy rim decorated with fine vertical lines, wheel-engraved marks, American, 1905–33, 10½in (26.5cm) high.
£750–950 ⚒ S(O)

Art Nouveau Jewellery

A pendant/brooch, designed as a winged dragon, the wings set with green *plique-à-jour* enamel, the body with paste highlights and red stone eyes, c1900.
£160–200 B(Ba)

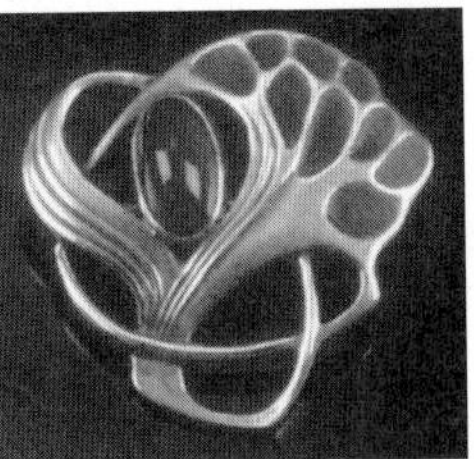

A sterling silver brooch, decorated with green *plique-à-jour* enamel and a green chalcedony, hallmark for Fahrner, German, c1901.
£650–820 SK

An emerald, pearl and diamond clip, c1910.
£1,300–1,500 S

A necklace, by Gip, with a carved horn stylized butterfly pendant supporting a tear drop horn bead, with stained lilac hardstone beads interspersed with pierced scrollwork links, c1900.
£270–340 P(Ba)

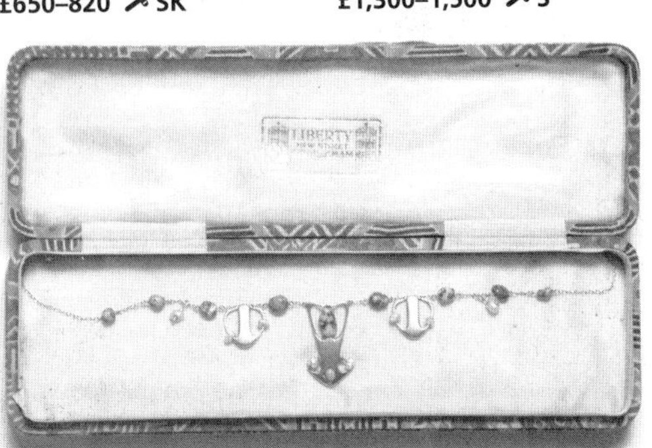

► A Liberty & Co 18ct gold, turquoise and pearl stone set necklace, c1900, in original case.
£3,000–3,250 SHa

Items in the Art Nouveau Jewellery section have been arranged in subject order.

Art Nouveau Lighting

A silver-plated oil lamp, with frosted glass shade etched with male profile medallions and Greek key band, with a removable glass oil font and Messenger's Patented burner surmounting an Art Nouveau Barbour Silverplate Co candlestick with iris decoration, early 20thC, 32in (81.5cm) high.
£250–300 SK

A leaded glass hanging light fixture, possibly by Chicago Mosaic Co, decorated with spring-green, butterscotch and white glass tiles, interspersed with bands of flowers, early 20thC, 29in (73.5cm) high including fittings.
£3,500–4,500 BB(S)

A Daum cameo glass *plafonnier*, the grey glass mottled with salmon and amber overlaid in dark and light burgundy and cut with a design of nicotiana blooms within gilt-cast mounts, signed, French, c1910, 20in (51cm) diam.
£2,700–3,000 JAA

A student's lamp, by Handel, the opalescent green glass shade on a bronze base, American, Meriden, Connecticut, c1900, 24in(61cm) high.
£1,800–2,200 JAA

► A pair of bronze wall lights, modelled as the heads of a boy and a girl with light fittings emanating from their mouths, signed 'G. de Kerveguen', Belgian, c1930, 8in 920.5cm) high.
£2,800–3,500 G(B)

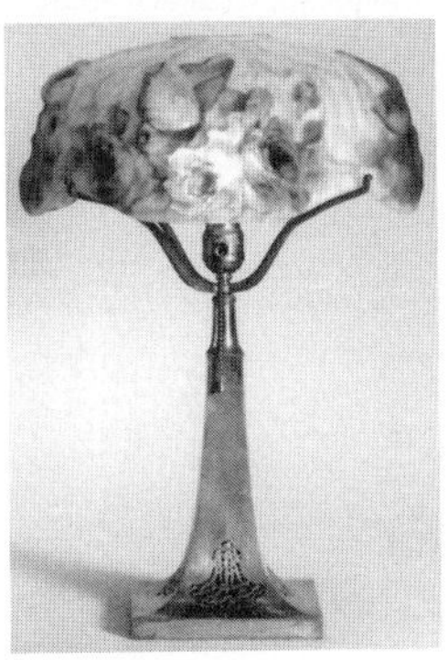

◄ A Pairpoint Puffy table lamp, the shade raised on a silver-coloured metal base, stamped and impressed marks, American, New Bedford, Massachusetts, early 20thC, 20½in (52cm) high.
£4,000–5,000 SK

A table lamp, by Pittsburgh Lamp, Brass and Glass Co, with frosted and textured glass shade, the interior painted with a mountainous landscape, the exterior painted with pine trees, the metal base with scroll, shield, floral and foliate motifs in relief, American, c1920, 27in (68.5cm) high.
£1,400–1,750 SK

A pair of Tiffany Favrile glass and patinated-bronze two-light sconces, shades signed, bronze unsigned, minor chips to rims, American, early 20thC, 9¾in (25cm) high.
£7,700–9,500 BB(S)

An Art Nouveau brass lantern, with vaseline glass insert, c1900, 15in 938cm) high.
£360–400 EAL

► **A patinated metal-mounted glass table lamp,** the shade with six striated caramel and white glass panels and red glass border panels, American, early 20thC, 24½in (62cm) high.
£600–700 SK

A gilded brass ceiling lamp, with original orange shade, signed Schneider, c1910, 29in (73.5cm) high.
£450–500 EAL

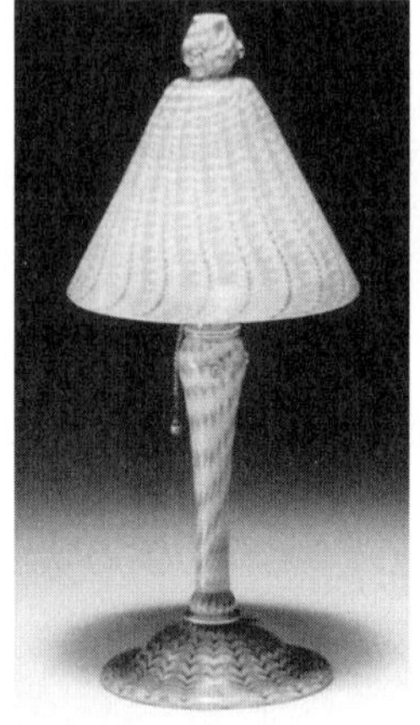

A Tiffany Favrile glass and gilt-bronze arabesque lamp, inscribed marks, American, 1899–1920, 14¾in (37.5cm) diam.
£4,000–5,000 S(NY)

A hall lantern, with brass mounts and frosted glass, c1900, 13in (33cm) high.
£140–175 SWO

A Tiffany Favrile glass shade, composed of radiating tiles in mottled amber and green glass, stamped mark, on an unmarked patinated-bronze lamp standard, early 20thC, 22½in (57cm) high.
£6,500–7,200 BB(S)

A Tiffany Favrile glass and bronze lamp with root base, inscribed mark, American, 1899–1920, 18in (45.5cm) high.
£3,750–4,750 S(NY)

A two-arm light fitting, in oxidized copper, with original frosted shade, c1900, 15in (38cm) wide.
£315–350 EAL

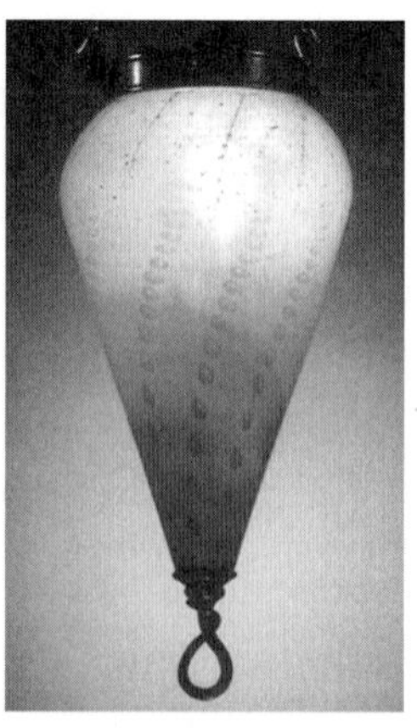

A Tiffany Favrile glass and bronze hanging lamp, American, 1899–1920, 35½in (90cm) high.
£6,000–7,500 S(NY)

A hammered-iron gas fitting, with original vaseline glass shade, c1900, 26in (66cm) high.
£360–400 EAL

A table lamp, the frosted glass shade interior-painted with trees and foliage silhouetted against a yellow/orange shaded sky and water, on a patinated cast-metal base, the base marked 'A. & R. Co', early 20thC, 23¾in (60.5cm) high.
£675–850 SK

◄ **An Art Nouveau polished brass gas lamp,** with green glass shades, c1900, 34in (86.5cm) high.
£360–400 EAL

Art Nouveau Metalware

A silver bowl, by Frank Brothers, with a repoussé floral pattern on four legs, one side with a handle moulded as a flower stem, marked, Austrian, Vienna 1900–10, 12¼in (31cm) wide, 32oz.
£1,200–1,500 DORO

A silver and agate three-handled sugar basin, by Omar Ramsden and Alwyn Carr, c1906, 5in (12.5cm) high.
£1,600–1,750 DAD

A sterling silver *martelé* fairy comport, by Clemens Friedell, the hammered dish chased with fairies and poppies, the base with chased poppy and foliate decoration, signed and dated, Pasadena 1914, 10½in (26.5cm) diam.
£7,000–8,750 SK

Collectors in California are great fans of Friedell and fight for his designs, particularly those with fairies.

A Liberty & Co Cymric silver coffee spoon, the handle cast with stylized leaves and picked out in coloured enamels, Birmingham 1904, 4½in (11.5cm) long.
£150–220 LFA

A two-handled silver bowl, by The Goldsmiths & Silversmiths Co, embossed with stylized floral decoration, London 1909, 11in (28cm) wide.
£550–700 Bon

A silver bowl, with *martelé* decoration, London 1912, 11¾in (30cm) wide.
£300–375 RTo

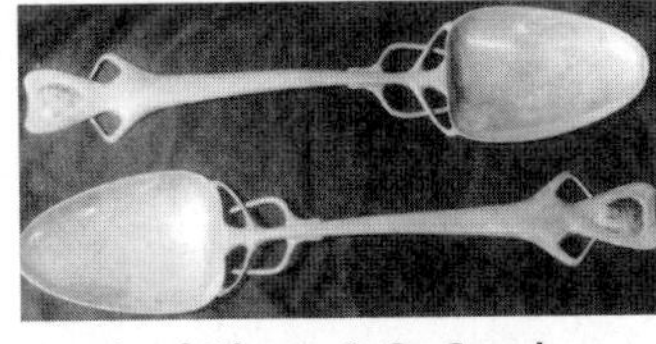

An Orivit pewter and glass-lined centrepiece, stamped mark, German, early 20thC, 11½in (29cm) wide.
£300–350 S(O)

A pair of Liberty & Co Cymric silver serving spoons, the ends set with turquoise blue and green enamel, Birmingham 1902, in a case.
£560–700 LVS

A silvered-pewter four-division figural tray, by WMF, stamped mark, German, early 20thC, 10¼in (26cm) high.
£700–800 S(O)

► **A Liberty & Co Tudric pewter matched five-piece tea service,** stamped marks, early 20thC, tray 18in (45.5cm) wide.
£525–575 S(O)

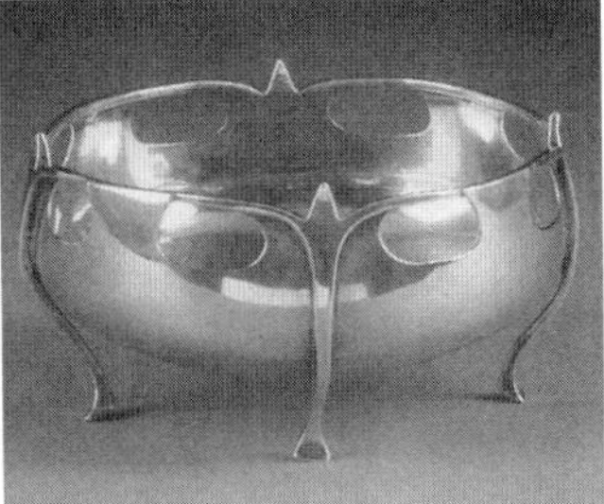

A Liberty & Co Cymric silver bowl, the exterior applied with four stylized scroll legs, the rim pierced with asymmetrical oval forms, one leg damaged, Birmingham 1901, 4½in (11.5cm) diam.
£520–650 Bon

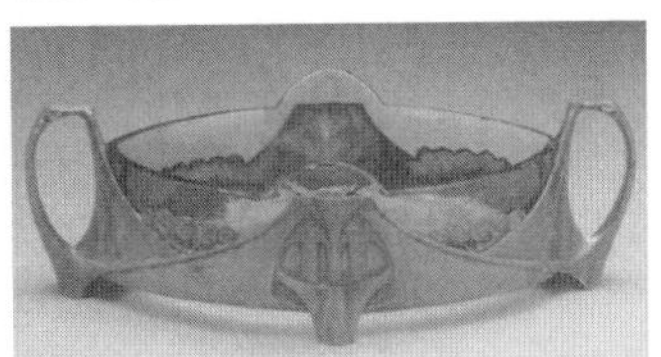

A pewter and green glass-lined centrepiece, by WMF, stamped mark, German, early 20thC, 14½in (37cm) wide.
£400–450 S(O)

A gilt-bronze dish, by Albert Marionnet, French, c1905, 8in (20.5cm) wide.
£1,150–1,300 MI

A Viennese .800 silver tray, decorated with whiplash lines and curves and repoussé waterlilies, maker 'CA' possibly Carl Altgrüber, Austrian, 11¾in ((30cm) wide.
£600–660 NOA

Art Deco

The Art Deco world was dominated by the desire for speed, luxury and opulence. It was a world of changing social attitudes, where liberated young women drank cocktails, listened to jazz and danced till dawn. Nicknamed the Roaring Twenties, it was a world where the chains of the past were thrust aside and all eyes were raised eagerly to the future.

The term Art Deco only came into general use in the 1960s, but it refers back to the great exhibition of Decorative Arts held in Paris in 1925, which presented to the world a dazzling new style that was to be the successor of Art Nouveau: the style of modernism, the Jazz Age, ocean liners, cinemas and skyscrapers.

The Art Deco movement became all the rage in France, and other countries including the USA, Britain and Germany, produced their own, often equally successful, versions of the style. In furniture especially, the French predominated with the virtuoso cabinet-making of Ruhlmann and Primavera, and the brilliant originality of Gray and Royère.

Glass was regarded highly by both connoisseurs and collectors, and many factories were created, producing thousands of items designed by such great names as Gallé, Schneider, Baccarat, Lalique, Daum, Argy-Rousseau and Tiffany.

The 1925 Paris exhibition was an important event for ceramics manufacturers such as Longwy, Goldscheider, Boch Frères, Clarice Cliff, Susie Cooper and Carlton Ware. All experimented with new techniques as well as previously unseen designs and textures.

One of the most expressive mediums of the Art Deco period was sculpture. Bruno Zach, Paul Philippe, Otto Poertzel, Ferdinand Preiss, Alexandre Kélety and Rembrandt Bugatti are among the recognized masters of this category, but one artist, Demêtre Chiparus, stands out for his sheer craft, sense of design and huge output.

Recent sales in Paris have achieved record-breaking prices for the designs of the best cabinet makers, and also for those of lesser known names. As Georgian and French Empire pieces become mainly the preserve of the wealthy, Art Deco furniture is coming in to fill the gap. The style is particularly popular with the young these days, as the functional, clean lines enhance today's life styles. They are keen to acquire useful items such as dining room suites, bookcases, cocktail cabinets and bergères, and also light fittings, mirrors, bronzes and porcelain to enhance the overall effect.

Anne B. Mitofsky-Citron & Laurance B. Citron

Art Deco Ceramics

An Augarten modernistic design porcelain vase, by Franz von Zülow, Vienna, polychrome-decorated with gilt rims, marked, Austrian, designed c1925, 9¼in (23.5cm) high.
£2,800–3,500 DORO

A Boch Frères, Keramis, glazed stoneware vase, by Charles Catteau, signed, incised and printed marks, Belgian, c1925, 12½in (32cm) high.
£2,200–2,750 S(NY)

A Boch Frères, Keramis, stoneware vase, by Charles Catteau, glazed in shades of *eau-de-nil* and brown/black with a frieze of flamingos, signed, incised mark, Belgian, c1925, 11in (28cm) high.
£2,750–3,500 S

A Boch Frères, Keramis, earthenware vase, designed by Jules-Ernest Chaput, signed, Belgian, c1930, 19¼in (49cm) high.
£8,750–11,000 S(NY)
In 1927 at the age of 15 Jules-Ernest Chaput joined the firm of Boch Frères, Keramis, where he quickly excelled and began working with the team headed by Charles Catteau.

Boch Frères, Keramis

The Belgian firm Boch Frères was founded in 1767 at Sept Fontaines in the Saarland, but by the mid-19th century, following a split, part of the firm established the manufactory, Boch Frères, Keramis, in Belgium, to produce earthenware vases, tablewares and candlesticks. Their wares of the mid-1920s to the 1940s represent the most important Belgian contribution to Art Deco. Some stonewares were also produced. All their pieces from this period are white-bodied.

The English artist Arthur Finch worked for Boch Frères as a decorator until 1930. His vases employ the large, swollen shape typical of the factory, but he used a red background in slip and glazed ochre to the dark green and blue motifs.

A Bretby dented vase, with jade green matt glaze, 1931–35, 9in (23cm) high.
£150–165 ⊞ HUN

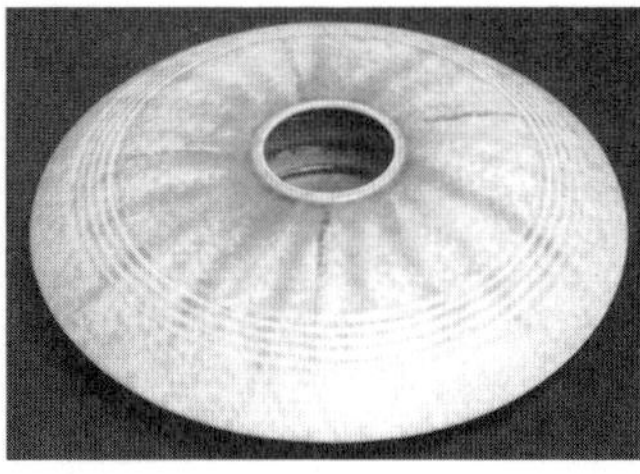

A Bretby disc-shaped posy vase, decorated with a grey speckled glaze with green and yellow stripes, c1932, 9½in (24cm) high.
£100–120 ⊞ HUN

A Carlton Ware lustre bowl, the exterior decorated with butterflies on a rich blue ground, the interior with an apricot glaze, c1930, 10in (25.5cm) high.
£440–550 ⚒ G(L)

A Foley bone china pink lustre part tea service, comprising 19 pieces, designed by Laura Knight, 1932–34, cake plate 9¼in (23.5cm) diam.
£525–575 ⚒ S(O)

A Gouda Zuid-Holland earthenware bowl, hand-painted, Dutch, c1924, 2½in (6.5cm) high.
£215–240 ⊞ MI

An Elton Ware pottery three-handled vase, with embossed flower decoration, signed, c1930, 10in (25.5cm) high.
£240–265 ⊞ RUSK

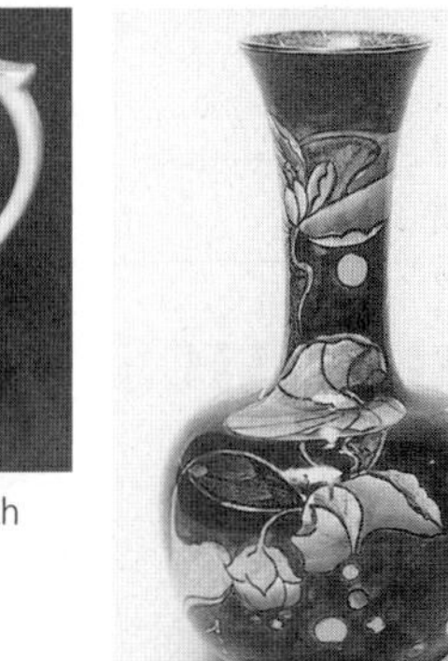

A T. G. Green jug, with painted and stencilled decoration, 1930s, 7in (18cm) high.
£120–150 ⊞ CAL

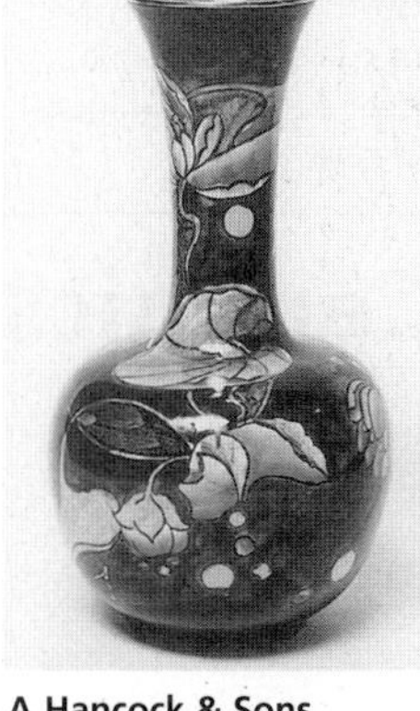

A Hancock & Sons Coronaware vase, decorated with Waterlily pattern, signed by Molly Hancock, c1924, 8in (20.5cm) high.
£200–225 ⊞ PIC

A Longwy pottery vase, decorated with cobalt-blue, cream and yellow diamonds with incised outlines on a turquoise ground, printed mark, French, 1930s, 9½in (24cm) high.
£350–400 ⚒ RIT

◄ **A Maling bowl,** with scaled green decoration and Garland pattern to rim, standing on three feet, 1940s, 9¼in (23.5cm) high.
£110–140 ⚒ PFK

► **A Shelley Vogue trio,** decorated with Blocks pattern, c1930, plate 7in (18cm) square.
£270–300 ⊞ RH

A pair of Pilkington's Royal Lancastrian vases, c1920, 10in (25.5cm) high.
£160–175 ⊞ RUSK

A Poole Pottery plaque, Summer Flowers, by Carter, Stabler and Adams, c1921, 10½in (26.5cm) high.
£200–240 ⚒ G(B)

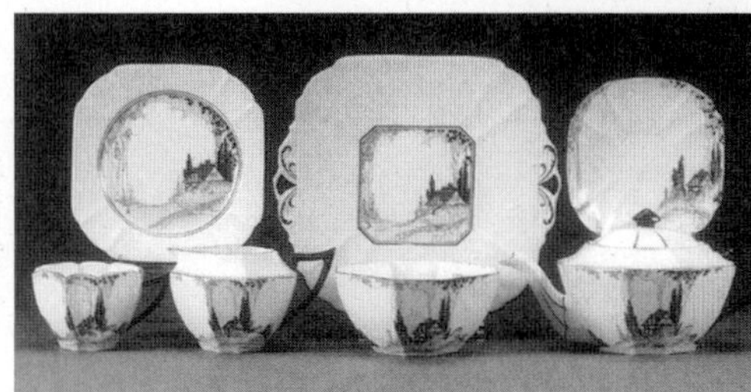

A Shelley Queen Anne-shape tea service, comprising 24 pieces, decorated with a cottage among trees, printed marks, 1930s.
£850–950 ⚒ S(O)

Clarice Cliff

◀ **A Clarice Cliff Inspiration basket,** decorated with Lily pattern, c1930, 15in (38cm) high.
£900–1,000 ⊞ RH

▶ **A Clarice Cliff My Garden biscuit barrel and cover,** c1930, 7½in (19cm) high.
£130–160 ⚒ G(L)

A Clarice Cliff Newport Bizarre bowl, decorated with Crocus pattern, c1930, 8¼in (21cm) diam.
£180–225 ⚒ BBR

A Clarice Cliff conical bowl, decorated with Bobbins pattern on a *cafe au lait* ground, c1930, 9¾in (25cm) diam.
£800–1,000 ⚒ LAY

A Clarice Cliff daffodil bowl, decorated with Secrets pattern, with a chromium-plated stand, printed mark, 1933–37, 13½in (34.5cm) wide.
£400–500 ⚒ S(O)

Items in the Clarice Cliff section have been arranged in alphabetical order.

A Clarice Cliff Bizarre centrepiece/candleholder, decorated with Limberlost pattern, comprising two semi-circular flower troughs and two cube candlesticks painted with white flowers, green foliage and red trees, c1932, 2¼in (5.5cm) high.
£600–750 ⚒ P

A Clarice Cliff Fantasque cake plate, decorated with Melon pattern, with a chrome handle, printed marks, 1930–31, 8½in (21.5cm) diam.
£270–325 ⚒ S(O)

A Clarice Cliff cocoa pot, in the shape of a chicken, c1930, 6in (15cm) high.
£400–450 ⊞ RH

▶ **A Clarice Cliff floral coffee pot,** c1930, 8in (20.5cm) high.
£135–150 ⊞ RH

A pair of Clarice Cliff Gayday bookends, c1930, 6in (15cm) high.
£765–850 ⊞ RH

A Clarice Cliff Newport ribbed bowl, with embossed and painted floral decoration on a cream ground, marked, stamped and impressed marks, c1930, 7in (18cm) diam.
£85–110 ⚒ DA

Moulded Clarice Cliff designs do not command as high prices as the painted, highly Art Deco patterns.

A Clarice Cliff Petunia pattern daffodil bowl, base rim chip, c1930, 13in (33cm) wide.
£250–320 ⚒ G(L)

A Clarice Cliff Fantasque conical coffee can and saucer, decorated with Picasso Flower pattern in red, green and black, 1929–34, cup 2¼in (5.5cm) high.
£380–475 ⚒ B

A Clarice Cliff hors d'oeuvres dish, decorated with Applique Idyll pattern, chrome handle, c1930, 8½in (21.5cm) wide.
£190–228 G(L)

A Clarice Cliff fern pot, decorated with Crocus pattern, c1930, 4in (10cm) high.
£225–250 RH

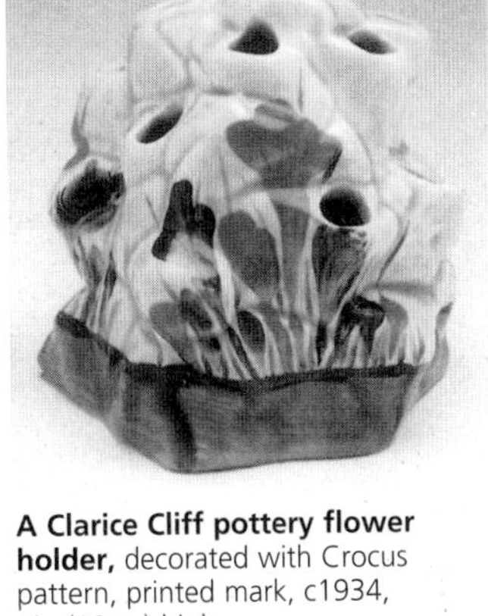

A Clarice Cliff pottery flower holder, decorated with Crocus pattern, printed mark, c1934, 4in (10cm) high.
£70–90 RFA

A Clarice Cliff Bizarre lotus jug, decorated with Aurea pattern, printed mark, c1935, 10in (25.5cm) high.
£320–385 LJ

A Clarice Cliff plate, decorated with brown Cowslip pattern, c1930, 7in (18cm) diam.
£315–350 RH

A pair of Clarice Cliff cruiseware palette-shaped buffet plates, c1930, 11in (28cm) wide.
£170–220 G(L)

► **A Clarice Cliff Fantasque preserve pot,** decorated in orange, pink, yellow and green on a cream ground, printed mark, 1929–34, 3in (7.5cm) high.
£120–150 BBR

◄ **A Clarice Cliff Biarritz side plate,** decorated with Idyll pattern, printed and impressed marks, 1931–36, 6½in (16.5cm) wide.
£425–500 S(O)

► **A Clarice Cliff Trieste tea-for-two set,** comprising seven pieces, decorated with banding in green, yellow, grey and black, c1934, teapot 5¼in (13.5cm) high.
£550–700 P

A Clarice cliff Bonjour sugar sifter, decorated with Idyll pattern, c1930, 5in (12.5cm) high.
£500–600 G(L)

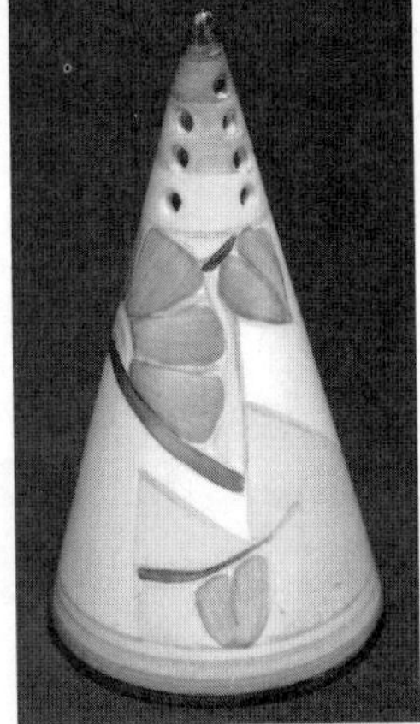

A Clarice Cliff conical sugar sifter, decorated with Moonflower pattern, c1930, 5in (12.5cm) high.
£720–800 RH

◄ **A Clarice Cliff Isis vase,** painted with daffodils and leaves in yellow, orange, silver and green on a goldstone ground, 1933–35, 9½in (24cm) high.
£320–400 P
Goldstone is a very matt 'gold-effect' mottled glaze and is often less popular with the public.

Miller's is a price GUIDE not a price LIST

Susie Cooper

A Susie Cooper banded hot water pot, c1930, 7in (18cm) high.
£80–90 ⊞ RH

A Susie Cooper Patricia Rose plate, c1930, 9in (23cm) diam.
£85–95 ⊞ RH
The Patricia Rose range was reaching much higher prices in the mid-1990s when it was favoured by Japanese collectors.

A Susie Cooper carved ware jug, decorated with a green glaze, incised signature, c1930, 8in (20.5cm) high.
£150–200 ⚒ RTo
Carved ware is the title of a range of wares that appear to have been carved out of clay.

A Susie Cooper hand-carved vase, depicting squirrels on a pink glaze, incised signature, c1932, 13¾in (35cm) high.
£160–200 ⚒ P(B)

◀ **A Susie Cooper trio,** decorated with Feather pattern, c1930, plate 5in (12.5cm) diam.
£75–85 ⊞ RH

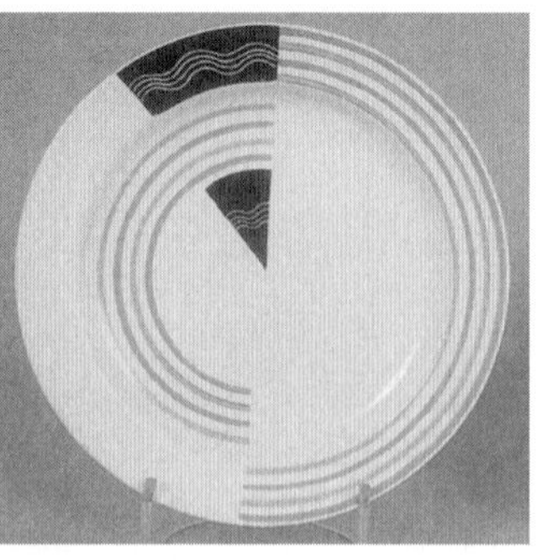

A pair of Susie Cooper Art Deco plates, for Crown Works, Burslem, decorated with bands of colours and shapes in black with wavy bands, printed mark, c1930, 8¾in (22.5cm) diam.
£140–175 ⚒ P(B)

A Susie Cooper pink teapot, decorated with Dresden Spray pattern, c1930, 5in (12.5cm) high.
£135–150 ⊞ RH

A Susie Cooper pottery vase, decorated in orange, red, black and brown, with silvered hoops to the shoulder, on a cream ground, c1930, 6in (15cm) high.
£180–225 ⚒ Mit

Charlotte Rhead

A Charlotte Rhead Crown Ducal ware jug, with tube-lined decoration on a metallic, orange and cream ground, 1930s, 8¾in (22cm) high.
£70–90 ⚒ WilP

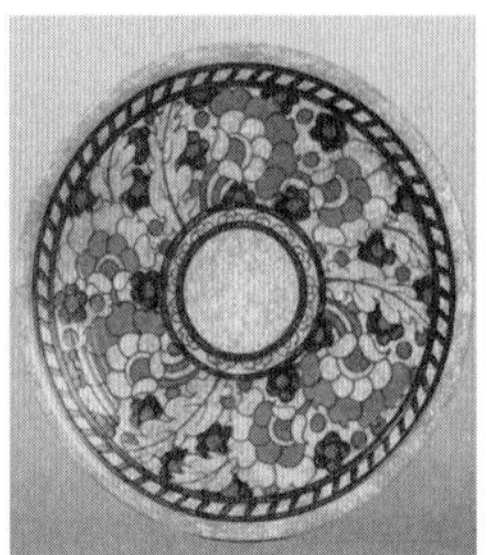

A Charlotte Rhead wall plaque, decorated with Byzantine pattern, with tube-lined decoration in blue and orange, signed, printed mark, 1930s, 12¾in (32.5cm) diam.
£230–280 ⚒ Mit

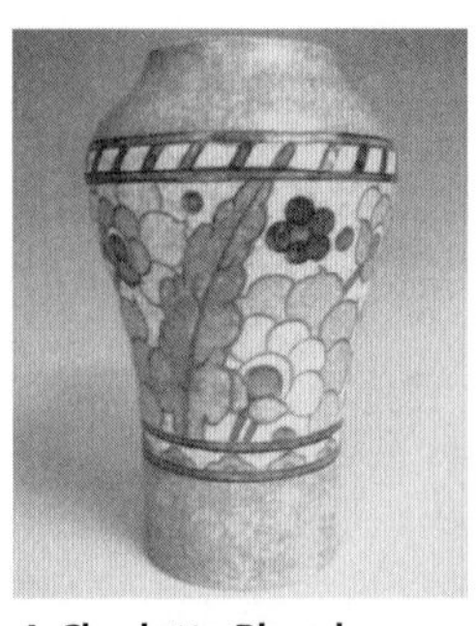

A Charlotte Rhead vase, with tube-lined decoration of flora in orange, yellow and blue on a green and cream ground, 1930s, 8in (20.5cm) high.
£115–150 ⚒ Pott

A Charlotte Rhead Crown Ducal vase, decorated with Byzantine pattern, with washed puce and green borders, signed, printed mark, 1930s, 8½in (21.5cm) high.
£140–175 ⚒ GAK

Art Deco Clocks & Watches

An Edgar Brandt wrought-iron and marble mantel clock, stamped mark, c1925, 13in (33cm) high.
£18,000–22,000 S(NY)

◄ **A sycamore and ebonized mantel clock,** with eight-day chime movement, on chrome feet, c1930, 10¼in (26cm) high.
£300–375 BLH

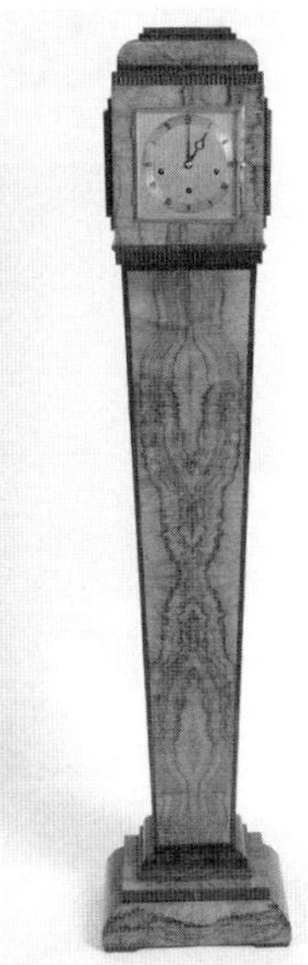

A walnut longcase clock, with eight-day chiming movement, c1930, 64in (162.5cm) high.
£2,400–2,650 MTay

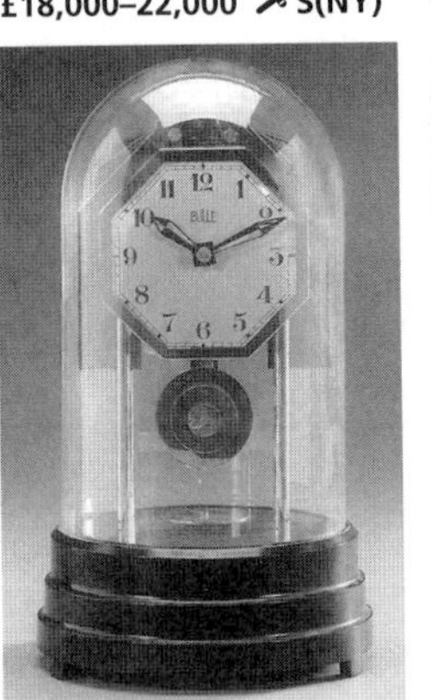

A Bulle electric mantel timepiece, with silvered dial, Bakelite base and glass dome, c1930, 10¼in (26cm) high.
£525–625 S(O)

A lady's sapphire and diamond wristwatch, c1925.
£1,200–1,500 S

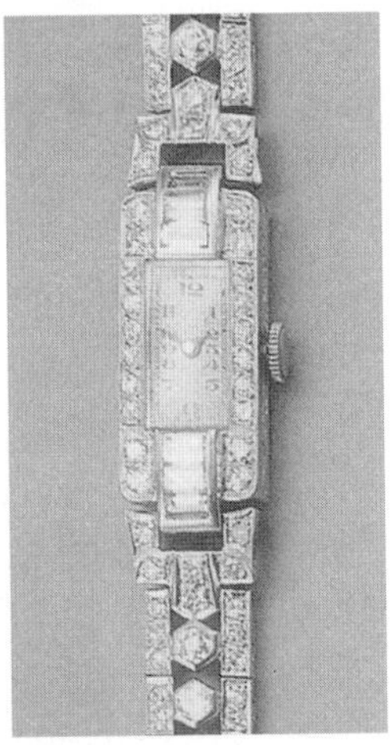

A lady's diamond wristwatch, c1930, 6¾in (17cm) long.
£2,400–3,000 S

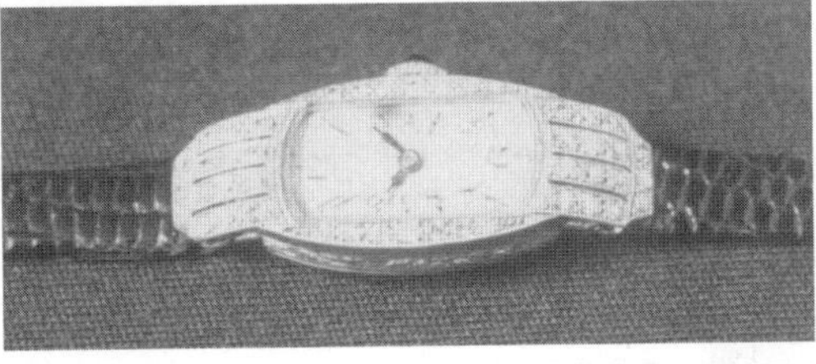

► **A diamond wristwatch,** with 15-jewelled movement, Swiss, c1930, ¾in (2cm) wide.
£600–700 GLa

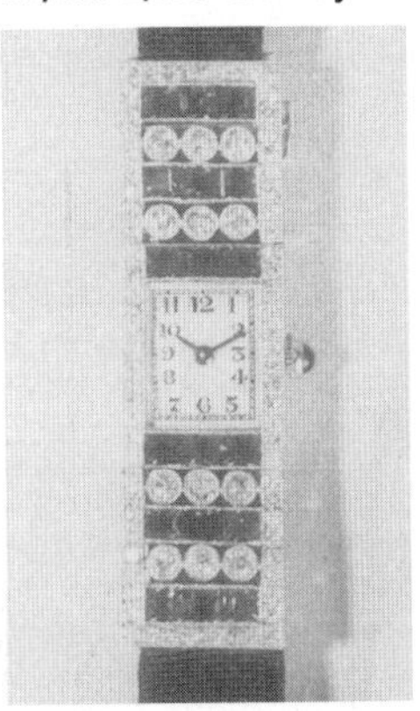

A sapphire and diamond cocktail watch, c1930.
£2,800–3,500 HYD

Art Deco Figures

A bronze and ivory figure of a Russian dancing girl, by S. Bertrand, on an onyx pedestal, signed, c1930, 8¾in (22cm) high.
£2,200–2,500 S

A French School bronze group of Diana the Huntress, by G. Daverny, on a marble base, signed, c1930, 41in (104cm) wide.
£1,200–1,400 S(O)

A ceramic figure of a dancer, by Goldscheider, wearing a green outfit and shoes, factory stamp and impressed number, Austrian, Vienna, c1939, 12½in (32cm) high.
£1,400–1,750 DORO

◄ **A silvered-bronze hunting dog,** by Franz Hagenauer, stamped mark, c1930, 18½in (47cm) wide.
£3,250–4,000 S

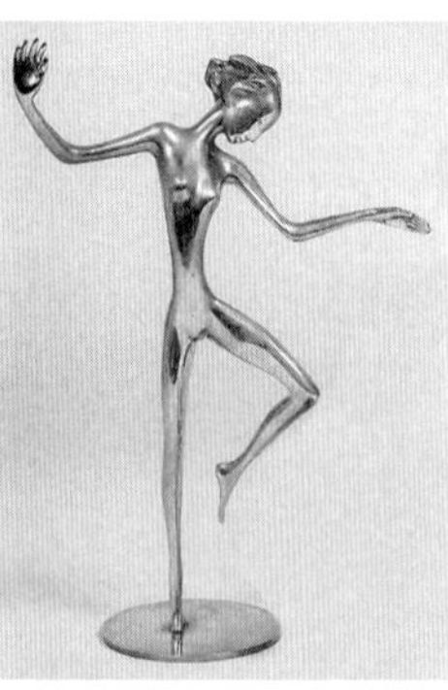

A brass figure of a dancer, by Karl Hagenauer, marked, Vienna, designed 1940–50, 10¼in (26cm) high.
£850–1,100 DORO

◀ **A metal figure of a dancer,** by Karl Hagenauer, on a wooden plinth, marked, Vienna, c1930, 23in (58.5cm) high.
£3,500–4,000 MI

A pottery figure of a woman dancer, by Joseph Lorenzl for Goldscheider, wearing a blue floral dress, printed marks, Vienna, c1930, 13¼in (33.5cm) high.
£700–875 P(B)

A gilt-bronze and carved ivory figure, by Ferdinand Preiss, on a black marble base, German, c1920, 12¼in (31cm) high.
£2,300–2,800 B

A ceramic figure of a woman holding a football, by Schaubachkunst, German, 1930s, 9in (23cm) high.
£160–200 G(L)

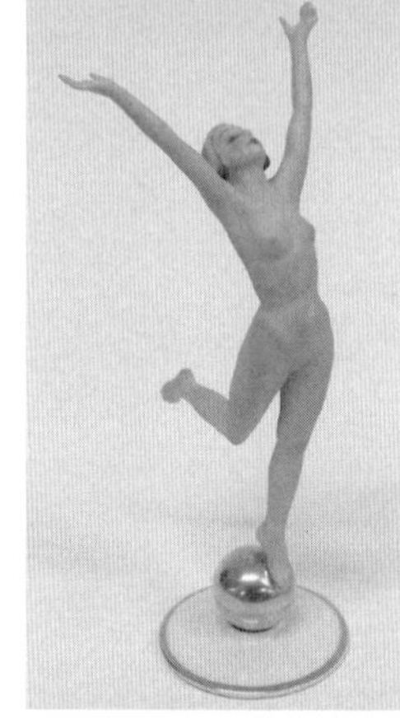

◀ **A porcelain figure of a female nude,** standing on a gilt ball, German, c1930, 8½in (21.5cm) high.
£140–175 G(L)

▶ **A porcelain figure of a musician,** impressed and printed marks, Continental, 1930–50, 8¾in (22cm) high.
£220–275 RFA

Art Deco Furniture

A Waring & Gillows bedroom suite, comprising a wardrobe, dressing table, pair of bedroom chairs, tallboy, bedside cabinet and single bed, veneered in light burr-walnut, rosewood, ebony and satinwood, label, c1925, wardrobe 73¾in (187.5cm) high.
£800–1,000 P(B)

A green stained-oak bedroom suite, comprising a wardrobe, tallboy, dressing table with silvered reeded detail and painted with a small panel of stylized leafage, and a pair of 36in (91.5cm) bed ends, c1936, wardrobe 74¼in (188.5cm) high.
£500–600 DD

► **A set of six upholstered dining chairs,** in the style of Dominique, French, c1925.
£5,750–6,250 S(NY)

A burr-walnut cocktail cabinet, the top with a central hinged lid and fall-front, enclosing a fitted and illuminated interior, above double doors, flanked by two further doors, c1930, 59½in (151cm) wide.
£100–125 P(Ba)

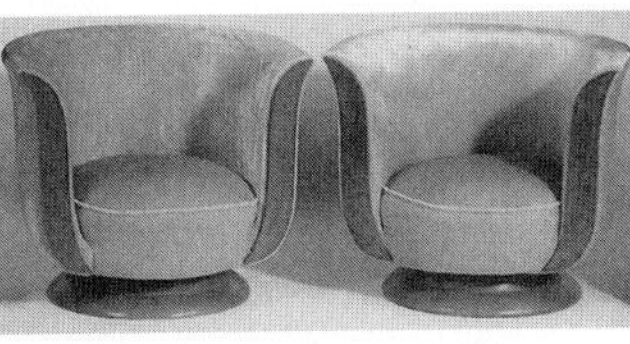

A pair of burr-walnut salon chairs, upholstered in beige velvet, French, c1945.
£1,600–1,800 SK

A Betty Joel hardwood chest of drawers, by C. Hall for Token Handmade Furniture, with carved walnut handles and plate-glass inset top, 33in (84cm) high.
£2,000–2,400 RUSK

A burr-walnut cocktail cabinet, possibly by Epstein and Goldman, the top with a mirror-lined fitted interior, the lower section with two doors enclosing pierced apertures for bottles, c1935, 48in (122cm) wide.
£1,500–1,800 B

A Betty Joel Indian laurel chest, the top inset with plate glass, above two short and three long drawers with ebonized pulls, c1932, 39¼in (99.5cm) high.
£1,200–1,500 B

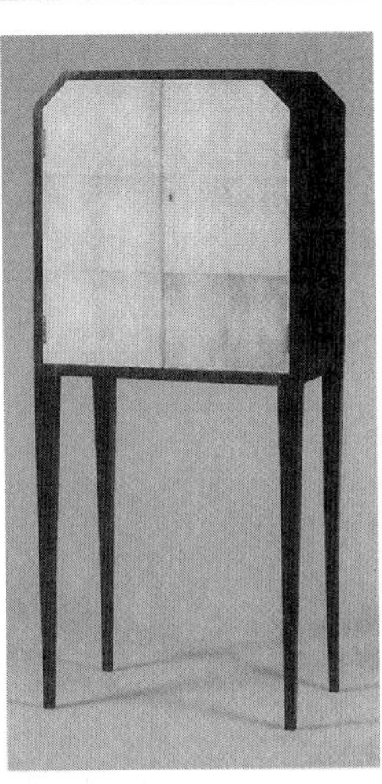

► **An ebonized, shagreen and ivory inlaid cocktail cabinet,** the cupboard doors enclosing a fitted interior, French, c1920, 25½in (65cm) wide.
£4,500–5,000 S(O)
The use of shagreen in this cabinet emphasizes the quality of manufacture.

A pair of Betty Joel armchairs, with ebonized wood surrounds, upholstered in white calico, c1930.
£2,000–2,200 RUSK

Betty Joel (English 1896–1984)

Betty Joel established her furniture workshop in 1921 in Hayling Island, followed by a factory in Portsmouth, a shop in London and another factory in Kingston. Much of her work was commissioned – for example, designs for film sets and some exclusive dwellings. Many pieces, especially bedroom furniture and wall cabinets, are built-in. Joel's furniture is large in size, as it was intended for the spacious rooms of London mansion flats. It is usually highly practical, versatile, simple and unfussy and mainly devoid of carved decoration and painted finishes. Some pieces are lacquered, but Joel had a strong preference for featuring the wood grain as the main, or sole, decorative element. Alternatively, she used contrasting veneers to produce an attractive effect. All pieces are hand-finished, although some machinery was used in the construction. The quality of the craftsmanship is excellent – for example, drawers are likely to fit very snugly, so that air rushes out when they are closed.

A limed oak corner unit, by Heals, the two corner cupboards flanked by a lower open bookshelf to the right and a cupboard with a fall-front to the left, c1930, 52¾in (134cm) high.
£320–400 ⚒ P(B)

This type of corner unit, which could be made up from different components to a client's specification, was available from Heals throughout the 1930s in many styles and woods and features in their catalogues of living room and dining room furniture during this period.

A Jean Prouvé oak and enamelled steel kneehole desk and chair, French, c1940, 60in (152.5cm) wide.
£12,000–15,000 ⚒ S(NY)

An upholstered four-piece matched lounge suite, comprising a sofa and three open armchairs of different design, two of these chairs are known to have been supplied by Betty Joel in 1935, c1938, sofa 79in (200.5cm) wide.
£1,300–1,600 ⚒ P

A limed oak four-piece office suite, comprising a desk, armchair and two side chairs upholstered in a grey patterned fabric, French, c1935, desk 58in (147.5cm) wide.
£6,000–7,500 ⚒ S(NY)

An Egyptian revival three-panel screen, the giltwood-framed canvas panels with a hand-painted scene, c1930, 60in (152.5cm) wide.
£2,500–2,750 ⚒ JAA

A rosewood sideboard, the glazed panel door flanked by cupboard doors and curved end sections, hinged to reveal shelves, French, c1930, 87in (221cm) wide.
£450–550 ⚒ P(B)

A black lacquered U-shaped sideboard, by Hille, with chrome handles and blondwood base, c1930, 65in (165cm) wide.
£1,100–1,200 ⊞ JAZZ

A wrought-iron and slate low table, in the style of Gilbert Poillerat, French, c1930, 37in (94cm) wide.
£5,250–6,500 ⚒ S(NY)

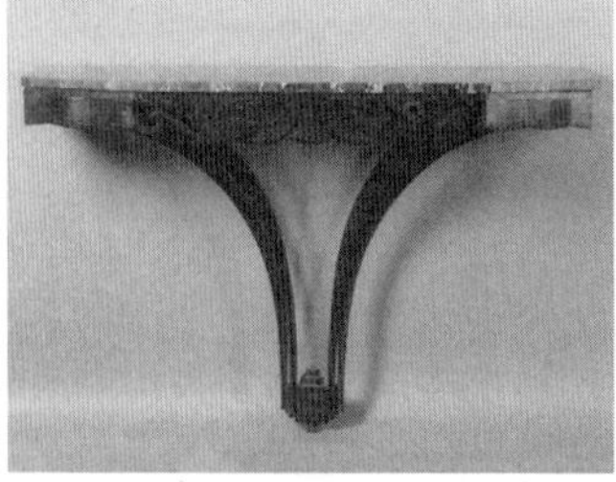

A wrought-iron and marble-topped console table, c1930, 62in (157.5cm) wide.
£900–1,000 ⚒ S(O)

A Heals walnut side table, with two frieze drawers, ivorine Heals trade label, c1936, 35¾in (91cm) wide.
£400–500 ⚒ B

◄ **A walnut three-tier tea trolley,** c1930, 28in (71cm) wide.
£150–200 ⚒ DA

A Betty Joel black walnut double wardrobe, by E. W. Kemp for Token Handmade Furniture, with two fall-front drawers to the base, c1928, 60in (152.5cm) wide.
£3,800–4,200 ⊞ RUSK

Art Deco Glass

A René Lalique clear, frosted and green-stained bowl, Gui No. 1, the underside moulded with fruiting mistletoe, wheelcut mark, after 1921, 9½in (24cm) diam.
£350–450 Bon

René Lalique

Starting his career as an innovative jewellery designer in the 1890s, René Lalique was to gain international recognition in the 1920s as a designer of beautiful mould-blown glass. His designs spanned both the Art Nouveau and Art Deco styles and embraced images from nature, the female form and some religious subjects.

Perhaps most recognized for his opalescent glassware, it is his coloured pieces, particularly in black or electric blue, that collectors seek out. Prices for Lalique glass stagnated in the early 1990s when the Japanese economy took a downwards turn. Today prices are stable once more, but collectors are particularly critical of polished areas where damage has been removed.

A René Lalique clear and frosted etched glass Naiade ashtray, signed, French, c1930, 4½in (11.5cm) high.
£160–200 G(L)

A René Lalique blue-tinted glass bowl, *Poissons*, moulded with spiralling fish blowing bubbles, incised mark, mid-20thC, 11in (28cm) wide.
£325–360 WL

► **A WMF Myra Kristal iridescent glass bowl,** the clear glass washed with amber-coloured iridescence, German, after 1925, 6in (15cm) diam.
£235–260 S(O)

A René Lalique moulded amethyst glass car mascot, modelled as a falcon, engraved marks, French, c1930, 6in (15cm) high.
£1,500–2,000 G(L)

A René Lalique clear and frosted glass panel, *Faune et Vigne*, relief-moulded with a faun holding fruit, between vine borders, chips, French, after 1929, 12in (30.5cm) high.
£1,200–1,500 Bon

A cocktail set, by Thomas Webb, comprising a jug and six glasses with engraved spiral decoration to the outer surface, marked with manufacturer's acid-stamp, c1930, jug 10¾in (27.5cm) high.
£400–500 P

Miller's is a price GUIDE not a price LIST

► **A René Lalique press-moulded and frosted car mascot,** *Victoire,* modelled as The Spirit of the Wind, moulded mark, 1928, 10in (25.5cm) wide.
£2,000–2,500 B
This model had some trimming to the hair, otherwise it would have sold for £6,000–8,000.

A pink glass scent atomiser, with silk tassel bulb, French, c1930, 3½in (9cm) high.
£65–75 JAZZ

A René Lalique glass scent bottle, modelled as a poppy pod with a female figure finial, moulded mark, French, 4in (10cm) high.
£700–875 ⚒ TEN

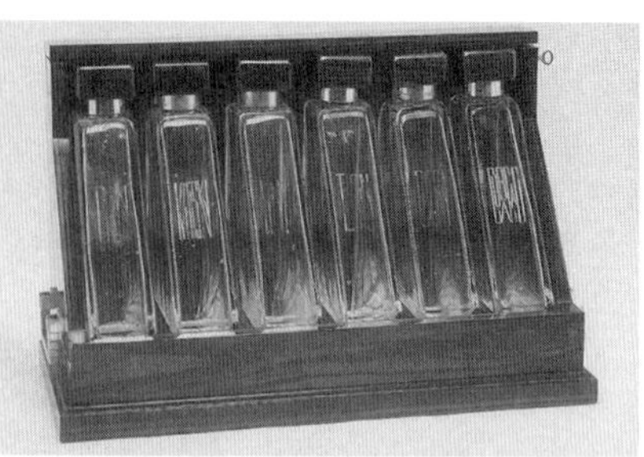

A glass and silvered-metal three-bottle tantalus stand, the decanters by Baccarat, two with etched mark, French, c1930, 13½in (34.5cm) wide.
£800–900 ⚒ S(O)

A Marcel Goupy *ebène-de-macassar,* enamelled glass and silvered-bronze tantalus, each bottle labelled in gilt-enamel, French, c1928, 17in (43cm) wide.
£3,000–3,750 ⚒ S(NY)

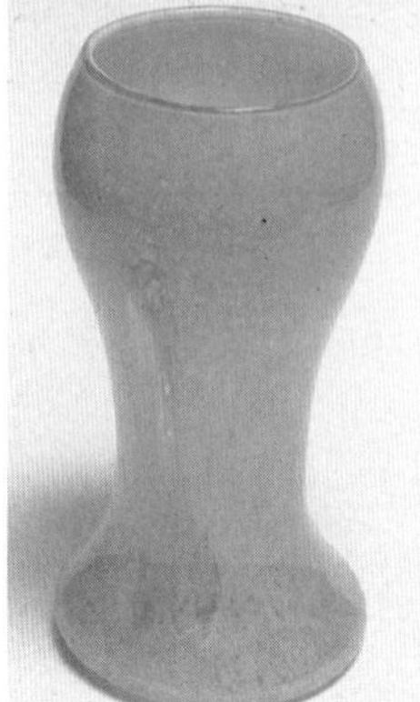

A Daum clear glass vase, with horizontal bands of acid-etching, engraved mark, French, 1920s, 10½in (26.5cm) high.
£450–550 ⚒ S(O)

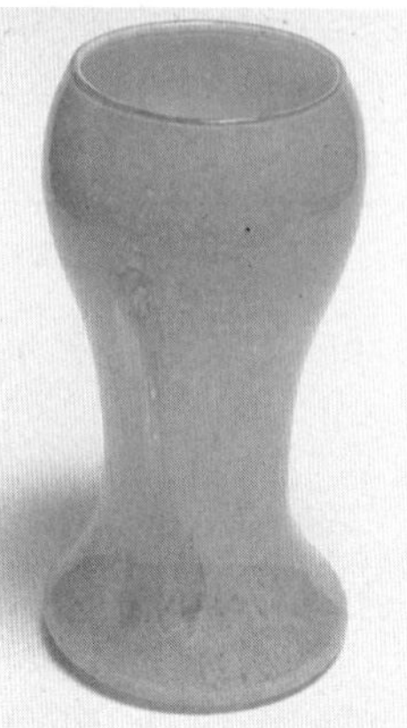

A Gray-Stan vase, decorated with apricot marbled swirls, engraved mark, c1930, 9in (23cm) high.
£250–280 ⊞ RUSK

A René Lalique clear glass vase, Lagamar, the frosted exterior moulded with bands and abstract decoration heightened with black enamel, wheel cut mark, French, 17¼in (44cm) high.
£9,500–12,000 ⚒ S
This is a very rare model and it is heavily moulded and spectacular.

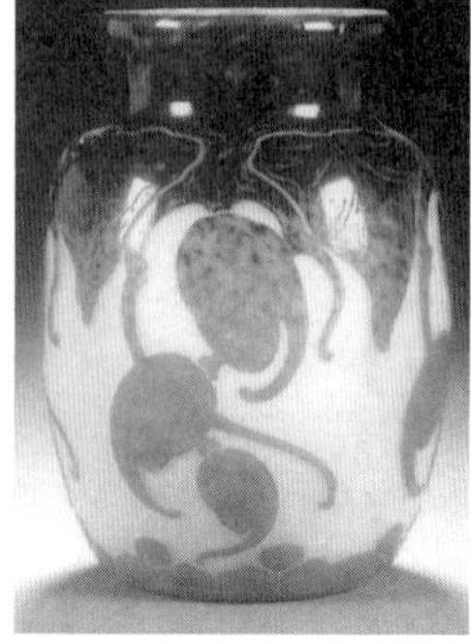

A Le Verre Français cameo glass vase, decorated with sprays of fruit pendant from a leafy band, incised signature, French, 10¾in (27.5cm) high.
£950–1,200 ⚒ S(O)

Art Deco Jewellery

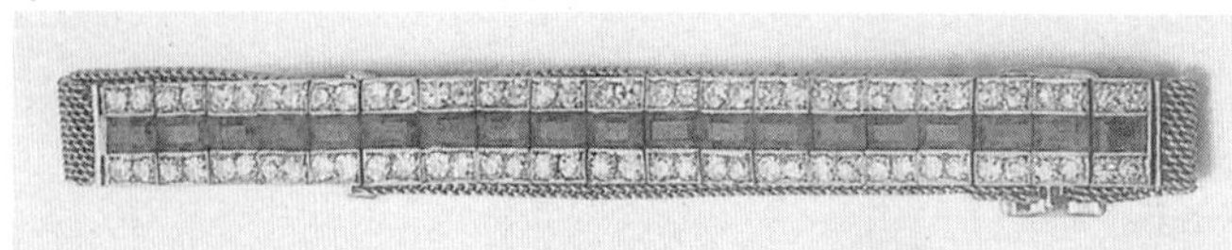

A natural spinel and diamond bracelet, c1920.
£1,200–1,500 ⚒ P(Ba)

An emerald, ruby and diamond clip brooch, set in platinum, c1930.
£2,200–2,750 ⚒ HYD

An onyx and diamond brooch, by Janesich, signed, French, 1920s.
£3,400–4,250 ⚒ S

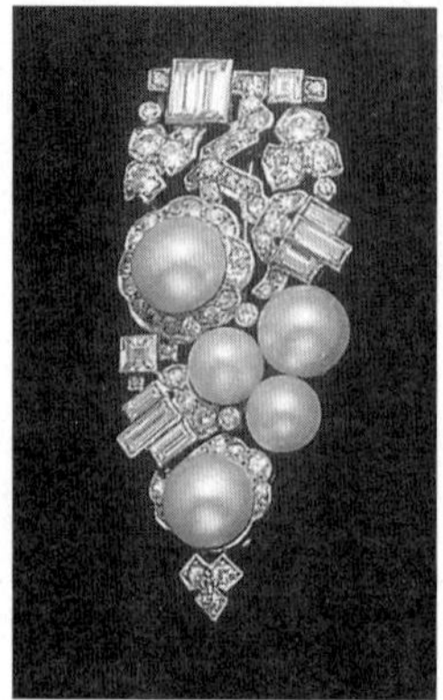

A pearl and diamond brooch, French, c1925.
£1,500–2,000 ⚒ B

A diamond necklace, c1935.
£3,300–4,200 ⚒ HAM

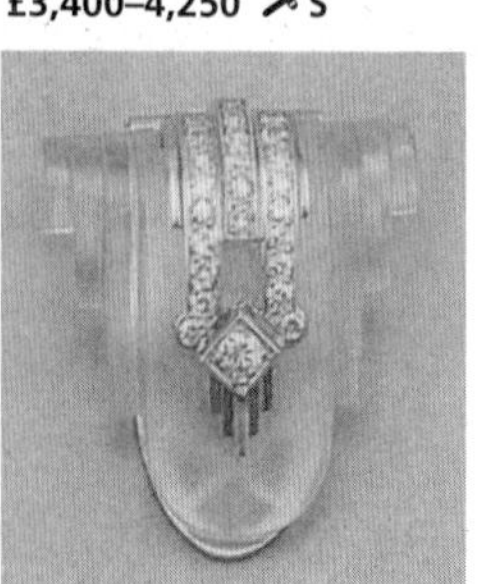

A Cartier rock crystal and diamond clip, designed as a stylized buckle, French, c1925.
£5,000–5,500 ⚒ S

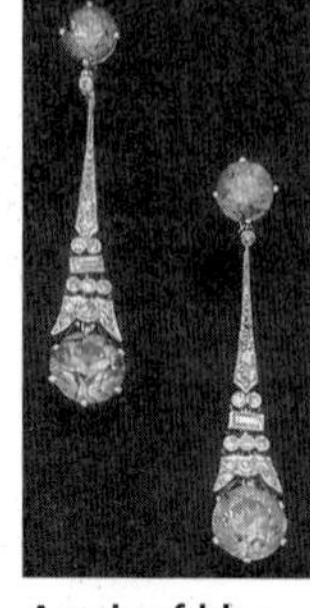

A pair of blue zircon and diamond pendant earrings, c1925, 1¾in (4.5cm) long.
£1,600–2,000 ⚒ B

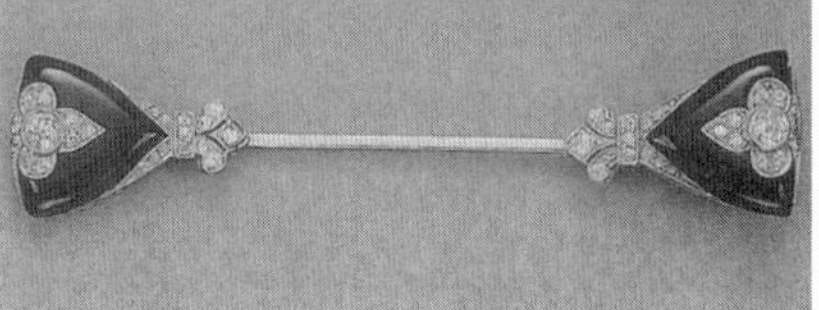

► **An onyx and diamond *sûreté* pin,** French, 1920s.
£2,700–3,000 ⚒ S

A Gabriel Argy-Rousseau *pâte-de-verre* pendant, decorated with a blue cornflower, c1920.
£775–975 SWO

A tourmaline, sapphire and diamond cluster ring, on a white metal shank, c1930.
£1,000–1,250 HYD

◄ **A sapphire and diamond ring,** c1930.
£1,300–1,600 P(Ba)

A sapphire and diamond ring, French, c1930.
£400–500 B(Ba)

An emerald and diamond ring, c1935.
£550–650 S

A gentleman's platinum and mother-of-pearl suite, comprising a pair of double cufflinks, four button covers and two shirt studs, hallmarked and boxed by William Drummond & Co, Melbourne, Australian, c1920.
£340–425 LJ

Art Deco Lighting

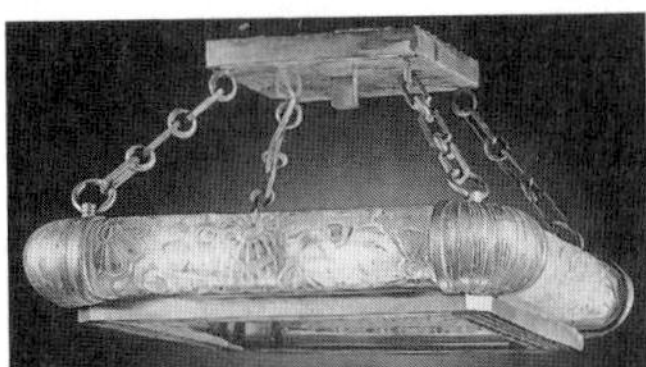

A Genet & Michon frosted and moulded glass and silvered-bronze chandelier, moulded mark, French, c1925, 19½in (49.5cm) wide.
£4,250–5,250 S(NY)

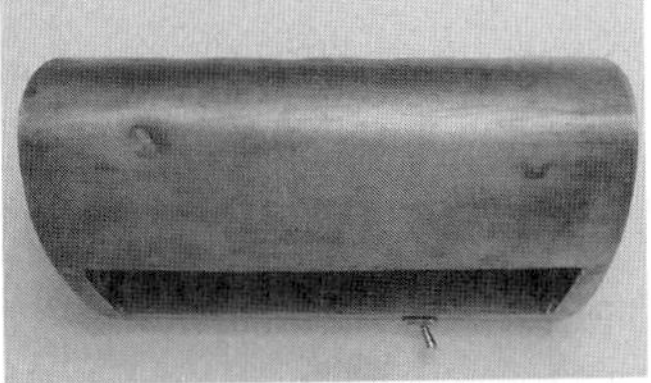

A pair of Le Corbusier fabricated metal sconces, French, c1935, 5¾in (14.5cm) wide.
£7,000–8,750 S(NY)

A pair of painted plaster appliqués, by Serge Roche, modelled as stylized leaves, French, early 1930s, 9¾in (25cm) high.
£3,200–3,500 S

A frosted glass and gilt-bronze chandelier, by Sabino, Paris, in the shape of a twelve-point star, 1925–50, 35in (89cm) diam.
£2,850–3,200 NOA

A Schneider glass and gilt-bronze chandelier, with mottled yellow and purple shades, engraved mark, French, c1920, 35½in (90cm) high.
£1,200–1,400 B

A brass wall light, c1930, 21¼in (54cm) high.
£220–275 P(B)

A Schneider glass and silvered-bronze table lamp, the moulded and frosted glass shade in a layered design, on an embossed and silvered base, French, c1925, 21in (53.5cm) high.
£500–550 JAA

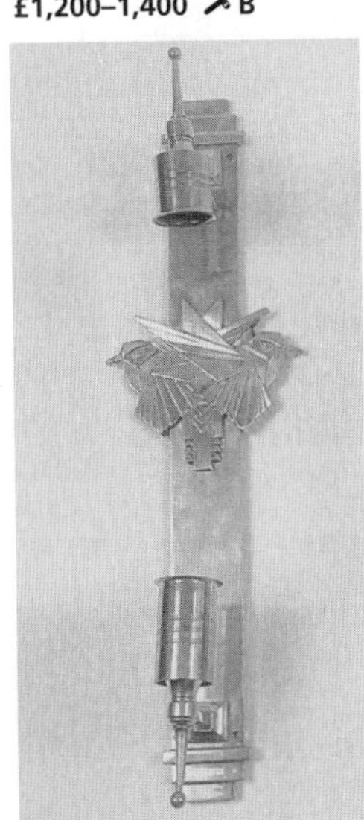

◄ **A pair of brass wall lights,** the backplate mounted with stylized doves, c1930, 19¾in (50cm) high.
£500–600 P(B)

► **A frosted glass and bronze chandelier,** the shades with moulded geometric floral designs, c1930, 20½in (52cm) high.
£1,700–2,200 SK

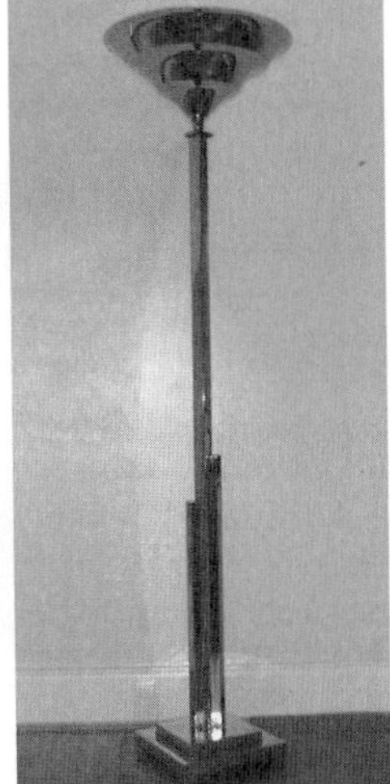

A chrome standard lamp, with replacement top, c1930, 74in (188cm) high.
£270–300 JAZZ
This lamp could originally have had a parchment shade.

Art Deco Metalware

A pair of cast brass andirons, the stems surmounted by stylized lion head finials and mounted with pierced radiating sun motifs, early 20thC, 26in (66cm) high.
£400–500 S(S)

A box, by Mappin & Webb, the blue *guilloche* enamel cover with applied carved coral and marcasite motif, on an engine-turned base, the gilded interior with inscription, London import marks for 1931, 3¼in (8cm) long, in a leather slip case.
£200–250 P(E)

A silver butter dish and cover, by Jean E. Puiforcat, Paris, with reeded rim, the domed cover with a hardstone finial, c1930, 4½in (11.5cm) diam, 6oz.
£525–650 S(O)

A silver bowl, with ropework borders, Austro-Hungarian, c1920, 10in (25.5cm) high.
£950–1,100 S(O)

A silver cocktail shaker and 12 goblets, by Tiffany & Co, New York, all engraved with initials, American, c1930, shaker 10¼in (26cm) high.
£3,500–4,500 S(NY)

► **A Dirk van Erp hammered-bronze jardinière,** impressed mark, American, c1920, 24in (61cm) wide.
£5,250–6,500 S(NY)

A silver christening mug, possibly by Keith Murray, for Mappin & Webb, the sides engraved with a frieze of four fishes swimming among undulating waves, 1935, 3¼in (8cm) high, 6oz.
£320–400 B(Ba)

◄ **A Josef Hoffman hammered and embossed brass vase,** by the Wiener Werkstätte, restored, impressed marks, Austrian, 1927, 7in (18cm) high.
£1,000–1,250 DORO

► **A silver vase,** with *martelé* decoration and a rosewood stem, maker's mark, French, Paris c1930, 5½in (14cm) high.
£330–400 S(O)

A silver powder box, by Jean E. Puiforcat, Paris, with wood finial and base, stamped mark, c1927, 4in (10cm) high, 3oz.
£2,000–2,200 S(O)

A Josef Hoffman brass dish, by the Wiener Werkstätte, impressed monogram and mark, Austrian, 1920–25, 12½in (32cm) diam.
£1,000–1,250 DORO

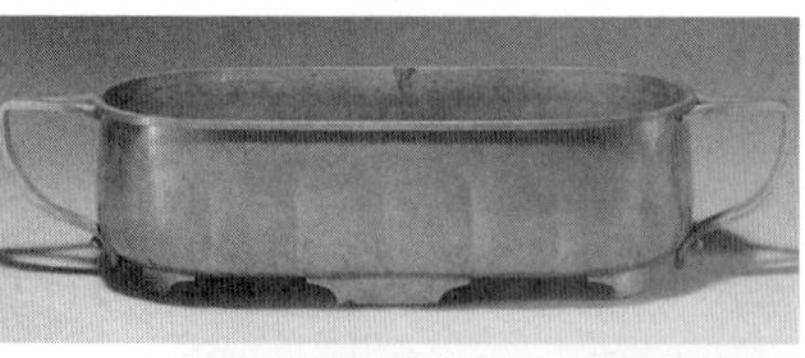

A silver three-piece tea service, by E. Viner, the teapot with an ivory finial and ivory scroll handle, London 1934, teapot 6in (15cm) high, 18oz.
£350–450 Bon

Art Deco Rugs & Textiles

A hand-tufted wool and cotton carpet, Continental, c1920, 198 x 132in (503 x 335.5cm).
£8,000–10,000 ⚒ S(NY)

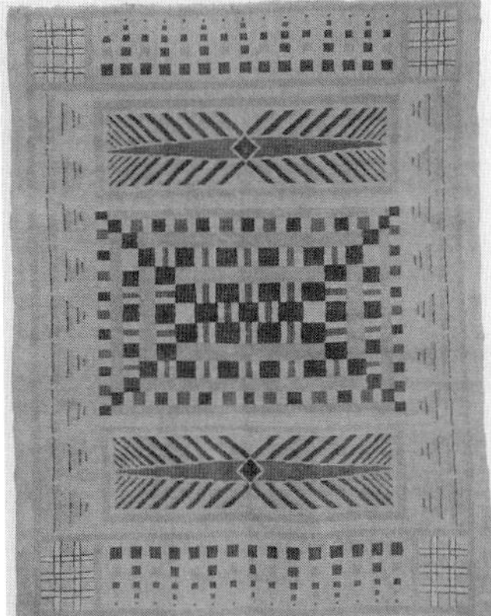

A wool carpet, woven in shades of brown and black, French, c1930, 106 x 80in (269 x 203cm).
£6,000–7,500 ⚒ S(NY)

A Marion Dorn silk batik fabric, with a linear and square pattern in shades of red, orange, yellow and white, now cut and made into a curtain, c1925, 49½ x 31in (125.5 x 78.5cm).
£620–775 ⚒ P

Marion Dorn was American but worked in England from the 1920s until WWII broke out, when she returned to the United States. She designed rugs, carpets and other textiles, manufactured by Edinburgh Weavers and other companies. She also produced collections for Fortnum & Mason and Claridge's.

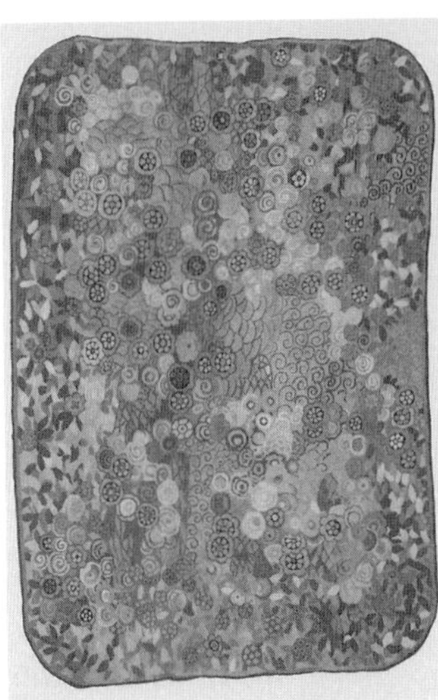

A woollen carpet, by Edouard Bénédictus, woven in shades of orange, pink, brown, green, mauve, white, black and blue with stylized flowers and leaves within a mauve and black border, French, c1925, 146 x 95½in (371 x 242.5cm).
£8,500–11,000 ⚒ S

A carpet, Chinese, c1930, 152 x 120in (386 x 305cm).
£9,500–12,000 ⚒ S(NY)

A woven wool tapestry, depicting Adam and Eve, c1930, 49 x 64in (124.5 x 162.5).
£3,750–4,500 ⚒ S(NY)

► **A black felt, diamond and rock crystal evening bag,** with a black enamel and diamond bar-and-hoop clasp and a black cord handle, c1920, 5½in (14cm) long.
£3,000–3,750 ⚒ B

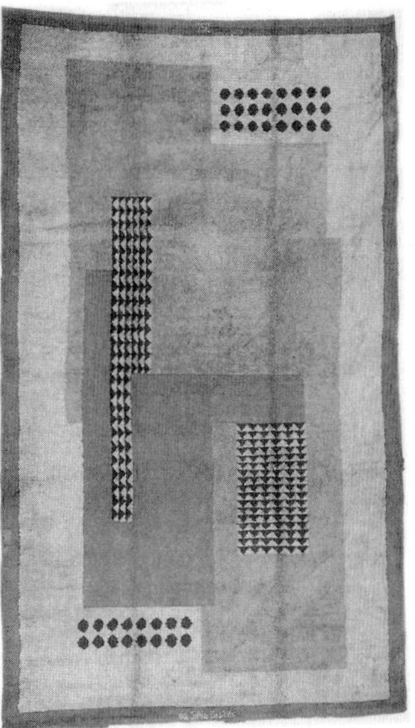

A Modernist carpet, by da Silva Bruhns, repiling, signed, French, c1925, 166 x 100in (420 x 254cm).
£13,000–16,000 ⚒ S(NY)

Ivan da Silva Bruhns (1881–1980) is regarded as the foremost French Modernist carpet designer. This carpet with its sparse, stylized geometric design and minimalist palette is one of his Synthetic Cubist weavings. Although da Silva Bruhns designed many carpets on commission for the Savonnerie and Aubusson manufactories amongst others, this carpet was woven at his own workshop, the Manufacture de Tapis de Savigny, which he set up in 1925 in Orge. This period of carpet production is identified by the appearance of both an inscription 'da Silva Bruhns' and the monogram 'IDSB'.

A Jean Lurçat wool tapestry, probably woven in Aubusson, woven signature, French, c1947, 50 x 73in (127cm x 185.5cm).
£4,500–5,500 ⚒ S(NY)

Twentieth-Century Design
Ceramics

A Katherine Pleydell-Bouverie stoneware vase, impressed seals, c1926, 7½in (19cm) high.
£450–565 ⚒ Bon

A Keith Murray white-glazed fruit bowl, 1930s, 14in (35.5cm) diam.
£585–650 ⊞ JAZZ

An Ernst Hubert vase, decorated with stylized flowers in blue and manganese with a crackle glaze, c1940, 6¾in (17cm) high.
£280–350 ⚒ DORO

A Ruskin Pottery crystalline vase, decorated with a trailing turquoise and blue crystalline glaze, above a green glaze, impressed mark, c1930, 12¼in (31cm) high.
£280–350 ⚒ P(B)

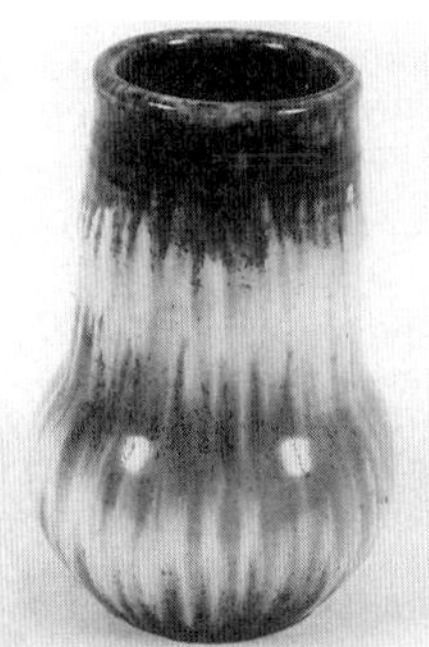

A Ruskin Pottery vase, decorated with an abstract-style blue wash design, signed, impressed mark, dated 1931, 8½in (21.5cm) high.
£160–200 ⚒ GAK

Ruskin Pottery (English 1898–1933)

William Howson Taylor, an English art potter, set up his art pottery in West Smethwick, Birmingham, and began commercial production in 1901 under the trade name of Ruskin Pottery. For an initial three-year period Taylor produced a lot of experimental pieces, and it was not until 1909 that he was officially allowed to trade as Ruskin. His range of wares includes his 'soufflé' pieces in a mottled, monochrome glaze, and lustre-decorated wares (both in earthenware),as well as an eggshell-thin bone china in crystalline glaze, and his keenly sought-after high-fired stonewares.

A Wedgwood mug, designed by Keith Murray, decorated with a straw matt glaze, c1930, 5in (12.5cm) high.
£70–80 ⊞ RUSK

A Bernard Leach stoneware tile, painted in brown and grey with a leaping deer, on a mottled grey and salmon pink ground, with a blue and brown speckled border, enamelled and impressed seals, c1947, 6in (15cm) high.
£500–625 ⚒ Bon

◄ **A Pablo Picasso earthenware ashtray,** Bird on a Branch, with oxidized paraffin decoration and oxidized marks, limited edition of 500, introduced 1952, 6in (15cm) square.
£380–475 ⚒ Bon

A pair of David Leach porcelain bowls, with iron rust decoration over a celadon glaze, c1960, 4½in (11.5cm) diam.
£110–125 ⊞ RUSK

A Pablo Picasso pottery dish, *Visage De Femme*, decorated in black, blue, green and cream, impressed marks, limited edition of 400, 1953, 15in (38cm) wide.
£3,200–4,000 ⚒ WW

A Bernard Rooke studio pottery vase, signed, 1970s, 7in (18cm) high.
£75–100 ⚒ DA

◄ **A Katherine Pleydell-Bouverie stoneware dish,** the brown-glazed interior with a cream-glazed radiating design, impressed seal, c1956, 12in (30.5cm) diam.
£270–340 ⚒ P(B)

Furniture

An Easiwork oak kitchen cabinet, with a two-door cupboard above tambour-fronted shelves flanked by a glazed cupboard door and a drawer, the lower section fitted with a pull-out enamelled surface and ironing board above an arrangement of drawers flanked by a cupboard, c1935, 63½in (161.5cm) wide.
£400–500 M
This cabinet was purchased at the 1936 Ideal Home Exhibition.

An Ernest Race dining table and three *en suite* BA chairs, with cast-aluminium frames, the table with a mahogany-veneered top, paper label, 1946, 48in (122cm) wide.
£575–720 S(S)

An L. M. 'Lizardman' Dutton of Huby oak dining room suite, comprising refectory table, five dining chairs with leather-upholstered seats, including one carver, and a sideboard, with carved Yorkshire rose detail, c1950, sideboard 54in (137cm) wide.
£800–1,000 DD

A Zoureff blackbean wood dining suite, comprising a dining table and ten chairs, and a sideboard with stylized geometric panelling, Australian, c1960, sideboard 141in (358cm) wide.
£2,800–3,200 LJ

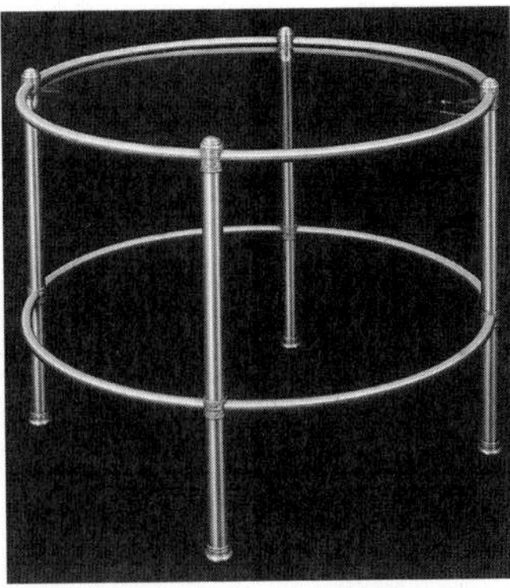

A prototype coffee/occasional table, by Warren McArthur Corporation, the original glass top in a tubular anodized aluminium frame, 1934, 13¼in (33.5cm) diam.
£1,800–2,250 TREA
Warren McArthur moved his furniture operation from Los Angeles to Rome, New York, in 1933 and as part of the compensation package for moving to the East Coast, McArthur gave his foreman a group of furniture including this table. The business closed in 1948 and the drawings, blueprints, photographic records and much of the furniture were taken to the local dump and burned, while unused or obsolete parts were shipped to a warehouse on Lake Erie. In the early 1970s the warehouse went up in flames and in order to contain the fire the building and the remaining McArthur wares were bulldozed into the water.

Condition

The condition is absolutely vital when assessing the value of an antique. Damaged pieces on the whole appreciate much less than perfect examples. However a rare desirable piece may command a high price even when damaged.

A Charles and Ray Eames oak-faced plywood LCW chair, for Herman Miller, designed 1945, manufactured 1949–58.
£1,100–1,200 ⊞ ORI

A pair of beech armchairs, with rope upholstery, French, c1950.
£585–650 ⊞ SIE

A Herman Miller coffee table, by George Nelson, American, c1954, 29in (73.5cm) diam.
£270–300 ⊞ ZOOM

George Nelson (American 1908–86)

- Studied architecture at Yale University from 1924–31.
- Won the prestigious Rome prize and from 1932–34 was in Italy where he was introduced to the work of key early Modernist designers such as Le Corbusier and Ludwig Mies van der Rohe.
- On his return to the United States he took up writing about architecture and design and became assistant editor of *Architectural Forum*.
- Set up an architectural practice with William Hamby in 1936; later joined the Faculty of Architecture at Yale.
- Collaborated with designer Henry Wright in 1946 on a book called *Tomorrow's House* which brought Modernist design to a wider American audience.
- From 1946–72 was director of design at the Herman Miller manufacturing firm, and from 1947 also had his own design office, George Nelson & Co, in New York.

A Hille set of four dining chairs, by Robin Day, with teak-faced moulded plywood seats and backs, on a blackened tubular steel frame, c1960.
£320–400 ⚒ P(B)

A C & B Italian UP2 armchair, by Gaetano Pesce, the moulded polyurethane foam with original orange/red stretch fabric cover, designed 1969, produced 1970–73.
£1,500–2,000 ⚒ DORO

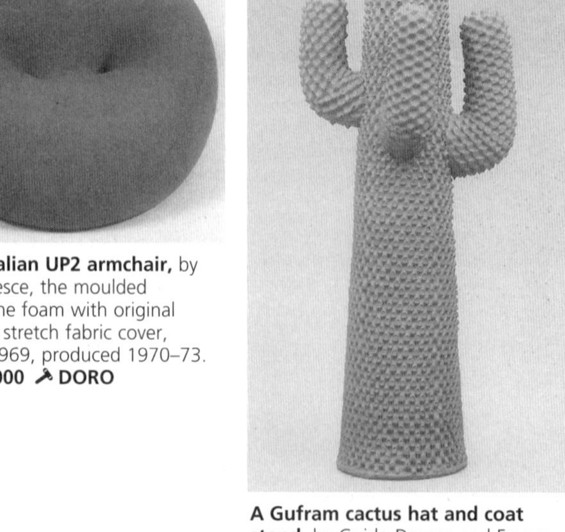

A Gufram cactus hat and coat stand, by Guido Drocco and Franco Mello, the moulded foam covered in green rubber, Italian, 1970s, 65¾in (167cm) high.
£2,200–2,750 ⚒ BUK

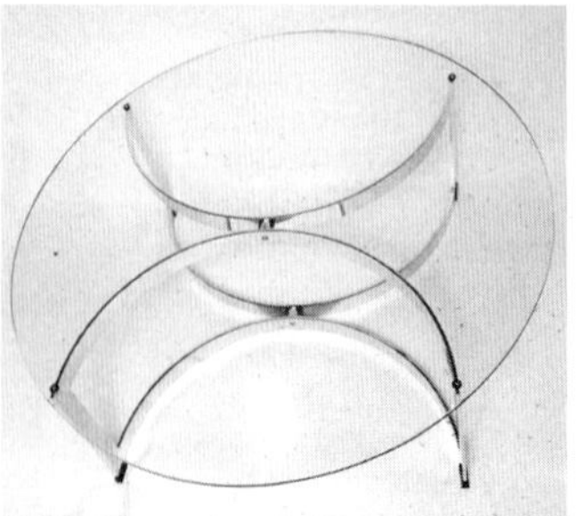

◀ **A glass and chrome coffee table,** by William Plunkett, c1968, 36in (91.5cm) diam.
£250–300 ⊞ MARK

Glass

An Irene Stevens glass bowl, by T. Webb & Corbett, the body with horizontal undulating mitre cuts intersected by concaved discs, on a star-cut foot, 1946, 10in (25.5cm) high.
£500–625 ⚒ P

A Vistosi stylized glass model of a bird, *Pulcino*, by Alessandro Pianon, with orange relief decoration, on copper legs, Italian, Venice, designed 1962, 8¾in (22cm) high.
£720–900 ⚒ BUK

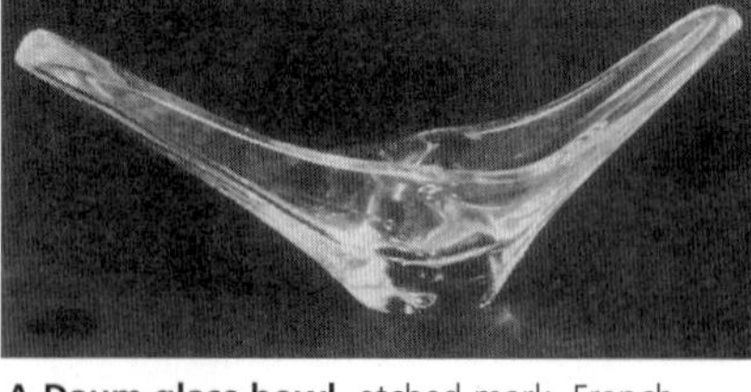

A Daum glass bowl, etched mark, French, mid-20thC, 23½in (59.5cm) wide.
£80–100 ⚒ WL

An Aureliano Toso Oriente glass bowl, by Dino Martens, internally decorated in colours, 1950s, 6¾in (17cm) wide.
£380–475 ⚒ BUK

Jewellery

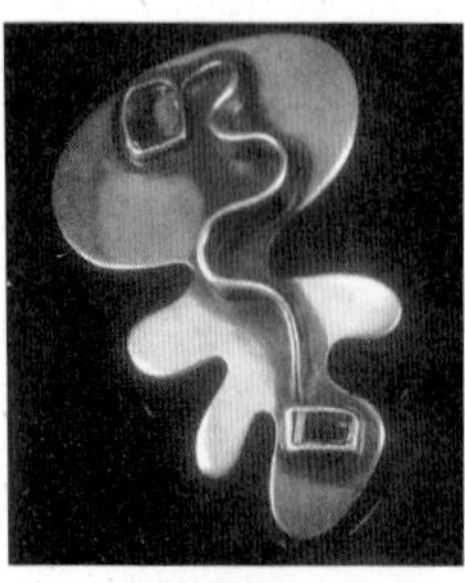

A sterling silver brooch, set with green and pink stones, hallmark for Sam Kramer, c1950.
£800–1,000 ⚒ SK

A Van Cleef & Arpels brooch, *Jeune Fille de Saint-Germain*, the head of rock crystal with sapphire eyes, ruby mouth and a sapphire and diamond collar, French, c1950.
£1,300–1,500 ⚒ S

Cross Reference
See Colour Review (page 503)

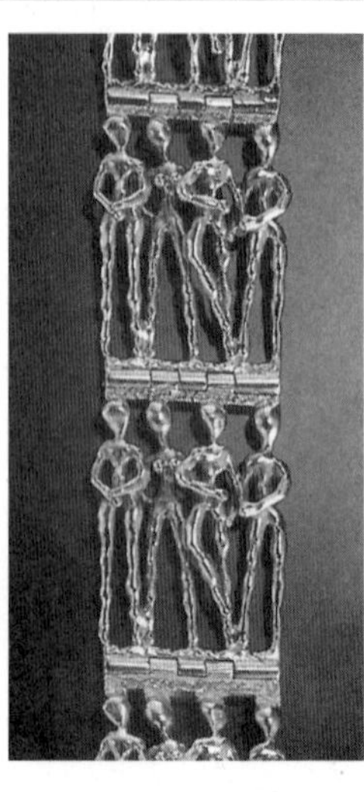

▶ **A Stuart Devlin 18ct gold bracelet,** each link worked to form a series of standing figures with interlocking arms, stamped mark, 1974, 7in (18cm) long, with original box.
£850–1,100 ⚒ P

The human figure was a frequent source of inspiration for many of Stuart Devlin's designs.

Lighting

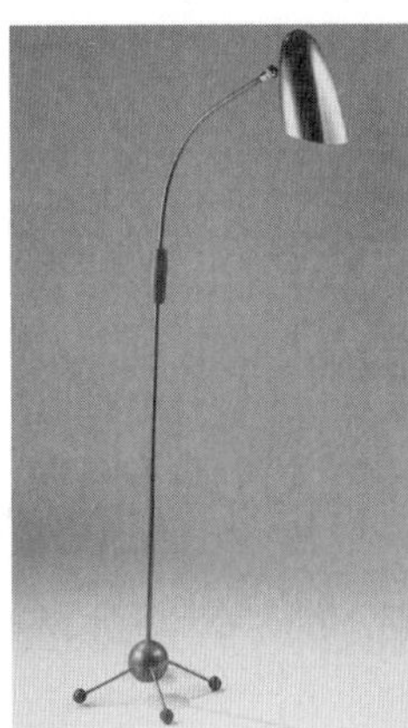

◄ **A Professor Nicholson standard lamp,** the copper body with cylindrical teak collar and a cone-shaped aluminium shade which may be articulated at a 360° angle, on four copper rod legs with spherical black rubber boots, designed 1945–46, 48½in (123cm) high.
£850–1,100 P

A Vallauris ceramic fish lamp, decorated in turquoise and gilt on red, French, c1950, 12in (30.5cm) high.
£70–78 ⊞ MLL

A Murano glass chandelier, Italian, c1960, 18in (45.5cm) high.
£1,100–1,250 ⊞ DOA

An Arteluce Flos chrome chandelier, by Gino Sarfatti, designed 1950, produced 1980s, 24½in (62cm) high.
£425–530 DORO

A Torretta Luci lamp, 1960s, 26in (66cm) high.
£450–500 ⊞ ZOOM

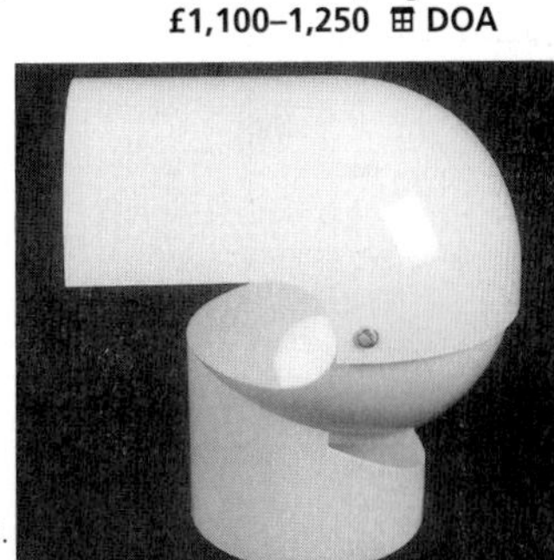

► **A Gae Aulenti Pileo lamp,** by Artemide, moulded white plastic, with adjustable top and chrome fittings, signed, Italian, 1970s, 17½in (44.5cm) high.
£450–550 TREA

Metalware

A silver-plated five-piece tea and coffee service, by Christofle & Co, French, c1960.
£1,200–1,400 ⊞ DID

A silver tazza, by Albert Frederick Baker, engraved with a sunburst, the tapering foot with a band of engraved flame decoration, on a polished onyx base, Birmingham 1969, 9½in (24cm) diam.
£340–425 P(L)

A Driade silver-plated candelabrum, by Borek Sipek, the seven branches with central flower vase, Italian, designed 1988, produced from 1989, 18½in (47cm) high.
£470–600 BUK

Wireless & Television

A Phillips 930A wireless, in a simulated rosewood case, c1930, 18½in (46.5cm) high.
£330–420 BLH

A Kuba de Luxe wooden radio/television combination, 1962.
£5,500–6,000 KOLN

A Keracolour white moulded plastic television, 20in (51cm) screen, not in working order, 1970s, 37in (94cm) high.
£360–450 DD

Miller's Price Guides

Miller's best-selling price guides are the ultimate reference books, ideal for both the experienced dealer and the first time collector. Completely new each year, Miller's price guides offer expert advice, thousands of new photographs, independently assessed price ranges, insider collecting tips and essential background information.

isbn 1 84000 612 9

isbn 1 84000 543 2

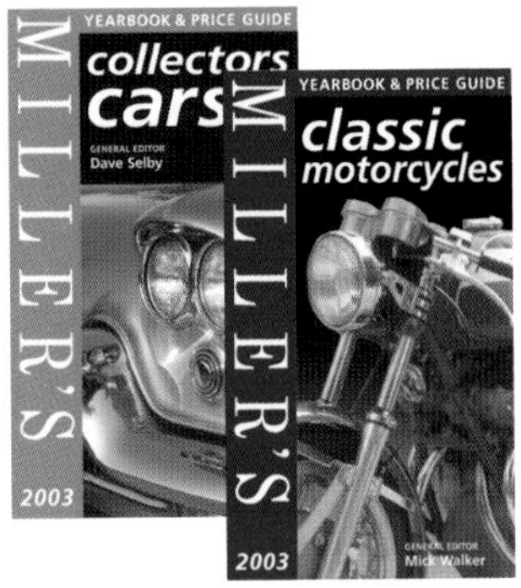

isbn 1 84000 631 5 isbn 1 84000 632 3

Antiques Price Guide 2003
UK £22.99 AU $59.95

Collectables Price Guide 2002/3
UK £17.99 AU $49.95

Classic Motorcycles Yearbook and Price Guide 2003
UK £14.99 AU $39.95

Collector's Cars Yearbook and Price Guide 2003
UK £19.99 AU $49.95

Miller's Buyer's Guides

The Miller's Buyer's Guide series provides invaluable reference material for the enthusiast as well as the experienced collector. Each guide concentrates on a popular area of collecting and features thousands of examples, which are illustrated, authenticated and given an up-to-date price range by a team of top dealers and auction house specialists.

isbn 1 84000 583 1

isbn 1 84000 555 6

isbn 1 84000 375 8

Art Nouveau & Art Deco
Ceramics
Chinese & Japanese Antiques
Clocks & Barometers
Glass
Late Georgian to Edwardian Furniture
Pine & Country Furniture
Silver & Plate

UK £19.99 AU $59.95

Miller's Collector's Guides

Miller's Collector's Guides provide an essential introduction to popular subjects for the budding collector. Reflecting the growing trend in the antiques market towards 'collectables' – small, often affordable items – these practical guides are filled with ideas on how to form a collection, what to specialise in and how to identify objects.

isbn 1 84000 538 6

isbn 1 840000 539 4

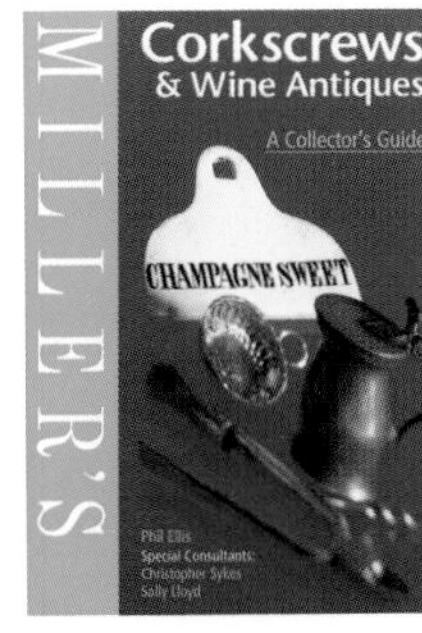

isbn 1 84000 439 8

Advertising Tins
Blue & White Pottery
Bottles & Pot Lids
Ceramics of the '20s & '30s
Ceramics of the '50s & '60s
Costume Jewellery
Glass of the '20s & '30s
Glass of the '50s & '60s
Goss & Crested China
Handbags
Paperweights
Pens & Writing Equipment
Perfume Bottles
Popular Glass
Postcards
Powder Compacts
Sewing Accessories
Smoking Accessories
Soft Toys
Staffordshire Figures
Watches
Corkscrews & Wine Antiques

UK £5.99 AU $17.95

Miller's Collecting....

Fascinating and informative guides on specific areas of collecting. These guides cover a wide range of topics on a particular subject, providing a price guide, and information on items worth thousands of pounds to pieces that can be picked up for less than £10. These guides have something for all collectors with an excellent range of interesting and affordable items from across the field.

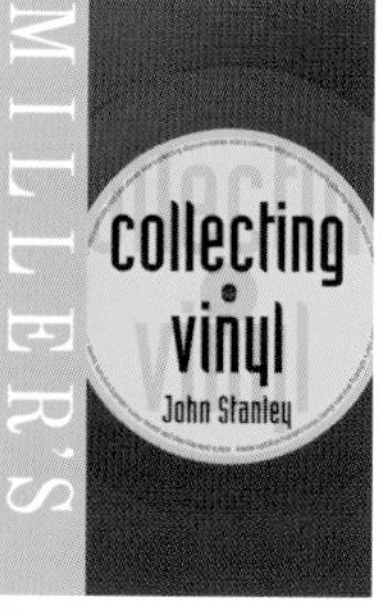

isbn 1 84000 511 4

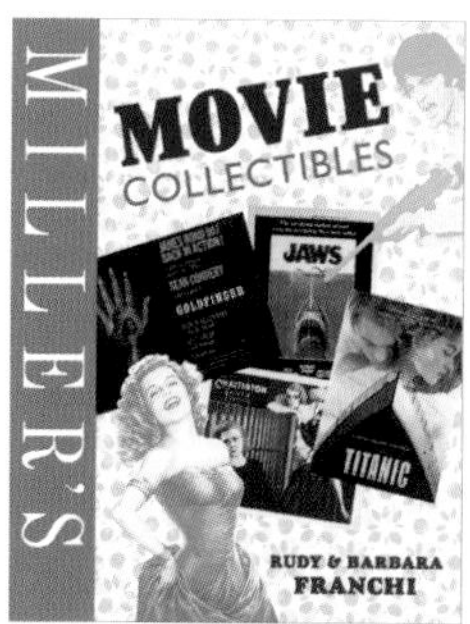

isbn 1 84000 510 6

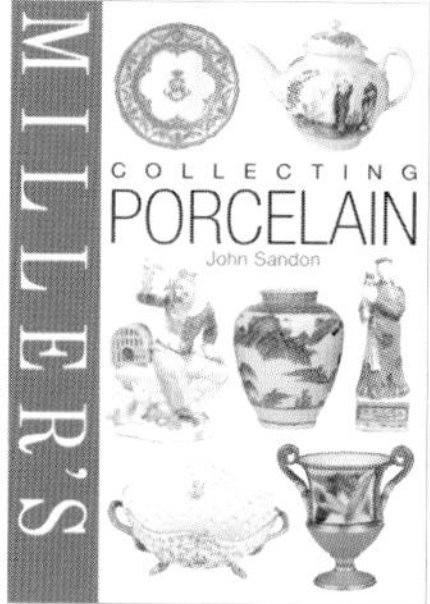

isbn 1 84000 613 7

Collecting the 1950s
Collecting the 1960s
Collecting the 1970s
UK £15.99 AU $45.00

Collecting Books
Collecting Science & Technology
Collecting Textiles
UK £19.99 AU $59.95

Collecting Fashion & Accessories
Movie Collectibles
UK £15.99 AU $49.95

Collecting Modern Design
UK £25.00 AU $70.00

Collecting Porcelain
UK £19.99 AU $59.95

Collecting Prints & Posters
UK £18.99 AU (na)

Collecting Vinyl
UK £12.99 AU $39.95

Miller's The Facts At Your Fingertips

These best-selling guides to popular collecting subjects combine historical background with practical advice for the collector by focusing on items that are available and affordable. They also look at identifying and dating pieces, assessing condition and recognising maker's marks. Each item is given a realistic price range while Fact Boxes highlight key collecting areas.

isbn 1 85732 898 1

isbn 1 84000 191 7

isbn 1 84000 143 7

Glass
Collecting Furniture
Collecting Silver
Teddy Bears & Dolls
Antiques & Collectables
Pottery & Porcelain
UK £12.99 AU $39.95

Two new series from Miller's

Introducing two brand new series from Miller's with a decidedly American accent. The insider's guides concentrate more on hints and techniques for assessing condition, avoiding fakes, spotting bargains and estimating fair value. The How to Compare & Value series helps the collector to develop an appraiser's eye and a connoisseur's knowledge, looking specifically at age, rarity, tricacy of design, maker, marks and other factors which define price.

isbn 1 84000 379 0

isbn 1 84000 380 4

isbn 1 84000 541 6

isbn 1 84000 542 4

Ameriaun Insider's Guide to
Toys & Games
Furniture
UK £17.99 AU $49.95

How to Compare & Value
American Art Pottery
American Quilts
UK £16.99 AU $49 .95

Art Glass
Samplers
UK £17.99 AU $49 .95

Miller's Checklists & Fact Files

Two invaluable pocket size series. Miller's Pocket Fact Files are compact reference guides for the specialist collector and enthusiast providing excellent identification and dating information. Miller's Antiques Checklists provide simple question-and-answer lists, advising what to look for and how to distinguish between the genuine article and a fake, an original and a copy.

isbn 1 84000 280 8

isbn 1 85732 273 8

isbn 1 84000 429 0

isbn 0 85533 689 7

Checklists

Art Deco	Porcelain
Art Nouveau	Pottery
Clocks	Silver & Plate
Furniture	Toys & Games
Glass	Victorian
Jewellery	
UK £9.99	**AU $29.95**

Fact Files

Antiques

A-Z Glass

Pottery & Porcelain Marks*

Silver & Sheffield Plate Marks

UK £7.99 **AU $24.95**

***UK £9.99**

Other Miller's Titles

No antiques lover should be without the classic *Miller's Antiques Encyclopedia*. Two titles that are also proving invaluable for the collector are *Miller's Antiques Shops, Fairs & Auctions*, an essential guide to fairs, dealers, auction houses, insurance valuers, repairers, restorers, packers and shippers, and *Miller's Antiques Art & Collectables on the Web*, featuring over 1000 websites from around the world. And for all those teddy bear enthusiasts, we have the irresistable *Miller's Teddy Bears: A Complete Collector's Guide*. These titles are just a selection from our Miller's list. To see the complete range of titles available, visit our website **www.millers.uk.com**

Antiques Encyclopedia
UK £40.00 **AU $120.00**

Teddy Bears:
A Complete Collector's Guide
UK £18.99 **AU $39.95**

Antiques Shops, Fairs & Auctions
UK £12.99 **AU $42.95**

Antiques, Art & Collectables on the Web
UK £9.99 **AU $29.95**

isbn 1 85732 747 0

isbn 1 84000 391 X

isbn 1 84000 569 6

isbn 1 84000 570 X

How to Order

To buy online visit our website www.millers.uk.com

To order in the UK, please contact: *LBS, PO Box 4264, Durrington, Worthing, West Sussex, BN13 3TG. tel: +44 (0)1903 828503*

To order in Australia, please contact: *Bookwise International Pty Ltd, 174 Cormack Road, Wingfield, SA 5013. tel: +618 8268 8222*

To order in New Zealand, please contact: *Reed Publishing NZ Ltd, 39 Rawene Road, Private Bag, Birkenhead, Auckland 10. tel: +64 9480 6039*

www.millers.uk.com

Colour Review

An Ault pottery moulded grotesque fish mask, attributed to Dr Christopher Dresser, c1900, 7½in (19cm) high.
£630–700 ⊞ HUN

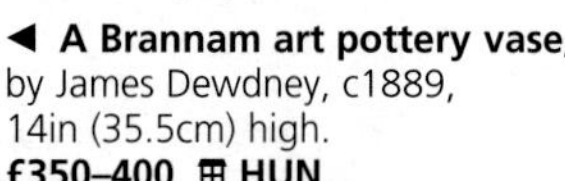

A Burmantofts faïence grotesque bulb vase, modelled as a three-legged toad, c1890, 7in (18cm) high.
£260–325 ⚒ G(L)

◄ A Brannam art pottery vase, by James Dewdney, c1889, 14in (35.5cm) high.
£350–400 ⊞ HUN

◄ A Burmantofts faïence tile, stamped mark, c1890, 11¾in (30cm) square.
£130–170 ⚒ DD

► A Burmantofts faïence jardinière and stand, minor chips, impressed marks, 1880s, 40in (101.5cm) high.
£400–500 ⚒ S(O)

A studio pottery 'Persian' vase, probably by William de Morgan, neck glued, c1880, 20½in (52cm) high.
£3,800–4,750 ⚒ TEN

Cross Reference
See Decorative Arts (page 444–476)

A pair of Linthorpe baluster vases, attributed to Dr Christopher Dresser, base chip, c1880, 19in (48.5cm) high.
£2,800–3,250 ⊞ HUN

A Maw & Co Swans vase, designed by Walter Crane, painted mark, c1890, 9¼in (23.5cm) high.
£8,000–10,000 ⚒ S(O)
This was a particularly strong price for this piece. Art pottery is very popular at the moment, perhaps as a result of the Harriman-Judd sales in New York, which created a renewed interest in this type of ceramic.

◄ A Bernard Moore flambé jardinière, painted by Dora M. Billington, painted marks, c1910, 11½in (29cm) high.
£2,500–3,300 ⚒ S(NY)
Ex-Harriman Judd Collection.

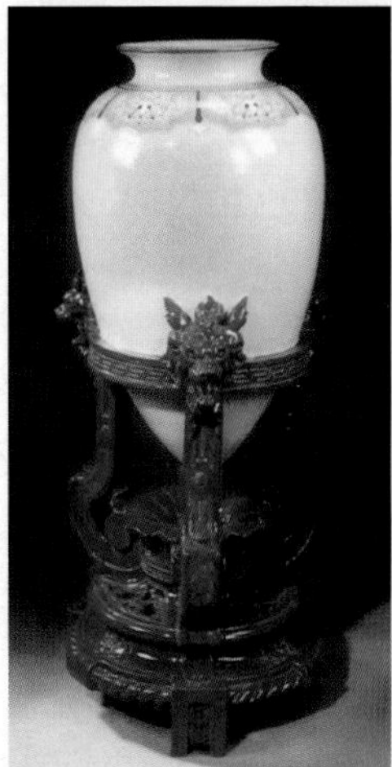

A Minton Chinese vase, after a design attributed to Dr Christopher Dresser, retouched, 1873, 35in (89cm) high.
£6,250–7,000 ⚒ S

A pair of art pottery candlesticks, Belgian, 1910–20, 16in (40.5cm) high.
£250–275 ⊞ DOA

An Arts and Crafts oak bureau bookcase, early 20thC, 31½in (80cm) wide.
£575–725 L&E

A set of 12 Morris & Co oak dining chairs, possibly designed by William Lethaby, including two carvers, c1870.
£7,500–8,500 PVD

A Heal's St Ives oak bedroom chair, c1885.
£135–150 NAW

A set of six Arts and Crafts oak dining chairs, by James Shoolbred & Co, including one armchair, c1905.
£625–800 TMA

An Arts and Crafts oak side chair, attributed to Leonard Wyburd, early 20thC.
£400–500 MAR

A pair of Wylie & Lockhead, Glasgow, oak and leather armchairs, c1905.
£1,200–1,500 PVD

A pair of oak chairs, with copper panels, by Norman and Stacey, c1905.
£600–700 PVD

A Liberty & Co oak breakfront dresser, by Shapland & Petter, c1900, 55in (139.5cm) wide.
£5,500–6,000 PVD

A John Broadwood & Sons Arts and Crafts oak piano, designed by Hugh Mackie Baillie Scott, c1885, 56in (142cm) wide.
£4,500–5,500 M

An Arts and Crafts walnut sideboard, by Shapland and Petter, c1900, 64in (162.5cm) wide.
£4,275–4,750 DOA

A screen, with Arts and Crafts-style machine-woven panels, c1900, 65in (165cm) high.
£240–275 NAW

An Arts and Crafts-style oak sideboard, with mirror back, early 20thC, 60in (152.5cm) wide.
£1,000–1,200 PFK

A Liberty & Co Arts and Crafts oak side cabinet, in the style of Leonard Wyburd, with painted walnut panels, early 20thC, 72in (183cm) wide.
£3,500–4,000 S(O)

An Arts and Crafts Moorish-style occasional table, with Celtic decoration, Irish, c1890, 15in (38cm) wide.
£2,000–2,500 B

An Arts and Crafts carved wooden box, The Four Seasons, by Kate M. Eadie, 6in (15cm) high.
£500–625 ⚒ DN

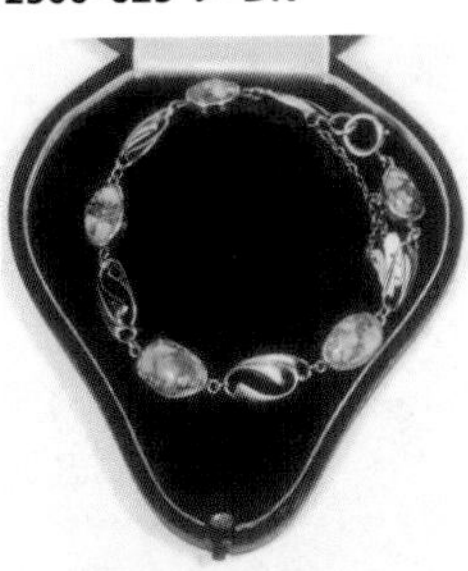

An Arts and Crafts gold and turquoise bracelet, designed by Murrle, Bennett & Co, c1900, in original box.
£700–1,000 ⊞ ASA

An Arts and Crafts copper coal bucket, c1900, 20in (51cm) high.
£380–425 ⊞ MTay

A Liberty & Co silver Cymric jug, by Archibald Knox, Birmingham 1901, 8¼in (21cm) high.
£7,000–8,750 ⚒ P

An Arts and Crafts Celtic-style silver three-handled bowl, by West & Son, Irish, Dublin 1911, 7in (18cm) wide.
£2,000–2,400 ⊞ SIL

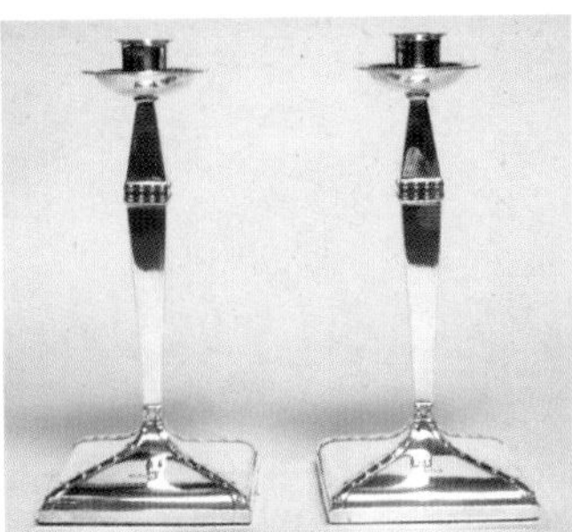

A pair of silver candlesticks, by H. Wilkinson, with loaded bases, Sheffield c1908, 9in (23cm) high.
£2,000–2,250 ⊞ DAD

A set of four Arts and Crafts hammered silver sweetmeat dishes, by Hamilton & Inches, Edinburgh 1905–06, 3in (7.5cm) high, 20.5oz.
£1,600–1,750 ⊞ NS

An Arts and Crafts hammered silver inkwell, by A. E. Jones, 1890–1910, 3in (7.5cm) high.
£300–400 ⊞ ASA

An Arts and Crafts *plique-à-jour* enamelled caddy spoon, c1900, 4in (10cm) long.
£850–950 ⊞ SHa

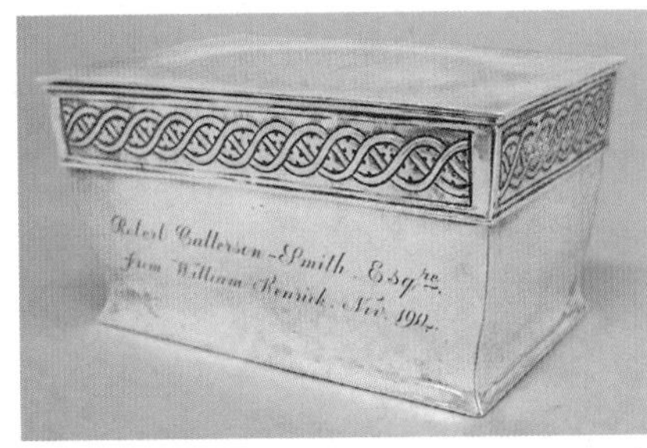

A Birmingham Guild of Handicraft Arts and Crafts silver casket, with presentation inscription, 1902, 5½in (14cm) wide, 18oz.
£1,500–1,800 ⚒ G(L)

A Newlyn-style copper chamberstick, decorated with repoussé mythical fishes, c1905, 8in (20.5cm) square.
£225–250 ⊞ RUSK

A silvered-metal and enamelled desk set, by Louis Comfort Tiffany, comprising seven pieces, American, early 20thC.
£3,400–3,750 ⚒ S(O)

An Arts and Crafts copper jardinière, with Ruskin plaques, c1900, 12in (30.5cm) diam.
£675–750 ⊞ SHa

◄ **An Arts and Crafts brass jardinière,** in the style of Margaret Gilmour, c1910, 9in (23cm) high.
£300–350 ⊞ RUSK

An Art Nouveau oak bookcase, by J. S. Henry, London, inlaid with metal and coloured wood, c1900, 44½in (113cm) wide.
£1,100–1,400 ⚒ DMC

An Art Nouveau walnut bookcase, with carved and gilt stylized floral panels, c1910, 32in (81.5cm) wide.
£2,500–3,200 ⚒ JAA

A mahogany 'peacock' display cabinet, by Shapland and Petter, inlaid with marquetry and mother-of-pearl, c1902, 54¾in (139cm) wide.
£4,500–5,750 ⚒ P

An Art Nouveau mahogany and satinwood inlaid cabinet, c1910, 36¼in (92cm) wide.
£1,300–1,600 ⚒ WL

An oak canterbury, with Art Nouveau-style carved decoration, early 20thC, 22¾in (58cm) wide.
£300–375 ⚒ L&E

A set of eight Art Nouveau mahogany and green leather dining chairs, c1900.
£2,000–2,250 ⊞ MTay

An oak and marquetry 'peacock' hall cupboard, by Shapland and Petter, towel rail supports missing, c1902, 72in (183cm) high.
£1,500–2,000 ⚒ B

An Emile Gallé fruitwood marquetry jardinière, signed, French, c1900, 16in (40.5cm) wide.
£2,700–3,300 ⚒ S(NY)

► A brass-inlaid mahogany jewel box, by Erhard & Sons, German, 1915–20, 11¾in (30cm) wide.
£165–200 ⚒ DORO

An Edwardian mahogany drawing room suite, comprising seven pieces, with marquetry Art Nouveau-style floral panels inlaid with bone, 37¾in (96cm) wide.
£1,800–2,250 ⚒ AH

A Vienna Secessionist bent beechwood eight-piece salon suite, attributed to Josef Hoffmann, Austrian, c1910, settee 51in (129.5cm) wide.
£8,000–10,000 ⚒ S(NY)

A Léon Bénouville mahogany dining table and six side chairs, French, c1900, 50½in (128.5cm) wide.
£10,500–13,000 ⚒ S(NY)

A Carlo Bugatti ebony and vellum-covered centre table, decorated with inlaid pewter, applied copper and ivory, Italian, c1900, 49¼in (125cm) wide.
£15,000–18,000 ⚒ B

A Hector Guimard painted-iron and agate table, French, c1900, 21in (53.5cm) diam.
£11,500–14,000 ⚒ S(NY)

A pair of Doulton Lambeth candlesticks, by Bessie Newbery, Emma Marriot and Agnes S. Horne, c1885, 7¾in (19.5cm) high.
£500–600 WilP

A Doulton Lambeth vase, by Hannah Barlow, 19thC, 12½in (32cm) high.
£900–1,000 TMA

A Royal Doulton Morrisian ware vase, c1900, 9in (23cm) high.
£350–400 GAA

A Royal Doulton Titanian ware bowl, c1920, 9in (23cm) diam.
£600–700 DSG

A Doulton Burslem earthenware vase, by D. Dewsberry, cracked, signed, impressed marks, c1889, 25¾in (65.5cm) high.
£2,200–2,750 S(NY)
The raised gilding on this piece is particularly fine and complex and this, coupled with the size of the vase, would suggest that it may have been intended for exhibition.

A Doulton Lambeth stoneware vase, by Mark Marshall, c1890, 12in (30.5cm) high.
£775–850 GAA

A Royal Doulton stoneware vase, impressed mark and number, incised monogram, early 20thC, 21in (53.5cm) high.
£2,000–2,500 S(NY)
Ex-Harriman Judd Collection.

A Doulton Lambeth stoneware vase, by Florence Barlow, 1890, 17in (43cm) high.
£2,250–2,500 GAA

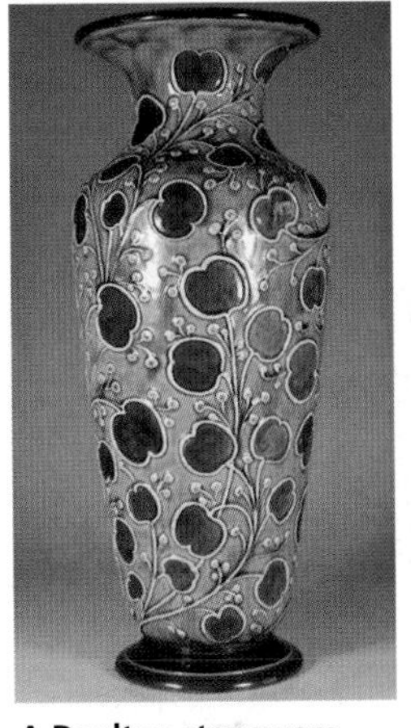

A Doulton stoneware vase, by Frank Butler, impressed and incised marks, late 19thC, 16in (40.5cm) high.
£600–750 WW

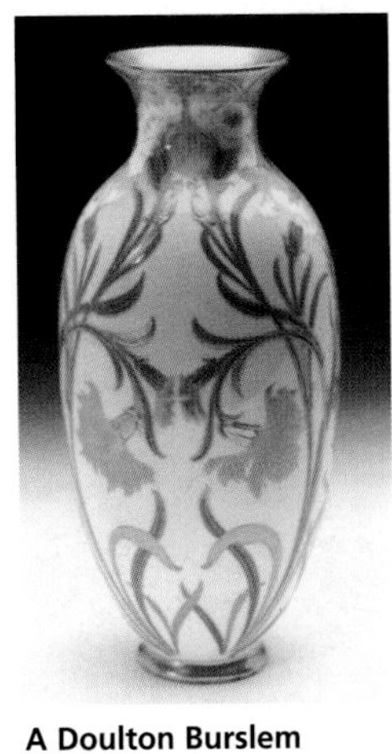

A Doulton Burslem Lactolian ware vase, by Walter Slater, signed, printed mark, c1890, 11½in (29cm) high.
£3,400–3,750 SHSY

A Doulton Lambeth Slaters patent vase, late 19thC, 16¼in (41.5cm) high.
£130–165 MAR

► **A Royal Doulton pottery toilet set,** comprising four pieces, basin with hairline cracks, printed marks, c1900.
£1,600–1,800 S

A Royal Doulton tyg, stamped marks, c1925, 7in (18cm) high.
£200–240 SWO

◄ **A Royal Doulton stoneware vase,** c1910, 9¾in (25cm) high.
£100–120 G(L)

A Martin Brothers stoneware incised dragon ewer, inscribed mark, dated 1893, 9½in (24cm) high.
£3,300–4,200 S(NY)
Ex-Harriman Judd Collection.

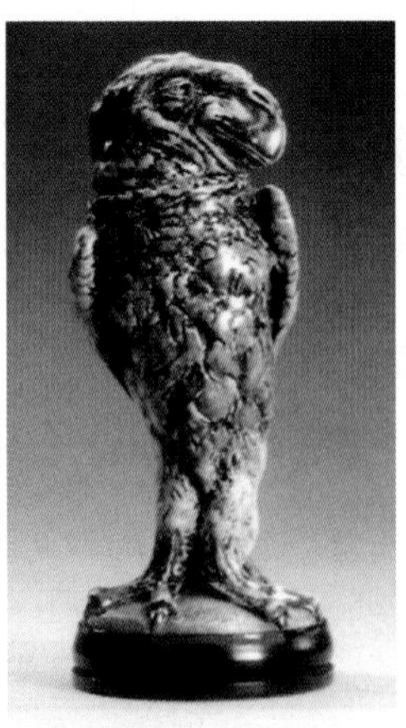

A Martin Brothers stoneware bird, incised mark, on a wooden base, 1914, 9in (23cm) high.
£9,500–12,000 TEN

A Martin Brothers stoneware vase, incised mark, dated October 1893, 9in (23cm) high.
£4,000–4,500 S(O)

A Moorcroft biscuit barrel and silver-plated cover, c1900, 6in (15cm) high.
£480–600 G(L)

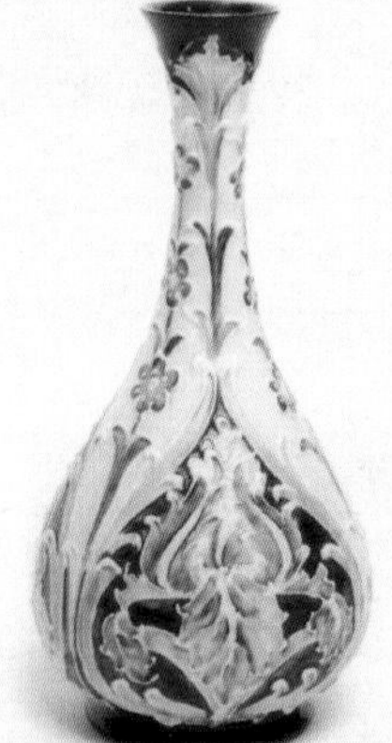

A Moorcroft Macintyre Florian ware vase, signed 'William Moorcroft', c1900, 8in (20.5cm) high.
£1,100–1,200 GAA

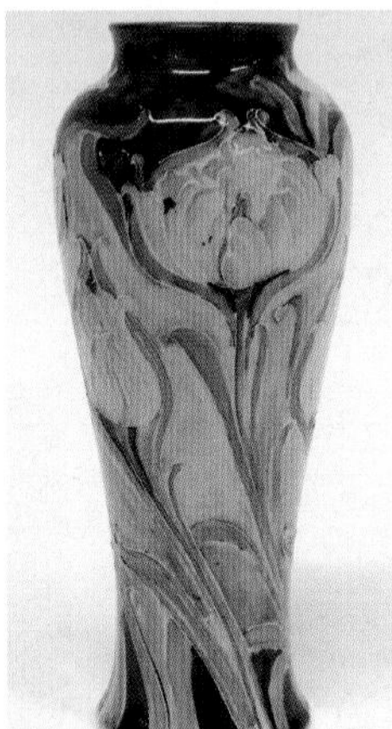

A Moorcroft Macintyre three-piece coffee set, spout restored, 1906–10, teapot 10in (25.5cm) high.
£3,400–3,750 Lan

◄ **A Moorcroft Macintyre Florian ware vase,** marked, c1900, 8¾in (22cm) high.
£2,700–3,400 G(L)

A Moorcroft white pansy vase, c1914, 10in (25.5cm) high.
£3,000–3,400 Lan

A Moorcroft pottery vase, decorated with Pomegranate pattern, impressed marks, painted signature, c1920, 10in (25.5cm) high.
£800–1,000 PFK

◄ **A pair of Moorcroft flambé vases,** decorated with Leaf and Berry pattern, 1918–26, 10in (25.5cm) high.
£1,800–2,200 TWr

An Emile Gallé faïence cat, minor losses, marked, late 19thC, 13in (33cm) high.
£2,000–2,500 ⚒ BWe

A Wedgwood lustre bowl, decorated with Butterfly pattern, c1900, 7in (18cm) diam.
£380–475 ⚒ G(L)

A Royal Dux figural centrepiece bowl, Bohemian, late 19thC, 21in (53.5cm) high.
£1,400–1,750 ⚒ TMA

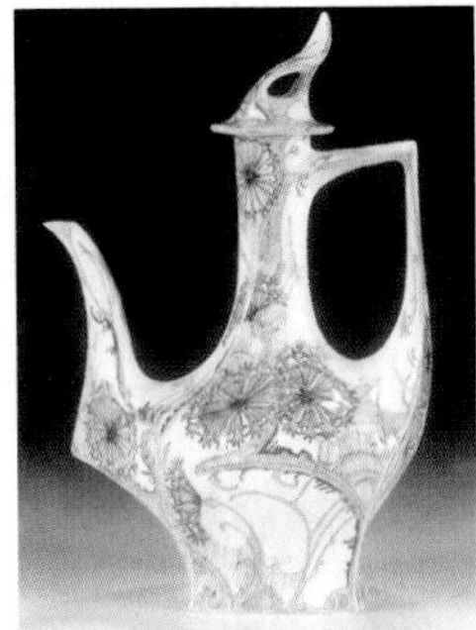

A Rozenburg eggshell porcelain coffee pot, decorated by Schellink, small chips, printed and painted marks, Dutch c1900, 9½in (24cm) high.
£2,300–2,850 ⚒ Bon

A Pilkington's Royal Lancastrian jar and cover, by Richard Joyce, impressed and painted marks, c1913, 9¼in (23.5cm) high.
£3,500–4,500 ⚒ TEN

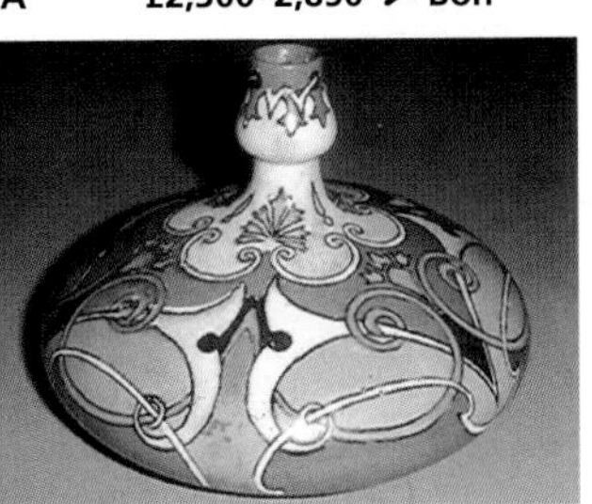

► **A Shelley Intarsio spill vase,** printed marks, early 20thC, 5½in (14cm) diam.
£140–175 ⚒ PFK

◄ **A Zsolnay Pecs earthenware and ebonized wood pedestal,** printed factory marks, Hungarian, early 20thC, 40¼in (102cm) high.
£600–700 ⚒ S(S)

► **An Art Nouveau relief-moulded tile,** c1905, 8in (20.5cm) square.
£80–100 ⊞ DAD

A Zsolnay Pecs iridescent-glazed ceramic umbrella stand, impressed marks, Hungarian, c1900, 26¾in (68cm) high.
£10,500–13,000 ⚒ S(NY)

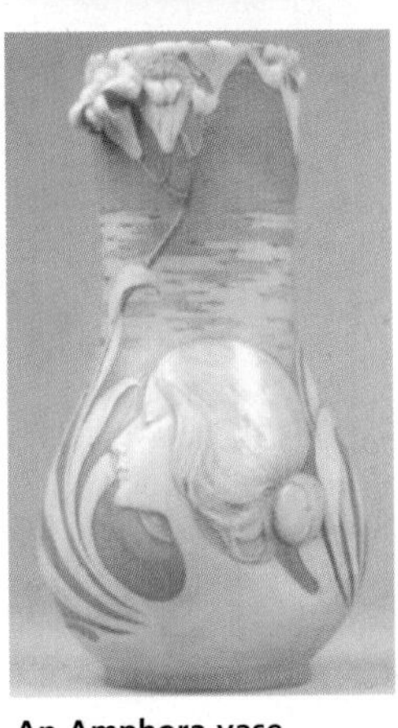

An Amphora vase, impressed and stamped marks, Bohemian, c1905, 18in (45.5cm) high.
£2,350–3,000 ⚒ DORO

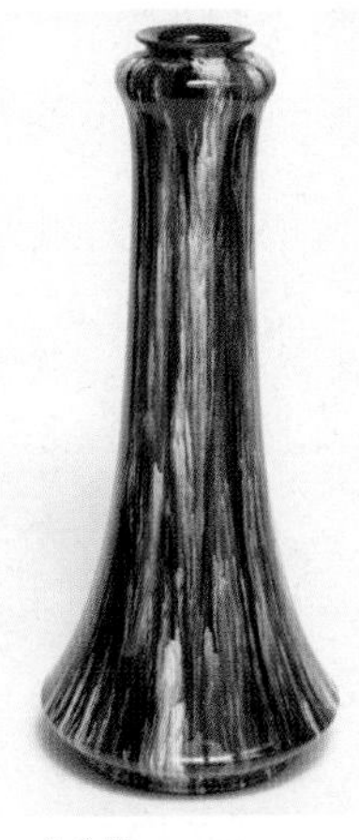

An Art Nouveau Bretby vase, c1913, 14½in (37cm) high.
£350–385 ⊞ HUN

A Rookwood vase, by F. Rothenbusch, impressed marks, American, 1918, 15in (38cm) high.
£3,500–4,500 ⚒ TREA

◄ **An Art Nouveau glazed pottery vase,** c1900, 14in (35.5cm) high.
£120–135 ⊞ DHA

◄ **A Tiffany Favrile pottery vase,** restored, incised monogram, American, 1904–10, 10in (25.5cm) high.
£5,000–6,000 ⚒ S(NY)

A Burgun & Schverer wheel-carved cameo glass vase, with silver mount, signed, French, c1895, 7in (18cm) high.
£5,000–6,250 S(NY)

A Daum acid-etched and enamelled glass vase, French, c1900, 6in (15cm) high.
£1,450–1,600 ART

An Emile Gallé cameo glass vase, raised signature, early 20thC, 7¾in (19.5cm) high.
£300–375 TEN

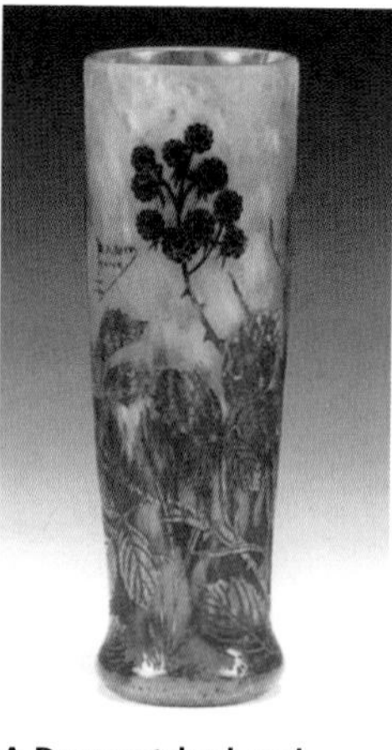

A Daum etched and enamelled glass vase, decorated with blackberries, French, c1900, 12½in (32cm) high.
£1,400–1,750 BERN

A de Vez cameo glass vase, signed, French, c1910, 12in (30.5cm) high.
£1,100–1,300 JAA

A pair of Loetz iridescent glass vases, in silver-plated mounts, Austrian, c1898, 15in (38cm) high.
£4,250–5,250 DORO

◄ **A Tiffany Favrile wheel-carved cameo glass vase,** inscribed mark, American, c1903, 4½in (11.5cm) high.
£11,500–14,000 S(NY)

A Daum cameo glass crocus vase, signed, French, c1900, 5½in (14cm) high.
£8,500–10,000 S(NY)

A pair of Emile Gallé enamelled glass vases, painted signature, late 19thC, 6in (15cm) high.
£3,750–4,500 S(O)

An iridescent glass vase, possibly Loetz, damaged, Continental, c1900, 18¼in (46.5cm) high.
£240–300 RTo

► **A Henri Bergé *pâte-de-verre* aquatic vase,** for Almeric Walter, marked, French, c1910, 8in (20.5cm) high.
£2,300–2,750 S

A Daum glass vase, the faceted form with acid-etched decoration depicting a dawn winter landscape, French, c1900, 4½in (11.5cm) high.
£2,800–3,200 OND

An Emile Gallé acid-etched and enamelled glass vase, engraved mark, c1890, 28¼in (72cm) high.
£6,500–8,000 B

A Quezal iridescent glass Jack-in-the-pulpit vase, inscribed mark, American, c1920, 12in (30.5cm) high.
£6,000–7,500 S(NY)

COLOUR REVIEW

An Art Nouveau silver bowl, by The Guild of Handicrafts, London 1904, 9¼in (23.5cm) wide.
£4,000–5,000 RTo

A WMF silver-plated centrepiece, c1890, 16in (40.5cm) wide.
£1,100–1,250 SHa

◄ **A Kate Harris silver-mounted copper casket,** set with chrysoprase cabochons, c1905, 6in (15cm) wide.
£2,000–2,250 DAD

A Ramsden & Carr Art Nouveau silver bowl and cover, with enamelled finial, inscribed, London 1910, 4¼in (11cm) high.
£1,800–2,200 S(O)

A Tiffany gilt-bronze seven-piece desk set, decorated with Pine Needle pattern, impressed marks and numbers, 1898–1928, pen tray 9¾in (25cm) wide.
£1,700–2,000 BB(S)

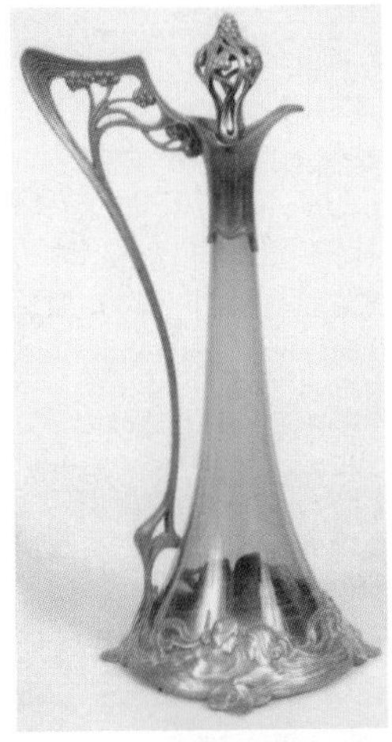

► **A WMF Art Nouveau glass claret jug and stopper,** with electroplate mounts, stamped to base, German, 14in (35.5cm) high.
£750–900 BWe

A gilt-bronze Art Nouveau Butterfly Lady dish, by Alexandre Vibert, Paris, signed, 5½in (14cm) wide.
£1,100–1,300 MI

A WMF pewter claret jug, German, c1906, 15in (38cm) high.
£1,500–1,700 OND

A copper jardinière, with brass lion mask handles and paw feet, c1900 9in (23cm) diam.
£130–150 DHA

A silver and mixed metal tray, by Whiting Manufacturing Co, Providence, Rhode Island, c1900, 7½in (19cm) wide.
£2,000–2,400 S

An Art Nouveau silver photograph frame, by Charles S. Green & Co, Birmingham 1901–02, 9in (23cm) high.
£675–750 NS

A Georg Anton Scheidt silver and enamel smelling salts bottle, Vienna c1900, 3½in (9cm) high.
£700–800 DAD

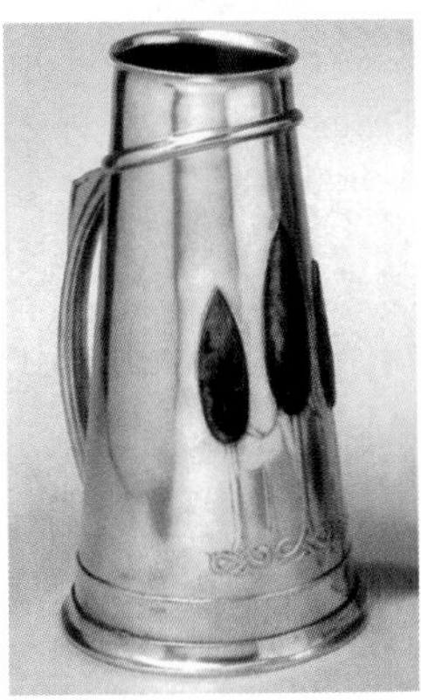

A Liberty & Co pewter and enamel tankard, stamped mark, c1900, 12¾in (32.5cm) high.
£2,200–2,700 B

A pair of Margaret Gilmour Art Nouveau embossed brass wall sconces, c1900, 14in (35.5cm) hight.
£3,550–4,000 DAD

A cold-painted bronze and ivory figure of a girl archer with a bow, 1890–1910, 15in (38cm) high.
£4,000–5,000 ⊞ ASA

An bronze bust of a young woman, by Emmanuel Villanis, entitled 'Capture', signed, French, 1880–1920, 23½in (59.5cm) high.
£2,250–2,500 ⚒ S(O)

A patinated and painted bronze figure of a dancer with a feather headdress, by Bergman, Vienna, inscribed and stamped marks, Austrian, 1910–20, 15½in (39.5cm) high.
£2,000–2,200 ⚒ DORO

A gilt-bronze and ivory figure of a girl, by Dominique Alonzo, entitled 'Young Girl', signed, French, c1920, 11in (28cm) high.
£2,000–2,500 ⚒ B

An Art Deco silvered-bronze figure of a dancing girl, by Marcel Bouraine, on an ebonized wood plinth, signed, French, early 20thC, 13in (33cm) high.
£2,250–2,500 ⚒ S(O)

A bronze and ivory figure of a dancer, by Demêtre H. Chiparus, French, 1890–1910, 19½in (49.5cm) high.
£20,000–25,000 ⊞ ASA

A cold-painted bronze and ivory figure, by Demêtre H. Chiparus, entitled 'After Reading', signed, French, c1920, 9¾in (25cm) high.
£4,500–5,500 ⚒ B

◄ An Art Nouveau carved ivory and bronze figure of a woman, by Josef Lorenzl, signed, Austrian, 7½in (19cm) high.
£2,800–3,200 ⚒ S(O)

A bronze figure, by Demêtre H. Chiparus, entitled 'Balancing', on a marble base, French, c1930, 18in (45.5cm) high.
£6,500–7,500 ⊞ OND

A gilt-bronze and carved ivory figure, by Affortunato Gory, entitled 'Danseuse Arabe', on a marble base, signed, French, c1920, 18in (45.5cm) high.
£4,000–5,000 ⚒ B

A cold-painted bronze and ivory figure of an archer, by Ferdinand Preiss, marked, German, c1930, 8½in (21.5cm) high.
£14,000–17,000 ⚒ S

A cold-painted bronze and carved and stained ivory figure, by Ferdinand Preiss, entitled 'The Stile', German, c1930, 9¾in (25cm) high.
£8,000–10,000 ⚒ B

A silvered-bronze, ivory and jewelled figure of a dancer, by Robert Ullmann, signed, Austrian, c1930, 9¾in (25cm) high.
£3,500–4,000 ⚒ S(O)

A Linthorpe lamp, c1881, 10in (25.5cm) high. **£550–650 ⊞ HUN**

A silvered-brass table oil lamp, by W. A. S. Benson, stamped, c1895, 26in (66cm) high. **£1,400–1,700 ⚒ S(O)**

► A mosaic leaded glass and bronze hanging shade, American, c1920, 29in (73.5cm) diam. **£2,300–2,750 ⚒ JAA**

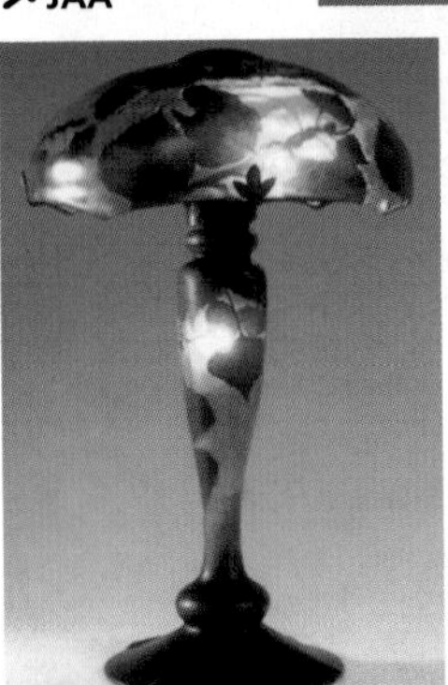

A Daum cameo glass table lamp, signed, French, c1910, 18½in (47cm) high. **£3,200–3,800 ⚒ JAA**

An Emile Gallé cameo glass ceiling light, cameo signature, c1900, 17½in (44.5cm) diam. **£4,500–5,000 ⚒ S(O)**

An Emile Gallé cameo glass and bronze table lamp, signed, c1900, 20in (51cm) high. **£4,250–4,750 ⚒ JAA**

A silvered-metal and shell Nautilus lamp, attributed to Gustave Gurschner, German, c1900, 10¾in (27.5cm) high. **£3,000–3,750 ⚒ B**

A Handel leaded glass and bronze table lamp, impressed mark, Meriden, Connecticut, early 20thC, 28in (71cm) high. **£6,000–7,000 ⚒ SK**

An enamelled glass and bronzed table lamp, attributed to Handel, American, c1920, 23½in (59.5cm) high. **£1,200–1,500 ⚒ JAA**

A Muller Frères glass and wrought-iron chandelier, marked, French, c1910, 29in (73.5cm) high. **£1,850–2,200 ⚒ JAA**

A Tiffany Fleur-de-Lys leaded glass and bronze table lamp, impressed mark, American, c1900, 21½in (54.5cm) high. **£13,500–17,000 ⚒ JAA**

A Tiffany Favrile glass and bronze geranium lamp, impressed mark, American, 1899–1920, 23in (58.5cm) high. **£10,500–13,000 ⚒ S(NY)**

A Tiffany Favrile glass and bronze Daffodil lamp, impressed mark, American, 1899–1918, 21in (53.5cm) high. **£16,000–17,500 ⚒ S(NY)**

A Tiffany Favrile glass and bronze Turtleback tile chandelier, hardware replaced, American, 1899–1920, 18in (45.5cm) diam. **£11,500–14,000 ⚒ S(NY)**

◄ A Tiffany Favrile glass and gilt-bronze Spider Web lamp, base regilt, impressed marks, American, 1899–1920, 17in (43cm) high. **£18,000–22,000 ⚒ S(NY)**

LOCATE THE SOURCE

The source of each illustration in Miller's can be found by checking the code letters below each caption with the Key to Illustrations, pages 794–800.

A Gabriel Argy-Rousseau *pâte-de-verre veilleuse,* *Rosaces*, on a wrought-iron base, moulded mark, French, 1923, 7in (18cm) high.
£5,000–6,000 S

A wrought-iron and etched Daum glass chandelier, in the style of Edgar Brandt, shade signed, c1930, 24in (61cm) diam.
£1,300–1,500 S(O)

A Handel reverse-painted glass and enamelled-metal Birds of Paradise lamp, enamelled by George Palme, shade signed, American, c1923, 23½in (59.5cm) high.
£17,500–20,000 S(NY)

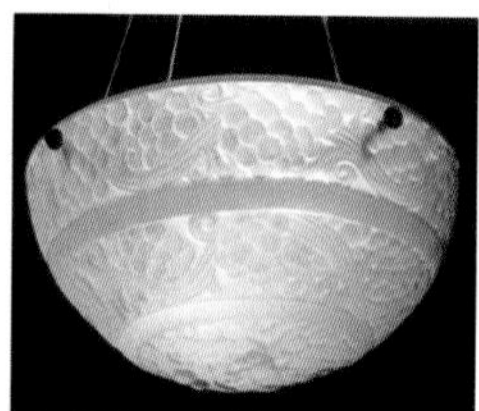

A René Lalique Saint-Vincent *plafonnier,* moulded mark, French, 1926, 13½in (34.5cm) diam.
£1,200–1,500 B

► **A bronzed-spelter and alabaster figural table lamp,** c1930, 16in (40.5cm) high.
£440–530 G(L)

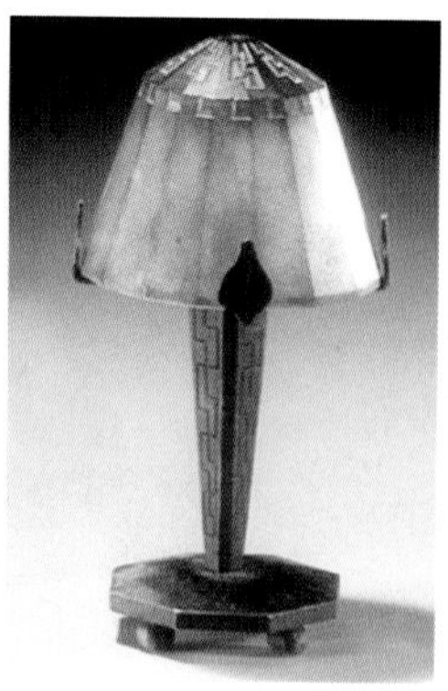

A Gabriel Argy-Rousseau *pâte-de-verre* and wrought-iron *veilleuse,* *Géometrique*, moulded mark, French, c1930, 6¾in (17cm) high.
£3,000–3,500 S(NY)

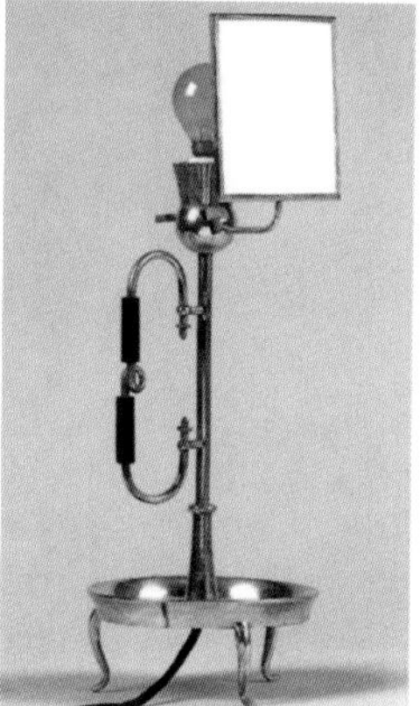

A Josef Frank brass table lamp, Vienna, c1925, 16½in (42cm) high.
£2,200–2,700 DORO

A Josef Riedel glass ceiling light, with nickeled-metal mounts, German, c1920, 13¾in (35cm) high.
£200–250 DORO

A Donald Deskey burr-maple and black lacquer five-piece bedroom suite, by Widdicomb, refinished, American, 1930, bed 41¼in (105cm) wide.
£3,000–3,750 TREA

A Betty Joel and David Joel rosewood eight-piece bedroom suite, c1939, dressing table 50¾in (129cm) wide.
£12,000–15,000 P

A burr-walnut cocktail cabinet, c1925, 56in (142cm) high.
£2,200–3,000 ASA

A Betty Joel silky oak Token secrétaire and open bookcase, 1932, 72in (183cm) wide.
£600–750 WW

► An Epstein bird's-eye maple and peach-mirror glass cocktail cabinet, c1938, 65in (165cm) wide.
£1,350–1,700 B

A walnut display cabinet, c1930, 50in (127cm) wide.
£340–375 NAW

A walnut, calamander and chrome vitrine, c1930, 49¼in (125cm) wide.
£550–700 B

A walnut display cabinet, c1930, 48in (122cm) wide.
£675–750 JAZZ

A Josef Frank walnut open armchair, Austrian, c1920.
£850–1,100 DORO

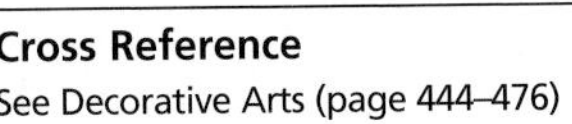

Cross Reference
See Decorative Arts (page 444–476)

► An ebony and bronze kneehole desk, French, c1925, 39½in (100.5cm) wide.
£4,500–5,500 S(NY)

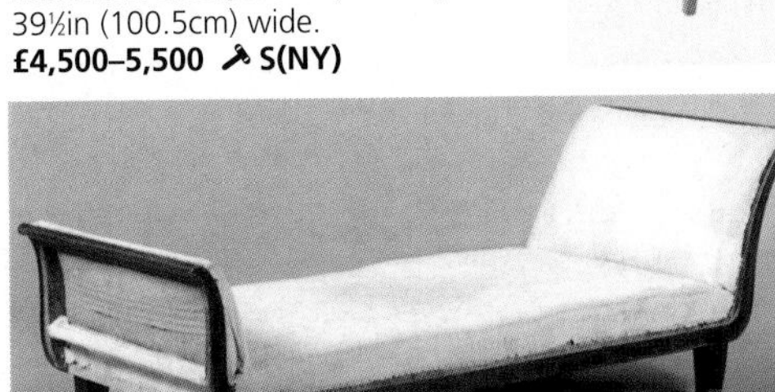

◄ An Adolf Loos mahogany daybed, by F. O. Schmidt, with original horse-hair upholstery, Austrian, 1918, 87in (221cm) wide.
£3,000–3,750 S

A Charlotte Chauchet-Guillère commode, made from ebony, ivory and various African woods, for Primavera, c1920, 82in (208.5cm) wide.
£20,000–22,000 MI

A Betty Joel silky oak dresser, dated 1929, 60in (152.5cm) wide.
£1,500–1,650 ⊞ ChC

A settee, c1930, 84in (213.5cm) wide.
£5,250–5,850 ⊞ RAN

A sycamore and ebonized three-piece lounge suite, c1930, sofa 68in (172.5cm) wide.
£2,600–3,250 ⚒ B

A Josef Frank linen-covered screen, c1925, 78¾in (200cm) wide.
£1,000–1,250 ⚒ DORO

A buttoned-leather three-piece suite, c1930.
£3,200–3,500 ⊞ ChC

An Edgar Brandt wrought-iron mirror, 'Biches', impressed mark, French, c1925, 42in (106.5cm) high.
£10,500–13,000 ⚒ S(NY)

A satin birch nine-piece dining suite, c1930.
£3,300–4,200 ⚒ JM

► **An Emile-Jacques Ruhlmann oak desk,** designed for l'Université de la Cité, Paris, branded mark, French, 1930, 47½in (120.5cm) wide.
£5,250–6,500 ⚒ S(NY)

A Bretby bowl, c1930, 4in (10cm) high.
£130–145 ⊞ HUN

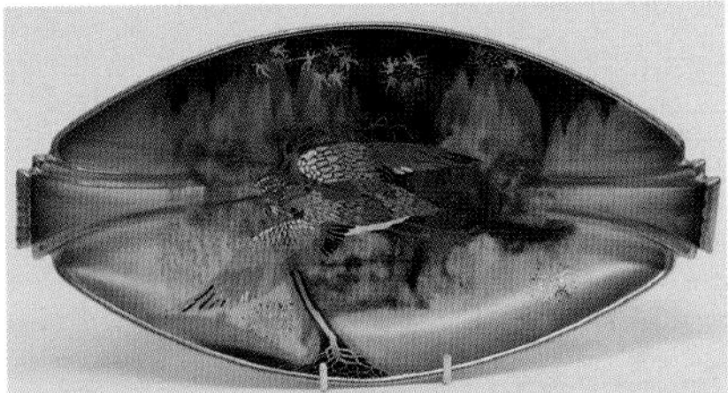

A Carlton Ware dish, decorated with Sketching Bird pattern, c1930, 12¼in (31cm) wide.
£320–400 ⚒ G(L)

A Carlton Ware vase, decorated with Gumflower Pattern, interior repainted, 1930s, 4¼in (11cm) high.
£270–300 ⊞ StC

A Susie Cooper four-piece part tea service, by Gray's pottery, decorated with Moons and Mountains pattern, enamel worn, c1930, teapot 3in (7.5cm) wide.
£650–800 ⚒ G(L)

A Gouda faïence ewer and stopper, Dutch, c1923, 11in (28cm) high.
£150–185 ⊞ DSG

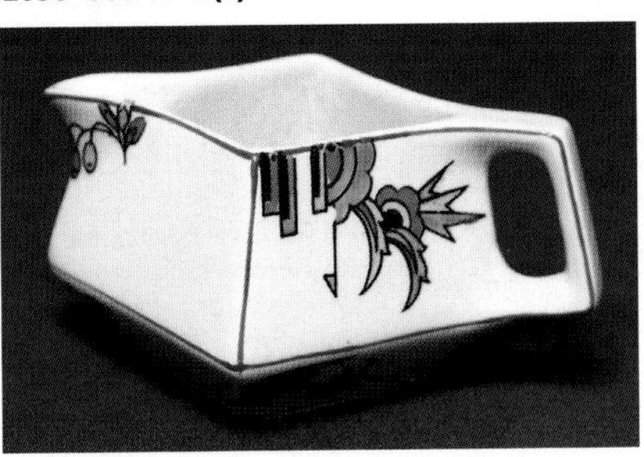

A T. G. Green Alpha design cream jug, 1930s, 2in (5cm) high.
£70–80 ⊞ CAL

A Hancock Coronaware vase, by F. X. Abraham, decorated with Spring Time pattern, signed, 1924, 8in (20.5cm) high.
£200–225 ⊞ PIC

A pair of earthenware Gouda Zuid-Holland vases, by Katy, Dutch, 1921, 3in (7.5cm) high.
£630–700 ⊞ MI

A Pilkington's Royal Lancastrian dish, decorated by William S. Mycock, impressed and painted marks, c1935, 11¾in (30cm) diam.
£200–250 ⚒ WW

A pair of Pilkington's Royal Lancastrian candlesticks, c1920, 12in (30.5cm) high.
£160–175 ⊞ RUSK

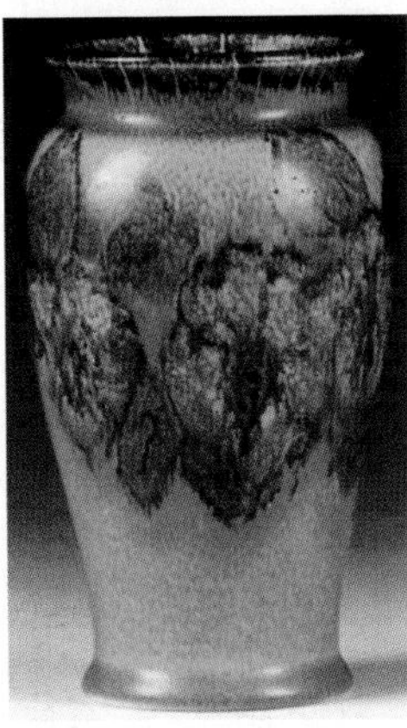

A Rookwood Pottery vase, designed by Vera Tischler, impressed and painted marks, American, dated 1925, 6½in (16.5cm) high.
£320–400 ⚒ Bon

A Poole Pottery vase, c1934, 5½in (14cm) high.
£280–325 ⊞ MI

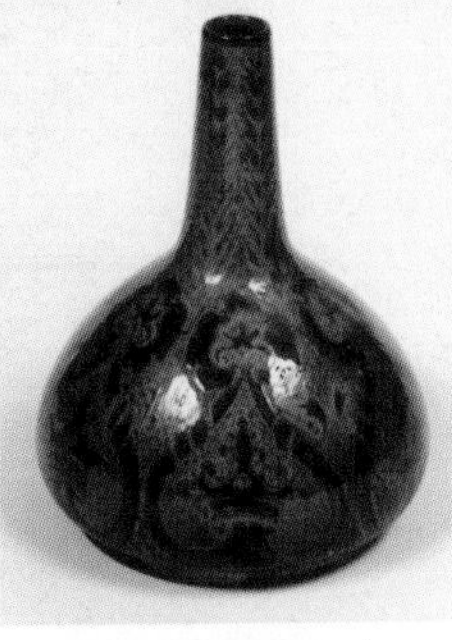

A Pilkington's Royal Lancastrian vase, with lustre glaze, 1930s, 7in (18cm) high.
£500–700 ⊞ ASA

A Pilkington's Royal Lancastrian vase, c1920, 10in (25.5cm) high.
£90–100 ⊞ RUSK

A Clarice Cliff biscuit barrel, decorated with Gayday pattern, painted and printed marks, 1930–34, 6¼in (16cm) high.
£270–330 S(O)

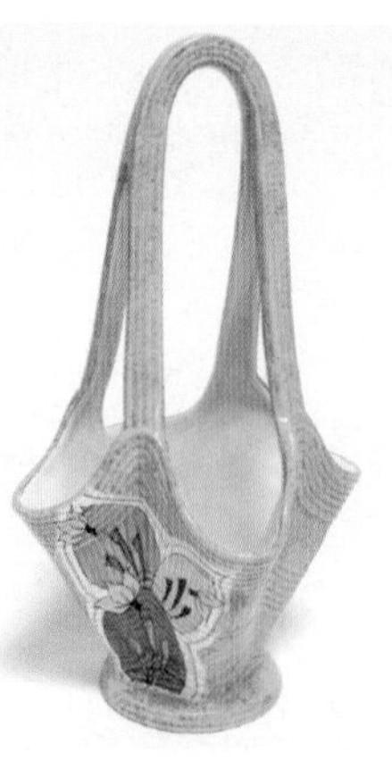

A Clarice Cliff basket-shape vase, decorated with Cowslip pattern, the interior with a pottery flowerholder, c1930, 13in (33cm) high.
£850–950 ⊞ RH

► **A Clarice Cliff Newport Pottery bowl,** decorated with Crocus pattern, marked, c1930, 12in (30.5cm) diam.
£200–250 DMC

◄ **A Clarice Cliff Newport Pottery Bizarre bowl,** decorated with Melon pattern, printed mark, c1930, 8¾in (22cm) diam.
£300–375 WL

A Clarice Cliff Bizarre figural centrepiece, Age of Jazz, broken and glued, marked, 8in (20.5cm) high.
£6,500–8,250 B

► **A Clarice Cliff Circus plate,** designed by Dame Laura Knight, c1930, 7in (18cm) diam.
£315–350 ⊞ RH

◄ **A Clarice Cliff Bizarre candle-stick,** modelled as a maiden with a bouquet of flowers, c1930, 7¼in (18.5cm) high.
£350–450 TMA

A Clarice Cliff jug, decorated with Melon pattern, c1930, 4in (10cm) high.
£675–750 ⊞ RH

A Clarice Cliff Bizarre sandwich plate, decorated with Sandon pattern, c1935, 9in (23cm) diam.
£260–325 G(L)

◄ **A Clarice Cliff Newport Pottery Fantasque beehive honey pot and cover,** decorated with Secrets pattern, marked, c1933, 2¾in (7cm) high.
£300–375 RFA

A Clarice Cliff Lotus jug, decorated with Blue Crocus pattern, c1930, 11½in (29cm) high.
£3,200–4,000 G(L)

A Clarice Cliff Newport Pottery Bizarre vase, c1930, 8in (20.5cm) high.
£500–650 PFK

◄ **A Clarice Cliff Stamford teapot,** decorated with Canterbury Bells pattern, c1930, 4¾in (12cm) high.
£420–525 G(L)

A Clarice Cliff Meiping vase, decorated with Inspiration Caprice pattern, painted marks, c1932, 9in (23cm) high.
£3,400–4,250 P

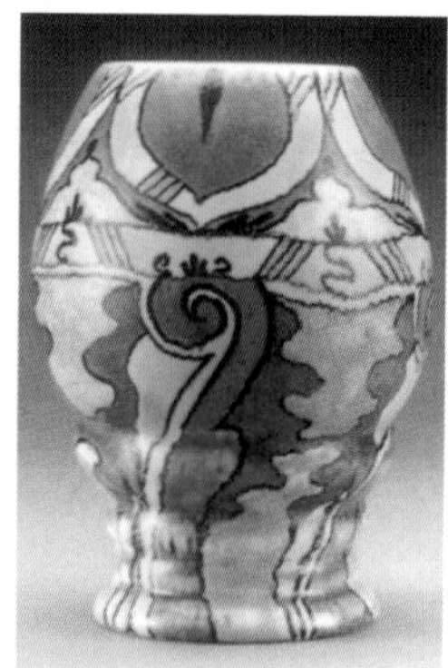

A Clarice Cliff pottery vase, decorated with Persian pattern in Inspiration glaze, marked, 1930–31, 8in (20.5cm) high.
£1,500–1,800 S(O)

Miller's is a price GUIDE not a price LIST

A Gabriel Argy-Rousseau *pâte-de-verre* vase, *Tragi-comique*, French, c1922, 10in (25.5cm) high.
£5,000–6,000 ⚒ S(NY)

An André Delatte cameo glass vase, signed, French, c1921, 10½in (26.5cm) high.
£1,000–1,200 ⚒ JAA

A René Lalique glass beaker, signed, French, c1930, 3in (7.5cm) high.
£220–275 ⚒ G(L)

A René Lalique Sauterelles glass vase, incised mark, French, after 1913, 10¾in (27.5cm) high.
£3,400–4,250 ⚒ Bon

◄ A Lune overlaid glass vase, French, c1930, 8¼in (21cm) high.
£200–250 ⚒ TRM

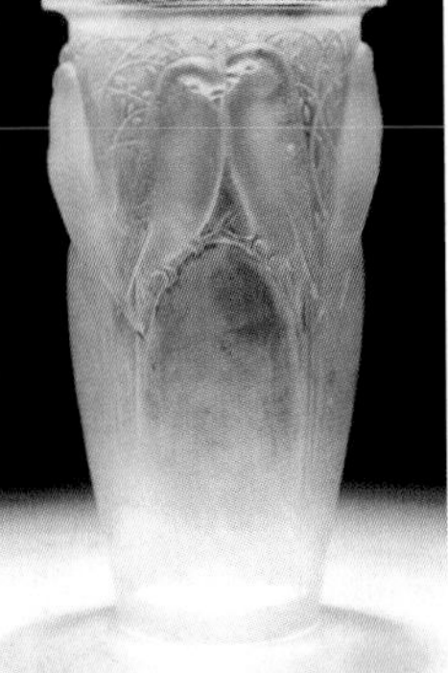

A René Lalique Ceylan glass vase, small rim chips, signed, French, designed 1924, produced pre-1945, 9½in (24cm) high.
£3,000–3,750 ⚒ RFA

A Schneider Bijou glass vase, signed, French, c1922, 4¼in (11cm) high.
£2,500–2,850 ⊞ MI

► A glass vase, Continental, c1930, 8¼in (21.5cm) high.
£135–150 ⊞ BEV

A Tiffany Favrile iridescent glass vase, signed, American, c1925, 9in (23cm) high.
£750–950 ⚒ DORO

◄ A Venini Murano amethyst vase, signed, Italian, c1930, 10in (25.5cm) high.
£340–375 ⊞ RUSK

A chrome coal bin, c1939, 19in (48.5cm) wide.
£550–700 ⚒ P

A silver-plated cocktail set, by Keith Murray, comprising eight pieces, c1935, tray 15¼in (38.5cm) wide.
£550–700 ⚒ P

The Lingford silver table service, by Omar Ramsden, comprising 168 pieces, 1912 and 1927–39, in an oak-veneered cabinet.
£52,000–65,000 ⚒ TEN
This service was bought via a personal friend of the Ramsdens. Some of the spoons are engraved with the initials D-B, for Downes-Butcher, Mrs Ramsden's previous married name, indicating that the service was originally made for her and then added to by Ramsden after their marriage.

A silver tea service, by A. E. Jones, Birmingham 1934, teapot 6in (15cm) wide.
£2,000–2,250 ⊞ SHa

◄ A pair of silver vases, by Tiffany & Co, marked, New York c1930, 20in (51cm) high.
£16,000–18,000 ⚒ S(NY)

A St Ives earthenware jug, by Shoji Hamada, two cracks, impressed seals, c1923, 4¼in (11cm) high.
£1,000–1,250 Bon

A St Ives earthenware slipware dish, attributed to Bernard Leach, impressed seal, c1933, 10¾in (27.5cm) diam.
£800–1,000 Bon

A ceramic wall plaque, by Sylvia Schleiss, after 1940, 11in (28cm) diam.
£1,300–1,600 DORO

A Leach Pottery St Ives porcelain bottle vase, decorated with a tree design, c1960, 3½in (9cm) high.
£45–50 RUSK

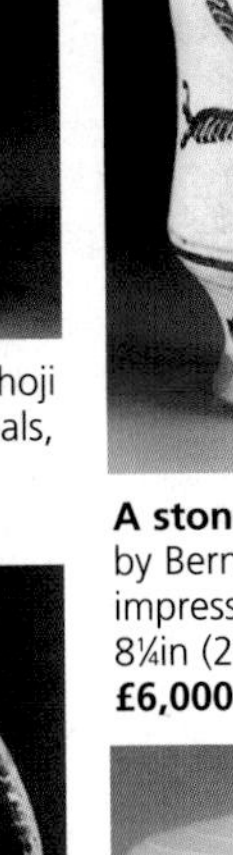

A stoneware *albarello*, by Bernard Leach, impressed seals, c1928, 8¼in (21cm) high.
£6,000–7,500 Bon

A vase, polychrome-decorated with abstract leaf motifs, after 1940, 11¾in (30cm) high.
£120–150 DORO

A Wedgwood green-glaze bowl, designed by Keith Murray, with early signature and registration numbers, 1930s, 9½in (24cm) diam.
£270–300 JAZZ

An earthenware teapot, by Michael Cardew, impressed initials and seal, c1935, 9½in (24cm) wide.
£320–400 Bon

◄ **A Wedgwood earthenware vase,** designed by Keith Murray, minor damage, impressed and printed marks, facsimile signature, after 1933, 11½in (29cm) high.
£470–600 S(O)

A Dame Lucie Rie pouring vessel, seal marks, c1960, 3in (7.5cm) high.
£300–325 RUSK

A Poole Pottery ceramic wall plaque, by Robert Jefferson, decorated with textured glazes, c1965, 15in (38cm) diam.
£3,400–4,250 P

◄ **A Troika Pottery vase,** decorated by Penny Black, chip, painted mark and monogram, c1970, 13¾in (35cm) high.
£530–600 S(O)

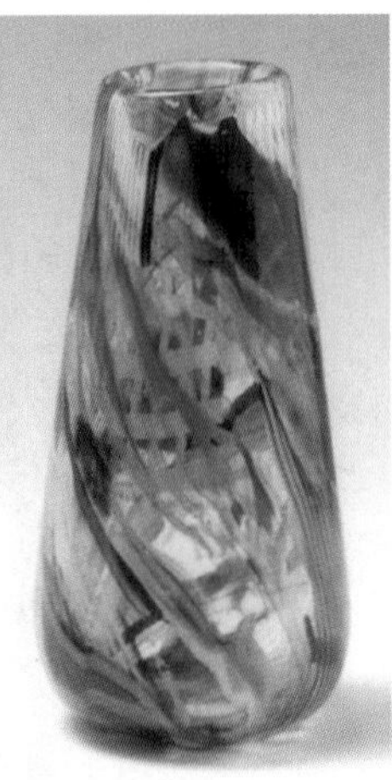

A Dino Martens glass vase, produced by Aureliano Toso, Italian, c1955, 9¾in (25cm) high.
£3,000–3,750 S(NY)

A Dame Laura Knight glass exhibition vase, produced by Stuart & Sons, manfacturer's and designer's acid stamp, 1934, 10¾in (27.5cm) high.
£700–875 P
This piece was designed for the Design in Industry exhibition at Harrods department store, London, in 1934. Stuart & Sons were the only glassmakers to be commissioned by the government to produce pieces for the exhibition.

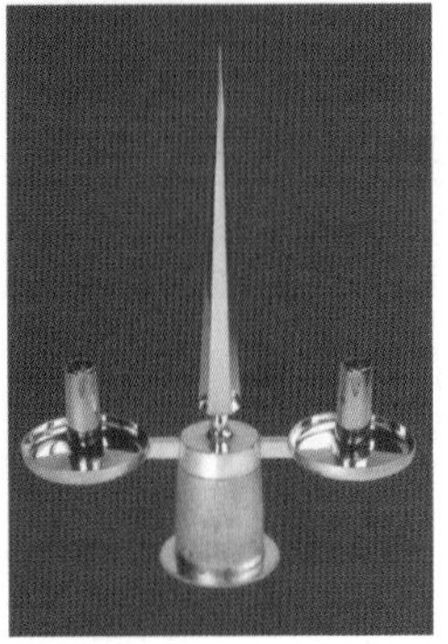

◄ **A silver candelabrum,** by Gerald Benney, maker's stamp, with original presentation case, 1961, 15½in (39.5cm) high.
£3,000–3,750 P

A Barovier & Toso glass bowl, incised signature, Italian, Murano, designed c1955, 16in (40.5cm) high.
£1,800–2,250 DORO

A chrome centre light, Italian, 1960s, 26in (66cm) wide.
£650–750 ⊞ ZOOM

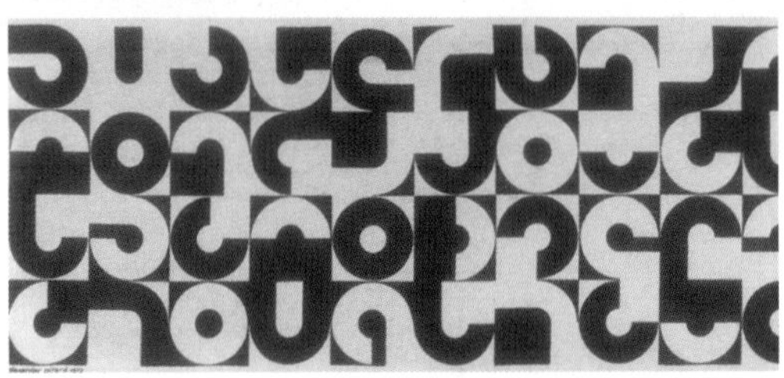

A fabric panel, Circle Sections A, by Alexander Girard, signed, 1972, 22½ x 64¾in (57 x 164.5cm).
£350–450 TREA

A white birch and aluminium prototype tall chest, by Warren McArthur Corporation, American, 1934, 34in (86.5cm) wide.
£6,500–8,000 TREA

A Charles and Ray Eames birch storage unit, ESU 200, by Herman Miller, with laminate interior shelves, signed, American, c1950, 47in (119.5cm) wide.
£3,200–4,000 TREA

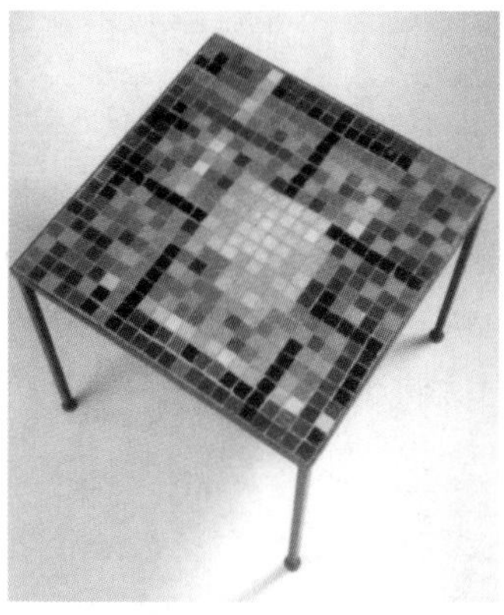

A John Piper mosaic glass occasional table, Terence Conran, on a stove-enamelled steel frame, c1955, 18½in (47cm) square.
£1,700–2,200 P

A Shiro Kuramata occasional table, Nana, for Memphis, Milan, Italian, 1983, 23¾in (60.5cm) wide.
£1,200–1,500 DORO

A Marcel Breuer long chair, by Isokon, the moulded plywood seat within a laminated birch frame, the seat covered with padding and upholstered in velvet, old restoration, designed 1935–36, produced 1936.
£4,700–6,000 P

A Robert Heritage screen-printed sideboard, by A. G. Evans, with an ebonized top and sides, the three frieze drawers veneered in pale birch, on metal rod legs, 1950s, 54in (137cm) wide.
£3,000–3,750 DN

A George Nelson walnut Swag-leg home desk, by Herman Miller, with a white laminate top, on chrome legs, American, c1956, 39in (99cm) wide.
£2,800–3,500 TREA

An Alessandro Mendini lacquered and veneered wood sideboard, Cantaride, for Nuova Alchimia, produced by Zabro, the front with painted decoration, limited production, Italian, 1984, 57in (145cm) wide.
£1,200–1,500 S(O)

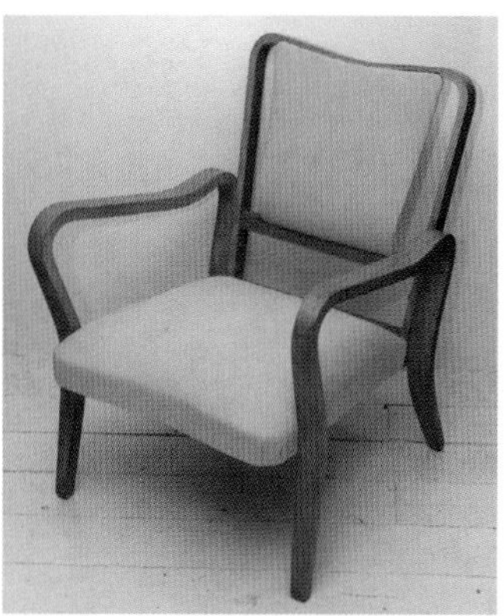

A pair of armchairs, French, c1950.
£850–950 SIE

A Piero Fornasetti reversible four-panel screen, *Libraria/Instrumenti Musicali*, with tranfer-printed decoration, Italian, c1950, 72in (183cm) wide.
£6,500–8,000 S(NY)

A David Bartlett flat-pack paper tab chair, c1963.
£650–820 P

A Ron Arad steel-framed rocking armchair, Soft Heart, for Morosa, upholstered in a wool fabric over foam, Italian, 1989.
£1,200–1,500 DORO

Lamps & Lighting
Ceiling & Wall Lights

A Regency bronze three-branch chandelier, with glass fittings, 30in (76cm) high.
£630–700 ⊞ EAL

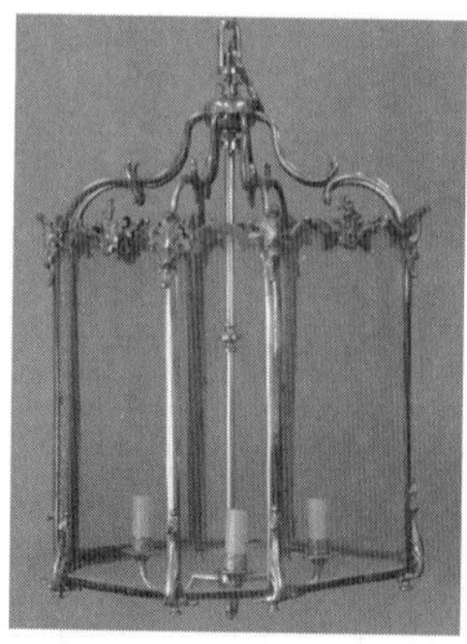

A brass and gilt-bronze-mounted octagonal hall lantern, early 19thC, 24in (61cm) high.
£600–750 ⚒ SWO

A sheet iron pierced pendant lantern, early 19thC, 14in (35.5cm) high.
£430–475 ⊞ SEA

A hall lantern, 19thC, 16½in (42cm) high.
£550–700 ⚒ CGC

Always check that electric lighting conforms to the current safety regulations.

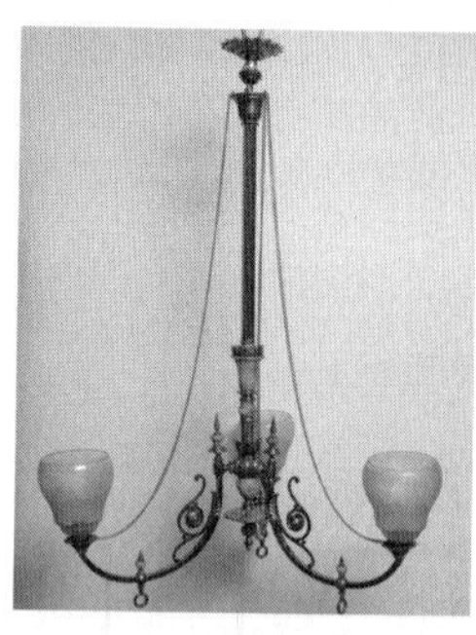

► **A mid-Victorian gilt-bronze gas lamp,** with alabaster fittings and etched glass shades, 39in (99cm) high.
£720–800 ⊞ EAL

A pair of glass lantern shades, 19thC, 10¾in (27.5cm) diam.
£600–750 ⚒ B(Ed)

A metal hexagonal hall lantern, 19thC, 29in (73.5cm) high.
£750–950 ⚒ MEA

A pair of brass wall lights, c1880, 17in (43cm) high.
£450–500 ⊞ JPr

A patent design rise and fall gas lamp, in original brass finish, with opaque glass shade, c1870, 43in (109cm) high.
£550–600 ⊞ EAL

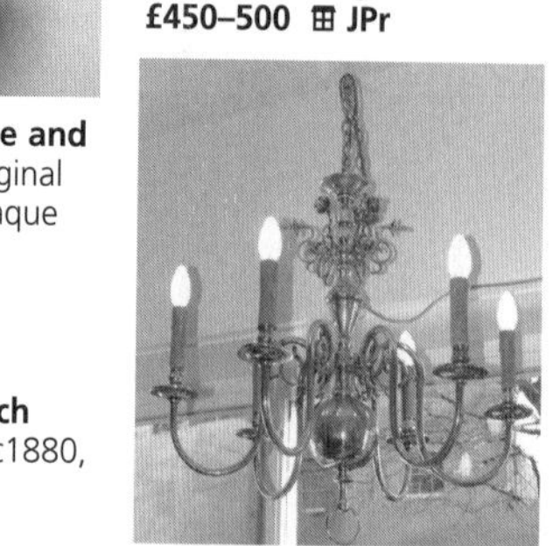

► **A brass six-branch chandelier,** French, c1880, 14in (35.5cm) wide.
£720–800 ⊞ OLA

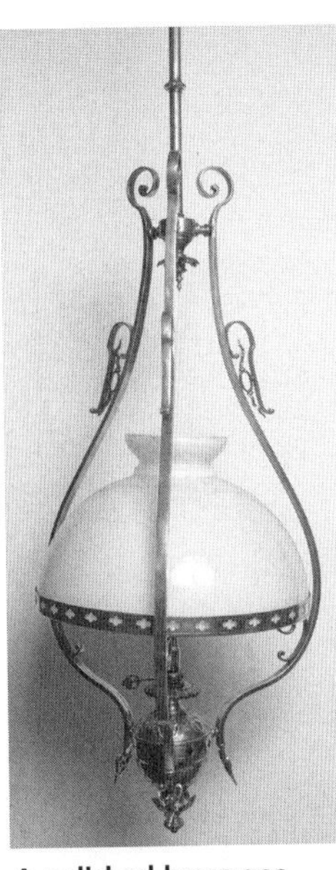
A polished brass gas lamp, with original opaque shade, French, c1880, 55in (139.5cm) high.
£315–350 ⊞ EAL

A brass and wrought-iron Louis XVI-style six-branch chandelier, fitted for electricity, French, c1900, 34in (86.5cm) high.
£2,000–2,200 ⚒ NOA

A pair of carved and green-painted wood mirrored three-light girandoles, rococo style, Italian, early 20thC, 43¼in (110cm) high.
£1,250–1,500 ⚒ P(Ba)

A brass and copper oil lamp, by Hinks, Birmingham, c1890, 36in (91.5cm) high.
£225–250 ⊞ EAL

A silver-plated six-branch chandelier, c1900, 25in (63.5cm) wide.
£720–800 ⊞ EAL

A set of three Edwardian brass twelve-light electroliers, with four spare arms, 40in (101.5cm) wide.
£900–1,100 ⚒ G(L)

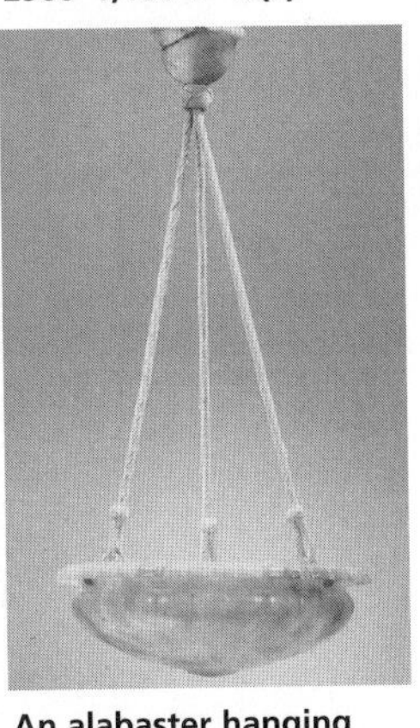
An alabaster hanging dish light, suspended by ropes, Italian, c1900, 15¾in (40cm) diam.
£470–600 ⚒ S(Am)

► A pair of brass Davey lamps, 1910–20, 15in (38cm) high.
£380–425 ⊞ PEZ

A pair of wall lights, with hand-cut drops, late 19thC, 14in (35.5cm) high.
£450–550 ⊞ JPr

A set of eight ormolu Louis XVI-style wall lights, by Raingo Frères, the backplate of spiralling cornucopia form with flowers and fruits suspended from ribbon-tied drapery, fitted for electricity, stamped, French, late 19thC, 24½in (62cm) high.
£7,000–8,750 ⚒ N

A pair of gilt-metal and frosted glass ceiling lights, early 20thC, 11½in (29cm) high.
£1,200–1,400 ⚒ S(O)

A set of three silver-plated wall lamps, with original cut-glass shades by Osler, c1900, 12in (30.5cm) high.
£1,350–1,500 ⊞ EAL

A pair of bronze wall lights, French, c1900, 23¾in (60.5cm) high.
£385–475 ⚒ LCM

A gilt-metal chandelier, with original glass pendants and eight electric candles, minor damage, Vienna, early 20thC, 41¼in (105cm) high.
£425–525 ⚒ DORO

A white glass pendant lamp, with brass gallery and chain, c1930, 16in (40.5cm) diam.
£180–200 ⊞ EAL

Table & Standard Lamps

A Regency metal oil lamp, with a fluted cut-glass font, now fitted for electricity, 19¾in (50cm) high.
£1,500–1,800 P(S)

A pair of porcelain oil lamps, the oil fittings signed 'Tucker and Son, Arundel Works, London', c1840, 28in (71cm) high.
£770–850 S(O)

A Victorian brass gas table lamp, with alabaster fittings and original amber glass shade, 22in (56cm) high.
£225–250 EAL

A brass Colza lamp, with a brass label 'Perry & Co, 72 New Bond St', early 19thC, 20in (51cm) high.
£550–700 PF

A pair of silver oil lamps, with plated fittings and spiral-moulded glass shades, marked 'Sener 900', probably American, 19thC, 11in (28cm) high, 17oz.
£300–375 F&C

A Victorian brass and glass well oil lamp, with an etched glass shade, 20½in (52cm) high.
£100–120 SWO

► **A Victorian paraffin lamp,** with a gadrooned cistern and a Hinks's No. 2 burner, shade and chimney missing, later adapted for electricity, 18in (45.5cm) high.
£90–120 PFK

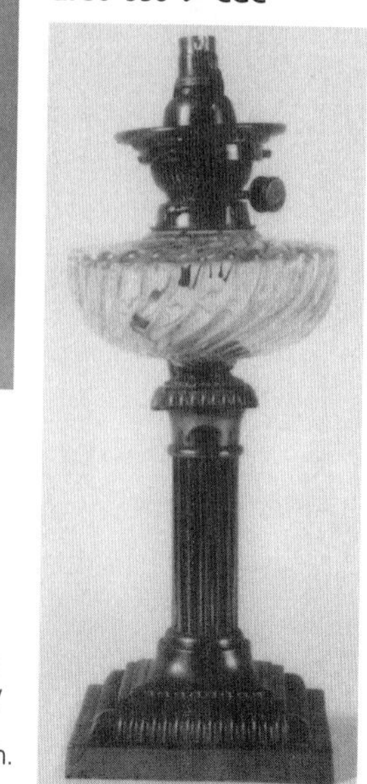

An Empire ormolu candle stand, with a stiff-leaf, stylized flowerhead and acanthus-cast baluster column, now fitted for electricity, stamped 'Thomire à Paris', French, early 19thC, 14¼in (36cm) high.
£3,000–3,750 DN

An ormolu-mounted Paris porcelain lamp, French, mid-19thC, 21in (53.5cm) high.
£750–950 CGC

A brass oil lamp, with embossed decoration of sailing boats and windmills, Dutch, early 19thC, 14½in (37cm) high.
£175–220 P

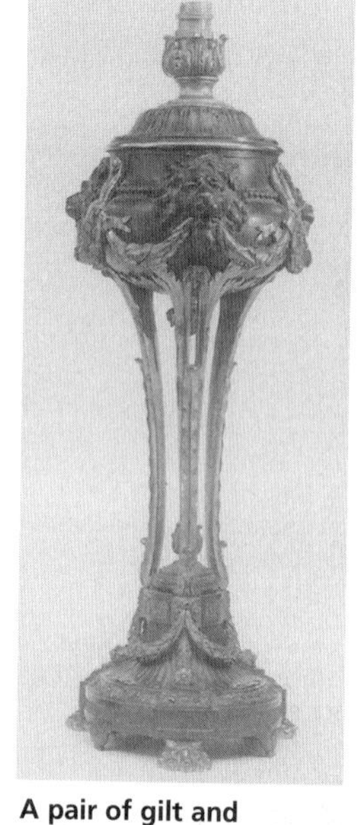

A pair of gilt and patinated-bronze oil lamp bases, the reservoirs with beaded girdles and lion's mask mounts, fitted for electricity, French, 1850–75, 21in (53.5cm) high.
£1,250–1,500 P(Ba)

A Victorian gilt-brass oil lamp, by Whitfield and Hughes, London, 33¾in (85.5cm) high.
£900–1,150 DN

A pair of Victorian brass oil lamps, on stepped plinths with cast-iron lion mask feet, fitted for electricity, 31½in (80cm) high.
£1,700–2,200 ⚒ B(Ed)

A silver-plated oil lamp, with original etched glass shade, c1880, 30in (76cm) high.
£400–450 ⊞ EAL

A late Victorian silver-plated table lamp, with a central flame finial and two acanthus spray side paraffin lights with ruby glass shades, the foot with a French inscription, base 7in (18cm) high.
£75–95 ⚒ WW

A black-painted patinated-bronze Renaissance revival four-light torchère, the central griffin above stylized griffin's heads, on a reeded standard ending in a seated griffin, fitted for electricity, late 19thC, 45in (114.5cm) high.
£2,200–2,500 ⚒ SK

A pair of bronze and rouge marble table lamps, on three monopodia lion paw supports, surmounted by gilt and black shades, late 19thC, 30in (76cm) high.
£1,800–2,200 ⚒ MEA

An original gas table lamp, on a Corinthian column, with period clear and etched glass shade, fitted for electricity, c1900, 26¾in (68cm) high.
£500–600 ⊞ CHA

An Edwardian electro-plated oil lamp, on a Corinthian column, with a clear cut-glass reservoir, 23¼in (59cm) high.
£400–500 ⚒ CGC

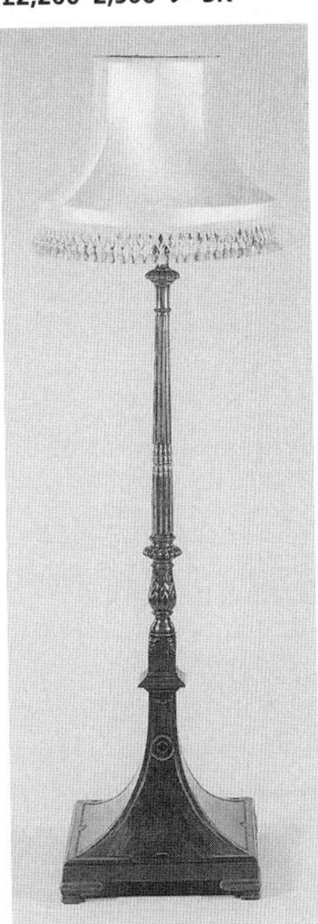

A mahogany standard lamp, with a stop-fluted baluster stem, c1910, 63in (160cm) high.
£3,200–3,500 ⚒ S

An ebony and brass lamp, on a Corinthian column, c1910, 22in (56cm) high.
£350–400 ⊞ HUM

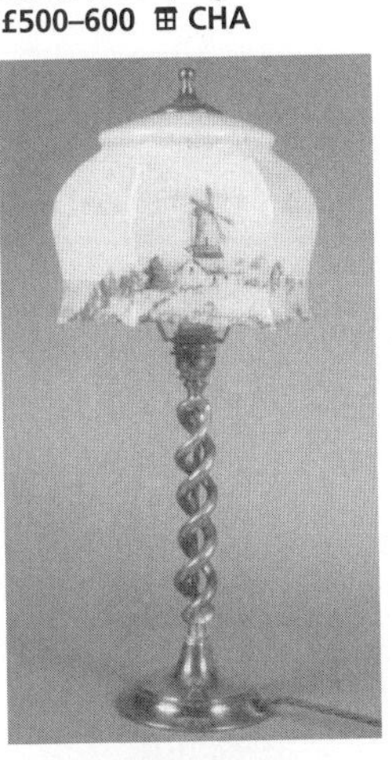

A brass table lamp, with hand-painted period shade, c1920, 17¾in (45cm) high.
£180–225 ⊞ CHA

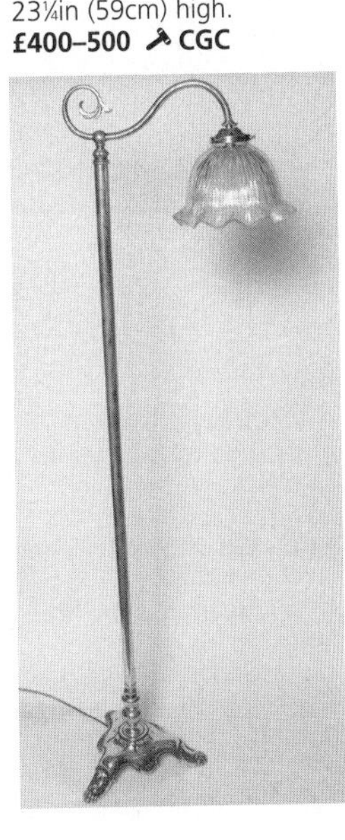

◄ **A brass reading lamp,** with lion's paw feet and replacement glass shade, German, c1930, 66in (167.5cm) high.
£315–350 ⊞ EAL

Rugs & Carpets

A Cuenca carpet, with four cruciform symbols in ivory, golds and tan on a mid-blue field enclosed by a meander border in similar colours, repiled and rewoven areas, Spanish, 17thC, 97 x 67in (246.5 x 170cm).
£4,500–5,500 ⚒ S(NY)

An Aubusson carpet, with a rococo design in ivory, gold, celadon green, red and dark brown, with festoons of pink roses, French, c1880, 198 x 167in (505 x 426cm).
£7,750–9,750 ⚒ NOA

A needlework rug, worked in coloured wools with a central flowerhead medallion on a dark brown field, with an all-over design of scrolling flowers, and an outer border of diaper panels and leaves, 18thC, 134 x 100in (340.5 x 254cm).
£48,000–60,000 ⚒ DN

Although catalogued as 'European' and conservatively estimated at £600–800 because of its worn condition, this rug was fought over by two telephone bidders who took the price up to £48,000. It was considered that it is, in fact, 18th century and English, making it a very desirable item.

A rug, the coral field with an all-over sea-green lattice enclosing stylized indigo palmettes and framed by an indigo palmette border, Spanish, dated 1955, 66 x 52in (167.5 x 132cm).
£1,000–1,200 ⚒ P

A Savonnerie carpet, with a concentric design of swirling leaves and roses in greens, blues, ivory and rose pink on a dark gold field, enclosed by an inner rose spray and flowerhead gold border and outer lozenge gold and green border, French, early 20thC, 118¼ x 121in (300.5 x 307.5cm).
£11,000–14,000 ⚒ S(NY)

A Mujur prayer rug, the purple-red field with a sprigged and serrated ivory frame and prayer arch on an olive green field, enclosed by a diamond and ivory inner border and red, orange, olive and ivory flowerhead outer border, slight wear, damaged, central Anatolian, late 19thC, 61 x 48in (155 x 122cm).
£180–225 ⚒ WW

An Aubusson rug, with a shaped medallion in ivory and gold with crimson sprays on a dark gold ground with ivory sprays, enclosed by a crimson and gold border, French, mid-19thC, 95 x 79in (241.5 x 200.5cm).
£700–800 ⚒ S(O)

The rugs in this section have been arranged in geographical sequence from west to east, in the following order: Europe, Turkey, Anatolia, Caucasus, Persia, Turkestan, India and China.

A Donegal rug, the all-over design of large flowers, stems and leaves in golds, dark red and ivory on a blue/black field, enclosed by dark gold borders, Irish, c1920, 101¼ x 72¾in (257 x 185cm).
£400–500 ⚒ S(O)

A Bergama rug, the light red field with 12 quartered *güls* interspersed with hooked cruciform devices in gold, light red and ivory, enclosed by multiple floral hooked and banded borders, and a running dog outer border, Anatolian, c1900, 74 x 47in (188 x 119.5cm).
£700–800 ⊞ DNo

A Yürük bag face, with a red and purple star on an ivory and red serrated hexagon on a dark blue field, with multi-coloured flowerheads and hooked and diamond symbols, enclosed by an arrowhead, the red border with a multi-coloured flowerhead on a purple bottom panel, slight wear, damaged, east Anatolian, late 19thC, 24 x 23in (61 x 58.5cm).
£300–375 WW

A Lori Pambak rug, the madder field centred by an ivory octagonal medallion enclosing a sea-green heraldic motif, flanked by hooked stellar panels and framed by triple narrow borders of running dog motifs, southwest Caucasian, late 19thC, 93¾ x 65½in (238 x 166.5cm).
£1,750–2,000 P

A Shirvan rug, with *Lesghi* medallions in blues and pale orange, the central one in an ivory panel, all on a dark blue field decorated with multi-coloured flowerheads and other devices, enclosed by five narrow flowerhead and ribbon borders in ivory, blue and pale orange, east Caucasian, c1900, 56 x 43in (142 x 109cm).
£820–900 S(O)

A Karachov rug, the sky-blue field with alternating madder cruciform and ivory rectangular medallions flanked by polychrome panels of hooked motifs, framed by an ivory stylized *kufic* border, southwest Caucasian, c1880, 99¼ x 63in (252 x 160cm).
£1,850–2,200 P

A rug, with a mid-blue pole medallion within a dark blue main border of naïve human, animal and geometric figures, south Caucasian, dated 1910, 58 x 39in (147.5 x 99cm).
£400–500 DN

A Shirvan rug, the field with a trellis design of flowerheads and serrated stems in light brown, blues, gold and ivory on a navy field, enclosed by a floral ivory frame, a main pale brown wine-glass-and-leaf border and two carnation subsidiary borders, outer border missing at both ends, east Caucasian, c1870, 58 x 45in (147.5 x 114.5cm).
£600–650 DNo

▶ **A Soumakh rug,** with geometric shapes of dark and light blue, light green, yellow, red and ivory on a brick-red ground, some wear, east Caucasian, c1865, 141 x 106in (358 x 269cm).
£850–1,000 JAA

A Kazak rug, the red field with all-over *boteh* design in gold and blue, enclosed by red and ivory reciprocal trefoil inner and outer frames, flanking the blue and green main border with stylized flowerheads, southwest Caucasian, c1910, 58 x 35in (147.5 x 89cm).
£575–625 S(O)

A Chichi rug, the indigo field with an all-over design of rosettes and hooked geometric motifs, framed by a charcoal rosette and slant-leaf border, east Caucasian, late 19thC, 76 x 50in (193 x 127cm).
£2,300–2,750 P

A Veramin carpet, with an all-over design of swags of flowerheads and leaves in pale green, red and blue on a dark brown field, enclosed by a narrow floral border, north Persian, c1920, 109 x 70in (277 x 178cm).
£1,500–1,700 S(O)

A Bakshaish rug, the light red field with a hexagonal medallion in pale blue and red with vertical columns terminating in stylized flowerheads, enclosed by triple floral borders in similar colours, some wear, northwest Persian, c1890, 75 x 40in (190.5 x 101.5cm).
£600–680 ⊞ DNo

A Bidjar rug, the hexagonal pale red medallion with lobed motifs at each end in light blue on a midnight blue field, enclosed by a scrolled ribbon, red main border and two light blue floral subsidiary borders, northwest Persian, c1900, 80 x 52in (203 x 132cm).
£1,100–1,250 ⊞ DNo

History of rugs & carpets

It is not known for sure exactly when people first began to practise pile weaving, but so far the earliest known hand-knotted rug dates from the 3rd–5th centuries BC, and was found in southern Siberia. Fragments from the 3rd–6th centuries AD have also been found in Xinjian in eastern Turkestan. Persian carpets are mentioned in 10th century Arab records and by the 13th century rug-weaving was well established in Anatolia. Fourteenth and 15th century paintings depict weavings similar to early Turkish carpets.

A Heriz rug, with hexagonal anchor medallions in red and gold on navy on a light red field decorated with flowerheads, enclosed by ivory and flowerhead spandrels and triple floral borders, northwest Persian, c1910, 49 x 30in (124.5 x 76cm).
£350–400 ⊞ DNo

A Karadja carpet, the abrashed indigo field with three columns of hooked palmettes and stellar medallions interspersed by angular floral motifs, framed by a madder samovar border, northwest Persian, c1900, 132 x 102½in (335.5 x 260.5cm).
£1,850–2,200 P

A Serapi carpet, with a radiating plant ivory medallion with a blue and rust on gold surround on a rust field with serrated ivory and blue spandrels, enclosed by a polychrome palmette on a navy main border, northwest Persian, c1890, 156 x 116in (396 x 294.5cm).
£1,700–2,000 S(O)

A Kurdish long rug, the pole medallions with flowerheads and branches and small *boteh* on a dark blue field, enclosed by a triple floral border in gold, blue and brown, slight wear, northwest Persian, probably Veramin area, late 19thC, 98 x 49in (249 x 124.5cm).
£680–850 WW

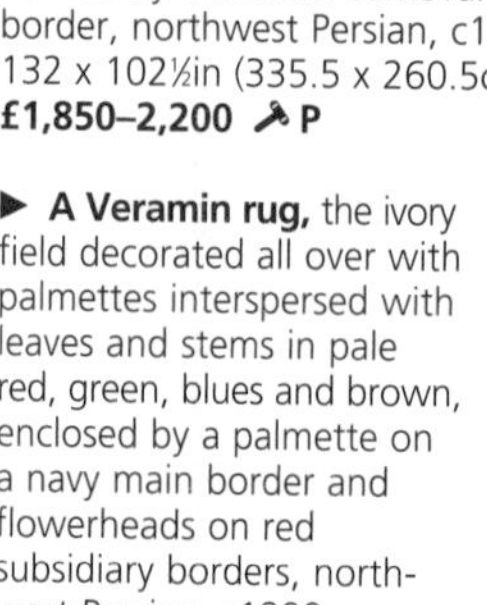

► **A Veramin rug,** the ivory field decorated all over with palmettes interspersed with leaves and stems in pale red, green, blues and brown, enclosed by a palmette on a navy main border and flowerheads on red subsidiary borders, northwest Persian, c1900, 80¾ x 57in (205 x 145cm).
£2,300–3,000 WW

Value of a carpet

Condition is crucial to the value of a rug or carpet. A pleasing balance of colours is also important, and an allover pattern is preferable to a medallion design, except for Heriz, or very old, pieces. Age is naturally an important factor, and examples dating from before c1880 are sought-after. Fine quality wool is generally more desirable than silk, which is prone to corrosion.

A Bakhtiyari rug, the pale blue field with repeating red and black *gül* pattern featuring birds and flowers in green, yellow, blue and red, within a brown border with stylized foliage, west Persian, early 20thC, 75 x 54in (190.5 x 137cm).
£500–600 AH

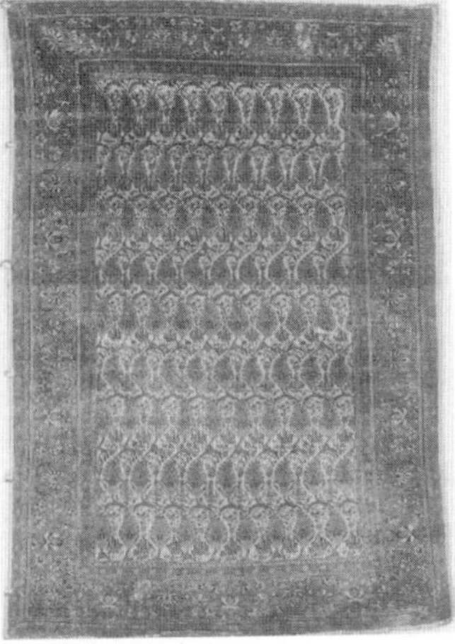

A Feraghan silk rug, the ivory field decorated with linked reciprocal *boteh* in reds, blues and brown, enclosed by a dark red floral main border and thin red and pale blue subsidiary borders, west Persian, c1920, 78¾ x 50¾in (200 x 129cm).
£800–1,000 S(O)

A Jaf Kurdish rug, the field with a madder diamond lattice design, enclosing hooked motifs, framed by an ivory cruciform border and running dog guard stripes, west Persian, late 19thC, 85¾ x 43in (218 x 109cm).
£700–800 P

◀ **A Jaf Kurdish bagface,** the red and blue twin panels with diamond medallions, with a flowerhead on a gold frame, within a flowerhead on navy border above a polychrome curled-leaf bottom panel, northwest Persian, c1900, 26 x 44in (66 x 112cm).
£260–325 WW

A Jaf Kurdish bagface, decorated with blue hooked diamonds within a dark brown trellis, enclosed by a red and blue floral on ivory border and a reciprocal trefoil frame, some damage, west Persian, early 20thC, 31¼ x 41in (79.5 x 104cm).
£60–75 WW

A Hamadan runner, with two ivory lotus flowers and a gold and ivory branch design on an abrashed rust-red field, some repairs and wear, west Persian, c1880, 117 x 40in (297 x 101.5cm).
£850–950 ⊞ DNo
The branch design included in this runner is usually found in Karagashli Caucasian rugs.

A Senneh Hamadan rug, the central ivory medallion decorated with stylized floral symbols, birds and scorpions in light reds, indigo and green on a light red field with dark blue spandrels decorated with floral symbols, enclosed by a flowerhead floral red main border and two guard stripes, west Persian, c1920, 56 x 43in (142 x 109cm).
£400–460 ⊞ DNo

A Lilihan rug, the burgundy ground decorated with a floral pattern in ivory, blue, green, cobalt and red, west Persian, c1930, 55 x 38in (139.5 x 96.5cm).
£230–275 JAA

A Kurdistan rug, the red hexagonal medallion with turquoise anchor pendants on a blue-black field on an ivory ground, all-over decorated with a polychrome *herati* design, enclosed by a floral meander red main border, west Persian, 1900–20, 79 x 51in (200.5 x 129.5cm).
£1,000–1,200 ⊞ LIN

A Shiraz rug, with a triple-pole medallion in pale red, browns, blues and ivory on a pale orange-red field decorated with stylized plants and birds, enclosed by triple geometric and floral borders, repairs, southwest Persian, c1900, 52 x 33in (132 x 84cm).
£235–260 ⊞ DNo

Layout of a carpet

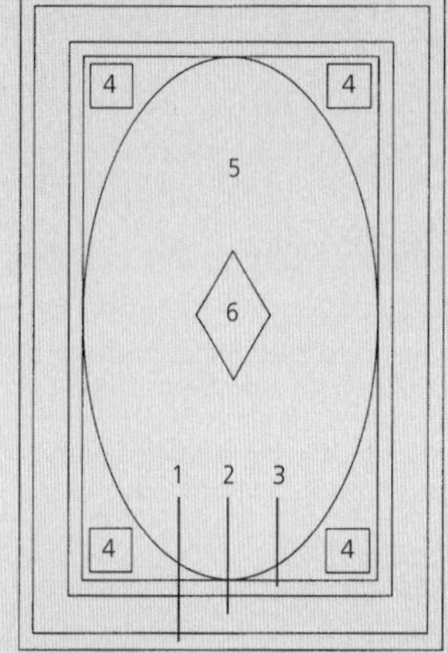

1 Outer guardstripe or minor border
2 Main border
3 Inner guardstripe or border
4 Spandrel
5 Field or ground
6 Medallion

A Maslaghan rug, the central medallion in blues, gold, ivory and red-brown containing a stylized peacock on a red-brown field decorated with flowers and peacocks, enclosed by a zigzag frame in bue and ivory and dark blue spandrels with multi-coloured flowerheads and triple floral borders, central Persian, c1920, 47 x 33in (119.5 x 84cm).
£500–550 ⊞ DNo

An Afshar rug, the indigo field of stylized plants centred by a stellar medallion and flanked by vases issuing flowers, framed by a terracotta floral vine border, south Persian, late 19thC, 73 x 61in (185.5 x 155cm).
£800–950 ⚒ P

A Kurk Kashan rug, the indigo field of floral vines centred by a madder floral cusped medallion, enclosed by an indigo border of lozenge motifs and interlocking tendrils, central Persian, c1910, 81¼ x 51¼in (206.5 x 130cm).
£3,200–4,000 ⚒ P

A Nejefabad *pushti*, decorated with a sprigged yellow and floral medallion on an oval shaded red field, enclosed by a yellow main border and reciprocal guard stripes, central Persian, c1930, 32 x 26in (81.5 x 66cm).
£400–450 ⊞ LIN

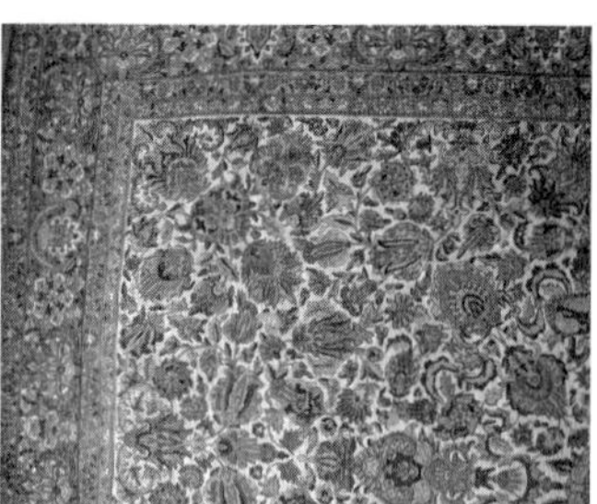

A Kerman carpet, with an all-over pattern of palmettes, leaves and flowers in reds, greens, blues and gold on an ivory field, enclosed by a similar floral main border and two pairs of floral subsidiary borders, south Persian, c1900, 168 x 123½in (426.5 x 313.5cm).
£1,850–2,200 ⚒ SWO

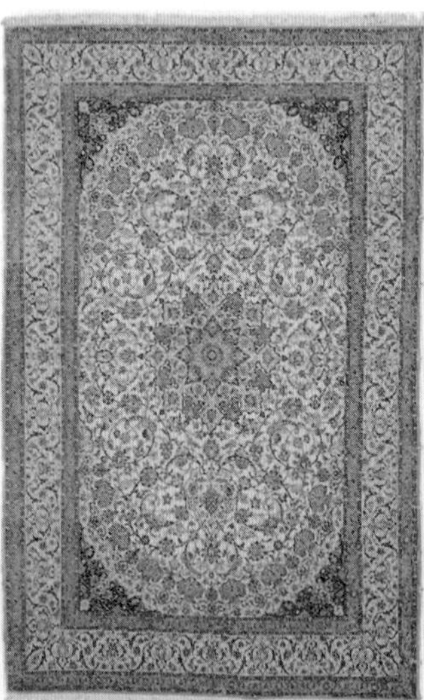

A part-silk Nain carpet, the central star medallion with a formal curvilinear scrolling stem and flower design, all in pale and dark blues on an oval field with dark blue spandrels, enclosed by a floral ivory main border and twin subsidiary borders, central Persian, 1900–25, 134¾ x 87in (342.5 x 221cm).
£1,350–1,500 ⚒ S(O)

A Ziegler Mahal *wagireh*, with a design of curling stems, leaves and palmettes in gold, ivory and blue on an orange-red field, enclosed by triple narrow borders, central Persian, c1900, 44 x 42½in (112 x 108cm).
£2,500–3,000 ⚒ S(O)

A *wagireh* is a knotted sampler used by weavers showing part of the field design and a section of the border and guard stripe.

A Belouch prayer rug, the camel-coloured field decorated with stylized Tree of Life, leaves and shrubs in reds, brown and indigo, enclosed by a double ivory frame and a red, brown and ivory main border, northeast Persian, c1880, 58 x 36in (147.5 x 91.5cm).
£280–325 DNo

A Belouch bagface, with a design of trellised diamonds in diagonal rows of red, pink and brown, two ivory frames contain triple geometric borders, slight wear and damage, northeast Persian, Khorasan, c1900, 34 x 42¼in (86.5 x 107.5cm).
£80–100 WW

An Afshar rug, with linked and stylized floral forms in red, brown and blue in horizontal rows on an ivory field, enclosed by triple floral borders, slight wear, southeast Persian, Kerman area, c1920, 60 x 50in (152.5 x 127cm).
£100–125 WW

Prayer rugs

Prayer rugs are highly regarded by collectors of tribal and village rugs. They were traditionally used by Muslims for prayer, the *mihrab* (triangle- or square-shaped prayer niche) at the top being pointed towards Mecca. The person praying would then kneel, placing his hands in the spandrels and his head within the *mihrab*. When not in use, these rugs would be rolled up in order to keep them clean.

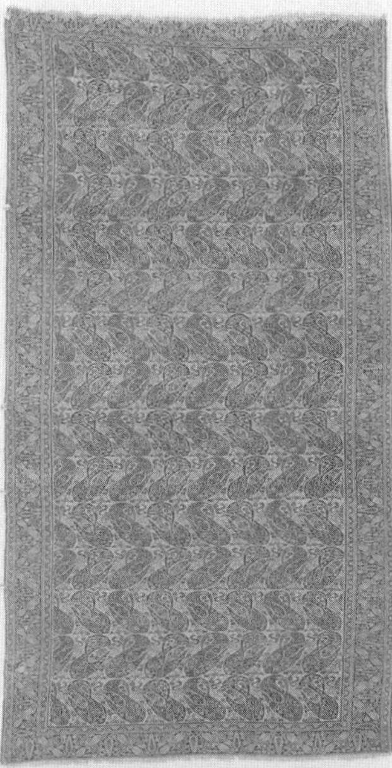

An Afshar rug, the midnight-blue field decorated with a stepped anchor medallion in pink, ivory, rust and blues with matching spandrels, enclosed by an ivory and floral border, southeast Persian, c1930, 55 x 42in (139.5 x 106.5cm).
£280–325 DNo

A Belouch rug, the light red field decorated with *boteh* in navy, blues, ivory and red, enclosed by a blue and lilac hooked frame, a main ivory Afshar border and a red trefoil outer border, northeast Persian, c1900, 60 x 42in (152.5 x 106.5cm).
£550–650 DNo

An Afshar rug, with *boteh* surrounded by scattered stylized animals, birds and other symbols in pale colours on an ivory field, enclosed by triple geometric and floral borders, some reweaves and wear, southeast Persian, c1890, 72 x 56in (183 x 142cm).
£350–400 DNo

◀ **A Doroksh long rug,** with rows of reciprocal leaves in blues, reds and gold on an ivory ground, enclosed by a miniature leaf main border and twin guard stripes, northeast Persian, c1880, 116¼ x 61½in (295.5 x 156cm).
£1,200–1,500 S(O)

A Laver Kerman carpet, the classic workshop design with curvilinear medallion and spandrel layout in reds, blues and ivory, enclosed by triple complementary borders, southeast Persian, c1890, 163 x 111¾in (414 x 284cm).
£3,700–4,000 S(O)

◀ **A Kerman rug,** with a closely detailed petal and star medallion in reds, blues and gold on a pale lemon field, with a formal curvilinear floral design overall, enclosed by a red, blue and gold floral main border and two flowerhead subsidiary borders, southeast Persian, c1900, 88¼ x 54¼in (224 x 138cm).
£500–600 S(O)

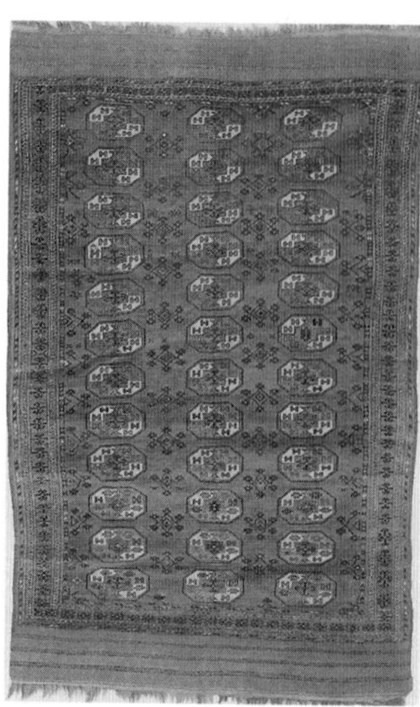

A Kizyl Ayak main carpet, the madder field with 36 *güls* in three columns, framed by a stellar border and long-banded and fringed *kilim* ends, west Turkestani, late 19thC, 115¾ x 72in (294 x 183cm).
£1,400–1,700 P

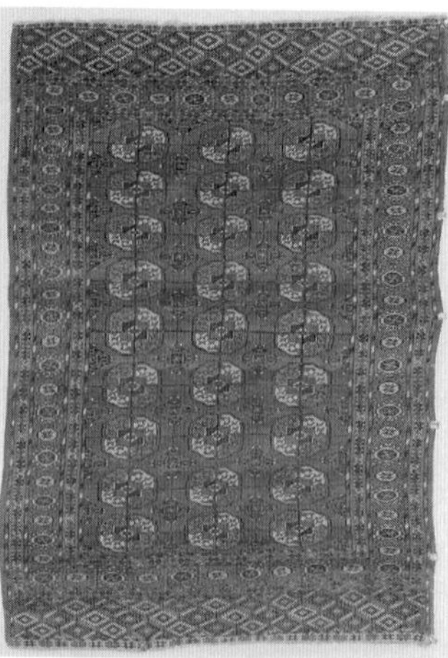

A Tekke rug, with 27 quartered *güls* in three columns interspersed with Kurbaka minor *güls* in navy, crimson, red and ivory on a madder field, enclosed by a main starburst border and with hooked diamond lattice *elem* panels at each end, west Turkestani, c1890, 83½ x 59¾in (212 x 152cm).
£1,000–1,100 S(O)

A Tekke Turkman rug, with 12 *güls* in two columns of six in ivory, reds and indigo on a madder field, enclosed by multiple borders with fringed diamond *elem* panels at each end, west Turkestani, c1910, 79¼ x 53¼in (201.5 x 135.5cm).
£100–125 WW

A Tekke Turkman rug, with 14 *Salor güls* in two columns of seven and Tekke minor *güls* between, in ivory, blues and red on a raspberry red field, enclosed by multiple borders, wear, some damage, west Turkestani, 1910–20, 78 x 61in (198 x 155cm).
£140–170 WW

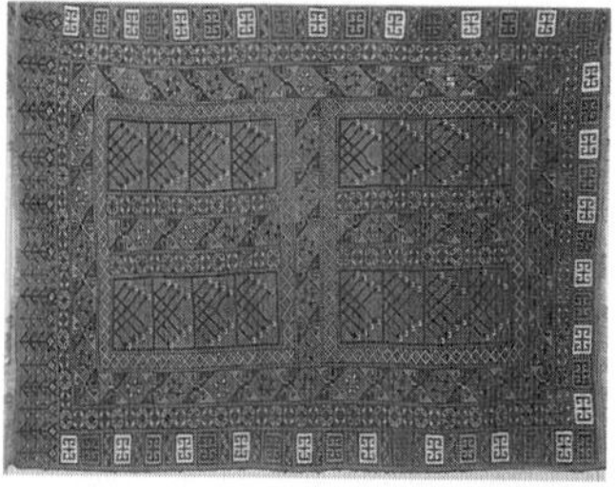

An Ersari tent doorway hanging, the four panels with the *Insikush* design divided by geometric bands forming the main border, enclosed by an outer flowerhead border and *sainlak* frame, the lower panel decorated with rows of plants, all in pale reds, browns, ivory and navy, southwest Turkestani, c1910, 80 x 57in (203 x 145cm).
£850–950 ⊞ DNo

A Tekke Turkman rug, the four-panel field decorated in blue on crimson, enclosed by an ivory frame and panels of trees in reds, green, blues and ivory, the bottom panel composed of figures-of-eight rosettes, west Turkestani, c1940, 58 x 42in (147.5 x 106.5cm).
£500–550 ⊞ DNo

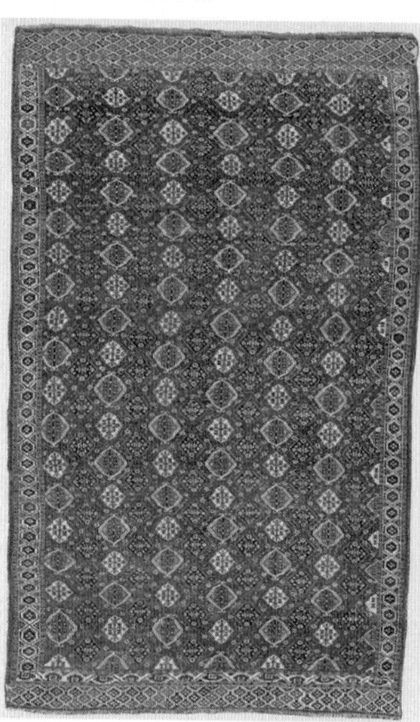

A Chodor main carpet, decorated with *güls* in red, ivory and navy, enclosed by a lozenge floral main border and with diagonal rosette *elem* panels at each end, minor reweaves, north Turkestani, c1875, 176 x 105¼in (447 x 267.5cm).
£4,500–5,500 S(NY)

A Yomut carpet, the aubergine field with staggered columns of *dyrnak güls*, framed by an ivory border of hooked rosettes and leaf motifs with stepped rosette *elems*, northwest Turkestani, late 19thC, 107½ x 65½in (273 x 166.5cm).
£1,600–2,000 P

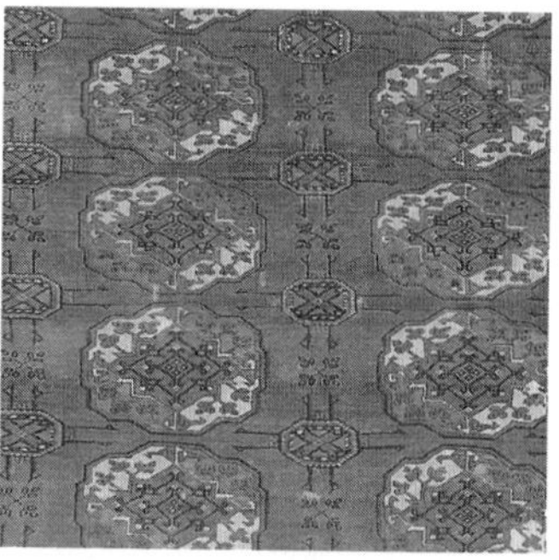

An Ersari small carpet, the deep terracotta field with three columns of nine *güls*, supported by cruciform octagonal *güls* and ivory stepped *gül* border, northwest Afghani, c1870, 95¼ x 86½in (242 x 219.5cm).
£3,500–4,500 S

A carpet, with an all-over floral design in pale blues, green, ivory and sage on a deep rose field, enclosed by a floral and blue main border, sage and ivory subsidiary borders and plain red margin, overall wear, Indian, possibly Agra, c1930, 141 x 111in (358 x 282cm).
£120–150 ⚒ WW

A Hassanpur Jail *miqrazi* (cotton piled) rug, northwest Indian, Punjab, mid- to late 19thC, 71 x 45in (180.5 x 114.5cm).
£420–525 ⚒ WW
Cotton-piled rugs of good age are now rare as they were not made for export.

A carpet, with sprays of flowers in many pale colours on a mid-blue field and beige border, Chinese, 1930–50, 117 x 86in (297 x 218.5cm).
£110–140 ⚒ WW

A carpet, with a large blue-black, tan and ivory pole medallion with matching spandrels on a foliage-filled pale red field, enclosed by triple complementary floral borders, Indo-Persian, c1920, 194 x 143¾in (493 x 365cm).
£5,000–5,500 ⚒ S(O)

An Amritsar carpet, with concentric floral medallions in pale lilac and browns on a cream field, with conforming triple floral borders, north Indian, c1910, 137½ x 105¼in (349.5 x 267.5cm).
£820–900 ⚒ S(O)

A silver-thread carpet, decorated with dragons and stylized rivers, in shades of orange, red, ivory and indigo, with inscription in cartouche, Chinese, 18thC, 96 x 62in (244 x 157.5cm).
£9,500–12,000 ⚒ S(P)

► **A rug,** the pink and yellow field decorated with five blue Buddhist medallions on a lattice key pattern ground within a main matching border, Chinese, late 19thC, 68¼ x 50in (173.5 x 127cm).
£580–725 ⚒ DN

An Amritsar carpet, with a delicate outline pattern of stellar medallions, matching spandrels, leaves and flowerheads throughout the field and main border, all on a pale gold ground, losses and moth damage, north Indian, c1900, 118¼ x 95in (300.5 x 241.5cm).
£4,500–5,500 ⚒ S(NY)

A Ninghsia rug, with an all-over concentric floral design in pale red, grey and navy on a pale jade-green field, enclosed by a pearl and T-border and an outer floral meander ivory border, north Chinese, 19thC, 120½ x 55¼in (306 x 140.5cm).
£1,100–1,300 ⚒ S(O)

Textiles
Covers & Quilts

A patchwork coverlet, worked in polychrome-striped, checked and floral printed fabric stripes, the back plain, 19thC, 90½ x 74½in (230 x 189cm).
£350–450 PFK

A cotton quilt, with orange and green sunflowers with brown centres, green leaves and stems, with orange and green meandering vine and flower border, American, 19thC, 72 x 89in (183 x 226cm).
£4,000–4,500 SK(B)

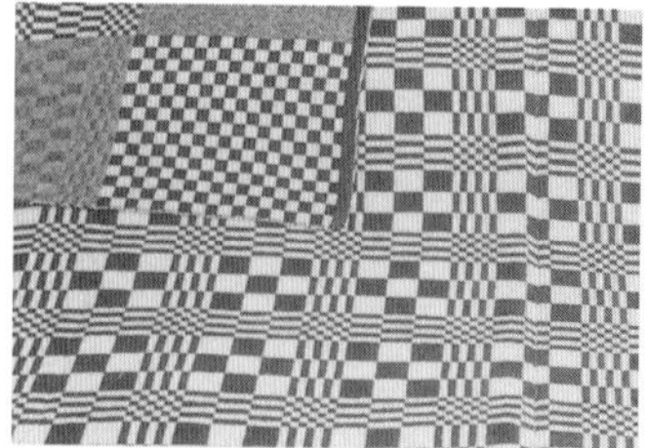

A narrow loom wool tapestry bed cover, in black and white, 19thC, Welsh, 73 x 92in (183.5 x 233.5cm).
£180–200 JJ

Narrow loom covers were made in two pieces and then seamed together, 19th century looms being narrower than modern ones. The word tapestry is used in Wales to describe a double-cloth fabric where two cloths are woven simultaneously.

A cotton patchwork coverlet, the centre panel printed with blooms, the surround of plain and printed hexagonal pieces worked in a lattice pattern, the border with chevron motifs, cotton lined, c1840, 56 x 35¾in (142 x 91cm).
£350–450 B

◄ **A hand-stitched silk patchwork coverlet,** in multi-colours, mid-19thC, 54in (137cm) square.
£315–350 JPr

An embroidered cover, worked on a loosely woven ground in green, terracotta, blue and cream silks in a chequered design with geometric motifs, French, mid-19thC, 72½ x 74¾in (184 x 190cm).
£800–1,000 B

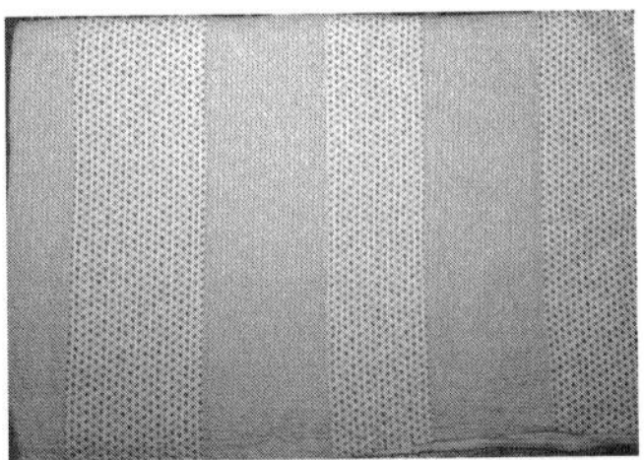

A Durham strip quilt, hand-stitched, late 19thC, 84 x 94in (213.5 x 239cm).
£360–400 JPr

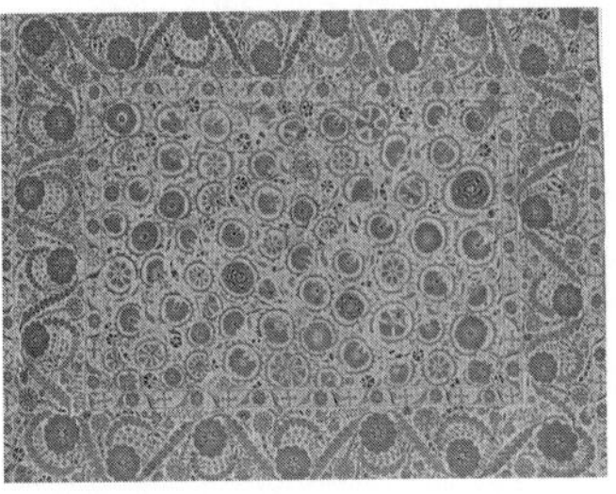

A Bokhara *susani*, embroidered with red flowers on a camel ground, Uzbekistanian, late 19thC, 92 x 75in (233.5 x 190.5cm).
£2,200–2,500 S(O)

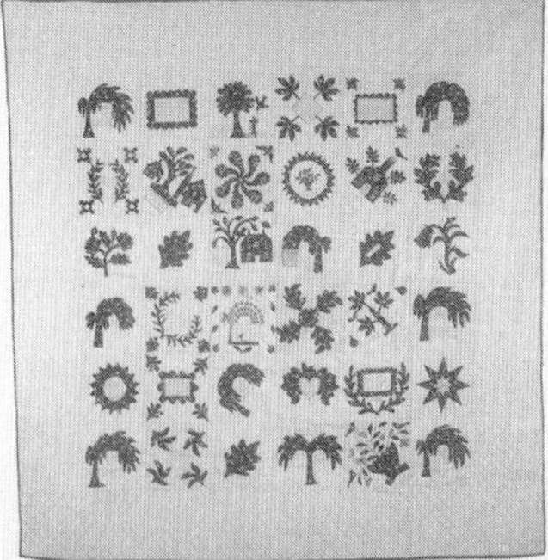

A cotton friendship quilt, with 36 hand-sewn squares appliquéd, embroidered and inscribed by members of the Baptist Church for Reverend William A. Sargent, American, Louden, New Hampshire, c1850.
£1,350–1,500 SK(B)
Reverend Sargent's daughter assembled the squares into a quilt with a border and binding in the 1930s.

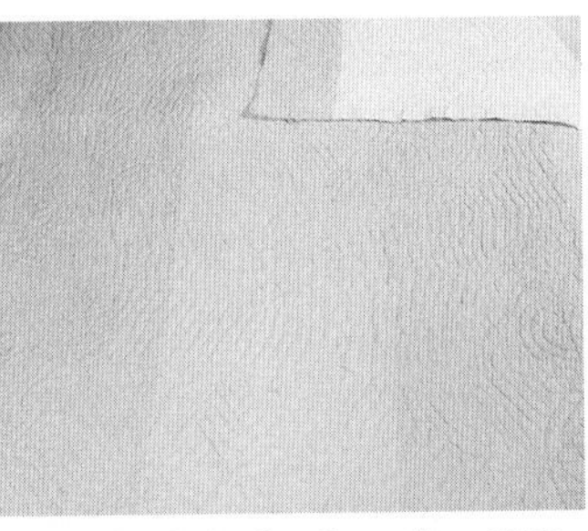

A hand-stitched strip quilt, c1890, 68 x 66in (172.5 x 167.5cm).
£240–300 JJ
A strip quilt, or 'Strippy', is composed of alternating strips of different fabrics, either solid colours or prints. It is very often used as the back of a patchwork or floral quilt.

► **A handmade silk and bobbin lace bed cover,** c1920, 108in (274.5cm) square.
£400–450 JPr

A North Country whole cloth stitched quilt, small repair, c1880, 83 x 82in (211 x 208.5cm).
£275–300 JJ
Each side of this quilt is composed of the same fabric, the artistry lying in the stitching rather than the piecing.

An embroidered black wool cloth cover, applied with coloured wool cloth designed with a central medallion of flowerheads, the border with roundels of a vase of flowers, late 19thC, 63in (160cm) square.
£350–400 P

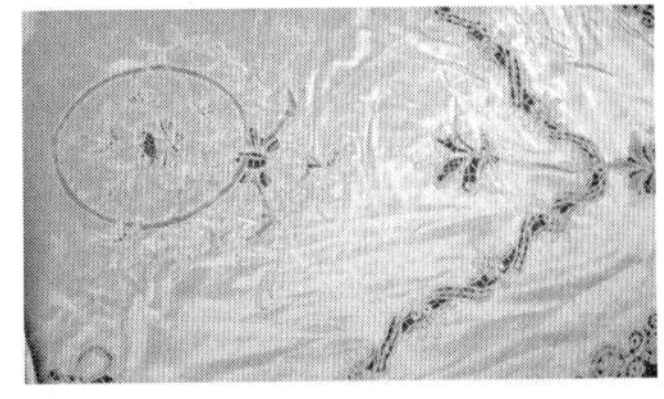

Embroidery & Needlework

A fragment of *Opus Anglicanum* English Work, worked in silks and metal threads, 1400–25, 6¾ x 6½in (17 x 16.5cm).
£1,300–1,500 S(S)
English Work was the name given to ecclesiastical embroidery which gained fame throughout Europe by the middle of the 13th century.

◄ **A crewelwork hanging,** decorated in red, green, brown and yellow on a cream ground, late 17thC, 75 x 37in (190.5 x 94cm).
£4,500–5,500 MGa

Cross Reference
See Colour Review (page 605)

A joined crewelwork panel, worked in shades of red and indigo, with flowering shrubs sprouting from hillocks, late 17th–early 18thC, 18 x 50in (45.5 x 127cm), framed and glazed.
£500–625 TMA

A beadwork picture, depicting a landscape with ruined castles among streams, a waterfall and fields, ships, animals and people, some restoration to the sky, possibly Flemish, late 17th–early 18thC, 21¼ x 30¾in (54 x 78cm), in a 19thC ebonized frame.
£2,400–3,000 S

An embroidered picture, on ivory satin, depicting Charity feeding two children fruits from a cornucopia, Faith to one side and Hope to the other, some wear at top, c1700, 12 x 16in (30.5 x 40.5cm), in an ebonized frame.
£1,300–1,500 S

A pair of silkwork panels, worked in coloured thread, one with a young lady holding a bird, the other with an exotic bird, 18thC, 9 x 7in (23 x 18cm).
£2,200–2,750 HYD

◄ **A bolster cover,** undyed linen embroidered with crimson silk in a lattice pattern, faults, Greek, Naxos, 18thC, 19 x 42in (48.5 x 116.5 cm).
£400–450 P

A canvaswork chair cover, French, mid–18thC, 18 x 19in (45.5 x 48.5cm).
£1,500–1,800 MGa

A silk picture, sewn in shades of blue, russet, green and pink, depicting a family scene with a cottage in the background, with a painted background, late 18thC, 11 x 13in (28 x 33cm).
£550–650 WWo

A silkwork picture, depicting a boy with a dog, late 18thC, 15 x 17in (38 x 43cm).
£400–450 JPr

A silk needlework map of England and Wales, by Mary Goodwin, Walton School, 1795, 20½ x 16½in (52 x 42cm), framed.
£400–500 N

A needlework map, worked in silk threads within a running floral border, inscribed 'England & Wales', c1810, 19 x 17in (48.5 x 43cm), framed.
£420–525 DD

An embroidered silk picture of Moses in the Bulrushes, the contemporary costumes embroidered in blue and pink silk, the hands and faces painted, late 18thC, framed.
£300–370 WWo

A Regency embroidered silkwork picture, the faces and arms painted in watercolours, 7¼in x (18.5cm) wide, in a gilt frame, glazed.
£420–525 MCA

A silk needlework picture, depicting a religious subject, c1810, 11 x 14in (28 x 35.5cm).
£375–425 PSC

A Regency needlework and painted silk picture, depicting a girl in a landscape, with black and gilt *verre églomisé* surround, 13¾ x 11¼in (35 x 28.5cm), in a gilt frame.
£300–375 AH

A woolwork picture, worked in shades of beige, tan, dark green and pink on silk, depicting a shepherdess, with painted faces, hands and background, early 19thC, 12 x 10in (30.5 x 25.5cm).
£450–550 ⊞ WWo

A woolwork picture, depicting two children crossing a stream, a cottage in the distance, 19thC, 10 x 12¼in (25.5 x 31cm), in a mahogany frame.
£200–250 AH

A Victorian embroidered print, *La Mode Illustrée*, 10 x 14in (25.5 x 35.5cm).
£80–100 GAK

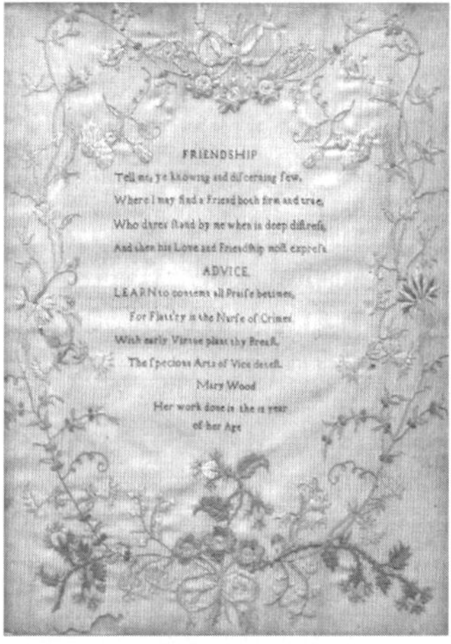

A Regency silkwork panel, by Mary Wood, aged 11, with verses entitled Friendship and Advice, surrounded by a floral border, 16 x 12in (40.5 x 30.5cm).
£1,150–1,500 BR

An early Victorian woolwork picture, depicting two figures with linked arms holding a trail of flowers, with a bird and trees above, within a stylized floral border, 15in (38cm) square, in a rosewood and gilt frame.
£150–200 CDC

A woolwork picture, by Caroline Adshead, aged 10, depicting a Swiss boy and St Joseph, with flower detail, 1851, 19 x 17¼in (48.5 x 44cm), in a later frame.
£65–80 L&E

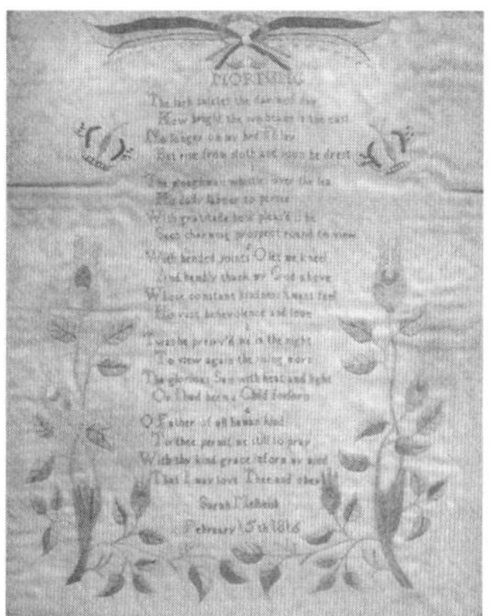

A needlework picture , by Sarah Melhuish, entitled 'Morning', embroidered in coloured silks on a linen ground with verse, bordered by butterflies and flower sprays, 1816, 15¼ x 12¼in (38.5 x 31cm), framed and glazed.
£270–340 F&C

◄ **A pair of Regency silk pictures,** depicting figures in garden settings, with painted faces, minor damage, 7½ x 5½in (19 x 14cm), in gilt frames, glazed.
£250–320 TMA

A woolwork picture of a fisher-woman, 19thC, 16 x 18in (40.5 x 45.5cm), framed.
£200–225 ⊞ DHA

A silk and woolwork picture, worked in brown, red and green silks and wools, depicting a family at rest under an oak tree, 19thC, 13½ x 18½in (34.5 x 47cm), in a gilt frame.
£280–350 Bea(E)

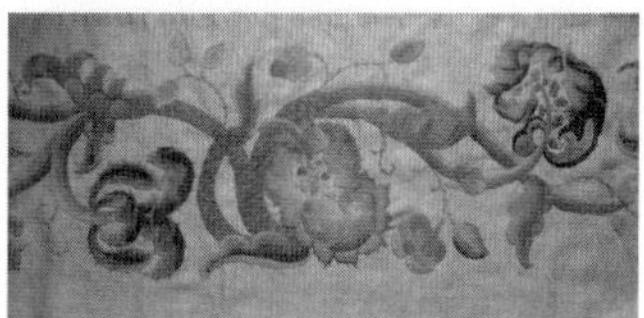

A crewelwork pelmet, late 19thC, 8 x 18in (20.5 x 45.5cm).
£450–500 ⊞ JPr

Lace

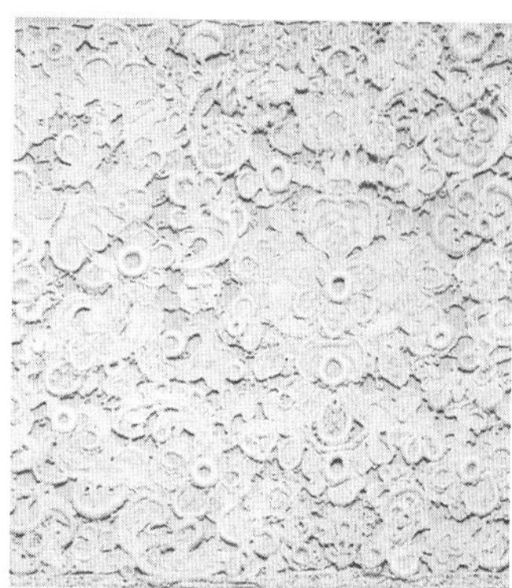

A gros-point Venetian needlelace panel, designed with a flower bloom and a profusion of flowerheads and scrolling leaves, faults, Italian, mid-17thC, 9½ x 45¼in (24 x 115cm), mounted on saffron cotton.
£170–220 B

A panel of Point de France needle-lace, designed with vases of flowers under canopies, the surround with scrolling flowers and leaves, curling tendrils and blossom, faults, French, c1720, 23¾ x 27½in (60.5 x 70cm).
£450–550 B

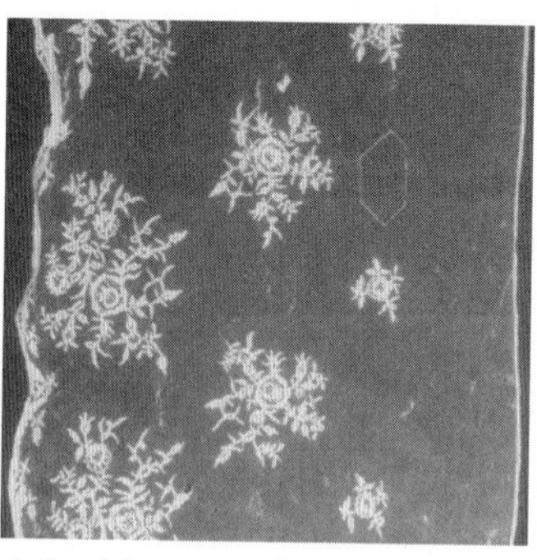

A Carrickmacross flounce and sleeves, c1870, Irish, 137¾ x 12in (350 x 30.5cm).
£80–100 JuC

A tape lace cloth, c1920, 36in (91.5cm) square.
£25–30 AL

A border of needlelace, in the style of Venetian gros point, designed with flower blooms and scrolling leaves, Irish, late 19thC, 4 x 42½in (10 x 108cm).
£300–375 B

Samplers

An embroidered long sampler, by Mary Cox, worked in brown, ivory and green silks with alphabet tests, honeysuckle and other floral borders, late 17thC, 26 x 8¼in (66 x 21cm).
£530–600 S(S)

◄ **A strip sampler,** worked with the alphabet and numerals, inscribed and dated 'AR 1712', 20 x 5½in (51 x 14cm).
£520–650 LFA

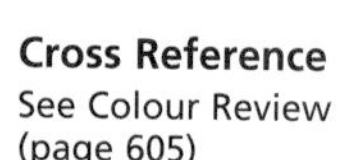

Cross Reference
See Colour Review (page 605)

A silkwork sampler, by Mary Toulmin, worked with alphabet and numbered bands above central verse, within a strawberry zigzag border, 1767, 11¾ x 8¾in (30 x 22cm).
£800–1,000 CGC

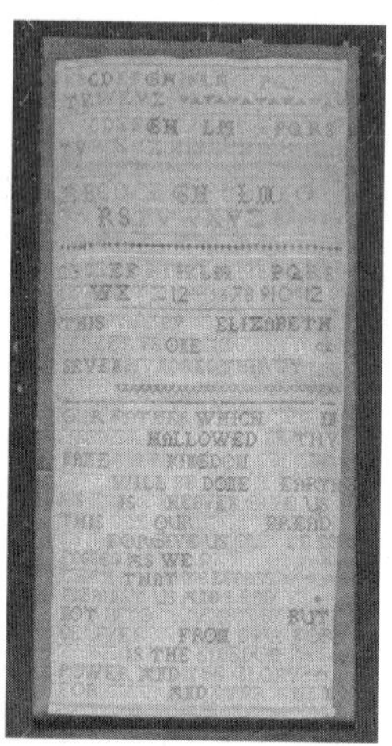

A strip sampler worked in silks, 1735, 18 x 8in (45.5 x 20.5cm).
£800–900 JPr

A needlework sampler, by Mary Hafline, embroidered in silk on linen with Jacob meeting Rebecca at the well, American, Pennsylvania, c1780, 12½in (32cm) square.
£4,500–5,500 S(NY)

A sampler, by Rachel Tatum, worked in coloured silks of greens, browns and greys with alphabet verse and floral sprays, 1789, 13¾ x 12¼in (35 x 31cm).
£360–450 Bea(E)

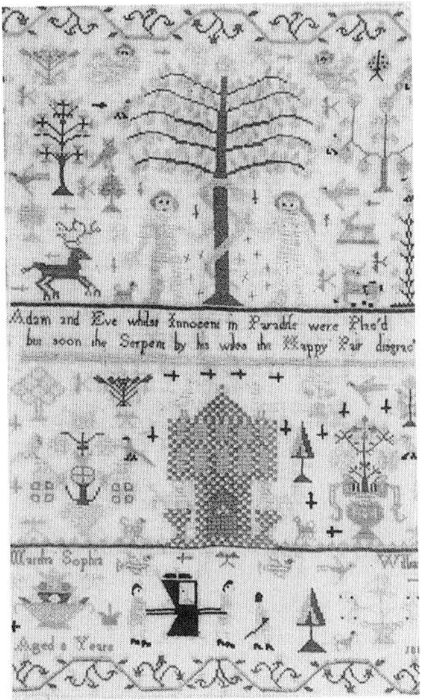

A needlework sampler, by Martha Sophia Williams, aged eight, worked with Adam and Eve, a house, sedan chair, black-faced figure and a verse, 1804, 13 x 10¾in (33 x 27.5cm), framed and glazed.
£1,700–2,200 CAG

A needlework sampler, by Sarah Boynton, aged 13, worked in coloured threads and wool with the alphabet and text above a stylized garden with flower-filled urns, within a Greek key border, 1827, 16¼ x 12¼in (41.5 x 31cm), in a bird's-eye maple frame.
£420–525 RTo

A sampler, by Mary Allcock, worked with the alphabet, American, dated 1790, 14 x 12in (35.5 x 30.5cm).
£1,600–1,800 HCFA

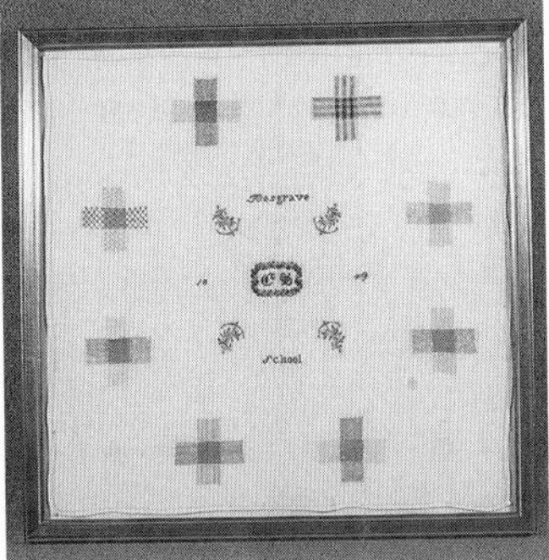

A darning sampler, worked at Kexgrave School, early 19thC, 14in (35.5cm) square.
£700–800 WiA

A sampler, by Mirah Johnson, worked with alphabets, numerals, religious verse and text in black silks, polychrome patterns and motifs within a geometric border, damaged, c1829, 13 x 12in (33 x 30.5cm).
£300–375 G(L)

A needlework sampler, by Sarah Goodwin, decorated with a seated lady within an arbour between stylized apple trees above a Georgian house, dated 1798, 17 x 12½in (43 x 32cm).
£1,150–1,500 BR

A needlework sampler, by Jane Coulsons, aged 13, Salmonfield, 'The Dedication of Solomon's Temple', with decorated text, temple, birds, shrubs and butterflies, early 19thC, 25 x 21in (63.5 x 53.5cm), in a stained wood frame.
£500–550 AG

◄ **An Adam and Eve sampler,** by Elizabeth Smith, worked in wools, 1827, 16 x 13in (40.5 x 33cm).
£600–670 HIS

A sampler, by Ann Sreham, depicting a red brick house flanked by fir trees and deer above text and three potted plants, 1829, 17¾ x 15½in (45 x 39.5cm).
£360–450 CDC

Collecting samplers

Early fine-quality examples in good condition are the most desirable. Condition is critical – check for moth or mould damage, faded colours and run-stained grounds. Professional cleaning and restoration are advisable, and original frames and backboards add to the value.

A miniature sampler, by M. F. Godfrey, 1830, 5 x 6in (12.5 x 15cm).
£330–360 ⊞ HIS

A woolwork sampler, by Emily Mayler, 1830, 10 x 11in (25.5 x 28cm).
£270–300 ⊞ JPr

A needlework sampler, by E. M. Worsham, worked in polychrome threads on a linen ground with rows of the alphabet above a building and a pious verse, losses, American, possibly Danville, Virginia, 1836, 16 x 16½in (40.5 x 42cm), framed.
£3,000–3,500 ⚒ WcH

A commemorative woolwork sampler, by Alice Alcock, depicting a Sunday School surrounded by inscriptions, 1846, 22 x 20in (56 x 51cm).
£650–800 ⊞ WiA

A silk sampler, by Charlotte Thornton, depicting a house with verse and trees within a floral border, dated 1848, 13 x 17in (33 x 43cm).
£1,300–1,450 ⊞ HIS

A woolwork sampler, by Charlotte Edwards, 19thC, 16 x 11½in (40.5 x 29cm), in an oak frame.
£200–240 ⚒ AH

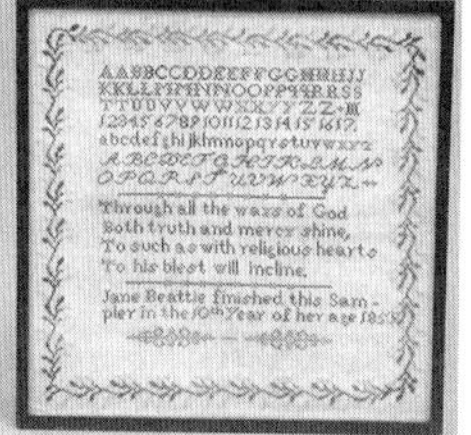

A needlework sampler, by Jane Beattie, aged nine, worked in black thread with alphabets and numerals above a verse, within a border of pink flowering plants, 1859, 12 x 12½in (30.5 x 32cm), in an ebonized frame.
£180–225 ⚒ PFK

A school sampler, by Anna Williamson, 1879, 6in (25cm) square.
£165–185 ⊞ HIS

► **An embroidered sampler,** with geometric patterns and a landscape, South African, with initials M. H. and dated 1943, 19 x 10½in (48.5 x 26.5cm).
£170–220 ⚒ RBB

Tapestries

A tapestry, depicting a bear hunt, surrounded by a border of fruit and foliage, wear and restoration, probably reduced in size, re-woven areas, Flemish, probably Oudenaarde, early 17thC, 114¼ x 98¼in (290 x 249.5cm).
£4,600–5,500 S(P)

A tapestry fragment, possibly the Story of Troy, woven in shades of blue, green and brown, with figures flanking an old man with books, a ship being unloaded in the distance, Flemish, probably Oudenaarde, early 17thC, 88¼ x 61in (224 x 155cm).
£2,200–2,750 S(Am)

An Aubusson Old Testament tapestry fragment, from the story of Judith, depicting two women assuring the Jews of the deliverance of the City of Bethulia, late 17thC, 89½ x 77¼in (227.5 x 196cm).
£2,700–3,400 S(Am)

A wool tapestry, depicting trees and foliage, with a peacock to the foreground, a castle to the background, with black cotton backing, Continental, 17th–18thC, 107 x 106in (272 x 269cm).
£2,700–3,000 SK

An Aubusson chinoiserie tapestry, depicting exotic birds in the foreground before three flowering trees, a pagoda in the clearing, within a scrolling vine border, 18thC, 111 x 143in (282 x 363cm).
£4,200–5,250 S(NY)

A tapestry panel, depicting a courting couple in a landscape, with a temple folly in the distance, within ribbon *guilloche* and a flowerhead border, Continental, 18thC, 70 x 58¼in (178 x 148cm).
£2,700–3,000 SK

A tapestry panel, depicting the Wolf and the Lamb from the *Fables* of La Fontaine, attributed to the Fulham manufactory of Peter Parisot, c1750, 27½ x 22¾in (70 x 58cm), in a carved giltwood frame.
£3,500–4,500 S

Miller's is a price GUIDE not a price LIST

◄ **A tapestry,** depicting Ulysses planning the construction of the Trojan horse, minor restoration, Spanish, 18th–19thC, 84¾ x 82¾in (215.5 x 210cm).
£4,500–5,750 LCM

A tapestry panel, French, c1850, 26in (66cm) square, framed.
£800–900 KA

► **An Aubusson metal-thread tapestry *portière*,** depicting a hanging basket of flowers and floral trophies on an ivory field framed by bulrushes, c1850, 132in x 44in (335.5 x 112cm).
£1,300–1,500 S(S)

Costume

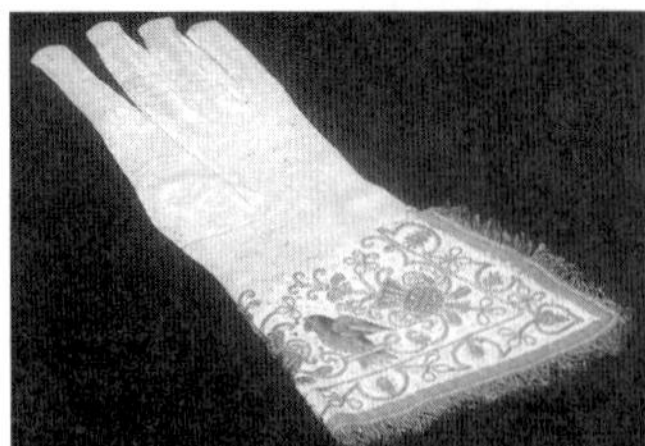

A buff leather glove, the cuff embroidered with coloured silks and applied gold and silver thread, with parrots and vases of flowers, c1640.
£1,100–1,200 ⚒ B

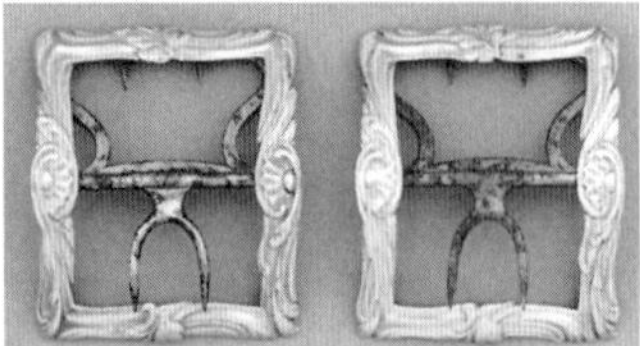

A pair of gold shoe buckles, with shell and scroll repoussé work, base metal backs, French, c1750, 2in (5cm) wide.
£600–750 ⚒ Bon

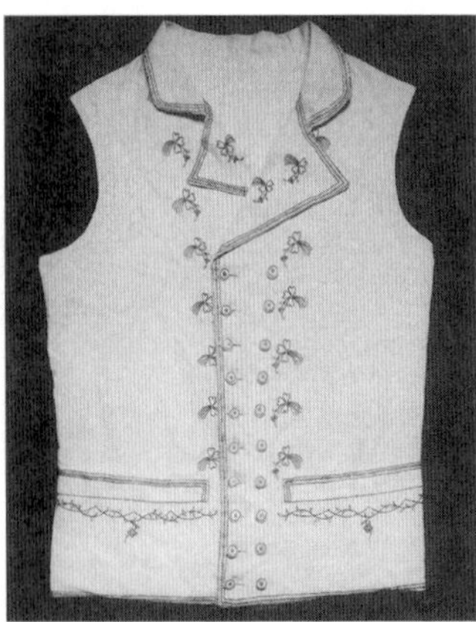

A gentleman's undyed linen waistcoat, the border and buttons embroidered in tan and silver thread, the back embroidered with initials, lined, faults, c1800.
£220–275 ⚒ B

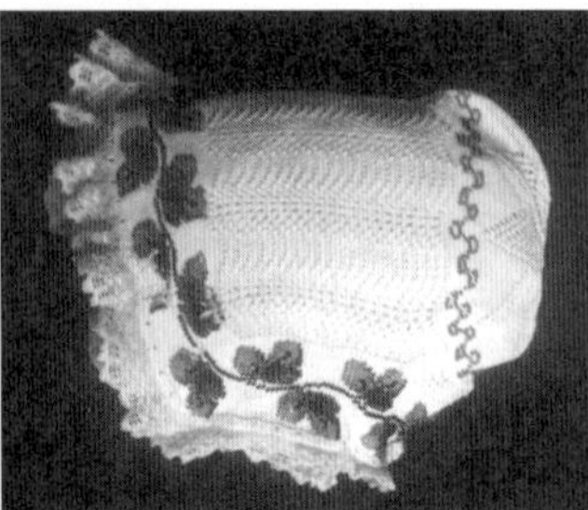

A beaded bonnet, Swiss or German, c1820, 11in (28cm) high.
£160–180 ⊞ JuC

► **A woven-wool long shawl,** in green, brown, golden yellow, pale blue and cream, with initials 'TM' woven to each corner, faults, French, c1850, 116¼ x 55¼in (295.5 x 140.5cm).
£300–375 ⚒ B

A gentleman's Ottoman-style undress hat, embroidered in gold and silver on a leather ground, lined with satin, 18thC.
£160–200 ⚒ HYD

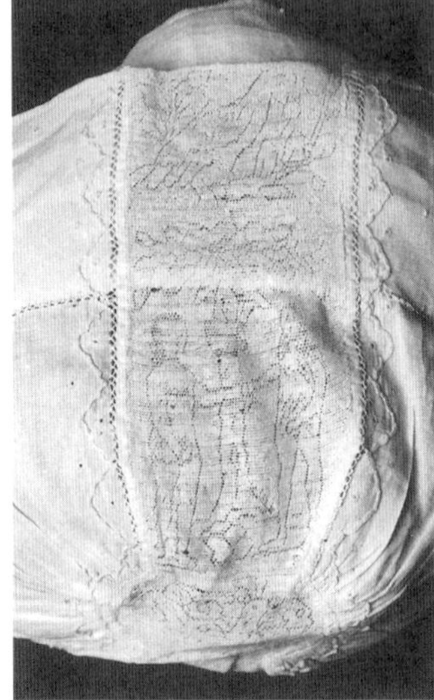

A linen baby bonnet, designed with a peacock, a bird holding a cherry in its beak, and Adam and Eve standing beside the apple tree, with a needlelace insertion from the forehead to the nape, c1760.
£900–1,100 ⚒ B

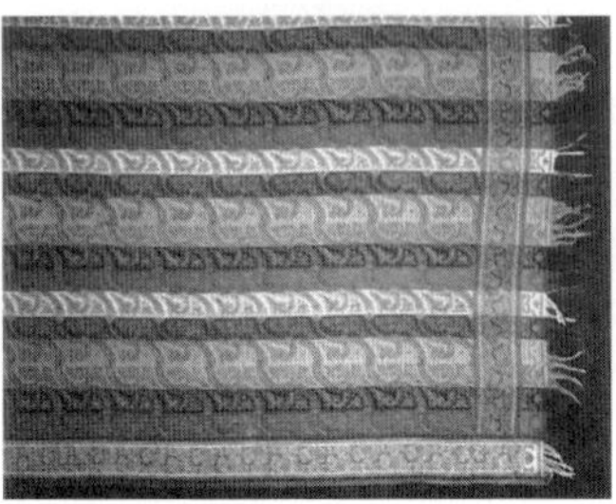

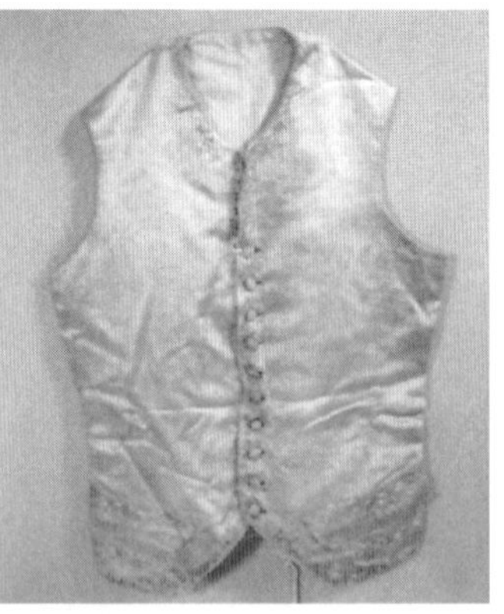

A gentleman's waistcoat, in canary-yellow silk with floral silk embroidery, 1740–50.
£200–250 ⚒ WW

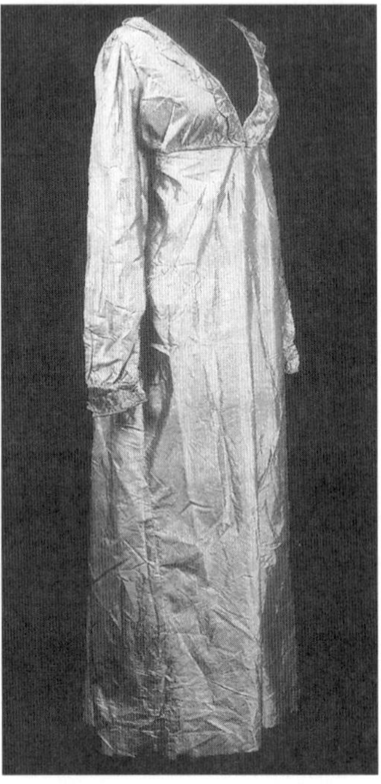

A grey silk dress, the bodice and cuffs with ruched frill and lilac braid trim, altered, c1800.
£600–750 ⚒ B

◄ **A beaded bag,** with a gilt frame, early 19thC, 4in (10cm) long.
£100–120 ⊞ JPr

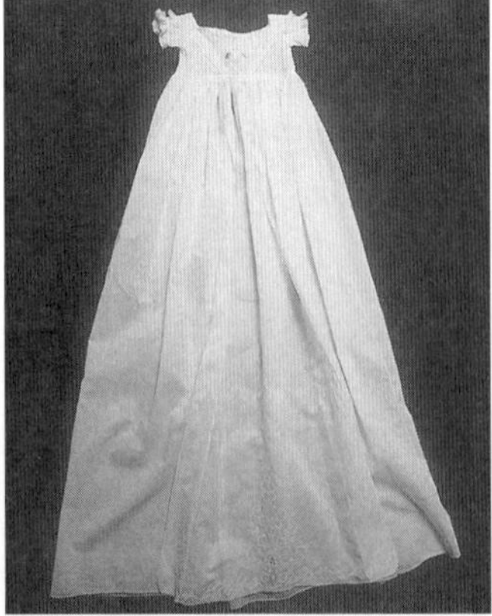

An Ayrshire embroidery christening robe, c1840, 46in (117cm) long.
£100–110 ⊞ JuC

A shop sample silk dress, 1850–60, 18in (45.5cm) long.
£325–360 ⊞ JPr

A Victorian woven-silk Paisley shawl, 68 x 72in (173 x 183cm).
£350–400 ⊞ DE

A pair of wood and leather clogs, c1900, 12in (30.5cm) long.
£80–90 ⊞ MLL

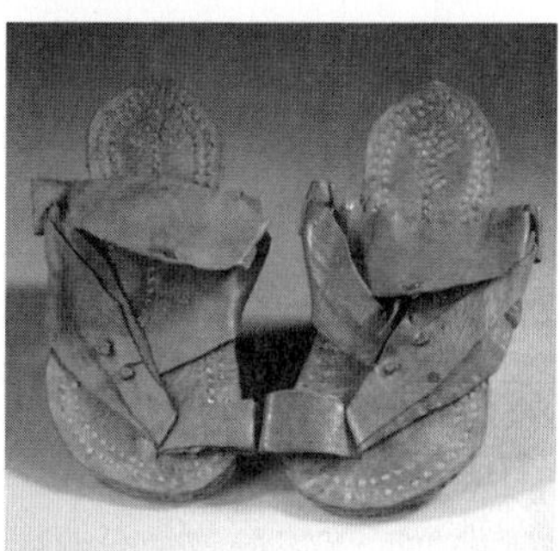

A pair of T. E. Lawrence's tan leather desert sandals, with embroidered detailing to the soles, c1917, 10½in (26.5cm) long.
£2,000–2,200 ⚒ S

A pair of lady's black-beaded satin shoes, c1920, 9in (23cm) long.
£60–70 ⊞ BaN

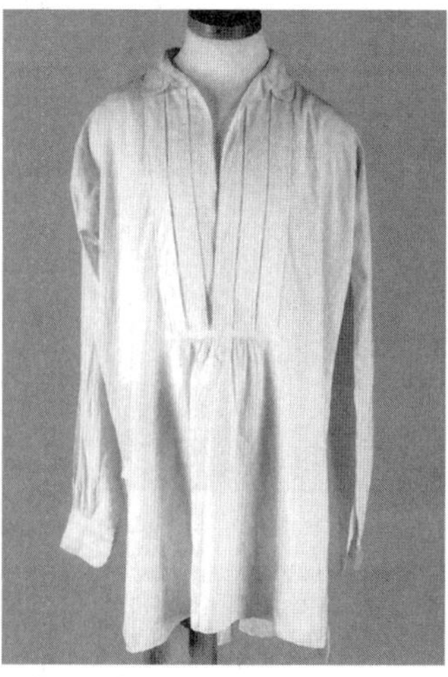

A linen shirt, owned by Prince Albert, with blind tucks to the front, embroidered to one hip in blue silks with the royal crown, initial 'A' and dated 1854.
£700–900 ⚒ S

A Paisley shawl, Kashmiri, late 19thC, 76in (193cm) square.
£800–1,000 ⚒ S(O)

A cocktail dress, worked with silver bugle beads on a black ground, with label 'Made in France', 1920s.
£200–240 ⚒ HYD

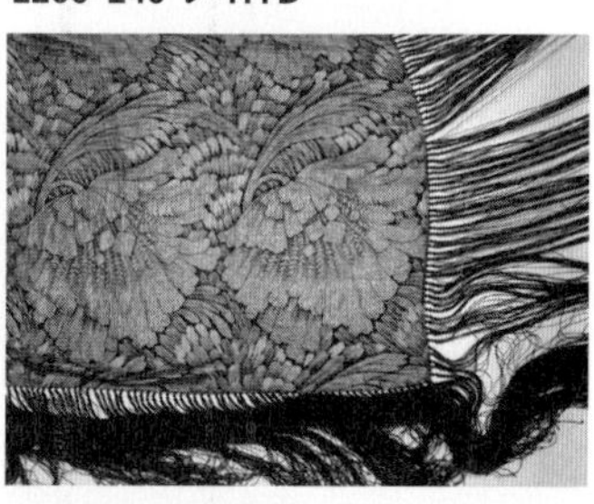

A silk lamé shawl, 1930s, 24 x 48in (61 x 122cm).
£315–350 ⊞ JPr

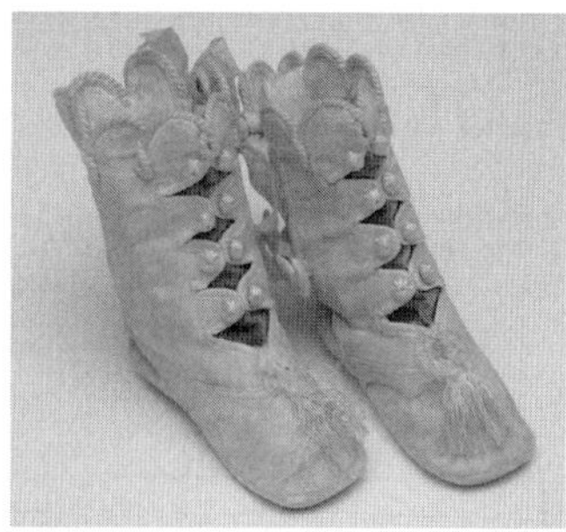

A child's pair of silk shoes, c1860, 5in (12.5cm) high.
£160–180 ⊞ JPr

A pair of lady's silk bootees, c1880.
£115–130 ⊞ JPr

An Edwardian evening dress, with black beading and a turquoise underskirt.
£120–140 ⚒ SWO

A Jax pale pink shantung silk outfit, worn by Marilyn Monroe in *The Seven Year Itch*, American, 1955.
£18,000–22,000 ⚒ S

Fans

A fan, the paper leaf painted with a shepherd shearing a sheep, a lady and her male companion seated nearby, the carved ivory sticks and guards with piqué work and mother-of-pearl appliqué, faults, Italian, c1720.
£300–375 B

A fan, the paper leaf painted with children and adults in the countryside, with carved and painted ivory sticks, French, late 18thC, 10in (25.5cm) long, with a satin-lined card box.
£300–375 B

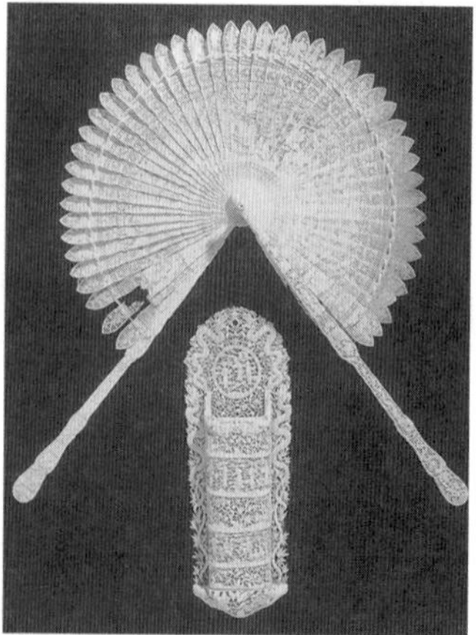

A Chinese export ivory cockade fan, the sticks carved and pierced with figures at leisure and play in garden scenes, sticks missing, faults, early 19thC, 12½in (32cm) long, with carved ivory wall case.
£1,000–1,250 B

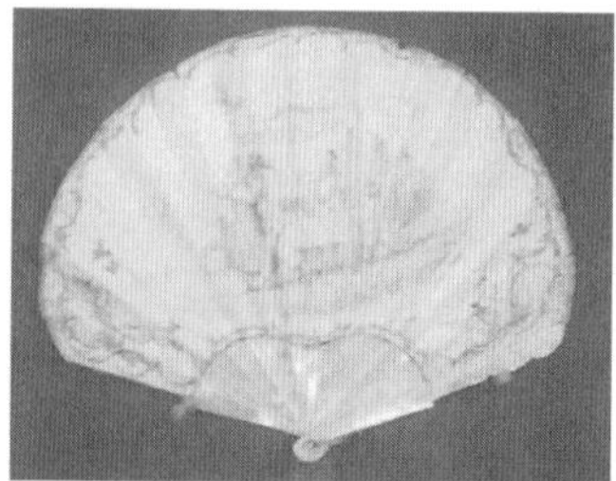

A fontange fan, the chicken skin leaf painted with figures revelling in a landscape, mother-of-pearl sticks and guards, 19thC, 6¼in (16cm) long, in a Duvelleroy box.
£100–120 WW

A fan, the paper leaf painted with a shepherd and his lady in a pastoral landscape, carved ivory sticks and guards, probably German, c1765, 10½in (26.5cm) long.
£170–200 S(Am)

A Chinese export ivory brisé fan, the sticks carved and pierced with rosettes, birds and shells below a swag border suspending from bat motifs, the centre with an oval medallion reserving a vacant shield, minor damage, c1800, 7½in (19cm) long, boxed.
£100–125 B(Ba)

A hand-coloured print fan, with pierced ivory sticks, c1830, 10in (25.5cm) long.
£235–260 JPr

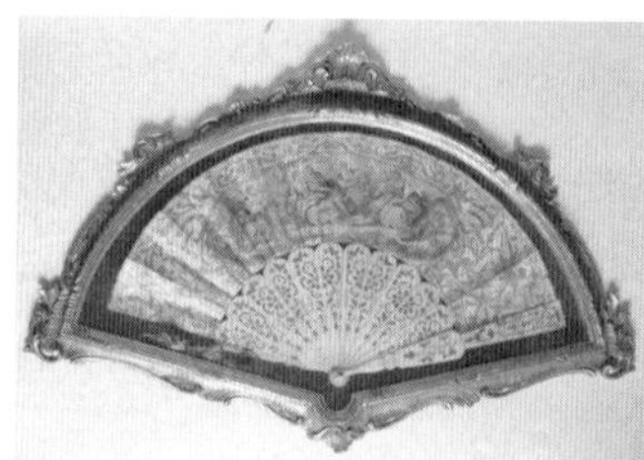

A cased fan, with a gilded and hand-coloured leaf and pierced ivory sticks, French, 19thC, 25in (63.5cm) wide.
£400–450 JPr

► **A fan,** the printed and painted leaf designed with the family of Darius before Alexander, the gorge with companions, the reverse with a group kneeling before a shrine in black, grey and white, with carved, pierced and silvered mother-of-pearl sticks, faults, probably French, c1860, 11¼in (28.5cm) long, with a velvet-covered box.
£200–250 B

A chinoiserie fan, the painted leaf decorated with appliqué ivory, fabric, and feathers, red lacquer sticks, c1780, 10¾in (27.5cm) long.
£380–420 S(Am)

A fan, decorated with figures, phoenixes and other birds, minor damage, Chinese, Qing dynasty, early 19thC, 9in (23cm) long.
£350–450 BUK

A Chinese export tortoiseshell brisé fan, the sticks carved and pierced with figures at leisure in garden scenes, the surround with flowers and blossom, c1840, 7½in (19cm) long.
£650–800 P

A cased fan, with painted leaf and carved and pierced ivory sticks, French, mid-19thC, 24in (61cm) wide.
£315–350 JPr

A Chinese export tortoiseshell brisé fan, the shaped sticks carved with horses, boats, bridges and garden scenes, the guards with figures, trees and flowers, c1870, 9½in (24cm) long, with a carved sandalwood box.
£1,200–1,350 B

A Bruges lace fan, with painted and carved mother-of-pearl and ivory sticks, c1880, 9in (23cm) long.
£145–160 JPr

A fan, the Brussels *point de gaze* needlelace leaf designed with a dog and birds before a cottage, with horn sticks, faults, Belgian, c1890, 8in (20.5cm) long.
£340–425 B

A Japanese export fan, the paper leaf painted with peasants in the countryside, the reverse with wisteria and chrysanthemums, with bamboo sticks, the ivory guards and *ojime* with *shibayama* decoration, late 19thC, 15in (38cm) long.
£500–625 P

An Edwardian bone, lace and gauze fan, hand-painted with apple blossom, 14in (35.5cm) long.
£75–85 JPr

A Chinese export fan, the painted paper leaf with groups of scholars and dignitaries, with applied ivory and silk with pierced ivory sticks and carved guards, Chinese, c1870, 10¾in (27.5cm) long, with a black and gilt lacquer box.
£450–550 P

A Brussels mixed-lace fan, with tortoiseshell sticks, c1880, 9in (23cm) long.
£145–160 JPr

A fan, the Empress Calendar 1898, the 12 card sections pierced and chromolithographed with children, flowers and birds representing the months of the year, 17in (43cm) wide.
£85–100 DW

A fan, the black gauze leaf with gilt spangle and green silk appliqué designed with scrolls, flowers and leaves, the green-stained carved bone sticks decorated with ribbons and flowers, c1900, 8¾in (22cm) long, with a satin-lined card box.
£300–375 B

► **A fan,** with paper-card leaves colour printed with the heads of European statesmen and military leaders, cane guards, facsimile signatures, Austrian, c1914, 7in (18cm) long.
£100–125 DW

A Chantilly lace fan, the black leaf mounted onto plain tortoiseshell sticks and guards, one stick broken, c1880, 10¼in (26cm) long, with a white card J. Duvelleroy box.
£3,500–4,000 S
This fan belonged to Alice Liddell, who was immortalized by Lewis Carroll in *Alice in Wonderland*.

A lacquered ivory fan, decorated on both sides with a pheasant beside a rose mallow shrub among autumn grasses, the guard with birds and insects, all in gold-coloured *takamakie, hiramakie* and *e-nashiji*, minor inlay loss, Japanese, Meiji period, 1868–1911, 20in (51cm) wide.
£3,400–4,250 S

A fan, the Brussels *point de gaze* needlelace leaf inset with a central gauze panel painted with a nymph, a panel to each reserve of dancing *amoretti*, with mother-of-pearl sticks, signed 'M. Rodigue', French, c1890, 14¼in (36cm) long.
£300–375 B

A fan, the paper leaf painted on both sides with figures on terraces with borders of animals, buildings and flowers, with carved ivory sticks and guards, Chinese, early 20thC, 13in (33cm) long.
£250–320 PF

Jewellery
Bangles & Bracelets

A gold seven-row bracelet, with citrine clasp, 19thC, 6¼in (16cm) long.
£350–450 S(S)

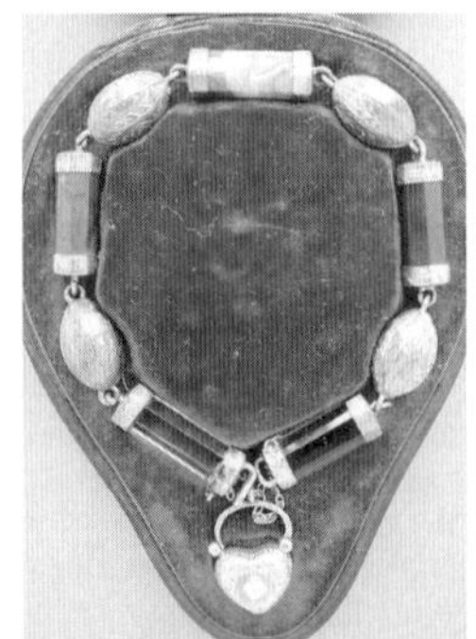

A pair of Victorian 14ct gold bangles, with a black-enamelled Greek key pattern.
£600–750 SLN

◀ **A Victorian gold-mounted bracelet,** set with hardstone and semi-precious stones spaced by engraved gold links, with a pearl-set padlock clasp, Scottish, 6¼in (16cm) long, with fitted case.
£480–600 G(L)

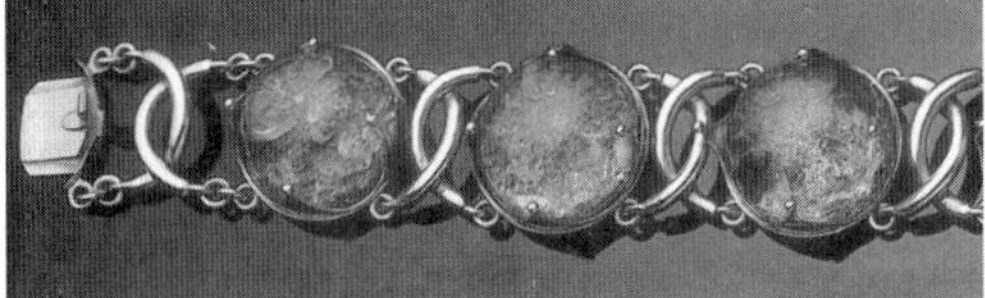

A Victorian rock crystal bracelet, mounted in gold, c1870, 8in (20.5cm) long, in a fitted case by Marshall & Sons, Edinburgh.
£1,600–2,000 P(Ed)

A *pietra dura* and gold-mounted bracelet, with seven panels, 19thC.
£1,300–1,600 E

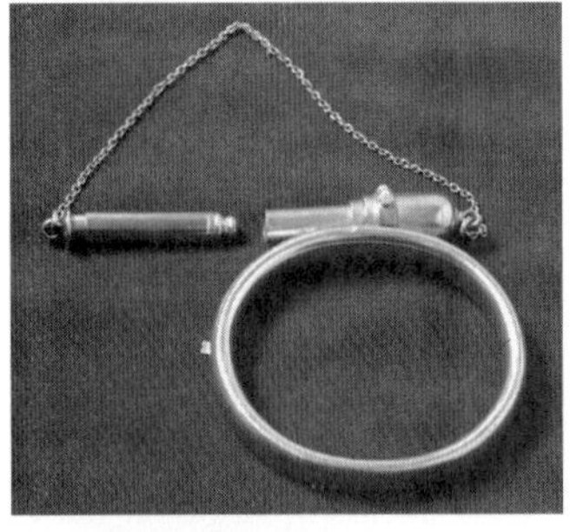

An 18ct gold bangle, mounted with a telescopic pencil modelled as a cannon, c1880, 2½in (6.5cm) wide.
£1,500–1,650 ⊞ NBL

An 18ct gold openwork navette-shape panel bracelet, c1880, 7in (18cm) long.
£800–900 ⊞ NBL

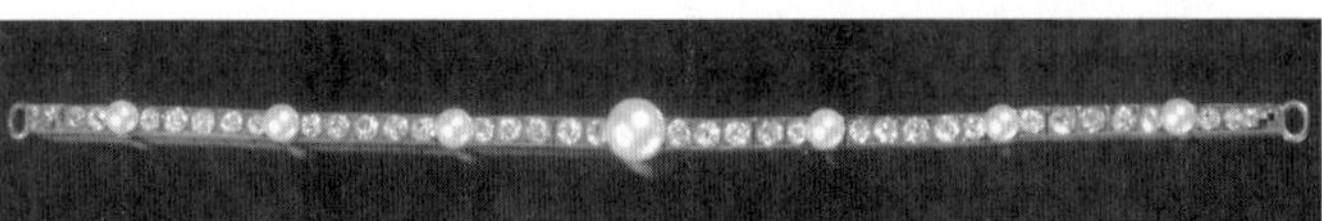

A gold, silver, diamond, pearl and cultured pearl bracelet, with clasp conversion fitments for wear as a choker or bandeau, late 19thC.
£3,700–4,700 Bea(E)

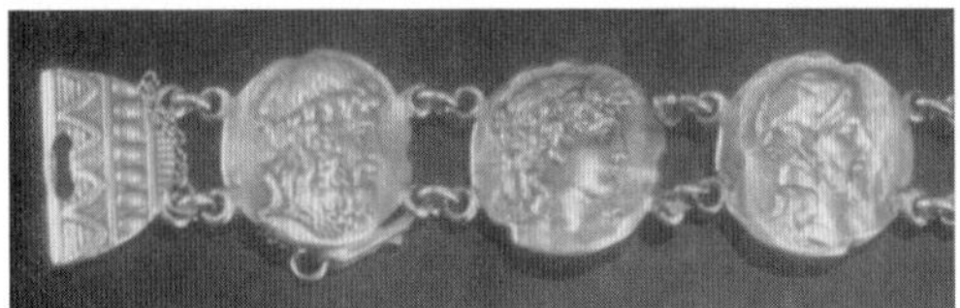

A sterling silver link bracelet, comprising six medallions depicting the profiles of classical figures, hallmark for Shiebler, c1900, 7½in (19cm) long.
£350–450 SK

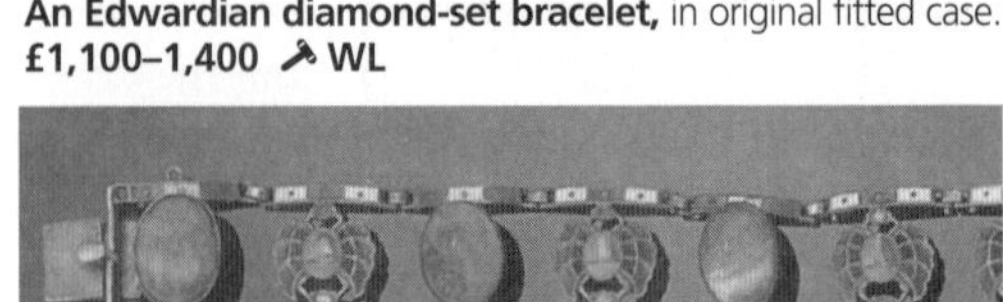

An Edwardian diamond-set bracelet, in original fitted case.
£1,100–1,400 WL

A 15ct gold nautical pennant alphabet bracelet, set with flags, each representing a letter of the alphabet and spelling out 'Remembrance', c1920, 8in (20.5cm) long.
£675–750 ⊞ TGL

▶ **A 14ct gold bracelet,** set with diamonds and synthetic sapphires, c1935.
£1,000–1,200 BUK

An Egyptian revival bracelet, with alternating carved amethyst cabochons in the shape of scarab beetles and turquoise enamel scarabs with *plique-à-jour* detailing, Cairo, Egyptian, c1920, in maker's original cardboard box for R. Sednaoui.
£225–275 LJ

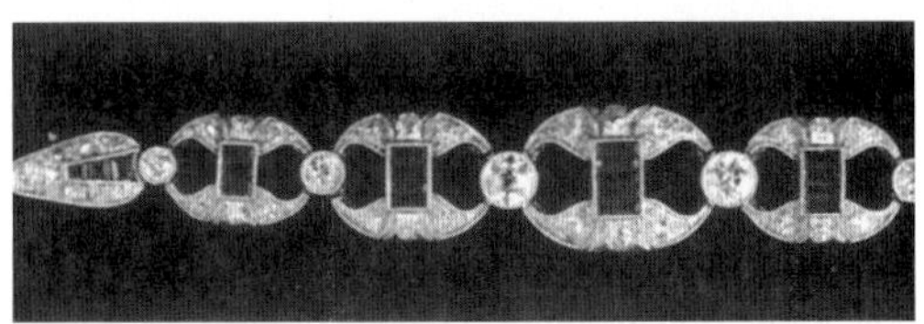

Brooches

A chrysoberyl brooch, in a gold foliate and cannetille mount, early 19thC, in a fitted case.
£360–450 ⚒ L

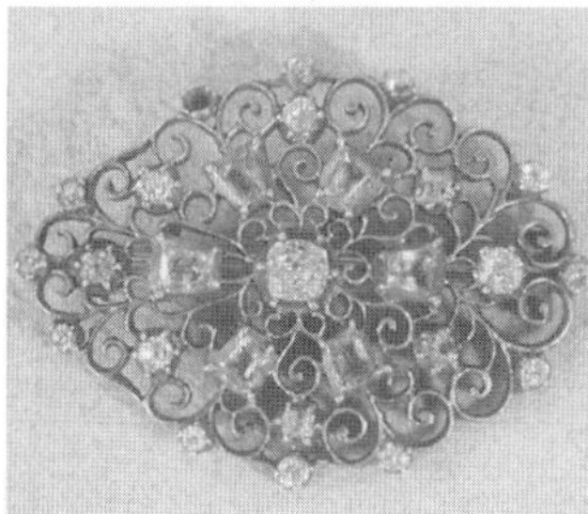

An open-scrolled brooch, set with diamonds and green stones, 19thC, 1½in (4cm) wide.
£340–425 ⚒ CGC

A Victorian pebble brooch, set with various agates and part floral engraved, Scottish.
£170–220 ⚒ DN

A Victorian mosaic brooch, set with semi-precious stones, Scottish, 3½in (9cm) wide.
£100–125 ⚒ WBH

A suite of brooch/pendant and earrings, the painted, enamelled, mother-of-pearl plaques surrounded by cut steel, slight damage, early 19thC.
£280–350 ⚒ WL

Cut steel jewellery was extremely popular in France and Britain from the 18th century. The facetted steel studs produce a rich, sparkling effect. The industry originated in Woodstock, Oxfordshire, and was developed by the famous engineer and manufacturer Matthew Boulton in the second half of the 18th century.

Agate jewellery

Scottish agate jewellery was very popular in the last quarter of the 19th century, the more so because it was very affordable. Pieces normally incorporate different coloured stained agate and carnelian, with the natural grain of the stone showing through. Settings are generally silver or gilt metal. There is still a lot of this type of jewellery in existence and it is keenly collected, but bracelets in good condition are getting harder to find. It is important to check that all the agate pieces are intact and undamaged as missing or broken pieces are expensive to replace or restore.

A Victorian 15ct gold brooch, of flower-burst design, set with turquoises and diamonds, 1¼in (3cm) wide.
£300–325 ⊞ ReJ

◄ **A pebble brooch,** set with a citrine, surrounded by a border of foil-backed quartz and agate panels, mounted in silver with engraved borders, Scottish, c1880, 2in (5cm) diam.
£270–340 ⚒ P(Ed)

A brooch, painted with a landscape on mother-of-pearl, 19thC, 2¾in (7cm) wide.
£110–140 ⚒ SWO

A Neapolitan coral brooch, carved with Bacchus in a vine and ram's head border, 19thC, 1¾in (4.5cm) high.
£340–425 ⚒ G(L)

A 15ct gold and silver brooch, in the shape of a wild rose, set with diamonds, c1880, 1in (2.5cm) wide.
£900–985 ⊞ WIM

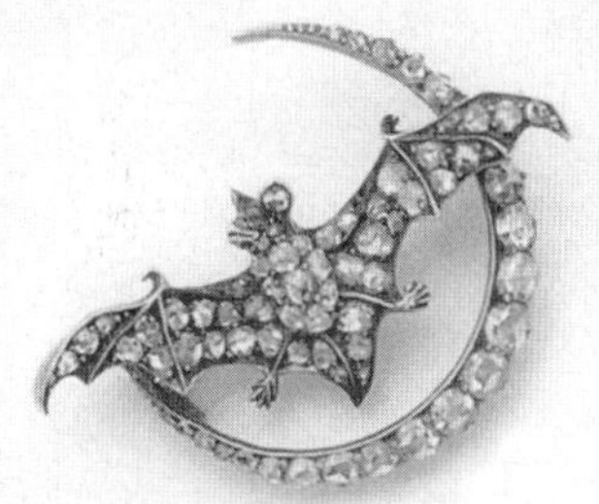

A diamond brooch, in the shape of a crescent moon and flying bat, mounted in silver and gold, c1870, 1¾in (4.5cm) wide.
£2,000–2,400 ⚒ B

LOCATE THE SOURCE
The source of each illustration in Miller's can be found by checking the code letters below each caption with the Key to Illustrations, pages 794–800.

JEWELLERY

Cameos

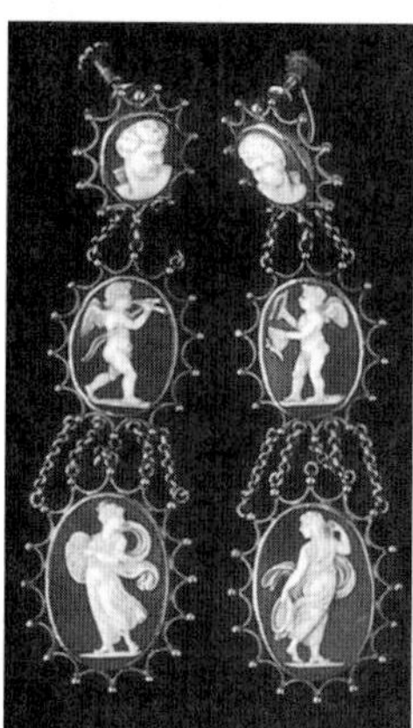

A pair of shell cameo earrings, depicting classical figures, three chains broken, early 19thC, 3in (7.5cm) long.
£700–850 L

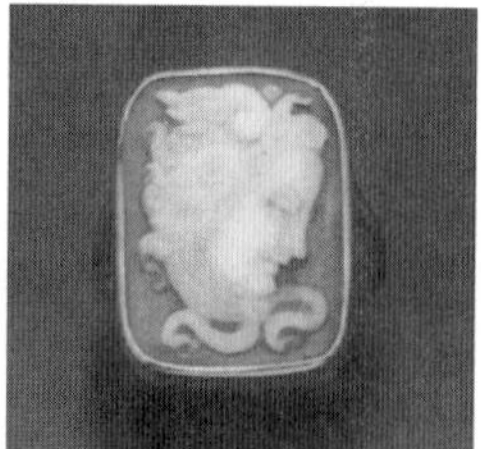

An early Victorian shell cameo ring, carved to depict the head of Medusa.
£180–225 B(Ba)

An early Victorian black opal cameo ring, carved to depict the face of a monkey, with red cabochon-cut eyes.
£500–625 B(Ba)

A shell cameo brooch, carved to depict the Three Graces, c1850.
£220–275 B(Ba)

► **A lava cameo pendant,** carved to depict a Bacchante, set in a contemporary mount with box-link chain, c1860.
£250–320 B(Ba)

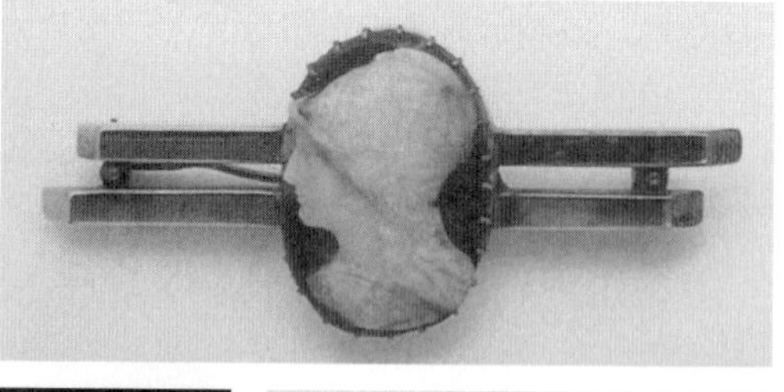

A lava cameo bracelet, with portrait cameos mounted in gold and engraved to the reverse with the names of each character, including Dante and Macchiavelli, 19thC, 7in (18cm) long.
£600–725 L

A Victorian shell cameo brooch, depicting a profile of Zeus within a gold foliate-engraved border, 2in (5cm) wide.
£230–280 S(S)

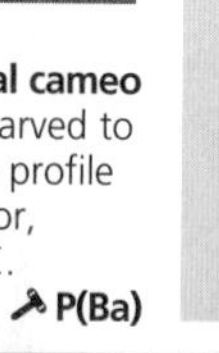

► **An opal cameo brooch,** carved to depict the profile of a warrior, late 19thC.
£700–875 P(Ba)

A Victorian carved shell cameo brooch, depicting the profile of a girl, with fruiting vine decoration to her hair, the frame with wirework decoration, 2¼in (5.5cm) high.
£550–700 L

A Victorian gold-framed shell cameo brooch, depicting Roman figures, 3in (7.5cm) wide.
£200–250 GAK

A late Victorian shell cameo brooch, carved to depict a female classical figure, with floral bouquets to her hair.
£260–325 P(S)

A late Victorian shell cameo brooch, carved to depict a maiden in profile, within a bead and wirework surround, cased.
£220–275 Bon

A lava cameo brooch, relief-carved with two figures and a goose in clouds, surrounded by a twisted 14ct gold-work border, c1890.
£460–575 NOA

Cufflinks

► **A pair of diamond cufflinks,** and three matching studs, 19thC.
£1,500–1,800 S

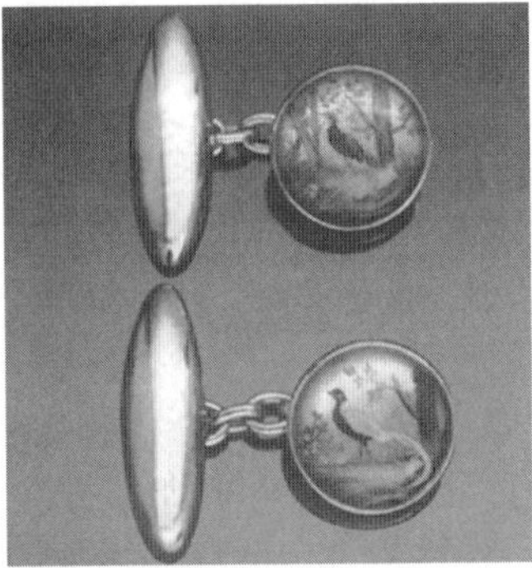

A pair of late Victorian painted reverse intaglio cufflinks, depicting pheasants.
£380–475 Bon

A pair of enamel and gold Royal Presentation cufflinks, the plaques decorated with the monogram of Edward VII in black and white opaque enamel, c1910.
£1,100–1,400 B
Probably made to commemorate the death of Edward VII on 6 May 1910.

Miller's is a price GUIDE not a price LIST

◄ **A pair of cufflinks,** decorated in enamel with a rose motif, within a border of diamonds, 1920s.
£3,350–4,000 S

Earrings

A pair of amethyst pendant earrings, mid-19thC.
£280–350 B(Ba)

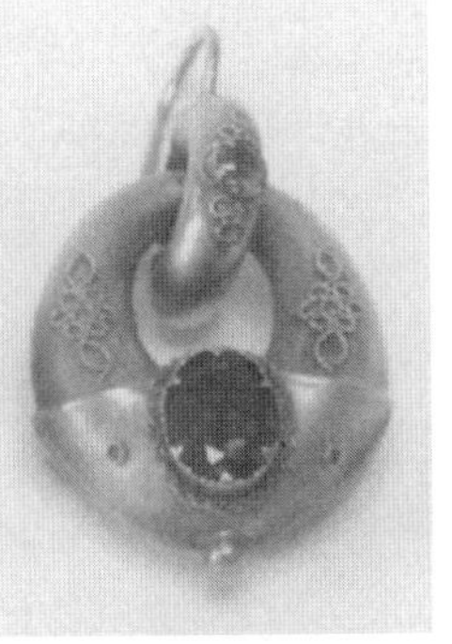

A pair of Victorian gold earrings, set with amethysts.
£150–200 LFA

A pair of Victorian hair pendant earrings, c1850.
£380–475 P(Ba)

A pair of turquoise and pearl earrings, set in 15ct gold, with black enamel detail, c1860, 1¼in (3cm) long.
£800–875 WIM

A pair of garnet pendant earrings, late 19thC, 1¾in (4.5cm) long.
£350–450 Bon

A pair of white gold, pearl and diamond pendant earrings, c1900.
£650–820 LCM

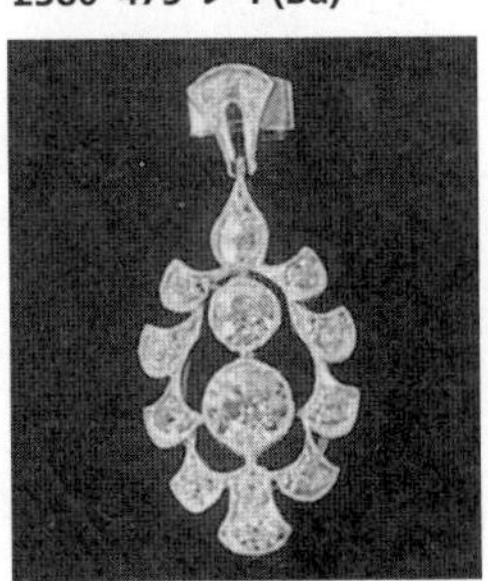

A pair of Edwardian diamond-set pendant earrings, of pierced leaf design.
£1,700–2,200 GAK

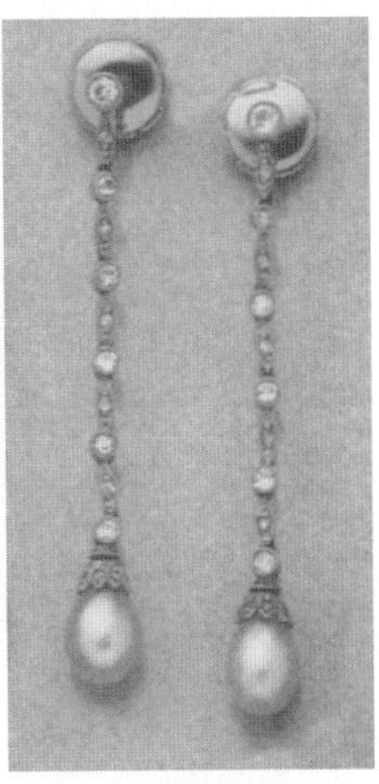

A pair of Belle Epoque pearl and diamond pendant earrings, c1910.
£1,300–1,500 SHSY

Cross Reference
See Colour Review (page 609)

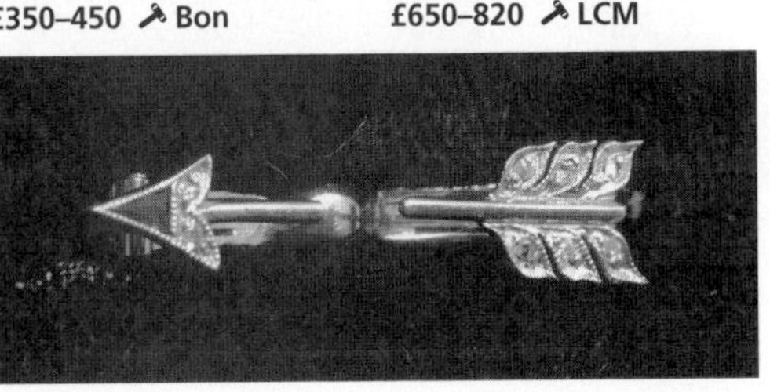

◄ **A pair of 18ct gold and platinum arrow earrings,** set with rubies and diamonds, 1930s, 1in (2.5cm) long.
£580–650 TGL

JEWELLERY

Necklaces

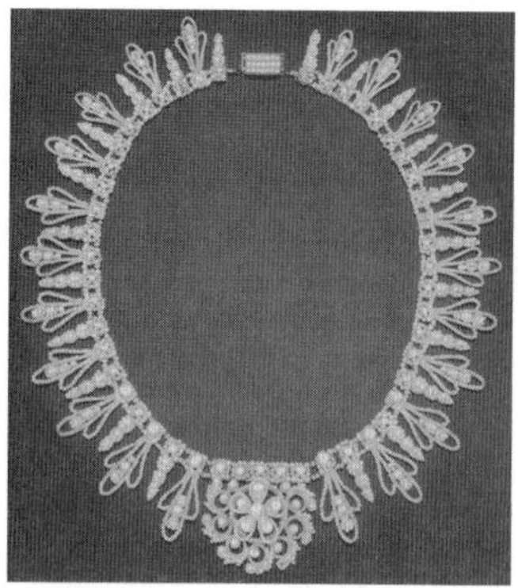

A seed pearl collar, c1800, in a red leather presentation case.
£700–800 ⚒ LJ

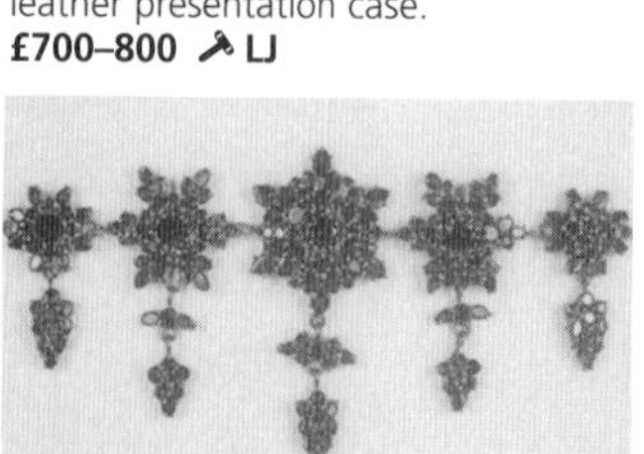

A Victorian necklace, with garnet-set flowerheads and pendant clusters.
£800–1,000 ⚒ B&L

► A 15ct gold bead-chain necklace, c1880, 18in (45.5cm) long.
£1,700–1,875 ⊞ WIM

A Regency seed pearl rope necklace, the clasp formed from two portrait miniatures of gentlemen in uniform.
£300–375 ⚒ HYD

A tortoiseshell necklace, suspending a locket with an applied cluster of turquoises in the shape of a flower.
£150–200 ⚒ B(Ba)

A half-pearl and pink topaz necklace, c1890, cased.
£1,350–1,700 ⚒ P(Ba)

◄ A silver, shell and pearl necklace, each shell with a button pearl to centre, suspending a removable pendant cross, stamped 'TTJ & Son, Sydney', Australian, c1890, 18in (45.5cm) long.
£1,300–1,500 ⚒ SK

► A gold, half-pearl and sapphire necklace, probably by S. Smith, c1900.
£1,000–1,250 ⚒ TEN

An Edwardian 15ct gold necklet, set with turquoise and seed pearls, stamped, in original fitted case.
£500–600 ⚒ WL

JEWELLERY

Pendants

A jewelled and enamelled gold-mounted pearl pendant, modelled as a salamander encircling a ruby, with cabochon-set eyes and opaque white enamel mouth, the reverse with green *champlevé* enamelled scale decoration, 17thC.
£1,400–1,700 ⚒ B

The mythological salamander, which thrives as it burns, is representative of passionate love. This pendant was probably intended as a gift of fidelity and may have originally formed part of a Renaissance ear pendant. The colour combination of red and green is typically found in Renaissance objects, while the workmanship and subject matter are possible indications of Spanish or Portuguese origin.

► **A silver and metal locket,** the Japanese-style decoration depicting a crane flying over a pool at sunset, on a gold guard chain, late 19thC.
£400–500 ⚒ Bea(E)

An Edwardian gold pendant, modelled as a diamond-set bar and two knife-edge suspensions with a single pear-shaped sapphire drop and a larger pear-shaped drop set with three diamonds, on a trace link chain, 2¾in (7cm) long.
£850–1,100 ⚒ G(L)

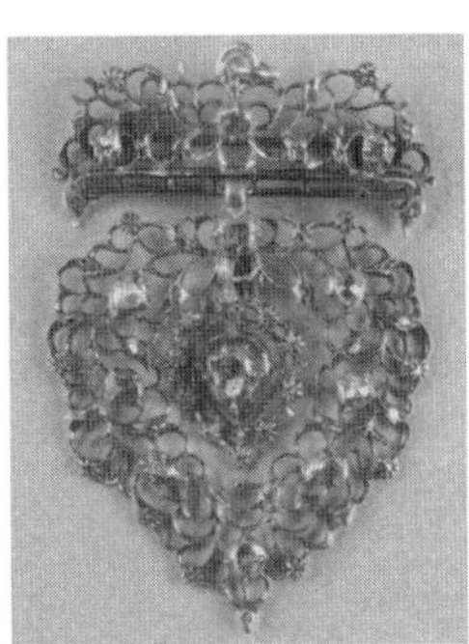

A gold and silver Flemish heart pendant, set with diamonds, marks for 1815–32.
£550–650 ⚒ BERN

A cross pendant, set with diamonds, Continental, c1820, 1¾in (4.5cm) long.
£500–550 ⊞ NBL

A coral and gold cross pendant, with an ivory centre, c1820, 2in (5cm) long.
£115–130 ⊞ JSM

Care of jewellery

Keep items of jewellery separately in small boxes or suede or felt pouches – heaping them together in a jewellery box will damage them. Pearls should always be kept separately from gemstones, because the metal claws of gem settings can scratch a pearl and ruin its surface lustre. Rings should not be allowed to knock against each other as this can result in chipped stones and scratched or dented settings. Intense heat can dry out or crack organic materials such as tortoiseshell, ivory, coral and opals.

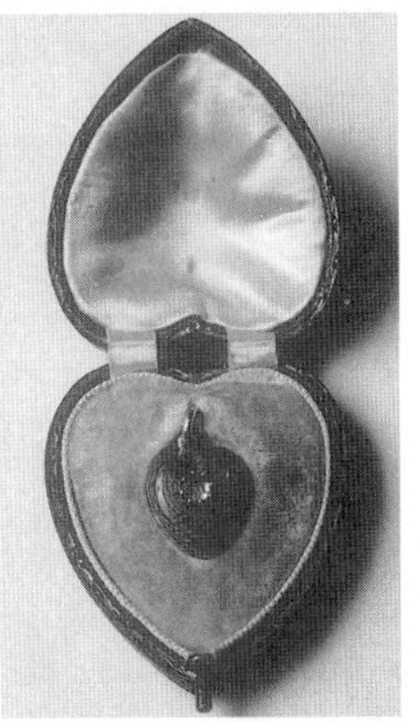

A red enamel heart pendant, centred with a diamond, c1880, ½in (2cm) long, in original box.
£1,600–1,800 ⊞ BeE

An Edwardian gold double-heart locket and bow, set with diamonds, turquoise and pearls, with a 15ct gold chain necklet.
£270–340 ⚒ F&C

An Edwardian aquamarine and diamond necklet, ½in (1.25cm) long.
£800–900 ⊞ GLa

An Edwardian platinum and diamond pendant/brooch, on a platinum-topped 14ct gold mount.
£4,700–6,000 ⚒ SK

An Edwardian pendant/brooch, designed as a garland of flowers descending from scroll-work, with diamond and pearl drops.
£520–650 ⚒ HYD

An Edwardian amethyst and pearl pendant, on a fine link chain.
£110–140 ⚒ LFA

JEWELLERY

Pins

A stick pin, the hardstone plaque carved to depict the profile of a lady, within a surround of diamonds in box settings, mid-19thC, cased.
£280–350 P(Ba)

A reverse intaglio crystal stick pin, with a monogram of Frederick of Prussia, c1880, 4in (10cm) long.
£1,450–1,600 NBL
Frederick of Prussia was the husband of Princess Victoria, Queen Victoria's eldest daughter.

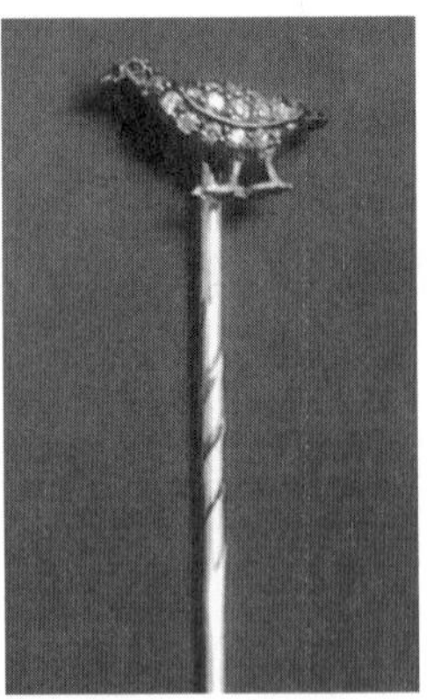

A diamond stick pin, modelled as a bird set with rose-cut diamonds, c1890, cased.
£200–250 B(Ba)

An Edwardian stick pin, with a diamond set within a ruby surround and seed pearl bezel.
£170–220 B(Ba)

An Edwardian pearl and diamond stick pin, with an 18ct gold mount.
£230–275 SK

Rings

An enamelled gold mourning ring, for Spencer, Earl of Northampton, in black enamel with a white border, the interior with a memorial inscription, 1796.
£320–400 Bon

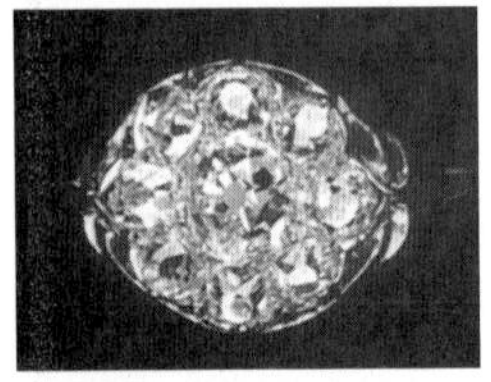

A gold cluster ring, set with diamonds, 19thC, cased.
£650–820 L

A Victorian diamond ring, set in silver on gold, engraved, with stylized fleur-de-lys shanks.
£550–700 L

► **A gold ring,** set with diamonds and a pearl, late 19thC.
£1,200–1,500 Bea(E)

An enamelled gold and diamond ring, with a diamond-set monogram 'RH' on a mauve enamel ground, the reverse with hair compartment, 1775–1825.
£700–875 Bea(E)

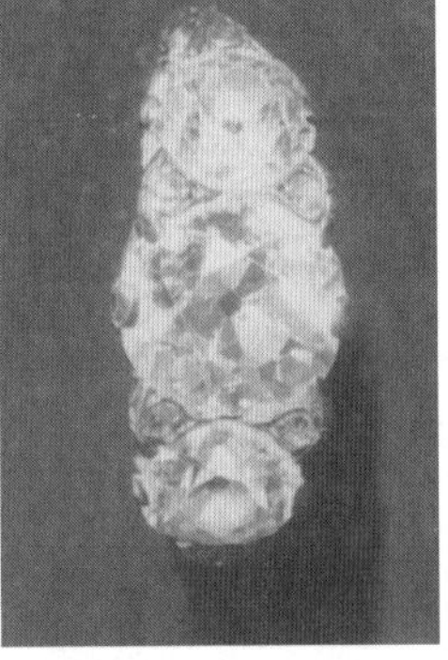

A Victorian three-stone diamond ring, on a chased gold shank.
£5,500–7,000 HYD

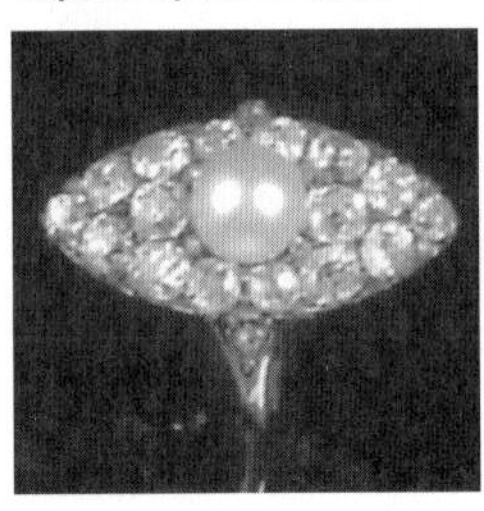

An intaglio ring, the oval cornelian carved to depict Hope, early 19thC.
£250–320 B(Ba)

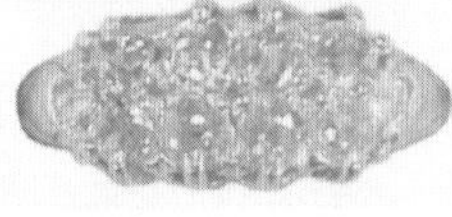

A Victorian 18ct gold ring, set with two rows of four diamonds.
£200–250 F&C

A diamond ring, c1890.
£1,750–2,200 B(Ba)

A memorial ring, set with a diamond within a black enamel panel enclosed by a surround of half pearls, the mount inscribed to the interior, c1830.
£320–400 B(Ba)

A Victorian 15ct gold black-enamelled memorial ring, centred with a Latin cross set with seed pearls, the reverse with a hair compartment, one pearl missing.
£170–220 G(L)

An 18ct gold ring, set with natural pearls, c1890.
£1,100–1,250 TGL

◄ **An Edwardian pearl and diamond ring,** set with one white and one pink pearl, in a platinum-topped 14ct gold mount.
£400–500 SK

Enamel

An enamel beaker, displaying the Imperial double-headed eagle and cypher of Tsar Nicholas II above the date 1896, 4in (10cm) high.
£600–700 JAA

According to Russian custom, after a coronation there was an outdoor fête for the people, where free food, sweets and presents, such as this beaker, were given out. It is thought that over half a million people congregated to receive their free gifts. As the crowds pushed forwards an estimated 2,000 people died in the crush. Nicholas was apparently not even present, and instead danced the night away with his wife Alexandra at a ball hosted by the French Ambassador, an act that infuriated the people, and led to these beakers being known as 'blood cups'.

A Bilston enamel bodkin case, the white ground polychrome-decorated with sprays of flowers and enriched with gilding, inscribed *'Sincer en Amitie'*, with gilt-metal mounts, 18thC, 5¼in (13.5cm) high.
£1,100–1,400 HYD

A Birmingham enamel box, the hinged cover printed in black, with a metal mount, hinge broken, c1760, 2¾in (7cm) wide.
£250–300 P

► **A gilt-metal and enamel box,** the hinged lid painted with a couple, the interior painted in puce with a man on horseback, German, 18thC, 3½in (9cm) wide.
£360–450 AH

Cross Reference
See Colour Review (page 611)

A gilded-silver and enamel *kovsh*, enamelled with colourful stylized foliage, with a border of white circles, Russian, c1900, 7½in (19cm) long.
£2,500–3,250 S(NY)

A pair of Imperial cloisonné enamel salts, Russian, St Petersburg, c1890, 2in (5cm) diam.
£750–850 SHa

◄ **A silver-gilt and cloisonné enamel vodka tot,** by Ivan Khlebnikov, Russian, Moscow c1917, 2in (5cm) high.
£1,000–1,100 MIR

► **A silver wager cup,** enamelled with dancing couples in an architectural landscape, with a silver-gilt-lined pivotal bowl, some wear, Continental, probably German, 19thC, 5in (12.5cm) high.
£750–825 RIT

A cloisonné enamel cigarette case, decorated with flowers, foliage and stylized feathery wings in shaded enamels on a pale blue ground, edged with a lavender-blue border with pink flowers and green leaves, minor chips, Russian, 1908–17, 4in (10cm) long.
£1,000–1,250 P

A south Staffordshire *étui*, with silver mounts, the hinged cover painted with a small landscape, a panel of flowers on a grey ground on the top, with panels of rural landscapes, reserved on a white ground with *bianco-sopra-bianco* decoration, chip, fine cracking, late 18thC, 4in (10cm) high.
£1,400–1,600 P

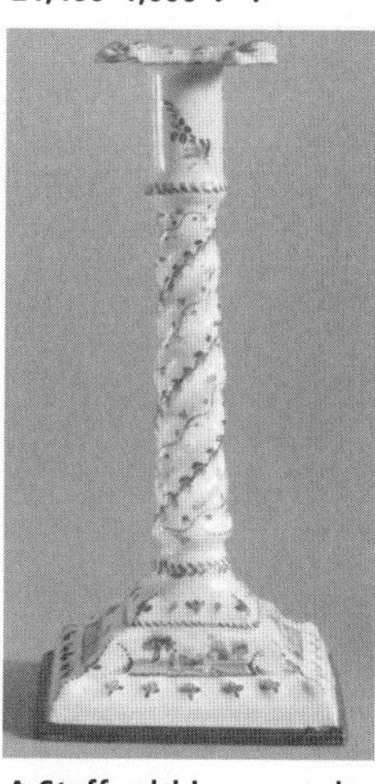

A Staffordshire enamel taperstick, slight damage, c1775, 6¼in (16cm) high.
£470–600 S(O)

Fabergé

A Fabergé brass ashtray, chased with the Imperial eagle and inscribed in Russian 'War 1914' and 'Fabergé', c1915, 4¼in (11cm) diam.
£780–975 S

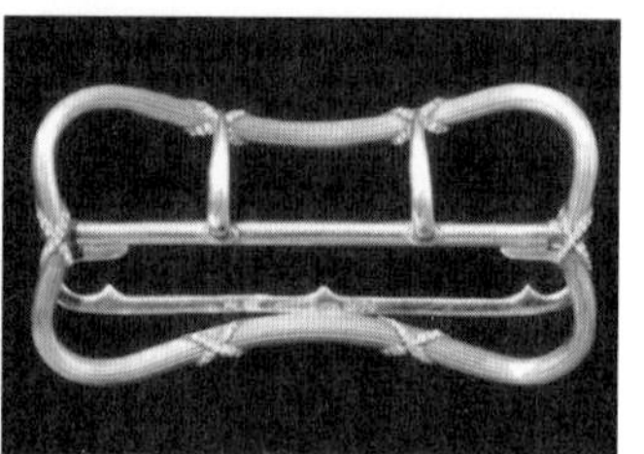

A Fabergé gold and jewelled buckle, workmaster Henrik Wigström, the reeded gold sides with diamond-set ribbon ties, St Petersburg, c1900, 2½in (6.5cm) wide.
£2,400–3,000 S

A Fabergé silver bowl, Moscow 1894, 6¾in (17cm) wide.
£2,700–3,400 BUK

A Fabergé moonstone and gold floral spray brooch, c1910, ¾in (2cm) long, in original holly wood box.
£1,700–2,200 B

► A Fabergé silver pocket case, with 15ct gold fittings and a cabochon sapphire button, St Petersburg, 1896–1908, 2in (5cm) wide.
£2,700–3,000 MIR

A Fabergé brooch, workmaster August Hollming, the translucent red enamel set with a flower spray set with six diamonds, the back engraved 14ct gold, Russian, 1899–1908, in original holly wood box.
£5,300–6,500 Bri

► A Fabergé silver lidded tankard, with engraved floral decoration and a central cartouche, gilt interior, workmaster's mark 'AA', Moscow 1895, 6¼in (16cm) high, 20.25oz.
£1,800–2,250 DORO

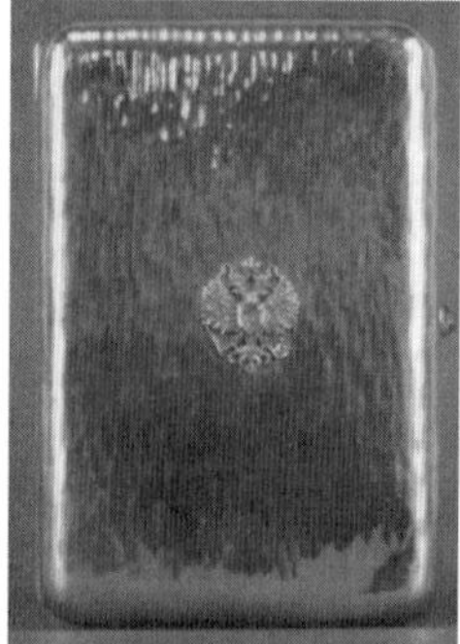

A gold and diamond cigarette case, probably Fabergé, with a textured finish, the front applied with the Romanov twin-headed eagle, set with rose diamonds, the thumbpiece set with a cabochon ruby, St Petersburg marks and engraved presentation inscription to interior, late 19thC, 3¾in (9.5cm) high, in a green leather case inscribed 'Wartski Ltd ... London'.
£1,600–2,000 RTo

A Fabergé silver-mounted glass vase, Moscow, 1908–17, 12in (30.5cm) high.
£5,200–5,750 SHa

Gold

A gold-mounted mother-of-pearl commemorative box, the hinged lid engraved with a coat-of-arms, the sides inlaid with vertical gold borders, inset with a glazed panel of plaited hair, the interior with a memorial inscription, c1780, 3¼in (8.5cm) wide.
£2,300–2,800 Bon

An Imperial gold cigarette case, Russian, St Petersburg, 1908–17, 4in (10cm) wide.
£2,500–2,750 SHa

A 9ct gold engine-turned cigarette case, Birmingham 1929, 5in (12.5cm) wide.
£320–400 Bon

An 18ct gold dressing table set, by The Goldsmiths & Silversmiths Co, comprising 16 pieces, engine-turned decoration, Sheffield 1906, brushes 4¼in (11cm) wide.
£1,700–2,000 S(O)

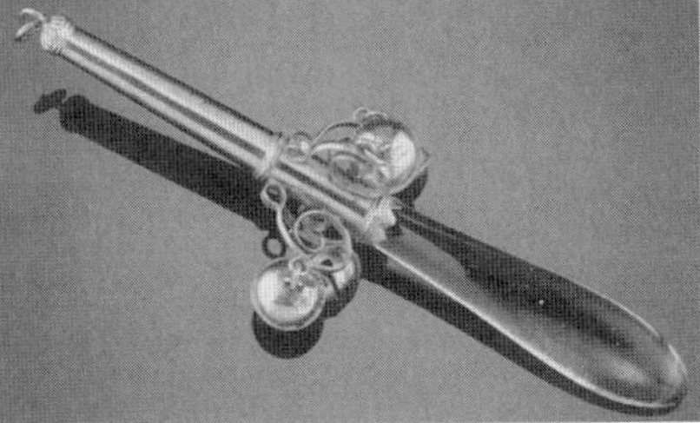

A child's gold rattle, probably by Otto Knoop, Amsterdam, with a glass handle, Dutch, c1735, 5¾in (14.5cm) long.
£550–600 S(Am)

A gold snuff box, by Peter Werritzer, with a gold-mounted agate cover, basketweave sides and agate base, 1744, 3¼in (8.5cm) diam.
£6,000–7,250 Bon

◄ **A three-colour gold snuff box,** maker's mark 'LC' in a rectangle, probably Swiss, c1785, 2¾in (7cm) wide.
£1,300–1,500 S(O)

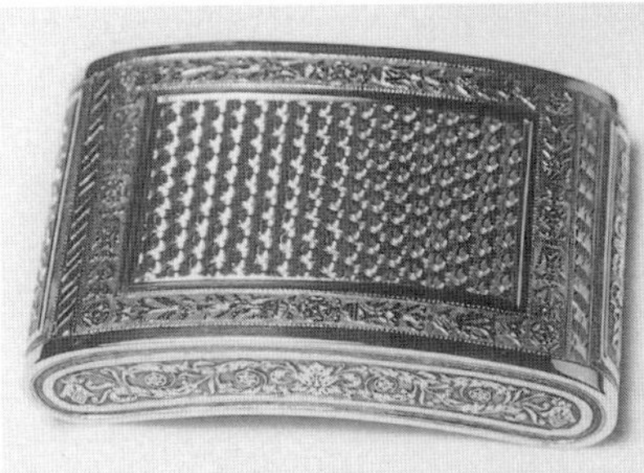

◄ **An 18ct gold snuff box,** French, Paris, 1809–19, 3½in (9cm) wide.
£3,500–4,000 BEX

A gold vinaigrette, with concentric engine-turned decoration and circular punched borders, early 19thC, 1¼in (3cm) wide.
£250–320 Bon

A gold-mounted citrine vinaigrette, the sides and base with engine-turned decoration, the grille pierced with a lyre flanked by laurel leaves, c1840, 1¼in (3cm) long.
£750–950 Bon

A gold vinaigrette, decorated in black, white and green enamels, French, 1819–38, 1in (2.5cm) high.
£280–350 F&C

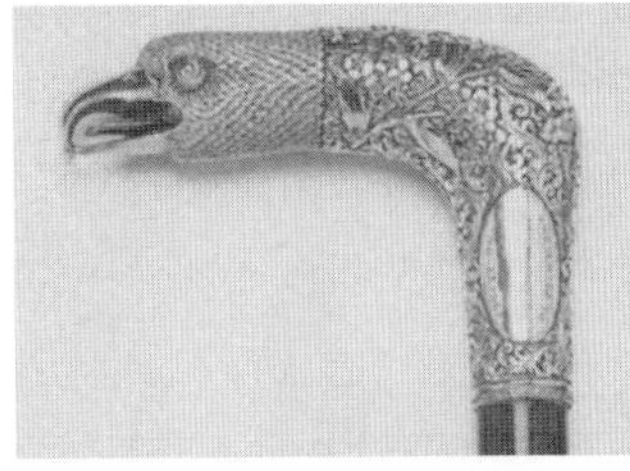

A gold-mounted eagle walking stick, the handle chased with scrolling foliate and floral decoration and an eagle's head finial, with presentation inscription, on a snakewood shaft, American, c1889, 34¼in (87cm) long.
£800–1,000 B

GOLD

Asian Works of Art
Cloisonné & Enamel

A *plique-à-jour* bowl, decorated with butterflies, roses, peonies and other flowers on a green ground, with a silver rim, chip and crack, Japanese, Meiji period, 1868–1911, 5½in (14cm) diam.
£3,500–4,000 S

A cloisonné box and cover, decorated with lotus scrolls, the lid applied with five gilt-bronze plaques, Chinese, 18thC, 13in (33cm) wide, with a carved wood stand.
£1,300–1,600 WW

A cloisonné enamelled box, depicting Jurojin and the white deer of immortality on a pale yellow/green ground, signed 'Hayashi Tanigoro', Japanese, early 20thC, 5¼in (13.5cm) wide.
£2,000–2,400 BB(S)

A cloisonné enamel and gilt-bronze jar, with two bands of scrolling lotus-headed foliage divided by a raised band of daisy cartouches on a dark blue ground, with two gilt cloud-scroll handles and wood cover and stand, small dent, incised Qianlong mark, Chinese, 1736–95, 4½in (11.5cm) high.
£1,350–1,700 P(Ba)

A cloisonné enamel bowl, decorated with flowering and fruiting branches on a blue ground, Chinese, 19thC, 28¾in (73cm) diam.
£2,000–2,400 S(Am)

A gilt-mounted cloisonné teapot and lid, decorated with phoenix and auspicious objects, Japanese, Meiji period, 1868–1911, 6¼in (16cm) wide.
£220–275 WW

◄ **A pair of cloisonné vases,** decorated with insects and flowers on a blue ground with geometric borders, Chinese, 19thC, 13in (33cm) high.
£400–500 GAK

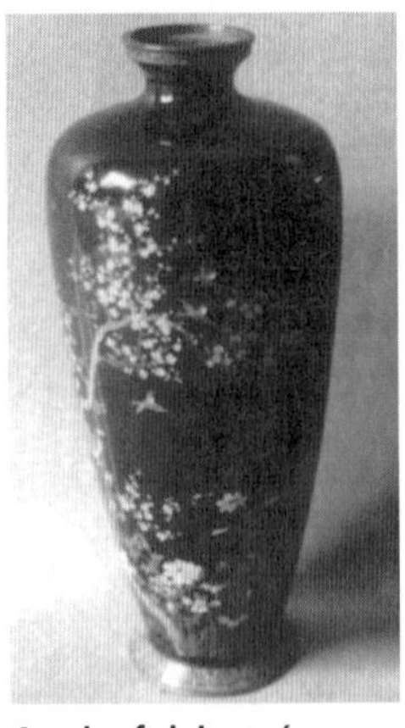

A pair of cloisonné vases, decorated with silver wire with cherry blossom, birds, lilies and other flowers on a dark blue ground, signed, one damaged, Japanese, 19thC, 9½in (24cm) high.
£140–175 TRM

An enamelled gilt-copper vase, with twin handles, decorated in turquoise and cobalt-blue enamel with floral trellis design, Indian, Kashmir, late 19thC, 14¾in (37.5cm) high.
£650–820 Bon(C)

A pair of cloisonné enamel vases, mounted as lamps, Japanese, Taisho period, 1912–26, 15in 938cm) high.
£630–700 WcH

A cloisonné vase, decorated with silver wire depicting cranes on a dark blue ground, slight damage, Japanese, c1920, 7in (18cm) high.
£230–255 FU

Glass

An olive-green glass dish, Qianlong mark and period, Chinese, 1736–95, 6½in (16.5cm) diam.
£5,000–5,500 ⚒ S(O)

Miller's is a price GUIDE not a price LIST

A lobed amber Peking glass dish, Chinese, 19thC, 10in (25.5cm) diam.
£600–670 ⊞ GLD

A glass painting, depicting a lady wearing an ivory-trimmed blue silk coat, Chinese, 19thC, 12¼in (31cm) wide, in a gilt composition frame.
£300–375 ⚒ Bon(C)

Jade

An enamelled silver and jade-inset bracelet, the nine panel links inset with gods of good fortune, Chinese, early 20thC.
£400–500 ⚒ CGC

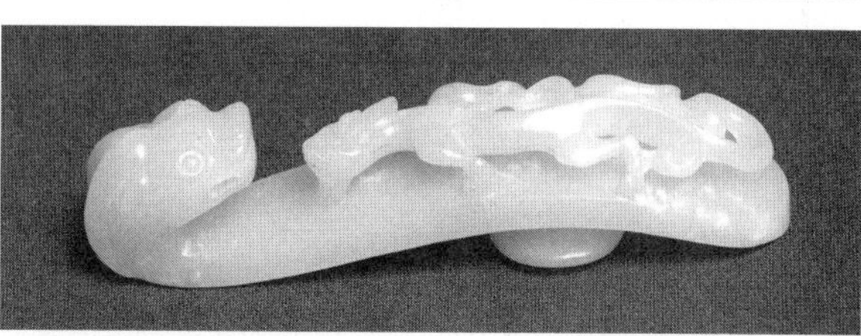

A jade belt buckle, Chinese, 19thC, 4in (10cm) wide.
£315–350 ⊞ GLD

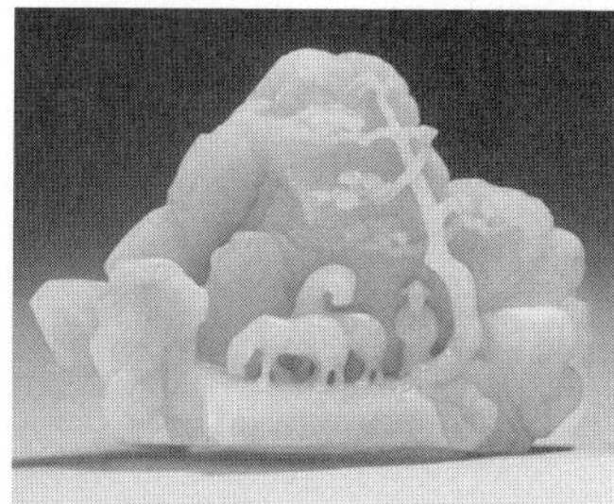

A white jade boulder carving, carved with a travelling scholar and his two horses standing beneath a pine tree on a cliff, the reverse with a pavilion above a waterfall, Chinese, early 18thC, 7in (18cm) wide.
£5,000–6,000 ⚒ S(NY)

► **A celadon green jade boulder carving,** carved with a scholar and attendant in a mountain landscape, Chinese, 19thC, 4in (10cm) high.
£675–850 ⚒ SK

A jade tripod censer, the body carved with twin mythical beast mask ring handles, the cover with a Buddhistic lion and cub, slightly chipped, 19thC, 6¾in (17cm) high.
£300–360 ⚒ P(Ba)

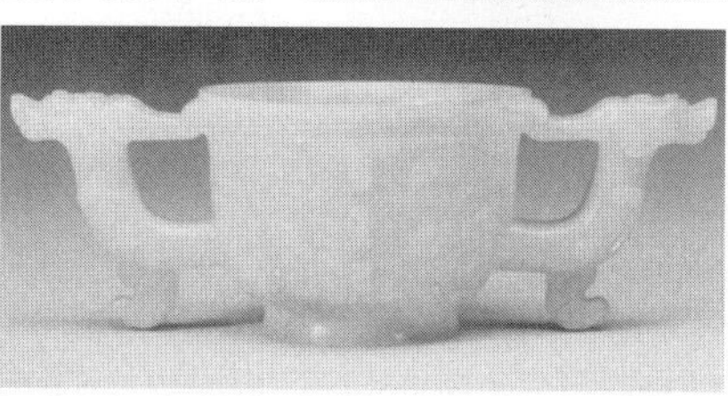

A celadon jade carving of a *gui*, in the shape of an archaic bronze ritual vessel, the body with carved *taotie* motifs and flanges, the handles modelled as stylized dragons, Chinese, 18thC, 2½in (6.5cm) high.
£2,200–2,700 ⚒ S

A pale green jade vase and cover, the reticulated body carved with peonies and other foliage, the handles similarly carved, Chinese, Qianlong period, 1736–95, 6½in (16.5cm) wide.
£3,500–4,500 ⚒ HYD

◄ **A white jade vase,** carved as an open lotus flower surrounded by smaller flowers and buds, Chinese, 19thC, 6in (15cm) high, on a wooden stand.
£1,200–1,500 ⚒ WW

A Moghul-style grey jade vase, with elephant head handles suspending loose rings, Chinese, 19thC, 6¼in (16cm) high, on a *zitan* stand.
£1,800–2,200 ⚒ S(Am)

Lacquer

A lacquer scroll box and cover, with floral decoration, Japanese, late 19thC, 23in (58.5cm) wide.
£440–550 ⚒ G(B)

A black lacquer fruit dish, with decorated handle, Chinese, provincial, 19thC, 14in (35.5cm) diam.
£70–80 ⊞ OE

A lacquer perfume cabinet, the door opening to reveal three drawers, the sides lacquered with birds among flowering branches, Japanese, Meiji period, 1868–1911, 13¼in (33.5cm) wide.
£1,200–1,500 ⚒ SLN

A lacquer *shikishibako*, decorated in gold and multi-coloured *togidashi* with figures picnicking beneath a willow on the river bank, on a faded *nashiji* ground, Japanese, 8 x 7in (20.5 x 18cm), in a fitted case.
£4,000–5,000 ⚒ DN
A *shikishibako* was used to store poem papers.

A *Shibayama* brooch and earring set, Japanese, c1900.
£500–600 ⊞ Ma

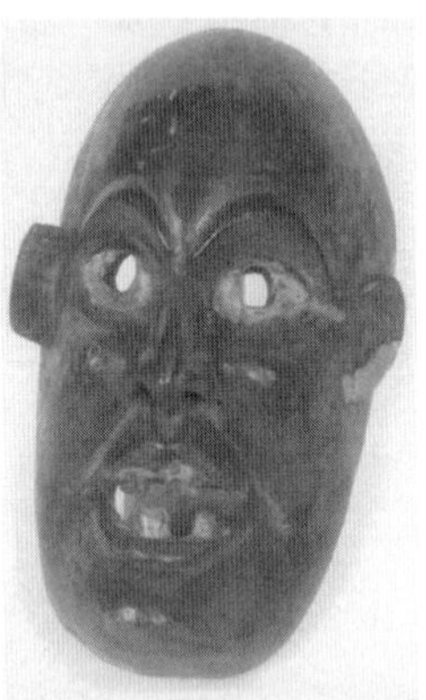

A lacquered writing table, decorated in gold and silver *hiramakie*, *takamakie* and foil, applied in gold and silver with a building surrounded by pine trees and a mountainous landscape, minor wear, Japanese, Meiji period, 1868–1911, 23¾in (60.5cm) wide.
£400–500 ⚒ B(Ba)

A lacquer photograph album, the cover decorated with an exotic bird among branches, contains approximately 50 coloured photographs, Japanese, early 20thC.
£1,400–1,750 ⚒ EH

◀ **A red lacquer clown mask,** Tibetan, 1875–1925, 12in (30.5cm) high.
£120–150 ⚒ L&E

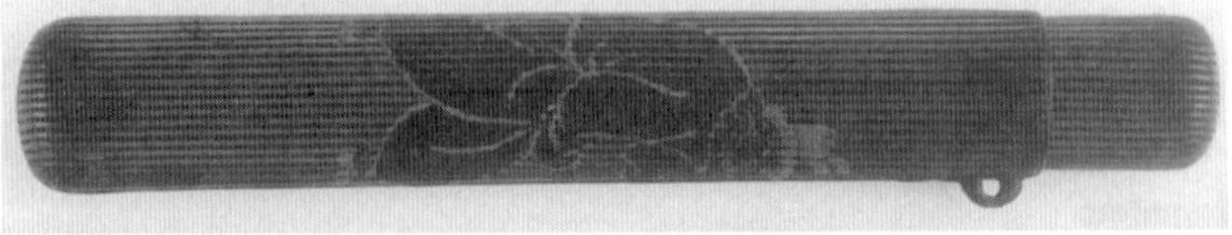

A lacquered pipecase, the shaft with vertical grooves and decorated in red and black lacquer with a Portuguese sailor giving direction to his seated hound, Japanese, 19thC, 8¼in (21cm) wide.
£1,000–1,200 ⚒ BB(S)

A lacquer writing utensil box, depicting Daruma in gold and red lacquered relief on a ground of crushed *aogai*, the *nashiji* interior shows *kiku* beside a winding stream in silver and gold *takamakie* and *hiramakie*, fitted with ink stone and water dropper, Japanese, 17thC, 9½ x 9in (24 x 23cm).
£1,600–2,000 ⚒ DN
Daruma was the founder of Zen Buddhism.

A lacquered vessel in five sections, decorated with a figure of Shojo drinking from a charger and a man with a fan, Japanese, c1900, 8in (20.5cm) high.
£2,000–2,200 ⚒ S
Shojo was a sake-loving elf.

Metalware

A silver footed bowl, Japanese, 1900-50, 9in (23cm) diam, 34.5oz.
£460–575 WcH

A silver comport, the everted rim with embossed leaf decoration, the stem surrounded by fronds and reeds, the edges supported by three egrets, Chinese, Sunshing, Hong Kong, 1860–90, 9¾in (25cm) high, 45oz.
£3,200–3,500 SK

A bronze hanging incense burner, modelled as a five-petalled lotus flower, the reticulated cover surmounted by a *shishi*, Japanese, 19thC, 8in (20.5cm) wide.
£230–280 WW

A *shakudo* box and cover, decorated in *iroe takazogan* with birds and flowers, signed, Japanese, Meiji period, 1868–1911, 4¼in (11cm) diam.
£6,000–7,500 Bon(C)

A pewter and jade ewer, with jade handle and spout, incised with floral detail, Chinese, 18th–19thC, 3½in (9cm) high.
£200–250 S(O)

A silver coffee percolator, by Grostate & Co, engraved with a crest above an armorial shield, with wooden handle and knop, Indian, Madras, c1820, 9½in (24cm) high, 34oz.
£2,000–2,500 P

A brass incense burner, Indian, early 19thC, 6in (15cm) diam.
£340–375 SEA

A silver tray, by Luen Wo, Shanghai, the corners embossed with figures in landscapes, the sides applied with Chinese hieroglyphics enclosing a chased floral-patterned ground, Chinese, 1890–1900, 28in (71cm) wide, 136oz.
£1,600–2,000 CGC

◄ **A pair of cast-bronze incense burners and covers,** with Dog of *Fo* finials and opposing loop handles entwined with dragons, the body decorated with cast and applied birds and animals, probably Chinese, late 19thC, 32in (81.5cm) high, on a pair of late 19thC ebonized hardwood torchères, 48in (122cm) high.
£1,100–1,400 AAR

◄ **A bronze vase with two mask handles,** inlaid in gold- and silver-coloured metals and moulded in relief with birds in flowering branches, dent, Japanese, 19thC, 14½in (37cm) high.
£380–475 DN

► **A bronze vase,** cast with an eagle worked in *shibuichi* and *shakudo*, signed in gilt 'IKKO', Japanese, Meiji period, 1868–1911, 9½in (24cm) high.
£2,500–2,800 LBO

A bronze and iron *katri*, Tibetan, late 19thC, 6in (15cm) high.
£200–220 FU
This is a ceremonial piece originally used for chopping medicinal herbs.

ASIAN WORKS OF ART

Stone

A grey schist reliquary, carved in the shape of a lotus, Indian, Gandhara, 2nd–4thC AD, 5½in (14cm) diam.
£320–350 ⚒ SK

A red sandstone balustrade section, depicting an elephant with two *mahouts*, Indian, Mughal, 17thC, 23¾in (60cm) high.
£800–1,000 ⚒ Bon(C)

► **A granite lantern,** Japanese, Meiji period, 1868–1911, 72in (183cm) high.
£3,200–4,000 ⚒ S(S)

Wood

A cypresswood and iron well bucket, Chinese provincial, mid-19thC, 14in (35.5cm).
£180–200 ⊞ FU

Cross Reference
See Colour Review (page 612)

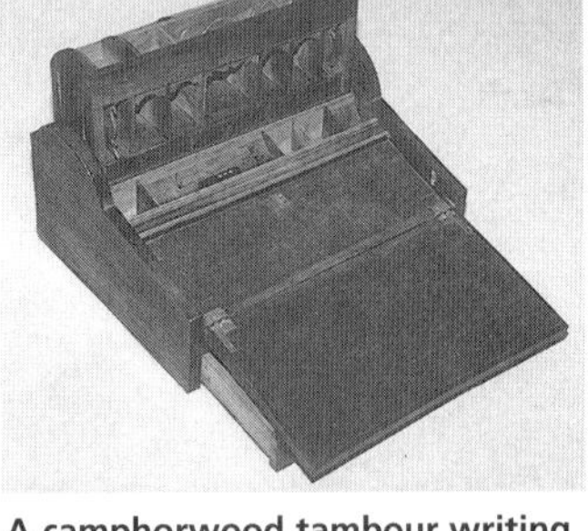

A camphorwood tambour writing box, probably Chinese, made for the western market, c1860, 19in (48.5cm) wide.
£850–950 ⊞ TWh

◄ **A wood hand-operated automaton,** Japanese, c1890, 5in (12.5cm) high.
£270–300 ⊞ AUTO

A carved wood jewellery box, the doors and apron with carving of dragons, Chinese, 19thC, 15¾in (40cm) wide.
£1,700–2,200 ⚒ NOA

A hardwood jardinière, carved and pierced all over with foliage and fruit, with a removable brass liner, Indian, 19thC, 15½in (39.5cm) high.
£360–430 ⚒ S(S)

A pair of carved wood and lacquered jardinières, the exteriors carved in bas-relief with butterflies, chrysanthemums and other flowers and foliage, picked out in gold and coloured lacquers and inlaid with abalone, with fitted copper liners, Japanese, early 20thC, 8¾in (22cm) high.
£400–500 ⚒ P(Ba)

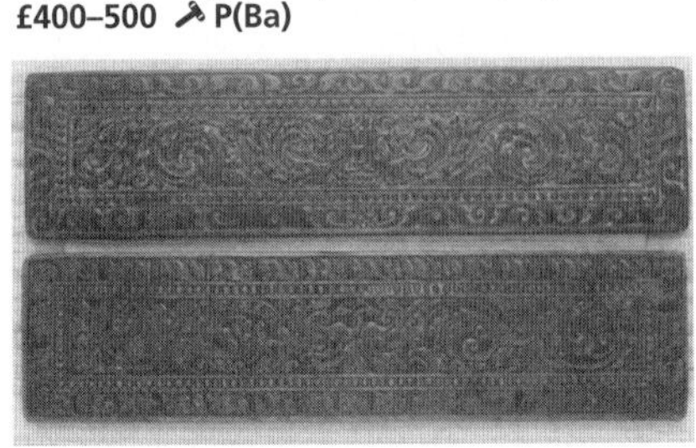

► **A pair of carved wood *sutra* covers,** the front cover with a seated Buddha set between heads of Buddhist spirits attached to long foliate scrolls framed by leaf scroll borders, the reverse with a pair of intertwined birds with foliate scrolls forming their tails enclosed by a scrolling border, Tibetan, 14th–15thC, 21½in (54.5cm) high, now mounted on a cloth-covered board.
£1,000–1,200 ⚒ BB(S)
A *sutra* is a narrative part of Buddhist literature, a brief prayer.

Arms & Armour

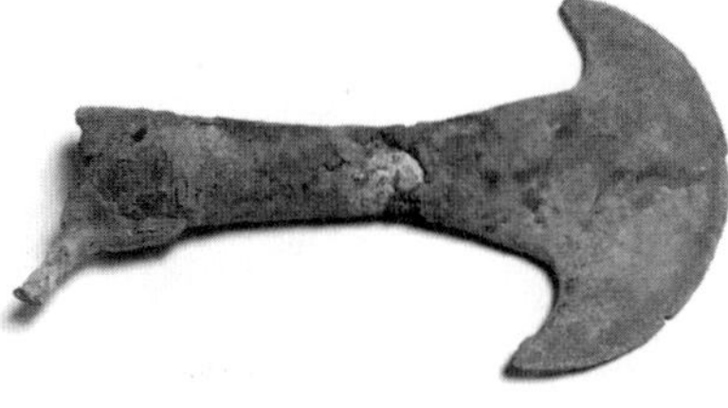

A ceremonial bronze axe head, Chinese, Shang Dynasty, 16th century–c1050 BC, 6in (15cm) high.
£675–750 GLD

A *katana* blade, the *saya* with bands of *aogai-nashiji* and black *ishime*, decorated in gold *takamakie* with butterflies and dragonflies above grasses, the iron *tsuba* signed *'Goshu ju Masatsugu saku'*, gilt *mino-goto fuchi-kashira* with flowers and insects and *shakudo* and gilt floral *menuki*, Japanese, Bizen, blade 16thC, mounts 19thC, 27in (68.5cm) long.
£3,800–4,200 S

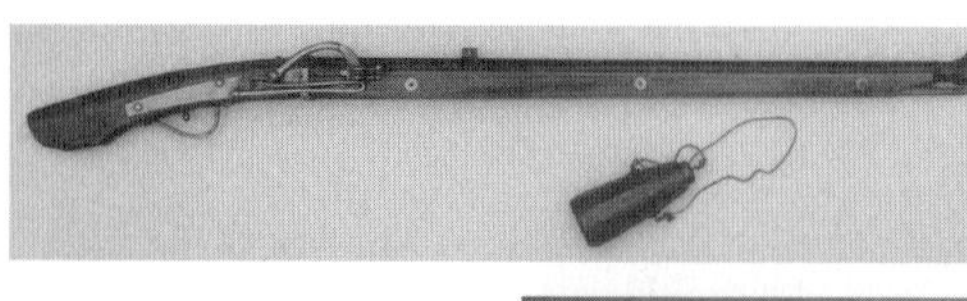

◄ **A matchlock,** with a wooden powder flask, Japanese, Edo period, 18thC, 37½in (95.5cm) long.
£1,400–1,700 BB(S)

A black-lacquered iron samurai armour, Japanese, c1800.
£1,700–2,200 Herm

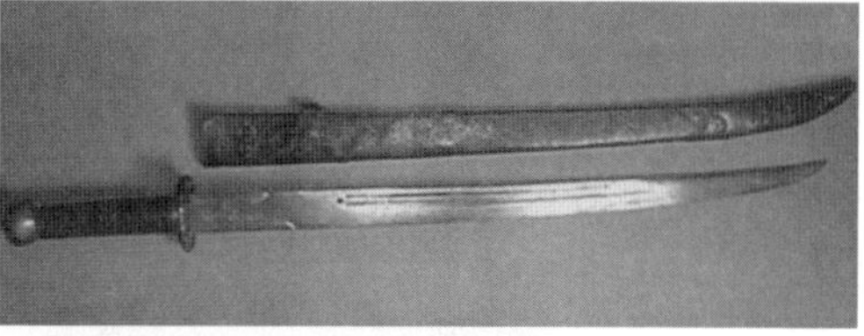

► **A back sword,** the brass hilt mounts with cash motif decoration, with leather-covered grip and leather scabbard blind-pierced with cash motifs, Chinese, 19thC, 33¼in (84.5cm) long.
£170–220 PFK

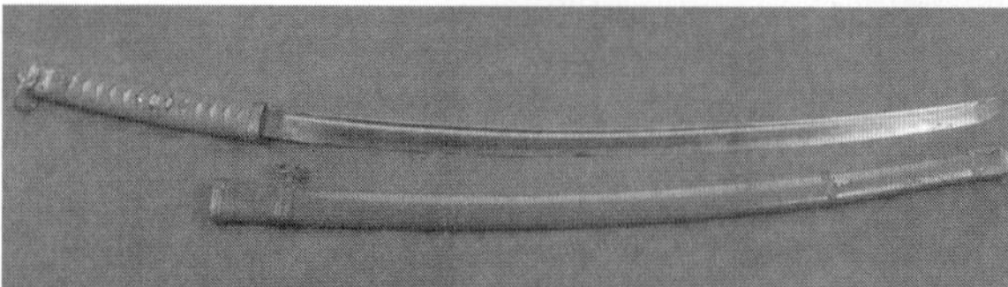

◄ **A *katana*,** with a brown lacquer *saya* blade, Japanese, 19thC, 28½in (72.5cm) long.
£330–420 SLN

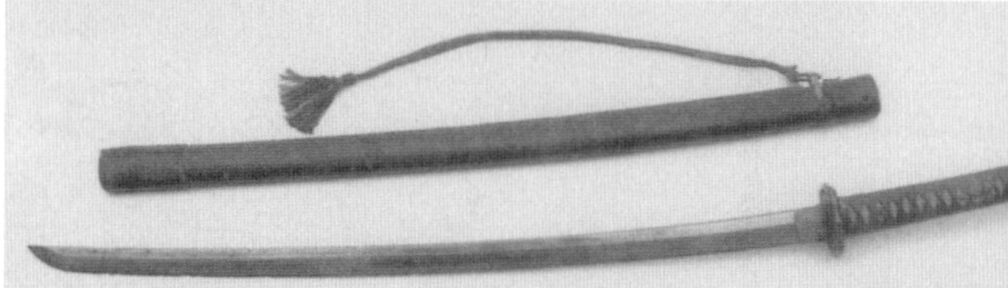

► **A WWII *katana*,** with a bronze pierced floral *tsuba* and a leather-bound *saya*, Japanese, blade 27½in (70cm) long.
£340–425 Bea(E)

Tsuba

► **A *shibuichi tsuba*,** cut and infilled with *shakudo*, with gilt fan-shaped decoration containing birds, clouds and a silver moon, inscribed 'Kofu-Ju', Japanese, Akaokichi, 18thC, 2¾in (7cm) high.
£260–325 CGC

An iron *tsuba*, cast and worked in the shape of a Buddhist rosary, two of the beads gilt, probably inscribed 'Kofu No Ju', Japanese, Ushinaga, 18thC, 3in (7.5cm).
£180–225 CGC

An iron *tsuba*, carved with a recumbent tiger turning and raising its paw, the stripes in gold, signed 'Manzaiju Katsuhiro', dated 1858, 2½in (6.5cm) high.
£2,200–2,750 S(NY)

◄ **An iron *tsuba*,** from the Bishu School of Artists, inlaid with various metals depicting rabbits at play, unsigned, Japanese, mid-19thC, 3in (7.5cm) high.
£450–500 KIE

Clocks

A japanned metal *faux* tortoiseshell clock and stand, with 3in (7.5cm) enamel dial set in a pink and gilt arched surround decorated with flower sprays, centre seconds, two train bell striking fusee and chain movement with cylinder escapement, Chinese, c1800, 11½in (29cm) high.
£1,750–2,000 S(O)

LOCATE THE SOURCE

The source of each illustration in Miller's can be found by checking the code letters below each caption with the Key to Illustrations, pages 794–800.

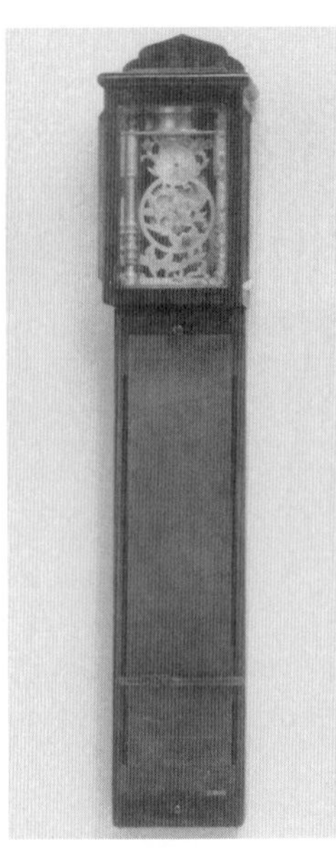

► **A pillar timepiece,** the front plate pierced and engraved with chrysanthemums, subsidiary seconds calibrated from one to six, with verge and balance escapement, the case with a brass plate engraved with a scale showing Japanese time, Japanese, 19thC, 15½in (39.5cm) high.
£3,000–3,750 S(NY)

A travelling clock, the revolving dial with fixed hand and 12 movable hour plaques, set on a flower-engraved brass surround with two calendar apertures above, the movement with fusee and chain for the going train with verge and balance escapement, Japanese, 19thC, 7¾in (19.5cm) high, with a hardwood case and travelling clock.
£3,800–4,200 S

Figures & Models

A grey schist figure of a standing Buddha, Indian, Gandhara, 3rd–4thC AD, 34½in (87.5cm) high.
£6,000–6,600 WcH

A marble figure of a Buddha, wearing a gilded lacquer robe decorated with coloured stones, Indian, 19thC, 11½in (29cm) high.
£250–320 F&C

◄ **A wooden juggernaught carving of demi-god Garuda in praying posture,** south Indian, Tamali Nadu, 1675–1725, 20in (51cm) high.
£2,500–2,800 GRG

A black lacquer torso of Buddha, Burmese, 18thC, 15¾in (40cm) high.
£1,350–1,500 LOP

◄ **A carved ivory figure of a maiden,** holding a fan and cups as two attendants serve her tea and play music, Chinese, 19thC, 19¾in (50cm) high.
£2,200–2,500 JAA

A carved ivory figure, depicting a seated female holding a sheaf of corn in one hand, Goanese, 18thC, 3¼in (8cm) high.
£900–1,150 P

An ivory figure, modelled as a tradesman carrying gourds and a basket, Japanese, 19thC, 12in (30.5cm) high, on a hardwood base.
£600–750 WL

A gilded-bronze figural group, the dancing figure wearing a gilded robe and holding aloft airbells, his companion playing a horn, Japanese, 19thC, 18½in (47cm) high, on a base decorated with gold-lacquered scrolling foliage.
£12,000–15,000 LVS

This piece was almost certainly by a famous maker, which resulted in it selling for nearly four times the lowest estimate, despite minor damage to the stand. Maker's marks are usually small and hidden away and can easily be missed.

A cast-bronze seated Buddha, the hair tinted with blue pigment and the remaining surfaces showing remains of black pigment over a layer of gold lacquer, Korean, Chosen Dynasty, 19thC, 15¾in (40cm) high.
£3,700–4,000 BB(S)

A wood carving of Buddha, depicted on a lotus throne with two acolytes, Chinese, c1850, 14in (35.5cm) high.
£145–160 FU

An ivory *okimono*, depicting a turtle catcher dragging a snapping turtle, signed 'Mitsunari', Japanese, c1850, 6in (15cm) high.
£900–1,000 AMC

A carved ivory group of monkeys and an octopus, the octopus with inlaid wood eyes, all details picked out in a brown wash, minor losses and repairs, one monkey missing, Japanese, Meiji period, 1868–1911, 5½in (14cm) high.
£380–475 B(Ba)

A bronze and ivory fisherman with his catch, signed 'Jonan', Japanese, Meiji period, 1868–1911, 12in (30.5cm) high, on a carved wooden base.
£4,000–4,500 LBO

An ivory *okimono*, in the form of a Chinese man struggling in the wind as arrows fly at him, stepping over wrapped packages, signed 'Gyokusan', Japanese, Meiji period, 1868-1911, 7½in (19cm) high.
£450–500 AMC

◄ **A bronze model of a tiger,** Japanese, c1880, 4½in (11.5cm) high.
£550–650 GLD

A carving of an *oni*, with mother-of-pearl eyes, signed in a seal 'Akikuni', Japanese, Meiji period, 1868-1911, 3½in (9cm) high.
£2,000–2,200 LBO

A bronze group of an elephant and two tigers, signed 'Seiya', Japanese, Meiji period, 1868–1911, 17in (43cm) wide.
£2,100–2,350 FU

A bronze lidded censer, in the shape of an elephant, south-east Asian, c1880, 9in (23cm) wide.
£200–220 FRY

An ivory *okimono* of a ship, crewed by the seven gods of Felicity, with phoenix head prow, signed 'Kakihan', minor damage and some losses, Japanese, early 20thC, 21¾in (55.5cm) wide.
£2,000–2,500 TEN

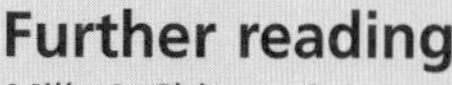

Further reading

Miller's Chinese & Japanese Antiques Buyer's Guide, Miller's Publications, 1999

A table decoration of a pair of silvered-bronze pigeons, on a black lacquered stand, Japanese, c1920, stand 15½in (39.5cm) wide, with original travelling case.
£1,100–1,250 JC

Furniture

Asian furniture has always had its admirers in the West. After the great exhibitions of the 19th century there was a surge of interest in all things Oriental, and large numbers of display cabinets, chests and screens were imported. However, it is only recently that functional domestic furniture, and in particular Chinese provincial, has been brought over in any great quantity to meet the demands of the decorators and a fashion for the exotic. Although such pieces can be very decorative they may not be a good investment. Much of it is poor quality, in both the workmanship and the woods used, and has often been altered to meet the needs of the western market. For example, altar tables have been cut down to coffee table height, bed panels turned into wall mirrors, and old bamboo furniture disassembled and remade into items such as magazine racks, baby's cots and cradles and clothing and towel stands.

Classic Chinese furniture of the Ming (1368–1644) and Qing (1644–1916) dynasties is much admired in the West for its simplicity of form combined with strong but elegant construction. Most pieces are made from *huanghuali*, a hard, close wood with a beautiful grain, which is quite distinct and varied and polishes to a light red with darker grain. The furniture is made up without the use of nails, the use of a minimal amount of glue being secondary to the intricate and exact joinery. Classic *huanghuali* furniture is now quite rare: since the export of such furniture from China is banned, pieces already in the West are fast disappearing into museums and private collections. As a result, prices continue to rise. However, it is still very good value compared to western furniture, considering its age, quality and workmanship.

Oriental lacquerwork furniture was imported into the West in large quantities from the end of the 17th century. Mainly from Japan and China, this export furniture was made specifically for the western taste and includes display cabinets, chests, screens, work and writing boxes, bureaux and tea tables. It is often highly ornate and embellished with bone, ivory and mother-of-pearl. Most of the larger specimen cabinets sit on contemporaneous western chinoiserie stands: this is not considered detrimental to the value of the chest.

As empires expanded in the 19th century, western expatriates living in the colonies ordered local manufacturers to supply their furniture: much of this was a curious mix of Asian and western tastes. Locally made copies of fine western furniture are now very sought after, particularly if of high quality and rare woods. Anglo-Indian pieces of simple form were always well made from the best local woods so attract a high price. Over-ornate, highly carved furniture is not as desirable, even if of high quality but is good value if that is your taste. **Peter Wain**

A pair of elm benches, Chinese provincial, 19thC, 42in (106.5cm) wide.
£650–700 ⊞ TQM

A hardwood cabinet, with latticework shelves, Chinese, 19thC, 41in (104cm) wide.
£1,100–1,400 ⚒ SLN

A pair of rosewood bookcases, with softwood inset shelves, 1875–1900, 34½in (87.5cm) wide.
£925–1,150 ⚒ NOA

► **A lacquer table cabinet,** Japanese, c1880, 12in (20.5cm) high.
£350–400 ⊞ DJH

A lacquer table bureau, with a shaped drawer, lacquer restored, Chinese Export, 18thC, 28in (71cm) wide, on a later stand.
£400–500 ⚒ P(O)

A black lacquer cabinet, the doors decorated with tree peonies, jardinières and perching birds, the fitted interior with ten drawers decorated in shades of gilt and bronze with pavilion landscapes, the door interiors with bamboo, butterflies and birds, distressed, Chinese, mid-18thC, 38in (96.5cm) wide, on a mid-18thC English black-japanned chinoiserie stand.
£2,000–2,400 ⚒ N

◄ **A painted cabinet,** decorated on three sides with Lohan and Buddhist symbols, Tibetan, 19thC, 16¼in (41.5cm) wide.
£1,800–2,000 ⊞ LOP

A teak cabinet, with two drawers over two doors, with carved panels, traces of black lacquer on door panels, Chinese provincial, early 20thC, 32in (81.5cm) high.
£500–550 ⊞ OE

A pair of hardwood and mother-of-pearl-inlaid armchairs, decorated throughout with trailing foliage and birds, the pierced backs and arms above solid seats, Chinese, 19thC.
£700–800 ⚒ S(S)

A set of four carved hardwood dining chairs, the stylized lyre-shaped backs carved throughout with leaf decoration, Anglo-Indian, 1800–50.
£800–900 ⚒ S(S)

A carved hardwood armchair, the top-rail in the shape of a dragon above a pierced foliate splat back, on four dragon legs, Chinese, early 20thC.
£370–470 ⚒ RTo

An elm side chair, with a rattan seat and curved rest, Chinese, 19thC.
£1,300–1,500 ⊞ GRG

A pair of ebony armchairs, with caned seats, Anglo-Indian, 1825–50.
£18,000–20,000 ⚒ S
Although they are in the style of a Sheraton prototype, these chairs are commonly referred to as 'Raffles chairs' after Sir Stamford Raffles, Governor of Java and founder of Singapore, during whose administration they first became popular in the former Dutch colonies. This style of chair is very fashionable with decorators at present, and their value is enhanced because they are constructed of solid ebony.

◀ **An ebony chair,** with cane seat, carved in low relief with scrolling and flowering foliage, south Indian, 1650–1700.
£2,200–2,600 ⚒ SWO

A pair of black-lacquered elm armchairs, lacquer worn, Chinese provincial, 19thC.
£765–850 ⊞ OE

A carved hardwood nursing chair, the open foliage-decorated high back over a drop-in seat, Anglo-Indian, 19thC.
£130–160 ⚒ WW

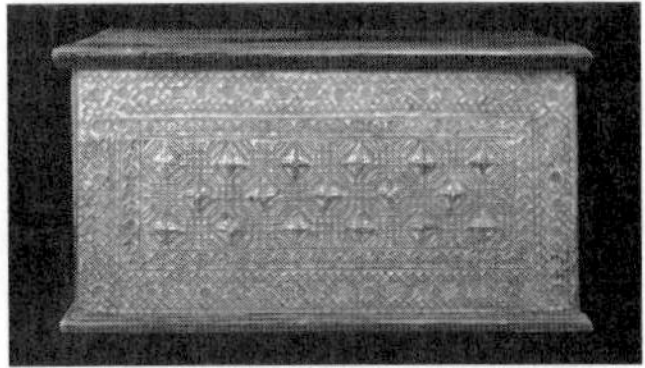

A gilded teak *sadaik* chest, Burmese, 19thC, 43¼in (110cm) wide.
£3,500–4,000 ⊞ LOP
A *sadaik* is a Buddhist scripture chest. A library where Buddhist scriptural texts are kept is essential to every monastery and the texts are arranged in chests or cabinets called *sadaik*. The importance of these chests is expressed through their excellent craftsmanship.

◀ **A black lacquer and wood chest,** with painted front panel and original brass clasp, Mongolian, late 19thC, 34in (86.5cm) wide, on a later stand.
£585–650 ⊞ OE

An elm cupboard, with black lacquer panels, Chinese, 1850–99, 44in (112cm) wide.
£5,750–6,500 ⊞ GRG

A hardwood cupboard-on-stand, with pierced brass fret hinges and escutcheons, the base with two drawers, Indo-Portuguese, 19thC, 43in (109cm) wide.
£360–450 ⚒ WW

A *tieli* desk, with original metalwork and broken-ice foot rest, Chinese, Canton, 47in (119.5cm) wide.
£3,000–3,400 ⊞ GRG

Items in the Asian Works of Art section have been arranged in subject order.

► **A black lacquer and parcel-gilt four-fold screen,** polychrome-decorated to one side with figures, pagodas, insects, wild beasts, exotic birds and foliage, the reverse with scenes of torture, faults, Chinese, late 19thC, 93¼in (237cm) high.
£2,600–3,250 ⚒ S(S)
It was common for expatriates to bring back 'novelty' screens, boxes, works of art, etc, which on the outside had the appearance of normality but on the inside showed erotic, torture and similar scenes of so-called Chinese exotic life.

◄ **A four-fold carved screen,** each black and red lacquer panel decorated with birds and foliage in bone, ivory and mother-of-pearl, surmounted by a carved dragon panel, Japanese, 19thC, 72¾in (185cm) high.
£600–750 ⚒ TRM

Authenticating Asian lacquer furniture

The huge demand for lacquerwork in Europe in the 17th and 18th centuries resulted in a great traffic of craftsmen between west and east, as well as pieces of furniture being constructed in Europe in order to be sent to China or Japan to be lacquered before being returned to be sold. It can therefore be quite difficult to differentiate between eastern and western lacquering, but the following pointers will give an indication:

- Japanese lacquerwork is usually on a black background, with sparse, uncluttered, intricate, stylized, asymmetrical designs
- Predominant colours in eastern lacquerwork are black, brown, dark green, ochre, purple, red, vermilion, yellow.
- Predominant colours in English lacquerwork are black, blue, transparent brown, chestnut, olive, red.
- Predominant colours in French lacquerwork are blue, green, reddish-orange, white, yellow.
- European craftsmen failed to represent Asian facial features, dress and gestures, accurately although the surrounding landscapes will appear eastern.
- Symmetrical designs are a western concept. The (symmetrical) borders frequently used by English craftsmen would never have appeared on Asian work.

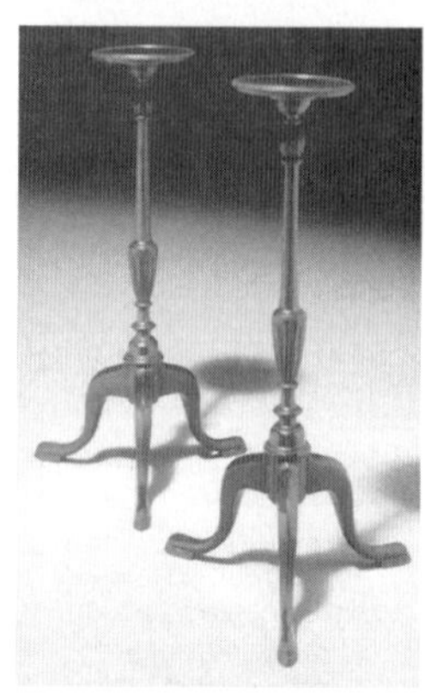

A pair of calamander candle stands, Ceylonese, 1775–1825, 9¾in (25cm) diam.
£5,500–6,000 ⚒ Bon

◄ **A hardwood sideboard,** the back carved with sages and dragons, the carved panel doors decorated with dragons among clouds, Chinese, 19thC, 62¼in (158cm) wide.
£1,000–1,250 ⚒ P(E)

► **A pair of ju wood stands,** Chinese, 19thC, 21in (53.5cm) high.
£500–600 ⊞ TQM

ASIAN WORKS OF ART

A carved rosewood torchère stand, the top with a border of carved fruit and flora, Burmese, late 19thC, 17¼in (44cm) high.
£800–975 P

A carved stand with inset marble top, Chinese, c1910, 24in (61cm) high.
£340–375 ⊞ MTay

► **A carved *zitan* and hardwood stool,** the apron carved with detached archaistic scrolls flanking a stylized mask, with traces of black lacquer overall, Chinese, 18thC, 24in (61cm) wide.
£2,500–3,000 S(NY)

Cross Reference
See Colour Review (page 616–617)

► **A carved *huanghuali* table,** the apron carved with confronting sinuous dragons flanking leaf scrolls, Chinese, 17thC, 37½in (95.5cm) wide.
£8,500–10,000 S(NY)

An ebony footstool, with caned seat, Anglo-Indian, c1830, 16in (40.5cm) wide.
£600–680 ⊞ DJH

A tortoiseshell and carved walnut games table, the shaped tilt-top centred by a chess board within engraved sprays of flowers and thistles, surrounded by an ebonized moulded border, Anglo-Indian, c1860, 17¼in (44cm) wide.
£5,000–6,000 S

A low table, with latticework apron, Chinese, 1775–1825, 29in (73.5cm) wide.
£1,150–1,300 ⊞ GRG

An elm table, with three drawers, Chinese, 19thC, 65in (165cm) wide.
£1,000–1,250 SLN

A teak centre table, the waved frieze and triform base carved with leaves and fruit, Indian, 19thC, 46¾in (119cm) diam.
£800–1,000 P(S)

Insurance values

Always insure your valuable antiques for the cost of replacing them with similar items, regardless of the original price paid. Both dealers and auctioneers can provide a valuation service for a fee.

A *tieli* altar table, with a pierced and scrolling frieze, height lowered, Chinese, c1880, 32in (78.5cm) high.
£800–875 ⊞ JC

A pair of stools, Chinese, 19thC, 9in (23cm) high.
£600–680 ⊞ RAN

A lacquer tray, decorated in *iroe/hiramakie* and *takamakie*, losses, corners cracked, Japanese, Meiji period, 1868–1911, 33½in (85cm) wide, on a later stand.
£1,100–1,300 WcH

Inro

A four-case lacquer *inro*, decorated in gold and silver *togadashi*, on a black ground, with a pair of sparrows perched on leaves among wild chrysanthemums and reeds, the reverse with a moon, Japanese, 19thC, 3in (7.5cm) high.
£2,400–3,000 S(NY)

A two-case patinated-brass *inro*, with foliate motif, on a cord with silvered *ojime* slide-bead and clam-shell-shaped metal *netsuke*, Japanese, Meiji Period, 1868–1911, 1½in (4cm) high.
£170–200 RIT

A four-case lacquer *inro*, decorated in gilt, silver and red lacquer on a *nashiji* and black ground, depicting stylized flowers among foliage, Japanese, Meiji Period, 1868–1911, 3¼in (8.5cm) high.
£500–600 P(Ba)

A four-case black and gilt lacquer *inro*, decorated with branches of bamboo to one side, the reverse with a four-character poem against prunus in flower, and pine boughs growing along a riverbank in gold *hiramakie*, with a coral bead *ojime* and a 20thC marine ivory *netsuke* of a *karako* crawling over a garden rock, signed Ichino, Japanese, 19thC, 3¼in (8.5cm) high.
£1,400–1,700 BB(S)

Netsuke

A lacquered wood *netsuke* of Shoki, the warrior holding his blade as he leans into the wind searching for demons, signed Shuzan, Japanese, 18thC, 3½in (9cm) high.
£1,300–1,500 BB(S)

◄ **An ivory seal *netsuke* of a dromedary with a foreigner,** the camel with inlaid eyes, ivory slightly stained, Japanese, probably Osaka, 19thC, 1½in (4cm) high.
£1,600–1,800 S

A carved red lacquer netsuke of figures drinking among pine trees, the sides with lotus flowers divided by shaped apertures lined with mother-of-pearl, Japanese, 19thC, 1½in (4cm) wide.
£220–275 P(Ba)

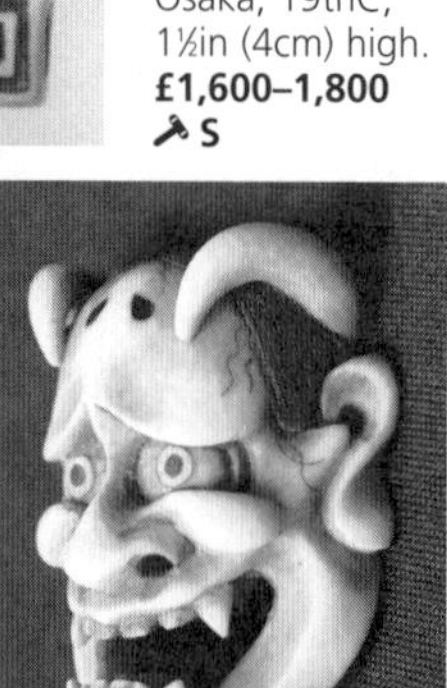

► **A carved ivory *netsuke* of a mask of Hannya,** signed Koichi, Japanese, Meiji period, 1868–1911, 2in (5cm) high.
£450–500 AMC

A carved ivory *netsuke* of a group of horses, signed Tomochika, Japanese, 19thC, 1½in (4cm) high.
£820–900 BB(S)

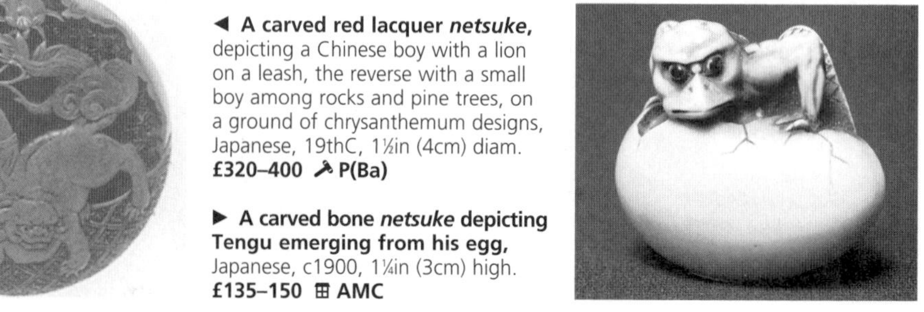

◄ **A carved red lacquer *netsuke*,** depicting a Chinese boy with a lion on a leash, the reverse with a small boy among rocks and pine trees, on a ground of chrysanthemum designs, Japanese, 19thC, 1½in (4cm) diam.
£320–400 P(Ba)

► **A carved bone *netsuke* depicting Tengu emerging from his egg,** Japanese, c1900, 1¼in (3cm) high.
£135–150 AMC

Robes & Costume

An embroidered robe, decorated with dragons and *shou* medallions worked in metallic gold couched threads, on a blue satin ground, Chinese, 19thC, 55in (139.5cm) long.
£1,700–2,000 BB(S)

A formal court robe, the Prussian blue silk embroidered throughout in couched gilt threads with nine dragons among cloud scrolls and auspicious symbols, Chinese, late 19thC.
£750–950 Bon(C)

An official's wardrobe of clothes and accessories, Chinese, late 19thC.
£2,000–2,500 Bon(C)

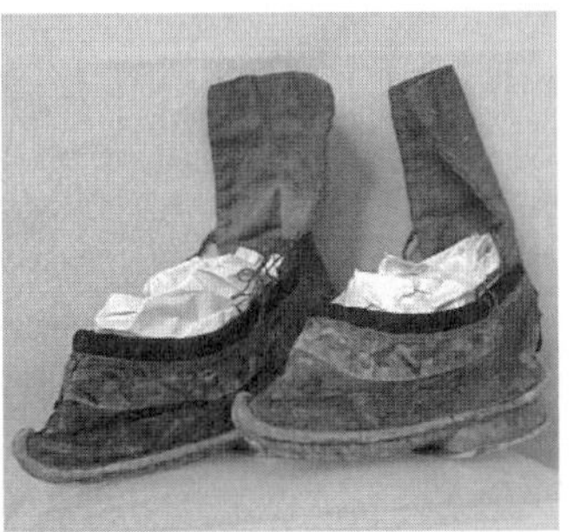

► **A dragon robe,** decorated with a brocade of dragons and Buddhist emblems on a purple ground, Chinese, 1900–25.
£400–450 SK
Condition of textiles determine price. This robe had possibly sustained more damage than the other robes pictured on this page.

◄ **A pair of lotus bud shoes,** in pale blue and ivory silk embroidered with flowers, Chinese, late 19th–early 20thC.
£25–30 WW

Snuff Bottles

◄ **A mustard-yellow glass snuff bottle,** 18thC, 2in (5cm) high.
£720–800 RHa

An interior-painted snuff bottle, by Ma Shaoxuan, with a portrait of the Beijing Opera actor Tan Xinpei, the reverse with an inscription and date, signed, Chinese, Beijing, dated 1900, 2½in (6.5cm) high.
£4,500–5,500 S(NY)

A nephrite snuff bottle, with a russet inclusion forming a raised archaic dragon, with jadeite stopper, Chinese, mid-18thC, 3¼in (8.5cm) high.
£420–525 TEN

► **A green overlay glass snuff bottle,** the overlay carved with a grasshopper resting on two peapods, the reverse with a dragonfly and a fruiting plant on a mottled white ground, with cracked amethyst stopper, Chinese, 18th–19thC, 2½in (6.5cm) high.
£350–450 B(Ba)

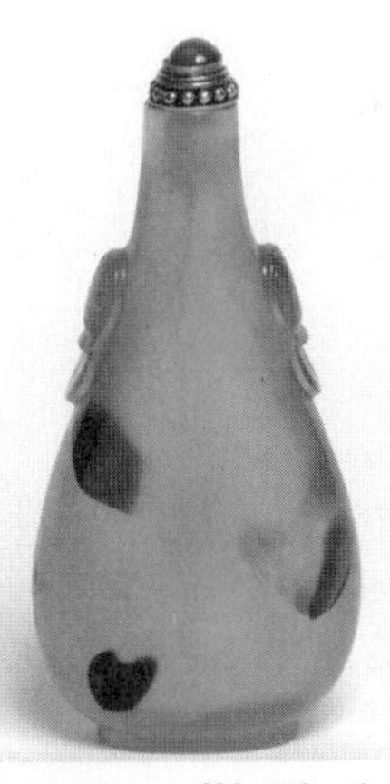

An agate snuff bottle, the sides carved with mask-and-ring handles, with imitation-jade glass stopper, Chinese, 1780–1850, 4in (10cm) high.
£1,000–1,100 RHa

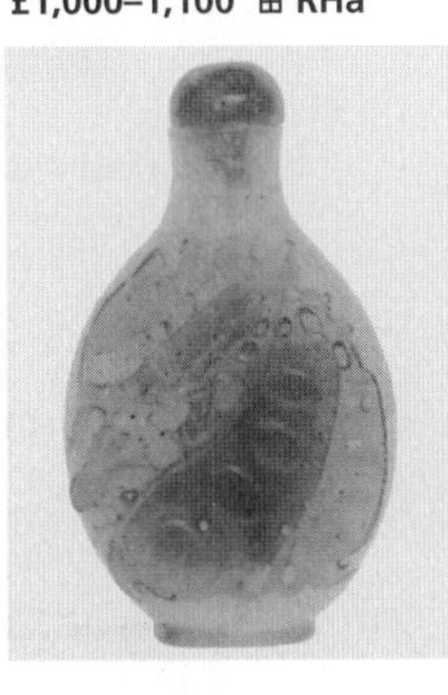

An amber snuff bottle, Chinese, 1780–1850, 2½in (6.5cm) high.
£2,500–2,750 S(NY)

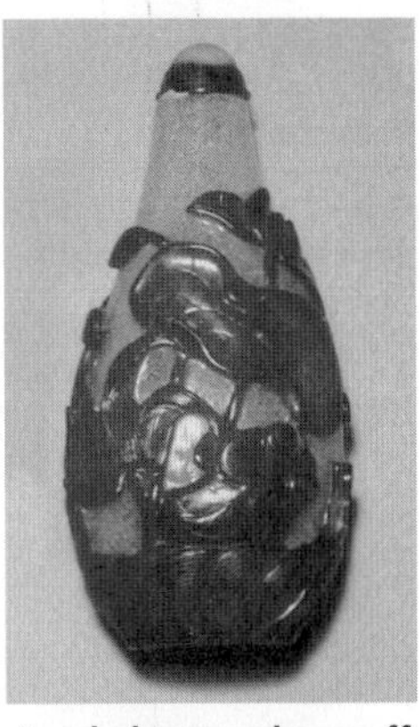

A red glass overlay snuff bottle, the sides carved with carp among blossoming and leafy lotus plants, on a snowflake ground, Chinese, 1780–1850, 3in (7.5cm) high.
£1,600–2,000 S(NY)

A nephrite snuff bottle, the ochre skin remaining in one area, with imitation-jade glass stopper, Chinese, 1780–1850, 2¾in (7cm) high.
£1,400–1,600 ⊞ RHa

A white nephrite snuff bottle, carved with figures on a sampan floating beneath a gnarled tree, with an inscription to one side, Chinese, 1780–1850, 3in (7.5cm) high.
£1,440–1,600 ⊞ RHa

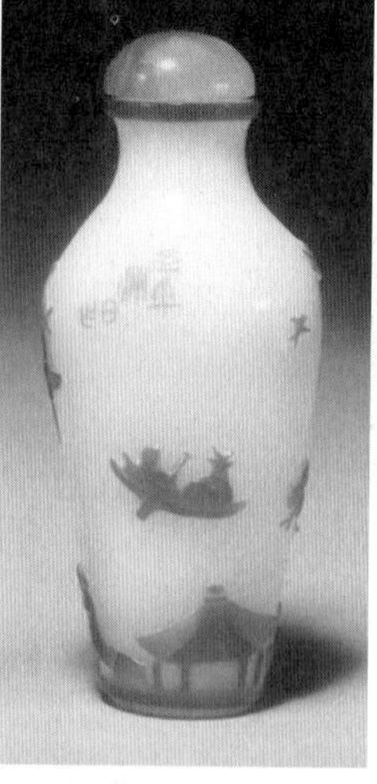

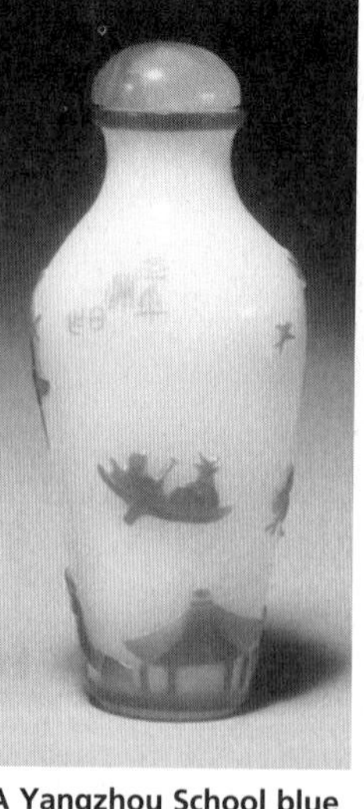

A Yangzhou School blue overlay glass snuff bottle, decorated with a scene of a scholar crossing a bridge, a figure ferrying an ox across the lake below, and a soaring crane, the shoulder with date inscription, Chinese, dated 1822, 2½in (6.5cm) high.
£4,500–5,000 ⚒ S(NY)

A red overlay glass snuff bottle, carved with squirrels and grapes, Chinese, 1780–1850, 3½in (9cm) high.
£900–1,000 ⊞ RHa

An agate double-gourd snuff bottle, Chinese, 1800–80, 3in (7.5cm) high.
£1,000–1,100 ⊞ RHa

A cinnabar lacquered snuff bottle, relief-carved with figures on riverside pagoda terraces and piers overlooking the lapping waves, beneath pine trees, *ruyi* and foliate borders, with stopper, c1900, 3in (7.5cm) high.
£300–375 ⚒ P(Ba)

► **A chalcedony snuff bottle,** carved as a jujube fruit studded with ochre-coloured peanuts, Chinese, 1840–1900, 2½in (6.5cm) high.
£750–825 ⚒ S(NY)
The combined depiction of both jujube and peanut forms the rebus *Zaozi*, 'early arrival of male offspring'.

Textiles

An ivory satin coverlet, embroidered in silks, with cupids and cupid masks amid strapwork, acanthus scrolls and exotic birds, re-lined, missing two corners, produced for the European market, Chinese, early 18thC, 87½ x 89in (222.5 x 226cm).
£2,200–2,700 ⚒ S(O)

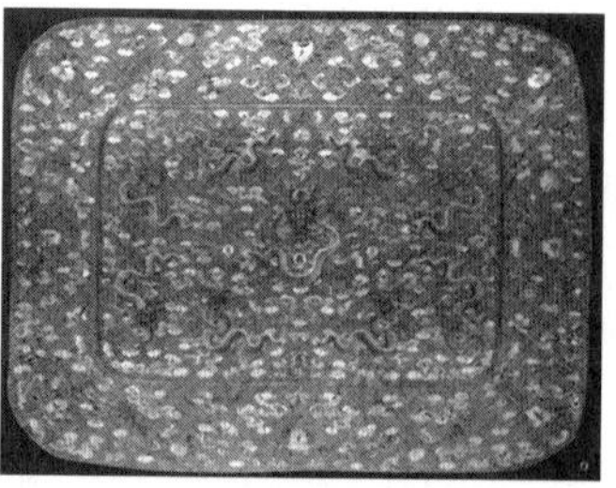

An embroidered satin Nine Dragon *kang* cover, minor losses, Chinese, 19thC, 39½ x 51½in (100.5 x 131cm), framed and glazed.
£2,000–2,400 ⚒ BB(S)
A *kang* is a raised bed or bench found in large Chinese halls and palaces. In winter it is heated from underneath with coals.

A pair of embroideries, in mainly pale cream, green and yellow, depicting phoenix surrounded by butterflies and flowering prunus, Chinese, 19thC, 19in (48.5cm) diam, in glazed ebony frames.
£250–320 ⚒ TRM
The phoenix was the symbol of the ladies' court.

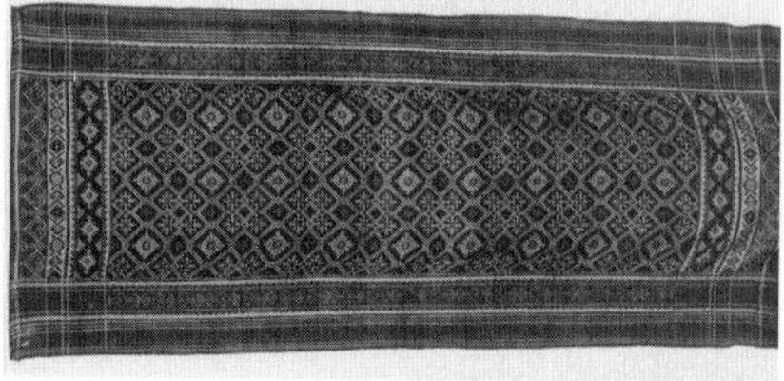

► **A silk *ikat* cloth,** Indian, Gujarat, 19thC, 33 x 39in (84 x 99cm).
£500–600 ⚒ SK
In this type of cloth the warp and weft threads are tie-dyed before weaving.

Islamic Works of Art

Arms & Armour

An ornamental dagger, with an agate hilt, the silvered- and gilded-bronze scabbard decorated with Greek mythological and battle scenes, with two accessories for cutting and piercing, Persian, 19thC, 13½in (34.5cm) long, boxed.
£900–1,150 LCM

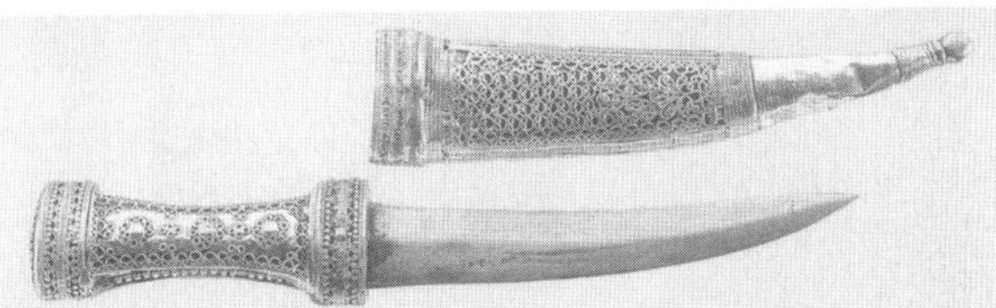

An Ottoman *khanjar*, the silver grip with floral filigree decoration, with a silver-plated, decorated scabbard *en suite*, minor repairs to *khanjar*, Turkish, c1900, 14¼in (36cm) long.
£200–250 Herm

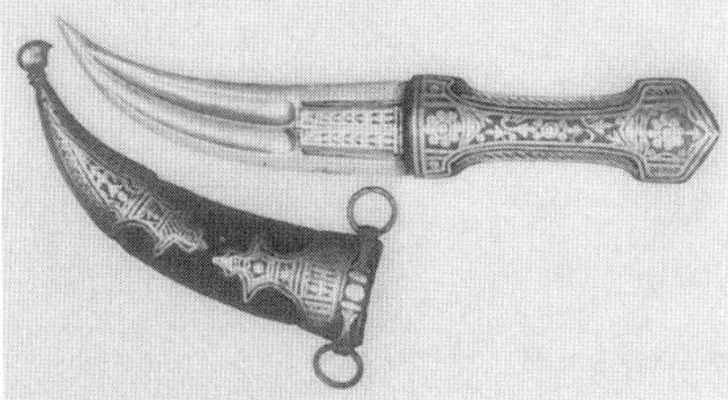

A *jambiya*, the steel hilt and sheath mounts silver damascened with flowers, foliage and geometric ornament, with red velvet-covered sheath, Syrian, 19thC, 11½in (29cm) long.
£360–450 WAL

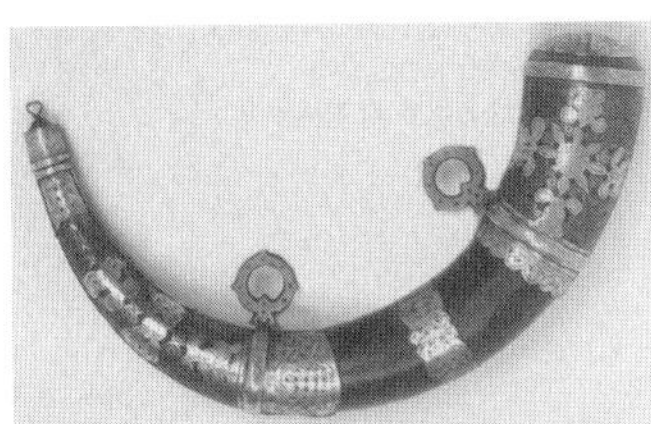

A powder horn, the body with brass mounts faced with sheet silver, engraved overall and chiselled with geometric scrolled designs, Moroccan, 19thC, 13¼in (33.5cm) long.
£280–350 WAL

▶ **An Ottoman powder primer and strap,** the wooden body encased in sheet silver, with a cast silver cap and steel arm and a pair of brass hinges attached to a leather strap, repoussé decoration of roccoco scrolls, rosettes and fronds, signed Mahmud, Turkish, dated AH1192/AD1778, 8in (20cm) long.
£400–500 Bon

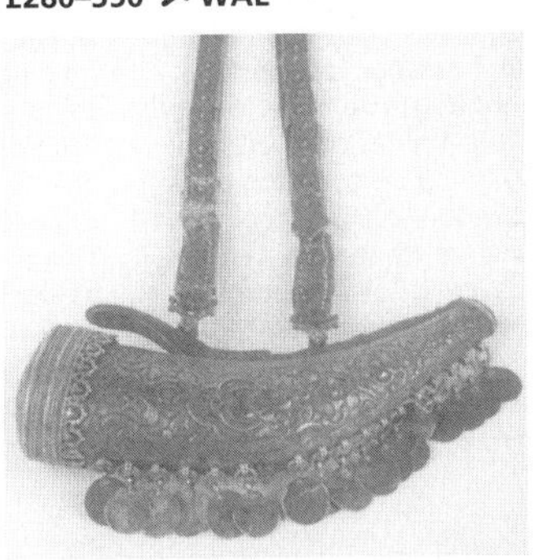

A damascened-steel *khula khud* and armguards, Persian, 19thC, helmet 27¼in (69cm) high.
£1,600–2,000 Herm

Ceramics

▶ **A pottery dish,** decorated in mustard and cream slip, on a raised pedestal foot, Persian, 10th–11thC, 7¼in (18.5cm) diam.
£130–145 CrF

A blue and white ewer, painted in underglaze blue and outlined in black with a pattern of stylized foliage within *ruyi* borders, with metal spout and rim mounts, some damage and restoration, Middle Eastern, 18th–19thC, 8¼in (21cm) high.
£180–225 P(Ba)

A Nishapur slip-painted pottery bowl, decorated in mustard, red, manganese/brown and white with a band of stylized *kufic* inscription between two panels, both depicting an animal, with *kufic* inscription to the rim band, Persian, 9th–10thC, 9in (23cm) diam.
£1,000–1,250 Bon

◀ **A Channakale pottery lion,** decorated with green splashes on a yellow ground, with moulded, applied detailing, Turkish, 19thC, 6¼in (16cm) high.
£700–875 Bon(C)

Furniture

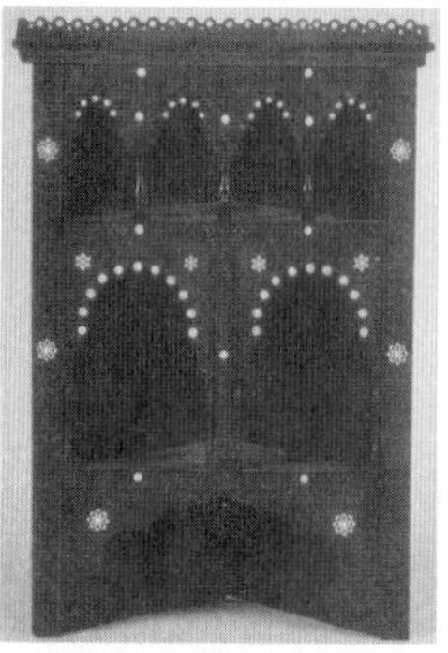

A parquetry wood corner cabinet, relief-carved with arabesques and inlaid with mother-of-pearl rosettes, Syrian, Damascus, 19thC, 24¼in (61.5cm) high.
£550–700 Bon

A mother-of-pearl parquetry table, the decagonal top centred by a flowerhead-inlaid roundel, Egyptian or Syrian, 19thC, 16½in (42cm) wide.
£2,300–2,700 S

A parquetry wood hexagonal table, decorated with mother-of-pearl and wood with lozenges centred on a decorative *tughra*, Syrian, Damascus, late 19thC, 23½in (59.5cm) high.
£400–500 Bon

A Moresque marquetry and mother-of-pearl-inlaid games table, the hinged top inlaid with various woods in geometrical patterns, enclosing a green gaming surface within a marquetry-inlaid border, opening to reveal a tric-trac board, Spanish, c1900, 31in (82¼cm) wide.
£1,800–2,200 S(Am)

Glass

A green glass beaker, the impressed decoration of repeated bands of *kufic* script alternating with pairs of lozenges, Syrian, Egyptian or Iraqi, 9th/10thC, 3¼in (8.5cm) high.
£5,000–5,500 S
The inscription reads 'Blessing upon its owner'.

A mould-blown turquoise glass bottle, the body impressed with a honeycomb design, Persian, 11th/12thC, 3¾in (9.5cm) high.
£500–625 Bon

A millefiori glass gaming piece, the turquoise body with red, yellow, green and white insets, and a black and white band, Mesopotamian or Persian, 8th/9thC, 1¼in (3cm) high.
£1,000–1,250 Bon

◄ **A free-blown green glass bottle,** the body impressed with a frieze of ribs, Persian, 11th/12thC, 10¼in (26cm) high.
£1,100–1,300 Bon

Manuscripts

◄ **A Koran,** in Arabic manuscript on gold-sprinkled paper, 324 leaves, bearing the signature of Abdullah al-Tabakh, in brown morocco binding with stamped floral decoration, repaired, some worming, Persian, 15th/16thC, 13¼ x 8¾in (33.5 x 22cm).
£9,000–11,500 P(Ba)

A calligraphy panel, ink on paper, Turkish, c1920, 27½ x 16in (70 x 40.5cm), framed and glazed.
£250–300 SK

◄ **An Ottoman Koran fragment,** four handwritten sheets embellished in gold and polychrome, with a gold-embossed leather cover, 18th/19thC, 5 x 7¾in (12.5 x 19.5cm), with embroidered 19thC case.
£330–420 Herm

Metalware

A bronze inkwell, engraved with three arched cartouches containing two confronted birds and flanked by floral roundels, late 12th–13thC.
£1,600–2,000 ⚒ S(NY)

A brass footed bowl, engraved with floral decoration and courtly persons, Persian, 19thC, 8½in (21.5cm) diam.
£200–250 ⚒ Herm

► **A Khorasan bronze mortar,** incised with a frieze of birds against palmettes, bands of *kufic* inscription around the base and a frieze of cursive inscription around the mouth, Persian, 12thC, 7¼in (18.5cm) diam, with pestle.
£1,600–2,000 ⚒ Bon

► **A silver pomander,** the top with pierced foliate design, the bowl engraved on the exterior with foliate designs, Persian, c1800, 3in (7.5cm) diam.
£450–550 ⊞ CoHA

Wood

► **An Ottoman wood casket,** inlaid with mother-of-pearl and tortoiseshell, Turkish, 18thC, 13½in (34.5cm) wide.
£730–900 ⚒ Herm

◄ **A lacquered wood covered box,** the body encircled by a solid red band above two black bands, a black band with a reserved *kufic* inscription below the mouth, the lid with a reversed cable band between yellow bands, the underside of the lid embellished green, Persian, 11th–12thC, 3¾in (9.5cm) high.
£1,500–1,800 ⚒ Bon

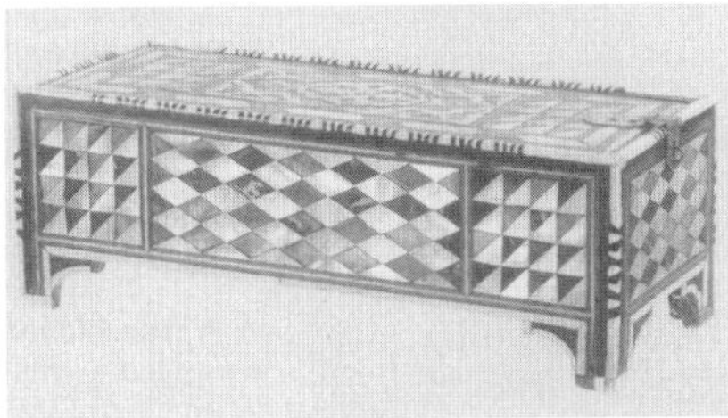

A Qajar pearwood casket, relief-carved with a portrait of Nasr-al-Din Shah, surrounded by putti among foliage, the border with floral sprays, the sides with further portraits, Persian, late 19thC, 18¼in (46.5cm) wide.
£2,800–3,500 ⚒ Bon

Textiles

An Anteri robe, the midnight blue velvet worked with silver thread, decorated with vases of flowers to the hem and cuffs, the whole with tendril-and-flower spray motifs, Turkish, late 19thC.
£370–420 ⚒ P

Cross Reference
See Colour Review (page 618)

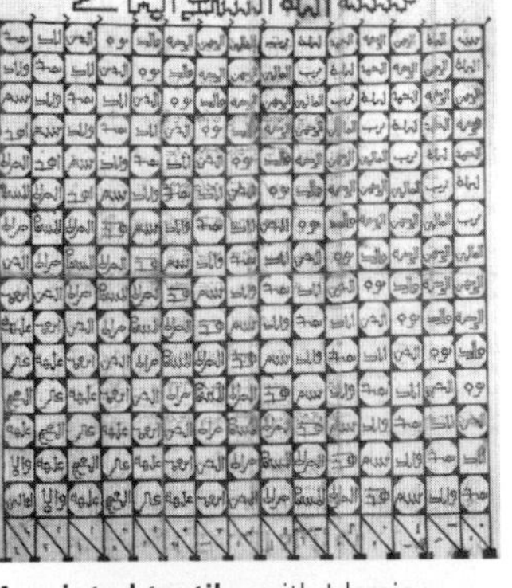

A painted textile, with Islamic inscription in *kufic* form, Indian, 19thC, 16 x 17in (40.5 x 43cm), framed and glazed.
£550–600 ⚒ SK

A Kirman cover, the cream wool embroidered in coloured wools with a central medallion, the inner border with a stylized cone motif, the outer border with flowers and leaves, Persian, late 19thC, 54 x 38in (137 x 96.5cm)
£250–275 ⚒ P

Architectural Antiques

One of the greatest joys of garden statuary and architectural items lies in the enormous variety of objects that fall into these categories. There is always something fresh to be discovered or learned. It is also an area that is relatively new in the antiques world. While it is true that there has been garden statuary and architectural items of merit from the early days of civilization and that Classical or Renaissance pieces can change hands for considerable sums of money, the 'golden age' of enormous production and tremendous variety and invention was between 1860 and 1900. Many wonderful pieces from this era and often earlier ones can be found for modest sums when compared to other fields of antiques, which can only add to the attraction.

The past year has been an interesting one – as this area of collecting matures and continues to grow, trends are becoming discernible. The most notable, and one which very much reflects the entire antiques trade, is that the best examples by well-known makers are the surest bets for investments. Pieces bought five years ago can have doubled or even trebled in the price that a dealer asks or an auction house achieves. These pieces are however the exceptional ones and for the serious collector or wealthy speculator, but wonderful pieces by good makers can still be found for relatively modest sums.

There are however a few areas that seem to have peaked over the last couple of years, for instance cast-iron seats, especially Coalbrookdale pieces. Some extraordinary prices were fetched at auction for rare patterns such as Passion-flower or Medallion and this skewed people's expectations for the more common patterns and increased the number of reproductions on the market. Interest in genuine examples continues to be high but it is unlikely that prices will be as high as they were two years ago. Eighteenth century lead-work is similarly depressed and currently isn't fetching as much as it was five to ten years ago. Wirework furniture and planters still have not recovered the prices that were realized in the late '80s and early '90s, although scarcity of unusual patterns will perhaps prompt a revival of interest.

Bargains can be found in all sorts of places from car boot sales to dealers and auction houses. What used to be the preserve of a few top London dealers is now enjoyed by an increasing number of people and the opportunities for finding and buying pieces has grown correspondingly. One word of caution though: beware the modern reproduction! After an item has been outside for a number of years and has been exposed to the ravages of the British climate it can look a lot older than it actually is. If you only want a piece for its decorative appeal that is fine, but if you are specifically looking for antiques it is always worth consulting a specialist. **Rupert van der Werff**

Iron

A Val d'Osne Foundry cast-iron fountain, modelled as a child holding a duck, with bill plumbed for water, after Mathurin Moreau, French, c1870, 34in (86.5cm) high.
£2,500–2,750 ⚒ S(S)

► A pair of cast-iron gates, with three tiers of gilt spear finials, late 19th–early 20thC, 142in (360.5cm) high.
£5,750–7,000 ⚒ S(S)

A cast-iron fountain, on a stoneware pedestal, 1850–1900, 38in (96.5cm) diam.
£600–720 ⚒ S(S)

◄ A late Georgian cast-iron fire insurance plaque, Shaw Walker & Co, Union Street, Glasgow, centred by a thistle, 6¼in (16cm) high.
£75–95 ⚒ PFK

A Victorian wrought-iron gate, 36in (91.5cm) wide.
£720–800 ⊞ OIA

◄ A cast-iron hitching post, surmounted by a lion's head painted tan, brown and black above a green collar, the column with gilt embellishments, some repainting, American, late 19thC, 45in (114.5cm) high.
£1,850–2,200 ⚒ SK(B)

A wrought-iron jardinière, the frame decorated with trailing roses and sunflowers, possibly 18thC, 59in (150cm) wide.
£4,500–5,750 S(S)

A painted cast-iron lion wall plaque, late 18thC, 19in (48.5cm) wide.
£750–850 ⊞ ChC

◄ **A pair of bronzed and cast-iron lamp posts,** the copper lantern with crown finial, French, c1870, 160in (406cm) high.
£3,700–4,000 S(S)

A pair of cast-iron planters, 18th–19thC, 18in (45.5cm) high.
£2,000–2,400 S(S)

A cast-iron plant stand, with six circular pot stands, late 19thC, 40½in (103cm) high.
£575–700 S(S)

A cast-iron radiator, French, c1900, 26in (66cm) high.
£350–400 ⊞ C&R

► **A cast-iron garden armchair,** probably by Robert Wood Foundry, Philadelphia, with traces of white paint, American, 1845–55.
£300–360 WcH

A set of five panels of wrought-iron and bronze railing, with barley-twist uprights and scroll decoration applied with bronze foliate mounts, 27in (68cm) high.
£700–800 S(S)

A Regency wrought-iron garden chair, early 19thC.
£425–525 Bon(C)

◄ **A set of four Victorian cast-iron garden chairs.**
£550–700 MEA

A Coalbrookdale cast-iron seat, in Water Plant pattern, the back pierced with geometric flowers, c1870, 75in (190.5cm) wide.
£850–1,000 S(S)

A cast-iron seat, in Medallion pattern, the back centred with a panel of a seated classical maiden, possibly American, late 19thC, 58in (147.5cm) wide.
£900–1,150 S(S)

A cast-iron seat, in Fern and Blackberry pattern, the seat pierced with interwoven geometric decoration, American, late 19thC, 58in (147.5cm) wide.
£900–1,150 S(S)

A wrought-iron conversation seat, the three chairs with simulated caned backs flanked by scrolls, the top with maker's stamp 'Tonchon', French, c1900, 58in (147.5cm) wide.
£2,000–2,200 S(S)

◀ **A wrought-iron tree bench,** mid-19thC, 78in (198cm) diam.
£2,000–2,200 S(S)

A pair of cast-iron urns on pedestals, 1870–80, 44in (112cm) high.
£750–950 WL

A Victorian cast-iron garden urn, with applied rosettes and acanthus scrolls, mask-and-loop handles, 23in (58.5cm) diam.
£530–670 DD

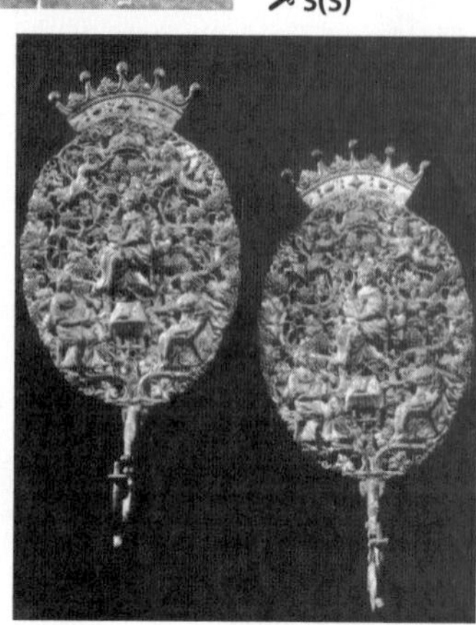

A pair of gilt cast-iron wall sconces, the backs pierce-decorated with Virgin and Child and saints against fruiting vine, each surmounted by a coronet, Continental, 18thC, 17in (43cm) high.
£750–950 P(O)

Lead

A Georgian lead cistern, 47in (119.5cm) wide.
£2,400–2,700 ⊞ L(sm)

A lead cistern, the front and one side decorated with strapwork panels, the front with ownership initials and putti cartouches, dated 1749, 44in (112cm) wide.
£3,000–3,750 S

A pair of lead urns, the acanthus-cast bodies decorated with vignettes of classical scenes and with grotesque bird handles, early 20thC, 22in (56cm) high.
£1,750–2,000 S(S)

Prices

The price ranges quoted in this book reflect the average price a purchaser might expect to pay for a similar item. The price will vary according to the condition, rarity, size, popularity, provenance, colour and restoration of the item, and this must be taken into account when assessing values. Don't forget that if you are selling it is quite likely that you will be offered less than the price range.

A lead hopper, the up pipe moulded with putti and initials and dated 1776, 53½in (136cm) high.
£525–600 S(S)

Marble

A white marble terrier, late 19thC, 15¾in (40cm) high.
£1,200–1,500 S(S)

A marble horse, 1920s, 23in (58.5cm) high.
£350–400 OLA

An English School white marble figure of a nymph gazing into a stream, late 19thC, 33¼in (84.5cm) high.
£6,000–7,500 S

A variegated pink marble column, 19thC, 44¼in (112.5cm) high.
£350–450 F&C

A pair of marble tritons, late 19thC, 49in (124.5cm) high.
£12,500–15,000 S(NY)
Marble tritons are very rare and even more so if they are a pair.

A pair of Carrara marble pedestals, Italian, c1780, 55in (139.5cm) high.
£12,500–14,000 W&C
Eighteenth-century pedestals sell for a premium, particularly if the surface is good.

A white marble figure of Venus, after Canova, mid-19thC, 67in (170cm) high.
£1,200–1,500 S(S)

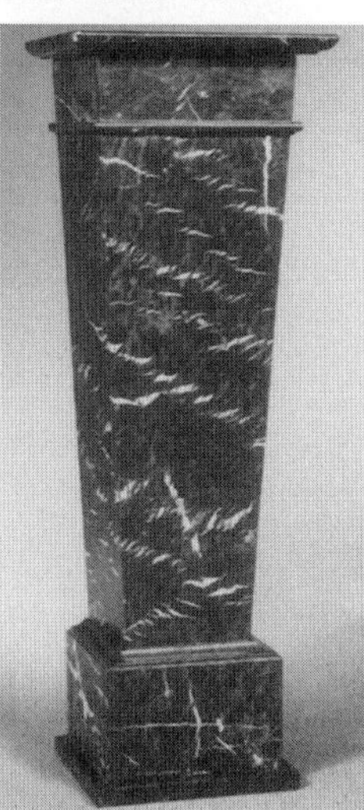

A red and black marble Louis XVI-style pedestal, French, 1875–90, 47in (119.5cm) high.
£1,400–1,700 NOA

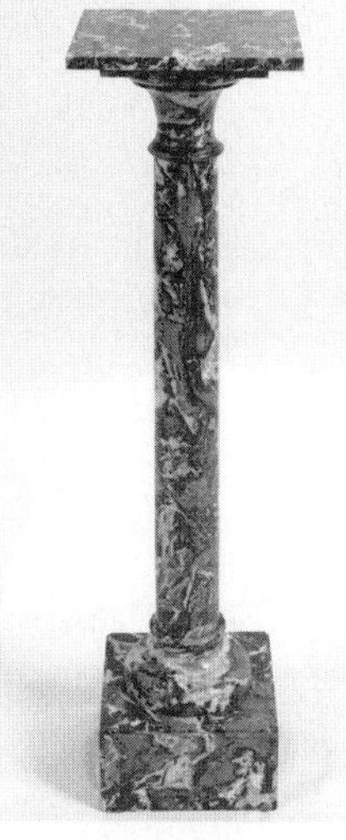

A marble pedestal, with swivel top, c1920, 43in (109cm) high.
£700–785 MTay

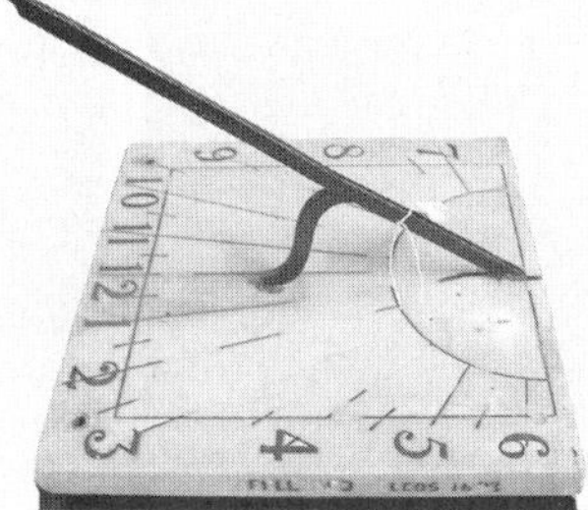

◄ **A marble wall-mounted sundial,** inscribed 'Appleyard, Leeds 1893', 18in (45.5cm) high.
£160–200 G(L)

► **An Istrian marble sundial,** the bronze dial with cockerel gnomon support, inscribed 'John P. White and Sons Ltd, London and Bedford', supported by three herm figures, early 20thC, 48in (122cm) high.
£1,850–2,200 S(S)

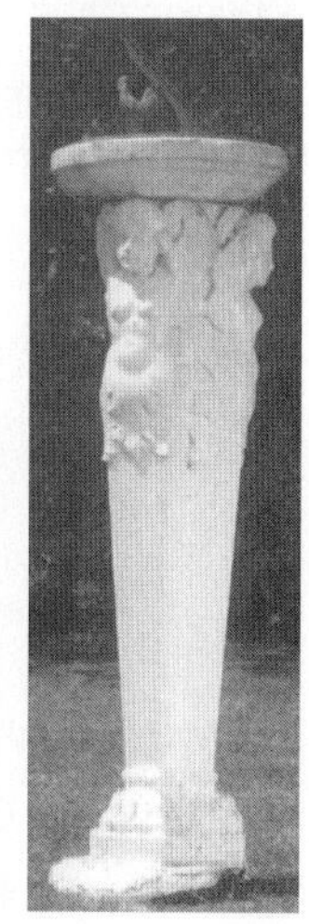

► **A pair of white marble troughs,** with drainage holes, late 19thC, 36in (91.5cm) wide.
£800–900 S(S)

Stone & Composition Stone

A pair of carved Portland stone corbel heads, in the shape of lions' heads with ferocious expressions, 17thC, 17in (43cm) high.
£1,400–1,600 S(S)

A pair of carved limestone lions, mid-18thC, 45in (114.5cm) wide.
£2,500–3,000 S(S)

A pair of sandstone lions, 19thC, 35½in (90cm) wide.
£3,500–4,500 P(Ed)

A pair of 16thC-style composition stone lions, 19thC, 42in (106.5cm) wide.
£1,200–1,500 S(S)

A sandstone keystone, carved in high relief with the head of a statesman resembling Abraham Lincoln, c1860, 24in (61cm) high.
£700–850 S(S)

A stone bust of Lord Palmerston, by John Edward Jones, signed and indistinctly dated, some damage, probably 1861, 25½in (65cm) high.
£100–125 F&C

A pink sandstone decorative piece, Scottish, 1890, 13in (33cm) high.
£180–200 OLA

A composition stone planter, 1920s, 29in (73.5cm) high.
£550–600 OLA

A composition stone figure of a young boy, the base moulded with a lizard, c1930, 32in (81.5cm) high.
£420–460 S(S)

A neo-classical-style cast-stone wall fountain, mounted with wrought-iron rings, 67in (170cm) long.
£2,800–3,500 BB(S)

◄ **A granite fruit mill trough,** 19thC, 38in (96.5cm) diam.
£675–750 WRe
These are commonly throught to have been used for pressing apples when making cider.

A carved Bath stone urn, the body with a frieze of foliage and flowerheads, c1870, 29in (73.5cm) high.
£575–720 S(S)

A Portland stone sundial, the bronze dial bearing the date 1723, early 20thC, 47in (119.5cm) high.
£1,200–1,500 S(S)

Terracotta

A late Victorian terracotta garden urn, with a detachable foot, on a flowerhead panelled plinth, small chips, 36in (91.5cm) high.
£260–325 WW

A pair of Victorian terracotta urns, stamped 'Pulham's Terracotta London and Broxbourne', 25½in (65cm) diam.
£700–875 P(Ed)

A pair of Doulton terracotta urns on plinths, c1920, 35½in (90cm) high.
£1,600–1,800 OLA

◄ **A terracotta figure of a huntress representing America,** wearing an animal pelt and a feather head-dress and holding a bow and quiver of arrows, the base stamped 'A Tarres, Alfareria, Barcelona', Spanish, late 19thC, 34in (86.4cm) high.
£2,400–2,700 S(S)

Wood

A medieval oak wood carving, of the bust of a lady with elaborate chignon, probably 14thC, now contained within a 19thC parcel-gilt oak wall bracket, 17½in (44.5cm) high.
£430–550 F&C

Three Gothic carved oak tracery panels, 15th/16th century, 7½in (19cm) square.
£875–975 SEA

A pair of oak carvings of birds, c1670, 5in (12.5cm) square.
£150–165 TRI

► **A carpenter's carved oak armorial shield,** c1880, 13in (33cm) high.
£135–150 HUM

A pair of carved oak pilasters, 17thC, 25in (63.5cm) high.
£1,150–1,275 SEA

A wooden carving of a lion, from a coat-of-arms, 17thC, 13in (33cm) high.
£850–950 TRI

A pair of giltwood terms, the female heads mounted on flower-encrusted tapering columns, Italian, 18thC, 15¾in (40cm) high.
£750–825 P

A wooden rustic summer house, with tile-hung roof, the interior fitted with benches, applied overall with branch sections, early 20thC, 96in (244cm) wide.
£4,500–5,000 S(S)

Bathroom Fittings

A Victorian corner basin, with decorative cast-iron support, 24in (61cm) wide.
£500–550 ⊞ DOR

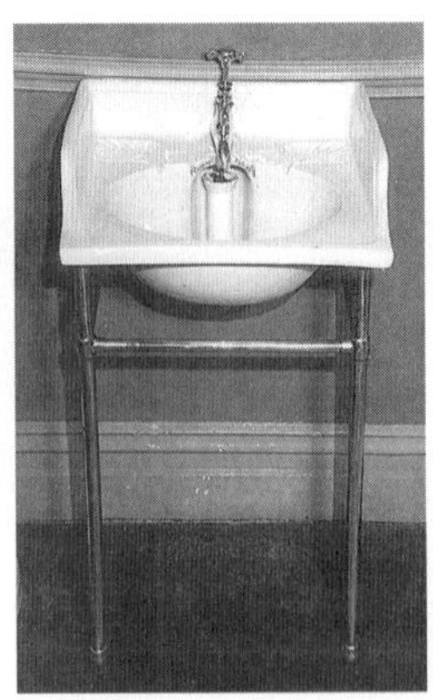

A Cardinal patent basin and wash stand, c1887, 19in (48.5cm) wide.
£1,500–1,700 ⊞ WRe

A basin, c1900, 15in (38cm) square.
£450–500 ⊞ C&R

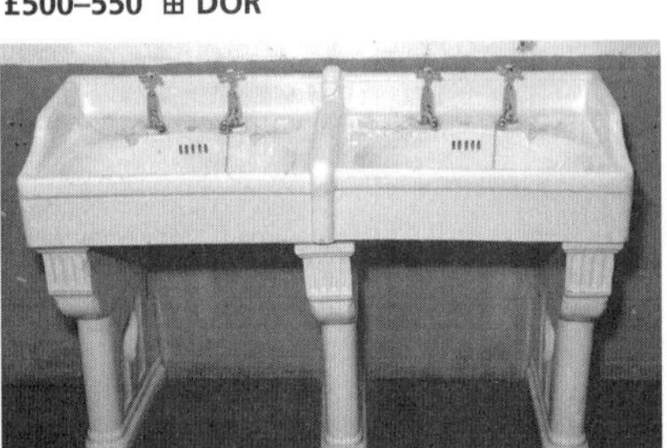

A Twyfords Adamant double basin, with legs, c1915, 49in (124.5cm) wide.
£1,100–1,250 ⊞ WRe

► **A pedestal basin,** with taps and pop-up plug, c1920, 31in (78.5cm) wide.
£1,100–1,200 ⊞ OIA

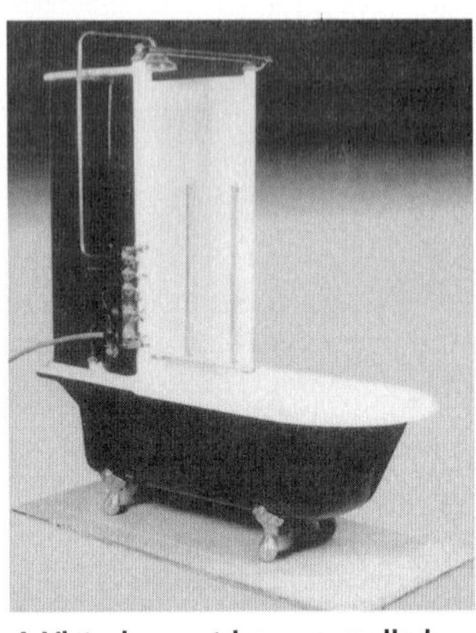

A Victorian cast-iron enamelled bath/shower, with five various taps, claw-and-ball feet, on a marble plinth, 76in (193cm) long.
£1,800–2,250 ⚒ P(Ed)

◄ **A Falkirk Iron Co roll-top bath,** with original nickel taps and plunger, Scottish, c1880, 78in (198cm) long.
£2,700–3,000 ⊞ L(r)

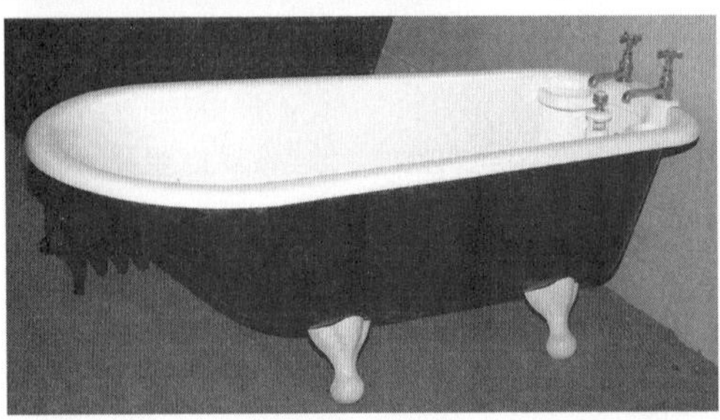

A cast-iron plunger bath, c1900, 66in (167.5cm) long.
£2,250–2,500 ⊞ C&R

► **A bidet,** French, c1900, 25in (63.5cm) long.
£400–500 ⊞ C&R

A cast-iron high-level cistern, French, c1900, 16in (40.5cm) wide.
£500–600 ⊞ C&R

A Doulton Simplicitas lavatory pan, c1900, 16in (40.5cm) high.
£1,800–2,000 ⊞ C&R

► **A Porcher lavatory pan,** French, c1900, 15in (38cm) high.
£320–400 ⊞ C&R

A pair of Victorian nickel-plated globe bath taps, refurbished, 5in (12.5cm) high.
£160–180 ⊞ OLA

► **A pair of Edwardian nickel-plated bath taps,** reconditioned, 7in (18cm) high.
£270–300 ⊞ WRe

A pair of Row Brothers nickel-plated bath taps, reconditioned, c1901, 5in (12.5cm) high.
£225–250 ⊞ WRe

► **A pair of brass sink taps,** refurbished, 1940–50, 9in (23cm) high.
£145–160 ⊞ OIA

A Librex washdown lavatory pan, 1890–1910, 16in (40.5cm) high.
£350–400 ⊞ DOR

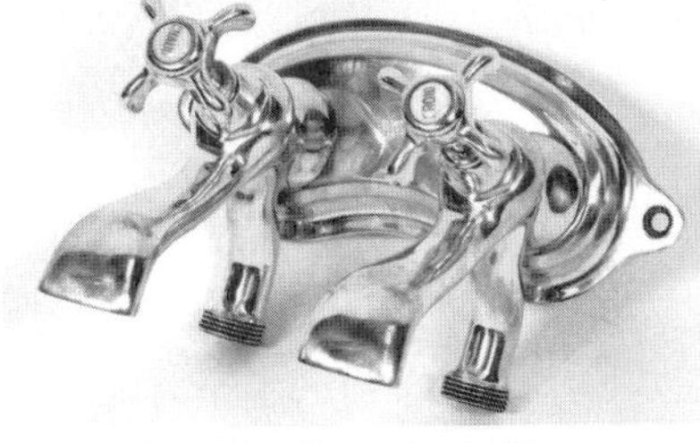

A pair of polished brass bath filler taps, c1900, 22in (56cm) wide.
£675–750 ⊞ C&R

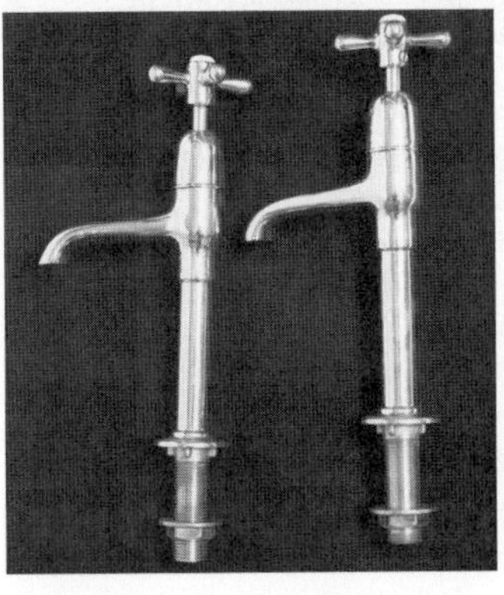

A Laydas lavatory pan, by John Bolding, with mahogany seat and cistern, c1900, 42in (106.5cm) high.
£1,500–1,800 ⊞ C&R

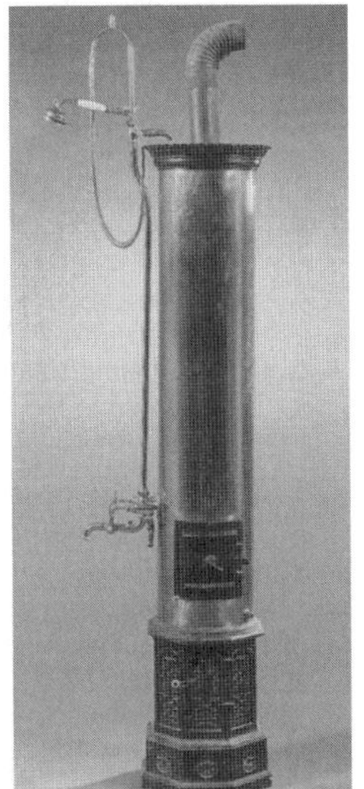

A cast-iron and copper boiler with shower, cast with arabesque ornaments, 1875–1925, 92½in (235cm) high.
£300–375 ⚒ S(Am)

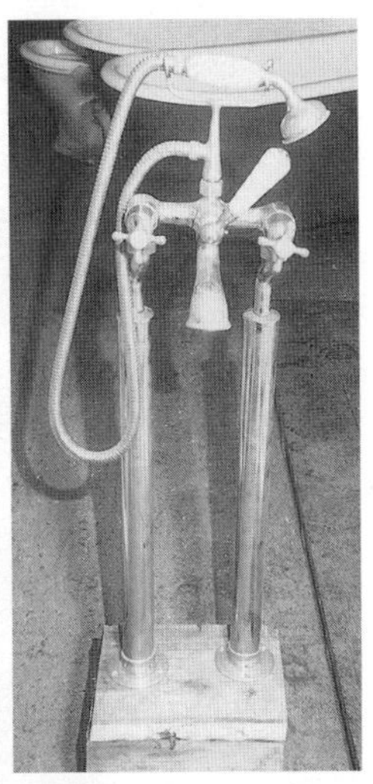

An Edwardian nickel-plated mixer and hand set, on floor-standing pipes, 37in (94cm) high.
£500–600 ⊞ DOR

Doors & Door Furniture

A Regency pine six-panel front door, 85in (216cm) high.
£115–130 ⊞ WRe

A front door, with bowed-glass inset in the shape of an eye, 1930s, 78in (198cm) high.
£115–130 ⊞ WRe

A Victorian hand-painted glass over-door panel, 38in (96.5cm) wide.
£225–250 ⊞ OLA

A pair of Edwardian brass door knobs, 3in (7.5cm) wide.
£30–35 ⊞ WRe

◀ **A brass dolphin door knocker,** c1825, 9in (23cm) wide.
£380–425 ⊞ RGe

▶ **An iron letter plate and handle,** design registered 1936, 7in (18cm) wide.
£60–70 ⊞ WRe

Fireplaces

A George III pine and gesso fire surround, attributed to Ramage and Fergusson, Leith, the frieze centred by a basket with thistles and a rose flanked by further panels with baskets of flowers, Scottish, 71¾in (182.5cm) wide.
£5,500–7,000 ⚒ P(Ed)

A George II pine and gesso fire surround, 56in (142cm) wide.
£5,000–5,600 ⊞ HA

A Renaissance-style Istrian stone fire surround, the frieze carved with *amorini* and foliate arabesques, the jambs modelled as composite pilasters decorated with classical urns filled with fruit and torchères issuing grotesques and foliage, Italian, early 19thC, 70in (178cm) wide.
£7,000–9,000 ⚒ Bon

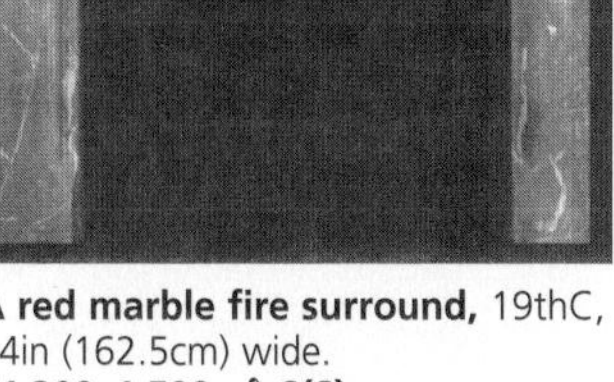

A red marble fire surround, 19thC, 64in (162.5cm) wide.
£1,200–1,500 ⚒ S(S)

A carved oak Renaissance-style fire surround, the carved frieze over half-fluted Corinthian columns decorated at the base with foliate carving, on lion's head plinth bases, French, c1840, 72¾in (185cm) wide.
£10,000–11,000 ⊞ W&C

A marble fire surround, with fluted jambs, c1840, 66in (167.5cm) wide.
£2,800–3,200 ⊞ ASH

► **A Carrara marble fire surround,** carved with garlands of fruit and flowers, with decorated key stone, c1850, 76in (193cm) wide.
£5,750–6,500 ⊞ ASH

A mahogany fire surround, with a mirror back and shelved superstructure, the mirror flanked by concave apertures, 19thC, 74¾in (190cm) wide.
£2,300–2,800 ⚒ P(Ba)

A Louis XVI-style *brêche violette* marble fire surround, the plain panelled frieze flanked by flowerheads, 19thC, 61½in (156cm) wide.
£2,750–3,500 ⚒ S(S)

► **A majolica fire surround,** the frieze with grotesque mask surrounded by scrolling foliage, the corners with terms, Italian, 19thC, 33in (84cm) wide.
£1,250–1,500 ⚒ S(Am)

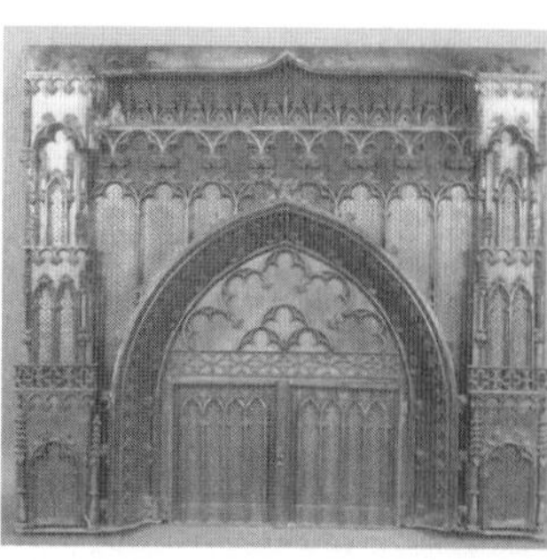

A Victorian Gothic revival brass and japanned fire grate façade, cast with spires, pinnacles and tracers with stylized oak leaves, the central arch flanked by outset towers and pilasters, and enclosed by two doors, 44in (112cm) wide.
£750–950 N

A grey/white marble Louis XV-style fire surround, the frieze centred by a seashell and foliate decoration, the jambs decorated with foliage, with a marble hearth, late 19thC, 59in (150cm) wide.
£2,400–3,000 B

A carved oak Jacobean-style fire surround, 1875–1925, 65½in (166.5cm) wide.
£300–375 Bon(C)

A painted slate fire surround, c1900, 62in (157.5cm) wide.
£550–600 WRe

A brass and iron fire grate, the brass uprights cast with a shell between C-scrolls and surmounted by urn finials issuing flames, mid-18thC, 22¾in (58cm) wide.
£8,500–11,000 S

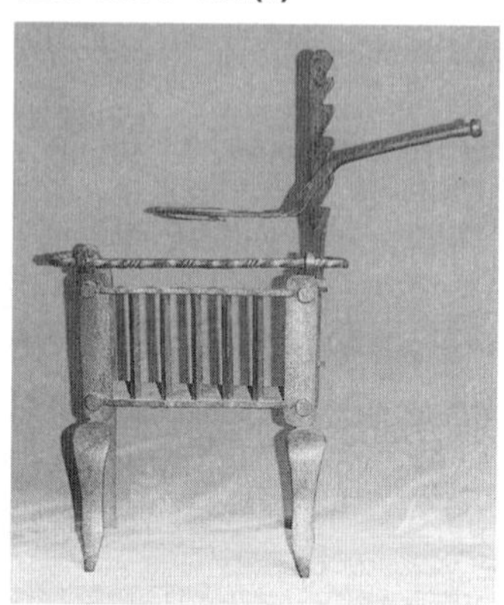

A coal grate, French, c1870, 27¼in (69cm) high.
£450–500 AMS
This was for use in a hearth and never became popular due to the abundance of wood in most parts of France.

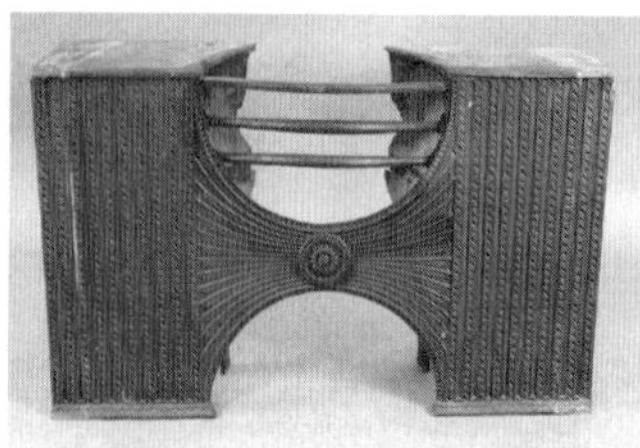

◄ **A George III cast-iron fire grate,** 37in (94cm) wide.
£220–275 SWO

A cast-iron decorated fireplace, c1810, 36in (91.5cm) wide.
£1,350–1,500 WRe

A pair of register grates, by Thomas Elsley, London, c1890, 36in (91.5cm) wide.
£5,700–6,350 L(sm)

A cast-iron and brass fire grate, the baluster-knopped brass finials mounted on scrolling bracket feet, c1910, 35½in (90cm) wide.
£850–1,100 B

Fireplace Accessories

A pair of wrought-iron andirons, with mushroom finials, late 17thC, 21in (53.5cm) high.
£2,700–3,000 ⚒ S

A pair of cast-iron andirons, French, mid-19thC, 20½in (52cm) high.
£145–160 ⊞ AMS

A pair of brass and wrought-iron fire dogs, c1870, 32in (81.5cm) high.
£1,000–1,150 ⊞ HA

An armorial cast-iron fire back, 1850–90, 26in (66cm) high.
£700–775 ⊞ SEA

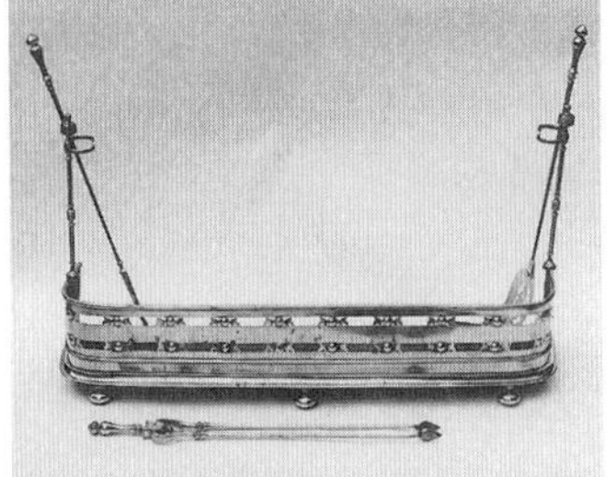

A cut polished steel fender, with supports to house steel fire irons, c1810, 42in (106.5cm) wide.
£600–725 ⊞ ASH

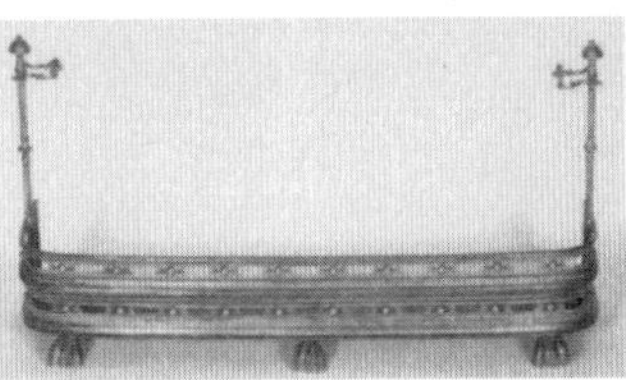

A pierced D-shaped brass fender, 46½in (118cm) wide.
£200–250 ⚒ DMC

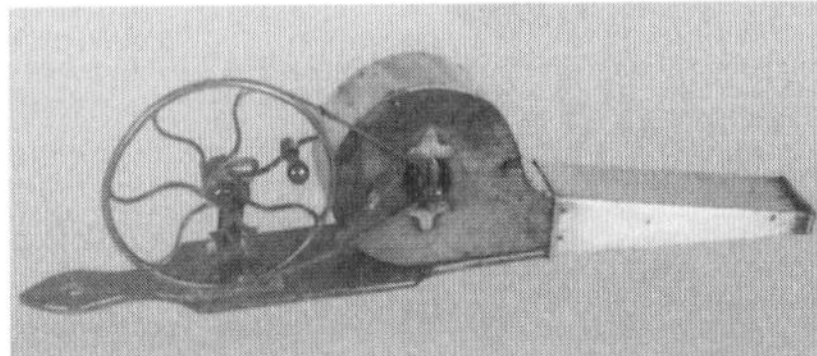

◄ **A set of George III Westmorland bellows,** with mahogany casework, brass bindings and cast-brass wheel, 28in (71cm) long.
£500–625 ⚒ Mit

A spark guard, with wirework front and brass rail and base, c1815, 34in (86.5cm) wide.
£350–380 ⊞ ASH

A set of iron fire irons, French, c1770, 30in (76cm) long.
£560–625 ⊞ SEA

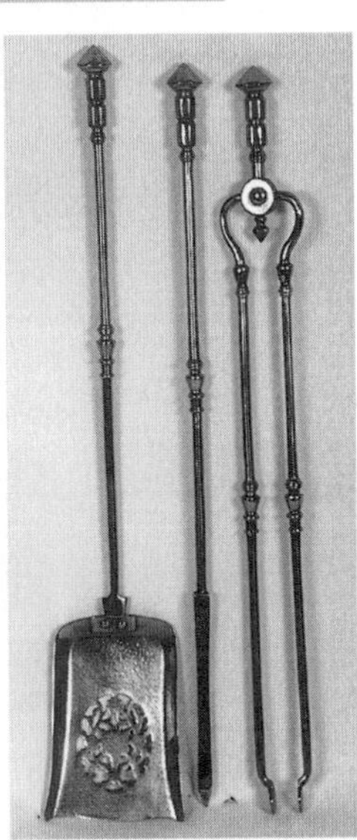

A set of steel fire irons, 19thC, 30in (76cm) long.
£280–325 ⊞ RPh

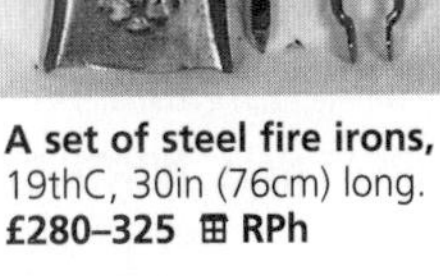

A copper and steel footman, c1840, 14in (35.5cm) wide.
£190–210 ⊞ PICA

Cross Reference
See Colour Review (page 619)

An oak log bin, with three brass bands and bar handles, late 19thC, 22in (56cm) high.
£550–700 ⚒ N

► **A pair of William IV/early Victorian iron coal boxes,** with lion's mask handles and paw feet, black-japanned with gilt-line borders, 17in (43cm) wide.
£450–550 ⚒ PFK

Sculpture – Focus on bronze

Sculpture is unusual among art forms for two reasons. Firstly, it is tactile: touching is part of the enjoyment. Secondly, since each piece is not unique, we can buy museum-quality works for less than museum-quality prices. As far as bronzes are concerned, the great century of bronze sculpting from 1830–1930 saw figural work evolve from the classical masters through Art Nouveau and Art Deco to the modernism of Dalou and Rodin, and the *animalier oeuvre* from Antoine-Louis Barye in the late 19th century to Bugatti in the early 20th century.

Production of bronzes is complex and costly. They are cast using either sand or 'lost wax'. Both techniques produce top quality results, but sand requires less bronze and more manual chasing. In the 19th century sand was more commonly used until labour became more expensive than the bronze itself in around 1900, when the lost wax process became the norm. With each method the foundry duplicates the artist's clay model and dismembers the copy to cast in several hollow pieces. The pieces (sometimes up to 30) are pinned together, the holes and imperfections corrected and all the detail rechiselled as needed by an unsung hero-craftsman called a 'chaser' ('*ciseleur*' in French). Finally patina, usually a chemical soup depending on which colour is sought, is applied in several layers under considerable heat.

French foundries produced the majority of the bronzes, turning art into a successful commerce with finely finished and detailed models. Other styles of sculpture worth getting to know include English (simple, romantic and rare), German (starkly simple), Italian (often portraying more of the emotion behind the piece), Russian (extraordinary understanding of horses) and Belgian (powerful early 20th-century social comments).

Don't be put off because you know nothing about the subject. Ask yourself these questions as you look at a piece:

- Do I like it and will it grow on me?
- If bronze, is it a good cast and how many were made? Often, no-one knows. Perhaps the more useful question is 'when will I see another one that I like as much?' Imagine how much it would cost if it were unique: all bronzes would be in museums. Look at the hands and feet (paws and collars of animals). If the small details are well executed, so too are the larger.
- Is it in original condition? Not always easy to see, so don't be shy – ask the dealer or auction house staff. Remember it is old, so signs of past love are normal.

Finally, there is no 'right' price for most sculpture. Compare the one you like with others. If the price is fair, your enjoyment of it will rightly make you forget what you invested in it. **William Bevan**

► **A turned pearwood bowl,** the centre with a carved pine head of John the Baptist, Austrian, south Tyrol, c1500, 14½in (37cm) diam.
£1,100–1,300 ⚒ DORO

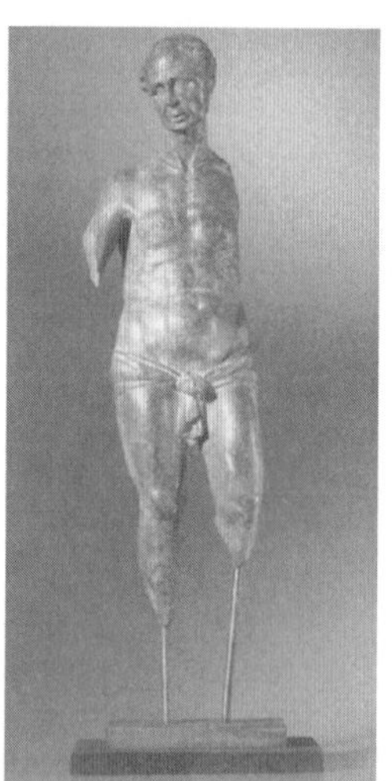

► **A softwood male torso,** with traces of original paint, probably Alpine, 16thC, 27½in (70cm) high.
£2,000–2,500 ⚒ S(Z)

An ivory portrait plaque, by Jean Cavalier, depicting a nobleman, signed, Anglo-French, c1680, 3in (7.5cm) high.
£2,500–2,800 ⊞ AEF

A relief-carved ivory flat-back figure group of the Madonna and Child, German, 17thC, 5in (12.5cm) high.
£2,700–3,400 ⚒ HOLL

A carved wooden plaque of topers and musicians at a table, losses, woodworm damage, Dutch/Flemish, c1700, 11in (28cm) wide.
£850–1,100 ⚒ Bon(C)

An ivory figural group of Abraham sacrificing Isaac, with a ram in the background, south German, 18thC, 3in (7.5cm) high.
£750–950 ⚒ DORO

A carved wood figure of a young peasant boy, 1875–1925, 34in (86.5cm) high.
£460–575 HYD

A plaster library bust of Charles James Fox, with bronze patination, inscribed 'Pubd by M. Hauswirth Dec. the 2nd 1811, 19 Mount Street, Grosvenor Sq. London', 11½in (29cm) high.
£420–525 WW

A bronze model of a dachshund, by Pierre Jules Mêne, French, c1850, 29½in (75cm) wide.
£3,500–4,000 ⊞ BeF

◄ **A carved wood polychrome group of St Anthony and the Infant Christ,** losses, Italian, 19thC, 33in (84cm) high.
£500–625 Bon(C)

Bronze

Bronze is an alloy of 90 per cent copper, seven per cent tin and three per cent zinc, but individual foundries varied in what they added (eg mercury) and even if they tried, no two batches of bronze for casting would be exactly the same.

A bronze bust of Princess Victoria, by William Behnes, mid-19thC, 10½in (26.5cm) high.
£600–700 S(S)

◄ **A bronze figure of a convivial friar,** on a later yew wood socle, mid-19thC, 10in (25.5cm) high.
£750–850 RGa

An ivory bust of Oliver Cromwell, by Matthew Noble, signed, dated 1860, on a yellow-veined marble pillar base, 10¼in (26cm) high overall.
£1,700–2,200 TEN
Matthew Noble was born in Hackness near Scarborough in 1818 and died in London in 1876. He exhibited at the Royal Academy between 1845 and 1876.

A Dieppe ivory triptych, the central panel carved with a scene from the Battle of Naseby beneath a royal coat-of-arms surmount, the left panel carved with Charles I bidding farewell to his children, the right carved with the Execution of Charles I, above a scroll cartouche inscribed with the title of each panel, French, 19thC, 10in (25.5cm) high, with an oak and brown velvet frame.
£1,600–2,000 RTo

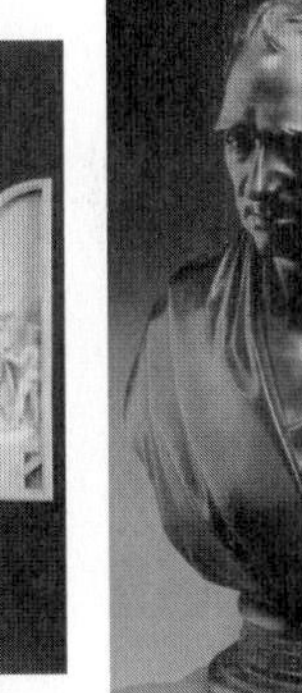

A bronze bust of George Stephenson, by Edward William Wyon, signed, dated 1858, 12¾in (32.5cm) high.
£620–750 P
Son of the chief engraver of seals, Wyon studied at the Royal Academy schools. He first exhibited at the Royal Academy in 1831 with a bust of General Maitland and specialized in portrait busts of famous contemporaries.

◄ **A bronze figure of a Toltec priest,** wearing a feathered headdress and skirt and holding a parakeet, c1860, 11½in (29cm) high.
£280–320 ⊞ NAW
Toltecs were a native central American people who lived 10–12th century AD.

A pair of Elkington & Co bronze models of jockeys, horses and their trainers, by John Willis Good, signed, 12in (30.5cm) high.
£18,000–20,000 P

Two Victorian ivory figures of Nathaniel Winkle and Mr Wardle, from Charles Dickens's *Pickwick Papers*, 6in (15cm) high.
£320–350 each LBO

A group of a hunter with a lion cub, by Auguste de Wever, signed, Belgian, c1875, 34½in (87.5cm) high.
£3,300–3,750 BeF

◄ A bronze figure of Ceres, after the Antique, French, 19thC, 15½in (39.5cm) high.
£700–850 JAA

A white marble bust of Apollo, on a turned marble base, 19thC, 30in (76cm) high.
£3,800–4,750 SWO

A pair of bronze models of Summer and Autumn, French, 19thC, 25in (63.5cm) high.
£5,250–5,850 RAN

Patinating & gilding

In sculpture, as opposed to furniture, patina is not the natural process of aging, but rather the application of one of a variety of chemical 'soups' under heat. Different chemicals give different colours. A. L. Barye's first great patina was the leaves of autumn, being red, green and brown. Black became more common in the mid-19th century, but Art Nouveau ushered in lighter tones; until this century we see green, red and today even blue. Nineteenth century gilding was the application of a very hot paste of powdered gold and mercury. It ages to a lovely greenish satin. Contemporary gilding is much more garish.

◄ A gilded-bronze figure of St George slaying the dragon, by Emmanuel Fremiet, French, c1876, 23in (58.5cm) high.
£3,200–3,500 RGa

A marble bust of a boy, inscribed 'P Dal Necho F Milano 1874', 19thC, 20in (51cm) high.
£800–1,000 SLN

A bronze bust of a young woman, by Leopold Harze, entitled 'Dorine', foundry seal of J. Peterman, Brussels, c1875, 13¾in (35cm) high.
£2,500–2,800 G&H

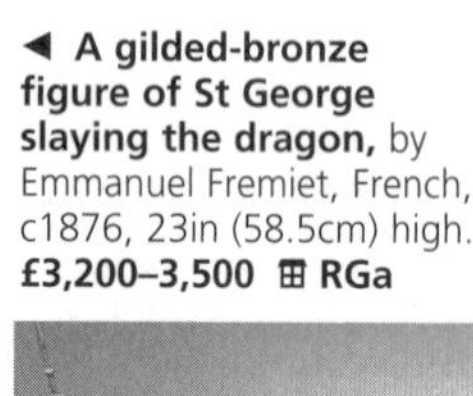

A bronze group of a seated classical female figure, reading a book, personifying the Arts, the base inscribed 'J. C. de Blezer', French, 19thC, 11½in (29cm) high.
£320–400 WW

A bronze model of a Tartar warrior, by Alfred Barye, signed, late 19thC, 14¼in (36cm) high.
£900–1,150 P
The son of Antoine Louis Barye, Alfred also produced animalier bronzes, working in his father's studio, He made his Paris Salon début in 1864.

A plaster figure of a barrel organ player, by John Rogers, entitled 'School Days', signed, American, dated 1877, 23in (58.5cm) high, on a wooden base.
£850–1,100 ⚒ S

An ivory group of Pan with a cherub, signed 'L. Küchler', on a marble base, German, 19thC, 17in (43cm) high.
£1,650–1,850 ⊞ LBO

► A bronze model of a woman, by Mage, French, c1880, 17in (43cm) high.
£1,700–2,000 ⊞ G&H

A cold-painted bronze Arab female figure, on a marble base, 19thC, 9½in (24cm) high.
£230–280 ⚒ AG

A bronze figure, by Adrien Etienne Gaudez, entitled 'Minstrel', French, c1880, 15in (38cm) high.
£3,000–3,400 ⊞ G&H
Gaudez studied under Jouffroy and began exhibiting at the Salon from 1864, winning a 1st class medal in 1881.

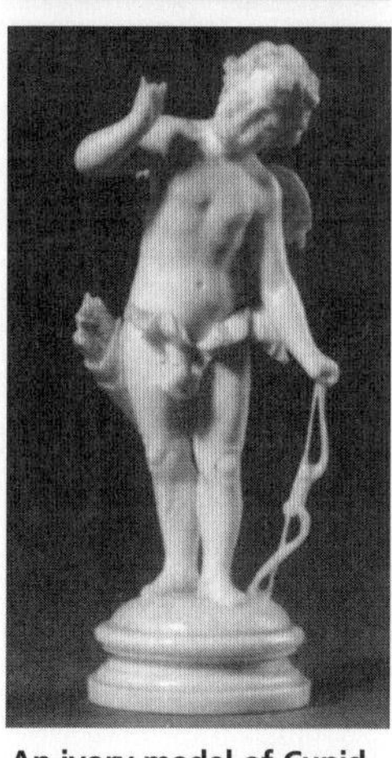

An ivory model of Cupid, Austrian, Vienna, 1880–90, 4¼in (11.5cm) high.
£425–525 ⚒ DORO

Signatures & foundry marks

From about 1820, most non 'after the Antique' bronzes are signed. Not all, however, have foundry marks. It depended who was in charge of production and marketing. Successful sculptors, like A. L. Barye and P. J. Mêne, would have their own foundry and would place no mark, whereas J. B. Carpeaux placed his own mark. Emile Picault, Ferdinand Pautrot and the Comte du Passage are examples of sculptors who were either so well-to-do or so marketable that they never seem to have foundry marks. Many others, like Van der Straeten signed production contracts with the foundries and their work is stamped. The depth and clarity of the impressions of signature and foundry marks are a good way of judging the quality of the cast.

A Victorian bronze figure of Hippocrates, resting against a bookcase, 16¼in (41.5cm) high.
£1,200–1,500 ⚒ LJ

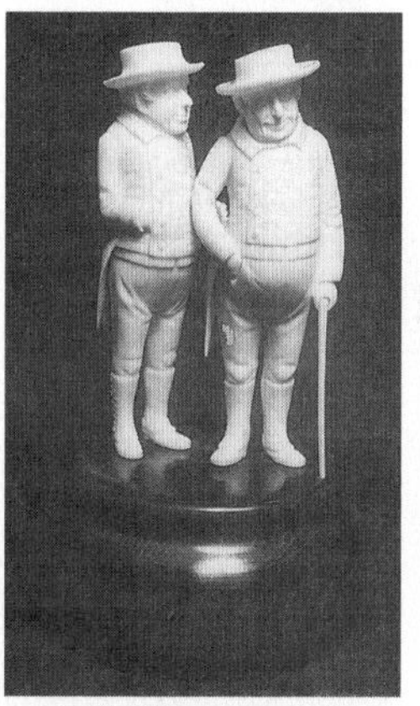

Two carved ivory caricature figures, of gentlemen wearing period costume, late 19thC, 6in (15cm) high.
£1,100–1,200 ⊞ LBO

A bronze figure of an African slave in chains, inscribed 'Am I not a man and a brother?', late 19thC, 5in (12.5cm) high.
£260–325 ⚒ G(L)

A pair of polychrome-painted wooden figures of Nelson and Wellington, late 19thC, 15½in (39.5cm) high.
£320–400 ⚒ S(S)

A cold-painted bronze penwipe, modelled as a recumbent Great Dane, 19thC, 7in (18cm) wide.
£330–420 ⚒ TMA

A bronze figure of an Arab girl, by Antoine Bofill, entitled 'Mendiante Arabe', foundry marks for Pinedo, Paris, signed, French, late 19thC, 10¾in (27.5cm) high.
£600–750 ⚒ **BLH**

Miller's is a price GUIDE not a price LIST

A bronze figure of Mignon, by Adrien Etienne Gaudez, leaning against a rock, a mandolin in her hand, signed, lacking patination, on an associated damaged and repaired pedestal, French, late 19thC, 43¾in (111cm) high.
£1,800–2,250 ⚒ **P(WM)**
Gaudez studied at the Ecole des Beaux Arts in Paris, making his début at the Salon in 1870. Mignon is the eponymous heroine of the opera, by Ambroise Thomas. The character is a young maiden kidnapped as a child by gypsies, and the story is a popular subject in both French art and sculpture.

◀ **A group of a boy pulling a goat by its horns,** by Hans Latt, signed, German, c1890, 11½in (29cm) high.
£3,000–3,300 ⊞ **BeF**

▶ **A terracotta figure of a mariner,** by J. Dommisse, on a polished slate base, French, c1890, 19in (48.5cm) wide.
£575–650 ⊞ **HUM**

A cold-painted composition figure of a Nubian slave descending steps, after J. Koenig, carrying a gilt vase and bowl, repaired, late 19thC, 39in (99cm) high.
£450–550 ⚒ **N**

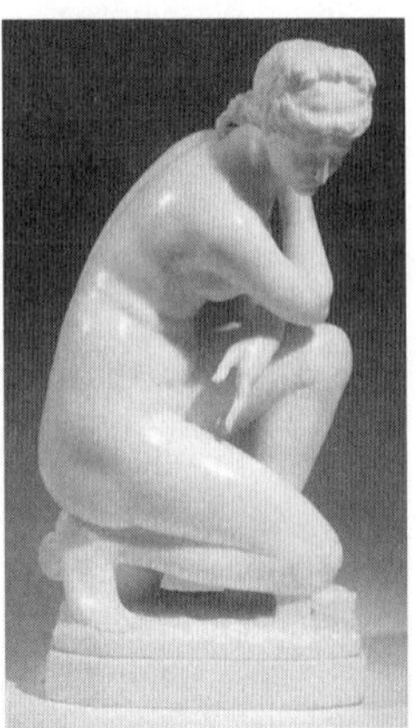

An alabaster model of the crouching Venus, by L. Pampeloni, on a conforming alabaster base, signed, Italian, late 19thC, 20in (51cm) high.
£1,000–1,300 ⚒ **P**

A bronze model of *Lutin des Bois*, by Luca Madrassi, the winged figure of a boy standing on a naturalistically cast base, two birds at his feet, signed, Italian, late 19thC, 33½in (85cm) high.
£1,850–2,200 ⚒ **P**
Madrassi began his training in Italy, continuing to study at the Ecole des Beaux Arts after moving to Paris and becoming a French citizen. He worked in Carrier Belleuse's studio, exhibiting at the Salon from 1881 to 1885. He is perhaps better known in England for his association with Lord Ronald Gower and his involvement with works by Gower, such as the Shakespeare memorial at Stratford-upon-Avon.

▶ **An alabaster figure of Joan of Arc,** after Chapu, French, late 19thC, 14in (35.5cm) high.
£900–1,000 ⚒ **S(O)**
Chapu exhibited the marble Joan of Arc in the Salon of 1872.

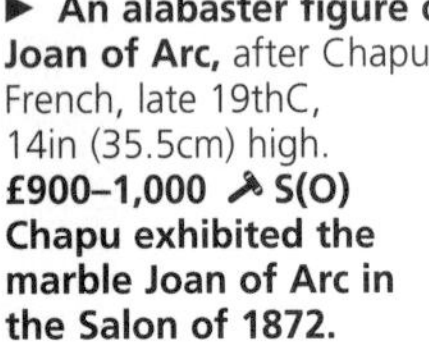

A bronze figure of a classical lady, leaning beside a column, inscribed 'F Barbedienne Fondeur', impressed seal, French, late 19thC, 11¼in (28.5cm) high.
£600–750 ⚒ **WL**

A Dieppe ivory figure of Mary Queen of Scots, her dress opening to reveal a triptych depicting an angry encounter with Queen Elizabeth I, the back inscribed 'Sahrada', French, late 19thC, 6¾in (17cm) high.
£1,750–2,200 ⚒ **P(Ed)**
The French town of Dieppe produced a large number of ivory triptych figures in the 19th century and Mary Queen of Scots was a popular subject, representing the 'Auld Alliance' between Scotland and France. The interior scene with the Catholic Mary berating the Protestant Elizabeth with her low-cut bodice is fictional but fitted in with the romantic French mood towards Scotland at the time.

◄ **A cast-iron model of a borzoi,** by A. Jiccodo, Continental, probably French, c1900, 7in (18cm) high.
£380–425 ⊞ ChC

► **A pair of cold-painted spelter figures of Arabs,** one holding a staff and bowl, a gong suspended from his waist, the other a staff and a woven bag, Continental, c1900, 23¼in (59cm) high.
£620–775 ⚒ P(Ba)

A cold-painted bronze figure of an Arab praying, Austrian, early 20thC, 5½in (14cm) high.
£800–1,000 ⚒ G(L)

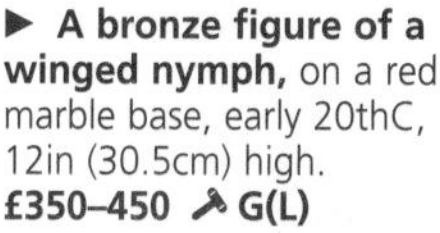

► **A bronze figure of a winged nymph,** on a red marble base, early 20thC, 12in (30.5cm) high.
£350–450 ⚒ G(L)

◄ **A bronze model of a Native American on horseback,** by Edouard Drouot, Etling foundry stamp, French, c1910, 21in (53.5cm) high.
£5,500–6,200 ⊞ RGa

A bronze model of a golden pheasant, by R. Pollin, with silver-gilt patina, on a mottled black marble plinth, Continental, c1920, 26¼in (66.5cm) wide.
£550–700 ⚒ S(S)

► **A marble group of two children,** entitled 'Affortunato Gory', Italian, c1925, 18½in (47cm) high.
£4,300–4,700 ⊞ G&H

A bronze model of a stag, by Thomas Cartier, French, c1900, 19¾in (50cm) high.
£2,650–3,000 ⊞ G&H

A bronze bust of Abraham Lincoln, by John Gutzon Mothe Borglum, American, signed and dated 1908, 38in (96.5cm) high.
£17,000–20,000 ⚒ S(NY)
Born near Bear Lake, Idaho, Gutzon Borglum was educated at St Mary's College, Kansas. He studied sculpture in San Francisco and later at the Académie Julian in Paris. He exhibited at the St Louis World's Fair in 1904 and he was a member of the Société Nationale des Beaux-Arts in Paris. He is best known for the group of heads of Washington, Jefferson, Lincoln and Theodore Roosevelt at Mt Rushmore, which his son, Lincoln Borglum, completed after his death.

A painted plaster portrait head of a youth, after the Antique, c1900, 26¾in (68cm) high.
£270–340 ⚒ RTo

A bronze figure of a laughing young woman, K.K.K. Vienna foundry mark, Austrian, c1910, 10¼in (26cm) high.
£1,000–1,100 ⊞ BeF

A model of a standing nude, by Gerhard Schliepstein, signed, German, c1920, 15½in (39.5cm) high.
£1,800–2,000 ⊞ BeF

Metalware

Brass

A pair of rococo-style, patinated-brass five-branch appliques, French, c1900, 19¾in (50cm) high.
£550–650 ⊞ AMS

A pair of brass petal-base candlesticks, c1740, 8in (20.5cm) high.
£700–775 ⊞ SEA

A pair of brass candlesticks, the columns supported by eagles, French, 19thC, 8in (20.5cm) high.
£240–300 🔨 Bea(E)

A brass coffee urn, Dutch, c1800, 11¾in (30cm) high.
£550–620 ⊞ JC

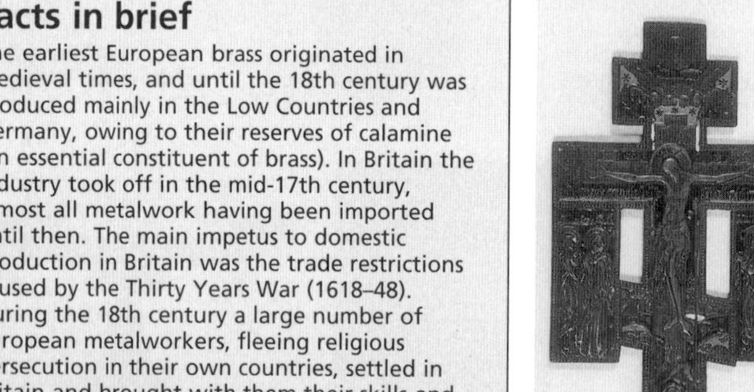

Facts in brief

The earliest European brass originated in medieval times, and until the 18th century was produced mainly in the Low Countries and Germany, owing to their reserves of calamine (an essential constituent of brass). In Britain the industry took off in the mid-17th century, almost all metalwork having been imported until then. The main impetus to domestic production in Britain was the trade restrictions caused by the Thirty Years War (1618–48). During the 18th century a large number of European metalworkers, fleeing religious persecution in their own countries, settled in Britain and brought with them their skills and knowledge. With the advances in mechanization and mass-production in the 19th century, many of the small metalworkers were incapable of keeping up with the demand for wares and were supplanted by factories.

A brass and multi-coloured enamel crucifix, Russian, 19thC, 6in (15cm) high.
£200–220 ⊞ ICO

A brass door stop, with maker's mark WT & S, c1850, 11in (28cm) high.
£300–325 ⊞ RGe

► A Victorian brass desk stand, with glass inkwell, 8¾in (22cm) wide.
£140–175 🔨 WilP

A Victorian brass pen stand, 9in (23cm) high.
£100–115 🔨 SWO

◄ A brass samovar, with various marks, including reference to the International Exhibition in Paris 1878, Russian, c1880, 25½in (65cm) high.
£265–325 🔨 Herm

► A Victorian gilt-brass photograph frame, with a pierced and engraved leaf scroll border, 9¼in (23.5cm) high.
£170–220 🔨 LFA

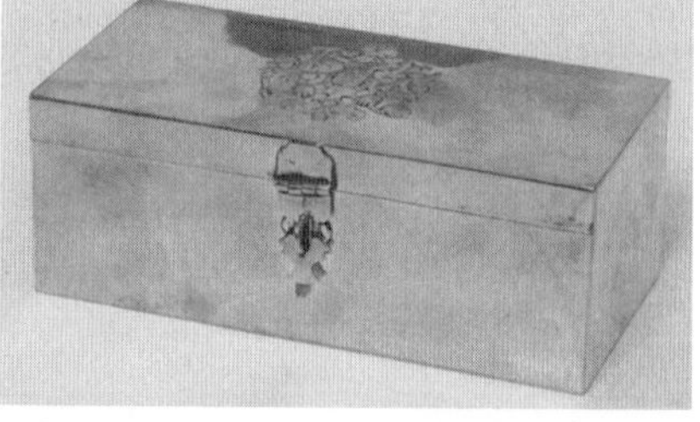

A brass tea caddy, the hinged lid repoussé-decorated with the Russian Imperial double-headed eagle, Russian, 19thC, 6¾in (17cm) wide.
£250–320 🔨 JAA

Bronze

A bronze pilgrim's bell, 17th/18thC, 4in (10cm) high.
£200–225 ⊞ SEA

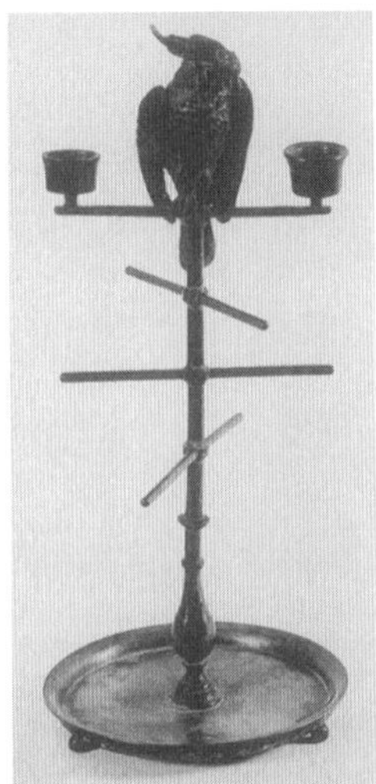

A bronze candelabrum/ jewellery stand, the centre with a container modelled as a cockatoo, flanked by two sconces, 1875–1925, 13½in (34.5cm) high.
£150–180 ⚒ GAK

A patinated and gilt-bronze four-light candelabra, after Moreau, on a classical maiden support, impressed mark, late 19thC, 15¾in (40cm) high, on an ebonized plinth base.
£450–565 ⚒ P(Ba)

◄ **A pair of bronze altar candlesticks,** Italian, 18thC, 41in (104cm) high.
£1,100–1,200 ⊞ DJH

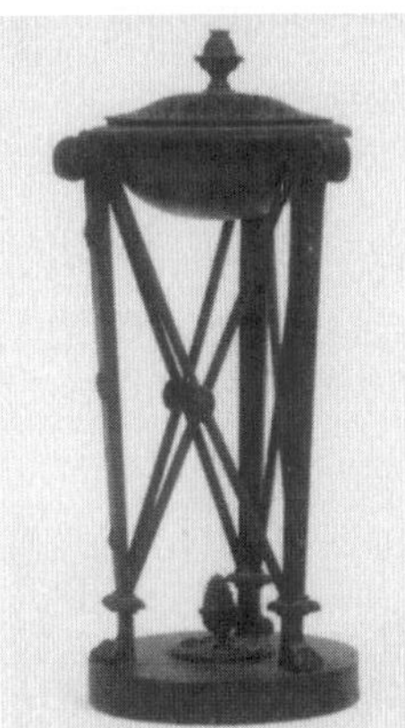

A pair of bronze incense burners, the detachable circular vessels with pierced covers, 19thC, 10½in (26.5cm) high.
£480–600 ⚒ DMC

A gilt-lacquered bronze lustre garniture, comprising three pieces, the bases formed as a figural group of an old man, his dog and a female companion, American, probably Boston, 1875–1900, 16½in (42cm) high.
£400–500 ⚒ NOA

A Victorian bronze comport, applied with dragon handles, 10in (25.5cm) high, on a stepped oak base.
£150–180 ⚒ G(L)

A gilt-bronze boat-shaped inkstand, with fitted interior and classical relief-cast sides, supported by a dragon on an associated rococo foot, 19thC, 9in (23cm) high.
£540–675 ⚒ S

A bronze inkwell, with a central urn-shaped well, hinged lid and crenellated edges, 19thC, 6¼in (16cm) high.
£130–160 ⚒ SWO

A bronze mortar, dated 1692, 4in (10cm) high.
£875–975 ⊞ SEA

A bronze 16thC-style mortar, the body etched with stylized arabesque scrolls and with two shields enclosing a bird and a gryphon, maker's initials S and C, German, possibly Nuremberg, 18thC, 3¾in (9.5cm) high.
£700–800 ⚒ S(O)
Ex-Rudolf Just Collection.

◄ **A pair of Grand Tour bronze vases,** cast with friezes of classical figures, the handles formed as winged infant demi-figures playing pan pipes, on Siena marble pillars with bronze and black slate bases, 19thC, 11½in (29cm) high.
£480–600 ⚒ N

◄ **A bronze watch stand,** 1790–1810, 8in (20.5cm) high, on a stepped base.
£850–950 ⊞ RGe

Copper

A cut silvered-copper book-cover, c1780, 5 x 6in (12.5 x 15cm)
£315–350 ⊞ HUM

A pair of copper altar pricket candlesticks, chased and embossed with lobed knops, cherub masks, the tripartite bases with heraldic crests, crucifix and cherub masks, Continental, 18thC, 33in (84cm) high.
£140–175 ⚒ TMA

◄ **A late Georgian copper tea kettle, stand and burner,** stamped 'Hodges & Sons, Dublin', 17in (43cm) high.
£170–220 ⚒ TMA

A copper alloy footed dish, decorated in relief with classical-style figures, the underside engraved 'Art Union of London 1857', mid-19thC, 16½in (42cm) diam.
£100–125 ⚒ PFK

A copper hot water urn, with ivory grips, early 19thC, 17¾in (45cm) high.
£100–120 ⚒ L&E

A copper measure, c1870, 15in (38cm) high.
£360–400 ⊞ HA

Iron

A cast-iron boot scraper, c1840, 18in (45.5cm) wide.
£315–350 ⊞ RGe

An iron Armada chest, with a false front escutcheon, the lock plate decorated with mermen, 17thC, 30½in (77.5cm) wide.
£1,300–1,600 ⚒ SWO

► **An iron candlestick,** 18thC, on a turned wooden base, 6¾in (17cm) high.
£150–200 ⚒ PFK

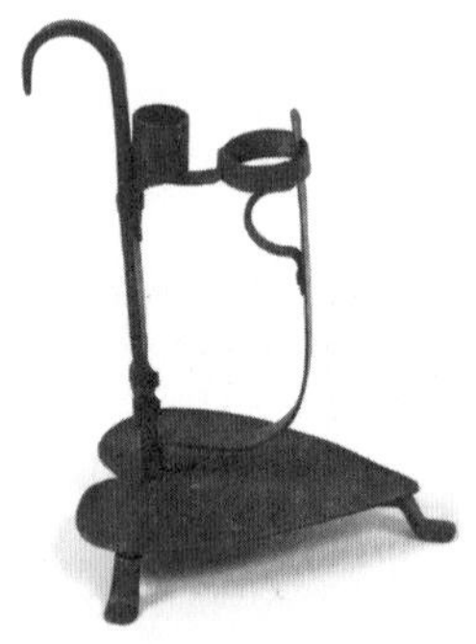

An iron rush light, with candle holder, on a heart-shaped base, c1770, 9in (23cm) high.
£300–325 ⊞ RGe

► **A Victorian painted cast-iron doorstop,** modelled as a pineapple with foliage, 14in (35.5cm) high.
£75–95 ⚒ WW

A cast-iron door stop, modelled as a lion, 19thC, 15in (38cm) high.
£430–475 ⊞ SEA

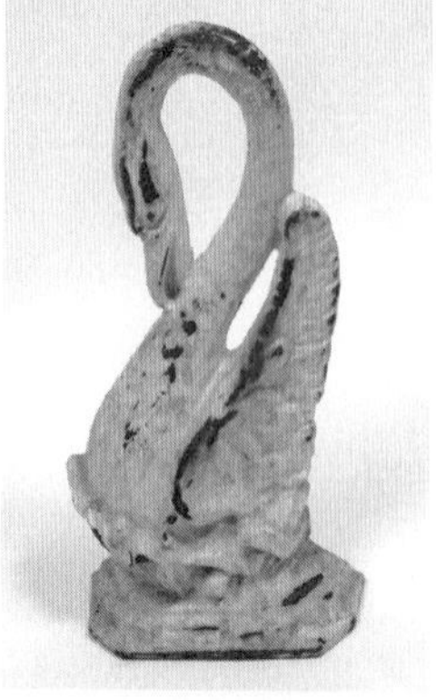

A cast-iron doorstop, modelled as a swan, 19thC, 15in (38cm) high.
£115–125 ⊞ PICA

Ormolu

A pair of ormolu two-branch candelabra, in the form of winged female figures, on engraved circular mother-of-pearl bases, French, early 19thC, 14¾in (37.5cm) high.
£1,100–1,400 ⚒ F&C

A pair of cast-ormolu rococo candelabra, the branches embellished with leaf and trailing vine, 19thC, 16½in (42cm) high.
£280–350 ⚒ L&E

A pair of porcelain and ormolu-mounted candlesticks, decorated with hand-painted floral panels, Continental, 19thC, 7in (18cm) high.
£150–180 ⚒ Mit

A pair of rococo-style ormolu candelabra, with central twin flowerhead motif, converted to electricity, 19thC, 10in (25.5cm) high.
£380–475 ⚒ DML

► **An ormolu photograph frame,** with a floral-cast and ribbon-tied surround, the shagreen centre with three initialled heart-shaped apertures, early 20thC, 5¼in (13.5cm) wide.
£600–700 ⚒ DMC

Pewter

A pewter charger, with ownership triad to the rim and touchmark to the reverse, maker's mark SB, c1690, 18in (45.5cm) diam.
£700–800 ⚒ S(O)

A pewter dish, with touchmark of Tudor roses, c1730, 13½in (34.5cm) diam.
£180–200 ⊞ SEA

A pewter dish, the rim engraved with flowers and ownership initials, the centre with a mounted huntsman, maker's marks to the reverse, Bohemian, Eger, c1746, 14in (35.5cm) diam.
£600–700 ⚒ S(O)
Ex-Rudolf Just Collection.

A pewter half pint measure, with maker's touchmark RS to the lip, c1690, 4¾in (12cm) high.
£400–450 ⚒ S(O)

◄ **A pewter flagon,** 18thC, 11½in (29cm) high.
£500–550 ⊞ SEA

A George IV pewter gallon measure, by Yates, 10½in (26.5cm) high.
£1,250–1,500 ⚒ RBB

Miller's is a price GUIDE not a price LIST

A pewter lidded tankard, on cherub mask-head feet with triple-cusp thumbpiece, German, 18thC, 6¼in (16cm) high.
£550–700 ⚒ P

METALWARE

Toleware

A hatter's tole trade sign, French, c1860, 8in (20.5cm) high.
£315–350 ⊞ RGe

◀ **A Victorian tole bird cage,** painted in blue and gilt, on three ball-and-claw feet, 61in (155cm) high.
£700–850 ⚒ DN

▶ **A tole tea canister,** painted with a Chinese man, now converted as a lamp, early 20thC, 15in (38cm) high.
£450–550 ⚒ CGC

An Empire tole tray, gilt-decorated with scrolling leaves, cornucopiae and eagles within laurel wreaths, French, early 19thC, 20½in (52cm) wide.
£675–850 ⚒ SK

A toleware tray, with painted decoration of exotic birds and butterflies among floral sprays and fruit, heightened with gilt scroll and foliate decoration, 19thC, 30¾in (78cm) wide.
£280–350 ⚒ Bea(E)

A Pontypool-type toleware tray, painted with flowers and gilded grapevine against a green ground, 19thC, 17½in (44.5cm) diam.
£200–250 ⚒ G(L)

Miscellaneous

A pair of gilt-metal candlesticks, French, c1870, 33in (84cm) high.
£800–880 ⊞ RAN

▶ **A pair of Victorian cast-metal photograph frames,** embellished with maidens, cherubs and scrolls, 14in (35.5cm) high.
£100–120 ⚒ FHF

A pair of gilt-metal six-light candelabra, cast with foliate scrolls and cherub columns, French, late 19thC, 21¼in (54cm) high.
£500–625 ⚒ P(S)

A woven-steel dog collar, the central plaque engraved with the owner's details, original lock and later key, 18thC, 5in (12.5cm) diam.
£300–350 ⚒ S(S)

A pair of Edwardian polished steel nut crackers, 10in (25.5cm) long.
£145–160 ⊞ PICA

A pressed metal paperclip, showing postal rates, c1880, 6in (15cm) high.
£125–140 ⊞ HUM

Leather

A leather ***aide-mémoire,*** by Palais Royale, with gilt corners and a central view painted on glass, French, c1860, 3 x 5in (7.5 x 12.5cm).
£1,100–1,250 ⊞ SHa

A leather blackjack, stamped 'Ross, Winchester', the silver rim Sheffield 1936, 9¼in (23.5cm) high.
£75–100 ⚒ LFA

A painted and decorated leather fire bucket, inscribed 'Friendship in Adversity I. Foster', one handle strap broken, American, dated 1802, 11¾in (30cm) high.
£1,400–1,600 ⚒ WcH

A painted leather fire bucket, with brass-studded rim, and two handles cast with masks, 19thC, 10¼in (26cm) diam.
£420–525 ⚒ DN

◄ **A stitched leather bucket,** 19thC, 11in (28cm) high.
£200–240 ⚒ Bea(E)

A George I tooled-leather dispatch box, with steel carrying handle, decorated with four crowns with 'GR' below each, and rondel and stellar motifs, with tooled floral decoration to the sides, 16¼in (41.5cm) wide.
£300–375 ⚒ Bea(E)

► **A Victorian leather fire bucket,** with original paint, 11in (28cm) high.
£280–320 ⊞ SPT

A polychrome embossed leather Royal coat-of-arms, 1775–1825, 30in (76cm) square, in a later wooden frame.
£800–1,000 ⚒ Bon(C)

A leather display trunk, by Joseph Walker, Liverpool, with original hardware and maker's label, c1810, 12in (30.5cm) wide.
£585–650 ⊞ DeG

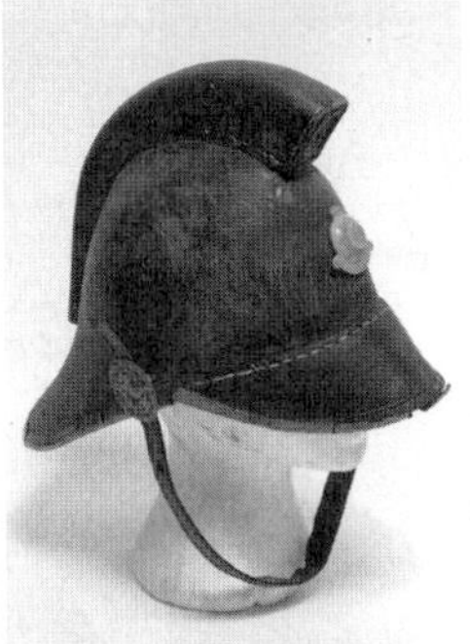

A fireman's leather helmet, c1900, 10in (25.5cm) high.
£55–60 ⊞ Q&C

A leather boot trunk, by Insall, Bristol, late 19thC, 27in (68.5cm) wide.
£675–750 ⊞ ChC

► **A brass-studded leather trunk,** c1880, 29in (73.5cm) high.
£600–650 ⊞ MLL

Papier Mâché

A black-lacquered papier mâché cabinet, inlay to the lid, apron and feet with mother-of-pearl, the body with gilt decoration and raised green-painted panels with applied brass cruciform foliate motifs, the hinged lid enclosing lidded and open compartments, the doors to the front enclosing mother-of-pearl-inlaid long and short drawers around a central recess, lid and one foot detached but present, 19thC, 12½in (32cm) wide.
£150–200 PFK

An early Victorian papier mâché workbox, the doors inlaid with mother-of-pearl and painted with flowers, opening to three interior drawers with gilt borders on a key-pattern-painted base, 9½in (24cm) high.
£380–475 HYD

► **A pair of papier mâché face screens,** painted in the style of Richard Ansell with hunting groups, on turned giltwood handles, early 19thC, 9½in (24cm) high.
£500–625 P(Ed)

A papier mâché box, with painted lid, c1890, 5in (12.5cm) wide.
£145–160 HUM

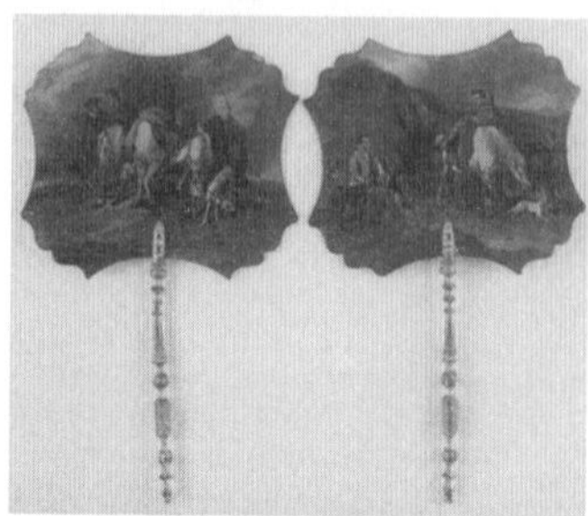

A Victorian papier mâché snuff box, with white metal inlay, 2½in (6.5cm) wide.
£20–22 JOA

A papier mâché stationery folder, the front painted with heathers, c1860, 12in (30.5cm) wide.
£135–150 HUM

A papier mâché tray, by Henry Clay, polychrome-decorated on a maroon ground, c1820, 27in (68.5cm) wide.
£1,700–1,850 S

The firm of Clay was established in 1772 by Henry Clay, a leading japanner and papier mâché manufacturer who worked at various times for George III, the Prince of Wales, Horace Walpole and the dukes of Bedford and Northumberland. Originally based in Birmingham, Clay transferred his business to London around 1785, and despite his death in 1812, the firm continued to trade from Covent Garden under his name until 1822. After this date they stamped objects 'W Clay & Co' at an address in Fenchurch Street, before finally closing in 1860.

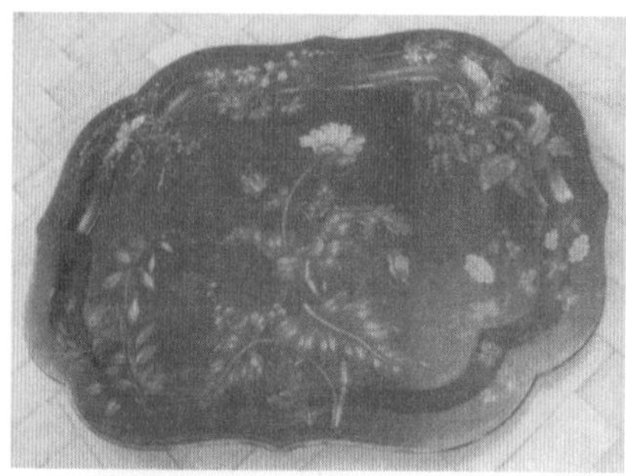

◄ **An early Victorian papier mâché tray,** painted in coloured enamels with flowers and leaves, and picked out in gilt with leaf sprays, 31in (78.5cm) wide.
£600–750 LFA

A Victorian papier maché tray, by Jennens & Bettridge, with scroll border, painted with flowers and two birds, impressed mark, 31in (78.5cm) wide.
£350–450 G(L)

A Victorian papier maché tray, painted with a central vase of summer flowers on a brown ground, the back stamped 'R Walton & Co', 33in (84cm) wide.
£425–525 P(O)

A papier mâché writing slope, inlaid with mother-of-pearl, the fall-front painted with flowers within gilt spandrels, the slope inset with pink velvet, mid-19thC, 12¼in (31cm) wide.
£240–300 CG

Treen

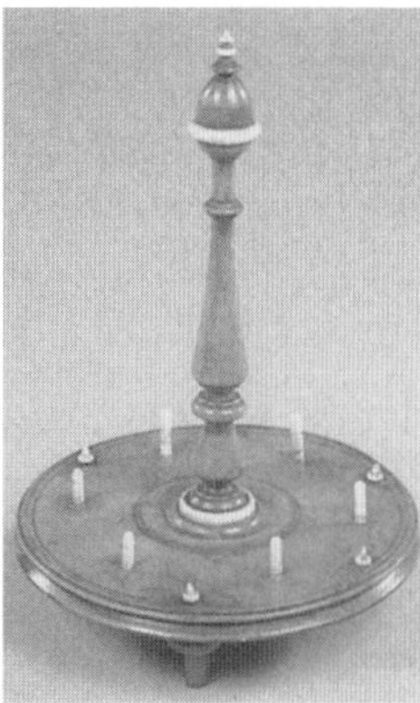

A treen bobbin stand, possibly walnut, with acorn finial and bone spindles, 19thC, 12¼in (31cm) high.
£160–200 ⚒ PFK

A mahogany book press, early 19thC, 14in (35.5cm) high.
£400–450 ⊞ F&F
This was used to flatten books that were warping.

A mahogany book stand, the stepped edge decorated with an applied reel and turned quarter moulding, c1835, 18in (45.5cm) wide.
£470–520 ⊞ JC

A mahogany candle stand, 18thC, 16in (40.5cm) high.
£600–680 ⊞ DJH

A dug-out boat-shaped bowl, with original orange and blue paint, early 19thC, 21in (53.5cm) long.
£300–340 ⊞ NEW

A fruitwood box, the lid decorated with a nativity scene, with brass hinges, c1740, 4in (10cm) wide.
£225–250 ⊞ RGe

A Georgian *lignum vitae* cruet, with five facet-cut glass condiments, the rotating stand with silver mounts and handles, minor damage, some mounts later, c1750, 12¼in (31cm) high.
£400–500 ⚒ TEN

A turned birchwood egg cup stand, and six egg cups, c1830, 7in (18cm) high.
£220–250 ⊞ F&F

A set of four mahogany egg cups, c1840, 3½in (9cm) high.
£340–375 ⊞ RGe

A *lignum vitae* coffee grinder, with metal handle, cracks, 18thC, 7in (18cm) high.
£160–200 ⚒ RTo

► **A penwork face screen,** the birch or satinwood screen decorated with chinoiserie scenes, the handle mahogany, c1810, 14in (35.5cm) high.
£180–200 ⊞ F&F

A *lignum vitae* and bellmetal hand bell, c1820, 14in (35.5cm) high.
£130–145 ⊞ F&F

A *lignum vitae* inkstand, in the shape of a beehive with a concealed central glass inkwell and three pen holders, 19thC, 3¼in (8cm) high.
£80–100 ⚒ PFK

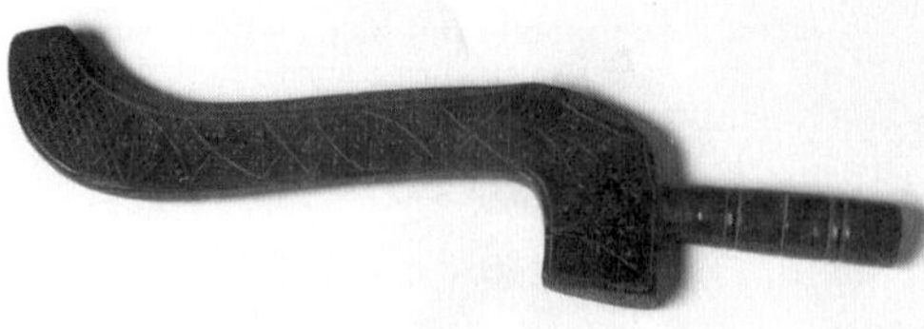

A treen knitting sheath, Welsh, c1840, 10in (25.5cm) high.
£160–180 ⊞ HUM

◀ **A sycamore love spoon,** the yellow-stained handle pierce-carved with heart, soul and roundel motifs, Welsh, 19thC, 7¾in (19.5cm) high.
£430–550 ⚒ PF

A mahogany Grand Tour mirror, with boxwood stringing, c1880, 8in (20.5cm) high.
£180–200 ⊞ ChC

A carved wood nutcracker, in the shape of a goat, c1900, 7in (18cm) high.
£160–180 ⊞ MLa

A turned muffineer, probably birchwood, with repair to foot, c1825, 5in (12.5cm) high.
£115–125 ⊞ F&F

◀ **An elm panel,** carved in high relief with figures dancing to a man playing a pipe, 19thC, 16 x 14in (40.5 x 35.5cm).
£180–200 ⊞ AMR

◀ **A carved and painted wood model of an owl,** on a wooden base, American, 1850–1900, 11in (28cm) high.
£950–1,100 ⚒ BB(S)

A carved oak portrait of Flavius Josephus, in primitive style, backing damaged, early 18thC, 10 x 6in (25.5 x 15cm).
£450–500 ⊞ HUM

A George III crossbanded figured walnut pin cushion, with gadroon moulding, lion mask ring handles and cast-metal rococo-style feet, 6½in (16.5cm) wide.
£170–220 ⚒ TMA

A turned fruitwood salt, c1820, 5in (12.5cm) high.
£225–250 ⊞ SEA

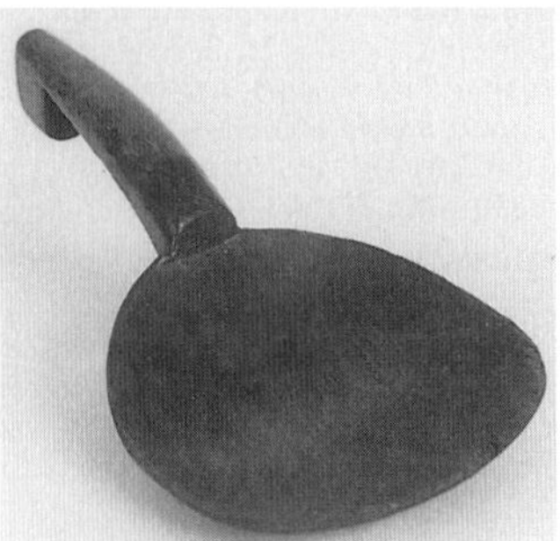

A wooden paddle/scoop, c1860, 9in (23cm) long.
£115–130 ⊞ MSB

A wooden smoker's stand, modelled as a dog's head, with composition eyes, an ashtray and match compartment between the paws, the head lifting to reveal a tobacco compartment, late 19th/early 20thC, 6½in (16.5cm) high.
£850–1,100 ⚒ GAK

A Georgian mahogany salt box, with inlaid decoration, some damage, 18in (45.5cm) high.
£130–160 ⚒ FHF

A coquilla nut snuff man, 18thC, 3in (7.5cm) high.
£550–700 ⚒ BAG

◄ **A rootwood snuff box,** the push-on cover impressed with a Masonic temple medallion, inscribed underneath 'Gloire du Grand Architecte de L'Univers', French, 19thC, 3¼in (8.5cm) diam.
£400–500 ⚒ PFK

► **A wooden trick snuff shoe,** with a biting snake, c1890, 4in (10cm) high.
£160–180 ⊞ HUM

A George III fruitwood spinning wheel, with bone turnings, 50in (127cm) high.
£250–320 ⚒ F&C

A cherrywood spinning wheel, French, c1780, 55in (139.5cm) high.
£350–385 ⊞ TDS

A turned wood storage jar, 19thC, 4½in (11.5cm) high.
£160–175 ⊞ SEA

A mahogany veneered tea canister, with satinwood banding and inlaid stringing, the cover inlaid with a quatrefoil motif, early 19thC, 4¼in (11cm) high.
£60–75 ⚒ WW

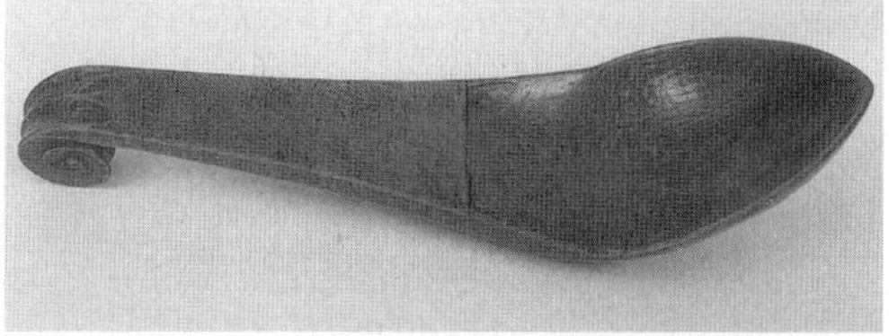

A fruitwood spoon, 18thC, 8in (20.5cm) long.
£250–280 ⊞ AEF

A carved wood tobacco stand, modelled as a bear carrying a basket with a hinged lid on his back, German, Black Forest, late 19thC, 13½in (34.5cm) high.
£850–1,100 ⚒ RIT

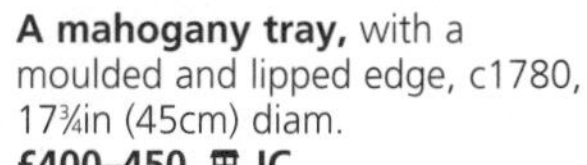

A mahogany tray, with a moulded and lipped edge, c1780, 17¾in (45cm) diam.
£400–450 ⊞ JC

An Edwardian mahogany tea tray, decorated in coloured woods with musical instruments, bow and arrows, within a foliate scrolled surround, 26in (66cm) wide.
£400–500 ⚒ TMA

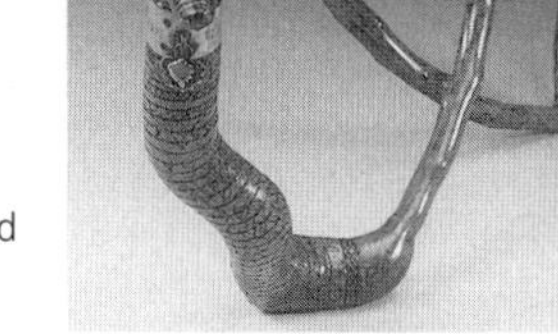

► **An Edwardian carved root walking stick,** the handle carved as the head of a dachshund, 30in (76cm) long.
£380–475 ⚒ TMA

Tunbridge Ware

A pair of painted Tunbridge ware bellows, c1815, 14in (35.5cm) long.
£70–80 ⊞ F&F

A Tunbridge ware blotter cover, decorated with central panels of birds within patterned borders, c1860, 11in (28cm) wide.
£200–240 ⚒ G(L)

A Tunbridge ware box, decorated with a bird, replaced knob, 19thC, 4in (10cm) wide.
£100–125 ⊞ PSA

LOCATE THE SOURCE
The source of each illustration in Miller's can be found by checking the code letters below each caption with the Key to Illustrations, pages 794–800.

A Tunbridge ware box, decorated with a mosaic of a dog, c1870, 3½in (9cm) wide.
£200–220 ⊞ AMH

A Tunbridge ware magnifying glass, 19thC, 6in (15cm) long.
£520–575 ⊞ PSA

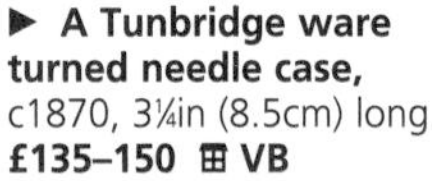

► **A Tunbridge ware turned needle case,** c1870, 3¼in (8.5cm) long.
£135–150 ⊞ VB

A Tunbridge ware pen box, 7in (18cm) wide.
£80–100 ⊞ VBO

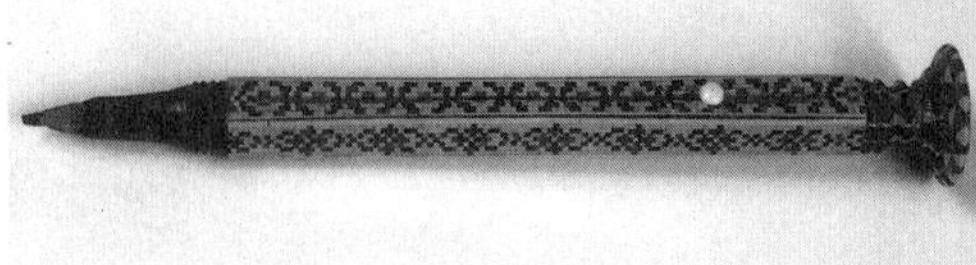

A Tunbridge ware propelling pencil, c1870, 4in (10cm) long.
£270–300 ⊞ AMH

► **A Tunbridge ware sewing box,** the central panel with floral decoration and floral banding, 19thC, 9½in (24cm) wide.
£340–425 ⚒ Mit

A Tunbridge ware snuff box, c1850, 2¾in (7cm) diam.
£150–170 ⊞ AMH

A Tunbridge ware stamp box, decorated with a mosaic of the head of Queen Victoria, c1850, 1½in (4cm) wide.
£180–200 ⊞ AMH

A miniature Tunbridge ware table, for storing pins, c1860, 3¼in (8.5cm) diam.
£320–350 ⊞ VB

A Tunbridge ware tea caddy, with two compartments, the hinged cover decorated with a castle view and bands of geometric and foliate inlay, 19thC, 10½in (26.5cm) wide.
£800–1,000 ⚒ TMA

A Tunbridge ware tea caddy, the lid decorated with a floral panel within a similar border, void interior, 19thC, 6in (15cm) wide.
£110–140 ⚒ GAK

A Tunbridge ware bird's-eye maple tea caddy, the top with tessera view of Eridge Castle, the interior with two lidded divisions, the sides with a band of tessera roses, restored, 19thC, 26in (66cm) wide.
£500–625 ⚒ BR

A Victorian Tunbridge ware tea chest, the hinged cover inlaid with parquetry, the interior with a lid, the sides decorated with flowers, 5in (12.5cm) high.
£180–225 ⚒ WW

A Tunbridge ware rosewood tray, the centre with a gaugework view of a cottage within half-square borders, some edge moulding missing, 19thC, 10in (25.5cm) wide.
£600–725 ⚒ BR

A Tunbridge ware tray, c1870, 7in (18cm) wide.
£180–200 ⊞ AMH

A Tunbridge ware rosewood writing slope, decorated with panels of Balmoral Castle, with fruit and floral banding, fitted interior, c1850, 12½in (32cm) wide.
£620–775 ⚒ G(L)

A Victorian Tunbridge ware rosewood workbox, the hinged cover inlaid with a panel depicting a castle among trees, within stylized foliate borders, the sides with a band of flowers and foliage, 10½in (26.5cm) wide.
£500–625 ⚒ P(S)

A Tunbridge ware ebonized workbox, with central floral panel and banding, c1860, 10½in (26.5cm) wide.
£440–550 ⚒ G(L)

► **A Tunbridge ware rosewood writing slope,** with tessera view of Eridge Castle, the lid opening to reveal an inkwell and pen box, 19thC, 30in (76cm) wide.
£1,150–1,380 ⚒ BR

Boxes

A mahogany tea caddy, with inlaid fan paterae, c1790, 5in (12.5cm) square.
£1,300–1,450 ⊞ BBo

A Georgian rosewood tea caddy, with mother-of-pearl inlay, the interior fitted with two lidded containers and a glass mixing bowl, some damage, 13½in (34.5cm) wide.
£170–220 ⚒ FHF

A Tartan ware tea caddy, by Charles Stiven, Laurencekirk, enclosing three caddies with wooden hinged tops decorated with ink drawings of scenes from Sir Walter Scott's novels, the side decoration with vermilion wrigglework, 19thC, 12in (30.5cm) wide.
£5,000–6,000 ⚒ P(Ed)

The records show that Charles Stiven (1753–1820) was an established box maker in the small Aberdeenshire village of Laurencekirk and that unusually his premises doubled as the stagecoach booking office. After his death in 1820, his son Alexander took over the business and was to hold a Royal Warrant.

A Regency tortoiseshell tea caddy, the interior fitted with two compartments, on ivory feet, 6in (15cm) wide.
£600–700 ⚒ DD

◀ **A prisoner of war straw workbox,** French, c1810, 3in (7.5cm) wide.
£145–160 ⊞ HUM

► **A burr-yew campaign writing slope,** early 19thC, 10in (25.5cm) wide.
£675–750 ⊞ ChC

◀ **A satinwood workbox,** the top outlined with cut-steel marcasite decoration, with triangular lidded compartments flanking a central pin cushion, above a mahogany-lined drawer, c1820, 11in (28cm) wide.
£520–575 ⊞ JC

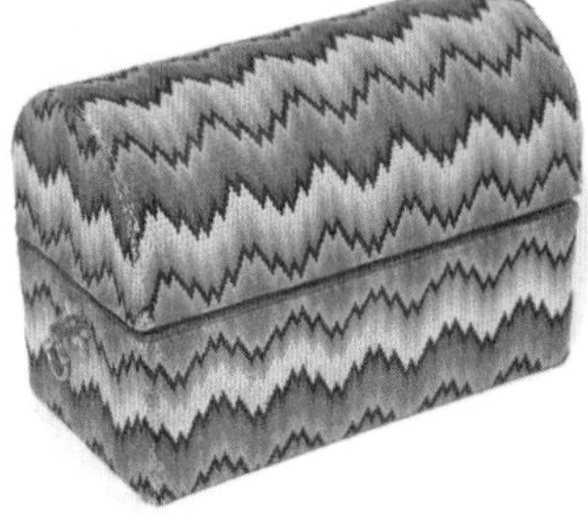

► **A casket,** covered in silk Florentine flame-stitch embroidery, with later silk lining, 19thC, 11in (28cm) wide.
£165–185 ⊞ HA

A tortoiseshell tea caddy, with pewter and ivory stringing, Dutch, c1850, 4½in (11.5cm) wide.
£1,800–2,000 ⊞ AKS

► **A rosewood and parquetry workbox,** the lid opening to reveal a crimson velvet and morocco interior, c1860, 13in (33cm) wide.
£700–780 ⊞ RAN

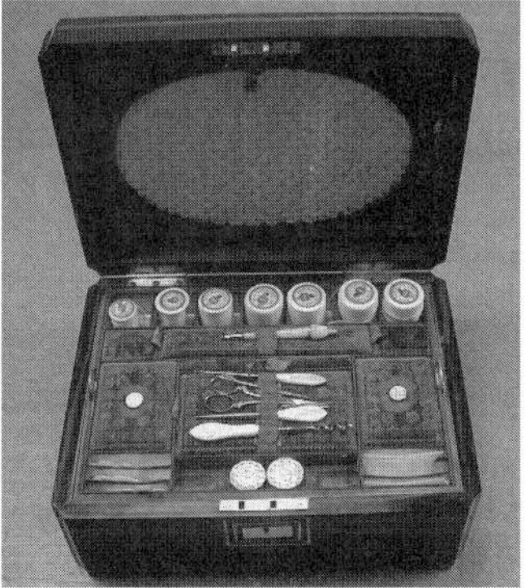

A Victorian coromandel needlework box, by Gay & Son, London, with mother-of-pearl detail and original wine-coloured stamped velvet interior, the lift-out tray with fitted boxes and containing mother-of-pearl needlework accessories, 11¾in (30cm) wide.
£620–700 ⚒ TMA

A brass-banded walnut writing slope, c1880, 15½in (39.5cm) wide.
£200–220 ⊞ TO

A mahogany and satinwood jewellery box, the lid opening to release a fall-front, the interior with three drawers and a tray lined with red velvet, late 19thC, 13½in (34.5cm) wide.
£380–480 ⚒ CGC

A black and gilt-decorated steel strong box, with satin-lined interior and chinoiserie decoration, 19thC, 8in (20.5cm) wide.
£170–220 ⚒ LFA

A Victorian burr-walnut-veneered glove box, with pierced fret brass and ivory mounts and escutcheon, with a mauve silk-lined interior, 10in (25.5cm) wide.
£100–120 ⚒ WW

A mahogany jewellery box, inlaid with walnut, satinwood, maple and mahogany, banded in rosewood, with boxwood stringing, with original velvet lining, c1880, 11in (28cm) wide.
£380–420 ⊞ JC

An oyster-veneered olivewood lace box, c1690, 11in (28cm) wide.
£900–1,000 ⊞ F&F

A red boullework stationery box, with original silk-lined interior and fitted compartments, stamped 'A Vickery, Regent Street', mid-19thC, 8½in (21.5cm) wide.
£850–1,100 ⚒ TMA

A marquetry-inlaid jewellery box, Continental, c1860, 7in (18cm) square.
£235–260 ⊞ HA

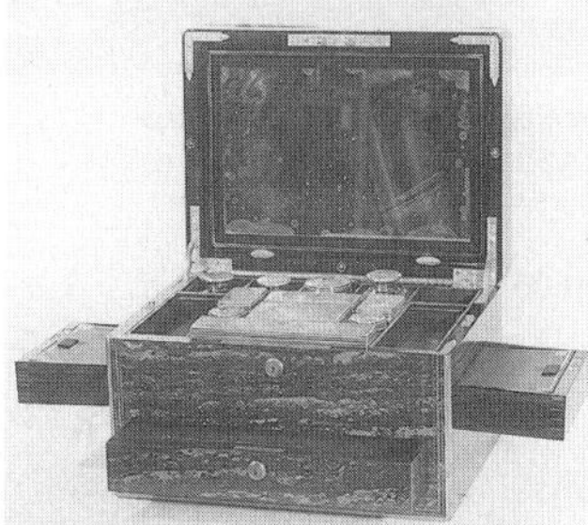

A Victorian coromandel dressing case, with brass stringing, the interior fitted with cut-glass and silver-mounted accessories, and removable lid mirror enclosing stationery compartment, one bottle missing, 14in (35.5cm) wide.
£600–700 ⚒ AH

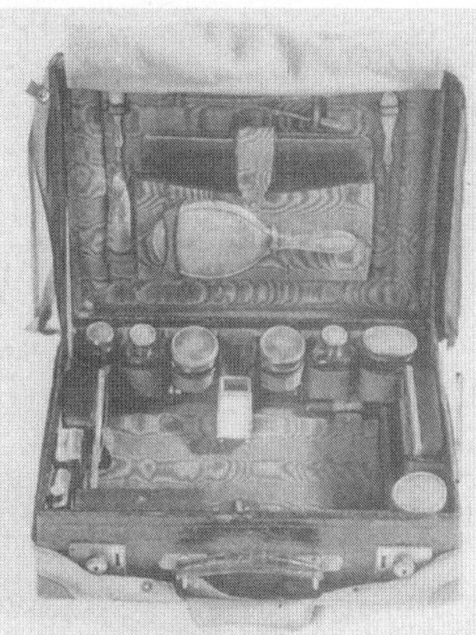

A gentleman's snakeskin dressing case, by Drew & Sons, London, with silver-mounted glass fittings, including a miniature silver carriage timepiece, some pieces missing, hallmarked London 1908, 20in (51cm) wide.
£750–900 ⚒ Bri

Music

Cylinder Musical Boxes

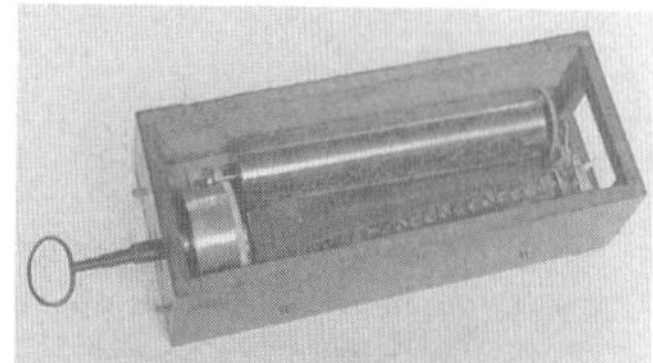

A sectional comb cylinder musical box, playing four airs, the comb with 20 tooth sections, external controls, the walnut case missing lid, early 19thC, 11½in (29cm) wide.
£500–600 P(WM)

A Victorian ebonized and painted cylinder musical box, playing four airs, Swiss, 12in (30.5cm) wide.
£400–450 TMA

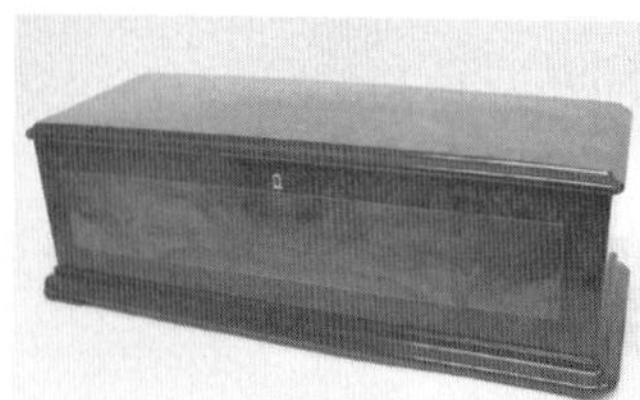

A cylinder musical box, by Nicole Freres, playing 12 airs, in a walnut case, Swiss, late 19thC, 28¾in (53.5cm) wide.
£1,200–1,500 G(L)

A cylinder musical box, playing 12 airs, the rosewood lid with marquetry musical trophies, stamped 'GB&Co', Swiss, late 19thC, 22¾in (58cm) wide.
£800–1,000 CGC

LOCATE THE SOURCE
The source of each illustration in Miller's can be found by checking the code letters below each caption with the Key to Illustrations, pages 794–800.

A 'Bells in Sight' musical box, playing 10 airs, in a rosewood case inlaid with floral sprays and crossbanded in kingwood, with ebonized borders, Swiss, mid-19thC, 23¼in (59cm) wide.
£1,800–2,250 TEN

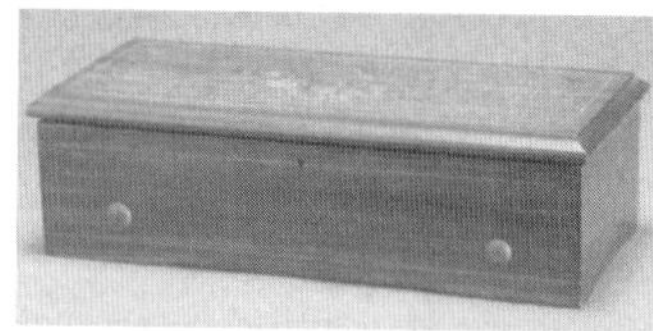

A rosewood cylinder musical box, inlaid with marquetry and grain-painted, playing ten airs, Swiss, c1870, 20¼in (51.5cm) wide.
£800–950 WcH

An orchestrion cylinder musical box, by Charles Ullmann, playing six tunes, Swiss, c1880, 19¼in (49cm) wide.
£3,000–3,300 KOLN

A cylinder musical box, by Lepee, playing 12 tunes, French, c1890, 26in (66cm) wide.
£2,250–2,500 ⊞ AUTO

A cylinder musical box, by Nicole Frères, playing eight airs, fully restored, Swiss, c1865, 21in (53.5cm) wide.
£3,400–3,800 ⊞ KHW

An Ami Rivenc musical box, playing 20 airs, the rosewood-veneered case inlaid with musical trophies within a vine leaf and floral border, 1894, 25¼in (65cm) wide.
£2,400–3,000 P(WM)

A cylinder musical box, by Paillard, playing six airs, in a burr-walnut and ebonized case, Swiss, c1885, 25in (61cm) wide.
£4,800–5,300 ⊞ RGa

A cylinder musical box, by B. A. Bremond, Geneva, playing ten airs, contained in an ebonized and bird's-eye maple case on stand, Swiss, c1900, 47in (119.5cm) wide.
£4,000–5,000 IM

Disc Musical Boxes

A Regina disc musical box, with 27 discs, in a mahogany case, the base containing an additional 17 discs, American, c1898, 42in (106.5cm) wide.
£16,000–18,000 JAA
This was purchased new from the Regina Factory in Rahway, New Jersey in 1898 and remained in the original family until it sold recently.

► **A Symphonion disc musical box,** contained in a fruitwood case, with original disc tin, German, c1900, 10in (25.5cm) wide.
£675–750 ⊞ AUTO

A Polyphon coin-operated disc musical box, with one disc, contained in a walnut case, German, c1900, 21¼in (54cm) wide.
£2,800–3,200 KOLN

A Polyphon disc musical box, with approximately 50 discs, contained in a walnut case, the lid with marquetry floral panel, the interior with a print of putti playing musical instruments, German, late 19thC, 18in (45.5cm) wide.
£800–1,000 AH

► **A Symphonion disc musical box,** with one disc, contained in a rosewood-veneered case, the lid inlaid with a marquetry panel of flowers, lid interior with applied prints of cherubs, German, c1900, 19½in (49.5cm) wide.
£700–800 AG

A Symphonion coin-operated disc musical box, with a quantity of discs, German, c1900, 36in (91.5cm) high.
£1,800–2,200 N

Mechanical Music

A mahogany barrel piano, unrestored, Spanish, c1860, 48in (122cm) wide.
£630–700 ⊞ PG

A cabinet roller organ, by The Autophone Co, the walnut case with stencilled decoration, American, late 19thC, 18¼in (46.5cm) wide.
£370–470 P(WM)

A singing bird ornament, by Bontems, Paris, in a porcelain jardinière with ormolu mounts and celadon flowers, c1870, 18in (45.5cm) high.
£4,000–5,000 ⊞ GWe

◄ **A singing bird in a cage automaton,** by Bontems, Paris, c1900, 11in (28cm) high.
£1,350–1,500 ⊞ KHW

► **A singing birds in a cage automaton,** c1920, 12in (30.5cm) high.
£350–400 ⊞ Beb

A singing bird filigree metal snuff box, German, c1950, 3in (7.5cm) wide.
£1,600–1,750 ⊞ AUTO

Phonographs

An Edison home phonograph, with tin horn, c1900, 14in (35.5cm) wide.
£700–875 ⚒ BLH

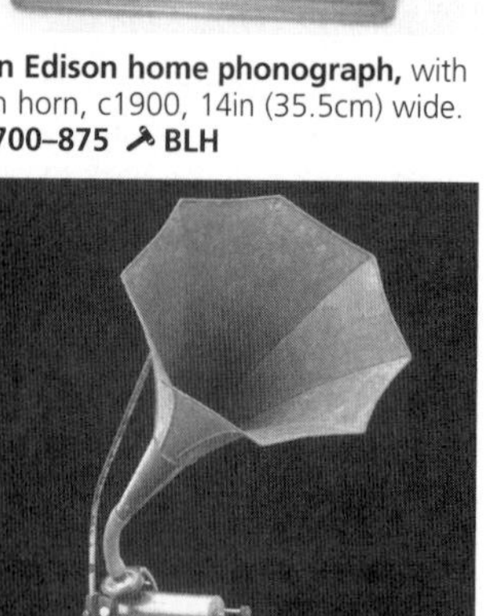

An Edison Gem phonograph, in an oak case, with 18 cylinders, c1905, horn 20½in (52cm) long.
£500–600 ⚒ LJ

A Loiret No.2 phonograph, with a reproduction celluloid horn, in a paper-covered wood carrying case, with four cylinders, case water damaged, French, c1900, 14¾in (37.5cm) wide.
£3,000–3,300 ⚒ SK(B)

An Edison home phonograph, in original wooden case with gilt banner and lettering, with black-japanned horn and two Edison Bell cylindrical records, late 19thC, 18in (45.5cm) wide.
£320–400 ⚒ PFK

A Heywood-Wakefield Perfektone phonograph, by Gardners, with a mahogany frame and wicker body, American, 1920s, 43in (109cm) high.
£520–620 ⚒ SK(B)

◀ **An Edison standard phonograph,** c1920, 16in (40.5cm) wide.
£450–480 ⊞ KHW

Gramophones

A Berliner Type A gramophone, No. 6475, in an oak case, Canadian, c1905, horn 14in (35.5cm) diam.
£3,000–3,300 ⚒ SK(B)

A Pathé gramophone, in a mahogany case, with blue-painted horn, c1910, 11½in (29cm) wide.
£330–400 ⚒ P(WM)

◀ **A Paillard Ecophone gramophone,** in a carved walnut case, with replacement soundbox, Swiss, 1910–20, 13¾in (35cm) wide.
£500–600 ⚒ P(WM)

A Decca Salon gramophone, in an oak cabinet, c1930, 20in (51cm) wide.
£180–200 ⊞ CBGR

Miller's is a price GUIDE not a price LIST

Musical Instruments

The collector of musical instruments can be presented with an enormous challenge: deciding whether to spend £150 on a late 19th-century mandolin, £1,000,000 on a Stradivarius violin, or anything in between. What sets musical instruments apart from other collectable items is the extra dimension of sound. They not only can be a feast to the eye, but to the ear as well. A historical instrument with an important provenance can be seen as an antique recording device that lets us not only see but also hear the past.

The collector can take advantage of the regular musical instrument sales that are offered by many leading auction houses, or purchase from the specialist dealers who offer instruments restored to playing condition. A look through this guide will give some idea of the range of instruments available.

The market for stringed instruments in the violin family has always been strong and no doubt will continue to be so. The world record auction price for a violin (a Stradivarius) is £947,500, and the next comparable example could no doubt break the £1,000,000 barrier. For keyboard instruments the traditional area of growth has been for rare 17th- and 18th-century harpsichords, with a recent auction price reaching £267,500 for a 1679 Couchet single manual. There has also been a rise in prices for art-case pianos – particularly for those with an important provenance or casework designed by a well-known artist. Markets to watch in the future are Italian violins of the late 19th or early 20th century, and American guitars of the 1940s and 1950s. Some of the guitars, if they have associations with a famous musician, can now fetch enormous prices.

With musical instruments it is important to always take expert advice, particularly when venturing into the upper reaches of the market. Take the time to find a reputable dealer who can guide you and also provide some guarantees. Some of the auction houses now provide what is virtually a retail service with stringed instruments, allowing prospective purchasers to take the instruments away and try them before bidding. When purchasing an instrument from an auction house, ask for a condition report if you are uncertain. For example, a crack in the back of a stringed instrument, even if well repaired, can considerably reduce its value. With a keyboard instrument, it is important to take into account the cost of restoration if you are going to keep it as a playing instrument. High-quality restoration is time consuming and expensive. Above all, keep in mind why you are buying the instrument: just for the pleasure of ownership; as an instrument to be used regularly; or as an investment. **David Winston**

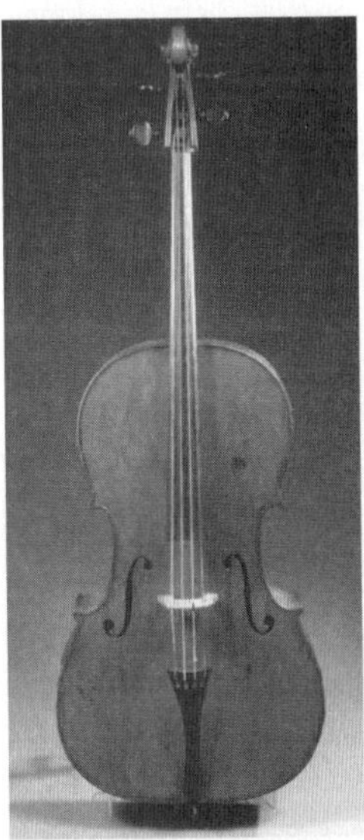

A cello, by Nicolas Augustin Chappuy, French, c1770, old table restorations, length of back 28¼in (72cm), in fitted case.
£5,500–6,500 P

A cello, by the school of Thomas Dodd, London, c1820, length of back 29¼in (74.5cm).
£7,000–8,500 Bon

A cello, German, c1830, length of back 29¼in (74.5cm).
£3,200–4,000 Bon

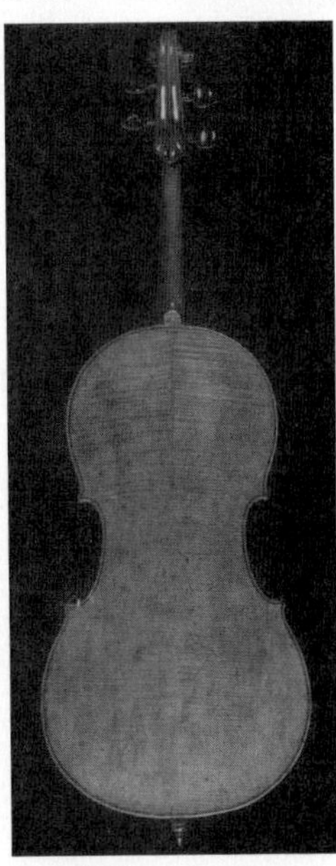

A cello, by William Tarr, Manchester, c1840, length of back 29¼in (74.5cm).
£9,000–11,000 Bon

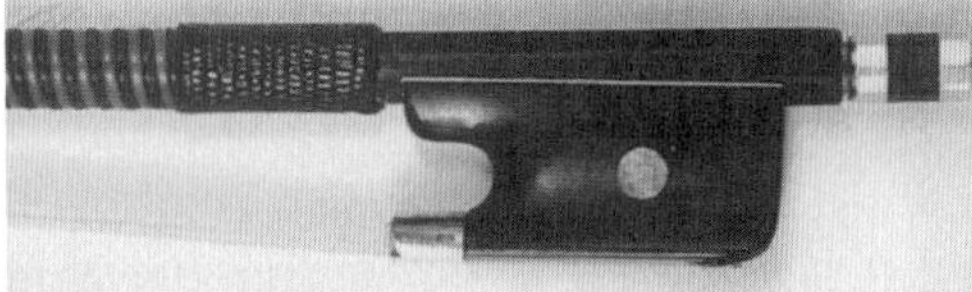

A gold-mounted cello bow, by J. Dodd, London, 1820, gold mounts later, 87g.
£1,400–1,700 Bon

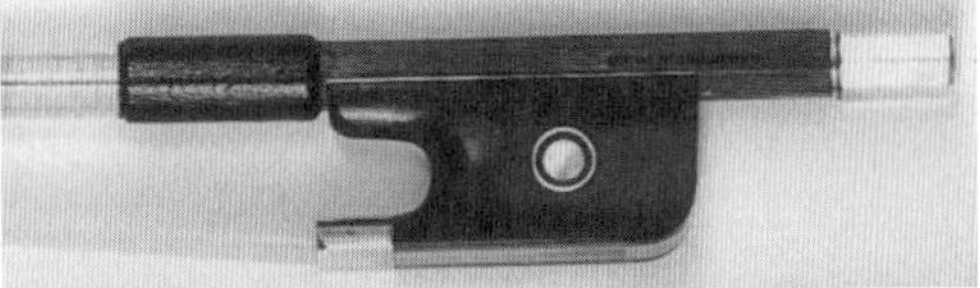

A silver-mounted cello bow, by E. Sartory, French, stamped, c1920, 79g.
£5,000–6,000 Bon

A silver-mounted cello bow, by F. N. Voirin, no hair, cloth lapping, stamped, French, c1920, 61g.
£2,000–2,400 ⚒ Bon

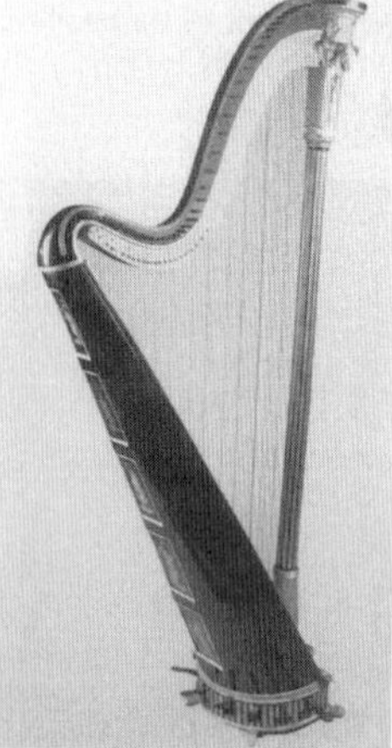

A Regency-style ebonized and gilt harp, by Sebastian Erard, the main stem decorated with griffins, lyres and foliate and ram-mask decoration above caryatids, and a fluted ebonized and gilt stem, leading to winged seahorses to the base, the sound-box decorated in gilt with symbolic muses, 19thC, 67in (170cm) high.
£2,000–2,500 ⚒ Mit

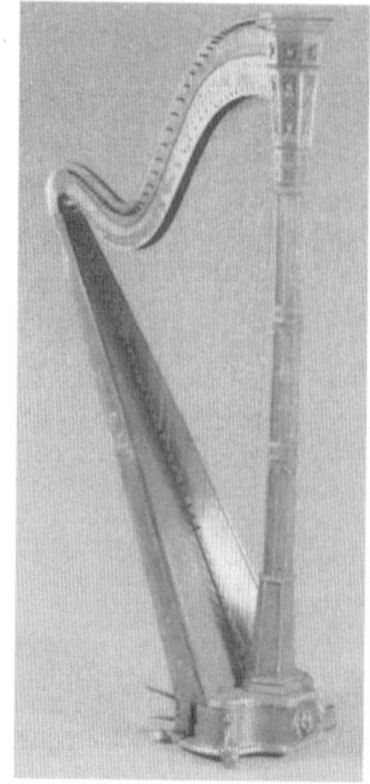

A double-action pedal harp, by Alexander Blazell, London, the lacquered body with gilt line decoration, later soundboard, the column in Gothic style with gilded mouldings and headed by strapwork panels, 19thC, 69½in (176.5cm) high.
£6,250–7,000 ⚒ S

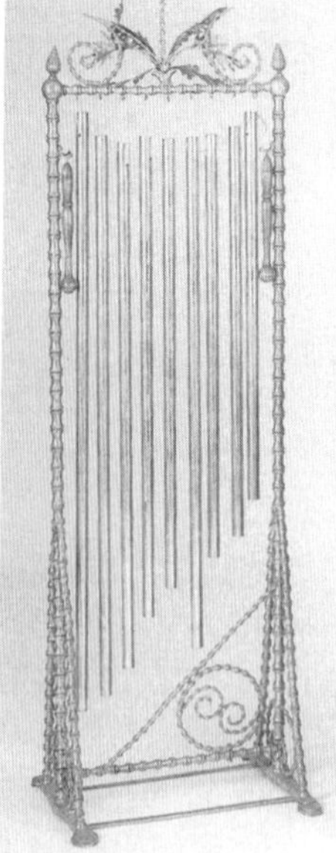

A set of late Victorian brass and plated standing chimes, stamped Harringtons Patent 'Tubular Bells', Coventry, 64¼in (163cm).
£500–600 ⚒ P(NW)

► A black-lacquered harp lute, by Barry, London, the table with inset rose pierced and gilded with the Royal Arms and edged in gilt with a band of honeysuckle and foliage, the column headed by gilt gesso acanthus leaves, early 19thC, 34¾in (88.5cm) high.
£500–600 ⚒ S

A guitar, by Gibson Inc, Kalamazoo, with two-piece maple back and ebony fingerboard, American, 1947, length of back 21in (53.5cm), with original case.
£3,200–3,500 ⚒ SK

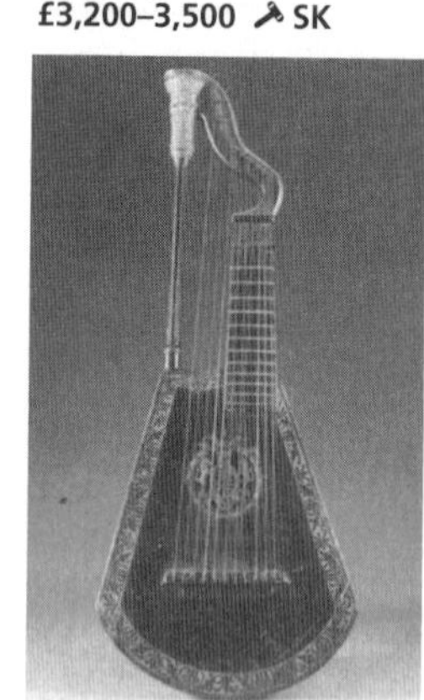

◄ A George III mahogany and painted keyed metallophone, by Broderip & Wilkinson, with original decoration on the soundboard, the remaining decoration of a later date, formerly with an undertier, 38¼in (97cm) wide.
£5,500–6,000 ⚒ S

This keyed metallophone, a keyboard instrument with tuned metal bars struck with hammers, and a predecessor of the celesta or dulcitone, is highly unusual in being so early. This type is generally associated with the latter part of the 19th century, when its characteristic of remaining in tune made it popular with missionaries. However, the partnership of Broderip & Wilkinson, based in the Haymarket, London, only existed between 1798 (when Longman & Broderip went bankrupt) and 1807 (when Broderip died). Although the firm continued under Wilkinson for another two years after Broderip's death, it was styled Wilkinson & Co and this piano can be confidently dated to these nine years spanning the turn of the 19th century.

A George III mahogany square piano, by Thomas Tomkison, London, with rosewood crossbanding and foliate brass mounts, the keyboard surround with pierced fretwork and brass inlay, 67in (170cm) wide.
£475–550 ⚒ AH

A Federal mahogany and rosewood-crossbanded square piano, by Charles Albrecht, Philadelphia, with brass mounts, the keyboard above three drawers, minor damage, American, c1825, 66¾in (169.5cm) wide.
£600–700 ⚒ WcH

Cross Reference
See Colour Review (page 724)

A fortepiano, by Maximilian Schott, Vienna, veneered in Hungarian ash, with four pedals, Austrian, c1828, 96in (244cm) long.
£18,000–20,000 ⊞ PPC

A walnut fortepiano, by Mayer & Heitzmann, Vienna, with two pedals, original condition, Austrian, c1840, 99in (251.5cm) wide.
£12,500–14,000 ⊞ PPC
A fortepiano is an early type of piano.

A rosewood grand piano, by Bechstein, German, c1888, 72in (183cm) wide.
£4,500–5,000 ⊞ PG

A burr-walnut grand piano, by Bechstein, German, c1900, 93¼in (230cm) long.
£6,000–7,000 ⊞ PEx

A fiddle-back mahogany-veneered grand piano, by Pleyel, French, c1905, 72in (183cm) long.
£5,500–6,000 ⊞ PG

A burr-walnut grand piano, by John Brimsmead & Sons, London, c1860, 79in (200.5cm) wide, with bench.
£1,850–2,200 ⚒ WcH

An upright piano, by Joseph Gramer, American, c1890, 56½in (143.5cm) wide.
£2,700–3,000 ⊞ PG

A model A grand piano, by Bechstein, in original ebony case, German, c1900, 90½in (230cm) long.
£2,800–3,500 ⊞ PEx

An upright piano, by Erard, the Art Nouveau case inlaid with marquetry figures, chequered inlay banding and pierced chrome fretwork detail, restored, French, c1904, 51in (129.5cm) wide.
£18,000–20,000 ⊞ PPC

A rococo revival ebonized square grand piano, by Hazelton Brothers, American, 1875–1900, 83½in (212cm) wide.
£1,500–2,000 ⚒ NOA

An ebonized upright piano, by Bechstein, German, c1900, 48in (122cm) high.
£3,200–3,500 ⊞ PG

An inlaid rosewood upright piano, by Bechstein, inlaid with three panels of Art Nouveau-style flowers between reeded uprights, German, 61in (155cm) wide.
£500–600 ⚒ PFK

Cross Reference
See Colour Review (page 726)

A Louis XVI-style plum-pudding mahogany grand piano, by Erard, with bronze mounts, French, early 20thC, 84in (213.5cm) long.
£17,500–20,000 ⚒ S(NY)

A mahogany model O grand piano, by Steinway, American, c1912, 90½in (230cm) long.
£6,500–8,000 ⊞ PEx

A mahogany baby grand piano, by Steinbech, German, c1915, 64in (162.5cm) wide.
£2,700–3,000 ⊞ PG

A mahogany baby grand piano, by Kirkman, London, 1915–18, 52in (132cm) wide.
£2,700–3,000 ⊞ PG

A mahogany baby grand piano, by Bentley, 1915–18, 58in (147.5cm) wide.
£2,700–3,000 ⊞ PG

A mahogany grand piano, by Steinway, German, c1916, 89in (226cm) long, with bench.
£6,300–7,000 ⚒ WcH

A 'sunburst' rosewood-veneered grand piano, by Gaveau, restored, French, c1925, 60in (152.5cm) wide.
£19,000–21,000 ⊞ PPC

Prices

The price ranges quoted in this book reflect the average price a purchaser might expect to pay for a similar item. The price will vary according to the condition, rarity, size, popularity, provenance, colour and restoration of the item, and this must be taken into account when assessing values. Don't forget that if you are selling it is quite likely that you will be offered less than the price range.

► A mahogany cottage upright piano, by W. H. Barnes, c1930, 43in (109cm) high.
£900–1,000 ⊞ PG

A mahogany mini piano, by Eavestaff, 1930s, 51in (129.5cm) wide, with matching stool.
£400–450 ⊞ JAZZ

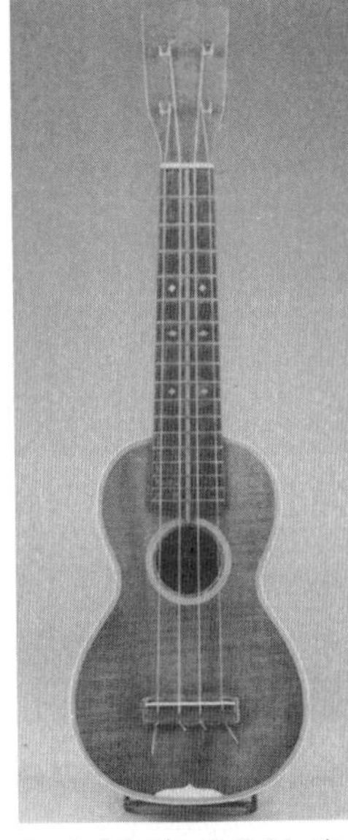

A ukulele, by C. F. Martin & Co, Nazareth, with mahogany neck and ebony fingerboard, American, c1930, length of back 9½in (24cm), with original case.
£2,000–2,500 SK

A viola, by Charles Buthod, Mirecourt, French, c1880, length of back 15¾in (40cm).
£1,400–1,750 Bon

A violin, by Antonius Venaccia, Naples, Italian, 1764, length of back 14in (35.6cm).
£9,000–11,000 Bon

A violin, by Tomasso Eberle, Naples, Italian, c1770, length of back 14in (35.5cm).
£10,000–12,000 Bon

A violin, c1770, length of back 14¼in (36cm).
£1,400–1,750 Bon

A violin, attributed to Vincenzo Panormo, London/Dublin, c1800, length of back 14in (35.5cm), in fitted case.
£7,000–8,500 P

A violin, of the Guadagnini School, Italian, mid-19thC, length of back 14in (35.5cm), with bow and case.
£2,200–2,600 GH

A violin, by George Craske, London, c1859, length of back 14¼in (36cm).
£3,200–3,800 Bon

A violin, in a Biedermeier brass-mounted fruitwood-veneered case, 19thC, 30¼in (77cm) long.
£350–450 NOA

◀ **A violin,** with paper label inscribed 'Giovanni Paolo Maggini, Deutsche Arbeit', German, 19thC, length of back 24in (61cm), with case and bow.
£320–400 SWO

▶ **A violin,** after Del Gesu, c1880, length of back 14in (35.5cm).
£850–1,000 Bon

A violin, by Gand & Barnardel, Paris, French, 1890, length of back 14in (35.5cm).
£12,000–14,000 ⚒ SK

A violin, from the workshop of Vincenzo Sannino, Naples, Italian, 1911, length of back 14in (35.5cm).
£7,500–9,000 ⚒ SK

A violin, by Benigno Saccani, Milan, Italian, 1909, length of back 14in (35.5cm), with case.
£3,800–4,500 ⚒ SK

A violin, possibly by Giovanni Pistucci, Naples, Italian, c1918, length of back 14in (35.5cm).
£4,500–5,500 ⚒ Bon

A J. B. Vuillaume reproduction violin, 1928, length of back 14in (35.5cm).
£550–650 ⚒ GH

A violin, c1920, length of back 14in (35.5cm).
£3,000–3,500 ⚒ Bon

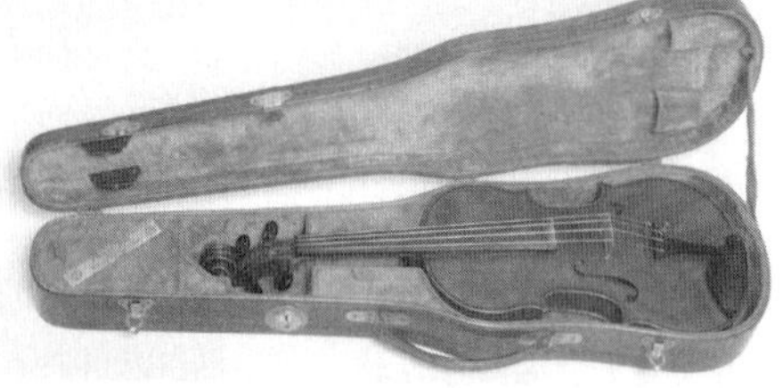

A violin, by Pierre Hel, French, 1918, length of back 14in (35.5cm), with original case.
£4,500–5,500 ⚒ GH

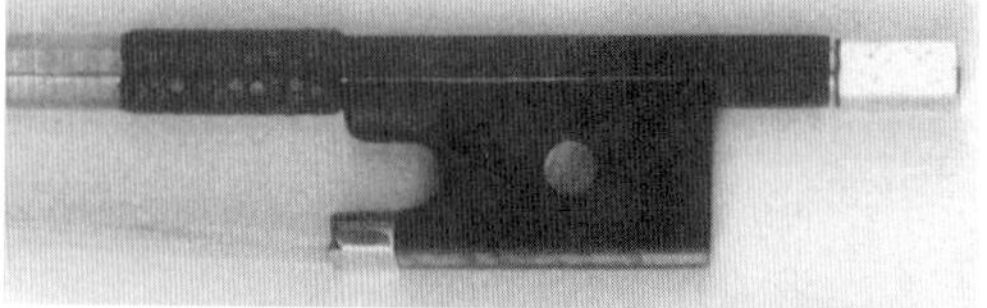

A silver-mounted violin bow, by Auguste Barbe, French, c1870, 61g.
£1,000–1,200 ⚒ Bon

A gold and ivory-mounted violin bow, by W. E. Hill & Sons, stamped, 1951, 63g.
£3,800–4,500 ⚒ Bon
This bow was made for the 1951 Festival of Great Britain and is sold with a letter from W. E. Hill & Sons and the photocopy of the Official 1951 Certificate from the Festival of Britain.

Icons

An icon of the Smolensk Mother of God with St Kiril, Russian, 16thC, 12¾ x 10½in (32.5 x 26.5cm).
£3,400–4,250 JAA

A Stroganov School icon of the Virgin Comforter to those who Grieve, Russian, 17thC, 12 x 10in (30.5 x 25.5cm).
£7,500–8,500 ICO

An icon of the Tikhvin Mother of God, Russian, 17thC, 12¼ x 11in (31 x 28cm).
£1,500–1,700 JAA

► **A pair of icons from an iconostas,** one depicting Prince Vladimir with St Anna, the other with Cappadocian Heirarchs with the Virgin and Christ, Russian, probably 18thC, 50 x 28in (127 x 71cm).
£6,000–7,500 S
An iconostas is a screen bearing icons at the head of the nave in an Eastern church.

An icon of The Pokrov, egg tempera on wood panel, northern Russian, 16thC, 28¼ x 20¼in (72 x 51.5cm).
£7,000–8,000 RKa

An icon of the Dormition, the borders covered with a silver metal oklad, Russian, 17thC, 12¼ x 10½in (31 x 26.5cm).
£2,700–3,000 JAA

An icon of the Saviour, Russian, Moscow, 16th/17thC, 12¼ x 10½in (31 x 26.5cm).
£2,500–3,000 JAA

An icon of The Last Judgement, egg tempera on wood panel, Russian, 17thC, 15¼ x 12½in (39.5 x 32cm).
£6,000–7,000 RKa

Cross Reference
See Colour Review (page 727)

An icon of the Hodgeteria, the Virgin and Child painted on a gilt ground within an integral arched wood frame relief-carved with flowers and foliage, Greek, late 17thC, 9¾ x 8in (25 x 20.5cm).
£2,500–3,000 Bon

An icon of Metropolitan George, in a silver-gilt and enamel oklad, Russian, early 19thC, 14 x 12in (35.5 x 30.5cm).
£5,000–5,500 S

A bronze travelling icon of Sts Ulita and her son Kyric, Zossima and Savaati, with female martyrs, Russian, 19thC, 2½ x 2in (6.5 x 5cm).
£25–30 ⊞ ICO

An icon of St Alexander Nevsky, with silvered metal oklad not pictured, Russian, 19thC, 12 x 10in (30.5 x 25.5cm).
£750–900 JAA

St Alexander defeated an invasion of the Swedes in the river Neva from whence he took the name 'Neva' – 'Nevskiy'.

An icon painted with a figure of Christ, covered by a silver oklad, Russian, 19thC, 4¼ x 3½in (11 x 9cm).
£70–80 G(L)

An icon of the Tolga Mother of God, with gilded-silver and enamel oklad, the beadwork pearl robes set with jewels, Russian, 1895, 12 x 10½in (30.5 x 26.5cm).
£5,250–6,000 S(NY)

An icon of the Resurrection of Christ, surrounded by 12 festival scenes, egg tempera and gilt, Russian, 19thC, 13¾ x 12in (35 x 30.5cm).
£750–900 BUK

A brass triptych of Christ with the Virgin and St John, Russian, 19thC, 6 x 7in (15 x 18cm).
£225–250 ⊞ ICO

An icon of Christ Emmanuel, with gilded silver and jewelled oklad, set with simulated diamonds, Russian, 1819, 13 x 10½in (33 x 26.5cm).
£3,500–4,000 S(NY)

An icon of the translation of the relics of St John Chrysostom, Russian, c1890, 10½ x 8¾in (26.5 x 22cm).
£700–800 JAA

◀ **An icon of the Mother of God,** the Virgin depicted with three hands and wearing a purple maphorion over a cream cap and chemise, eastern European, 19thC, 19¾ x 16¼in (50 x 41.5cm).
£180–225 Bea(E)

An icon of the Resurrection, surrounded by 12 festival scenes, the background and borders incised, gold-leafed and with *faux* enamelling, Russian, c1890, 12¼ x 10½in (31 x 26.5cm).
£900–1,200 JAA

An icon of St Nicholas, with partly gilded silver and enamel oklad, the borders enamelled with colourful foliage, Russian, c1900, 8¾ x 7in (22 x 18cm).
£3,500–4,500 S(NY)

An icon of the Vladimir Virgin and Child, covered by an engine-turned silver oklad, Russian, c1900, 6 x 7in (15 x 18cm).
£350–400 ICO

► **An icon of St Nicholas,** with a silver oklad, Russian, c1910, 12¼ x 10½in (31 x 26.5cm).
£700–850 SLN

A silver-gilt-mounted icon of Christ Pantocrator, damage to oklad, Russian, 7 x 5½in (18 x 14cm).
£170–220 WcH

An icon of the Kazan Mother of God, with gilded silver enamel oklad, Russian, c1900, 10½ x 8¾in (26.5 x 22cm).
£3,500–4,500 S

A miniature icon of Christ Pantocrator, covered by a silver oklad, Russian, c1900, 4in (10cm) high.
£350–400 ICO

An icon of the Kievan Virgin and Child, covered by a silver oklad, Russian, c1900, 3in (7.5cm) high.
£450–500 ICO

◄ **An icon of St Seraphim of Sarov,** the borders gilded, incised and with colourful decoration, Russian, c1903, 10½ x 9in (26.5 x 23cm).
£630–700 JAA

An icon of selected saints, by Nicholai Zverev, with gilded silver and shaded enamel oklad, the robes of filigree silver, Russian, c1910, 12½ x 10½in (32 x 26.5cm).
£2,200–2,700 S(NY)

Colour Review

A brass gas table lamp, with period shade, now converted to electricity, c1890, 23½in (59.5cm) high.
£500–600 ⊞ CHA

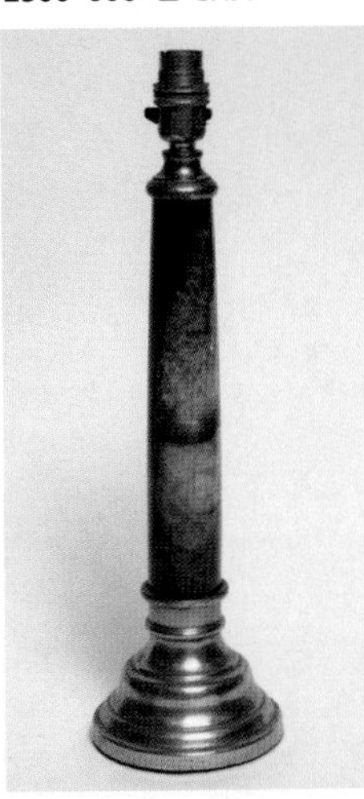

A brass and blue john electric lamp stand, c1910, 16in (40.5cm) high.
£720–800 ⊞ HUM

A gilt-metal seven-light chandelier, Continental, 19thC, 17in (43cm) high.
£3,000–3,750 ⚒ DN

► **A brass four-arm chandelier,** French, c1880, 18in (45.5cm) wide.
£720–800 ⊞ OLA

An electric table lamp, with vaseline glass shade, c1890, 17in (43cm) high.
£450–500 ⊞ CHA

A brass electric table lamp, with opaline glass shades, c1910, 21½in (54.5cm) high.
£700–800 ⊞ CHA

A pair of verdigris bronze gas wall lamps, c1870, 13in (33cm) wide.
£1,350–1,500 ⊞ EAL

A brass gasolier, now converted to electricity, c1900, 30in (76cm) high.
£600–650 ⊞ CHA

A gilded brass table lamp, with original shade, French, c1900, 17in (43cm) high.
£180–200 ⊞ EAL

A Colza gilt-bronze oil hanging light, now converted to electricity, c1835, 18¼in (46.5cm) diam.
£350–420 ⚒ S(S)

A pair of ormolu and bronze wall lights, late 19thC, 19in (48.5cm) high.
£7,000–8,750 ⚒ DN

A Colza brass oil lamp, with original opaline shade, now converted to electricity, c1900, 26in (66cm) high.
£800–900 ⊞ CHA

A brass gas lamp, with original shade, c1870, 34in (86.5cm) wide.
£400–450 ⊞ EAL

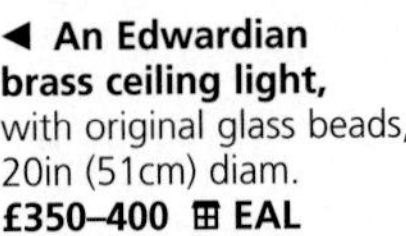

A gilt-metal and coloured opaline glass chandelier, probably Austrian, c1900, 69in (175.5cm) high.
£5,300–6,000 ⚒ S(O)

◄ **An Edwardian brass ceiling light,** with original glass beads, 20in (51cm) diam.
£350–400 ⊞ EAL

A carpet, with a French Savonnerie design, Irish, Donegal, c1930, 276 x 180in (700 x 457cm).
£17,000–20,000 ⚒ S

A Victorian needlework carpet, 138 x 114in (350.50 x 289.5cm).
£1,800–2,000 ⚒ S(O)

An Aubusson rug, French, 1850–75, 73 x 71in (185.5 x 180.5cm).
£6,500–8,250 ⚒ S(NY)

A needlework carpet, worked in gros and petit point, European, 18thC, 108 x 121¼in (274.5 x 308cm).
£9,500–12,000 ⚒ DN

An Axminster carpet, 1770–90, 170 x 167in (432 x 424cm).
£73,000–90,000 ⚒ P

A Panderma prayer rug, north-west Turkish, early 19thC, 55¼ x 45in (140.5 x 114.5cm).
£700–875 ⚒ DN

A Yürük prayer rug, repaired crease, east Anatolian, c1870, 68 x 39in (172.5 x 99cm).
£200–220 ⊞ DNo

A Kirshehir funeral rug, central Anatolian, c1900, 63 x 41in (160 x 104cm).
£320–350 ⊞ DNo

A Chelaberd rug, south-west Caucasian, late 19thC, 109 x 60in (277 x 152.5cm).
£2,400–3,000 ⚒ P

A Shirvan rug, east Caucasian, c1880, 79 x 49in (200.5 x 124.5cm).
£3,200–3,500 ⊞ DNo

A rug, south Caucasian, Karabagh, early 20thC, 68 x 51in (172.5 x 129.5cm).
£500–600 ⚒ AH

A Gendje runner, west Caucasian, c1880, 138 x 40in (350.5 x 101.5cm).
£2,700–3,000 ⊞ LIN

A Gendje rug, some wear, west Caucasian, c1850, 77 x 49in (195.5 x 124.5cm).
£765–850 ⊞ DNo

A Teheran carpet, north Persian, 1900–25, 111 x 75in (282 x 190.5cm).
£6,200–7,750 S(NY)

An Agra carpet, repiled and rewoven areas, north-west Indian, c1900, 172 x 143in (437 x 363cm).
£11,000–13,000 S(NY)

A Bidjar rug, minor damage, north-west Persian, c1890, 78 x 52in (198 x 132cm).
£675–850 JAA

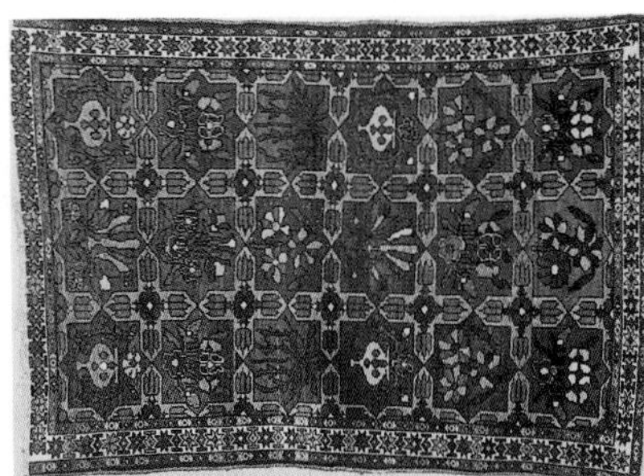

A Bakhtiyari rug, west Persian, c1920, 78 x 56in (198 x 142cm).
£420–460 DNo

A Maslaghan rug, central Persian, c1920, 76 x 51in (193 x 129.5cm).
£900–1,100 DNo

◄ **A Senneh rug,** west Persian, 19thC, 72¾ x 55¼in (185 x 140.5cm).
£1,800–2,250 B&L

◄ **A Malayer carpet,** west Persian, c1900, 95 x 81in (241.5 x 205.5cm).
£800–950 SLN

An Afshar rug, south-east Persian, c1900, 67 x 52in (170 x 132cm).
£1,100–1,250 DNo

A Yomut *chuval*, south-west Turkestani, c1880, 47 x 33in (119.5 x 84cm).
£900–1,000 LIN

◄ **A Ninghsia lion-dog carpet,** repiled and rewoven, west Chinese, c1800, 161in (409cm) square.
£8,000–10,000 S(NY)

A Khamseh rug, south-west Persian, c1870, 74 x 41in (188 x 104cm).
£5,250–5,750 P

An Amritsar carpet, north Indian, c1890, 136 x 101in (345.5 x 256.5cm).
£4,500–5,500 P

A patchwork and appliqué quilted double bedcover, embroidered with the maker's name, and dated 1848, 105 x 95in (266.5 x 241.5cm).
£800–1,000 DN

A northern England 'Strippy' reverse patchwork quilt, c1890, 81 x 75in (205.5 x 190.5cm).
£320–400 JJ

An appliquéd cotton flag quilt, the reverse printed with reserves of George Washington and the shield of the United States, 1875–1900, 92 x 69in (233.5 x 175.5cm).
£3,200–3,500 BB(S)

A quilt, incorporating Confederate and southern political themes, American, New Orleans, c1895, 86 x 82in (218.5 x 208.5cm).
£4,000–4,500 NOA

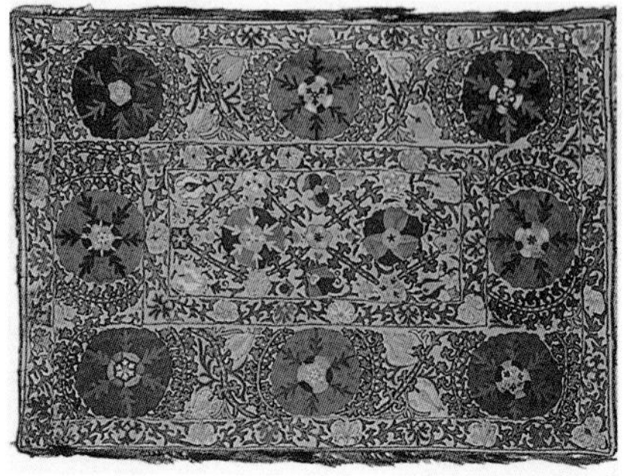

A Bokhara *susani*, Uzbekistani, late 19thC, 38 x 54in (96.5 x 137cm).
£2,000–2,200 P

► **An appliqué pillar silk-on-silk runner,** Italian, 17thC, 112 x 22in (284.5 x 56cm).
£2,800–3,400 MGa

A pair of quilts, American, early 20thC, 89 x 65in (226 x 165cm).
£450–550 S(O)

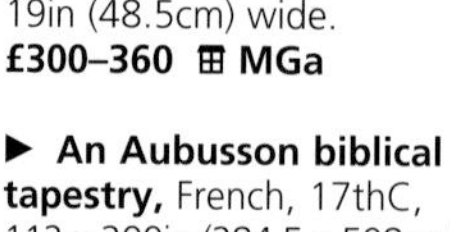

A brocaded silk panel, French, Lyon, 18thC, 19in (48.5cm) wide.
£300–360 MGa

► **An Aubusson biblical tapestry,** French, 17thC, 112 x 200in (284.5 x 508cm).
£6,500–8,200 S(NY)

An Aubusson tapestry, French, 17thC, 112 x 95in (284.5 x 241.5cm).
£3,500–4,200 Bon

An Aubusson tapestry panel, French, 19thC, 44½ x 41in (113 x 104cm).
£1,300–1,600 RIT

A tapestry, Flemish, Brussels, early 18thC, 118¼ x 149½in (300.5 x 380cm).
£13,000–16,000 DN

◄ **An embroidery picture,** The Judgement of Paris, some wear and repairs, 17thC, 14 x 18in (35.5 x 45.5cm).
£3,800–4,750 ⚒ TMA

► **A wool and silk petit point panel,** 18thC, 17in (43cm) wide.
£3,400–4,250 ⚒ Gam

A pair of silk pictures, in their original frames, late 18thC, 8½ x 7½in (21.5 x 19cm).
£900–1,100 ⊞ WWo

A woolwork picture, 19thC, 13 x 16½in (33 x 42cm), in a rosewood frame.
£650–820 ⚒ AH

A sampler, worked in coloured silks, Scottish, early 19thC, 20 x 14in (51 x 35.5cm).
£4,500–5,500 ⊞ WiA

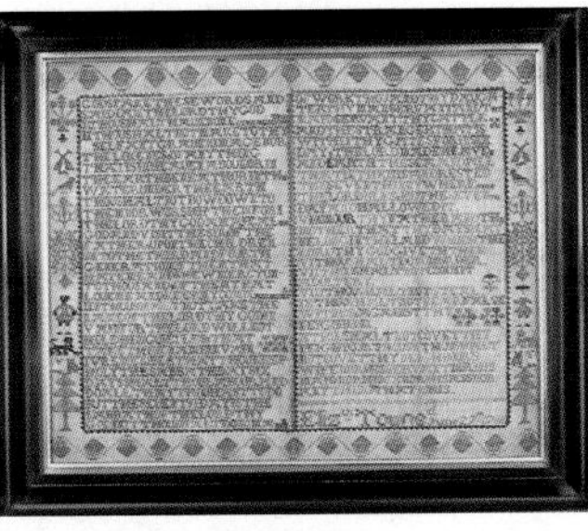

A silk and chenille embroidered mourning picture, American, c1805, 16 x 14in (40.5 x 35.5cm).
£3,500–4,500 ⚒ BB(S)

A sampler, dated 1720, 18 x 13in (45.5 x 33cm).
£5,000–5,500 ⊞ WiA

A needlework sampler, by Sarah Smith, American, probably Plymouth, Massachusetts, dated 1813, 16¼ x 17¼in (41.5 x 44cm).
£8,750–11,000 ⚒ S(NY)

◄ **A wool and linen needlework sampler,** by Eliza Mitchell, American, 1846, 24 x 23in (61 x 58.5cm).
£3,500–4,500 ⚒ BB(S)

► **A wool needlework sampler,** by Sarah Jane Evans, dated 1865, 12½ x 12in (32 x 30.5cm), in a partially gilt wooden frame.
£130–160 ⚒ PFK

A feltwork picture, c1820, 19 x 16in (48.5 x 40.5cm).
£350–400 ⊞ PSC

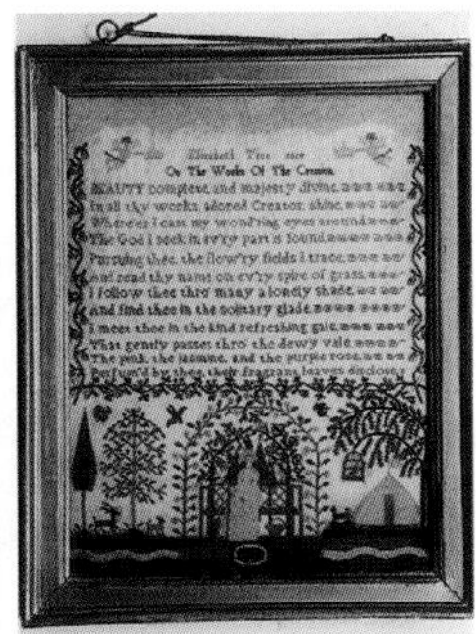

A sampler, by Elizabeth Tice, dated 1810, 16 x 13in (40.5 x 33cm).
£4,500–5,000 ⊞ HIS

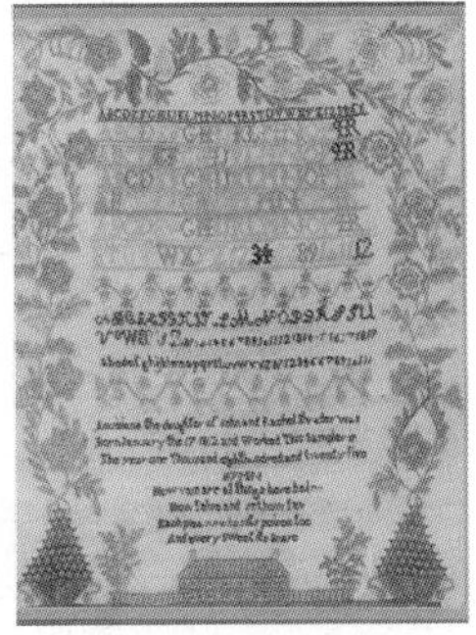

A needlework sampler, by Louisiana Shrader, American, Kentucky, 1825, 21 x 17½in (53.5 x 44.5cm).
£13,000–15,000 ⚒ SLN

A filigreework bracelet, the centre set with Brazilian topaz, 1820–30, 7in (18cm) long.
£4,000–4,500 ⊞ WIM

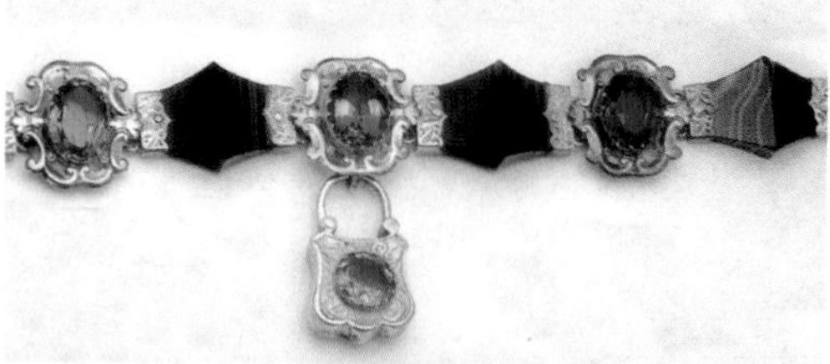

A banded agate and citrine bracelet, c1860.
£300–375 ⚒ B(Ba)

A gold-mounted pebble bracelet, Scottish, c1870, 8¾in (22cm) long.
£1,100–1,200 ⚒ P(Ed)

A ruby and diamond bracelet, late 19thC.
£750–950 ⚒ B(Ba)

A diamond, emerald and platinum bracelet, Austrian, c1910, ¾in (2cm) wide.
£14,000–15,500 ⊞ NBL

An amethyst bangle, c1890.
£400–500 ⚒ B(Ba)

A Georgian 18ct gold filigree love brooch, with glazed panel enclosing a lock of hair, 1in (2.5cm) wide.
£520–575 ⊞ TGL

A gold shell cameo, with serpent surround, 19thC, 23½in (59.5cm) wide.
£950–1,100 ⚒ S(S)

A flowerhead and stem brooch, set with rubies, sapphires and diamonds, mounted with an *en tremblant* pearl- and diamond-set butterfly, c1840, 4½in (11.5cm) long.
£7,000–7,700 ⊞ NBL

A ruby, diamond and enamel brooch, by Philibert-Honoré Audoard, French, c1850, 2in (5cm) square.
£9,000–9,850 ⊞ NBL

A mid-Victorian amethyst brooch/pendant, in a cannetille mount, 3½in (9cm) long.
£7,000–7,700 ⊞ NBL

A micro mosaic brooch, c1860.
£1,100–1,400 ⚒ B(Ba)

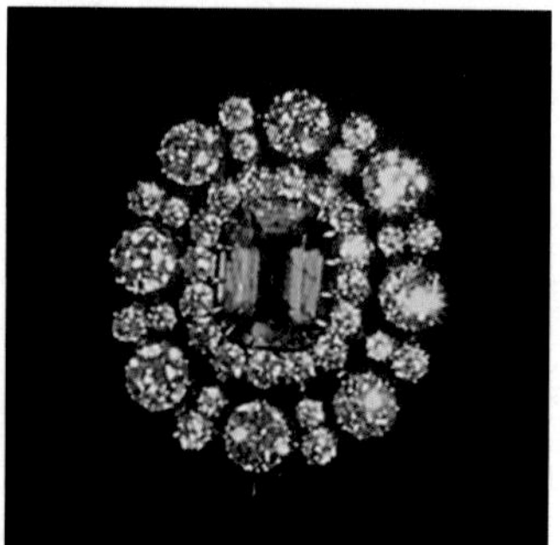

◄ A Victorian emerald and diamond brooch/pendant.
£16,000–20,000 ⚒ HYD

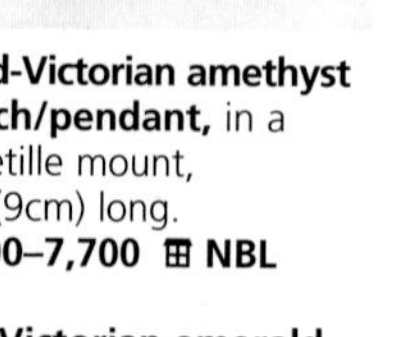

► A 15ct gold, pearl and turquoise locket brooch, c1860, 1½in (4cm) wide.
£700–785 ⊞ WIM

A cameo brooch, depicting Bacchus, 1870, 2¾in (7cm) wide.
£2,200–2,450 ⊞ WIM

A hardstone brooch, mounted with bloodstone and agate, Scottish, c1870, 2¼in (5.5cm) high.
£1,750–1,950 ⊞ TGL

A Victorian gold and white-enamelled brooch, the centre set with an amethyst, the reverse with a locket, 1½in (4cm) wide.
£150–200 ⚒ G(L)

A Victorian gold brooch, set with an amethyst within a border of split pearls, 1¼in (3cm) high.
£150–200 ⚒ G(L)

A 15ct gold amethyst brooch, c1880, 2in (5cm) high.
£800–900 ⊞ WIM

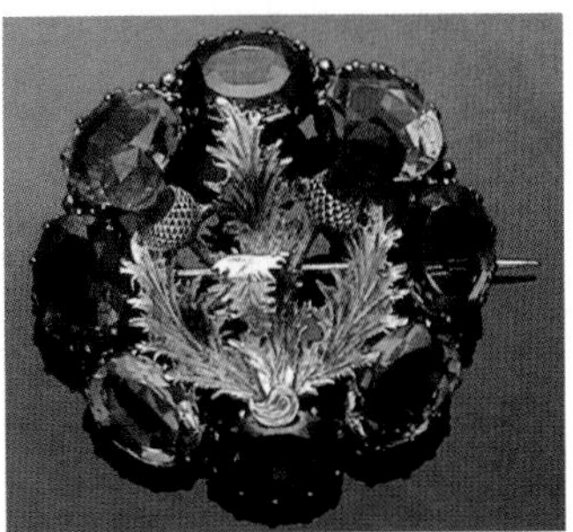

A citrine and amethyst brooch, the centre with engraved silver foliage, c1890, 1¾in (4.5cm) high.
£520–650 ⚒ P(Ed)

A diamond and peridot brooch/pendant, c1890, 2½in (6.5cm) high.
£11,000–12,500 ⊞ NBL

◀ **A late Victorian opal and diamond brooch,** by Hancock & Co, in original presentation box.
£2,400–3,000 ⚒ AG

A 15ct gold brooch, the centre set with a cluster of diamonds and with locket back, hallmarked Birmingham 1904.
£270–340 ⚒ WL

A demantoid garnet brooch/pendant, Russian, c1890.
£6,000–7,000 ⊞ NBL

A black opal and diamond brooch, c1925, 1½in (4cm) high.
£3,400–4,250 ⚒ SHSY

A white gold brooch, set with sapphires and diamonds, c1930.
£3,000–3,750 ⚒ LCM

A ruby and diamond brooch, c1940.
£2,000–2,500 ⚒ HAM

A pair of beryl, ruby and gold earrings, four stones missing, one paste replacement, c1830.
£650–820 P(S)

A pair of 18ct gold shell cameo earrings, c1860.
£470–570 LJ

A pair of micro-mosaic earrings and pendant, the pendant with glazed locket reverse, c1875.
£1,700–2,200 B

A late Victorian gold necklace, the pendants set with amethysts, citrines and aquamarines.
£700–875 G(L)

A 15ct gold brooch and earrings, set with garnets, c1860, in original box.
£2,000–2,350 WIM

A pair of sapphire and diamond cluster earrings, suspended from a diamond fleur-de-lys, c1870, 1in (2.5cm) long.
£4,500–5,000 NBL

A topaz necklace, c1825, 17in (43cm) long.
£2,800–3,500 B

A silver-gilt and enamel pendant necklace, gemset with scrolls and flowers, with a pair of matching pendant earrings, 19thC, pendant 4¾in (4.5cm) long.
£350–425 CGC

A pair of coral earrings, carved with shells and crustaceans, c1860, in a fitted box.
£1,250–1,375 TGL

A gold, turquoise, enamel and diamond demi-parure, c1870, earrings 2½in (6.5cm) long.
£1,000–1,200 S(S)

A citrine pendant, c1850.
£320–400 B(Ba)

A tourmaline, aquamarine and peridot necklace, c1895.
£1,400–1,750 B(Ba)

An opal and diamond necklace, by J. E. Caldwell & Co, the diamond bow swag later, signed, American, c1905, 16¾in (42.5cm) long.
£2,750–3,500 SK

An 18ct gold locket, mounted with a Wedgwood cameo surrounded by natural pearls, c1830, 1¾in (4.5cm) long, in original box.
£1,575–1,750 TGL

A locket pendant, set with gems and cultured pearls, the reverse with a hairwork panel, c1830.
£2,800–3,500 P(Ba)

A Victorian micro-mosaic locket pendant, in original case.
£680–850 RBB

A late Victorian gold and silver pendant, set with rose-cut diamonds, the centre with two amethysts, 2in (5cm) high.
£500–625 G(L)

A gold locket, mounted with rubies and diamonds, late 19thC.
£650–820 Bea(E)

An enamel and half pearl locket, the reverse with glass locket, c1890.
£500–625 P(Ba)

A pendant, by Saunders & Sheppard, set with pearls and aquamarines, c1910, 1¾in (4.5cm) long.
£900–1,000 WIM

An amethyst and pearl pendant, c1910.
£500–625 B

A George III diamond and blue enamel ring.
£850–1,100 HYD

A diamond and blue enamel ring, c1800.
£800–1,000 P(L)

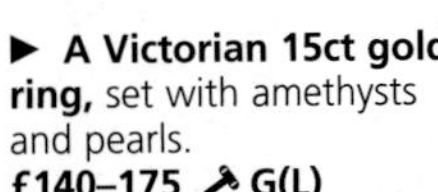

► A Victorian 15ct gold ring, set with amethysts and pearls.
£140–175 G(L)

A ruby and diamond ring, c1880.
£1,250–1,400 TGL

An 18ct gold and platinum ring, set with a natural pearl, rubies and diamonds, French, c1910.
£3,400–3,750 WIM

A ruby and natural pearl ring, c1920.
£3,200–3,500 NBL

A Birmingham leopard bonbonnière, some damage, late 18thC, 1½in (4cm) diam.
£1,800–2,200 TMA

A silver-gilt and cloisonné enamel bowl, by Ivan Khlebnikov, Moscow, Russian, c1888, 4in (10cm) diam.
£1,500–1,650 MIR

An enamel box and cover, modelled as a chaffinch, c1760, 1½in (4cm) wide.
£440–550 WW

A gilt-mounted Limoges enamel box, decorated with portrait medallions of saints, French, 19thC, 1½in (4cm) diam.
£400–480 G(L)

A silver-gilt enamel dish, maker's mark 'IS', Russian, Moscow, 1896–1907, 10in (25.5cm) diam.
£3,250–4,000 BUK

A Fabergé jewelled silver-gilt and enamel pill box, workmaster F. Afanassiev, Russian, St Petersburg, 1908–17, 1½in (4cm) square.
£5,000–5,500 S

A Limoges pre-Raphaelite-style enamel plaque, French, c1900, 3½ x 2½in (9 x 6.5cm).
£400–450 WAC

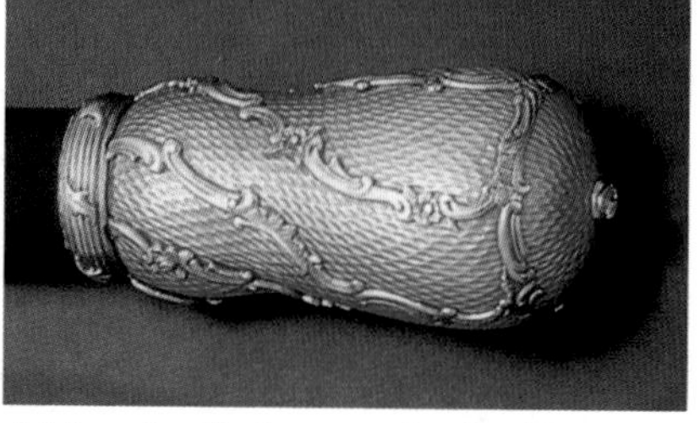

A Fabergé *guilloche* enamel and gold rococo-style handle, with a diamond terminal, later mounted as a paper knife with ebony blade, Russian, c1890, handle 2in (5cm) long.
£7,000–8,000 B

A Fabergé lapis lazuli egg pendant, mounted with a gold cipher set with rubies, 1896–1907, ¾in (2cm) high.
£4,000–4,500 SHa

► **A four-colour gold snuff box,** French, c1780, 3in (7.5cm) diam.
£4,500–5,000 BEX

► **A jewelled gold and enamel snuff box,** maker's mark 'AP', Swiss, Geneva, c1790, 2¼in (5.5cm) wide, in original tooled leather case.
£2,200–2,500 S(O)

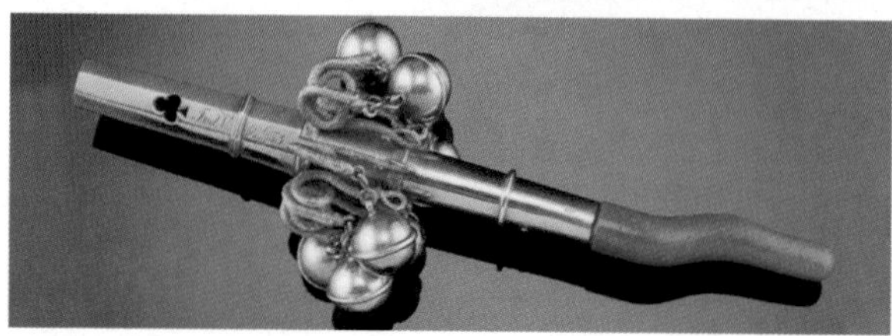

A gold and coral rattle, assay master Jan Berend Schöne Jnr, Dutch, Amsterdam, c1817, 6in (15cm) long.
£950–1,200 S(Am)

An 18ct gold assembled dressing table set, by Tiffany & Co, comprising 16 pieces, engraved with monograms, New York, 1920–30, powder jar 6¾in (17cm) diam.
£7,000–8,750 S(NY)

A pair of cloisonné vases, on wooden base, Japanese, Meiji period, 1868–1911, 12in (30.5cm) high.
£2,200–2,700 ⚒ G(L)

An overlay glass bottle, Chinese, 18thC, 4in (10cm) high.
£4,000–5,000 ⚒ S(NY)

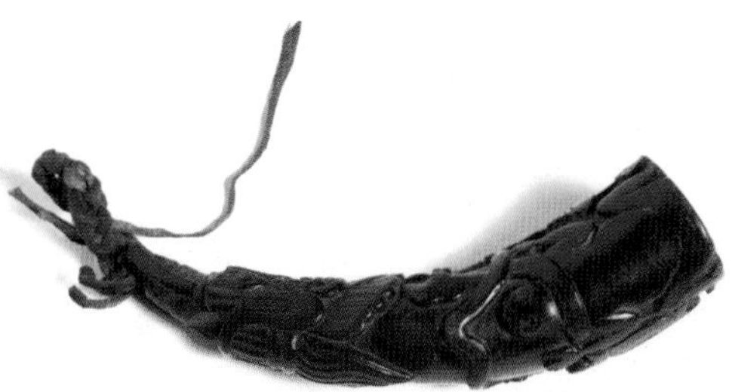

A horn seed sprinkler, repaired, Tibetan, early 19thC, 5in (12.5cm) long.
£225–250 ⊞ FU

◀ A lacquer box and cover, slight damage, Chinese, Ming Dynasty, 16thC, 3in (7.5cm) diam.
£1,850–2,250 ⚒ BUK

A Chinese export lacquer tea caddy, with three engraved pewter canisters, mid-19thC, 19¾in (50cm) wide.
£2,200–2,750 ⚒ S

A lacquer chest, with gilt-metal mounts, Japanese, Meiji period, 1868–1911, 25in (63.5cm) wide.
£500–625 ⚒ G(L)

A carved and painted portable wooden altar, some wear and losses to paint, Tibetan, 18thC, 5¼in (13.5cm) diam.
£4,500–5,500 ⚒ S(P)

A *hongmu* wood brushpot and tray, inlaid in soapstone, jade and mother-of-pearl, Chinese, 18th–19thC, 12¾in (32.5cm) diam.
£1,300–1,500 ⚒ S(Am)

A gilded belt hook, China, BC 475–AD 8, 6in (15cm) long.
£585–650 ⊞ GLD

A gilt-lacquer stationery box, Japanese, early 20thC, 12¼in (31cm) wide.
£3,500–4,250 ⚒ BB(S)

A bronze vase, Japanese, 19thC, 9in (23cm) high.
£1,100–1,300 ⚒ DN

◀ A painted wood hat box, Chinese, c1920, 14in (35.5cm) diam.
£135–150 ⊞ OE

A bronze vase, cast and chased with a fierce Shi Shi, with gilt eyes, signed Kozan Zo, dents, Japanese, Meiji period, 1868–1911, 8¾in (22cm) high.
£200–240 ⚒ WW

A lacquered wood elephant, Chinese, Qianlong period, 1736–95, 13½in (34.5cm) high.
£6,000–7,500 S(NY)

A giltwood Buddha, on a later carved teak base, Thai, 18thC, 37¾in (96cm) high.
£1,400–1,700 LJ

A carved ivory figure of Weituo, cracks, repair, 18th–19thC, 8½in (21.5cm) high.
£1,600–2,000 BB(S)

A bronze and copper Buddha, Burmese, Mandalay, 19thC, 25½in (65cm) high.
£7,500–8,500 LOP

A stone Nat, Burmese, 19thC, 11¾in (30cm) high.
£1,250–1,400 LOP

A carved wood figure of Buddha, traces of paint, Sino-Tibetan, 19thC, 42in (106.5cm) high.
£4,500–5,750 G(B)

► A pair of red lacquered wood kneeling disciples, Burmese, Mandalay, 19thC, 9¾in (25cm) high.
£750–850 LOP

An ivory *okimono* of a man with a broom, signed 'Gyokuichi', Japanese, Meiji period, 1868–1911, 4in (10cm) high.
£450–500 AMC

A wood and ivory group of a Karako boy and *oni*, signed 'Toryo' in a red seal, early 20thC, 7in (18cm) high.
£4,500–5,000 LBO

A wood and ivory figure of a Samurai, Japanese, Meiji period, 1868–1911, 14in (35.5cm) high.
£2,200–2,500 S

A carved ivory and wood figure of a Bijin, old damage, minor losses, signed, Japanese, Meiji period, 1868–1911, 8in (20.5cm) high.
£1,100–1,400 P(Ba)

A bronze model of a tiger, signed 'Seiya', Japanese, Meiji period, 1868–1911, 22in (56cm) wide, on a hardwood stand.
£2,400–3,000 AH

► A coral group, Chinese, late Qing Dynasty, early 20thC, 14½in (37cm) high.
£3,200–4,000 B

A *Tosei-Gusoku*, with earlier red-lacquered iron mempo, possibly before 1600, and gilt-bronze cuirass, Japanese, early 19thC.
£1,700–2,200 Herm

A Bizen shinshinto yokoyama *katana* and mounts, Japanese, 19thC, 27¼in (69cm) long.
£4,000–5,000 S(NY)

A two-case wood *inro*, signed Nobuaki-to, Japanese, 19thC, 4in (10cm) high.
£4,250–5,250 S(NY)

A five-case gilt-lacquer *inro*, Shibayama School, Japanese, Meiji period, 1868–1911, 3¾in (9.5cm) high.
£5,500–7,000 BB(S)

A stained ivory *netsuke* of a musician playing his drum, Japanese, Meiji period, 1868–1911, 1½in (4cm) high.
£225–250 AMC

◄ An agate snuff bottle, Chinese, 1780–1850, 2¾in (7cm) high.
£1,450–1,600 RHa

A carnelian snuff bottle, Chinese, 1780–1850, 2½in (6.5cm) high.
£1,450–1,600 RHa

A glass snuff bottle, Chinese, 1780–1850, 3in (7.5cm) high.
£1,700–2,000 RHa

A five-colour overlay glass snuff bottle, Chinese, 1780–1860, 2½in (6.5cm) high.
£7,000–8,750 S(NY)

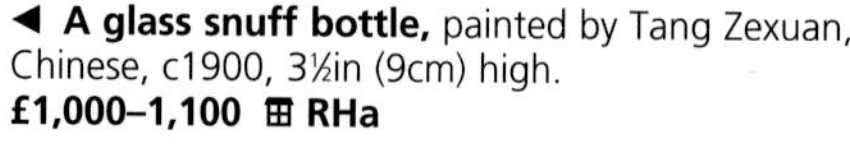

◄ A glass snuff bottle, painted by Tang Zexuan, Chinese, c1900, 3½in (9cm) high.
£1,000–1,100 RHa

A silk *tchuba*, Tibetan, silk c1700, robe 19thC.
£3,500–4,500 B

A Ming *kesi* woven silk cover, faults, 16th–17thC, 14½in (37cm) square.
£380–475 B

An embroidered wool opera curtain, Chinese, late 19thC, 137¾ x 69¾in (350 x 177cm).
£1,800–2,200 S(O)

An ebony cabinet bookcase, of exhibition quality, Anglo-Indian, Ceylon, 1850–90, 49½in (125.5cm) wide.
£23,000–26,000 ⊞ RMi

A *huanghuali* wood six-poster canopy bed, restored, 17th–18thC, 80in (203cm) wide.
£15,000–18,000 ⚒ BB(S)

► A black lacquered cabinet-on-stand, decorated with gilt chinoiserie, on an associated carved giltwood stand, Chinese, late 17thC, 46½in (118cm) wide.
£12,000–15,000 ⚒ P

A black and gilt lacquered cabinet-on-stand, Japanese, cabinet late 17thC, stand c1770, 38in (96.5cm) wide.
£12,000–15,000 ⚒ S

A pair of black and red lacquered side cabinets, Chinese, 18thC, 23in (58.5cm) wide.
£11,000–13,500 ⚒ S

A gilt-bronze-mounted papier-mâché cabinet, on a later base, Chinese, 18th–19thC, 60in (152.5cm) wide.
£3,300–4,000 ⚒ S(O)

A padouk, mother-of-pearl, ivory and brass marquetry side cabinet, Indo-Portuguese, 17thC, 44½in (113cm) wide.
£9,500–12,000 ⚒ B

A pair of Chinese black lacquered apothecary cabinets, 1790s, 74in (188cm) wide.
£11,000–12,500 ⊞ GRG

A lacquered pine cabinet, Chinese, 1875–1900, 36½in (92.5cm) wide.
£600–700 ⚒ NOA

A provincial pine kitchen cabinet, with black lacquered panels, Chinese, early 20thC, 42in (106.7cm) wide.
£1,000–1,150 ⊞ OE

A penwork table cabinet, some losses, Anglo-Indian, early 19thC, 12½in (32cm) wide.
£1,100–1,300 ⚒ P(Ba)

◄ A painted gesso cabinet, decorated with dragon medallions, Tibetan, 18thC, 38¼in (97cm) wide.
£2,700–3,000 ⊞ LOP

A brass-mounted lacquered cabinet, on an ebonized stand, Japanese, c1900, 30¼in (77cm) wide.
£2,000–2,500 ⚒ NOA

A lacquered display cabinet, inlaid with bone and mother-of-pearl, Japanese, Meiji period, c1900, 47¾in (121.5cm) wide.
£3,200–4,000 ⚒ TEN

A brass-mounted elm folding chair, Chinese, early 19thC.
£3,000–3,450 ⊞ GRG

A carved hardwood folding armchair, with metal fittings, replaced leather seat, Chinese, late 19thC.
£2,000–2,500 ⚒ RIT

A pair of elm provincial armchairs, with carved backs, Chinese, late 19thC.
£1,100–1,200 ⊞ OE

A pair of lacquered storage cabinets, with original paintwork and lacquer, Chinese, early 18thC, 44in (112cm) wide.
£11,000–12,500 ⊞ GRG

A carved and lacquered chest of drawers, Chinese, 18thC, 34in (86.5cm) wide.
£1,650–1,850 ⊞ NAW

An Indian export lacquered chest and stand, c1820, 35in (89cm) wide.
£3,400–3,800 ⊞ DJH

An *icri* wood chest of drawers, with locking safe and original wrought-iron metalwork, Japanese, c1860, 21in (53.5cm) wide.
£1,500–1,700 ⊞ GRG

A painted chest, with iron mounts, 18thC, 36¼in (92cm) wide.
£2,000–2,250 ⊞ LOP

An elm desk, with a secret compartment, Chinese, 19thC, 44in (112cm) wide.
£1,100–1,250 ⊞ OE

A mirror painting, in an associated carved giltwood and gesso frame altered to accommodate the plate, Chinese, 1750–75, 27½in (70cm) wide.
£17,000–20,000 ⚒ S

A *huanghuali* wood table, Chinese, 17thC, 36¾in (93.5cm) wide.
£8,750–11,000 ⚒ S(NY)

A carved ebony and satinwood console table, Ceylonese, 19thC, 55½in (141cm) wide.
£10,000–12,500 ⚒ Bon

◄ **A painted table,** Tibetan, 19thC, 32¼in (82cm) wide.
£1,800–2,000 ⊞ LOP

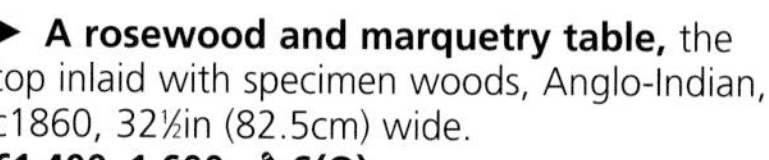

► **A rosewood and marquetry table,** the top inlaid with specimen woods, Anglo-Indian, c1860, 32½in (82.5cm) wide.
£1,400–1,600 ⚒ S(O)

◀ **A bone- and brass-inlaid Miquelet-lock flintlock rifle,** mid-18thC, Ottoman, 47¼in (120cm) long.
£2,300–3,000 ⚒ Herm

A Safavid pottery dish, hairline cracks, seal marks, 17thC, 17in (43cm) diam.
£5,200–6,500 ⚒ WW

A Nishapur buff ware pottery bowl, Persian, 9th–10thC, 7¼in (18.5cm) diam.
£2,000–2,500 ⚒ Bon

A Safavid *cuerda seca* pottery tile, Persian, 16thC, 9½ x 7½in (24 x 19cm), framed.
£3,000–3,750 ⚒ Bon

A parcel-gilt and green-painted Venetian-style cabinet-on-stand, Turkish, 1750–75, 39¾in (101cm) wide.
£30,000–37,000 ⚒ S

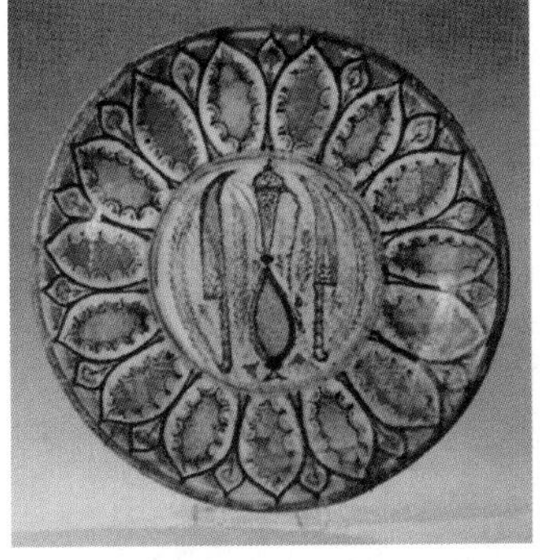

A pottery dish, minor damage, repairs, probably Persian/Samarkand, 18th–19thC, 23in (58.5cm) diam.
£1,250–1,500 ⚒ BUK

◀ **An Iznik pottery vase,** 19thC, 11in (28cm) high.
£280–350 ⚒ CGC

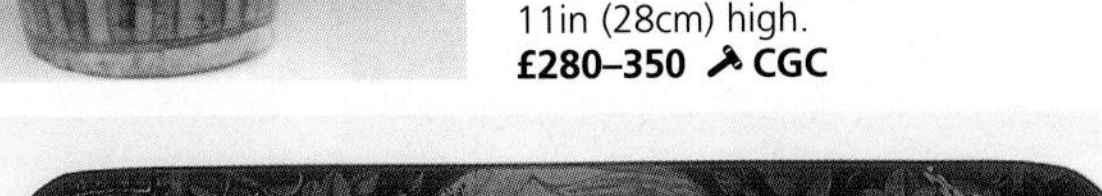

A lacquered pen box, signed by Abu'l-Hassan Afshar, Persian, Qajar, dated 'A.H.1275' (AD1858), 8½in (21.5cm) long.
£3,200–4,000 ⚒ S

A parquetry wood sofa and four chairs, inlaid with mother-of-pearl, Syrian, Damascus, late 19thC, sofa 67¼in (171cm) wide.
£2,600–3,250 ⚒ Bon

A gold-damascened steel begging bowl (*kashkul*), Persian, 19thC, 10in (25.5cm) wide.
£1,700–2,000 ⚒ BB(S)

A Khorasan copper and bronze bucket, with incised and inlaid decoration, Persian, 12thC, 8in (20.5cm) diam.
£6,000–7,500 ⚒ Bon

A silk-embroidered wool panel, Turkish, 19thC, 54¼ x 52in (138 x 132cm).
£2,800–3,500 ⚒ Bon

A copper horse weather vane, by J. W. Fiske, late 19thC, 33in (84cm) long.
£2,400–2,800 ⊞ DRG

◄ **A composition stone jardinière,** by Maniffatura di Signa, Italian, c1900, 48¾in (124cm) wide.
£8,000–8,800 ⊞ L(sm)

A Puritas lavatory pan, c1900, 16in (40.5cm) high.
£1,800–2,000 ⊞ C&R

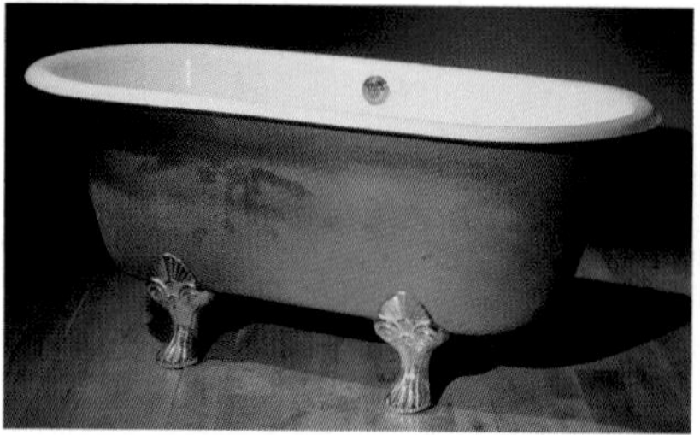

A double-ended bath, French, c1890, 28¾in (73cm) wide.
£2,400–2,700 ⊞ L(r)

A painted and parcel-gilt overdoor, Austrian, c1800, 53¼in (135.5cm) wide.
£4,500–5,000 ⚒ S(Am)

A George III white and Siena marble fire surround, 73in (185.5cm) wide.
£70,000–77,000 ⊞ L(sm)

A set of polished brass bath taps, with integral soap dish, French, c1900, 11in (28cm) wide.
£1,350–1,500 ⊞ C&R

A set of carved oak swing doors, French, c1890, 90in (228.5cm) wide.
£1,350–1,500 ⊞ OLA

A cast-iron fire grate, in the style of George Bullock, early 19thC, 34½in (87cm) wide.
£5,250–6,000 ⚒ Bon

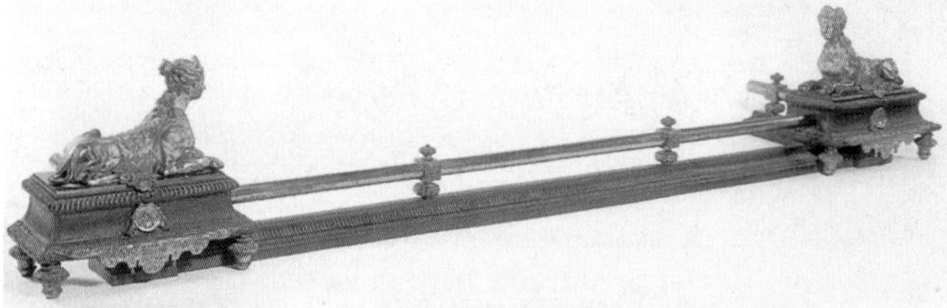

A cast-iron and gilt-metal fender, 19thC, 79½in (202cm) wide.
£3,400–4,250 ⚒ DN

A pair of Louis XV-style bronze lion andirons, on a gilt rococo scroll base, mid-19thC, 18in (45.5cm) high.
£2,400–3,000 ⚒ S(S)

◄ **A pair of lacquer bellows,** with chinoiserie decoration, c1810, 14in (35.5cm) long.
£150–165 ⊞ F&F

A Victorian painted and gilt tin purdonium, the hinged cover with a picture of *The Monarch of the Glen*, Birmingham, 12in (30.5cm) high.
£260–325 ⚒ WW

A carved stone head of a young man, c1720, 25in (63.5cm) high.
£3,700–4,000 ⊞ W&C

A pair of sandstone lions, North Country, 18th–19thC, 20in (51cm) high.
£4,500–5,750 ⚒ S(S)

A white marble figure of Eve, some damage, dated 1881, 72in (183cm) high.
£5,200–6,500 ⚒ LFA

A pair of cast-iron lions, probably American, 1850–90, 40in (101.5cm) high.
£4,500–5,750 ⚒ S(S)

► **A pair of black-painted cast-iron statues,** modelled as retrievers, American, possibly New York, 1850–75, 29in (73.5cm) high.
£11,000–13,000 ⚒ S(NY)

► **A composition stone eagle owl,** possibly by Austin and Seeley, 1850–90, 33in (84cm) high.
£1,400–1,700 ⚒ S(S)

A terracotta group of lovers, base stamped 'W Wilkes, Leeds', late 19thC, 49in (124.5cm) high.
£2,000–2,200 ⚒ S(S)

A pair of spelter busts of Bacchus and Hebe, by Miroy Frères, Paris, stamped, late 19thC, 22½in (57cm) high.
£9,000–10,000 ⊞ W&C

A zinc fountain, modelled as a heron clutching a serpent in its beak, the bronze head plumbed for water, American, late 19thC, 51in (129.5cm) high.
£7,000–8,500 ⚒ S(S)

A pair of Travertine marble lions, Italian, late 19thC, 38in (96.5cm) high.
£9,500–12,000 ⚒ S

A statuary marble head of a woman, after Rodin, French, c1900, 14in (35.5cm) high.
£3,700–4,000 ⊞ W&C

A cast stone model of a bear, restored, French, 1875–1925, 26in (66cm) high.
£1,700–2,000 ⚒ BB(S)

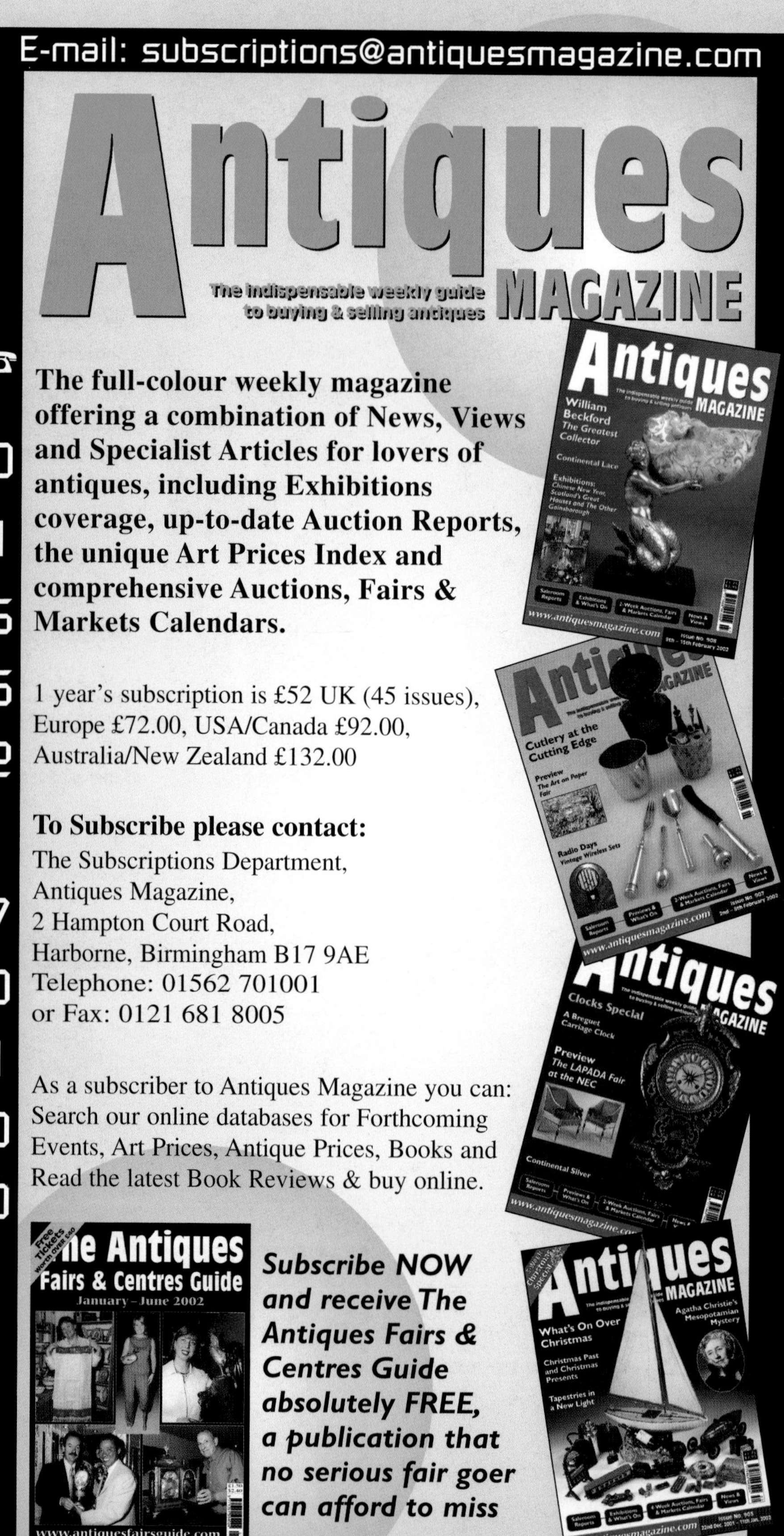
E-mail: subscriptions@antiquesmagazine.com
Antiques MAGAZINE
The indispensable weekly guide to buying & selling antiques
01562 701001
The full-colour weekly magazine offering a combination of News, Views and Specialist Articles for lovers of antiques, including Exhibitions coverage, up-to-date Auction Reports, the unique Art Prices Index and comprehensive Auctions, Fairs & Markets Calendars.
1 year's subscription is £52 UK (45 issues), Europe £72.00, USA/Canada £92.00, Australia/New Zealand £132.00
To Subscribe please contact:
The Subscriptions Department,
Antiques Magazine,
2 Hampton Court Road,
Harborne, Birmingham B17 9AE
Telephone: 01562 701001
or Fax: 0121 681 8005
As a subscriber to Antiques Magazine you can: Search our online databases for Forthcoming Events, Art Prices, Antique Prices, Books and Read the latest Book Reviews & buy online.
The Antiques Fairs & Centres Guide
January – June 2002
www.antiquesfairsguide.com
Subscribe NOW and receive The Antiques Fairs & Centres Guide absolutely FREE, a publication that no serious fair goer can afford to miss
William Beckford The Greatest Collector
Continental Lace
Cutlery at the Cutting Edge
Radio Days
Clocks Special
A Breguet Carriage Clock
Preview The LAPADA Fair at the NEC
Continental Silver
What's On Over Christmas
Agatha Christie's Mesopotamian Mystery
Tapestries in a New Light
www.antiquesmagazine.com
Website: http://www.antiquesmagazine.com

A carved polychrome group of the Pietà, damaged, repaired, north Italian, early 16thC, 32¼in (82cm) high.
£2,500–3,250 Bon(C)

A gilt-bronze angel, on a marble base, Italian, Venice, late 16thC, 2½in (6.5cm) high.
£850–1,000 S

A polychrome and partially gilded wooden carving of a cherub kneeling on a cloud, 17thC, 22in (56cm) high.
£3,400–3,800 RAN

A painted terracotta figure of a girl, defects, Italian, Venice, c1800, 26¾in (68cm) high.
£6,750–8,500 S(Mi)

A plaster figure of an Egyptian, attributed to Humphrey Hopper, c1820, 55in (139.5cm) high.
£2,700–3,000 NAW

A pair of walnut and ivory figures of pedlars, some losses, German, 19thC, 10in (25.5cm) high.
£1,000–1,250 Bon

A group of a stag and hounds, *'Chasse au Cerf'*, by Pierre Jules Mêne, signed, French, c1850, 17¾in (45cm) wide.
£7,000–8,000 BeF

A pair of carved and painted figures, German, Bavaria, mid-19thC, 10in (25.5cm) high.
£1,750–2,000 ChC

A bronze figure of a bull, by Isidore Bonheur, Peyrol foundry stamp, c1870, 22in (56cm) wide.
£10,000–11,500 RGa

A gilt-bronze woodcock, by Alfred Dubucand, French, c1880,12½in (32cm) high.
£1,900–2,100 BeF

◄ **A bronze group,** by Edouard Drouot, entitled *Lutte pour la Vie*, French. c1895, 19¾in (50cm) high.
£4,200–4,500 G&H

► **An alabaster figure of a dancing girl,** c1900, 24in (61cm) high.
£575–720 P

A cold-painted bronze model of a native American, by Carl Kauba, Vienna, c1900, 11½in (29cm) high.
£3,700–4,200 P

A pair of carved wood *epergne* vases, modelled as deer standing before trees, German, Black Forest, c1870, 15in (38cm) high.
£340–375 ⊞ PICA

► **A Victorian wooden nutcracker,** modelled as a squatting figure wearing a cloak and tricorn hat, 5¼in (13.5cm) high.
£180–225 ⚒ G(L)

A coquilla nut pomander, with screw-on lid, c1850, 2in (5cm) diam.
£400–450 ⊞ LBr

A turned *lignum vitae* pounce pot, c1760, 4in (10cm) high.
£240–270 ⊞ F&F

A wooden snuff box, in the shape of bellows, 19thC, 5in (12.5cm) long.
£585–650 ⊞ RGe

A carved coquilla nut snuff box, French, c1790, 4in (10cm) high.
£850–950 ⊞ AEF

A wooden snuff box, in the shape of a shoe, with brass inlay, Continental, c1850, 5¼in (13.5cm) long.
£315–350 ⊞ HUM

A fruitwood watch holder, c1780, 16in (40.5cm) high.
£1,800–2,000 ⊞ SEA

A Tunbridge ware rosewood bookrest, on a telescopic stand with loaded foot, c1860, 11¼in (28.5cm) high.
£400–480 ⚒ G(L)

A Tunbridge ware blotter, by Thomas Barlow, c1870, 9½in (24cm) wide.
£500–550 ⊞ VB

► **A Tunbridge ware rosewood wine table,** with a view of Hever Castle, early 19thC, 20in (51cm) wide.
£1,200–1,500 ⚒ BR

A Tunbridge ware stationery box, inner divisions removed, 19thC, 8¼in (21cm) wide.
£800–1,000 ⚒ TMA

A brass-mounted casket, enclosing a scarlet damask-lined interior, French, late 19thC, 20½in (52cm) wide.
£550–650 HAM

An iron-handled brass warming pan, engraved with the Vintners' Arms and three barrels motif, dated 1661, 42in (106.5cm) long.
£750–850 F&F

A gilt and patinated-bronze jardinière, inscribed La Fée aux Paons, late 19thC, 17in (43cm) wide.
£5,700–7,000 S(NY)

A red boullework inkstand, French, 19thC, 8in (20.5cm) wide.
£420–500 TMA

A brass coffee pot, with a wooden handle, traces of silvering, minor dents, c1755, 9½in (24cm) high.
£4,700–5,200 S(S)

A pair of gilt-bronze candelabra, 19thC, 27in (68.5cm) high.
£5,800–6,500 RAN

A pair of Louis XVI white and black marble, ormolu and patinated-bronze candelabra, 25in (63.5cm) high.
£13,000–15,000 RGa

◀ **A papier mâché tray,** c1830, 16in (40.5cm) wide.
£350–400 PICA

A gilt-brass inkstand cast as a galleon, on a marble base, c1820, 7in (18cm) high.
£1,500–1,650 NAW

A pair of gilt-bronze and agate candlesticks, probably German, early 19thC, 7in (18cm) high.
£3,800–4,200 S

A pair of gilt-bronze tazze, in the form of a kneeling mermaid holding aloft a shell, French, 19thC, 11½in (29cm) high.
£2,300–2,800 DN

A blue john chalice, 19thC, 6½in (16.5cm) high.
£2,000–2,400 AH

Portrait Miniatures

A portrait miniature of Sir Kenelm Digby, wearing a black doublet with a lace-edged white lawn collar, by Bernard Lens III after Peter Oliver, inscribed on reverse with artist's and subject's details, c1730, 3in (7.5cm) high, in a gilt-metal frame.
£350–450 Bon
Bernard Lens is known to have copied works by many of the early miniaturists.

► **A portrait miniature of a lady,** possibly Hélène Fourment, wearing a black cap adorned with a pink ribbon and a blue dress, by Heinrich von Hurter, signed and dated 1777, 3¼in (8.5cm) diam.
£2,800–3,500 S

A portrait miniature of a young woman, wearing a blue dress and red shawl, English School, on ivory, c1760, 3in (7.5cm) high, in a turned ivory frame.
£380–440 LFA

A portrait miniature of a gentleman, wearing a blue coat, watercolour on ivory, 1770, 2in (5cm) high, in original shagreen case.
£280–320 ⊞ PSC

► **A portrait miniature of a gentleman,** wearing a blue coat, white waistcoat and lace cravat, by John Bogle, the reverse with a lock of hair backed with ivory, signed with initials, dated 1794, 2in (5cm) high, in a gold frame.
£2,000–2,400 Bon

A portrait miniature of the Reverend Sir William Henry Clerke, wearing a black coat and white cravat, by Philip Jean, in original gold frame with blue glass back, c1792, 2¼in (5.5cm) high.
£1,900–2,100 ⊞ EFA

A portrait miniature of a gentleman, English School, watercolour on ivory, the reverse with a lock of hair, in a gilt locket frame, late 18thC, 2½in (6.5cm) high.
£220–275 G(L)

Cross Reference
See Colour Review
(page 728)

◄ **A portrait miniature of a gentleman,** by William Court, London, the reverse with plaited hair and inscription, c1795, in a rolled gold frame, 2¾in (7cm) high.
£470–550 S(O)
William Court exhibited at the Royal Academy between 1785 and 1823.

A portrait miniature of a gentleman, wearing a blue coat, white waistcoat, stock and lace cravat, by Charles Shirreff, the reverse glazed to reveal seed-pearl monogram 'FN' and a lock of hair tied with split seed pearls on blue glass bordered by seed pearls, c1795, 2in (5cm) high, in a gold frame.
£1,300–1,600 Bon

A portrait miniature of a gentleman, wearing a blue coat, yellow waistcoat, white stock and cravat, attributed to John Thomas Barber Beaumont, the reverse glazed to reveal gold monogram on plaited hair, in a gold frame, c1800, 2½in (6.5cm) high.
£425–500 Bon

A portrait miniature of a gentleman, by Archer James Oliver, signed, the reverse inscribed with the artist's London address, in a gold frame with a blue and opalescent white glass reverse, dated 1802, 3in (7.5cm) high.
£1,000–1,100 S(O)

A portrait miniature of a young boy, wearing a blue coat with red collar, white waistcoat, shirt and stock, English School, c1795, 1¾in (4.5cm) high, in a Continental ormolu frame with a gilt-metal stand.
£550–650 P

A portrait miniature of a child, wearing a white dress with a blue sash, holding a red gun, by Matthias Finucane, c1800, 2¼in (65.5cm) high, in a gilt-mounted papier mâché frame.
£850–1,100 Bon

A portrait miniature of a young naval officer, wearing a navy and gold coat, English School, on ivory, the reverse with plaited hair panel, in a yellow metal frame with blue enamelled back, c1800, 2½in (6.5cm) high, in original red morocco case.
£750–900 LFA

A portrait miniature of a gentleman, wearing a blue coat, white waistcoat and frilled cravat, by Horace Hone, in a gold frame with blue glass reverse, signed with monogram, dated 1796, 3in (7.5cm) high.
£1,800–2,200 Bon

A portrait miniature of a gentleman, wearing a yellow waistcoat, attributed to Roger Jean, the reverse with a lock of hair, in a locket frame, c1800, 3in (7.5cm) high.
£1,250–1,400 ⊞ BHa

A portrait miniature of a gentleman, wearing a blue coat and white stock, English School, indistinctly signed with initials 'H?', the reverse with hair plait, c1800, 3in (7.5cm), in a gold frame.
£280–350 Bea(E)

A portrait miniature of a gentleman, English School, watercolour on ivory, late 18thC, 2¾in (7cm) high.
£240–280 G(L)

A portrait miniature of a gentleman, wearing a blue coat, English School, the reverse with a lock of hair and seed pearls with monogram, on opaline glass, in original gold locket frame, c1800, 3in (7.5cm) high.
£1,600–1,800 ⊞ BHa

A portrait miniature of a lady, wearing a white dress and cap, French School, in a corded gilt-metal frame, c1800, 3½in (9cm) high.
£1,750–2,000 S(O)

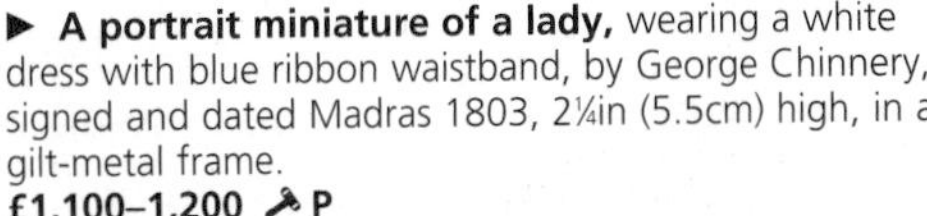

► **A portrait miniature of a lady,** wearing a white dress with blue ribbon waistband, by George Chinnery, signed and dated Madras 1803, 2¼in (5.5cm) high, in a gilt-metal frame.
£1,100–1,200 P
Chinnery sailed from England in 1802 to Madras, where he settled until he moved to Calcutta in June 1807.

A portrait miniature of an infantry officer, wearing a dark blue coat with red collar and lapels, German School, the glazed reverse containing a lock of hair, c1805, 2¾in (7cm) high, in a silver-gilt frame.
£300–375 P

A portrait miniature of Mary, Marchioness of Downshire, wearing a black dress with white lace collar and white lace bonnet, by Mrs Anne Mee, c1810, 4¾in (12cm) high, in a gilded wood frame.
£500–600 Bon

A portrait miniature of a gentleman, wearing a black coat and a white stock, English School, on ivory, the reverse with plaited hair, in a yellow metal frame, c1820, 2¾in (7cm) high.
£200–250 LFA

► **A portrait miniature of Count Frederic Antoine Marie de Goltstein,** wearing Hussars uniform, in a brass-mounted, formerly gilt, rosewood frame, dated 1829, 9¼in (23.5cm) high.
£350–400 Herm

A portrait miniature of a young man, wearing a blue jacket with lace jabot, by Alexander Gallaway, the reverse inscribed 'Edin-r', signed and dated 1807, 2¾in (7cm) high
£500–600 Bea(E)

A portrait miniature of a young man, wearing a dark jacket and white stock, French School, c1810, 2¾in (7cm) high, in a moulded brass frame.
£350–450 Bea(E)

A portrait miniature of a lady, wearing a white dress and a blue shawl, by Ferdinand Machera, signed and dated 1809, in a gilt-metal frame, 4in (10cm) high.
£400–500 P

A portrait miniature of Mary Spencer Wynter, wearing a white dress with pale blue waistband, by Thomas Richmond, signed and dated 1814, 3¼in (8.5cm) high, in a fitted leather case.
£600–700 P

◄ **A portrait miniature of Louise Barretto,** by Adam Buck, watercolour on card, signed and dated 1827, 5in (12.5cm) high.
£1,000–1,100 EFA

A pair of portrait miniatures of Mr and Mrs Lucas, she wearing a white mob cap and black dress, he wearing a dark coat, waistcoat, white shirt and cravat, by J. W. Childe, in leather frames, signed and dated 1831 on reverse, 4¼in (11cm) high.
£750–900 S(S)

A portrait miniature of a young lady, wearing a white lace gown with scarlet ribbons in her hair and dress, English School, watercolour on paper, c1835, 5¼in (13.5cm) high, in a gilt engine-turned mount and mahogany frame.
£110–140 P(EA)

A portrait miniature of a gentleman, wearing a black coat, waistcoat and a white shirt, attributed to George W. Stevens, the reverse glazed to reveal locks of hair, in a gold frame, American, c1845, 2½in (6.4cm) high.
£380–450 Bon
Stevens was active in Boston, Massachusetts, between 1845 and 1850 and is listed in the city directory as a miniaturist between 1840 and 1843. He exhibited at the Boston Mechanic's Association in 1841, 1844 and 1850.

A portrait miniature of a young gentleman, on ivory, inscribed on reverse, dated 1853, 2¼in (5.5cm) high.
£150–200 F&C

A portrait miniature of a young lady, wearing a white dress and floral-trimmed hair decoration, French School, in a gilt locket frame with vacant reverse, c1840, 2½in (6.5cm) high.
£1,750–2,000 ⊞ BHa

A portrait miniature of Empress Josephine, on a porcelain plaque, 19thC, 3¼in (8.5cm) high.
£270–340 SWO

A portrait miniature of a lady, wearing a pale green dress trimmed with black ribbon, by Hugh Nicolson, in a gilt-metal frame, the reverse with blue glass, signed and dated 1896, 3½in (9cm) high.
£750–900 P
Nicolson exhibited at the Royal Academy from 1893 to 1896.

A portrait miniature of an army officer, wearing the Victoria Cross and India Mutiny medals, English School, watercolour on ivory, 19thC, 1¼in (3.5cm) high.
£450–575 G(L)

Insurance values

Always insure your valuable antiques for the cost of replacing them with similar items, regardless of the original price paid. Both dealers and auctioneers can provide a valuation service for a fee.

A portrait miniature of a lady, wearing a blue shawl, white ruff and flower-decorated bonnet, 19thC, 2in (5cm) high, in a foliate-decorated brass frame.
£80–100 PFK

A portrait miniature of a lady, wearing a pink-lined black dress with white lace collar and a black hat, English School, c1900, 6¾in (17cm) high, in a gold-plated frame.
£400–500 P

Silhouettes

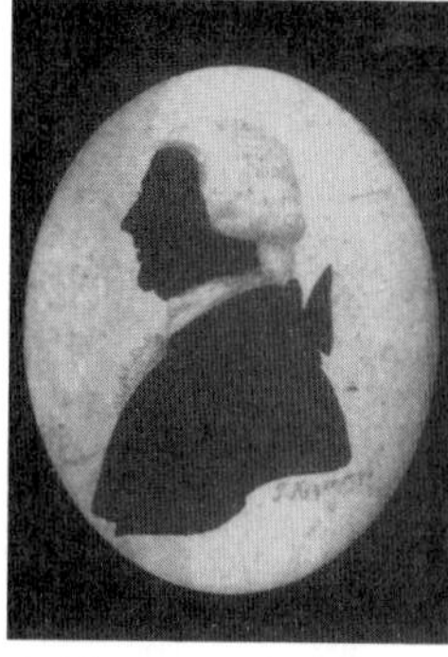

A silhouette of a gentleman, by Jeremiah Meyer, painted on card, signed and dated 1746, 2¾in (7cm) high, in a gilt-mounted papier mâché frame.
£140–175 Bon
This would have been executed when Meyer was just 11 years old, prior to his arrival in England and subsequent formal training as a miniaturist and enameller. His father was also a portrait painter, so it is unsurprising that the young Meyer would have experimented with portraits at an early age.

A silhouette of a gentleman, by A. Charles, Strand, London, painted on card, signed, c1790, 5¼in (13.5cm) high, in a turned pearwood frame.
£350–450 Bon
This is an unusually large example of Charles' work.

► **A multicoloured silhouette of a lady,** watercolour on ivory, c1825, 6½in (16.5cm) high.
£130–145 PSC

A pair of silhouettes of a husband and wife, with bronzing, 19thC, 3½ x 2½in (9 x 6.5cm).
£100–120 BR

► **A silhouette of a child,** attributed to Merryweather, cut-out on card heightened with gold on a watercolour background, c1830, 5¼in (13.5cm) high, in a wood frame.
£550–650 Bon

A silhouette of a lady, by George Atkinson, painted on card and highlighted with gold, c1825, 2½in (6.5cm) high, in a gilt-mounted papier mâché frame.
£240–300 Bon
This portrait shows Atkinson's particular skill at depicting ladies' fashions of the period.

A gilded silhouette of a gentleman, watercolour on card, c1835, 14in (35.5cm) high.
£150–175 PSC

◄ **A silhouette portrait of a young boy and girl,** in a maple frame, c1850, 6¾in (17cm) high.
£160–200 LFA

A pair of silhouette portraits of a gentleman and a lady, by Dempsey, with gilt highlights, label on reverse, mid-19thC, 4in (10cm) high, within bird's-eye maple frames.
£450–500 WcH

A silhouette of a gentleman, by P. Osborn, painted on paper, signed and dated 1857, 5½in (14cm) high, in a veneered maplewood frame with gilded border.
£320–400 P

A silhouette portrait, probably of the artist's son, Claude, attributed to Mortimer Menpes, cut black paper laid down on white paper, signed, early 20thC, 6¼in (16cm) high.
£140–175 L

Artists' Materials

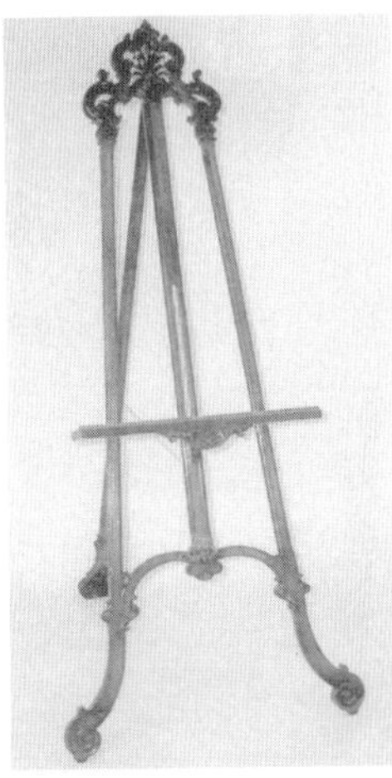

A Victorian walnut adjustable easel, the pierced and S-scroll carved crest on three moulded supports and scrolled front legs, 71in (180.5cm) high.
£500–600 CGC

An ebonized easel, the broken arch crest centred by a carved palmetto above a spindled gallery, with brass hardware, French, 1850–75, 75in (190.5cm) high
£630–700 NOA

An oak studio easel, late 19thC, 89¼in (226.5cm) high, unextended.
£600–700 Bon(C)

An oak easel, late 19thC, 102in (259cm) high extended.
£500–600 DN

A parcel-gilt and black-painted display easel, early 20thC, 80in (203cm) high.
£600–700 Bon(C)

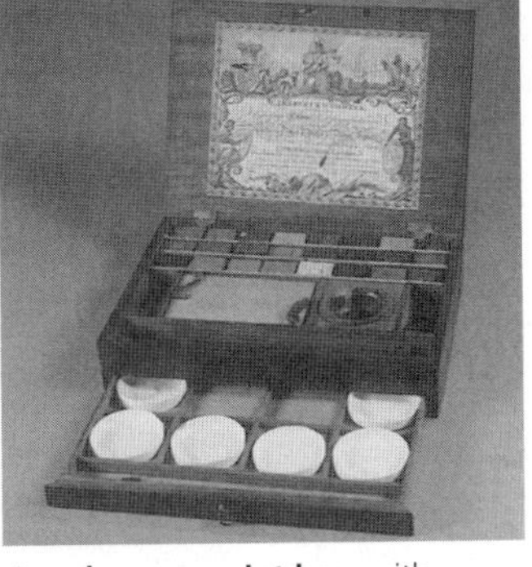

A mahogany paint box, with original paper label for Reeves & Son, with frieze drawer, early 19thC, 11in (28cm) wide.
£470–550 S(O)

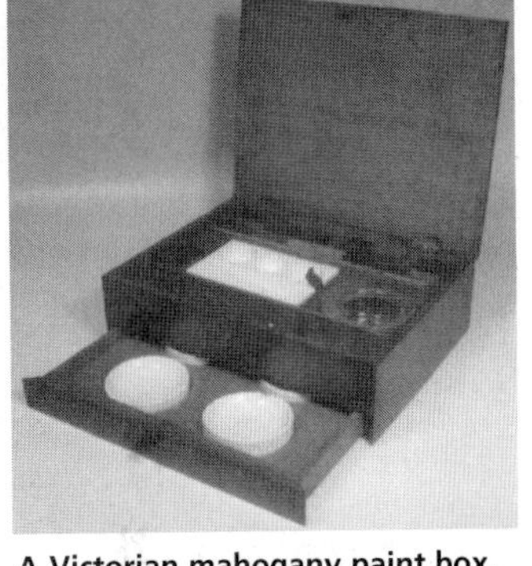

A Victorian mahogany paint box, the lid with ebonized stringing, with fitted interior, the frieze drawer with ceramic mixing palettes, 9in (23cm) wide.
£200–250 WW

A Victorian mahogany paint box, the fitted interior with a trade label for Reeves & Son, London, with frieze drawer, 9¼in (23.5cm) wide.
£280–350 WW

An artist's mahogany table, the frieze drawer with a sliding panel centred by a hinged flap rising on a ratchet with open compartment below, the frieze centred by a carved chieftain mask and leaf scrolls, the sides with two pairs of opposing frieze drawers, Irish, c1750, 37¼in (94.5cm) wide.
£75,000–95,000 S
Because of the buoyant Irish market and the enthusiasm with which Irish Americans collect examples of their heritage, any Irish pieces of good quality, particularly those dating from the 18th century, are selling for very high prices.

An Aesthetic Movement cherrywood print rack, the rail embellished with foliate- and floral-inlaid panels of ebony and walnut on a maple field, the back rack with a folding compartment for the vertical display of prints, American, 1875–1900, 34¼in (87cm) wide.
£1,500–1,650 NOA

Antiquities

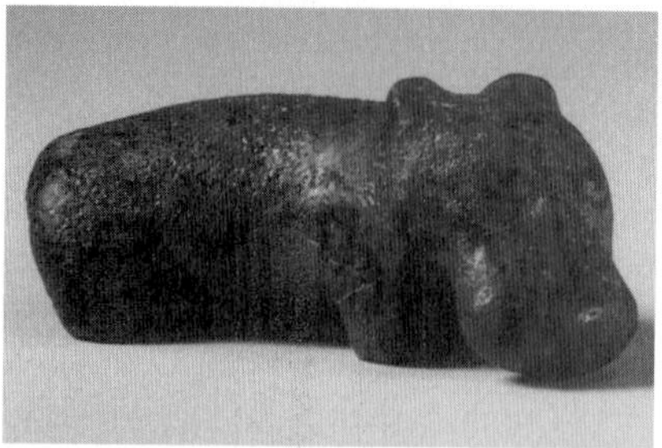

A blue faïence model of a hippopotamus, painted in black with intersecting lotus flowers and buds, Egyptian, 12th Dynasty, 1938–1759 BC, 4¼in (11.cm) wide.
£7,000–8,000 S(NY)

A limestone offering table, Middle Kingdom, 12th Dynasty, 1900–1700 BC.
£3,400–3,750 S(Z)

A bronze model of a cat, Egyptian, 10th–16th Dynasty, c1190–525 BC, 3½in (9cm) high.
£730–900 SLN

The items in this section have been arranged chronologically in sequence of civilisations, namely Egyptian, Near Eastern, Greek, Roman, Byzantine, western European, British, Anglo-Saxon and Medieval.

A bronze protome, in the shape of a lion emerging from a rectangular sockle, with engraved whiskers and ears, Egyptian, 21st–26th Dynasty, 1075–525 BC, 2¾in (7cm) high.
£1,750–2,000 S(NY)
A protome is usually a head and shoulders bust often with a flat back.

◄ **A silver amulet of Bastet,** the lion-headed goddess wears the disc and uraeus, Egyptian, 3rd Intermediate Period, 1069–747 BC, 2½in (6.5cm) high, with later suspension loop and modern silver chain.
£400–500 B

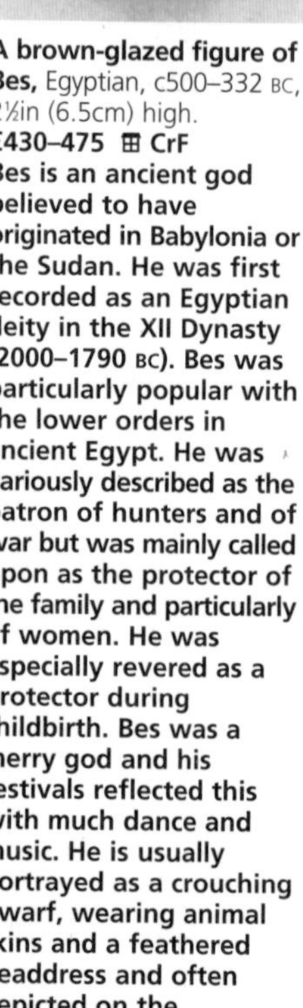

A brown-glazed figure of Bes, Egyptian, c500–332 BC, 2½in (6.5cm) high.
£430–475 CrF
Bes is an ancient god believed to have originated in Babylonia or the Sudan. He was first recorded as an Egyptian deity in the XII Dynasty (2000–1790 BC). Bes was particularly popular with the lower orders in ancient Egypt. He was variously described as the patron of hunters and of war but was mainly called upon as the protector of the family and particularly of women. He was especially revered as a protector during childbirth. Bes was a merry god and his festivals reflected this with much dance and music. He is usually portrayed as a crouching dwarf, wearing animal skins and a feathered headdress and often depicted on the headboards of beds or as a figurine used to adorn the birthing places and ward off evil spirits.

An engraved colourless glass vase, with a wheel-engraved horizontal latticework frieze framed above and below with wheel-engraved lines and bunches of grapes and festoons, probably Egyptian, AD 4th–5thC, 9in (23cm) high.
£4,800–6,000 S(NY)

A Coptic terracotta vase, the shoulder decorated in umber slip with two birds flanking a basket of fruit, restored, some repainting, the reverse of the vase replaced, Egyptian, 6th–7thC AD, 11½in (29cm) high.
£575–720 B
If in good condition this piece would fetch in the region of £1,000.

A votive bronze figure of Osiris, wearing the atef crown, with incised collar and holding the crook and flail, Egyptian, Late Period, post-600 BC, 10¾in (27.5cm) high.
£2,000–2,200 B

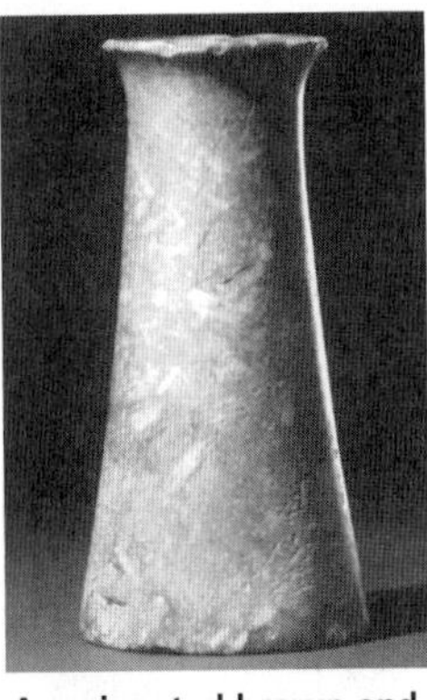

A variegated brown and white stone ritual object, Bactrian, late 3rd–early 2nd milliennium BC, 6in (15cm) high.
£1,700–2,000 ⚒ S

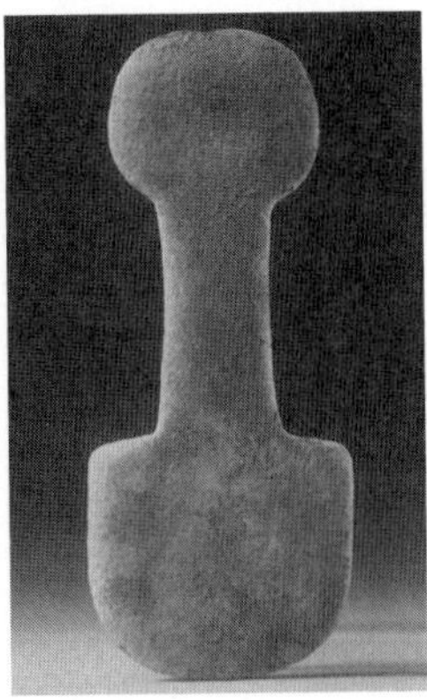

A marble idol, Cycladic, early Bronze Age, c2700–2400 BC, 6¾in (17cm) high.
£3,000–3,600 ⚒ S(NY)

A spouted jar, decorated in cream slip with red bands around the lower neck and extended rays towards the base, the rim damaged and repaired, small chip to spout, Near Eastern, 1st millennium BC, 8½in (21.5cm) high.
£585–650 ⊞ CrF

A Master-of-Animals finial, modelled as the mirrored bodies of two mythological creatures extending from two janus-headed figures, Luristani, 8th–7thC BC, 6½in (16.5cm) high.
£585–650 ⊞ CrF

The use of these finials has been interpreted in many ways such as totem symbols, deity standards, cult idols or chariot fittings.

◄ **A bronze horse-bit,** each cheek-piece in the shape of a horse or mule walking on a bar, Luristani, c8thC BC, 7in (18cm) wide.
£3,000–3,500 ⚒ S(NY)

A silver spoon, the twisted handle terminating in the stylized head of a horned creature, Sasanian, c5th–6thC BC, 7½in (19cm) long.
£620–720 ⚒ Bon

A glass head pendant, restored, Phoenician, c6th–4thC BC, 1¼in (3cm) high.
£600–700 ⚒ Bon

A four-handled stamnos, decorated in orange/brown bands and four pairs of stylized flowers on the shoulder, some repairs and restoration, rim chip, Mycenaean, c12thC BC, 13in (33cm) high.
£3,400–3,750 ⊞ CrF

► **An Attic/Rhodian pottery vase,** in the form of a female head, wearing a headdress decorated with a black-glazed vine trail, neck and handle broken, chipped, Greek, c7th–6thC BC, 4in (10cm) high.
£350–450 ⚒ Bon(C)

A hollow terracotta head of a kore, Greek, c6thC BC, 4¼in (11cm) high.
£450–550 ⚒ Bon(C)

A kouros is a model of naked standing youth dating from the Greek Archaic Period (660–480). Kore is the female counterpart. Typically, kore display a general eastern influence and a rather stiff 'archaic' smile.

A pottery model of a horse and rider, Greek, Geometric Period, 6thC BC, 4¾in (12cm) high.
£550–600 ⊞ HEL

An early Iron Age limestone figure of a draped male, Greek Cypriot, 1050–650 BC, 12¼in (31cm) high.
£720–800 ⊞ HEL

◄ **A Corinthian pottery aryballos,** incised and highlighted in red with a central scale pattern, cmid–6thC BC, 4in (10cm) high.
£875–1,100 ⚒ S(NY)

► **A Corinthian votive dish,** decorated on the rim with encircling bands and linked dots, c6thC BC, 6¼in (16cm) diam.
£300–345 ⊞ CrF

► **An Attic lekythos,** the white ground body decorated with ivy leaf and lattice bands, handle repaired, Greek, 5thC BC, 9¼in (23.5cm) high.
£300–360 ⚒ B

A pottery figure of the goddess Demeter, Greek, Archaic Period, 550–520 BC, 9¾in (25cm) high.
£1,350–1,500 ⊞ HEL

A Hellenistic terracotta figure of a woman, Boeotian, cmid-4thC BC, 8in (20.5cm) high.
£1,750–2,000 ⚒ S(NY)

A Hellenistic bronze model of a deer, one ear missing, c2ndC BC, 3¾in (9.5cm) high.
£4,500–5,500 ⚒ S(NY)

◄ **An Apulian Red Figure epychisis,** the body decorated with bejewelled Eros, a rosette and other motifs in the field, a plant to either side, the details added in white and yellow, 330–320 BC, 7in (18cm) high.
£1,750–2,000 ⚒ S(NY)

An Apulian skyphos, decorated on both sides with a representation of Athena's owl standing between two palm fronds, repaired, Greek South Italian, c4thC BC, 3¼in (8.5cm) high.
£700–785 ⊞ CrF

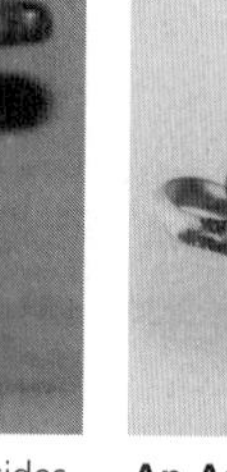

An Apulian Red Figure lekanis, the lid decorated on one side with a bejewelled and chiton-clad seated lady and on the other with bejewelled Eros in flight, the details added in white and yellow, the reserved areas covered in a red wash, 350–330 BC, 10¼in (26cm) wide.
£1,100–1,200 ⚒ S(NY)

A Red Figure askos, decorated with a maenad on one side, the reverse with a goose, a worn stylized palmette beneath the spout, Greek South Italian, c4thC BC, 2in (5cm) high.
£450–550 ⚒ Bon(C)

◄ **A Gnathia Ware kylix,** the rim decorated in white slip with a band of tongues and ivy leaf with some red incised detail, Greek, 4thC BC, 3¾in (9.5cm) diam excluding handles.
£250–300 ⚒ B

A Daunian storage jar, the dark umber slipware decorated with encircling dark bands, some chipping, Greek South Italian, 5th–4thC BC, 4¾in (12cm) high.
£165–185 ⊞ CrF

► **A black glazed kylix,** Greek South Italian, 4thC BC, 10¼in (26cm) wide.
£400–450 ⊞ HEL

An Etruscan pottery amphora, decorated in orange-brown and cream slip with banded lines and inverted triangles, two stylized ducks on each side of the shoulder, minor restoration, 7th–6thC BC, 16in (40.5cm) high.
£1,900–2,100 ⊞ CrF

An Etruscan black-glazed oinochoe, some glaze flaked, c6thC BC, 14¼in (36cm) high.
£675–750 ⊞ CrF

A Roman pottery figure of Zeus, seated on a throne, 1st–2ndC AD, 4in (10cm) high.
£225–250 ⊞ HEL

A Roman terracotta bust of the goddess Aphrodite, 1st–2ndC AD, 7in (18cm) high.
£1,500–1,650 ⊞ CrF

A Roman bronze lar, dressed in a short flowing gown and holding a patera in his left hand, the right arm mostly missing, 1st–3rdC AD, 3¼in (8.5cm) high.
£500–550 ⊞ ANG
Lares were household gods who were supposed to ensure the family always had sufficient food. This figure would have held a cornucopia in his right hand. This was found in Carnuntum, the military town on the Danube founded by Antoninus Pius.

A Roman bronze figure of Mercury, wearing a winged helmet and holding a purse in his right hand with his cloak and caduceus in his left, 1st–2ndC AD, 3¼in (8.5cm) high.
£1,400–1,600 ⊞ CrF
This is a particularly elaborate votive bronze.

A Roman bronze strigil, 2ndC AD, 75in (190cm) long.
£400–450 ⊞ ANG
This was found in Carnuntum. Strigils were used in the bathing process to scrape sand, oil and dirt off the body.

A Roman pale green glass ewer, with applied handle and threaded decoration around the lip and neck, broken foot rim, 2ndC AD, 9in (23cm) high.
£400–450 ⚒ SK

A carved sandstone bust of a woman, Syrian, Palmyra, 2ndC AD, 21in (53.5cm) high.
£5,250–6,000 ⚒ SK

A Roman glass stem cup, 3rd–4thC AD, 3½in (9cm) high.
£1,100–1,200 ⊞ JHa

A Roman white marble head of the god Mercury, 2ndC AD, 4¼in (11cm) high.
£550–600 ⊞ HEL

► **A Roman gold bracelet,** composed of spiral-wound strips terminating in confronted ram heads, with repoussé and chased details, Egyptian, c3rdC AD, 2¼in (5.5cm) diam.
£1,750–2,000 ⚒ S(NY)

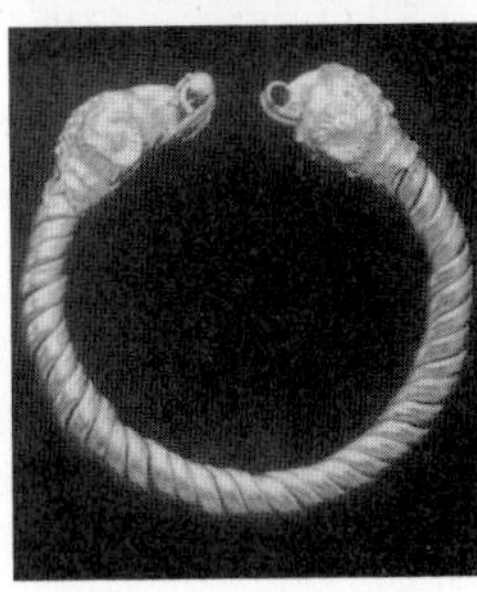

A Roman red slipware bowl, the interior decorated with three running wild boars, a seated leopard and a leafy tree, repaired, with small amounts of infill in places, north African, 3rd–4thC AD, 7in (18cm) diam.
£1,500–1,800 ⚒ Bon

A Byzantine colourless glass lamp, covered with milky iridescence, rim slightly chipped, eastern Mediterranean, c6th–7thC AD, 3¾in (9.5cm) wide.
£650–800 Bon
This kind of glass receptacle would have fitted into a bronze hanging lamp holder and would have been filled with oils that were burnt for lighting.

A late Bronze Age sickle, with moulded decoration, from south-east England, 900–800 BC, 6in (15cm) long.
£120–135 ANG

A Danubian bronze figure of a Celtic rider, holding a short sword in his hand, right leg missing, 2nd–1stC BC, 2½in (6.5cm) high.
£110–125 ANG

Cross Reference
See Colour Review (page 729)

A Visigothic radiate-head bronze brooch, 5th–7thC AD, 3¼in (8.5cm) long.
£85–100 ANG

► **A Frankish polychrome glass bead necklace,** with modern clasp, some beads replaced, 6th–7thC AD, 18½in (47cm) long.
£380–420 CrF

An Anglo-Saxon grey burnished pottery urn, decorated with six chevrons above arched grooves, neck area repaired, c6thC AD, 9in (23cm) high.
£700–800 Bon

An Anglo-Saxon bronze long brooch, with double axe-shaped head, the borders with punched decoration, 4½in (11.5cm) long.
£480–530 B

An Anglo-Saxon iron spearhead, 8thC AD, 7¾in (19.5cm) long.
£130–145 CrF

► **A medieval pottery floor tile,** decorated with a buff-green fleur-de-lys, c1350, 9in (23cm) square, in an oak frame.
£270–300
HUM

Tribal Art

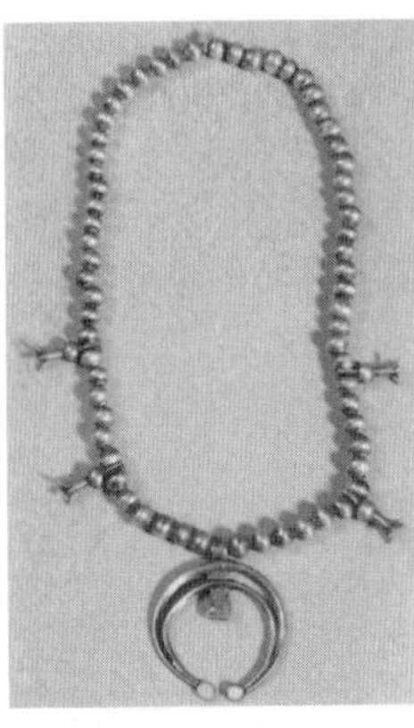

A Southwest silver and turquoise squash blossom necklace, Native American, Navajo, late 19thC, 15½in (39.5cm) long.
£1,850–2,000 SK(B)
Most Navajo jewellery on the market dates from the 1920s–40s and therefore is worth considerably less than this 19th-century example.

A Southwest painted wood box, painted with Kachina images in black on a yellow ochre ground, Native American, probably Hopi, late 19thC, 13½in (34.5cm) wide.
£4,700–5,500 SK(B)
Kachinas are supernatural ancestor figures.

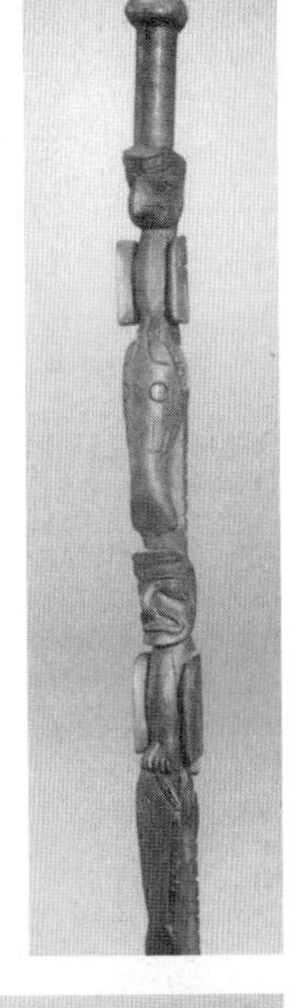

► **A Northwest coast cane,** carved in the shape of various totemic creatures, traces of pigment, Native American, late 19thC, 36½in (92.5cm) high.
£1,000–1,200 SK(B)

Items in the Tribal Art section have been arranged geographically from west to east.

A Plains hide bag, applied with seed beads, decorated on one side with a stellar design within a medallion, the reverse with four chequered cruciform motifs on a blue ground, Native American, 4¾in (12cm) wide.
£575–700 P

◄ **A Southwest coiled basketwork tray,** Native American, Pima, early 20thC, 12¼in (31cm) diam.
£550–600 SK(B)

A Central Plains child's trade blue cloth dress, sewn with six rows of dentilia shells around the collar and further decorated with sequins, brass bells and ribbons, Native American, Lakota, late 19thC, 30in (76cm) long.
£2,700–3,000 SK(B)

A Central Plains beaded cloth and hide doll, Native American, probably Arapaho, late 19thC, 15½in (39.5cm) high.
£1,350–1,500 SK(B)

A Plateau beaded hide bag, decorated with coloured beads on a light blue ground, Native American, c1900, 16 x 9½in (40.5 x 24cm), framed.
£1,250–1,500 SK(B)

Miller's is a price GUIDE not a price LIST

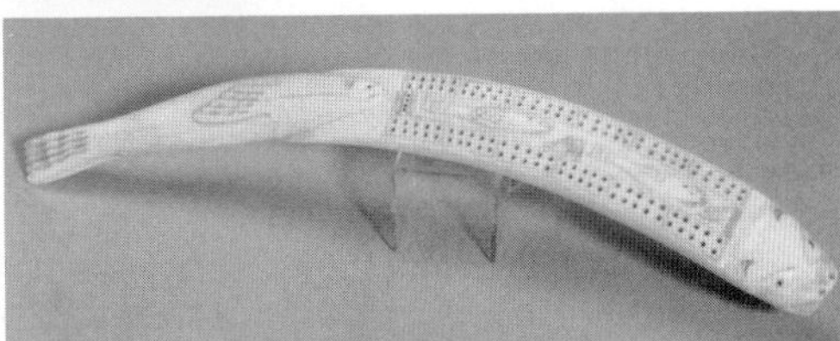

An Inuit ivory tusk cribbage board, carved in the shape of a seal with a bear's head and two smaller relief-carved seals, engraved walrus and floral details, with black, green and red pigments, missing peg support, 16in (40.5cm) long.
£750–850 SK(B)

► **A Great Lakes birch bark and porcupine quill box,** Native American, c1910, 6in (15cm) diam.
£120–140 HUM

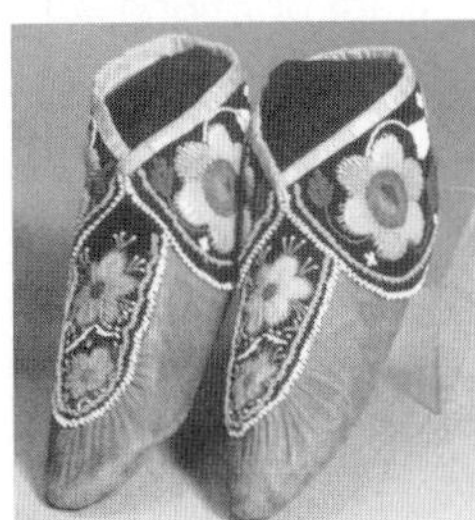

◄ **A pair of Northeast beaded cloth and hide moccasins,** the black velvet vamps and cuffs partially beaded with multicoloured floral devices, Native American, Iroquois, c1870, 9½in (24cm) long.
£1,600–2,000 SK(B)

TRIBAL ART

A carved wood mask, African, Sierra Leone, 7½in (18.5cm) high.
£600–650 SK(B)

► **A black-painted Mende Sande society sowei mask,** African, Sierra Leone/Liberia, 17¼in (44cm) high.
£500–600 Bon(C)

The sowei mask is unique in sub-Saharan Africa in that it is the only documented instance of masks commissioned and worn by women. The Sande society is a multi-ethnic association responsible for the socialization of young women, in which they undergo strict tutorial and surgical procedure as part of their initiation, ending with celebration and dancing with sowei masks. As the embodiment of Sande ideals, the mask illustrates the standards of beauty and morality: neck folds, a broad smooth forehead (intelligence), slit eyes, small nose and closed mouth (small is beautiful) and a shiny black patina (purity and association with the original ancestor who emerges from dark water).

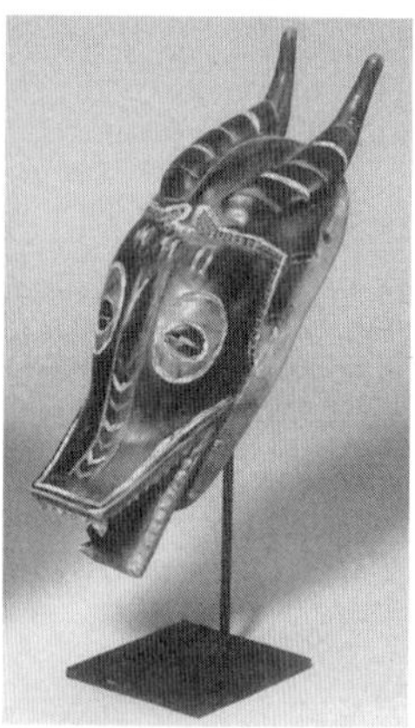

A Guro carved wood antelope mask, with red, black and white pigments, African, Ivory Coast, 13½in (34.5cm) wide.
£230–280 SK(B)

A Baule wood female figure, the lips accentuated by vertical scarifications, African, Ivory Coast, 15¾in (40cm) high.
£575–720 P

A cloth and cowrie shell shirt and headdress, repairs, African, Bamama, headdress 35in (89cm) long.
£420–500 SK(B)

A Dan Wé wooden mask, with exaggerated zoomorphic features, decorated with kaolin, African, Ivory Coast, 10½in (26.5cm) high.
£1,400–1,750 S(NY)

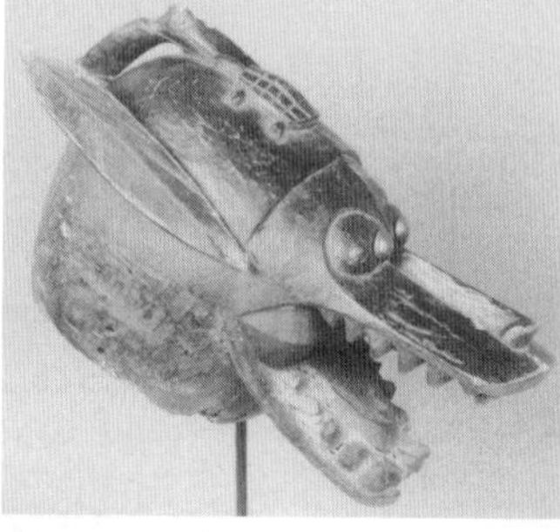

◄ **A Senufo wooden helmet mask,** in the shape of a bush cow, the forehead carved with a bird and a turtle, with brass stud eyes, some termite damage, African, Ivory Coast, 21¼in (54cm) long.
£230–280 P

A Guro wooden female figure, seated on a tall stool, strands of white beads encircling the neck, African, Ivory Coast, 12in (30.5cm) high.
£2,000–2,500 S(NY)

◄ **A terracotta storage vessel,** the shoulders with incised decoration, Burkina Faso, Dagari, 17in (43cm) wide.
£2,200–2,750 S(NY)

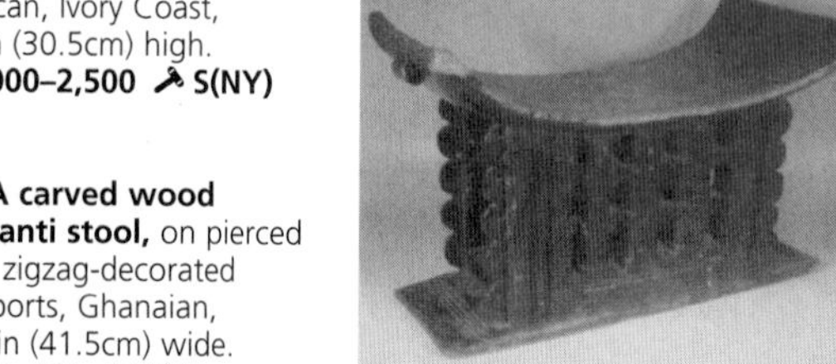

► **A carved wood Ashanti stool,** on pierced and zigzag-decorated supports, Ghanaian, 16¼in (41.5cm) wide.
£150–180 WW

A Benin wood table, with two legs carved in relief with a stylized soldier and two carved with figures in European dress, the stretchers carved with hunting leopards, a repeat scroll motif and an equestrian figure in European dress, Nigerian, 41in (104cm) wide.
£1,500–1,650 P

◄ **A Calabar mask,** with black pigment, applied kaolin and hair, Nigerian, Benue River, early 20thC, 12in (30.5cm) high.
£650–720 ⊞ GRG

A Yoruba wooden house post, composed of a female figure standing above a male half length figure, each with traces of red and yellow pigment, Nigerian, Ikelu Londo State, 52in (132cm) high.
£150–220 ⚒ P

An Ibo masquerade crest, carved as a human head, painted with white and black scarifications, the neck applied with bands of colour, Nigerian, 33in (84cm) high.
£220–250 ⚒ P

A wooden Gelede mask, Nigerian, 9¾in (25cm) high.
£635–700 ⚒ BERN

A Songye wood and raffia fetish, Congo region, 8¼in (21cm) high.
£530–600 ⚒ BERN

◄ **A Hemba carved wood Janus figure,** insect damage, central African, Congo region, 9½in (24cm) high.
£420–520 ⚒ SK(B)

A pair of Yoruba Ibeji figures, the female with domed coiffure rising to a point, the male with cap-shaped coiffure, his chest carved with a triangular pectoral, both with strands of cowrie shells attached to the wrists, Nigerian, 9¾in (25cm) high.
£450–575 ⚒ P

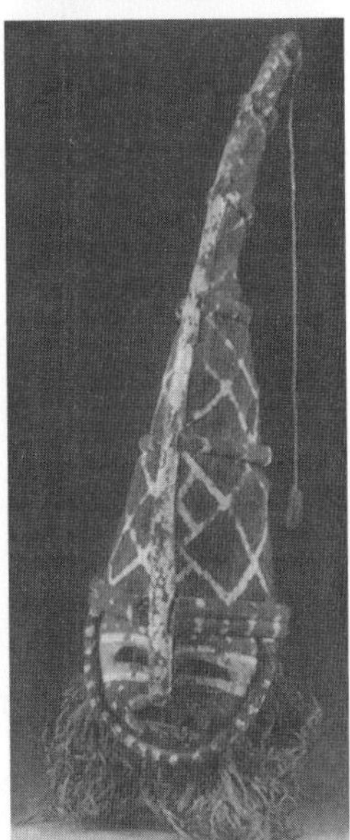

A Luvale fibre mask , painted with pink, white and black pigment, composed of bark cloth over a wicker frame with a raffia fringe, Zambian/Angolan, 45¼in (115cm) high.
£300–375 ⚒ Bon(C)

A Yoruba shrine sculpture or stool, enclosing a male and female, she stands wearing a skirt and breast scarf, he is seated wearing western clothes, with grey and white paint, Nigerian, 17¾in (45cm`) high.
£220–270 ⚒ Bon(C)

◄ **An Akan wooden tribal lion,** resting on the back of a turtle, with stippled decoration, damaged, west African, 11in (28cm) high.
£150–220 ⚒ DD

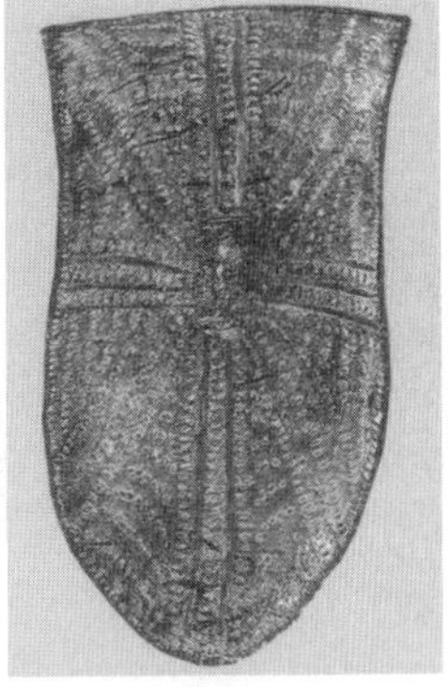

A Mofu leather shield, embossed with a geometric design edged with fur on the outer side, west African, north Cameroon, c1900, 37½in (97.5cm) high.
£200–250 ⚒ Herm

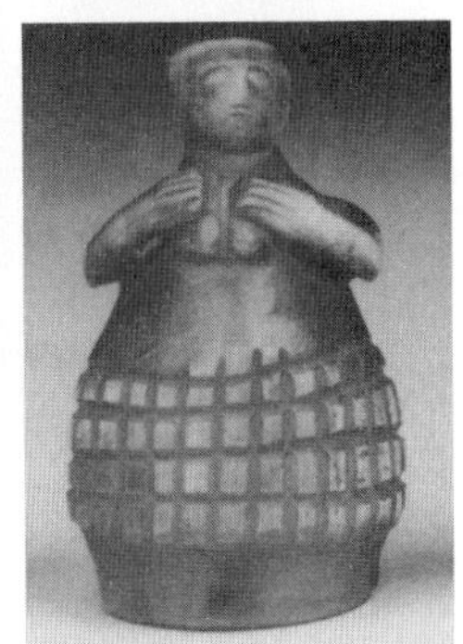

A horn snuff container, carved as a woman, with incised lattice skirt, stopper missing, South African, 3¼in (8.5cm) high, on a wooden base.
£160–200 ⚒ P

◄ **An Ifugao wood carving,** the base carved with four lizards in relief, Philippines, 11¼in (28.5cm) high.
£230–280 SK(B)

A carved hardwood figure of a Raksha, Balinese, 1875–1925, 12½in (32cm) high.
£230–260 SK

A coconut shell, the rim on one side carved as a bird-like heart-shaped face, the whole incised with abstract faces, curvilinear and chevron motifs, Sepik River, Wosera, Papua New Guinea, 4¾in (12cm) diam.
£1,750–2,000 S(NY)

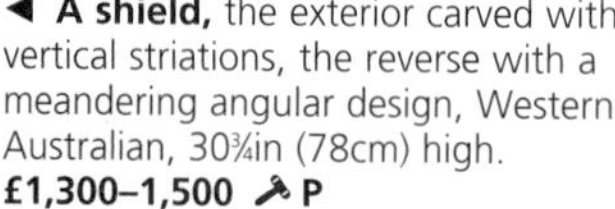

◄ **A shield,** the exterior carved with vertical striations, the reverse with a meandering angular design, Western Australian, 30¾in (78cm) high.
£1,300–1,500 P

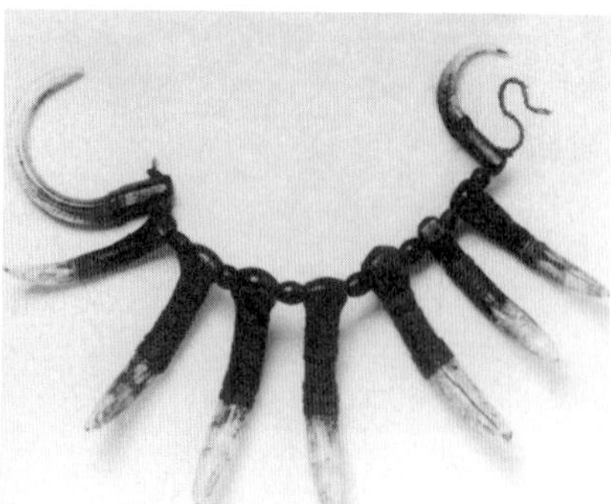

A Toradja necklace, composed of seven crocodile teeth, secured to geometric decorated wood terminals with bands of plaited fibre binding, flanked by two boars' teeth, Indonesian, 13in (33cm) long.
£670–750 P

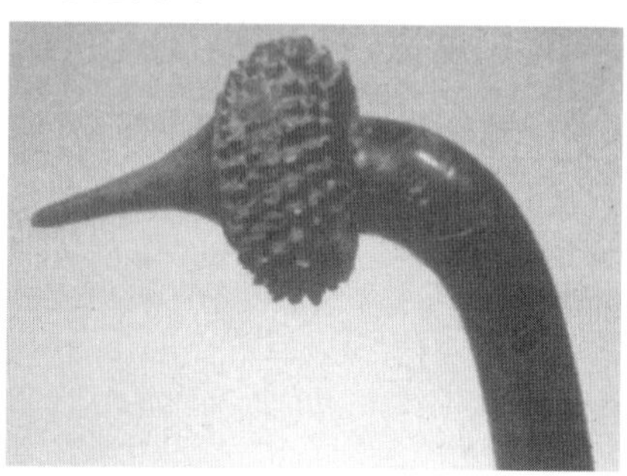

A pineapple club, with burrwood knop and geometric carved grip, Fijian, 40in (101.5cm) long.
£300–375 CDC

A priest's wooden oil dish, the handle decorated with panels edged by zigzag motifs, Fijian.
£2,200–2,750 S(NY)

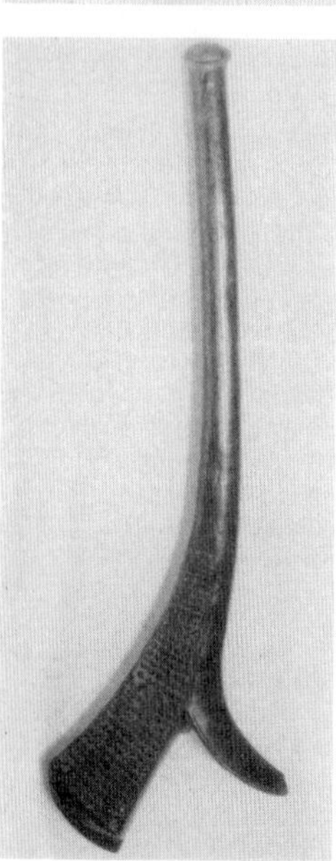

► **A carved wood stilt step,** decorated with a crouching tiki figure, Polynesian, Marquesas Island, late 18thC, 14in (35.5cm) high.
£2,500–2,750 SK(B)
Tiki are stylized human figures representing ancestors.

◄ **A gunstock club,** the butt carved in relief with dot surface, Fijian, 45in (114.5cm) long.
£450–500 P
This club is of particularly large size.

A Maori wooden post figure, the face incised with scrolling tattoos, New Zealand, 30¾in (78cm) high.
£250–275 P

Books & Book Illustrations

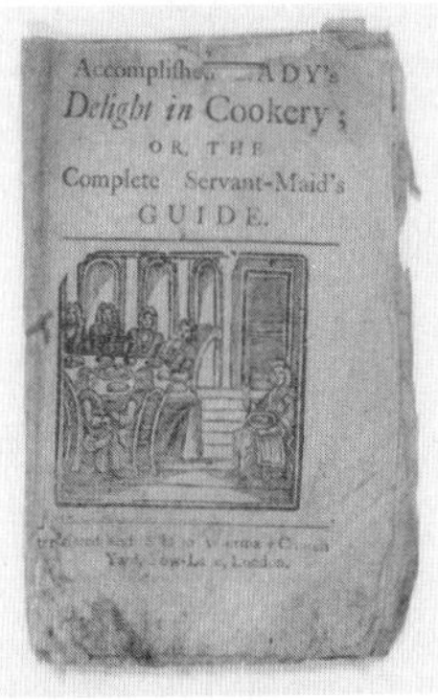

Accomplished Lady's Delight in Cookery; or, the Complete Servant-Maid's Guide, London, c1780, 12°, 24 pages, crude woodcut to title, some loss of lettering.
£900–1,100 ⚒ DW

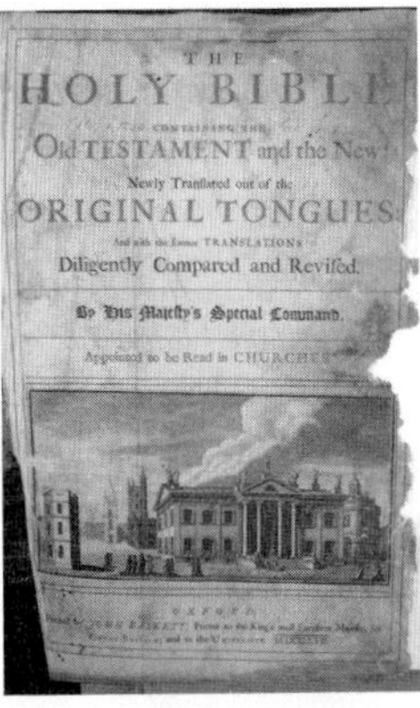

The Holy Bible, printed by John Basket, Oxford, 1717, 2°, illustrated with engraved vignettes, missing frontispiece, severe fore-edge damage, full reversed calf.
£360–440 ⚒ N

William Burroughs, *Junkie: Confessions of An Unredeemed Drug Addict*, by William Lee, Ace Double Books, New York, 1953, bound with **Maurice Helbrandt,** *Narcotic Agent*, original printed wrappers.
£720–850 ⚒ DW

John Angell, *Stenography; or, Short-hand Improved*, first edition, c1758, 8°, signed by the author, engraved title and 21 plates, bound in contemporary calf.
£500–600 ⚒ Bon
A list of subscribers in this book includes Samuel Johnson.

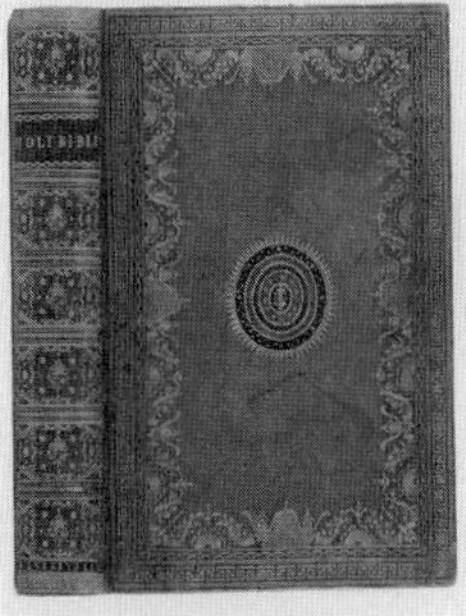

The Holy Bible, printed by John Baskerville, Cambridge, 1763, 2°, full morocco binding, gilt extra by Kalthoeber.
£1,250–1,500 ⚒ WW

John Cassin, *Illustrations of the Birds of California, Texas, Oregon, British and Russian America*, published by J. B. Lippincott & Co, Philadelphia, 1862, large 8°, 50 hand-coloured lithographed plates, spine and edges gilt, original blind-tooled brown morocco.
£4,500–5,500 ⚒ S(NY)

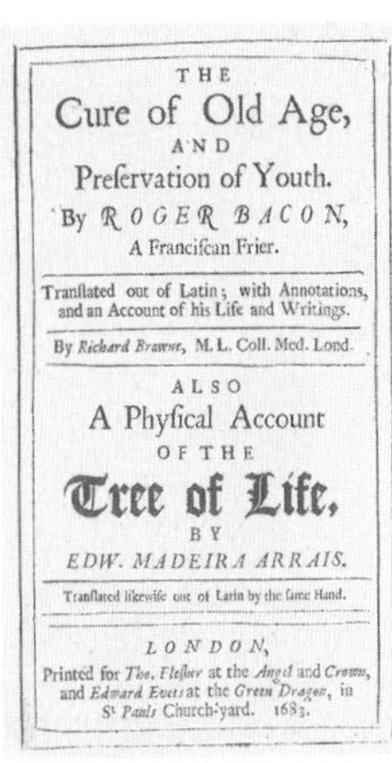

Roger Bacon, *The Cure of Old Age, and Preservation of Youth*...also **Edw. Madeira Arrais,** a physical account of the *Tree of Life*, published by Thomas Flesher and Edward Evets, first edition in English, 1683, 8°, translated by Richard Brawne, two parts in one volume, rebacked, contemporary calf.
£1,000–1,250 ⚒ Bon

Giovanni Boccaccio, *Le Decameron*, published by E. Roffet, Paris, 1548, 8°, wood-engraved title and ten folding illustrations, later green crushed morocco by Rivière, gilt.
£600–700 ⚒ P

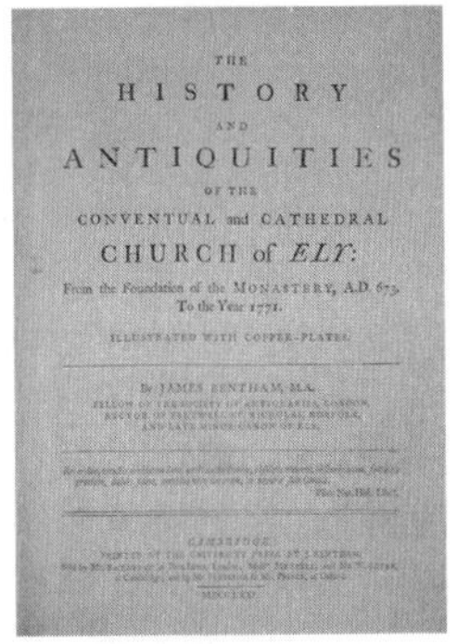

James Bentham, *The History and Antiquities of the Conventual and Cathedral Church of Ely*, Cambridge, 1771, 4°, engraved plates, with Supplement by William Stevenson, rebacked calf.
£280–350 ⚒ CGC

George Bradshaw, *Bradshaw's Map of the Railways, Canals, Navigable Rivers and Mineral Districts of Great Britain, reduced from the Ordnance Survey*, engraved and printed by John Dower, c1853, large 8°, hand-coloured folding map, on linen, in a contemporary gilt-decorated morocco slipcase.
£360–440 ⚒ DW

◄ **Agatha Christie,** *The Hound of Death, and other stories*, Odhams Press, first edition, 1933, 8°, original cloth.
£200–250 ⚒ BBA

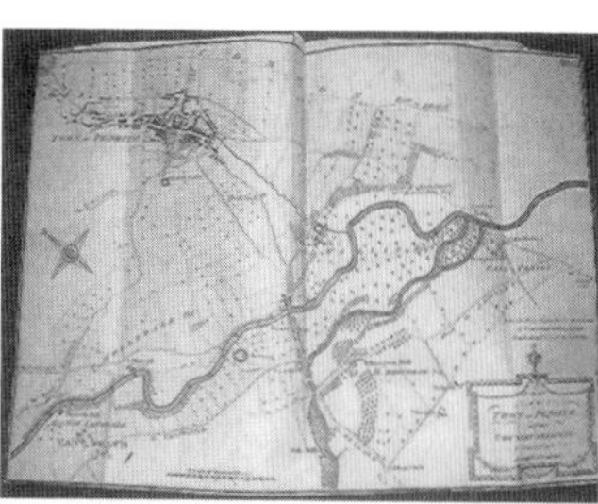

James Clarke, *A Survey of the Lakes of Cumberland, Westmorland and Lancashire*, printed for the author, first edition, 1787, 2°, with 11 large folding maps and two plates, repairs, full panelled calf binding.
£850–1,100 PFK

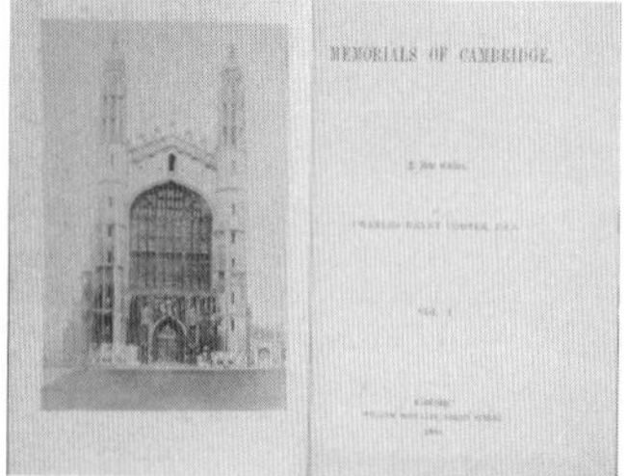

Charles Henry Cooper, *Memorials of Cambridge*, new edition, 1860–66, 4°, three volumes, mounted photographic plates, gilt lettered spines, half bound.
£380–450 CGC

► **James Fenimore Cooper,** *The Pilot*, published by John Miller, London, first edition, 1824, three volumes, gilt contemporary calf, 5 x 7in (12.5 x 18cm).
£180–200 BAY

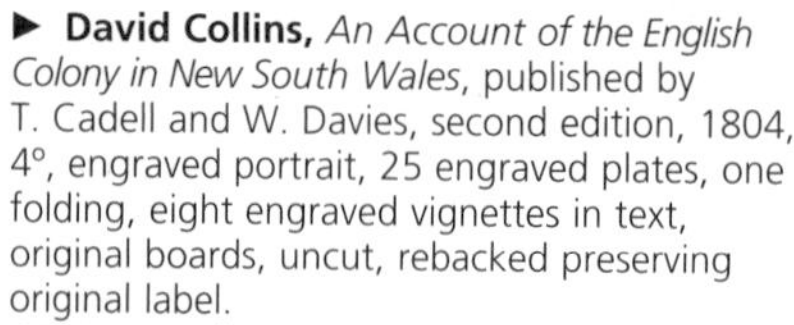

► **David Collins,** *An Account of the English Colony in New South Wales*, published by T. Cadell and W. Davies, second edition, 1804, 4°, engraved portrait, 25 engraved plates, one folding, eight engraved vignettes in text, original boards, uncut, rebacked preserving original label.
£400–500 P

Matthew Consett, *A Tour through Sweden, Swedish-Lapland, Finland and Denmark*, 1789, 4°, with seven engraved plates and one woodcut by Bewick, spine defective, upper cover near detached, contemporary boards, in modern cloth bookbox.
£250–300 DW

Edward J. Detmold (Illustrator), *The Fables of Aesop*, published by Hodder & Stoughton, London, New York & Toronto, c1909, 4°, colour frontispiece, 22 colour plates, publisher's original decorated cloth.
£70–85 RTo

Rev Charles Lutwidge Dodgson (Lewis Carroll), *The Hunting of the Snark*, with nine illustrations by Henry Holiday, first edition, 1876, 8°, with black and white wood-engraved plates, original black endpapers, original gilt-decorated red cloth.
£270–340 DW
This is a very early issue, in the variant red cloth.

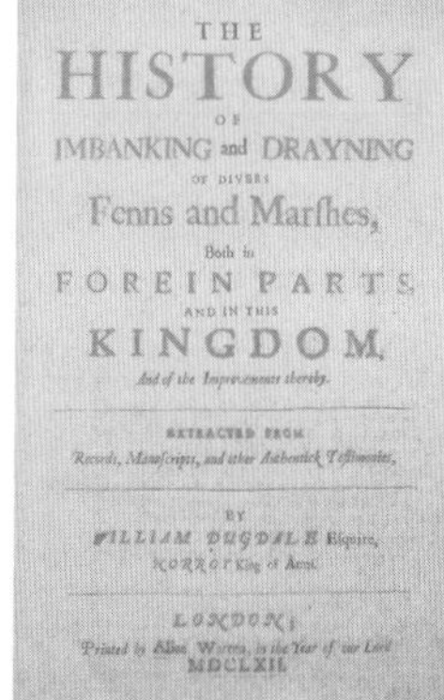

William Dugdale, *The History of Imbanking and Drayning of Divers Fenns and Marshes*, first edition, London, 1662, 4°, 11 folding illustrations, later gilt full calf.
£1,650–2,000 CGC

► **Ebenezer Emmons,** *Agriculture of New York*, part III, Albany, 1851, 4°, two additional engraved titles, 100 hand-coloured lithographed plates, bound in contemporary half calf.
£550–600 BBA

Henry Fielding, *The History of The Adventures of Joseph Andrews*, first edition in two volumes, 1742, 6½ x 4in (16.5 x 10cm), rebound leather by Bayntun.
£675–750 BAY

Ioan de Grijalva, *Chronicle of the Order of Our Father St. Augustine*, Mexico, 1624, 7¾ x 6¾in (19.5 x 17cm), restored, missing front cover and first and last pages.
£1,700–2,200 LCM

▶ **Augustus Grimble,** *The Salmon and Sea Trout Rivers of England and Wales*, published by Kegan Paul, first edition, 1904, 4°, two volumes, one of 350 large paper copies, 2 folding maps, numerous plates and illustrations, vellum-backed boards.
£600–700 BBA

Ian Fleming, *The Man with the Golden Gun*, first edition, 1965, 8°, original boards with gold-embossed design on front cover, dust-jacket.
£2,000–2,400 BBA
This is the very scarce issue with the gold gun on the upper cover, considered by the publishers inadequate and subsequently reissued in plain boards.

Graham Greene, *The Little Fire Engine*, colour illustrations and pictorial endpapers by Dorothy Craigie, first edition, 1950, long oblong 8°, original cloth in dust-jacket.
£350–450 DW

John Gould, FRS, an illustration entitled 'Paradisea Decora. Grey-chested Bird of Paradise', original hand-coloured lithographed plate from *The Birds of New Guinea and the adjacent Papuan Islands including many new species recently discovered in Australia*, c1880, 21¾ x 14¼in (55.5 x 36cm).
£850–1,100 DW

Anna C. Hartshorne, *Japan and her People*, published by Kegan Paul, French, Trubner & Co, Philadelphia, 1902, 8°, two volumes, numerous black and white illustrations from photographs, folding map, original gilt-decorated crimson cloth, with original linenized protective wrappers.
£200–250 DW

Ernest Hemingway, *The Old Man and the Sea*, published by Charles Scribner's Sons, New York, 13th edition, 1956, 12°, with dedicatory inscription from the author, original blue cloth and dust-jacket.
£1,850–2,250 WcH

Cross Reference
See Colour Review (page 731)

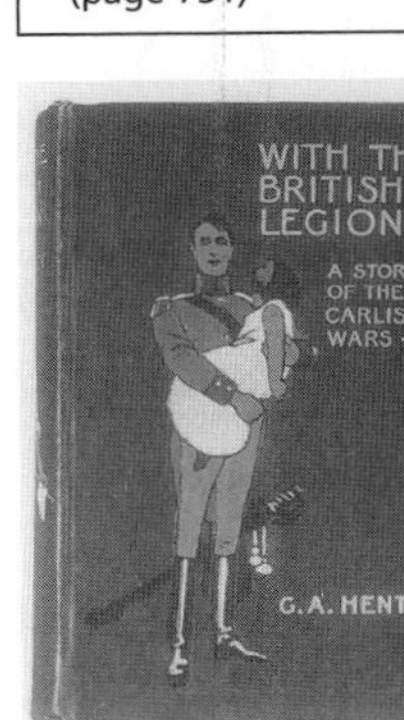

G. A. Henty, *With the British Legion*, first edition, 1903, 8°, with 10 plates by Wal Paget, original blue pictorial cloth.
£115–150 BBA

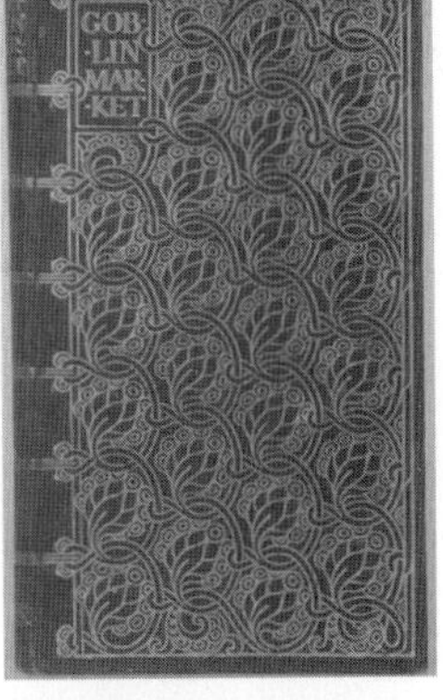

Laurence Housman, (Illustrator), *Goblin Market*, by Christina Rossetti, no date, c1893, tall 12°, 12 plates and numerous illustrations and decorations, original green cloth, stamped in gilt after a design by Housman.
£175–200 RTo

Charles Mason Hovey, *The Fruits of America*, New York, 1853, 4°, 48 chromo-lithograph plates, in contemporary gilt-decorated dark green morocco.
£350–400 DW

H. N. Humphreys and J. O. Westwood, *British Moths and their Transformations*, published by William S. Orr & Co, London, 1851, 4°, 2 volumes, 124 hand-coloured plates, gilt-lettered green half morocco.
£600–660 ⚒ RTo

Thomas Kentish, *The Pyrotechnist's Treasury; or, Complete Art of Making Fireworks*, first edition, 1878, 8°, 16 plates, original decorated cloth.
£575–675 ⚒ BBA

William Lambard, *A Perambulation of Kent*, published by Ralphe Newberie, first edition, 1576, small 4°, engraved map of the Heptarchy with early hand-colouring, without the folding map, in modern half-crushed morocco.
£900–1,100 ⚒ Bon

Miller's is a price GUIDE not a price LIST

C. S. Lewis, *Out of the Silent Planet*, published by The Bodley Head, first edition, 1938, 7½ x 5in (19 x 12.5cm), original purple cloth with gilt titles on spine, with pictorial dustwrapper by Harold Jones.
£3,800–4,200 ⊞ JON

Captain Frederick Marryat, *Newton Forster*, published by James Cochrane & Co, London, first edition, 1832, 8 x 5in (20.5 x 12.5cm), three volumes, bound in contemporary gilt calf.
£340–380 ⊞ BAY

Gregory M. Mathews, *A Supplement to the Birds of Norfolk & Lord Howe Islands*, first edition, 1936, 2°, 24 hand-finished colour plates, six black and white, original green card wrappers in contemporary cloth.
£200–250 ⚒ DW

A. A. Milne, *The House at Pooh Corner*, illustrated by E. H. Shepard, 1928, 4°, No. 313 of 350 large paper copies on hand-made paper signed by the author and artists, largely unopened, original cloth-backed boards, paper label on upper cover.
£1,100–1,400 ⚒ P

James Morier, *The Adventures of Hajji Baba of Ispahan*, published by John Murray, London, first edition, 1824, 7 x 4in (18 x 10cm), 3 volumes, bound in half calf.
£270–300 ⊞ BAY

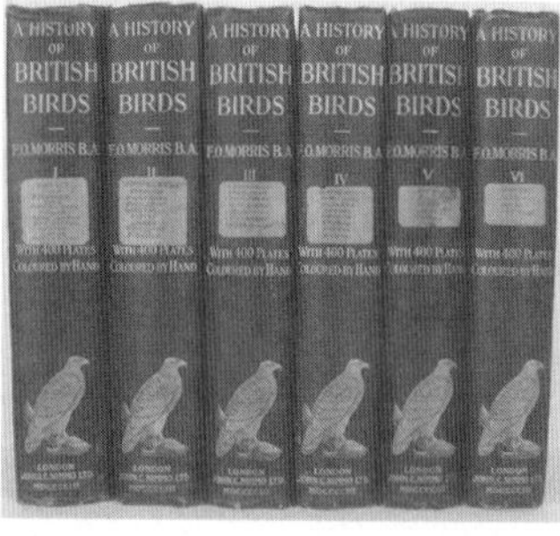

◄ **Rev Francis Orpen Morris,** *A History of British Birds*, London, fifth edition, 1903, 4°, 6 volumes, 400 plates printed in colours from woodblocks and finished by hand, extra-illustrated with numerous coloured illustrations from other later publications, original gilt green cloth, later paper labels stuck on spines.
£380–460 ⚒ RTo

► **Kay Nielsen, (Illustrator),** *Fairy Tales*, by Hans Andersen, published by Doran, New York, 1924, 4°, 12 tipped-in colour plates, black and white illustrations, bound in original pictorial cloth.
£250–320 ⚒ DW

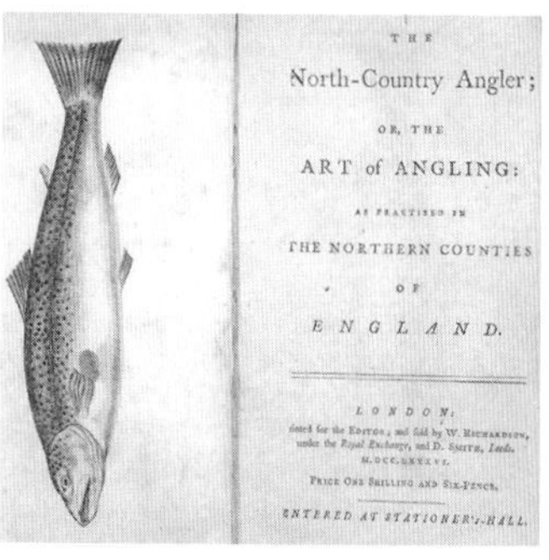

The North Country Angler; or, The Art of Angling, printed for the editor, 1786, 12°, engraved frontispiece, later calf-backed marbled boards.
£1,200–1,400 ⚒ BBA

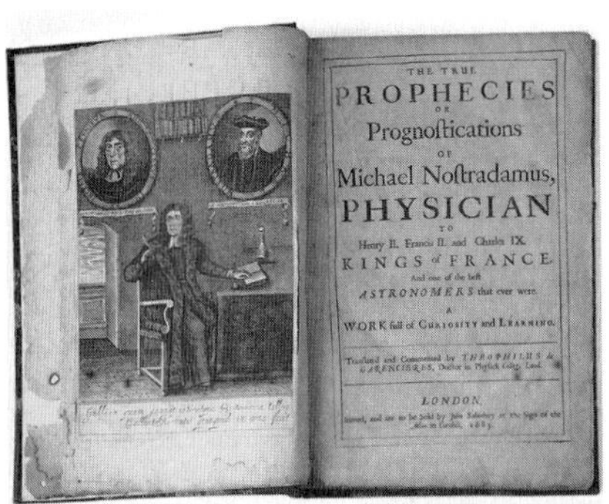

◀ **Michael Nostradamus,** *The True Prophecies or Prognostications of Michael Nostradamus, Physician to Henry II, Francis II and Charles IX, Kings of France*, translated and commented by Theophilus de Garencières, London, 1685, 2°, portrait frontispiece, modern half-buckram.
£850–1,100 ⚒ G(L)

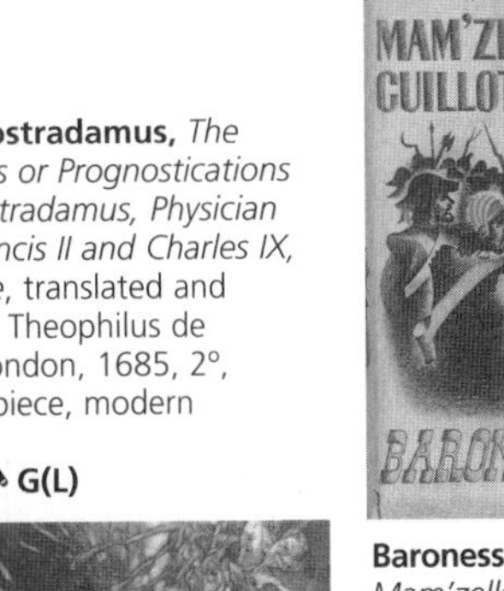

Baroness Emmuska Orczy, *Mam'zelle Guillotine*, first edition, 1940, 8°, original cloth, dust-jacket.
£800–900 ⚒ BBA

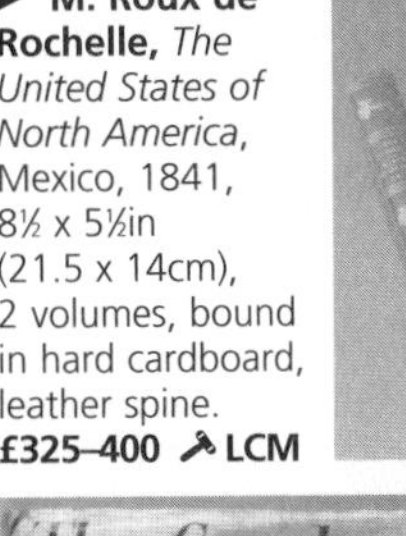

◀ **Arthur Rackham,** illustrator of *A Midsummer Night's Dream*, by William Shakespeare, London and New York, 1908, 4°, 39 colour plates, frontispiece and one plate detached, original cloth, spine missing.
£100–125 ⚒ RTo

Louis Philippe, Duke of Orleans, *A Travers la Banquise de Spitzberg au Cap Philippe*, Paris, 1907, Imperial 8°, presentation inscription from the author on front fly, portrait, vignette title, 10 coloured plates, large folding map, folding chart and panorama, in contemporary half russia.
£250–300 ⚒ F&C

A pique tortoiseshell copy of The Prayer Book, French, 19thC, 4 x 3in (10 x 7.5cm).
£1,100–1,250 ⊞ SHa

▶ **M. Roux de Rochelle,** *The United States of North America*, Mexico, 1841, 8½ x 5½in (21.5 x 14cm), 2 volumes, bound in hard cardboard, leather spine.
£325–400 ⚒ LCM

▶ **Salman Rushdie,** *The Satanic Verses*, published by Viking, first edition, 1988, 8°, signed by the author in ink to the title, original gilt cloth, dust-jacket.
£135–170 ⚒ DW

J. D. Salinger, *The Catcher in the Rye*, first UK edition, 1951, 8°, original cloth, dust-jacket.
£340–380 ⚒ DW

Margaret Tempest, original artwork for *Little Grey Rabbit*, c1940, watercolour on paper, 4in (10cm) diam.
£4,250–5,000 ⊞ BRG

Ipswich born Margaret Tempest (1892–1982) studied at the Ipswich School of Art, then the Westminster School of Art. To supplement her income she taught, among others, the naturalist and artist Peter Scott. She illustrated 66 books, the most famous being the *Little Grey Rabbit* series written by Allison Uttley, but also 20 of her own, some of which are in the Ipswich Museum.

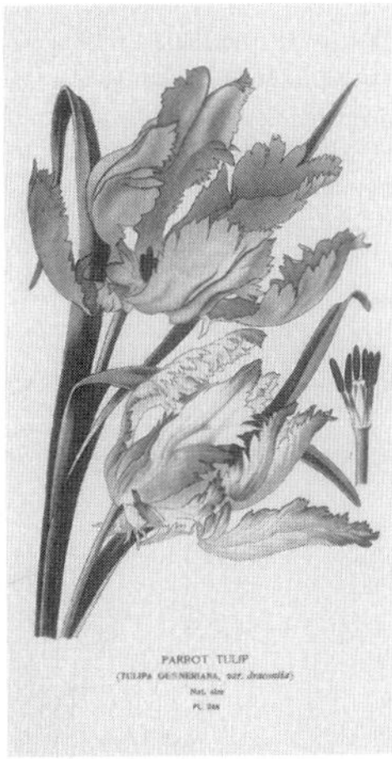

Edward Step, *Favourite Flowers of Garden and Greenhouse*, published by Frederick Warne, 1896–97, 8°, four volumes, 316 chromolithographed plates, bound in contemporary half green calf.
£800–1,000 ⚒ Bon

Jonathan Swift, *Voyages de Gulliver*, published by G. Martin, Paris, second edition, in French, 1727, 8°, two volumes, 4 engraved plates, bound in contemporary calf, spine gilt.
£200–250 ⚒ P

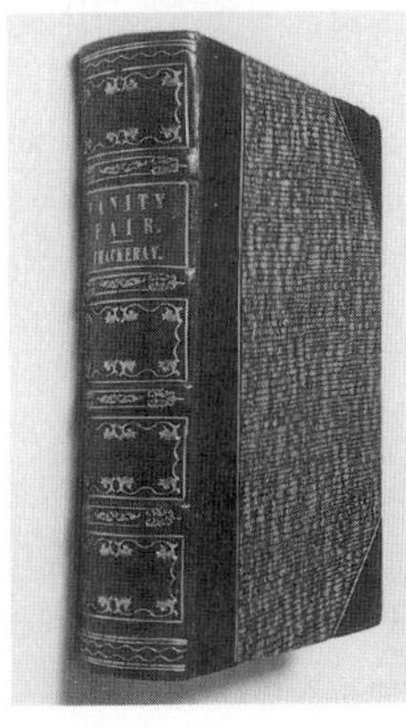

◀ **William Makepeace Thackeray,** *Vanity Fair*, published by Bradbury & Evans, London, first edition, 1849, 9 x 6in (23 x 15cm), contemporary half calf, gilt.
£250–300 ⊞ BAY

Tourist's Guide to Mexico City, 1854, 6 x 4in (15 x 10cm), bound in stiff cardboard, with leather back.
£220–275 LCM

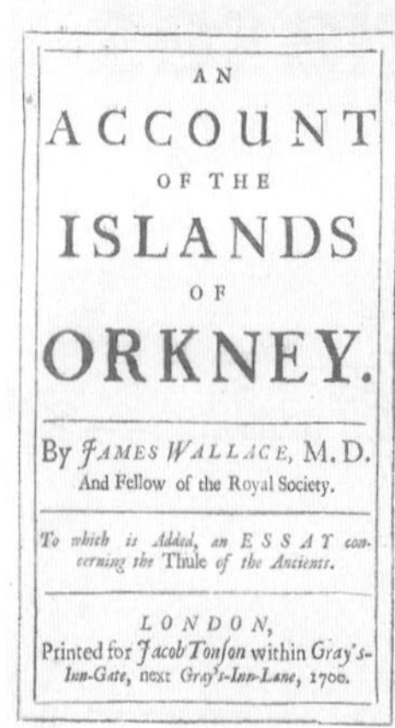

AN
ACCOUNT
OF THE
ISLANDS
OF
ORKNEY.

By JAMES WALLACE, M.D.
And Fellow of the Royal Society.

To which is Added, an ESSAY concerning the Thule of the Ancients.

LONDON,
Printed for Jacob Tonson within Gray's-Inn-Gate, next Gray's-Inn-Lane, 1700.

James Wallace, *An Account of the Islands of Orkney*, published by J. Tonson, 1700, 8°, folding engraved map and plate, bound in contemporary panelled calf, rebacked.
£380–450 Bon

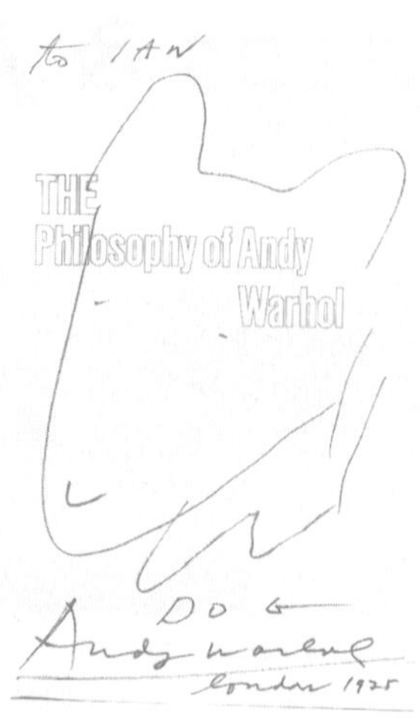

Andy Warhol, *The Philosophy of Andy Warhol*, published by Cassell, London, 1975, 8°, signed and dated by the author, with an original drawing of a dog's head, publisher's cloth, dust-jacket.
£700–800 Bon

◄ **Evelyn Waugh,** *Brideshead Revisited*, first edition, published by Chapman & Hall, London, 1945, 8°, dust-jacket.
£550–650 HAM

► **John Wood,** *An Essay Towards a Description of Bath in Four Parts*, second edition, 1749, 8 x 6in (20.5 x 15cm), rebound in period style.
£750–850 BAY

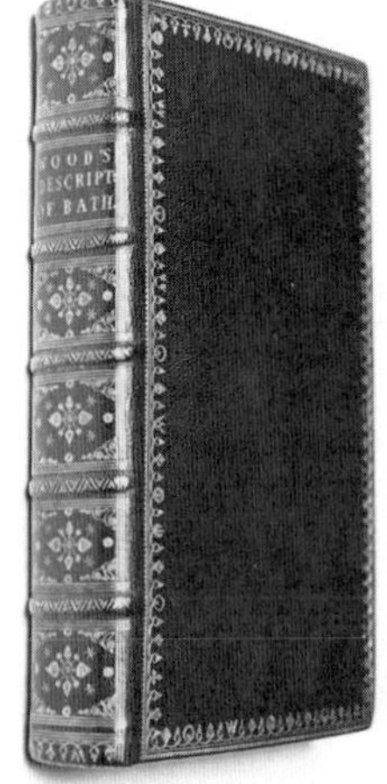

Virginia Woolf, *Monday or Tuesday*, published by Leonard & Virginia Woolf at The Hogarth Press, Richmond, first edition, 1921, 8°, four full-page woodcuts by Vanessa Bell, 1000 copies printed, original cloth-backed pictorial boards designed by Vanessa Bell.
£1,200–1,400 S

Oscar Wilde, *The Happy Prince and other Tales*, illustrated by Walter Crane and Jacomb Hood, 1888, 4°, No. 71 of numbered limited edition of 75, illustrations mounted on rice paper, original printed Japanese vellum, in a modern quarter morocco slipcase.
£1,500–2,000 DW

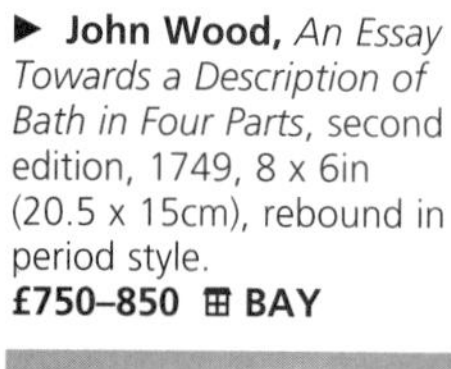

P. G. Wodehouse, *Heavy Weather*, first edition, London, 1933, 8°, dust-jacket.
£420–500 HAM

Virginia Woolf, *The Years*, first edition, London, 1937, 8°, dust-jacket.
£700–850 HAM

The Yellow Book, An Illustrated Quarterly, published 1894–97, small 4°, 13 volumes, plates by Beardsley, Sickert, Beerbohm, Crane and others, original pictorial cloth.
£750–825 BBA

A. Yosy, *Switzerland as now divided into nineteen Cantons...with picturesque Representation of the Dress and Manners of the Swiss*, published by J. Booth and J. Murray, London, 1815, 8°, 50 hand-coloured aquatint plates, lithographed plate of music, bound in modern half morocco.
£1,100–1,200 S

Niceto de Zamcois, *History of Mexico, from its earliest times to our own days*, published by J. F. Parres & Co, Barcelona and Mexico, 1876–82, 9 x 6¼in (23 x 16cm), bound in stiff card, leather spine.
£160–200 LCM

Maps & Atlases

World

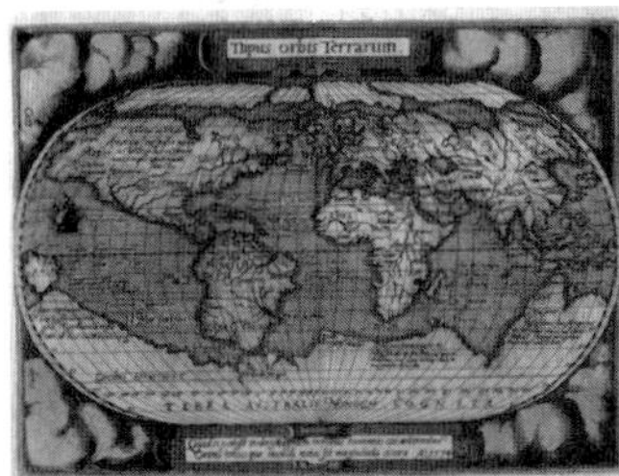

Abraham Ortelius, *Tiipus Orbis Terrarum*, Antwerp, 1574, coloured, 6¼ x 8¾in (16 x 22cm).
£1,500–1,650 ⊞ JOP
This is a very scarce miniature map of the world, prepared for the first edition of Ortelius' *Epitome*. Engraved at a larger size (8°) than the book (16°) and requiring folding, damage often resulted. Because of the map's unwieldy and consequently fragile nature it was used only until 1585 when it was replaced by a smaller plate. This example has a protective upper margin where the original was trimmed close.

▶ **James Wyld,** *A New General Atlas of Modern Geography*, with 66 plans, tables and maps, most maps coloured and either folding or double-page, title and index damaged and loose, covers detached, c1851, 23¼ x 17¾in (59 x 45cm).
£1,800–2,200 ⚒ CGC

Adam Friedrich Zürner, *Planisphaerium terrestre cum utroque coelesti hemisphaerio, sive diversa orbis terraquei*, double-page engraved twin hemispherical map, original outline colour, Pieter Schenk, Amsterdam, c1700, 19¾ x 22½in (50 x 57cm).
£2,200–2,750 ⚒ Bon

Items in the Maps & Atlases section have been arranged in date order within each sub-section.

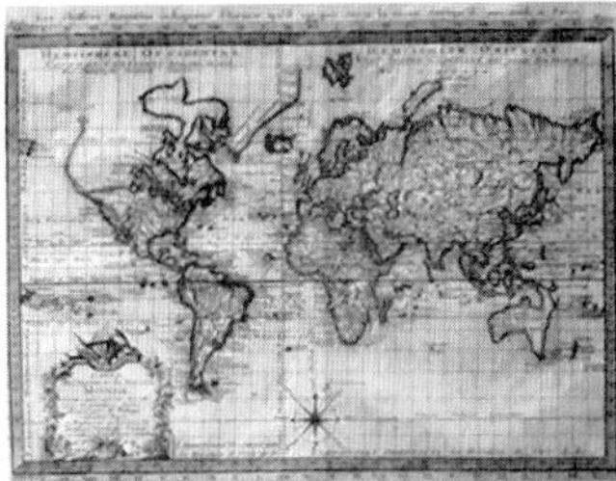

E. A. Philippe de Pretôt, *Carte de l'Ancien et du Nouveau Monde*, a Mercator projection of the world, Paris, 1771, 16¼ x 11½in (41.5 x 29cm).
£585–650 ⊞ JOP

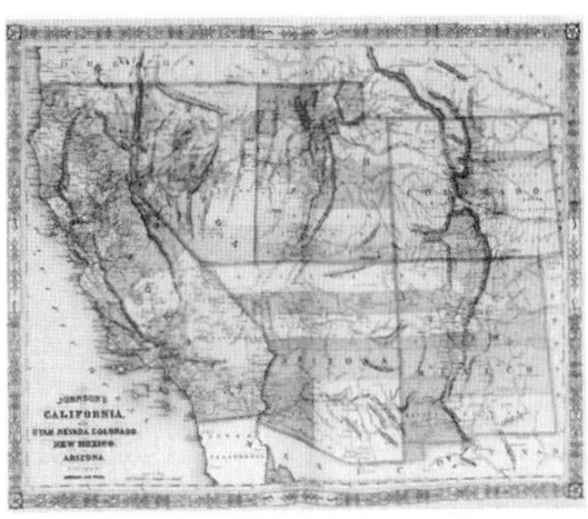

J. Alvin Johnson, *Johnson's New Illustrated Family Atlas of the World*, 105 hand-coloured engraved maps and town plans, publisher's green half morocco, green cloth boards stamped with gilt, Johnson & Ward, New York, 1866, 2°.
£1,200–1,500 ⚒ Bon

Africa & Arabia

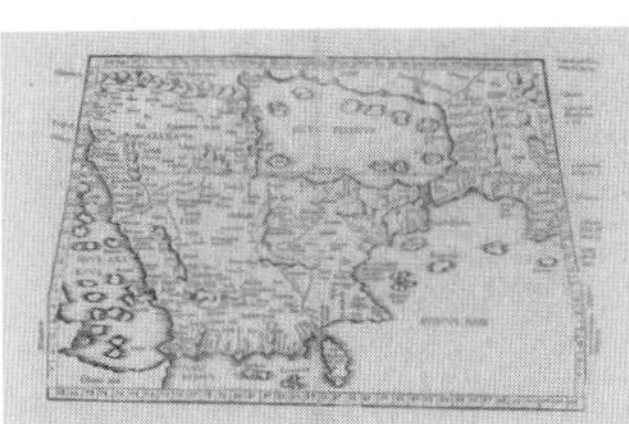

C. Ptolemaeus, untitled map of the Arabian peninsula, double-page woodcut map, G. Tredschel, Vienna, 1541, 10¾ x 17¾in (27.5 x 45cm).
£470–550 ⚒ S

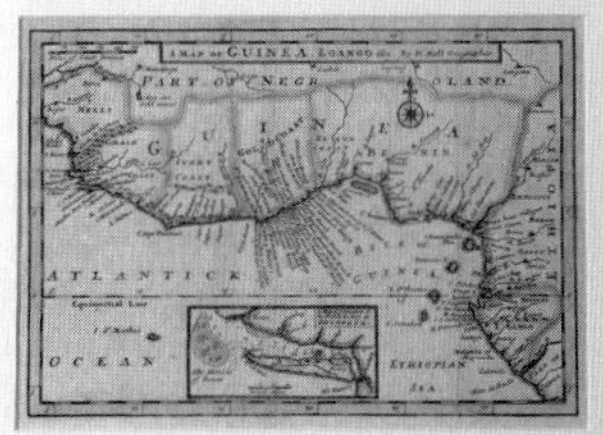

Hermann Moll, *A Map of Guinea*, 1719, 8 x 11in (20.5 x 28cm).
£80–90 ⊞ MAG

▶ **Hermann Moll,** *A Map of Africa*, 1719, 10 x 9in (25.5 x 23cm).
£135–150 ⊞ MAG

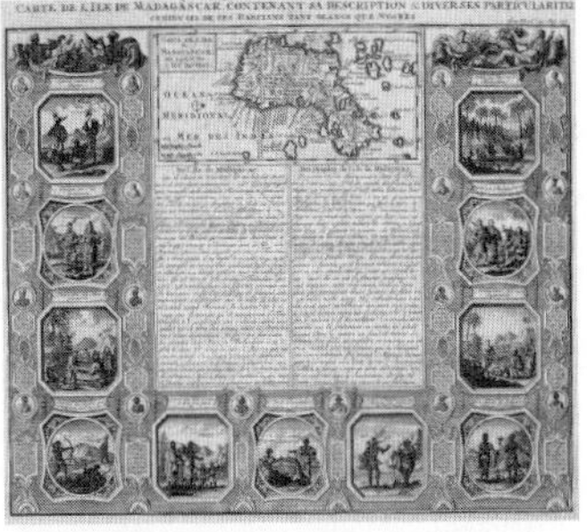

H. A. Chatelain, *Carte de l'Ile de Madagascar*, uncoloured, with descriptive text, bordered with 11 native scenes, Amsterdam, 1719, 17¼ x 15in (44 x 38cm).
£160–180 ⊞ JOP

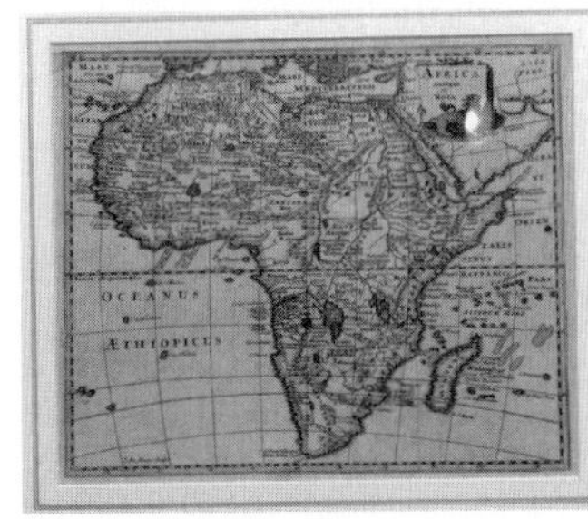

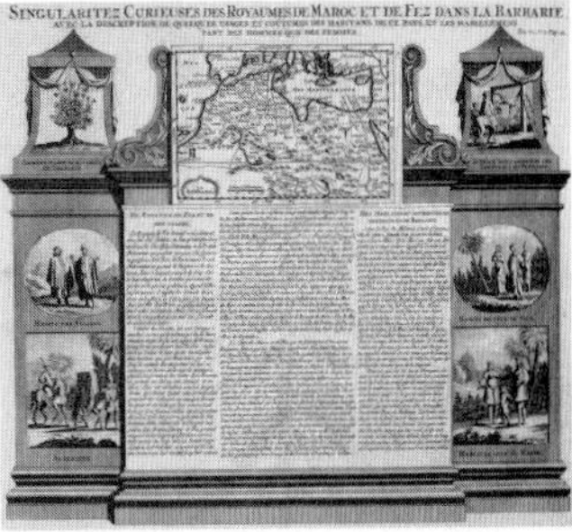

H. A. Chatelain, *Singularitez Curieuses des Royaumes de Maroc et de Fez dans la Barberie*, uncoloured, bordered by illustrations of native life, with text description, Amsterdam, 1719, 17 x 14¼in (43 x 36cm).
£145–160 ⊞ JOP

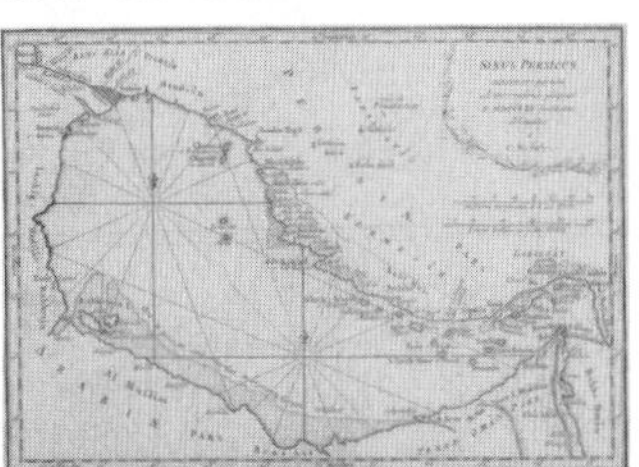

Carsten Niebuhr, *Sinus Persicus*, a map of the Persian Gulf, Copenhagen, 1772, 8 x 11½in (20.5 x 29cm), framed and glazed.
£425–500 ⚒ S

Americas

◀ **Abraham Ortelius,** *Americae sive Novi Orbis, Nova Descriptio*, engraved map of the American continent in early hand colouring, 1587, but issued 1603–12, 14 x 19in (35.5 x 48.5cm).
£2,750–3,000 ⚒ BBA

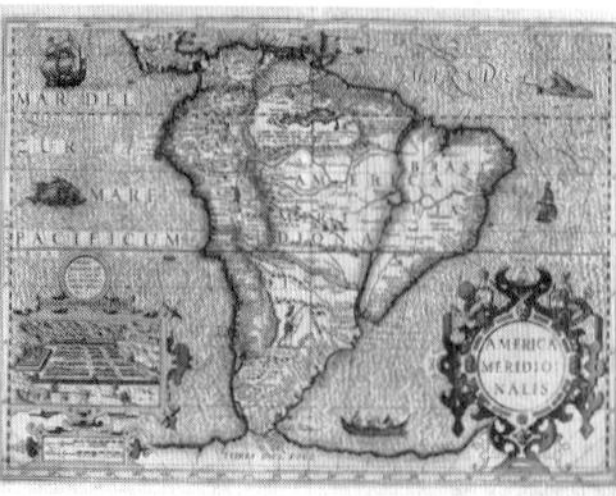

Jodocus Hondius, *America Meridionalis*, original outline colour, centrefold split, repaired, Amsterdam, 1606–22, 19¼ x 14in (49 x 35.5cm).
£1,100–1,200 ⊞ JOP

Mercator/Hondius, *America sive India nova*, double-page engraved hemispherical map of North and South America, Amsterdam, c1609, 14¼ x 18in (36 x 45.5cm).
£2,800–3,500 ⚒ Bon

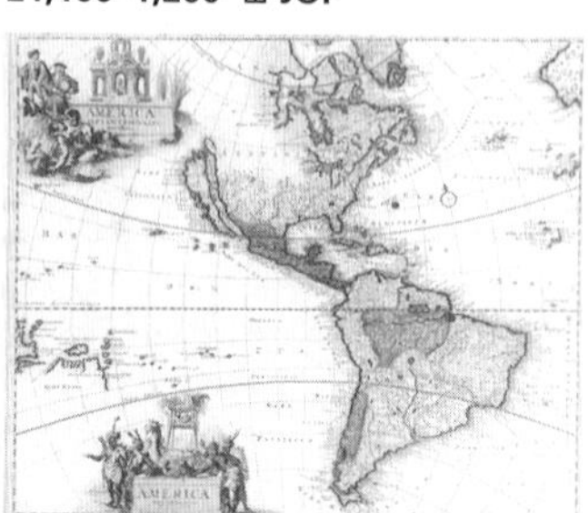

Nova Virginia Tabula, a map of Virginia, hand-coloured, printed by Willem Blaeu, 1640, 14¾ x 19in (37.5 x 48.5cm), framed.
£950–1,200 ⚒ SLN

Pieter Schenk, *America septentrionalis ... America meridionalis*, hand-coloured double-page engraved map with California as an island, c1690, 18¾ x 22¼in (47.5 x 56.6cm).
£950–1,200 ⚒ Bon

Nicolas de Fer, *L'Amérique, Meridionale et Septentrionale*, double-page engraved map of the Americas with California as an island, original outline colour, the lower border repaired, Paris, 1705, 18¼ x 21in (46.5 x 61cm).
£1,400–1,600 ⚒ S

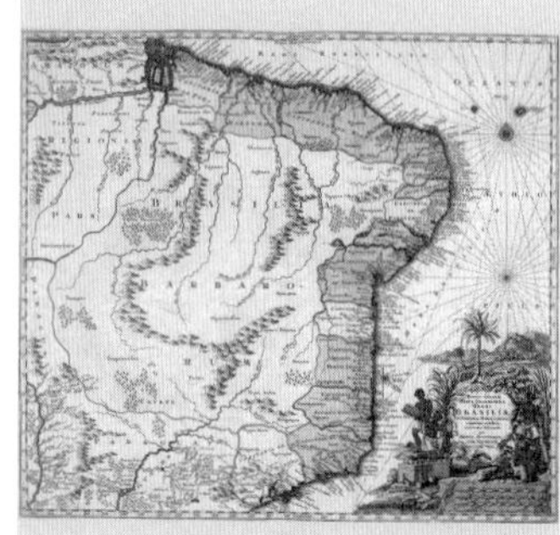

G. M. Seutter, *Recens Elaborata Mappa Geographica Regni Brasiliae*, with original colour, the title decoration showing native figures with tobacco pipes, decorated with produce and foliage set against a mountainous background, Augsburg, c1735, 21¾ x 19¼in (55.5 x 49cm).
£550–620 ⊞ JOP

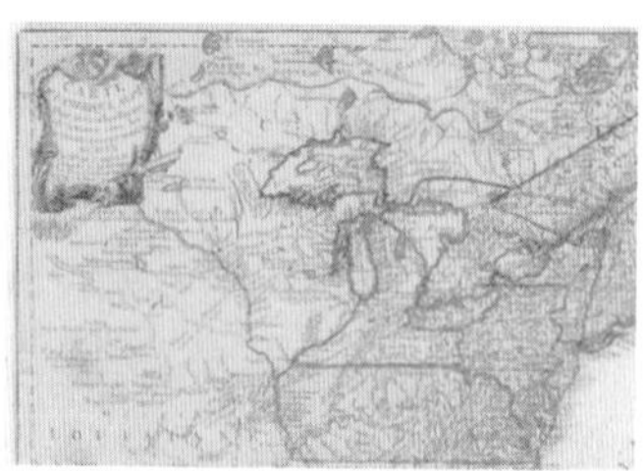

Jean de Beaurain, *Carte de l'Amérique Sept.*, double-page engraved map, original hand colour, trimmed close, Paris, 1777, 16¼ x 24½in (41.5 x 62cm).
£2,700–3,000 ⚒ S
This was published as France was entering the Revolutionary War. The large inset depicts the province of New York, extending north to the Great Lakes and St Lawrence River.

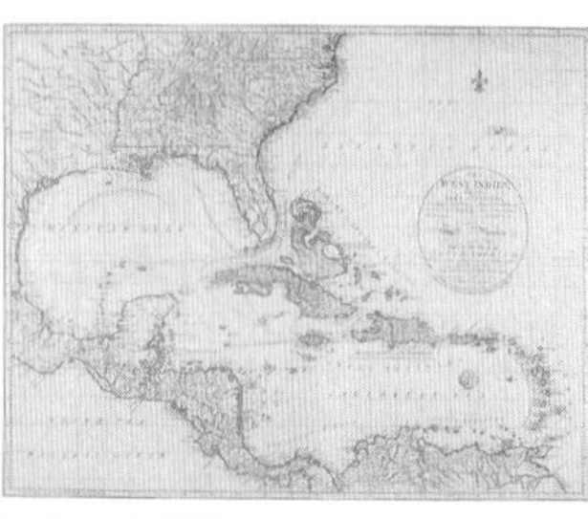

Robert Wilkinson, *The West Indies, including part of Virginia, North Carolina, South Carolina, Georgia, East Florida, West Florida, Louisiana and the Gulf of Mexico*, double-page engraved map, trimmed close to border, several short tears, London, 1782, 22¾ x 28¼in (58 x 72cm).
£950–1,200 ⚒ S

J. Thomson, a map of the United States, c1820, 20 x 24in (51 x 61cm).
£180–200 ⊞ MAG

Franz Anton Schraembl, *Generalkarte von Nordamerica samt den Westindischen Inseln*, uncoloured engraved map, with inset plans of Hudson Bay and the Gulf of California, Vienna, 1788, 39¾ x 45in (101 x 114.5cm).
£1,100–1,200 ⚒ DW

Asia & Australasia

Sebastian Munster, *Tabula Orientalis Regionis, Asiae Scilicet Extremas Complectens Terras & Regna*, uncoloured woodcut map, c1550, 10¼ x 13¾in (26 x 35cm).
£260–320 DW

Abraham Ortelius, *Chinae, olim Sinarum regionis, nova descriptio, auctore Ludovico Georgio*, double-page engraved map, hand-coloured, Antwerp, 1584, 14¼ x 18¼in (36 x 46.5cm).
£1,500–2,000 Bon

H. A. Chatelain, *Nouvelle Carte de l'Ile de Ceylon*, uncoloured, Amsterdam, 1719, 17¼ x 15½in (44 x 39.5cm).
£215–240 JOP
Unusually for a map of this period, roads are shown and miniature Dutch flags identify the locations of the Dutch trading interests.

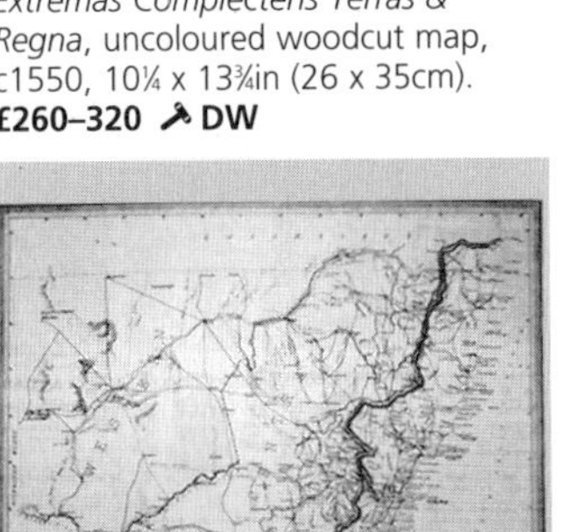

◀ **Skinner,** a map of New South Wales, uncoloured, Sydney, c1885, 17¼ x 15in (44 x 38cm).
£160–180 JOP
This was issued in a directory or gazeteer and the reverse has advertisements for numerous local services and businesses, a theatre guide and also wharfage and tonnage rates.

▶ **Andrew Garran,** *Picturesque Atlas of Australasia*, three volumes, 40 plates, 19 maps, contemporary morocco, Sydney, 1886, 2°.
£150–200 BBA

Europe

Sebastian Munster, *Italia XIIII Nova Tabula*, uncoloured woodcut of Italy showing Corsica, Sardinia and Sicily, c1545, 10¾ x 13½in (27.5 x 34.5cm).
£200–240 DW

▶ **Joannes Jansson,** a map of Greece, published by Hornius, 1652, 19 x 15in (48.5 x 38cm).
£450–500 MAG

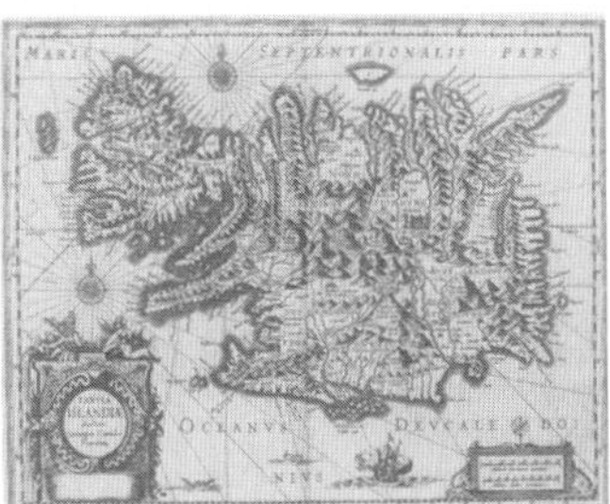

Joannes Blaeu, *Tabula Islandiae*, engraved map of Iceland, after Joris Carolus, Amsterdam, c1630, 15 x 19½in (38 x 49.5cm).
£400–500 BBA

LOCATE THE SOURCE

The source of each illustration in Miller's can be found by checking the code letters below each caption with the Key to Illustrations, pages 794–800.

◀ **Pieter Schenk,** *Carte des Courones du Nord*, a map of Scandinavia, Amsterdam, 1708, 25¼ x 35½in (64 x 90cm).
£500–600 BUK

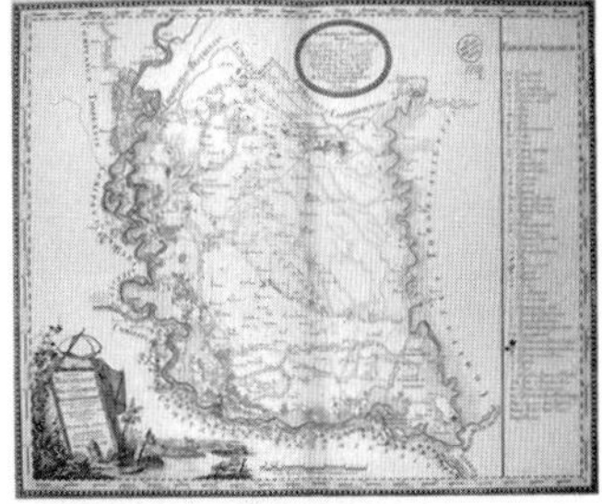

J. M. von Lichternstern, *Comitatus Bacsiensis*, a map of Hungary, uncoloured, Vienna, 1793, 22½ x 18½in (57 x 47cm).
£415–460 JOP
This is a very unusual thematic map of the once Hungarian region of Bacs, the area between the Danube and the Theis rivers, with Stadt Maria Theresiopolis – modern Subotica – prominent. An extensive key identifies a variety of features, including the economic activities of the region.

Great Britain & Ireland

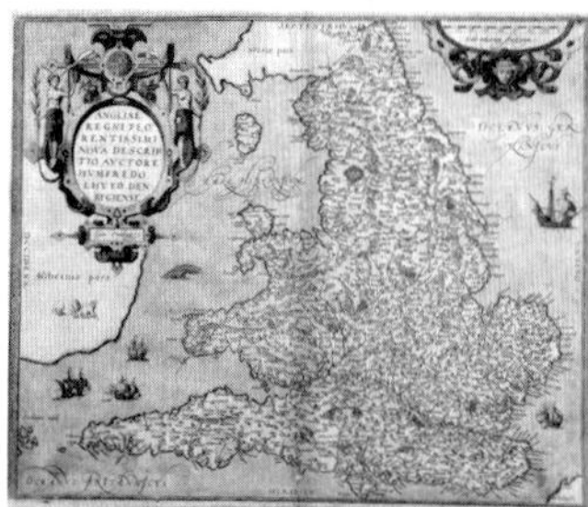

Humphrey Lluyd, *Angliae Regni Florentissimi Nova Descriptio*, a double-page map of England and Wales, early hand colouring, some damage and repair, 1573, 15 x 18½in (38 x 47cm).
£400–500 N
This is the first printed map of England, drawn in 1568 and first published in the 1573 supplement to Abraham Ortelius' *Theatrum Orbis Terrarum*.

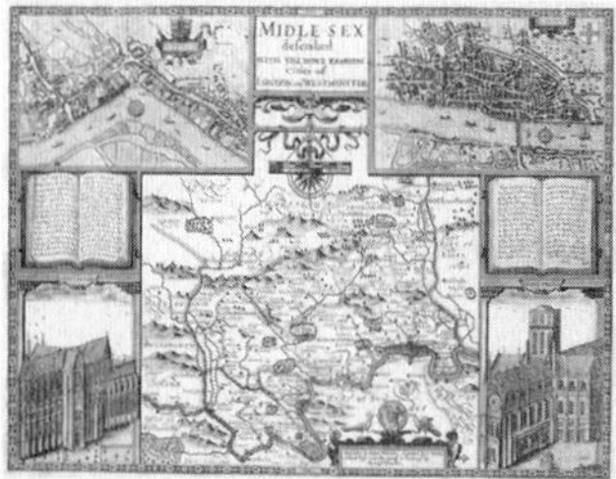

John Speed, *Midle-Sex Described, with the most famous Cities of London and Westminster*, hand-coloured, double-page map, inset with bird's-eye views of London and Westminster, and elevations of St Paul's and St Peter's, printed by George Humble, 1610 but later, 15 x 20in (38 x 51cm).
£700–850 Bon

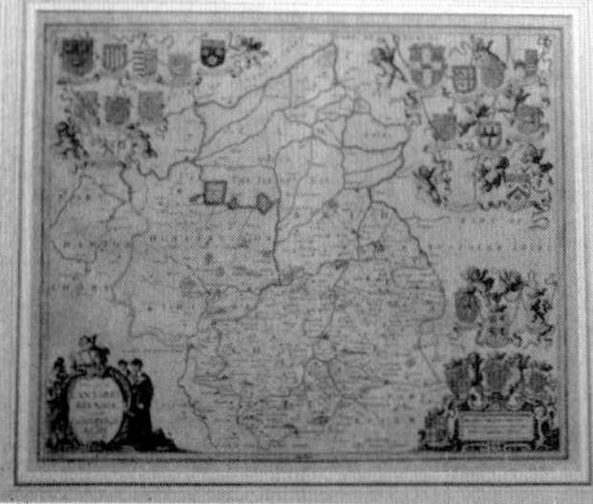

Joannes Jansson, *Cantabri Giensis*, a map of Cambridgeshire, c1645, 16 x 21in (40.5 x 53.5cm).
£550–600 MAG

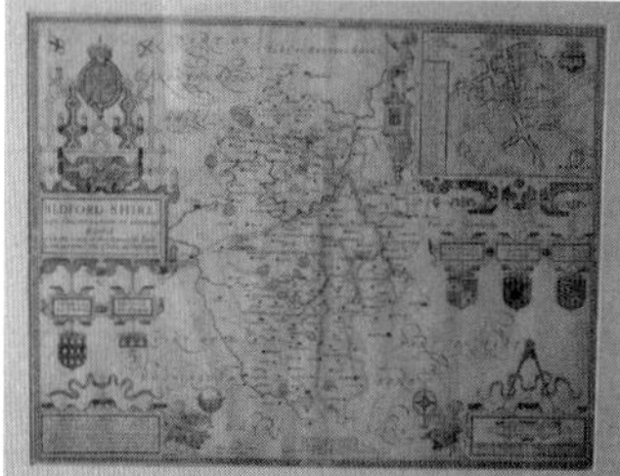

John Speed, *Bedford Shire*, a hand-coloured map, Henry Overton edition, 1713, 20 x 16in (51 x 40.5cm).
£600–675 MCC

Christopher Saxton, a double-page engraved map of Lincolnshire, with original hand colour, the royal arms heightened with gold, 1579, 16 x 21in (40.5 x 53.5cm).
£2,000–2,400 Bon

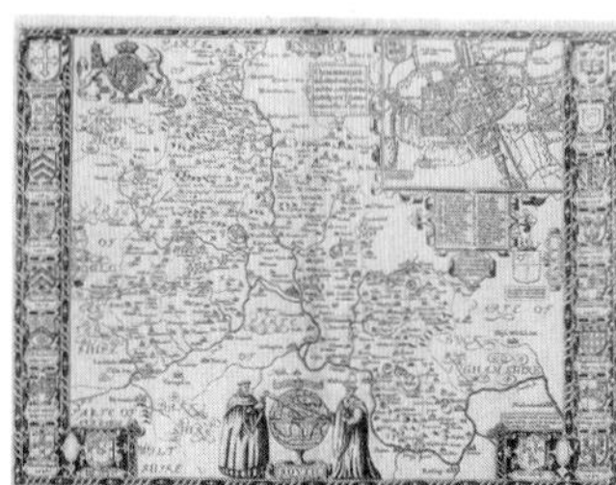

John Speed, *Oxfordshire Described, with ye Citie and the Armes of the Colledges of ye famous University*, engraved map, trimmed close at sides, printed by Sudbury & Humble, 1611, 15¼ x 20¾in (38.5 x 52.5cm).
£1,000–1,200 BBA

Joannes Jansson, a map of Northamptonshire, 1646, 22 x 17in (56 x 43cm).
£420–465 MCC

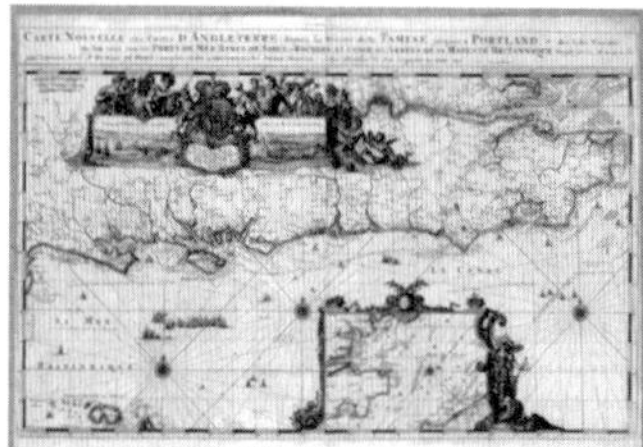

R. de Hooghe/P. Mortier, *Carte Nouvelle des Costes d'Angleterre*, a chart of the coast of southeast England, with original outline colour, Amsterdam, 1693, 37½ x 19¾in (95.5 x 50.cm).
£2,000–2,200 JOP

▶ **Emanuel Bowen,** a map of Northamptonshire, hand-coloured, 1753, 22 x 29in (56 x 73.5cm).
£380–420 MCC

Humphrey Lhuyd/J. Hondius, *Cambriae*, a map of Wales, copperplate, with original outline colour, engraved by Pieter van den Keere for Jodocus Hondius' editions of Mercator's *Atlas*, Amsterdam, 1607–23, 19½ x 13¾in (49.5 x 35cm).
£600–680 JOP
Lhuyd, antiquary and philosopher, is regarded as the first Welsh cartographer and his map of Wales as the first of the country.

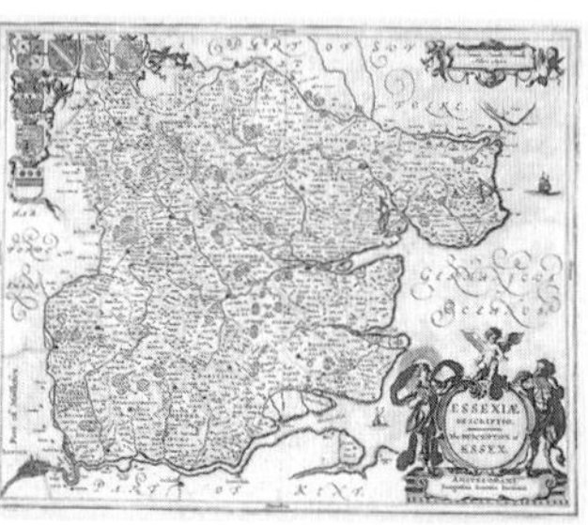

Joannes Jansson, *The Description of Essex*, hand-coloured engraved map, French text to verso, small repair, 1640s, 15½ x 19¼in (39.5 x 49cm).
£140–175 DW

T. Danckerts, *Angliae*, a map of the British Isles, 1690, 19 x 23in (48.5 x 23cm).
£550–600 MAG

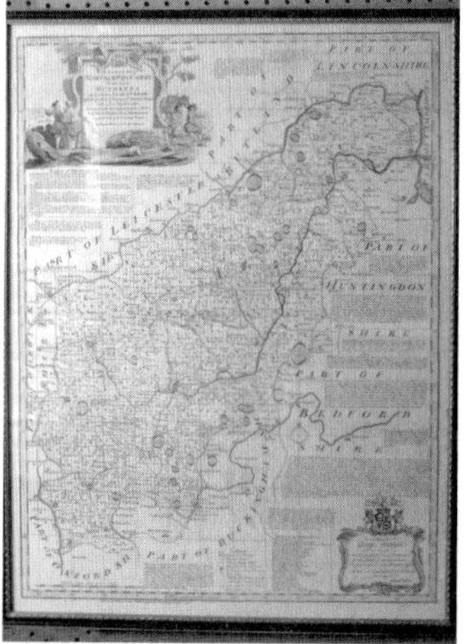

◀ **Johann Baptist Homan,** a map of Ireland, hand coloured and engraved, c1730, 23¼ x 19¼in (59 x 49cm).
£300–400 DW

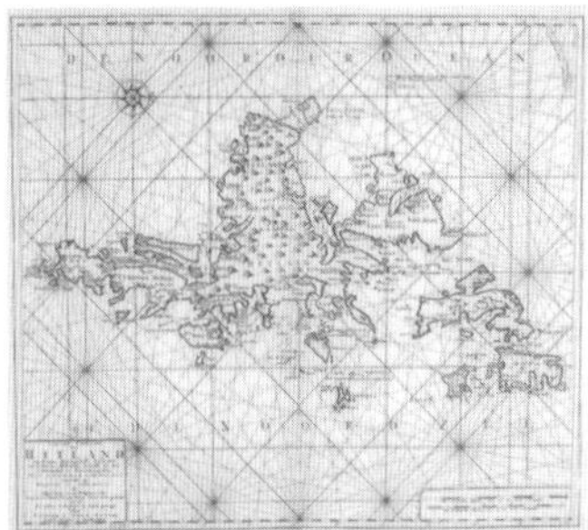

Reiner and Joshua Ottens, a map of the Shetland Islands, a hand-coloured engraved map, rhumb lines and compass rose, text to verso in Dutch, Amsterdam, c1730, 19 x 22½in (48.5 x 57cm).
£280–350 DW

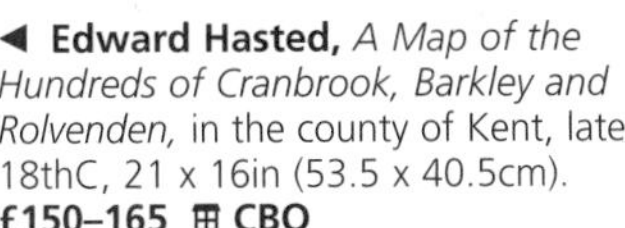

◀ **Edward Hasted,** *A Map of the Hundreds of Cranbrook, Barkley and Rolvenden,* in the county of Kent, late 18thC, 21 x 16in (53.5 x 40.5cm).
£150–165 CBO

▶ **William Camden,** *Britannia*, three vols, edited by Richard Gough, with 97 plates and 56 maps, mostly folding, uncut in original boards, 1789, 2°.
£2,000–2,200 BBA

Emanuel & Thomas Bowen, a map of Oxfordshire, 1777, 19 x 13in (48.5 x 33cm).
£225–250 MAG

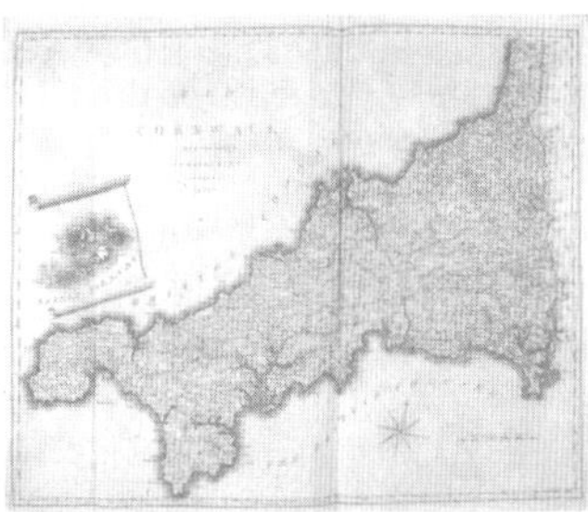

Town & City Plans

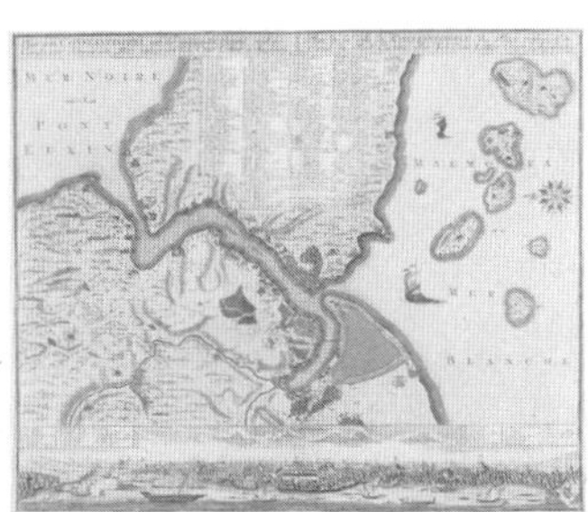

T. C. Lotter, *Plan von Constantinople*, double-page engraved map with panorama of the city below, map hand-coloured, panorama plain, Augsburg, 1735, 19 x 21¼in (48.5 x 54cm).
£1,100–1,300 S

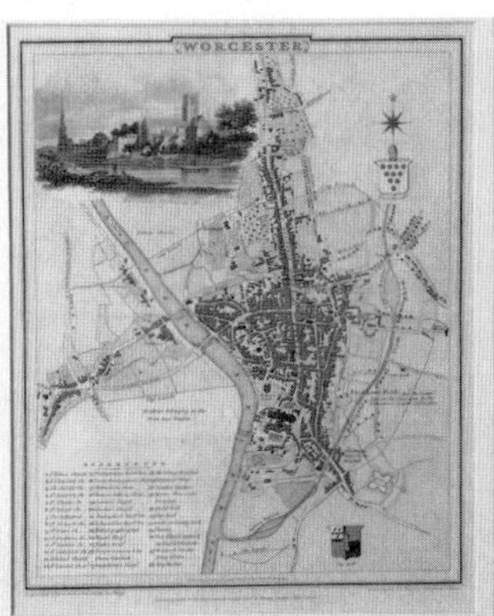

Cole & Roper, *Worcester*, a town plan, 1808, 10 x 8in (25.5 x 20.5cm).
£80–90 MAG

Lodovico Ughi, a folding engraved plan of Venice, letterpress key printed from a separate plate pasted below, original outline colour, laid on canvas, evidence of waterstaining to upper border, Luigi Lurlanetto, Venice, 1787, 24½ x 25¾in (62.5 x 68cm).
£1,100–1,200 S

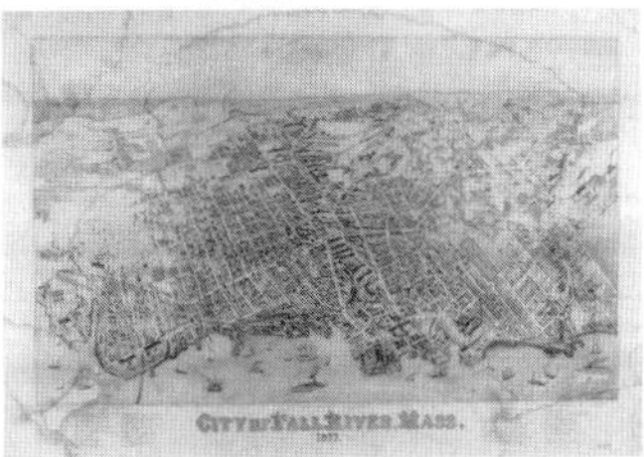

C. H. Vogt, *City of Fall River, Mass*, lithograph with hand colouring on paper, published by O. H. Bailey and J. C. Hazen, 1877, 28¾ x 45½in (73 x 115.5cm).
£320–380 SK(B)

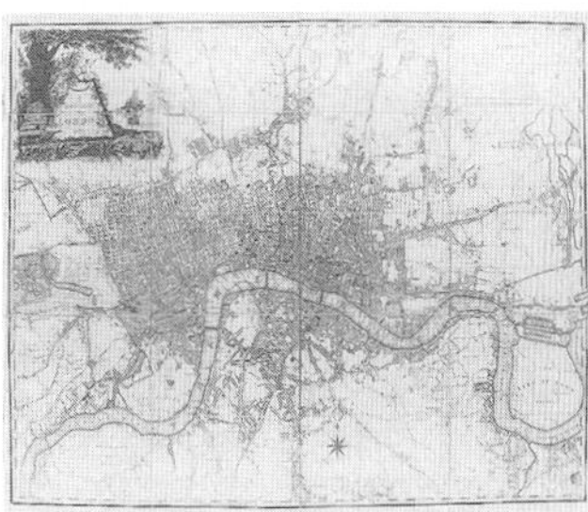

A New Map of London, including the Wet-Docks, and the Villages Round London, a hand-coloured engraved map, third edition, sectionalized on linen, with original card slipcase, published by Laurie & Whittle, 1805, 23¾ x 31¼in (58 x 79.5cm).
£370–470 DW

Winnipeg, Canada, a lithographed bird's-eye view/plan of Winnipeg, surrounded by 23 vignette views, including a prospect of the city in 1871, apparently laid down, Mortimer & Co for W. G. Fonseca, Ottawa, 1884, 30½ x 40¼in (77.5 x 102cm), framed and glazed.
£600–700 S

Dolls
Selected Makers

An Alexander Doll Co hard plastic Cinderella doll, with blue lashed eyes and blonde hair, wearing a blue satin ball gown, stockings and carrying glass slippers, American, c1950, 18in (45.5cm) high.
£220–250 SK(B)

An Allwin felt and velvet Dutch boy doll, wearing a blue top and orange trousers, with label to left foot, 1930s, 18in (45.5cm) high.
£225–250 Beb

A C. M. Bergmann bisque-headed doll, with weighted blue eyes, original wig and jointed composition body, German, c1910, 26in (66cm) high.
£450–550 BaN

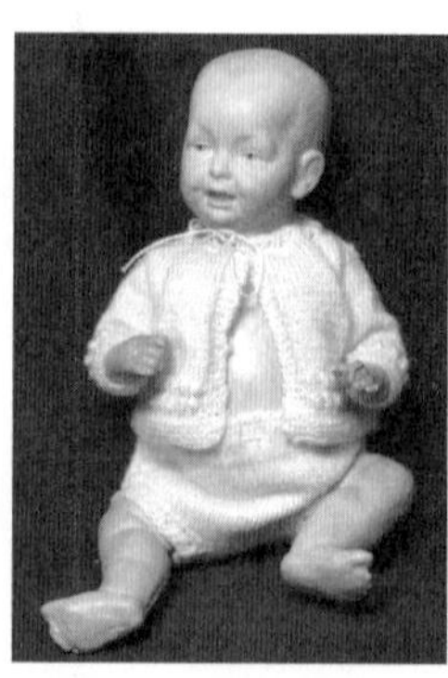

A Fritz Bierschenk bisque-headed character baby doll, with painted blue eyes and a five-piece composition body, German, c1915, 11in (28cm) high.
£300–350 BaN

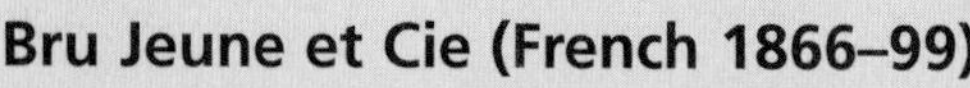

Bru Jeune et Cie (French 1866–99)

Bru Jeune et Cie was founded in Paris in 1866 by Léon Casimir Bru and until 1883 made bisque-headed fashion dolls with heads supplied by the Barrois company. Bru, Jumeau's chief competitor, was famed for the quality and innovative designs of his dolls. In 1877, the firm was dissolved but reformed under the name Bru Jeune and in 1883 it was sold to Henri Chevrot. From 1883 the company produced only *bébés*, most of which were expensive, luxury items that won numerous awards.

Paul Eugène Girard, a friend of Chevrot, took over the factory in 1889 and due to competition from German companies he began producing novel and less expensive products. He also introduced the first open-mouthed doll, a talking *bébé* and dolls that breathed and blew kisses. Despite his innovations, the business did not improve and in 1899 it amalgamated with the Société Français de Fabrication de Bébés et Jouets, an association of leading French doll manufacturers formed to challenge the threat from German competition.

Early Bru dolls were sometimes marked 'Déposé', 'BJ' and/or 'Bru Jne & Cie', and a rare type made from 1879 to 1894 has a circle and dot mark on the back of the head. Later dolls may be inscribed with a letter (A – M) which relates to the doll's size. A new type introduced by Girard was marked 'Bru Jne R'.

A Bru Jeune bisque-headed smiler doll, with blue-lined paperweight eyes and blonde mohair wig, kid body, wearing a white cotton dress with blue ribbon trim, impressed 'C' on head and right shoulder, French, c1870, 13in (33cm) high
£2,500–2,750 SK(B)

A Bru Jeune walking, talking, kiss-throwing bisque-headed doll, with weighted brown glass eyes, blonde wig and composition body, pull-string cord activating the right arm, with incised 'R', French, c1890, 21in (53.3cm) high, with a leatherette-covered trunk containing dolls clothes.
£2,000–2,400 S(S)

Cross Reference
See Colour Review (page 732)

► **A character doll,** possibly Chad Valley, with painted eyes and original clothing, c1930, 19in (48.5cm) high.
£150–200 WilP

◄ **A Chad Valley 'Happy' dwarf doll,** the felt face with painted features and white beard, original blue and yellow costume, c1935, 9½in (24cm) high.
£100–125 VEC

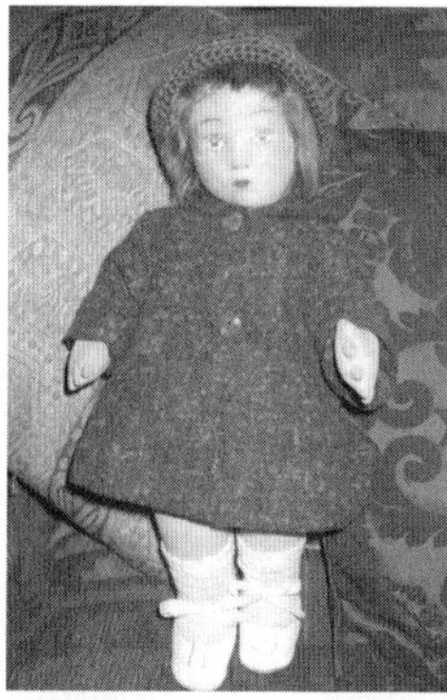

A felt doll, probably Deans, wearing original coat, c1930, 17in (43cm) high.
£225–250 Beb

A Helen Jenson Gladdie character doll, the biscoloid head with open/closed mouth, two teeth and glass eyes, the cloth body with composition arms and legs, wearing original clothes, c1929, 16½in (42cm) high.
£1,000–1,100 DOL

The Gladdie doll was designed c1928 by the American Helen Jensen and manufactured by the German company Borgfeldt, who called it Happy Ann even though it was dressed either as a girl or a boy. It was made in various sizes, the largest being 24in (61cm) high.

A Jumeau bisque-headed *bébé* doll, with composition body and original blue silk dress, French, c1885, 22½in (57cm) high.
£2,250–2,500 Beb

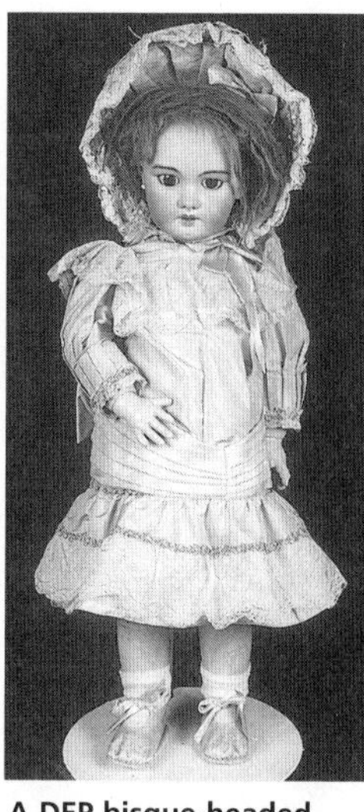

A DEP bisque-headed doll, with a composition body, made for the French market, German, c1890, 27in (68.5cm) high.
£800–875 PSA

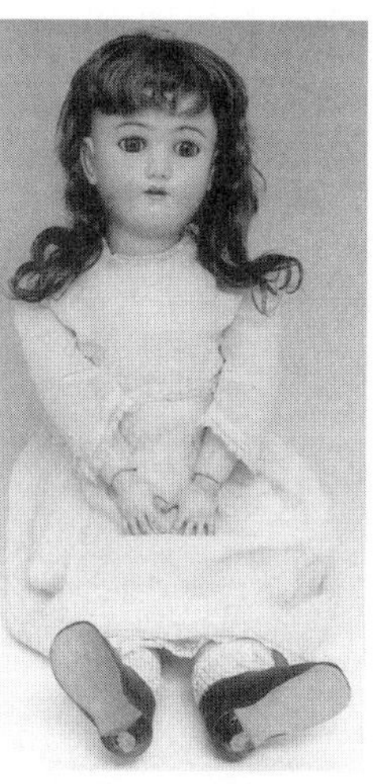

A Heinrich Handwerck bisque-headed doll, with weighted blue glass eyes and brown mohair wig, ball-jointed composition body, wearing a lace panelled dress and undergarments, impressed mark, German, c1910, 26in (66cm) high.
£350–400 B(WM)

A Cuno and Otto Dressel doll, with fixed glass eyes, inserted hair, cloth body and wax lower arms and legs, stamped maker's mark, German, c1875, 31½in (80cm) high.
£1,200–1,400 BaN

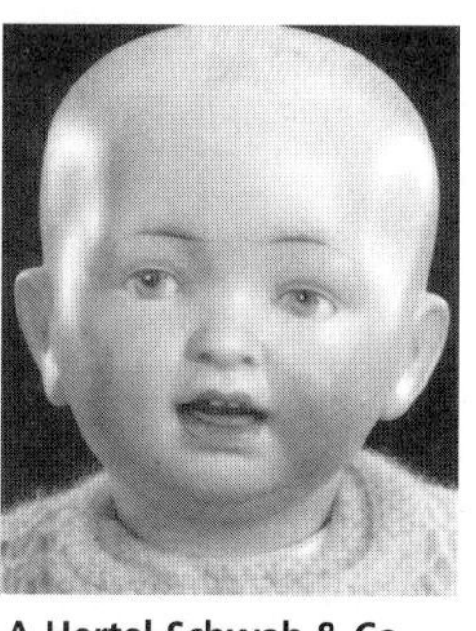

A Hertel Schwab & Co bisque-headed character doll, with painted blue eyes, brush-stroke head and curved limb composition body, impressed '3 151', German, c1912, 11½in (29cm) high.
£230–285 S(S)

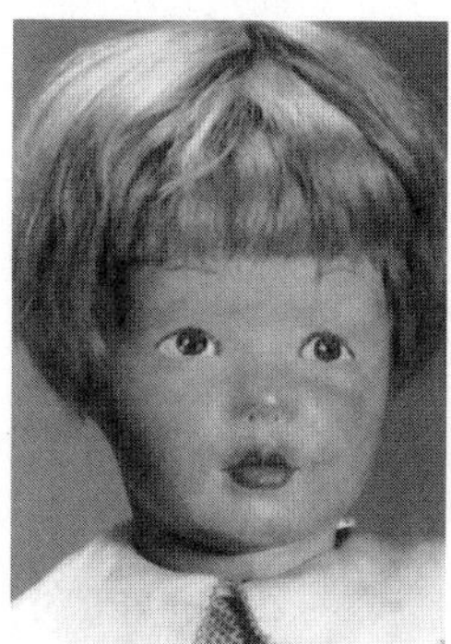

A Kamkins cloth doll, with painted blue eyes, a blonde mohair wig and wearing a red and white printed cotton dress and black and white shoes, stamped, American, early 20thC, 19in (48.5cm) high.
£730–850 SK(B)

◄ **A Jumeau *bébé* doll,** size seven, wearing a white dress and drawers, French, c1890, 18in (45.5cm) high.
£1,500–1,700 Beb

An Ideal Shirley Temple composite doll, with sleeping eyes and applied wig, wearing original costume, c1935, 20½in (52cm) high.
£170–220 WilP

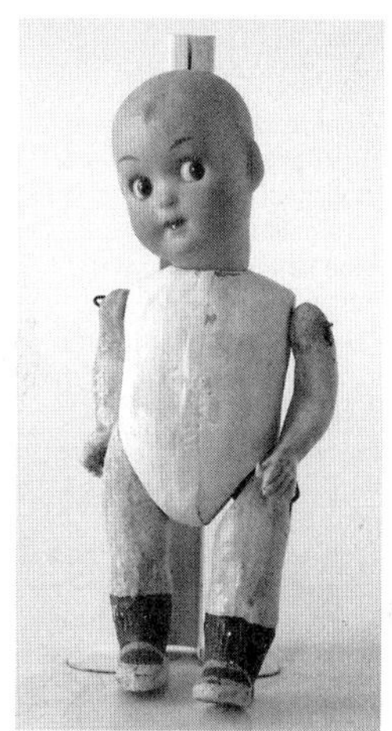

A Gebrüder Heubach bisque-headed doll, with brown eyes, five-piece composition body and painted socks and shoes, impressed mark '6 OD 95-94-30', German, 6¾in (17cm) high.
£120–150 G(B)

A Kämmer & Reinhardt/ Simon & Halbig bisque-headed doll, with weighted blue glass eyes, blonde mohair wig and ball-jointed composition body, wearing some original costume, impressed '76' and 'W' on forehead, German, c1898, 30in (76cm) high, in original cardboard box with extra clothes and accessories.
£1,000–1,200 S(S)

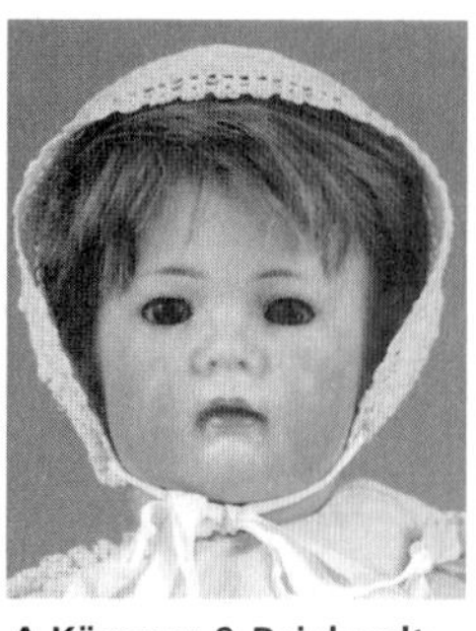

A Kämmer & Reinhardt bisque-headed doll, No. 115A, with weighted brown glass eyes and short brown wig, wood and composition baby body, wearing a pink dress and bonnet, body incorrect, German, c1908, 14in (35.5cm) high.
£650–750 ⚒ Bon(C)

A bisque-headed googly character doll, possibly Kestner, style 217, with glass eyes and five-piece toddler body, German, c1910, 7in (18cm) high.
£750–850 ⊞ Beb

Character dolls with round or googly eyes and impish expressions are known as googlies. They first came to the market c1911 and were produced for over 20 years by various German factories.

Miller's is a price GUIDE not a price LIST

An Armand Marseille bisque shoulder-headed doll, mould 370, with original wig, kid body and bisque lower arms, German, c1900, 19in (48.5cm) high.
£300–350 ⊞ BaN

A Käthe Kruse doll, 'Kathleen' doll VIII 161, with hazel eyes, blonde wig and disc-joined cloth body, wearing original red print cotton dress, white lawn pinafore and white socks and shoes, German, c1950, 20in (51cm) high.
£730–800 ⚒ SK(B)

A Kestner character baby doll, with flirty eyes, wearing white clothes and bonnet, German, 1915–20, 17in (43cm) high.
£900–1,000 ⊞ Beb

An Armand Marseille bisque-headed straight-leg walker doll, mould 390, with original wig and composition body, German, c1900, 23¼in (59cm) high.
£300–350 ⊞ BaN

► **A Kestner bisque-headed doll,** with blue sleeping eyes, blonde mohair wig and fully articulated composition and wood body, wearing a blue striped woven cotton dress and brown shoes, impressed '143', German, early 20thC, 21in (53.5cm) high.
£950–1,150 ⚒ SK(B)

A Kestner bisque-headed child doll, mould 171, German, c1890, 19in (48.5cm) high.
£750–875 ⊞ Beb

A Charles Marcoux character child doll, French, c1900, 13in (33cm) high.
£1,100–1,200 ⊞ Beb

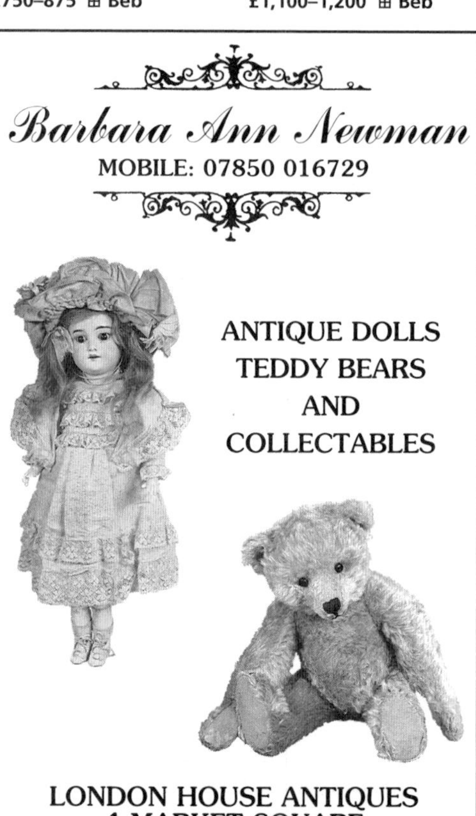

DOLLS

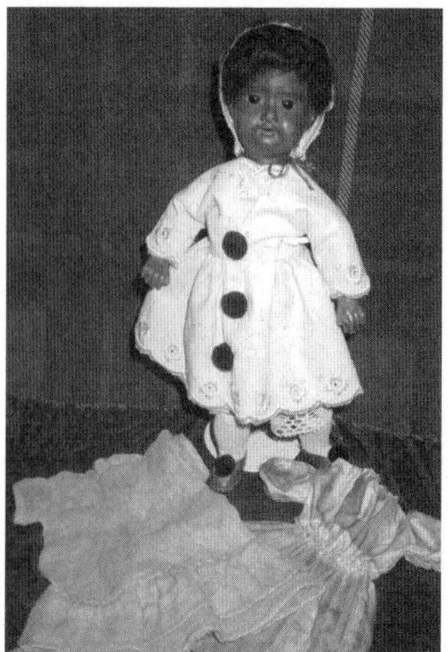

An Armand Marseille child doll, mould 390, with three outfits, German, c1910, 13in (33cm) high.
£350–400 ⊞ Beb
Black dolls by Armand Marseille are rarely seen.

An Armand Marseille bisque-headed doll, mould 390, with a composition body, clothes remade, German, c1915, 18in (45.5cm) high.
£270–300 ⊞ PSA

An Armand Marseille solid dome bisque-headed doll, mould 970, with blue sleeping eyes, painted hair and composition body, German, c1922, 9¾in (25cm) high.
£275–325 ⊞ BAN

An Armand Marseille bisque-headed googly doll, mould 323, with weighted blue glass eyes and a composition toddler body, hairline crack to face, German, c1910, 12in (30.5cm) high.
£450–550 ⊞ BaN

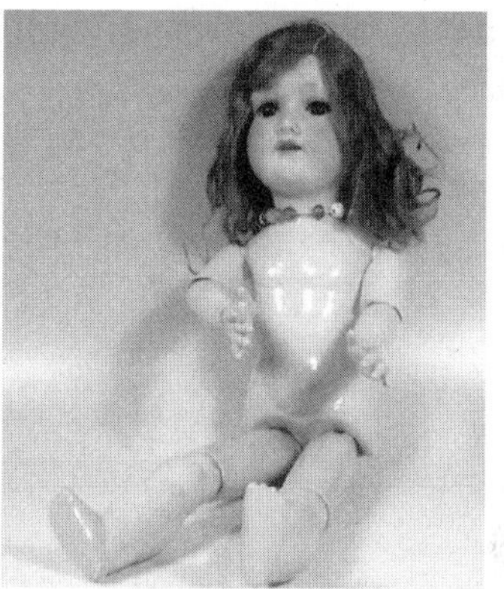

An Armand Marseille bisque-headed doll, mould 390n, with brown sleeping eyes, brown wig, and composition body with jointed wooden limbs, upper legs possibly replaced, German, 1915–20, 20in (51cm) high.
£100–125 ⚒ WW

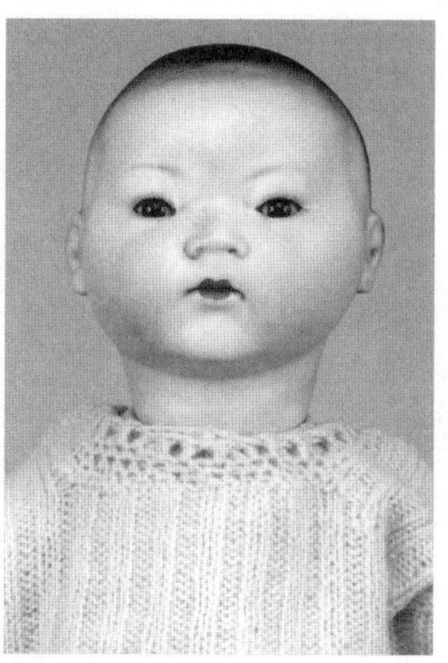

An Armand Marseille bisque-headed Oriental My Dream Baby doll, with weighted brown eyes and curved limb composition body, requires re-stringing, impressed '353/4K', German, c1926, 15¾in (40cm) high.
£600–700 ⚒ VEC

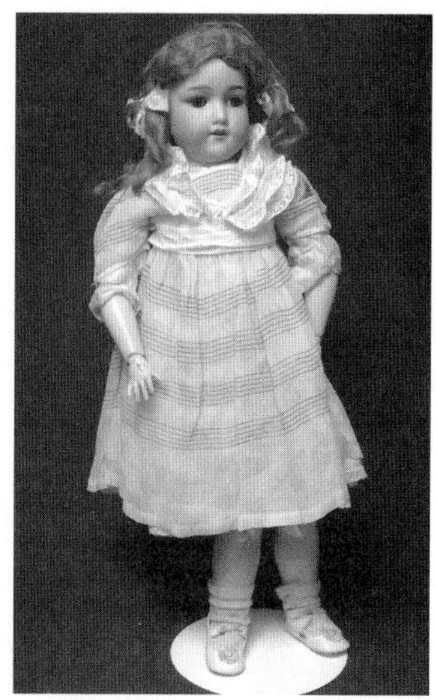

An Armand Marseille bisque-headed doll, mould 390, with original wig and clothes, German, c1910, 24¾in (63cm) high.
£275–325 ⊞ BaN

An Armand Marseille bisque-headed googly doll, with jointed composition body, wearing a white cotton dress, German, c1920, 8in (20.5cm) high.
£550–600 ⊞ PSA

A Mattel Barbie doll, Fashion Queen, No. 870, wearing a gold and cream striped swimsuit and matching head scarf, with a stand and three wigs, American, c1963, 11½in (29cm) high, in original box.
£250–300 ⚒ P(WM)

A Nymphenburg china shoulder-headed doll, with blue painted downcast eyes, and moulded blonde hair, with fabric body to waist, long china hands, wearing original court dress of brown velvet, on a wire cage base, German, 1875–1925, 19in (48.5cm) high.
£950–1,100 ⚒ SK(B)

An S.F.B.J. *bébé* doll, mould 60, with small wooden chair, French, c1900, 14in (35.5cm) high.
£650–750 ⊞ Beb

An S.F.B.J. bisque-headed doll, with blue sleeping eyes and jointed composition body, wearing contemporary clothes, impressed '60 1 1/2', French, early 20thC, 19in (48.5cm) high.
£240–280 ⚒ G(L)

A Schilling shoulder-headed doll, with glass eyes and wax-over-composition body, German, 1875–80, 12in (30.5cm) high.
£350–400 ⊞ Beb

An S.F.B.J. *bébé* doll, mould 60, French, c1900, 13in (33cm) high.
£600–700 ⊞ Beb

A Simon & Halbig bisque-headed child doll, with painted face, mobile eyes and composite jointed body, impressed 'No. 1078', German, c1890, 35in (89cm) high, seated in a bentwood chair.
£1,100–1,400 ⚒ HYD

A Bruno Schmidt bisque-headed character doll, mould Z072, with bent limb composition baby body, c1910, 14in (35.5cm) high.
£1,200–1,400 ⊞ BaN

An S.F.B.J. bisque-headed doll, with weighted blue glass eyes, brown mohair wig and fully jointed composition body, wearing a blue silk dress, bonnet, underclothes and leather shoes, French, c1910, 16in (40.5cm) high.
£220–275 ⚒ Bon(C)

An Schönau & Hoffmeister bisque doll, in a plush bunny suit, attached to working tricycle, pedals when pushed, German, c1930, 10in (25.5cm) high.
£450–500 ⊞ Beb

◄ **An S.F.B.J. bisque-headed doll,** mould 236, with open/closed mouth and a composition baby body, French, c1910, 22¾in (58cm) high.
£1,000–1,200 ⊞ BaN

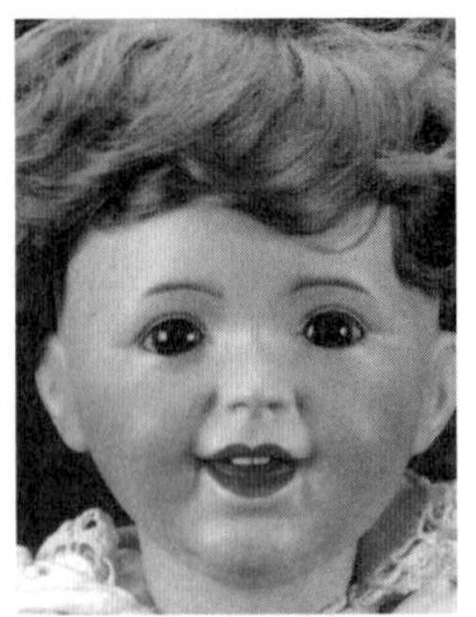

An S.F.B.J. bisque-headed doll, with weighted brown glass eyes and five-piece curved limb composition body, replacement wig, fingers chipped, French, c1910, 26in (66cm) high.
£700–800 ⚒ S(S)

LOCATE THE SOURCE
The source of each illustration in Miller's can be found by checking the code letters below each caption with the Key to Illustrations, pages 794–800.

◄ **A Simon & Halbig Kämmer & Reinhardt bisque-headed doll,** No. 117, with weighted blue glass eyes, real lashes, brown wig and a fully jointed composition flapper body, wearing a brown knitted jumper, tunic and leather shoes, with a blue smock dress, German, c1910, 14in (35.5cm) high.
£550–650 ⚒ Bon(C)

A Simon & Halbig bisque-headed doll, with blue glass sleeping eyes, brown mohair wig and jointed composition limbs and body, wearing a cream broderie anglaise dress and brown leather shoes, marked '1078', German, 1910, 14½in (37cm) high.
£800–1,000 AH

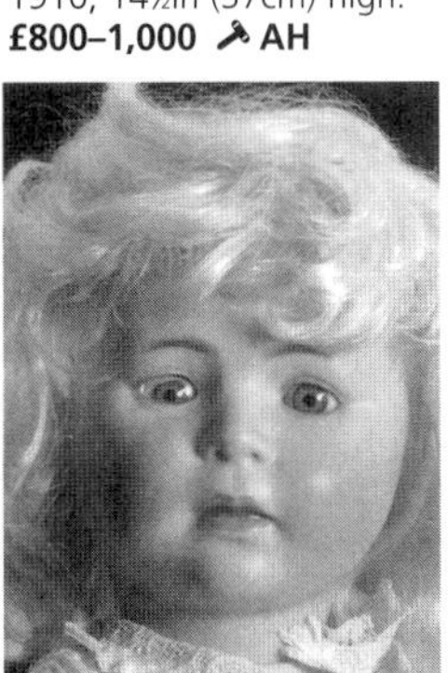

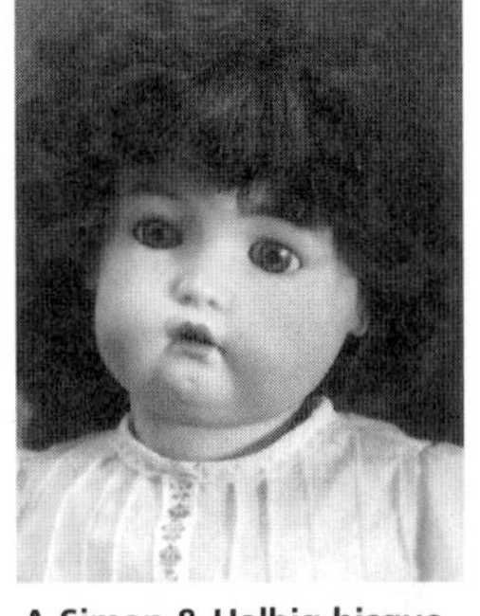

A Simon & Halbig bisque-headed character doll, with blue sleeping eyes, dark brown wig and fully articulated composition body, wearing a pink organdy dress and blue hat, repainting to body, impressed marks '1299', German, early 20thC, 25in (63.5cm) high.
£950–1,200 SK(B)

◄ **A Simon & Halbig bisque-headed character doll,** with weighted blue glass eyes, open/closed mouth, and composition body, wearing a whitework dress, with one additional whitework dress, replacement blonde wig, one finger repaired, impressed mark '1488 15' German, c1920, 21¾in (55.5cm) high.
£2,000–2,200 S(S)

A Simon & Halbig Kämmer & Reinhardt bisque-headed doll, No. 122, with weighted blue glass eyes, blonde wig and fully jointed composition toddler body, wearing a white dress, underclothes, bonnet and shoes, German, c1910, 19in (48.5cm) high, in original box with My Little Darling Kämmer & Reinhardt paper label.
£650–820 Bon(C)

Simon & Halbig made heads for other German makers including Kämmer & Reinhardt, Schmidt and Dressel and some of the best French makers including Jumeau, Roulet and Decamps. These usually carry the marks of both firms.

A Simon & Halbig bisque-headed Oriental doll, with brown sleeping eyes, original black mohair wig and fully articulated composition body, wearing a possibly original mulberry and ivory floral print cotton kimono, one finger reglued, German, early 20thC, 17½in (44.5cm) high.
£1,400–1,700 SK(B)

Simon & Halbig (German c1869–1930)

Simon & Halbig was one of the most prolific German manufacturers of china and bisque shoulder-heads. Early examples had solid domed heads with fixed glass eyes, flat, painted brows and lashes and a closed mouth. They were attached to a gusseted kid or composition body. Later dolls had socket heads with an open crown and cardboard pate, moulded painted brows, real hair lashes and an open mouth. The company also specialized in Oriental and black dolls.

Dolls are often collected according to their mould number which is usually included in the impressed mark SH and a number relating to size on the back of the head or the shoulder plate.

A Sheppard & Co Philadelphia Baby cloth doll, with painted head and shoulders, brown painted eyes, light brown hair and painted lower limbs, wearing a white batiste dress and white cotton undergarments, American, c1900, 21in (53.5cm) high.
£2,200–2,500 SK(B)

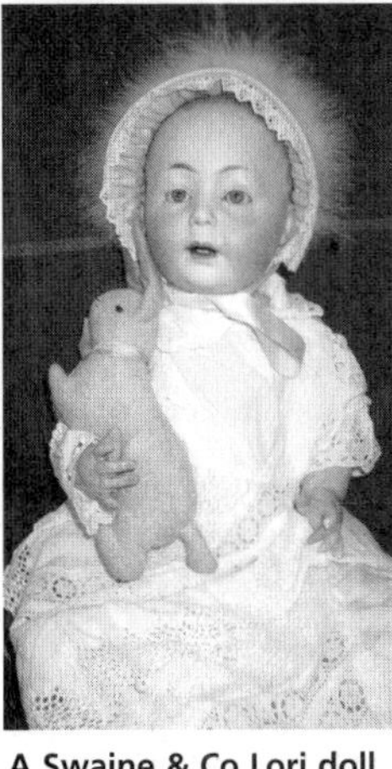

A Swaine & Co Lori doll, with five-piece baby body, extra clothes and toy rabbit, German, c1915, 24in (61cm) high.
£2,250–2,500 Beb

Cross Reference
See Colour Review (page 732)

◄ **A Jules Steiner *bébé* doll,** with fixed blue eyes and five-piece composition body, some fingers missing, damage to toes and heels, requires restringing, impressed 'A7', French, c1889, 15in (38cm) high.
£1,500–2,000 VEC

► **A Jules Steiner bisque-headed *bébé* doll,** with brown paperweight eyes, dark-brown human hair wig over original grey cardboard human pate and fully articulated composition body, wearing a new outfit of silky salmon and lace, impressed 'A7', French, c1890, 14in (35.5cm) high.
£1,700–2,000 SK(B)

Unknown Makers

A wooden doll, the painted face with inset black pupil-less eyes, nailed real hair wig and wood jointed arms, the legs joined at knee and hip, with block feet, wearing a Spitalfields dusky pink brocaded silk robe with quilted red silk underskirt, cotton petticoat, cotton stockings and yellow silk quilted shoes and satin lace-trimmed headdress, c1750, 17in (43cm) high.
£8,000–10,000 Gam
This doll, dating from c1750, was part of a large consignment from a deceased estate that had lain in storage for at least five years. Being of such an early date, wearing a beautiful Spitalfields silk dress which dated from some 20 years earlier, and being moreover fresh to the market, it created great excitement with collectors and dealers and sold for a hammer price of £8,000.

A wooden doll, with enamelled black pupil-less eyes, original nailed real hair wig, squared hips with jointed legs and kid leather arms with separately stitched fingers, wearing a 1830s cream tulle dress over a cotton chemise, one foot restored, one foot repainted, arms not stuffed and reattached to the torso, c1760, 15½in (39.5cm) high.
£1,000–1,200 S(S)

A poured wax shoulded-headed doll, with fixed brown glass eyes, real hair wig and later cloth body with wax lower arms, dressed as an Abbess, fingers missing, mid-19thC, 14½in (37cm) high.
£230–280 S(S)

A Parian doll with moulded snood, with blue painted eyes, moulded blonde hair, cloth body and Parian lower limbs, wearing a brown silk dress, German, c1870, 13½in (43.5cm) high.
£380–450 SK(B)

► **A set of three stone bisque dolls,** probably German, c1890, 5½in (14cm) high.
£200–250 Beb
Stone bisque is a heavy bisque which has a marble-like finish.

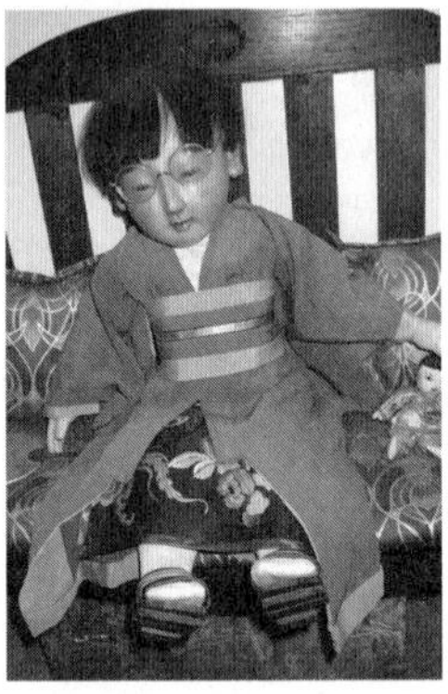

A Japanese gofun-headed girl doll, with floating limbs and wearing original kimono, with spare outfit, c1890, 22in (56cm) high.
£800–900 Beb
Gofun is a Japanese type of composition made from crushed oyster shells.

◄ **A wax-over-papier-mâché doll,** wearing a tartan outfit, c1890, 9in (23cm) high.
£90–100 Beb

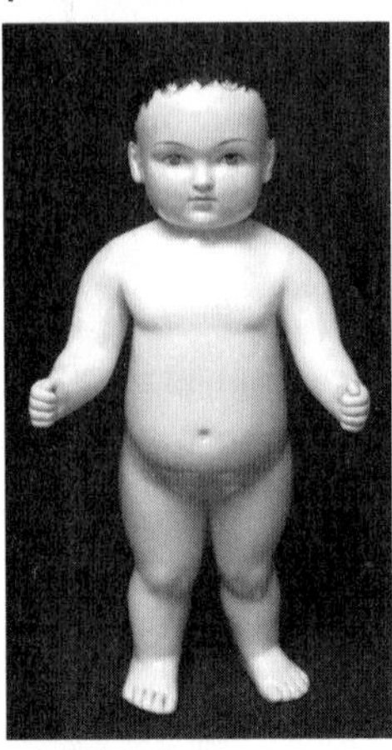

A Frozen Charlotte china doll, with painted brown eyes and moulded black hair, German, c1890, 15in (38cm) high.
£280–350 BaN
The Frozen Charlotte dolls were made by various German manufacturers around the turn of the 19th century.

A pair of Munich art doll-style dolls, a Dutch boy and girl, with composition bodies, c1900, 12in (30.5cm) high.
£280–350 Beb
This type of art doll was first made in Munich c1900.

A bisque shoulder-headed doll, with fixed blue glass eyes, blonde mohair wig, a waisted kid leather body and bisque lower arms, wearing a cream linen gown, possibly German, 1900–10, 11¼in (28.5cm) high, with a painted wooden armoire and a collection of dolls' clothes and effects.
£450–550 P(WM)

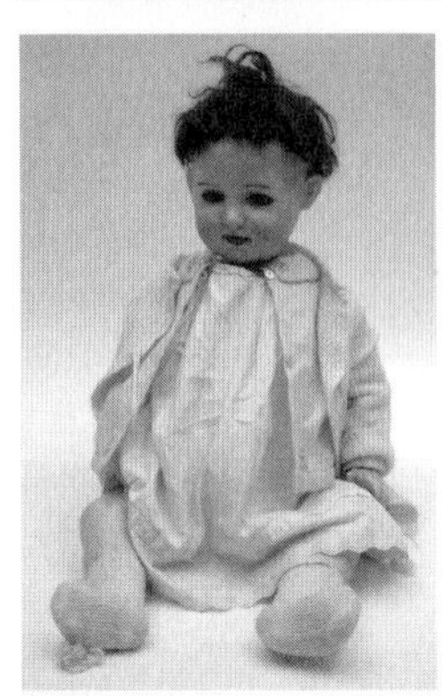

◄ **A bisque-headed character baby doll,** with brown sleeping eyes and a five-piece composition body, marked PT 924.14, German, early 20thC, 26in (66cm) high.
£240–280 G(L)

Dolls' Houses & Accessories

A painted wooden doll's house, early 19thC, 23in (58.5cm) wide.
£380–425 ⊞ PICA

A doll's house, made from a plan published in *Hobbies of Dereham* magazine, 1920s, 32in (81.5cm) wide, with a later garage extension.
£160–200 ⚒ DA

A doll's house, with furniture, labelled 'An O.D. product, made in Scotland', c1950, 15in (38cm) wide.
£90–100 ⊞ Beb

A late Victorian painted wooden doll's house, with a green mock tiled roof and cream-painted opening front, on a green-painted stand, 49½in (125.5cm) wide.
£400–500 ⚒ WW

► A Tri-ang Ultra Modern series Art Deco doll's house, with two storeys, the flat roof with sun deck and removable sun room, the exterior painted cream with green detailing, the integral garage with room over, 1930s, 40in (101.5cm) wide.
£600–700 ⚒ WAL

A Tri-ang Tudor-style doll's house, the single front opening to reveal two rooms with furniture and fittings, with porch/garage, 1950s, 11in (28cm) wide.
£125–160 ⚒ WAL

A painted wooden doll's house, comprising two storeys and an attic, with opening roof and front, early 20thC, 40in (101.5cm) wide.
£600–750 ⚒ AH

A one-room doll's house, with original papered floor and walls, on a green base, French, 1930s, 14in (35.5cm) wide.
£150–180 ⚒ G(L)

A Victorian doll's house doll, with bisque head and shoulder plate and fabric body and limbs, wearing a cotton print dress and sun bonnet with lace cap, 7in (18cm) high.
£220–270 ⚒ LFA

A doll's house cabinet, with chromolithographs of children at play and a boy drummer, 19thC, 4in (10cm) wide.
£200–250 ⚒ DA

A doll's house hall table, with mirror over and chromolithograph to base showing a child with a dog, 19thC, 2½in (6.5cm) wide.
£100–140 ⚒ DA

A doll's house gilt stick-stand, c1880, 3in (7.5cm) high.
£120–135 ⊞ PSA

DOLLS' HOUSES & ACCESSORIES

Teddy Bears

A Chad Valley mohair teddy bear, with glass eyes and Rexine pads, 1940–50s, 19in (48.5cm) high.
£240–280 ⚒ VEC

A Chiltern golden plush teddy bear, with reverse-painted amber and black glass eyes, stitched claws and velvet pads, eyes loose, restored mouth, c1930, 24in (61cm) high.
£420–500 ⚒ B(WM)

A Chiltern teddy bear, with cinnamon nose and velvet pads, c1930, 13in (33cm) high.
£270–300 ⊞ Beb

A Chiltern Hugmee mohair plush teddy bear, with glass eyes, 1930s, 16in (40.5cm) high.
£340–375 ⊞ Beb

Chiltern Toys (1920–67)

The Chiltern Toys works was established in Chesham, Buckinghamshire in 1908 and at first mainly produced wooden toys and fabric dolls with china heads. Their first teddy bear, Master Teddy, appeared in 1915. He had googly eyes, his head and limbs were made of mohair, his body of fabric, and he wore trousers and a jacket. The name Chiltern Toys was officially registered in 1924, the year their Hugmee teddy bears were first introduced. These were particularly successful and continued to be made until 1967, when the company became a subsidiary of Chad Valley.

◄ **A Gabrielle cream plush Paddington Bear,** wearing a blue felt coat, fawn hat and red Dunlop wellington boots, with original tag, 1970s, 20in (51cm) high.
£180–225 ⚒ VEC

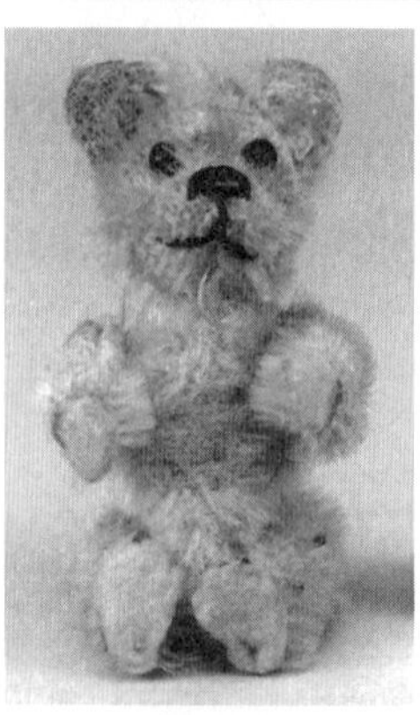

◄ **A Schuco Piccolo beige mohair teddy bear,** with black eyes and cream felt hands and feet, 1930s, 2½in (6.5cm) high.
£120–150 ⚒ VEC

► **A plush teddy bear,** fully jointed, c1900, 23in (58.5cm) high.
£340–425 ⚒ BR

A Merrythought Cheeky art silk teddy bear, with glass eyes, fully jointed, with label, holes in felt pads, 1950s, 11½in (29cm) high.
£270–340 ⚒ VEC

A gold mohair teddy bear, with original black boot button eyes, fully jointed, nose missing, pads replaced, American, c1910, 11in (28cm) high.
£260–320 ⚒ VEC

A pale mohair plush teddy bear, with pink pads, in good condition, c1920, 14in (35.5cm) high.
£500–550 ⊞ Beb

A beige plush teddy bear, with boot button eyes, growler and stitched black nose, mouth and claws, 1900–50, 17in (45.5cm) high.
£100–120 ⚒ WW

► **A fluffy mohair cub teddy bear,** with glass eyes and shortened limbs, c1930, 14in (35.5cm) high.
£320–350 ⊞ Beb

Soft Toys

A Chad Valley cream velvet Bonzo dog, with painted features, stitched nose and claws and Chad Valley button on collar, with spring-coiled legs, one leg restored, 1920s, 12in (30.5cm) long.
£700–800 ⚒ P(WM)

A Merrythought grey velvet Jerry mouse, with stitched eyes, nose and claws, c1940, 9in (23cm) high.
£225–250 ⊞ Beb

A Schuco red mohair monkey perfume bottle, with felt hands and feet, fully jointed, 1920s, 3½in (9cm) high.
£300–375 ⚒ VEC

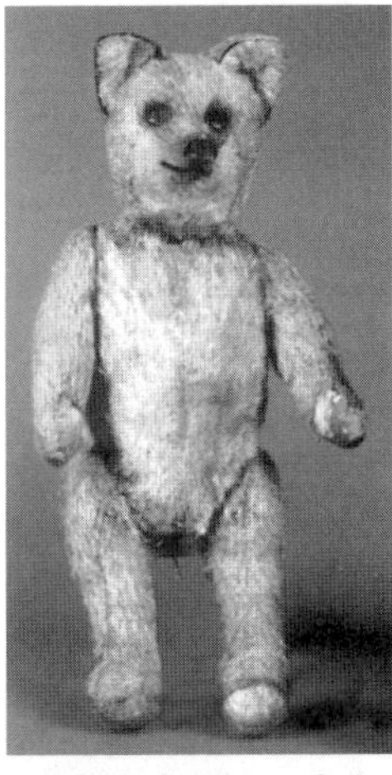

A Schuco brown mohair Yes/No fox, with metal-cased red glass eyes, stitched nose and mouth and straw-filled body, leather paw pads and long tail operating Yes/No head movement, paw pads recovered, German, c1920, 9in (23cm) high.
£170–220 ⚒ Bon(C)

l. A Steiff cinnamon mohair plush monkey, wearing original waistcoat and fez, with ear button, 1920–30, 12in (30.5cm) high.
£440–450
r. A Steiff pale brown mohair plush monkey, with ear button, 1920–30, 15in (38cm) high.
£500–550 ⊞ Beb

A Steiff lamb, in good condition, c1950, 12in (30.5cm) high.
£270–300 ⊞ Beb

A Steiff dachshund, Bazi, with original collar, bell and chest tag, without ear button, c1960, 4in (10cm) high.
£35–45 ⊞ TED

A black and white plush toy dog, probably German, c1920, 20in (51cm) long.
£225–250 ⊞ Beb

A felt Felix the Cat, with glass eyes and stitched black mouth, with wire body and long tail, c1935, 13¾in (35.cm) high.
£240–280 ⚒ VEC

A Pekinese toy dog, 1920s, 12in (30.5cm) high.
£270–300 ⊞ Beb

A felt Mickey Mouse, with boot button eyes, printed face and jointed body, wearing red shorts and yellow shoes, c1930, 8in (20.5cm) high.
£100–125 ⚒ BLH

Toys
Aeroplanes

A Dinky Toys No. 60 aeroplane set, comprising Percival Gull, Cierva Autogiro, DH Leopard Moth, Imperial Airways liner, low-wing monoplane and General Monospar, 1930s, in original display box with instructions.
£1,200–1,500 WAL

A Dinky Supertoys No. 701 Shetland Flying Boat, painted silver with black propellers, 1947–49, with original box.
£420–525 VEC

A Tippco clockwork high-wing single engine monoplane, with four dropping bombs suspended under the wings, lithographed in grey with black/brown detailing, German, late 1930s, 10in (25.5cm) wide.
£550–650 B(WM)

Boats

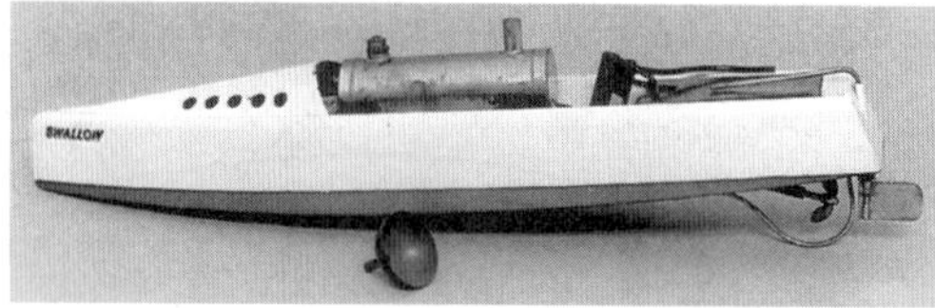

A Bowman live steam speedboat, *Swallow,* painted in cream and red, c1930, 20in (51cm) wide, in original wooden box.
£260–325 B(WM)

A Dent cast-iron paddle-wheeler, *Adirondack*, finished in white with yellow top, with articulated rocker arm that moves up and down as toy is pulled forward, wear, American, c1905, 15in (38cm) wide.
£1,250–1,500 S(NY)

A Trix tinplate clockwork two-funnel liner, *Windsor Castle*, with a red and grey hull and beige and yellow superstructure, 1930–40, 17¾in (45cm) wide.
£180–225 VEC

► **A wooden boat and tender,** *The Scotland*, by Claude Lovat Fraser for the author Naomi Mitchison, with four wooden sailors and cargo, c1910, boat 23in (58.5cm) long.
£630–700 Beb

Mechanical Toys

◄ **A Daiya tinplate battery-operated Space Conqueror robot,** finished in blue with yellow battery pack, rotating antennae missing, Japanese, mid-1950s, 16in (40.5cm) high.
£370–470 VEC

► **A Fernand Martin clockwork violin-playing figure,** with painted tin face, marked, replacement jacket, French, c1900, 7in (18cm) high.
£250–320 AH

A clockwork bisque-headed musical dancer, Giselle, French, 1890, 11in (28cm) high.
£1,100–1,200 AUTO

A musical automaton of a rabbit in a cabbage, by Roullet & Decamps, French, c1895, 7in (18cm) high.
£2,250–2,500 ⊞ KHW

An automaton of a jumping tiger, probably by Decamps, skin-covered with simulated stripes, with yellow and black glass eyes, the clockwork mechanism causing it to shake its head, crouch and spring, French, early 20thC, 15¾in (40cm) long.
£450–550 ⚒ Bea(E)

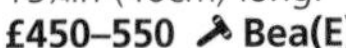

A T. N. clockwork Ko Ko the Sandwich Man, Japanese, c1960, 8in (20.5cm) high.
£160–175 ⊞ GTM

TOYS

A Webb's patent Jubilee Dancer, with articulated wood figure and spring motor, 1870s, 10in (25.5cm) high on a walnut base.
£850–1,000 ⚒ SK(B)

◄ **An automaton of a country gentleman,** his head moving from side to side and his right arm up and down, needing restoration, French, 19thC, 15½in (39.5cm) high.
£160–200 ⚒ FHF

► **A mechanical papier mâché nodding clown,** with fixed blue glass eyes, painted smile and green, red and blue face paint, orange curly wig and composition lower arms, wearing a red and white costume and green felt pointed hat, with original key, two fingers damaged, probably French, late 19thC, 24in (61cm) high.
£700–800 ⚒ Bon(C)

Money Boxes

◄ **A Creedmore metal money box,** modelled as a soldier firing the coin towards a tree stump, late 19thC, 10in (25.5cm) wide.
£300–360 ⚒ G(L)

A Victorian painted wood money box, modelled as a house with red brickwork, 11in (28cm) wide.
£1,300–1,600 ⚒ HYD

◄ **An iron bear money box,** 19thC, 6in (15cm) high.
£50–60 ⚒ SWO

Noah's Arks

A straw-work Noah's Ark, with sliding door revealing a collection of carved wood animals, French, 19thC, 14in (35.5cm) wide.
£900–1,100 ⚒ S(S)

A painted wooden Noah's Ark, the sliding side panel revealing a quantity of carved and painted wooden animals, late 19thC.
£700–875 ⚒ LFA

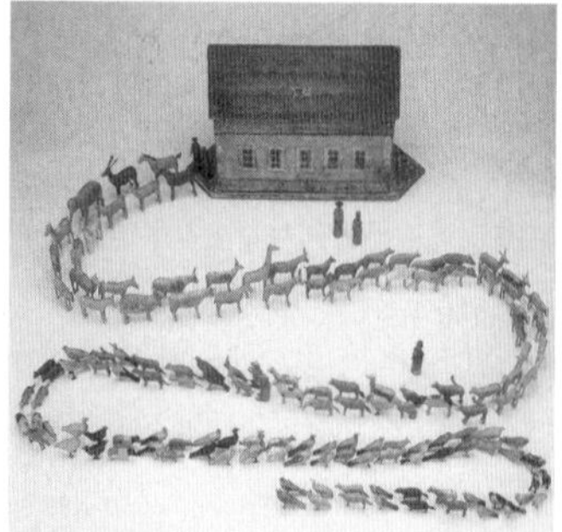

A hand-painted Noah's Ark, with animals and figures, German, c1860, 15in (38cm) wide.
£2,250–2,500 ⊞ RYA

Rocking Horses

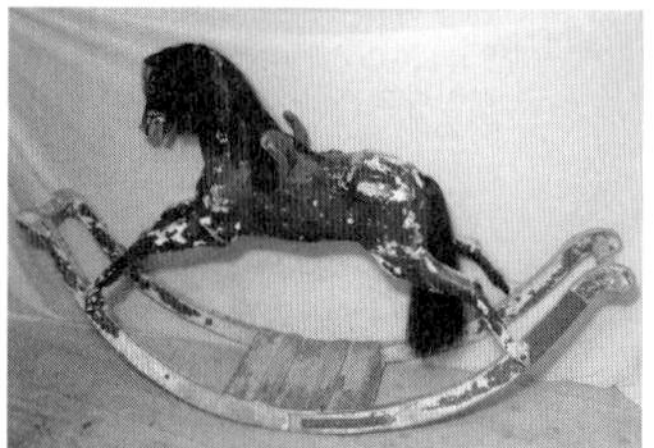

A wooden rocking horse, in need of restoration, c1820, 45¾in (116cm) high.
£4,500–5,000 ⊞ AQ

A Victorian dapple grey rocking horse, with leather tack, on traditional rocker base, 87in (221cm) long.
£1,000–1,250 ⚒ G(L)

A black and white rocking horse, with grey mane and tail and leather saddle and bridle, on slatted pine rockers, 19thC, 76in (193cm) long.
£400–500 ⚒ E

Cross Reference
See Colour Review (page 735)

◄ **A Lines rocking horse,** painted dapple grey with pale blue saddle cloth, on a safety stand, restored, c1900, 36in (91.5cm) high.
£2,300–3,100 ⊞ RGa

► **A Lines rocking horse,** painted dapple grey with blue saddle cloth, on a safety stand, restored, early 20thC, 38 in (96.5cm) long.
£2,000–3,100 ⊞ RGa

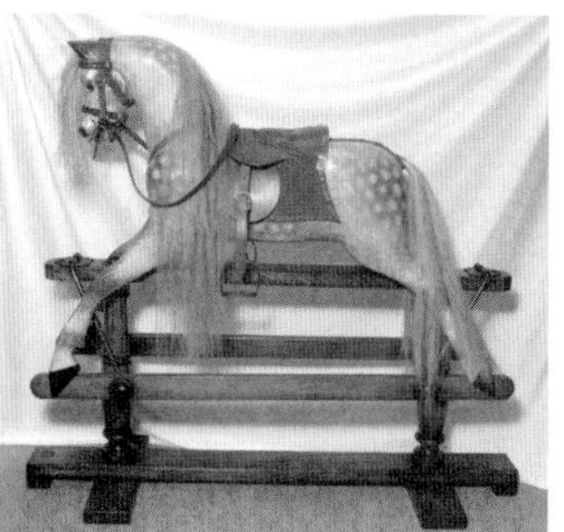

◄ **A Lines rocking horse,** painted dapple grey with red saddle cloth, on a safety stand, restored, c1920, 37in (94cm) long.
£3,200–3,500 ⊞ RGa

Soldiers & Accessories

◄ **A Britains set of 12 Lancers,** set No. 8, with four Lancers and Officer in blue jackets with red plumes, on 'pony' horses, one Lancer's arm and one sword missing, c1897.
£270–300 S(S)

A Britains French Infantry open supply wagon, with two horses, driver wearing blue uniform with red trousers, two seated orderlies and grey four-wheel wagon, dated 14.3.06.
£500–650 VEC

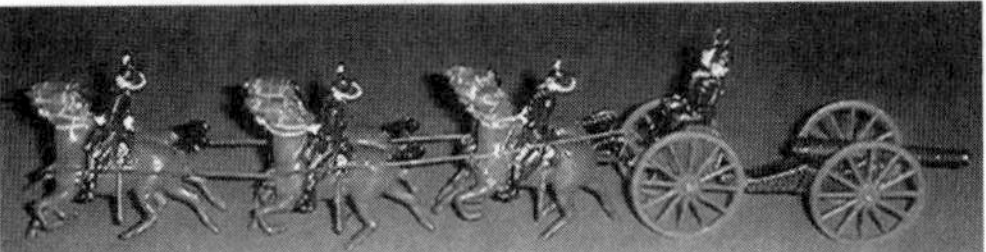

A Crescent Toys hollow-cast lead Royal Horse Artillery group, comprising six horses, three with riders and two loose figures seated on a gun carriage, hand-painted, 1930s–40s, 14½in (37cm) long with original box.
£170–220 PFK

A Tipp & Co/Elastolin tinplate and composition camouflage half-track vehicle, with nine composition storm troopers, towing a searchlight, late 1930s, 17in (43cm) long.
£520–650 P(WM)

◄ **An M & C tinplate coastal/naval gun,** with revolving gantry and steps, German, c1905, 7½in (19cm) high.
£400–500 IM

A set of Cycle Corps figures, possibly by Hanks Bros of London, comprising five khaki troops with bicycles, one lower leg detached, one bicycle missing, c1916, in original box.
£380–475 S(S)

Trains

A Bing gauge I LMS brake/corridor coach, late 1920s.
£340–425 B(WM)

A Bing for Basset-Lowke gauge I clockwork 4–4–0 LNWR precursor 513, with tender, repainted, c1930.
£500–600 B(WM)

The German toy train manufacturer Gebrüder Bing supplied the British company Bassett-Lowke with trains for sale through its retail outfit in London and its mail-order catalogue from c1900 until Bing's closure in 1933.

A Bing gauge I live steam spirit-fired 4–4–0 County of Northampton locomotive, RN 3410, with tender, finished in green, maroon and black Great Western livery, 1930s, 25in (63.5cm) long.
£550–650 WAL

An Exley LMR wagon, c1938, 17in (43cm) long, with original box.
£350–400 ⊞ HOB

► **A J. Falk live steam stork leg locomotive,** hand-enamelled in green livery with pale green and cream lining, with tender, German, c1910–20, 11¾in (30cm), over buffers.
£350–450 S(S)

TOYS

A Fleischmann metal-bodied locomotive, finished in red, German, 1955, 9in (23cm) long.
£65–75 ⊞ VJ

A Hornby No. 2 Pullman coach, finished in dark brown and cream livery, with detachable roof and brass buffers, mid–1920s, boxed.
£70–90 ⚒ WAL

A Hornby clockwork Metropolitan train set, consisting of locomotive, first coach, brake/third coach and track, late 1920s, in original box.
£330–420 ⚒ B(WM)

► **A Hornby gauge 0 McAlpine & Sons rotary tipping wagon,** c1925, 6in (15cm) long, boxed.
£70–80 ⊞ GTM

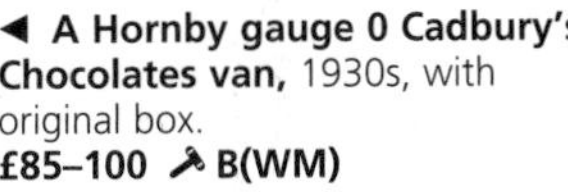

A Hornby gauge 0 No. 0 milk traffic van, c1930, 6in (15cm) long, with original red box.
£70–80 ⊞ GTM

◄ **A Hornby gauge 0 Cadbury's Chocolates van,** 1930s, with original box.
£85–100 ⚒ B(WM)

► **A Hornby gauge 0 Southern Railways gun powder van,** 1935, 7in (18cm) long.
£400–500 ⊞ HOB

A Hornby gauge 0 BP motor spirit tanker, c1920, 6in (15cm) long, with original red box.
£70–80 ⊞ GTM

A Hornby M3 locomotive, finished in maroon and black LMS livery, early 1930s, 7in (18cm) long, with original box.
£75–85 ⊞ VJ

A Hornby gauge 0 No. 1 passenger train set, comprising 0–4–0 No. 1 locomotive and tender in green LNER livery, RN 2810, three coaches and a guard's van, in light brown livery with dark grey roofs, with a quantity of curved rails, 1930s, in original box.
£300–375 ⚒ WAL

A Hornby clockwork 0–4–0 No. 1 locomotive and tender, No. 2251, finished in Great Western green livery, and clockwork 0–4–0 No. 1 Tank locomotive No. 6600 finished in Great Western green, wheels replaced, mid–late 1930s, with empty box for No. 1 Special Tender.
£160–200 ⚒ VEC

► **A Hornby gauge 0 No. 2 Pullman coach,** Loraine, finished in brown and cream livery with dark grey roof and Mansell wheels, c1935, 12in (30.5cm) long, boxed.
£120–150 ⚒ WAL

TOYS

◄ **A Hornby Dublo diesel electric locomotive,** finished in green, c1950, 8in (20.5cm) long.
£100–120 ⊞ GTM

A Lionel gauge I Classic train set, comprising a heavy diecast and sheet steel 2–4–2 locomotive and bogie tender No. 390E, finished in blue, with parlour cars 183 with baggage end, 184 passengers only and observation car 185, finished in Lionel Lines orange and cream livery, American, c1970, boxed.
£250–320 ⚒ WAL

◄ **A Märklin gauge I clockwork 4–4–0 George V locomotive,** No. 2663, with tender, finished in black and cream and red-lined livery, tender relined, German, c1920.
£280–350 ⚒ Bon(C)

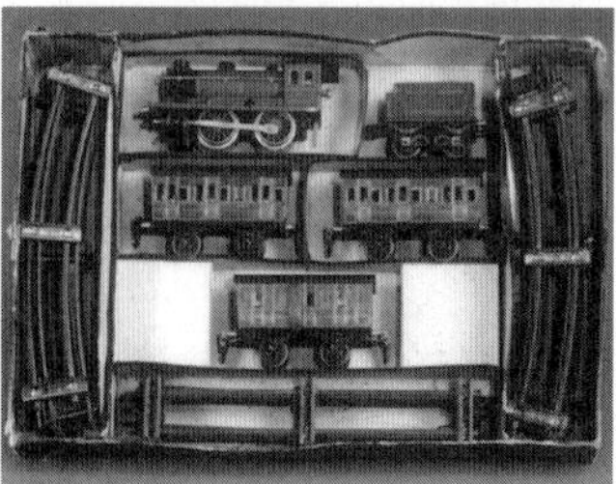

A Märklin gauge 0 passenger train set, comprising a clockwork 0–4–0 engine and tender R950, finished in maroon livery, with three LMS coaches in teak livery, track and instructions, German, c1930, boxed.
£250–320 ⚒ Bon(C)

A Tri-ang gauge 00 plastic train set, comprising electric locomotive, observation carriage, baggage car and a small quantity of track, 1960s.
£40–50 ⚒ DA

A Trix Express Southern Railway motor coach 11081, with restaurant car 7621, parts of rear bogie replaced by wooden pieces, in box marked 'Trix Express', mid–1930s.
£170–220 ⚒ P(WM)

◄ **A Trix Twin Diesel Flier two coach set,** c1950, with box base only.
£85–100 ⚒ B(WM)

Trix trains

Originally established in 1934 in Germany by Stefan and Franz Bing, Trix developed a British company named Trix Twin in 1935 with Winteringham, Bassett-Lowke's manufacturing arm. It was later renamed Precision Models. Trix Twin also had access to the original German factory, with many parts sourced in Germany. Their production consisted of the Trix Express range of trains to complement the British range.

► **A Trix Diesel Flier two coach set,** c1955, each car 8½in (21.5cm) long, with original box.
£100–120 ⊞ VJ

Vehicles

An Alps tinplate Lincoln Futura experimental car, finished in silver, with battery-operated remote control, Japanese, 1950s.
£320–400 ⚒ VEC

A Corgi Toys The Saint's car, No. 258, c1960, 4in (10cm) long.
£100–110 ⊞ GTM
This is merchandizing from the popular 1960s TV series *The Saint*, starring Roger Moore.

A Dinky Toys Pickfords removal van, No. 28b, finished in blue with gold lettering, c1930.
£250–320 ⚒ VEC

A Bing clockwork open tourer with driver, finished in light blue with grey interior, 1920s.
£1,600–2,000 ⚒ VEC

A Corgi *The Man from U.N.C.L.E.* Thrush-Buster car, No. 497, finished in white, 1966, with pictorial stand and box.
£460–575 ⚒ VEC

A Dinky Toys fire engine with ladder, No. 32D, French, c1950, 6in (15cm) long, with original box.
£160–195 ⊞ GTM

A Chad Valley clockwork games van, marked 'The Chad Valley Co Ltd, Harborne, England', rear door detached, c1950.
£250–320 ⚒ B(WM)

A Corgi James Bond 007 Aston Martin D.B.5, No. 270, 1969, 4in (10cm) long, in unopened box.
£450–500 ⊞ UCO

A Dinky Supertoys gift set, No. 990, comprising a 982 Pullmore car transporter, a 154 Hillman Minx in light green and cream, a 156 Rover 75 in cream and blue, a 161 Austin Somerset in red and yellow, a 162 Ford Zephyr in green and cream, and a 794 loading ramp, 1956–58, with box.
£650–820 ⚒ Bon(C)

► **A Dinky Toys Bedford ten hundredweight van,** No. 482, 1950s, 3½in (9cm) long, with original box.
£150–175
⊞ UCO

A J. Distler tinplate clockwork sports coupé, finished in pink, c1950, 10in (25.5cm) long.
£85–100 ⚒ G(L)

A Günthermann clockwork record car, Campbell's Bluebird, lithographed in blue with yellow lining, British and US flags to tail fin and radiator cowling, German, c1930, 20in (51cm) long.
£450–500 ⚒ S(S)

A Kenton cast-iron Yellow Cab, finished in orange and black with ventilator glass windows at front, missing spare tyre and driver, American, C1925, 7½in (19cm) long.
£1,000–1,100 ⚒ S(NY)
American toys are keenly collected in the home market.

A Kingsbury tinplate clockwork Sunbeam landspeed attempt car, finished in red with British and American flags and 'Sunbeam' to the front, 1930s, 18in (45.5cm) long.
£160–200 Bon(C)

A Shackleton clockwork Foden flat-bed lorry, finished in blue and red, with key and spanner, c1950, boxed.
£280–350 AH

A Tri-ang Minic clockwork Paterson & Pickfords van, No. 22M, finished in red and green livery, late 1940s, boxed.
£150–180 WAL

A Matchbox Hillman Minx, No. 43, 1958–62, with original box.
£200–250 VEC

◄ **A Mettoy clockwork racing car,** finished in red and yellow, with replacement driver, 1950s, 15in (38cm) long.
£160–200 P(WM)

A Morestone's *Noddy* gift set, comprising Noddy's car, Big Ears on his bicycle, and Mr Plod the policeman, c1960, boxed.
£280–350 VEC
Morestone was the brand name used by toy wholesalers Morris & Stone. They marketed their toys as Modern Products.

◄ **A Tri-ang Scalextric Auto Union,** No. C/71, finished in yellow with green-spoked wheels, mid-1960s, with original box.
£380–475 VEC

► **A Wells Toys tin and plastic friction drive GPO repair lorry,** finished in green, complete with accessories, c1960, boxed.
£135–150 GTM

A wooden pull-along model of a London stage coach, painted in red and black, with four white plaster horses, figures, luggage and two dogs, mid-19thC, 35½in (90cm) long.
£400–500 DD

Miscellaneous Toys & Games

A child's teaching alphabet, in a wooden case, c1820, 3in (7.5cm) high.
£135–150 ⊞ HUM

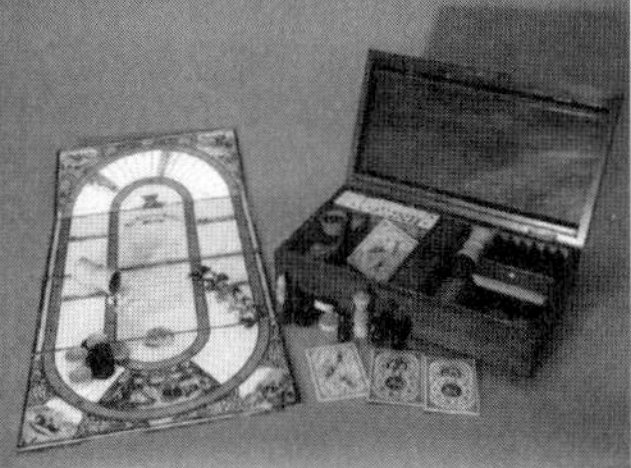

A mahogany games compendium, containing a folding board for backgammon, chess and draughts, and 'the steeplechase', with various games pieces and score cards, 19thC.
£200–240 ⚒ WilP

A fruitwood collapsible bagatelle table, c1890, 35in (89cm) wide.
£360–400 ⊞ ChC

► **A mahogany ball game,** c1900, 12in (30.5cm) high.
£80–100 ⊞ ChC

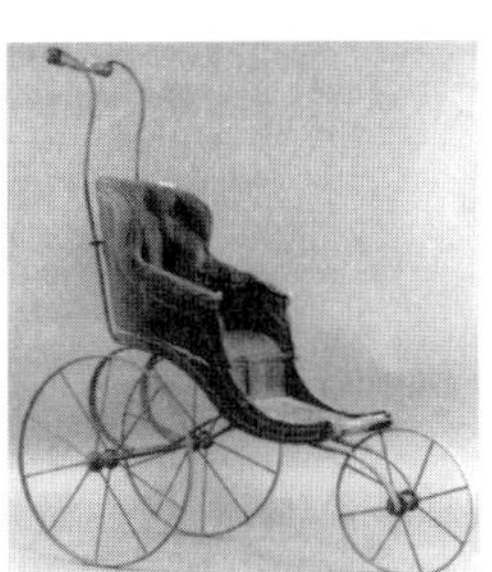

A bone Barleycorn pattern chess set, one side stained red, the other left natural, 19thC, King 5in (12.5cm) high.
£185–225 ⚒ Bea(E)

◄ **A Victorian doll's bath chair perambulator,** with a buttoned-leather upholstered back and black-painted body, on three wrought-iron wheels, 30in (76cm) high.
£400–500 ⚒ RTo

An Oak Tree Series Pixie Pin Game, c1930, 21in (53.5cm) wide.
£225–250 ⊞ ChC

► **A Pelham Puppets Pinocchio string puppet,** Type SS, wearing a pale blue shirt, red shorts, yellow braces and a green hat, c1950, 10in (25.5cm) high.
£170–220 ⚒ Bon(C)

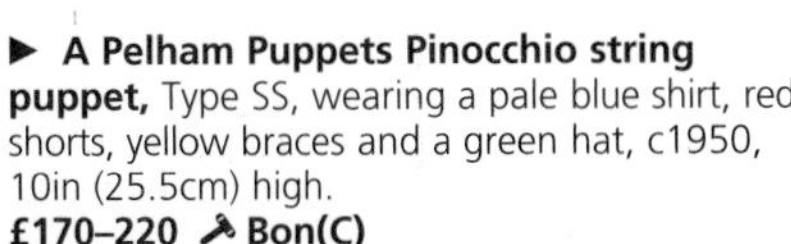

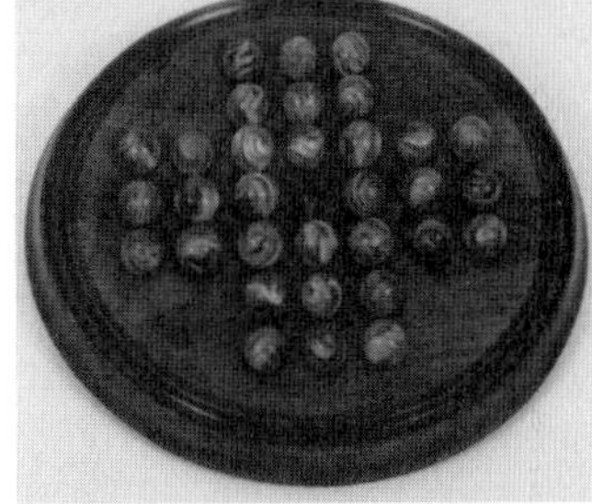

A Victorian mahogany solitaire board, on three button feet, with 32 original swirl-centre glass marbles, 11in (28cm) diam.
£240–300 ⊞ DMC

A Victorian wood and metal tricycle horse, 30in (76cm) wide.
£430–480 ⊞ PICA

A Merit Dan Dare walkie-talkie set, as new, c1953.
£240–270 ⚒ CBP

◄ **A toy ventriloquist's dummy,** by the Reliable Toy Co, Canadian, c1910, 24in (61cm) high.
£270–300 ⊞ AUTO

Ephemera

Annuals, Books & Comics

Toby, issue No. 1, part illustrated by W. Heath Robinson, published by J. Waddington, tear to back cover, 1921.
£120–140 ⚒ CBP

The Beano, issue No. 75, second Xmas comic, 1939.
£450–550 ⚒ CBP

The Avengers, issue No. 1, 1963.
£220–250 ⚒ CBP

◀ ***The Felix Annual,*** issue No. 1, published by E. Hulton & Co, four colour plates, 1924.
£100–125 ⚒ CBP

Radio Fun Annual, issue No. 1, 1940.
£160–200 ⚒ CBP

The Broons, fourth bi-annual, 1950.
£900–1,000 ⚒ CBP

Star Trek, issue No. 1, published by Gold Key, 1967.
£100–120 ⚒ CBP

◀ ***Lois Lane,*** issue Nos. 46–53, complete year, 1964.
£120–150 ⚒ CBP

The Skipper, issue No. 1, 1930.
£200–250 ⚒ CBP

Triumph, issue Nos. 637–88, complete year, 1937.
£150–180 ⚒ CBP

▶ ***Mickey Mouse's Summer Vacation,*** Walt Disney, published by Whitman Publishing Co, USA, 1948, 7 x 5in (18 x 12.5cm).
£35–40 ⊞ SDP

EPHEMERA

Autographs

Queen Victoria, a signed photograph by W. & D. Downey, Ebury St, London, 1895, 13 x 7in (33 x 18cm).
£1,600–1,750 AEL

Miller's is a price GUIDE not a price LIST

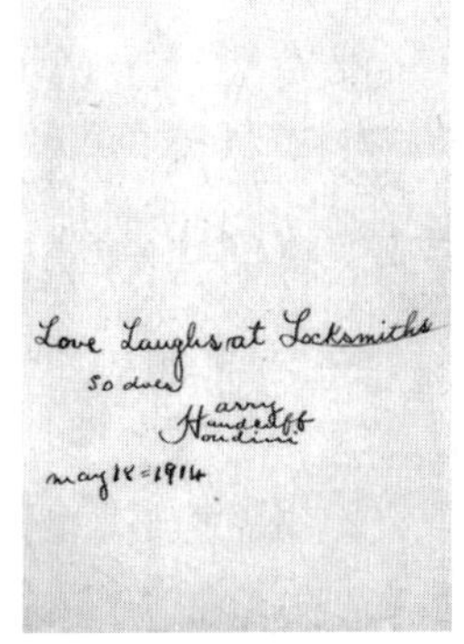

Love Laughs at Locksmiths
so does
Harry
Handcuff
Houdini
may 18=1914

Harry Houdini, an album page, 'Love laughs at locksmiths, so does Harry Handcuff Houdini', dated in his hand 18 May 1914, date partially inked over in a different hand and colour, 8 x 4¾in (20.5 x 12cm).
£800–900 VS

► **Marie Curie,** an autograph letter to an unidentified correspondent, dated Paris 1915, 8 pages, 8°.
£900–1,150 WcH

◄ **Enrico Caruso,** an autograph and signed photograph, c1915, 6 x 4in (15 x 10cm).
£320–350 SDP

George V, a photograph of his children, David, Bertie, Mary, Harry, George and John, signed by each of them, dated 1916 by Mary, later Princess Royal, 5¼ x 3½in (13 x 9cm).
£750–950 Bon

Sir John Alcock, snapshot photograph of an early biplane, signed by Alcock, c1919.
£160–200 DW
Alcock's signature is perhaps the rarest of all the early aviators as he was tragically killed six months after his epic flight with Sir Arthur Brown in June 1919 - the first men to fly across the Atlantic, presumably in the biplane in the photograph shown here.

Ernest Shackleton, an autograph on feint ruled paper, laid down to album page with magazine photo beneath, dated Eastbourne 26 July 1918.
£160–200 VS

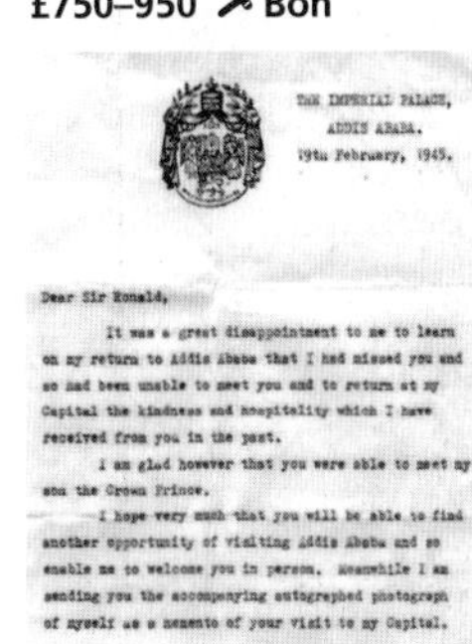

THE IMPERIAL PALACE,
ADDIS ABABA.
19th February, 1945.

Dear Sir Ronald,

It was a great disappointment to me to learn on my return to Addis Ababa that I had missed you and so had been unable to meet you and to return at my Capital the kindness and hospitality which I have received from you in the past.

I am glad however that you were able to meet my son the Crown Prince.

I hope very much that you will be able to find another opportunity of visiting Addis Ababa and so enable me to welcome you in person. Meanwhile I am sending you the accompanying autographed photograph of myself as a memento of your visit to my Capital.

Yours sincerely,

► **Haile Selassi, Emperor of Ethiopia,** a typed letter, signed, one page, 4°.
£450–550 F&C
From The Imperial Palace, Addis Ababa, dated 19 February 1945, with the Crown Prince's gold-embossed and signed visiting card.

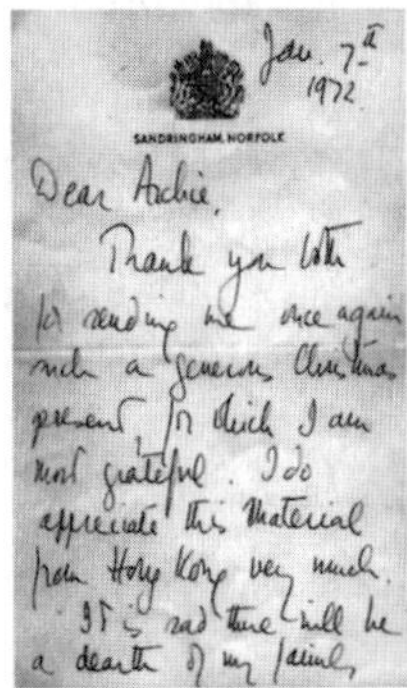

SANDRINGHAM, NORFOLK

Jan. 7th 1972

Dear Archie,

Thank you both for sending me once again such a generous Christmas present, for which I am most grateful. I do appreciate this material from Hong Kong very much. It is sad there will be a dearth of my family

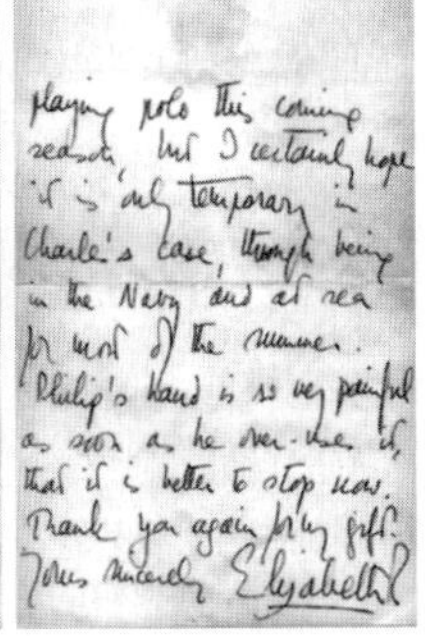

playing polo this coming season, but I certainly hope it is only temporary in Charles's case, through being in the Navy and at sea for most of the summer. Philip's hand is so very painful as soon as he over-uses it, that it is better to stop now. Thank you again for my gift, Yours sincerely Elizabeth R

Queen Elizabeth II, a signed letter to Major A. David, the Queen's Polo Manager, thanking him for a Christmas present remarking 'there will be a dearth of my family playing polo this coming season but I certainly hope it is only temporary in Charles's case, through being in the Navy and at sea for most of the summer. Philip's hand is so very painful as soon as he over-uses it, that it is better to stop now', two pages, Sandringham, 7 January 1972.
£420–525 VS

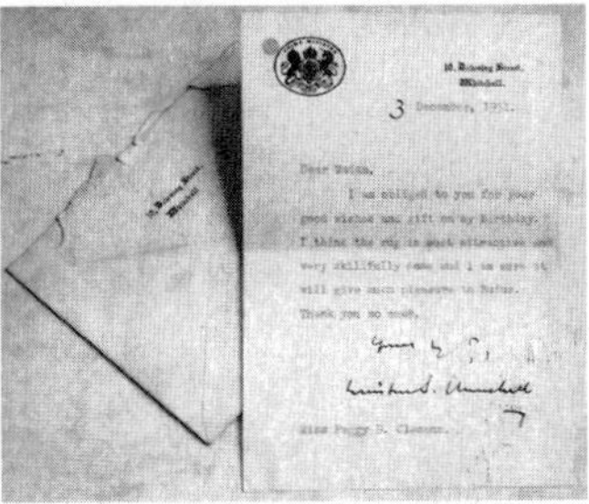

Winston Churchill, A 'thank you' letter from the Prime Minister, to a Miss Peggy D. Clements, regarding a gift, dated 3 December 1951.
£650–820 BLH

► **Laurence Olivier and Vivien Leigh,** a signed photograph, late 1950s, 5 x 3in (12.5 x 7.5cm).
£300–340 SDP

Cigarette Cards

Churchman, The Story of London, showing London from c50 BC, set of 50, 1934.
£55–60 ⊞ MUR

Hignett, Greetings of the World, set of 25, 1907.
£55–63 ⊞ MUR

Lambert & Butler, Motors, set of 25, 1908.
£160–200 ⚒ Bon

John Player & Sons, Motor Cars, set of 50, 1937.
£45–50 ⊞ LCC

John Player & Sons, Country Sports, complete set of 25, 1930.
£115–140 ⚒ VS

Taddy, Heraldry Series, set of 25, 1911.
£140–175 ⚒ P

Wills, Air Raid Precautions, set of 50, 1938.
£30–35 ⊞ LCC

Postcards

◄ **A Lincoln typhoid postcard,** depicting people drawing water at Midland Station, 1905.
£60–75 ⚒ VS

► **A suffragettes postcard,** Bristol, Varsity Students' Revenge, depicting wrecked suffragette head-quarters, 1910.
£250–320 ⚒ VS

An LB & SC postcard, depicting Seaford railway station, 1913.
£18–20 ⊞ JMC

A suffragettes postcard, by Graham, showing the funeral at Morpeth of Miss E. W. Davison, 1913.
£300–375 ⚒ VS
Emily Davison was a member of the Women's Social and Political Union who was frequently imprisoned, often resorting to hunger strikes. In 1913, she famously threw herself under the King's horse at the Derby and was trampled underfoot, dying several days later.

◀ **A postcard,** showing a railway smash, Northern Camp, Yorkshire, 15th May 1917.
£50–60 ⚒ VS

Further reading

Miller's Postcards, A Collector's Guide, Miller's Publications, 2000

▶ **A set of six signed Oilettes,** by Harry Payne, showing the police, c1918.
£55–65 ⚒ SpP
Oilette is the trade name Tuck used to distinguish their various series.

Posters

A poster for the Moulin Rouge, by Jules Chéret, printed by Chaux, Paris, linen-backed, a few repaired tears and losses, 1890, 23¾ x 16¼in (60.5 x 41.5cm).
£500–550 ⚒ BBA

A Columbia Pictures poster, for *Jolson Sings Again*, colour lithograph, Argentinian, c1930, 43 x 29½in (109 x 74cm).
£80–125 ⚒ DW

◀ **A Gilbert's Circus pictorial poster,** with a portrait of Zette Handel above an illustration of her Ladies Orchestra, colour lithograph, printed by Creber, Plymouth, c1900, 19¾ x 15in (50 x 38cm).
£180–225 ⚒ Bon

A Royal Air Force recruitment poster, by Ernest Oker, lithograph, minor damage and some tape repairs, signed and dated '20', c1920, 20 x 30in (51 x 76cm).
£320–350 ⚒ S(S)

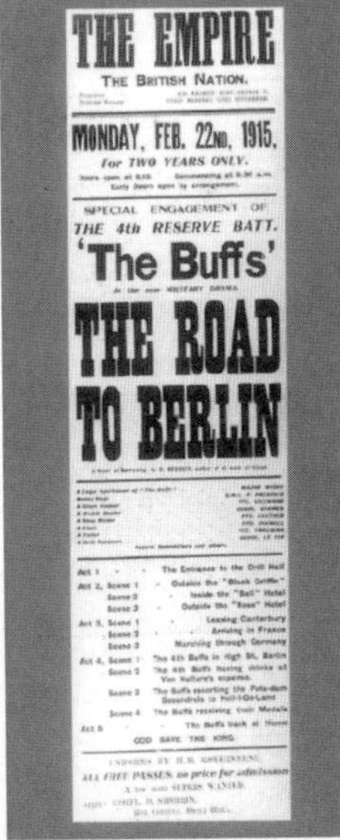

A Land and Water magazine poster, by Cecil Aldin, printed by Bemrose, Derby, 1900, 30 x 20in (76 x 51cm).
£550–700 ⚒ ONS

◀ **A WWI recruitment poster,** designed as a theatre poster for 'The Empire - The British Nation', entitled 'The Buffs - The Road to Berlin - A Play in Five Acts, apply to Corporal D. Sherrin ...Drill Hall...Canterbury', dated Monday, February 22nd 1915, 29½ x 9½in (75 x 24cm), framed and glazed.
£200–240 ⚒ CAG

▶ **A Great Western Railway and London, Midland and Scottish Railway poster,** by Claude Buckle, advertising Ireland's Mansion, Shrewsbury, c1935, 39½ x 24¾in (100 x 63cm).
£300–375 ⚒ Bea(E)
Ireland's Mansion was built in 1575 and is probably the most notable black and white Elizabethan building in Shropshire.

An Italian Line Genua poster, Expresse-Dienst Zuid-Afrika, by G. Patrone, mounted on linen, 1935, 37½ x 24½in (95.5 x 62cm).
£100–125 ⚒ ONS

EPHEMERA

A Bertram Mills' Circus poster, with illustration of Les Kimris aerial act at Olympia, colour lithograph, some tears, 1936, 30 x 20in (76 x 51cm).
£240–300 Bon

A Shell poster, by Siono, Italian, 1949, 39½ x 27½in (100.5 x 70cm).
£240–300 ONS

Cross Reference
See Colour Review (page 740)

A British Railways poster, by Paul Henry, Ireland for Holidays – Lough Derg, c1949, 39¾ x 24¾in (101 x 63cm).
£500–650 Bea(E)

A British Railways poster, by Frank Sherwin, advertising Bexhill, slight tear, 1950s, 40¼ x 25¼in (102 x 64cm).
£270–340 P(WM)

A Warner Brothers poster, advertising *Rebel Without a Cause*, laid down to board, some creasing and tears to corners, 1955, 36¼ x 26¾in (92 x 68cm), framed and glazed.
£100–120 VS

A film poster, advertising *The Big Lift*, 1959, 30 x 40in (76 x 101.5cm).
£160–175 SDP

A United Artists film poster, advertising *Dr No*, two-colour version, 1962, 30 x 40in (76 x 101.5cm).
£180–225 Bon(C)

A Mirisch Corporation poster, advertising *The Thomas Crown Affair*, 1960s, 30 x 20in (76 x 51cm).
£115–140 DW

An Amicus Productions poster, advertising *The Five Keys of Terror*, two-sheet, 1965, 55 x 38in (139.5 x 96.5cm).
£145–160 SDP

A British Railways poster, by Norman Wilkinson, Service to Industry – Steel, c1963, 39¾ x 49¾in (101 x 126cm).
£280–350 Bea(E)

A Universal poster, advertising *Fahrenheit 451*, Australian, 1966, (101 x 68cm).
£80–125 DN

◀ **An *Oz* magazine poster,** Plant a Flower Child, in copper/gold and black, with 'Special Surprise' *Oz* magazine issue No. 5 printed on the reverse, tears in four places, 1967, 45¼ x 30¼in (115 x 77cm).
£250–320 Bon(C)
***Oz* Issue 5 was published as a fold-out poster in an ingenious, but ultimately unsuccessful, attempt to circumvent the Wilson government's introduction of a purchase tax levied on magazines but not on posters. *Oz* reverted to the original format for Issue 6.**

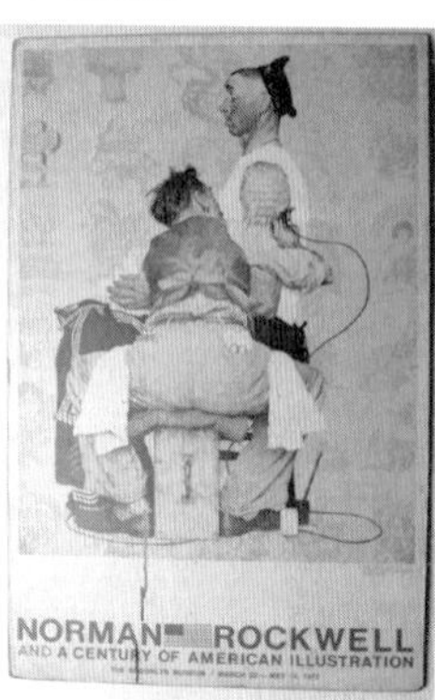

A poster, by Norman Rockwell, advertising an exhibition of his work at the Brooklyn Museum, laminated onto board, 1972, 37 x 24in (94 x 61cm).
£315–350 Ram

Rock & Pop

Elvis Presley, a black and white limited edition photograph of Elvis Presley entering the Cleveland Arena, Ohio, November 1956, signed and titled in pencil by the photographer, Lew Allen, 14 x 11in (35.5 x 28cm).
£220–275 ⚒ FO
Lew Allen was the only professional photographer to document this concert.

A Cunard menu, for the RMS *Queen Elizabeth*, the front cover signed by Bill Haley and one other, tear, Friday 1st February 1957, 10½ x 8in (26.5 x 20.5cm).
£80–100 ⚒ VS

A Jimi Hendrix black and white portrait promotional poster, late 1967, 29½ x 19in (74.5 x 48.5cm).
£400–500 ⚒ Bon

A 12-page programme for The Beatles Show, at the Odeon Cinema, Llandudno, 12–17 August 1963, purple cover, 10 x 8in (25.5 x 20.5cm).
£120–150 ⚒ FO

◄ **A Beatles pottery mug and associated saucer,** with transfer-printed named portraits of the four band members, mug impressed 'Jocque Tams England 64', saucer with printed marks of Washington Pottery, Hanley, 1960s, mug, 4in (10cm) high.
£70–90 ⚒ PFK

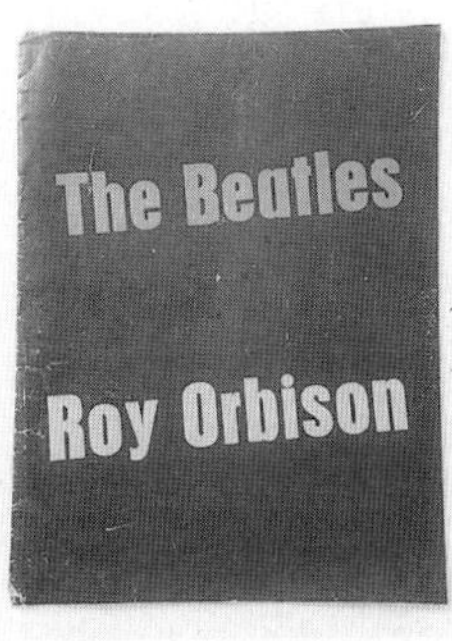

◄ **A Beatles and Roy Orbison UK Tour programme,** 1963, 10 x 8in (25.5 x 20.5cm).
£40–50 ⊞ CTO

Big Brother & The Holding Company mono LP record, 1967.
£30–35 ⊞ TOT

marquee club

10th NATIONAL JAZZ, BLUES & POP MUSIC FESTIVAL PLUMPTON

FIRST FESTIVAL APPEARANCES

1970 CLASSIFIED INFORMATION

A double-sided handbill, from the Marquee Club, London, listing the programme for June 1970 which includes Humble Pie, Elton John and Slade, the front with editorial on the 10th National Jazz, Blues & Pop Music Festival, Plumpton Racecourse, listing the festival line up which includes Alexis Corner, the Rolling Stones, Manfred Mann, Yardbirds, Eric Clapton, Small Faces and Fleetwood Mac, 9 x 6in (23 x 15cm).
£130–160 ⚒ FO

Queen
Invite You To
A Night At The Opera

A Queen autographed programme, 'Queen Invite You To A Night At The Opera', in pink ballpoint, on the front cover, 1975–76, 8¼ x 10½in (21 x 26.5cm).
£360–450 ⚒ Bon(C)

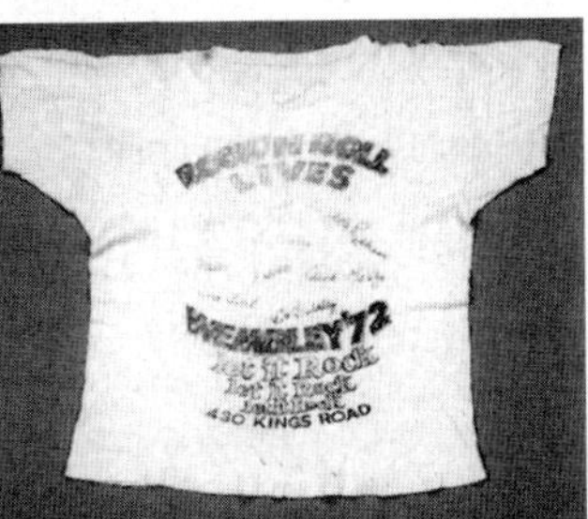

A Rock'N'Roll Lives T-shirt, by Westwood/McLaren, Let It Rock, 1972.
£950–1,200 ⚒ S(O)

◄ **A Linda McCartney portrait poster of Pete Townshend,** the colour screen-print on cartridge paper signed by the photographer in pencil, mid-1970s, 21¾ x 17¼in (55.5 x 44cm), framed.
£160–200 ⚒ Bon(C)

Insurance values

Always insure your valuable antiques for the cost of replacing them with similar items, regardless of the original price paid. Both dealers and auctioneers can provide a valuation service for a fee.

Printed sheet music of 'Mull of Kintyre', front cover signed by Paul McCartney and Denny Laine, 1977.
£100–125 DW

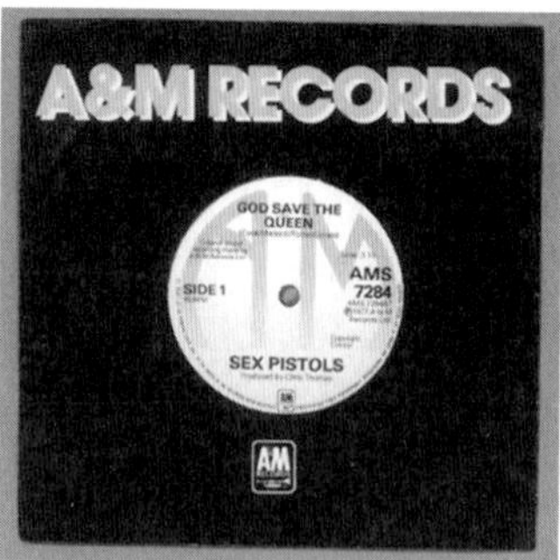

A copy of the withdrawn A & M single 'God Save The Queen'/'No Feeling', by the Sex Pistols, with original sleeve, 1977.
£2,800–3,200 S(O)

A battery-operated tinplate Monkee-mobile, by ASC, with four figures of The Monkees, late 1960s, boxed.
£800–1,000 VEC

◄ **A GRAMMY nomination plaque,** presented to the Bee Gees, 1978, in original box with accompanying letter dated February 1979.
£220–275 FO

A photograph of The Who, signed by all four members, 1960s.
£100–120 VS

A Sex Pistols press kit, from Warner Brothers, with nine photographs and a cartoon poster of Malcolm McLaren's story of the Sex Pistols, 1978, 10 x 8in (25.5 x 20.5cm).
£250–300 IQ

► **A scratch plate,** autographed by John Lee Hooker, Robert Plant, Phil Collins, Mark Knopfler and Brian May, 1980s–90s.
£280–325 Bon(C)

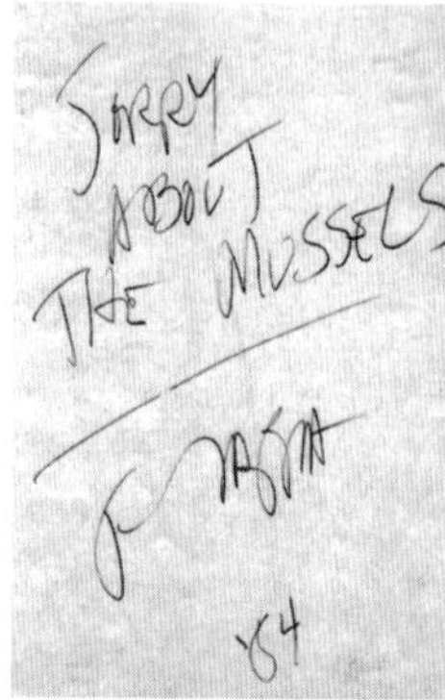

Frank Zappa, a signed page, removed from a visitors' book, annotated in his hand 'Sorry about the Mussels', 1984.
£70–90 VS

A David Bowie autograph, on a clipped piece of paper mounted with a photograph of David Bowie performing on stage, signed 'best wishes from the Glass Spider Tour! Bowie 87', 5¼ x 4in (13.5 x 10cm).
£120–150 Bon(C)

Scientific Instruments

Calculating Instruments & Machines

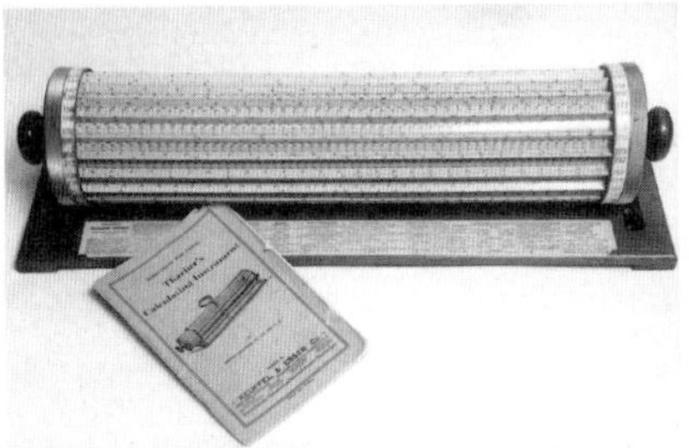

A Thacher's calculating instrument, patented by Edwin Thacher and made by Keuffel & Esser, American, 1881, 24in (61cm) wide, with original case and instructions.
£2,300–2,600 ⊞ ETO

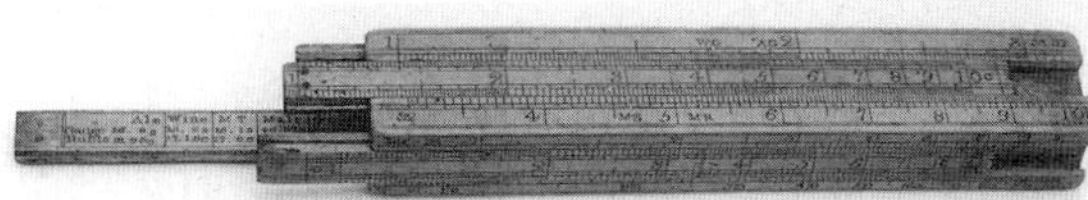

A boxwood four-slide gauger's rule, by William Lewis, London, 1780–90, 6in (15cm) wide.
£250–300 ⊞ TOM

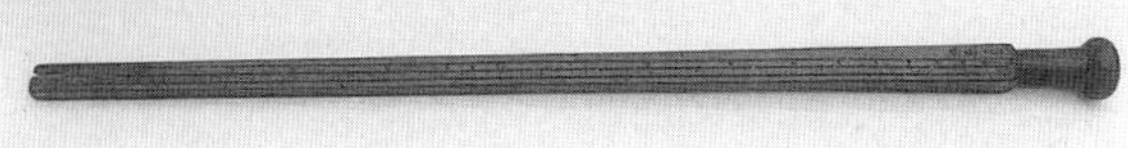

A yew wood measuring rule, dated 1705, 31in (78.5cm) long.
£300–360 ⊞ TOM

► **A Locke adder,** Kensett, Iowa, with nine sliding coloured indices and embossed tin case, American, early 20thC, 10¾in (27.5cm) wide.
£320–380 ⚒ SK(B)

Compasses & Dials

A brass sundial, by Dollond, London, c1770, 9in (23cm) diam.
£320–350 ⊞ RGe

A mahogany-cased compass, late 18thC, 5in (12.5cm) square.
£450–500 ⊞ DJH

A compass, in a gold case, the hinged cover engraved with a flowerhead and a border of foliage, with bright-cut sides, French, early 19thC, 1in (2.5cm) diam.
£200–250 ⚒ WW

A brass mining dial, by Troughton & Simms, London, the compass set with a steel needle, stop lever and two levels, signed, 19thC, 4¾in (12cm) diam.
£240–300 ⚒ B(Ba)

► **A brass equinoctial horizontal compass/ sundial,** French, 19thC, 4in (10cm) square, in a mahogany carrying case.
£420–525 ⚒ SWO

A compass/sundial, c1880, 5in (12.5cm) wide, with original wooden case.
£475–525 ⊞ PHo

► **A brass sundial,** the bottom inscribed 'Ade R, McNair, U.S. Navy, Saratoga Springs, N.Y.', with finger and suspension rings, American, 19thC, 2½in (6.5cm) wide.
£200–240 ⚒ SK(B)

Globes & Armillary Spheres

An armillary sphere, by Luigi Cervellati, Bologna, paper on board, on an octagonal stand supported by four walnut legs with stretchers, minor damage, Italian, late 18thC, 19¼in (49cm) high.
£9,500–12,000 ⚒ S(O)

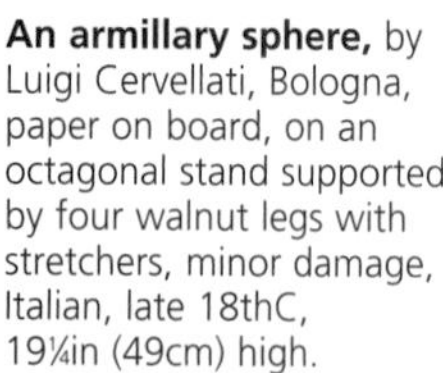

A terrestrial pocket globe, by William King, Irish, c1750, 3in (7.5cm) diam, with fishskin case, the interior with celestial charts.
£2,500–3,200 ⚒ MEA

A mahogany globe, entitled 'Kirkwoods New Terrestrial Globe', with brass meridian, early 19thC, 11¾in (30cm) diam.
£2,200–2,750 ⚒ B(EA)

A Malby's terrestrial globe, mounted on stained wood stand, published by Edward Stanford 1860, 17¾in (45cm) high.
£950–1,200 ⚒ L&E

A terrestrial table globe, by Merzbach and Falk, Brussels, on an ebonized wood stand, showing the months and the signs of the zodiac, Belgian, signed and dated 1881, 20in (51cm) high.
£1,100–1,200 ⚒ NOA

A collapsible terrestrial globe, by George Phillip & Son, after the design by Betts, c1880, 15in (38cm) diam.
£500–600 ⊞ ChC

A globe, on a cast-iron stand, French, late 19thC, 23in (58.5cm) high.
£450–500 ⊞ PICA

► **A Phillips globe,** on a cast-iron base, c1920, 20in (51cm) high.
£380–430 ⊞ ETO

A Trippensee planetarium, with brass sun, earth with coloured gores and geared moon, on brass base with calendar, season and zodiac circle, American, Detroit, c1920, 20in (51cm) wide, possibly in original storage case.
£950–1,100 ⚒ SK(B)

The globe has been annotated with the routes of the Graf Zeppelin's around-the-world flight, the Lindbergh trans-Atlantic flight, and Admiral Byrd's Antarctic flight, all important aviation highlights of the 1920s.

Medical & Dental

An apothecary's wooden box, with screw top and base, 1800–20, 5½in (14cm) high.
£430–475 ⊞ RGe

A doctor's wooden box, with copper and brass trim and rope handles, painted green with red and white motifs, the walnut flame-veneered door enclosing an interior compartment, 19thC, American, 18¼in (46.5cm) wide.
£800–900 ⚒ SK(B)

A brass-bound mahogany medicine chest, 19thC, 7½in (19cm) wide.
£270–340 ⚒ Bea(E)

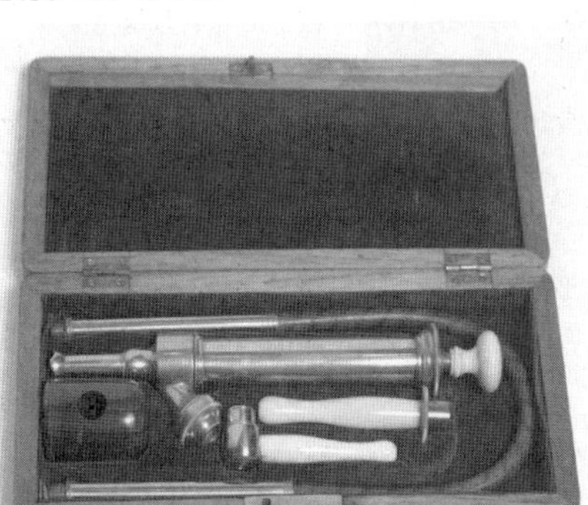

A brass and ivory enema set, by Coreter, c1860, 9in (23cm) wide, in a fitted mahogany case.
£250–300 ⊞ ETO

A wood, bronze and aluminium articulated prosthetic hand, c1910, 7in (18cm) long.
£1,100–1,250 ⊞ AUTO

A pair of silvered ear horns, in a fitted silk and velvet-lined case signed for John Bell & Croydon, Wigmore Street, London, early 20thC, 2½in (6.5cm) high.
£150–180 ⚒ B(Ba)

Items in the Medical & Dental section have been arranged in alphabetical order.

A Dr Dudgeon's sphygmograph, by J. Ganter, retailed by Salt & Son, Birmingham, wrist strap and box missing, 19thC, ½in (1.5cm) wide.
£225–250 ⊞ PHo
This is used to record variations in blood pressure and pulse.

▶ **A glass specie jar,** the white ground with a gilt and blue label, 19thC, 23½in (59.5cm) high.
£250–320 ⚒ DW
These were used to contain various human, animal and plant species and specimens.

A post-mortem set, by Down Bros, late 19thC, 13¼in (33.5cm) wide, in a mahogany case.
£330–420 ⚒ DW

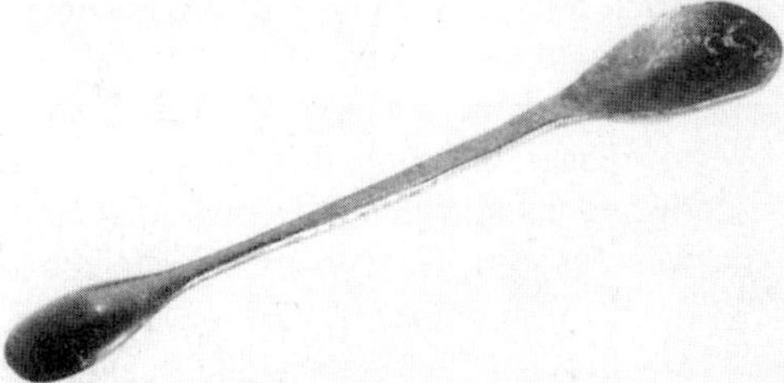

An apothecary's bronze double measuring spoon, for measuring and mixing medicine, 17thC, 15¼in (38.5cm) long.
£115–140 ⚒ Herm

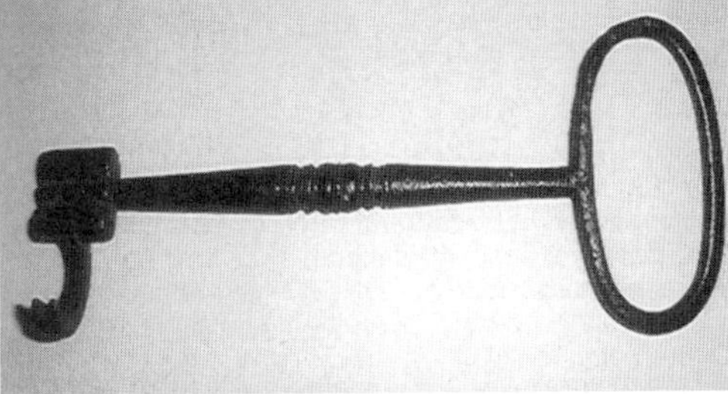

An iron dental toothkey, mid-18thC, 5¾in (14.5cm) long.
£80–100 ⚒ PFK

Meteorological

A Campbell Stokes sunshine recorder, with a black lacquered frame, eastern European, c1960, 8in (20.5cm) high.
£700–800 ⊞ RTW

A brass thermometer, by T. C. Salter, c1823, 8in (20.5cm) high.
£315–350 ⊞ RGe

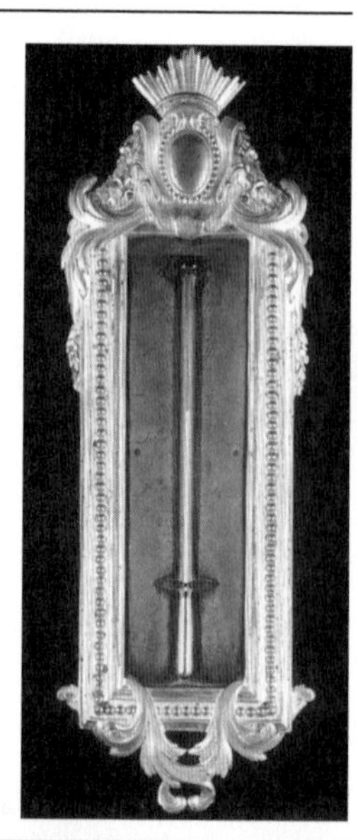

► **A gilt-brass thermometer,** by H. Comyns, Chelsea, 1800–1850, 15¼in (38.5cm) high.
£1,300–1,500 ⚒ S
Henry Comyns is recorded as an optical, mathematical and philosophical instrument maker working at 17 King's Road, Chelsea, London, between 1820 and 1845.

Microscopes

A Culpeper-style microscope, by R. Huntley of Holborn, in original mahogany box complete with accessories, c1810, 17½in (44.5cm) high.
£1,600–1,750 ⊞ PHo

A Ross compound monocular microscope, signed, with accessories, c1850, 17¾in (45cm) high unextended.
£650–720 ⚒ S(O)

Cross Reference
See Colour Review (page 738)

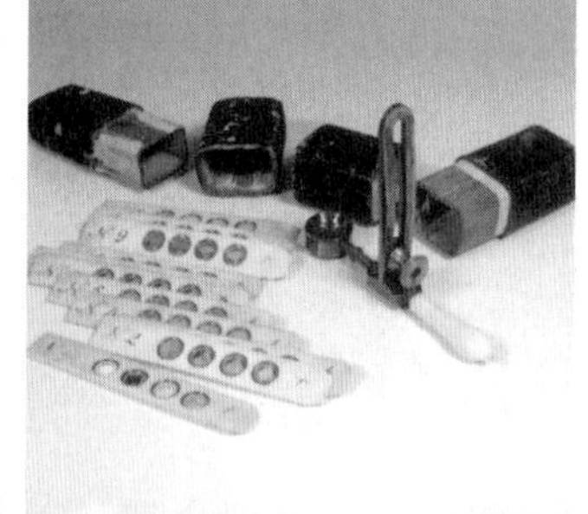

► **A brass botanical pocket microscope,** with an ivory handle and 12 ivory slides, 19thC, 3in (7.5cm) high, microscope and slides both cased.
£320–400 ⚒ WW

A lacquered brass Continental-style microscope, by L. Schrauer, New York, with rack-and-pinion and micrometer fine focusing, signed, with accessories, in a fitted mahogany case, American, late 19thC, 12½in (32cm) high.
£850–950 ⚒ SK(B)

A brass and metal microscope, by E. Leitz, Wetzlar and London, c1920, 11in (28cm) high.
£280–320 ⊞ BoC

Surveying & Drawing Instruments

A compass and clinometer, by J. Hicks, c1885, 3in (7.5cm) diam, with original case.
£180–200 ⊞ PHo

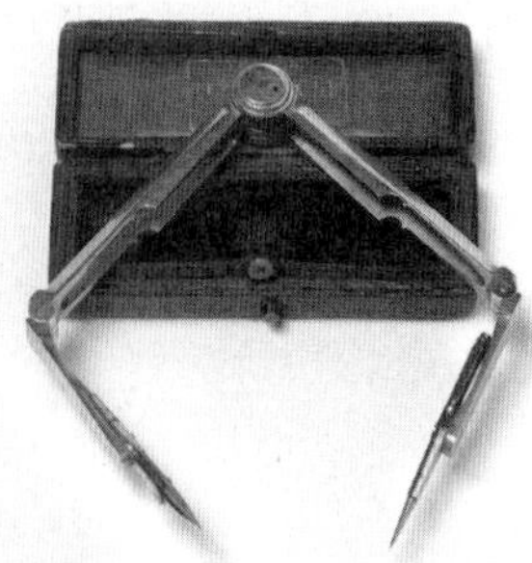

◄ **A folding compass,** by Halden & Co, c1910, 2½in (6.5cm) wide, in original red morocco case.
£70–80 ⊞ PHo

A set of silver, steel and ivory drawing instruments, in a wooden box with an escutcheon engraved with the name 'W. M. Beaufort', German, 19thC, 14in (35.5cm) wide.
£450–550 ⚒ Bon
William Morris Beaufort was born in 1823, son of Rear Admiral Francis Beaufort, inventor of the Wind Scale which bears his name.

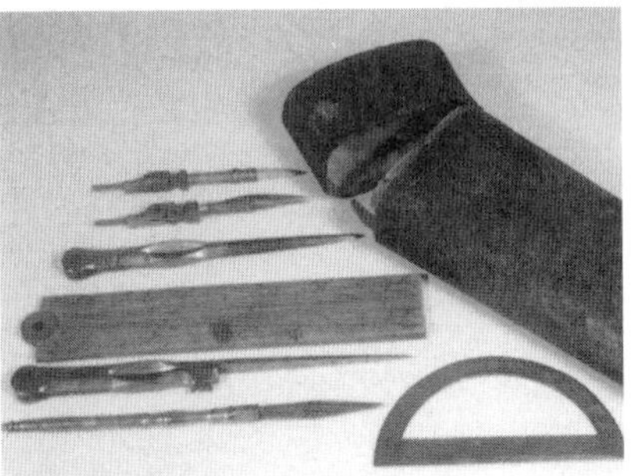

A set of brass drawing instruments, 19thC, 7in (18cm) long, in a sharkskin case.
£80–100 ⚒ WW

A set of drawing instruments, by B. J. Hall & Co, Birmingham, c1920, 14in (35.5cm) long, cased.
£380–420 ⊞ ETO

A brass eidograph, by Arch Butt, London, c1880, 38in (96.5cm) long, in original box.
£500–550 ⊞ HUM
This is used for reducing or enlarging drawings.

► **A surveyor's brass level,** one support replaced, early 19thC, 12in (30.5cm) long, with a folding mahogany stand.
£200–250 ⚒ WW

Telescopes

A 1½ inch table reflecting telescope, with shagreen-covered brass tube on a similar base mounted onto a later brass plate, probably French, 1725–50, 6¼in (16cm) high.
£4,750–6,000 ⚒ S(O)
Small 'salon' table reflectors of this kind, produced for the luxury market, are very uncommon.

A mahogany-barrelled refracting telescope, on a brass stand, c1795, 25in (63.5cm) long.
£900–1,000 ⊞ HUM

A brass and mahogany telescope, by Worthington and Allan, London, c1810, 29in (73.5cm) long, on a brass stand.
£550–600 ⊞ PHo

Miller's is a price GUIDE not a price LIST

► **A baleen-covered telescope and stand,** by A. Abraham, c1830, 4½in (11.5cm) wide, in original case.
£430–475 ⊞ PHo

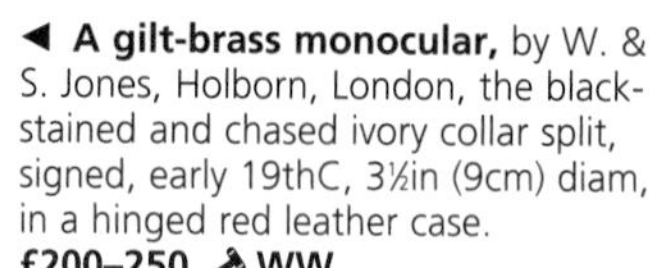

◄ **A gilt-brass monocular,** by W. & S. Jones, Holborn, London, the black-stained and chased ivory collar split, signed, early 19thC, 3½in (9cm) diam, in a hinged red leather case.
£200–250 WW

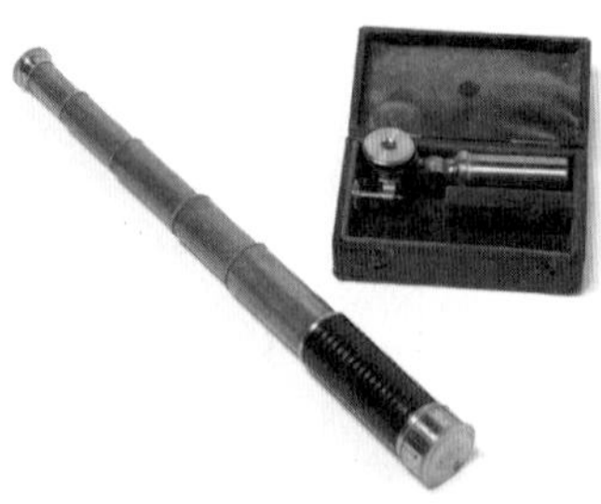

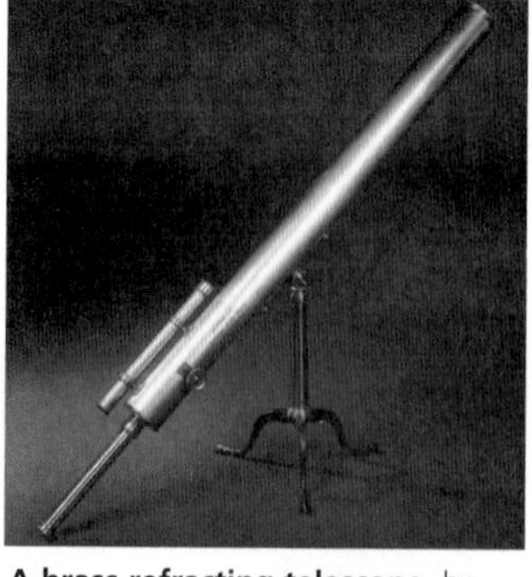

A brass refracting telescope, by Newton & Co, Fleet Street, London, with a 3½in lens, on a tripod stand, 19thC, 52½in (133.5cm) long, in a mahogany case.
£650–800 B(Ed)

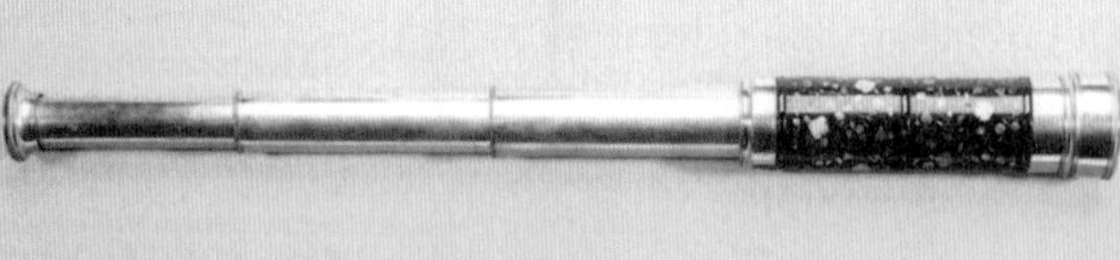

A brass 2inch refracting telescope, by Lerebours, the three-draw body of the tube decorated with two bands of tortoiseshell inlaid with mother-of-pearl and brass foliate decoration interspersed with horn, French, c1870, 21½in (54.5cm) long, extended.
£2,500–3,000 S(O)

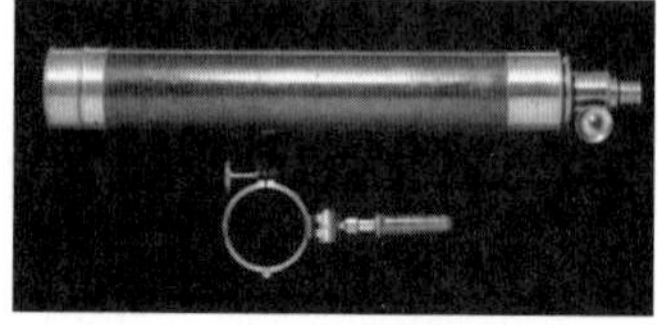

A brass- and mahogany-bound 4inch refracting telescope, by G. & S. Merz, Munich, in a fitted stained case with sliding cover, with accessories, signed, German, c1870, 26½in (67.5cm) unextended.
£820–900 S(O)

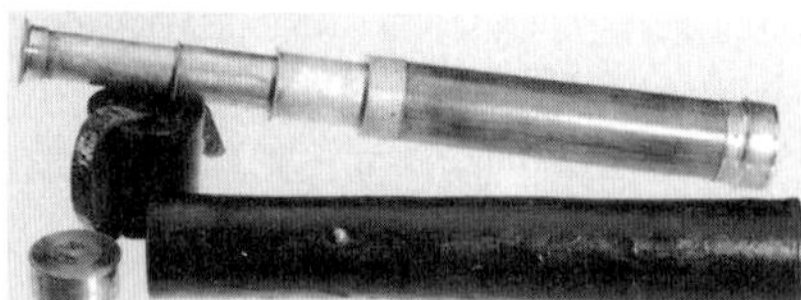

A three-draw brass and wood telescope, by Utzschneider & Fraunhofer, German, 19thC, 32in (81.5cm) extended, in a leather case.
£150–200 Herm

A lacquered and enamelled brass 4inch refracting telescope and stand, by Ross, London, late 19thC, body tube 47in (119.5cm) long, with a cased set of lenses.
£1,200–1,400 B

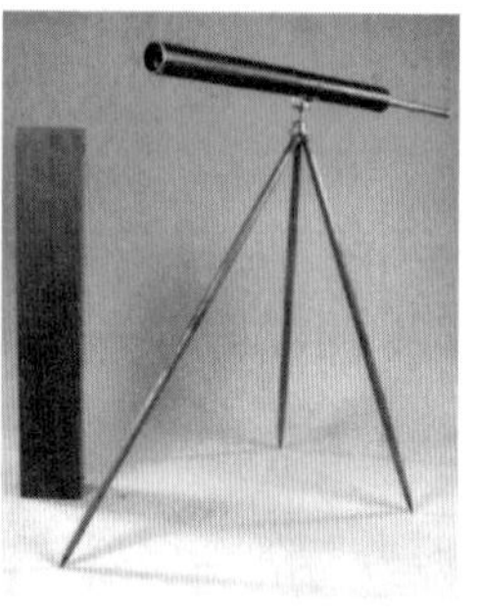

◄ **A late Victorian/ Edwardian refracting telescope,** by S. B. Solomons, London, the black leather-covered barrel with screw-on brass fittings, barrel 42½in (108cm) long and 3in (7.5cm) diam, on a wooden tripod 54½in (138.5cm) high, in original pine case.
£220–275 PFK

A brass and iron astronomical telescope, by G. & S. Merz, Munich, with equatorial mount and original case and paperwork, German, c1900, 27in (68.5cm) long.
£720–800 ⊞ PHo

Weights & Measures

A copper four gallon measure, 19thC, 14in (35.5cm) high.
£185–225 GAK

A set of diamond scales, by De Grave & Son, with weights, c1820, 5¼in (13.5cm) wide, in a mahogany box.
£200–220 ⊞ PHo

A George II mahogany waywiser, with turned wooden handle and brass scales, 48¾in (124cm) high.
£620–775 Bea(E)

Marine

Barometers

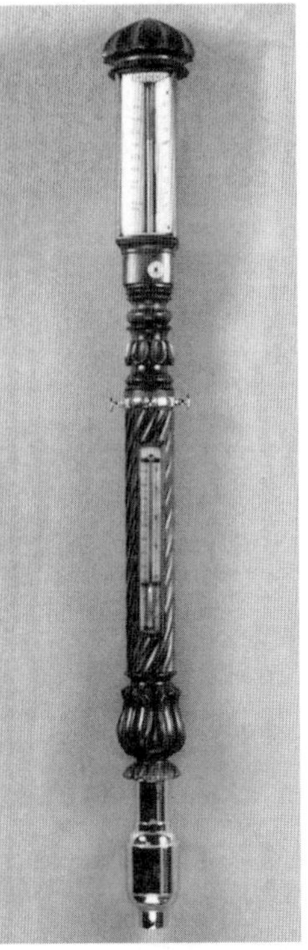

A mahogany marine barometer, by David W. Laird, Leith, the concealed tube with bone plates and vernier, the spiral trunk inset with a thermometer above a chromed-brass cistern cover, signed, c1850, 37½in (95.5cm) high.
£3,300–3,700 ⚒ S(O)

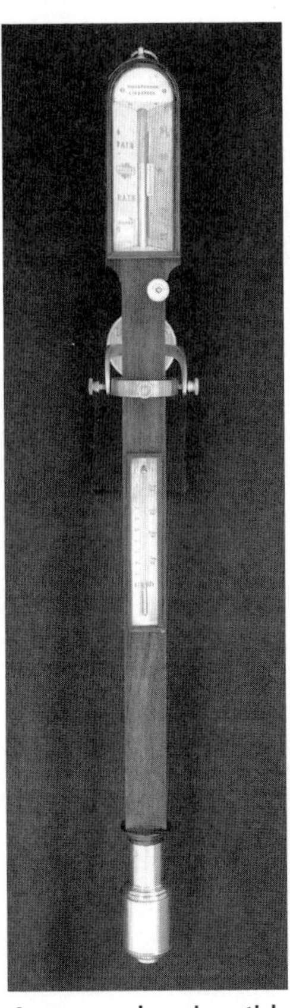

A rosewood marine stick barometer, by Keen & Frodsham, with ivory register plates, c1850, 36in (91.5cm) high.
£2,500–3,000 ⊞ AW

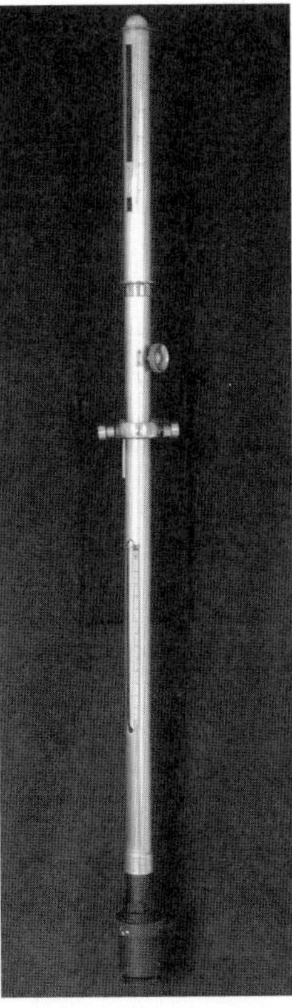

A Kew-Pattern brass-cased marine barometer, by Patrick Adie, London, retailed by Richard Adie, Liverpool, c1870, 36in (91.5cm) high.
£2,000–2,400 ⊞ AW

A brass presentation aneroid barometer/clock desk piece, in the shape of a ship's wheel, the wheel engraved 'Beaumaris Regatta July 30 1877 won by Coral Charles H. Beloe', on a red marble base, French, dated 1877, 11½in (29cm) high.
£1,500–1,700 ⚒ S(O)

Insurance values

Always insure your valuable antiques for the cost of replacing them with similar items, regardless of the original price paid. Both dealers and auctioneers can provide a valuation service for a fee.

Chronometers & Timekeepers

A one-day marine chronometer, by R. Arnold, London, the 4in (10cm) silvered dial with subsidiary seconds dial, in a brass-bound mahogany box, signed, some alteration and restoration, early 19thC, 7¼in (18.5cm) square.
£550–675 ⚒ Bea(E)

A brass-cased bulkhead wall timepiece, by Hallett, Brighton, the painted dial with subsidiary seconds dial, the single fusee movement with a lever escapement and maintaining power, mid-19thC, 10in (25.5cm) diam.
£400–500 ⚒ Bon

Cross Reference
See Colour Review (page 739)

An eight-day marine chronometer, by T. S. Negus, New York, the 4¾in (12cm) silvered dial with gold hands and subsidiaries for seconds and state of wind, in a distressed rosewood-veneered box with later mahogany upper tier, American, mid-19thC, 9in (23cm) square.
£1,500–2,000 ⚒ B

Miller's Compares

I. A brass-bound rosewood two-day marine chronometer, by John Poole, London, the 4in (10cm) silvered dial with subsidiary up-and-down and seconds dials and gold hands, with outer wood travelling case, signed, c1880, 7½in (19cm) high.
£3,000–3,300 S(O)

II. A mahogany two-day marine chronometer, by John Poole, London, the 4in (10cm) silvered dial with subsidiary up-and-down and seconds dials and gold hands, signed, c1870, 7in (18cm) square.
£2,000–2,400 S(O)

Item I is a superior piece to Item II because of the box in which it is housed. It is made of rosewood, a relatively rare and therefore desirable timber, and is brass bound, which helps to keep its shape and protect it from knocks. It also comes with a further wooden travelling case. Item II, while a standard piece of good quality, is contained in a mahogany box without any of the finer features of Item I.

A silver freesprung deck watch, by H. White & Co, London, the white enamel dial with subsidiary seconds, signed, hallmarked London 1910, 2¼in (5.5cm) diam, in a mahogany box.
£1,700–2,000 PT

A naval ship's chronometer, by Lange & Söhne Glashütte, in a mahogany box, German, c1940, 7in (18cm) wide.
£3,400–3,750 AGR

► **An eight-day marine chronometer,** by Waltham Watch Co, Massachusetts, the silvered dial with subsidiaries for seconds and state of wind, in a brass-bound mahogany case, signed, American, c1919, 5in (12.5cm) high.
£950–1,100 P(Ba)

MARINE

Model Ships

◄ **A marine diorama,** in a rosewood frame, c1840, 23in (58.5cm) wide.
£630–700 NoC

A shipbuilder's model of fast steel screw steamer *Bawean*, by James Lang, Sunderland, built for the Netherlands India Steam Navigations Co, in original glazed case, 1886, 40¼in (102cm) long.
£3,000–3,750 BAG

A carved bone and brass-mounted painted wood model of an American frigate, with an American schooner, enclosed in a turned mahogany showcase, 1850–1900, 22¼in (56.5cm) wide.
£2,700–3,000 WcH

A sailor-made waterline model of a clipper, with painted wooden hull and paper sails, mounted on a simulated sea, in a glazed showcase, late 19thC, 21¾in (55.5cm) wide.
£350–420 S(O)

A Victorian live model of a steam ship, *Nautilus*, the wooden hull enclosing the cylinder, 49in (124.5cm) long.
£325–400 F&C
This was built in the last years of Queen Victoria's reign by Samuel Neville Shaw Mee when he was 14–15 years of age.

◄ **A wooden schooner-rigged pond yacht,** with brass rudder, bowsprit, anchor, chains and pulleys, on a wooden stand, early 20thC, 68½in (174cm) long.
£750–950 Bon

Nautical Handicrafts

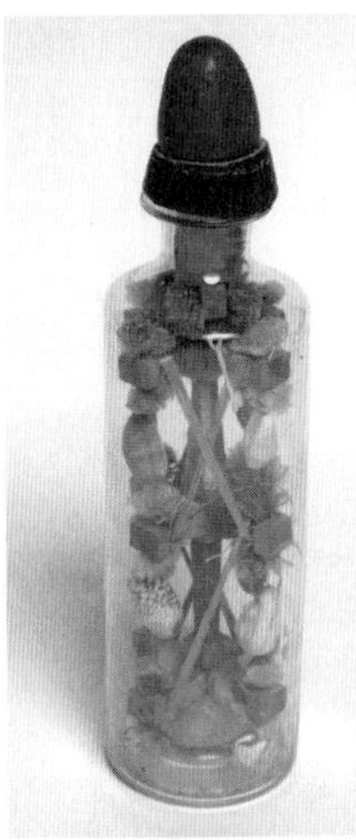

A bone prisoner-of-war games box, the lid sliding to reveal dominoes and dice in three compartments, the sides inscribed 'Forever' and 'Fidelity', one foot missing, 19thC, 11¾in (30cm) wide.
£400–500 Bon

◄ **A sailor's love token in a bottle,** made with wood, silk and shells, early 19thC, 10in (25.5cm) high.
£200–220 ⊞ HUM

A sailor's pine sewing casket, carved with geometric patterns, the compartment interior with a hand-painted maritime scene applied to the interior lid, French, early 19thC, 12½in (32cm) wide.
£400–500 S(O)

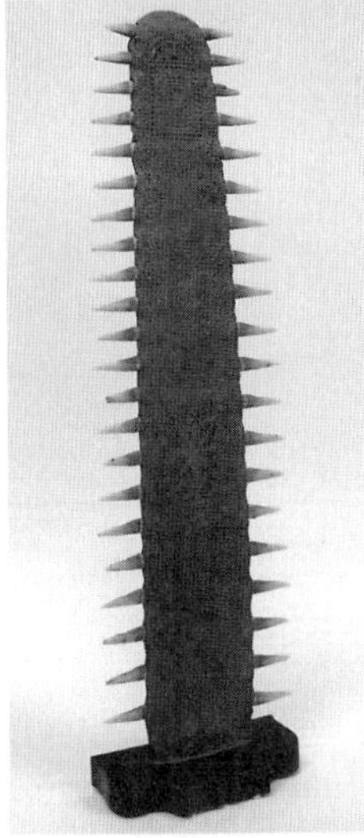

A straw-work picture of the steamer *The Greast Eastern*, Welsh, c1880, 32½ x 24½in (82.5 x 62cm).
£1,450–1,600 ⊞ DeG

◄ **A scrimshaw swordfish bill,** engraved with various motifs including an anchor and an all-seeing eye, on a hardwood stand with bone feet, 19thC, 25in (63.5cm) high.
£320–400 G(L)

A collage and raised textile naval panel, inscribed '*Dieu et Mon Droit*' below a lion, unicorn and crowned shield with flags and ship sails beyond, worked in coloured wool and threads, in a bird's-eye maple frame, late 19thC, 15¼ x 13¾in (38.5 x 35cm).
£180–225 RTo

Navigational Instruments

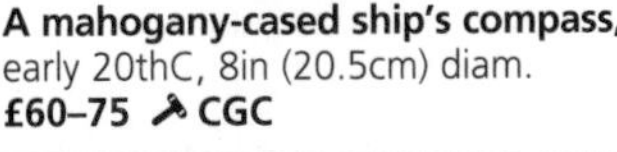

A mahogany-cased ship's compass, early 20thC, 8in (20.5cm) diam.
£60–75 CGC

◄ **A naval compass,** by Kelvin, Bottomley and Baird, in a mahogany box, c1915, 10in (25.5cm) square.
£315–350 ⊞ PHo

A ship's brass inclinometer, c1930, 15in (38cm) high.
£125–140 ⊞ PHo

Sextants & octants

Octants (so-called because their frame is one eighth of a circle) and sextants (one sixth of a circle) measure angular distance by means of reflective mirrors. Octants usually have wooden frames - mahogany, boxwood or ebony are typical. Sextants were usually brass-framed and more accurate than octants and are therefore often more expensive.

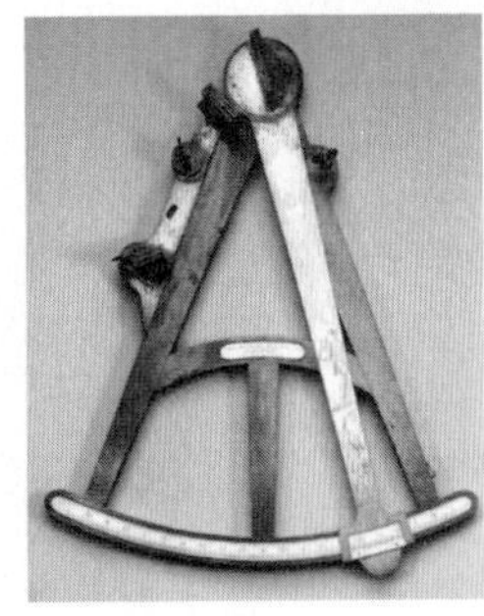

◄ **An ebony octant,** by John Thornton, with ivory scale and vernier, the brass index arm engraved with a figure of a sailor using the octant, dated 1780, radius 17¾in (45cm).
£2,200–2,500 S(O)

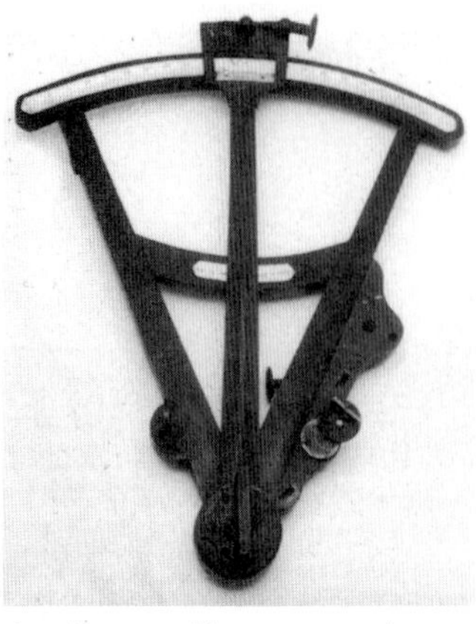

An ebony and brass octant, by Spencer, Browning & Rust, 19thC, 11½in (29cm) radius.
£240–300 Bon

◄ **A reflecting circle,** by Troughton & Simms, London, with two additional telescopes and a magnifier, signed, c1880, 10½in (26.5cm) diam, in a fitted case.
£2,200–2,500 S(O)
Troughton first produced his own design of a three-arm reflecting circle in 1796. He remained the leading maker of such instruments, which never attained the same level of popularity as they did in France where the design had originated.

► **A ship's station pointer,** by Cooke, Troughton & Simms, in original brass and mahogany case, c1920, 20in (51cm) wide.
£270–300 PHo

A pewter and brass parallel rule, engraved 'Thos. Williams'. c1780, 14in (35.5cm) long.
£315–350 RGe

Ships' Fittings

A brass ship's bell for the *Princess Royale*, c1912, 16in (40.5cm) diam.
£950–1,150 S(O)

A ship's saloon chair, with carved and incised mahogany back-rail and arms, on a cast-iron tripod base, c1900.
£700–800 S(O)

A pair of Cunard oak deckchairs from the *Mauritania*, one stamped on the reverse 'Cunard', with folding foot rest and original canvas cushions/lifesavers, 1920s, 63in (160cm) long.
£800–900 S(O)

A brass mast-head lamp, converted to electricity in the early 20thC, c1890, 11in (28cm) high.
£220–245 PEZ

► **A brass-mounted copper ship's lantern,** by William Hardie, Glasgow, early 20thC, 12in (30.5cm) high excluding handle.
£80–100 PFK

A set of mahogany yacht hanging shelves, with apertures for glasses and a decanter, c1850, 19in (48.5cm) wide.
£150–165 F&F

► **A Victorian brass-mounted oak ship's wheel,** 41in (104cm) diam.
£300–360 G(L)

Miscellaneous

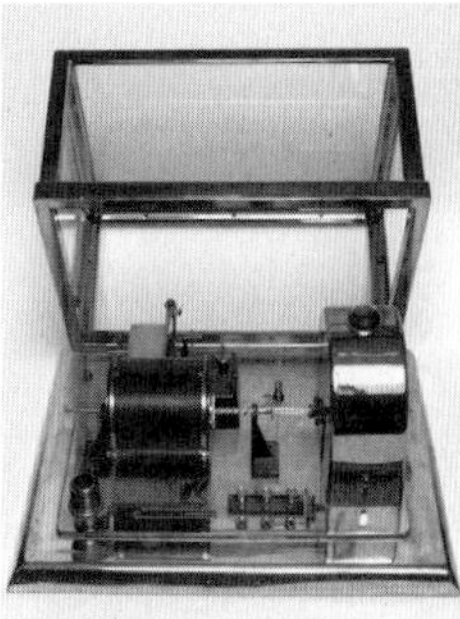

A US naval recording anemometer, the seven-day clockwork mechanism on an electroplated metal frame, in a glass case, c1944, 15in (38cm) wide.
£450–500 ⊞ RTW

A waterman's decorated prize backboard, for Greenwich Regatta 1853, painted with scrolling acanthus leaves tipped with dragons' heads surrounding a shield surmounted by a crown, 57in (145cm) wide.
£2,700–3,500 ⚒ Bon

A biscuit from the departure of RMS *Titanic*, the impressed image of the Olympic/Titanic surrounded by 'White Star Steamers Olympic/Titanic each 45000 tons, Carr Carlise', with signs of mould, c1912, 2½in (6.5cm) diam.
£3,500–4,000 ⚒ S(O)
Captain Morris Harvey-Clarke was the Clearing Officer in Southampton during the time of 1912. It is believed that he probably picked up this biscuit from on board the liner shortly before she departed from Southampton for New York and it has been handed down through his family.

A chain, suspending six enamelled semaphore flag message plaques, the reverse of each engraved with a translation, c1890, 17in (43cm) long.
£2,500–2,750 ⊞ NBL

An ivory compass and thermometer, by William Gardner, Glasgow, modelled as a lighthouse, on a mahogany base with glass dome cover, signed, c1850, 8¼in (21cm) high.
£600–650 ⚒ S(O)

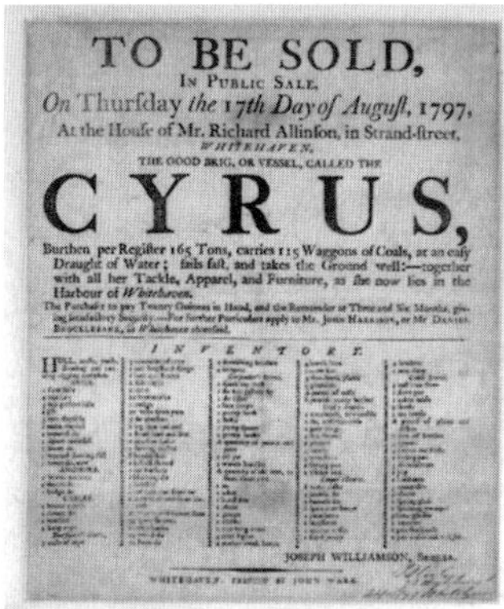

TO BE SOLD,
IN PUBLIC SALE.
On Thursday the 17th Day of August, 1797,
At the House of Mr. Richard Allinson, in Strand-street,
WHITEHAVEN,
THE GOOD BRIG, OR VESSEL, CALLED THE
CYRUS,
Burthen per Register 165 Tons, carries 115 Waggons of Coals, at an easy Draught of Water; sails fast, and takes the Ground well:—together with all her Tackle, Apparel, and Furniture, as she now lies in the Harbour of Whitehaven.

INVENTORY.

JOSEPH WILLIAMSON, Broker.

A printed broadsheet of the auction of the brigg *Cyrus*, framed and mounted, dated 1797, 15 x 12in (38 x 30.5cm).
£525–575 ⚒ S(O)

A White Star Line silver-plated bread roll dish, by Elkington, with crests on each side incorporating the house flag, the rim displaying the star and rib design, the base stamped 'White Star Line', 12¾in (32.5cm) wide.
£420–525 ⚒ SRA

A pair of English School hand-coloured mezzotints, entitled 'The Midshipmen's Berth', and 'A Scene on the Main deck', 19thC, 11½in x 18in (29 x 45.5cm).
£500–600 ⚒ DN

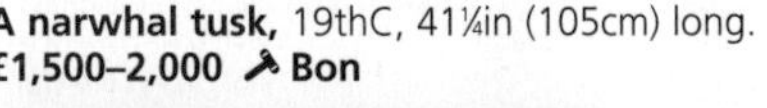

A narwhal tusk, 19thC, 41¼in (105cm) long.
£1,500–2,000 ⚒ Bon

A gardener's mahogany boat-shaped trug, inscribed 'Fred of Cowes' to the bow, late 19thC, 14½in (37cm) long.
£550–700 ⚒ S(O)

◀ **A plate from the British Antarctic Expedition,** 1903–13, aboard the *Terra Nova*, with navy blue rim and blue transfer-printed 'British Antarctic Expedition' insignia, c1910, 9in (23cm) diam.
£2,000–2,200 ⚒ S(O)
The *Terra Nova* was a three-masted barque aboard which Captain Scott took his second expedition to the Antarctic. This plate was given to the father of the vendor in Cardiff in 1910 by Captain Scott.

Cameras

A Pecrops mahogany and brass field camera, by R. & J. Beck, London, half-plate, numbered '509', 1890s, in a fitted box with two DDs.
£250–320 P(WM)

A Blair stereo Weno camera, with f/8 Bausch & Lomb lenses in a brass stereo shutter, 1902–03.
£200–250 B(WM)
This is an original Blair manufactured Weno, made before Kodak took over the company.

A Houghton's Triple Diamond half-plate field camera, with Wray London 8 x 5 lens in brass barrel with cap, triple extension mahogany and brass tapered folding bellows, c1900.
£200–250 P(WM)

A Kershaw Peregrine III camera, No. 4/25807, with f/2.8 coated Taylor Hobson Adotal lens in Talykron shutter 1 to 1/400 sec. B, lens locking mechanism requires adjustment, c1950.
£270–340 P(WM)

◄ **A Kine Exakta camera,** with an Ihagee Anastigmat Exaktar 5.4cm f/3.5 lens and a Tele Megor 4in f/4 helically-focussed lens, and various extension tubes and adaptors, c1936.
£450–550 P(WM)
This was possibly the first 35mm SLR camera in production.

A Kodak No. 2 stereo camera, with twin rapid rectilinear lenses, c1901.
£150–200 B(WM)
Kodak made only this one model of stereo box for twin 3½in square images or single exposure 3½in square.

A Lancaster Instantograph mahogany and brass half-plate field camera, pre-1887.
£200–250 P(WM)
The camera has to be dismantled to change from horizontal to vertical format and vice versa. From 1887, the Instantograph design was changed to the more common drop bed field camera.

A Microflex twin-lens reflex camera, No. 15154, with an MPP Micronar 77.5mm f/3 taking lens in a Prontor SVS shutter in maker's box, with instructions and two maker's leather cases, c1950.
£120–150 P(WM)

A Rolleiflex 28C twin-lens reflex camera, German, c1954, 8in (20.5cm) high.
£240–300 ⊞ VCL

A Zeiss Ikon Adoro 230/5 Tropical camera, with teak body and tan bellows, Dominar-Anastigmat 13.5cm f/4.5 lens, c1930, in a Nagel case.
£350–450 P(WM)

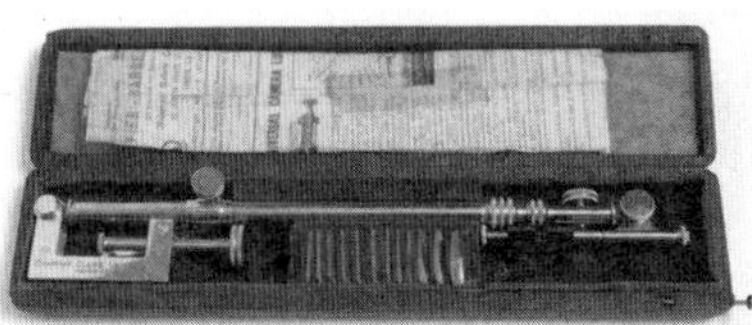

A wooden half-plate camera, with red bellows and brass trim, Thornton Pickard shutter, 1890–1900, 12in (30.5cm) high.
£130–150 ⊞ HEG

◄ **A Chambre Claire Universelle Universal camera,** with instructions, French, c1920, 11in (28cm) wide, cased.
£115–130 ⊞ GAC

Optical Devices & Viewers

A mahogany framed fly-eye mirror, the reverse with magnifying mirror, c1820, 5in (12.5cm) diam.
£270–300 ⊞ HUM
This is a scientific curiosity, designed to give the impression of a fly's vision - that is, multi-image.

A folding stereo graphoscope, the stereo viewer folding into a walnut-veneered box with brass inlay, French, c1870, 8in (20.cm) wide closed.
£350–400 ⊞ APC

A tinplate and brass magic lantern, with three-wick spirit burner, chimney and slide holder, c1910, in original tin case, 15¾in (40cm) wide.
£130–160 ⊞ APC

A chromotrope mechanical magic lantern slide, c1890, 7in (18cm) wide.
£125–140 ⊞ AUTO

◄ An Ernst Planck child's Cinematographe magic lantern, supplied by Gamages, London, for still and moving pictures, blue enamel finish, with films and slides, German, c1910, 9¾in (25cm) high.
£250–300 ⊞ APC

A salesman's sample case, by H. C. White Co, North Bennington, Vermont, including a perfescope, two cartons of slides, catalogues and literature, dated 1907.
£650–720 ⚒ SK(B)

◄ A Richard Frères mahogany slide automatic stereoscope, Le Taxiphote, No. 11204, with a mahogany box containing glass slides, French, c1920.
£450–550 ⚒ WW

A Smith, Beck and Beck mahogany and brass New Achromatic stereoscope, No. 1706, with matching storage cabinet forming a plinth for the viewer, introduced 1858, cabinet 13½in (34.5cm) high.
£650–820 ⚒ B(WM)

A Richard Frères mahogany stereoscope, Le Taxiphote, with rack-and-pinion focussing lenses and ocular adjustment and lever-operated changing mechanism, with a quantity of glass slides, French, early 20thC, 19¼in (49cm) high.
£320–400 ⚒ P(WM)

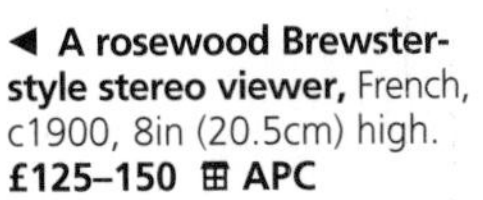

◄ A rosewood Brewster-style stereo viewer, French, c1900, 8in (20.5cm) high.
£125–150 ⊞ APC

A walnut stereo pedestal viewer, the sliding box with rack-and-pinion focussing operated by brass side wheels, with wire frames for approximately 50 stereo views, minor damage, 1850–90, 16½in (42cm) high.
£250–320 ⚒ P(WM)

A burr-walnut and ebonized floor-standing stereo card and photograph viewer, takes 100 stereo cards on a wire revolving magazine, French, c1890, 47¼in (120cm) high.
£1,200–1,500 ⊞ APC

Photographs

Although photographs have been collected ever since they were invented, the modern approach to the collection and care of historically and artistically important photographs only began in the 1970s, when Christie's and Sotheby's began to hold regular sales devoted to the subject. The 150th anniversary of the birth of photography in 1989 was marked by special exhibitions in the UK and USA and attracted huge audiences, fashion photography and photo-journalism having been made into prominent art forms by newspaper colour supplements.

A recognition of the historical importance and rarity of photographs dating from the mid-19th century onwards led to a growth in prices for this material during the 1980s and 1990s. This was in part linked to the creation of new collections of historical material by institutions, particularly American museums.

Paper-based photographs were invented by William Henry Fox-Talbot in England in the 1830s, and techniques were improved in France and England during the next two decades. Much of this material resurfaced during the 1970s and 1980s and was sold at auction, often going abroad or to institutions.

Louis-Jacques-Mandé Daguerre, a Frenchman, invented simultaneously to Fox-Talbot a different form of photography, based on a unique image on a silvered-copper base, known as a daguerreotype. It proved more popular and long lasting in the USA than anywhere else and thus there are more examples to be found there, and consequently a larger collecting interest.

Because much of the history and art of photography in the 20th century is dominated by US photographers, the American market for 20th-century images has been stronger than that in the UK. Vintage prints, that is those made by the photographer on or around the date of taking the photograph, sell for a premium, whereas those made in subsequent years are usually of lower value (see the Cartier-Bresson and Brett Weston prints illustrated on pp 692 and 694).

The recent landmark sale in Paris of the stunning collection of rare 19th-century and vintage 20th-century photographs formed by Marie-Thérèse and André Jammes shows that the best and rarest images can command prices of £500,000 plus. Nevertheless it is still possible to collect rare, unusual and beautiful images for much less, and to put together exciting specialist collections. Over the past 20 years photographs have more than held their own against equities in value terms. Moreover, much material remains to be discovered: there are exciting times ahead.

Richard Meara

◄ **Ansel Adams,** 'Sierra Nevada, Winter Evening from the Owens Valley, California', plate 15 from Portfolio IV, mounted and signed, No. 90 of 260, in original printed wrapper, American, San Francisco, 1963, 11½ x 9in (29 x 23cm).
£3,300–4,200 ⚒ S(NY)

Beken & Son, 'Valsheda', silver print, signed and titled, mounted, c1935, 11 x 4¼in (28 x 11cm).
£575–700 ⚒ S(O)

Items in the Photographs section have been arranged in alphabetical order according to the photographer.

◄ **Felix Bonfils,** 'Seller of Date Cakes, Jaffa', albumen print, French, c1880, 9½ x 8in (24 x 20.5cm).
£150–200 ⊞ RMe

Hippolyte Bayard, 'Eglise de St-Pierre à Louviers', Blanquart-Evrard process print from a paper negative, edge-mounted on card, French, pre-1853, 7¾ x 10in (19.5 x 25.5cm).
£1,000–1,200 ⚒ BBA

S. T. Blessing, 'Mardi Gras, New Orleans', stereographic albumen photograph, American, c1880, 3¼ x 3in (8.5 x 7.5cm).
£150–180 ⚒ NOA
Stereocard collecting tends to be very country specific, and prices for many cards are higher in the US than in the UK.

Bill Brandt, 'Beyond the Fringe' captioned 'Jonathan Miller, Alan Bennett, Peter Cook, Dudley Moore' and titled by the photographer, 1961, 9 x 7¾in (23 x 19.5cm).
£2,200–2,750 S(NY)

Joseph Cundall, 'Royal Sappers and Miners 1856', lightly albumenized salt print, 8½ x 7½in (21.5 x 19cm).
£650–800 RMe
One of a series of soldiers taken for Queen Victoria when the men had returned after the Crimean War.

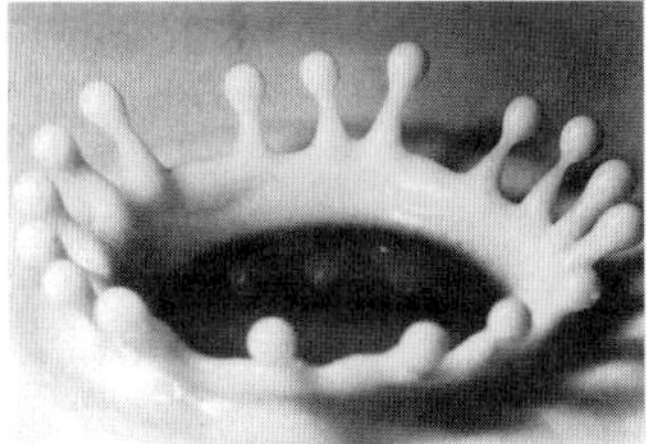

Harold Edgerton, 'Milk Drop Coronet', the reverse with Milk Industry Foundation credit stamp, signed, American, c1935, 6½ x 9½in (16.5 x 24cm).
£5,250–6,500 S(NY)

Francis Frith, 'Crocodile on a Sandbank', albumen print from wet collodian negative, from the publication *Egypt and Palestine Photographed and Described*, 1858, 6 x 9in (15 x 23cm).
£500–600 RMe

Julia Margaret Cameron, 'Alfred, Lord Tennyson', albumen print, signed by the photographer and by Tennyson, 1869, 11½ x 9in (29 x 23cm).
£8,750–11,000 S(NY)

Charles Lutwidge Dodgson (Lewis Carroll), 'Alice Liddell as The Beggar-Maid', albumen print, 1858, 5¼ x 6in (13.5 x 15cm).
£180,000–200,000 S
This is Carroll's most celebrated image of Alice Liddell, the little girl who was the inspiration for *Alice in Wonderland* and *Alice Through the Looking Glass*. An inherent flaw, or perhaps careless handling, resulted in the loss of a small area of emulsion beside Alice's left knee. This is visible as a small dark patch on the print. Carroll scored a line across the plate, just below the mark, thereafter making prints from only the newly cropped negative.

Colonel Joseph Gale, 'Evening Gleams', printing out paper print, c1890, 8 x 6in (20.5 x 15cm).
£500–600 RMe
Joseph Gale was a member of the Linked Ring pictorialist group.

Henri Cartier-Bresson, 'Siphnos, Greece', signed, French, 1961, printed later, 9½ x 14in (24 x 35.5cm).
£3,000–3,750 S(NY)

Edward S. Curtis, 'Lahkedup-Skokomish', photogravure, American, c1912, 8½ x 6in (21.5 x 15cm).
£340–425 NOA

Dolamore & Bullock, 'Paddington Station, The Inauguration of the Metropolitan Line', albumen print, mounted on card, photographer's printed label to verso, probably 1862, 10¾ x 14¼in (27.5 x 36cm).
£500–600 BBA
This was the first underground passenger railway in the world. The occasion is almost certainly the first trial run on 24 May 1862 when the passengers included Gladstone, at that time Chancellor of the Exchequer, and later to become Prime Minister, and his wife.

Colonel Joseph Gale, 'St Paul's from the Thames', printing out paper print, c1900, 5 x 6in (12.5 x 15cm).
£400–500 RMe

John Wheeley Gough Gutch, Dr Gully's house and douche baths from the Swan's Pool, Great Malvern April 1856, lightly albumenized salt print, 6 x 8¼in (15 x 21cm).
£650–800 ⊞ RMe

◄ **Mr Kilburn,** Regent St, London, a daguerreotype, framed and contained in a red morocco-covered case with photographer's details, c1850, 5 x 4in (12.5 x 10cm).
£650–800 ⚒ B(WM)

Jacques-Henri Lartigue, 'My First Photo of my Cousin Simone Roussel', signed, French, c1902, printed later, 10¼ x 14in (26 x 35.5cm).
£2,600–3,250 ⚒ S(NY)
Lartigue took this photograph when he was about 8 years old.

◄ **Robert Mapplethorpe,** 'Irises', plate No. 2 from the 'Y' Portfolio, mounted, signed and numbered, 16 of 31, American, 1978, 7½ x 8½in (19 x 21.5cm).
£2,200–2,750 ⚒ S(NY)

► **Helmut Newton,** 'Upstairs at Maxim's', signed, titled and dated, French, 1978, printed before 1990, 14¼ x 9½in (36 x 24cm).
£2,200–2,750 ⚒ S(NY)

David Octavius Hill and Robert Adamson, 'Miss Rigby' or Miss Glynne, actress and dramatic reader, photogravure on tissue, by Thomas Annan, from the original salted paper print by Hill and Adamson, c1845, 8 x 5½in (20.5 x 14cm).
£320–400 ⊞ RMe

Kusakabei Kimbei, Japanese Geisha, hand-tinted albumen print, Japanese, c1890, 10 x 8in (25.5 x 20.5cm).
£120–130 ⊞ RMe

► **Helen Levitt,** Two Boys Smoking, signed and dated, American, c1934, 7½ x 6¾in (19 x 17cm).
£4,500–5,500 ⚒ S(NY)

Karl Moon, 'Navaho Boy', orotone, photographer's name etched into the plate, studio stamp on the mat, the reverse with photographer's stamp, American, 1907, 13½ x 10½in (34.5 x 26.5cm), in a contemporary gilt frame.
£7,000–8,750 ⚒ S(NY)
An orotone photograph is printed on a glass plate, the back of which is then painted with gold mixed with banana oil.

W. H. Jackson, 'The Royal Gorge - Grand Canyon of the Arkansas', on original mount, American, Denver, Colorado, c1880, 21¼ x 16½in (54 x 42cm).
£1,300–1,600 ⚒ Bon

Dorothea Lange, 'Tenant Farmers without Farms, Hardman County, Texas', the reverse with photographer's studio stamp, American, 1937, printed 1950s, 7½ x 9½in (19 x 24cm).
£2,400–3,000 ⚒ S(NY)

Angus McBean, John Gielgud as Prospero, gelatin silver print, 1957, 9½ x 7½in (24 x 19cm).
£100–120 ⊞ RMe

Nicéphore Niépce, 'A Man Leading a Horse', a heliographic print on paper from a copper plate, with correspondence addressed to his cousin, French, 1825, 4 x 5¾in (10 x 14.5cm).
£305,000+ S(P)
This is the first photographically produced image, dated to two years earlier than any previously known example. 'Photograph' as a word hadn't been invented, so Niépce called it a heliograph, literally 'sun writing'.

◄ **Roland W. Reed,** Three Piegan Warriors at a Lakeside, American, 1912, 9½ x 7¼in (24 x 18.5cm).
£450–575 SK(B)

Wilhelm Von Gloeden, 'Boy with Fish', albumen print, Sicilian, Taormina, c1890, 5 x 7½in (12.5 x 19cm).
£1,000–1,200 RMe

Anon, 'Jog Jakarta', from an album of 50 gelatin silver prints of Indonesian dancers, printed c1920, negative may be earlier, 8½ x 11in (21.5 x 28cm).
£1,800–2,000 RMe

Herbert Ponting, 'Terra Nova at Cape Evans', The Fine Art Society No. 27, with Ponting's embossed mark, 1910, 30 x 24in (76 x 61cm), in a glazed wood frame.
£1,500–2,000 N
Herbert Pointing was the official photographer on Captain Scott's last expedition to the Antarctic in 1910–13. The Fine Art Society show of 1913–14 exhibited a selection of 200 images by Ponting which were available for sale.

Jan Saudek, 'Boy and Airplane', Czechoslovakian, dated 1968, 10½in (26.5cm) square.
£800–1,000 DuM

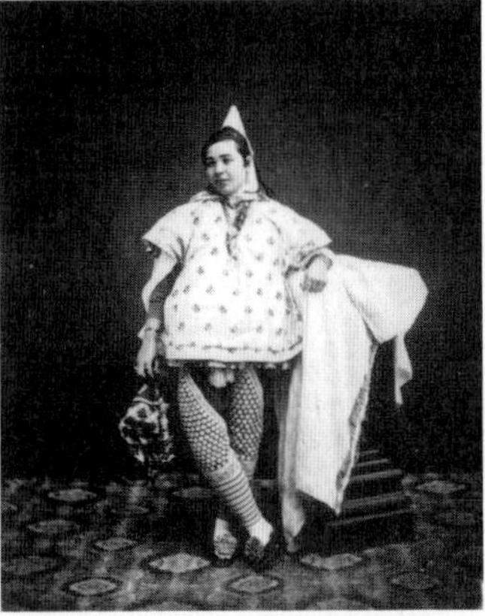

Anon, 'Jewess of Tunis', albumen print from wet collodion negative, c1880, 10 x 8in (25.5 x 20.5cm).
£180–220 RMe

► **Anon,** European in oriental costume, albumen print, c1890, 11 x 8in (28 x 20.5cm).
£100–150 RMe

Man Ray, 'Gertrude Stein', titled by the photographer and with his Paris studio stamp and a Condé Nast stamp, American, 1926–29, printed before September 1934, 8½ x 6½in (21.5 x 16.5cm).
£5,250–6,500 S(NY)

Brett Weston, 'Dune, Oceano', mounted to board, signed, American, dated 1934, printed later, 9½ x 7½in (24 x 19cm).
£2,850–3,500 S(NY)

Anon, 'Alice and Ivo Bligh', children of the 6th Earl of Darnley, albumen print from wet collodian negative, c1865, 8 x 6in (20.5 x 15cm).
£280–350 RMe

Arms & Armour

Armour

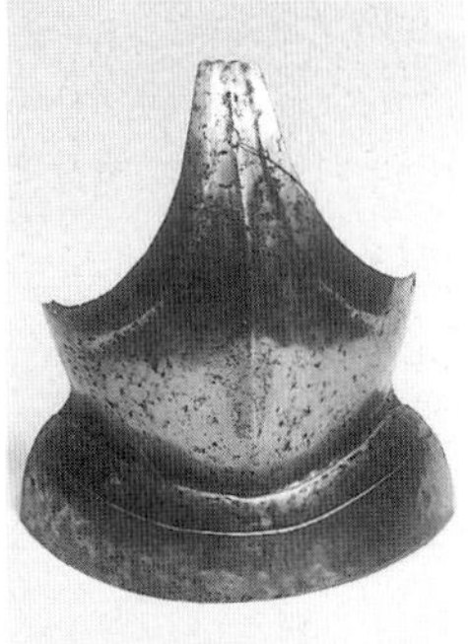

A steel plackart, from the island of Rhodes, German/Austrian, c1480, 15in (38cm) high.
£2,700–3,000 ⊞ ARB
A plackart is placed over the breastplate for extra protection.

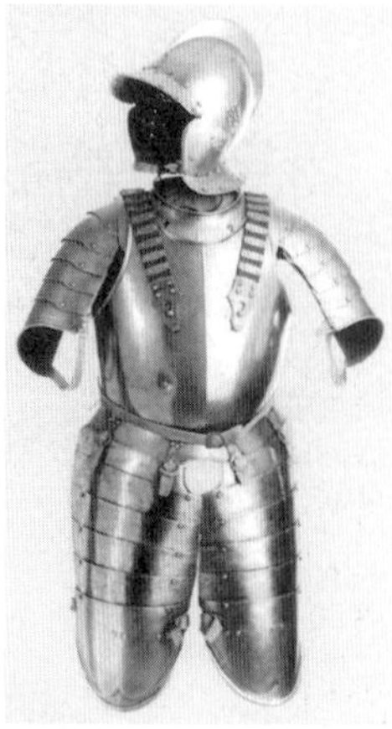

A foot soldier's suit of armour, on a modern iron stand, Vienna, c1600.
£6,000–7,500 ⚒ Herm

A cavalry trooper's armour, c1640.
£3,500–4,500 ⊞ ARB

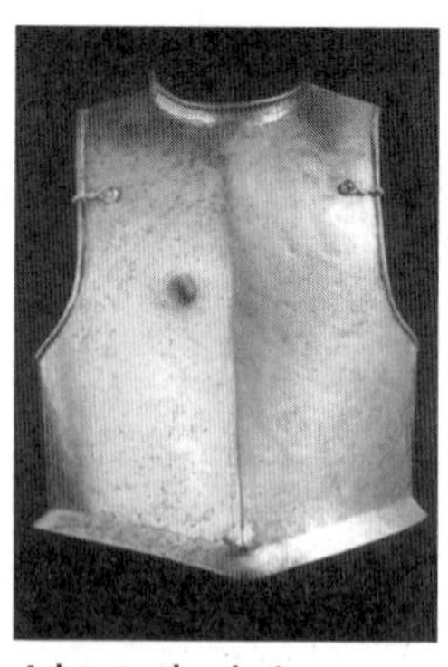

A harquebusier's cuirass, with ordnance mark for the reign of Charles II and armourer's mark 'WM', associated backplate, c1670, 16½in (42cm) high.
£2,000–2,400 ⚒ S(O)

A mail and lamella shirt, Indian, 17thC.
£500–625 ⚒ WAL
The inscription in Devangri script inside this shirt indicates that it was taken at the Siege of Adoni in 1689.

A trooper's breastplate, painted black, pitted, north European, late 17thC, 15½in (39.5cm) high.
£800–900 ⚒ S(O)

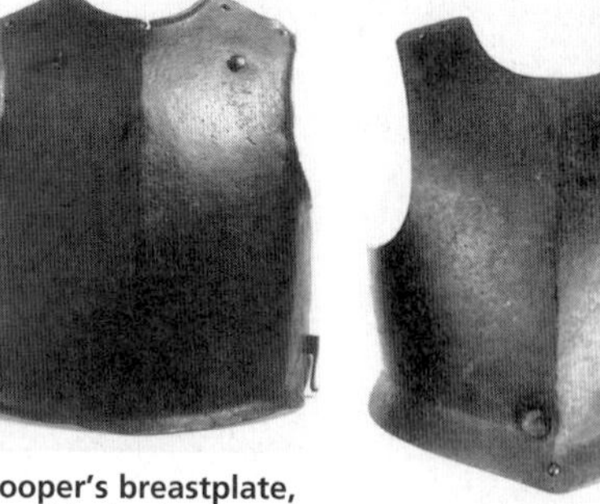

A forged iron breastplate, German, 18thC, 13¾in (35cm) high.
£400–500 ⚒ Herm

◄ A cuirassier's breast- and backplate, faced with brass, the rayed backplate retaining traces of plating, with leather-backed brass shoulder chains and leather waist strap, leather straps replaced, French, c1830.
£1,000–1,250 ⚒ WAL

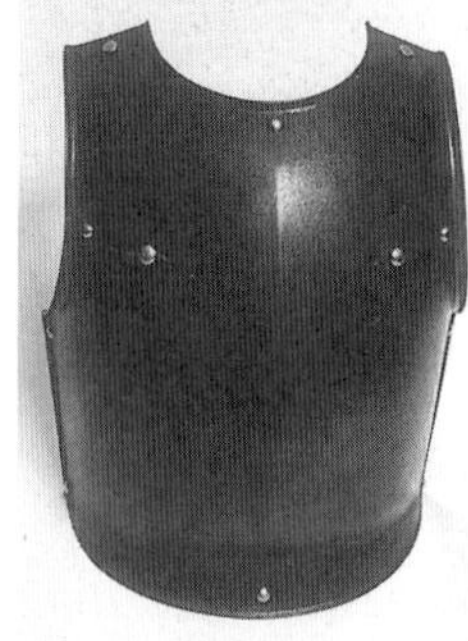

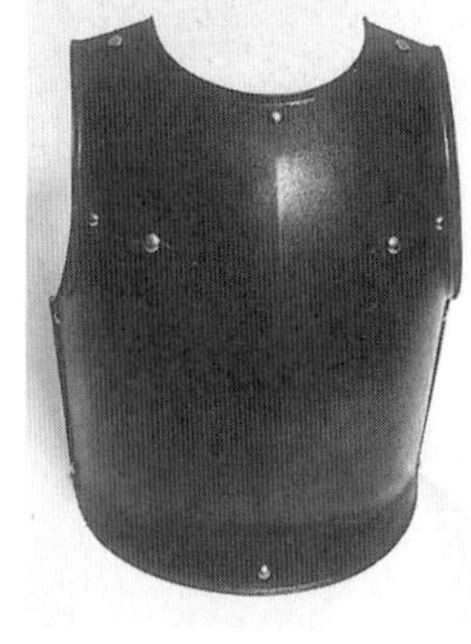

A steel breastplate, with brass rivets, French, c1840, 17in (43cm) high.
£350–400 ⊞ ARB

A cavalry trooper's breastplate, with brass-rimmed borders, studded with brass rivets and retaining much nickel-plated finish, 19thC, 17½in (44.5cm) high.
£150–180 ⚒ S(O)

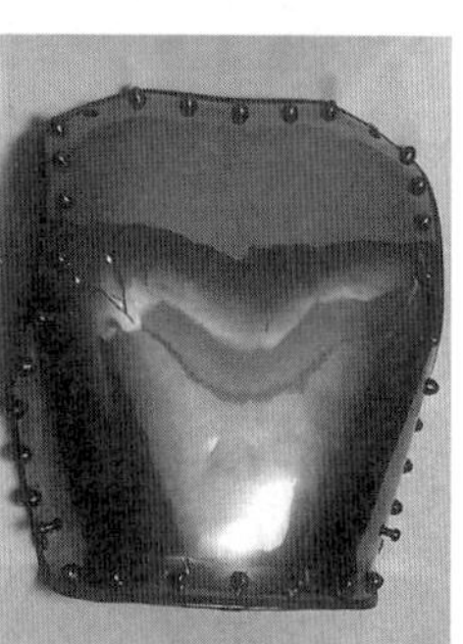

A nickel-plated backplate, with brass edges and rivets and original leather liner, c1890.
£450–500 ⊞ ARB

A copper and steel cuirassier's ceremonial breast- and backplate, with brass straps, on a wooden stand, breastplate damaged, 19thC.
£2,200–2,500 ⚒ S(Am)

Cross Reference
See Colour Review (page 742)

◄ A morion, German, c1600, 14in (35.5cm) high.
£1,850–2,200 ⚒ Herm

Cannons

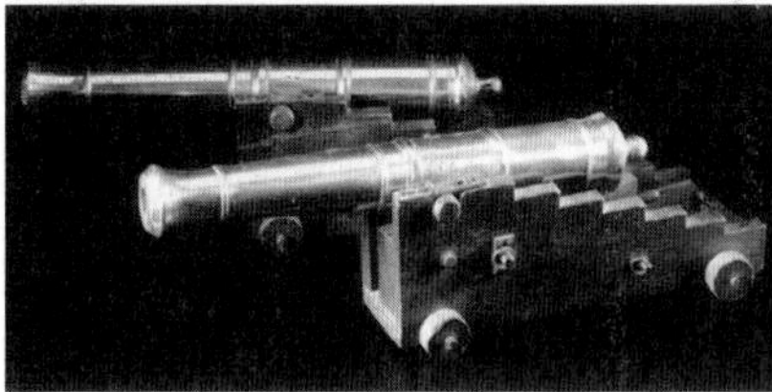

A pair of brass saluting cannons, with multi-stage barrels, one cut for an ignition device, the other filled, on later stepped wooden carriages, 18thC, 17in (43cm) long to vent.
£2,400–3,000 S

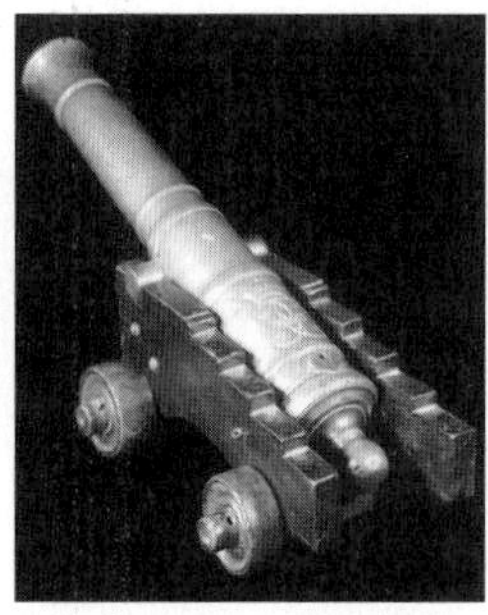

A bronze saluting cannon, with multi-stage barrels, cast with the letters 'GG' beneath a coronet, on a later stepped wooden carriage, 1750–90, barrel 20¼in (51.5cm) long.
£1,750–2,000 S(O)

A carronade, on a stepped wooden carriage, 18thC and later, barrel 34¼in (87cm) long.
£300–375 WL

◄ **A cast-iron table cannon,** cast in two stages, on a wooden trillion with brass wheels and ramrod, early 20thC, 12in (30.5cm) long.
£180–225 G(L)

A model field gun, cast in three stages, the mahogany split trail with metal mounts, 19thC, 16in (40.5cm) long.
£1,200–1,500 WAL

Edged Weapons

A hangar, with German blade and cast-brass hilt, running wolf mark, c1690, 32in (81.5cm) long.
£1,100–1,400 ⊞ ARB

A stiletto, with iron grip and quillon, Italian, c1600, 9¾in (25cm) long.
£350–400 Herm

A cavalry trooper's backsword, the straight single-edged blade with spear point, brass hilt, grip replaced, blade 33in (84cm) long.
£350–400 ⊞ ASB

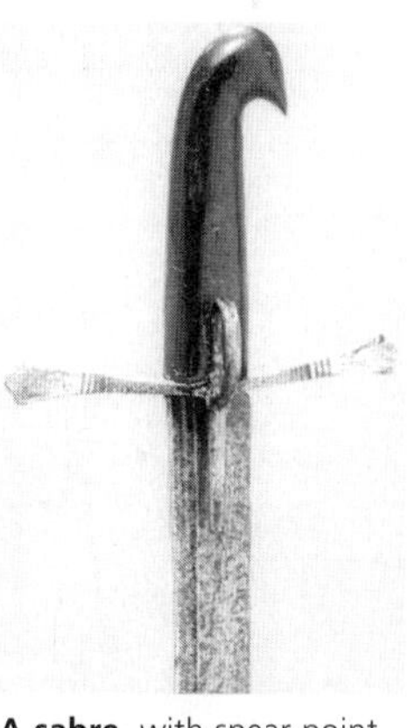

A sabre, with spear point and brass-plated quillon, wooden grip, Hungarian, 1700–50, 36½in (93cm) long.
£630–800 Herm

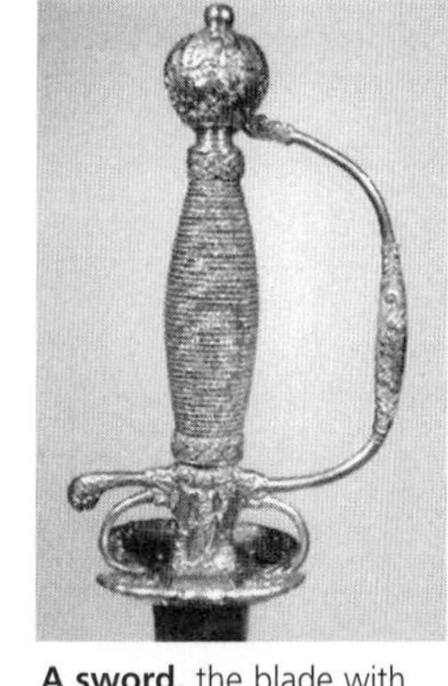

A sword, the blade with brass inlay, the silver-gilt hilt embossed with classical figures, maker's mark 'RG', Dutch, c1730, blade 27¼in (69cm) long.
£620–775 WW

A *schiavona*, with double-edged blade and fish-tail pommel, bracket hilt, Italian, Venice, c1720, 45in (114.5cm) long.
£1,500–1,650 ⊞ GV

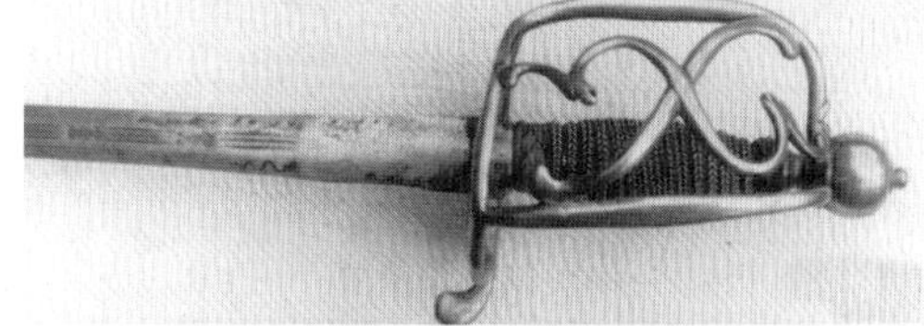

A cavalry officer's sword, with straight double-edged blade decorated with flowers and geometric patterns at the forte, the brass basket hilt with intertwining bars modelled as a serpent, c1730, blade 33½in (85cm) long.
£750–850 ⊞ ASB

Garth Vincent
Antique Arms and Armour
LAPADA
MEMBER
THE GUN TRADE ASSOCIATION
I have customers worldwide
and I am interested in purchasing
single items or complete collections,
advice freely given
Dealer in antique and reproduction
arms and armour for the collector,
investor and interior decorator
Commission buying at auction
Access & Visa accepted
Brochure available
The Old Manor House
Allington, Nr Grantham
Lincolnshire NG32 2DH
Telephone: 01400 281358
Fax: 01400 282658
Mobile: 07785 352151
Email: garthvincent@aol.com
Website: http://www.guns.uk.com

A rapier, with basket hilt, mid-18thC, 29½in (75cm) long.
£400–500 DN

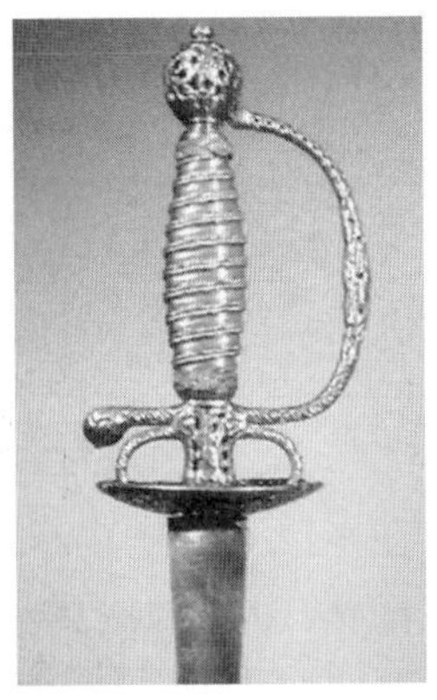

A sword, the blade by Christopher Day, with a pierced and chiselled steel hilt, Belgian, Brussels, c1760, 30in (76cm) long.
£400–500 WW

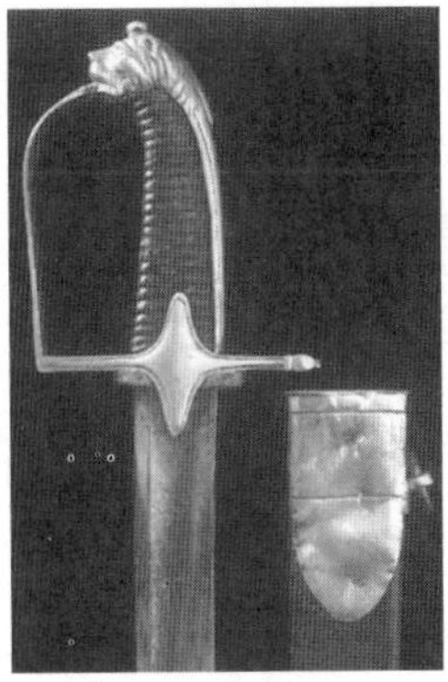

An officer's sword, the curved regulation blade etched with foliaged lion's head and a crowned 'MK', brass hilt including lionhead pommel, in a brass-mounted leather scabbard, German, Bavaria, 1850–90, blade 31in (78.5cm) long.
£250–300 S(O)

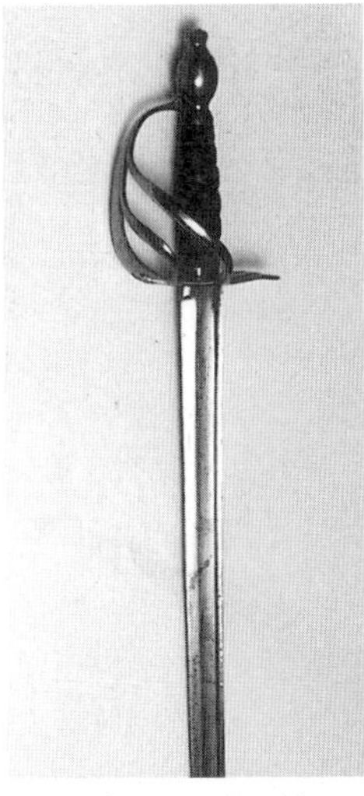

A cavalry sword, with half-basket hilt, c1788, 43in (109cm) long.
£1,000–1,200 ARB

A backsword, made in Birmingham for Highland regiments of the government service, the straight single-edged blade with fuller and spear point, the basket hilt comprising five plates pierced with a pattern of circles and triangles, late 18thC, blade 32in (81.5cm) long.
£1,150–1,300 ASB

A sabre, the blade with five short fullers, engraved with royal cypher and monogram, the ivory and wire-bound grip with lion's head pommel, the leather scabbard signed 'Foster, Sword Cutler to his Majesty, Prince of Wales, St James Street', late 18thC, blade 24¾in (63cm) long.
£800–1,000 Bea(E)

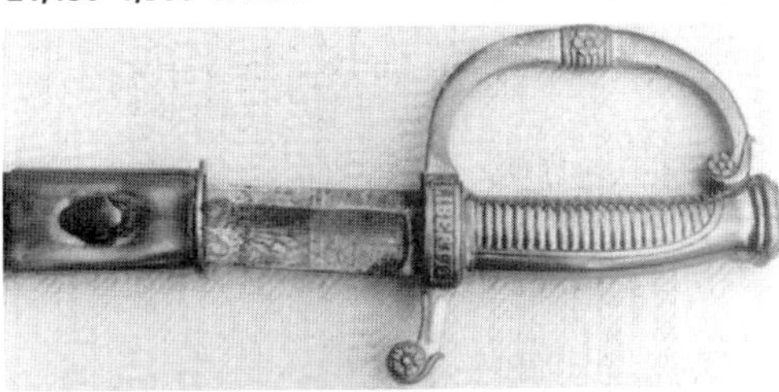

A Revolutionary infantryman's sabre, the curved single-edged blade with broad fuller etched 'Liberté, ordre public' and 'J.L. Pascal' to the reverse, the brass stirrup hilt with grooved grip and traces of original gilding, decorated with rosettes and incorporating 'Liberté' on the guard, in original brass-mounted black leather scabbard, French, c1790, blade 24½in (62cm) long.
£700–800 ASB

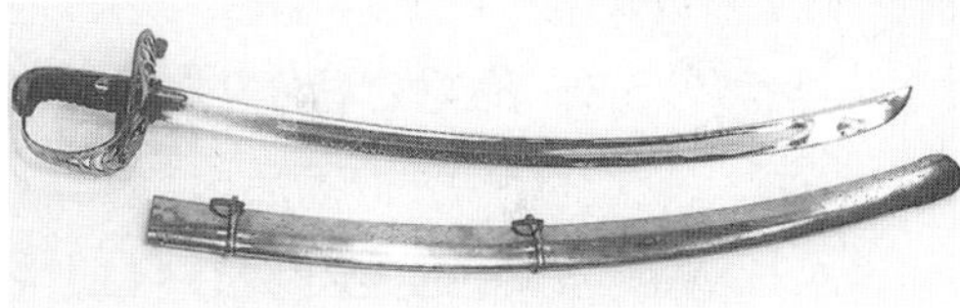

A cavalry officer's sabre, the curved blade engraved with the royal cypher and 'Drawn In My Country's Cause', c1796, 38in (96.5cm) long.
£1,400–1,600 GV

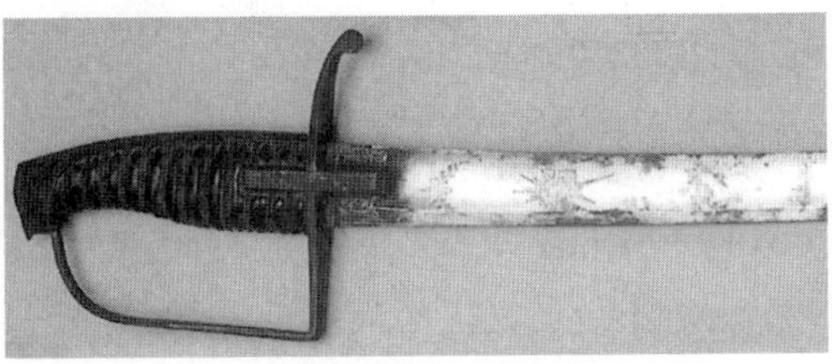

Directoire/First Empire officer's sabre, the etched blade with some bluing and gilding remaining, with stirrup hilt and wired grip, in a leather and metal-mounted scabbard, end section missing, French, early 19thC, 29½in (75cm) long.
£260–325 DN

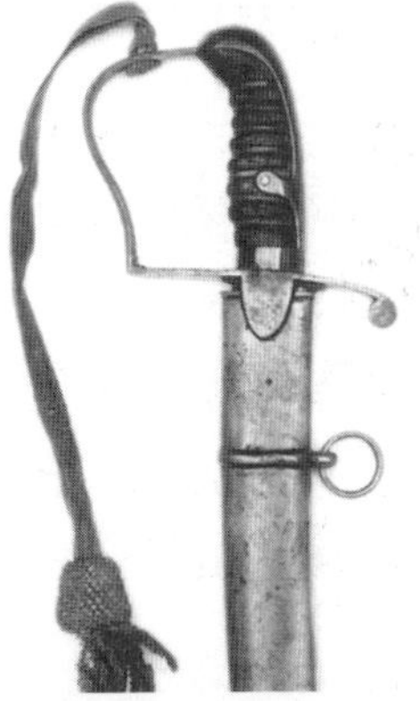

◄ **A 1796 pattern Light Cavalry officer's sabre,** by Osborn & Gunby, with curved single-edged blade double-edged towards the point and fullered over most of its length along the back edge on each side, the forte etched and gilt with decoration, the leather-covered wooden grip bound with twisted silver wire, in original steel scabbard, warranted, early 19thC, blade 32¾in (83cm) long.
£850–1,100 Bon

► **A hilted broadsword,** with double-edged blade, the brass basket with one bar fractured, working replacement pommel, wooden grip, Scottish, c1810, blade 31in (78.5cm) long.
£600–650 GV

An officer's mameluke, the plain single-edged blade with reinforced point, with gilt hilt and ivory grips with rosettes, two missing, in a leather scabbard with embossed and engraved gilt mounts, c1815, 36in (91.5cm) long.
£1,100–1,200 ⊞ WSA

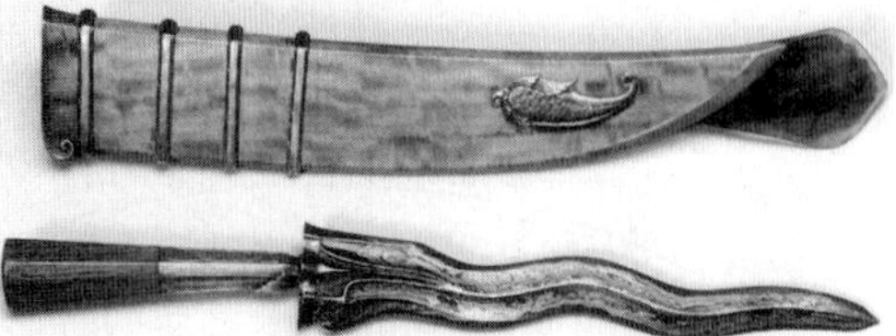

A ceremonial knife, with kris form steel blade, engraved silver-gilt mounts and sandalwood scabbard, Javanese, possibly Surakarta, 19thC, 17½in (44.5cm) long.
£900–1,150 ⚒ SK

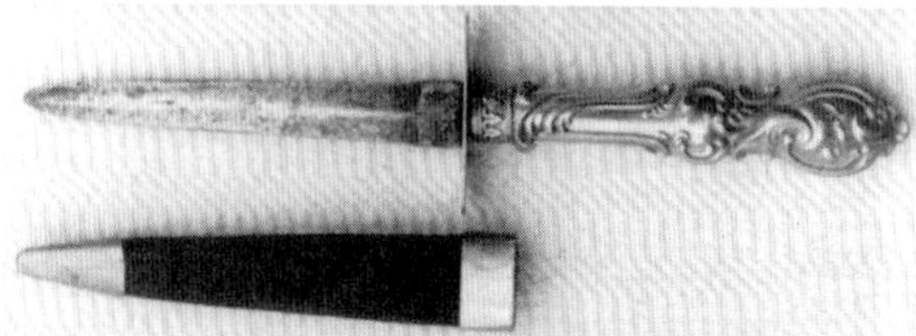

A dirk, by Lingard, Peacroft, Sheffield, for the American market, with straight double-edged blade, the nickel silver handle decorated with rococo scrolls, in a nickel silver-mounted sheath, mid-19thC, blade 4¾in (12cm) long.
£125–140 ⊞ ASB

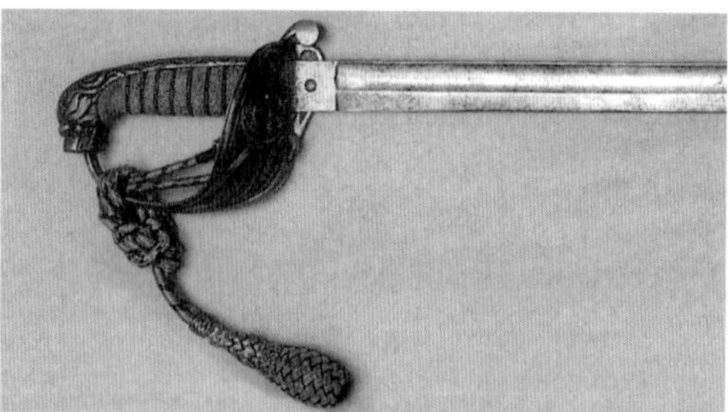

A late Victorian Royal Navy officer's sword, by Kenning, Little and Britain, London, with etched blade, regulation gilt-metal guard with lion's head pommel, in a gilt-metal-mounted leather scabbard, blade 30¾in (78cm) long.
£260–325 ⚒ DN

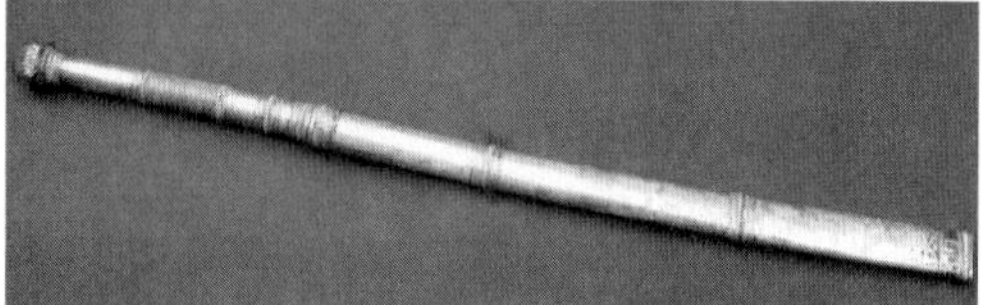

A silver-mounted *dha*, the wooden silver-wrapped hilt with embossed pommel and cord-bound grip, the hilt mounting and silver-sheathed wooden scabbard with beaded decoration, pommel split and reattached, Burmese, 19thC, 32in (81.5cm) long.
£315–350 ⊞ CrF

A sword, the slightly curved fullered single-edged blade engraved with Chinese characters, with brass stirrup hilt, horn grip and lion's head brass pommel, in a wooden sheath with brass mounts, Vietnamese, 19thC, blade 22in (56cm) long.
£240–300 ⚒ WAL

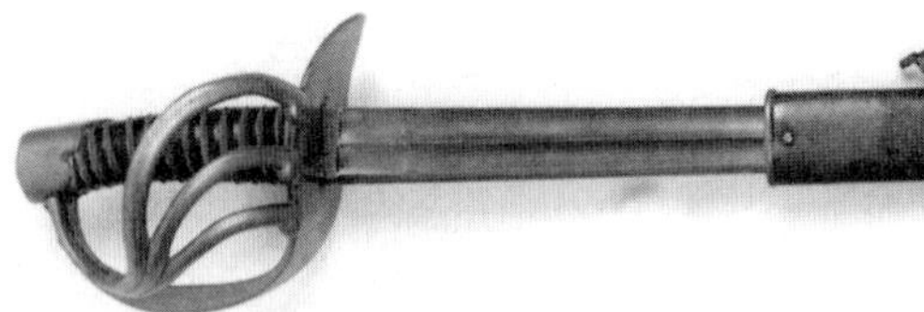

A cavalry trooper's sword, the straight bi-fullered blade etched 'Manufre Rale de Klingenthal Fev 1830 sa', with regulation brass hilt and wire-bound leather-covered grip, in a steel scabbard, French, 1830.
£320–400 ⚒ WAL

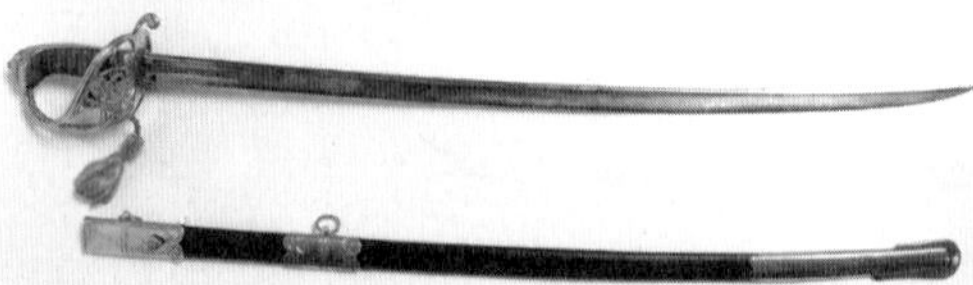

A William IV infantry officer's sword, 14in (35.5cm) long.
£500–550 ⊞ Q&C

A Civil War period non-regulation pattern staff and field officer's sword, by H. Sauerbier, Newark, New Jersey, with single-edged blade, the forte etched with scrolling foliage, the three-bar basket guard modelled as scrolling acanthus foliage, with wire-bound leather-covered grip, in original brass-mounted steel scabbard, blade 32in (81.5cm) long.
£1,350–1,500 ⊞ ASB

Firearms

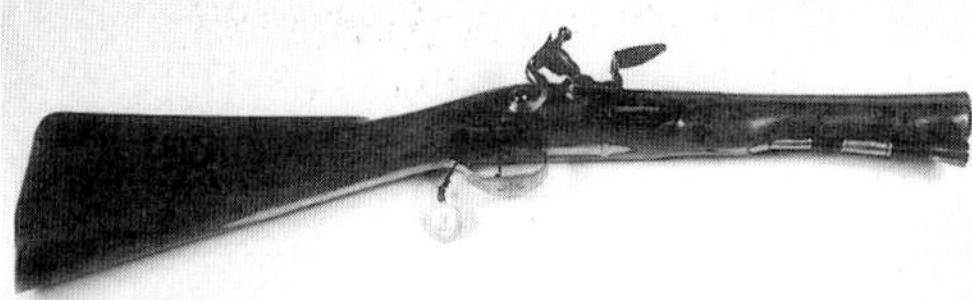

A flintlock blunderbuss, by Steele, with flared brass barrel, London proofs, engraved at breech, the walnut stock with engraved brass mounts, barrel lock and sideplate c1710, remainder c1760, barrel 9¾in (25cm) long.
£2,000–2,250 ⊞ WSA

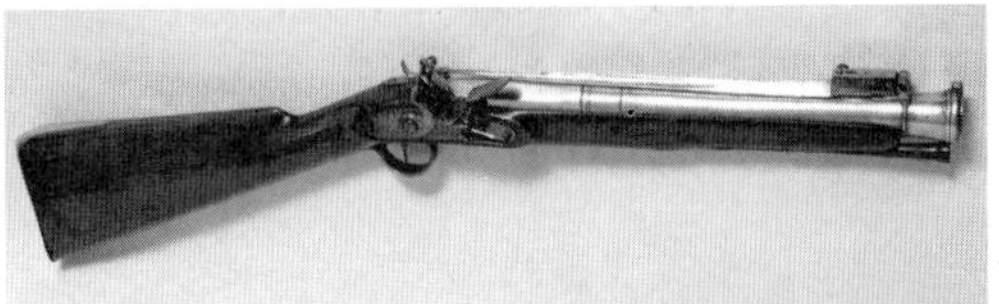

A brass-barrelled coaching blunderbuss, by Twigg, London, from the London to Dover route, c1775, 30in (76cm) long.
£1,850–2,000 ⊞ DJH

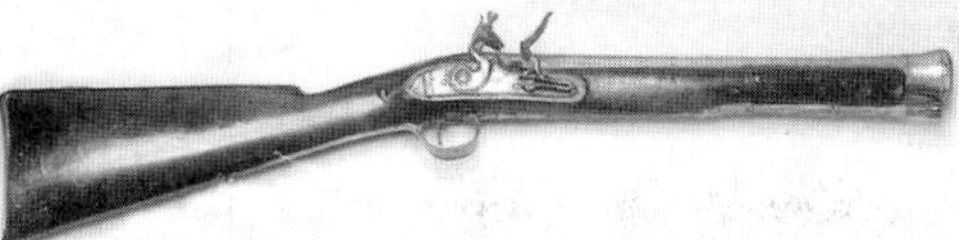

A brass-barrelled flintlock blunderbuss, by Parr, London, with proof marks, walnut stock and brass mounts, bone-tipped wooden ramrod, late 18thC, 30in (76cm) long.
£600–725 ⚒ DN

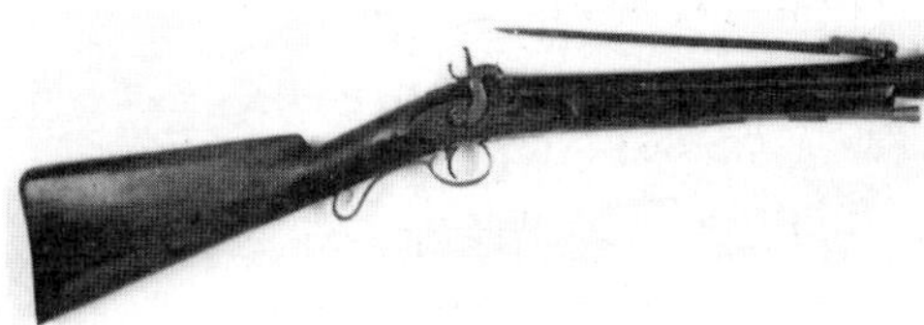

A steel-barrelled percussion blunderbuss, by Hole, Bristol, Birmingham proved, the walnut full stock with steel mounts, the top spring bayonet released by thumb catch, with incorrect brass-tipped ramrod, early 19thC, 30½in (77.5cm) long.
£850–1,000 ⚒ WAL

A .450 Westley Richards patent Monkey-Tail breech-loading percussion saddle carbine, with Birmingham proof marks, figured walnut full stock, steel mounts and original steel ramrod, with calibrated folding adjustable back-sight, and original leather cover, dated 1862, barrel 19½in (49.5cm) long.
£600–750 ⚒ Bon

► **A Remington-Elliott .32 four-shot rimfire derringer,** American, c1870, 5in (12.5cm) long.
£700–900 ⚒ Mit

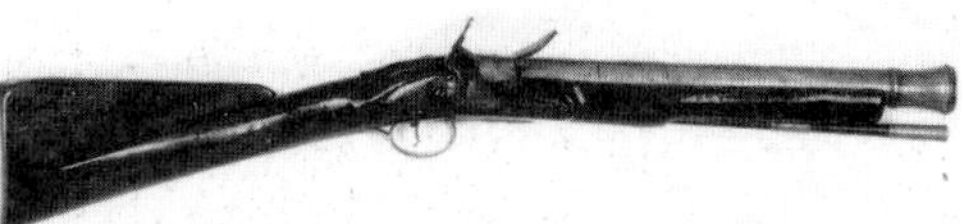

A brass-barrelled flintlock blunderbuss, by Brander, London proved, with full walnut stock and later brass-tipped wooden ramrod, stock refinished with some repairs, c1770, 31¾in (80.5cm) long.
£1,000–1,200 ⚒ WAL

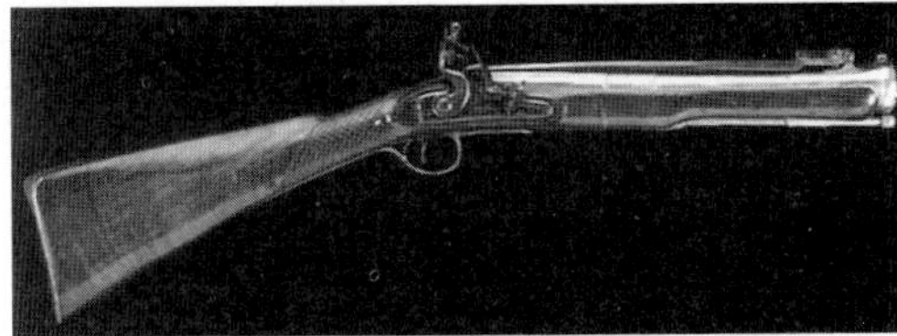

A brass-barrelled flintlock blunderbuss, by Walklate, London, Tower private proof marks, fitted with spring bayonet above a figured-walnut full stock, fore-end repaired, with associated steel ramrod, c1790, 29½in (75cm) long.
£1,650–1,800 ⚒ S(O)

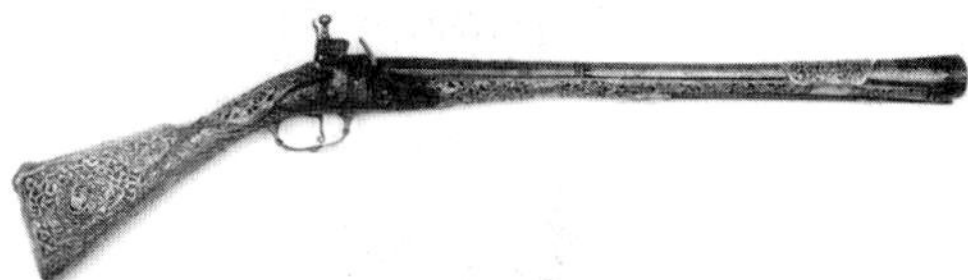

A silver-gilt-mounted flintlock blunderbuss, the wooden full stock decorated with symmetrical designs of pierced, embossed and chased foliate strapwork, with later wooden ramrod, Balkan, 1775–1825, 31¼in (79.5cm) long.
£4,000–4,750 ⚒ Bon

A flintlock blunderbuss, signed 'Scott', with Birmingham proof marks, the two-stage steel barrel fitted with a sprung folding bayonet above, the figured walnut full stock with foliate-engraved brass mounts, brass-tipped ramrod, possibly original, early 19thC, 30in (76cm) long.
£1,000–1,250 ⚒ Bon

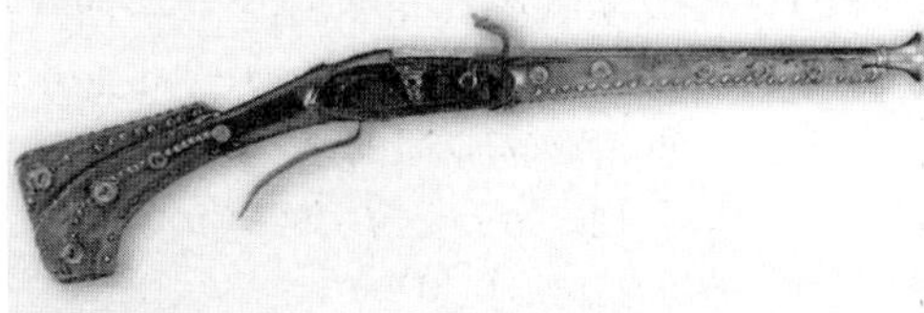

An iron-barrelled matchlock carbine, the figured hardwood full stock with Catalan-style butt enriched over its surface with domed brass nails and discs in imitation of coins, South American, 18thC, 22in (56cm) long.
£700–875 ⚒ S(O)

A .750 flintlock musket, by Thomas Staton, with figured walnut full stock and regulation-style plain brass mounts, original steel ramrod, 1775–85, barrel 39in (99cm) long.
£950-1,200 ⚒ S(O)
Thomas Staton was gunmaker to the East India Company c1778–89 and also worked for the Hudson's Bay Company c1775–81.

A Short Land pattern flintlock musket, with ordnance proofs, walnut full stock and regulation brass furniture, butt stamped 'Queens, 21 Bat, NSM (Nova Scotia Militia) 200', c1780, barrel 42in (106.5cm).
£3,200–3,500 ⊞ WSA

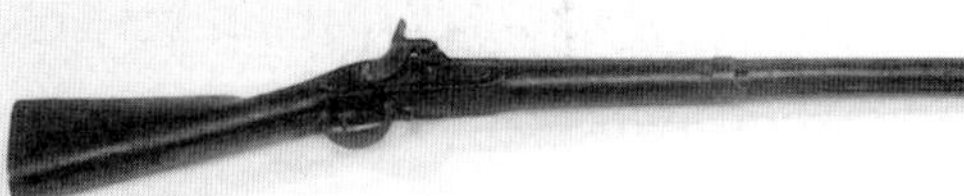

A contract musket, lockplate marked 'U.S. Springfield 1816', left side of butt stock with cheek scoop, American, 57½in (146cm) long.
£370–470 SLN

A gentleman's brass-mounted flintlock pistol, by T. Probin, with walnut full stock, steel barrel and lock, badly pitted, c1750, 16in (40.5cm) long.
£650–750 ⊞ ARB

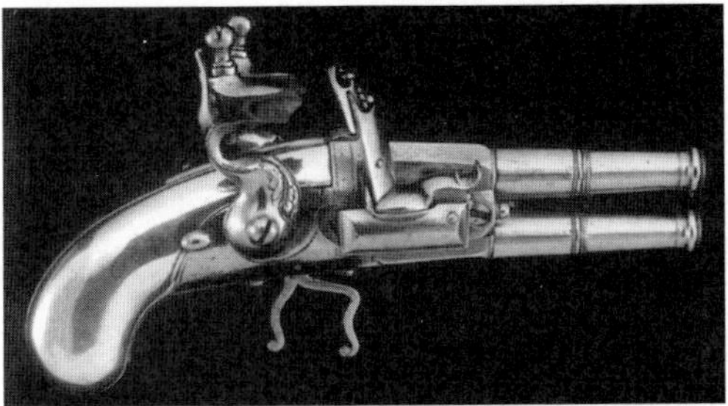

An all-metal over-and-under flintlock pocket pistol, the pans with rainproof covers released by a chiselled spring-catch concealed within the steel, the silver butt decorated with engraved and gilt ornament, Russian, Tula, dated 1750, 6in (15cm) long.
£3,000–3,300 S(O)
The Tula ironworks were founded in central Russia by Peter the Great to make small arms, but by 1725 it had been partly converted into a factory making steel furniture and ornaments. Tula pieces were very expensive and because of their rarity and desirability they still command a premium today.

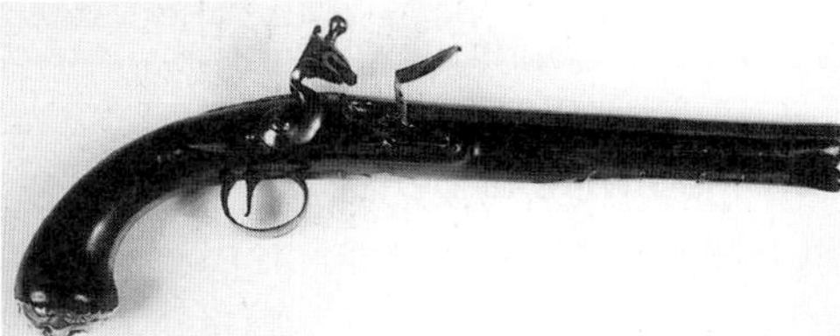

A silver and iron-mounted flintlock holster pistol, by Griffin, London, with Irish registration marks, London proofs and maker's mark, walnut full stock, horn-tipped ramrod, c1760, barrel 9in (23cm) long.
£1,450–1,600 ⊞ WSA

▶ **A percussion pistol,** with walnut stock and gilt-bronze mounts, signed 'Lazaro Lazarino' under powder chamber, lockplate marked 'Fromery, Berlin', German, c1760, 15½in (39.5cm) long.
£470–600 Herm

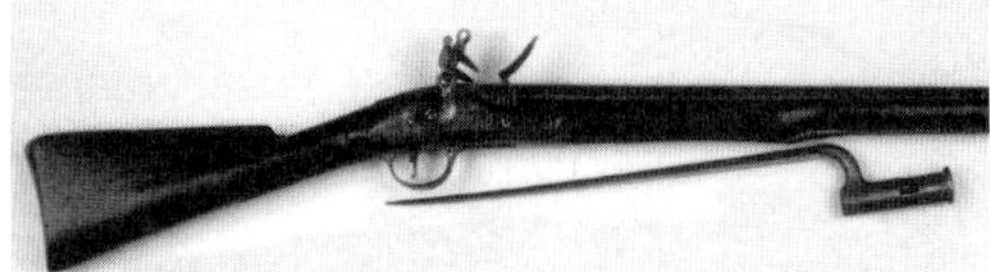

A 10 bore India pattern volunteer Brown Bess flintlock musket, with Tower private proofs, the walnut full stock with regulation brass mounts, steel ramrod, with original triangular socket bayonet by Woolley & Deakin dated 1803, action requires attention, c1800, 55in (139.5cm) long.
£100–125 WAL

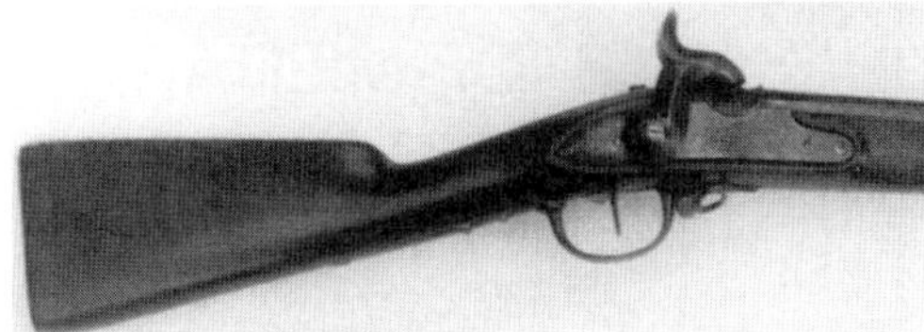

An 18mm three-band percussion musket, with brass fore sight, left side of walnut stock with cheek scoop, steel furniture, Swiss, c1840, barrel 40½in (103cm) long.
£700–780 ⊞ ASB

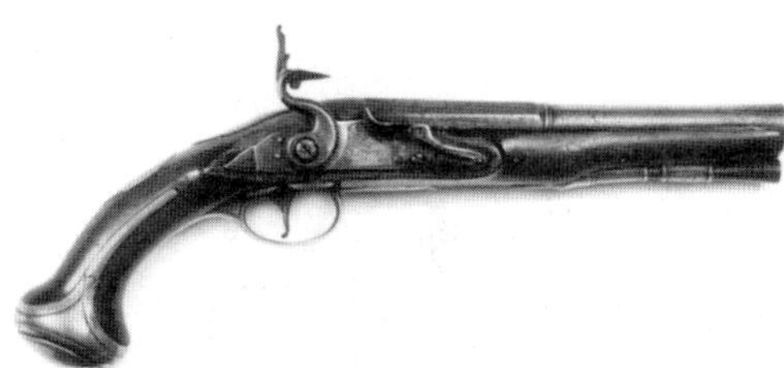

A pair of 20 bore brass-mounted flintlock pistols, by Lowe, London, with London proof marks, figured-walnut full stocks and engraved brass mounts, one later wooden ramrod, the other missing, mid-18thC, 12½in (32cm) long.
£720–900 Bon

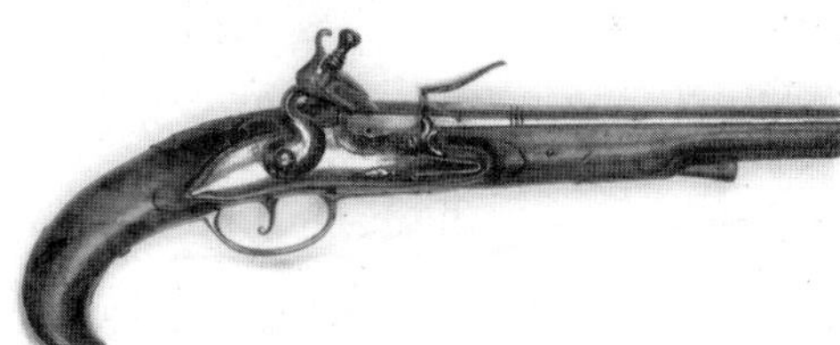

A 20 bore flintlock holster pistol, with walnut full stock and plain brass mounts, shortened during its working life, short replacement ramrod, Continental, mid-18thC, 14½in (37cm) long.
£430–540 WAL

A pair of brass-barrelled flintlock blunderbuss pistols, by John Joyner, Holborn, London, with Tower proofs, engraved with acanthus foliage, walnut full stocks, brass furniture, rosewood ramrods, one later, c1760, barrels 7½in (19cm) long.
£4,000–5,000 WD

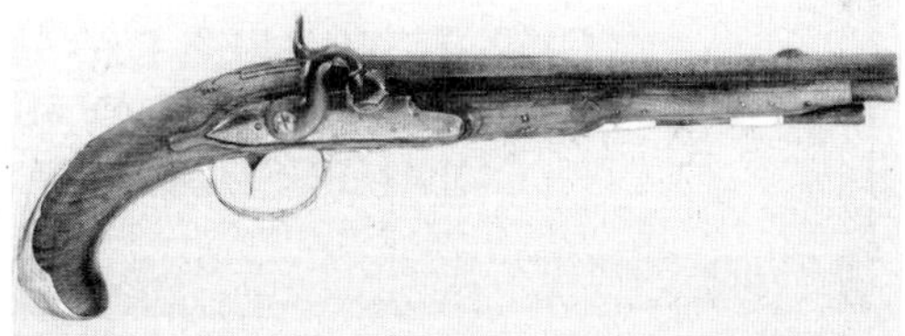

► **A flintlock duelling pistol,** by Ketland & Co, with Tower private proofs, walnut full stock with shell carved around barrel tang, engraved iron mounts and horn-tipped wooden ramrod, c1785, barrel 9in (23cm) long.
£1,350–1,500 ⊞ WSA

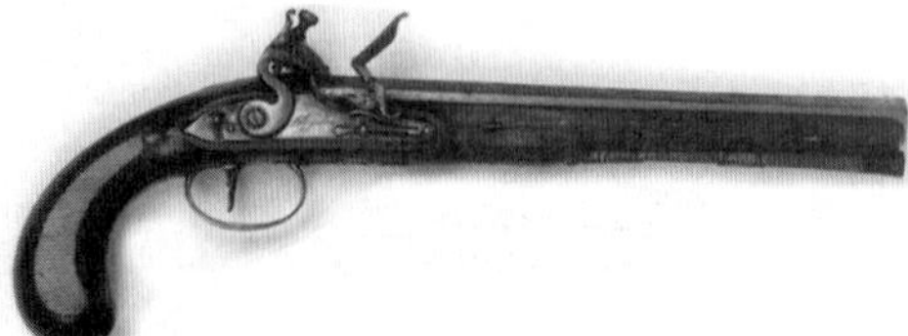

A 24 bore flintlock duelling pistol, by Wogdon, with octagonal barrel and full stock, area of fore-end missing, some restoration, c1780, 15in (38cm) long.
£675–850 WAL

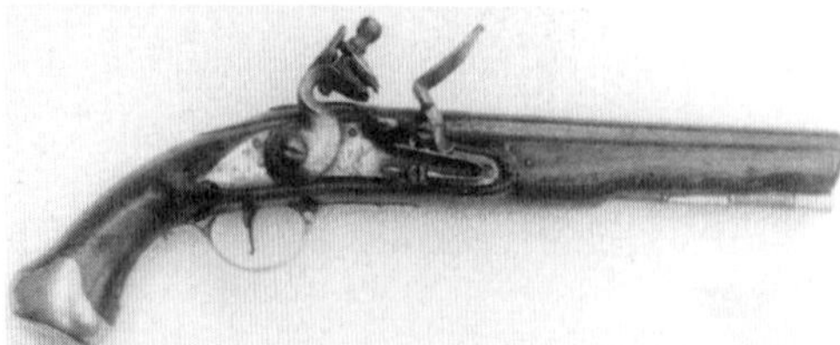

A 16 bore Light Dragoon flintlock holster pistol, inscribed 'York Hussars', the repaired walnut stock with brass furniture, early 19thC, barrel 9in (23cm) long.
£750–850 ⊞ ASB

The York Hussars were one of the many yeomanry cavalry units that were founded to protect Britain during the Napoleonic emergency. Firearms which bear original marks of yeomanry regiments are very rare.

A gentleman's flintlock pocket pistol, by Richards, London, with folding trigger and rifle barrel, c1810, 8in (20.5cm) long.
£700–800 ⊞ ARB

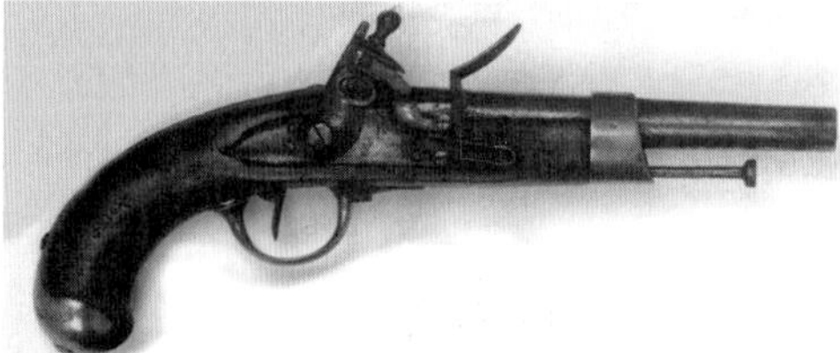

A 13 bore AN 9 flintlock holster pistol, with half stock, regulation brass mounts and pan, steel gripstrap, grip stamped 'GB 1810', stockmaker's stamp 'G Morel', restored ramrod, French, dated 1810, 14in (35.5cm) long.
£450–565 WAL

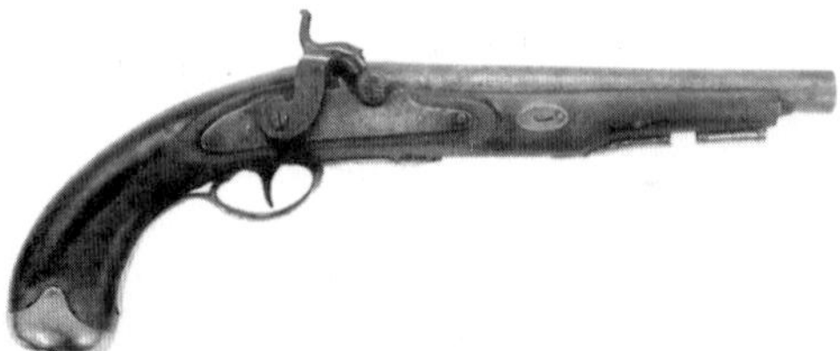

A flintlock holster pistol, converted to percussion, the walnut stock with brass butt cap and guard, the lockplate engraved 'Dublin Castle', with G.R. and crown, ramrod and end cap missing, early 19thC, 15½in (39.5cm) long.
£150–200 F&C

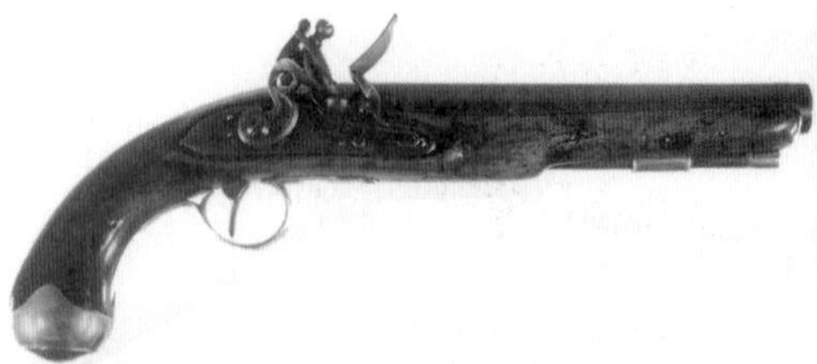

A 16 bore Light Dragoon-type flintlock holster pistol, by Rigby & Son, Dublin, with repaired walnut full stock and brass regulation furniture, later ramrod, barrel pitted, Irish, c1800, barrel 9in (23cm) long.
£650–820 WD

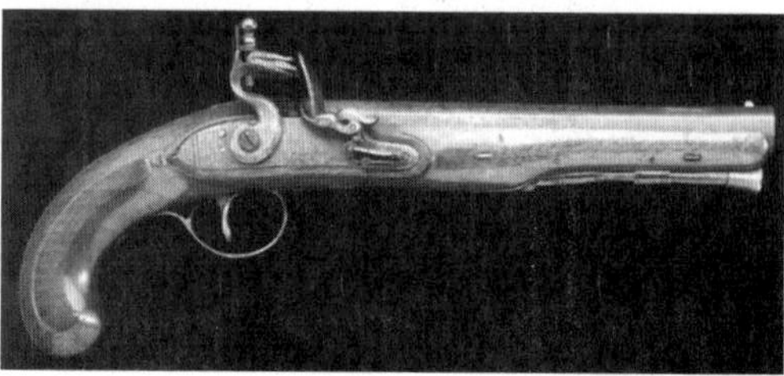

A flintlock duelling pistol, by Calverts, Leeds, Birmingham private proof marks, with figured walnut full stock and steel trigger-guard with pineapple finial, signed, associated ramrod, c1810, 14in (35.5cm) long.
£600–650 S(O)

A pair of flintlock blunderbuss pistols, by Cox & Co, with Derby and Birmingham proofs, with brass two-stage barrels and walnut full stocks, engraved brass trigger guards and ramrod pipes, wooden ramrods, one cock and both ramrods replaced, c1815, 9in (23cm) long.
£3,300–3,650 ⊞ WSA

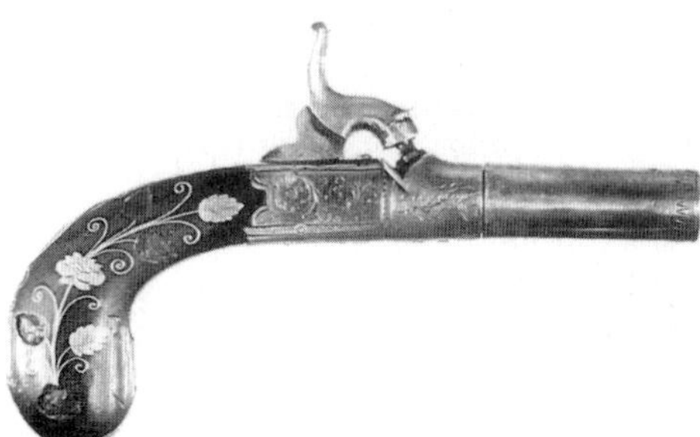

A pair of 48 bore percussion pocket pistols, by C. Adams & Son, London, the walnut grips inlaid with silver wire flowers and foliage, the silver butt caps with iron-hinged trap covers, some inlay missing, c1830, barrels 2¾in (7cm) long.
£400–500 ⚒ WD

A sea-service pistol, with ordnance proofs, the walnut full stock with regulation brass furniture, swivel ramrod, c1830, 15in (38cm) long.
£1,450–1,600 ⊞ WSA

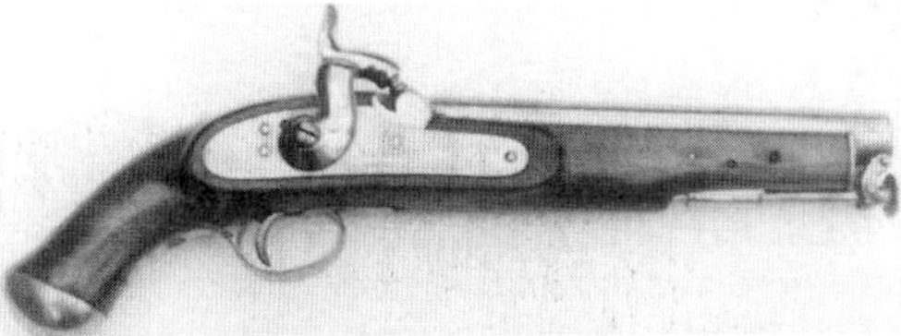

A 12 bore percussion cavalry pistol, by Lacy & Co, London, with London proof marks, with swivel rammer and Lovell's patent lock and walnut stock with brass furniture, c1840, barrel 9¼in (23.5cm) long.
£450–500 ⊞ ASB
Cavalry pistols of musket bore are very rare.

A 24 bore percussion coastguard pistol, by Lacy & Co, London, the walnut full stock with brass regulation furniture and iron lanyard loop, c1840, barrel 6in (15cm) long.
£360–450 ⚒ WD

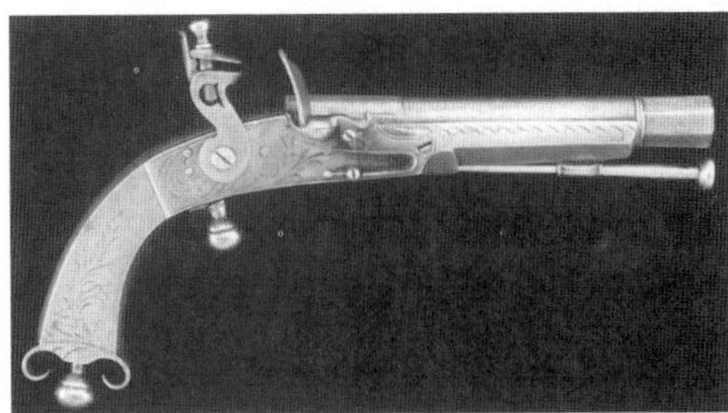

A steel flintlock Highland dress pistol, with Birmingham proof marks, with engraved stock and ram's horn butt engraved with thistle sprays, 1825–30, 10¼in (26cm) long.
£820–1,000 ⚒ S(O)

A flintlock cavalry pistol, designed by Henry Nock, made for the East India Co, with walnut full stock, brass mounts and swivel ramrod, c1830, 16in (40.5cm) long.
£750–850 ⊞ ARB

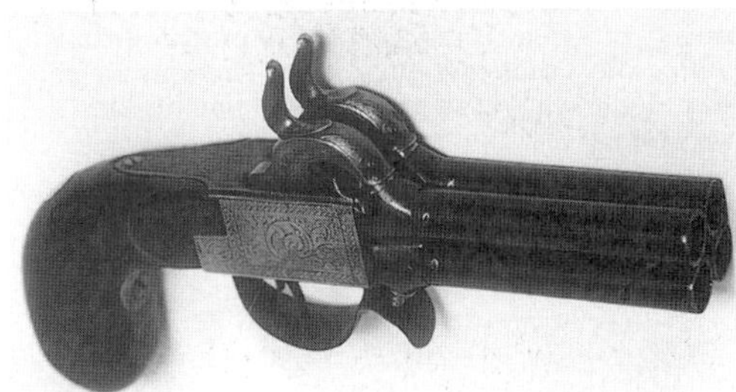

A four-barrel over-and-under pistol, with dolphin hammer and trigger guard lock, 1840–50, 9in (23cm) long.
£900–1,000 ⊞ SPA

A 6 shot hand-rotated pepperbox pistol, by W. Hole, Bristol, c1840, 9½in (24cm) long.
£850–950 ⊞ SPA

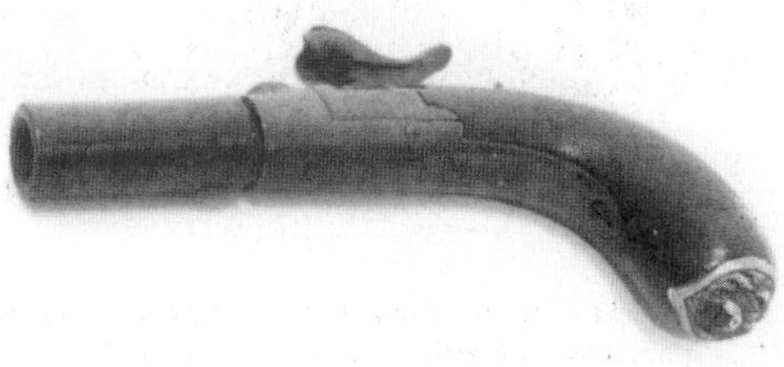

A percussion muff pistol, the engraved lock plates with proof mark, with dolphin cock, folding trigger and screw-on barrel, signed 'Boston, Wakefield', 19thC, 6in (15cm) long.
£260–325 ⚒ DA

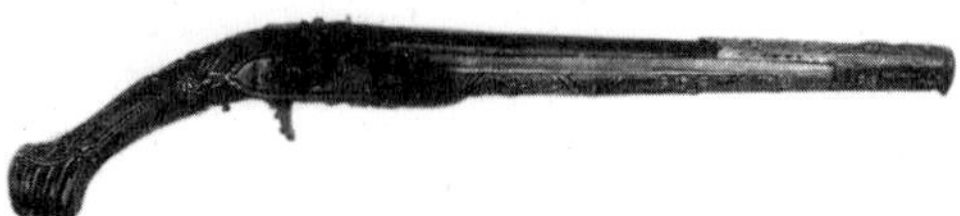

A 20 bore flintlock holster pistol, the iron barrel inlaid with designs of silver strapwork at the breech, the tang overlaid with punched silver, silver full stock and butt cast and chased overall in relief with flowering foliage and trophies of arms, false ramrod, trigger-guard missing, Balkan, 19thC, 20½in (52cm) long.
£500–625 Bon

A double-barrelled sidehammer travelling pistol, Birmingham proved, the walnut butt with vacant white metal escutcheon, steel ramrod, c1850, 8½in (21.5cm) long.
£270–300 CrF

A 31 calibre Colt London pocket model 1849 pistol, serial No. 1402, with London proofs, octagonal barrel and varnished walnut grip, 1854, barrel 5in (12.5cm) long.
£550–700 WD

A six-shot pepperbox percussion revolver, by T. Thomson, Aberdeen, with foliate-engraved nickel mounts and rosewood handle, 19thC, 8in (20.5cm) long.
£375–475 F&C

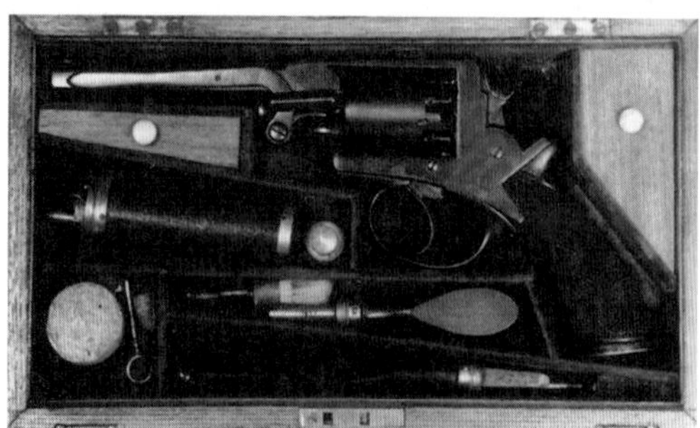

A 54 bore Beaumont-Adams patent five-shot double action percussion revolver, retailed by Deane & Son, London, with London proof marks, refinished chequered walnut butt, rammer possibly replaced, in a later lined and fitted wooden case with reproduction accessories, c1860, 11¾in (30cm) long.
£750–950 Bon

A 15 bore officer's percussion pistol, the octagonal sighted barrel inlaid with silver foliage, with walnut full stock, foliate-engraved steel mounts and stirrup ramrod, Spanish, dated 1845, 12½in (32cm) long.
£320–400 Bon

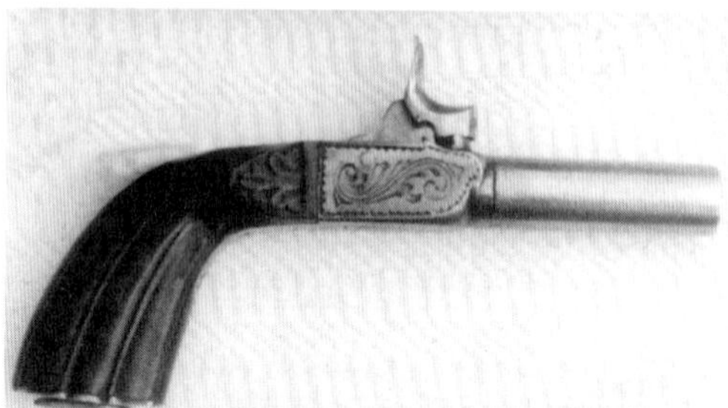

A pair of 60 bore boxlock percussion pistols, with scroll-engraved frames, concealed triggers, fluted walnut grips and nickel silver grip caps, barrels unscrew for loading, Belgian, c1850, barrels 2in (5cm) long.
£600–650 ASB

A six-shot pepperbox percussion revolver, the octagonal barrel signed 'Chas Osborne', the lock, trigger guard and butt with scroll-engraved decoration, the wooden sides to the grip with cross-hatched decoration, 19thC, 8¼in (21cm) long.
£200–250 RTo

An Adams-style self-cocking open-frame percussion cap revolver, with restored ramrod plunger, 1850–55, 8in (20.5cm) long.
£225–250 CrF

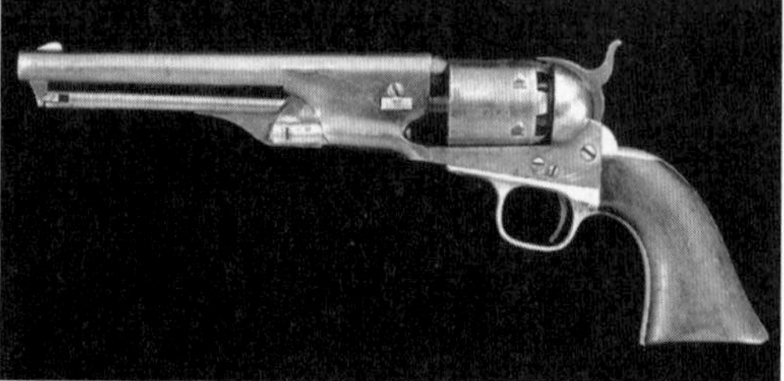

A .36 calibre Colt model 1861 Navy percussion revolver, No. 4161, 1861, 13in (33cm) long.
£1,400–1,600 S(O)

A Colt model 1860 Army percussion revolver, No. 2067, the sighted barrel with New York address, replaced walnut grips, 1861, 13¾in (35cm) long.
£550–700 Bon

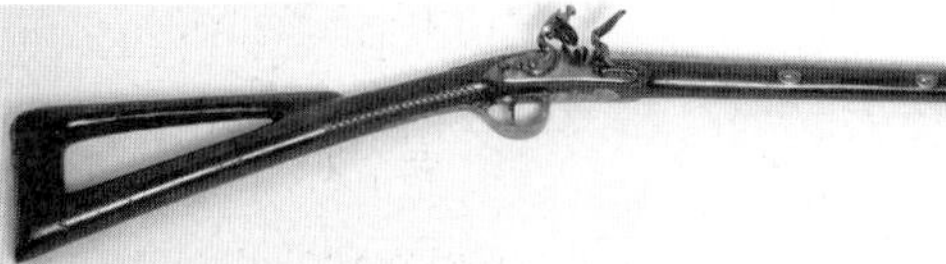

A rifle, by Bate, late 18thC, 39in (99cm) long.
£2,700–3,000 DJH
This rifle was upgraded to waterproof lock by Bate approximately 20 years after manufacture.

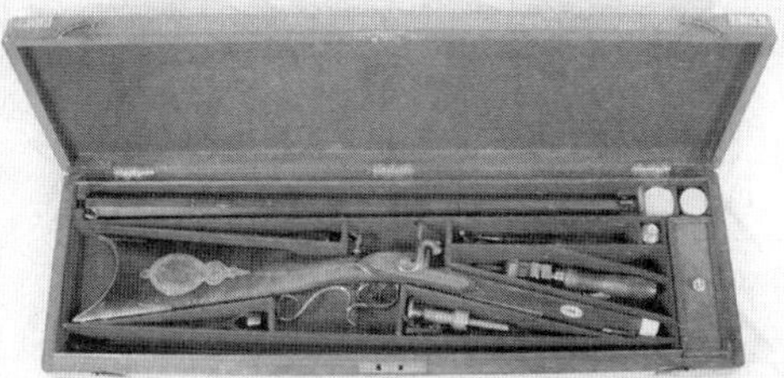

A 100 bore percussion rifle, with octagonal barrel, the walnut half stock with adjustable peep hole rearsight at the wrist, in a period mahogany case relined in green baize with accessories, American, c1860, barrel 26¾in (68cm) long.
£2,000–2,400 WD

A .36 calibre Colt model 1851 Navy six-shot single action percussion revolver, the octagonal barrel with Colt's New York address, with plain walnut grips, refinished by nickel plating, manufactured 1869, barrel 7½in (19cm) long.
£675–750 ASB

An 8 bore breech-loading percussion wall rifle, with folding long-range back-sight, walnut butt, steel butt-plate and trigger guard, folding peg mount, French, dated 1831, barrel 47in (119.5cm) long.
£800–1,000 Bon

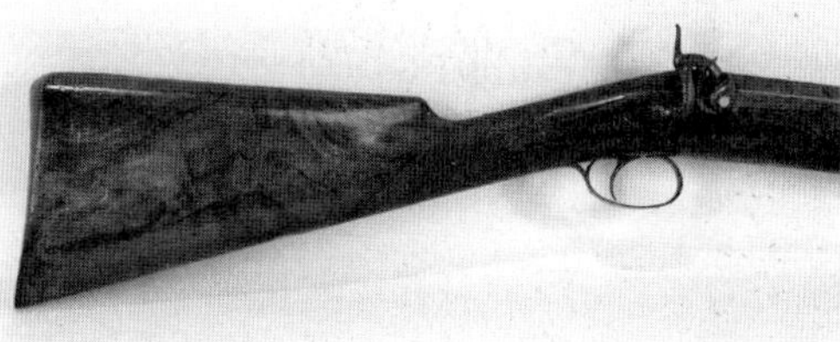

A muzzle-loading percussion rifle, by William Weston, Brighton, with walnut stock and engraved decoration, 19thC, barrel 30in (76cm) long.
£340–425 SWO

Polearms

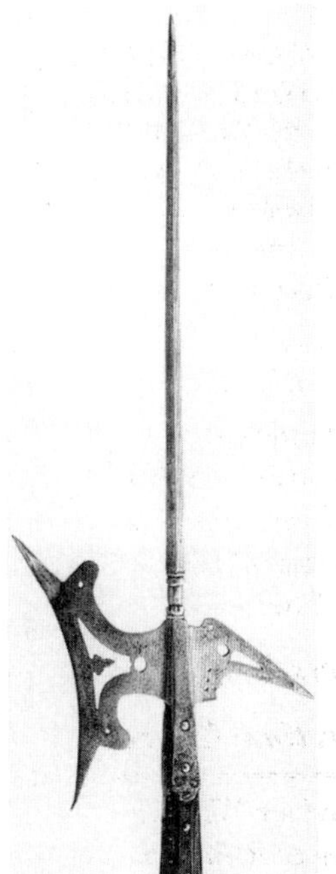

A halberd, German, 16thC, 98in (249cm) long.
£500–625 Herm

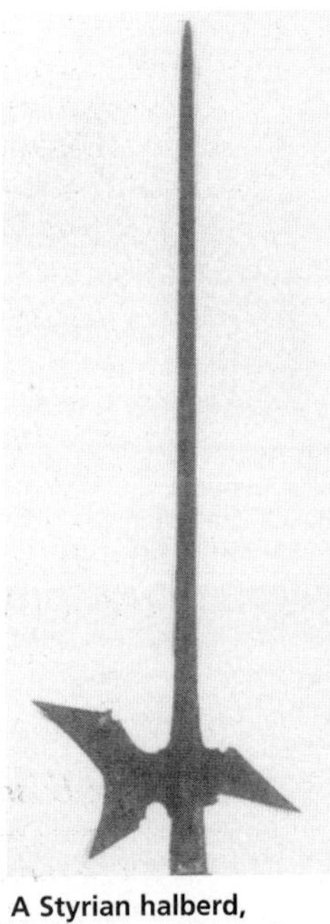

A Styrian halberd, on a later wooden haft, Austrian, 1575–1600, head 50½in (128.5cm) long.
£765–900 S(O)

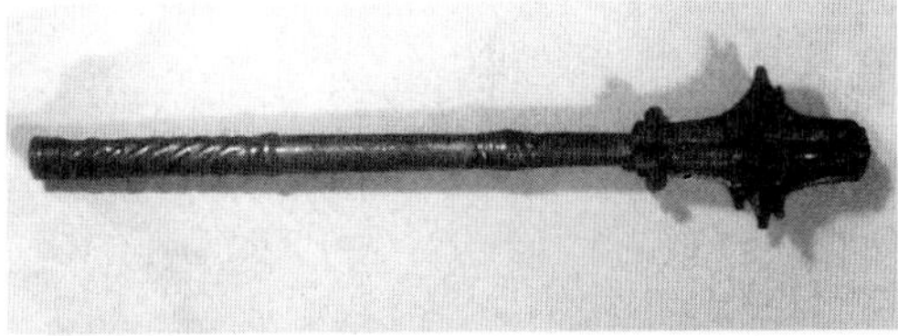

A mace, the head with seven flanges, three-stage steel haft, probably German, mid-16thC, 22in (56cm) long.
£1,200–1,500 WW

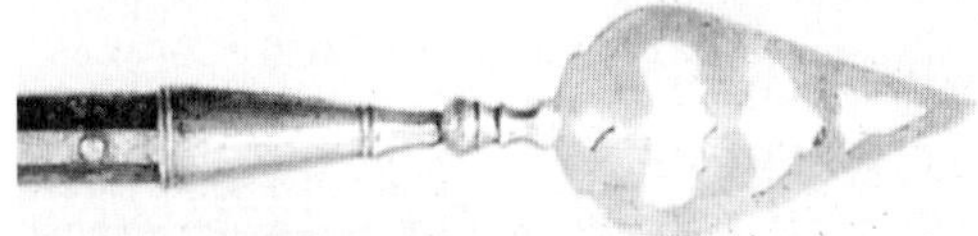

An officer's spontoon, with wrought-iron blade, on a wooden shaft, 18thC, 78¾in (200cm) long.
£270–340 Herm

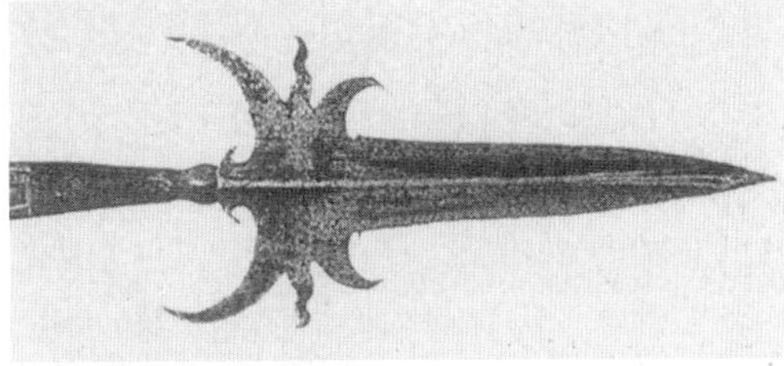

An officer's spontoon, with an iron blade on a wooden shaft, south German, 18thC, 20¼in (51.5cm) long.
£115–140 Herm

Militaria

Badges

A Victorian 3rd Battalion Northumberland Fusiliers plaid brooch, 4in (10cm) diam.
£250–300 ⊞ Q&C
This was the only English regiment to have a Scottish pipe band.

A Victorian other ranks' gilt-metal South Australian Defence Force helmet plate.
£200–240 WAL

A Victorian West York Artillery Volunteers officer's white metal sabretache badge.
£150–200 WAL

◄ A Royal Marine Light Infantry officer's helmet plate, 1902–05.
£320–400 DNW

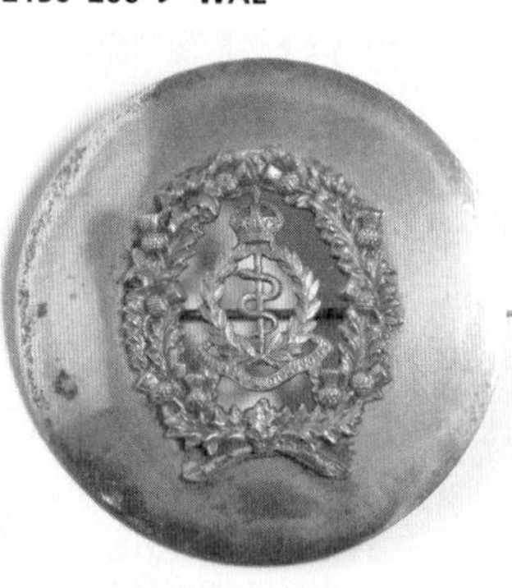

► A George VI silver-plated plaid brooch, 4½in (11.5cm) diam.
£115–125 ⊞ Q&C

Costume

A Victorian Bedfordshire Regiment officer's blue cloth helmet, together with red mess jacket, trousers and other mess-style dress.
£725–900 HOLL

A uniform, belonging to a high-ranking officer or military official, German, Baden, 1806–11.
£3,300–4,200 Herm

► A Victorian Royal Scots Greys Bandmaster full dress uniform, comprising scarlet tunic and yellow-striped blue breeches, with black doeskin inside leg pads.
£350–450 WAL

A London Scottish Volunteers Lieutenant's uniform, comprising cap, tunic, kilt, cloak, socks, mittens, belts and sporran, grey with blue facings and beige piping, in a tin trunk, 19thC.
£525–650 Bri

A 7th (the Princess Royal's) Dragoon Guards captain's full dress scarlet tunic, c1900.
£220–275 WAL

A military tunic and breeches, in blue with red velvet and silver braid cuffs, German, 1910–11.
£400–450 S(Am)

Miller's is a price GUIDE not a price LIST

A Border Regiment Band Sergeant Major's uniform, c1950.
£90–100 Q&C

Helmets & Headdresses

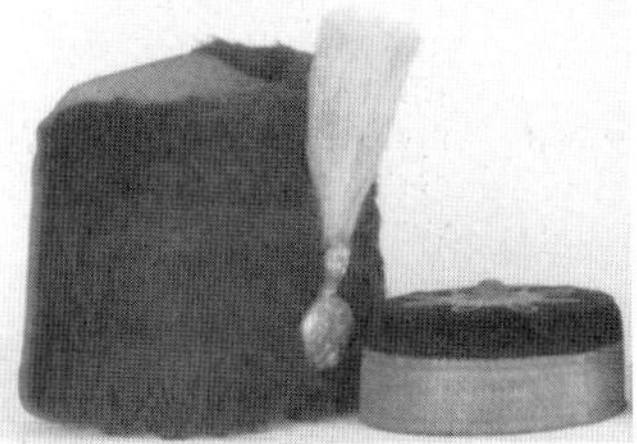

A Victorian Volunteer Artillery officer's busby, with white hair plume and companion pill box hat, both in their japanned tin cases.
£350–450 WAL

A Victorian Queen's Westminster Volunteers other ranks' grey felt slouch hat, with scarlet lace headband and white metal badge on scarlet backing.
£380–475 WAL

A Victorian 5th Royal Hussars Shako, 9in (23cm) high.
£800–900 Q&C

MILITARIA

A Victorian 24th Middlesex Rifle Volunteers officer's astrakhan busby, the rifle green cloth top with braided ornament and a feather plume.
£400–500 WAL

A 19th Hussars officer's busby, with hat box and plume holder, late 19hC.
£675–750 Q&C

A No. 5 Company 1st Volunteer Battalion The Royal Scots (Queen's Rifle Volunteer Brigade) non-commissioned officer's fur busby, the rifle green cloth top with black hair/vulture feather plume, c1888.
£425–525 WAL

A Royal Hungarian Guard brass-mounted steel helmet, 1892–1912.
£2,200–2,750 Herm

► **A Victorian 3rd Volunteer Battalion The Lancashire Fusiliers officer's blue peaked forage cap,** with black lace headband and silver-embroidered peak.
£220–260 WAL

An Imperial *Pickelhaube*, with leather skull, brass fittings, helmet plate for Württemberg, and liner, slight damage, German, c1910.
£250–285 TOB

Orders & Medals

A Military General Service medal, awarded to Sergeant William Fulton, Grenadier Guards, 1793–1814.
£800–900 ⊞ Q&C

A Scinde medal, awarded to Captain F. W. Follett, 25th Regiment, fitted with replacement claw and suspension, Meeanee/Hyderabad,1843.
£550–700 ⚒ Gle

A Canada General Service medal, awarded to Private R. H. Bescoby, Ontario Regiment, one bar, Red River 1870, 1866–70.
£900–1,150 ⚒ Gle
Three hundred and sixty five medals were issued with the single bar Red River 1870.

A WWI National Canine Defence League silver medal, awarded to Bobs, in a contemporary box with a photograph of the dog.
£1,800–2,250 ⚒ Gle
This WWI award was awarded to Bobs, a fox terrier who was a ship's pet, who saved ten men of HMS *Tornado* after attack by German submarines. Bobs' persistent barking attracted the notice of HMS *Radient,* which rescued the half-frozen and unconscious condition survivors from a raft.

A group of seven medals, awarded to Lieutenant Colonel R. F. D. De F. Berrange, Queen's Regiment and South African Forces, Military Cross, G.V.R., with Second Award Bar, 1914–15 Star, British War and Victory Medals, War Medal, Africa Service Medal, Belgian Croix de Guerre.
£1,350–1,700 ⚒ DNW

A group of four medals, awarded to Private G. Final, killed in action December 1914, 1st Battalion Grenadier Guards, Queen's South Africa medal two clasps, 1914 Star and bar, British War and Victory medals.
£500–550 ⊞ Q&C

A WWI M.C. group of five medals, awarded to Lieutenant Colonel H. Stedman, 4th Gurkhas, Military Cross, G.V.R., 1914–15 Star, British War and Victory medals, India General Service 1908–35, with two clasps, Waziristan 1919–21, Waziristan 1921–24, with oak leaf.
£600–725 ⚒ DNW

A gallantry and meritorious service group of five medals, awarded to Lieutenant J. F. Warren, Royal Engineers, Member of the British Empire, 1914–18 War medal, Victory medal, General Service medal, one bar, Defence medal.
£250–275 ⊞ RMC

A group of five medals, awarded to Major Ellison, Grenadier Guards, Military Cross 1917, 1914–15 Star, British War medal, Victory medal with oak leaf, WWII Defence Medal.
£900–1,000 ⊞ Q&C

► A WWI pair of medals and photograph, awarded to Private H. A. Woodcock, 3rd Battalion Grenadier Guards, killed in action 5 December 1917, Arras, 14 x 13in (35.5 x 33cm), framed.
£135–150 ⊞ Q&C

A group of nine medals, Ferdinand I 1914–27 bronze medal, Order of the Crown, type II breast badge, 1913 Red Cross medal, Carol I medal for bravery with swords, commemorative Cross 1916–18 with bar, Victory medal, 1883–1933 Anniversary medal, 1839–1939 Anniversary medal, Serbia Order of St Sava breast badge, Rumanian.
£280–350 ⚒ Gle

A George V Military Cross and Pair, awarded to Captain E. Neville Ashe, 16th Manchester Regiment, in a velvet- and silk-lined display case covered in purple leather, dated 1917.
£600–725 ⚒ Bon

A Campaign Group of five medals, awarded to F. R. Woodward, Royal Navy, 1939–45 Star, Atlantic Star, Africa Star, Pacific Star with bar, 1939–45 War Medal with two named sports medallions.
£70–75 ⊞ RMC

A Long Service and Commemorative group of five medals, awarded to Captain F. J. Towell, Indian Army Ordinance Corps, 1939–45 Star, Burma Star, 1939–45 War medal, India Service medal, Army Long Service and Good Conduct medal with bar.
£330–365 ⊞ RMC

Powder Flasks

An iron-mounted flattened cowhorn powder flask, engraved with a battle scene between two soldiers and a lion, the reverse with concentric circles, German, 1600–50, 11in (28cm) long.
£280–350 ⚒ Herm

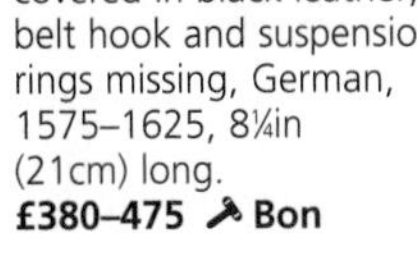

A musketeer's powder flask, the wooden body covered in black leather, belt hook and suspension rings missing, German, 1575–1625, 8¼in (21cm) long.
£380–475 ⚒ Bon

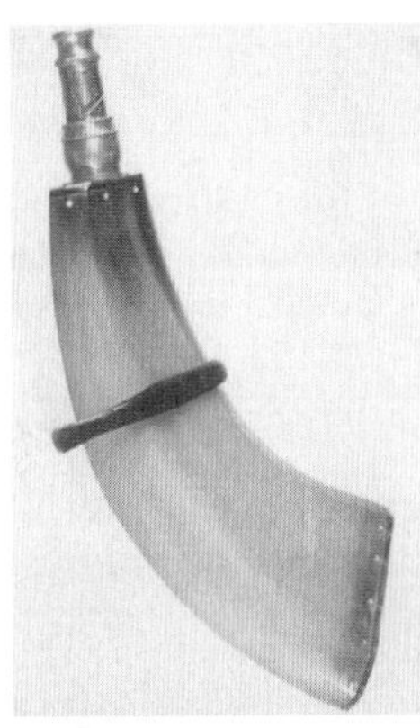

A powder horn, the flattened body with iron belt hook, the white metal top with push-in charger, probably French, c1780, 9½in (24cm) long.
£220–275 ⚒ WD

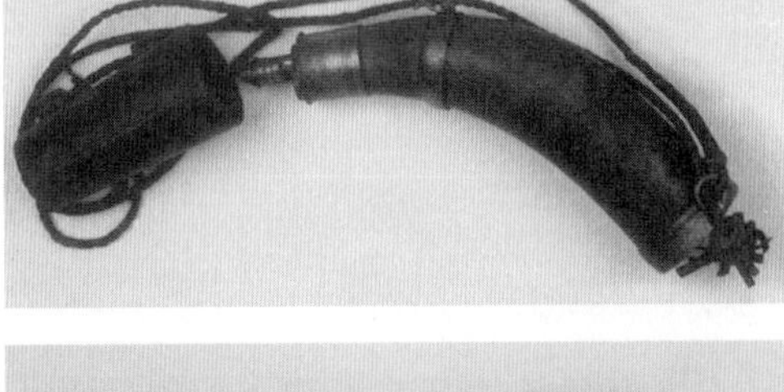

◀ **A brass-mounted cowhorn powder flask,** probably for rifle volunteers, with original leather charger cover, late 18thC, 11in (28cm) long.
£230–280 ⚒ WAL

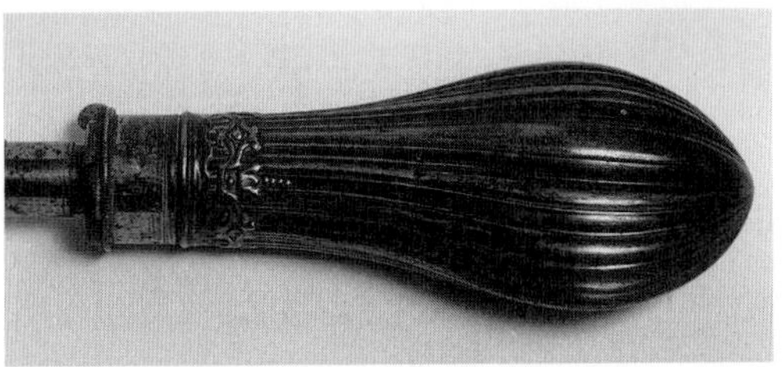

A copper and brass powder flask, by Hawksley, 1820, 8¼in (21cm) long.
£100–125 ⊞ SPA

A copper powder flask, marked 'B à Paris' and decorated with laurel and oak leaves and acorns enclosing a crossed pair of pistols, a crossed pair of swords, and a pike, French, c1840, 4½in (11.5cm) long.
£160–180 ⊞ ASB

Miscellaneous

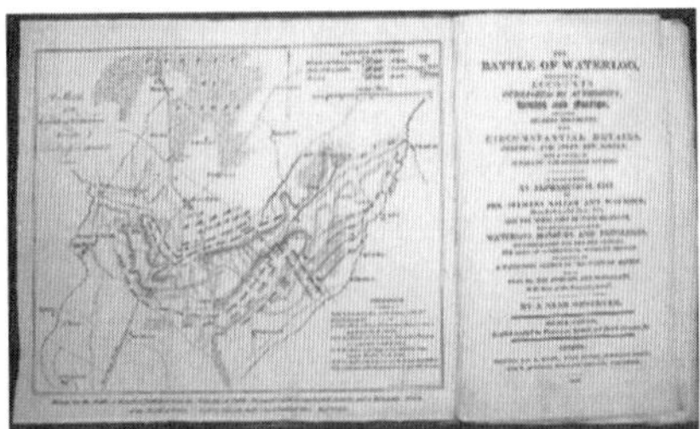

The Battle of Waterloo, by a near observer, containing the accounts published by authority ...to which is added an alphabetical list of the officers killed and wounded, published by J. Booth *et al*, London, 4th edition, 8°, in publisher's printed blue paper boards.
£125–150 PFK

A Rifle Brigade officer's cross belt, silver badge hallmarked 1898, the furniture 1952, 42in (106.5cm) long.
£360–400 Q&C

Badges such as the one on this cross belt would be passed from father to son which is why it bears an earlier date. The rest of the silver mounts date from the period of manufacture of the belt.

A group photograph, of eight officers of the 58th Foot, wearing full scarlet dress tunics, at Sunderland Barracks, 7 October 1861, 10¾ x 8¾in (27.5 x 22cm).
£260–325 Gle

An epovette, calibrated to 5, 1750–1800, 9½in (24cm) long.
£400–450 SPA

An epovette was used to test gun powder and determine how much to load into the pistol.

► **A Victorian Royal Scots Greys officer's gilt and silver-plated waist belt plate.**
£170–220 WAL

► **A pair of military range-finding binoculars,** French, c1910, 4¼in (11.5cm) long.
£80–90 PHo

A Lynn Loyal Volunteers officer's copper gilt gorget, engraved with the Royal Arms of Great Britain before 1801, with faded blue or black silk rosettes, 1794–1801.
£400–500 DNW

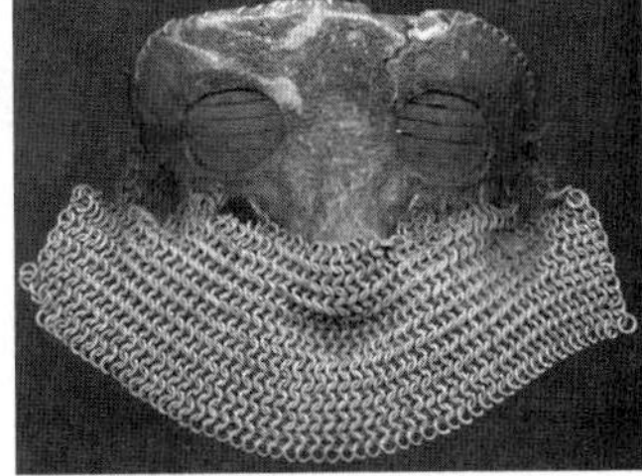

A WWI British tank crew mask, c1917.
£120–150 N

A WWI officer's trench periscope, by R. & J. Beck, with wood hand grip, the copper and brass case with gun-metal finish, with adjustable lens, French, 18in (45.5cm) long.
£150–200 WW

A 49th (Hertfordshire) Regiment officer's shoulder belt plate, 1843–55.
£300–375 DNW

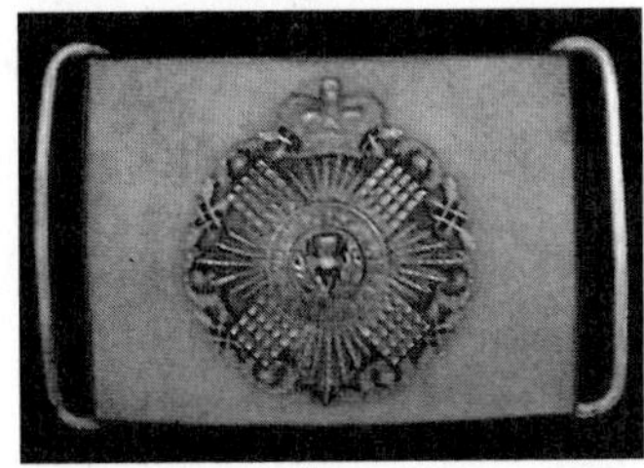

A brass and copper three-way pistol flask, 1820–50, 4½in (11.5cm) high.
£200–235 SPA

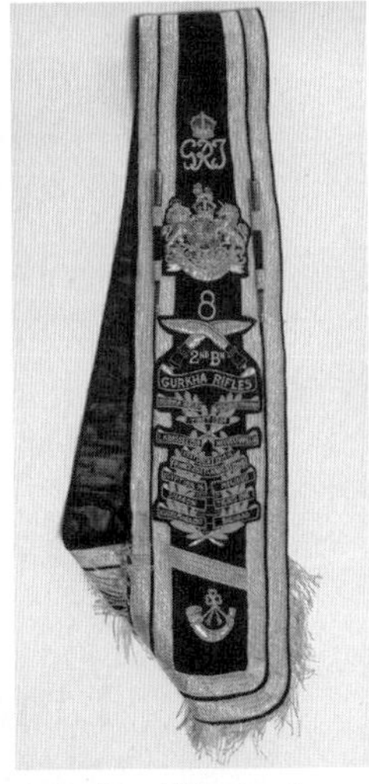

A Gurkha Rifles 2nd Battalion Drum Major's sash, pre-1947, 37in (94cm) long.
£350–400 Q&C

MILITARIA

Sport
Billiards

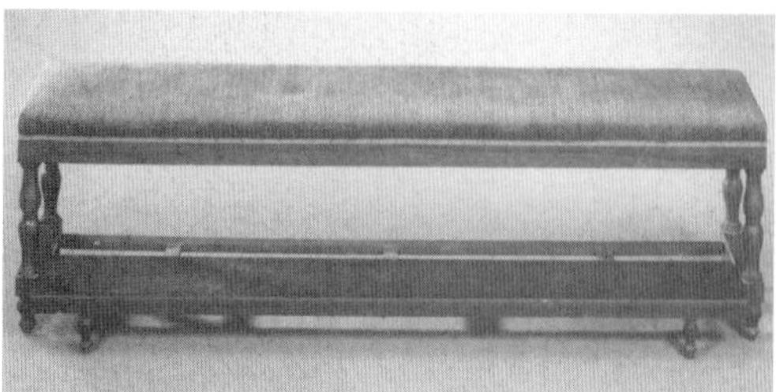

A mahogany billiards room bench, with woven upholstery and a sliding footstool, French, c1840, 82¾in (210cm) wide.
£1,500–2,000 ⚒ S(Am)

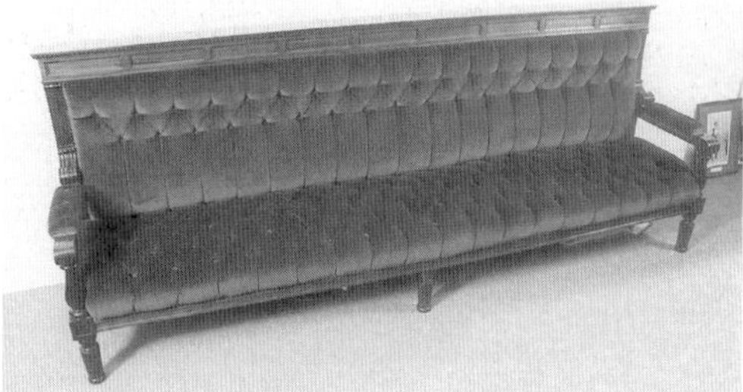

A pair of George Wright billiards room benches, upholstered in green velvet, c1880, 96in (244cm) wide.
£4,000–5,000 ⊞ WBB

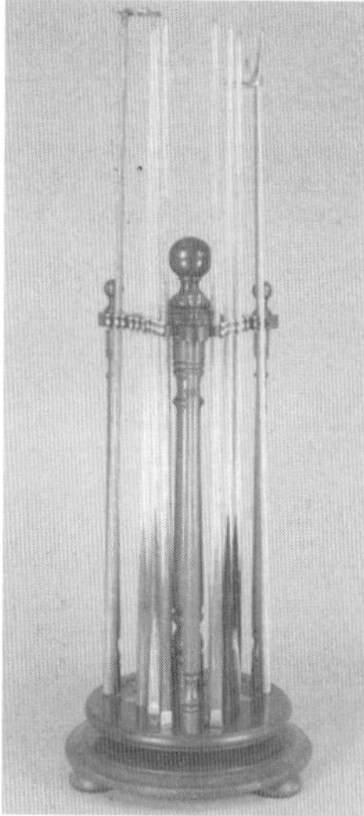

► **A mahogany revolving cue stand,** the three sides fitted with six metal cue brackets, with ten cues and accessories, late 19thC, 47in (119.5cm) high.
£1,200–1,500 ⚒ S

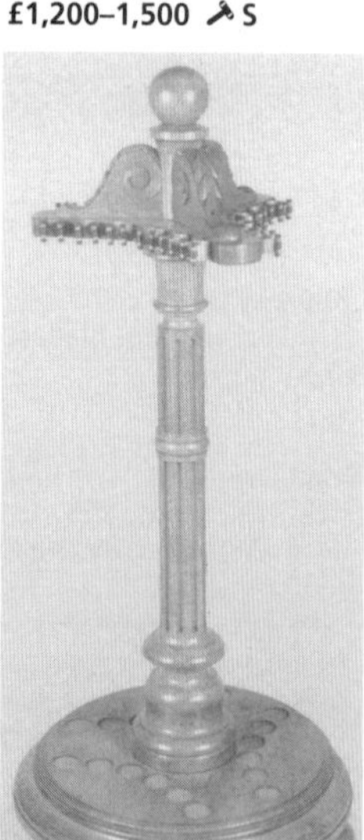

An oak revolving billiard cue stand, with apertures for 18 cues, late 19thC, 47in (119.5cm) high.
£700–850 ⚒ Mit

► **A Palmer & Sons revolving cue stand,** with ebony clips, c1890, 48in (122cm) high.
£1,350–1,500 ⊞ WBB

► **A Victorian mahogany cue stand,** 14in (35.5cm) wide.
£300–375 ⚒ SWO

An oak marker cabinet, incorporating hidden mechanism to transform cabinet into multi-function use, 18thC, 72in (183cm) high.
£7,500–8,500 ⊞ WBB

► **A George Wright mahogany static round cue stand,** c1875, 48in (122cm) high.
£1,100–1,300 ⊞ WBB

A colour lithograph, by Thackeray, entitled 'A Billiard Match – Snookered', published by Landeker & Brown, London, 1902, 27½ x 21¼in (70 x 54cm), framed and glazed.
£60–75 ANA

◄ **A Raper & Sons oak scoreboard,** with dogtooth inlay, ivory slider and mother-of-pearl markings, c1865, 48in (122cm) wide.
£1,200–1,500 WBB

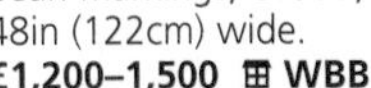

A William Morris oak scoreboard, 1881, 72in (183cm) high.
£7,000–8,000 WBB

► **A Burroughes & Watts scoreboard,** with centre blackboard and rotating score indicators, late 19thC, 36in (91.5cm) wide.
£425–525 Mit

An E. Thurston burr-yew billiards table, 1845, 144 x 72in (366 x 183cm).
£20,000–25,000 WBB

A G. Ashcroft burr-walnut billiards table, 1865, 144 x 172in (366 x 183cm).
£20,000–25,000 WBB

A Victorian snooker table, 144 x 72in (366 x 183cm).
£1,200–1,500 MAR

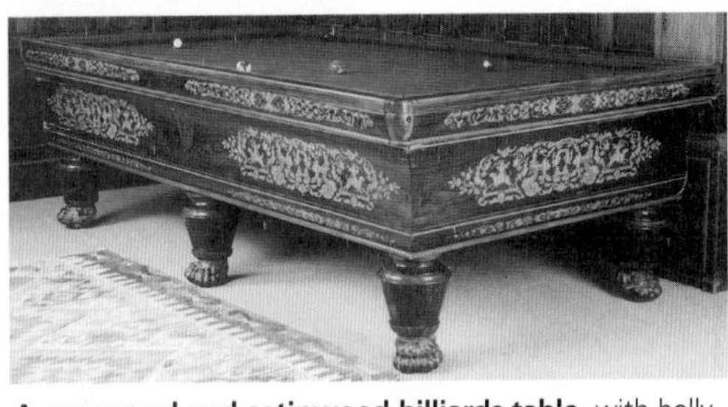

A rosewood and satinwood billiards table, with holly and kingwood inlay and marquetry, in need of restoration, French, c1850, 108 x 54in (274.5 x 137cm).
£30,000–35,000 WBB

◄ **A Burroughes & Watts oak billiards table,** labelled, with modern canopy light, a set of cues and other accessories, late 19thC, 144 x 72in (366 x 183cm).
£1,400–1,750 Mit

An Orme & Sons oak billiards table, 1890, 144 x 72in (366 x 183cm).
£40,000–45,000 WBB

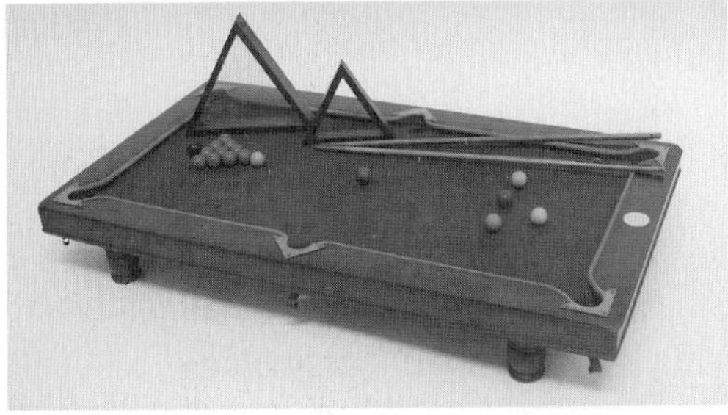

◄ **A mahogany miniature snooker table,** with baize-lined slate bed, on four legs, with balls, triangle and two spring-loaded brass cues, 1875–1925, 20in (51cm) wide.
£600–700 G(L)

Boxing

Two pairs of children's boxing gloves, c1930, largest 8in (20.5cm) long.
£45–50 ⊞ SA

A training shirt from the Big Bear Camp, signed by Lennox Lewis and four others, white with navy blue, 1997.
£170–200 ⚒ ANA

Pierce Egan, *Boxiana; or Sketches of Antient Modern Pugilism,*1840s, large 8°, with engraved frontispiece and title page and 62 uncoloured engraved plates, bound in contemporary quarter morocco, hinges repaired.
£230–280 ⚒ DW

A World Heavyweight Boxing Championship pennant, Muhammad Ali v Sonny Lewis, Lewiston, Maine, 25 May 1965, blue and yellow felt, 25½in (65cm) long.
£180–225 ⚒ ANA

Henry Alken, 'A Prize Fight', from The National Sports of Great Britain series, aquatint by I. Clark, with original hand colouring, published by T. McLean, 1820, 10¾ x 14½in (27.5 x 37 cm).
£170–200 ⚒ BBA

◄ **A signed photograph,** Muhammad Ali and The Beatles, 1964, 25 x 28in (63.5 x 71cm), framed and glazed.
£7,000–7,750 ⊞ SMW

Cricket

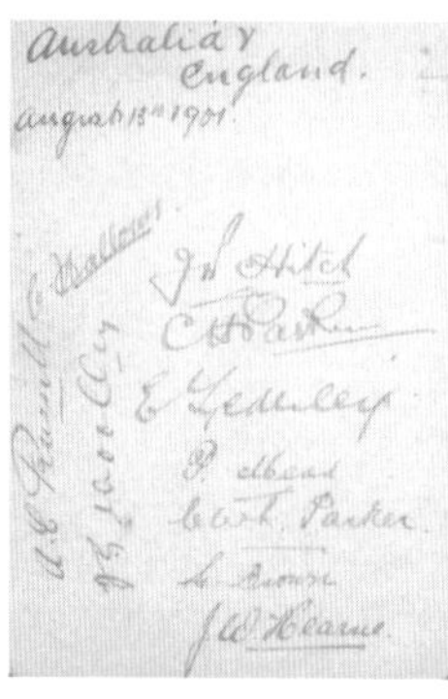

A collection of ten autographs, from the England Test Team against Australia, 13 August 1921, ink signatures on an autograph album leaf.
£85–100 ⚒ DW

Cross Reference
See Colour Review (page 743)

► **Don Bradman,** *'Flicker' No. 1, On Drive and Off Drive,* published by Flicker Production, 1930s, 16°, with wrappers.
£120–140 ⚒ P(Ba)

Alfred Taylor, *Cheltenham Cricket Week,* softback brochure, 62 pages, 1905, 6 x 9½in (15 x 24cm).
£180–225 ⚒ VS

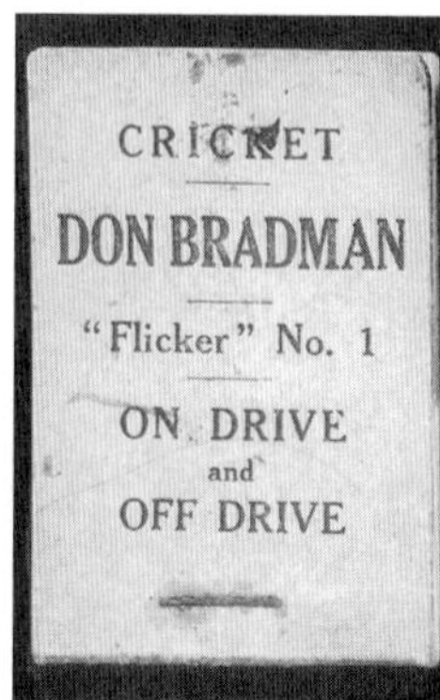

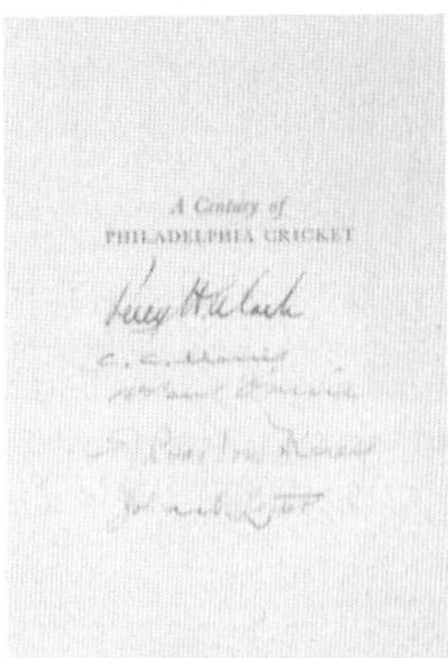

John Lester, *A Century of Philadelphia Cricket*, hardback edition, 1951, signed to half-title page by C. C. Morris, W. P. O'Neill, Percy Clark, J. B. King and J. A. Lester, with dust jacket, tape repairs.
£260–325 VS

A cricket ball, commemorating Fred Trueman's first hat-trick in First Class cricket, mounted with a silver band with presentation inscription 'Yorkshire v Nottinghamshire, Trent Bridge 1951'.
£550–700 S

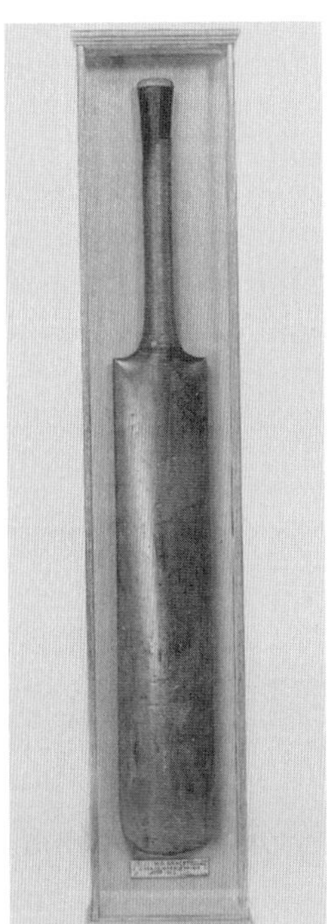

► **A Crawford Exceller cricket bat,** with signed inscription from W. G. Grace, handle grip worn, some woodworming, dated 1909, in a wooden and perspex display case with inscribed plaque.
£900–1,100 P(Ba)

A cricket bat, signed by the England v West Indies teams, including Malcolm Marshall, 1988, 31in (78.5cm) long.
£150–200 SMW

A Parian bust of W. G. Grace, by Robinson & Leadbeater, c1890, 6½in (16.5cm) high.
£600–700 RdV

A menu card, for the dinner commemorating the retirement from County cricket of Jack Hobbs held at the Dorchester Hotel on 17 July 1935, with signed portrait of Hobbs loosely inserted and coloured pictorial covers, 16 pages.
£380–430 P(Ba)

A pair of cricketing interest spill vases, after Kinsella, entitled 'The Hope of his Side' and 'The Boss', German, c1910, 5in (12.5cm) high.
£180–200 PEZ

A photograph of the Yorkshire County cricket team, 1903, 18 x 15in (45.5 x 38cm), framed and glazed.
£75–85 SA

A Victorian silver lustre mug, decorated with three cricketers on a beige stoneware body, 4in (10cm) high.
£180–220 G(L)

A commemorative cricket mug, transfer-printed in black and white with Herbert and W. Sutcliffe, inscribed 'Pudsey Corporation Test Records...1924–1925', retailed by W. Ellis Moorcroft of Bramley, c1925, 4in (10cm) high.
£320–400 DD

◄ **A *carte-de-visite* portrait photograph of W. G. Grace,** by Elliot & Fry, showing Grace aged about 30 years, with his pencil signature on the reverse, c1878, 4 x 2½in (10 x 6.5cm).
£220–270 DW

► **Two sets of four picture postcards,** entitled 'Portraits of the Complete English Team who Brought Home the Ashes' and 'Portraits of the Australian Team, 1905', published by A. C. Cricket Rhymester.
£100–125 F&C

SPORT

Croquet

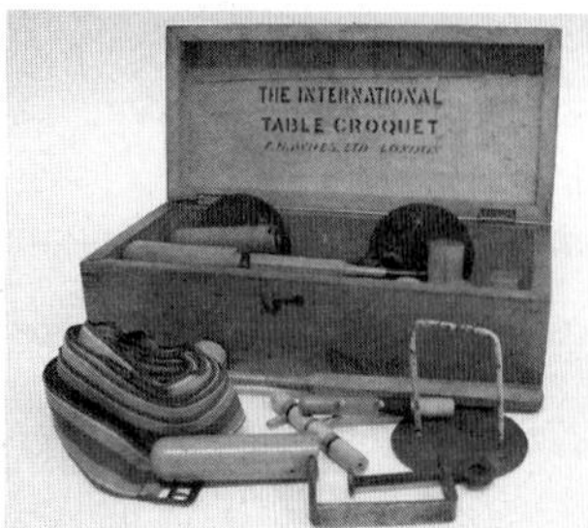

A table croquet set, by F. H. Ayres, London, with rules booklet, c1906, 12in (30.5cm) long, in original pine box.
£100–125 ⚒ G(L)

A brass carrier for four croquet balls, with loop handle, 19thC.
£160–200 ⚒ LFA

A tile, depicting a couple playing croquet, c1890, 6in (15cm) square.
£50–60 ⊞ WAB

Equestrian

A pair of black leather riding boots, with trees, 24in (61cm) high, early 20thC.
£100–125 ⊞ SPT

A bamboo riding crop, with an antler handle, silver collar and a leather loop end, c1910, 32in (81.5cm) long.
£90–105 ⊞ GBr

◄ A *Vanity Fair* cartoon, by Spy, entitled 'The Favourite Jockey', original lithographed caricature of Fred Archer, 1881, 2°, in a glazed maplewood frame.
£100–120 ⚒ DW

A set of four lithographs, by Spy, depicting steeple chase scenes, hand-coloured, heightened with varnish, published by F. Sala & Co, Berlin, c1860, 17¼ x 22in (44 x 56cm), mounted.
£400–500 ⚒ DW

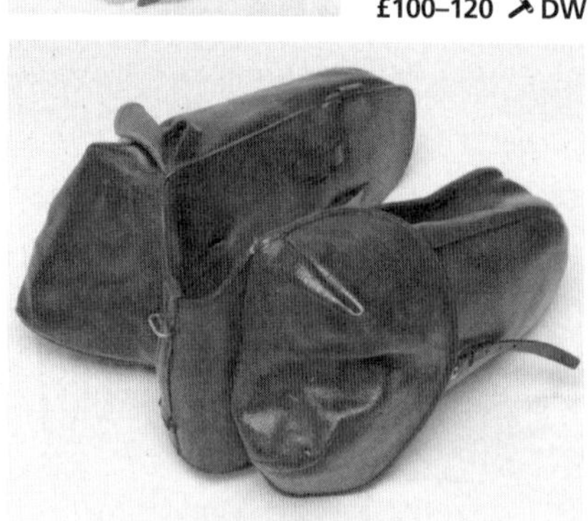

A leather saddle bag, for hunting and shooting equipment, c1930, 15in (38cm) high.
£70–75 ⊞ SA

A papier mâché veterinary model of a horse's hoof and fetlock, dissecting and unhooking to reveal named and numbered parts, French, 19thC, 12½in (32cm) high.
£370–470 ⚒ CGC

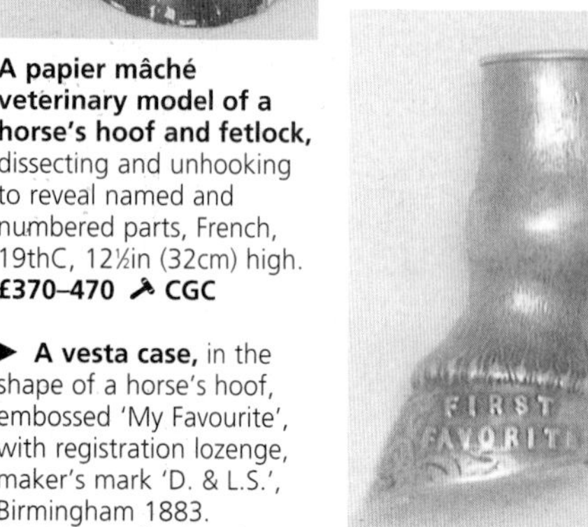

► A vesta case, in the shape of a horse's hoof, embossed 'My Favourite', with registration lozenge, maker's mark 'D. & L.S.', Birmingham 1883.
£450–550 ⚒ B(WM)

A pearlware Prattware horse racing jug, decorated in blue, brown, orange, yellow and green, c1800, 8in (20.5cm) high.
£750–850 ⊞ RdV

► A rosewood snuff mull, the hinged lid carved as the underside of a horse's hoof, 19thC, 4¼in (11cm) wide.
£1,000–1,200 ⚒ Bea(E)

Fishing

An angler's leather-bound reed creel, with offset hole for catch and original strap, 1930s, 13in (33cm) high.
£100–120 ⊞ PEZ

► **A painted wood and metal fish decoy,** in the shape of a turtle, with metal fins and bead inset eyes, American, early 20thC, 8in (20.5cm) wide.
£650–800 ⚒ BB(S)

A pair of stuffed and mounted tench, in a bowfronted case, 1900–20, case 32½in (82.5cm) wide.
£650–800 ⚒ CGC

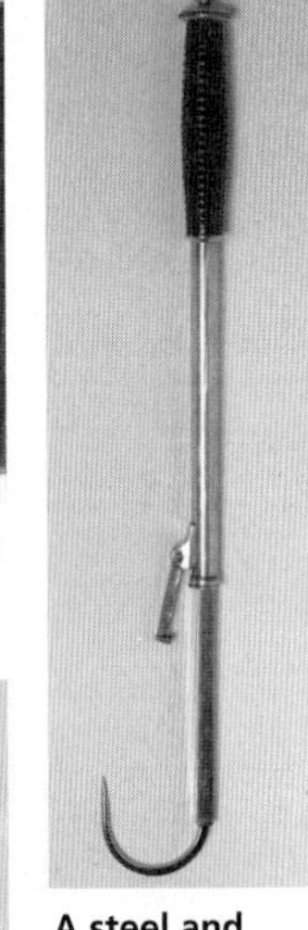

A steel and bass gaff, with mahogany belt hook, c1930, 21in (53.5cm) long.
£115–130 ⊞ PEZ

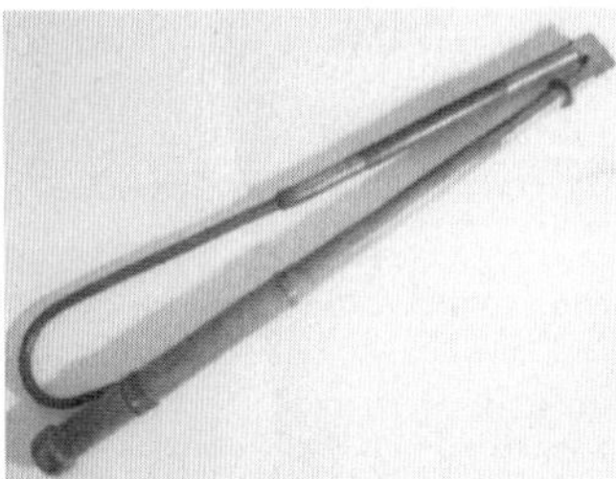

A wood, brass and steel folding gaff, The Dawson, by C. Farlow & Co, London, with brass spring folding latch and sliding ferrule point protector, 1885–94, 37in (94cm) long.
£260–325 ⚒ MUL

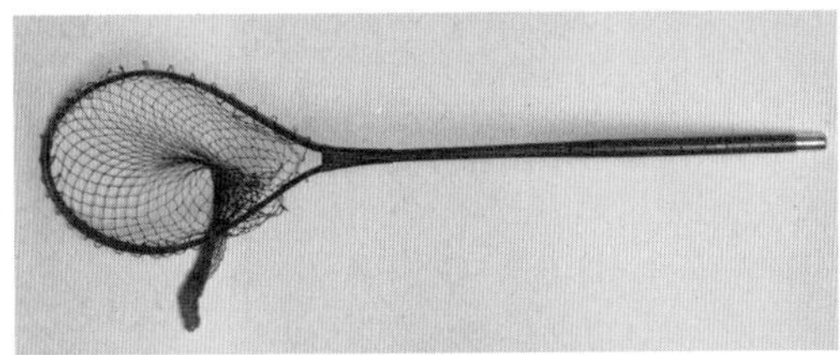

A wood hoop landing net, with belt clip and brass end cap, 1880–1900, 37in (94cm) long.
£100–125 ⊞ PEZ

► **A wood-handled trout landing net, The Gye,** by C. Farlow & Co, London, the greenheart shaft and pear-shaped sliding head with original net, 1885–94.
£100–125 ⚒ MUL

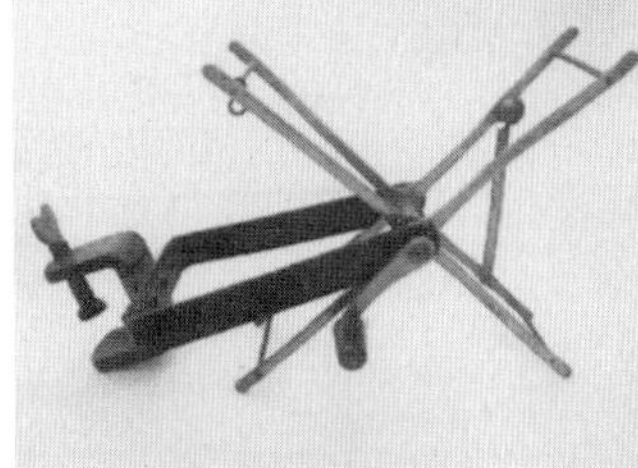

◄ **A brass and steel clamp table line drier,** by C. Farlow & Co, London, with adjustable arm and curved brass crank wind handle, 1885–94.
£200–250 ⚒ MUL

An Allcock Coxon Aerial 4inch reel, with six spokes, walnut backplate and ebonite drum, one spoke bent, c1910.
£500–625 ⚒ Bon(W)

An Allcock Aerial Popular 4inch alloy reel, with solid front and rear drum, c1930.
£130–160 ⚒ MUL

An Allcock Aerial 4inch laminated Bakelite sea reel, with weight regulator, twin xylonite handles and optional check, c1940.
£230–280 Bon(W)

An Army & Navy 4½inch Perfect-style salmon fly reel, with rim-mounted drag adjustment and brass foot, 1930–40.
£100–120 PEZ

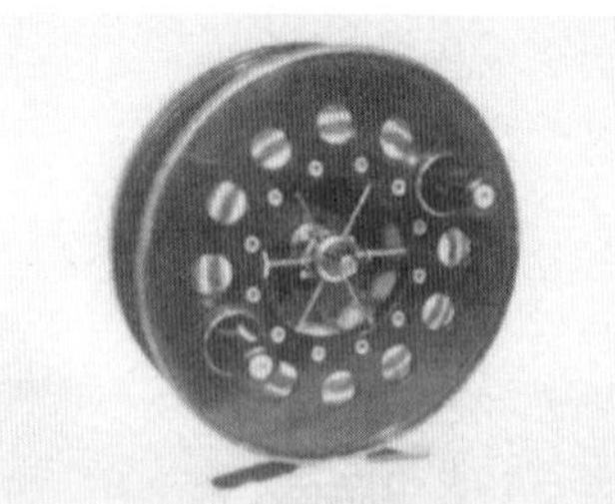

An Allcock Aerial 4½inch centre pin reel, with black bubble finish, c1953.
£110–140 MUL

An Eaton & Deller 2¾inch Hercules-style trout fly reel, with nickel silver fittings, c1910.
£140–180 OTB

LOCATE THE SOURCE
The source of each illustration in Miller's can be found by checking the code letters below each caption with the Key to Illustrations, pages 794–800.

An Army & Navy 4¼inch brass platewind reel, with fixed check, raised winding plate, ebonized handle and Hercules-style foot, c1930.
£145–160 PEZ

A Hardy Birmingham 2¾inch brass platewind reel, with constant check, two-pillar construction and bridged foot, c1900.
£300–375 MUL

A Hardy Silex No. 2 3½inch alloy casting reel, with rim tension regulator, ivorine bar latch, twin handles, three-screw drum release latch and chrome foot, 1914–22.
£130–160 MUL

A Hardy Perfect 3⅜inch trout fly reel, plain bearing model with 1917 check, ivorine handle and alloy foot, c1920.
£130–160 EP

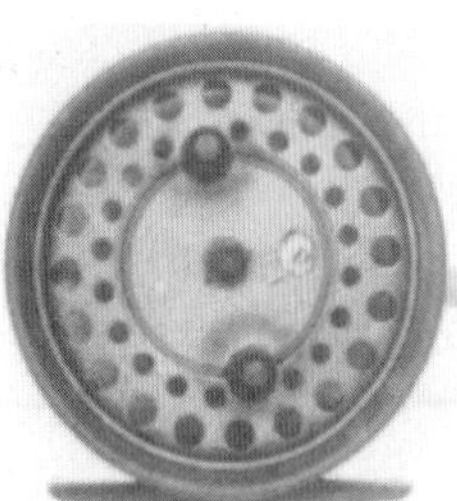

A Hardy Silex Major 4inch alloy reel, with ivorine rim lever, nickel silver backplate, tension button, twin black ebonite handles and smooth brass foot, 1923–28.
£170–220 MUL

A Hardy Super Silex 3¾inch casting reel, with twin black handles, white indicator dial, ivorine brake handle and grooved brass foot, 1920s.
£140–175 EP

A G. Little & Co 3¾inch brass and ebonite salmon reel, with nickel silver rims, five-pillar construction with constant check, three-screw drum latch and bridged foot, some rust, 1839–74.
£165–220 MUL

A Moscrop Patent 3inch gunmetal trout fly reel, with perforated drum, patented U-shaped wire clip drum release and matt black finish, c1895.
£60–70 OTB

A 4inch brass and ebony wide drum salmon reel, c1900.
£150–165 SPA

A 5inch walnut and brass starback Nottingham reel, with on and off check, all-wood spool and Bickerdyke line guard, c1890.
£80–90 PEZ

A Malloch 2¼inch brass and ebonite trout fly wheel, with nickel silver rims, brass handle plate, ivorine handle, ebonite backplate and fixed check, c1900.
£150–200 EP

An F. T. Williams & Co 2¼inch brass platewind trout fly reel, with fixed check and three brass pillars, c1875.
£100–120 EP

A 6inch mahogany and brass starback sea reel, with offset optional check and 1903 Preedy Patent No. 303965 brake system to backplate, rear brass drum flange and twin wooden handles, button missing from backplate.
£70–90 MUL

A 5inch mahogany and brass Nottingham-style reel, with wheel back brass-lined backplate and optional check, c1910.
£200–250 Bon(W)

A Millwards 4inch walnut Nottingham-style frog-back reel, with Bickerdyke line guide, brass wing nut, black composition handles and optional check, 1920s–30s.
£200–250 Bon(W)

A 3inch clamp winch Nottingham reel, with perforated iron collar and lyre tail locking screw, late 19thC.
£400–500 OTB

A Victorian 2¼inch crankwind fly reel, with 2in wide drum, curved winch arm fitted with turned ivory handle and three-pin brass bridged foot.
£100–120 MUL

A 4½inch casting reel, with ebonite faceplate, twin horn handles on brass oval mounts, six perforations, Slater latch, alloy rear drum plate, ebonite backplate with brass starback and optional check button, c1910.
£180–225 EP

A walnut and olivewood oyster-veneered lace box, c1690, 21½in (54.5cm) wide.
£5,500–6,000 ⊞ REI

► **A walrus ivory box,** with incised decoration, minor damage, Russian, Archangel, 1725–75, 7in (18cm) wide.
£3,400–4,250 ⚒ BUK

A kingwood, amaranth and marquetry tea caddy, with a gilt-bronze handle and Japanese Imari bowls and covers, the caddy Italian, probably Rome, 1725–50, 12½in (32cm) wide.
£18,000–20,000 ⚒ S

An olivewood oyster-veneered lace box, c1690, 11in (28cm) wide.
£900–1,000 ⊞ F&F

A laburnum-veneered tea caddy, c1780, 10in (25.5cm) wide.
£2,500–2,800 ⊞ HA

A kingwood strong box, on a later stand, French, c1690, 20in (51cm) wide.
£4,750–5,250 ⊞ REI

An inlaid walnut knife box, 18thC, 16in (40.5cm) high.
£700–785 ⊞ DJH

A painted satinwood work box, with brass carrying handles, late 18thC, 10¾in (27.5cm) wide.
£650–800 ⚒ CGC

A tortoiseshell travelling desk set, French, early 19thC, 3in (7.5cm) high.
£320–400 ⚒ G(L)

► A provincial *papier peint* lady's box, French, c1825, 12½in (32cm) wide.
£2,600–3,250 ⚒ S(NY)

A lacquer and steel box, with a miniature of the Marquise de Talhoet, French, c1790, 3in (7.5cm) diam.
£2,500–2,750 ⊞ SHa

A tortoiseshell tea caddy, the cover with later silver spandrels and cartouche, dated Birmingham 1876, caddy early 19thC, 5in (12.5cm) wide.
£2,000–2,200 ⚒ TMA

An embossed tortoiseshell tea caddy, c1830, 6½in (16.5cm) wide.
£7,500–8,000 ⊞ AKS

A boullework tea caddy, c1830, 9in (23cm) wide.
£700–785 ⊞ RAN

A tortoiseshell and mother-of-pearl tea caddy, c1840, 8in (20.5cm) wide.
£2,700–3,000 ⊞ BBo

► A lacewood writing slope, c1850, 20in (51cm) wide.
£325–360 ⊞ PICA

A tortoiseshell tea caddy, with mother-of-pearl floral inlay and white metal stringing, c1860, 8in (20.5cm) wide.
£3,200–3,500 ⊞ BBo

A heart-shaped shell box, c1860, 6in (15cm) wide.
£90–100 ⊞ F&F

◄ A Mauchline ware tea caddy, the lid painted with a cottage interior, 19thC, 9½in (24cm) wide.
£900–1,100 ⚒ B(Ed)

A brass-mounted coromandel writing compendium, by Jenner and Knewstub, with a satinwood and leather interior, c1865, 19in (48.5cm) wide.
£3,200–3,500 ⊞ F

A Victorian burr-walnut desk set, by Hall, Belgravia, with gilt-metal hinges and inset porcelain roundels, letter box 9in (23cm) wide.
£2,000–2,500 AH

A Victorian mahogany writing box, 15in (38cm) wide.
£200–250 SWO

◀ **A child's walnut writing slope,** c1870, 12in (30.5cm) wide.
£500–550 ⊞ OTT

A coromandel dressing case, with brass trim and silver and glass toilet jars, London 1876, 12¼in (31cm) wide.
£2,000–2,500 AH

An inlaid souvenir box, with a secret compartment, Italian, c1900, 9in (23cm) wide.
£165–185 ⊞ MLL

◀ **A brass-mounted malachite box,** minor repairs, Russian, c1900, 6¾in (17cm) wide.
£500–625 BUK

◀ **A four-stringed bass,** probably by Cole of Manchester, c1880, length of back 45¼in (115cm).
£11,000–14,000 ⚒ Bon

A guitar, by C. F. Martin & Co, Nazareth, with rosewood back and sides and ebony fingerboard, American, c1930, length of back 19¼in (49cm), with case.
£7,500–8,250 ⚒ SK

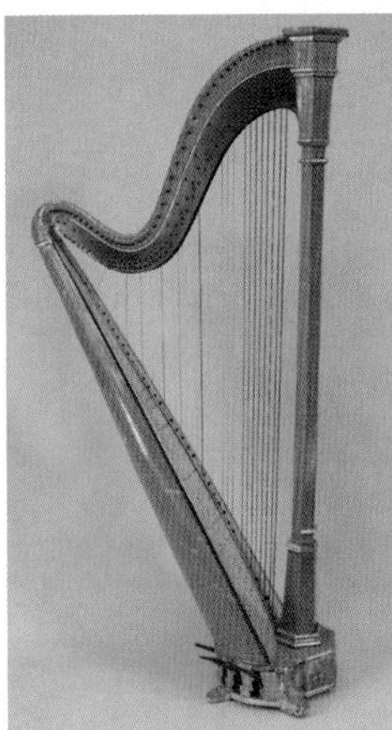

◀ **A parcel-gilt simulated satinwood harp,** by E. Serquet, Cavendish Square, London, 19thC, 68in (172.5cm) high.
£1,500–2,000 ⚒ G(L)

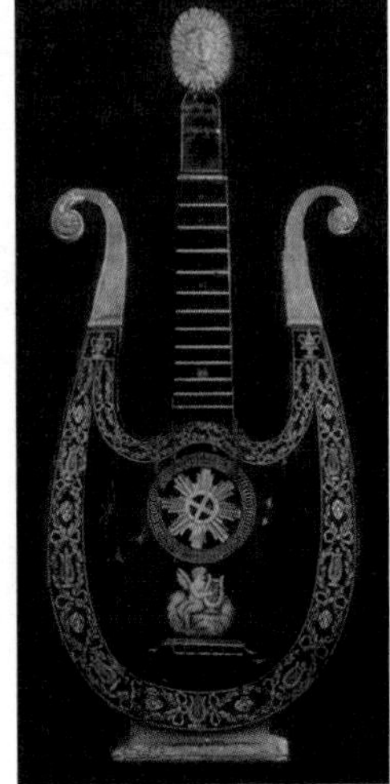

A harp-lyre, possibly by Edward Light, London, c1810, 23in (58.5cm) high.
£1,600–2,000 ⚒ Bon

◀ **A flatback bass hurdy-gurdy,** by Caron, Versailles, with maple back and ribs, c1780.
£1,800–2,250 ⚒ P

◀ **A mandolin,** by Angara and D'Isanto, Naples, with maple body, the table inlaid with tortoiseshell, Italian, c1893, 23½in (59.5cm) long.
£160–200 ⚒ DN

A brass-inlaid mahogany square piano, by A. Babcock, Boston, American, c1830, 66in (167.5cm) wide.
£1,250–1,600 ⚒ SLN

A grand piano, by Bechstein, German, 1859, 75in (190.5cm) wide.
£22,500–25,000 ⊞ PPC
This is the oldest-known surviving piano by this maker.

A satinbirch and carved boxwood upright piano, by H. W. Batley, the case by James Shoolbred & Co, the movement by Collard & Collard, with an octagonal adjustable music stool *en suite*, c1878, 63in (160cm) wide.
£50,000–60,000 ⚒ S

◀ **An amaranth, kingwood and tulipwood marquetry piano,** by T. Probst, Lyon, French, 19thC, 56in (142cm) wide.
£7,000–8,750 ⚒ S(Am)

► **A tulipwood marquetry grand piano,** the case by François Linke, Paris, the works by Steinway & Sons, New York, with gilt-bronze and porcelain mounts, with an associated Louis XVI-style walnut piano stool, late 19th–early 20thC, 77in (195.5cm) long.
£180,000–200,000 ⚒ S(NY)
This piano is typical of the exceptionally high quality of Linke's work.

A tulipwood parquetry Louis XVI-style grand piano, by Erard, with gilt-bronze mounts, late 19thC, 72in (183cm) long.
£20,000–24,000 ⚒ S(NY)

A boulle and ebonized wood upright piano, with adjustable, ebonized piano stool, French, 19thC, 51¼in (130cm) wide.
£4,500–5,500 ⚒ LCM

A grand piano, by Broadwood, in a satinwood case with ormolu relief, c1890, 108in (274.5cm) wide.
£5,000–6,250 ⚒ P(Ba)

A concert grand piano, by Steinway, in a rosewood case, with ivory keys, c1890, 90½in (230cm) wide.
£12,000–15,000 ⊞ PEx

A grand piano, by Blüthner, in fiddle-back veneered mahogany, German, c1910, 72in (183cm) wide.
£5,850–6,500 ⊞ PG

A grand piano, by Erard, Paris, the case in figured mahogany with boxwood and ebony banding, with brass-inlaid legs, restored, 1914, 84in (213.5cm) wide.
£40,000–45,000 ⊞ PPC

An Art Deco grand piano, by Strohmenger, in a burr-walnut and figured maple case, 1930s, 51in (129.5cm) wide.
£6,000–7,500 ⚒ P(Ba)

◀ **A violin,** by John Johnson, London, labelled, dated 1759, length of back 14in (35.5cm).
£4,800–6,000 ⚒ GH

A violin, by J. B. Vuillaume, Paris, after Stradivarius, 1860, length of back 13¾in (35cm).
£32,000–40,000 ⚒ Bon
A letter accompanying this violin describes it as 'one of the Artist's (Vuillaume) oldest and most beautiful specimens'.

◀ **A violin,** by Gustav Bernardel, Paris, 1894, length of back 14in (35.5cm), cased.
£10,000–12,500 ⚒ P

A violin, by Giulio Degani, Venice, 1895, length of back 14in (35.5cm).
£12,500–16,000 ⚒ Bon

◀ **A violin,** by Carl Becker, Chicago, American, 1940, length of back 14in (35.5cm).
£18,000–20,000 ⚒ SK

◀ **A viola,** by Camillo Mandelli, Buenos Aires, Argentinian, 1906, length of back 15¾in (40cm).
£10,000–12,500 ⚒ Bon

An icon of the Seven Sleepers of Ephesus, egg tempera on a wooden panel, Cretan, early 16thC, 10¾ x 8¾in (27.5 x 22cm).
£7,000–7,600 ⊞ RKa

An icon of Saint Nicholas surrounded by scenes from his life and miracles, egg tempera on a wooden panel, Russian, 16thC, 38½ x 32½in (98 x 82.5cm).
£45,000–50,000 ⊞ RKa

An icon of The Coronation of the Virgin by The Holy Trinity, with embossed silver and gilded oklad, probably Bolivian, 18thC, 10¼ x 7½in (26 x 19cm), framed.
£1,500–2,000 ⚒ LCM

An icon of the Virgin and Child, Greek, 18thC, 9½ x 6¾in (24 x 17cm).
£200–250 ⚒ Bea(E)

An icon of the Tikhvin Mother of God, Russian, c1800, 24 x 18in (61 x 45.5cm).
£2,700–3,000 ⚒ JAA

An icon of the Anastasis with Feasts, Russian, 19thC, 17¾ x 15in (45 x 38cm).
£3,500–4,500 ⚒ S(NY)

◀ **An icon triptych,** overlaid with decorative metal covering, Russian, 19thC, 26 x 25in (66 x 63.5cm), open.
£5,000–5,500 ⚒ JAA

An icon of St Nicholas, in brass and enamel, Russian, c1860, 4in (10cm) square.
£100–120 ⊞ ICO

An icon of Simeon the God-receiver, with gilded background and borders, c1890, 8½ x 7in (18 x 21.5cm).
£1,100–1,200 ⚒ JAA

A miniature icon of Saints Samon, Gury and Aviv, in silver and blue enamel oklad, Russian, c1900, 3 x 2½in (7.5 x 6.5cm).
£800–900 ⊞ ICO

▶ **An icon of Christ Pantocrator,** gilded silver and enamel oklad, Russian, Moscow, c1900, 12¼ x 10½in (31 x 26.5cm).
£8,000–9,000 ⚒ S

A portrait miniature of a gentleman, by Richard Cosway, RA, in a pearl frame, c1790, 3½in (9cm) high.
£9,000–10,000 ⊞ EFA

A portrait miniature of a lady, signed Mlle Antoinette Louise Damarcy, dated 1822, in an ormolu frame, 2½in (6.5cm) high.
£1,600–2,000 ⚒ P

A portrait miniature of a lady, attributed to George Engleheart, watercolour on ivory, late 18th–early 19thC, 2½in (6.5cm) high, in a red leather case.
£2,600–3,250 ⚒ G(L)

A portrait miniature of a lady, by Charles Hayter, in a gold frame, the reverse with locks of hair, signed, dated 1796, 2½in (6.5cm) high.
£2,000–2,500 ⚒ P

A portrait miniature of a gentleman of the Berkley family, by Jeremiah Meyer, c1780, 1½in (4cm) wide.
£10,000–11,500 ⊞ BHa

A portrait miniature of Lady Caroline Lamb, by Mrs Anne Mee, signed, c1815, 3¼in (8.5cm) high, in a red leather case.
£9,000–11,000 ⚒ Bon

A portrait miniature of Mrs David Wedderburne, by Andrew Plimer, dated 1787, 2¾in (7cm) high.
£5,000–6,250 ⚒ Bon

A portrait miniature of an officer, English School, c1808, 2¾in (7cm) high.
£320–400 ⚒ Bea(E)

A portrait miniature of a lady, by F. T. Rochard, in a gilt locket frame, c1835, 4in (10cm) wide.
£2,700–3,000 ⊞ BHa

A pair of miniature bust portraits of Colonel and Mrs Ezekiel Fisk How, of Massachusetts, attributed to Rufus Porter, watercolour and pen and ink on paper, in original frames, 1810, 4½in (11.5cm) high.
£5,250–6,500 ⚒ S(NY)

A portrait miniature of a gentleman, by John Smart, signed and dated 1778, 1½in (4cm) high, in a gold-trimmed tortoiseshell box.
£13,500–15,000 ⊞ EFA

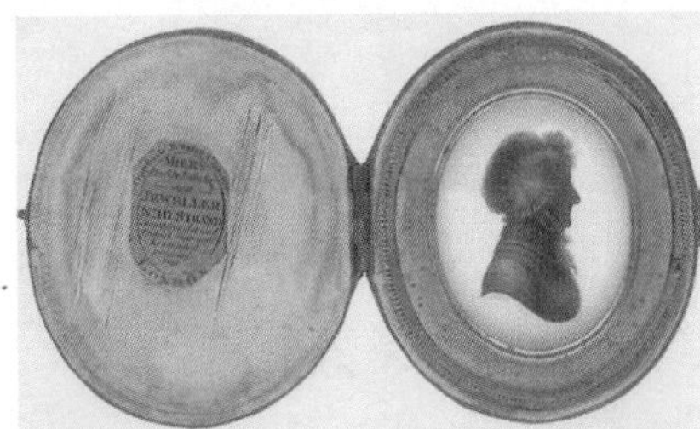

A bronzed silhouette of a lady, from the studio of John Miers, signed, in a leather case, 1½in (4cm) high.
£450–565 ⚒ Bea(E)
This is likely to have been painted by John Field.

◄ A silhouette of an Officer of Volunteers, by Charles Buncombe, (fl1795–1830), painted in colour on card, in a hammered brass frame, 4¼in (11cm) high.
£3,000–3,750 ⚒ P

A pair of silhouette portraits of Rev John Lamb and Maria Lamb, English School, in original maple frames, dated 1840, 10in (25.5cm) high.
£500–600 ⚒ L&E

A buff ware jar, Egyptian, Predynastic Period, c3400–3200 BC, 8in (20.5cm) high.
£10,000–12,500 S(NY)

A gessoed and painted wood mummy mask, Egyptian, 730–332 BC, 11¾in (30cm) high.
£720–800 HEL

A composition amulet of Thoth, Egyptian, Late Period, c664–525 BC, 3¼in (8.5cm) high.
£600–725 Bon

A polychrome and giltwood figure of Ptah-Seker-Osiris, Egyptian, Ptolemaic Period, 304–30 BC, 21¼in (54cm) high.
£6,500–8,200 S(NY)

◄ **An Attic Red-Figure krater,** Greek, c470 BC, 11in (28cm) high.
£8,750–11,000 S(NY)

A pottery stirrup vessel, with ochre-painted geometric decoration, Mycenaean, 1300–1200 BC, 3½in (9cm) high.
£450–500 HEL

An Apulian Red-Figure bell krater, repaired, Greek, 4thC BC, 11¾in (30cm) high.
£1,600–1,800 B

An Apulian two-handled vase, Greek, 4th–2ndC BC, 10½in (26.5cm) high.
£750–950 TEN

A gold pendant with chain, Greek, c325 BC, pendant 1½in (4cm) high.
£11,000–14,000 S(NY)

A Hellenistic core-formed glass amphoriskos, 2nd/mid-1stC BC, 6¼in (16cm) high.
£2,700–3,200 S(NY)

◄ **A gold ring,** Celtiberian, c5th–4thC BC, ¾in (2cm) diam.
£1,300–1,600 Bon

A glass jug, Roman, 1st–2ndC AD, 9½in (24cm) high.
£1,350–1,500 HEL

A core-formed glass aryballos, rim chipped, Etruscan, late 6th/early 5thC BC, 1¾in (4.5cm) high.
£500–600 Bon

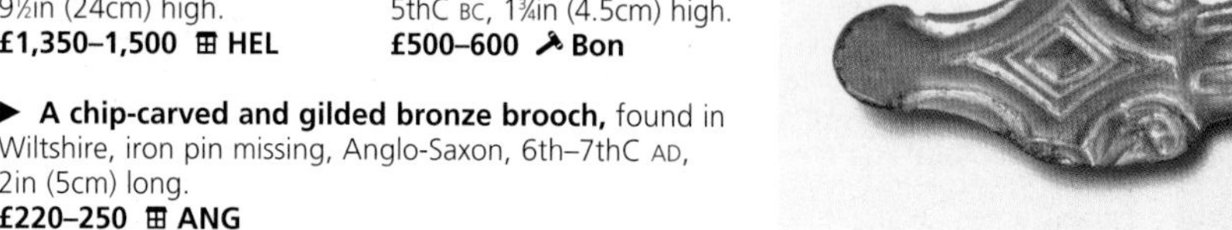

► **A chip-carved and gilded bronze brooch,** found in Wiltshire, iron pin missing, Anglo-Saxon, 6th–7thC AD, 2in (5cm) long.
£220–250 ANG

A pair of Arapaho woman's beaded high-top moccasins, Native American, c1880, 19in (48.5cm) high.
£7,000–8,000 SK(B)

A Micmac quillwork blotter, Native American, 15¾in (40cm) wide.
£1,400–1,600 P
Collected c1850. This is a tribal art term for saying when the piece was acquired, which indicates a possible date.

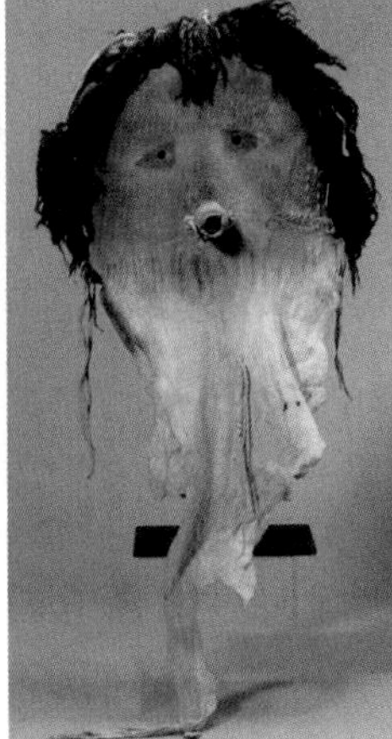

◄ A Navajo buckskin Yeibichai dancer's mask, Native American, 32in (81.5cm) long.
£5,000–5,500 SK(B)

A Malinke mask, covered with a mud matrix inset with abrus seeds and cowrie shells, Mali, 8¾in (22cm) high.
£2,600–3,250 S(NY)

◄ A Yoruba carving of a mother and baby, Nigerian, 1900–25, 24in (61cm) high.
£1,500–1,700 GRG

An Ekoi skin-covered headdress, on a basketry base, Nigerian, late 19thC, 19in (48.5cm) high.
£1,200–1,500 TeW

◄ A Baule carved wood mask, with applied kaolin, Ivory Coast, 1900–20, 18in (45.5cm) high.
£2,800–3,200 GRG

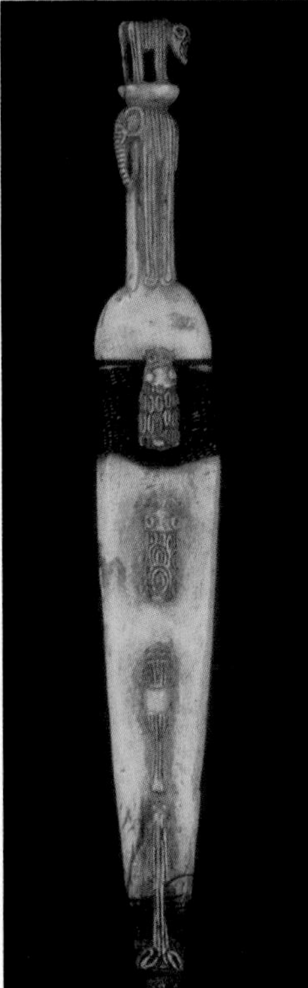

A paint-decorated wooden Galowa mask, Gabonese, 11½in (29cm) high.
£425–530 BERN

◄ A carved ivory and wood Tswana knife, South African, 9in (23cm) long.
£8,700–9,500 P

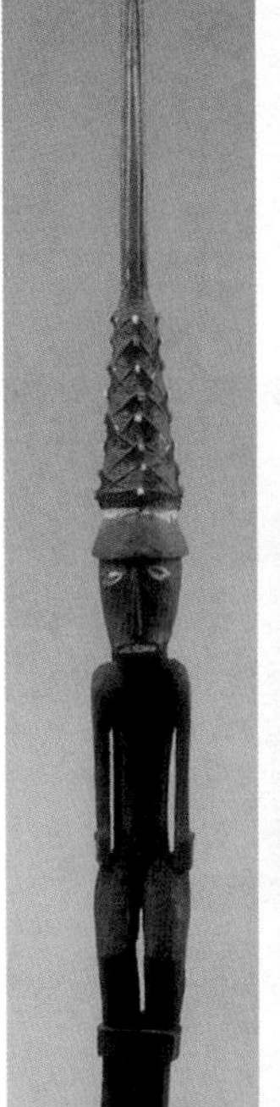

► An Admiralty Islands fish spine spear tip, the wooden handle in the form of an abstract figure with incised eyes beneath the headdress, decorated with beads and inset with a ray-spine, 15¾in (40cm) high.
£2,000–2,400 S(NY)

A Tsonga staff-headrest, the base cracked and re-joined to the support, South African, 25½in (65cm) wide.
£3,300–4,000 P

A Mahakala wooden mask, with painted decoration, northeast Indian, Sikkim, 19thC, 20½in (52cm) high.
£5,250–6,500 S(NY)

◀ **John James Audubon,** Yellow Breasted Chat, Plate 244 of the Bein edition of *Birds of America,* American, executed 1860, 40in (101.5cm) high, in a gilt-lined hardwood frame.
£2,200–2,500 NOA

John Gibson Lockhart, *Memories of the Life of Sir Walter Scott,* published by Robert Scott, Edinburgh, full leather, with fore-edge painting, 1842, 8°.
£750–950 RIT

Henry John Elwes and Augustine Henry, *The Trees of Great Britain and Ireland*, privately printed in seven volumes, 1906–13, 4°.
£1,700–2,200 CGC

Thomas L. McKenney and James Hall, *History of the Indian Tribes of North America,* three volumes, American, Philadelphia, 1854, 8°.
£9,500–12,000 BBA

Sir Samuel Rush Meyrick, *A Critical Inquiry into Antient Armour, as is Existed in Europe*, three volumes, second edition, red half-morocco, 1842, folio.
£1,200–1,400 DW

Peter Weink, original artwork from *Noddy Goes to the Fair,* by Enid Blyton, 1960, 6½in (16.5cm) high.
£1,300–1,450 BRG

Lewis Wright, *The New Book of Poultry*, London, printed by Cassell & Co, 1902, half-roan, 4°.
£150–180 RTo

A papier mâché shoulder-headed doll, wearing original clothes, French, c1850, 22½in (57cm) high.
£2,500–3,250 Bon(C)

A Max Oscar Arnold bisque shoulder-headed fashion doll, with bisque arms, wearing original two-piece silk outfit, c1890, 14in (35.5cm) high.
£550–600 Beb

An Armand Marseille bisque googly doll, all original, German, c1915, 12in (30.5cm) high.
£720–800 Beb

A bisque-headed doll, impressed 'Darling', 1875–1925, 20in (51cm) high.
£125–160 DMC

An F. Gaultier *bébé* doll, with blue paperweight eyes, wearing an antique outfit, French, c1885, 17½in (44.5cm) high.
£3,500–4,000 Beb

◄ **A Jumeau bisque-headed *bébé* doll,** with jointed composition and wood body, French, c1880, 15½in (39.5cm) high.
£3,700–4,500 SK(B)

A bisque-headed *bébé* doll, all original, Paris, c1900, 24in (61cm) high.
£1,650–1,850 Beb

A Goebel Fly on Nose bisque-headed doll, with metal fly attached through a special hole on the nose, German, early 20thC, 17in (43cm) high.
£900–1,000 Beb

A Gebrüder Kuhnlenz bisque-headed doll, missing two fingers, German, c1910, 18in (45.5cm) high.
£400–500 Bon(C)

◄ **A May Frères Mascotte *bébé* doll,** all original, French, c1885, 19in (48.5cm) high.
£3,600–4,000 Beb

A bisque-headed gypsy *bébé* doll, c1900, 30in (76cm) high.
£1,800–2,000 Beb

A Heinrich Handwerck bisque-headed doll, mould No. 174, with composition body, German, c1900, 29¼in (74.5cm) high.
£1,000–1,200 BaN

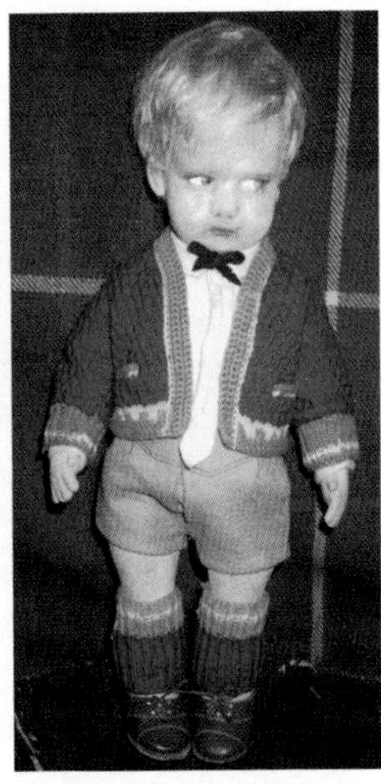

A Lenci felt boy doll, all original, Italian, c1930, 18in (45.5cm) high.
£800–900 Beb

A Chiltern mohair teddy bear, c1930, 16in (40.5cm) high.
£220–275 Bon(C)

A Farnell mohair teddy bear, c1918, 14in (35.5cm) high.
£1,100–1,300 Bon(C)

A Hermann teddy bear, with growler, German, 1930s, 20in (51cm) high.
£400–450 Beb

A Steiff teddy bear, German, c1905.
£850–950 Beb

A teddy bear, 1915–20, 18in (45.5cm) high.
£400–450 Beb

A plush teddy bear, c1915, 22in (56cm) high.
£350–450 WW

A Märklin clockwork tinplate liner, German, mid-1930s, 16in (40.5cm) long.
£2,000–2,400 WAL

► **A steam-power model ocean liner,** with wooden hull and tinplate upper decks, 1950s, 24in (61cm) long.
£100–125 Bon(C)

◄ **A Kenton cast-iron cabriolet,** minor replacement, American, c1905, 15½in (39.5cm) long.
£3,300–4,200 S(NY)

◄ **A battery-operated tinplate bulldozer,** Japanese, c1950, 10in (25.5cm) long.
£200–225 GTM

► **A Günthermann tinplate car,** with clockwork motor and electric lights, German, c1930, 14in (35.5cm) long.
£550–600 GTM

A Dent cast-iron Mack dump truck, American, c1923, 15in (38cm) long.
£8,000–10,000 S(NY)

► **A Dinky Toys Big Bedford van,** No. 925, c1950, 6in (15cm) long.
£320–350 GTM

A Dinky Toys racing cars gift set, No. 249, 1955–58, boxed.
£700–900 Bon(C)

A Jouets en Paris tinplate clockwork Citroën car, 1930s, 12in (30.5cm) long.
£150–200 Bon(C)

A Hornby 0 gauge Royal Scot locomotive and tender, slight imperfections, c1920.
£300–360 N

► **A Märklin 0 gauge steam locomotive,** with original tender, German, 1935, 20in (51cm) long.
£2,700–3,500 KOLN

A Hornby No. 1 passenger train set, 1930s, boxed.
£300–375 WAL

► **A Wilkins cast-iron floor train,** locomotive with old repair, American, c1890, 54in (137cm) long.
£3,300–4,200 S(NY)

A carved wood and plaster butcher's shop model, in a glazed mahogany frame, mid-19thC, 20 x 28in (51 x 71cm).
£4,500–5,750 ⚒ S(S)

A simulated stonework painted wooden dolls' house, with a quantity of dolls' house furniture, c1900, 47¼in (120cm) wide.
£3,000–3,600 ⚒ B&L

A wooden dolls' house, with detachable roof and sliding back opening, c1920, 33in (84cm) high, on a later stand.
£120–150 ⚒ SWO

A dolls' house, with removable rear panel and electric lighting, with period furniture and fittings, late 1920s, 30in (76cm) wide.
£270–350 ⚒ WAL

◄ A Gustave Vichy automaton banjo player, with two-air musical movement, Paris, c1890, 19in (48.5cm) high.
£4,500–5,000 ⊞ KHW

A Gustave Vichy automaton monkey harpist, Paris, c1890, 16in (40.5cm) high.
£8,500–9,500 ⊞ AUTO

◄ An Ives clockwork churning toy, mechanism in working order, American, c1880, 11in (28cm) wide.
£3,750–4,750 ⚒ S(NY)

A clockwork bar billiards player, possibly Continental, early 20thC, 6in (15cm) long.
£240–300 ⚒ AH

A wooden rocking horse, possibly Irish, c1880, 45in (114.5cm) high.
£4,850–5,400 ⊞ RGa

A tinplate battery-operated gear robot, Japanese, c1960, 11in (28cm) high.
£180–200 ⊞ GTM

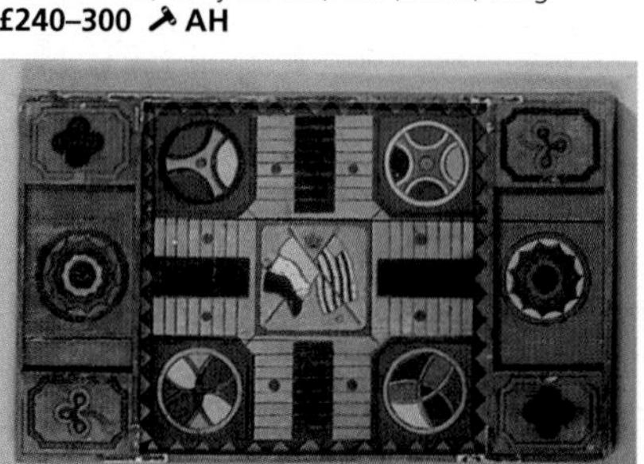

A polychrome-incised and painted game board, possibly Canadian, early 20thC, 19in (48.5cm) wide.
£4,200–5,250 ⚒ SK(B)

A mid-Victorian walnut games compendium, label for Stephenson, Oxford St, London, 12½in (32cm) wide.
£1,350–1,700 ⚒ B(Ed)

A Phillips boxwood photographic exposure meter slide rule, c1880, 4in (10cm) wide, in original box.
£250–300 ⊞ TOM

A univeral equinoctial dial, by G. S. Wood, late Abraham & Co, Liverpool, in a leather-covered case, late 19thC, 2½in (6.5cm) diam.
£400–500 B(Ed)

An orrery, by W. Jones, signed, on a mahogany base, c1812, 7¾in (19.5cm) diam, in a fitted mahogany case.
£9,000–11,500 S(O)

A Jordan photographic sunshine recorder, by Negretti and Zambra, c1880, 8in (20.5cm) high.
£800–900 ⊞ RTW

◄ **A lacquered brass universal equinoctial ring dial,** by Butterfield, Paris, mid-18thC, 5in (12.5cm) diam.
£5,000–5,500 B

A pocket terrestrial globe, by Nathaniel Hill, dated 1754, 3in (7.5cm) diam, in a ray-skin case.
£2,300–2,800 G(L)

A pair of celestial and terrestrial pocket globes, by Newton, 1800–50, 4¼in (11cm) high.
£8,500–10,000 S(P)

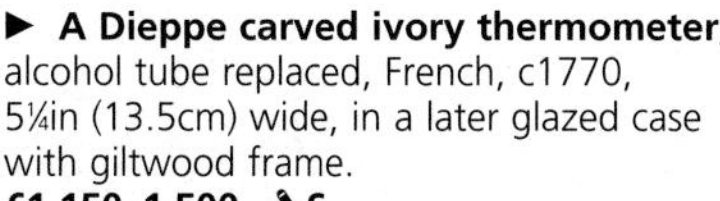

► **A Dieppe carved ivory thermometer,** alcohol tube replaced, French, c1770, 5¼in (13.5cm) wide, in a later glazed case with giltwood frame.
£1,150–1,500 S
This thermometer was formerly in the collection of Queen Mary at Marlborough House, London.

► **A brass pantograph,** by Davies, Derby, with ivory wheels, c1860, 40in (101.5cm) long.
£315–350
⊞ HUM

A boxwood compass sundial, signed 'PPB', c1800, 2¼in (5.5cm) long.
£240–265 ⊞ PHo

A bronze water meter timepiece, by George Kent, London and Kent, the enamel chapter ring flanked by a water flow dial, early 20thC, 26in (66cm) high.
£350–450 Bon

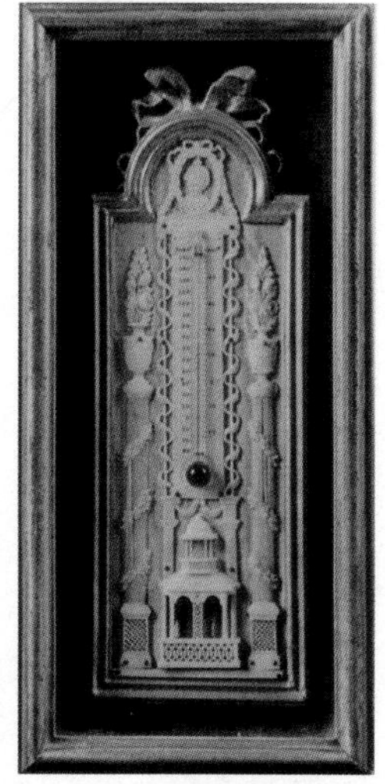

◄ **A Victorian brass binocular microscope,** by Henry Crouch, London, 18¼in (46.5cm) high, in a mahogany case fitted with accessories.
£1,200–1,500 AH

A two-day marine chronometer, signed 'Tobias and Livitt, 31 Minories, London', in a brass-bound rosewood case, c1820, dial 4in (10cm) diam.
£2,200–2,600 GH

A brass astral seven-day naval clock, by Smith, c1955, 8in (20.5cm) diam.
£350–400 RTW

A carved and painted pine model of a boat, c1860, 20in (51cm) long.
£1,100–1,250 RYA

► **A model of a three-masted paddle steamer,** *City of Baltimore*, 19thC, in original glazed wood case, 44½in (113cm) long.
£2,000–2,500 BAG

A woolwork picture of a man-of-war, flying British and American flags, 19thC, in a bird's-eye maple frame, 17 x 25in (43 x 63.5cm).
£1,700–2,200 BR

A woolwork picture, entitled 'The English Fleet leaving Spithead in 1855 for the Baltic', 19thC, 44in (112cm) wide, unframed.
£7,000–8,750 Bon

A gilt-brass pocket nocturnal, the handle incorporating a magnetic compass, needle missing, French, dated 1597, 2in (5cm) diam.
£20,000–22,000 S(O)

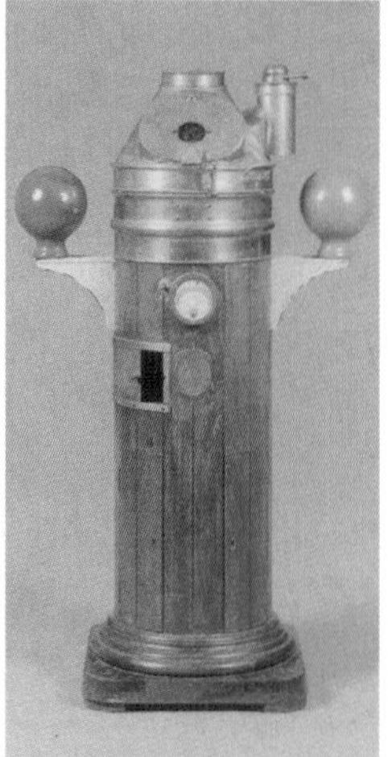

A brass binnacle compass, by Kelvin Bottomley & Baird, on a teak column, early 20thC, 57½in (146cm) high.
£800–1,000 S(O)

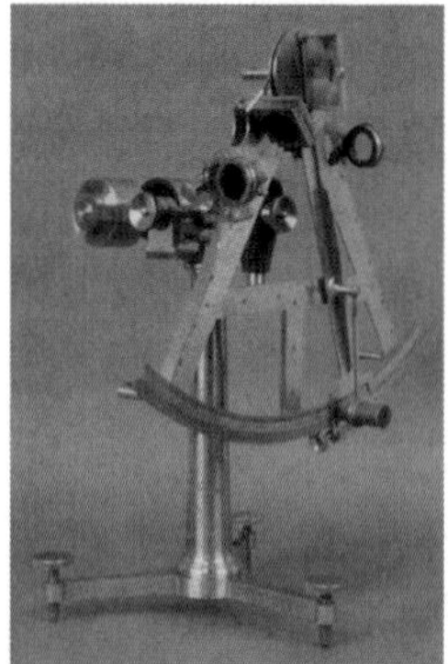

◄ **A lacquered brass sextant,** by Cary, London, early 19thC, 17½in (44.5cm) high, with a mahogany case and a later case for the stand.
£1,000–1,250 RTo

A bell-framed sextant, in original mahogany box complete with accessories, c1900, 10in (25.5cm) wide.
£720–800 PHo

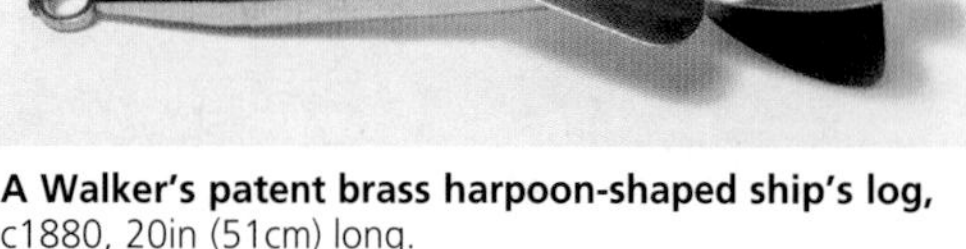

A Walker's patent brass harpoon-shaped ship's log, c1880, 20in (51cm) long.
£405–450 PHo

◄ **A carved and painted pine figurehead,** mid-19thC, 60in (152.5cm) high.
£5,300–6,500 S(O)

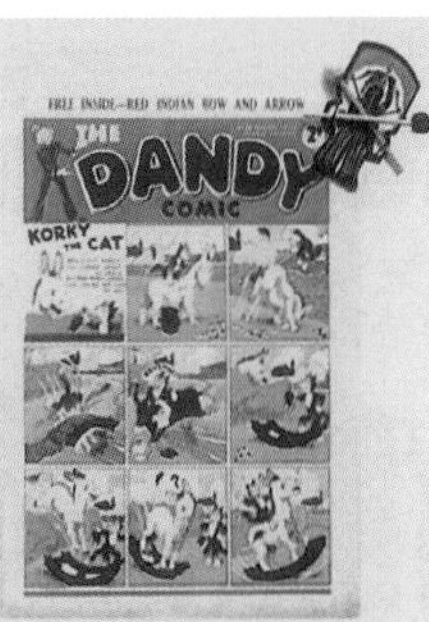

The Dandy Comic, with free gift Red Indian bow and arrows, issue No. 39, 1938.
£400–450 CBP

Cohen, Weenen & Co, Victoria Cross Heroes, set of 50 cigarette cards, 1916.
£215–230 RTo

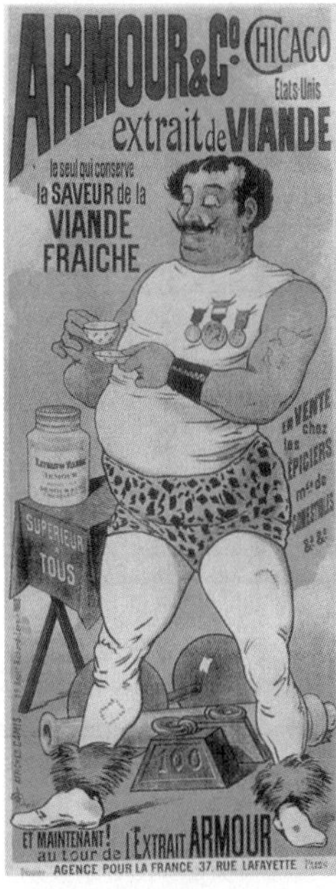

A Guillaume Armour & Co poster, by Affiches Camis, Paris, advertising Extrait de Viande, backed and edged with japan paper, c1895, 112¼ x 42½in (285 x 108cm).
£350–450 BBA

► **A Paul Lengell poster,** *Le Grand Cirque*, printed by Hartfort, Paris, mounted on linen, French, 1940s, 60 x 45in (152.5 x 114.5cm).
£300–375 DW

Film Fun Annual, issue No. 1, 1938.
£340–375 CBP

Thomson & Porteus, Arms of British Towns, set of 50 cigarette cards, 1905.
£265–300 P

A Midland Great Western Railway of Ireland poster, by F. Hugo d'Alesi, advertising tours in Connemara, Galway, Achill and west of Ireland, mounted on linen, c1900, 48½ x 34¾in (123 x 88.5cm).
£3,000–3,750 ONS

The Beano Book, issue No. 3, 1942.
£850–950 CBP

Franklyn Davey, Football Club Colours, set of 50 cigarette cards, 1901.
£420–460 P
Loadstone is a brand of cigarettes manufactured by Franklyn Davey.

BAT, Indian Chiefs, set of 50 cigarette cards, 1930.
£240–270 P

Wills, The Life of King Edward VIII, set of 50 cigarette cards, 1937.
£160–200 Bon
These were never issued with cigarettes.

◄ **A British Railways poster,** by Harry Riley, advertising Coney Beach, Porthcawl, 1950s, 40¼ x 25¼in (102 x 64cm).
£360–450 P(WM)

An Edo von Handel-Mazzetti poster, advertising The Grossglockner, lithograph, Berlin, c1930, 39½ x 24¾in (100.5 x 63cm).
£160–200 DW

◄ **A Metro-Goldwyn-Mayer poster,** advertising *Blow-Up*, 1966, 39¾ x 26¾in (101 x 68cm).
£120–150 DN

◀ ***Beach Boys' Party* album,** mounted and framed, c1965.
£220–275 ⚒ Bon(C)

A poster, advertising Fleetwood Mac at Southampton Guildhall, silkscreen, 1970, 30 x 20in (76 x 51cm).
£250–320 ⚒ FO

A Saville Theatre poster, by Hapshash & The Coloured Coat, advertising The Who and Junior Walker, published by Osiris Visions, 1967, 30 x 19¼in (76 x 49cm).
£180–225 ⚒ Bon(C)

▶ **Johnny Rotten's Anarchy shirt,** 1976.
£4,000–4,500 ⚒ S(O)

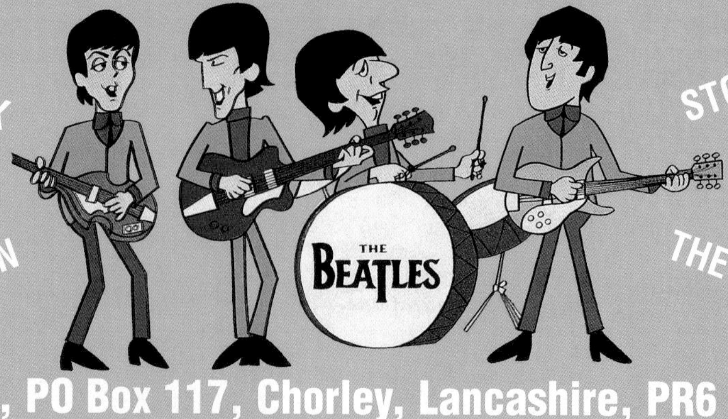

A Corgi Toys Yellow Submarine, c1969, 7in (18cm) long, boxed.
£400–450 ⊞ GTM

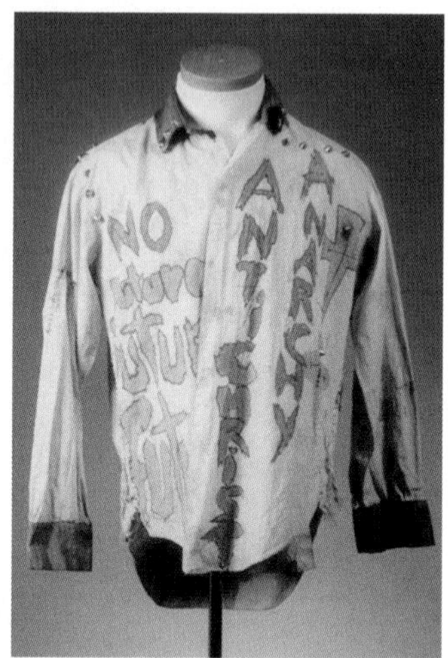

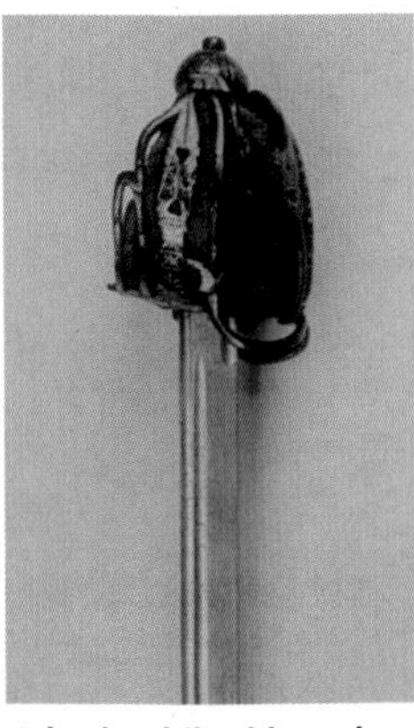

A basket-hilted broad-sword, the handle with japanned decoration and velvet liners, Scottish, c1700, 38¼in (97cm) long.
£8,000–9,000 ⊞ NS

◄ **A stirrup-hilted sabre,** with gilt-bronze hilt and scabbard, c1805, blade 27in (68.5cm) long.
£1,600–1,800 ⊞ ASB

A naval civil war cutlass, by Ames of Chicopee, Massachusetts, American, dated 1862, 32in (81.5cm) long, with leather scabbard.
£450–550 ⚒ SLN

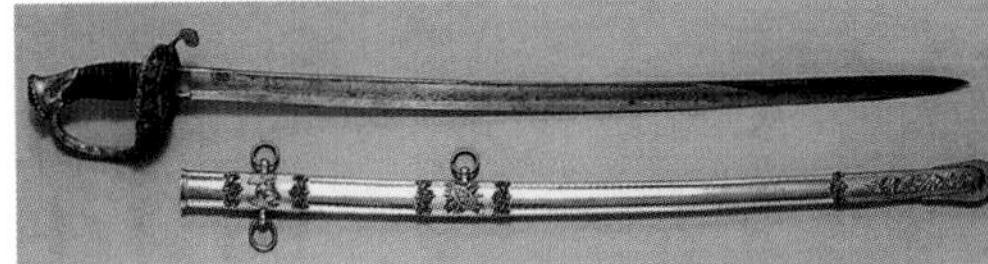

A Civil War presentation sword, by Ames of Chicopee, Massachusetts, with a gilt-brass guard and nickel-plated scabbard, inscribed 'Presented to Lieut. Louis N. Stodder by the Citizens of Boston Feby. 23, 1863', American, 1862–63, 38in (96.5cm) long.
£13,000–16,000 ⚒ S(NY)

A brass-inlaid maple full stock wheel lock rifle, by Christian Koppler, Linz, dated 1696, 37½in (95.5cm) long.
£2,000–2,500 ⚒ Herm

A pair of flintlock pistols, by Wheatley, original condition, 18thC, 15in (38cm) long.
£3,500–4,000 ⊞ DJH

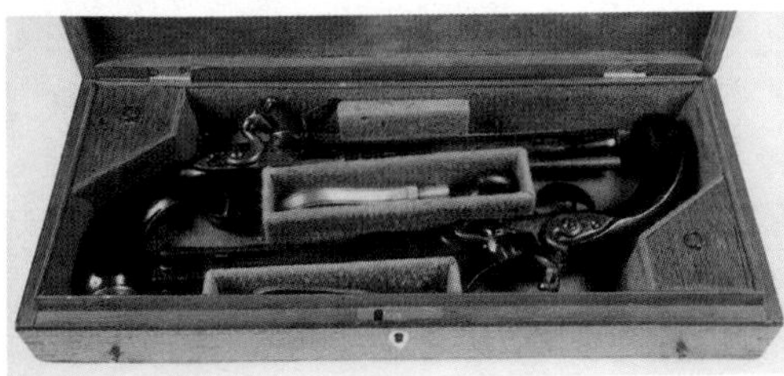

◄ **A pair of flintlock duelling pistols,** by Wogdon, with walnut full stocks, c1790, in a baize-lined oak case 18½in (47cm) wide.
£7,000–8,000 ⊞ WSA

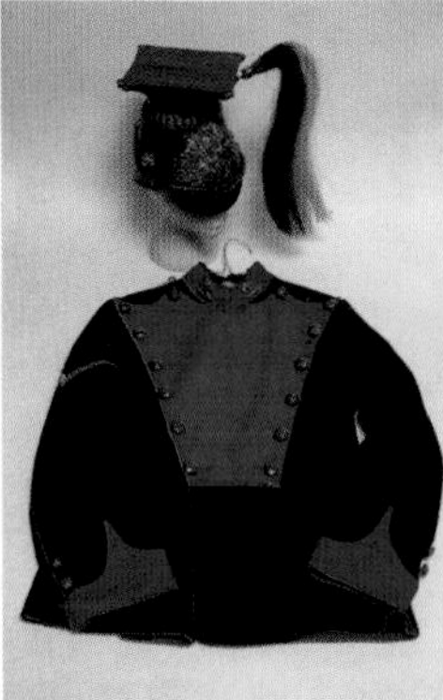

A 12th Lancers uniform and helmet, c1912.
£1,100–1,200 ⊞ Q&C

A Victorian 12th Lancers other ranks' lance cap, the plate with battle honours to Sevastopol, chin chain replaced.
£550–700 ⚒ WAL

A WWII group of 12 medals, awarded to Air Vice-Marshal H. V. Champion de Crespigny, CB, Great War Pilot's MC, DFC, C. B. neck badge not shown.
£6,000–7,750 ⚒ DNW

◄ **A Georgian 39th Regiment painted wood side drum,** c1800, 16in (40.5cm) high.
£1,500–2,000 ⚒ WAL

► **A George IV brass-mounted mahogany campaign box,** by Palmer, London, 22¼in (56.5cm) wide.
£1,800–2,250 ⚒ TEN

An oak billiard table, inlaid with marquetry, with score cabinet, 1858, 72in (183cm) wide.
£68,000–75,000 ⊞ WBB

A Victorian mahogany revolving snooker cue stand, 48in (122cm) high.
£2,000–2,400 ⚒ MAR

A Doulton Lambeth stoneware jug, decorated with applied vignettes of batsman, bowler and wicket-keeper within incised stylized flower borders, impressed and incised marks, c1900, 8in (20.5cm) high.
£650–800 ⚒ RTo

A Coalport porcelain trophy, for Pains Lane races, chips to knop, 1842, 13in (33cm) high.
£8,000–9,500 ⚒ S
Coalport made a speciality of racing trophies.

A bronze group of a mounted polo player, by Isidore Bonheur, signed, with Peyrol foundry stamp, French, c1875, 14¼in (36cm) high.
£22,000–25,000 ⊞ RGa

A carved and painted salmon, c1954, 46¾in (119cm) wide.
£2,200–2,750 ⚒ P(Ed)

◄ **A trinket box,** by George Heath, the cover enamelled with a day at the races, 1887, 3¾in (9.5cm) wide.
£2,000–2,400 ⚒ B

► **A stuffed and mounted perch,** by J. Cooper & Sons, in a bowfronted case, 1892, 19in (48.5cm) wide.
£900–1,100 ⚒ CGC

◄ **A boy's football cap,** 1875–1900, 6½in (16.5cm) interior diam.
£85–100 ⚒ PFK

A walnut and brass frog-back Nottingham sea reel, c1890, 6in (15cm) diam.
£270–300 ⊞ PEZ

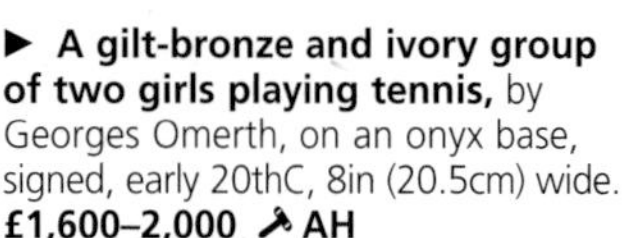

► **A gilt-bronze and ivory group of two girls playing tennis,** by Georges Omerth, on an onyx base, signed, early 20thC, 8in (20.5cm) wide.
£1,600–2,000 ⚒ AH

A Burnley No. 8 shirt, worn by Jimmy McIlroy during the European Cup tie at Turf Moor, with an official programme and three French magazines reporting the ties, 1960.
£3,500–4,250 ⚒ Bon(C)

A pair of porcelain Copenhagen plates, Danish, 1779, 9½in (24cm) diam.
£1,000–1,200 ⊞ US

A giltwood cartel timepiece, by A. J. Biurman, Norrköping, the movement with later anchor escapement, Swedish, c1790, 33in (84cm) high.
£10,000–12,000 ⊞ JIL

A painted pine cupboard, Swedish, c1770, 30in (76cm) wide.
£2,700–3,000 ⊞ JF

► **An Empire mahogany tallboy,** Swedish, c1820, 40¾in (103.5cm) wide.
£5,500–6,000 ⊞ CAV

A faïence vase and pedestal, painted with the seated figure of Queen Louise below the arms of Charles XV of Sweden and Norway, Swedish, Gustafsberg, c1870, 91¾in (233cm) high.
£24,000–30,000 ⚒ S
It is believed that this was made for one of the International Exhibitions in the second half of the 19th century.

An Empire mirror and console table, with gilt and bronzed decoration, the table with a limestone top, Finnish, early 19thC, 89½in (227.5cm) high.
£2,400–3,000 ⚒ BUK

► **A pair of gilded armchairs,** the moulded frame with harebell carving, the arms supported with *faux* bronze carved griffins, Swedish, Gothenberg, c1870.
£17,500–19,500 ⊞ HA

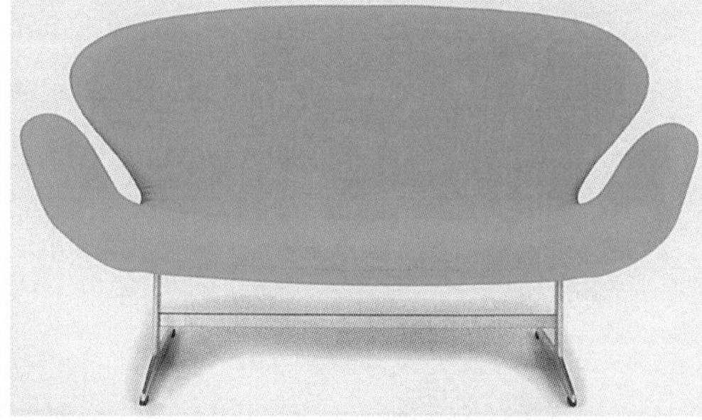

An Arne Jacobsen Swan settee, for Fritz Hansen, Danish, 1950s.
£1,600–2,000 ⚒ TREA

An Orrefors Kraka vase, designed by Sven Palmqvist, Swedish, c1954, 14in (45.5cm) high.
£600–650 ⊞ RUSK

A silver covered bowl and cover, by Georg Jensen, the cover set with carnelian, glass liner, Danish, post-1945, 6¾in (17cm) diam.
£8,000–10,000 ⚒ S(O)

► **A matched pair of gilt-bronze-mounted porphyry lidded urns,** lid finial missing, Swedish, early 19thC, largest 21in (53.5cm) high.
£23,000–28,000 ⚒ P
Porphyry was commercially mined on a large scale in Alvdalen, Sweden from the end of the 18th century until the mid-19th century.

◄ **A sampler,** worked in silk, metal thread and beads, Swedish, dated 1785, 12½ x 10¾in (32 x 27.5cm).
£4,000–5,000 ⚒ WW

Football

A child's leather football, size 3, c1920.
£150–175 ⊞ SMW

An FFF Allen World Cup leather football, autographed by Marcel and Kopa, with the French magazine *Sport & Vie*, June 1958, the cover picture signed by Kopa, 1958.
£350–450 ⚒ Bon(C)

An Ireland International blue wool jersey, worn by Billy Gillespie, 1928.
£700–800 ⚒ S(O)
This jersey was gained as a swap from the Irish captain Billy Gillespie of Sheffield United following the match at Goodison Park, 22 October 1928.

A 15ct gold and enamel Scottish FA Cup winner's medal, inscribed 'Won by Rangers FC, J Macpherson', 1897–98.
£900–1,100 ⚒ S(O)

TOTTENHAM HOTSPUR.

A Southampton v Tottenham Hotspur match card, 3 October 1906.
£1,100–1,200 ⚒ S(O)

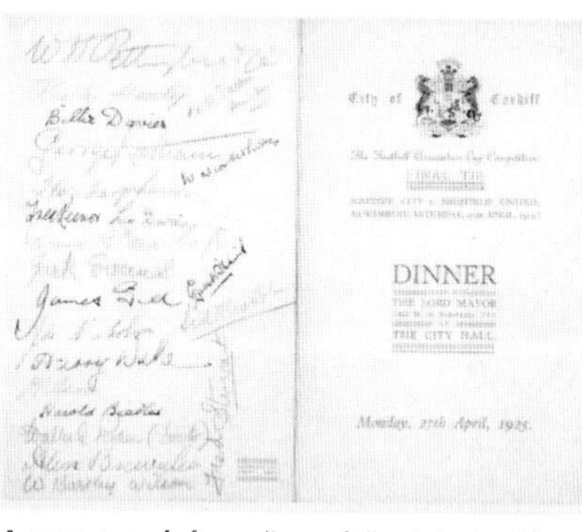
City of Cardiff

DINNER

A menu card, for a dinner following the FA Cup Final between Cardiff City and Sheffield United on 27 April 1925, signed in ink and pencil on the back cover by 22 of the Cardiff City team and management.
£1,500–2,000 ⚒ ANA

◄ **A black and white postcard of Cardiff City Football Club,** by Wilkes of West Bromwich, signed in ink on the reverse by the 11 members of the Cup-winning side, 1927.
£500–600 ⚒ ANA

A signed colour photograph of Bobby Moore, 1966, 5 x 8in (12.5 x 20.5cm).
£150–200 ⊞ EE

Miller's is a price GUIDE not a price LIST

A black and white postcard, depicting the Arsenal v Manchester United cup tie, Manchester, 10 March 1906, 3 x 6in (7.5 x 15cm).
£320–380 ⊞ EE

THE MANCHESTER UNITED
OFFICIAL PROGRAMME
THE NEW PALACE
GEORGE GRAVES
FRED KITCHEN

A Manchester United v Newcastle United programme, 28 November 1914, inner page loose.
£820–900 ⚒ S(O)

► **A Bolton Wanderers v West Ham United FA Cup Final programme,** for the first Wembley final, 28 April 1923.
£650–800 ⚒ Bon(C)

BRITISH EMPIRE EXHIBITION
PROGRAMME & SOUVENIR
FINAL TIE
THE EMPIRE STADIUM
WEMBLEY
BOLTON WANDERERS
WEST HAM UNITED

Golf

A George Bussey & Co patent automaton Caddie golf bag, with canvas club and ball bags applied to the main wooden structure, c1905, 35½in (90cm) long.
£900–1,100 S

A draw sheet, for The First Amateur Championship Golf Tournament at the Royal & Ancient Club, St Andrews, September 1886, with printed list of players and names of clubs from which they were entered, single sheet, oblong 2°.
£1,250–1,500 F&C

A brown-glazed stoneware sand holder, with two shell handles, the front with a shield and hole number, c1890, 10in (25.5cm) high.
£450–565 Bon(C)

Prior to the era of wooden tee pegs, a sand holder would be placed on the border of the teeing area and held sand from which the players took a pinch to tee up the golf ball. The number of the hole is incised on the holder and the grooves filled with sand in order that the number could be read.

Bernard Darwin and others, *History of Golf in Britain*, first edition, 1952, 4°, with colour frontispiece, black and white illustrations and golf course plans, containing 46 ink signatures obtained at the British Open at Royal Lytham, bound in original cloth with gilt morocco label and dust-jacket.
£500–625 DW

An Open Golf Championship match programme, St Andrews, July 1960, centenary issue, with order of play sheet.
£130–160 ANA

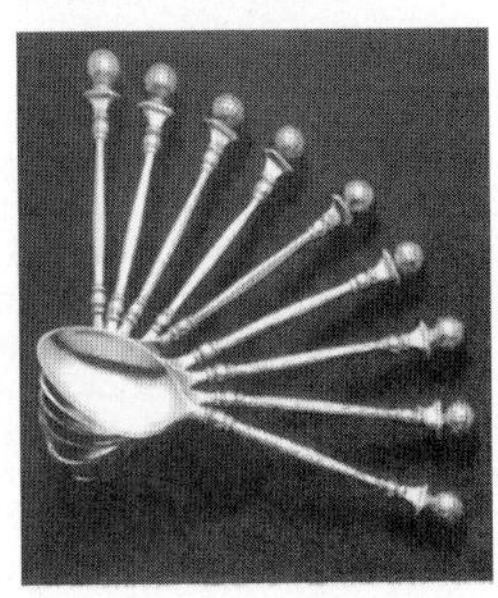

A Wood & Co biscuit barrel, printed and painted with golfing scenes, with pewter rim, swing handle and matched silver-plated lid, printed factory marks, early 20thC, 7in (18cm) high.
£950–1,200 FHF

◄ **A brassie,** The Jimmy, made for Alex Patrick, with hickory shaft and leather grip, c1915, 36in (91.5cm) long.
£80–90 PEZ

A WMF pewter inkwell, modelled with a golfing scene, German, c1905, 7in (18cm) wide.
£400–440 PEZ

An 18ct gold half hunter pocket watch, owned by Arnaud Massey, with initials 'A. M.' engraved on the rear cover, the inside engraved 'Open Golf Championship 1906, presented by James Carter & Co', 1906, 1¾in (4.5cm) diam.
£650–820 Bon(C)

Arnaud Massey was French Open champion in 1906 and again in 1907.

◄ **A set of 12 silver teaspoons,** with golf ball terminals, Birmingham 1930–40, 4½in (11.5cm) long.
£350–400 S

SPORT

Rugby

◄ **A Five Point laced rugby ball,** with 52 ink signatures of former rugby players, including 30 members from the 1977 British Lions Touring Party, and A. T. Reid (New Zealand, 1935–37) and C. E. O. Badeley, (New Zealand 1920–24), c1950.
£125–150 DW

A Yorkshire Rugby League cap, worn by George Todd, maroon velvet with gilt-wire tassel, white rose and gilt-metal badge, with a photograph of Todd and an embroidered badge for Yorkshire County Rugby League, 1929.
£320–400 Bon(C)

A Welsh International rugby jersey, red, with embroidered badge, 'C' to back, the name Bowcott to neck label, 1928–32.
£200–250 ANA

◄ **A menu card** for a dinner held after the France v Wales match on 27 March 1957, signed by the French XV and 12 Welsh players.
£120–140 ANA

► **A black and white team photograph of Hunslet Rugby Club,** mounted above a menu card, signed by 19 of the team and officials, for a dinner held in honour of the team following the 1965 Rugby League Cup Final at Wembley, framed and glazed.
£75–95 ANA

A Halifax football team pottery mug, printed in blue with the players' names and inscribed 'Winners of Northern Rugby League, 1st Division' and 'Winners of Northern Union, Challenge Cup', c1902, 4in (10cm) high.
£240–300 SAS

A Wales v France match programme, 28 February 1925, at Cardiff Arms Park, punched holes to upper margin.
£160–200 ANA

Shooting

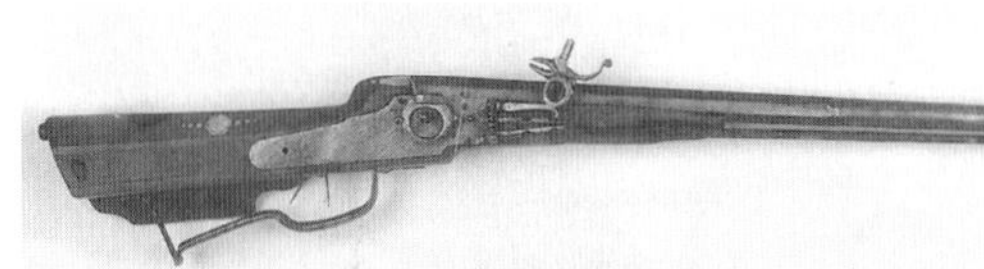

A 20 bore wheel lock sporting gun, with later Tower proofs, half octagonal barrel, walnut half stock inlaid with engraved staghorn silhouettes and various motifs, wooden ramrod, some restoration, stock refinished, German, 17thC, 38½in (98cm) long.
£725–900 WAL

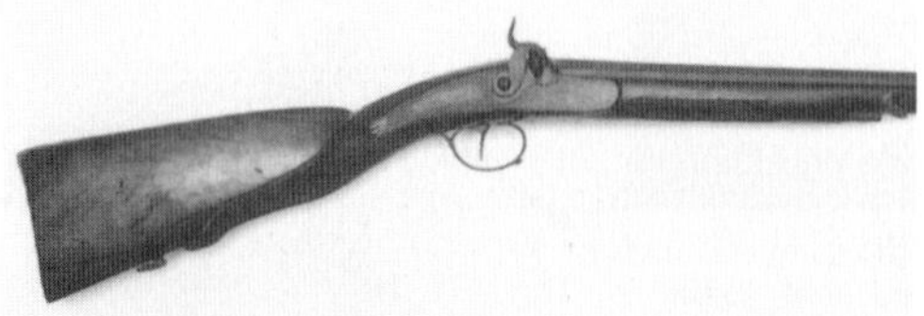

An 18 bore percussion sporting gun, by P. Petri, Lucca, the Spanish two-stage barrel with silver fore-sight between gold foliage, with figured walnut half stock, the breech inlaid with gold motifs, steel mounts, ramrod missing, Italian, 1836–39, barrel 35in (89cm) long.
£280–350 Bon

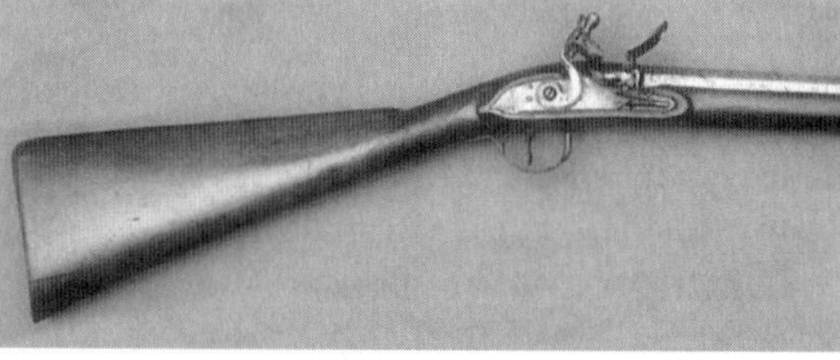

A flintlock sporting gun, with sighted two-stage barrel, the breech signed 'D. Scott, Edinr', half stock with horn fore-end cap and engraved steel mounts, with brass-tipped ramrod, c1810, 37¼in (94.5cm) long.
£500–625 P(Ed)

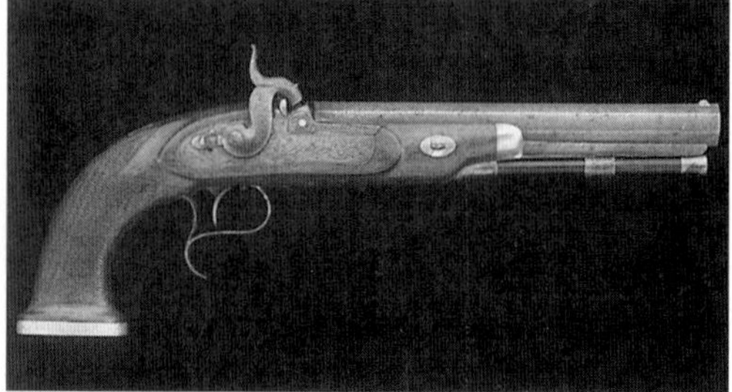

A percussion target pistol, by Sherwood, Portsmouth, Birmingham proof marks, with signed octagonal twist-sighted barrel, figured walnut half stock and later ramrod, steel refinished, 1843–48, 14½in (37cm) long.
£770–850 S(O)

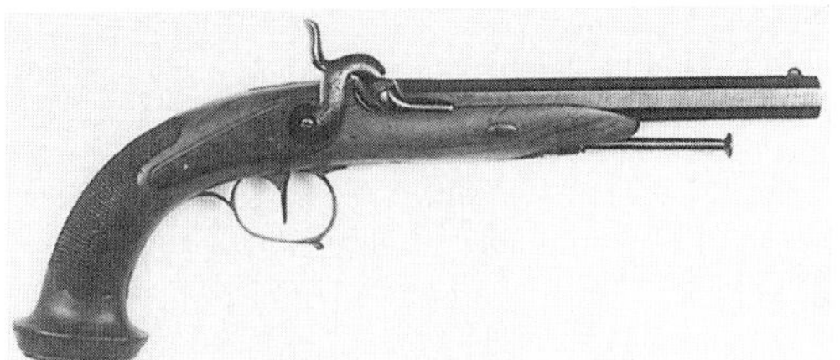

A pair of 32 bore percussion target pistols, by P. Collette, Paris, with rebrowned twist octagonal sighted polygroove rifled barrels, figured walnut half stocks, foliate engraved steel mounts and steel ramrods, signed, steel parts refinished, 1850–1900, 14in (35.5cm) long.
£550–700 ⚒ Bon

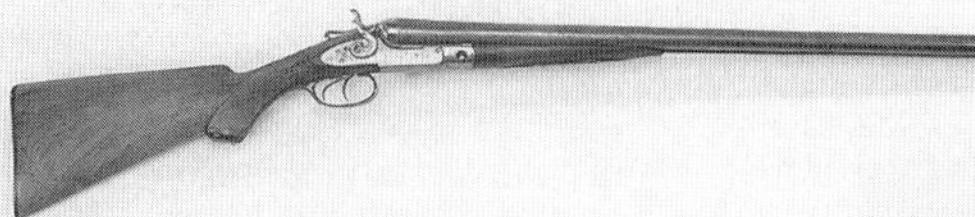

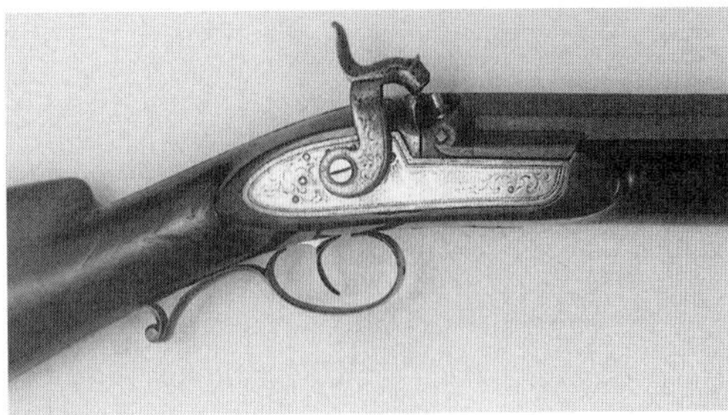

A 4 bore percussion fowling gun, by Cogswell & Harrison, with browned two-stage barrel, brass-tipped wooden ramrod and scroll engraved lockplate, c1870, barrel 36in (91.5cm) long.
£500–600 ⚒ EP

◄ **A hammer shotgun,** by Parker Bros, Serial No. 34917, with damascus barrels, 10 gauge, 1883, barrels 29in (73.5cm) long.
£330–420 ⚒ SLN

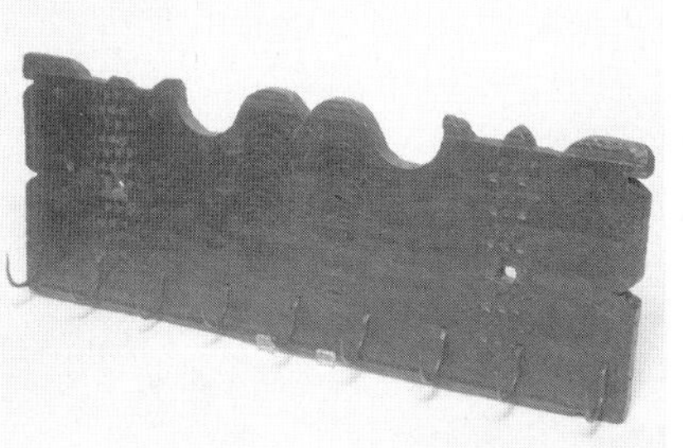

A carved oak hook plate for hanging game, c1680, 22in (56cm) long.
£430–475 ⊞ SEA

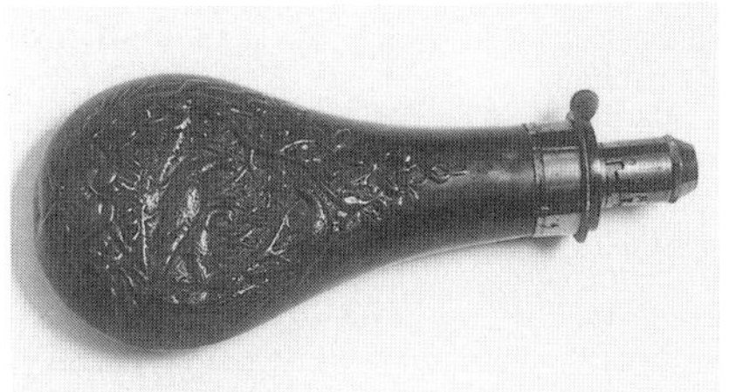

A Prattware jug, decorated with hunting scenes, c1820, 8in (20.5cm) high.
£600–675 ⊞ SEA

◄ **A brass and copper powder flask,** by Bartram & Co, with variable nozzle, c1850, 8in (20.5cm) long.
£120–150 ⊞ ARB

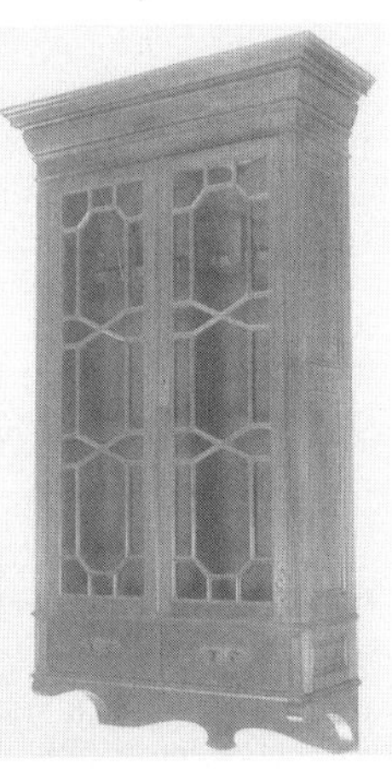

A late Victorian walnut gun cabinet, with two astragal-glazed doors enclosing a baize-lined fitted interior, above two drawers, 40in (101.5cm) wide.
£450–565 ⚒ DN

Tennis

A teak bench, with gilt-metal plaque inscribed 'Original teak bench seat from Centre Court, Wimbledon, installed 1922 removed 1983', 66in (167.5cm) long.
£1,500–1,800 ⚒ S

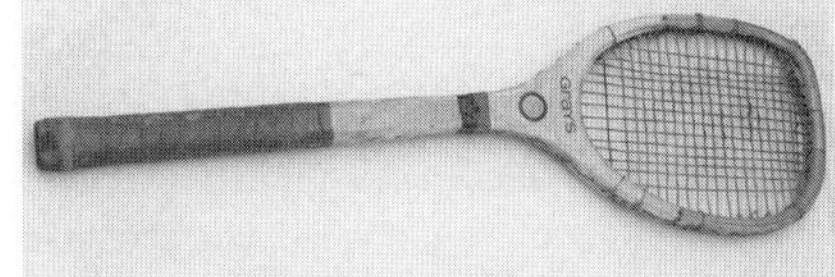

A Gray's real tennis racket, c1960, 26in (66cm) long.
£30–35 ⊞ SA

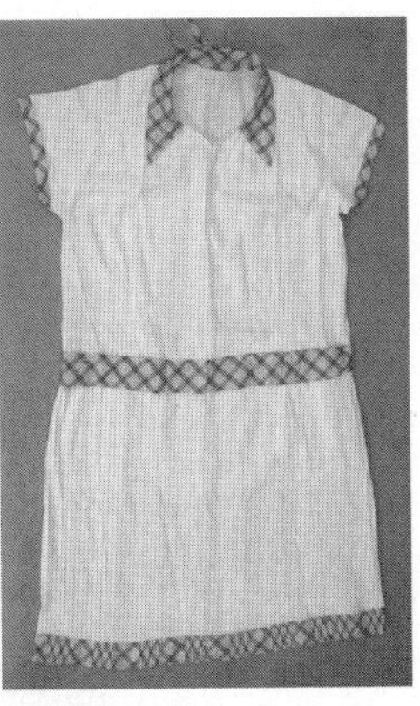

A tennis dress, in cream silk with blue trim, 1920s.
£100–120 ⚒ SWO

► **A mahogany multiple tennis press,** by Williams, Paris, c1910, 12in (30.5cm) wide.
£160–175 ⊞ SA

A wooden box, to contain an Army & Navy lawn tennis compendium set, c1885, 39in (99cm) long.
£150–200 ⊞ SA

Focus on Scandinavia

Swedish styles were greatly influenced by the French since, from the time of Louis XIV, Sweden enjoyed a special relationship with France. All leading architects and artists travelled to Paris to study and some continued to Italy as well. When the Swedish Royal Palace was being built in the 1730s and 1740s, a large number of French craftsmen and artists were employed to decorate and make much of the furniture. Workshops were set up and the French masters trained Swedish apprentices there.

The elaborate Louis XV or rococo style was popular in aristocratic circles but did not make an impression beyond the grander houses. In the 1770s there was a change towards a stricter neoclassical fashion, the style named 'Gustavian' after the King. The simple but elegant furniture is still popular today with designers and interior decorators in Britain, America, France and of course Sweden. It is usually painted in cool grey or white and chairs were often inspired by Hepplewhite designs. Gustavian furniture continued to be made by local craftsmen in the provinces during the early 19th century and the style experienced a revival in the early 20th century, largely due to the Swedish painter Carl Larsson whose watercolours of his own house, which contained many pieces, exerted great influence. Swedish rococo and Gustavian furniture is very popular not only in Scandinavia, where the highest prices are generally paid for good, signed pieces, but also very popular in America, England and France.

During the Empire period (1800–1820) many grand pieces such as giltwood mirrors with matching console tables were produced in Sweden, mainly for the aristocracy and the royal palaces. From the 1820s the Biedermeier style became very popular in Scandinavia. Made in indigenous blond woods like birch this furniture has recently become sought after in Europe and America.

The great Stockholm exhibition in 1930 was a landmark when the new Functionalist style was introduced in architecture and furniture design. New exciting designs were presented, some in new materials like chrome, but also in the more traditional oak and blond woods. Modern Scandinavian furniture (1930–50) is becoming increasingly popular in Scandinavia attracting high prices as a result. There is also great interest in other countries, many pieces currently being exported to Australia.

The glass industry enjoyed a tremendous upswing from the 1920s as manufacturers like Orrefors and Kosta employed artists such as Edvard Hald, Simon Gate and Vicke Lindstrand as designers. Many of their items are collectors' pieces and fetch high prices at auction, especially in Sweden.

Håkan Groth

Furniture

A birchwood bench, Swedish, c1800, 43½in (110.5cm) wide.
£2,400–2,700 ⊞ CAV

A bronze-mounted elm rococo bureau, with fitted interior, restored, Stockholm, mid-18thC, 41¼in (105cm) wide, with keys.
£2,500–3,000 ⚒ BUK

A brass-mounted mahogany secretaire, Stockholm, c1800, 36½in (93cm) wide, with keys.
£3,300–4,200 ⚒ BUK

◄ A baroque burr-thuja and ebonized cabinet, the two doors inlaid with a star motif, above one drawer, the ebonized lower part with square-shaped supports on a potboard base, 18thC, 53¼in (135cm) wide.
£2,500–3,000 ⚒ S(Am)

► A bronze-mounted walnut cabinet, Stockholm, 1750–1800, 61in (155cm) wide.
£3,800–4,750 ⚒ BUK

A blue-painted pine cabinet, Swedish, 1800–10, 44½in (113cm) wide.
£2,250–2,500 ⊞ CAV

A pine cabinet, the two panelled doors opening to four shelves above two drawers, painted in yellow and brown to simulate wood, with green and red marbleized detail, some damage, date 1815, 62¼in (158cm) wide.
£1,700–2,000 ⚒ SK(B)

A Biedermeier mahogany cabinet, with satinwood inlay, Danish, c1815, 21¼in (54cm) wide.
£4,500–5,000 ⊞ CAV

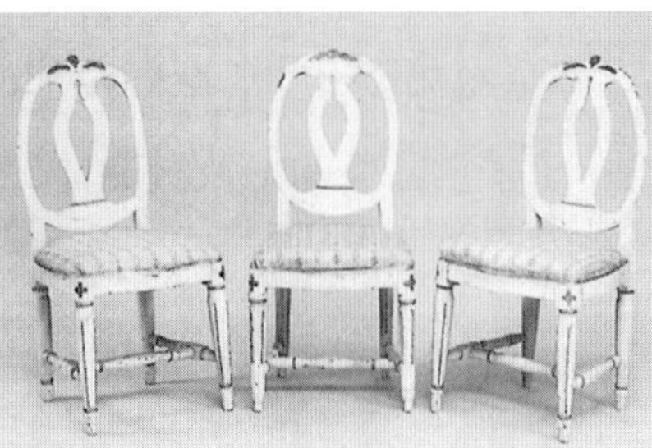

A set of three white-painted chairs, with bronzed, carved decoration, damaged, Swedish, 1800–20.
£1,500–2,000 ⚒ BUK

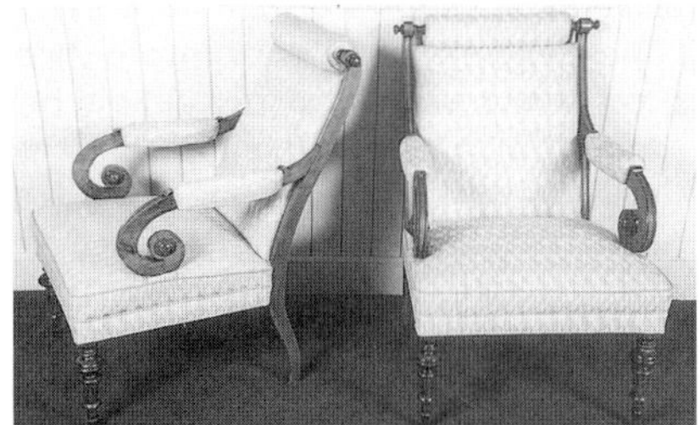

► **A pair of oak-framed armchairs,** c1890.
£1,500–1,700 ⊞ RPh

A miniature walnut chair, with a leather-covered seat, the seat-rail carved with the initials 'A. C. H.' and dated 1799, the arms missing the upholstered elbow rests, 11½in (29cm) high.
£1,400–1,750 ⚒ CGC

A mahogany commode, with damaged grey limestone top, Stockholm, 1800–20, 43in (109.5cm) wide.
£1,400–1,750 ⚒ BUK

A white-painted pine secretaire chest, Swedish, 1820–30, 46in (117cm) wide.
£2,000–2,300 ⊞ CAV

◄ **A mahogany secretaire,** with gilt-bronze mounts, keys missing, Stockholm, c1820, 47¾in (121.5cm) wide.
£3,500–4,500 ⚒ BUK

A Biedermeier masur birch and birchwood secretaire, Swedish, c1830, 43in (109cm) wide.
£3,500–4,000 ⊞ CAV

◄ **A mahogany mirror,** with a later painted glass panel, c1840, 14in (35.5cm) wide.
£240–300 ⚒ S(O)

A carved giltwood mirror, by Carl Gustaf Fyrwald, Master in Stockholm 1774–1816, signed, hall-marked Stockholm 1785, 1800–20, glass of later date, 54¼in (138cm) high.
£2,700–3,500 ⚒ BUK

A white-painted pine country sideboard, with reeded doors, Swedish, c1790, 49in (124.5cm) wide.
£1,800–2,000 ⊞ JF

A mahogany Empire-style sofa, with cream and green upholstery, Swedish, 1900–10, 50in (127cm) wide.
£1,500–1,650 ⊞ CAV

A Biedermeier mahogany sofa, the side cabinets inlaid with urns and maidens, with cream and orange upholstery, Danish, c1890, 82in (208.5cm) wide.
£1,350–1,500 ⊞ RAN

A pair of white-painted stools, bronzed, with upholstered seats, Stockholm, c1790.
£1,200–1,500 ⚒ BUK

A pair of Biedermeier birchwood stools, Swedish, 1820–30, 15½in (39.5cm) wide.
£3,000–3,400 ⊞ CAV

A pair of late Gustavian-style white-painted stools, bronzed, with stuff-over seats, damaged, Swedish, mid-19thC.
£600–750 ⚒ BUK

A demi-lune console table, in carved and bronzed giltwood, with grey limestone top, Stockholm, 1800–20, 33¾in (86cm) wide.
£2,500–3,000 ⚒ BUK

A white-painted console table, with bronzed, carved detail, damaged, top of later date, c1800, 30¼in (77cm) wide.
£650–820 ⚒ BUK

A mahogany side table, with drawer, Stockholm, 1775–1800, 29½in (75cm) wide.
£1,400–1,700 ⚒ BUK

A mahogany demi-lune games table, with fold-over top, minor damage, Swedish, 1800–20, 20½in (52cm) wide.
£600–750 ⚒ BUK

An alder root-veneered tilt-top table, Swedish, early 19thC, 37½in (95.5cm) diam.
£550–700 ⚒ BUK

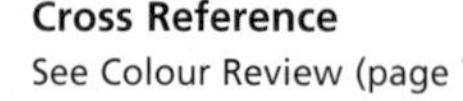

Cross Reference
See Colour Review (page 744)

A Biedermeier-style birchwood dining table, Swedish, 1900–10, 56¼in (143cm) diam.
£5,300–6,000 ⊞ CAV

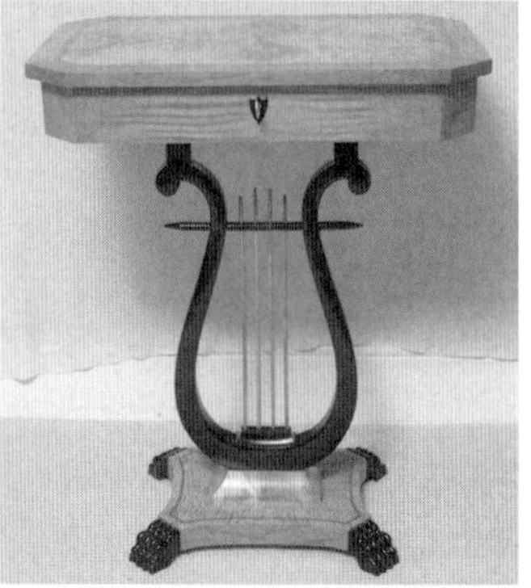

A Biedermeier-style birchwood lyre table, Swedish, 1910–20, 29¼in (74.5cm) high.
£2,500–3,000 ⊞ CAV

Twentieth-Century Furniture

A Finmark Constructivists birch-wood chair, by Alvar Aalto, the seat of laminated ply, Finnish, early 1930s.
£765–850 ⊞ ORI

A set of six Series 7 chairs, by Arne Jacobsen, in bent plywood on chrome legs, Danish, designed in 1955, manufactured 1980–90.
£400–450 ⊞ MARK

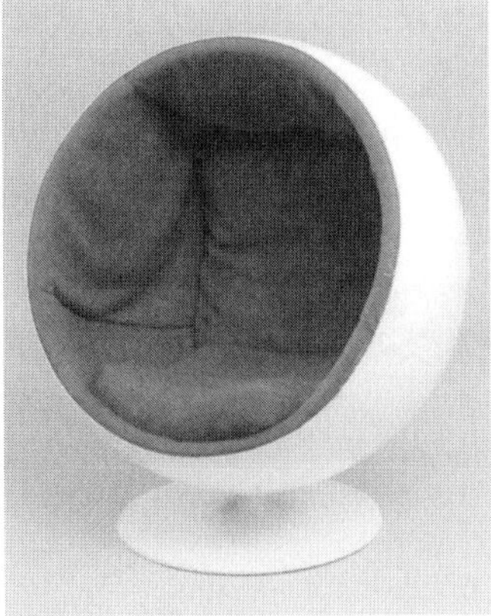

An Eero Aarnio Thunderball chair, by Asko, in white plastic upholstered in red, the cloth partly damaged, Finnish, c1963.
£1,000–1,250 ⚒ BUK

► An Arbe steel Parrot chair, by Ib Arberg, on a black angular metal stand, Swedish, c1970.
£320–400 ⚒ BAG

A set of eight Fritz Hansen 3100 Ant chairs, by Arne Jacobsen, rosewood-veneered plywood, Danish, stamped, designed 1951–52.
£1,100–1,300 ⚒ S(O)

A Fog and Morup orange plastic tub chair, designed by Ole Gjerlov-Knudsen, with loose circular brown corduroy cushion, marked and labelled, Danish, c1960.
£50–60 ⚒ BAG

A set of five Fritz Hansen 3107 armchairs, by Arne Jacobsen, with brown enamelled plywood seats and arms on chrome legs, marked, Danish, c1955.
£500–600 ⚒ BAG

◄ A Fritz Hansen Bachelor lounge chair, by Verner Panton, the chromed metal frame with a sling seat and yellow cloth cushions, Danish, designed 1955.
£145–180 ⚒ BAG

An Eero Aarnio Bubble chair, by Asko, the clear plastic seat with chrome trim, over a chrome base with a loose red seat cushion, Finnish, 1960s.
£1,100–1,300 ⚒ TREA

A wire Cone chair, by Verner Panton, Danish, c1960.
£1,000–1,200 ⊞ MARK

A pair of Fritz Hansen Pantonova chrome chairs and ottoman, by Verner Panton, cushions of later date, Danish, c1971.
£550–700 BUK

► **A Fritz Hansen System 123 fabric and chrome screen,** by Verner Panton, Danish, designed and produced 1972.
£600–700 MARK

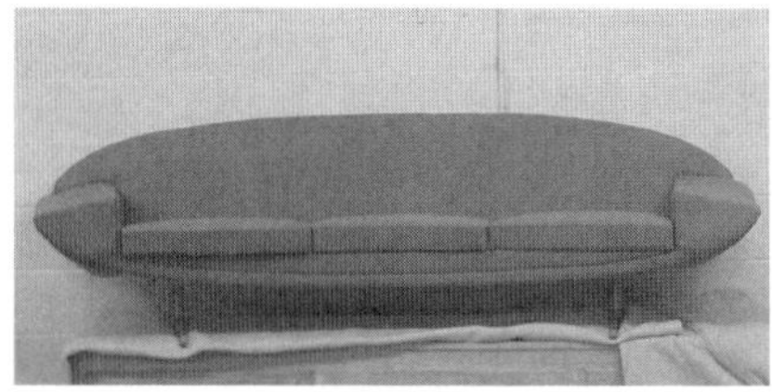

A Trendsum Capri upholstered settee, designed by Jos Andersen, with gold-coloured upholstery on polished metal legs, Swedish, c1960, 86½in (219.5cm) wide.
£675–850 BAG

A Hanaen & Sörensen sofa, by Finn Juhl, upholstered in an orange woollen fabric with yellow woollen cushions, Danish, designed 1957, 93in (236cm) wide.
£1,100–1,400 BUK

A satin walnut and calamander Poiret-style bedroom suite, with applied ebonized motifs, comprising a pair of single beds uniting to form a double bed, a dressing table, a pair of bedside cupboards, a pair of chairs, and a chest of drawers, Stockholm, c1925.
£1,600–2,000 B

A lounge suite, by Hans Wegner, comprising two oak armchairs with green and brown cushions and an oak table, branded mark, Danish, c1955, table 35in (89cm) square.
£230–275 JAA

A Fritz Hansen breakfast suite, by Arne Jacobsen, comprising a table and three 3101 Ant chairs in rosewood-face veneer, on tubular steel uprights, marked, Danish, c1955, table 45¼in (115cm) wide.
£900–1,000 P(B)

A Nordiska Kompaniet jacaranda and walnut Typenco table, by Axel Einar Hjort, with a metal base, restored, minor damage, Stockholm, early 1930s, 31½in (80cm) diam.
£1,000–1,250 BUK

A Fritz Hansen sofa table, by Arne Jacobsen, with mahogany top and aluminium base, Danish, 1958, 51½in (131cm) long.
£850–1,100 DORO

A Nordiska Kompaniet sofa table, by Stig Lindberg and David Rosen, the enamel top polychrome-decorated with a dining scene, marked, Gustavsberg, Swedish, 1952.
£800–1,000 BUK

A rosewood gateleg dining table, the crossbanded top with integral interlocking hinge, on V-shaped legs, Danish, c1970.
£350–450 BAG

An Art Deco chrome drinks trolley, Swedish, c1920, 17½in (44.5cm) wide.
£530–600 CAV

Ceramics

A Royal Copenhagen biscuit bust of the Apotheosis of Napoleon, after Berthel Thorwaldsen, minor chips, factory mark, impressed marks, Danish, early 20thC, 10in (25.5cm) high.
£400–450 ⚒ S(O)

A faïence butter-box, in the shape of a partridge sitting on a yellow and green base, Swedish, Marieberg, 1758–66, 6in (15cm) long.
£2,800–3,200 ⚒ BUK

A hand-painted porcelain cream cup, with blue flowers and gilt-line detail, Swedish, c1775, 3in (7.5cm) high.
£600–700 ⊞ US

A blue and white faïence jug, painted with birds and flowers, with painter's initial 'D', Swedish, Rörstrand 1740-50, 4¾in (12cm) high.
£1,200–1,400 ⚒ BUK

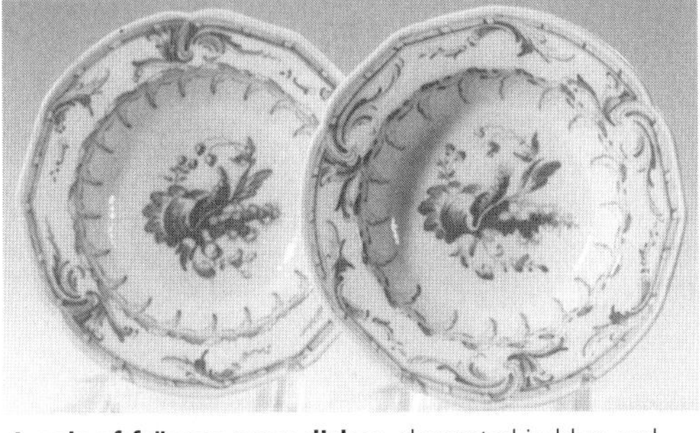

A pair of faïence soup dishes, decorated in blue and white with the Rhenish pattern on a *bianco-sopra-bianco* ground, Swedish, c1765, 8¾in (22cm) diam.
£800–950 ⚒ BUK

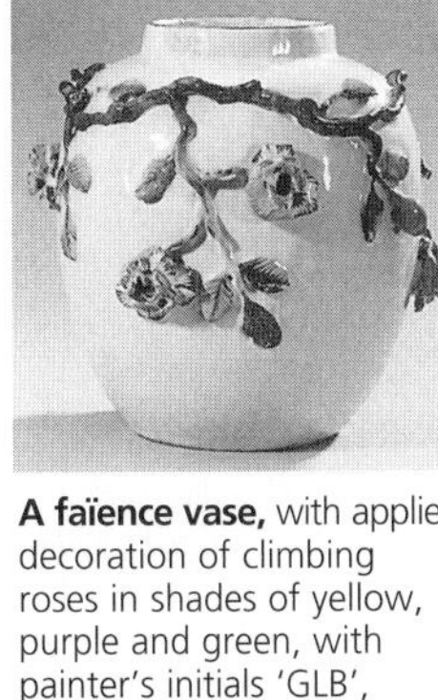

A faïence vase and cover, painted with birds and flowers in blue, yellow and manganese, chips, Swedish, Rörstrand, 1752, 14½in (37cm) high.
£850–1,100 ⚒ BUK

A faïence vase, with applied decoration of climbing roses in shades of yellow, purple and green, with painter's initials 'GLB', slight damage, restoration, Swedish, Marieberg, 1758–66, 8¾in (22cm) high.
£900–1,100 ⚒ BUK

A Royal Copenhagen figure of a fisherman, modelled by Carl Martin-Hansen, wearing a yellow sou'wester and brown trousers, with a net in his hand, marked and impressed Skagen, Danish, 1910–20, 13in (33cm) high.
£250–300 ⚒ B

A faïence tea canister, with blue chinoiserie decoration of flowers issuing from rockwork on a white ground, Swedish, Rörstrand, 1740–50, 5in (12.5cm) high.
£350–420 ⚒ BUK

► A Gustavsberg Vaga vase, by Wilhelm Kåge, in a matt white glaze, impressed mark and gold label, Swedish, c1940, 9¾in (25cm) high.
£170–220 ⚒ BAG

A Gustavsberg stoneware vase, by Stig Lindberg, with impressed chequered decoration glazed in blue, green and brown, signed, Swedish, 1963, 14½in (37cm) high.
£1,100–1,400 ⚒ BUK

A neo-classical vase, signed 'Ibsen', Danish, mid-19thC, 16½in (42cm) high.
£900–980 ⊞ CAV

Glass

A glass beaker, probably Henrikstorp, with engraved decoration of a stylized basket of flowers, 1700–50, 7in (18cm) high.
£425–550 BUK

An Iittala Kanterelli vase, by Tapio Wirkkala, with clear glass linear-cut decoration, Finnish, designed 1946, produced 1948–60, 3½in (9cm) high.
£200–250 BAG

A presentation glass goblet, the bell-shaped bowl engraved with a crowned inscribed cartouche, the reverse with a rose branch, the composite stem with a bladed knop between two beaded knops, above a spiral air-twist section with a wide shoulder knop and small basal knop, the foot engraved with a border of formal flowers, Norwegian, dated 1771, 9¾in (25cm) high.
£675–800 P

A pair of blue glass footed bowls, probably Gjövig, Norwegian, 1800–50, 6¾in (17cm) diam.
£800–1,000 BUK

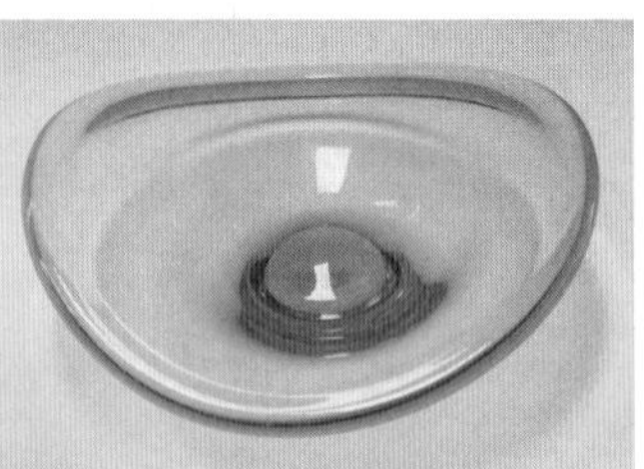

▶ **A Holmegaard freeform glass bowl,** by Per Lutken, signed, Danish, 1950–60, 12½in (32cm) high.
£100–120 ORI

▶ **An Orrefors clear glass vase,** Swedish, 1950s, 11in (28cm) high.
£100–120 MCC

A Kosta Glasbruk Träd i Dimma vase, by Vicke Lindstrand, the clear glass decorated with stylized trees in violet/black against an opalescent white background, incised signature, Swedish, designed 1950–51, 12½in (32cm) high.
£1,500–2,000 DORO

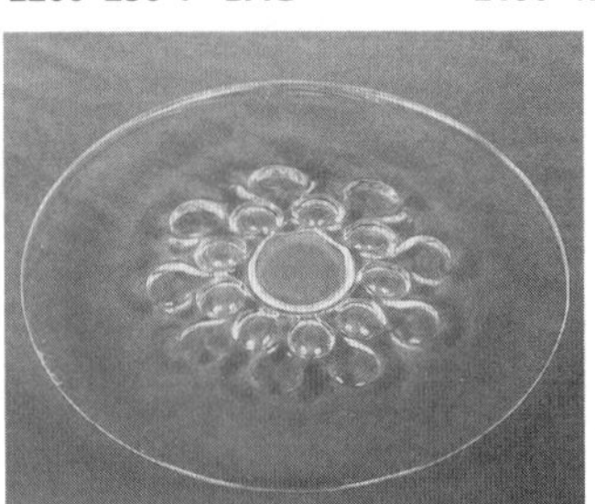

An Orrefors glass dish, signed and stamped, Swedish, 1970s, 15½in (39.5cm) diam.
£175–200 ZOOM

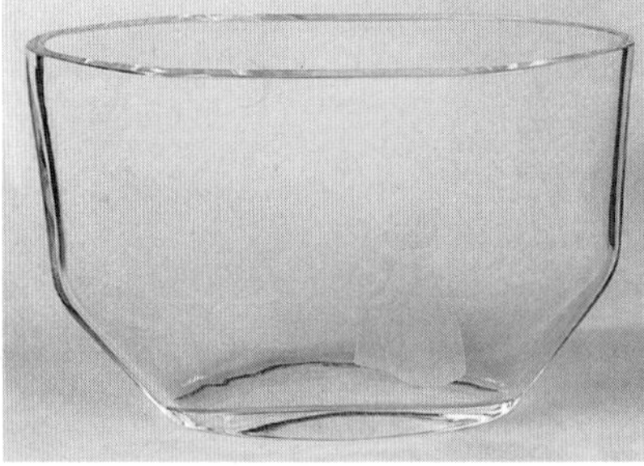

An Orrefors glass vase, etched with a young girl looking at the moon and stars, Swedish, c1950, 6in (15cm) high.
£300–325 MI

A Nuutajarvi Notsjo glass U-shaped vase, by Mikko Merikallio, with a blue interior cased in clear glass, marked and dated 1964, Finnish.
£80–100 BAG

▶ **An Iittala glass vase,** with textured exterior, signed, Finnish, 1960s, 7in (18cm) high.
£130–160 G(L)

A Holmegaard blue glass gulvase, by Otto Breuer, Danish, 1960s, 15in (38cm) high.
£90–100 ORI

Silver

A silver beaker, possibly Joen Andersen, chased with scrolling leaves and flowerheads, with inscribed initials and date, Danish, c1670, 3½in (9cm) high, 4oz.
£425–500 S(O)

A silver beaker, engraved with initials and later embossed with a band of flowers and leaf scrolls on a matt ground, makers mark 'I.PB.?', Swedish, Norrköping, 18thC, 3½in (9cm) high, 2oz.
£200–240 DN

A silver snuff box, by Andreas Öhrman, with chased and engraved decoration of the Imperial orb on a pedestal and the North Star, surrounded by volutes, rocaille and shells, with gilt interior, decoration worn, Stockholm 1765, 2¾in (7cm) wide.
£650–800 BUK

► **A hammered silver box and cover,** by Gran and Lagyle, with an amber ball finial in a foliage bud calyx, marked 'GL', Copenhagen 1917, 4in (10cm) diam.
£400–450 DAD

A silver sugar box, by Johan Jacob Lihr, supported on two swans, the lid decorated with a recumbent lion, Finnish, Tammisaari 1830, 7in (18cm) diam.
£2,000–2,500 BUK

A hammered silver caddy spoon, by Georg Jensen, with beaded end, import marks for 1927, Danish, 1¼in (3cm) long.
£270–300 DAD

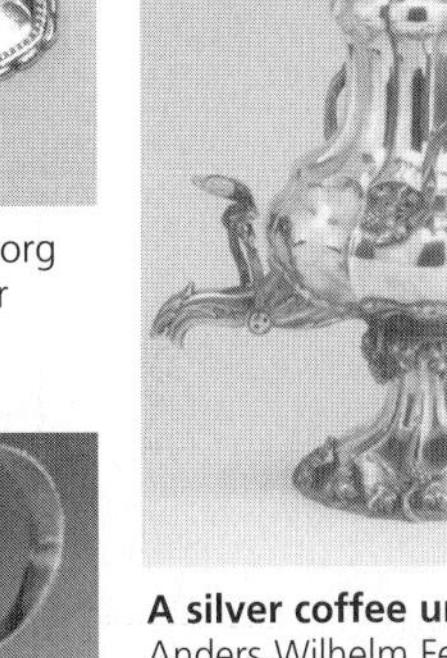

A silver coffee urn, by Anders Wilhelm Felixsson, decorated with applied vines, the knop in the shape of a flower, Finnish, Loviisa 1857, 11½in (29cm) high.
£2,000–2,500 BUK

A silver coffee pot, by Arvid Floberg, with a flower finial and ebonized handle, on paw feet, Stockholm 1785, 8¼in (21cm) high.
£2,000–2,500 BUK

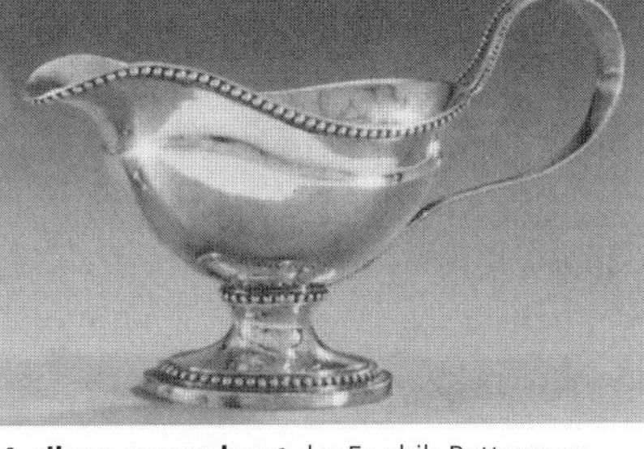

A silver cream boat, by Fredrik Pettersson Ström, with beaded edge and gilt interior, Stockholm 1789, 7in (18cm) wide.
£650–800 BUK

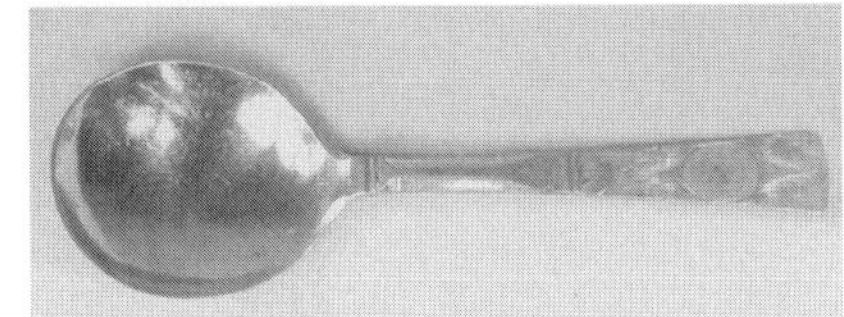

A parcel-gilt spoon, partially foliate engraved, inscribed on reverse of stem 'ROS 1710', 18thC, 7½in (19cm) long, 1.5oz.
£160–200 CGC

◄ **A set of six silver-gilt and coloured enamel coffee spoons,** by J. Tolstrup, Norwegian, Kristiania c1900, 3oz, cased.
£100–120 WW

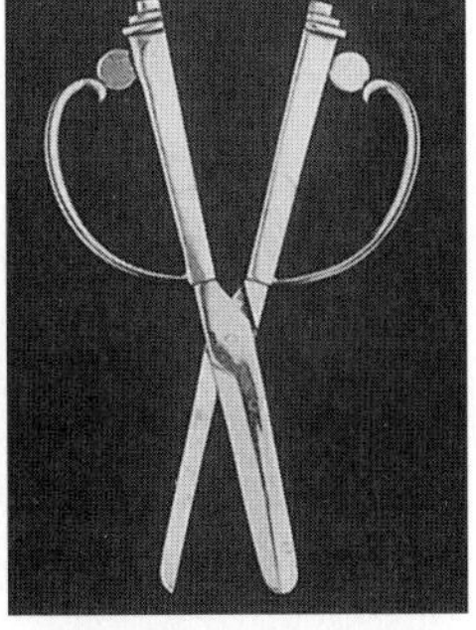

A pair of Georg Jensen silver grape scissors, designed by Harald Nielsen, Pyramid pattern, with stainless steel blades, import marks for London 1931, Danish, 5in (12.5cm) long.
£450–565 Bon

Clocks & Watches

A walnut and parcel-gilt longcase clock, by H. Wolffenberg, with eight-day rack and bell-striking movement, Danish, Haderslev, c1775, 88½in (225cm) high.
£1,250–1,500 S(O)

◄ **A wall clock,** by Per Henrik Beurling, the giltwood case flanked by flowers, Swedish, c1800, 32¾in (83cm) high.
£1,300–1,500 BUK
Beurling was a Master Clockmaker from 1783–1806 in Stockholm.

► **A giltwood Gustavian-style wall clock,** by E. Uddholm, Stockholm, c1910, 31¾in (80.5cm) high.
£1,500–1,650 CAV

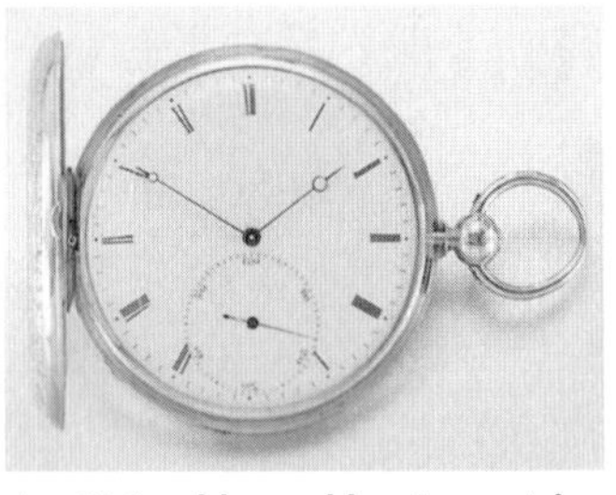

An 18ct gold cased hunter watch, by Jules Jürgensen, with subsidiary seconds dial, and key-wound lever movement, engraved, Copenhagen, c1860, 1¾in (4.5cm) diam.
£1,200–1,400 S(G)
An accomplished watchmaker and a student of physics, mathematics and astronomy, Jules Jürgensen (1808–1877) came from a family of chronometer and watchmakers, including his father, the famous chronometer maker Urban Jürgensen. By 1826, just two years after he established his own firm at his birth place, Le Locle, Switzerland, Jules was awarded the title Watchmaker to His Majesty the King of Denmark. He was also honoured with the titles Knight of the Légion d'Honneur and Knight of the Royal Order of Daneborg. Amongst his innovations, Jules had patents for keyless watch winding and for a hand-setting mechanism. His skill gained him much recognition, and his watches frequently won awards from the 1860s onwards.

Lighting

A brass lamp, with pierced decoration of trailing flowers, on three feet, Swedish, 1650–1700, 29in (73.5cm) high.
£2,350–3,000 BUK

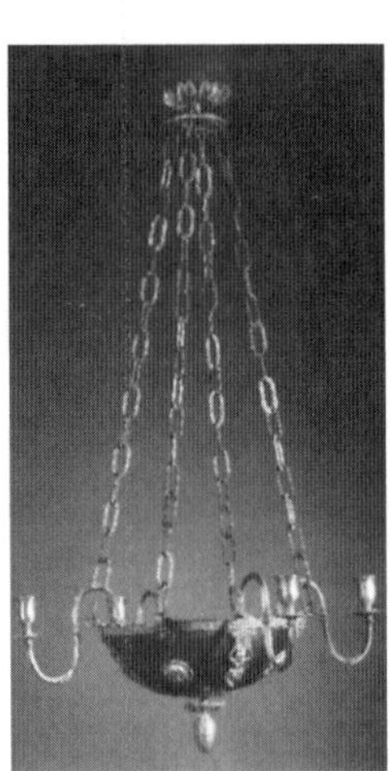

◄ **A patinated-brass four-light chandelier,** one arm missing, Swedish, 19thC, 47¼in (120cm) high.
£950–1,100 S(Z)

► **A pair of gilt-metal wall lights,** Swedish, early 20thC, 36½in (92.5cm) high.
£2,200–2,500 S(O)

► **A Louis Poulsen Artichoke ceiling light,** by Poul Henningsen, the graduated brushed-steel reflectors with reflective internal surface, with hanging system, Danish, designed 1958, 25½in (65cm) high.
£2,350–2,600 PLB

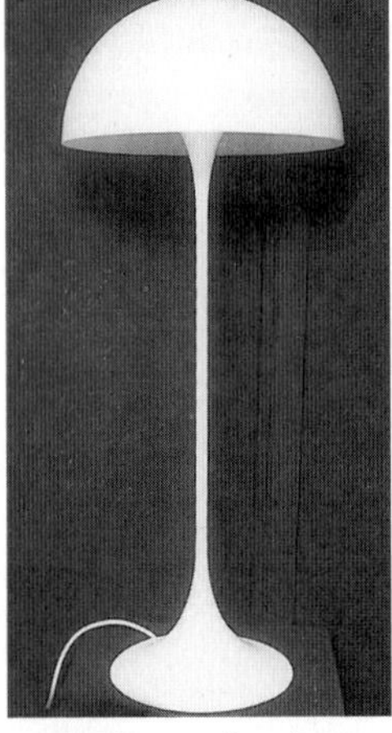

A plastic standing lamp, by Verner Panton, Danish, 1960–70, 46in (117cm) high.
£500–550 ZOOM

A Louis Poulsen VP-Globe ceiling light, by Verner Panton, clear Plexiglas with coloured reflectors, slight damage, Danish, designed 1975, no longer in production, 19¾in (50cm) high.
£850–1,100 BUK

Rugs & Textiles

◄ **A hooked rug,** with flowers and geometric motifs in pastel colours on a blue ground, the main border with similar decoration on a green ground, restored, Finnish, Huittinen, dated 1822, 73½in x 56in (186.5 x 142cm).
£750–950 ⚒ BUK

A cover, with four rows of stylized motifs in yellow, light red, beige, pale green and shades of blue, the zigzag border decorated with birds and flowers, signed with initials and date, slight damage and repairs, 1825, Swedish, Skåne, 78¼ x 49½in (199 x 125.5cm).
£1,250–1,500 ⚒ BUK

A red ground carpet, with a crown motif stitched to the back of one corner, Danish, c1920, 161½ x 157in (410 x 398cm).
£900–1,000 ⚒ S(O)

◄ **A cushion cover,** woven in Rose and Grapevines pattern, Swedish or Norwegian, late 18thC, 20 x 23in (51 x 58.5cm).
£950–1,200 ⚒ WW
This is an important and rare early piece.

A hooked rug, by Sigvard Bernadotte, in shades of blue, beige, red, yellow, pink and mauve, slight damage, signed, 1940s, 66 x 42in (167.5 x 106.5cm).
£275–350 ⚒ BUK

A flatweave side-saddle cover, woven with initials and date, 1882, Icelandic, 61½ x 34in (156 x 86.5cm).
£240–300 ⚒ WW

Jewellery

► **An 18ct gold filigree bracelet,** with a diamond and pearl plaque, Stockholm, 1807.
£825–1,000 ⚒ BUK

► **A silver brooch,** by Georg Jensen, depicting two birds with an ear of wheat, stamped import mark for London 1967, Danish, 1½in (4cm) square.
£180–225 ⚒ Bea(E)

A Lapponia 14ct gold necklace, Tenochtitlan, by Björn Weskström, Norwegian, Helsinki, 1980s.
£1,000–1,250 ⊞ DID

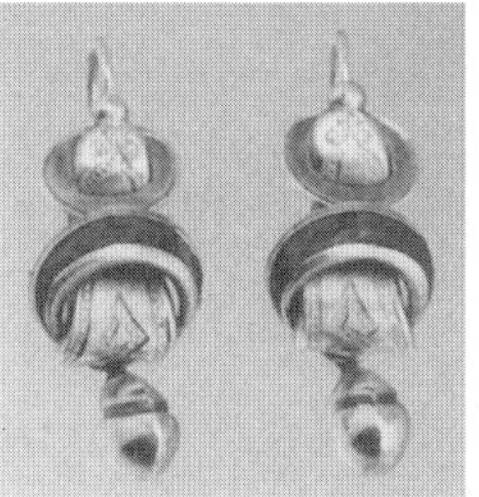

A pair of 18ct gold and enamel earrings, by R. Mellin, Finnish, Helsinki, 1858.
£450–550 ⚒ BUK

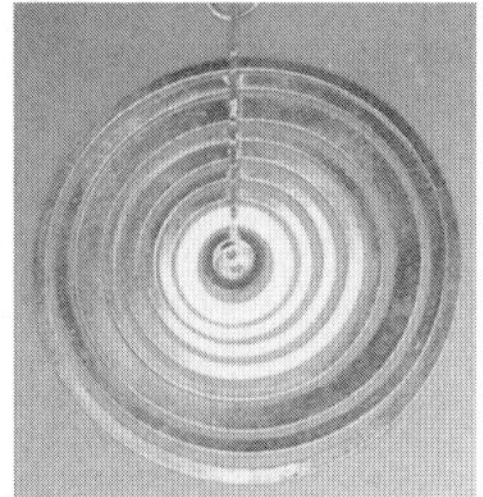

A sterling silver pendant, by Tapio Wirkkala, Silver Moon, Finnish, 1974, 2½in (6.5cm) diam.
£250–320 ⚒ BUK

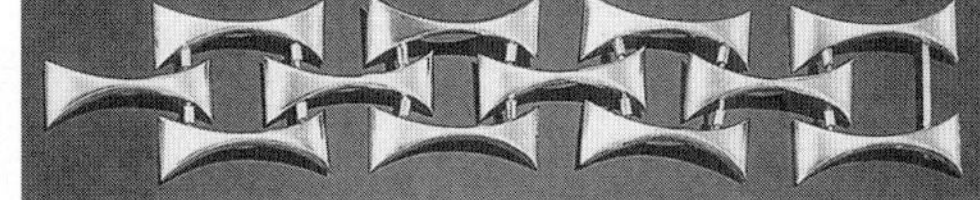

A sterling silver bracelet, by Tostrup, hallmarked, Norwegian, c1960.
£225–275 ⚒ LJ

► **A Sheherazade sterling silver necklace,** by Kristian Nilsson, Stockholm, 1982, 17¾in (45cm) long.
£550–700 ⚒ BUK

Metalware

A pair of brass candlesticks, 19thC, 5¾in (14.5cm) high.
£140–175 SWO

A Svenskt Tenn pewter bowl, by Anna Petrus, the interior with engraved decoration, stamped mark, Swedish, 1944, 9¼in (23.5cm) diam.
£620–775 BUK

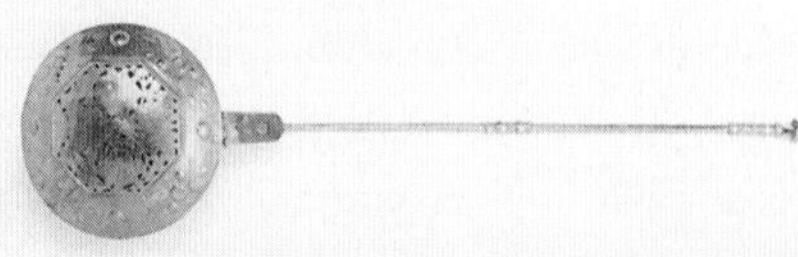

A pair of brass wall sconces, the convex plates decorated with flowers and bosses, Swedish, 18thC, 13¾in (35cm) high.
£2,500–3,250 BUK

◄ **A brass warming pan,** with pierced floral decoration, Swedish, 18thC, 43¾in (111cm) long.
£400–500 BUK

Treen

A carved butter tub, with cylindrical lift-off cover, Norwegian, mid-19thC, 11½in (29cm) diam.
£770–850 S(O)

► **A burr-birch lidded tankard,** Norwegian, 1750–1800, 8in (20.5cm) high.
£800–900 S

► **Two carved wood tally boards,** the faces ornamented with chip carving, 18thC, largest 30in (76cm) long.
£130–200 each TMA

A carved oak foot warmer, with brass handle, the base carved with the owner's name and date, 1759, 9in (23cm) high.
£1,000–1,100 ⊞ TRI

Miscellaneous

A pallash, with brass half-basket hilt, c1740, 38¾in (98.5cm) blade.
£800–975 WW

A terracotta bust, by Rasmus Peter Ipsen, Copenhagen, mid-19thC, 18½in (47cm) high.
£2,300–2,600 ⊞ G&H

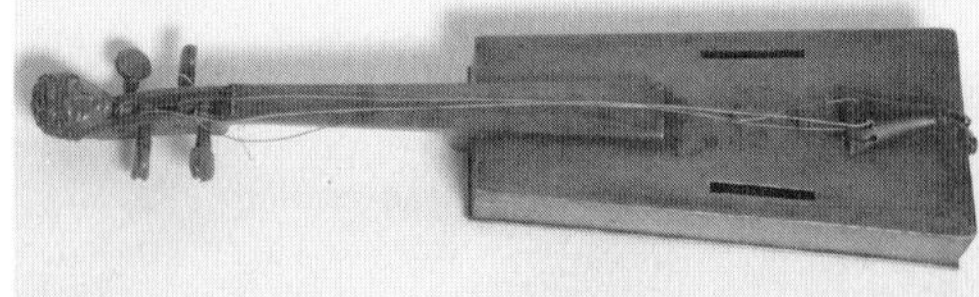

A carved cedarwood fiddle, c1860, 22in (56cm) long.
£400–450 ⊞ DJH

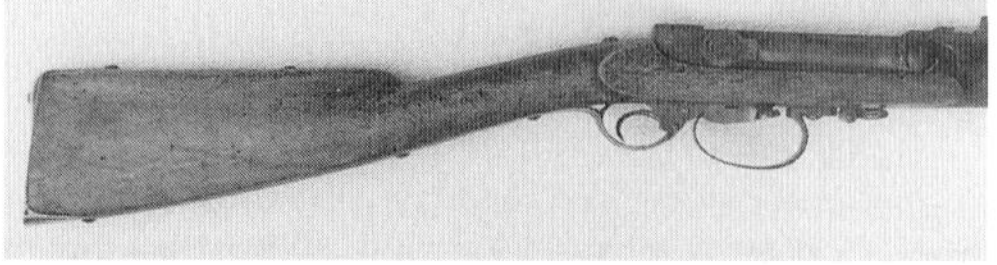

A .451 Lobnitz breech loading capping-under-hammer percussion rifle, Danish, dated 1861, barrel 36in (91.5cm) long.
£1,100–1,200 ⊞ ASB
This example is fitted with Whitworth's hexagonal rifling and is probably an experimental arm designed for troop trials for sharp-shooters. Danish military arms on the Lobnitz system are rare, and a combination with Whitworth's rifling appears to be unheard of.

Glossary

We have defined here some of the terms that you will come across in this book. If there are any terms or technicalities you would like explained or you feel should be included in future, please let us know.

agate ware: 18thC pottery, veined or marbled to resemble the mineral agate.
albarello: Pottery vessel used for storing pharmaceutical ingredients.
amboyna: Yellowish-brown burred wood imported from the West Indies and used as a veneer.
anchor escapement: Said to have been invented c1670 by Robert Hooke or William Clement. A type of escape mechanism shaped like an anchor, which engages at precise intervals with the toothed escape wheel. The anchor permits the use of a pendulum (either long or short), and gives greater accuracy than was possible with the verge escapement.
***aogai*:** Japanese lacquer technique.
arabesque: Scrolling foliate decoration
aryballos: Ancient bottle-shaped vessel.
askos: Small ancient Greek vessel to contain liquids, in the shape of a closed pot with a spout.
associated: Term used in antiques, in which one part of an item is of the same design but not originally made for it. See marriage.
atlas (pl. atlantes): Column in the form of a male figure.
automaton: Any moving toy or decorative object, usually powered by a clockwork mechanism.
bezel: Ring, usually brass, surrounding the dial of a clock, and securing the glass dial cover.
Biedermeier: Style of furniture made principally in the 1820s and 1830s in Austria, Germany and parts of Scandinavia and characterized by simple, heavy Classical forms. It is named after a fictional character who symbolized the German bourgeoisie of the early 19thC.
bijin: A Japanese term for a beautiful woman.
bisque: French term for biscuit ware, or unglazed porcelain.
***blanc-de-chine*:** Translucent white Chinese porcelain, unpainted and with a thick glaze, made at kilns in Dehua in the Fujian province from the Song Dynasty and copied in Europe.
***boteh*:** Stylized design of a floral bush found on rugs, similar to a Paisley design.
bracket clock: Originally a 17thC clock which had to be set high up on a bracket because of the length of the weights; now sometimes applied to any mantel or table clock.
Britannia Standard: Higher standard of silver required between 1697 and 1720. Denoted by Britannia and a lion's head in profile on the hallmark.
***bureau de dame*:** Writing desk of delicate appearance and designed for use by ladies. Usually raised above slender cabriole legs and with one or two external drawers.
***bureau plat*:** French writing table with a flat top and drawers in the frieze.
cabaret set: Tea set on a tray for three or more people.
calamander: Hardwood, imported from Sri Lanka (of the same family as ebony), used in the Regency period for making small articles of furniture, as a veneer and for crossbanding.
***camaieu*:** Porcelain decoration using different tones of a single colour.
cameo glass: Two or more layers of coloured glass in which the top layer/s are then cut or etched away to create a multi-coloured design in relief. An ancient technique popular with Art Nouveau glassmakers in the early 20thC.
candle slide: Wooden slide to hold a candlestick.
cartouche: Ornate tablet or shield surrounded by scrollwork and foliage, often bearing an inscription, monogram or coat-of-arms.
cavetto: Quarter-round concave moulding
celadon: Chinese stonewares with an opaque grey-green glaze, first made in the Song Dynasty and still made today, principally in Korea.
cellaret: Lidded container on legs designed to hold wine. The interior is often divided into sections for individual bottles.
***champlevé*:** Enamelling on copper or bronze, similar to cloisonné, in which a glass paste is applied to the hollowed-out design, fired and ground smooth.
chapter ring: Circular ring on a clock dial on which the hours and minutes are engraved, attached or painted.
character doll: One with a naturalistic face, especially laughing, crying, pouting, etc.
***chilong*:** Chinese mythical dragon-type lizard.
Chinese Imari: Chinese imitations of Japanese blue, red and gold painted Imari wares, made from the early 18thC.
chinoiserie: The fashion, prevailing in the late 18thC, for Chinese-style ornamentation on porcelain, wall-papers, fabrics, furniture and garden architecture.
***chuval*:** Turkic word meaning bag.
cistern tube: Mercury tube fitted into stick barometers, the lower end of which is sealed into a boxwood cistern.
clock garniture: Matching group of clock and vases or candelabra made for the mantel shelf. Often highly ornate.
cloisonné: Enamelling on metal with divisions in the design separated by lines of fine metal wire. A speciality of the Limoges region of France in the Middle Ages, and of Chinese craftsmen to the present day.
coin silver: Silver of the standard used for coinage, ie .925 or sterling.
coromandel: Imported wood from the Coromandel coast of India, of similar blackish appearance to calamander and used from c1780 for banding, and for small pieces of furniture.
countwheel: Wheel with segments cut out of the edge or with pins fitted to one face, which controls the striking of a clock. Also known as a locking plate.
***cuerda seca*:** Tile-making technique, developed in Iran in the 15thC, whereby the colours of the design were separated by an oily substance which leaves a brownish outline.
***cwpwrdd deuddarn*:** Welsh variety of the press cupboard with two tiers.
cyma: Double-curved moulding. Cyma recta is concave above and convex below; cyma reversa the other way round. Also known as ogee and reverse ogee moulding. Popular with 18thC cabinet-makers.

Cymric: Trade-name used by Liberty & Co for a mass-produced range of silverware inspired by Celtic art, introduced in 1899 and often incorporating enamelled pictorial plaques.

deadbeat escapement: Type of anchor escapement, possibly invented by George Graham and used in precision pendulum clocks.

Delft: Dutch tin-glazed earthenwares named after the town of Delft, the principal production centre, from the 16thC onwards. Similar pottery made in England from the late 16thC is also termed 'delft' or 'delftware'.

***deutsche Blumen*:** Naturalistically painted flowers, either single or tied into bunches, used as a popular decorative motif on 18thC pottery and porcelain.

diaper: Surface decoration composed of repeated diamonds or squares, often carved in low relief.

ding: Chinese three-legged vessel.

diorama: Miniature three-dimensional scene.

dog of *Fo*: Buddhist guardian lion.

doucai: Decoration on Chinese porcelain using five colours.

***écuelle*:** 17th and 18thC vessel, usually of silver, but sometimes ceramic, for serving soup. Has a shallow, circular bowl, two handles and a domed cover. It often comes complete with a stand.

***elem*:** End panels or skirts of Turkoman carpets.

***ensi*:** Rug used as a tent door by Turkoman tribes.

EPNS: Electroplated nickel silver.

escapement: Means or device which regulates the release of the power of a timepiece to its pendulum or balance.

faïence: Tin-glazed earthenwares named after the town of Faenza in Italy, but actually used to describe products made anywhere but Italy, where they are called maiolica.

***famille jaune/noire/rose/verte*:** Chinese porcelain in which yellow, black, pink or green respectively are the predominant ground colours.

***fauteuil*:** French open-armed drawing room chair.

fielded panel: Panel with bevelled or chamfered edges.

filigree: Lacy openwork of silver or gold thread, produced in large quantities since end 19thC.

flatware (1): Collective name for flat pottery and porcelain, such as plates, dishes and saucers.

flatware (2): Cutlery.

fluted: Border that resembles a scalloped edge, used as a decoration on furniture, glass, silver and porcelain items.

fusee: 18thC clockwork invention; a cone-shaped drum, linked to the spring barrel by a length of gut or chain. The shape compensates for the declining strength of the mainspring thus ensuring constant timekeeping.

gadroon: Border or ornament comprising radiating lobes of either curbed or straight form. Used from the late Elizabethan period.

girandole: Carved and gilt candle sconce incorporating a mirror.

***goncalo alves*:** Brazilian timber sometimes mistaken for rosewood.

***grisaille*:** Monochrome decoration, usually grey, used on ceramics and furniture during the 18th and 19thC.

***guéridon*:** Small circular table designed to carry some form of lighting.

***guilloche*:** Pattern of twisting bands, spirals, double spirals or linked chains.

***gül*:** From the Persian word for flower – usually used to describe a geometric flowerhead on a rug.

halberd: Spear fitted with a double axe.

hard paste: True porcelain made of china stone (petuntse) and kaolin; the formula was long known to, and kept secret by, Chinese potters but only discovered in the 1720s at Meissen, Germany, from where it spread to the rest of Europe and the Americas. Recognized by its hard, glossy feel.

harewood: Sycamore which has been stained a greenish colour. It is used mainly as an inlay and was known as silverwood in the 18thC.

***herati*:** Overall repeating design of a flowerhead within a lozenge issuing small leaves. Used in descriptions of rugs.

***hiramakie*:** Japanese term for sponged gold applied level with the surface.

***hirame*:** Japanese lacquer decorated with gold and silver leaf.

***hongmu*:** Type of wood used in the manufacture of Chinese furniture.

***ho-o*:** Mythical Chinese bird, similar to a phoenix, symbolizing wisdom and energy.

***huanghuali*:** Type of Oriental wood, much admired for its colour.

Imari: Export Japanese porcelain of predominantly red, blue and gold decoration which, although made in Arita, is called Imari after the port from which it was shipped.

***indianische Blumen*:** Indian flowers; painting on porcelain in the Oriental style, especially on mid-18thC Meissen.

***inro*:** Japanese multi-compartmental medicine or seal container, carried suspended from the sash of a kimono.

***iroe takazogan*:** Inlay in relief decoration on Japanese items.

ironstone: Stoneware, patented 1813 by Charles James Mason, containing ground glassy slag, a by-product of iron smelting, for extra strength.

jadeite: Type of jade, normally the best and most desirable.

Kakiemon: Family of 17thC Japanese porcelain decorators who produced wares decorated with flowers and figures on a white ground in distinctive colours: azure, yellow, turquoise and soft red. Widely imitated in Europe.

***katana*:** Long Japanese sword

***kejebe gül*:** Cruciform medallion based on the eight-pointed star, usually in navy or ivory, most commonly found in Salor Turkoman rugs.

***kiku mon*:** Japanese stylized chrysanthemum.

***kilin*:** Chinese mythical beast with a lion's tail, cloven hooves and the scales of a dragon.

***kinrande*:** Japanese brocade decoration.

***kiri*:** Japanese name for the Paulownia flower.

***kirin*:** Japanese mythical beast.

knop: Knob, protuberance or swelling in the stem of a wine glass, of various forms which can be used as an aid to dating and provenance.

***koro*:** Japanese incense burner.

***kovsh*:** Russian vessel used for measuring drink, often highly decorated for ornamental purposes.

***kraak porselein*:** Dutch term for porcelain raided from Portuguese ships, used to describe the earliest Chinese export porcelain.

krater: Ancient Greek vessel for mixing water and wine in which the mouth is always the widest part.

***kufic*:** Arabic angular script – used in rugs to refer to stylized geometric calligraphy.

kylix: Ancient Greek shallow two-handled drinking vessel.

latticinio: Fine threads of white or clear glass forming a filigree mesh effect enclosed in clear glass.

lekythos: Ancient Greek flask used for oil perfume.

***lingzhi*:** Type of fungus or mushroom, used as a motif on Chinese works of art.
Lithyalin: Polished opaque glass resembling hardstones, patented by Friedrich Egermann in 1829 at his factory in Haida, northern Bohemia.
loaded: In silverware, a hollow part of a vessel, usually a candlestick, filled with pitch or sand for weight and stability.
Long Eliza: Elongated female figure found on Kangxi blue and white export porcelain. The name derives from the Dutch 'lange lijsen'.
lunette: Semi-circular decorative motif popular for carved friezes in the Jacobean and Victorian periods.
made up: Piece of furniture that has been put together from parts of other pieces of furniture. See marriage.
maiolica: Tin-glazed earthenware produced in Italy from the 15thC to the present day.
majolica: Heavily-potted, moulded ware covered in transparent glazes in distinctive, often sombre colours, developed by the Minton factory in the mid-19thC.
manjua: Japanese bun filled with sweet bean paste, now applied to the shape of a netsuke.
marriage: Joining together of two unrelated parts to form one piece of furniture. See associated and made up.
***martelé*:** Term for silverware with a fine, hammered surface, first produced in France and later revived by the American silversmiths Gorham Manufacturing Co during the Art Nouveau period.
merese: Flat disc of glass which links the bowl and stem, and sometimes the stem and foot, of a drinking glass.
***mihrab*:** Prayer niche with a pointed arch; the motif which distinguishes a prayer rug from other types.
millefiori: Multi-coloured, or mosaic, glass, made since antiquity by fusing a number of coloured glass rods into a cane, and cutting off thin sections; much used to ornament paperweights.
***nashiji*:** Multitude of gold flakes in Japanese lacquer.
***netsuke*:** Japanese carved toggles made to secure sagemono (hanging things) to the obi (waist belt) from a cord; usually of ivory, lacquer, silver or wood, from the 16thC.
nulling: Decorative carving in the form of irregular fluting which is usually of ivory, lacquer, silver or wood, from the 16thC.
niello: Black metal alloy or enamel used for filling in engraved designs on silverware.
oinochoe: Small ancient Greek jug with handles.
***ojime*:** Japanese word meaning bead.
***okimono*:** Small, finely carved Japanese ornament.
oklad: Silver or gold icon cover, applied as a tribute or in gratitude for a prayer answered. Also known as a riza or basma.
olpe: Type of ancient Greek jug.
ormolu: Strictly, gilded bronze but used loosely for any yellow metal. Originally used for furniture handles and mounts but, from the 18thC, for inkstands, candlesticks etc.
overlay: In cased glass, the top layer, usually engraved to reveal a different coloured layer beneath.
palmette: In rugs, a cross-section through a stylized flowerhead or fruit.
***pâte-de-cristal*:** Glass that is crushed into fine crystals and and then bound together so that it can be moulded rather than having to be worked in its molten state.
***pâte-de-verre*:** Translucent glass created by melting and applying powdered glass in layers or by casting it in a mould.
***pâte-sur-pâte*:** 19thC Sèvres porcelain technique, much copied, of applying coloured clay decoration to the body before firing.
penwork: Type of decoration applied to japanned furniture, principally in England in the late 18th/early 19thC. Patterns in white japan were applied to a piece which had already been japanned black, and then the details and shading were added using black Indian ink with a fine quill pen.
pier glass: Mirror designed to be fixed to the pier, or wall, between two tall window openings, often partnered by a matching pier table. Made from mid-17thC.
***pietra dura*:** Italian term for hardstone, applied to a mosaic pattern of semi-precious stones and marble.
***plique-à-jour*:** Enamelling technique in which a structure of metal strips is laid on a metal background to form enclosed areas which are then filled with transparent enamels. When the backing is removed, a transparent 'stained glass' effect is achieved.
plum pudding: Type of figuring in some veneers, produced by dark oval spots in the wood. Found particularly in mahogany.
pole screen: Small adjustable screen mounted on a pole and designed to stand in front of an open fire to shield a lady's face from the heat.
***poudreuse*:** French dressing table.
powder flask: Device for measuring out a precise quantity of priming powder, suspended from a musketeer's belt or bandolier and often ornately decorated. Sporting flasks are often made of antler and carved with hunting scenes.
powder horn: Cow horn hollowed out, blocked at the wide end with a wooden plug and fitted with a measuring device at the narrow end, used by musketeers for dispensing a precise quantity of priming powder.
printie: Circular or oval scoop out of glass, sometimes called a lens.
prunt: Blob of glass applied to the stem of a drinking vessel both as decoration and to stop the glass from slipping in the hand.
Puritan spoon: Transitional style of silver spoon, linking early English to modern types. Similar to a slip top but with a broader stem, its name derives from its plain form.
pushti: Rug measuring approximately 3ft x 2ft.
qilin: Alternative spelling of kilin - a Chinese mythical beast.
quarter-veneered: Four consecutively cut, and therefore identical, pieces of veneer laid at opposite ends to each other to give a mirrored effect.
register plate: Scale of a barometer against which the mercury level is read.
regulator: Clock of great accuracy, thus sometimes used for controlling or checking other timepieces.
rocaille: Shell and rock motifs found in rococo work.
rummer: 19thC English low drinking goblet.
***ruyi*:** Chinese presentation sceptre.
***sancai*:** Three-colour decoration on Chinese porcelain.
***sang-de-boeuf*:** (lit. ox-blood) A bright red glaze used extensively on Chinese ceramics during the Qing Dynasty.

S.F.B.J.: Société de Fabrication de Bébés et Jouets; association of doll makers founded 1899 by the merger of Jumeau, Bru and others.
sgraffito: Form of ceramic decoration incised through a coloured slip, revealing the ground beneath.
***shakudo*:** Japanese term for an alloy of copper and gold.
***Shibayama*:** Lacquer applied with semi-precious stones and ivory.
***shibuichi*:** Japanese term for an alloy of copper and silver.
***shinshinto*:** Japanese term meaning 'new new', referring to edged weapons produced between 1800 and 1868.
***shishi*:** Japanese mythical beast, a lion-dog.
***shou* symbol:** Formal, artistic version of the Chinese character shou, meaning long-life.
shoulder-head: Term for a doll's head and shoulders below the neck.
shoulderplate: Area of a doll's shoulder-head below the neck.
siphon tube: U-shaped tube fitted into wheel barometers where the level of mercury in the short arm is used to record air pressure.
soft paste: Artificial porcelain made with the addition of ground glass, bone-ash or soap-stone. Used by most European porcelain manufacturers during the 18thC. Recognized by its soft, soapy feel.
spadroon: Cut-and-thrust sword.
spandrel: Element of design, closing off a corner.
spelter: Zinc treated to look like bronze and much used as an inexpensive substitute in Art Nouveau appliqué ornament and Art Deco figures.
spontoon: Type of halberd often carried by junior infantry officers and senior non-commissioned officers.
stamnos: Large ancient Greek jar that would have contained liquids or solids, characterized by a short neck and two horizontally applied handles.
strapwork: Repeated carved decoration suggesting plaited straps.
stuff-over: Descriptive of upholstered furniture where the covering extends over the frame of the seat.
stumpwork: Embroidery which incorporates distinctive areas of raised decoration, formed by padding certain areas of the design.
susani: Central Asian hand-embroidered bridal bed-cover.
sympiesometer: Instrument that uses a gas and coloured oil to record air pressure.
***takamakie*:** Technique used in Japanese lacquerware in which the design is built up and modelled in a mixture of lacquer and charcoal or clay dust, and then often gilded.
***Taotie*:** Chinese mythical animal which devours wrong-doers.
tassets: Overlapping plates in armour for the groin and thighs.
tazza: Wide but shallow bowl on a stem with a foot; ceramic and metal tazzas were made in antiquity and the form was revived by Venetian glassmakers in 15thC. Also made in silver from 16thC.
teapoy: Piece of furniture in the form of a tea caddy on legs, with a hinged lid opening to reveal caddies, mixing bowl and other tea drinking accessories.
tear: Tear-drop shaped air bubble in the stem of an early 18thC wine glass, from which the air-twist evolved.
term: Pillar or pedestal terminating in a carving of a human head or torso, usually armless.
tester: Wooden canopy over a bedstead supported on either two or four posts. It may extend fully over the bed, known as a full tester, or only over the bedhead half, known as a half tester.
tête-à-tête: Tea set for two people.
***tieli*:** Chinese hardwood
***togidashi*:** Japanese lacquer technique in which further layers of lacquer are added to *hiramakie.*
thuyawood: Reddish-brown wood with distinctive small 'bird's-eye' markings, imported from Africa and used as a veneer.
timepiece: Clock that does not strike or chime.
tin glaze: Glassy opaque white glaze of tin oxide; re-introduced to Europe in 14thC by Moorish potters; the characteristic glaze of delftware, faïence and maiolica.
touch: Maker's mark stamped on much, but not all, early English pewter. Their use was strictly controlled by the Pewterer's Company of London: early examples consist of initials, later ones are more elaborate and pictorial, sometimes including the maker's address.
trumeau: Section of wall between two openings; a pier mirror.
***tsuba*:** Guard of a Japanese sword, usually consisting of an ornamented plate.
Tudric: Range of Celtic-inspired Art Nouveau pewter of high quality, designed for mass-production by Archibald Knox and others, and retailed through Liberty & Co.
tulipwood: Yellow-brown wood with reddish stripe, imported from Central and South America and used as a veneer and for inlay and crossbanding.
tyg: Mug with three or more handles.
verge escapement: Oldest form of escapement, found on clocks as early as 1300 and still in use in 1900. Consisting of a bar (the verge) with two flag-shaped pallets that rock in and out of the teeth of the crown or escape wheel to regulate the movement.
vernier scale: Short scale added to the traditional 3in (7.5cm) scale on stick barometers to give more precise readings than had previously been possible.
***verre églomisé*:** Painting on glass. Often the reverse side of the glass is covered in gold or silver leaf through which a pattern is engraved and then painted black.
vesta case: Ornate flat case of silver or other metal for carrying vestas, an early form of match. Used from mid-19thC.
vitrine: French display cabinet which is often of bombé or serpentine outline and ornately decorated with marquetry and ormolu.
Vitruvian scroll: Repeated border ornament of scrolls that resemble waves.
WMF: Short for Württembergische Metallwarenfabrik, a German foundry that was one of the principal producers of Art Nouveau metalware.
***wucai*:** Type of five-colour Chinese porcelain decoration.
yen yen: Chinese term for a long-necked vase with a trumpet mouth.
***yingqing*:** Type of Chinese porcelain from Jingdezhen, Jianxi Province, first produced during the Song Dynasty.
zitan: Type of dense wood used for making Chinese furniture.

Directory of Specialists

If you wish to be included in next year's directory, or if you have a change of address or telephone number, please contact Miller's Advertising Department by April 2003. We advise readers to make contact by telepone before visiting a dealer, therefore avoiding a wasted journey.

20th Century Design

Kent
20th Century Marks, 12 Market Square, Westerham TN16 1AW
Tel: 01959 562221
Mobile: 07831 778992
lambarda@btconnect.com
www.20thcenturymarks.co.uk
20th century furniture and design.

Kent
Catchpole & Rye, Saracens Dairy, Jobbs Lane, Pluckley, Ashford TN27 0SA
Tel: 01233 840840
info@crye.co.uk www.crye.co.uk

Surrey
Drummond's Architectural Antiques Ltd, The Kirkpatrick Buildings, 25 London Road (A3), Hindhead GU26 6AB
Tel: 01428 609444
www.drummonds-arch.co.uk
Open 7 days.

Americana

U.S.A.
American West Indies Trading Antiques, 27315 Barbuda Lane, Summerland Key, Florida 33042
Tel: 305 872 3948
awindies@worldnet.att.net
www.eBay.com
Also *Ethnographic art, Folk Art, Art Deco.*

Allan Katz Americana, 25 Old Still Road, Woodbridge, Connecticut 06525
Tel: 001 203 393 9356
Folk Art, trade signs and weather vanes.

Antique Dealers' Association

T.V.A.D.A., The Old College, Queen Street, Dorchester-on-Thames OX10 7HL
Tel/Fax: 01865 341639
antiques@tvada.co.uk
www.tvada.co.uk

Antiquities

Dorset
Ancient & Gothic
Tel: 01202 431721
Architectural Antiques.

Architectural Antiques

Cheshire
Nostalgia, Hollands Mill, 61 Shaw Heath, Stockport SK3 8BH
Tel: 0161 477 7706
www.nostalgia-uk.com

Devon
Ashburton Marbles, Great Hall, North Street, Ashburton TQ13 7QD
Tel & Fax: 01364 653189
enquiries@adrianager.co.uk
www.adrianager.co.uk
Antique fireplaces, surrounds and accessories.

Dorset
Dorset Reclamation, Cow Drove, Bere Regis, Wareham BH20 7JZ
Tel: 01929 472200
info@dorsetrec.u-net.com
www.dorset-reclamation.co.uk

Gloucestershire
Minchinhampton Architectural Salvage Company, Cirencester Road, Chalford, Stroud GL6 8PE
Tel: 01285 760886
masco@catbrain.com
www.catbrain.com
Architectural antiques, garden statuary, bespoke chimney pieces and traditional flooring. MASCo specialises in large architectural features and garden ornaments. The company also carries extensive stocks of hard and soft wood flooring as well as reclaimed building materials.

Olliff's Architectural Antiques 19–21 Lower Redland Road, Redland, Bristol BS6 6TB
Tel: 0117 923 9232
marcus@olliffs.com www.olliffs.com

Arms & Militaria

Cheshire
Armourer - The Militaria Magazine, Published by Beaumont Publishing Ltd, 1st floor Adelphi Mill, Bollington SK10 5JB
Tel: 01625 575700
editor@armourer.co.uk
www.armourer.co.uk
A bi-monthly magazine for military antique collectors and military history enthusiasts offering hundreds of contacts for buying and selling, articles on all aspects of militaria collecting plus the dates of UK militaria fairs and auctions. Available on subsription.

Gloucestershire
Q & C Militaria, 22 Suffolk Road, Cheltenham GL50 2AQ
Tel/Fax: 01242 519815
Mobile 07778 613977
john@qc-militaria.freeserve.co.uk
www.qcmilitaria.com

Kent
Sporting Antiques, 10 Union Square, The Pantiles. Tunbridge Wells TN4 8HE
Tel: 01892 522661
Specialist dealers in antique arms, armour, pistols - sporting & military inclusive of all accessories & tools. Books & prints. We buy & sell.

Lincolnshire
Garth Vincent, The Old Manor House, Allington, Nr Grantham NG32 2DH Tel: 01400 281358
garthvincent@aol.com
www.guns.uk.com

London
James Booth, 7 Nottingham Street, Bingham Place W1M 3FG
Tel: 0207 935 3153
james@arms-armour-militaria.com
www.arms-armour-militaria.com

Surrey
West Street Antiques, 63 West Street, Dorking RH4 1BS
Tel/Fax: 01306 883487
weststant@aol.com
www.antiquearmsandarmour.com

East Sussex
Wallis & Wallis, West Street Auction Galleries, Lewes BN7 2NJ
Tel: 01273 480208
auctions@wallisandwallis.co.uk
www.wallisandwallis.co.uk
Auctioneers of militaria, arms and armour and medals.

Warwickshire
London Antique Arms Fairs Ltd, 15 Burbury Court, Emscote Road, Warwick CV34 5LD
01432 355416 & 01926 499022
www.antiquearmsfairsltd.co.uk

Asian

Buckinghamshire
Glade Antiques, PO Box 939, Marlow SL7 1SR
Tel: 01628 487255
Mobile: 07771 552 328
sonia@gladeantiques.com
www.gladeantiques.com
Oriental ceramics, bronzes and jades.

Somerset
Lopburi Art & Antiques, 5/8 Saville Row, Bath BA1 2QP
Tel/Fax: 01225 322947
mail@lopburi.co.uk
www.lopburi.co.uk

U.S.A.
Mimi's Antiques, 8763 Carriage Hills Drive, Columbia MD 21046
Tel: 001 410 381 6862/ 443 250 0930
mimisantiques@comcast.net
www.mimisantiques.com
www.trocadero.com/mimisantiques
18th and 19th century Chinese Export porcelain, American and English Furniture, Continental porcelain, paintings, Sterling, Oriental rugs.

Barographs

Somerset
Richard Twort
Tel/Fax 01934 641900
Mobile 07711 939789

Barometers

Berkshire
Alan Walker, Halfway Manor, Halfway, Nr Newbury RG20 8NR
Tel/Fax: 01488 657670
Mobile: 07770 728397
www.alanwalker-barometers.com

Cheshire
Derek & Tina Rayment Antiques, Orchard House, Barton Road, Barton, Nr Farndon SY14 7HT
Tel: 01829 270429
Mobiles: 07860 666629 / 07702 922410
raymentantiques@aol.com
Also repair & restoration.

Somerset
Knole Barometers, Bingham House, West Street, Somerton TA11 7PS
Tel: 01458 241015
Mobile: 07785 364567
dccops@btconnect.com

Wiltshire
P A Oxley, The Old Rectory, Cherhill, Nr Calne SN11 8UX
Tel: 01249 816227
info@paoxley.com
www.british-antiqueclocks.com

West Yorkshire
Weather House Antiques, Kym S. Walker, Foster Clough, Hebden Bridge HX7 5QZ
Tel: 01422 882808/886961
Mobile: 07889 750711
kymwalker@btinternet.com

U.S.A.
Barometer Fair, PO Box 22502, Sarasota, Florida 34277
Tel/Fax: 941 923 6136
john@barometerfair.com
Buys, sells and restores antique barometers.

Beds

Cheshire
Victorian Imports, Mac House, St Thomas's Place, Stockport SK1 3TZ
Tel: 07940 719256 / 07946 417074
victorianimports@btinternet.com
www.welcome.to/victorianimports

Worcestershire
S W Antiques, Abbey Showrooms, Newlands, Pershore WR10 1BP
Tel: 01386 555580
sw-antiques@talk21.com
www.sw-antiques.co.uk

Wales
Seventh Heaven, Chirk Mill, Chirk, Wrexham, County Borough LL14 5BU
Tel: 01691 777622/773563
requests@seventh-heaven.co.uk
www.seventh-heaven.co.uk

Billiard Tables

Berkshire
William Bentley Billiards, Standen Manor Farm, Hungerford RG17 0RB
Tel: 01488 861711
www.billiards.co.uk

Books

London
Bloomsbury Book Auctions, 3 & 4 Hardwick Street, Off Rosebery Avenue EC1R 4RY
Tel: 0207 833 2636/7 & 0207 923 6940
info@bloomsbury-book-auct.com
www.bloomsbury-book-auct.com

Middlesex
John Ives, 5 Normanhurst Drive, Twickenham TW1 1NA
Tel: 020 8892 6265
jives@btconnect.com
Reference books on antiques and collecting.

Somerset
Bookbasket.co.uk, 30A Monmouth Street, Bath BA1 2AN
Tel: 01225 484877
bookbasket@btconnect.com
www.bookbasket.co.uk
Books on antiques and collectable subjects at discount prices.

Surrey
David Aldous-Cook, PO Box 413, Sutton SM3 8SZ
Tel: 020 8642 4842
Reference books on antiques and collectables.

Wiltshire
Dominic Winter Book Auctions, The Old School, Maxwell Street, Swindon SN1 5DR
Tel: 01793 611340
info@dominicwinter.co.uk
www.dominicwinter.co.uk

Boxes & Treen

Berkshire
Mostly Boxes, 93 High Street, Eton, Windsor SL4 6AF
Tel: 01753 858470
Open Mon–Sat 10am–6.30pm

London
Gerald Mathias, Antiquarius, 135–142 Kings Road, Chelsea SW3 4PW
Tel/Fax: 020 7351 0484
fineantiqueboxes@geraldmathias.com
www.geraldmathias.com

Somerset
Alan & Kathy Stacey
Appointment only
Tel: 01963 441333
sales@antiqueboxes.uk.com

www.antiqueboxes.uk.com
Tea caddies and fine boxes. Specialist dealers in tortoiseshell, ivory, mop, shagreen, exotic timber pieces. Professional conservation services, consultancy, valuations. Members of LAPADA & BAFRA.

British Antique Furniture Restorers' Association

BAFRA Head Office, The Old Rectory, Warmwell, Dorchester, Dorset DT2 8HQ
Tel/Fax: 01305 854822
headoffice@bafra.org.uk

Bedfordshire
Duncan Michael Everitt, DME Restorations Ltd, 11 Church Street, Ampthill MK45 2PL
Tel: 01525 405819
duncan@dmerestorations.com
www.dmerestorations.com
A full restoration service of furniture.

Berkshire
Ben Norris & Co., Knowl Hill Farm, Knowl Hill, Kingsclere, Newbury RG20 4NY
Tel: 01635 297950
Gilding, carving & architectural woodwork.

Cambridgeshire
Ludovic Potts, Unit 1 & 1A, Haddenham Business Park, Station Road, Ely CB6 3XD
Tel: 01353 741537
mail@restorers.co.uk
www.restorers.co.uk
Traditional repairs, boulle, walnut, oak, veneering, upholstery, cane, rush & gilding.

Derbyshire
Anthony Allen, Antique Restorers & Conservators, The Old Wharf Workshop, Redmoor Lane, New Mills, High Peak SK22 3JS
Tel: 01663 745274

Devon
Tony Vernon, 15 Follett Road, Topsham, Exeter EX3 0JP
Tel: 01392 874635
tonyvernon@antiquewood.co.uk
www.antiquewood.co.uk
All aspects of conservation and restoration including gilding, carving, upholstery, veneering and polishing. Accredited member of BAFRA; the British Antique Furniture Restorers' Association.

Dorset
Philip Hawkins, Glebe Workshop, Semley, Shaftesbury SP7 9AP
Tel: 01747 830830
hawkinssemley@hotmail.com
Early oak restoration specialist.

Essex
Clive Beardall, 104B High Street, Maldon CM9 5ET
Tel: 01621 857890
www.clivebeardall.co.uk
Open Mon–Fri 8am–5.30pm Sat 9am–3pm.

Gloucestershire
Alan Hessel, The Old Town Workshop, St George's Close, Moreton-in-Marsh GL56 0LP
Tel: 01608 650026

Hampshire
John Hartley, Johnson's Barns, Waterworks Road, Sheet, Petersfield GU32 2BY Tel: 01730 233792
tankerdale@aol.com
Comprehensive furniture restoration. Large workshops.

David C. E Lewry, Wychelms, 66 Gorran Avenue, Rowner, Gosport PO13 0NF Tel: 01329 286901
Furniture.

Hertfordshire
John B Carr, Charles Perry Restorations Ltd, Praewood Farm, Hemel Hempstead Road, St Albans AL3 6AA Tel: 01727 853487
cperry@praewood.freeserve.co.uk
Specialists in restoration and conservation.

Clifford J Tracy Ltd, Unit 3 Shaftesbury Industrial Centre Icknield Way, Letchworth SG6 1HE
Tel: 01462 684855
Restoration of antique furniture, marquetry, inlaid ivory, brass and tortoiseshell, woodturning, polishing, gilding, general cabinetmaking and complete re-upholstery service. Worm-infested furniture is guaranteed clear by non-toxic methods. Free estimates.

Kent
Timothy Akers, The Forge, 39 Chancery Lane, Beckenham BR3 6NR Tel: 020 8650 9179
www.akersofantiques.com
Longcase and bracket clocks, cabinet-making, French polishing.

Benedict Clegg, Rear of 20 Camden Road, Tunbridge Wells TN1 2PT Tel: 01892 548095

Bruce Luckhurst, Little Surrenden Workshops, Ashford Road, Bethersden, Ashford TN26 3BG
Tel: 01233 820589
restoration@woodwise.newnet.co.uk
www.bruceluckhurst.co.uk
1 Year Course Available, also weekend and 5 day courses.

Lancashire
Eric Smith Antique Restorations, The Old Church, Park Road, Darwen BB3 2LD Tel: 01254 776222
Furniture, vernacular furniture, longcase clocks. Registered with Museums & Galleries Commission London.

Lincolnshire
Michael Czajkowski BSc, E. Czajkowski & Son, 96 Tor O Moor Road, Woodhall Spa LN10 6SB
Tel: 01526 352895
michael.czajkowski@ntlworld.com
Conservation and restoration of antique furniture, clocks (dials, movements and cases) and barometers. Skills include: marquetry Buhle and inlay work; carving & gilding; lacquer work, re-upholstery and upholstery conservation; clockwork & associated metal work. Regular collection service to the East Midlands and London. Member of BAFRA and Accredited Member United Kingdom Institiute of Conservation.

London
Sebastian Giles, Sebastian Giles Furniture, 11 Junction Mews W2 1PN Tel: 020 7258 3721
Comprehensive.

Rodrigo Titian, Titian Studio, 32 Warple Way, Acton W3 0DJ
Tel: 020 8222 6600
enquiries@titianstudios.co.uk
www.titianstudios.co.uk
Carving, gilding, lacquer, painted furniture and French polishing. Caning & rushing.

Norfolk
Michael Dolling, Church Farm Barns, Glandford, Holt NR25 7JR
Tel: 01263 741115
Also at: 44 White Hart Street, East Harling NR16 2NE
Restoration of Antique and fine furniture including marquetry, carving, gilding, upholstery and caning.

Roderick Nigel Larwood, The Oaks, Station Road, Larling, Norwich NR16 2QS Tel: 01953 717937
rodlar@tinyworld.co.uk
Restorers of fine antiques and traditional finishers.

Shropshire
Richard Higgins Conservation, The Old School, Longnor, Nr Shrewsbury SY5 7PP Tel: 01743 718162
All fine furniture, clocks, movements, dials and cases, casting, plating, boulle, gilding, lacquerwork, carving, period upholstery.

Somerset
Stuart Bradbury, M & S Bradbury, The Barn, Hanham Lane, Paulton, Bristol BS39 7PF Tel: 01761 418910
Antique furniture conservation and restoration.

Robert P Tandy, Unit 5, Manor Workshops, West End, Nailsea, Bristol BS48 4DD
Tel: 01275 856378
robertptandy@hotmail.com
Traditional antique furniture restoration & repairs.

Staffordshire
Stefan Herberholz, Middleton Hall, Middleton B78 2AE
Mobile: 07973 151681

Surrey
Hedgecoe & Freeland, Antique Furniture Restoration and Upholstery, 21 Burrow Hill Green, Chobham, Woking GU24 8QP
Tel: 01276 858206
Mobile: 07771 953870
hedgecoefreeland@aol.com

Timothy Naylor, 24 Bridge Road, Chertsey KT16 8JN
Tel: 01932 567129

West Sussex
Simon Paterson, Whitelands, West Dean, Chichester PO18 0RL
Tel/Fax: 01243 811900
hotglue@lineone.net
Boulle work, marquetry, clock case & general restoration & repair.

Albert Plumb, Albert Plumb Furniture Co, Briarfield, Itchenor Green, Chichester PO20 7DA
Tel: 01243 513700
Cabinet making, upholstery.

West Midlands
Phillip Slater, 93 Hewell Road, Barnt Green, Birmingham B45 8NL
Tel: 0121 445 4942
Inlay work, marquetry.

Wiltshire
William Cook, High Trees House, Savernake Forest, Nr Marlborough SN8 4NE Tel: 01672 513017
william.cook@virgin.net

Worcestershire
Jeffrey Hall, Malvern Studios, 56 Cowleigh Road, Malvern WR14 1QD Tel: 01684 574913

Scotland
William Trist, 135 St Leonard's Street, Edinburgh EH8 9RB
Tel: 0131 667 7775
Antique furniture restoration. Cabinet and chairmakers, cane & rush seating, upholstery.

Cameras

Lincolnshire
Antique Photographic Co Ltd
Tel: 01949 842192
alpaco47@aol.com

Ceramics

Hampshire
Rick Hubbard Art Deco, 3 Tee Court, Bell Street, Romsey SO51 8GY
Tel: 01794 513133
Mobile: 07767 267607
rick@rickhubbard-artdeco.co.uk
www.rickhubbard-artdeco.co.uk
Large selection of Clarice Cliff, Shelley, Susie Cooper plus many more and furniture.

Clocks

Buckinghamshire
Carlton Clocks, Station Road, Little Chalfont HP7 9PP
Tel: 01494 763793
info@ukclocks.com
www.ukclocks.com

Cheshire
Coppelia Antiques, Holford Lodge, Plumley Moor Road, Plumley WA16 9RS Tel: 01565 722197
www.coppeliaantiques.co.uk
Open 7 days by appt.

Cumbria
G. K. Hadfield, Beck Bank, Great Salkeld, Penrith CA11 9LN
Tel/Fax: 01768 870111
gkhadfield@dial.pipex.com

Devon
Musgrave Bickford Antiques, 15 East Street, Crediton EX17 3AT
Tel: 01363 775042

Essex
Bellhouse Antiques
Tel/Fax: 01268 710415
Bellhouse.antiques@virgin.net

It's About Time, 863 London Road, Westcliff on Sea SS0 9SZ
Tel/Fax: 01702 472574
sales@antiqueclock.co.uk
www.antiqueclock.co.uk

Gloucestershire
Jonathan Carter, PO Box 212, Stroud GL6 0YW
Tel: 01453 839150
Mobile: 07968 267528
www.carterclocks.com

Jeffrey Formby, Orchard Cottage, East Street, Moreton-in-Marsh GL56 0LQ Tel/Fax: 01608 650558
www.formby-clocks.co.uk
Visitors by appointment.

The Grandfather Clock Shop, Styles of Stow, The Little House, Sheep Street, Stow-on-the-Wold GL54 1JS Tel/Fax: 01451 830455
info@stylesofstow.co.uk
www.stylesofstow.co.uk
Open all day Mon–Sat or by appt.

Jillings Antique Clocks, Croft House, 17 Church Street, Newent GL18 1PU Tel: 01531 822100
Mobile: 07973 830110
clocks@jillings.com
www.Jillings.com
Open Fri & Sat or by appt.

Greater Manchester
Northern Clocks, Boothsbank Farm Worsley, Manchester M28 1LL
Tel: 0161 790 8414
Mobile: 07970 820258
info@northernclocks.co.uk
www.northernclocks.co.uk
Open Thurs, Fri, Sat 10am–5pm or by appointment.

Hampshire
Bryan Clisby, Antique Clocks at Andwells Antiques, High Street, Hartley Wintney RG27 8NY
Tel: 01252 716436 or 842305
www.bryanclisby-antiqueclocks.co.uk

The Clock-Work-Shop (Winchester), 6A Parchment Street, Winchester SO23 8AT Tel: 01962 842331
Mobile: 07973 736155
www.clock-work-shop.co.uk

Kent
Campbell & Archard Ltd, Lychgate House, Church Street, Seal TN15 0AR Tel: 01732 761153
campbellarchard@btclick.com
www.campbellandarchard.co.uk
Open by appointment.

Gaby Gunst, 140 High Street, Tenterden TN30 6HT
Tel: 01580 765818
Closed Sundays.

The Old Clock Shop, 63 High Street, West Malling ME19 6NA
Tel/Fax: 01732 843246
www.theoldclockshop.co.uk
Open Mon–Sat 9am–5pm.

Derek Roberts, 25 Shipbourne Road, Tonbridge TN10 3DN
Tel: 01732 358986
drclocks@clara.net
www.qualityantiqueclocks.com

London
The Clock Clinic Ltd, 85 Lower Richmond Road, Putney SW15 1EU
Tel: 020 8788 1407
clockclinic@btconnect.com
www.clockclinic.co.uk
Open Tues–Fri 9am–6pm Sat 9am–1pm Closed Mondays.

Gavin Douglas Fine Antiques Ltd, 75 Portobello Road W11 2QB
Tel: 01825 723441 / 0207 221 1121
Mobile: 07860 680521
gavin@antique-clocks.co.uk
www.antique-clocks.co.uk

Pendulum, King House, 51 Maddox Street W1R 9LA
Tel: 020 7629 6606
www.pendulumofmayfair.co.uk

Roderick Antique Clocks, 23 Vicarage Gate W8 4AA
Tel: 020 7937 8517
rick@roderickantiqueclocks.com
www.roderickantiqueclocks.com

W. F. Turk, 355 Kingston Road, Wimbledon Chase SW20 8JX
Tel/Fax: 020 8543 3231
www.wfturk.com

Oxfordshire
Craig Barfoot Antique Clocks, Tudor House, East Hagbourne OX11 9LR Tel: 01235 818968
Mobile: 07710 858158
craigb@tinyworld.co.uk

Somerset
Kembery Antique Clocks, Bartlett Street Antiques Centre, 5 Bartlett Street, Bath BA1 2QZ
Tel: 0117 956 5281
kembery@kdclocks.co.uk
www.kdclocks.co.uk

Surrey
Antique Clocks by Patrick Thomas, 62a West Street, Dorking RH4 1BS
Tel: 01306 743661
clockman@fsmail.net
www.antiqueclockshop.co.uk

The Clock House, 75 Pound Street, Carshalton SM5 3PG
Tel: 020 8773 4844
Mobile: 07850 363 317
markcocklin@theclockhouse.co.uk
www.theclockhouse.co.uk
Open Tues–Fri 9.30am–4.30pm Sat 9am–6pm or by appointment.

The Clock Shop, 64 Church Street, Weybridge KT13 8DL
Tel: 01932 840407/855503
Open Mon–Sat 10am–6pm Closed Wed.

Horological Workshops, 204 Worplesdon Road, Guildford GU2 9UY Tel: 01483 576496
enquiries@horologicalworkshops.com
www.HorologicalWorkshops.com

East Sussex
Sam Orr Antique Clocks, 34–36 High Street, Hurstpierpoint, Nr Brighton BN6 9RG Tel: 01273 832081
Mobile: 07860 230888
clocks@samorr.co.uk
www.samorr.co.uk

Warwickshire
Summersons, 172 Emscote Road, Warwick CV34 5QN
Tel/Fax: 01926 400630
clocks@summersons.com
www.summersons.com
We offer a complete restoration service for antique clocks & barometers. We also undertake the following: Dial restoration, cabinetwork & French polishing, wheel cutting, one-off parts made, clock hands cut, fretwork, silvering/gilding, polishing/laquering, restoration parts & materials, insurance valuations, free estimates & advice. WANTED: Clocks & barometers purchased in any condition.

West Midlands
Woodward Antique Clocks, 14 High Street, Tettenhall, Wolverhampton WV6 8QT
Tel: 01902 745608

Wiltshire
P A Oxley Antique Clocks, The Old Rectory, Cherhill, Nr Calne SN11 8UX Tel: 01249 816227
info@paoxley.com
www.british-antiqueclocks.com
Open Mon–Sat 9.30am–5pm Closed Wed or by appt.

Allan Smith Clocks, Amity Cottage, 162 Beechcroft Road, Upper Stratton, Swindon SN2 7QE
Tel/Fax: 01793 822977
Mobile: 07778 834342
allansmithclocks@lineone.net
www.allan-smith-antique-clocks.co.uk

Yorkshire
Time & Motion, 1 Beckside, Beverley HU17 0PB
Tel: 01482 881574

North Yorkshire
Brian Loomes, Calf Haugh Farm, Pateley Bridge HG3 5HW
Tel: 01423 711163
www.brianloomes.com

Republic of Ireland
Jonathan Beech, Westport, Co. Mayo Tel: 00 353 98 28688
www.antiqueclocks-ireland.com
Member of the Irish Antique Dealers' Association.

Scotland
John Mann Antique Clocks, The Clock Showroom, Canonbie, Near Carlisle, Galloway DG14 OSY
Tel: 013873 71337/71827
Mobile: 07850 606 147
jmannclock@aol.com
www.johnmannantiqueclocks.co.uk

U.S.A.
R. O. Schmitt Fine Art, Box 1941, Salem, New Hampshire 03079
Tel: 603 893 5915
bob@roschmittfinearts.com
www.antiqueclockauction.com
Specialist antique clock auctions.

Comics
London
Comic Book Postal Auctions Ltd, 40–42 Osnaburgh Street NW1 3ND Tel: 020 7424 0007
comicbook@compuserve.com
www.compalcomics.com

Decorative Arts
Gloucestershire
Ruskin Decorative Arts, 5 Talbot Court, Stow-on-the-Wold, Cheltenham GL54 1DP
Tel: 01451 832254
Specialising in the Decorative Arts 1860–1930. Arts & Crafts, Art Nouveau & Art Deco items. Cotswold School Movement incl. Guild of Handicraft, Gordon Russell & Gimson & The Barnsleys, etc.

Greater Manchester
A S Antiques, 26 Broad Street, Pendleton, Salford M6 5BY
Tel: 0161 737 5938
Mobile: 07836 368230
as@sternshine.demon.co.uk
Open Thurs, Fri & Sat or by appt.

London
20th Century Glass, Kensington Church Street Antique Centre, 58–60 Kensington Church Street W8 4DB Tel: 020 7938 1137
Tel/Fax: 020 7729 9875
Mobile: 07971 859848
Glass. Open Thurs, Fri & Sat 12noon–6pm or by appointment.

Artemis Decorative Arts Ltd, 36 Kensington Church Street W8 4BX
Tel/Fax: 020 7376 0377
Artemis.w8@btinternet.com
www.artemisdecorativearts.com

Rumours, 4 The Mall, Upper Street, Camden Passage, Islington N1 0PD Tel: 020 7704 6549
Mob: 07836 277274/07831 103748
Rumdec@aol.com
Moorcroft.

Shapiro & Co, Stand 380, Gray's Antique Market, 58 Davies Street W1Y 5LP Tel: 020 7491 2710
Faberge.

Staffordshire
AD Antiques, PO Box 1623, Woodseaves, Stafford ST20 0SF
Tel: 01785 284815
Mobile: 07939 508171
www.adantiques.com
Ceramics, glass and metals from the Art Nouveau, Arts & Crafts and Secessionist Movements.

Surrey
Gooday Gallery, 14 Richmond Hill, Richmond TW10 6QX
Tel: 020 8940 8652
Mobile: 077101 24540
goodaygallery@aol.com
Decorative antiques 1880–1980.

Republic of Ireland
Mitofsky Antiques, 8 Rathfarnham Road, Terenure, Dublin 6
Tel: 00 353 1 492 0033
info@mitofskyartdeco.com
www.mitofskyartdeco.com

Scotland
decorative arts@doune, Scottish Antique and Arts Centre, Carse of Cambus, Doune, Perthshire FK16 6HD Tel: 01786 461439
Mobile: 07778 475974
decorativearts.doune@btinternet.com

U.S.A.
JMW Gallery, 144 Lincoln Street, Boston MA02111
Tel: 001 617 338 9097
www.jmwgallery.com
American Arts & Crafts, Decorative Arts, American Art Pottery, Mission furniture, lighting, colour block prints, metalwork.

Treadway Gallery, Inc., and John Toomey Gallery, 2029 Madison Road, Cincinnati, Ohio 45208
Tel: 001 513 321 6742
treadway2029@earthlink.net
www.treadwaygallery.com
Arts & Crafts, Art Nouveau, American & European paintings, Art Deco, 1950s/modern.

Dolls
Kent
Barbara Ann Newman, London House Antiques, 4 Market Square, Westerham TN16 1AW
Tel: 01959 564479
Mobile: 07850 016729

Ephemera
Nottinghamshire
T. Vennett-Smith, 11 Nottingham Road, Gotham NG11 0HE
Tel: 0115 983 0541
info@vennett-smith.com
www.vennett-smith.com
Ephemera auctions

Exhibition & Fair Organisers
Devon
Trident Exhibitions, West Devon Business Park, Tavistock PL19 9DP
Tel: 01822 614671
info@trident-exhibitions.co.uk
www.tridentexhibitions.co.uk
www.interfine.co.uk

Warwickshire
London Antique Arms Fairs Ltd, 15 Burbury Court, Emscote Road, Warwick CV34 5LD
Tel: 01926 499022
www.antiquearmsfairsltd.co.uk

U.S.A.
Forbes & Turner, 45 Larchwood Road, South Portland, Maine 04106
Tel: 001 207 767 3967
LindaT@aol.com
www.ForbesandTurner.com

Exporters
Devon
Pugh's Antiques, Pugh's Farm, Monkton, Nr Honiton EX14 9QH
Tel: 01404 42860
sales@pughsantiques.com
www.pughsantiques.com
Open Mon–Sat.

Nottinghamshire
Antiques Across the World, James Alexander Buildings, London Road/Manvers Street, Nottingham NG2 3AE
Tel: 0115 979 9199
tonyrimes@btinternet.com

Staffordshire
Acorn G.D.S. Ltd
Tel: 01538 399670
acorn@acorn-freight.co.uk
www.acorn-freight.co.uk

East Sussex
International Furniture Exporters, The Old Cement Works, South Heighton, Newhaven BN9 0HS
Tel: 01273 611251
www.cisweb.co.uk/ife

The Old Mint House, High Street, Pevensey BN24 5LF
Tel/Fax: 01323 762337
antiques@minthouse.co.uk
www.minthouse.co.uk
Open Mon–Fri 9am–5.30pm Sat 10.30am–4.30pm or by appt.

Wiltshire
North Wilts Exporters, Farm Hill House, Brinkworth SN15 5AJ
Tel: 01666 510876
Mobile: 07836 260730
mike@northwilts.demon.co.uk
www.northwiltsantiqueexporters.com
Open Mon–Sat 8am–6pm or by appt.

Fishing
Hampshire
Evans & Partridge, Agriculture House, High Street, Stockbridge SO20 6HF Tel: 01264 810702
Sporting auctions.

London
Angling Auctions, P O Box 2095 W12 8RU Tel: 020 8749 4175
neil@anglingauctions.demon.co.uk

Furniture
Bedfordshire
Transatlantic Antiques and Fine Art Ltd, 101 Dunstable Street, Ampthill MK45 2NG
Tel/Fax: 01525 403346
transatlantic@talk21.com
www.transatlantic.com

Berkshire
Hill Farm Antiques, Hill Farm, Shop Lane, Leckhampstead, Nr Newbury RG20 8QG
Tel: 01488 638541/ 638361
Mobile: 07836 503561
Specialists in antique dining tables.

The Old Malthouse, Hungerford
Tel/Fax: 01488 682209
hunwick@oldmalthouse30.freeserve.co.uk

Cumbria
Anthemion, Cartmel, Grange Over Sands LA11 6QD
Tel: 015395 36295
Mobile: 07768 443757

Derbyshire
Spurrier-Smith Antiques, 28, 30, 39 Church Street, Ashbourne DE6 1AJ Tel: 01335 343669/342198/ 344377

Devon
Musgrave Bickford Antiques, 15 East Street, Crediton EX17 3AT Tel: 01363 775042

Pugh's Antiques, Pugh's Farm, Monkton, Nr Honiton EX14 9QH Tel: 01404 42860 sales@pughsantiques.com www.pughsantiques.com *Open Mon–Sat.*

Dorset
Michael Barrington, The Old Rectory, Warmwell, Dorchester DT2 8HQ Tel: 01305 854822 *The conservation and restoration of antique & fine furniture & clocks. Clock dials and movements, barometers, upholstery, mechanical music, automata and toys, antique metalwork ferrous and non-ferrous.*

Essex
F. G. Bruschweiler (Antiques) Ltd, 41–67 Lower Lambricks, Rayleigh SS6 8DA Tel: 01268 773 761 info@fgbantiques.com www.fgbantiques.com *Member of LAPADA*

Gloucestershire
Berry Antiques, 3 High Street, Moreton in Marsh GL56 0AH Tel: 01608 652929 chris@berryantiques.com berryantiques.com berryantiques.co.uk *Open Mon–Sat 10am–5.30pm Sun 11am–5pm Closed Tues.*

Hertfordshire
Collins Antiques, Corner House, Wheathampstead AL4 8AP Tel: 01582 833111 www.antique-finder.co.uk

Kent
Flower House Antiques, 90 High Street, Tenterden TN30 6HT Tel: 01580 763764

Langton Green Antiques, Langton Road, Langton Green, Tunbridge Wells TN3 0HP Tel/Fax: 01892 862004 antiques@langtongreen.fsbusiness.co.uk www.langtongreenantiques.co.uk

Gillian Shepherd, Old Corner House Antiques, 6 Poplar Road, Wittersham, Tenterden TN30 7PG Tel: 01797 270236 *Open Weds–Sat 10am–5pm.*

Sutton Valence Antiques, North Street, Sutton Valence, Nr Maidstone ME17 3AP Tel: 01622 843333/01622 675332 svantiques@aol.com www.svantiques.co.uk

Lincolnshire
David J Hansord & Son, 6 & 7 Castle Hill, Lincoln LN1 3AA Tel: 01522 530044 Mobile: 07831 183511

Seaview Antiques, Stanhope Road, Horncastle LN9 5DG Tel: 01507 524524 tracey.collins@virgin.net www.seaviewantiques.co.uk

London
Oola Boola, 139–147 Kirkdale SE26 4QJ Tel: 0208 291 9999 Mobile: 07956 261252 oola.boola@telco4u.net

Middlesex
Phelps Antiques, 133–135 St Margaret's Road, Twickenham TW1 1RG Tel: 020 8892 1778/7129 antiques@phelps.co.uk www.phelps.co.uk *Mon–Fri 9am–5.30pm Sat 9.30am–5.30pm Sun 12am–4pm.*

Nottinghamshire
Ranby Hall-Antiques, Barnby Moor, Retford DN22 8JQ Tel: 01777 860696 Mobile: 07860 463477 paul.wyatt@virgin.net www.ranbyhall.antiques-gb.com

Oxfordshire
The Chair Set, 18 Market Place, Woodstock OX20 1TA Tel: 01428 707301 Mobile: 07711 625 477 algjames@btopenworld.com www.thechairset.com *Specialists in sets of chairs, furniture and accessories for the dining room.*

Rupert Hitchcox Antiques, The Garth, Warpsgrove, Nr Chalgrove, Oxford OX44 7RW Tel/Fax: 01865 890241

Georg S. Wissinger Antiques, Georgian House Antiques, 2, 21 & 44 West Street, Chipping Norton OX7 5EU Tel/Fax: 01608 641369

Surrey
The Dorking Desk Shop, 41 West Street, Dorking RH4 1BU Tel: 01306 883327 www.desk.uk.com *Antique desks.*

J Hartley Antiques Ltd, 186 High Street, Ripley GU23 6BB Tel: 01483 224318

Ripley Antiques, 67 High Street, Ripley GU23 6AN Tel: 01483 224981 Also at: Palladio, Petworth, Sussex.

East Sussex
David Cardoza Antiques, Lewes Road, Laughton, Lewes BN8 6BN Tel: 01323 811162 Mobile: 07855 835991 sales@davidcardozaantiques.co.uk www.davidcardozaantiques.co.uk *French antiques and decorative items.*

The Old Mint House, High Street, Pevensey BN24 5LF Tel/Fax: 01323 762337 antiques@minthouse.co.uk www.minthouse.co.uk *Open Mon–Fri 9am–5.30pm Sat 10.30am–4.30pm or by appt.*

West Sussex
British Antique Replicas, School Close, Queen Elizabeth Avenue, Burgess Hill RH15 9RX Tel: 01444 245577 *Antique replica furniture.*

Dycheling Antiques, 34 High Street, Ditchling, Hassocks BN6 8TA Tel: 01273 842929 Mobile: 07785 456341 www.antiquechairmatching.com

Stable Antiques, Adrian Hoyle, 98a High Street, Lindfield RH16 2HP Tel: 01444 483662 Mobile: 07768 900331 madhoyle@aol.com *Regency furniture.*

Warwickshire
Apollo Antiques Ltd, The Saltisford, Birmingham Road, Warwick CV34 4TD Tel: 01926 494746/494666 www.apolloantiques.com

Coleshill Antiques & Interiors, 12–14 High Street, Coleshill B46 1AZ Tel: 01675 467416 enquiries@coleshillantiques.com www.coleshillantiques.com

West Midlands
Martin Taylor Antiques, 323 Tettenhall Road, Wolverhampton WV6 0JZ Tel: 01902 751166 Mobile:07836 636524 enquiries@mtaylor-antiques.co.uk www.mtaylor-antiques.co.uk

Wiltshire
Cross Hayes Antiques, Units 6–8 Westbrook Farm, Draycot Cerne, Chippenham SN15 5LH Tel/Fax: 01249 720033 david@crosshayes.co.uk www.crosshayes.co.uk *Shipping furniture.*

U.S.A.
Antique Associates at West Townsend, PO Box 129W, 473 Main Street, West Townsend MA 01474 Tel: (978) 597 8084 drh@aaawt.com

Axe Antiques, 275 Alt. A1A (SR811), Jupiter, Florida 33477, Palm Beach County Tel: 001 561 743 7888/1 877 689 1730 www.axeantiques.com *Also stocks fine art, vintage pillows, seals, militaria and architectural elements.*

Dragonflies Antiques & Decorating Center, Frank & Cathy Sykes, New England Events Mgt., PO Box 678, 24 Center Street, Wolfeboro, New Hampshire 03894 Tel: 001 603 569 0000 Dragonflies@metrocast.net *Also Folk Art, mahogany speed boat models, maps and antiquarian books.*

Douglas Hamel Antiques, 56 Staniels Road, Chichester, New Hampshire 03234 Tel: 001 603 798 5912 doughamel@shakerantiques.com www.shakerantiques.com *We buy, sell & locate Shaker antiques.*

Frank & Barbara Pollack, 1214 Green Bay Road, Highland Park, Illinois 60035 Tel: 001 847 433 2213 fpollack@compuserve *American antiques & art, American primitive paintings, furniture, toleware, Folk Art & accessories of 18th, 19th & 20thc.*

Warehouse Provence, 1120 Massachusetts Ave, (Rte 111) Boxborough, Maine. MA 01710, (Rte.111), Boxborough, Maine MA 01719 Tel: 001 978 266 0200 warehouseprovence@aics.net www.warehouseprovence.com

Glass

Somerset
Somervale Antiques, 6 Radstock Road, Midsomer Norton, Bath BA3 2AJ Tel: 01761 412686 Mobile: 07885 088022 ronthomas@somervaleantiquesglass.co.uk www.somervaleantiquesglass.co.uk

Insurance

London
Aon Ltd, 8 Devonshire Square EC2M 4PL Tel: 020 7882 0374 private-clients@ars.aon.co.uk

Irish Antique Dealers Association

The Irish Antique Dealers Association, Adare, Co. Limerick Tel: 061 364409 irantda@eircom.net

Ivory & Tortoiseshell

Somerset
Alan & Kathy Stacey (Appt. only) Tel: 01963 441333 sales@antiqueboxes.uk.com www.antiqueboxes.uk.com *Tea caddies and fine boxes. Specialist dealers in tortoiseshell, ivory, mop, shagreen, exotic timber pieces. Professional*

conservation services, consultancy, valuations. Members of LAPADA & BAFRA.

Jewellery

London

Wimpole Antiques, Stand 349, Grays Antique Market, 58 Davies Street W1K 5LP
Tel/Fax: 020 7499 2889
WimpoleAntiques@compuserve.com

Kitchenware

Gloucestershire

Bread & Roses, Durham House Antique Centre, Sheep Street, Stow on the Wold GL54 1AA
Tel: 01926 817342/01451 870404

Lincolnshire

Skip & Janie Smithson Antiques
Tel/Fax: 01754 810265
Mobile: 07831 399180
Dairy bygones, enamel wares, laundry items and advertising.

East Sussex

Ann Lingard, Ropewalk Antiques, Rye TN31 7NA Tel: 01797 223486
ann-lingard@ropewalkantiques.freeserve.co.uk

Lighting

Devon

The Exeter Antique Lighting Co, Cellar 15, The Quay, Exeter EX2 4AP
Tel: 01392 490848
Mobile: 07702 969438
www.antiquelightingcompany.com
Antique lighting and stained glass specialists.

London

Dernier & Hamlyn Ltd, 3 Egerton Terrace, Knightsbridge SW3 2EX
Tel: 020 7225 5030
info@dernier-hamlyn.com
www.dernier-hamlyn.com
Bespoke lighting manufacturers and restoration specialists.

Somerset

Joanna Proops, Antique Textiles & Lighting, 34 Belvedere, Lansdown Hill, Bath BA1 5HR Tel: 01225 310795
antiquetextiles@uk.online.co.uk
www.antiquetextiles.co.uk

U.S.A.

Lamps: By The Book, Inc., 514 14th, West Palm Beach, Florida 33401 Tel: 001 561 659 1723
booklamps@msn.com
www.lampsbythebook.com
Gift lamps.

Markets & Centres

Derbyshire

Chappells Antiques Centre - Bakewell, King Street, Bakewell DE45 1DZ Tel: 01629 812496
ask@chappellsantiquescentre.com
www.chappellsantiquescentre.com
30 established dealers inc. BADA & LAPADA members. Quality period furniture, ceramics, silver, plate, metals, treen, clocks, barometers, books, pictures, maps, prints, textiles, kitchenalia, lighting and furnishing accessories from the 17th–20thC, scientific, pharmaceutical and sporting antiques. Open Mon–Sat 10am–5pm Sun 12noon–5pm. Closed Christmas Day, Boxing Day & New Year's Day. Please ring for brochure, giving location and parking information.

Matlock Antiques, Collectables & Riverside Café, 7 Dale Road, Matlock DE4 3LT Tel: 01629 760808
Proprietor W. Shirley. Over 70 dealers. Open 7 days 10am–5pm including Bank Holidays.

Devon

Colyton Antiques Centre, Dolphin Street, Colyton EX24 6LU
Tel: 01297 552339
colytonantiques@modelgarage.co.uk

Essex

Debden Antiques, Elder Street, Debden, Saffron Walden CB11 3JY
Tel: 01799 543007
info@debden-antiques.co.uk
debden-antiques.co.uk
Mon–Sat 10am–5.30pm Sun and Bank Hols 11am–4pm. 30 quality dealers in a stunning 17th century Essex barn. Large selection of 16th–20th century oak, mahogany and pine furniture, watercolours and oil paintings, rugs, ceramics, silver and jewellery. Plus garden furniture and ornaments in our lovely courtyard.

Gloucestershire

The Antiques Emporium, The Old Chapel, Long Street, Tetbury GL8 8AA Tel: 01666 505281
Open Mon–Sat 10am–5pm, Sun 1–5pm. 38 dealers. Jewellery, clocks, Art Deco, books, furniture, treen, flatware, glass, china, porcelain and decorative accessories.

Durham House Antiques Centre, Sheep Street, Stow-on-the-Wold GL54 1AA Tel: 01451 870404
30+ dealers with an extensive range of town and country furniture, metalware, books, pottery, porcelain, kitchenware, silver, jewellery and art. Mon–Sat 10am–5pm Sunday 11am–5pm. Stow-on-the-Wold, Cotswold home to over 40 antique shops, galleries and bookshops.

Gloucester Antiques Centre, The Historic Docks, 1 Severn Road, Gloucester GL1 2LE
Tel: 01452 529716
www.antiques.center.com
The Gloucester Antiques Centre makes a fine day out, with antiques and collectibles of every description. There is something for everyone, even those that are not antiques collectors will find items to decorate any home. Collectors of modern items are catered for. Open Mon–Sat 10am–5pm Sun 1pm–5pm.

Jubilee Hall Antiques Centre, Oak Street, Lechlade GL7 3AY
Tel: 01367 253777
mail@jubileehall.co.uk
www.jubileehall.co.uk

Kent

Malthouse Arcade, High Street, Hythe CT21 5BW
Tel: 01303 260103

Lancashire

The Antique Centre, 56 Garstang Road, Preston PR1 1NA
Tel: 01772 882078
Open 7 days a week.

GB Antiques Centre, Lancaster Leisure Park, (the former Hornsea Pottery), Wyresdale Road, Lancaster LA1 3LA
Tel: 01524 844734
Over 140 dealers in 40,000 sq. ft. of space. Showing porcelain, pottery, Art Deco, glass, books and linen. Also a large selection of mahogany, oak and pine Furniture. Open 7 days a week 10am–5pm.

Kingsmill Antique Centre, Queen Street, Harle Syke, Burnley BB10 2HX Tel: 01282 431953
Open 7 days 10am–5pm, 8pm Thurs. 8,500 sq ft.

Lincolnshire

Hemswell Antique Centres, Caenby Corner Estate, Hemswell Cliff, Gainsborough DN21 5TJ
Tel: 01427 668389
info@hemswell-antiques.com
www.hemswell-antiques.com
Open 7 days 10am–5pm.

London

Antiquarius Antiques Centre, 131/141 King's Road, Chelsea SW3 5ST Tel: 020 7351 5353
antique@dial.pipex.com
Open Mon–Sat 10am–6pm.

Atlantic Antiques Centres, Chenil House, 181–183 Kings Road SW3 5EB Tel: 020 7351 5353
antique@dial.pipex.com

Bond Street Antiques Centre, 124 New Bond Street W1Y 9AE
Tel: 020 7351 5353
antique@dial.pipex.com
Open Mon–Sat 10am–5.30pm.

The Mall Antiques Arcade, Camden Passage, Islington, N1 Tel: 020 7351 5353
antique@dial.pipex.com
Open Tues, Thurs & Fri 10am–5pm Wed 7.30am–5pm Sat 9am–6pm.

Nottinghamshire

Castlegate Antiques Centre, 55 Castlegate, Newark NG24 1BE
Tel: 01636 700076
Mobile: 07860 843739

Dukeries Antiques Centre, Thoresby Park, Budly, Newark NG22 9EX Tel: 01623 822252
Mobile: 07836 635312

Newark Antiques Centre, Regent House, Lombard Street, Newark NG24 1BX Tel: 01636 605504

Newark Antiques Warehouse, Old Kelham Road, Newark NG24 1BX
Tel: 01636 674869
Mobile: 07974 429185
enquiries@newarkantiques.co.uk

No.1 Castlegate Antiques, 1–3 Castlegate, Newark NG24 1AZ
Tel: 01636 701877
Mobile: 07850 463173

Oxfordshire

Antiques on High, 85 High Street, Oxford OX1 4BG
Tel: 01865 251075
Open 7 days a week 10am–5pm. Sun & Bank Holidays 11am–5pm. 35 dealers with a wide range of quality stock.

The Arbery Centre, Market Place, Wantage OX12 8AB
Tel: 01235 767331

Chipping Norton Antiques Centre, Ivy House, Middle Row, Market Place, Chipping Norton
Tel: 01608 644212

Deddington Antiques Centre, Market Place, Bull Ring, Deddington, Nr Banbury OX15 0TT
Tel: 01869 338968
4 floors of antiques including period furniture, silver, porcelain, oils and watercolours, jewellery and much more. Ample free parking. Open 7 days Mon–Sat 10am–5pm, Sun 11am–5pm.

Lamb Arcade Antiques Centre, 83 High Street, Wallingford OX10 0BS Tel: 01491 835166
10am–5pm daily, Sat till 5.30pm. Bank Hols 11am–5pm. Furniture, silver, porcelain, glass, books, boxes, crafts, rugs, jewellery, brass bedsteads and linens, pictures, antique stringed instruments, sports and fishing items, decorative and ornamental items. Coffee shop and wine bar.

Somerset

Bartlett Street Antiques Centre, 5–10 Bartlett Street, Bath BA1 2QZ
Tel: 01225 466689/469998
info@antiques-centre.co.uk
www.antiques-centre.co.uk
Bath's largest antiques centre. Open Mon–Sat 9.30am– 5pm Weds 8am–5pm. Over 200 dealers selling all manner of antiques & collectables.

East Sussex

Church Hill Antiques Centre, 6 Station Street, Lewes BN7 2DA
Tel: 01273 474 842
www.church-hill-antiques.co.uk

Warwickshire

Barn Antiques Centre, Station Road, Long Marston, Nr Stratford-upon-Avon CV37 8RB
Tel: 01789 721399
www.barnantique.co.uk
Huge old barn crammed full of affordable antiques. Over13,000 sq ft and 50 established dealers. Open 7 days 10am–5pm. Large free car park. Licensed French bistro.

Granary Antiques Centre, Ansley Road (B4114), Nuneaton CV10 OQL
Tel: 024 76395551
www.gbsgranary.com
(Part of Hoar Park Craft Village) Open Tues–Sun and Bank Holidays 10am to 5pm. Porcelain, pottery, kitchenware, collectables, Victorian and Edwardian furniture. Masons Ironstone specialist. Licensed tearooms.

Worcestershire

Worcester Antiques Centre, Reindeer Court, Mealcheapen Street, Worcester WR1 4DF
Tel: 01905 610680
Monday to Sunday 10am–5pm. Open Sundays in December. 45 dealers. Worcester and English furniture, porcelain, silver, Art Nouveau, Arts & Crafts, jewellery, Also scientific instruments, glass, period watches, antique boxes and treen, ephemera and stamps. Full restoration services on the above.

Yorkshire

Cavendish Antique & Collectors Centre, 44 Stonegate, York YO1 8AS Tel: 01904 621666
sales@yorkantiquescentre.co.uk
www.yorkantiquescentre.co.uk
Open 7 days 9am–6pm. Over 50 dealers.

Chapel Antiques Centre, 99 Broadfield Road, Heeley, Sheffield S8 0XQ Tel: 0114 258 8288
info@antiquesinsheffield.com
www.antiquesinsheffield.com
Open 7 days. English & French furniture, gardenalia, beds, mirrors, chandeliers, fabrics. Services offered include restoration French polishing, upholstery & paint effects.

Sheffield Antiques Emporium, 15–19 Clyde Road, (off Broadfield Road), Heeley, Sheffield S8 0YD
Tel: 0114 258 4863
info@sheffieldantiquesemporium.com
www.sheffieldantiquesemporium.com
Open 7 days. 50+ dealers with specialists in Art Deco, Militaria, Retro clothing, linens, furniture, clocks & pictures. Cafe & parking.

Stonegate Antiques Centre, 41 Stonegate, York YO1 8AW
Tel: 01904 613888
sales@yorkantiquescentre.co.uk
www.yorkantiquescentre.co.uk
Open 7 days 9am–6pm. Over 110 dealers on 2 floors.

Wales

Afonwen Craft & Antique Centre, Afonwen, Nr Caerwys, Nr Mold, Flintshire CH7 5UB
Tel: 01352 720965
Open all year Tues–Sun 9.30am to 5.30pm, closed Mondays, open Bank Holidays. The largest centre in North Wales and the borders.

14,000 sq ft, 40 dealers. Fabulous selection of antiques, china, silver, crystal, quality collectables, fine furniture, oak, walnut, mahogany, pine from around the world. Excellent restaurant.

Offa's Dyke Antique Centre, 4 High Street, Knighton, Powys LD7 1AT
Tel: 01547 528635/528940
Open Mon–Sat 10–1, 2–5. 12 dealers in 18th–20th century ceramics including Delft and slipware, glass, books on antiques, general antiques and collectables.

Medals

Hampshire
Romsey Medal Centre, PO Box 169, Romsey SO51 6XU
Tel: 01794 324488/322125
post@romseymedals.co.uk
www.romseymedals.co.uk

Miniatures

Gloucestershire
Judy & Brian Harden Antiques, PO Box 14, Bourton on the Water, Cheltenham GL54 2YR
Tel/Fax: 01451 810684
Mobile: 07831 692252
harden@portraitminiatures.co.uk
www.portraitminiatures.co.uk
Portrait miniatures.

Money Boxes

Yorkshire
John & Simon Haley, 89 Northgate, Halifax HX1 1XF
Tel: 01422 822148/360434
toysandbanks@aol.com

Musical Instruments

Nottinghamshire
Turner Violins, 1–5 Lily Grove, Beeston NG9 1QL
Tel: 0115 943 0333
turnerviolins@compuserve.com

Oak & Country

Cambridgeshire
Mark Seabrook Antiques, Huntingdon
Tel: 01480 861935
Mobile: 07770 721931
enquiries@markseabrook.com
www.markseabrook.com

Cheshire
Adams Antiques, Churche's Mansion, 150 Hospital Street, Nantwich CW5 5RY
Tel: 01270 625643/07901 855200
Early oak, walnut and country furniture.

Kent
Douglas Bryan Antiques, The Old Bakery, St Davids Bridge, Cranbrook TN17 3HN
Tel: 01580 713103

London
Robert Young Antiques, 68 Battersea Bridge Road SW11 3AG
Tel: 020 7228 7847
Country furniture & Folk Art.

Northamptonshire
Paul Hopwell, 30 High Street, West Haddon NN6 7AP
Tel: 01788 510636
Mobile: 07836 505950
paulhopwell@antiqueoak.co.uk
www.antiqueoak.co.uk

Oxfordshire
Key Antiques of Chipping Norton
Tel/Fax: 01608 644992

Surrey
Anthony Welling, Broadway Barn, High Street, Ripley GU23 6AQ
Tel/Fax: 01483 225384

The Refectory, 38 West Street, Dorking RH4 1BU
Tel/Fax: 01306 742111
www.therefectory.co.uk
Refectory table specialist.

Packers & Shippers

Dorset
Alan Franklin Transport, 26 Blackmoor Road, Ebblake Industrial Estate, Verwood BH31 6BB Tel: 01202 826539

Gloucestershire
The Shipping Company, Bourton Industrial Park, Bourton on the Water, Cheltenham GL54 2HQ
Tel: 01451 822451
enquiries@theshippingcompanyltd.com
www.theshippingcompanyltd.com

A. J. Williams (Shipping), 607 Central Park, Petherton Road, Hengrove, Bristol BS14 9BZ
Tel: 01275 892166
aj.williams@btclick.com

Paperweights

Cheshire
Sweetbriar Gallery, Sweetbriar House, Robin Hood Lane, Helsby WA6 9NH Tel: 01928 723851
Mobile: 07860 907532
sweetbr@globalnet.co.uk
www.sweetbriar.co.uk

Northern Ireland
Marion Langham Limited, Claranagh, Tempo, County Fermanagh BT94 3FJ
Tel: 028 895 41247
marion@ladymarion.co.uk
www.ladymarion.co.uk

U.S.A.
The Dunlop Collection, P.O. Box 6269, Statesville, NC 28687
Tel: (704) 871 2626 or Toll Free Telephone (800) 227 1996

Photographs

London
Jubilee Photographica, 10 Pierrepoint Row, Camden Passage N1 8EE Mobile: 07860 793707
Specialist shop and gallery dealing in rare and collectable photographs from the 19th and 20th centuries. We sell and hold a large and constantly changing stock of cartes de visite, stereocards, daguerreotypes and ambrotypes, albums of travel, topographical and ethnic photographs, art photographs,and a range of books on the art and history of photography. We also have magic lanterns and lantern slides, and stereoscopic viewers. Open Wednesdays and Saturdays 10am to 4pm.

Pianos

Gloucestershire
Piano-Export, Bridge Road, Kingswood, Bristol BS15 4FW
Tel: 0117 956 8300
Open Mon–Fri.

Pine

Cornwall
Julie Strachey, Trevaskis Barn, Gwinear Road, Nr Hayle TR27 5JQ
Tel: 01209 613750
Antique farm & country furniture in pine, oak, etc. Ironwork & interesting pieces for the garden (no repro). By appointment.

Cumbria
Ben Eggleston Antiques, The Dovecote, Long Marton, Appleby CA16 6BJ
Tel/Fax: 01768 361849
ben@beneggelstonantiques.co.uk
www.beneggelstonantiques.co.uk
Trade only.

Essex
English Rose Antiques, 7 Church Street, Coggeshall CO6 1TU
Tel: 01376 562683
Tel: 07770 880790 & 0049 (0)1719 949541
englishroseantiques@hotmail.com
www.Delta-Line-Trading.de

Large selection of English and Continental pine furniture. Open Mon–Sun 10am–5.30pm Closed Wed.

Hampshire
Pine Cellars, 39 Jewry Street, Winchester SO23 8RY
Tel: 01962 777546/867014

Kent
Up Country, The Old Corn Stores, 68 St John's Road, Tunbridge Wells TN4 9PE Tel: 01892 523341
www.upcountryantiques.co.uk

Lancashire
David Roper Antiques, Hill View Farm, Gill Lane, Longton, Preston PR4 4ST Tel: 01772 615366
Mobile: 07803 134851
davidroper@supanet.com
Mostly English 18th, 19th and early 20th Century pine and country furniture. Also decorative accessories and collectables. No reproductions.

Nottinghamshire
A. B. Period Pine, The Barn, 38 Main Street, Farnsfield, Newark NG22 8EA Tel: 01623 882288
www.abperiodpine.co.uk

Harlequin Antiques, 79–81 Mansfield Road, Daybrook, Nottingham NG5 6BH
Tel: 0115 967 4590
sales@antiquepine.net
www.antiquepine.net

Somerset
Gilbert & Dale Antiques, The Old Chapel, Church Street, Ilchester, Nr Yeovil BA22 8ZA
Tel: 01935 840464
Painted pine & country.

Westville House Antiques, Westville House, Littleton, Nr Somerton TA11 6NP
Tel/Fax: 01458 273376
Mobile: 07941 510823
antique@westville.co.uk
www.westville.co.uk

East Sussex
Ann Lingard, Ropewalk Antiques, Rye TN31 7NA
Tel: 01797 223486
annlingard@ropewalkantiques.freeserve.co.uk

Graham Price, Apple Store, Chaucer Industrial Estate, Dittons Road, Polegate BN26 6JF
Tel: 01323 487167
www.grahampriceantiques.co.uk

Warwickshire
Pine & Things, Portobello Farm, Campden Road, Nr Shipston-on-Stour CV36 4PY
Tel: 01608 663849

Wiltshire
North Wilts Exporters, Farm Hill House, Brinkworth SN15 5AJ
Tel: 01666 510876
Mobile: 07836 260730
mike@northwilts.demon.co.uk
www.northwiltsantiqueexporters.com
Open Mon–Sat 8am–6pm or by appointment.

Republic of Ireland
Delvin Farm Antiques, Gormonston, Co Meath
Tel: 00 353 1 841 2285
info@delvinfarmpine.com
john@delvinfarmpine.com
www.delvinfarmpine.com

Porcelain

Bedfordshire
Transatlantic Antiques and Fine Art Ltd, 101 Dunstable Street, Ampthill MK45 2NG
Tel/Fax: 01525 403346
transatlantic@talk21.com
www.transatlantic.com

Gloucestershire
Judy & Brian Harden Antiques, PO Box 14, Bourton on the Water, Cheltenham GL54 2YR
Tel: 01451 810684
harden@meissenfigures.co.uk
www.meissenfigures.co.uk
Meissen figures.

Hampshire
Goss & Crested China Club & Museum, incorporating Milestone Publications, 62 Murray Road, Horndean PO8 9JL
Tel: (023) 9259 7440
info@gosschinaclub.demon.co.uk
www.gosscrestedchina.co.uk

London
Huntley, Diana Antiques, 8 Camden Passage, Islington N1 8ED
Tel: 020 7226 4605
diana@dianahuntleyantiques.co.uk
www.dianahuntleyantiques.co.uk

Marion Langham Limited
Tel: 020 7730 1002
marion@ladymarion.co.uk
www.ladymarion.co.uk
Belleek.

Shropshire
Vanessa Harvey, 30A Corve Street, Ludlow SY8 1GB
Tel: 01584 876375

Somerset
Andrew Dando, 4 Wood Street, Queen Square, Bath BA1 2JQ
Tel: 01225 422702
www.andrewdando.co.uk
English, Oriental and Continental porcelain.

East Sussex
Tony Horsley, PO Box 3127, Brighton BN1 5SS
Tel: 01273 550770
Candle extinguishers, Royal Worcester and other fine procelain.

Warwickshire
Coleshill Antiques & Interiors, 12–14 High Street, Coleshill B46 1AZ
Tel: 01675 462931
enquiries@coleshillantiques.com
www.coleshillantiques.com

Yorkshire
The Crested China Co, Station House, Driffield YO25 6PX
Tel: 01377 257042
dt@thecrestedchinacompany.com
www.thecrestedchinacompany.com

Pottery

Berkshire
Special Auction Services
The Coach House, Midgham Park Reading RG7 5UG
Tel: 0118 971 2949
www.invaluable.com/sas/
Specialist auctions of commemoratives, pot lids & Prattware, Fairings, Goss & Crested, Baxter & Le Blond prints.

Buckinghamshire
Gillian Neale Antiques, PO Box 247, Aylesbury HP20 1JZ
Tel: 01296 423754/07860 638700
gillianneale@aol.com
www.gillianneaeantiques.co.uk
Blue & white transfer printed pottery 1780–1860.

Cheshire
Moorcroft Pottery Chester
Tel: 01244 301800
Sales@Moorcroftchester.co.uk
www.Moorcroftchester.co.uk

Dorset
Greystoke Antiques, 4 Swan Yard, (off Cheap Street), Sherborne DT9 3AX Tel: 01935 812833
Adjacent to town centre car park. 10am to 4.30pm daily, closed wednesday. Blue transfer printed pottery 1790–1850. Always some 200 to 300 pieces in stock.

Hampshire
Millers Antiques Ltd, Netherbrook House, 86 Christchurch Road, Ringwood BH24 1DR
Tel: 01425 472062
mail@millers-antiques.co.uk
www.millers-antiques.co.uk

Kent
Serendipity, 125 High Street, Deal CT14 6BB
Tel: 01304 369165/01304 366536
dipityantiques@aol.com
Staffordshire pottery.

Gillian Shepherd, Old Corner House Antiques, 6 Poplar Road, Wittersham, Tenterden TN30 7PG
Tel: 01797 270236
Open Weds–Sat 10am–5pm.

London
Jonathan Horne, 66 Kensington Church Street W8 4BY
Tel: 020 7221 5658
JH@jonathanhorne.co.uk
www.jonathanhorne.co.uk
Early English pottery.

Somerset
Andrew Dando, 4 Wood Street, Queen Square, Bath BA1 2JQ
Tel: 01225 422702
www.andrewdando.co.uk
English, Oriental and Continental pottery.

Tyne & Wear
Ian Sharp Antiques, 23 Front Street, Tynemouth NE30 4DX
Tel: 0191 296 0656
iansharp@sharpantiques.demon.co.uk
www.sharpantiques.demon.co.uk
Tyneside & Wearside ceramics.

Publication

London
Antiques Trade Gazette, 115 Shaftesbury Avenue WC2H 8AD
Tel: 0207 420 6646

West Midlands
Antiques Magazine, H.P. Publishing, 2 Hampton Court Road, Harborne, Birmingham B17 9AE Tel: 0121 681 8000
Subs 01562 701001
subscriptions@antiquesmagazine.com
www.antiquesmagazine.com

France
Guide Emer, 23 rue des Jeûneurs, 75002 Paris
Tel: 00 33 (0) 1 44 07 31 66
guidemer@wanadoo.fr
www.franceantiq.fr/guide.emer
Guide of French and European antiques.

Restoration

London
Oliver Clarke, Heritage Restorations, 96 Webber Street SE1 0QN Tel: 020 7928 3624
18th & 19th century furniture specialist.

Northamptonshire
Leather Conservation Centre, University College Campus, Boughton Green Road, Moulton Park, Northampton NN2 7AN
Tel: 01604 719766
icc@northampton.ac.uk
Conservation and restoration of leather screens, wall hangings, car, carriage and furniture upholstery, saddlery, luggage, firemens' helmets and much, much more. The Centre is included on the Register maintained by the United Kingdom Institute for Conservation.

Rock & Pop

Cheshire
Collector's Corner, PO Box 8, Congleton CW12 4GD
Tel: 01260 270429
dave.popcorner@ukonline.co.uk

Lancashire
Tracks, PO Box 117, Chorley PR6 0UU Tel: 01257 269726
sales@tracks.co.uk
Beatles and rare pop memorabilia.

Rocking Horses

Essex
Haddon Rocking Horses Ltd, 5 Telford Road, Clacton on Sea CO15 4LP Tel: 01255 424745
millers@haddonrockinghorses.co.uk
www.haddonrockinghorses.co.uk

Rugs & Carpets

Gloucestershire
Samarkand Galleries, 7–8 Brewery Yard, Sheep Street, Stow-on-the-Wold GL54 1AA Tel: 01451 832322
mac@samarkand.co.uk
www.samarkand.co.uk
Antique rugs from Near East & Central Asia. Antique Nomadic weavings. Decorative carpets. Tribal artefacts. Unique contemporary Rugs. Contact: Brian MacDonald FRGS.

Kent
Desmond & Amanda North, The Orchard, 186 Hale Street, East Peckham TN12 5JB
Tel: 01622 871353
Unusual, decorative and beautiful old & antique Tribal & Nomadic rugs, carpets, runners from Persia, The Caucasus, Anatolia, & Central Asia. Rugs, runners mostly £100–2000; carpets mostly £400–4000.

Scientific Instruments

Cheshire
Charles Tomlinson, Chester
Tel/Fax: 01244 318395
charles.tomlinson@lineone.net
www.lineone.net/-charles.tomlinson

Kent
Sporting Antiques, 10 Union Square, The Pantiles, Tunbridge Wells TN4 8HE
Tel: 01892 522661
Theodolites, sextants, levels, marine & military compasses, microscopes, telescopes & drawing instruments.

Surrey
Eric Tombs, 62a West Street, Dorking RH4 1BS
Tel/Fax: 01306 743661
ertombs@aol.com

Scotland
Early Technology, Monkton House, Old Craighall, Musselburgh, Midlothian EH21 8SF
Tel: 0131 665 5753
Mobile: 07831 106768
michael.bennett-levy@virgin.net
www.earlytech.com
Open any time by appointment.

Services

Hampshire
Securikey Ltd, P O Box 18, Aldershot GU12 4SL
Tel: 01252 311888
enquiries@securikey.co.uk
www.securikey.co.uk
Underfloor safes.

U.S.A.
Go Antiques, 2330 Aubin Lane, Baton Rouge, LA 70816
Tel: UK 01423 771122
US 1 877 481 5750
sales@goantiques.com
www.goantiques.com
AOL Keyword: GoAntiques
Antiques, art, collectables & more.

Silver

Bedfordshire
Transatlantic Antiques and Fine Art Ltd, 101 Dunstable Street, Ampthill MK45 2NG
Tel/Fax: 01525 403346
transatlantic@talk21.com
www.transatlantic.com

Dorset
Greystoke Antiques, 4 Swan Yard, (off Cheap Street), Sherborne DT9 3AX Tel: 01935 812833
Adjacent to town centre car park. 10am–4.30pm daily, closed wednesday. Georgian, Victorian and later silver.

London
Daniel Bexfield, 26 Burlington Arcade W1J 0PU
Tel: 020 7491 1720
antiques@bexfield.co.uk
www.bexfield.co.uk

The Silver Fund, 40 Bury Street, St James's SW1Y 6AU
Tel: 020 7839 7664
dealers@thesilverfund.com
www.thesilverfund.com

Shropshire
Vanessa Harvey, 30A Corve Street, Ludlow SY8 1GB
Tel: 01584 876375

U.S.A.
Antique Elegance
Tel: 001 617 484 7556
gloria415@aol.com
Also jewellery, pottery, porcelain, orientalia, cut-glass, paintings, rugs & furniture.

Imperial Half Bushel, 831 North Howard Street, Baltimore, Maryland 21201
Tel: 001 410 462 1192
patrick.duggan@worldnet.att.com
www.imperialhalfbushel.com

The Silver Fund, 1001 Madison Avenue at 77th Street, New York NY10021
Tel: 001 212 794 4994
dealers@thesilverfund.com
www.thesilverfund.com

Sports & Games

Kent
Sporting Antiques, 10 Union Square, The Pantiles, Tunbridge Wells TN4 8HE
Tel: 01892 522661
Fishing rods, reels, trophies, books & prints. Golf & general antique sporting goods.

Nottinghamshire
T. Vennett-Smith, 11 Nottingham Road, Gotham NG11 0HE
Tel: 0115 983 0541
info@vennett-smith.com
www.vennett-smith.com
Sporting auctions.

U.S.A.
Triple 'L' Sports, PO Box 281, Winthorp, Maine 04364
Tel: 001 207 377 5787
llsport@ctel.net
Winchester collectables, fishing, hunting, trapping, knives, primitives, baseball, football, golf, tennis, memorabilia and advertising.

Teddy Bears

Oxfordshire
Teddy Bears of Witney, 99 High Street, Witney OX28 6HY
Tel: 01993 702616/706616

Textiles

Lancashire
Decades, 20 Lord St West, Blackburn BB2 1JX
Tel: 01254 693320
Original Victorian to 1970s classic clothing, accessories, jewellery, textiles, lace, linen and much more.

London
Erna Hiscock & John Shepherd, Chelsea Galleries, 69 Portobello Road W11 Tel: 01233 661407
Mobile: 0771 562 7273
erna@ernahiscockantiques.com
www.ernahiscockantiques.com
Antique samplers. Sats 7am–3pm.

Somerset
Joanna Proops, Antique Textiles & Lighting, 34 Belvedere, Lansdown Hill, Bath BA1 5HR
Tel: 01225 310795
antiquetextiles@uk.online.co.uk
www.antiquetextiles.co.uk

U.S.A.
Antique European Linens, PO Box 789, Gulf Breeze, Florida 32562-0789
Tel: 001 850 432 4777
Cell 850 450 463
name@antiqueeuropeanlinens.com
www.antiqueeuropeanlinens.com

M. Finkel & Daughter, 936 Pine Street, Philadelphia, Pennsylvania 19107-6128
Tel: 001 215 627 7797
mailbox@finkelantiques.com
www.finkelantiques.com
America's leading antique sampler and needlework dealer.

Toys

Kent
The Collector's Toy & Model Shop, 52 Canterbury Road, Margate CT9 5BG
Tel: 01843 232301
Mobile: 07973 232778
www.collectorstoyandmodelshop.co.uk

London
Automatomania, Stand 124, Grays Antique Market, 58 Davies Street W1K 5LP
Tel: 020 7495 5259
Mobile: 07790 719097
magic@automatomania.com
www.automatomania.com
Automata, magic and fairground art.

East Sussex
Wallis & Wallis, West Street Auction Galleries, Lewes BN7 2NJ
Tel: 01273 480208
grb@wallisandwallis.co.uk
www.wallisandwallis.co.uk
Auctioneers of diecast toys, model railways, tin plate toys and models.

Yorkshire
John & Simon Haley, 89 Northgate, Halifax HX1 1XF
Tel: 01422 822148/360434
toysandbanks@aol.com

Tunbridge Ware

Kent
Bracketts, Auction Hall, Pantiles, Tunbridge Wells TN1 1UU
Tel: 01892 544500
www.bfaa.co.uk
Tunbridge ware auctioneers.

Watches

Kent
Tempus, Union Square, The Pantiles, Tunbridge Wells
Tel/Fax: 01932 828936
www.tempus-watches.co.uk

Lancashire
Brittons Jewellers, 4 King Street, Clitheroe BB7 2EP
Tel: 01200 425555
info@brittons-watches.co.uk
www.brittons-watches.co.uk
www.antique-jewelry.co.uk

London
Pieces of Time, (1–7 Davies Mews), 26 South Molton Lane W1Y 2LP
Tel: 020 7629 2422
info@antique-watch.com
www.antique-watch.com

Yorkshire
Harpers Jewellers Ltd, 2/6 Minster Gates, York YO1 7HL
Tel: 01904 632634
harpers@talk21.com
www.vintage-watches.co.uk

Directory of Auctioneers

Auctioneers who hold frequent sales should contact us by April 2003 for inclusion in the next edition.

Bedfordshire

W&H Peacock, 26 Newnham Street, Bedford MK40 3JR
Tel: 01234 266366

Berkshire

Dreweatt Neate, Donnington Priory, Donnington, Newbury RG14 2JE,
Tel: 01635 553553
fineart@dreweatt-neate.co.uk

Law Fine Art, Fir Tree Cottage, Church Lane, Brimpton RG7 4TJ
Tel: 0118 971 0353
info@lawfineart.co.uk
www.lawfineart.co.uk

Padworth Auctions, 30 The Broadway, Thatcham RG19 3H,
Tel: 01734 713772

Shiplake Fine Art, 31 Great Knollys Street, Reading RG1 7HU.
Tel: 01734 594748

Special Auction Services, The Coach House, Midgham Park, Reading, RG7 5UG
Tel: 0118 971 2949
www.invaluable.com/sas/

Buckinghamshire

Amersham Auction Rooms, 125 Station Road, Amersham HP7 0AH
Tel: 01494 729292
info@amershamauctionrooms.co.uk
www.thesaurus.co.uk/amersham

Bosley's, 42 West Street, Marlow SL7 2NB Tel: 01628 488188
Bourne End Auction Rooms, Station Approach, Bourne End SL8 5QH.
Tel: 01628 531500

Cambridgeshire

Cheffins, 2 Clifton Road, Cambridge CB2 4BW Tel: 01223 213343
www.cheffins.co.uk

Rowley Fine Art, The Old Bishop's Palace, Little Downham, Ely CB6 2TD Tel: 01353 699177
mail@rowleyfineart.com
www.rowleyfineart.com

Willingham Auctions, 25 High Street, Willingham CB4 5ES
Tel: 01954 261252

Channel Islands

Bonhams and Langlois, Westaway Chambers, 39 Don Street, St Helier, Jersey JE2 4TR, Tel: 01534 722441

Bonhams & Martel Maides Ltd, Allez St Auction Rooms, 9 High Street, St Peter Port, Guernsey GY1 4NY
Tel: 01481 713463/722700

Cheshire

Bonhams, New House, 150 Christleton Road, Chester CH3 5T,
Tel: 01244 313936
www.bonhams.com

Dockree's, Landmark House, 1st Floor, Station Road, Cheadle Hulme SK8 5AT
Tel: 0161 485 1258

Halls Fine Art Auctions, Booth Mansion, 30 Watergate Street, Chester CH1 2LA
Tel: 01244 312300/312112

Frank R Marshall & Co, Marshall House, Church Hill, Knutsford WA16 6DH
Tel: 01565 653284

Maxwells of Wilmslow inc Dockree's, 133A Woodford Road, Woodford SK7 1QD
Tel/Fax: 0161 439 5182

Wright Manley, Beeston Castle Salerooms, Tarporley CW6 9NZ
Tel: 01829 262150

Cleveland

Vectis Auctions Ltd/Barry Potter Auctions, Fleck Way, Thornaby, Stockton-on-Tees TS17 9JZ
Tel: 01642 750616
admin@vectis.co.uk
admin@barrypotterauctions.com
www.vectis.co.uk
www.barrypotterauctions.co.uk

Cornwall

Bonhams, Cornubia Hall, Eastcliffe Road, Par PL24 2AQ Tel: 01726 814047
www.bonhams.com

W H Lane & Son, Jubilee House, Queen Street, Penzance TR18 2DF
Tel: 01736 361447

David Lay, Auction House, Alverton, Penzance TR18 4RE
Tel: 01736 361414

Martyn Rowe, Truro Auction Centre, City Wharf, Malpas Road, Truro TR1 1QH
Tel: 01872 260020

Cumbria

Bonhams, 48 Cecil Street, Carlisle CA1 1NT Tel: 01228 542422
www.bonhams.com

Mitchells, Fairfield House, Station Road, Cockermouth CA13 9PY
Tel: 01900 827800

Penrith Farmers' & Kidd's plc, Skirsgill Salerooms, Penrith CA11 0DN
Tel: 01768 890781
penrith.farmers@virgin.net

Thomson, Roddick & Medcalf, Coleridge House, Shaddongate, Carlisle CA2 5TU
Tel: 01228 528939

Devon

Bearnes, St Edmund's Court, Okehampton Street, Exeter EX4 1DU
Tel: 01392 422800

Bonhams, Dowell Street, Honiton EX14 8LX Tel: 01404 41872
www.bonhams.com

Bonhams, 38/39 Southernhay East, Exeter EX1 1PE Tel: 01392 455 955
www.bonhams.com

Michael J Bowman, 6 Haccombe House, Netherton, Newton Abbot TQ12 4SJ
Tel: 01626 872890

Eldreds Auctioneers & Valuers, 13-15 Ridge Park Road, Plympton, Plymouth PL7 2BS Tel: 01752 340066

R A Fenner & Co, The Stannary Gallery, Drake Road, Tavistock PL19 0AX
Tel: 01822 617799/617800 Fax: 01822 617595 acroton@ rafenner.com
www.rafenner.com

S.J. Hales, 87 Fore Street, Bovey Tracey TQ13 9AB Tel & Fax: 01626 836684

The Plymouth Auction Rooms, Edwin House, St John's Rd, Cattedown, Plymouth PL4 0NZ Tel: 01752 25474

Rendells, Stonepark, Ashburton TQ13 7RH Tel: 01364 653017 stonepark@rendells.co.uk
www.rendells.co.uk

G S Shobrook & Co, 20 Western Approach, Plymouth PL1 1TG
Tel: 01752 663341

John Smale & Co, 11 High Street, Barnstaple EX31 1BG
Tel: 01271 42000/42916

Martin Spencer-Thomas, Bicton Street, Exmouth EX8 2SN Tel: 01395 267403

Taylors, Honiton Galleries, 205 High Street, Honiton EX14 8LF
Tel: 01404 42404

Dorset

Bonhams, Long Street Salerooms, Sherborne DT9 3BS Tel: 01935 815271
www.bonhams.com

Chapman, Moore & Mugford, 9 High Street, Shaftesbury SP7 8JB
Tel: 01747 852400

Cottees of Wareham, The Market, East Street, Wareham BH20 4NR
Tel: 01929 552826
www.auctionsatcottees.co.uk

Hy Duke & Son, Dorchester Fine Art Salerooms, Dorchester DT1 1QS
Tel: 01305 265080

Riddetts of Bournemouth, 1 77 Holdenhurst Road, Bournemouth BH8 8DQ
Tel: 01202 555686
auctions@riddetts.co.uk

Semley Auctioneers, Station Road, Semley, Shaftesbury SP7 9AN Tel/Fax: 01747 855122/855222

Essex

Ambrose, Ambrose House, Old Station Road, Loughton IG10 4PE
Tel: 020 8502 3951

Cooper Hirst Auctions, The Granary Saleroom, Victoria Road, Chelmsford CM2 6LH
Tel: 01245 260535

Leigh Auction Rooms, John Stacey & Sons, 88-90 Pall Mall, Leigh-on-Sea SS9 1RG
Tel: 01702 77051

Saffron Walden Auctions, 1 Market Street, Saffron Walden CB10 1JB
Tel: 01799 513281

Sworders, 14 Cambridge Road, Stansted Mountfitchet CM24 8BZ
Tel: 01279 817778 www.sworder.co.uk

Flintshire

Dodds Property World, Victoria Auction Galleries, 9 Chester Street, Mold CH7 1EB
Tel: 01352 752552

Gloucestershire

Bristol Auction Rooms, St John's Place, Apsley Road, Clifton, Bristol BS8 2ST
Tel: 0117 973 7201
www.bristolauctionrooms.com

Bruton, Knowles & Co, 111 Eastgate Street, Gloucester GL1 1PZ
Tel: 01452 521267

The Cotswold Auction Company Ltd, incorporating Short Graham & Co and Hobbs and Chambers Fine Arts, The Coach House, Swan Yard, 9-13 West Market Place, Cirencester GL7 2NH
Tel: 01285 642420
info@cotswoldauction.co.uk
www.cotswoldauction.co.uk

The Cotswold Auction Company Ltd, incorporating Short Graham & Co and Hobbs and Chambers Fine Arts, Chapel Walk Saleroom, Cheltenham GL50 3DS
Tel: 01242 256363
info@cotswoldauction.co.uk
www.cotswoldauction.co.uk

The Cotswold Auction Company Ltd, incorporating Short Graham & Co and Hobbs and Chambers Fine Arts, 4–6 Clarence Street, Gloucester GL1 1DX
Tel: 01452 521177
info@cotswoldauction.co.uk
www.cotswoldauction.co.uk

Mallams, 26 Grosvenor Street, Cheltenham GL52 2SG
Tel: 01242 235712

Moore, Allen & Innocent, The Salerooms, Norcote, Cirencester GL7 5RH Tel: 01285 646050 fineart@mooreallen.co.uk www.mooreallen.co.uk

Specialised Postcard Auctions, 25 Gloucester Street, Cirencester GL7 2DJ Tel: 01285 659057

Tayler & Fletcher, London House, High Street, Bourton-on-the-Water, Cheltenham GL54 2AP Tel: 01451 821666 bourton@taylerfletcher.com www.taylerfletcher.com

Wotton Auction Rooms, Tabernacle Road, Wotton-under-Edge GL12 7EB Tel: 01453 844733 info@wottonauctionrooms.co.uk www.wottonauctionrooms.co.uk

Greater Manchester

Bonhams, The Stables, 213 Ashley Road, Hale WA15 9TB Tel: 0161 927 3822 www.bonhams.com

Capes Dunn & Co, The Auction Galleries, 38 Charles Street, Off Princess Street, M1 7DB Tel: 0161 273 6060/1911

Hampshire

Bonhams, 54 Southampton Road, Ringwood BH24 1JD Tel: 01425 473333 www.bonhams.com

Bonhams, The Red House, Hyde Street, Winchester SO23 7DX Tel: 01962 862515 www.bonhams.com

Evans & Partridge, Agriculture House, High Street, Stockbridge SO20 6HF Tel: 01264 810702

Jacobs & Hunt, 26 Lavant Street, Petersfield GU32 3EF Tel: 01730 233933 www.jacobsandhunt.co.uk

George Kidner, The Old School, The Square, Pennington, Lymington, SO41 8GN Tel: 01590 670070 www.georgekidner.co.uk

May & Son, The Old Stables, 9A Winchester Road, Andover SP10 2EG Tel: 01264 323417 office@mayandson.com www.mayandson.com

D M Nesbit & Co, Fine Art and Auction Department, Southsea Salerooms, 7 Clarendon Road, Southsea PO5 2ED Tel: 023 9286 4321 auctions@nesbits.co.uk www.nesbits.co.uk

Odiham Auction Sales, Unit 4, Priors Farm, West Green Road, Mattingley RG27 8JU Tel: 01189 326824 auction@dircon.co.uk

Herefordshire

Brightwells Fine Art, The Fine Art Saleroom, Ryelands Road, Leominster HR6 8NZ Tel: 01568 611122 fineart@brightwells.com www.brightwells.com

Morris Bricknell, Stuart House, 18 Gloucester Road, Ross-on-Wye HR9 5BU Tel: 01989 768320

Nigel Ward & Co, The Border Property Centre, Pontrilas HR2 0EH Tel: 01981 240140

Hertfordshire

Brown & Merry, Tring Market Auctions, The Market Premises, Brook Street, Tring HP23 5EF Tel: 01442 826446 sales@tringmarketauctions.co.uk www.tringmarketauctions.co.uk

Sworders, The Hertford Saleroom, 42 St Andrew Street, Hertford SG14 1JA Tel: 01992 583508 www.sworder.co.uk

Humberside

Dickinson Davy & Markham, Wrawby Street, Brigg DN20 8JJ Tel: 01652 653666

Kent

Bonhams, 49 London Road, Sevenoaks TN13 1AR Tel: 01732 740310 www.bonhams.com

Bracketts, Auction Hall, Pantiles, Tunbridge Wells TN1 1UU Tel: 01892 544500 www.bfaa.co.uk

Calcutt Maclean Standen, The Estate Office, Stone Street, Cranbrook TN17 3HD Tel: 01580 713828

The Canterbury Auction Galleries, 40 Station Road West, Canterbury CT2 8AN Tel: 01227 763337 canterbury_auction_galleries@compuserve.com www.thecanterburyauctiongalleries.com

Mervyn Carey, Twysden Cottage, Benenden, Cranbrook TN17 4LD 01580 240283

Gorringes, 15 The Pantiles, Tunbridge Wells TN2 5TD Tel: 01892 619670 www.gorringes.co.uk

Ibbett Mosely, 125 High Street, Sevenoaks TN13 1UT Tel: 01732 456731

Lambert & Foster, 102 High Street, Tenterden TN30 6HT Tel: 01580 762083 saleroom@lambertandfoster.co.uk www.lambertandfoster.co.uk

Medway Auctions, 23 High Street, Rochester ME1 1LN Tel: 01634 847444 medauc@dircon.co.uk www.medwayauctions.co.uk

B J Norris, The Quest, West Street, Harrietsham, Maidstone ME17 1JD Tel: 01622 859515

Wealden Auction Galleries, Desmond Judd, 23 Hendly Drive, Cranbrook TN17 3DY Tel: 01580 714522

Lancashire

Smythe's, 174 Victoria Road West, Cleveleys FY5 3NE Tel: 01253 852184

Tony & Sons, 4-8 Lynwood Road, Blackburn BB2 6HP Tel: 01254 691748

Leicestershire

William H. Brown, Warner Auction Rooms, 16-18 Halford Street, Leicester LE1 6AS Tel: 0116 255 9900

Gildings, 64 Roman Way, Market Harborough LE16 7PQ Tel: 01858 410414 sales@gildings.co.uk www.gildings.co.uk

Heathcote Ball & Co, Castle Auction Rooms, 78 St Nicholas Circle, Leicester LE1 5NW Tel: 0116 253 6789 www.heathcote-ball.clara.co.uk

Lincolnshire

Thomas Mawer & Son, The Lincoln Saleroom, 63 Monks Road, Lincoln LN2 5HP Tel: 01522 524984

Marilyn Swain Auctions, The Old Barracks, Sandon Road, Grantham NG31 9AS Tel: 01476 568861

Walter's, No 1 Mint Lane, Lincoln LN1 1UD Tel: 01522 525454

London

Academy Auctioneers & Valuers, Northcote House, Northcote Avenue, Ealing W5 3UR Tel: 020 8579 7466 www.thesaurus.co.uk/academy/

Angling Auctions, P O Box 2095 W12 8RU Tel: 020 8749 4175 neil@anglingauctions.demon.co.uk

Bloomsbury Book Auctions, 3 & 4 Hardwick Street, Off Rosebery Avenue EC1R 4RY Tel: 020 7833 2636/7 & 0207923 6940 info@bloomsbury-book-auct.com www.bloomsbury-book-auct.com

Bonhams, Montpelier Street, Knightsbridge SW7 1HH Tel: 020 7393 3900 www.bonhams.com

Bonhams, 65-69 Lots Road, Chelsea SW10 0RN Tel: 020 7393 3900 www.bonhams.com

Bonhams, 101 New Bond Street W1S 1SR Tel: 020 7629 6602 www.bonhams.com

Bonhams, 10 Salem Road, Bayswater W2 4DL Tel: 020 7313 2700 www.bonhams.com

Christie, Manson & Wood Ltd, 8 King Street, St James's SW1Y 6QT Tel: 020 7839 9060 www.christies.com

Christie's South Kensington Ltd, 85 Old Brompton Road SW7 3LD Tel: 020 7581 7611 www.christies.com

Comic Book Postal Auctions Ltd, 40-42 Osnaburgh Street NW1 3ND Tel: 020 7424 0007 comicbook@compuserve.com www.compalcomics.com

Criterion Salerooms, 53 Essex Road, Islington N1 2BN Tel: 020 7359 5707

Dix-Noonan-Webb, 1 Old Bond Street W1S 4PB Tel: 020 7499 5022

Glendining's, (A division of Bonhams specialising in coins & medals), 101 New Bond Street W1S 1SR Tel: 020 7493 2445 www.bonhams.com

Harmers of London, 111 Power Road, Chiswick W4 5PY Tel: 020 8747 6100 auctions@harmers.demon.co.uk www.harmers.com

Lloyds International Auction Galleries, Lloyds House, 9 Lydden Road SW18 4LT Tel: 020 8788 7777 www.lloyds-auction.co.uk

Lots Road Galleries, 71-73 Lots Road, Chelsea SW10 0RN Tel: 020 7351 7771

Morton & Eden Ltd, in association with Sotheby's, 45 Maddox Street W1S 2PE Tel: 020 7493 5344 info@mortonandeden.com www.sothebys.com

Onslow's, The Depot, 2 Michael Road SW6 2AD Tel: 020 7371 0505

Proud Oriental Auctions, Proud Galleries, 5 Buckingham St WC2N 6BP Tel: 020 7839 4942

Rosebery's Fine Art Ltd, 74/76 Knights Hill SE27 0JD Tel: 020 8761 2522 auctions@roseberys.co.uk

Sotheby's, 34-35 New Bond Street W1A 2AA Tel: 020 7293 5000 www.sothebys.com

Sotheby's Olympia, Hammersmith Road W14 8UX Tel: 020 7293 5000 www.sothebys.com

Spink & Son Ltd, 69 Southampton Road, Bloomsbury WC1B 4ET Tel: 020 7563 4000

Merseyside

Cato Crane & Co, Liverpool Auction Rooms, 6 Stanhope Street, Liverpool L8 5RF 0151 709 5559 johncrane@cato-crane.co.uk www.cato-crane.co.uk

Outhwaite & Litherland, Kingsway Galleries, Fontenoy Street, Liverpool L3 2BE Tel: 0151 236 6561

Middlesex

West Middlesex Auction Rooms, 113-114 High Street, Brentford TW8 8AT Tel: 020 8568 9080

Norfolk

Garry M Emms & Co Ltd, Great Yarmouth Salerooms, Beevor Road (off South Beach Parade), Great Yarmouth NR30 3PS Tel: 01493 332668 g_emms@gt-yarmouth-auctions.com www.gt-yarmouth-auctions.com

Thomas Wm Gaze & Son, Diss Auction Rooms, Roydon Road, Diss IP22 3LN Tel: 01379 650306 www.twgaze.com

Keys, Aylsham Salerooms, Off Palmers Lane, Aylsham NR11 6JA Tel: 01263 733195 www.aylshamsalerooms.co.uk

Knight's, Cuckoo Cottage. Town Green, Alby, Norwich NR11 7HE Tel: 01263 768488

Northamptonshire

Merry's Auctioneers, Northampton Auction & Sales Centre, Liliput Road, Brackmills, Northampton NN4 7BY Tel: 01604 769990

Northern Ireland

Anderson's Auction Rooms Ltd, Unit 7, Prince Regent Business Park, Prince Regent Road, Castereagh, Belfast BT5 6QR Tel: 028 9040 1888

Nottinghamshire

Bonhams, 20 The Square, Retford DN22 6XE Tel: 01777 708633 www.bonhams.com

Bonhams, 57 Mansfield Road, Nottingham NG1 3PL Tel: 0115 947 4414 www.bonhams.com

Arthur Johnson & Sons Ltd, The Nottingham Auction Centre, Meadow Lane, Nottingham NG2 3GY Tel: 0115 986 9128

Mellors & Kirk, The Auction House, Gregory Street, Lenton Tel: 0115 979 0000

Neales, 192 Mansfield Road, Nottingham NG1 3HU Tel: 0115 962 4141 fineart@neales.co.uk www.neales-auctions.com

C B Sheppard & Son, The Auction Galleries, Chatsworth Street, Sutton-in-Ashfield NG17 4GG Tel: 01773 872419

T Vennett-Smith, 11 Nottingham Road, Gotham NG11 0HE Tel: 0115 983 0541 info@vennett-smith.com www.vennett-smith.com

Oxfordshire

Bonhams, 39 Park End Street, Oxford OX1 1JD Tel: 01865 723524 www.bonhams.com

Holloway's, 49 Parsons Street, Banbury OX16 5PF Tel: 01295 817777 enquiries@hollowaysauctioneers.co.uk www.hollowaysauctioneers.co.uk

Mallams, Bocardo House, 24 St Michael's Street, Oxford OX1 2EB Tel: 01865 241358 oxford@mallams.co.uk

Simmons & Sons, 32 Bell Street, Henley-on-Thames RG9 2BH Tel: 01491 612810 www.simmonsandsons.com

Soames County Auctioneers, Pinnocks Farm Estates, Northmoor OX8 1AY Tel: 01865 300626

Republic of Ireland

James Adam & Sons, 26 St Stephen's Green, Dublin 2 Tel: 00 3531 676 0261

Christie's Dublin, 52 Waterloo Road, Dublin 4 Tel: 00 353 1 6680 585 www.christies.com

Hamilton Osborne King, 4 Main Street, Blackrock, Co. Dublin Tel: 353 1 288 5011 blackrock@hok.ie www.hok.ie

Mealy's, Chatsworth Street, Castle Comer, Co Kilkenny Tel: 00 353 56 41229 info@mealys.com www.mealys.com

Whyte's Auctioneers, 38 Molesworth Street, Dublin 2 Tel: 00 353 1 676 2888 info@whytes.ie www.whytes.ie

Scotland

Bonhams, 65 George Street, Edinburgh EH2 2JL Tel: 0131 225 2266 www.bonhams.com

Bonhams, 176 St Vincent Street, Glasgow G2 5SG Tel: 0141 223 8866 www.bonhams.com

Christie's Scotland Ltd, 164-166 Bath Street, Glasgow G2 4TG Tel: 0141 332 8134 www.christies.com

William Hardie Ltd, 15a Blythswood Square, Glasgow G2 4EW Tel: 0141 221 6780

Loves Auction Rooms, 52 Canal Street, Perth PH2 8LF Tel: 01738 633337

Lyon & Turnbull, 33 Broughton Place, Edinburgh EH1 3RR Tel: 0131 557 8844

Macgregor Auctions, 56 Largo Road, St Andrews, Fife KY16 8RP Tel: 01334 472431

Shapes Fine Art Auctioneers & Valuers, Bankhead Avenue, Sighthill, Edinburgh EH11 4BY Tel: 0131 453 3222 auctionsadmin@shapesauctioneers.co.uk www.shapesauctioneers.co.uk

L S Smellie & Sons Ltd, Within the Furniture Market, Lower Auchingramont Road, Hamilton ML10 6BE Tel: 01698 282007

Sotheby's, 112 George Street, Edinburgh EH2 4LH Tel: 0131 226 7201 www.sothebys.com

Thomson Roddick & Medcalf, 60 Tel: 01387 255366

Thomson Roddick & Medcalf, 20 Murray Street, Annan DG12 6EG Tel: 01461 202575

Thomson Roddick & Medcalf, 44/3 Hardengreen Business Park, Eskbank, Edinburgh EH22 3NX Tel: 0131 454 9090

Shropshire

Halls Fine Art Auctions, Welsh Bridge, Shrewsbury SY3 8LA Tel: 01743 231212

McCartneys, Ox Pasture, Overture Road, Ludlow SY8 4AA Tel: 01584 872251

Mullock & Madeley, The Old Shippon, Wall-under-Heywood, Church Stretton SY6 7DS Tel: 01694 771771/07803 276394 auctions@mullockmadeley.co.uk www.mullockmadeley.co.uk

Nock Deighton, Livestock & Auction Centre, Tasley, Bridgnorth WV16 4QR Tel: 01746 762666

Walker Barnett & Hill, Cosford Auction Rooms, Long Lane, Cosford TF11 8PJ Tel: 01902 375555 wbhauctions@lineone.net www.walker-barnett-hill.co.uk

Welsh Bridge Salerooms, Welsh Bridge, Shrewsbury SY3 8LH Tel: 01743 231212

Somerset

Aldridges, Newark House. 26-45 Cheltenham Street, Bath BA2 3EX Tel: 01225 462830

Bonhams, 1 Old King Street, Bath BA1 2JT Tel: 01225 788 988 www.bonhams.com

Clevedon Salerooms, Herbert Road, Clevedon BS21 7ND Tel: 01275 876699

Gardiner Houlgate, The Bath Auction Rooms, 9 Leafield Way, Corsham, Nr Bath SN13 9SW Tel: 01225 812912 gardiner-houlgate.co.uk www.invaluable.com/gardiner-houlgate

Greenslade Taylor Hunt Fine Art, Magdelene House, Church Square, Taunton TA1 1SB Tel: 01823 332525

Lawrence Fine Art Auctioneers, South Street, Crewkerne TA18 8AB Tel: 01460 73041

Tamlyn & Son, 56 High Street, Bridgwater TA6 3BN Tel: 01278 458241

Staffordshire

Louis Taylor Auctioneers & Valuers, Britannia House, 10 Town Road, Hanley, Stoke on Trent ST1 2QG Tel: 01782 214111

Potteries Specialist Auctions, 271 Waterloo Road, Cobridge, Stoke on Trent ST6 3HR Tel: 01782 286622

Wintertons Ltd, Lichfield Auction Centre, Fradley Park, Lichfield WS13 6NU Tel: 01543 263256 enquiries@wintertons.co.uk www.wintertons.co.uk

Suffolk

Abbotts Auction Rooms, Campsea Ashe, Woodbridge IP13 0PS Tel: 01728 746323

Boardman Fine Art Auctioneers, Station Road Corner, Haverhill CB9 0EY Tel: 01440 730414

Bonhams, 32 Boss Hall Road, Ipswich IP1 5DJ Tel: 01473 740494 www.bonhams.com

Diamond Mills & Co, 117 Hamilton Road, Felixstowe IP11 7BL Tel: 01394 282281

Dyson & Son, The Auction Room, Church Street, Clare CO10 8PD Tel: 01787 277993 info@dyson-auctioneers.co.uk www.dyson-auctioneers.co.uk

Lacy Scott and Knight, Fine Art Department, The Auction Centre, 10 Risbygate Street, Bury St Edmunds IP33 3AA Tel: 01284 76353

Neal Sons & Fletcher, 2 6 Church Street, Woodbridge IP12 1DP Tel: 01394 382263

Olivers, Olivers Rooms, Burkitts Lane, Sudbury CO10 1HB Tel: 01787 880305 oliversauctions@btconnect.com

Vost's, Newmarket CB8 9AU Tel: 01638 561313

Surrey

Bonhams, Millmead, Guildford GU2 4BE Tel: 01483 504030 www.bonhams.com

Clarke Gammon, The Guildford Auction Rooms, Bedford Road, Guildford GU1 4SJ Tel: 01483 880915

Ewbank, Burnt Common Auction Rooms, London Road, Send, Woking GU23 7LN Tel: 01483 223101 www.ewbankauctions.co.uk

Hamptons International, Baverstock House, 93 High Street, Godalming GU7 1AL Tel: 01483 423567 fineartauctions@hamptons-int.com www.hamptons.co.uk/fineart

Lawrences Auctioneers Limited, Norfolk House, 80 High Street, Bletchingley RH1 4PA Tel: 01883 743323 www.lawrencesbletchingley.co.uk

John Nicholson, The Auction Rooms, Longfield, Midhurst Road, Fernhurst GU27 3HA Tel: 01428 653727

Richmond & Surrey Auctions Ltd, Richmond Station, Kew Road, Old Railway Parcels Depot, Richmond TW9 2NA Tel: 020 8948 6677

P F Windibank, The Dorking Halls, Reigate Road, Dorking RH4 1SG Tel: 01306 884556/876280 sjw@windibank.co.uk www.windibank.co.uk

East Sussex

Burstow & Hewett, Abbey Auction Galleries and Granary Salerooms, Lower Lake, Battle TN33 0AT Tel: 01424 772374

Gorringes Auction Galleries, Terminus Road, Bexhill-on-Sea TN39 3LR Tel: 01424 212994 bexhill@gorringes.co.uk www.gorringes.co.uk

Gorringes inc Julian Dawson, 15 North Street, Lewes BN7 2PD Tel: 01273 472503 auctions@gorringes.co.uk www.gorringes.co.uk

Gorringes inc Julian Dawson, 56 High Street, Lewes BN7 1XE Tel: 01273 478221 www.gorringes.co.uk

Graves, Son & Pilcher, Hove Auction Rooms, Hove Street, Hove BN3 2GL Tel: 01273 735266

Edgar Horns Fine Art Auctioneers, 46-50 South Street, Eastbourne BN21 4XB Tel: 01323 410419 www.edgarhorns.co

Raymond P Inman, The Auction Galleries, 35 & 40 Temple Street, Brighton BN1 3BH Tel: 01273 774777 www.raymondinman.co.uk

Rye Auction Galleries, Rock Channel, Rye TN31 7HL Tel: 01797 222124 sales@ryeauction.fsnet.co.uk

Wallis & Wallis, West Street Auction Galleries, Lewes BN7 2NJ Tel: 01273 480208 auctions@wallisandwallis.co.uk www.wallisandwallis.co.uk

West Sussex

Henry Adams Fine Art Auctioneers, Baffins Hall, Baffins Lane, Chichester PO19 1UA Tel: 01243 532223 enquiries@henryadamsfineart.co.uk www.henryadamsfineart.co.uk

John Bellman Auctioneers, New Pound Business Park, Wisborough Green, Billingshurst RH14 0AZ Tel: 01403 700858 jbellman@compuserve.com

Peter Cheney, Western Road Auction Rooms, Western Road, Littlehampton BN17 5NP Tel: 01903 722264 & 713418

Denham's, The Auction Galleries, Warnham, Horsham RH12 3RZ Tel: 01403 255699 Tel/Fax: 01403 253837 denhams@lineone.net

R H Ellis & Sons, 44-46 High Street, Worthing BN11 1LL Tel: 01903 238999

Sotheby's Sussex, Summers Place, Billingshurst RH14 9AD Tel: 01403 833500 www.sothebys.com

Stride & Son, Southdown House, St John's Street, Chichester PO19 1XQ Tel: 01243 780207

Rupert Toovey & Co Ltd, Star Road, Partridge Green RH13 8RA Tel: 01403 711744 auctions@rupert-toovey.com www.rupert-toovey.com

Worthing Auction Galleries Ltd, Fleet House, Teville Gate, Worthing BN11 1UA Tel: 01903 205565 info@worthing-auctions.co.uk www.worthing-auctions.co.uk

Tyne & Wear

Anderson & Garland (Auctioneers), Marlborough House, Marlborough Crescent, Newcastle-upon-Tyne NE1 4EE Tel: 0191 232 6278

Boldon Auction Galleries, 24a Front Street, East Boldon NE36 0SJ Tel: 0191 537 2630

Bonhams, 30-32 Grey Street, Newcastle Upon Tyne NE1 6AE Tel: 0191 233 9930

Sneddons, Sunderland Auction Rooms, 30 Villiers Street, Sunderland SR1 1EJ Tel: 0191 514 5931

Wales

Anthemion Auctions, 2 Llandough Trading Park, Penarth Road, Cardiff CF11 8RR Tel: 029 2071 2608

Morgan Evans & Co Ltd, 30 Church Street, Llangefni, Anglesey, Gwynedd LL77 7DU Tel: 01248 723303/421582 llangefni@morganevans.demon.co.uk www.morganevans.com

Rogers Jones & Co, The Saleroom, 33 Abergele Road, Colwyn Bay LL29 7RU Tel: 01492 532176 www.rogersjones.ukauctioneers.com

J. Straker Chadwick & Sons, Market Street Chambers, Abergavenny, Monmouthshire NP7 5SD Tel: 01873 852624

Wingetts Auction Gallery, 29 Holt St, Wrexham, Clwyd LL13 8DH Tel: 01978 353553 auctions@wingetts.co.uk www.wingetts.co.uk

South Wales

Peter Francis, Curiosity Sale Room, 19 King Street, Carmarthen SA31 1BH Tel: 01267 233456 Peterfrancis@valuers.fsnet.co.uk www.peterfrancis.co.uk

Warwickshire

Bigwood Auctioneers Ltd, The Old School, Tiddington, Stratford-upon-Avon CV37 7AW Tel: 01789 269415

Locke & England, 18 Guy Street, Leamington Spa CV32 4RT Tel: 01926 889100 www.auctions-online.com/locke

West Midlands

Biddle and Webb of Birmingham, Ladywood Middleway, Birmingham B16 0PP Tel: 0121 455 8042 antiques@biddleandwebb.freeserve.co.uk

Bonhams, The Old House, Station Road, Knowle, Solihull B93 0HT Tel: 01564 776151 www.bonhams.com

Frank H Fellows & Sons, Augusta House, 19 Augusta Street, Hockley, Birmingham B18 6JA Tel: 0121 212 2131

Weller & Dufty Ltd, 141 Bromsgrove Street, Birmingham B5 6RQ Tel: 0121 692 1414 wellerdufty@freewire.co.uk www.wellerandufty.co.uk

Wiltshire

Henry Aldridge & Son, Unit 1, Bath Road Business Centre, Devizes SN10 1XA Tel: 01380 729199 andrew.aldridge@virgin.net www.henry-aldridge.co.uk

Finan & Co, The Square, Mere BA12 6DJ Tel: 01747 861411

Kidson Trigg, Estate Office, Friars Farm, Sevenhampton, Highworth, Swindon SN6 7PZ Tel: 01793 861000

Dominic Winter Book Auctions, The Old School, Maxwell Street, Swindon SN1 5DR Tel: 01793 611340 info@dominicwinter.co.uk www.dominicwinter.co.uk

Woolley & Wallis, Salisbury Salerooms, 51-61 Castle Street, Salisbury SP1 3SU Tel: 01722 424500

Worcestershire

Andrew Grant, St Mark's House, St Mark's Close, Worcester WR5 3DJ Tel: 01905 357547

Philip Laney, The Malvern Auction Centre, Portland Road, off Victoria Road, Malvern WR14 2TA Tel: 01684 893933 PhilipLaney@compuserve.com

Philip Serrell, The Malvern Saleroom, Barnards Green Road, Malvern WR14 3LW Tel: 01684 892314

Yorkshire

BBR, Elsecar Heritage Centre, Wath Road, Elsecar, Barnsley S74 8HJ Tel: 01226 745156 www.onlinebbr.com

Bonhams, 17a East Parade, Leeds LS1 2BH Tel: 0113 2448011 www.bonhams.com

Boulton & Cooper, St Michael's House, Market Place, Malton YO17 7LR Tel: 01653 696151

H C Chapman & Son, The Auction Mart, North Street, Scarborough YO11 1DL Tel: 01723 372424

Cundalls, 15 Market Place, Malton YO17 7LP Tel: 01653 697820

Dee, Atkinson & Harrison, The Exchange Saleroom, Driffield YO25 6LD Tel: 01377 253151 exchange@dee-atkinson-harrison.co.uk www.dee-atkinson-harrison.co.uk

David Duggleby, The Vine St Salerooms, Scarborough YO11 1XN Tel: 01723 507111 auctions@davidduggleby.freeserve.co.uk www.davidduggleby.com also at: West End Rooms, The Paddock Whitby YO23 3DB

ELR Auctions Ltd, The Nichols Building, Shalesmoor, Sheffield S3 8UJ Tel: 0114 281 6161

Andrew Hartley, Victoria Hall Salerooms, Little Lane, Ilkley LS29 8EA Tel: 01943 816363 info@andrewhartleyfinearts.co.uk www.andrewhartleyfinearts.co.uk

Lithgow Sons & Partners, The Auction Houses, Station Road, Stokesley, Middlesbrough TS9 7AB Tel: 01642 710158 info@lithgowsauctions.com www.lithgowsauctions.com

Malcolm's No. 1 Auctioneers & Valuers Tel: 01977 684971 info@malcolmsno1auctions.co.uk www.malcolmsno1auctions.co.uk

Christopher Matthews, 23 Mount Street, Harrogate HG2 8DQ Tel: 01423 871756

Morphets of Harrogate, 6 Albert Street, Harrogate HG1 1JL Tel: 01423 530030

Tennants, The Auction Centre, Harmby Road, Leyburn DL8 5SG Tel: 01969 623780

Tennants, 34 Montpellier Parade, Harrogate HG1 2TG Tel: 01423 531661 enquiry@tennants-ltd.co.uk www.tennants.co.uk

Wilkinson & Beighton Auctioneers, Woodhouse Green, Thurcroft, Rotherham SY3 8LA Tel: 01709 700005

Wombell's Antiques & General Auction, The Auction Gallery, Northminster Business Park, Northfield Lane, Upper Poppleton, York YO26 6QU Tel: 01904 790777 www.invaluable.com/wombell

Austria

Dorotheum, Palais Dorotheum, A-1010 Wien, Dorotheergasse. 17 Tel: 0043 1 515 60 35

Australia

Bonhams, Level 1, 1111 High Street, Armadale 3143, Melbourne, Victoria NSW 2025 Tel: (613) 9823 1949

Leonard Joel Auctioneers, 333 Malvern Road, South Yarra, Victoria 3141 Tel: 03 9826 4333 decarts@ljoel.com.au *or*jewellery@ljoel.com.a www.ljoel.com.au

Shapiro Auctioneers, 162 Queen Street, Woollahra, Sydney NSW 2025 Tel: 00 612 9326 1588

Belgium

Horta, Hotel de Ventes, 16 Avenue Ducpetiaux 1060, Brussels Tel: 02 533 11 11

Canada

Bailey's Auctions, 467 Elmira Road North, Guelph, Ontario N1H 6J4 Tel: 001 519 823 1107 auctioneer@baileyauctions.com www.baileyauctions.com

Robert Deveau Galleries, Fine Art Auctioneers, 297-299 Queen Street, Toronto, Ontario M5A 1S7 Tel: 00 416 364 6271

Ritchies Inc., Auctioneers & Appraisers of Antiques & Fine Art, 288 King Street East, Toronto, Ontario M5A 1K4 Tel: (416) 364 1864 auction@ritchies.com www.ritchies.com

A Touch of Class Auctions, 92 College Crescent, Barrie, Ontario L4M 5C8 Tel: 001 705 726 2120 kristarichards@rogers.com www.atouchofclassauctions.com

Waddington's Auctions, 111 Bathurst Street, Toronto MSV 2RI Tel: 001 416 504 9100 vb@waddingtonsauctions.com www.waddingtonsauctions.com

When the Hammer Goes Down, 440 Douglas Avenue, Toronto, Ontario M5M 1H4 Tel: 001 416 787 1700 TOLL FREE 1 (866) BIDCALR (243 2257) BIDCALR@rogers.com www.bidcalr.com

China

Christie's Hong Kong, 2203-5 Alexandra House, 16-20 Chater Road, Hong Kong Tel: 00 852 2521 5396

Sotheby's, Li Po Chun Chambers, 18th Floor, 189 Des Vouex Road, Hong Kong Tel: 852 524 8121

Denmark

Bruun Rasmussen-Havnen, Pakhusvej 12, DK-2100, Copenhagen Tel: +45 70 27 60 80 havnen@bruun-rasmussen.dk www.bruun-rasmussen.dk

Finland

Bukowskis, Horhammer, Iso Roobertink, 12 Stora Robertsg, 00120 Helsinki Helsingfors Tel: 00 358 9 668 9110 www.bukowskis.fi

Hagelstam, Bulevardi 9 A, II kerros, 00120 Helsinki Tel: 358 (0)9 680 2300 www.hagelstam.fi

France

Sotheby's France SA, 76 Rue du Faubourg, Saint Honore, 75008 Paris Tel: 00 33 147 42 22 32

Germany

Auction Team Koln, Postfach 50 11 19, 50971 Koln Tel: 00 49 0221 38 70 49 auction@breker.com

Hermann Historica OHG, Postfach 201009, 80010 Munchen Tel: 00 49 89 5237296

Sotheby's Berlin, Palais amFestungsgraben, Unter den Linden, Neue Wache D-10117 Tel: 49 (30) 201 0521

Sotheby's Munich, Odeonsplatz 16, D-80539 Munchen Tel: 49 (89) 291 31 51

Israel

Sotheby's Israel, Gordon 38, Tel Aviv 63414 Tel: 972(3)522 3822

Italy

Christie's Rome, Palazzo Massimo, Lancellotti, Piazza Navona 114, Rome 00186 Tel: 00 396 687 2787

Sotheby's, Palazzo Broggi, Via Broggi 19, 20129 Milano Tel: 02 295001 www.sothebys.com

Sotheby's Rome, Piazza d'Espana 90, 00187 Rome Tel: 39(6) 69941791/6781798

Mexico

Galeria Louis C. Morton, GLC A7073L IYS, Monte Athos 179, Col. Lomas de Chapultepec CP11000 Tel: 52 5520 5005 glmorton@prodigy net.mx www.lmorton.com

Monaco

Sotheby's Monaco, Le Sporting d'Hiver, Place du Casino, 98001 Cedex Tel: 00 377 93 30 888

Christie's Monaco, S.A.M., Park Palace, 98000 Tel: 00 337 9325 1933

Netherlands

Christie's Amsterdam, Cornelis Schuystraat 57, 107150 Amsterdam Tel: (3120) 57 55 255

Sotheby's Amsterdam, De Boelelaan 30, 1083 HJ, Amsterdam Tel: 00 31 20 550 22 00

Van Sabben Poster Auctions, PO Box 2065, 1620 EB Hoorn Tel: 31 229 268203 uboersma@sabbenposterauctions.nl www.vsabbenposterauctions.nl

Singapore

Christie's, Unit 3 Park Lane, Goodwood Park Hotel, 22 Scotts Road Tel: (65) 235 3828

Sotheby's (Singapore) Pte Ltd, 1 Cuscaden Road, 01-01 The Regent Tel: (65) 732 8239

Sweden

Bukowskis, Arsenalsgatan 4, Stockholm - SE111 47 Tel: 00 46 (0)8 614 08 00 info@bukowskis.se www.bukowskis.se

Switzerland

Christie's (International) S.A., 8 Place de la Taconnerie, 1204 Geneva Tel: 00 4122 319 1766

Phillips, Kreuzstrasse 54, 8008 Zurich Tel: 00 41 1 254 2400

Phillips Geneva, 9 rue Ami-Levrier, CH-1201 Geneva Tel: 00 41 22 738 0707

Sotheby's, 13 Quai du Mont Blanc, Geneva CH-1201 Tel: 00 41 22 908 4800

Sotheby's Zurich, Gessneralee 1, CH-8021 Zurich Tel: 00 41 1 226 2200

U.S.A.

Frank H Boos Gallery, 420 Enterprise Court, Bloomfield Hills, Michigan 48302 Tel: 001 248 332 1500

Butterfields, 220 San Bruno Avenue, San Francisco CA 94103 Tel: 00 1 415 861 7500

Butterfields, 7601 Sunset Boulevard, Los Angeles CA 90046 Tel: 00 1 323 850 7500

Braswell Galleries, 125 West Ave, Norwalk CT06854 Tel: 001 203 899 7420

Butterfields, 441 W. Huron Street, Chicago IL 60610 Tel: 00 1 312 377 7500

Christie, Manson & Woods International Inc., 502 Park Avenue, (including Christie's East), New York 10022 Tel: 001 212 636 2000

Christie's East, 219 East 67th Street, New York NY10021 Tel: 001 212 606 0400

William Doyle Galleries, 175 East 87th Street, New York 10128 Tel: 212 427 2730

Du Mouchelles, 409 East Jefferson, Detroit, Michigan 48226 Tel: 001 313 963 6255

Eldred's, Robert C Eldred Co Inc, 1475 Route 6A, East Dennis, Massachusetts 0796 02641 Tel: 00 1 508 385 311

Freeman Fine Art Of Philadelphia Inc Philadelphia PA 19103 Tel: 001 215 563 9275The Great Atlantic Auction Company, 2 Harris & Main Street, Putnam CT 06260 Tel: 001 860 963 2234 www.thegreatatlanticauction.com

Gene Harris Antique Auction Center, 203 S. 18th Avenue, PO Box 476, Marshalltown, Iowa 50158 Tel: 641 752 0600 geneharris@geneharrisauctions.com geneharrisauctions.com

Hunt Auctions, 75 E. Uwchlan Avenue, Suite 130, Exton, Pennsylvania 19341 Tel: 001 610 524 0822 info@huntauctions.com www.huntauctions.com

Randy Inman Auctions Inc, PO Box 726, Waterville, Maine 04903-0726 Tel: 001 207 872 6900 inman@inmanauctions.com www.inmanauctions.com

James D. Julia Inc, Route 201, Skowhegan Road, Fairfield ME 04937 Tel: (207) 453 7125 www.juliaauctions.com

Jackson's Auctioneers & Appraise IA 50613 Tel: 00 1 319 277 Joy Luke, The Gallery, 300E Grove Street, Bloomington IL 61701 Tel: 001 309 828 5533 joyluke@aol.com www.joyluke.com

MastroNet, Inc, 1515 W.22nd Street, Suite 125, Oak Brook, Illinois 60523 Tel: 001 630 472 1200 lauraharden@mastronet.com www.mastronet.com

Paul McInnis Inc Auction Gallery, 21, Rockrimmon Road, Northampton, New Hampshire 03862-2336 Tel: 001 603 964 1301

New Orleans Auction Galleries, Inc, 801 Magazine Street, AT 510 Julia, New Orleans, Louisiana 70130 Tel: 00 1 504 566 1849

Northeast Auctions, 93 Pleasant St, Portsmouth NH 03810-4504 Tel: 001 603 433 8400 neacat@ttlc.net

Phillips New York, 406 East 79th Street, New York NY10021 Tel: 00 1 212 570 4830

R. O. Schmitt Fine Art, Box 1941, Salem, New Hampshire 03079 Tel: 603 893 5915 bob@roschmittfinearts.com www.antiqueclockauction.com

Skinner Inc, 357 Main Street, Bolton MA 01740 Tel: 00 1 978 779 6241

Skinner Inc, The Heritage On The Garden, 63 Park Plaza, Boston MA 02116 Tel: 001 617 350 5400

Sloan's Auctioneers & Appraisers, 4920 Wyaconda Road, North Bethesda MD 20852 Tel: 00 1 301 468 4911/800 649 5066 www.sloansauction.com

Sloan's Auctioneers & Appraisers, 2516 Ponce de Leon Boulevard, Coral Gables, Florida 33134 Tel: 305 447 0757 www.sloansauction.com

Sotheby's, 1334 York Avenue, New York NY 10021 Tel: 00 1 212 606 7000

Sotheby's, 9665 Wilshire Boulevard, Beverly Hills, California 90212 Tel: (310) 274 0340

Sotheby's, 215 West Ohio Street, Chicago, Illinois 60610 Tel: 00 1 312 670 0010

Swann Galleries,Inc, 104 East 25th Street, New York 10010 Tel: 00 1 212 2544710

Treadway Gallery, Inc and John Toomey Gallery, Treadway Gallery, Inc, 2029 Madison Road, Cincinnati, Ohio 45208 Tel: 001 513 321 6742 www.treadwaygallery.com

Wolfs Gallery, 1239 W 6th Street, Cleveland OH 44113 Tel: 216 575 9653

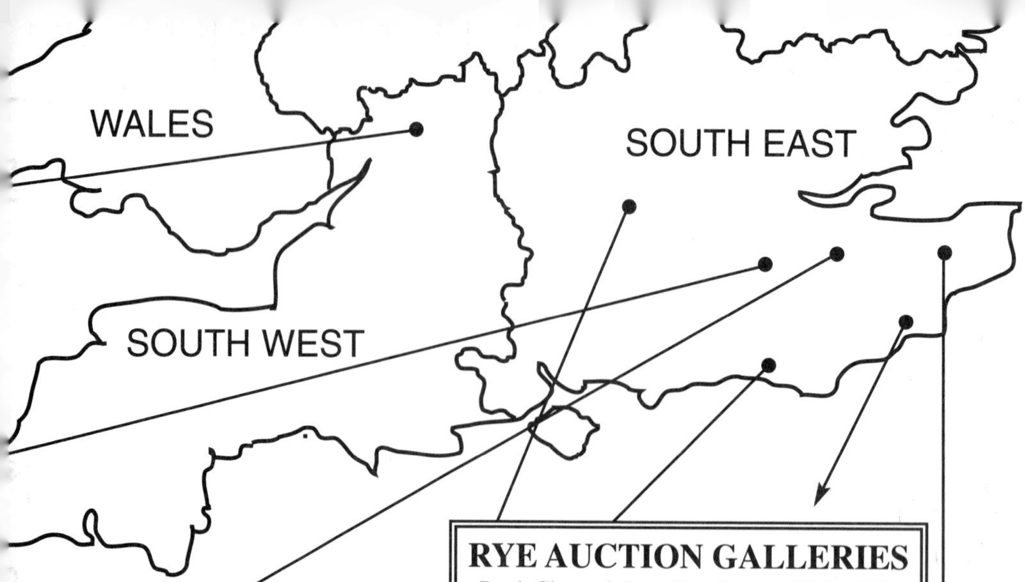

WALES
SOUTH EAST
SOUTH WEST

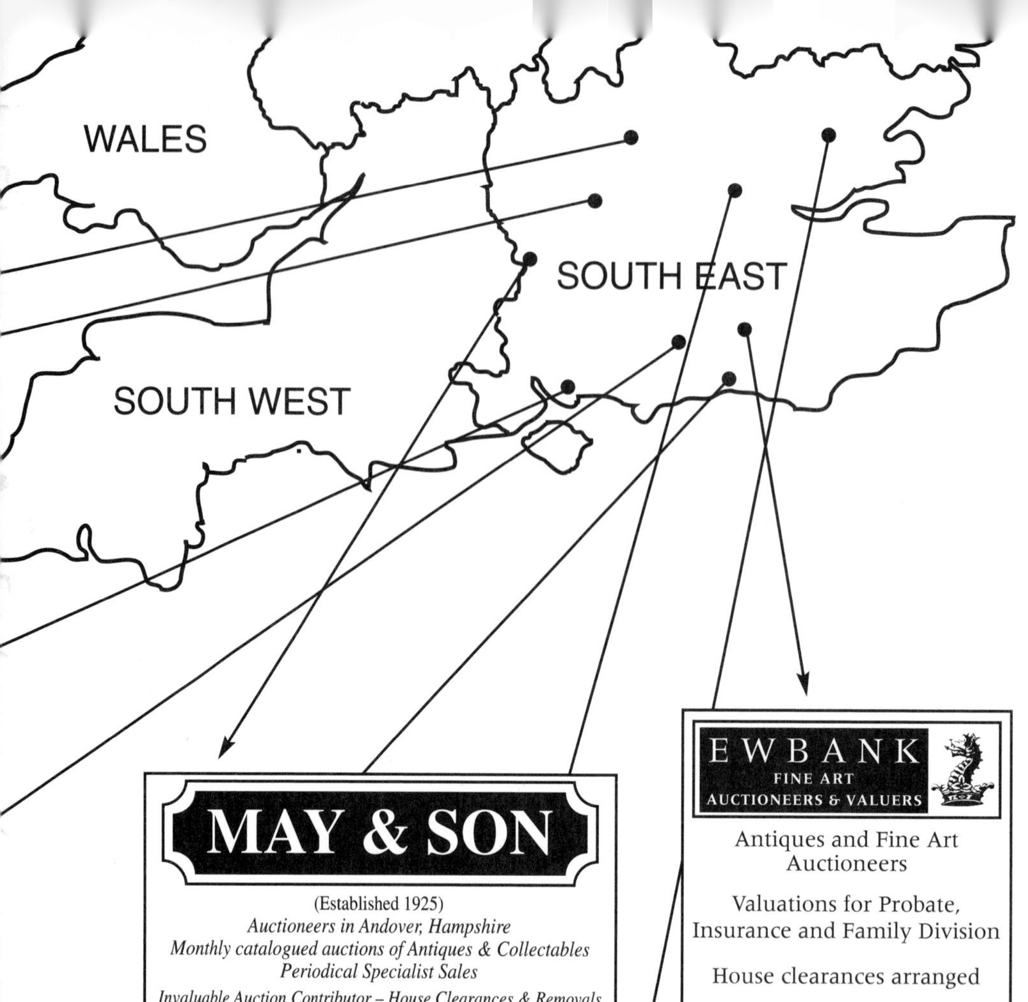
WALES
SOUTH EAST
SOUTH WEST

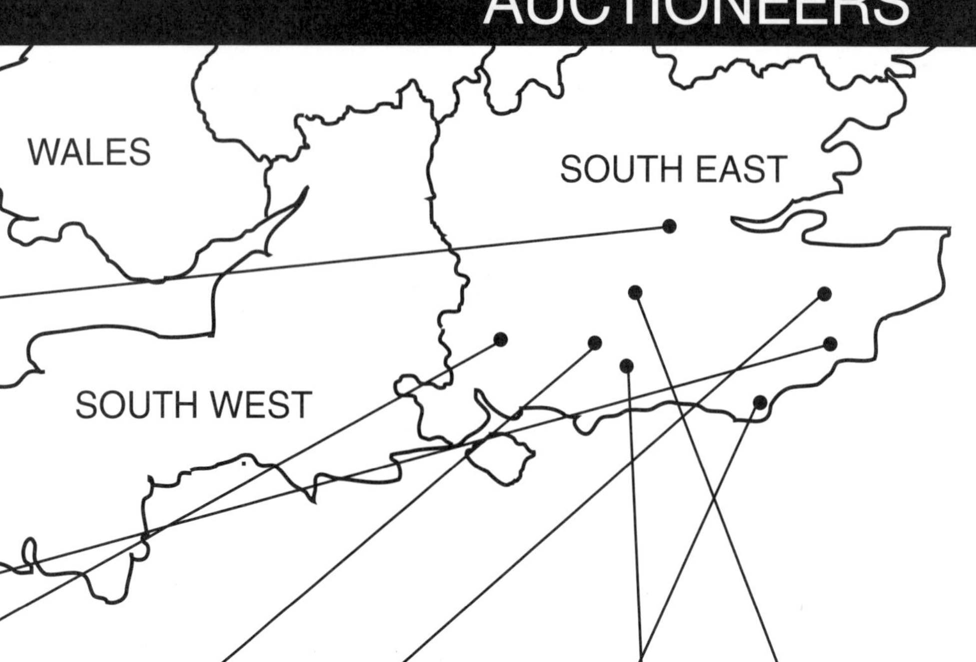

The Fine Art Auction Group
BRACKETTS
• AUCTIONEERS •

AUCTIONS AT TUNBRIDGE WELLS

Bi-monthly 2 day Antique Sales including Fine Furniture & Clocks, Ceramics & Glass, Prints Paintings & Books, Silver & Jewellery, Specialist & Tunbridge Ware

Fortnightly General Sales
Valuations for Probate, Insurance and Family Division

01892 544500

Auction Hall, The Pantiles
Tunbridge Wells, Kent TN2 5QL
www.bfaa.co.uk

P.F. WINDIBANK
FINE ART AUCTIONEERS AND VALUERS

The Dorking Halls,
Reigate Road, Dorking,
Surrey RH4 1SG

Tel: 01306 884556/876280
Fax: 01306 884669
Email: sjw@windibank.co.uk
Website: www.windibank.co.uk

Established 1945

Auctions at EASTBOURNE

Bi-monthly two-day Antique Sales including Fine Furniture & Clocks, Ceramics & Glass, Prints, Paintings & Books, Silver & Jewellery

Fortnightly General Sales

Valuations for Probate, Insurance & Family Division

01323 410419

The Fine Art Auction Group
EDGAR HORNS
• AUCTIONEERS •

46-50 South Street
Eastbourne, East Sussex
www.edgarhorns.com

RUPERT TOOVEY
AUCTIONEERS & VALUERS

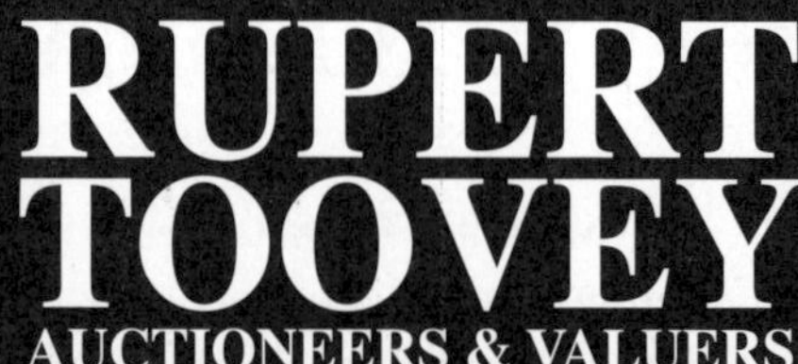

Professional Members of the Royal Institution of Chartered Surveyors

STAR ROAD
PARTRIDGE GREEN
WEST SUSSEX RH13 8RA
01403-711744
www.rupert-toovey.com

We are moving to new premises towards the end of 2002 ~ please ring or check our website for details.

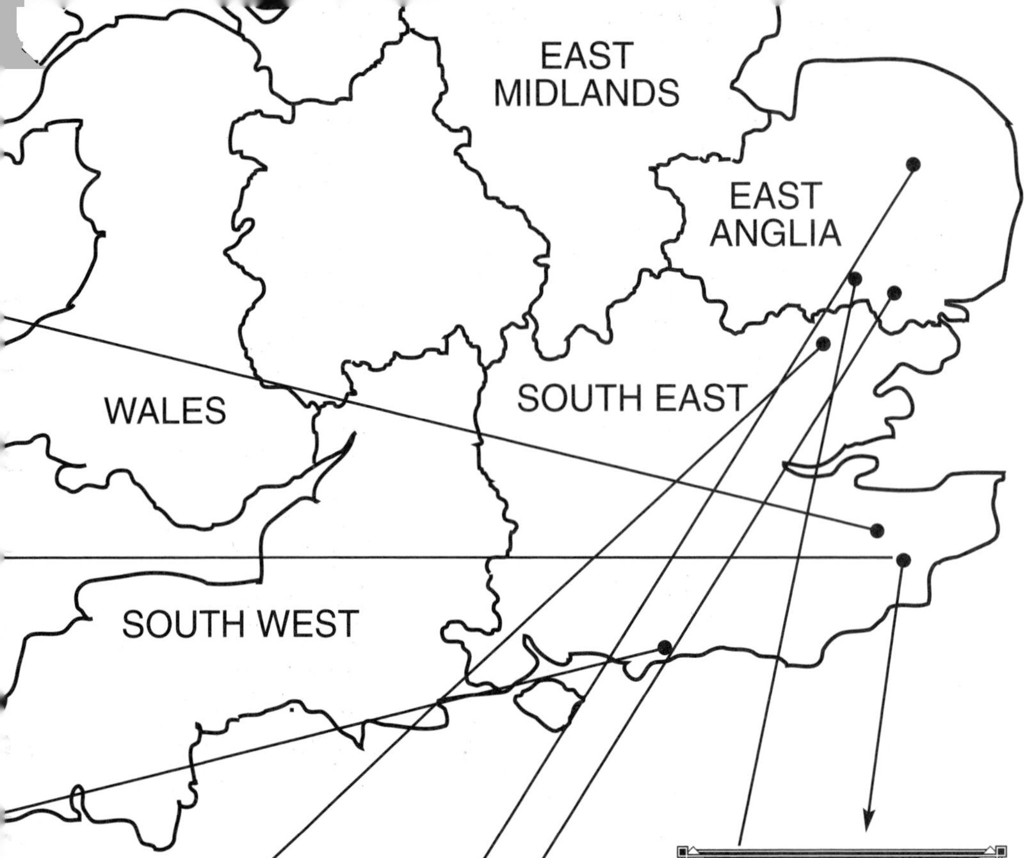

EAST
MIDLANDS
EAST
ANGLIA
WALES
SOUTH EAST
SOUTH WEST

WALES

SOUTH EAST

SOUTH WEST

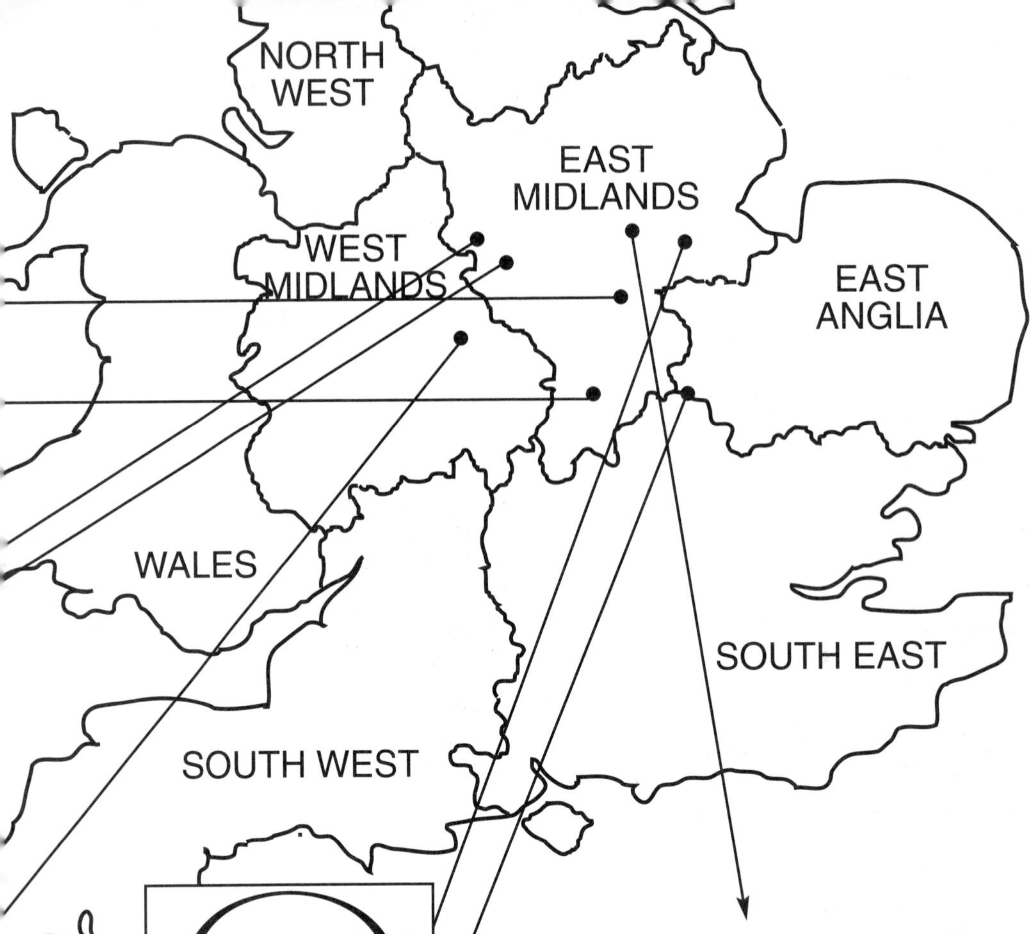

NORTH WEST
EAST MIDLANDS
WEST MIDLANDS
EAST ANGLIA
WALES
SOUTH EAST
SOUTH WEST

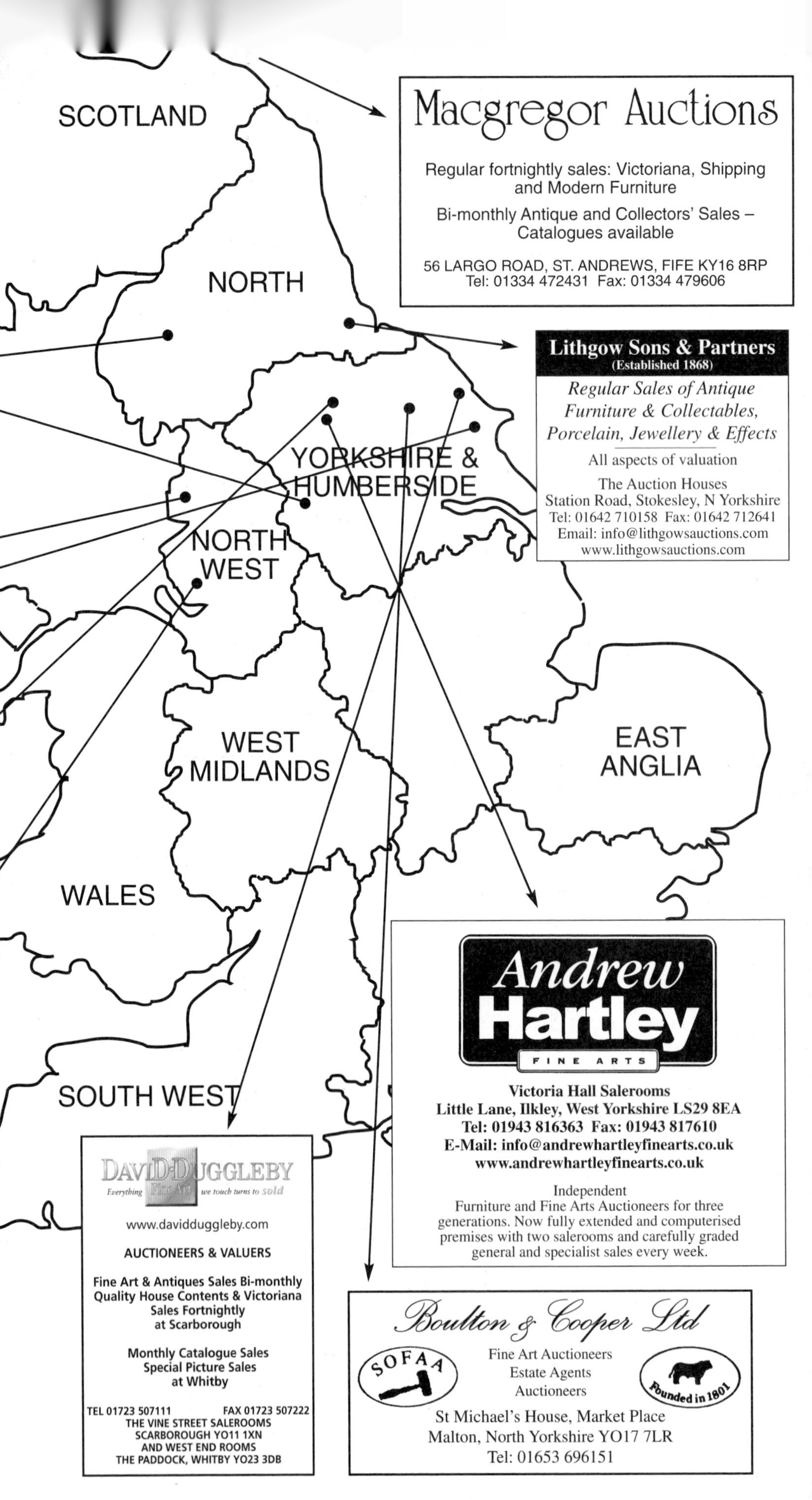

SCOTLAND
NORTH
YORKSHIRE & HUMBERSIDE
NORTH WEST
WEST MIDLANDS
EAST ANGLIA
WALES
SOUTH WEST
Macgregor Auctions
Regular fortnightly sales: Victoriana, Shipping and Modern Furniture
Bi-monthly Antique and Collectors' Sales – Catalogues available
56 LARGO ROAD, ST. ANDREWS, FIFE KY16 8RP
Tel: 01334 472431 Fax: 01334 479606
Lithgow Sons & Partners
(Established 1868)
Regular Sales of Antique Furniture & Collectables, Porcelain, Jewellery & Effects
All aspects of valuation
The Auction Houses
Station Road, Stokesley, N Yorkshire
Tel: 01642 710158 Fax: 01642 712641
Email: info@lithgowsauctions.com
www.lithgowsauctions.com
Andrew Hartley
FINE ARTS
Victoria Hall Salerooms
Little Lane, Ilkley, West Yorkshire LS29 8EA
Tel: 01943 816363 Fax: 01943 817610
E-Mail: info@andrewhartleyfinearts.co.uk
www.andrewhartleyfinearts.co.uk
Independent
Furniture and Fine Arts Auctioneers for three generations. Now fully extended and computerised premises with two salerooms and carefully graded general and specialist sales every week.
DAVID DUGGLEBY
Everything Fine Art we touch turns to sold
www.davidduggleby.com
AUCTIONEERS & VALUERS
Fine Art & Antiques Sales Bi-monthly
Quality House Contents & Victoriana Sales Fortnightly
at Scarborough
Monthly Catalogue Sales
Special Picture Sales
at Whitby
TEL 01723 507111 FAX 01723 507222
THE VINE STREET SALEROOMS
SCARBOROUGH YO11 1XN
AND WEST END ROOMS
THE PADDOCK, WHITBY YO23 3DB
Boulton & Cooper Ltd
SOFAA
Fine Art Auctioneers
Estate Agents
Auctioneers
Founded in 1801
St Michael's House, Market Place
Malton, North Yorkshire YO17 7LR
Tel: 01653 696151

NORTH WEST

EAST MIDLANDS

WEST MIDLANDS

WALES

SOUTH EAST

SOUTH WEST

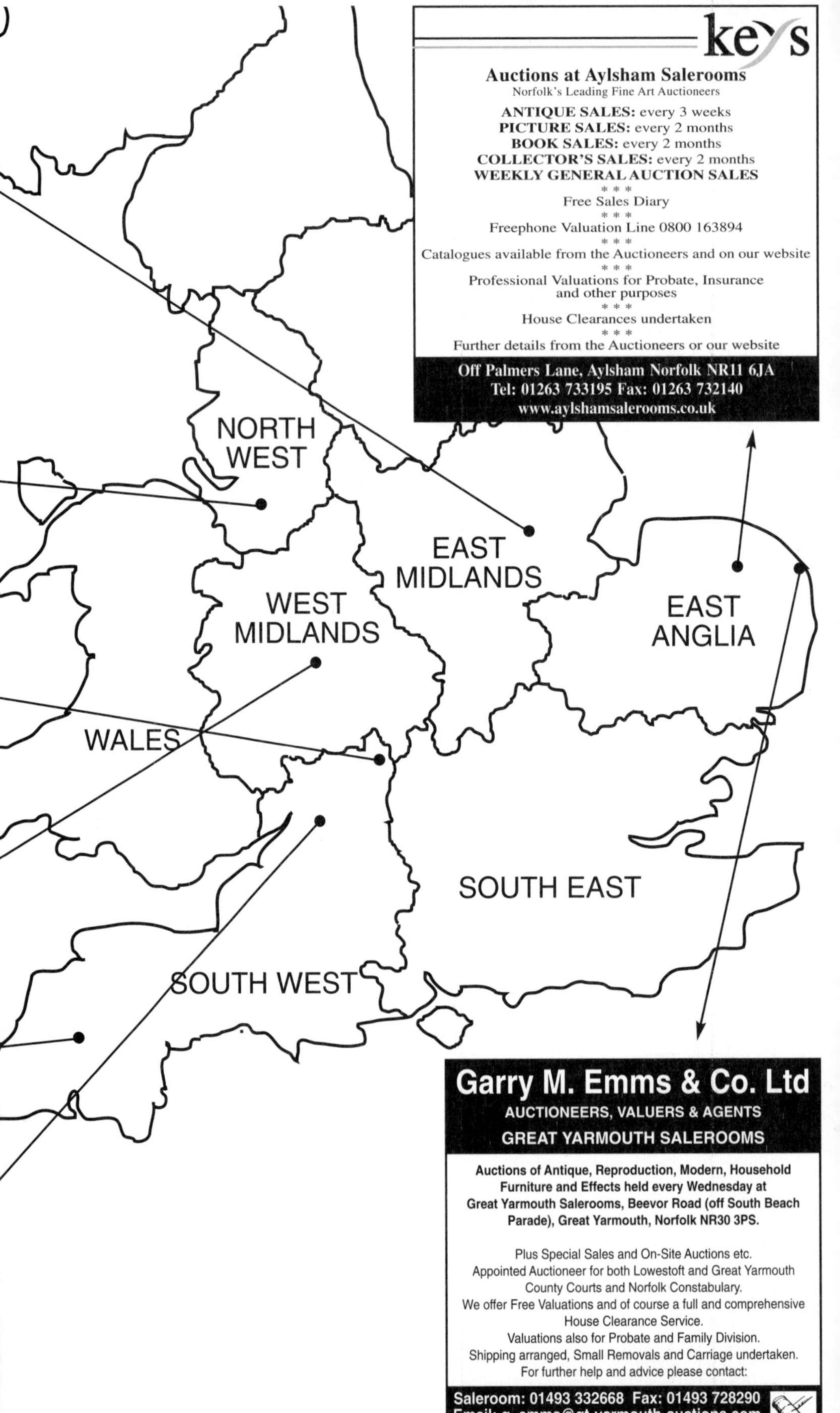

keys
Auctions at Aylsham Salerooms
Norfolk's Leading Fine Art Auctioneers
ANTIQUE SALES: every 3 weeks
PICTURE SALES: every 2 months
BOOK SALES: every 2 months
COLLECTOR'S SALES: every 2 months
WEEKLY GENERAL AUCTION SALES
Free Sales Diary
Freephone Valuation Line 0800 163894
Catalogues available from the Auctioneers and on our website
Professional Valuations for Probate, Insurance and other purposes
House Clearances undertaken
Further details from the Auctioneers or our website
Off Palmers Lane, Aylsham Norfolk NR11 6JA
Tel: 01263 733195 Fax: 01263 732140
www.aylshamsalerooms.co.uk
NORTH WEST
EAST MIDLANDS
WEST MIDLANDS
EAST ANGLIA
WALES
SOUTH EAST
SOUTH WEST
Garry M. Emms & Co. Ltd
AUCTIONEERS, VALUERS & AGENTS
GREAT YARMOUTH SALEROOMS
Auctions of Antique, Reproduction, Modern, Household Furniture and Effects held every Wednesday at Great Yarmouth Salerooms, Beevor Road (off South Beach Parade), Great Yarmouth, Norfolk NR30 3PS.
Plus Special Sales and On-Site Auctions etc.
Appointed Auctioneer for both Lowestoft and Great Yarmouth County Courts and Norfolk Constabulary.
We offer Free Valuations and of course a full and comprehensive House Clearance Service.
Valuations also for Probate and Family Division.
Shipping arranged, Small Removals and Carriage undertaken.
For further help and advice please contact:
Saleroom: 01493 332668 Fax: 01493 728290
Email: g_emms@gt-yarmouth-auctions.com
www.gt-yarmouth-auctions.com

Key to Illustrations

Each illustration and descriptive caption is accompanied by a letter code. By referring to the following list of auctioneers (denoted by *) and dealers (•) the source of any item may be immediately determined. Inclusion in this edition in no way constitutes or implies a contract or binding offer on the part of any of our contributors to supply or sell the goods illustrated, or similar articles, at the prices stated. Advertisers in this year's directory are denoted by †.

If you require a valuation for an item, it is advisable to check whether the dealer or specialist will carry out this service and if there is a charge. Please mention Miller's when making an enquiry. Having found a specialist who will carry out your valuation it is best to send a photograph and description of the item to the specialist together with a stamped addressed envelope for the reply. A valuation by telephone is not possible.

Most dealers are only too happy to help you with your enquiry; however, they are very busy people and consideration of the above points would be welcomed.

AAR *† Amersham Auction Rooms, 125 Station Road, Amersham, Buckinghamshire HP7 0AH Tel: 01494 729292

ACO • Angela & Clive Oliver, 68 Watergate Street, Chester CH1 2LA Tel: 01244 312306/335157

AdA •† Adams Antiques, Churche's Mansion, 150 Hospital Street, Nantwich, Cheshire CW5 5RY Tel: 01270 625643/07901 855200

AEF • A & E Foster, Buckinghamshire Tel: 01494 562024

AEL • Argyll Etkin Ltd, 1–9 Hills Place, Oxford Circus, London W1F 7SA Tel: 020 7437 7800 philatelists@argyll-etkin.com www.argyll-etkin.com

AG * Anderson & Garland (Auctioneers), Marlborough House, Marlborough Crescent, Newcastle-upon-Tyne, Tyne & Wear NE1 4EE Tel: 0191 232 6278

AGR • Anthony Green Antiques, Unit 39, The Bond Street Antique Centre, 124 New Bond Street, London W1S 1DX Tel: 020 7409 2854 vintagewatches@hotmail.com www.anthonygreen.com

AH *† Andrew Hartley, Victoria Hall Salerooms, Little Lane, Ilkley, Yorkshire LS29 8EA Tel: 01943 816363 info@andrewhartleyfinearts.co.uk www.andrewhartleyfinearts.co.uk

AKS •† Alan & Kathy Stacey. Appointment only Tel: 01963 441333 sales@antiqueboxes.uk.com www.antiqueboxes.uk.com

AL •† Ann Lingard, Ropewalk Antiques, Rye, East Sussex TN31 7NA Tel: 01797 223486 ann-lingard@ropewalkantiques.freeserve.co.uk

ALiN • Andrew Lineham Fine Glass, The Mall, Camden Passage, London N1 8ED Tel: 020 7704 0195 wed & sat 01243 576241 Mobile: 07767 702722 andrew@andrewlineham.co.uk www.andrewlineham.co.uk

ALS •† Allan Smith Clocks, Amity Cottage, 162 Beechcroft Road, Upper Stratton, Swindon, Wiltshire SN2 7QE Tel/Fax: 01793 822977 Mobile: 07778 834342 allansmithclocks@lineone.net www.allan-smith-antique-clocks.co.uk

AMC • Amelie Caswell Tel: 0117 9077960

AMH • Amherst Antiques, Monomark House, 27 Old Gloucester Street, London WC1N 3XX Mobile: 07850 350212 amherstantiques@monomark.co.uk

AMR • Amron Antiques Tel: 01782 566895

AMS • Andy & Margaret Shannan, 28 Plymouth Road, Buckfastleigh, Devon TQ11 0DB Tel: 01364 644624 Mobile: 07971 590395

ANA * Anthemion Auctions, 2 Llandough Trading Park, Penarth Road, Cardiff, Wales CF11 8RR Tel: 029 2071 2608

ANG •† Ancient & Gothic Tel: 01202 431721

APC • Antique Photographic Company Ltd Tel: 01949 842192 alpaco47@aol.com

APO •† Apollo Antiques Ltd, The Saltisford, Birmingham Road, Warwick, Warwickshire CV34 4TD Tel: 01926 494746/494666 www.apolloantiques.com

AQ • Antiquated, 10 New Street, Petworth, West Sussex GU28 0AS Tel: 01798 344011

ARB • Arbour Antiques Ltd, Poet's Arbour, Sheep Street, Stratford-on-Avon, Warwickshire CV37 6EF Tel: 01789 293453

ART •† Artemis Decorative Arts Ltd, 36 Kensington Church Street, London W8 4BX Tel/Fax: 020 7376 0377 Artemis.w8@btinternet.com www.artemisdecorativearts.com

ASA •† A. S. Antiques, 26 Broad Street, Pendleton, Salford, Greater Manchester M6 5BY Tel: 0161 737 5938 Mobile: 07836 368230 as@sternshine.demon.co.uk

ASB • Andrew Spencer Bottomley, The Coach House, Thongs Bridge, Holmfirth, Yorkshire HD7 2TT Tel: 01484 685234 andrewbottomley@compuserve.com

ASH •† Ashburton Marbles, Great Hall, North Street, Ashburton, Devon TQ13 7QD Tel & Fax: 01364 653189 enquiries@adrianager.co.uk www.adrianager.co.uk

AUTO • Automatomania, Stand 124, Grays Antique Market, 58 Davies Street, London W1K 5LP Tel: 020 7495 5259 Mobile: 07790 719097 magic@automatomania.com www.automatomania.com

AW •† Alan Walker, Halfway Manor, Halfway, Nr Newbury, Berkshire RG20 8NR Tel/Fax: 01488 657670 Mobile: 07770 728397 www.alanwalker-barometers.com

B(B) * Bonhams, 1 Old King Street, Bath, Somerset BA1 2JT Tel: 01225 788 988

B(Ba) * Bonhams, 10 Salem Road, Bayswater, London W2 4DL Tel: 020 7313 2700 www.phillips-auctions.com

B(E) * Bonhams, 38/39 Southernhay East, Exeter, Devon EX1 1PE Tel: 01392 455 955

B(EA) * Bonhams, 32 Boss Hall Road, Ipswich, Suffolk IP1 5DJ Tel: 01473 740494

B(Ed) * Bonhams, 65 George Street, Edinburgh, Scotland EH2 2JL Tel: 0131 225 2266

B(L) * Bonhams, 17a East Parade, Leeds, Yorkshire LS1 2BH Tel: 0113 2448011

B(NW) * Bonhams, New House, 150 Christleton Road, Chester, Cheshire CH3 5TD Tel: 01244 313936

B(O) * Bonhams, 39 Park End Street, Oxford, Oxfordshire OX1 1JD Tel: 01865 723524

B(S) * Bonhams, 49 London Road, Sevenoaks, Kent TN13 1AR Tel: 01732 740310

B(WM) * Bonhams, The Old House, Station Road, Knowle, Solihull, West Midlands B93 0HT Tel: 01564 776151

B&L * Bonhams and Langlois, Westaway Chambers, 39 Don Street, St Helier, Jersey, Channel Islands JE2 4TR Tel: 01534 722441

B&R •† Bread & Roses, Durham House Antique Centre, Sheep Street, Stow on the Wold, Gloucestershire GL54 1AA Tel: 01926 817342/01451 870404

B *† Bonhams, 101 New Bond Street, London W1S 1SR Tel: 020 7629 6602 www.bonhams.com

BAG * Boldon Auction Galleries, 24a Front Street, East Boldon, Tyne & Wear NE36 0SJ Tel: 0191 537 2630

BaN •† Barbara Ann Newman, London House Antiques, 4 Market Square, Westerham, Kent TN16 1AW Tel: 01959 564479 Mobile: 07850 016729

BAY • George Bayntun, Manvers Street, Bath, Somerset BA1 1JW Tel: 01225 466000 EBayntun@aol.com

BB(S) * Butterfields, 220 San Bruno Avenue, San Francisco CA 94103, U.S.A. Tel: 00 1 415 861 7500

BBA *† Bloomsbury Book Auctions, 3 & 4 Hardwick Street, Off Rosebery Avenue, London EC1R 4RY Tel: 020 7833 2636/7 & 0207923 6940 info@bloomsbury-book-auct.com www.bloomsbury-book-auct.com

BBo • Bazaar Boxes Tel: 01992 504 454 Mobile: 07970 909 206 bazaarboxes@hotmail.com

BBR * BBR, Elsecar Heritage Centre, Wath Road, Elsecar, Barnsley, Yorkshire S74 8HJ Tel: 01226 745156 www.onlinebbr.com

Bea(E) * Bearnes, St Edmund's Court, Okehampton Street, Exeter, Devon EX4 1DU Tel: 01392 422800

Beb • Bebes et Jouets, c/o Post Office, Edinburgh, Scotland EH7 6HW Tel: 0131 332 5650 Mobile: 0771 4374995 bebesetjouets@u.genie.co.uk you.genie.co.uk/bebesetjouets

BeE • Belle Epoque, 14 Herbert Street, Dublin 2, Republic of Ireland Tel: 07973 371909

BeF • Bevan Fine Art, PO Box 60, Uckfield, East Sussex TN22 1ZD Tel: 01825 766649 Mobile: 07711 262022 bevanfineart@quista.net

BELL •† Bellhouse Antiques Tel/Fax: 01268 710415 Bellhouse.antiques@virgin.net

BERA •† Berry Antiques, 3 High Street, Moreton in Marsh, Gloucestershire GL56 0AH Tel: 01608 652929 chris@berryantiques.com berryantiques.com berryantiques.co.uk

BERN * Bernaerts, Verlatstraat 18–22, 2000 Antwerpen/Anvers Tel: +32 (0)3 248 19 21 edmond.bernaerts@ping.be www.auction-bernaerts.com

BES • Bear Steps Antiques, Fish Street, Shrewsbury, Shropshire SY1 1UR Tel: 01743 344298/ 07720 675813 englishporcelain@aol.com www.bear-steps-antiques.co.uk

BEV • Beverley, 30 Church Street, Marylebone, London NW8 8EP Tel: 020 7262 1576

BEX •† Daniel Bexfield, 26 Burlington Arcade, London W1J 0PU Tel: 020 7491 1720 antiques@bexfield.co.uk www.bexfield.co.uk

BHa •† Judy & Brian Harden Antiques, PO Box 14, Bourton on the Water, Cheltenham, Gloucestershire GL54 2YR Tel/Fax: 01451 810684 Mobile: 07831 692252 harden@portraitminiatures.co.uk harden@meissenfigures.co.uk www.portraitminiatures.co.uk www.meissen.co.uk

BLH * Ambrose, Ambrose House, Old Station Road, Loughton, Essex IG10 4PE Tel: 020 8502 3951

BMi • Bobbie Middleton, 58 Long Street, Tetbury, Gloucestershire GL8 8AQ Tel: 01666 502761 Mob: 07774 192660 bobbiemiddleton@lineone.net

Bns •† Brittons Jewellers, 4 King Street, Clitheroe, Lancashire BB7 2EP Tel: 01200 425555 info@brittons-watches.co.uk www.brittons-watches.co.uk www.antique-jewelry.co.uk

BoC • Bounty Antiques Centre, 76 Fore Street, Topsham, Devon EX3 0HQ Tel: 01392 875007 Mobile: 07939 526504

Bon *† Bonhams, Montpelier Street, Knightsbridge, London SW7 1HH Tel: 020 7393 3900 www.bonhams.com

Bon(C) * Bonhams, 65–69 Lots Road, Chelsea, London SW10 0RN Tel: 020 7393 3900 www.bonhams.com

Bon(W) * Bonhams, Dowell Street, Honiton, Devon EX14 8LX Tel: 01404 41872

BONN • Bonnons Antique Glass Tel: 02380 273900 www.bonnonsantiqueglass.co.uk

BR *† Bracketts, Auction Hall, Pantiles, Tunbridge Wells Kent TN1 1UU Tel: 01892 544500 www.bfaa.co.uk

BRG • Brandler Galleries, 1 Coptfold Road, Brentwood, Essex CM14 4BN Tel: 01277 222269 john@brandler-galleries.com www.brandler-galleries.com

BrH • Bright Helm Antiques & Interiors, 40 Sydney Street, Brighton, East Sussex BN1 4EP Tel: 01273 572059 Mobile: 07973 558051 www.sexualpine.co.uk

Bri *† Bristol Auction Rooms, St John's Place, Apsley Road, Clifton, Bristol, Gloucestershire BS8 2ST Tel: 0117 973 7201 www.bristolauctionrooms.com

BRU • Brunel Antiques, Bartlett Street Antiques Centre, Bath, Somerset BA1 2QZ Tel: 0117 968 1734

BrW • Brian Watson Antique Glass BY APPOINTMENT, Foxwarren Cottage, High Street, Marsham, Norwich, Norfolk NR10 5QA Tel: 01263 732519

BUK * Bukowskis, Arsenalsgatan 4, Stockholm, Sweden-SE111 47 Tel: 00 46 (0)8 614 08 00 info@bukowskis.se www.bukowskis.se

BWe *† Biddle and Webb of Birmingham, Ladywood Middleway, Birmingham, West Midlands B16 0PP Tel: 0121 455 8042 antiques@biddleandwebb.freeserve.co.uk

Byl • Bygones of Ireland Ltd, Lodge Road, Westport, County Mayo, Republic of Ireland Tel: 00 353 98 26132/25701

C&A •† Campbell & Archard Ltd, Lychgate House, Church Street, Seal, Kent TN15 0AR Tel: 01732 761153 campbellarchard@btclick.com www.campbellandarchard.co.uk

C&R •† Catchpole & Rye, Saracens Dairy, Jobbs Lane, Pluckley, Ashford, Kent TN27 0SA Tel: 01233 840840 info@crye.co.uk www.crye.co.uk

CAG *† The Canterbury Auction Galleries, 40 Station Road West, Canterbury, Kent CT2 8AN Tel: 01227 763337 canterbury_auction_galleries@compuserve.com www.thecanterburyauctiongalleries.com

CAL • Cedar Antiques Ltd, High Street, Hartley Wintney, Hampshire RG27 8NY Tel: 01252 843222 or 01189 326628

CAT • Lennox Cato, 1 The Square, Church Street, Edenbridge, Kent TN8 5BD Tel: 01732 865988 Mobile: 07836 233473 cato@lennoxcato.com www.lennoxcato.com

CAV • Rupert Cavendish Antiques, 610 King's Road, London SW6 2DX Tel: 020 7731 7041 www.rupertcavendish.co.uk

CB • Christine Bridge, 78 Castelnau, London SW13 9EX Tel: 07000 445277

CBGR • Chris Baker Gramophones, All Our Yesterdays, 3 Cattle Market, Sandwich, Kent CT13 9AE Tel: 01304 614756 or 614756 cbgramophones@aol.com

CBO • The Chaucer Bookshop, 6–7 Beer Cart Lane, Canterbury, Kent CT1 2NY Tel: 01227 453912 chaucerbooks@canterbury.dialnet.com www.chaucer-bookshop.co.uk/main.html

CBP *† Comic Book Postal Auctions Ltd, 40–42 Osnaburgh Street, London NW1 3ND Tel: 020 7424 0007 comicbook@compuserve.com www.compalcomics.com

CDC * Capes Dunn & Co, The Auction Galleries, 38 Charles Street, Off Princess Street, Greater Manchester M1 7DB Tel: 0161 273 6060/1911

CG • The Canon Gallery, New Street, Petworth, West Sussex GU28 0AS Tel: 01798 344422

CGA •† Castlegate Antiques Centre, 55 Castlegate, Newark Nottinghamshire NG24 1BE Tel: 01636 700076 Mobile: 07860 843739

CGC * Cheffins, 2 Clifton Road, Cambridge, Cambridgeshire CB2 4BW Tel: 01223 213343 www.cheffins.co.uk

CHA • Chislehurst Antiques, 7 Royal Parade, Chislehurst, Kent BR7 6NR Tel: 020 8467 1530

ChC • Christopher Clarke, The Fosse Way, Stow-on-the-Wold, Gloucestershire GL54 1JS Tel: 01451 830476

CHE • Chelsea Clocks & Antiques, Stand H3–4, Antiquarius Market, 135 Kings Road, London SW3 4PW Tel: 020 7352 8646

CoA • Country Antiques (Wales), Castle Mill, Kidwelly, Carmarthenshire, Wales SA17 4UU Tel: 01554 890534

CoHA • Corner House Antiques and Ffoxe Antiques. By appointment Tel: 01793 762752 jdhis007@btopenworld

CrF • Crowdfree Antiques, PO Box 395, Bury St Edmunds, Suffolk IP31 2PG Tel: 0870 444 0791 info@crowdfree.com www.crowdfree.com

CTO •† Collector's Corner, PO Box 8, Congleton, Cheshire CW12 4GD Tel: 01260 270429 dave.popcorner@ukonline.co.uk

DA *† Dee, Atkinson & Harrison, The Exchange Saleroom, Driffield, Yorkshire YO25 6LD Tel: 01377 253151 exchange@dee-atkinson-harrison.co.uk www.dee-atkinson-harrison.co.uk

DAD • decorative arts @ doune, Scottish Antique and Arts Centre, Carse of Cambus, Doune, Perthshire, Scotland FK16 6HD Tel: 01786 461439 Mobile: 07778 475 974 decorativearts.doune@btinternet

DAN • Andrew Dando, 4 Wood Street, Queen Square, Bath, Somerset BA1 2JQ Tel: 01225 422702 www.andrewdando.co.uk

DD *† David Duggleby, The Vine St Salerooms, Scarborough, Yorkshire YO11 1XN Tel: 01723 507111 auctions@davidduggleby.freeserve.co.uk www.davidduggleby.com

DE • Decades, 20 Lord St West, Blackburn, Lancashire BB2 1JX Tel: 01254 693320

DeA • Delphi Antiques, Powerscourt Townhouse Centre, South William Street, Dublin 2, Republic of Ireland Tel: 00 353 1 679 0331

DeG • Denzil Grant, Suffolk Fine Arts, Drinkstone House, Drinkstone, Bury St. Edmunds, Suffolk IP30 9TG Tel: 01449 736576

Del • Delomosne & Son Ltd, Court Close, North Wraxall Chippenham, Wiltshire SN14 7AD Tel: 01225 891505

DFA •† Delvin Farm Antiques, Gormonston, Co Meath, Republic of Ireland Tel: 00 353 1 841 2285 info@delvinfarmpine.com john@delvinfarmpine.com www.delvinfarmpine.com

DHA • Durham House Antiques Centre, Sheep Street, Stow-on-the-Wold, Gloucestershire GL54 1AA Tel: 01451 870404

DHu • Diana Huntley Antiques, 8 Camden Passage, Islington, London N1 8ED Tel: 020 7226 4605 diana@dianahuntleyantiques.co.uk www.dianahuntleyantiques.co.uk

DID • Didier Antiques, 58–60 Kensington Church Street, London W8 4DB Tel: 020 7938 2537/078 36 232634

DJH •† David J Hansord & Son, 6 & 7 Castle Hill, Lincoln, Lincolnshire LN1 3AA Tel: 01522 530044 Mobile: 07831 183511

DLP •† The Dunlop Collection, P.O. Box 6269, Statesville, NC 28687 U.S.A. Tel: (704) 871 2626 or Toll Free Telephone (800) 227 1996

DMa • David March, Abbots Leigh, Bristol, Gloucestershire BS8 Tel: 0117 937 2422

DMC * Diamond Mills & Co, 117 Hamilton Road, Felixstowe, Suffolk IP11 7BL Tel: 01394 282281

DN * Dreweatt Neate, Donnington Priory, Donnington, Newbury, Berkshire RG14 2JE Tel: 01635 553553 fineart@dreweatt-neate.co.uk

DNo • Desmond & Amanda North, The Orchard, 86 Hale Street, East Peckham, Kent TN12 5JB Tel: 01622 871353

DNW * Dix-Noonan-Webb, 1 Old Bond Street, London W1S 4PB Tel: 020 7499 5022

DOA • Dorchester Antiques, 3 High Street, Dorchester-on-Thames, Oxfordshire OX10 7HH Tel: 01865 341 373

DOL • Dollectable, 53 Lower Bridge Street, Chester, Cheshire CH1 1RS Tel: 01244 344888/679195

DOR • Dorset Reclamation, Cow Drove, Bere Regis, Wareham, Dorset BH20 7JZ Tel: 01929 472200 info@dorsetrec.u-net.com www.dorset-reclamation.co.uk

DORO * Dorotheum Palais Dorotheum, A-1010 Wien, Dorotheergasse. 17, 1010 Austria Tel: 0043 1 515 60 354

DRG •† Dragonflies Antiques & Decorating Center, Frank & Cathy Sykes, New England Events Mgt., PO Box 678, 24 Center Street, Wolfeboro, New Hampshire 03894, U.S.A. Tel: 001 603 569 0000 Dragonflies@metrocast.net

DSG • Delf Stream Gallery, 14 New Street, Sandwich, Kent CT13 9AB Tel: 01304 617684 www.delfstreamgallery.com

DUK •† Dukeries Antiques Centre, Thoresby Park, Budby, Newark, Nottinghamshire NG22 9EX Tel: 01623 822252

DuM * Du Mouchelles, 409 East Jefferson, Detroit, Michigan 48226, U.S.A. Tel: 001 313 963 6255

DW *† Dominic Winter Book Auctions, The Old School, Maxwell Street, Swindon, Wiltshire SN1 5DR Tel: 01793 611340 info@dominicwinter.co.uk www.dominicwinter.co.uk

E *† Ewbank, Burnt Common Auction Rooms, London Road, Send, Woking, Surrey GU23 7LN Tel: 01483 223101 www.ewbankauctions.co.uk

EAL •† The Exeter Antique Lighting Co., Cellar 15, The Quay, Exeter, Devon EX2 4AP Tel: 01392 490848 Mobile: 07702 969438 www.antiquelightingcompany.com

EE • Empire Exchange, 1 Newton Street, Piccadilly, Manchester, Tel: 0161 2364445

EFA • Claudia Hill at Ellison Fine Art. By appointment only Tel: 01494 678880 Mobile: 077203 17899

EH *† Edgar Horns Fine Art Auctioneers, 46–50 South Street, Eastbourne, East Sussex BN21 4XB Tel: 01323 410419 www.edgarhorns.com

EP *† Evans & Partridge, Agriculture House, High Street, Stockbridge, Hampshire SO20 6HF Tel: 01264 810702

ESA • East Street Antiques, 42 East Street, Crewkerne, Somerset TA18 7AG Tel: 01460 78600

ETO • Eric Tombs, 62a West Street, Dorking, Surrey RH4 1BS Tel/Fax: 01306 743661 ertombs@aol.com

F • Freshfords, High Street, Freshford, Bath, Somerset BA3 6EF Tel: 01225 722111 Mobile: 07714 362 863 antiques@freshfords.com www.freshfords.com

F&C * Finan & Co, The Square, Mere, Wiltshire BA12 6DJ Tel: 01747 861411

F&F • Fenwick & Fenwick, 88–90 High Street, Broadway, Worcestershire WR12 7AJ Tel: 01386 53227/841724

FHF * Frank H Fellows & Sons, Augusta House, 19 Augusta Street, Hockley, Birmingham, West Midlands B18 6JA Tel: 0121 212 2131

FRY • Elizabeth Fry, The Bartlett Street Antiques Centre, Bath Tel: 07767 862733 liz@lizfry.co.uk www.lizfry.co.uk

FU • Fu Ts'ang Lung, Rotherham, Yorkshire Tel: 01709 829805 futsanglung@hotmail.com

G(B) * Gorringes Auction Galleries, Terminus Road, Bexhill-on-Sea, East Sussex TN39 3LR Tel: 01424 212994 bexhill@gorringes.co.uk www.gorringes.co.uk

G(L) * Gorringes inc Julian Dawson, 15 North Street, Lewes, East Sussex BN7 2PD Tel: 01273 472503 auctions@gorringes.co.uk www.gorringes.co.uk

G&CC •† Goss & Crested China Club & Museum, incorporating Milestone Publications, 62 Murray Road, Horndean, Hampshire PO8 9JL Tel: (023) 9259 7440 info@gosschinaclub.demon.co.uk www.gosscrestedchina.co.uk

G&H • Garret & Hazlehurst Mobile: 07976 247942 garhaz.com@btopenworld.com

GAA • Gabrian Antiques Tel: 01923 859675 gabrian.antiques@virgin.net

GAC • Gloucester Antiques Centre, The Historic Docks, 1 Severn Road, Gloucester, Gloucestershire GL1 2LE Tel: 01452 529716 www.antiques.center.com

GAK *† Keys, Aylsham Salerooms, Off Palmers Lane, Aylsham, Norfolk NR11 6JA Tel: 01263 733195 www.aylshamsalerooms.co.uk

Gam * Clarke Gammon, The Guildford Auction Rooms, Bedford Road, Guildford, Surrey GU1 4SJ Tel: 01483 880915

GBr • Geoffrey Breeze Antiques, 6 George Street, Bath, Somerset BA1 2EH Tel: 01225 466499

GD •† Gilbert & Dale Antiques, The Old Chapel, Church Street, Ilchester, Nr Yeovil, Somerset BA22 8ZA Tel: 01935 840464

GDO •† Gavin Douglas Fine Antique Ltd, 75 Portobello Road, London W11 2QB Tel: 01825 723441/ 0207 221 1121 Mobile: 07860 680521 gavin@antique-clocks.co.uk www.antique-clocks.co.uk

GH * Gardiner Houlgate, The Bath Auction Rooms, 9 Leafield Way, Corsham, Nr Bath, Somerset SN13 9SW Tel: 01225 812912 gardiner-houlgate.co.uk www.invaluable.com/gardiner-houlgate

GLa • Glassdrumman Antiques, 7 Union Square, The Pantiles, Tunbridge Wells, Kent TN4 8HE Tel: 01892 538615

GLD •† Glade Antiques, PO Box 939, Marlow, Buckinghamshire SL7 1SR Tel: 01628 487255 Mobile: 07771 552 328 sonia@gladeantiques.com www.gladeantiques.com

Gle * Glendining's (A division of Bonhams specialising in coins & medals), 101 New Bond Street, London W1S 1SR Tel: 020 7493 2445

GN •† Gillian Neale Antiques, PO Box 247, Aylesbury, Buckinghamshire HP20 1JZ Tel: 01296 423754/ 07860 638700 gillianneale@aol.com www.gillianneaeantiques.co.uk

GRG • Gordon Reece Galleries, Finkle Street, Knaresborough, Yorkshire HG5 8AA Tel: 01423 866219 www.gordonreecegalleries.com

GRI • Grimes House Antiques, High Street, Moreton-in-Marsh, Gloucestershire GL56 0AT Tel/Fax: 01608 651029 grimes_house@cix.co.uk grimeshouse.co.uk cranberryglass.co.uk

GS • Ged Selby Antique Glass. By appointment Tel: 01756 799673

GTM • Gloucester Toy Mart, Ground Floor, Antique Centre, Severn Road, Gloucester, Gloucestershire GL1 2LE Mobile: 07973 768452

GV •† Garth Vincent, The Old Manor House, Allington, Nr Grantham, Lincolnshire NG32 2DH Tel: 01400 281358 garthvincent@aol.com www.guns.uk.com

GWe • Graham Webb, 59 Ship Street, Brighton, East Sussex BN1 1AE Tel: 01273 321803

HA • Hallidays, The Old College, Dorchester- on-Thames, Oxfordshire OX10 7HL Tel: 01865 340028/68 Mobile: 07860 625917

Hal * Halls Fine Art Auctions, Welsh Bridge, Shrewsbury, Shropshire SY3 8LA Tel: 01743 231212

HAM *† Hamptons International, Baverstock House, 93 High Street, Godalming, Surrey GU7 1AL Tel: 01483 423567 fineartauctions@hamptons-int.com www.hamptons.co.uk/fineart

HCFA • Henry T Callan, 162 Quaker Meeting House Road, East Sandwich, MA 02537-1312, U.S.A. Tel: 508-888-5372

HEG • Stuart Heggie, 14 The Borough, Northgate, Canterbury, Kent CT1 2DR Tel: 01227 470422

HEL • Helios Gallery, 292 Westbourne Grove, London W11 2PS Tel: 077 11 955 997 heliosgallery@btinternet.com www.heliosgallery.cpm

Herm * Hermann Historica OHG, Postfach 201009, 80010 Munchen, Germany Tel: 00 49 89 5237296

HIS •† Erna Hiscock & John Shepherd, Chelsea Galleries, 69 Portobello Road, London W11 Tel: 01233 661407 Mobile: 0771 562 7273 erna@ernahiscockantiques.com www.ernahiscockantiques.com

HOA • Bob Hoare Antiques, Averys, Lewes/Uckfield Road (A26), Nr Ringmer, East Sussex Tel: 01273 814181 bob@antiquebob.demon.co.uk www.antiquebob.demon.co.uk

HOB • Hobday Toys Tel: 01895 636737 wendyhobday@freenet.co.uk

HOK * Hamilton Osborne King, 4 Main Street, Blackrock, Co. Dublin, Republic of Ireland Tel: 353 1 288 5011 blackrock@hok.ie www.hok.ie

HOLL *† Holloway's, 49 Parsons Street, Banbury, Oxfordshire OX16 5PF Tel: 01295 817777 enquiries@hollowaysauctioneers.co.uk www.hollowaysauctioneers.co.uk

HON • Honan's Antiques, Crowe Street, Gort, County Galway, Republic of Ireland Tel: 00 353 91 631407 www.honansantiques.com

HRQ •† Harlequin Antiques, 79–81 Mansfield Road, Daybrook, Nottingham, Nottinghamshire NG5 6BH Tel: 0115 967 4590 sales@antiquepine.net www.antiquepine.net

HUM • Humbleyard Fine Art, Unit 32 Admiral Vernon Arcade, Portobello Road, London W11 2DY Tel: 01362 637793 Mobile: 07836 349416

HUN • Huntercombe Manor Barn, Henley-on-Thames, Oxon, Oxfordshire RG9 5RY Tel: 01491 641349

HYD * Hy Duke & Son, Dorchester Fine Art Salerooms, Dorchester, Dorset DT1 1QS Tel: 01305 265080

ICO • Iconastas, 5 Piccadilly Arcade, London SW1 Tel: 020 7629 1433 iconastas@compuserve.com

IM *† Ibbett Mosely, 125 High Street, Sevenoaks, Kent TN13 1UT Tel: 01732 456731

IQ • Cloud Cuckooland, 12 Fore Street, Mevagissey, Cornwall PL26 6UQ Tel: 01726 842364 inkquest@dial.pipex.com www.inkquest.dial.pipex.com/

JAA *† Jackson's Auctioneers & Appraisers, 2229 Lincoln Street, Cedar Falls, IA 50613, U.S.A. Tel: 00 1 319 277 2256

JAK • Clive & Lynne Jackson Tel: 01242 254375 Mobile: 0410 239351

JAZZ • Jazz Art Deco Tel: 07721 032277 jazzartdeco@btinternet.com www.jazzartdeco.com

JBL • Judi Bland Tel: 01276 857576

JC • J Collins & Son, The Studio, 28 High Street, Bideford, Devon EX39 2AN Tel: 01237 473103

JF • Julia Foster. By appointment at 84 York Street, London W1H 1DP Tel: 07973 146610

JHa • Jeanette Hayhurst Fine Glass, 32a Kensington Church Street, London W8 4HA Tel: 020 7938 1539

JHo •† Jonathan Horne, 66 Kensington Church Street, London W8 4BY Tel: 020 7221 5658 JH@jonathanhorne.co.uk www.jonathanhorne.co.uk

JIL •† Jillings Antique Clocks, Croft House, 17 Church Street, Newent, Gloucestershire GL18 1PU Tel: 01531 822100 Mobile: 07973 830110 clocks@jillings.com www.Jillings.com

JJ • Jen Jones, Pontbrendu, LLanybydder, Ceredigion, Wales SA40 9UJ Tel: 01570 480610

JM *† Maxwells of Wilmslow inc Dockree's, 133A Woodford Road, Woodford, Cheshire SK7 1QD Tel/Fax: 0161 439 5182

JMC • J & M Collectables Tel: 01580 891657 jandmcollectables@tinyonline.co.uk

JNic * John Nicholson, The Auction Rooms, Longfield, Midhurst Road, Fernhurst, Surrey GU27 3HA Tel: 01428 653727

JOA • Joan Gale, Tombland Antiques Centre, 14 Tombland, Norwich, Norfolk NR3 1HF Tel: 01603 619129 joan.gale@ukgateway.net

JON • Jonkers, 24 Hart Street, Henley on Thames, Oxfordshire RG9 2AU Tel: 01491 576427 bromlea.jonkers@bjbooks.co.uk www.bjbooks.co.uk

JOP • Jonathan Potter Ltd, Antique Maps, 125 New Bond Street, London W1S 1DY Tel: 020 7491 3520 jpmaps@attglobal.net www.jpmaps.co.uk

JoV • Joe Vickers, Bartlett Street Antiques Market, Bath, Somerset BA1 2QZ Tel: 01225 466689

JPr • Joanna Proops Antique Textiles & Lighting, 34 Belvedere, Lansdown Hill, Bath, Somerset BA1 5HR Tel: 01225 310795 antiquetextiles@uk.online.co.uk www.antiquetextiles.co.uk

JRe • John Read, 29 Lark Rise, Martlesham Heath, Ipswich, Suffolk IP5 7SA Tel: 01473 624897

JSM • J & S. Millard Antiques, Assembly Antiques, 5–8 Saville Row, Bath, Somerset BA1 2QP Tel: 01225 469785

JuC • Julia Craig, Bartlett Street Antiques Centre, 5–10 Bartlett Street, Bath, Somerset BA1 2QZ Tel: 01225 448202/310457 Mobile: 07771 786846

JUP • Jupiter Antiques, P.O. Box 609, Rottingdean, East Sussex BN2 7FW Tel: 01273 302865

K&D •† Kembery Antique Clocks, Bartlett Street Antiques Centre, 5 Bartlett Street, Bath, Somerset BA1 2QZ Tel: 0117 956 5281/0850 623237 kembery@kdclocks.co.uk www.kdclocks.co.uk

KA • Kingston Antiques Centre, 29–31 London Road, Kingston-upon-Thames, Surrey KT2 6ND Tel: 020 8549 2004/3839 enquiries@kingstonantiquescentre.co.uk www.kingstonantiquescentre.co.uk

KHW • Keith Harding's World of Mechanical Music, The Oak House, High Street, Northleach, Gloucestershire GL54 3ET Tel: 01451 860181 keith@musicbox10.demon.co.uk www.mechanicalmusic.co.uk

KIE No longer trading

KOLN * Auction Team Koln, Postfach 50 11 19, 50971 Koln, Germany Tel: 00 49 0221 38 70 49 auction@breker.com

L * Lawrence Fine Art Auctioneers, South Street, Crewkerne, Somerset TA18 8AB Tel: 01460 73041

L(r) • LASSCO R. B. K., 41 Maltby Street, London SE1 3PA Tel: 020 7394 7788 www.lassco.co.uk

L(sm) • LASSCO St Michael's, Mark Street, London EC2A 4ER Tel: 020 7749 9944 www.lassco.co.uk

L&E * Locke & England, 18 Guy Street, Leamington Spa, Warwickshire CV32 4RT Tel: 01926 889100 www.auctions-online.com/locke

Lan • Lovejo Ann'tiques, PO Box 8289, Tamworth, West Midlands B79 9EE Tel: 01827 373254 Mobile: 07767 881161 joanne@lovejoanntiques.fsnet.co.uk

LAY * David Lay ASVA, Auction House, Alverton, Penzance, Cornwall TR18 4RE Tel: 01736 361414

LBO • Laura Bordignon Antiques, PO Box 6247, Finchingfield CM7 4ER Tel: 01371 811 791 Mobile: 07778 787929 laurabordignon@hotmail.com

LBr • Lynda Brine, Assembly Antiques Centre, 5–8 Saville Row, Bath, Somerset BA1 2QP Tel: 01225 448488 lyndabrine@yahoo.co.uk www.scentbottlesandsmalls.co.uk

LCC • The London Cigarette Card Co Ltd, Sutton Road , Somerton, Somerset TA11 6QP Tel: 01458 273452 www.londoncigcard.co.uk

LCM * Louis C. Morton, Galeria GLC A7073L IYS, Monte Athos, 179 Col. Lomas de Chapultepec, CP11000, Mexico Tel: 52 5520 5005 www.lmorton.com

LFA *† Law Fine Art, Firs Cottage, Church Lane, Brimpton, Berkshire RG7 4TJ Tel: 0118 971 0353 info@lawfineart.co.uk www.lawfineart.co.uk

LHO/ LHo • Lin Holroyd Antique Glass Tel: 01924 848780

LIN • Peter Linden, Georges Avenue, Blackrock, Dublin, Republic of Ireland Tel: 00 3531 288 5875 lind@indigo.ie www.peterlinden.com

LJ * Leonard Joel Auctioneers, 333 Malvern Road, South Yarra, Victoria 3141, Australia Tel: 03 9826 4333 decarts@ljoel.com.au or jewellery@ljoel.com.au www.ljoel.com.au

LOP •† Lopburi Art & Antiques, 5/8 Saville Row, Bath, Somerset BA1 2QP Tel/Fax: 01225 322947 mail@lopburi.co.uk www.lopburi.co.uk

LT *† Louis Taylor Auctioneers & Valuers, Britannia House, 10 Town Road, Hanley, Stoke on Trent, Staffordshire ST1 2QG Tel: 01782 214111

LVS * Loves Auction Rooms, 52 Canal Street, Perth, Scotland PH2 8LF Tel: 01738 633337

M * Morphets of Harrogate, 6 Albert Street, Harrogate, Yorkshire HG1 1JL Tel: 01423 530030

Ma • Marie Antiques, Stand G136–138, Alfie's Antique Market, 13–25 Church Street, London NW8 8DT Tel: 020 7706 3727 marie136@globalnet.co.uk www.marieantiques.co.uk

MAA • Mario's Antiques London Tel: 0207 226 2426 Mobile: 07956 580772 marwan@barazi.screaming.net www.marios_antiques.com

MAG • Magna Gallery, 41 High Street, Oxford, Oxfordshire OX1 4AP Tel: 01865 245805

MALC *† Malcolm's No. 1 Auctioneers & Valuers Tel: 01977 684971 info@malcolmsno1auctions.co.uk www.malcolmsno1auctions.co.uk

MAR * Frank R Marshall & Co, Marshall House, Church Hill, Knutsford, Cheshire WA16 6DH Tel: 01565 653284

MARK •† 20th Century Marks, 12 Market Square, Westerham, Kent TN16 1AW Tel: 01959 562221 Mobile: 07831 778992 lambarda@btconnect.com www.20thcenturymarks.co.uk

MAT * Christopher Matthews, 23 Mount Street, Harrogate, Yorkshire HG2 8DQ Tel: 01423 871756

MCA *† Mervyn Carey, Twysden Cottage, Benenden, Cranbrook, Kent TN17 4LD Tel: 01580 240283

MCC • M.C. Chapman Antiques, Bell Hill, Finedon, Northamptonshire NN9 5NB Tel: 01933 681260

MCN • MCN Antiques, 183 Westbourne Grove, London W11 2SB Tel: 020 7727 3796

MCO • Mary Cooke Antiques Ltd, 12 The Old Power Station, 121 Mortlake High Street, London SW14 8SN Tel: 020 8876 5777

MER • Mere Antiques, 13 Fore Street, Topsham, Exeter, Devon EX3 0HF Tel: 01392 874224

MGa • Marilyn Garrow Tel: 01728 648671 Mobile: 07774 842074 marogarrow@aol.com

MHB • M. H. Beeforth silver@meegan.co.uk www.antique-silverware.com www.antique-silverware.co.uk

MI •† Mitofsky Antiques, 8 Rathfarnham Road, Terenure, Dublin 6, Republic of Ireland Tel: 00 353 1 492 0033 info@mitofskyartdeco.com www.mitofskyartdeco.com

MIN • Ministry of Pine, The Ministry, St James Hall, Union Street, Trowbridge, Wiltshire BA14 8RU Tel: 01225 719500 Mobile: 07770 588536 ministryofpine.uk@virgin.net

MIR • Mir Russki Tel: 01506 843973/mob 07979 227779 info@russiansilver.co.uk www.russiansilver.co.uk

Mit * Mitchells, Fairfield House, Station Road, Cockermouth, Cumbria CA13 9PY Tel: 01900 827800

MLa •† Marion Langham Limited Tel: 020 7730 1002 marion@ladymarion.co.uk www.ladymarion.co.uk

MLL •† Millers Antiques Ltd, Netherbrook House, 86 Christchurch Road, Ringwood, Hampshire BH24 1DR Tel: 01425 472062 mail@millers-antiques.co.uk www.millers-antiques.co.uk

MPC •† Moorcroft Pottery Chester Tel: 01244 301800 Sales@Moorcroftchester.co.uk www.Moorcroftchester.co.uk

MSB • Marilynn and Sheila Brass, PO Box 380503, Cambridge, MA 02238-0503, U.S.A. Tel: 617 491 6064

MTay •† Martin Taylor Antiques, 323 Tettenhall Road, Wolverhampton, West Midlands WV6 0JZ Tel: 01902 751166/07836 636524 enquiries@mtaylor-antiques.co.uk www.mtaylor-antiques.co.uk

MUL * Mullock & Madeley, The Old Shippon, Wall-under-Heywood, Church Stretton, Shropshire SY6 7DS Tel: 01694 771771/ 07803 276394 auctions@mullockmadeley.co.uk www.mullockmadeley.co.uk

MUR • Murray Cards (International) Ltd, 51 Watford Way, Hendon Central, London NW4 3JH Tel: 020 8202 5688 murraycards@ukbusiness.com www.murraycards.com/

N *† Neales, 192 Mansfield Road, Nottingham, Nottinghamshire NG1 3HU Tel: 0115 962 4141 fineart@neales.co.uk www.neales-auctions.com

NAW •† Newark Antiques Warehouse, Old Kelham Road, Newark, Nottinghamshire NG24 1BX Tel: 01636 674869 Mobile: 07974 429185 enquiries@newarkantiques.co.uk

NBL • N Bloom & Son (1912) Ltd, Bond Street Antiques Centre, 124 New Bond Street, London W1S 1DX Tel: 020 7629 5060 nbloom@nbloom.co.uk www.nbloom.co.uk

NET • Nettlebed Antique Merchants, 1 High Street, Nettlebed, Henley on Thames, Oxfordshire RG9 5DA Tel: 01491 642062

NEW • Newsum Antiques, 2 High Street, Winchcombe, Gloucestershire GL54 5HT Tel: 01242 603446/07968 196668

NGO • King Ngo Antiques, Hoathwood House, Canterbury Road, Near Herne, Kent CT6 7LE Tel: 01227 372972

NMA • Noel Mercer Antiques, Aurora House, Hall Street, Long Melford, Sudbury, Suffolk CO10 9RJ Tel: 01787 311882/01206 323558

NOA * New Orleans Auction Galleries, Inc., 801 Magazine Street, AT 510 Julia, New Orleans, Louisiana 70130, U.S.A. Tel: 00 1 504 566 1849

NoC •† No.1 Castlegate Antiques, 1–3 Castlegate, Newark, Nottinghamshire NG24 1AZ Tel: 01636 701877 Mobile: 07850 463173

NOR • Nortonbury Antiques, BMC Box 5345, London WC1N 3XX Tel/Fax: 01984 631668 Mobile: 07774 174092 nortonbury.antiques@virgin.net www.antiquesweb.co.uk/nortonbury

NS • Nicholas Shaw Antiques, Great Grooms Antiques Centre, Parbrook, Billingshurst, West Sussex RH14 9EU Tel: 01403 786656/01403 785731 Mobile: 07785 643000 silver@nicholas-shaw.com www.nicholas-shaw.com

OE • Orient Expressions, Assembly Antiques Centre, 5–8 Saville Row, Bath, Somerset BA1 2QP Tel: 01225 313399 Mobile: 07747 691128

OFM • The Old French Mirror Company, Nightingales, Greys Green, Rotherfield Greys, Henley on Thames, Oxon, Oxfordshire RG9 4QQ Tel: 01491 628080 bridget@debreanski.freeserve.uk www.oldfrenchmirrors.com

OKK • Nadine Okker, 8 The Mall, 359 Upper Street, Islington, London N1 0PD Tel: 020 7354 9496 Mobile: 07740 027584

OLA/ • Olliff's Architectural Antiques, 19–21 Lower

OlA Redland Road, Redland, Bristol, Gloucestershire BS6 6TB Tel: 0117 923 9232 marcus@olliffs.com www.olliffs.com

Oli *† Olivers, Olivers Rooms, Burkitts Lane, Sudbury, Suffolk CO10 1HB Tel: 01787 880305 oliversauctions@btconnect.com

OND • Ondines Tel: 01865 882465

ONS * Onslow's, The Depot, 2 Michael Road, London SW6 2AD Tel: 020 7371 0505 Mobile: 078 31 473 400

ORI • Origin 101, Gateway Arcade, Islington High Street, London N1 Tel: 07769 686146/ 07747 758852 David @origin101.co.uk www.naturalmodern.com www.origin101.co.uk

OTB • Old Tackle Box, PO Box 55, Cranbrook, Kent TN17 3ZU Tel/Fax: 01580 713979 tackle.box@virgin.net

OTT • Otter Antiques, 20 High Street, Wallingford, Oxon Oxfordshire OX10 0BP Tel: 01491 825544

P see B

P(B) see B(B)

P(Ba) see B(Ba)

P(E) see B(E)

P(EA) see B(EA)

P(Ed) see B(Ed)

P(L) see B(L)

P(NW) see B(NW)

P(O) see B(O)

P(S) see B(S)

P(WM) see B(WM)

P&T • Pine & Things, Portobello Farm, Campden Road, Nr Shipston-on-Stour, Warwickshire CV36 4PY Tel: 01608 663849

PAO •† P A Oxley Antique Clocks, The Old Rectory, Cherhill, Nr Calne, Wiltshire SN11 8UX Tel: 01249 816227 info@paoxley.com www.british-antiqueclocks.com

PAY • Payne & Son, 131 High Street, Oxford, OX1 4DH Tel: 01865 243787 silver@payneandson.co.uk www.payneandson.co.uk

PCA • Patricia Cater Tel: 01451 830944 Patriciacaterorg@aol.com www.PatriciaCater-OrientalArt.com

PEx •† Piano-Export, Bridge Road, Kingswood, Bristol, Gloucestershire BS15 4FW Tel: 0117 956 8300

PEZ • Alan Pezaro, 62a West Street, Dorking, Surrey RH4 1BS Tel: 01306 743661

PF *† Peter Francis, Curiosity Sale Room, 19 King Street, Carmarthen, South Wales SA31 1BH Tel: 01267 233456 Peterfrancis@valuers.fsnet.co.uk www.peterfrancis.co.uk

PFK *† Penrith Farmers' & Kidd's plc, Skirsgill Salerooms, Penrith, Cumbria CA11 0DN Tel: 01768 890781 penrith.farmers@virgin.net

PG • Pianos Galore Ltd, Worth Farm, Little Horsted, Nr Uckfield, East Sussex TN22 5TT Tel: 01825 750567 info@pianosgalore.co.uk www.pianosgalore.co.uk

PHA •† Paul Hopwell, 30 High Street, West Haddon, Northamptonshire NN6 7AP Tel: 01788 510636 Mobile: 07836 505950 paulhopwell@antiqueoak.co.uk www.antiqueoak.co.uk

PHo • Paul Howard Mobile: 07881 862 375 scientificantiques@hotmail.com

PIC • David & Susan Pickles Tel: 01282 707673/0976 236983

PICA • Piccadilly Antiques, 280 High Street, Batheaston, Bath BA1 7RA Tel: 01225 851494 Mobile: 07785 966132 piccadillyantiques@ukonline.co.uk

PLB • Planet Bazaar, 149 Drummond Street, London NW1 2PB Tel: 0207 387 8326 Mobile: 07956 326301 info@planetbazaar.co.uk www.planetbazaar.co.uk

POT • Pot Board Tel: 01834 842699 Gill@potboard.co.uk www.potboard.co.uk

Pott * Potteries Specialist Auctions, 271 Waterloo Road, Cobridge, Stoke on Trent, Staffordshire ST6 3HR Tel: 01782 286622

PPC • Period Piano Company, Park Farm Oast, Hareplain Road, Biddenden, Nr Ashford, Kent TN27 8LJ Tel: 01580 291393 www.periodpiano.com

PSA • Pantiles Spa Antiques, 4, 5, 6 Union House, The Pantiles, Tunbridge Wells, Kent TN4 8HE Tel: 01892 541377 Mobile: 07711 283655 psa.wells@btinternet.com www.antiques-tun-wells-kent.co.uk

PSC • Peter & Sonia Cashman, Bartlett Street Antique Centre, 5–10 Bartlett Street, Bath, Somerset BA1 2QZ Tel: 01225 469497/mob 0780 8609860

PT •† Pieces of Time, (1–7 Davies Mews), 26 South Molton Lane, London W1Y 2LP Tel: 020 7629 2422 info@antique-watch.com www.antique-watch.com

PTh • Antique Clocks by Patrick Thomas, 62a West Street, Dorking, Surrey RH4 1BS Tel: 01306 743661 clockman@fsmail.net www.antiqueclockshop.co.uk

PVD • Puritan Values at the Dome, St Edmunds Business Park, St Edmunds Road, Southwold, Suffolk IP18 6BZ Tel: 01502 722211 Mobile: 07966 371676 sales@puritanvalues.com www.puritanvalues.com

Q&C •† Q & C Militaria, 22 Suffolk Road, Cheltenham, Gloucestershire GL50 2AQ Tel/Fax: 01242 519815 Mobile: 07778 613977 john@qc-militaria.freeserve.co.uk www.qcmilitaria.com

Ram • Rambo's Tattoo Studio, 42 Shudehill, Greater Manchester M4 1EY Tel: 0161 839 0090

RAN •† Ranby Hall-Antiques, Barnby Moor, Retford, Nottinghamshire DN22 8JQ Tel: 01777 860696 Mobile: 07860 463477 paul.wyatt@virgin.net www.ranbyhall.antiques-gb.com

RAP • Rapparee Antiques at Way Back When, 25 High Street, Edenbridge, Kent TN8 5AB Tel: 01732 868280 or 020 8777 4016

RAY •† Derek & Tina Rayment Antiques, Orchard House, Barton Road, Barton, Nr Farndon, Cheshire SY14 7HT Tel: 01829 270429 07860 666629/ 07702 922410 raymentantiques@aol.com

RBA • Roger Bradbury Antiques, Church Street, Coltishall, Norfolk NR12 7DJ Tel: 01603 737444

RBB *† Brightwells Fine Art, The Fine Art Saleroom, Ryelands Road, Leominster, Herefordshire HR6 8NZ Tel: 01568 611122 fineart@brightwells.com www.brightwells.com

RdeR • Rogers de Rin, 76 Royal Hospital Road, London SW3 4HN Tel: 020 7352 9007

RdV • Sudbury Antiques, Roger de Ville Tel: 01889 564311 Mobile: 07798 793857

REF •† The Refectory, 38 West Street, Dorking, Surrey RH4 1BU Tel/Fax: 01306 742111 www.therefectory.co.uk

REI • Reindeer Antiques Ltd, 43 Watling Street, Potterspury, Nr Towcester, Northamptonshire NN12 7QD Tel: 01908 542407 www.reindeerantiques.co.uk

ReJ • Regal Jewellery, 372 Sheffield Road, Chesterfield, Derbyshire S41 8LE Tel: 01246 233972 info@regaljewellery.com

RFA * Rowley Fine Art, The Old Bishop's Palace, Little Downham, Ely, Cambridgeshire CB6 2TD Tel: 01353 699177 mail@rowleyfineart.com www.rowleyfineart.com

RGa • Richard Gardner Antiques, Swanhouse, Market Square, Petworth, West Sussex GU28 0AN Tel: 01798 343411

RGe • Rupert Gentle Antiques, The Manor House, Milton Lilbourne, Nr Pewsey, Wiltshire SN9 5LQ Tel: 01672 563344

RH • Rick Hubbard Art Deco, 3 Tee Court, Bell Street, Romsey, Hampshire SO51 8GY Tel: 01794 513133 rick@rickhubbard-artdeco.co.uk www.rickhubbard-artdeco.co.uk

RHa • Robert Hall, 15c Clifford Street, London W1X 1RF Tel: 020 7734 4008

RIT *† Ritchies Inc., Auctioneers & Appraisers of Antiques & Fine Art, 288 King Street East, Toronto, Ontario M5A 1K4, Canada Tel: (416) 364 1864 auction@ritchies.com www.ritchies.com

RKa • Richardson & Kailas Tel: 020 7371 0491 By appt

RL • Roger Lamb Antiques, The Square, Stow-on-the Wold, Gloucestershire GL54 1AB Tel: 01451 831 371

RMC •† Romsey Medals, PO Box 169, Romsey, Hampshire SO51 6XU Tel: 01794 324488/322125 post@romseymedals.co.uk www.romseymedals.co.uk

RMe • Jubilee Photographica, 10 Pierrepoint Row, Camden Passage, London N1 8EE Mobile: 07860 793707

RMi • Richard Miles Tel: 020 8748 6385 rcmiles1@btclick.com www.richardmiles.net

ROSc *† R. O. Schmitt Fine Art, Box 1941, Salem, New Hampshire 03079, U.S.A. Tel: 603 893 5915 bob@roschmittfinearts.com www.antiqueclockauction.com

RPh •† Phelps Antiques, 133–135 St Margaret's Road, Twickenham, MiddlesexTW1 1RG Tel: 020 8892 1778/7129 antiques@phelps.co.uk www.phelps.co.uk

RTo *† Rupert Toovey & Co Ltd, Star Road, Partridge Green, West Sussex RH13 8RA Tel: 01403 711744 auctions@rupert-toovey.com www.rupert-toovey.com

RTW •† Richard Twort Tel/Fax: 01934 641900 Mobile: 07711 939789

RUSK • Ruskin Decorative Arts, 5 Talbot Court, Stow-on-the-Wold, Cheltenham, Gloucestershire GL54 1DP Tel: 01451 832254

RYA •† Robert Young Antiques, 68 Battersea Bridge Road, London SW11 3AG Tel: 020 7228 7847

S * Sotheby's, 34–35 New Bond Street, London W1A 2AA Tel: 020 7293 5000 www.sothebys.com

S(Am) * Sotheby's Amsterdam, De Boelelaan 30, 1083 HJ Amsterdam, Netherlands Tel: 00 31 20 550 22 00

S(G) * Sotheby's, 13 Quai du Mont Blanc, Geneva, Switzerland CH–1201 Tel: 00 41 22 908 4800

S(HK) * Sotheby's, Li Po Chun Chambers, 18th Floor, 189 Des Vouex Road, Hong Kong, China Tel: 852 524 8121

S(Mi) * Sotheby's, Palazzo Broggi, Via Broggi, 19, 20129 Milano, Italy Tel: 02 295001 www.sothebys.com

S(NY) * Sotheby's, 1334 York Avenue, New York NY 10021, U.S.A. Tel: 00 1 212 606 7000

S(O) * Sotheby's Olympia, Hammersmith Road, London W14 8UX Tel: 020 7293 5000

S(P) * Sotheby's France SA, 76 Rue du Faubourg, Saint Honore, 75008 Paris, France Tel: 00 33 147 42 22 32

S(S) * Sotheby's Sussex, Summers Place, Billingshurst, West Sussex RH14 9AD Tel: 01403 833500

S(Z) * Sotheby's Zurich, Gessneralee 1, CH–8021 Zurich, Switzerland Tel: 00 41 1 226 2200

SA • Sporting Antiques, St Ives, Cambridgeshire Tel: 01480 463891 john.lambden@virgin.net

SAS *† Special Auction Services, The Coach House, Midgham Park, Reading, Berkshire RG7 5UG Tel: 0118 971 2949 www.invaluable.com/sas/

SCO • Peter Scott, Stand 39, Bartlett Street Antiques Centre, Bath, Somerset BA1 2QZ Tel: 01225 310457/ 0117 986 8468 Mobile: 07850 639770

SDP • Stage Door Prints, 9 Cecil Court, London WC2N 4EZ Tel: 020 7240 1683

SEA •† Mark Seabrook Antiques, Huntingdon, Cambridgeshire Tel: 01480 861935 Mobile: 07770 721931 enquiries@markseabrook.com www.markseabrook.com

SeH •† Seventh Heaven, Chirk Mill, Chirk, Wrexham, County Borough, Wales LL14 5BU Tel: 01691 777622/773563 requests@seventh-heaven.co.uk www.seventh-heaven.co.uk

SER •† Serendipity, 125 High Street, Deal, Kent CT14 6BB Tel: 01304 369165/01304 366536 dipityantiques@aol.com

SH * Shapes Fine Art Auctioneers & Valuers, Bankhead Avenue, Sighthill, Edinburgh, Scotland EH11 4BY Tel: 0131 453 3222 auctionsadmin@shapesauctioneers.co.uk www.shapesauctioneers.co.uk

SHa •† Shapiro & Co, Stand 380, Gray's Antique Market, 58 Davies Street, London W1Y 5LP Tel: 020 7491 2710

SHSY * Shapiro Auctioneers, formerly Phillips, 162 Queen Street, Woollahra, Sydney NSW 2025, Australia Tel: 00 612 9326 1588

SIE • Sieff, 49 Long Street, Tetbury, Gloucestershire GL8 8AA Tel: 01666 504477 sieff@sieff.co.uk www.sieff.co.uk

SIL • The Silver Shop, Powerscourt Townhouse Centre, St Williams Street, Dublin 2, Republic of Ireland Tel: 00 3531 6794147

SK * Skinner Inc, The Heritage On The Garden, 63 Park Plaza, Boston MA 02116, U.S.A. Tel: 001 617 350 5400

SK(B) * Skinner Inc, 357 Main Street, Bolton MA 01740, U.S.A. Tel: 00 1 978 779 6241

SLN *† Sloan's Auctioneers & Appraisers, 4920 Wyaconda Road, North Bethesda, MD 20852, U.S.A. Tel: 00 1 301 468 4911/800 649 5066 www.sloansauction.com

SMI •† Skip & Janie Smithson Tel/Fax: 01754 810265 Mobile: 07831 399180

SMW • Sporting Memorabilia of Warwick, 13 Market Place, Warwick, Warwickshire CV34 4FS Tel: 01926 410600 Mobile: 07860 269340 sales@sportantiques.com sportsantiques.com

SO •† Sam Orr Antique Clocks, 34–36 High Street, Hurstpierpoint, Nr Brighton, East Sussex BN6 9RG Tel: 01273 832081 Mobile: 07860 230888 clocks@samorr.co.uk www.samorr.co.uk

Som •† Somervale Antiques, 6 Radstock Road, Midsomer Norton, Bath, Somerset BA3 2AJ Tel: 01761 412686 Mobile: 07885 088022 ronthomas@somervaleantiquesglass.co.uk www.somervaleantiquesglass.co.uk

SPA • Sporting Antiques, 10 Union Square, The Pantiles, Tunbridge Wells, Kent TN4 8HE Tel: 01892 522661

SpP * Specialised Postcard Auctions, 25 Gloucester Street, Cirencester, Gloucestershire GL7 2DJ Tel: 01285 659057

SPT • Sporting Times Gone By, Warehouse (Clubhouse) Tel: 01903 885656 Mobile: 07976 942059 www.sportingtimes.co.uk

SRA * Sheffield Railwayana Auctions, 43 Little Norton Lane, Sheffield, Yorkshire S8 8GA Tel: 0114 274 5085 ian@sheffrail.freeserve.co.uk www.sheffieldrailwayana.co.uk

SSW • Spencer Swaffer, 30 High Street, Arundel, West Sussex BN18 9AB Tel: 01903 882132

StC § St Clere Carlton Ware, P O Box 161, Sevenoaks, Kent TN15 6GA Tel: 01474 853630 stclere@aol.com www.stclere.co.uk

SuA • Suffolk House Antiques, High Street, Yoxford, Suffolk IP17 3EP Tel: 01728 668122 Mobile: 07860 521583

SWA •† S.W. Antiques, Abbey Showrooms, Newlands, Pershore, Worcestershire WR10 1BP 01386 555580 sw-antiques@talk21.com www.sw-antiques.co.uk

SWB •† Sweetbriar Gallery, Sweetbriar House, Robin Hood Lane, Helsby, Cheshire WA6 9NH Tel: 01928 723851 Mobile: 07860 907532 sweetbr@globalnet.co.uk www.sweetbriar.co.uk

SWG • Swan Gallery, High Street, Burford, Oxfordshire OX18 4RE Tel: 01993 822244

SWO *† Sworders, 14 Cambridge Road, Stansted Mountfitchet, Essex CM24 8BZ Tel: 01279 817778 www.sworder.co.uk

TDS • The Decorator Source, 39a Long Street, Tetbury, Gloucestershire GL8 8AA Tel: 01666 505358

TED •† Teddy Bears of Witney, 99 High Street, Witney, Oxfordshire OX28 6HY Tel: 01993 702616/706616

TEM •† Tempus, Union Square, The Pantiles, Tunbridge Wells, Kent Tel/Fax: 01932 828936 www.tempus-watches.co.uk

TEN *† Tennants, The Auction Centre, Harmby Road, Leyburn, Yorkshire DL8 5SG Tel: 01969 623780 enquiry@tennants-ltd.co.uk www.tennants.co.uk

TeW • Terry West, 2 Taylors Avenue, Cleethorpes, Lincolnshire DN35 0LD Tel: 01472 508729 Mobile: 07808 693287

TF *† Tayler & Fletcher, London House, High Street, Bourton-on-the-Water, Cheltenham, Gloucestershire GL54 2AP Tel: 01451 821666 bourton@taylerfletcher.com www.taylerfletcher.com

TGL • The Gilded Lily, 145/146 Gray's, 58 Davies Street, London W1K 5LP Tel: 020 7499 6260 jewellery@gilded-lily.co.uk graysantiques.com

TH •† Tony Horsley, PO Box 3127, Brighton, East Sussex BN1 5SS Tel: 01273 550770

TMA *† Brown & Merry, Tring Market Auctions, The Market Premises, Brook Street, Tring, Hertfordshire HP23 5EF Tel: 01442 826446 sales@tringmarketauctions.co.uk www.tringmarketauctions.co.uk

TO • Tombland Antique Centre, Augustine Steward House, 14 Tombland, Norwich, Norfolk NR3 1HF Tel: 01603 619129

TOB • The Old Brigade, 10A Harborough Road, Kingsthorpe, Northampton, Northamptonshire NN2 7AZ Tel: 01604 719389 theoldbrigade@easynet.co.uk www.theoldbrigade.co.uk

TOM •† Charles Tomlinson, Chester Tel/Fax: 01244 318395 Charles.Tomlinson@lineone.net charles.tomlinson@btinternet.com www.lineone.net/-charles.tomlinson

TOT • Totem, 168 Stoke Newington, Church Street, London N16 0JL Tel: 020 7275 0234 sales@totemrecords.com www.totemrecords.com

TPC •† Pine Cellars, 39 Jewry Street, Winchester, Hampshire SO23 8RY Tel: 01962 777546/867014

TQM • The Quiet Man, Core One, The Gasworks, 2 Michael Road, Chelsea, London SW6 2AN Tel: 020 7736 3384

TREA *† Treadway Gallery, Inc, 2029 Madison Road, Cincinnati, Ohio 45208, U.S.A. Tel: 001 513 321 6742 www.treadwaygallery.com

TRI • Trident Antiques, 2 Foundry House, Hall Street, Long Melford, Suffolk CO10 9JR Tel: 01787 883388 Mobile: 07860 221402 tridentoak@aol.com

TRL * Thomson, Roddick & Medcalf, Coleridge House, Shaddongate, Carlisle, Cumbria CA2 5TU Tel: 01228 528939

TRM * Thomson, Roddick & Medcalf, 60 Whitesands, Dumfries, Scotland DG1 2RS Tel: 01387 255366

TRM * Thomson Roddick & Medcalf, 20 Murray Street, Annan, Scotland DG12 6EG Tel: 01461 202575

TRM * Thomson Roddick & Medcalf, 44/3 Hardengreen Business Park, Eskbank, Edinburgh, Scotland EH22 3NX Tel: 0131 454 9090

TSC • The Silver Collection Ltd Tel: 01442 890954 Mobile: 07802 447813

TWh • Tim Wharton, 24 High Street, Redbourn, Nr St Albans, Hertfordshire AL3 7LL Tel: 01582 794371 Mobile: 07850 622880

TWr • Tim Wright Antiques, Richmond Chambers, 147 Bath Street, Glasgow G2 4SQ Tel: 0141 221 0364

UCO • Unique Collections, 52 Greenwich Church Street, London SE10 9BL Tel: 020 8305 0867 glen@uniquecollections.co.uk www.uniquecollections.co.uk

US • Ulla Stafford Tel: 0118 934 3208 Mobile: 07944 815104

VB • Variety Box, 16 Chapel Place, Tunbridge Wells, Kent TN1 1YQ Tel: 01892 531868

VBO/ VBo • Vernon Bowden, Bournemouth, Dorset Tel: 01202 763806

VCL • Vintage Cameras Ltd, 256 Kirkdale, Sydenham, London SE26 4NL Tel: 020 8778 5416 info@vintagecameras.co.uk www.vintagecameras.co.uk

VEC * Vectis Auctions Ltd/Barry Potter Auctions, Fleck Way, Thornaby, Stockton-on-Tees, Cleveland TS17 9JZ Tel: 01642 750616 admin@vectis.co.uk admin@barrypotterauctions.com www.vectis.co.uk www.barrypotterauctions.co.uk

VJ • Ventnor Junction, 48 High Street, Ventnor, Isle of Wight PO38 1LT Tel: 01983 853996 shop@ventjunc.freeserve.co.uk

VS *† T. Vennett-Smith, 11 Nottingham Road, Gotham, Nottinghamshire NG11 0HE Tel: 0115 983 0541 info@vennett-smith.com www.vennett-smith.com

W&C • Westland & Co, St Michael's Church, Leonard Street (off Great Eastern Street), London EC2A 4ER Tel: 0207 7398094 westland@westland.co.uk www.westland.co.uk

WAC • Worcester Antiques Centre, Reindeer Court, Mealcheapen Street, Worcester, Worcestershire WR1 4DF Tel: 01905 610680

WAL *† Wallis & Wallis, West Street Auction Galleries, Lewes, East Sussex BN7 2NJ Tel: 01273 480208 auctions@wallisandwallis.co.uk www.wallisandwallis.co.uk

WBB •† William Bentley Billiards, Standen Manor Farm, Hungerford, Berkshire RG17 0RB Tel: 01488 861711 www.billiards.co.uk

WBH *† Walker, Barnett & Hill, Cosford Auction Rooms, Long Lane, Cosford, Shropshire TF11 8PJ Tel: 01902 375555 wbhauctions@lineone.net www.walker-barnett-hill.co.uk

WcH * Weschler's, 909 E Street NW, Washington DC 20004 Tel: 202 628 1281/ 800 331 14630 www.weschlers.com

WD * Weller & Dufty Ltd, 141 Bromsgrove Street, Birmingham, West Midlands B5 6RQ Tel: 0121 692 1414 wellerdufty@freewire.co.uk www.welleranddufty.co.uk

WELD • J. W. Weldon, 55 Clarendon Street, Dublin 2, Republic of Ireland Tel: 00 353 1 677 1638

WELL •† Anthony Welling, Broadway Barn, High Street, Ripley, Surrey GU23 6AQ Tel/Fax: 01483 225384

WiA • Witney Antiques, 96–100 Corn Street, Witney, Oxfordshire OX8 7BU Tel: 01993 703902

WilP * W&H Peacock, 26 Newnham Street, Bedford, Bedfordshire MK40 3JR Tel: 01234 266366

WIM •† Wimpole Antiques, Stand 349, Grays Antique Market, 58 Davies Street, London W1K 5LP Tel/Fax: 020 7499 2889 WimpoleAntiques@compuserve.com

WL *† Wintertons Ltd, Lichfield Auction Centre, Fradley Park, Lichfield, Staffordshire WS13 6NU Tel: 01543 263256 enquiries@wintertons.co.uk www.wintertons.co.uk

WMa • William Macadam, Edinburgh, Scotland Tel: 0131 466 0343

WOM * Wombell's Antiques & General Auction, The Auction Gallery, Northminster Business Park, Northfield Lane, Upper Poppleton, York, Yorkshire YO26 6QU Tel: 01904 790777 www.invaluable.com/wombell

WRe • Walcot Reclamations, 108 Walcot Street, Bath, Somerset BA1 5BG Tel: 01225 444404

WSA •† West Street Antiques, 63 West Street, Dorking, Surrey RH4 1BS Tel/Fax: 01306 883487 weststant@aol.com www.antiquearmsandarmour.com

WV •† Westville House Antiques, Westville House, Littleton, Nr Somerton, Somerset TA11 6NP Tel/Fax: 01458 273376 Mobile: 07941 510823 antique@westville.co.uk www.westville.co.uk

WW * Woolley & Wallis, Salisbury Salerooms, 51–61 Castle Street, Salisbury, Wiltshire SP1 3SU Tel: 01722 424500

WWo • Woman's Work Tel: 020 8940 2589 Mobile: 07971 691748

WWW • WW Warner, The Forge, The Green, Brasted, Kent TN16 1JL Tel: 01959 563698

ZOOM • Zoom, Arch 65, Cambridge Grove, London W6 Tel: 07000 9666 2002 Mobile: 07958 372975 eddiesandham@hotmail.com www.retrozoom.com

Index to Advertisers

Index

Italic page numbers denote colour pages; **bold** numbers refer to information and pointer boxes

C

INDEX

INDEX

D

INDEX

INDEX

Q

R

S

INDEX